CW00661313

KAMIKAZE

The Story of
THE BRITISH PACIFIC FLEET

"In defeat, defiance; in victory, magnanimity; in peace, unity."

Winston Churchill

"One must not keep the past alive by giving it a place in the future through punishment."

Laurens van der Post

"Give wisdom to all in authority, bless Elisabeth our Queen and direct this nation and all nations in the ways of justice and of peace; that men may honour one another, and seek the common good."

The Book of Common Prayer
Alternative Service Book

OPERATION AREA, PACIFIC OCEAN

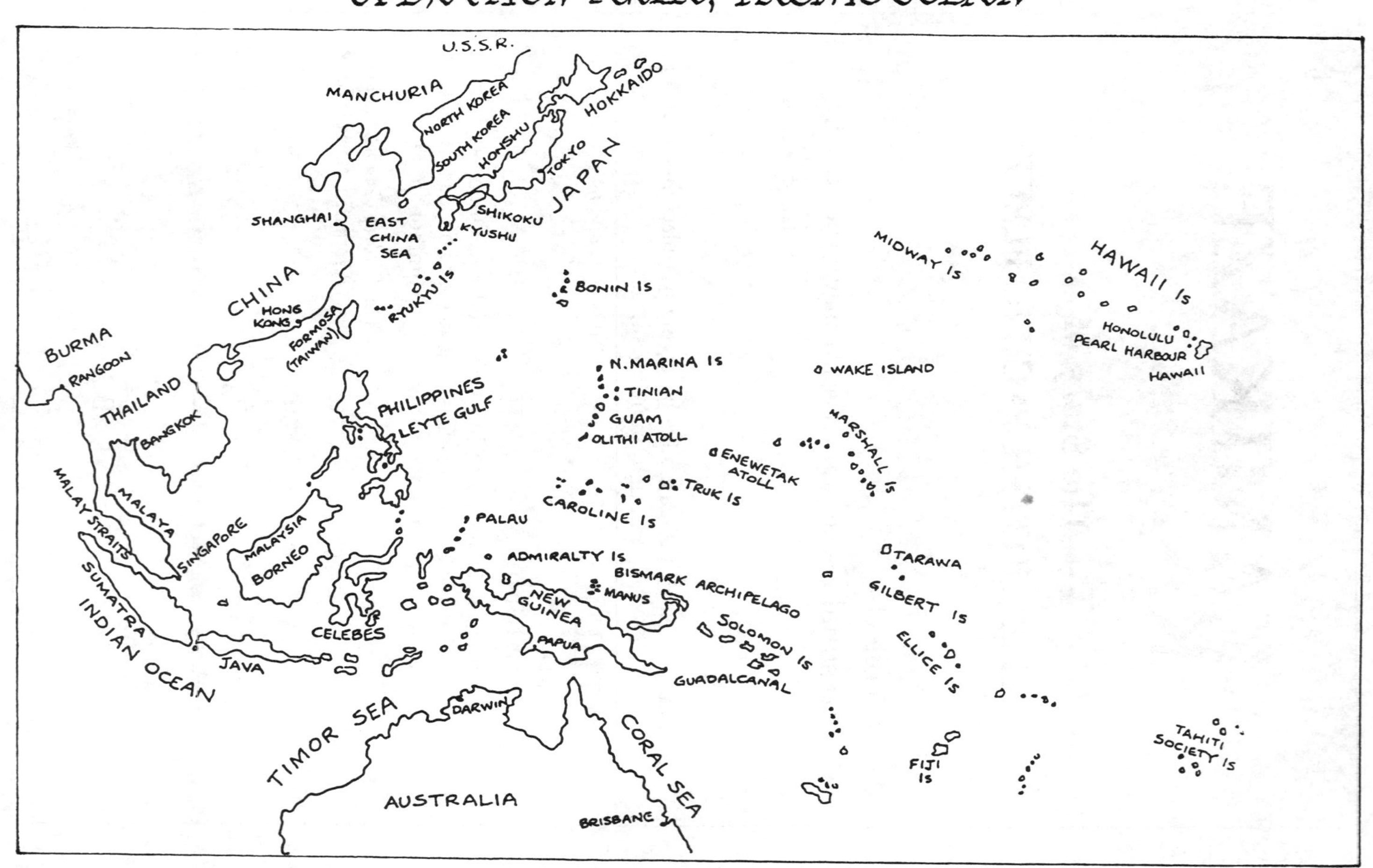

KAMIKAZE

The Divine Wind

•

A collection of extracts from authors with personal experiences as Prisoners of War

and

the memories of the men of

THE BRITISH PACIFIC FLEET,

who helped to bring them home

Edited by Stuart Eadon,
ex-Lieutenant, RNVR

Crécy Books

Revised Edition published by
Crécy Books Limited 1995
First published in 1991 by
Square One Publications

ISBN 0 947554 61 0

Printed and bound by Bookcraft (Bath) Ltd,
Midsomer Norton, Avon BA3 2BX

If my wife Rosamund had not encouraged me to write my own war story **Sakishima**, then **Kamikaze** would not have been published.

I was aware of the need to relate other men's stories also, and I realised that those men, like me, knew little of the war going on around them.

Thus I set out to discover what I could, on their behalf.

Part Two of **Kamikaze** is mainly written by the Men of the British Pacific Fleet, to whom it is dedicated—especially those who did not come home.

CONTENTS

FOREWORD

In writing a foreword to this book, I found myself in much the same position as a Theatre Critic who writes the Review of a play when he only saw the first minutes of the opening scene and the final curtain.

My part in the Pacific War was limited to the few disastrous months between the sinking of the *Prince of Wales* and *Repulse* and the Battles of the Java Sea in 1942 and the arrival of General MacArthur in Tokyo in 1945. Between those dates I was never in a POW camp which had a radio and relied for news upon the Japanese 'War News', occasional borrowed newspapers translated by amateur linguists and guesswork. I was not even aware that British ships were in the Pacific. Because of this I have devoured books and accounts of WW2 events and am happy to add **Kamikaze** to my list.

Stuart Eadon has given us a splendid companion to his previous book **Sakishima** and so puts into a worthy frame the picture he painted of Task Forces 57 and 37, The British Pacific Fleet in 1945. In so doing he, with the insight as it were of a Special Correspondent, reminds us of the magnitude of the Royal Navy's part in the Pacific and the courage and steadfastness of those latter 'Few' who went to fight that 'other war' after VE day.

The book will revive memories for many now ancient warriors, who played their part in the final defeat of Japan and illuminate events, some known and some unknown, of those crucial days.

Admiral Sir Frank Twiss KCB, KCVO, DSC

Admiral Sir Frank Twiss joined the Royal Naval College, Dartmouth in 1924 and was appointed to HMS *Revenge,* Flagship of the Atlantic Fleet in 1927. He served in HMS *Rodney,* HMS *Emerald,* HMS *Bideford,* HMS *Malaga,* HMS *Nelson* (Assistant Gunnery Officer), HMS *Grenville,* HMS *Trinidad* and as Gunnery Officer in HMS *Exeter.*

Exeter picked up survivors of the *Prince of Wales* and *Repulse* and then saw service at Singapore, Ceylon, Tanjong, Priok, Sourabaya and finally in the Task Force under ABDA Command, in defence of Java. HMS *Exeter* was in action in the Battle of the Java Sea and was eventually sunk on 1st March 1942.

For three and a half years, Admiral Twiss was a POW in Maccassar and Japan.

In 1946, he was appointed to HMS *Excellent* in charge of AA close range training and in November became Commanding Officer HMS *Porlock Bay* in the West Indies Squadron.

1947 saw him as Commander Atomic, Biological and Gas Training in HMS *Excellent* where he became Executive Officer in 1949. He was promoted Captain in 1950 and appointed Assistant Secretary, Chiefs of Staff Committee.

In 1953 he was Captain Fishery Protection and 5th Minesweeping Squadron in HMS *Coquette.*

After an Imperial Defence College Course in 1955, he became Captain RN Air Station, Bramcote, HMS *Gamecock.*

Three years later he was promoted to Rear Admiral and Naval Secretary to the First Lord until 1962.

Following his two years as Flag Officer Flotillas, Home Fleet, he was promoted to Vice Admiral in 1964 and became Commander Far East Fleet.

From 1967—70 he was Second Sea Lord and Chief of Naval Personnel.

Placed on the Retired List in 1970, he was made Black Rod until his retirement in 1978.

INTRODUCTION

After the publication of **Sakishima** in October 1988, I received over 100 letters and telephone calls thanking me for relating some of the little known activities of the British Pacific Fleet during 1945. These contacts, mainly from old shipmates, added further recollections of those momentous months Dec—Jan off Sumatra, March—June off Okinawa and between July and September off Japan.

When I wrote **Sakishima**, it was evident that to tell the full story of one aircraft carrier was an impossible task if the author was to do justice to all FAA Squadrons and Ships' Departments and relate all incidents. I could only include what I knew and what others told me—mistakes and all! A mere drop in the ocean, but nevertheless, better than nothing.

While writing I was, in my mind's eye, scanning and focussing through my binoculars again. This time not at the sky and the sea, but at the other ships in company, wondering what they had experienced. I thought too of the Fleet Train just over the horizon and of the oilers—the hospital ships and the men of the Merchant Navy.

Controlled by an unseen hand, all were joined in a common purpose. We were to get our Fleet Air Arm boys into the air and hopefully back again—to 'Find, Fix and Strike' the enemy, so that there would be peace for our children and grandchildren.

To achieve this required not only skill, but tedious mundane tasks carried out in unpleasant conditions, with 'simple' food and little sleep, in the knowledge that injury or death might result. The compensation was a comradeship indescribable to any succeeding generation.

Endeavouring to spread the canvas a little wider, **Kamikaze** provides some insight into the minds of our then enemies and, by first hand eye witness accounts of events from 'our side', reveals the hearts and minds of that rare breed 'The Men of The British Pacific Fleet'.

While compiling **Kamikaze**, I have endeavoured to include the stories of as many men and ships (60) as I could muster, while quoting extracts from authors with personal experience of events in order to provide a more complete picture.

Inevitably, these are recounted from different viewpoints and are therefore sometimes repeated, but it ensures an unbiased report of what really happened.

Outbreak of War

The broadcast given on the morning of 3 September 1939, in which the Rt Hon Neville Chamberlain announced that Britain was at war with Germany.

I am speaking to you from the Cabinet Room at 10 Downing Street. This morning the British Ambassador in Berlin handed the German Government a final note stating that, unless we heard from them by 11 o'clock that they were prepared at once to withdraw their troops from Poland, a state of war would exist between us. I have to tell you now that no such undertaking has been received, and that consequently this country is at war with Germany.

You can imagine what a bitter blow it is to me that all my long struggle to win peace has failed. Yet I cannot believe that there is anything more or anything different that I could have done and that would have been more successful.

Up to the very last it would have been quite possible to have arranged a peaceful and honourable settlement between Germany and Poland, but Hitler would not have it. He had evidently made up his mind to attack Poland whatever happened, and although he now says he put forward reasonable proposals which were rejected by the Poles, this is not a true statement.

The proposals were never shown to the Poles, nor to us, and, though they were announced in a German broadcast on Thursday night, Hitler did not wait to hear comments on them, but ordered his troops to cross the Polish frontier. His action shows convincingly that there is no chance of expecting that this man will ever give up his practice of using force to gain his will. He can only be stopped by force.

We and France are today, in fulfilment of our obligations, going to the aid of Poland, who is so bravely resisting this wicked and unprovoked attack on her people. We have a clear conscience. We have done all that any country could do to establish peace. The situation in which no word given by Germany's ruler could be trusted and no people or country could feel themselves safe, has become intolerable. And now that we have resolved to finish it, I know that you will all play your part with calmness and courage.

At such a moment as this, the assurances of support that we have received from the Empire are a source of profound encouragement to us.

You may be taking your part in the fighting services or as a volunteer in one of the branches of Civil Defence. If so you will report for duty in accordance with the instructions you have received. You may be engaged in work essential to the prosecution of war for the maintenance of the life of the people—in factories, in transport, in public utility concerns, or in the supply of other necessaries of life. If so, it is of vital importance that you should carry on with your jobs.

Now may God bless you all. May He defend the right. It is the evil things that we shall be fighting against—brute force, bad faith, injustice, oppression and persecution—and against them I am certain that the right will prevail.

Many books have been written about the war at sea, but very few have recounted the activities of the Royal Navy and Merchant Navy during the final months of the Second World War, six long years later, in the vast Pacific ocean . . .

. . . after the War in Europe had ceased!

Kamikaze is primarily intended for the survivors of the BPF and their families, to help them understand the important role they played in the overall operations in the Pacific. Over 220 men have contributed to Part Two and we are all grateful to them.

My only regret is that I have not been able to make contact with those who have other significant stories they could tell. Some have died, some have had the opportunity, but have not contributed and I respect their wishes.

Nevertheless, I hope you enjoy the book, and most of all, I hope it will make you think.

Stuart Eadon

PART ONE

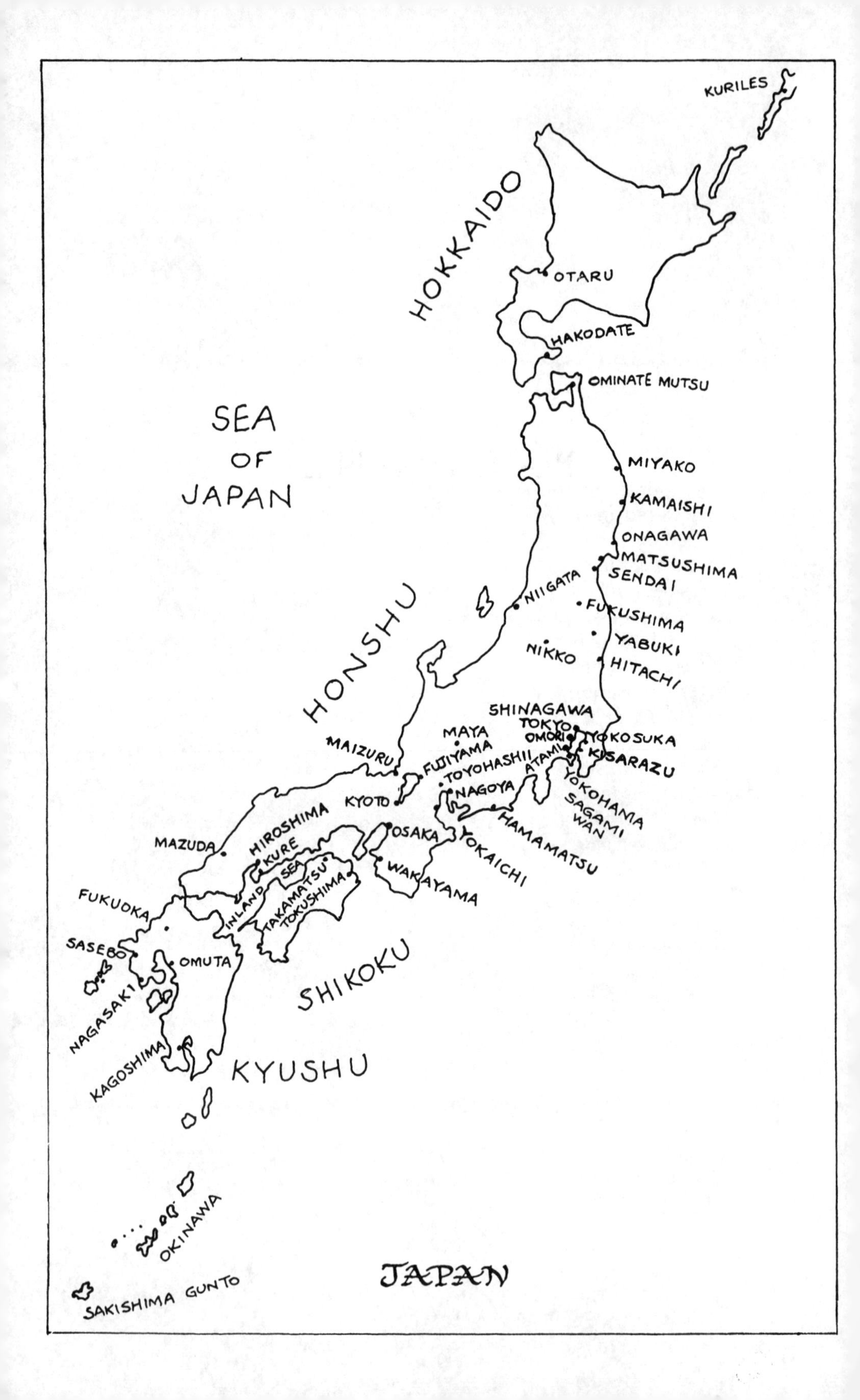
KURILES
HOKKAIDO
OTARU
HAKODATE
OMINATE MUTSU
SEA
OF
JAPAN
MIYAKO
KAMAISHI
ONAGAWA
MATSUSHIMA
SENDAI
NIIGATA
FUKUSHIMA
YABUKI
NIKKO
HITACHI
HONSHU
SHINAGAWA
TOKYO
MAYA
OMORI
YOKOSUKA
KISARAZU
MAIZURU
FUJIYAMA
TOYOHASHI
ATAMI
YOKOHAMA
SAGAMI
WAN
NAGOYA
KYOTO
HIROSHIMA
OSAKA
HAMAMATSU
YOKAICHI
MAZUDA
KURE
SEA
INLAND
TAKAMATSU
TOKUSHIMA
WAKAYAMA
FUKUOKA
SASEBO
OMUTA
SHIKOKU
NAGASAKI
KAGOSHIMA
KYUSHU
OKINAWA
JAPAN
SAKISHIMA GUNTO

CHAPTER ONE

The Other Hundred Years' War — Japan and her Destiny — The Naked Island — the Menacing Rise of Japan

'It had been a quiet night in 'A' Engine Room during the middle watch. I had shaved, showered and caught up on my dhobying when suddenly the tannoy was switched on. A very quiet voice said, "Anyone moving in the vicinity of the Flight deck at the moment will see a plane passing over. I cannot say what mission it is on, but I can say that it will create history." I went up on deck and watched a tiny lone speck in the morning sky. The next day, when the news broke about the Atom Bomb on Hiroshima, I knew I had seen The Enola Gay.'

ERA George Colling wrote this to me after reading my first book ***Sakishima****, which had brought the memories flooding back. We had both served on board HMS* Indefatigable, *the only British Aircraft Carrier to be left with the token Commonwealth Force when the rest of the British Pacific Fleet, duty done, had returned wearily to Sydney after months of strikes in the areas of Okinawa and the Japanese mainland.*

Now the end was in sight.

But what of the Beginning? Why and how had it all started? At the time, we didn't understand and candidly didn't care. We just wanted to go home.

Today, over 45 years later, most of us are little wiser. We have been busy getting on with our lives, bringing up our families and making our way in the world with varying degrees of so-called success.

Reaching the age of retirement, we have paused at last to reflect on our lives, to wonder whatever happened to old so-and-so. And then we remember that we have experienced very few friendships of such quality and depth since those 'dreadful times' and suddenly, in a life adjustment situation and a psychological need to feel fulfilled, we remember 'the good old days'. Reunions are rife. There is so little time left now to recapture that brand of comradeship which shines like a beacon in our youth. And no one, other than some of our own generation, knows about it. It is our secret and soon it will be dead.

'Nobody' understands us any more. Sometimes we feel like aliens in our own country. Maybe our old enemies feel the same.

Now at last we can relax and, if we want to, read about what we were really doing all those years ago. It's been quite a job finding out!

It was Ian Darby, ex Lieutenant (A) RNZNVR, who advised me to read 'The Rise and Fall of the Japanese Empire' by Captain D. H. James (1951) which 'opened the door' and helped me to really understand his *innermost feelings after being a Prisoner of War in Japan.*

When I read Russell Braddon's books 'The Naked Island' and 'The Other Hundred Years War 1941—2041', the whole scene of the BPF's involvement emerged for the first time and I had to write about its relevance.

But why did Japan want war so much? What made her attack Pearl Harbour without warning and bring America into the Second World conflict? We didn't understand it at the time and perhaps we will never know the full answer to that, but I trust that **Kamikaze** *will provide some insight and understanding, especially for those who were in the BPF.*

Captain James, a British Intelligence Officer, lived for much of his youth in Japan and could speak the language fluently. He was a Prisoner of War for three and a half years and yet, as you will see, he had a fair idea of what we *were up to out in the Pacific! (Chapter 2.)*

During the last weeks of the war, some of the BPF aircrews were imprisoned in the same POW camp as he, at Omori, where he was the Senior British Officer, in fact he mentions in his book two of my HMS Indefatigable *shipmates by name, Lieut. (A) Ian Darby RNZNVR and Lieut. Cdr. (A) Jimmy Crossman RNVR.*

But first, to set the scene, I quote from the brilliant writings of a man who has acquainted the world with his personal experiences, observations and research of the Japanese; famous author Australian Russell Braddon.

Of all the accounts I have read of the events leading up to Pearl Harbour, his is by far the easiest to understand:

'The Other Hundred Years War 1941—2041'

What with goddesses and dragons, divinely created islands and emperors, shoguns (who did the emperor's actual ruling) and the samurai (who did their shogun's dirty work) Japan's beginnings would have addled the brains of any Westerner. Indeed, Kenichi Yoshida (whose father was to become Japan's most famous Prime Minister in the early years of reconstruction after World War II) is very funny on the subject. 'Make believe' is what he calls it.

But first there had been the Emperor Meiji.

Meiji had set about modernizing and motivating a nation that was feudal. From 1890 onwards, therefore, and even after his death, until 1945, every school child in Japan, every school day of his life, dedicated himself to his Emperor.

Every morning of every school day every pupil bowed in the direction of the Imperial Palace—'Worshipping at a distance'—then repeated by heart the long Imperial Rescript on Education, and finally waited breathless for the question, 'What is your dearest ambition?'

To which, in passionate unison, the entire school responded, 'To die for the

Emperor'.

Meiji gave them their first opportunity to do so in 1894, when he allowed his Army to be provoked into occupying Seoul. This distressed not only the Emperor of Korea, who took prompt refuge in the Russian Embassy, but also the Emperor of China, who sent his navy to Korea's assistance. When the Japanese sank his navy, however, the Chinese sued for peace, and surrendered not only the island of Taiwan and the Manchurian peninsula of Kwantung, but the right to protect Korea as well.

Unfortunately, though, Korea's border touched that of Russia, and Czar Nicholas cared not at all for the idea of Japanese neighbours. With the full support of France and Germany, Nicholas required Japan to forego the fruits of her first foreign conquest. Explaining to his people that Japan may now 'eat stones and drink gall', indeed 'endure the unendurable', Emperor Meiji accepted the terms of this so called Triple Intervention. Japan could not defy the collective might of three great powers; but that was not to say that later she would be unable to pick them off one by one.

Russia's turn came surprisingly early. In 1904, without declaring war, the Japanese Navy made a daring raid on the Czar's Asiatic Fleet in Port Arthur, sank it and blockaded the Port while the Japanese Army laid seige to the Czar's Army in its formidable fortress.

Thus provoked, Nicholas dispatched his mighty Baltic Fleet three quarters of the way round the globe to raise the seige and punish the Japanese. Britain (with whom Japan had the forethought to sign an alliance in 1902) and America (whose President Theodore Roosevelt had promised his good offices should the Russians win) awaited the outcome, enthralled.

Just in time, Port Arthur's fortress fell. At a cost of 20,000 lives, the Japanese had captured 25,000 Russians (whom they treated with great chivalry) and 500 guns. Better still, they had freed Admiral Togo's fleet from its task of blockading the harbour. Togo at once sailed southwards, deployed his fleet in the Strait that separated Japan from Korea, and lay in wait.

The Czar's great Baltic Fleet steamed into the strait and was classically outmanouevred. The Japanese sank twenty capital ships, captured five more and drowned 12,000 Russians for the loss of 116 of their own sailors. Five years later, adding insult to injury, they annexed Korea. Russia's humiliation was complete; but the Triple Intervention had only been partially avenged, and the Japanese have long memories. Which did not fail them in 1914 when Britain declared war on Germany. As Britain's ally, Japan promptly seized the German leased port of Tsingtao and every German-held island in the Pacific. France's turn would come next. But not immediately. First, in 1915, while the rest of the world was preoccupied with Germany, Japan launched her second unprovoked attack on China, was swiftly victorious and marked her victory with a list of 21 demands to which the Chinese were required to accede promptly. Whereupon the British and Americans stepped in and virtually stripped Japan of the fruits of her second Chinese war. It was 1895 all over again; and worse was to come.

In 1921, Japan's alliance with Britain was due for renewal. Britain had already indicated that it was her intention to renew, and Hirohito's visit (as Crown Prince) to England had been such a success that the Japanese were confident that it would be renewed. After all, had not the Prince of Wales been his constant companion? Had not King George V himself been positively paternal? Had not Lloyd George, the Prime Minister, been both deferential and flattering?

But the Japanese had not given sufficient consideration to the role now being played in world affairs by America who, for the cost of a mere hundred thousand lives, was claiming to be the predominant victor of World War I. And America was displeased with Japan.

Displeased not only because of her recent adventure in China (for which, since it had lately had the good sense to become a Republic rather than an Empire, America now nursed an especially tender regard) but also because Japan was proving truculent on the subject of naval limitations. In point of fact, was even demanding the right to build the same tonnage of capital ships as America herself. Exerting all of its post-war influence, Washington therefore persuaded Whitehall to renege on the promised renewal of the Anglo-Japanese Alliance. The Japanese were outraged.

Washington, however had not finished demolishing Japan's pride. In 1924 it included the Japanese in the category of 'orientals' virtually banned from immigration into the United States. To have her would-be emigrants to California banned, was loss of face enough to Japan; but to have them labelled 'orientals', as if they were mere Chinese was intolerable.

Every Western nation, it now seemed to the Japanese, had the right to settle where it wished; they were denied the right because they were yellow. Every Western nation had had for centuries the right to seize foreign territory and colonise it; they, in the so-called interests of world peace, were denied it.

No wonder their Prince Konoye had recently written that 'Pacifism is by no means necessarily identified with justice and morality.' And how proper it was that he had also insisted upon 'the abolition of economic imperialism, and of discrimination between the yellow races and the white.'

By 1924, therefore, Japan (though by no means forgetful of France's thirty-year-old slight) had become obsessed with the idea that she was the victim of an Anglo-American conspiracy to keep her navy less prestigious than theirs, and to deny her the right of colonial expansion. Reminding herself that Britain's colonies studded the surface of the world, and that America's record in relation to the Mexicans, the Panamanians and the Hawaiians, to name only a few, was no more selfless than its recently acquired passion for the Chinese, Japan began to seethe.

China became the focal point of her rage. China was Japan's sister civilization. In decay and disarray, it was to Japan she should be looking for rescue from her own corruption, Soviet ambitions and Western exploitation.

China needed development, and Japan was the one nation entitled to help develop it—and, in the process, to provide herself with a huge colony for her would-be emigrants and a huge market for her exports, which the onset of the world depression had already decimated.

In 1931, therefore, Japan embarked on her third invasion of the Chinese mainland, describing her substantial campaign in Manchuria merely as an Incident, so as not to provoke the League of Nations unduly. At which America baldly declared her action to be a war of aggression and persuaded the League of Nations (of which it was not a member) to follow its example. Aware of the fact that this example might well be followed, Japan decided that, if the League of Nations were so 'rude' as to criticize her by name, she would leave it. She was criticised by name, and the rudeness of it infuriated her.

Preferring the million square miles of China she had virtually occupied, and the vast new market for her manufactured goods that she had thereby acquired, to international approbation, Japan ostentatiously resigned her membership of the League.

'What guarantee is there,' Matsuoka demanded of the League in his final address, 'that what you call world opinion is not mistaken? We Japanese are resigned to undergoing a period of tribulation. Certain people in Europe and America are seeking to crucify Japan here and now in the twentieth century.'

The period of tribulation that followed was China's, however, not Japan's; Manchuria being transformed into a puppet state and one Chinese city after another being put to the sword. Nanking fell on 7 December, 1937, after resistance as stubborn as Shanghai's had been. In the ensuing month, the 100,000 Japanese victors murdered and tortured to death 200,000 Chinese surrendered soldiers and civilians, and raped some 20,000 women. The western world was outraged.

Not everyone in Japan approved this policy of blatant aggression. Some even warned that it would lead to war with the United States and Britain. The militarists first silenced this body of opinion by assassinating its spokesmen, and then, adopting Hitler as their mentor, made adherence to their own philosophy obligatory. Any contrary opinions were branded 'wrong thinking'; and wrong thinking attracted the instant attentions of the Thought Police, whose methods were arbitrary and brutal.

Hitler's subsequent Blitzkrieg did nothing to undermine the overweening confidence of the militarists. Britain was on the brink of defeat, Europe had already succumbed, Russia had been invaded and America was palpably anxious *not* to go to war. There was no adventure that Japan could not now risk.

Should she so wish, and despite her Neutrality Pact with Russia, signed only months before, she could seize Siberia—and proposed doing so provided only that Hitler's march on Moscow did not falter. Or she could tighten the Navy's noose round the throat of Hong Kong (at whose border Japanese marines were impatiently awaiting the order to advance) and snuff out its life as a British colony. Or, easiest of all, she could at last avenge herself upon France, the third of 1895's insolent interventionists, by seizing its helpless colony in Indo China. Barely bothering to camouflage aggression as diplomacy, she persuaded the governor of northern Indo China (who could hope for no support from either Occupied France or its German masters) to allow her access to that province. And then, abandoning her plan to invade Siberia, because Hitler's offensive had stalled in the snow just outside Moscow, she began to move her massive Manchurian-based army southward, and brazenly occupied the whole of Indo China.

Three days later, Hitler agreed to the formation of a Tripartite Pact by which Japan's fate became inextricably linked with that of Italy and Germany. Implicit in that Pact was the understanding that, using Indo China as her spring board, Japan would immediately go to war with Germany's arch enemy, Britain. Japan, however, delayed—to discover whether Britain and America would offer her sufficient inducement to stay out of Hitler's war.

Churchill, preoccupied by the onslaughts of Germany and Italy, left the decision to Roosevelt; and Roosevelt decided that America, Britain and Holland should compel Japan's withdrawal from China and Indo China by denying her those supplies of oil, iron ore and scrap iron without which both her economy and her military machine would founder.

By late 1941, Japan thus found herself opposed by a second Triple Intervention a thousand times more deadly, and ten thousand times more provocative, than the first.

It left her with three options. To accept Roosevelt's terms, and die of shame. To ignore them, and watch her factories and war machines seize up. Or to reject them, go to war and take by force the oil and iron she needed.

I refer to: ***Japan and her Destiny*** *by Mamoru Shigemitsu which is self explanatory and provides an indication of the Japanese point of view.*

Edited by Major General F. S. G. Piggot and translated by Oswald White.

Author's Preface

The events which took place at home and abroad during some twenty years of the *Showa** Era formed the most turbulent epoch in the history of Japan; combined with her defeat in war, they brought about a revolution unprecedented since the opening of the country. This revolution still continues.

The storms and unrest were, from first to last, mainly in connection with the problem of China. As Minister at the outbreak of the Manchurian Crisis, and, later on, during the war as Ambassador, I represented Japan in China. Subsequent to the Manchurian Crisis I held posts whence I could observe clearly world tendencies: for three years at the nerve-centre as Vice-Minister for Foreign Affairs; from 1936 to the end of 1938 as Ambassador to the Soviet

---

* *(Name of the present era which began in 1926.)*

Union, the mainspring of world disturbance; then, until June 1941, as Ambassador in England, the political focus of Western Europe; and finally, after Japan's entry into the war, for two years as Foreign Minister.

Following on Japan's defeat I stood my trial for two and a half years at the International War Crimes Tribunal in Tokyo; during that time, day after day, I had the opportunity of listening to a great deal of evidence by the Prosecution, and rebuttals thereto by the Defence Counsel. Included in these exchanges were incidents of which up till then I had not known; also developments of many others which I had not previously fully understood and which became clear for the first time. If this was the case with me, who, throughout the whole turbulent period was in a position of considerable responsibility, both in home and foreign affairs, so much the more was it so with those without direct responsibility; they could not possibly comprehend the development of many of the internal and external events during these years. I believe that it is not only a matter of interest to myself to classify and unravel the evidence produced during the two and a half years of the Trial as objectively as possible; I am convinced also that the storms of *Showa*, being unique events in our history, should be studied carefully by my countrymen, for they contain much food for thought in connection with the future rebuilding of our country. These Memoirs are mainly based on knowledge acquired during my past appointments, supplemented by notes made at the Trial, and from memory. They contain also very valuable material heard from those of my fellow countrymen directly responsible for leading Japan in the past, who lived with me in prison for four years.

It is not easy to apportion fairly the responsibility for the turmoil in the *Showa* Era. I think it will be necessary for skilled historians to devote much time to the matter in the future. It is unnecessary to say that I am not attempting myself to make a considered historical judgment; I merely think it is my duty, as a participant in these events, to record accurately my own beliefs and to add some observations thereon, as a contribution to history.

The Tokyo War Crimes Tribunal was, of course, a military trial of the vanquished by the victors, one-sided, partisan and conducted by those against whom it was submitted that Japan had committed international crimes. The majority of judges recognized she had done so, but the minority (excluding the Philippine judge) in their judgment took an entirely contrary view; the Indian judge, Mr. Pal, in particular, considered the actions of Japan as being fully justified. As regards the Tokyo Trials themselves, world opinion has already been formed. Students of history must not overlook the minority judgment and concentrate merely on the decisions of the majority; furthermore, as regards the evidence at the Trial, it is important that full attention be paid to the submissions of the Defence Counsel, whether they were accepted by the Court or not.

The more the causes of the storms of *Showa*, their course and their influence on Japan are studied scientifically, the better it will be for the future of my countrymen.

Translator Oswald White wrote:

The Code of Military Honour

In Japan, poets and romantic writers likened the warrior to the cherry blossom. The cherry tree was cultivated not for its fruit, but for its flower, which the Japanese have taken to their hearts as the symbol of purity, of loyalty and of patriotism. Its beauty is short-lived. One moment the tree is decked out in ethereal beauty. The next a wind arises and the petals flutter to the ground. But there is no cause for tears because next year the tree will present the same brave display. The life of the warrior was like that of the cherry blossom. It was dedicated to his country and when the time came it was laid down without hesitation.

Political parties

There were at this time two—the Seiyu and the Minsei. They had no settled political principles, though the former tended to represent agricultural interests and the latter financial (the country *versus* the towns). The old Constitution seriously restricted the powers of the Diet. If I may be allowed to interpolate a personal opinion, it would be that many of the defects in the Japanese political system arose out of this denial of all real power to the Diet.

Author Shigemitsu continues:

It was the American policy to prevent the establishment by other powers of spheres of influence in China; the policy took its stand on the doctrine of the 'open door and equal opportunity for all'. The aim was to interpose a barrier against 'colonization' in East Asia. It had, therefore, become a positive policy that sounded a warning against power diplomacy and expressed sympathy with racial aspirations.

When Japan defended Manchuria from Russian inroads, the Americans sided with her. But when Japan herself adopted a forward policy in China, the attitude changed to one of firm opposition to 'aggression'. American policy had always as its objective the liberation of China. She sympathized with the revolutionaries and in view of her own past history carefully watched the awakening of the Chinese people. Her policy, therefore, was all too different from that of Japan, which thought only of temporary advantage and was swayed by the ideas of the party or faction in power at the moment.

Since the Opium War, Britain had enjoyed a paramount position in China and controlled East Asia. When Japan emerged as a Great Power, it became advantageous to join hands with her; hence the Anglo-Japanese Alliance. But the U.S. was not so well pleased that the Alliance should buttress Britain's vast possessions and enable Japan to make a forward move in China. The First World War caused a change. In East Asia Britain now had to collaborate with the U.S. and not with Japan, because this had become a first principle with America. The Alliance was abrogated and thenceforward Britain and the U.S. adopted a common policy in China.

After the 'Manchurian Incident' the Stimson doctrine declared that the U.S. could not recognize this alteration of the *status quo ante*. America announced her support of China and her opposition to Japan. As Japan plunged further and further into China, the U.S. attitude stiffened. She denounced her treaty of commerce, and enforced the 'freezing' order. During the Washington negotiations, the American attitude towards East Asia never wavered.

The American world policy under Roosevelt relied on her national strength to enable her to realize her ideals both in the East and in the West. She decided that the Axis powers were aggressors and joined forces with Britain, France, Russia and the Netherlands to resist them. Neither would she come to terms with aggressors nor yield ground to them.

As Japan advanced southward, so the A.B.C.D. encirclement was drawn tighter and left Japan no option but to state whether she wanted peace or War.

OPENING OF HOSTILITIES

The Cabinet's Attitude to the Negotiations

The world was waiting for the storm to break in the Pacific. The U.S. mustered her fleet in Pearl Harbour. The British and the Dutch hastened their preparations. In Japan the 'starvation' theory prevailed. The new Cabinet and the Supreme Command spent night and day at Headquarters studying and re-studying that important decision taken in the Imperial Presence and their talks revolved round the Washington negotiations.

The Government drew up two draft proposals, A and B, which were carried at a Council before the Throne on November 5th. Based on a resolve to make war, orders were issued that the negotiations were to terminate on November 25th, later postponed to November 29th.

In the negotiations, the Japanese Government had more than once repeated the same proposal in a different form but the two parties were thinking on different lines and their aims were so diametrically opposed that this method had not brought the American attitude any nearer to the Japanese. The Americans had broken the Japanese cyphers and the Secretary of State knew the Japanese intentions in advance and could plan his response accordingly.

War fever had grown in Japan and Nagano, Chief of the Naval General Staff, who had at one time said that war was out of the question, had been converted to the view that, if an initial victory led to the capture of oil and other resources from the Dutch East Indies, then Japan need not fear a long war. Since to an island country, victory or defeat rested on mastery at sea, the Navy's estimate of prospects and its decision had a decisive bearing on the question whether or not to fight. The bold policy won the day—there was nothing for it but to go all out for a final victory. Now that the Navy had stepped out of the confines of military strategy and invaded the field of politics, there was no one left to combat their views. The Army itself had long resolved on war and welcomed the Navy's new attitude.

As for the negotiations, there were limits to the concessions Japan could make. So long as the Army and Navy were confident of the issue, they could see no reason to compromise at the expense of their self-respect. The Japanese Government, therefore, made its last proposals to the U.S. Government, while in the Diet the Prime Minister and the Minister for Foreign Affairs adopted a firm attitude and indicated that there were limits beyond which concessions could not be made.

Final Negotiations

Proposal A made to the Americans was a final attempt at agreement on the lines of the preceding talks. If an understanding was not reached under A, then B proposed that Japan should withdraw her troops from South to North Indo-China, the U.S. should cease supporting Chiang Kai-shek and cancel the freezing order and a new point of departure could be found in the more cordial atmosphere that would result. In accordance with instructions, therefore, Nomura presented A.

There was a sense of urgency, since a time-limit had been decided upon. Nomura and Kurusu did their best and on November 20th presented B, as to which Togo had telegraphed them that it did not admit of compromise. The unconciliatory attitude was at once reflected in the American reaction and Cordell Hull, who understood the Japanese attitude from his intercepts, placed no faith in the protestations of the two diplomats. The Americans concluded that Japan was conceding nothing; in fact, judging from her deeds, she was becoming more stubborn than ever. Moreover they entertained doubts as to the reason why Kurusu had been sent, did not trust him and redoubled their suspicions.

The Secretary of State consulted with the signatories of the Nine Power Pact. By now the U.S. had abandoned procrastinating tactics and proposed to make certain of Japan's hostile intentions. They handed a reply on November 26th. It summarized the views of the associating powers and was firmer in tone than any previous communicaion. A *modus vivendi* had been drawn up at the request of the American Army but, in deference to the wishes of China and of Britain, this reply was presented instead. To put it briefly, the American reply demanded that the situation before the 'Manchurian Incident' should be restored. Japan had understood that she was being asked to withdraw her troops from Manchuria also, neither Roosevelt nor Hull imagined that Japan would comply. Indeed they both had a distinct impression that for Japan it would be the signal for war.

The vital point of the negotiations was really recognition of the state of Manchuokuo. That was the very minimum of what Japan had hoped to gain.

Withdrawal of troops from that country meant the dissolution of Manchoukuo. The Cabinet's attitude had already been determined in the Liaison Conference of November 15th and the Japanese Government interpreted the latest American proposal as an ultimatum demanding the impossible.

The negotiations had culminated in a crisis. According to official documents, the Americans regarded their proposal as the final stage in the negotiations, they anticipated that Japan would reject it and they ordered all Army and Navy stations in the Pacific to be alerted. Churchill announced that, if war broke out, Britain would join in within the hour. In Japan the Supreme Command and the Government had also made their decision.

From the beginning there had been fundamental misunderstandings on both sides. Many who took a hand in the negotiations had ideas different from those of Japan and their efforts had only added to the complications. The U.S. was determined to assist Britain to crush Nazi Germany and was prepared to go to war for the purpose. Had Japan been willing to liquidate her commitments under the Tripartite Alliance, to change over to a policy of collaboration with America and Britain and to withdraw her troops from China and Indo-China, then the U.S. might have made concessions in regard to Manchoukuo and striven for an understanding.

There is no reason to doubt the good intentions and zeal of Japan's representative* but the Army and Navy would not budge an inch from the stand they had taken. The Americans played for time to complete their preparations against attack. The Japanese Army and Navy bided their time to resort to direct action. From start to finish the negotiations were cumbered with contradictions and cross-purposes.

On December 1st a Council before the Throne deliberated upon a proposal to make war on the U.S., Britain and the Netherlands and finally decided on war.

Squadron sets out; Final Notification

A plan of operations was decided. A squadron was ordered to assemble at the Kuriles. 'If the U.S. remains obdurate and there is finally no hope of settlement, war opens on X Day and the enemy is to be "at once attacked".' The squadron would carry secret instructions but was to return if the negotiations were concluded satisfactorily. On X Day Nomura and Kurusu were to interview the Secretary of State before the attack and on Government instructions were to notify him that the negotiations were closed.

The Foreign Office regarded it as essential under The Hague Treaty that advance notice should be given of the opening of hostilities. The Supreme Command had no objection but the Navy insisted that the interval should be as short as possible in order to increase the advantage of a surprise attack. The point was left in the hands of the Supreme Command and the Foreign

---

* *Or representatives. There were two at the end.—Ed.*

Minister; on the insistence of the Naval General Staff, the interval was reduced to thirty minutes. The Foreign Office was to telegraph instructions to the Ambassadors by the close of the previous day. The notice was to be confined to a formal statement that the negotiations were closed and the essential details were to be telegraphed last. The Americans, however, read all the Government's important telegrams and knew beforehand.

Conference of Senior Statesmen

Preparations were made secretly and with despatch. A Military Council was held and, also, on November 29th, a conference of the senior statesmen. To the latter the Government explained the general circumstances and the course of the negotiations. Wakatsuki expressed concern at the economic situation but no particular questions were asked. Thereafter, the senior statesmen were summoned to an Audience and requested to give their views.

At this important meeting in the Palace no one opposed the war, no one advanced any considered views as to the future of the country. Public opinion was inflamed and thinking people had for days been dreading the outcome. In summoning the statesmen to the Palace and explaining the situation, the Government were already doing something out of the ordinary. The summons to an Audience at which they were invited to express their views was a complete break with precedent. Was it not because the Emperor was anxious to ascertain their views? They could not have doubted it. And yet, though the highest authority in the land, their Emperor, had given them this wonderful opportunity of expressing their views, why, if any one of them opposed the war (and actually they did), did not one single person summon all his courage and tell the naked truth? Perhaps they thought that they must go through with it now, that a *volte face* was impossible. Shall we say that they were impelled by the spirit of defeatism towards the Army?

Before this, H.I.H. Prince Takamatsu had suddenly, at the eleventh hour, informed the Emperor that the Navy still had misgivings and was opposed to war. H.I.M. had at once summoned the Minister Shimada and the Chief of the N.G.S. Nagano and had earnestly enquired what the Navy really thought. Both replied that the Navy's decision for war and its conviction of victory were exactly as had been decided by the Liaison Conference. Everything, therefore, was carried out as anticipated by the Liaison Conference, the Conference in the Imperial Presence was convened on December 1st, all arrangements were determined and the Emperor eventually approved the War Declaration.

The Surprise Attack of December 8th, 1941

In the early dawn of December 8th telephones in Tokyo were busy. The great success of the attack on Pearl Harbour was already known to those in the inner circles and communicated to their friends. The radio announced the outbreak of war and read the Imperial Decree. The citizens listened respectfully. They rejoiced at the good news and breathed a sigh of relief. It was not entirely due to the good news. They had been held in a state of suspense so long and now that waiting was over they sighed with relief, as a Japanese might well do, and as Japanese they resolved to go through with it to the end and smash the enemy. Nobody had time to reflect what it all meant.

The night before Ambassador Grew had received a personal message from the President to the Emperor urging peace and had requested Foreign Minister Togo to present it. But it was all too late. In the depth of the night Togo went to the Palace and delivered the President's telegram. By that time the attack had already begun. As the fateful day approached, delivery of telegrams to the British and American Embassies, including the President's appeal, had been delayed under instructions from Supreme Headquarters.

Togo called Grew to the Foreign Office at the same time as he had instructed Nomura and Kurusu to deliver the notice that negotiations were closed and handed him a copy. At that moment Grew thought that it was the reply to the President's appeal since he had not yet heard of the Pearl Harbour attack. When he returned to the Embassy outside communications had been cut.

There is no need for me to relate here the Japanese attack on Pearl Harbour. It has been well documented and publicised world wide. However, as we shall see later, it has become an impressive monument—not only to those who died that day, but to the thousands who died as a result of this specific attack over the next four years in the Pacific.

'The Other 100 Year War' *by Russell Braddon continues:-*

By 1937, Australia and New Zealand had become extremely anxious. In the event of war, Australia had enquired, would Britain be able to send a fleet to defend the Far East?

Why not station part of a fleet in Singapore even in peacetime? New Zealand had suggested.

Neither Dominion had been prepared to contribute a penny toward the cost of this aspect of Imperial Defence, of course, but both were determined constantly to remind Britain of her Imperial obligations; and it was then that the lies began.

If the Japanese should go to war with the British Empire, the British Government declared, a British fleet large and strong enough to contain the Japanese navy would instantly be despatched to the East—even though Britain might at the same time be involved in a war in Europe.

Worse, in 1938 Prime Minister Chamberlain of Britain had sought to dispel the nagging doubts of Australia's Prime Minister by insisting that: 'The idea that, in the event of war, we might not be able to defend our overseas possessions is entirely false.' Chamberlain had known at that time that the

Admiralty would have been able to despatch only one capital ship eastwards to deter an entire navy, but he had not hesitated to lie. And when Lieutenant General Sir William Dobbie, GOC in Malaya, had reported that *his* command was impressed with the performance of the Japanese in China; that he personally believed (contrary to expert opinion) that the end-of-year monsoon season could well be the time they would choose to invade Malaya; and that Singapore's air force was inadequate, he had promptly been relieved of his command.

Nevertheless, by 1939, far from rejecting the idea that Britain 'might not be able to defend her overseas possessions', Chamberlain's Government had come to accept the idea that they could *only* be held with the active co-operation of the United States of America—which co-operation seemed most unlikely to be forthcoming. The Dominions, however, were never appraised of this dismal fact.

Thus, by the time Italy had entered the war and France had surrendered, Singapore had become a naval base without a navy, and the Malayan Peninsula had become virtually indefensible. Chamberlain, however, had confided none of this to the Australian government; and his successor, Churchill, had merely asked Canberra to send one army division and two squadrons of aircraft to help strengthen Malaya's land and air defences.

Doubtless Chamberlain believed his lies justified, and Churchill could have cited the exigences both of war and of diplomacy to justify the despatch of British, Indian and Australian troops to a colony that was doomed.

As Admiral Sir Frank Twiss told me 'If anybody ever wanted to write a handbook for Staff College students on ''How NOT to run a Campaign'', they need look no further than the fall of Singapore and Java.'

This unhappy episode is fortunately too diverse and political to be other than 'referred to' in this volume!

Entitled READ THIS ALONE—AND THE WAR CAN BE WON, a Japanese booklet left the Emperor's soldiers (to each of whom it was issued) in no doubt as to why they must fight, whom they must fight and how they must fight them.

'The New Restoration of the 1930's has come about in response to the Imperial desire for peace in the Far East,' it began. 'Its task is the rescue of Asia from white aggression. Already Japan, the pioneer in this movement, has rescued Manchuria from the ambitions of the Soviets, and set China free from the extortions of the Anglo Americans.'

Having thus set the scene, the stage directions for the coming invasion of Malaya followed, succinct and explicit.

'Treat the natives with kindness,' the booklet commanded, 'but do not expect too much of them.'

'You may be killed in action,' it conceded, 'but don't die of disease.' Clearly, to allow oneself to die of disease was wrong thinking in its most reprehensible form. The author of the booklet, having given the matter further thought, reverted to it almost immediately. 'Do not,' he instructed, 'fall ill.'

The booklet was read by soldiers packed into the unventilated holds of ships that were sailing slowly towards Malaya through 120 degrees of tropical heat: it reminded them, though, that it was not only they who were suffering. 'Be kind,' it exhorted, 'to the horses.'

Nor would heat and disease be the sole dangers they would have to face once the voyage was over and the beach-head taken. 'If you discover a dangerous snake,' they were adjured, 'you must kill it. You should also swallow its liver raw, and cook and eat the meat. There is no better medicine for strengthening the body.'

Finally, as we who were already in Malaya had so often been told, there was the vexed subject of the jungle—into which, in our six wearisome months of training, we had ventured only once. About a mile. Just enough to demonstrate to us how disagreeable it was, and why our High Command had decided to meet any future invader either on Malaya's narrow roads or in the rubber plantations on either side of them. Where we would kindly not damage the trees because the sultans wouldn't like it. (Nor apparently did Hirohito, who enquired anxiously, once it had been decided to go to war, whether Malaya's rubber plantations would be damaged. He was doubtless reassured to learn that the Japanese Army intended to advance down Malaya's narrow roads only in small units led by a few tanks. 'That way,' he was told, 'there should be little danger of damaging the rubber forests.')

READ THIS ALONE was fatally perceptive on the aforesaid vexed subject of the jungle. 'By jungle is meant dense forest,' it said. 'This type of terrain is regarded by the weak-spirited as impenetrable, and for this very reason—in order to outmanoeuvre them—we must from time to time force our way through it. With proper preparation, and determination, it can be done.'

As if that simple truth were not damaging enough to our chances of victory, the booklet then drove a final nail into our coffin. 'If a man can pass,' it observed, 'so can a motor vehicle. If the road is too narrow, cut a way through. If there is a cliff in the way, let forty or fifty men in a bunch haul you up it.'

Haul you up it, indeed! *WE* had been conditioned to believe we'd done well if we succeeded in cajoling back on to the road a truck bogged twenty yards into a perfectly flat plantation. In all their planning, though, the Japanese were (and are again today) infinitely more positive than we. We aimed merely at halting them; they aimed at nothing less than our destruction.

'To check the withdrawal of enemy forces,' every third class private in the Japanese army read, 'one of your principal aims should be to outflank and gain control of catchment areas, wells and springs to his rear.' It was basic tactics like that that destroyed us.

And so, from mere tactics, to their morale.

'The long voyage, the sweltering march—all have been for this. When you encounter the enemy, after landing, regard yourself as an avenger come face to face at last with his father's murderer. The discomforts of a long sea voyage, and the rigours of the march, have all been but months of waiting for this moment when you may slay your enemy.

'Here before you is the man whose death will lighten your heart of its burden of brooding anger. Should you fail to destroy him, you may never rest in peace—and the first blow is always the vital one!'

And now came a morsel of that cheap invective that had been our staple diet. But it was only a morsel; and it came at exactly the right place in a heavy meal. 'Westerners,' the booklet jeered, 'being very superior people, very cowardly and effeminate, have an intense dislike of fighting in rain, mist or darkness. Night, though excellent for dancing, they cannot conceive of as a proper time for war. IN THIS, if we seize upon it, lies our great opportunity. The final realities of our holy crusade will come on the battlefield ahead.'

From Tokyo, General Tojo broadcast even more succinctly. Vowing that Japan had done all in her power to avert the war upon which she was now embarked, reminding his captive audience that in 2600 years Japan had never been defeated, he promised his fellow countrymen, 'Final victory'.

It is a miracle that Australian Russell Braddon is alive today. An extract from his experiences cannot be omitted from an appraisal of the evil we were fighting. Captured near Yong Peng in Malaya in 1941, Russell Braddon was a POW until August 1945. In his famous book **The Naked Island** *he recalls:*

'Stop there,' I heard the officer's clear voice directed as us, 'stop and surrender or we'll all be shot'—and my absurd Army training made me falter for a second and look back. I saw Herc already bleeding from a wound in the arm; and Sandshoes and the sergeant lying on the ground; and the officer standing quite still, the sigs looking at him questioningly and Harry in outrage. Just for a second we faltered. As in any race, when one falters, it was then too late. The path to the jungle was cut by a Jap soldier with a tommy gun. We stood still, our only chance lost. Then, very slowly, very foolishly and with a sense of utter unreality, I put up my hands.

At that moment all that occurred to me was that this procedure was completely disgraceful. I have not—since then—changed my mind. I have no doubt at all that I should have continued running. One does not win battles by standing still and extending the arms upwards in the hope that one's foes have read the Hague Convention concerning the treatment of prisoners of war. It was unfortunate that the Army had trained me sufficiently neither to disobey instantly and without hesitation, nor to obey implicitly and without compunction. Accordingly, I had done neither: and I now stood in the recognised pose of one who optimistically seeks mercy from a conqueror whose reputation is for being wholly merciless.

The enemy patrol closed in on us. Black-whiskered men, with smutty eyes and the squat pudding faces of bullies. They snatched off our watches first of all—and then belted us with rifle butts because these did not point to the north as they swung them around under the ludicrous impression that they were compasses, they made dirty gestures at the photographs of the women-folk they took from our wallets. They threw the money in the wallets away, saying, 'Dammé, dammé, Englishu dollars'; and pointing at the King's head on the notes, they commented: 'Georgey Six number ten. Tojo number one!' And all the time two Tamils stood in the background murmuring quietly to one another, their hips tight swathed in dirty check sarongs and their wide-splayed feet drawing restless patterns in the bare soil of the rubber plantation.

'Done a good job, haven't you, Joe?' demanded Harry savagely—but they wouldn't meet his eye. Just kept on drawing in the dirt with their toes.

Hugh picked up a $10 bill and stuffed it defiantly back in his pocket. Then they tied us up with wire, lashing it round our wrists, which were crossed behind our backs and looped to our throats. They prodded us on to the edge of a drain in the rubber. We sat with our legs in it, while they set their machine-guns up facing us and about ten yards away.

'That bloody intelligence officer would have to be right this time of all times, wouldn't he?' demanded Harry—we all knew that he referred to the 'Japanese take no prisoners' report, and Herc, bleeding badly, nodded rather wanly.

'We must die bravely,' said the officer desperately—at which the sergeant howled for mercy. Howled and pleaded, incredibly craven. Neither he nor Sandshoes had been hit at all when I had seen them prostrate on the ground, merely frightened. The sergeant continued to bawl lustily. We sat, the nine of us, side by side, on the edge of our ready-dug grave.

The Japanese machine-gunner lay down and peered along his barrel. It was my twenty-first birthday and I was not happy.

At the first long volley of shots I jerked rigid, dragging my right wrist out of its wire binding, but experiencing no emotion other than a faint surprise that I was still alive. A second volley rang out, and still the anticipated tearing of bullets into flesh was absent. Then I looked up and realised that the machine-gun was firing not at us in the trench but up the slight rise at a solitary figure who dashed across the skyline. Japanese soldiers were fanning quickly out through the rubber and his flight was obviously hopeless. In a few moments he was dragged down the hill to where we sat. He was an officer of our regiment, fair-haired, tall and lean. They tied him up with his own puttees, at which he protested indignantly. He wore that most useless of all weaons, a .45 revolver. His captors quickly took it from him.

Under cover of all this, I had untied Hugh, and he and the sigs were about to unloose Sandshoes, when the sergeant noticed what was happening and let out a wail of terror which got us all lashed up again, this time with a narrow, cutting rope. I was beginning not to love the sergeant.

The Japanese, of whom there were about fifteen, held a conference. They were squat, compact figures with coarse puttees, canvas, rubber-soled, web-toed boots, smooth brown hands, heavy black eyebrows across broad unintelligent foreheads, and ugly battle helmets. Each man wore two belts—one to keep his pants up and one to hold his grenades, his identity disc and his religious charm—and when they removed their helmets, they wore caps, and when the took off their caps, their heads had been shaved until only a harsh black stubble remained. They handled their weapons as if they had been born with them. They were the complete fighting animal.

Mopping his forehead with the silk scarf which they all carried—some painted with rising Suns, others with dirty pictures—their leader surveyed us morosely and idly waved the revolver he had taken from our latest recruit. They conferred in low voices of a pleasant tone, which contrasted strikingly with the screams and bellows they invariably used when speaking to us.

The leader addressed us, his left hand resting proudly on the hilt of a cheap-looking sword, his right clutching the revolver. He spoke little English.

'You,' he said, pointing to Roy, 'age-u?' Roy looked blank, so I told him that the little ape wanted to know how old he was.

'Twenty,' said Roy.

'Twenty-ka?' queried the leader and looked most surprised.

'You?' he said, pointing to Hugh.

'Twenty,' said Hugh.

'You?' continued the Jap to Rene.

'Twenty,' said Rene.

'You?' he demanded of me.

'Twenty-one,' I told him. He muttered to himself, then turned to his men and informed them, with a contemptuous gesture at us, 'Ni-ju.' They all registered astonishment.

'Baby,' he said. 'Twenty no good. Nippon soldier twenty-four. Nippon soldier Number One, Englishu soldier Number Ten.'

'Balls,' replied Hugh, whereupon the Jap—who did not understand the word but could not mistake the inflection—hit him with the butt of the revolver.

"You,' he pointed at me, 'wife-u-ka?'

'No wife,' I told him.

'Baby-ka?' he persisted.

'Not even any babies,' I assured him. He hit me with the revolver butt. He asked Rene and Roy the same questions; they gave the same answers—and received the same treatment. Harry, short, confident and thirty-ish, watched all this with his shrewd farmer's eye.

'You,' the Jap asked him, 'wife-u-ka?'

Harry, the bachelor, smiled his crooked smile. 'Yeah,' he said boldly.

'Yes?' questioned the Jap, delighted.

'Sure,' said Harry; and then, driving home is advantage, added: 'Three wives and eight babies.'

This information was received with open admiration by all the Japs who at once made lewd gestures in Harry's direction and give him a cigarette, placing it carefully in his mouth. Harry continued to smile—we had learnt our first lesson in Japanese psychology. Our execution was for the moment forgotten.

We marched the rest of that day and much of the night in grim silence. Marched with a speed and sureness that was astounding. We did not once see a road; we were usually in jungle; when we did hit a clearing, it came as no surprise to the Japs, who were instantly greeted by a Malay who had hot food ready. This clockwork organisation of fifth-column sympathisers and the time-table marching was almost incredible when one realised that the Japs who guarded us, had been in Malaya only six weeks and that they had spent the previous seven years fighting in China. It was explained only when one saw their cheap wrist-compasses (strapped on like watches) and the map by which they marched—a map which ignored all main routes and gave only creeks, padi tracks, jungle pads, native huts.

Every minute detail was there. Where our British maps would have marked nothing but jungle and a few contour lines, these Japs marched according to a plan that looked like a route through London. Every yard or so of their progress had been charted by twenty years or so of Japanese tailors, photographers, launderers, planters, miners and brothel-keepers in the period before the war. Now those years of work bore the fruits that were desired of them in the sure passage through the Malayan wilderness of this and a thousand other roving Japanese patrols.

At midnight we halted and the patrol slept—leaving us always heavily guarded. It was unnecessary. We slept, too. Nothing could have kept us awake.

Bound and force marched through the jungle barefoot we were severely manhandled and each of us was punched and kicked 100 times.

During those forty-eight hours we received one lot of water—about three mouthfuls each—and four coconuts. I managed also to scrape in a double handful of fly-blown rice off the Japs' garbage heap. This worked out at a spoonful each. We ate some of the drying copra but, though it makes good oil, it can hardly be described as appetising. Dysentry broke out, which was awkward . . . *they then joined other POWs—Ed.*

The new prisoners were all either English troops or Malay volunteers and were magnificent in their courage. During the night quite a few men were chosen by torchlight for questioning—mainly on the use of gas, about which none of us knew anything. They were taken outside and then, in the semi-gloom, just visible through the hole in the wall, stabbed and bashed to death. They died shouting defiance. At the end of the forty-eight hours, those of us who were left were herded into the truck—one of ours captured in the ambushed convoy—and driven off. We stood in sticky blood and the road on both sides for ten miles bore witness to the fury with which British troops had fought the enemy. No Japanese bodies remained—they were always swiftly removed—but the corpses of our own men lay everywhere, blackening and bloating in the sun like cattle in a drought.

The truck stopped suddenly. The driver had noticed an old Chinaman standing on the edge of the road. He was very old indeed and senile. The driver leapt out and with two other Japs battered him viciously. His cries brought more Nipponese troops to the scene. Soon there were hundreds. They decided to make a day of it and their preparations were soon complete. They set fire to the old man's head. As his hair blazed and he screamed the sort of screams that only burning men can scream they offered him water with which to extinguish the flames. When he seized the can of water it was boiling. He flung it over his head. The flames hissed out and he screamed even more piercingly. Petrol was poured on to the roasted scalp: a match applied: more boiling water offered. It was quite some time after he expired that the Japanese laughter and excitement died down. Rather like an English crowd at the conclusion of a closely-fought football match.

'Api,' they shouted in Malay to one another. *'Api: ayer panas. Api: ayer panas.'* Fire: hot water. Fire: hot water.

Chattering gaily, our driver got back into the truck. With a grind of gears and a jolt as the clutch was let carelessly up, we were on our way again.

We reached Ayer Hitham, where the superficially wounded were given some inadequate treatment by the Japanese and the seriously wounded were, we presumed, for no one ever saw them again, killed off. We slept the night in a school which reeked of death. In the morning one of the English soldiers produced a safety razor and blade. About thirty of us shaved with it. There was a well in the school yard which provided water for shaving and bathing and (in spite of rumours of a corpse in it), drinking. We were questioned, beaten up and moved to Batu Pahat.

At Batu Pahat we were questioned, beaten up and moved to Gemas. At Gemas we were questioned, beaten up (with especial fury because there the Australian 2/30th Battalion had staged a particularly successful ambush), and put into a cattle truck on a train. In all that time we had eaten only a few spoonfuls of rice. We had now been ten days with virtually no food at all and eight of us had marched about 180 miles in that time. It had become physically impossible any longer to attempt escape.

There was young Jimmy, then just eighteen years old, who had been collected with one hundred and thirty-four others of the wounded we abandoned at Parit Sulong and—having been tied up and knelt in the centre of the road—machine gunned. Jimmy's mate, also eighteen, and Jimmy himself (though both shot through the chest) still lived. Jimmy's mate writhed in pain and Jimmy lay across him, whispering frantically: 'Keep still, keep still.' But he could not keep still, so the Japanese noticed that he still lived and, tossing Jimmy off him and into the storm-water channel at the side of the road, lifted the slight figure to its feet and riddled it with tommy-gun bullets. Clinging to the weeds at the edge of the storm-water channel, Jimmy spent the next three hours in the black water. He saw the hundred and thirty-four machine-gunned men bayonetted and then set on fire with petrol and—after their incineration—systematically run over, backwards and forwards, by

Japanese-driven trucks.

Then the enemy marched out of Parit Sulong, stamping their feet and singing their Victory Song: but Jimmy found that he was too weak from his wounds and shock to clamber out of the canal. Too weak until wild pigs came out of the jungle onto the carnage of the moonlit road, and along with a few dogs, started eating the burnt flesh. Then, in horror, he leapt out of the channel and ran, mile after mile, through the night, until he collapsed in the jungle. For a week he wandered round, the bullet wound—which ran clean through his chest—full of swamp mud. Then he was captured: and although his chest seemed to be healing, in spite of the mud and the complete absence of treatment in our gaol, his eyes were constantly full of what he had seen. He and dozens of others had the same story to tell.

There was even Dusty Rhodes. Dusty was about five feet two inches tall, dark of complexion, strongly built in a squat kind of way, and not fearfully intelligent. He was in the middle thirties and tended not to understand things unless they were said slowly.

Dusty had escaped from Parit Sulong and had then swiftly become lost. Eventually he saw a British tank, so he knocked upon its side with his stick and, before it had occurred to him that the occupants who emerged from the tank looked strangely unlike Australians, had been captured by the Japanese. Here, however, native shrewdness intervened where intelligence could never shine. He, too, carried Mills bombs down his shirt front (a fact which the Japanese did not suspect in one who looked so harmless), so he shoved his stubby-fingered hand into his bosom, plucked out a grenade, deposited it carefully among his captors and then stepped smartly behind a rubber tree. When, after a shattering explosion, he deemed it safe to emerge, he was most gratified to observe that all the Japanese gentlemen were dead. He accordingly departed with great speed into the jungle and there, once more, lost himself.

Unfortunately, Dusty learnt only slowly. Two days later he came to another road and on it he observed another tank. Surely, thought Dusty, these are British tanks—with which he again rapped firmly on the side with his stick. To his astonishment he was instantly overwhelmed by what he declared roundly to be *'bloody battalions* of Japanese', who first relieved him of all his remaining Mills bombs, then treated him very roughly indeed and finally flung him into Pudu Gaol. By that time, it is regrettable to relate, Dusty had become firmly and irrevocably convinced that in Malaya *all* tanks were Japanese—and in this, of course, he was quite right.

It was the most apparent symbol of our greatest need—vitamins—and, at the same time, of the common man's indomitable humour under even the most humiliating of afflictions. For Rice Balls, to us, meant not one of the favourite dishes of the Japanese, but the ripping raw (by the denial of even a tiny quantity of Vitamin B2) of a man's scrotum and genitals. One felt first a faint discomfort, as of chafing. Then the skin split and peeled off an area which might spread from the genitals right down the inner thighs. This entire surface then became raw and sticky and painful. As one disconsolately surveyed the damage one could not help being reminded of our red-headed sergeant-major and his tinea that crept. By refusing us a spoonful each day of the worthless polishings taken off rice (and they could easily have given us a sackful), the Japanese wilfully condemned their prisoners to years of living with a scrotum that was red weeping flesh. It was a constant factor in one's life that varied between acute discomfort and acute pain. But it was always there—and it thereby had its effect upon everything one thought, everything one ate, everything one stole and upon every risk one was prepared to run to alleviate the avitaminosis of which it was the most degrading symptom. It was the outward and visible sign of a physical need which was to kill thousands and send hundreds of others blind, or near blind. And because the men who suffered this affliction ironically—and aptly—applied to it the name more commonly given to a food very close to the heart of every son of Nippon, it is fitting enough, however indelicate, to use it here. We ate rice. We ate rice only. Consequently we had Rice Balls.

Happy Feet were another symptom of the same thing—lack of vitamins. This scourge struck about half the men in gaol only, but made up the balance by striking them with a pain twice as severe as anything any of us had ever seen before. It inflicted them with a persistent series of searing stabs in the soles of their feet. The pain was like fire. But when they put their feet in water, the coolness immediately tore at them like ice, so that once again they moaned for warmth. As you looked at them, the flesh dropped off their bones, the light of youth from the eyes, the life from their faces. One was filled with a pity for them and a hatred for the enemy that nothing can remove.

Japanese Bastardry, as we Australians called it, applied to almost everything in our lives, but most of all because of the far-reaching effects it had—to our requests for drugs. Of these they had captured vast quantities and also had vast quantities of their own. Yet, despite the ready availability of emetin to cure dysentery, of quinine (the Dutch East Indies are the source of all quinine and the Japanese now owned all the Dutch East Indies) to quell our malaria, and of Vitamin B tablets (of which they had billions, for they are easy to manufacture) to counter the deficiencies of a rice diet, the little Nip constantly refused all requests for any of them. His best answer was: *'Ashita'*—'Tomorrow'—which, in the Jap mouth, means 'Never'; his more common reply was a savage bashing for him who was courageous enough to ask.

And, finally, with the introduction at this time of working parties, came that other Japanese refinement—food only for those who work. Needless to say, this did not mean that those men who lay ill and dying in the gaols and prison camps of Malaya starved, because whatever food the Japanese sent in as rations for the workers was at once distributed to all. The point was that the ration was wholly inadequate, even for the coolie standards to which we had been reduced; but when that ration had to stretch over an extra 20 per cent at least of our working population, then gradual starvation became a very real prospect.

The Japanese reasons for this policy were at times specious, at times brutal, but never convincing. They varied between the proposition that noble Nippon had much reconstruction work to do in wickedly exploited Malaya—wherefore we must be *encouraged* to work—and the ruthless statement that warlike Nippon did not greatly admire men who surrendered and that they had more than enough of us anyway. Anyhow, until the end of the war, rations were issued to us on the basis of Working Men only. Within a few weeks of the introduction of this generous catering system our M.O. pronounced that at the present rate of supply, with everything else in our favour—which he did not think a probable eventuality—we could only survive for a year. For some obscure reason, the verdict that in twelve months we would all be dead seemed to provide everyone with a perverse sense of hilarity and we felt happier than we had for days.

Only one other factor remains to complete the scene in which we were for the next nine months to live. This is the imprisonment, as well as ourselves, in our gaol, of political prisoners—mainly Chinese—seized by the Japanese for alleged British sympathies or rebel activities.

The right-hand leg of the two which, with our quarters, formed a triangle of buildings, was the one into which the Japanese herded these unfortunate natives. There they questioned, tortured, and murdered them. The process was noisy since the last thing any Oriental ever does is to endure physical pain or mental anguish in silence of the impassive nature invariably ascribed to them by writers who have never been to the East. When an Indian, Chinaman, Jap, Korean or Indonesian is in pain he screams and moans with an abandon which, to the European, is downright embarrassing. They are all of them admirably impassive about inflicting pain on others—being apparently immune to the European's ability to suffer vicariously—but when stung themselves they become most vociferous.

Thus, in the course of their questioning, when they were shipped on the gaol shipping triangle, or filled with water and jumped on, or made to stand for hours with a heavy stone held above their heads, or suspended by their ankles while urine was poured down their nostrils—Japanese refinements which I have seen British soldiers endure in stolid silence—the air was rent with their shrill screams. And when at last an entire cell of six natives was informed that at dawn *one* of the six, any one, would be taken out and executed, then the impassive Orientals really went to town. All six of them would maintain an uninterrupted vocal lament throughout the night. Then in the morning another head would appear on a pole in the streets and the surviving five would relapse into ecstatic silence, for they were still alive; whilst the native population outside would remain totally unmoved, for the head was not theirs; and we, who had so despised their screaming, would notice the head with shocked pity because a young man who had lived was now dead. All a matter of outlook—but, of the two, I preferred ours.

In spite of the horror of these heads as we marched out of the gaol each day, and in spite of the humiliation of natives watching us work for the Japanese, the working parties were—in those first weeks of captivity—a glorious release. It was delightful, even though the work was heavy and the Jap engineers in charge of us vicious to the point of insanity, to get out of those high walls with their layers of loose bricks on top so that escape over them was impossible. It was bliss to walk ten yards without, in that interval, having to cross twenty legs and smell the all-pervading smell of latrines. It was restoring to snatch a piece of frangipani off a tree as one passed—to smell its clean scent and carry it till the white petals went brown.

We worked for several weeks before this novelty wore off—worked, repairing Kuala Lumpur's demolished bridges, with that hysterical speed and to the accompaniment of those incessant hysterical screams and bellows that seem to be the main equipment of the Japanese engineer. Then one day we returned to the gaol and were told some good news—we were to move, all of us, out of the women's quarters designed for thirty, into the left wing of the two legs of the triangle. There we would live in supreme comfort, with only three men in each cell meant for one.

On the move being made, it was discovered that the V of the two cell blocks which, with our old quarters, made a triangle, was, in fact, an inverted Y and into the stem of the Y moved all the British troops. Thus in the Y we had Asiatic political prisoners screaming their heads off on one side, Australians on the other, and British in the stem.

I moved, with Hugh Moore and Arthur Farmer, into the cell nearest the junction of all three blocks and started at once drawing a full-scale map of the world over the whole of the left-hand wall so that we might the better follow the destruction of Nazidom in Europe and of Nippon in South-east Asia and the Pacific. Our life had begun to assume the shape and pattern which was to dominate the next four years—turning gaols and jungle into our home; living close to death by disease; working for the Japanese, and stealing from them.

After a small group had tried to escape, he wrote:

It became fairly obvious after two days in which they had been allowed no food, no water, and no latrine facilities that the Japanese were evilly disposed towards our escape party. Van Rennan himself sensed this and managed to throw a note into the main triangular courtyard urging us to ask for clemency towards Bell and Jan, both of whom were only in their very early twenties. This was done and the Japanese seemed agreeably inclined towards the request, nodding their heads and saying, 'Baby-ka' many times.

But, in spite of their head-noddings, the next morning we saw the whole party suddenly appear in the gaol's entrance just outside the guard-house. All their gear had been dumped near them—haversacks and clothing—but they themselves were still fiercely shackled and were filthy dirty. They looked very weak.

The Japanese motioned them towards the gaol gate. Inquiringly, Van Rennan gestured with his foot towards the pile of kit-bags. The Japanese nodded negatively, emphatically. It could mean only one thing. They knew it: and we knew it.

They were brave men, those eight. Their heads went up, and while we shouted cheerful remarks at them, trying not to let them know what we sensed, they grinned back at us so that we shouldn't sense what they knew. They went through the big gate. Whenever one of them turned our way, a mass smile would appear on all the strained faces that watched their departure. As soon as their backs were turned, the smile vanished. They were prodded and shoved, clumsy with their arms and legs bound, into a truck. They turned to face us; we smiled. The guard spoke to them: they looked down at him; our smiles vanished. The guard stopped speaking: they looked up; we smiled. Then the truck lurched off and the big gates shut. They were gone. 'There,' I thought with a lump in my throat, 'but for the grace of a mop of sun-bleached hair, goes Braddon.' The Indian who drove the truck told us later that they were taken to K.L. cemetery, there made to dig their own graves and then shot down into them. So ended the first, most promising and last escape plot of Pudu.

The Japanese declared generously that they would pay us for our work—10 cents a day. Thus, if one worked every day of the month, one earned the lavish sum of $3. This would buy a small handful of dried fish, a little coconut oil in which to fry it, and perhaps a banana or two. Bananas became almost a 'must' on one's shopping list, because they were reported to contain Vitamin E. And Vitamin E, we were told, combatted the sterility with which we were all threatened by our M.O. if the rice diet continued—which it gave every indication of doing for years.

As soon as we received our pay, we seized the opportunity to do something for the men who lay day after day in the hospital in our courtyard. We all gave 25 cents from our $3, and this Padre Duckworth took into town with him and with it bought soap and food and odd tit-bits. No money was ever better invested. It was sheer delight to see the faces of those near-corpses, who for weeks and months had been living a life of the most complete squalor, as the little Padre dished out his purchases to each one.

We resolved that we would make the same contribution each month. An officer, with the soul of a born Socialist pleasure-wrecker, suggested that the scheme was, in fact, a form of health insurance from which any man who fell ill would benefit. He was howled down with the greatest promptness. In our life, where we mostly had nothing to give, we were not thus lightly to be deprived of our once-monthly opportunity to be human. It remained a direct gift to the sick and after the first pay-day we were delighted when the Pommies announced their intention of 'being in it'. For the next six months there was always cash in hand to buy anything within reason for a sick man who needed it—whether it was black-market drugs or black-market food. . . .

In 1942 we were moved from Pudu to Changi. To the naïve Pudi-ite, Changi had other shocks. The docile acceptance of Tokyo time as the camp standard, rather than the old British time to which we in K.L. had clung so tenaciously. The ceremonial parades at which we were handed from N.C.O. to N.C.O. and officer to officer until, hours later, we were dismissed—all so that the Japanese might know how many of us still languished in their custody. The rash of concert parties and theatres—dozens of them playing each night: everything from *Androcles and the Lion* to Army smoke-ohs. The drug-selling ring which shamelessly traded M. & B. tablets from our own British hospital—tablets more priceless than diamonds—for bully beef from the Malays and Chinese. A ring which could not publicly be stamped out because, it was once rumoured, an M.O. was one of its members (he left the keys of the drug-store where the stooges could pick them up) and because some senior officers were also involved and to prosecute them would be 'bad for morale'. For whose? We Pudu-ites wondered.

Then there were the Spivs of Changi—men with courage and no scruples who went outside the wire each night to collect tinned food from old Army dumps in the rubber and then returned to sell their booty at black-market prices to their brethren back in camp. Every community has its villains—and Changi's preoccupation with such laudable though impractical conceptions as respect for officers and salutes thereto allowed its villains a scope which to those of us who had lived the fraternal life of K.L. was nauseating.

But if these follies and blacker sides of human nature became obvious to us for the first time in Changi, so did other things which were wholly delightful. For one thing, we hardly ever saw the Japanese (and the ideal life is, of course, one in which one *never sees any* Japanese). For another, the common man of Changi greeted us with overwhelming warmth. We had all been posted 'Missing, Believed Killed' for nine months and though, upon our return to the fold, we ruined many a model honour roll upon which we had optimistically been inscribed as 'dead', we were, nevertheless, made to feel most welcome.

Thus, all of us found ourselves equipped with a shirt and a pair of shorts and boots. And Piddington, whom I had last seen when I left him at Yong Peng at the beginning of the year, gave me a toothbrush and a pack of Gibbs' toothpaste—a delightful gift after so long using a finger and ground-up charcoal. The men of Changi were solid gold right through, as men, on the whole, always are.

Later, he wrote:

We crossed the Thailand border and found Thailand no different from Malaya except that its natives were rather more energetic—especially in their thieving, at which they were most adept. And eventually the train ground to a halt and we were ordered out, to the accompaniment of the usual endless bellowing, on to a rather dreary-looking platform.

Anxiously I took stock of my possessions. One water bottle, one mess tin, one spoon, toothbrush and razor; the complete works of G.B.S., *Mein Kampf* and an *Oxford Book of English Verse,* given to me just before our departure by Harry Witherford, the British officer who knew about the stars and turbo-jets. Having made certain that they were all there, I bundled them into the rice-bag I used as a haversack and, with the rest of the party, started off down a filthy dust track towards the promised convalescent camp.

As a nation we found the Thais excessively dishonest and thieving. We reciprocated wholeheartedly.

The Convalescent Camp turned out to be native huts made of attap, mud-floored, littered with excrement, seething with flies, and in that condition of unspeakable filth which only Asiatics can attain. It was bad enough for those of us who were fit, but for the men who had been uprooted from Changi's hospital it was like a death sentence. The five-day train trip had not improved their condition. The sour, fermented rice and the greasy water of those days had brought on fresh bouts of dysentery to almost all of them. They looked drawn and one felt fearful for them.

Without warning, the Japs swept down on the camp and searched it—searched it for everything from weapons to wireless sets. Though they found nothing, it was only at the expense of our dumping all grenades, bayonets, daggers and machine-gun parts (of which there were more than a few) down the camp well. The radio, being secreted in an accordion which the gentleman who owned it played gaily and with no tune at all throughout the search, was not discovered.

The Japanese, through Terai, then ordered us to fill our water bottles and fall in for a night march.

'How far?' we asked.

'Twenty miles,' was the answer.

All that night we marched with our respective sacks and packs on our backs; the qualis and dixies and axes and other tools slung on poles and carried by pairs of men in turn; the sick, as they collapsed, being supported by whoever was nearest. The Japs at the head of the column, marching with only a rifle, set a brisk pace which they refused to ease; and the Japs at the rear used a liberal rifle butt to ensure that this pace was maintained. I soon found myself slipping into my prison habit of counting. Each step I counted. Thousand after thousand—even though I determined dozens of times to stop—until I nearly went mad. The sun was scorching down again before we reached the next camp high on the water-eroded banks of a swift-running river. . . .

I urge you to read 'The Naked Island' for his experiences on the infamous Burma Railway.—Ed.

. . . The line was finished. From Bangkok to Rangoon it ran uninterruptedly—except that the Royal Air Force blew up the odd vital bridge at strategic intervals so that no train ever got through. But, for the moment, it was completed and the Japanese decided to open it with ceremony.

At this ceremony the senior British Officer on the line was invited to speak. He refused abruptly, saying that neither he nor any prisoner of war wished in any way to celebrate the official opening of a railway line whose every sleeper on its whole four-hundred-mile length had cost one human life. The Japanese were in no way put out.

The I.J.A. were now confronted with the problem of what to do with the wreckages of humanity who were the survivors of their Railway. These did not look like men; on the other hand, they were not quite animals. They had feet torn by bamboo thorns and working for long months without boots. Their shins had no spare flesh at all on the calf and looked as if bullets had exploded inside them, bursting the meat outwards and blackening it. These were their ulcers, of which they had dozens, from threepenny-bit size upwards, on each leg. Their thigh-bones and pelvis stood out sharply and on the point of each thigh-bone was that red raw patch like a saddle sore or monkey's behind. All their ribs showed clearly, the chest sloping backwards to the hollows of throat and collar-bone. Arms hung down, stick-like, with huge hands, and the skin wrinkled where muscle had vanished, like old men. Heads were shrunken on to skulls with large teeth and faintly glowing eyes set in black wells; hair was matted and lifeless. The whole body was draped with a loose-fitting envelope of thin purple-brown parchment which wrinkled horizontally over the stomach and chest and vertically on sagging fleshless buttocks.

That was what the Japanese and Koreans did to the men who went on Forces F and H and lived. Of the total number who left Singapore, about half had survived. Now, what to do with this wreckage? And when they looked at it, even the Nips were a little unnerved.

The first thing they did, therefore, was to collect most of the survivors at Kamburi—that same Kamburi which had been the last town before the jungle commenced on our march up. We were loaded on to trains and shipped down. There were several longish stops on the way to allow those who died to be buried.

Finally we steamed into the flat fields of Kamburi.

As I staggered off the train, cramped and ravenous, for we had had no food for two days, I noticed that beside the line ran long rows of huts separated into two areas. In the one were white men, in the other black men. Both lots looked shocking. The fence that marked the dividing line between Railway and camp was draped with white men only. The natives no longer took any interest in anything. Therein lay the difference. And, as I shambled towards this fence, one of the men on the other side crawled under it, dragged me through and greeted me with a warmth I had forgotten existed. It was Harry Witherford. I managed a feeble crack—'How's your turbo-jet?' I asked—but I was a bit overwhelmed. But he, good soul, knew what was required. Leading me firmly round the back of a hut he gave me bananas and boiled eggs—bought on the spot from a Thai—which I devoured frantically lest they vanish. Though I live to be a thousand the warmth of that greeting and the gift of that food after the sterile months of want that had gone before will never leave me. . . .

We moved into the huts. They had a raised platform on each side of the centre aisle—as our numbers increased so the amount of this platform available to one became steadily less. It was mathematical. Eventually we had nineteen inches a man and a line of men cross-wise at our feet. Nineteen inches is not enough for a man. To this the Japs pointed out that many died each day—soon there would be more room. In this, it seemed, there was a great truth, because the day did not seem to pass when twenty men were not buried. . . .

Ulcers were the main problem. They were attacked at once. Whilst Fagan operated all day on a bamboo table in a small cubicle kept free of flies by mosquito net (he cleaned out or amputated as many as forty legs a day, and always there was that gentle smile and the specialist's considerate manner), orderlies and volunteers, armed with common or garden spoons, which were sterilised in boiling water, cleaned out every ulcer in the camp at least once a day. The heroism of those men whose legs were so scooped clean—the flesh pared out like flesh from a melon—was incredible. It was not as if once done it was finished. There was invariably the next day. And the next day there was never any improvement. But always, when his turn came, each man would stretch his leg out flat for the orderly, raise himself slightly on his forearm and elbow and, with a friend ready to grab each shoulder should he move, say:

'O.K., mate, give her the works."

The the orderly would dig his spoon into the stinking pus until he had reached firm flesh and, having reached it, draw the spoon carefully down one side of the gaping wound and up the other. Swab it out; scoop out the few remaining mortified patches; put a bit of canvas soaked in acraflavine over the top and bind it up. Finished till tomorrow. The patient, who had lain straining rigidly backwards and not moving nor uttering more than a few small grunts, would then relax and crumple backwards, his forehead sweaty.

I cannot adequately describe the courage of those men because, having suffered only a few small ulcers myself, I shall never know the pain they bore so stoically. Let me hasten to state, however, that although I clung firmly to a bamboo upright for support I never once had the small craters round my ankle bones scooped clean with the fearsome spoon without either being sick, or fainting, or both. And had it not been for shame at the silence of those others, with the flesh from their knee to their ankle laid bare and their rigid straining backwards, I should have screamed with terror and with pain. . . .

So the day commenced. Next, the night's dead were collected from each ward and taken, in convoy, outside the camp and across the road to be buried. It was difficult not to count them each day: but counting them was depressing, and if one did succumb to the temptation, one pretended one hadn't.

After that the day was one's own, for there was no work to do. If one could walk, one went looking for friends: if not one lay hoping that some friends would come along instead. . . .

In Kamburi, water was always the difficulty. When it rained everyone crawled out and stood or lay under the pouring eaves of the huts and scrubbed themselves clean. But when it didn't rain, then even to get enough water to drink was a problem.

It was in this matter that a small group of officers started and carried out (always more difficult) a most generous scheme. Playfair, Le Maistre-Walker, Mackissack, MacLeod, Knox, Pockley and Gibson (there were others, doubtless, whose names I forget) collected a basin and a kerosene tin. They would fill the basin with clean, clear water collected from the well some distance outside the camp. Then they would send one of their number up to one of the huts and he would select someone to whom he would say, 'There's a tub of water for you down at our hut if you want it,' and that was all. When you went down to the hut, the basin stood outside with a small piece of soap. No one there. No questions asked. It was restoring, that free bath, after days of sweating with fever and parching heat.

Nor did the group stop there. With their limited officers' allowance, they made gifts of fruit, eggs and money—usually when one slept, so that one awoke to find it there beside one. They dropped in to each hut almost every day, each one of them, to yarn and see how things went. They pestered the hard-pressed medical staff if they saw a case that needed attention.

Let it be said here and now that almost all of us had experience of such groups and that without them things would have gone very hard indeed.

Russell Braddon describes far worse hardships than those retold here which are to illustrate the type of treatment endured and how our lads coped. For my part, I found the cold-blooded butchering of 230 patients and 93 Doctors and Nurses at Singapore Alexandra Hospital, one of the most appalling to absorb.—Ed.

These, then, were the men into whose hands we in Malaya, and the garrison of Hong Kong, had fallen. . . . as they swept apparently invincible through the Dutch East Indies, the Philippines and Burma, they would net hundreds of thousands more. Because we had surrendered, they took no pains at all to understand us: because it was essential to our survival, we took such pains as were necessary to understand them.

Addressing the House of Commons after the fall of Hong Kong, Anthony Eden accused them of 'nauseating hypocrisy' in their exaltation of bushido. Rather, he said, they had 'perpetrated against their helpless military prisoners, and the civil population, the same kind of barbarities as had aroused the horror of the civilised world at the time of the Nanking massacre of 1937.'

Eden, however, was wrong. Not even the Japanese have ever denied that the Nanking massacre of 200,000 Chinese civilians in 1937 was atrocious; but by 1942 the concept of bushido had been so distorted, yet so profoundly inculcated, that the Imperial Japanese Army (which is not to be confused with the Kempeitai) could justify atrocities committed in its name not only without a trace of hypocrisy, but even with total sincerity.

Extracts from* 'The Menacing Rise of Japan' *by Alexander Howard and Ernest Newman.

A bridge between Japan and Western civilization was opened in 1854, when Commodore Perry, an envoy of the United States of America, signed a treaty with the Bakufu (the military Government of the Shogun). This was the first stage in placing Japanese relations with the outside world on a reasonable basis and in opening up the country to foreign intercourse, which in reality proved to be the opening of the world to Japan.

I read elsewhere that Perry's message implied-Trade or be invaded.—Ed.

The history of Japan may be summarized in a few periods:

An era of transition, as mainland cultures and influences are slowly transplated and absorbed (about A.D. 300—700).

The Nara era—a golden age of Buddhist culture and of the rise of a specific Japanese civilization (seventh and eighth centuries).

The Heian era, marked by the rule of the aristocratic and feudal clans. This is the classical age of Japan, when Kyoto was the capital (ninth to thirteenth century).

The Kamakura era, characterized by the rise of feudalism and the rule of the Daimyo (military nobility), the coming of Zen Buddhism and a new virile age (thirteenth to fifteenth century).

The Ashikaga era, marking a further triumph of feudalism ending in an age of decorative profusion (fifteen to seventeenth centuries).

The Tokugawa era, representing the popularization of culture in Japan, the beginning of a commercial system (1603—1868).

The Meiji and post-Meiji eras, characterized by the changed policy towards intercourse with 'foreigners', expansion beyond the Japanese islands, the decision to industrialize the land, and the removal of the Court from the ancient city of Kyoto to the new and modern capital, Tokyo. A modern Constitution was introduced in 1889, followed by the reorganization of postal services, currency, and banking and educational systems, and the abolition of all special privileges hitherto accorded to foreigners, such as extra-territoriality.

Throughout the history of Japan in the past ninety years, which this book illustrates, there runs a note of duplicity and treachery which recalls Hitler at his worst. The contemptible tactics which sent a special Janapese Envoy with peace offers to Washington while at the same time the blow was being prepared and dealt at Pearl Harbour, were only the latest tricks employed by Japan to further her dream of world domination.

Immediately after Commodore Perry's visit in 1853, Shoin Yoshida, an Eastern forerunner of Hitler, founded a school, the *Matsushita Sonjuku,* the sum total of his teaching being tantamount to a Japanese *Mein Kampf*. In his lectures Yoshida laid down the grand strategy of Japanese Imperial expansion, which has been carried out so far to the letter. In 1927 General Bron Tanaka is said to have submitted to his Emperor the now famous secret 'Memorial' outlining the tactics to be employed for Japan's drive for world power. Although described at the time as a forgery—it probably was not written by Tanaka—it is a strange and grim fact that what has happened in the Pacific area during this generation has been in strict keeping with 'The Tanaka Memorial'.

Japan is unworthy to own colonies. Whatever blunders other nations may have committed in their colonies, they have usually honoured the conception of Justice. The Japanese have not. All who have come under the Japanese heel hate them bitterly, since they do not acknowledge that others can have views, let alone rights. After all, have they not been taught to believe that the Emperor of Japan is a god—and can the Emperor of Japan be a god to anyone but a Japanese?

There are horrible photographs—too gruesome to include. Here are some of the captions:—Ed.

The Gibbet Thousands of innocent Chinese have been hanged by the ruthless Japanese. A favourite practice of the preacher of 'Bushido' is to cut down the bodies, leaving the heads hanging—as an example.

Shades of our own 'Hanging, drawing and quartering' centuries before.—Ed.

Bayonet Practice One of the darkest deeds in a long chapter of unparalleled horrors. Japanese soldiers indulge in bayonet practice on unarmed Chinese prisoners.

Prisoners buried alive A harrowing incident after the capture of Nanking by the Japanese. Five Chinese prisoners were thrown alive into a grave for the amusement of the onlooking soldiers.

Punishment to fit the crime For accidentally tripping on a Japanese Army telegraph wire, this Chinese boy was bound to a post and had his head sawn off by the chivalrous Japanese invader.

CHAPTER TWO

The Rise and Fall of the Japanese Empire

I devote the second chapter to ***Captain D. H. James****, a brave, courageous leader of men who knew the Japanese people in peace and in war and who lets us share facts and experiences of which most of us were unaware.*

He wrote in ***'The Rise and Fall of the Japanese Empire'****, 1951:*

In 1937, Japan had decided to enlarge her Empire.

I hold no brief for the Japanese, who by their chicanery built up a national cult of militarism, based on mythology, and then sheltered behind the 'divinity' of the human pretender to the throne to sancify their vile projects of aggression at home and abroad, and I have nothing but contempt for the creatures who destroyed Japan and humiliated their 'sacred Emperor'. At the same time I am not so prejudiced as to ignore the history of the country and the abject conditions under which the masses were governed for centuries by a minority of sub-men. Sub-men who were steeped in a vile ideology; degenerates who were spawned by neoplatonism, posing before the world as direct descendents of KAMI (god) exclusive to the Japanese nation, a nation which for many generations had been inhabited by Ainu, Mongols, Malays, Koreans and Chinese of normal miscegnation.

Many and curious ideas have prevailed regarding the subjects of Tenno Heika. They have been described as a magnificent race, the true leaders of the Orient, progressive people with splendid patriotism and magnificent loyalty to the Emperor. Brave in war, tolerant in peace, proud and sensitive—fond of flowers and of children, simple in their habits, lovers of nature, efficient in trade and commerce—progressive in every way. Then again they have been referred to as people devoid of all morals destitute of finer feelings or religion—pagans who cut their bellies at the slightest provocation, fanatics, militarists, aggressors, petty imitators without imagination, liars in diplomacy, tricksters in trade—in short, the scum of Asia.

Between the extremes of adulation and contempt there is ample room for a middle course without destroying the basic truth which lays behind the various assertions.

One subject is uppermost in the minds of the Japanese—the pressure of living, the cost of rice. They are always most willing to discuss SEIKATSU—existence, livelihood, to keep one's pot boiling. And perhaps the problem of Japan, past and future, can best be expressed in terms of Rice, Population, Geography, Military Rule and a State Controlled Cult and Education.

The History of Japan affords ample evidence of the repression of the majority by a minority of soldiers and priests. The two-handed sword of despotism, which ruled by conveniently preserved Tennos, cloaked the real purpose of Shogun, Daimyo and hired Samurai. And, unfortunately the proletariat produced no leaders: they shirked civil war against the Shoguns and left the fighting to be done by rival bands of Samurai. This left them slaves and they were absorbed by the system in their struggle for existence even after the Restoration in 1868 when the intrusion of the western Powers indicated to them an alternative to feudalism and the law of the Samurai.

The physical and mental stagnation of the masses was due to centuries of under-nourishment and sub-normal living conditions: most of the time they existed near the border-line between malnutrition and health. And when the rice harvest failed they were reduced to geog aphy—living on root crops.

The food problems were not improved by the practice of destroying its vitamins when most of it was so low in nutritive value. Furthermore it was the habit in rural Japan to pay taxes, rents and wages in rice or other agricultural products: the ill-fed farmer had to feed the nation in addition to his own family and hired labourers as well as cater to the needs of the lazy priests.

The Japanese have multiplied too fast for the economics of the struggle for existence. Unconditional surrender saved the masses from destruction by high-explosives but it did not solve the food problem. True, there is—in addition to rice—some wheat, barley, oats and millet to go with varied vegetables and root crops, and a good supply of fish, but the standard of living is extremely low and the population, cooped up in the main islands, will not cease to multiply because there is a new Constitution framed by foreigners to replace that of Ito.

Japanese are more often than not regarded as part and parcel of the Chinese race but the bulk of the population, at present, are physically and psychologically different. Certainly they are a branch of the great yellow race, to which the Chinese in general belong, but they are by far the most highly specialized off-shoot of that race.

To destroy masses of Japanese, men, women and children by fire-raids, high-explosives and atom-bombs, was one way of exterminating a race of aggressors but it cannot be advanced that it was based on the teaching of Jesus Christ. On the contrary it was the triumph of western super-science over an inefficient eastern pupil; it was in no sense a victory of Christianity over Jinja-Shinto.

From the point of view of culture and democracy what was required was not the destruction of the people but the obliteration of basic anachronism by example and precept. But is western civilization not dangerously poised on the very pinnacle of blatant materialism and 'Thanks God' in an aside that the U.S.A. produced the atom-bomb ahead of her co-belligerents? Indeed there are many who say that our belief in an Almighty God is quite secondary to our blind faith in the scientist to whom we turn in the hour of danger and to whom we give praise and thanks for our preservation, past, present and future. In any case it may be well worth pondering over before we leap to conclusions, regarding the best way to convert the heathen to the democracy of present day western civilization, and destroy the temples and shrines of the wicked Shinto State of Japan.

It is claimed by Japanese, particularly by many of their eminent professors of ethology, that the characteristic spirit of the nation may be summed up in one word—Shinto. By 'Shinto' they mean 'kokumin dotoku' the modern national morality which is based on 'Sai-sei-itchi'—the fusion of a *state religion* with an *undemocratic government*: in short, the compulsory worship of a Divine Ruler and the compulsory obedience to an autocracy of military dictators. By 'Shinto' they mean *Jinja-Shinto*—Shrine Shinto—based on the twelve groups of shrines: Kampei-Sha, the Government Shrines, and all the Kokuhei-Sha, National Shrines, in Kensha (Prefecture), Gosha (District), Sonsha, (Village) and the 70,000 un-graded (Mukaku-sha) shrines, and the tens of thousand little shrines on hilltop and by the side of the road and on the kami-dana, the family god-shelf. And, above all, they mean the Ise Dai Jingu—and Amaterasu-o-mikami, the Sun Goddess.

However, the autochthons of Japan had a nameless religion until 6th Century A.D. when Chinese scholars (Buddhists and Confucianists) arrived in the country with the art of writing, and of cults and religions, for rulers and for people of the soil, and they soon had a name for the 'way of the gods' the religion of the natives.

Using three Chinese characters for 'follow', 'God' and 'way' they produced the combination meaning 'follow the will of the gods without question'. It was pronounced 'Shinto'.

According to Dr. Genji Kato, an authority on the subject—'Shinto is indeed a *religion* peculiar to and inherent in the Japanese mind, so that it cannot be displaced or eradicated by any conflicting religious powers from without.' And this is carried a stage further by the statement: 'Shinto is a thorough-going *national religion* throughout each and every phase of its long development, from the stage of nature religion to that of culture religion, with the Jinno or DIVINE RULER of the national at the centre of worship, keeping pace with the progress of Japanese civilization in general, so that in the mental texture of the people their religious faith and national consciousness have been so closely interwoven as now to be incapable of separation.'

That was Kato's opinion in 1935 but it is mentioned in the Nippon Shoki

(A.D. 720)—in connection with Kotoku Tenno (645—654)—that: 'We have commanded our son to rule according to the will of the kami and hereby the land has been ruled by a Tenno since the beginning of Heaven and Earth.'

Confucianism and Christianity were rejected by Japanese as unsuited to their needs. In Christianity the divine spirit dwells apart from the universe—mankind may acquire an element of divinity, or reject it—and nature, materiality and animals are excluded from possessing the divine nature. In Shinto there is no difference between divine spirit and any form of material being, for all is divinity.

The teaching of Confucious, like the teaching of Jesus, was plain and straightforward quite unlike Chinese-Buddhism the religion of monks and temples with grotesque and irrational observances. Jesus denounced patriotism and the ties of family loyalty. Jesus spread the gospel of universal brotherhood of mankind irrespective of colour or origin, He condemned the economics of capitalism, private wealth and personal advantage and for that reason His teaching was rejected by Tokugawa Iyemitsu the builder of the magnificent Nikko shrine.

The extent and nature of the criminal actions of Japanese soldiers, particularly their inhuman treatment of prisoners of war, came as an unpleasant surprise to the subjects of the United States of America and the British Empire. Not because war crimes are something new to modern civilization, or that they were considered the prerogatives of Nazism, but simply because of the documentary evidence regarding the samurai, bushido and other national characteristics of the Japanese submitted to the general public by so many native and foreign writers.

Japanese atrocities have their genesis in the hakko-ichi-u of the Nippon Shoki; the oneness of the Japanese national family—the unity of Tenno, State and People. No matter what a Japanese may do to a foreigner he acts as one of the national family. For that simple reason, one Japanese will refrain from interfering with the action of another Japanese even when he knows that it is immoral—even absolutely contrary to his own moralism.

Moral courage, to distinguish between right and wrong, is non-existent most of the time where a Japanese and a Foreigner's viewpoint is in conflict.

Thousands of allied prisoners of war were brutally over-worked and maltreated. Thousands were half-starved, tortured or bayonetted to death in cold blood. Yet, during my own three and a half years as a captive, I recall no instance when even an expression of disgust, or of mild regret, was made by a single Japanese, soldier or civilian, when an act of brutality was perpetrated in their presence.

If a Japanese private soldier killed a British prisoner of war by a blow of sword or iron bar, or killed him by slow torture, his superior officer may have asked for an explanation, but would not have considered it his duty to scold or punish his subordinate.

The Imperial General Staff issued orders that prisoners of war retaken after attempts to escape were to be shot. That was Japanese military law. I made two personal appeals to General Yamashita to reconsider the death penalty imposed on the first three young English soldiers retaken after escape from Changi Prisoner of War Camp on Singapore Island. I pointed out that there had been no notification of this drastic departure from International Law and that the three young men had never been informed by us, or by the Japanese, that the penalty for breaking out of camp was death.

I was informed that the matter was out of General Yamashita's hands. The men had been caught by the kempei, were tried by the kempei, and would be shot by the kempei who were resonsible for guarding the security of the state. I then appealed to the Singapore commander of the Kempeitai. He read my complaint, congratulated me on a 'good point' which should be rectified by an immediate notification of Japanese Military law to all prisoners of war.

The three soldiers were shot at sunset. They had waited outside the camp commandant's office for three hours sitting on spades and shovels to be used in digging their graves, while we tried to establish a very good point in international law.

I could fill pages with instances of similar crude and brutal mentality—I could fill pages with details of atrocities, but I refrain. My opinion, based on bitter experience, is that Japanese as a race are deficient in moral courage and proficient in killing in cold blood. I recollect no instance—during the Russo-Japanese War, Sino-Japanese Wars or in World Wars I and II—where a Japanese soldier or civilian was ever tried or punished for an act of murder or brutality committed outside of military action.

No doubt there are so-called progressive Japanese, and even sympathetic foreigners who have lived for years in Japan, who may consider my remarks as sweeping generalizations on Japan's moral code.

My critics may fall back on the delightful politeness, the valour, fortitude, bravery, fearlessness and courage of the nation and send me another copy of Bushido to revive my memories. But there were more British soldiers killed, or brutally treated, as prisoners of war than perished in fighting against the Japanese in battle during the entire campaign, and there are more Allied soldiers alive today who have suffered at the hands of the Japanese than the total number of foreigners who ever lived in Japan before 1941.

In 1941 at any rate, the first duty of a Japanese, in or out of his uniform—soldier or civilian, kempei or gorotsuki—was blind obedience to State Shintoism. There was no division of loyalties. Duty—in that sense—has nothing at all to do with conscience or their conduct towards foreigners.

When Kublai Khan attempted to conquer Japan a great storm destroyed his armade, KAMI (gods) in the shape of wind fought on Japan's side. Ever since then—1281—the divine wind, KAMI KAZE, is said to have sided with Japan when she was faced with any national adversity.

Japanese 'air-gods'—kami-kaze pilots—played a prominent part in the recent war. Their many exploits figured largely in national propaganda to uplift the morale of civilians: suicide-planes, human-torpedoes, were a real contribution to Japan's total-warfare and inflicted enormous damage on the allied fleet.

The spiritual home of Japanese national traditions and of kami-kaze, is the Imperial Shrine at Ise. This Shrine of Amaterasu-O-Mikami—the KO-DAI-JINGU—is rebuilt every twenty years. In it is enshrined the Sacred Mirror, one of the Sanshu-no-jingi—Three Sacred Treasures—supposed to have been given by Amaterasu to Ninigi-no-miko her grandson when she sent him to YAMATO, with these words:-

> '. . . The Luxuriant Land of Reed Plains is a country which our descendants are to inherit. Go therefore, Our Imperial Grandson and rule over it. And may our Imperial lineage continue unbroken and prosperous, coeternal with Heaven and Earth . . .'

By the end of September, 1943 all PoW Camps in Singapore, except Changi, had been closed. British, Australian, Indian, Dutch and Javanese Prisoners of War were sent up-country or overseas to Burma, Siam, Indo-China, Borneo, Formosa, China, Korea or to Japan's, or South Pacific Islands. They were to be brutally overworked, half-starved or beaten to death in order to bolster up Japan's all-in effort to conquer Greater East Asia.

From first to last, 87,000 allied Prisoners of War passed through Changi Camp. But of those who left Changi more than 30 per cent, died as a result of neglect or barbarity.

There was no lack of medical supplies or personnel when we surrendered. If Japan had observed the Geneva Conventions our total losses in 3½ years would not have exceeded 1,000 in Malaya, but the Japanese commandeered our medical stores and equipments and doled out inferior drugs and chemicals in minute quantities—they stole our X-ray equipment and they treated our medical personnel as sanitary squads. Despite their efforts to kill us off we managed to treat *80,000* patients in Changi Camp Hospitals between February, 1942 and September, 1945: *10,000* minor or major operations were performed and our total losses, from all causes, was 850 dead. We had to manage without mosquito nets and try and 'wash' linen and blankets without soap—we had more than one epidemic, we sent three complete hospital units to Siam and all the drugs and equipment the Japanese would allow us to send: we sent medical units with every draft, but despite it all we lost *16,000 Officers and men in Siam alone.*

No draft left Changi without a protest being lodged in writing by Malaya Command: I interpreted at dozens of our Command protest meetings with Camp Commandants and with Generals Fukuye and Arimura. But it was not the slightest use protesting for they were merely obeying their orders.

Nearly 50,000 prisoners of war were employed on the making of the Siam Railway—16,000 died of torture, disease or starvation. Major General Arimura, responsible for the movement orders, managed to surrender to the U.S.S.R. in Korea and up to July, 1948 all efforts to obtain his extradition have failed. General Fukuye shouted 'Banzai' just before being executed by a firing squad at Changi on 28th April, 1946: General Yamashita was executed for causing the death of 824 A.I.F. in the march-out from Sandakan.

Lt.-Colonel Satoishi with 33 of his officers and men were shot for herding 150 allied prisoners into an air-raid shelter on Palawan (P. Islands) 11th December 1944. They were drenched with petrol before the lighted torches were thrown among them.

The American Government secured posession of Japanese orders—issued between 12th January and March, 1944—which read 'By order of the Japanese Military authorities surrendered personnel captured, with the exception of individuals needed for minute investigation, *are to be put to death on the field of battle.'*

The part played by the Emperor received the condemnation of the President of the international military tribunal. In his opinion it was the Emperor who authorized war and could not be excused for doing so because his life was at stake—he was not bound to act on the advice of his ministers if he did not agree with it. The evidence proved that the Emperor accepted advice to make war against his better judgement.

But, in my opinion, it made no difference if Hirohito lived or died, the gumbatsu ruled the country absolutely through the Meiji Constitution, Shinto and Kodo. One Tenno more or less made no difference to the system or the working of it. Hirohito decided to live, for, like Premier Hara, there was a great deal he could do before he indulged in Tenno hari-kiri.

The Japanese who waged war in the Far East were not the men who were in the armed services when Meiji came to the throne in 1868. The senior officers dated from 1881, the conscripts, and the junior officers, dated from 1900; the first-line troops and their commanders dated from 1920. Between 1920 and 1941 the intake was at the rate of 300,000 per annum making a grand total of first-line troops and reserves under the age of 40 of 6,000,000 men. It was these men, between the ages of 20 and 40 who had been thoroughly drilled in kodo and State-Shinto by Araki and his kind who—no matter where they fought—had the same killing instincts in and out of action. They had exactly the same education from five years old to twenty years old when they joined the services. For that reason there was that common pattern of atrocity which appeared to surprise the Tribunal sitting in Tokyo.

Evidence before the court proved that Japanese medical officers removed hearts and livers from healthy prisoners while they were alive. Cannibalism was authorized—allied prisoners but not Japanese might be eaten even when other food was available.

One of General Tojo's earliest orders was to the effect that commandants of PoW Camps must not be obsessed by mistaken ideas of humanitarianism.

I was ordered to Japan under escort of Captain Shiono who had just arrived at Changi with a draft of prisoners of war from Java. There was no explanation—and in a few hours I boarded the 10,000 tonner *Ussuri Maru* with 500 other PoW's bound for Japan. Hardly had we piled aboard when kempei arrived and arrested four British officers—including W. Wooller the rugger international.

Then we tried to fit ourselves into the accommodation below deck. It was impossible until they agreed to our moving cargo, stowed on a hatch, and they chalked off another thirty foot alley-way. Our accommodation was now exactly 6-foot by 2-foot per man long or short, thick or thin. We were battened down in port and not allowed up on deck for about 24 hours after sailing.

Three days out from Singapore our convoy was attacked by American submarines. One 20,000 ton oil-tanker was destroyed but we evaded danger and made for Manila. During the attack we were battened-down, below deck in complete darkness. The only exit was guarded by bayonet-men. If we had been hit there would have been another *Lisbon Maru* disaster because it was impossible for more than a few men at a time to have mounted the narrow companion-way even if permitted by the squads of armed men posted at the exit and on deck.

En route I was fortunate in receiving only three thrashings from a mad 2/Lt. whom we named 'Basher'. But we all lost an average of 10 lbs. on account of the stifling atmosphere below deck with every porthole closed in the tropics. From morning to night perspiration oozed out of every pore and every few hours we would receive instructions on some subject or other. We had one set of latrines (over the scuppers) and these were 'out of bounds' after sunset unless I could persuade the armed guard that it was impossible for 500 men to regulate their bowels to order. Fifty per cent had diarrhoea: drinking water was limited to a mug or so a day and the voyage lasted a month.

I gained some information from 'friendly members' of the crew because I was the usual go-between PoW and captors and had opportunity to feel my way without being knifed. It was no longer a question of winning the war but: how can we bring the war to an end?

The crew of the *Ussuri Maru* had made too many trips to remain under any illusions regarding the blatant propaganda fed to the masses regarding the successes of Japan's invincible navy in the South Pacific Ocean. They were very dispirited and not at all impressed when the 'Basher' punched my nose because the black-out was not 100 per cent perfect in broad daylight.

When we docked at Moji, Japan in October 1943, the Kempei came aboard. They were not interested in the over five hundred PoWs but asked Shiono why I was sitting on my baggage watched by an n.c.o.? My escort explained and produced his authority for my journey to Tokyo—but they were not satisfied. They grilled me for an hour and then I was ordered to load my kit on to a truck and drag it through the streets to a PoW Camp in Moji where they locked me in a cell.

Soon, more kempei arrived with note-books and I was examined and cross-examined regarding my history from the early days of Meiji to the perplexed days of Showa Tenno. A bowl of rice followed the interrogation but, directly the kempei went, my own guards became pally. They admired my white hair and my Japanese—so I told them tales of old Japan and they produced sake and cigarettes, extra blankets, lots of tea and rice and tucked me in for the night.

Next morning I trundled my truck to the Railway Station followed by little boys and little girls who chanted merrily: 'Ojii-san! Ojii-San! Horyo ojii-san!': which was quite correct 'Grandpapa! Grandpapa! Prisoner of War Grandpapa!' and proper, but they ran away when I replied in Japanese that it was very rude to make fun of old people—very rude, and that they must be Chosen-jin (Koreans).

The train to Tokyo was crowded. Every seat occupied and corridors jammed with men, women and children. But they were quite polite and I was rammed into a corner seat and told by Shiono on no account to move or look out of the window. An armed n.c.o. sat with me and before we started another lot of kempei arrived with note-books and quizzed me for twenty minutes.

At Osaka, Captain Shiono was greeted by his family: he transferred all the loot he had brought over from Singapore—six large cases—and then paraded his 'special captive' for their close inspection. They were all extremely polite—one woman handed me some sweet cakes and a packet of peanuts but the approach of another kempei altered everything. Shiono yelled at me to get back into the train.

The kempei examined me and when he had finished said to my escort, 'Tell them at Kyoto if you want him taught a lesson, I'll inform them he's on this train.' But nothing happened at Kyoto because I was fast asleep.

At 8 a.m. we arrived at Tokyo. I was bundled into a car and taken by Shiono to Army Headquarters some miles away. At Hq. a Staff Colonel interrogated me—merely asking name, unit, rank, age, place of capture and nationality. As it checked up with the information on the movement order he passed me on to another room where I was interviewed by a General who did not give his name. He said that I had been brought to Japan to work at PoW Hq., but for the present the plan had been dropped and I would be taken to Omori PoW Camp until they were ready for me to start compiling a full list of all allied prisoners of war. But that I was not to worry about my future—nothing would happen to me at Omori.

Shiono came in, slipped me a packet of cigarettes, and then in a loud voice handed me over to an Eurasian with instructions to be careful and obey all Japanese orders.

A staff-car took us to Omori on the Tokyo-Yokohama main road and soon after we started, the Eurasian volunteered the information that I had been brought over from Malaya to act as Liaison Officer in Japan between PoW camps and Army Hq. and to compile a nominal roll. But I was more interested in the environment than in his remarks as we streaked past the rest of the mechanical traffic which spluttered along at ten to fifteen miles an hour propelled by charcoal-burning contraptions reminiscent of Heath Robinson's pictorial gadgets.

Japan was short of petrol. But what struck me most, after what I had seen in London, was the complete absence of air-raid shelters, or A.R.P. It was October, 1943 but the authorities in Tokyo were still confident that no allied bombers would be able to penetrate the ground and air defence of the capital.

Dolittle's solitary raid was made from an aircraft carrier and it was dismissed as a stunt although the captured airmen were murdered to discourage the others.

There were very few men on the streets, not one woman in a hundred wore native dress, they had discarded kimono, with yards of material, for overalls or baggy slacks fastened at the ankles with tape. Shops were open but very few goods were on sale—so far as I could see when we were held up by traffic.

The general impression was one of near bankruptcy after a dozen years of war in China and the South Pacific Ocean—it was indeed a shabby sight for the 'heart of the nation triumphant in war'—it was so unlike the colourful streets of Tokyo in pre-kodo days.

Omori is 7½ miles due south of the Imperial Palace and 12½ miles from Yokohama. When I was a boy it was a fashionable summer resort—a place to go to, to get away from stuffy Tokyo. Now, at the age of 63 I was going there as a Prisoner of War—a melancholy reflection. The Camp was situated at the north end of reclaimed land, not far from the old No. 4 Battery close to the mouth of Meguro-gawa flowing into Tokyo Bay.

A rickety wooden bridge spanned a tidal canal separating the island from the original coast line. It was this narrow strip of water which saved us from destruction more than once during the 1945 super fire raids on Tokyo by B 29's. We crossed the bridge on foot and when we reached the sentry at the gate my Eurasian gude, and the n.c.o. escort, snarled at me in the most approved yamato-damashi style to impress the sentry of the arrival of one more captive.

I was handed over to Major Hamada, assistant Camp Commandant who signed for me with his seal of office. Then I was handed a non-escape form to sign which reminded me of the way PoW's in Changi had been herded in a modern black-hole of Calcutta and told to sign or take the consequences.

After the signing I received the usual warnings, and the usual bit by bit search of my kit but Hamada refrained from taking any souvenirs. I repacked my kit, got on my feet and stood at attention for an hour when Private Kuriyama (o.c. discipline) took over. He made another thorough search of my kit telling me in gutter-Japanese that if I did not behave he would bushido me good and proper.

The numerous kit inspections and warnings occupied two hours then I was passed fit to join my comrades in No. 2 Barracks.

Omori Camp was two months old. When I arrived it was commanded by Lt.-Col. Suzuki and he was succeeded by a Colonel Sakeba an old-timer thoroughly steeped in kodo—one of the genuine war criminals, one-hundred per cent sadistic.

Five wooden barracks, 100 feet by 24 feet, housed 520 prisoners of war. Each prisoner had a bed space of 4 feet by 8 feet in the double-deckers, there was an 8 feet passage down the centre of each barrack; at each end were two 10 feet by 12 feet cubicles for officers.

Barracks were fitted with glassed-in sliding windows and there was ample ventilation. The quarters were tolerable in summer but ice-houses in winter because no heating of any description was provided or permitted and the flimsy structures were erected on wind-swept ground a few inches only above high tidemark.

There were three twenty-feet long wash-racks for 520 men but most of the time in summer there was a bare trickle of water—in winter the pipes were frozen. Latrines, on the same scale, were provided: there was no arrangement for disposal of sewage and the shallow concrete lined pits were filled to overflowing and alive with millions of white maggots.

Food was vile. There was no fixed ration scale, too few rice-boilers and the mixture of rice-sweepings and Kaoliang (the millet of Manchuria) topped with soya bean was never fully cooked. When it was 'cooked' (once a day) the mess was dumped into dirty tubs from which it was ladled into still dirtier serving-buckets: shortage of water prevented cleansing of anything from cooking utensils to a pocket handkerchief. The excess roughage, in every meal, was a constant irritant to the lining of the men's stomachs so the majority suffered from persistent diarrhoea.

Tenko!—roll-call—was at 5 a.m. in summer and 6.30 a.m. in winter: evening roll-call at any time between 6 p.m. and 10 p.m. according to the mood of the duty officer. Tenko was conducted according to Japanese rules of procedure and in Japanese. At tenko, boots had to be clean, tunic buttoned-up, bedding rolled-back, kit packed or piled in rows each 12 inches wide with items in their stipulated place in the pile. No clothing was allowed to hang in the barracks even if it was dripping wet at tenko hour.

Pushing, slapping and kicking was the immediate punishment for breach of tenko regulations. I was trounced because I blinked when the duty officer was speaking to me about not standing upright, when my feet were swollen with beri beri.

Most of the PoW at Omori were from Shinagawa Camp, a few miles away. At Shinagawa there was a 'hospital' run by Captain Tokuda the vilest type of 'doctor' to put on a Japanese uniform.

Omori and Shinagawa produced a full quota of war criminals who were tried and punished after the surrender. Both places are only a few miles from the Imperial Palace but they might have been three-thousand miles away for all the difference it made to the atrocious manner in which prisoners of war were treated.

In October, 1943, Omori camp news was obtained from the English editions of 'Japan Times' and 'Tokyo Mainichi'. There were no secret wireless-sets so the PoW had to depend entirely on Japanese versions of the progress of the war. In consequence of reading this enemy propaganda the general morale of the allied prisoners of war was extremely low. Most of them had already suffered at the hands of the Japanese and after eighteen months of captivity were pretty depressed by the 'news'.

As the latest arrival from overseas I was able to water down the propaganda with a few encouraging facts. And in order to keep informed of what was being written in the Japanese newspaper I decided to operate an undercover news service. It was just as well that I did so because after April, 1944 newspapers, Japanese or the foreign version were prohibited from being circulated in the camp.

Slowly I detected the first signs of discontent and disillusionment and a resignation to accept a long war if Germany was defeated in the west. It became evident, from editorial comment, that the propaganda of the official spokesmen to the effect that 'Japan was consolidating her gains preparatory to further occupation of enemy territory' was inconsistent with the known facts.

As early as November, 1943 there appeared hints of discord between Army and Navy about major strategy and there appeared demands for the dispersal of Tokyo population and the establishment of realistic air-raid precautions in vulnerable areas.

From October, 1943 (when General Tojo visited Singapore) to the end of the year the communiques repeatedly 'explained' the failures of the allies to reoccupy Japanese 'front-line bases' in the South Pacific despite the fact that Japan was waging war 4,000 miles from Tokyo. It was claimed that enormous losses were being inflicted on Australians and Americans in their vain attempts to take from Japan small islands thousands of miles from the homeland.

But all this did not explain the clamour for air-raid shelters, dispersal of population or the new restrictive food regulations.

On 7th December, 1943 (second anniversary of the attack on Pearl Harbour) I listened to a nation-wide broadcast by General Tojo. He said that Japan, in ninety days after bombing Pearl Harbour, had fanned out from Wake to Burma, from Gilberts to Solomons and even to the far Aleutians. War against the Allies was taken 5,000 miles away from Japan and her Navy was master of the seas from Honolulu to Ceylon. Now, on the threshold of a New Year, Japan would seek to consolidate her gains, and she would go on adding to those gains until ultimate victory was attained. Japan would win the war no matter how long it took and no matter what sacrifices had to be made.

He spoke well. There was no hesitation or faltering: he knew the truth, but the spirit of kodo urged him on—encouraged by the unconquerable spirit of the people in the homeland the armed forces were determined to vanquish the enemy in 1944. But—he warned—there must be no more slacking on the home front: more and still more planes and ships were wanted and a better output of munitions to ensure success against the material superiority of the enemy.

Loss of the Gilberts, in November, 1943, was reported as a minor incident: bombing of Paramushiro (Naval base on northerly point of Kuriles) on 13th September, 1943 had been dismissed as a 'silly tip-and-run affair' made to bolster up allied morale. Even the loss of Ley (16th September) had been explained away as part 'of our plan in New Guinea to whittle down allied land, sea and air forces before we make our attack on Australia.'

Previously (when I was in Malaya) the Coral Sea and Midway battles—May and June, 1942—were claimed as 'overwhelming victories of our peerless Navy' despite the actual results of the engagements.

We kept a list of these victories over the American Navy and the printed losses exceeded the total tonnage in 1941. But it was never explained how it was replaced, so often, after being sunk so statistically each time. Communiques were issued which detailed engagements but they hardly ever recorded Japanese naval losses or casualties. But they always referred to 'allied cowardice'.

No Japanese planes were shot down in combat—they failed to return after running out of petrol or they had crash-dived into an enemy target, generally a battleship, cruiser, destroyer or a 'large transport heavily laden with troops'.

The American Navy was 'useless during night engagements'—it was badly trained and the sailors were terrified when they sighted a Japanese warship, they became confused, panic ensued and they fired blindly at each other before fleeing from destruction. On land, in the air and on the sea, one Japanese warrior 'inspired by love of country and loyalty to Tenno Heika is more than a match for ten craven enemy fighting without a cause.'

The fight to finish on Attu and Kiska (May and June, 1943) was extolled and cited as evidence that 'the Spirit of Bushido and Yamato-damashi animated a mere handful of Japanese warriors who scorned to surrender. They fought to the end against overwhelming forces of the enemy. They died to a man. They shed their last drop of blood to prove to Americans the impossibility of inflicting final defeat on the 100 million loyal subjects of Japan.'

The main object of Japanese propaganda was to destroy the material advantages of the enemy by postulating the theory that the 'Japanese fighting spirit' completely discounted it. No matter how many aircraft, warships or soldiers were ranged against Japan she could not be defeated because the enemy lacked morale and were nothing but 'armed cowards'. To foster this thesis the communiques, and the broadcasts, stated whereas one or two Japanese destroyers had been destroyed ramming American aircraft carriers, for every minor loss of that kind at least ten enemy vessels were put out of action: for every aircraft lost the enemy lost twenty in the air or on the ground. Over and over again this nonsense was blared by Tokyo radio and re-broadcast in all asiatic and foreign languages from captured stations in occupied territory.

Despite this distortion of fact the truth began to make itself heard, at home and abroad; Japan was no longer winning the war—the official spokesman failed to explain the loss of Bougainville, Solomon Islands, or the naval disaster when an entire convoy—and escort—were destroyed by allied aircraft in the Bismark Sea.

This disaster ended the threat to Australia but the central theme was not the loss of men and ships but the heroic end of Admiral Yamamoto (C.-in-C. Navy) who set an example to all Japan by ji-metsu (self destruction) in atonement for failure in the service of Tenno Heika.

The decision of the Army to retain islands in the South Pacific, dominated by superior naval and air forces, could not be justified by the remote possibility of a dramatic success like the bombing of Pearl Harbour. Japan had not the yards or the raw material necessary to cope with the gigantic task of building up the naval or merchant tonnage required to support Tojo's military adventures 5,000 miles from his base of supply. The bid for an Empire in Greater East Asia had failed, the war was not lost and it was time to consider ending it in Japan's favour.

Akirameru is a word often used by Japanese to express the idea of abandoning all hope, relinquishing a plan or accepting the inevitable—resigning oneself to fate.

We had an interpreter named Ohnishi. He frequently gave me 'lectures' on culture and kodo. One day, during one of my many punishment periods (standing at attention for hours outside the camp office) he asked me if I understood the meaning of akirameru? I replied in the affirmative, adding that in my case it was no longer akirameru but 'temmei wo shiru'—taking life philosophically.

Ohnishi slapped me: 'I've told you before—the word of the Imperial Household is Law. Tenno Heika is greater than your God—there is no future for people like you.'

My crime, on that occasion was this. We were handed copies of the 'Japan Times' and ordered to comment on an official communique which announced a 'Great Victory'. In my 'report' I pointed out that many American battleships, aircraft carriers, cruisers and destroyers had been 'sunk' without the loss of a single Japanese warship—large or small. But, the Americans landed on Guadalcanal, Santa Isabel and Bougainville and the communique did not explain the arrival of the American troops to my satisfaction.

Such comment from a 'slave' infuriated the Camp Commandant—he had me on his shinto-mat and asked me to explain the swift and complete defeat of the British in Malaya. I did so. Then he said that as I had been afraid to die for my country I had lost my status as a soldier and should bow my head in shame and not be sarcastic.

The communique was issued by the Imperial Household and was not based on the theories of a coward. I expressed regret and was told to rewrite my report in Japanese! I did that and had to stand to attention for three hours until Lt.-Col. Suzuki accepted the translation—without comment.

To provide material for propaganda, Omori Camp was used as a show-place to demonstrate to young conscripts (en-route to the front) the degenerates they were fighting against. Time and again these groups would invade the camp led by guides and junior officers.

They would receive instructions regarding the habits of the captives, told to inspect them at close quarters and then to parade on the square where they were lectured by Staff-officers from the War Office. On all these occasions I was confined in one of the camp offices to prevent me from overhearing any of the 'secret instructions' being yelled at the youngsters on the square.

At other times mixed groups of newspaper men, artists, painters, authors, educationalists, members of the upper and the lower house visited us. I was confined to my cubicle but they interviewed, painted, sketched or photographed many of the others to obtain 'copy' and 'local colour' for magazines, newspapers and the movies.

But the most interesting person I met during my sojourn in Omori was Professor Fujisawa. Fujisawa was an associate of Dr. Nitobe and had been connected with the working of the League of Nations in Geneva. A brilliant scholar, widely travelled, he had mixed with the intelligentsia of America and Europe and his English was perfect. But his contact with 'western civilization' had convinced him that the salvtion of mankind could be only attained by its conversion to Shinto with Tenno Heika as the spiritual head and Tokyo as the centre of the universe having Japanese culture as the basis of international morality.

Fujisawa must not be confused with a babbler like Major Toyama of Changi. He came to Omori with the blessing of the War Office to lecture prisoners of war on Amaterasu, Jimmu Tenno, Shinto, Kodo and the divine Showa Tenno. Unfortunately the PoW officers who were ordered to attend his lecture in the cold bath-house were already half-starved, nearly frozen to death, bug-eaten and all too familiar with genuine Japanese culture to be interested in the mythology of the Yamato-jin.

Undismayed by his cool reception, Fujisawa changed his line of approach to the mass of unbelievers clad in rags and covered with boils and ulcers. He instructed Ohnishi to select a few beri-beri intellectual captives on which to try his new gospel of salvation. I was one of those ordered to attend Fujisawa's special lectures in a nice warm room in the Camp offices.

Fujisawa regaled us with tea, cakes and cigarettes and then—having set us at ease—explained the idea behind this fraternization. He wanted volunteers, candidates for intensive instruction in shinto, who would be taken from the camp and housed in comfortable surroundings where they would have leisure to meditate on the teaching of the thirteen sects of Shinto—twenty-million could not be wrong? 'Surely we did not want to miss this opportunity of learning about the great way of the gods—Kamu-nagara? And, he reminded me, one of the articles of faith of Konko-kyo—which was akin to Chrstianity—ran:

> 'If you would enter the WAY OF TRUTH, first of all drive away the clouds of doubt in your heart.'

I pointed out that Kawate Bunjiro founded Konko in 1859 and died in 1883—two years after I was born—whereas Christianity had existed for 1944 years and was introduced into Japan at about A.D. 1500. I preferred the revelation of Christ to that of Kawate Bunjiro or of any of the other Shinto sect founders.

Fujisawa was there to teach, not to argue. His opinion was that Japan was fighting a holy war against the materialism of western civilization: Christianity had failed and there were ethical advantages to mankind in Shinto. I agreed that there was quite a lot wrong with mankind, and the world, but doubted if the democratic nations would substitute Shinto for Christianity—for religious or administrative purposes. And I was quite sure neither the President of the United States, or King George VI of England would accept the Tenno as their spiritual father. Also, the nationalization of religion was out of fashion in the West: State-Shinto, with the Tenno venerated as divine, would not be acceptable to Christians or heathens in Europe or America. For better or for worse there could be no renunciation of Jesus Christ as the central figure in Christianity.

Fujisawa took the matter quite seriously—he wanted us as converts, so he was patient and tolerant. He agreed, it was not an easy problem to solve. It required serious study, it would take time—Rome was not built in a day. In his opinion a World Federation, based on Shinto, with Tenno the acknowledged spiritual head of a universal religion was by no means impossible. Already, Japan was the leader of Greater East Asia. Shinto, the basis of her success in arms, was spreading throughout China and India and it would reach Europe and America in time. Not in our time perhaps but in years to come when people had time and leisure to meditate on the real reason for strife and misery in the world.

We had three of these 'heart-to-heart' discussions behind closed doors. Shinto, he argued, must defeat Christianity in the end and pave the way for everlasting peace. We should welcome the opportunity to become missionaries of the true faith.

Suddenly, just as Fujisawa was about to close the third session, the door was flung open by Corporal Watanabe the n.c.o. responsible for discipline in Omori Camp. He demanded to know on whose authority Fujisawa, a civilian, was holding a meeting with prisoners of war behind a closed door?

Fujisawa was dumbfounded. He rushed out of the room to make his complaint to the Colonel: we were ordered back to barracks: that was the last we saw of Professor Fujisawa, but not of Corporal Watanabe.

No prisoner of war could fathom Watanabe's mentality: he was no killer with club, bayonet or sword but he superimposed a sustained mental intimidation and his persecution was planned to incite retaliation so that he could call in the guard to shed the blood of his victims. Many of my sturdy colleagues wanted to beat him to death and take the consequences but, I explained to them, that would only mean their own death and would have no effect on the fundamental principles of Japanese PoW administration.

Watanabe's first victims were men whose legs were covered with ulcers, or men who had walnut-sized boils—men with high fever, with lumbago or beri-beri—men who could hardly walk from bed to latrine. He would order them to stand upright in order to knock them down—for no reason at all. Just to show that he was 'Watanabe' responsible for discipline!

This animal was born in Kobe. I knew his family and his eldest sister was married to Lt. Okazaki who was the first Camp Commandant at Changi. He received a good education and was at Tokyo University before being conscripted and he came to Omori in November, 1943 and remained until the end of 1944.

The fame of this savage spread to every PoW camp in Japan and he was never restrained by any one, least of all by Lt.-Colonel Suzuki or Colonel Sakeba. For a few months I was able to check him. But, as interpreter and intercessor—between madman and victim—it was written in the stars that he would end by venting his spleen on me.

Not content with individual punishment he instituted his own system of collective punishment on the slightest provocation.

And when he was tired of swinging his club or fencing-stick he would retire to his room leaving us standing for hours watched by armed sentries. But he was not alone in his madness. His brutal methods were encouraged by Cadet Fuji, the M.O., 2/Lt. Kato, camp supervisor, and 'Dr.' Tokuda of Shinagawa Hospital.

Tokuda—'The Butcher'—never allowed a patient to remain in Hospital if there was a reason for discharging him. Fuji would never pass a man 'unfit for duty' unless he was on the verge of physical collapse, Watanabe saw to it that every man, sick or well, 'paraded' for work, and Kato included every man in

Omori Camp as 'fit for work', in camp or in a working party.

When a draft of PoW arrived,or semi-convalescents came in from Shinagawa, they were paraded for Watanabe. He knocked them down, used judo on them, punched and slapped them to 'correct bad attitude to Corporal Watanabe'. But he did nothing on the sly—it was done in the open with the knowledge and consent of all the camp staff from Colonel to office-girl. He boasted to me that his 'authority' transcended that of Colonel Sakeba and that all he did was in agreement with Japanese Military Law: even if he did kill one of us he could not be tried or punished.

British and American medical officers who protested against Tokuda's brutality were sent to Omori to be thrashed by Watanabe—and he told them so when they arrived. Suiting his words to his actions he thrashed them directly their kit had been inspected.

One American medical officer had 'bad attitude' so he was put on permanent 'benjo fatigue' and ordered to report each evening outside the camp office window. Watanabe would then come outside, walk up to the officer and punch him in the face. This went on, every day, for three weeks until the officer's face was black and blue and Watanabe could no longer make any impression on the pulpy flesh.

Perhaps there was epilepsy in his family to acount for the electrical activity of his brain for his bad spells, when he behaved like a raving lunatic, lasted best part of a week.

The 'attack' would come on suddenly. One moment he would be talking normally then he would see red, shriek like a fiend lashing out right and left and ordering 'all officers Tenko!'

But his most astonishing characteristic was vanity and his craving to be saluted! He issued 'orders' that he was to be saluted inside and outside barracks; when he was sighted by a PoW that individual must shout, 'Kei-rei! Kei-rei!' and all others in the vicinity must stop what they were doing, stand at attention and shout—loud and clear—Kei-rei! Kei-rei! and remain at attention until he said 'Yasume!' (stand at ease).

Not only that. But when they shouted 'Kei-rei!' they must bow in his direction, with the back inclined at an angle of 45 degrees, with eyes cast down in respect.

Nothing delighted him more than to rush into a full barrack and collect his quota of kei-rei's. Later on he issued further instructions: 'Corporal Watanabe's office-window, opened or closed, must be saluted by prisoners of war passing near to it or when it can be seen as they move about the camp.' The 'Bird' would take cover (outside the office) with a baseball-bat and wait to flog any person who failed to salute the window, so you had to salute shadow and substance of Watanabe.

Watanabe tried very hard for more than six-months to end my life. He would have succeeded but for the fact that in December, 1944 he was promoted to Sergeant and sent to another camp. For some time I had been suffering from beri-beri, yellow jaundice and diarrhoea and was down to 95 lbs. in weight. His favourite punishment for me was to have me shout 'Kei-rei!' and bow (outside his office window) five-hundred times and then to stand at attention for a few hours. But he tired of that. He caught me standing without my fingers fully stretched and set about me like a wild-cat. When he had finished my left eardrum was broken, both eyes closed and cut, face bruised, mouth and lips cut. I was in bed for a couple of weeks, then he returned to the attack.

He caught me with a lighted cigarette in the passage between the officers' cubicles. That was a serious crime—now he *would* teach me a lesson! I followed him inside the special-prisoners' compound—he closed the gate and then marked out a small square with his fencing-stick. I stood in the square while he beat me about the face and head with his stick. He resented the way I took that punishment so he started to ram the end of the stick into my throat which was much more painful.

Still he was not satisfied—my attitude was still bad—so he dropped his stick and tried to throttle me but I twisted clear and he fell headlong into a slit-trench.

I bent down and helped him out. He dusted his clothes and I handed him his fencing-stick, resuming my stance in the little square and waited for the next part of the performance. But he walked away, told me to follow, went into his office and left me to stand outside for an hour.

Nothing prevented millions of Japanese from knowing that, in turn, Nagasaki, Yawata, Sasebo, Omura, Musashima, Nagoya and Tokyo had been bombed regularly from June to December, 1944. They saw the damage to aircraft works and industrial areas, and—because the whole country knew about it—the newspapers were allowed to report the 'incidents' giving approximate number of the enemy aircraft shot down and brief mentions of damage and casualties.

Invasion by air was an accomplished fact. Invasion of the sacred soil of Japan was in the offing and it began to impress itself on the thoughts of the people and the Government. More than 2,000,000 of Tokyo's inhabitants were evacuated—dispersal of the population was ordered in Kobe, Osaka and Nagoya. A.R.P. was now of more importance than reliance on the 'Kamikaze Corps' althought the pilgrims flocked to the shrines, rang the bells and clapped their hands as in the days of the Mongol invasions.

In our district, thousands of houses were demolished to form fire-breaks; Omori—midway between Tokyo and Yokohama—was not a safe area. Repeated protests, regarding our safety, were made by the British and the American Governments but they were all ignored. Our camps were closed down *after* they had been destroyed by fire or bombing, and *after* we had suffered casualties. Not a single representative of the Red Cross—Japanese or Foreign—was allowed to visit Omori until late in 1945.

During World War II, frequent reference was made by many Japanese—including Emperor Hirohito—to the 100,0),000 people who would never surrender—the 100-million patriots who would defend the sacred soil of Japan. This figure refers to the total population of the 'Empire' which—according to the national census of October, 1935 was as follows:

Japan proper	69,251,265	
Korea	22,898,695	
Formosa	5,212,719	
Sakhalin	331,949	
Manchuria	1,656,763	(S.M. Ry. zone)
South Seas	102,238	
	99,453,629	
i. Residents Abroad	872,807	

Asia	339,998	Europe	2,954	N. America	174,230
Africa	201	Oceania	153,684	S. America	201,740

A point to remember about the 'unconditional surrender' is that in the total of 69,251,265 given above the proportion of men to women is about the same:

Men 34,731,860 Women 34,519,405

None of the women went through the conscript system and although they were not by any means free from kodoism they never were sadists like the men.

The air war, waged by U.S. Army and Navy Air Forces against the mainland of Japan, entered a definite offensive phase in November, 1944.

During November, 1944 the heaviest raid was staged by *100 B 29's* dropping *250* tons of bombs—on 1st August, 1945, *820 B 29's* unloaded *6,600* tons of explosives on five towns in North Kyushu. That was a week before the first atom-bomb was used against Hiroshima.

The object of all these raids was to slow down aircraft production, test air defences, and to train personnel for the pin-pointing raids which were to precede the saturation raids. According to newspapers I got hold of, 'few of the raiders returned to their base . . . many shot down by ground-defence or by combat in the air . . . very little damage done except to residential areas . . .'

We saw quite enough of the fires, and the destruction, in the Yokohama-Tokyo area. From the camp we did see at least six of the B 29's brought down in flames, and saw some of the crew bail out, but from the amount of criticism in the papers, regarding inefficient A.R.P., it was evident that damage had been heavy in the Capital.

Tinian and Saipan were available in January, 1945, but—according to the press

—were not used until middle of February for attacks on Japan by super-fortresses. This may have been correct because strikes from carrier-borne aircraft began early in the new year and the heavier B29 raids followed.

Soon after dawn, 15th February, dozens of navy-fighters and dive-bombers roared over Omori camp and we had a 'grandstand' view of overhead dog-fights and thrilling dives on the nearby aerodrome.

They were from U.S. carriers—hundreds of them and they continued their strike the next day on the Tokyo-Yokohama aerodromes with (according to the press) a loss of 'more than 200 planes'. We did not see more than a flash of the raids and saw only a few planes crash but an American report gave their losses as 49—all types—and claimed to have destroyed *659* enemy aircraft on the ground or in the air in addition to sinking 36 vessels. These 'figures' (on both sides) seemed to us rather exaggerated after the experience we had during the Battle of Britain.

On 18/19th there was a B 29 raid on Tokyo. This night-raid was followed on 19th by daylight attacks on Nakajima and Musashino aircraft plant (and industrial targets) in Tokyo area by more than 150 B 29's. Fires started during the night were plastered again and the fire-fighting services were occupied at full stretch for the remainder of the week. But the most destructive raid, to date, was on 25th February when *200 B 29's*, escorted by navy-fighters, pressed home attacks on military, air and naval installations in the Yokohama-Tokyo area.

So, long before the atom-bomb disintegrated them, their agony had been doubled by B 29's loads of *high-explosives* and *incendiaries*. From March to July, 1945, B 29's dropped *100,000 TONS* of incendiaries on 66 towns and cities wiping out 170 square miles of closely populated streets, more or less legitimate 'total-war targets'.

Planes were flying very low. A strong wind was fanning the fires as wave after wave came over and dropped 'baskets' of fresh incendiaries over the industrial districts north and east of the Imperial Palace and the factory area to the south-west, bordering Tokyo Bay. Wind direction was north to south. We were in the centre of the south-west coastal strip—between Sumidagawa and Tamagawa—and well inside the danger zone from the spreading fires.

Wave followed wave. Three hundred super-fortresses crossed the doomed City one early morning in March. They destroyed and then went on into the darkness beyond the flames, their bodies glistening as the beams of searchlights followed them until they were lost to sight in cloud. Wave followed wave. Like birds of ill omen, with widespread wings, they darted in and out of smoke and cloud to leave behind an incandescent holocaust.

Then I heard the tolling of bells and beating of drums in shrine and temple grounds of Omori where Shinto and Buddhist priest beckoned to the homeless victims of Araki's kodo. I stood on the bank and listened to the subdued voices of those across the narrow strip of water which divided friend and foe. It was as if mutual grief and sympathetic sadness was spreading the inspiration of the bells: there was no noise, no theological prayers, no calling to heaven for help in the hell of their surroundings. It was just the vibration of men, women and children whispering to comfort each other—that, and nothing more, could be heard.

Tokyo was burning! Tokyo was like the sounding board directing the emotions of the deluded to the ends of the Tenno's domain. Much water had passed under the Sumidagawa bridges since Tokugawa Hidetada banished Christians from Japan, and now—in the *yake-tsuchi Jidai,* western civilization was spreading the gospel of destruction and casting down the flaming torches into an ever-growing inferno. How times had changed!

In the early morning, hundreds of old men, women and young children from the Omori ward (now in flames) ferried themselves across the canal and took shelter on the seaward side of our wooden fence.

Clutching precious bundles they crouched down to avoid the heat from the raging furnace consuming their homes a few hundred yards away. We stared at them through knot-holes in the fence—they stared back at us. We smiled. There was so little between our chances of survival and theirs that we could only smile and hope for the best. Maybe they pinned their hope on the direction in which the wind was blowing for if it did change a few degrees the wooden fence which divided us would be our funeral bier.

Now and again we saw one of the super-fortresses stagger in flight, lose its place in the perfect formation, burst into flames, explode in the air or dive into the cauldron to become part and parcel of the inferno. Frequently we saw tiny dots float clear of a damaged plane and followed man and parachute drift to earth. More than once a suicide-plane would make its swift dive on its aerial target: a flash, momentary suspense after the impact, explosion in mid-air—then victor and vanquished crashed into fragments of metal and flesh and lost their identity in smoke and cloud.

Throughout the raid, ground-defence was active and accurate—the B 29's flew in low and bombed from about 10,000 feet as against the usual 20—24,000 feet of the daylight attacks on the same targets. But, considering the volume of flak, we counted less planes put out of action than there should have been in view of the close formation and bombing height. Not more than fourteen came down which was a small price to pay for the destruction of from *twelve to fifteen square miles of the City.*

Japanese casualties were heavy—the first reports were truly fantastic, but the official statement (after the surrender) did confirm the rumours: *83,000 were killed, 102,000 were injured*—making a total of 185,000 casualties, for one raid!

The American official report stated that 1,667 tons of incendiary bombs had been dropped from an altitude of 7,000 feet.

This raid was the most destructive, to life and property, so far recorded in history. It exceeded that at Hiroshima, or at Nagasaki, when the atom-bomb was used.

All day (10th March) an acrid smell filled our nostrils in Omori camp. When the tide lapped our fences it cast up hundreds of charred bodies. We stared through the knot-holes at the men, women and children sprawled in the mud or jammed against the logs from the demolished timber-yards—men, women and children, the remains of human beings remained there to rot alongside others who floated in after other raids on the Capital.

Nagoya, Osaka and Kobe were the next targets.

On 18th March the battered industrial area of *Nagoya* was visited by *300 B 29's* releasing *2,000 tons* of incendiaries.

Those who were directing the destruction of Japan's potentiality to wage war were determined to leave nothing to chance.

To complete the programme, for the time being, *Nagoya* was the objective on 25th March when *255 B 29's* plastered the Mitsubishi aero-engine plant with 1,500 tons of H.E., and on 30th March when a *smaller* formation of *200 B 29's* dropped a mixture of H.E. and fire-bomb.

Interlocked with this specific bombing, carrier-borne U.S. Navy aircraft struck at *Kure* Naval Yard and *Kobe* shipbuilding plant on 18th March, and on *Kyushu* aerodromes on 19th March. Land-based fighters retaliated by strikes against the U.S. Taskforce on 20th and 21st March, claiming numerous successes in 'a series of brilliant actions against superior forces of the enemy'.

Unfortunately, for Japan, these brilliant successes did not prevent large formations of B 29's from bombing industrial and military targets in *Kyushu* on 27th March or carrier-borne aircraft from raiding *Kyushu* air-bases on 29th and 30th March.

By now it was obvious to people and to politicians alike that the U.S.A. could force the surrender of Japan without the assistance of China, U.S.S.R., or the British Empire, and that they could do it without any slackening of her contribution to the utter destruction of Germany. And, what is more, the U.S.A. alone by the exercise of her sea and air-power could bring about defeat without the necessity to land troops on the main islands.

Those who were later on to be tried as 'War Criminals' had enough intelligence to arrive at a correct estimation of the extent of their failure to establish an Empire in Greater East Asia but they lacked the courage to sue for peace and thereby save the people from further slaughter.

The exit was marked 'Unconditional Surrender'. But it was easier for them to lead their dupes through Shinto gateways and to rely on kami-kaze for another 'miracle' than it was to agree to 'Unconditional Surrender' before the enemy was established on the sacred soil of Japan. Only the Tenno could help them now and he was still casting his net in shallow waters.

There was still 2,500,000 soldiers ready and willing to fight to preserve the Shinto State in all its theanthropic glory. To them, unconditional surrender did not square with Japanese ethics—it was a foreign idea linked with western civilization and, as such, beneath the contempt of the Japanese. No, it was not easy for the Tenno to lead sullen samurai, patriotic black-dragons—the protagonists of kodo—through the Torii of the Yasukini Shrine to clap their hands before the altar of the spirits of Japanese, who had laid down their lives for the country, and proclaim their disloyalty to Amaterasu.

Ogasawara, better known as Iojima or Iwojima, is one of the volcano islands, in the Bonins, about five hundred miles south of Japan. It was held by about 22,000 Japanese when first attacked by U.S. warships and B 29's on 8th November, 1944, and captured on 16th March, 1945. Japanese casualties were 21,000—mostly killed—and the American losses were 4,189 killed and 15,749 wounded according to official reports.

The first landing was made by Two Divisions of U.S. Marines on 18th February, 1945. Previously—25th—26th December, 1944, 24th January and 30th January—it had been bombed and shelled by B 29's, carrier-borne aircraft, and ships of the U.S. Pacific Fleet.

Iwojima was cited as *one example* of yamato-damashi; the garrison was isolated, they died to a man.

It was at this point that the B.P.F. following its success at Sumatra joined the U.S. Fleet.

Ten days later, U.S. Marines landed on Kerama Island 15 miles south-west of the Ryukyu Islands. This sounded the call to Japanese to 'rise as one man in defence of the sacred soil of Japan, inviolable by foreigners'. The response was magnificent, but the sacrifice was in vain.

On 1st April the advance guard of U.S. Infantry and Marines landed on the west coast of *OKINAWA*, the most important of the Ryukyu Islands. Okinawa was blockaded by the allied fleet and dominated by the allied airforce, but it held out for *92 days*.

Both sides flung everything they had into the contest—no quarter was asked for or given. It was a fight to the finish between 'uninspired conscripts' and yamato-damashi. The 'conscript' won but not until 115,853 Japanese had been killed and 7,902 of the inhabitants taken prisoner. American casualties were 85,000 (according to Japanese reports) killed and wounded in addition to heavy losses in aircraft, aircraft carriers, light and heavy warships, transports and landing craft. Japanese losses in the air were over 2,000 aircraft from April to the end of June when the battle for Okinawa was over.

Araki's kodo, the cult of brutality, should not be confused with yamato-damashi. The brutal fanatics, who delighted to torture their prisoners, were of the same stock but their inspiration was not the same. As soldiers, pure and simple, they were the 'sharpest steel' and lived and died in the true spirit of their code. To deny that is to detract from American heroism, on Iwojima or Okinawa, from British heroism and tenacity in the re-taking of Burma and the long period of 'blood, sweat and tears' during the South-West Pacific offensive of 1943—45.

These are but a few illustrations of the way in which the Japanese were bombed from the air, shelled from sea, battered and cut to bits. They fought bravely—it is a pity that their heroism contrasts so strangely with their atrocious behaviour to their captives. It is something in the blood 'which we ourselves are not always able to explain' as Harada puts it.

The population of Japan were told about the battles but not of the bloody details of the defeat. And, in order not to blunt the edge of yamato-damashi, the pilgrimages to Hachiman and Yasukuni Shrines were discouraged because of the vast crowds, of relatives of the forces overseas, who came to venerate the spirits of those who had died on the battlefield.

Attitude of the kodoites on the subject of ending the war was definite when Koiso resigned. They controlled an army of 2½ million men in Japan and an army of 3 million men overseas, they were in command of all the key points, dockyards, arsenals and munition factories. The sooner an invasion took place the better—it made no difference to them where the enemy landed, they had the soldiers, airmen and munitions necessary to inflict 500,000 casualties and still remain undefeated in the hills if not on the beaches. They had enough super-men in the Kamikaze Corps to man thousands of suicide-planes: what had been accomplished at Iwojima and Okinawa would be repeated on the soil of Japan.

After a few months of the 'blood-bath' the United States of America would hesitate to add to their casualties in order to bring about 'unconditional surrender'. Then, and then only, should Japan entertain the idea of a peace settlement.

There was no answer to the B 29's. But when the enemy did land they could strike back and inflict casualties—man for man—and that would be their answer, kill and be killed.

But the dupes of the Shinto State remained ignorant of the magnitude of Japan's defeat on the sea and in the air.

The leaders knew the truth and the Navy laboured under no illusions. All that was left of the battle-fleet was five battleships, three carriers and 12 cruisers. But, on 7th April, 1945, they made another desperate attempt to intervene in the Battle for Okinawa only to meet with another reverse in an action 60 miles off South Kyushu. Carrier-borne aircraft from Admiral Mitscher's task-force destroyed the 72,809 ton super-battleship *Yamato,* the escorting cruisers, *Isuzu* and *Yahagi* and the destroyer screen.

As usual the 'official spokesman' claimed a victory but the truth leaked out through the survivors and added to the general depression caused by the continuous bombing by the A.A.F.

However, the Japanese navy kept on fighting. Another naval and aerial counter-attack on the British and U.S. Naval units blockading Okinawa was carried out during the night of 12/13th April but the only news which was given out was, '120 of our suicide-planes failed to return from the Okinawa battlefield after inflicting enormous damage to the enemy fleet.'

Hirohito desired Peace—at any cost, but the Army was still determined 'to fight to the bitter end'. Hirohito could have sued for Peace and the chances are that his Edict would have been sufficient excuse for the Navy. But, in April, 1945, the country was at the mercy of the bayonet-men and civil war had to be avoided. To obtain 'Peace' by inciting his subjects to kill each other was out of the question for the Spiritual head of the Shinto State: Japan was not Italy and 'unconditional surender' was demanded by the Allies.

So Hirohito bided his time. He issued Edict after Edict—praised and rewarded thousands of his loyal subjects for their gallantry. He called on those who were not in the armed services to visit shrine and temple, to live abstemiously according to the traditions handed down from generation to generation. He made his own supplications before the Imperial Shrine in the grounds of the Palace littered with the debris of the air-raids; he neither abdicated nor precipitated civil war. No, Hirohito was no superman—he was not divine. He may have been weak or just a coward waiting for something to turn up. I do not know the answers but I do think that his methods, under the circumstances, suited Japanese. Few men in ancient or modern history had such a bloodless vindication of judgement when his last Edict was issued for it was obeyed by all his subjects and implemented by the machinery of a central government in full control of seventy million people.

What interested us most at this time (in the Yokohama-Tokyo area) was the absence of kami-kaze counter-attacks on the fighters or bombers. We put it down to shortage of petrol, or a plan to build up a strong reserve to deal with the 'invasion' but it served to reduce A.A.F. losses and enabled them to step-up their attacks from numerous new landing-strips on Bonins and Okinawa.

By the last week in April, air-warfare over Japan had reached the stage when the A.A.F. had 500 B 29's and 500 other types of bombers and fighters airborne at the same time. By calculating bomb-load—for B 29's—at five-ton it was possible to arrive at an estimate of tonnage being unloaded every day.

We had excellent maps of Japan, secured for us by chaps in working parties scrounging in bombed-out buildings; so it was not difficult to plot the day's havoc in any of the sixty odd target-areas.

Next, the aerial sledge-hammer, pounded Honshu airfields to bits on 11th, striking at Nagoya on 13th when *500 B 29's* discharged an explosive cargo of *3,600 tons* into a mass of debris. Two days later twenty airfields and aerodromes on Honshu and Shikoku were attacked by waves of carrier-borne aircraft.

Tokyo and Nagoya were the targets on 18th, and on 22nd 'coastal targets'—

shipping in Honshu and Kyushu—were hammered by B 29's and carrier-borne aircraft. There was also reports of mine-laying in the Sea of Japan between Moji and Fusan, in Korea.

'Photo Joe' came over again after the raid on 18th May: early on 23rd the sirens began to sound in Tokyo and Yokohama and in a few minutes the ground-defence was in action. Visibility was good and the first waves ran into a tremendous barrage of flak but the formations of from 20 to 30 B 29's—unaccompanied by fighters—pressed home their attack from the north, flying in exceedingly low for a daylight raid.

The noise from gun-fire and explosion of bombs exceeded anything we had heard before. In less than half an hour Tokyo was ablaze again; fire-fighters could do little as the successive waves dropped tons of H.E. and tons of incendiaries over a wide front.

There was little wind but the material damage was much greater than that done during the night raid of 9/10th March when 1,667 tons of incendiaries were expended on the target—now the raging furnace covered several square miles of the Capital and was still spreading when the last waves went over.

An American official report stated that *550 B29's* dropped *750,000 incendiary-bombs* in the total load of *4,500 tons* of explosives scattered on target that morning.

Not content with this demonstration of destructive power the A.A.F. sent over *500 B 29's with 4,000 tons of incendiaries* on the night of 25th/26th May, to make sure that Tokyo was really on fire! On 28th, *450 B 29's* escorted by P 51's and P 47's from 7th U.S.A.A.F., plastered Yokohama and Tokyo with a further *3,200 tons* of H.E.

Civilization 'measures war' by easily understood terms: *hundreds* of aircraft, thousands of tons of bombs, *hundreds of thousands of incendiaries, billions* of bullets, *millions* of men, *battleships* and *human-torpedoes*. To make it more readable, and not too boring, figures are explained by the enormous damage done, the great number of factories gutted, enemy 'potentiality for waging war' destroyed, and the number of casualties inflicted.

Number of casualties inflicted. Why not go into more detail for the benefit of the next generation? Why not put it bluntly: the number of men, women and children who have had their heads bashed in was greater during yesterday's attack than the number who had their stomach ripped open: the number who were trapped in buildings, crushed and roasted to death, was greater than those having arms and legs torn from their trunks: those receiving direct hits were scattered into smaller fragments than those pulverised by blast: the ratio, between the pulped and the calcinated, is as 1 is to 4: the new explosive, Mark VI, is more effective than Mark V, it strips hair, skin and flesh from bone much more neatly but we need something even better than Mark VI to increase casualties and reduce bomb-load.

On 31st May, *450 B 29's* with a strong fighter-escort from 7th U.S.A.A.F., unleashed another *3,200 tons* of H.E. on Osaka with the usual equilibrated damage to life and property.

Perhaps it is worth recording that, despite the heavy raids in the Yokohama-Tokyo area, the Omori camp staff and the numerous Japanese in daily contact with PoW working-parties, did not alter their behaviour to us for better or for worse. We still had Colonel Sakeba but 2/Lt. Kato and Sergeant Watanabe had left the camp: 'discipline' was maintained by a Sergeant-Major Oguri and he proved to be the most humane Japanese soldier I met from 1942 to 1945 and the morale in the camp (and the discipline) went up 100 per cent.

Unfortunately our personal treatment differed—during this period—from that accorded to allied airmen who bailed-out, or were shot-down, over Japan. They were treated by military and civilians with brutality equal to that accorded to army personnel by the major sadists.

Air-war, against Japan, was aided to a maximum point of destructiveness by the combined British and American naval action against Formosa, Okinawa, and the string of Islands from Kyushu to Ryukyus. In the beginning, B 24's and B 29's, striking from bases in China, dealt with airfields, ports and installations on Formosa which straddled the South Pacific. **Then from the second week in April, allied aircraft carriers closed in on Japan and hardly a day passed without hostile action being taken against land or sea targets by Anglo-American naval fighter-aircraft.**

From March to June, 1945, these task-forces staged more than fifty sorties against Formosa, Okinawa, Sakishima, Tokunoshima, Amamishima and Kikashima with concentrated attacks on the Amami and Saki group of islands.

On 4th and 5th May, battleships and cruisers of British Pacific Fleet shelled Miyakoshima, in the Sakishima group, while American task-forces operated inshore against the Kuriles—from Paramushiro down-coast to Saghalien—made nine strikes from carriers and six bombardments from surface craft.

But what interested me most was the 'secret lectures' given by Colonel Sakeba and Staff-officer from the War Office. I obtained my information from a Formosan anti-Jap in the special I. Corps. One lecture dealt with the subject of 'Disposing of PoW during the Invasion'. Omori was selected to illustrate the modus operandi.

> ...After all maps and documents likely to be of use to the invader are destroyed, muster PoW officers and hand over the camp to them. March out immediately but post machine-gun sections to cover the Omori bridge. When enemy troops appear the PoW will break camp and should be allowed to cross the bridge before machine-guns open fire and destroy them on the road which the enemy is attacking. If this way of disposing of them is not practicable other steps must be taken to prevent them escaping or joining incoming troops and helping them with local knowledge.

There was no invasion so we did not help the incoming troops with local knowledge. But, after each raid, our working-parties went over the Omori bridge to help in salvage operations. They worked alongside the natives, who searched in the gutted buildings for useful bits of property, and from first to last there was not a single incident involving civilians and prisoners of war. Truckloads of our chaps travelled over the bombed Omori-Yokohama-Tokyo area and, except for a few raised fists, no one expressed emotion one way or the other.

Some of our chaps had been in the Bataan death march, in which *10,000* Americans and Filipinos died, and for which crime General Kawan, Colonel Hirano and 13 others were duly hanged: others were picked out of the 'ditch' a few yards from the Camp or off a Pacific Island, some were from Hong Kong, Singapore or Java—we were a mixed lot of races from all the services but 'pigged-it' together very well indeed.

Carrier-borne planes from U.S. 3rd Fleet went north on 14th to bomb targets in North Honshu and Hokkaido while B 29's hammered the Kofu area.

On 16th, 17th and 18th there was a series of 'carrier raids' on Tokyo-Yokohama industrial-plant, airfields and harbour installations and for the first time the press admitted that British aircraft were operating against Japan. Coshu, Hitachi (N.E. of Tokyo), Fukui, Okasaki and other oil-refineries in the Osaka-Amagasaki area were raided on 16th and 19th by 600 B 29's.

According to the newspaper reports, the 'record strike' was carried out on 9th and 10th July when 2,000 aircraft, described as fighters, fighter-bombers, and super-fortresses, carried out simultaneous raids on Kyushu, Shikoku and Tokyo-Yokohama targets.

It was also stated, on the highest naval authority, that 14 enemy aircraft-carriers were operating in Japan's home waters.

There had been no secrecy displayed regarding the composition of the Anglo-American Fleet operating against Japan in July, 1945.

A few days later, *Hitachi*—only 75 miles North of Tokyo—was shelled from a 6-mile range by units of the British Pacific Fleet, including battleship *King George V*, and they had shelled the coast-line for about sixty-miles. There was no report of the damage caused by the shelling and no report of any counter-action by 'Baka' death-defying kamikaze pilots or by one of the many hundred one-man submarines based on Yokohama and Kure.

While these major naval operations were proceeding, British carrier-borne aircraft covered the action of the light-units of U.S. 3rd Fleet off the East coast of China prefecture.

While these naval operations were proceeding, official communiques were issued regarding the 'enormous successes against the enemy in the *OKINAWA*

BATTLE AREA!' According to these reports the Kamikaze corps brought down 500 British and American aircraft in addition to destroying a further 400 on the ground during the period 25—31st July. The communiques stated that 'enemy aircraft destroyed in air combat, or on the ground, during the Okinawa battles totalled 2,105.' Also—during the same period—'Kamikaze suicide-squads sank or damaged another 10 enemy warships bringing the grand-total (for the Okinawa battles) to 408 including battleships, cruisers, aircraft-carriers, destroyers, transports, tankers and landing-craft . . .' The final statement gave in tabular form the type and number of vessels sunk, damaged or slightly damaged between 1st April and 31st July.

Certainly the Kamikaze suicide-squads had enough 'floating targets' to aim for from mid-July the Anglo-American fleet consisted of 133 major units. The American Navy was represented by 8 battleships, 16 aircraft-carriers, 19 cruisers and 62 large destroyers: the British Navy by one battleship, 4 aircraft-carriers, 6 cruisers and 17 destroyers.

No doubt the combined fleet suffered heavy casualties and one report (in the *New York Times* of 12th August, 1945) stated that 'Baka kamikaze's' sank 20 and damaged 30 warships, with heavy loss of life. Vessels destroyed by the crash tactics of Japanese airmen included 11 destroyers, 3 escort-carriers, 2 minesweepers, and 2 ammunition ships; vessels damaged were 5 American and 3 British aircraft-carriers, 4 battleships, 2 escort-carriers, 3 American and 1 Australian cruiser, 11 destroyers and 1 hospital ship.

However, one thing was certain. Japan's Navy was now reduced to 'bits and pieces' and when the remnants were handed over, in September 1945, only 52 out of 380 major warships which were engaged on active service during World War II remained afloat.

It was the turn of the carrier-borne aircraft on 9th August: 1,200 planes, from combined fleet, operated against Koriyama, Masuda, Matsushima, Niigata, Sendai and Yabuki in North Honshu. Surface craft shelled Kamaishi steel-works.

In the report I circulated of that routine bombing of 'selected targets' included this item of later news . . . 'Two B 29's dropped a land-mine on Nagasaki. *150 B 29's* bombed Kurume, in West Honshu, dropping land-mines.' That was all I knew, at the time regarding the atom-bombing of Nagasaki.

Newspapers, which I got hold of, used the word *'ji-rai'*—land-mine—when reporting the damage at Hiroshima *until after* the atom-bomb had destroyed Nagasaki. It was then that the word *'gen-shi'*—atom—replaced the word *ji-rai*. The land-mine became *'Genshi-no-bakudan'*—atom-bomb, but I remained under the impression that numbers of *'ji-rai'* (or *'gensh-no-bakudan'*) had been dropped by B 29's. However, after Nagasaki had been dealt with, there was no confusion of thought in the mind of Japanese reporters for they commented freely on the *'gen-shi-no-boi'* (the great violence of the atom-bomb) when photographs of the Hiroshima damage were published in the newspapers.

At the time the atom bombs were dropped, the population of Hiroshima was (approximately) 320,000—including troops—and the population of Nagasaki about 260,000 of whom not more than half were in the industrial 'target' area of about *two square miles* which was also 'blasted out of recognition'.

The casualty figures, as given above, speak for themselves—grim statistics of the use of weapons of mass destruction, atomic energy applied to war. But I am tempted to make this comparison between the incendiary raid on Toyko (9/10th March, 1945) and the blast effects of the atomic bombs at Hiroshima and Nagasaki.

At Tokyo, 15.8 miles of the city were destroyed, *83,000* men, women and children were *killed* and *102,000* others *injured* by *1,667 tons* of incendiaries dropped from a bombing altitude of 7,050 ft., by *279 B 29's*. The raid on Tokyo lasted several hours. The 'raid' on Hiroshima and Nagasaki was by one machine over the towns for a few minutes and then the killing was *instantaneous* in the target areas of two square miles or so. The 'human target' at Tokyo was a million or more whereas at Hiroshima-Nagasaki it did not exceed 600,000 men, women and children.

From a purely scientific point of view the atom bombs were a success—a hideous, revolting success. The progress of our 'civilization', on its way to its own cremation, was facilitated by a 'secret weapon' of mass destruction. The team of scientific experts responsible for its perfection, no less than the politicians, have reason to be conscious of their successful collaboration in overcoming all the difficulties which confronted them before two atom bombs were used on the Japanese.

Only two atom bombs were in existence in August, 1945, and—from first to last—they cost the United States of America no less than $2,000,000,000. But the explosive energy of the bomb was equivalent to that of 20,000 tons of T.N.T., and never before could so many human beings be obliterated, or reduced to dust, in the fraction of the speed of sound. Never before was science so exact in its calculations to produce such a compact explosive—such a remarkable coercive bludgeon. Whether it was necessary to use the atom bomb against Japan in August, 1945, is a matter of opinion.

In June, 1945, President Truman and his advisers are said to have been in agreement not to use the atomic bomb. A policy committee, under Mr. Byrnes, it was stated, had prepared a report for President Truman and Mr. Churchill recommending that the bomb should not be used because it would not be wise for the United States of America to create a precedent for the use of such a terrible weapon.

A month later, during the Potsdam Conference, this wise decision was reversed after they had been informed of the success of the experiment carried out in the secrecy of the Mexican desert.

They also warned Japan, quite clearly, that 'The alternative for Japan is complete and utter destruction . . .' but did not specify the atomic bomb as the precise method of complete and utter destruction.

There was no need to. According to the 'rules of total-warfare' all weapons suitable for destruction are used by any without a declaration of intention. Japan was warned. In total warfare there is no room for sentiment. The objectives are clearly defined—complete and utter destruction at the earliest possible moment after the opening of hostilities. It was mere hypocrisy for Japan to cite 'International Law' after she had ignored it for twenty years and placed herself on record as the equal of the Huns in barbarity when she had 'residential centres' in China and elsewhere at the mercy of her indiscriminate bombers.

Hiroshima and Nagaski were *total-warfare* answers to the brutality of the Bataan death march and the 'polite bombing' of Pearl Harbour.

Mr. Winston Churchill (in the House on 16th August, 1945) stated quite clearly what Japan would have done had she been in possession of atomic bombs. Still, I shall never be convinced that it was necessary to use the atomic bomb, least of all on Nagasaki so soon after Hiroshima. Certainly not to 'prevent the sacrifice of a million American and a quarter of a million British lives in the desperate battles and massacres of an invasion of Japan.' Japan, *before the Potsdam Declaration*, had told the Soviet Union that she was ready to discuss terms of surrender with the allies.

There was almost as much secrecy observed about Japan's overtures for Peace as there was secrecy regarding the atomic bombs.

The Potsdam Three-Power Conference opened on 17th and closed on 25th July, 1945: the result of the British General Election was announced on 26th July—Mr. Attlee formed the Labour Government on 27th July and the atomic bomb was used on 6th August.

In a written reply to Mr. Horabin (Cornwall N. Ind. L.) Mr. Attlee in December, 1946, furnished this explanation:

> No overtures for peace were made by Japan to the countries *with which she was at war* prior to her acceptance of the terms of the Potsdam Declaration which she did not communicate to us until 10th August, 1945, 15 days after the declaration had been made and four days after the dropping of the first atomic bomb.
>
> It was known, however, that the Japanese leaders had previously been considering means of reaching a settlement more favourable to themselves than unconditional surrender.
>
> At Potsdam, on 28th July, Generalissimo Stalin informed President Truman and me *in strict confidence* that the Soviet Government, who had not at that time joined in the Far Eastern War, had received from the Japanese Government a proposal that they should act as mediators between the Japanese Government and the British and United States Government. According to Generalissimo Stalin, the Soviet Government interpreted this move as an attempt to obtain the collaboration of the Soviet Government in the furtherance of Japanese policy,

and they had therefore returned an unhesitating negative.

The information thus furnished by Generalissimo Stalin offered no new opportunity for hastening the conclusion of the war since the Japanese Government had already, by the Potsdam Declaration of 26th July, been invited in the most formal manner to surrender . . .

From this it is quite clear that nothing but unconditional surrender in advance of negotiations would be accepted, as a basis for restoration of peace, no matter how many millions of British or American lives were involved in the political decision, so the atomic bombs were used.

Mr. Churchill, speaking about Britain's share in atom-bomb research work, added—merely for dramatic emphasis: 'By God's mercy British and American science outpaced all German efforts'.

Deists and materialists, on the winning side in World War II, can thank their 'lucky stars' that we were not bombed into unconditional surrender by Hitler or Showa Tenno. Perhaps, Japanese first-hand experiences of atomic-energy applied to war will turn her from Shinto to Christianity in order to win in the next war.

On 10th August, 1,200 aircraft from combined fleet repeated the attacks of the previous day on the same targets in North Honshu.

Then on 11th and 12th hundreds of fighters and dive-bombers raided the Tokyo-area aerodromes: on 13th there was a mass demonstration over Tokyo—the record number of 1,600 strikes were made between sunrise and sunset on all the battered targets.

The end was in sight. On 14th August, 400 B 29's raided Kure and Hikari naval bases while a smaller formation struck at Osaka arsenal. In Omori we had another dawn to dusk spectacle of flight after flight of fighters and fighter-bombers machine-gunning the military targets to drive home the lessons of Hiroshima and Nagasaki.

Crowds continued to gather in the vicinity of the Imperial Palace on the 13th. The press contained no information of the progress of the peace overtures—the air-raid warnings heralded the approach of enemy aircraft. All day long the fighters and the fighter-bombers machine-gunned and bombed their targets in our area. What was happening?

Far into the night the Cabinet debated the implications of the Potsdam Declaration and its effect on the legal position of the Tenno. In the end, thirteen Ministers accepted the United Nation's conditions and three declined. Admiral Toyoda, Navy Chief of Staff, maintaining that the Allied reply avoided an answer to the main point, which was 'The Tenno is divine and could not accept orders from an earthly being'.

Admiral Suzuki, faced with opposition from General Anami, General Umezu (Chief of the General Staff) and Admiral Toyoda (Chief of Naval General Staff) who refused to sign the acceptance document, appealed to the

Tenno who convened an Imperial Conference for 10.00 hours 14th August. It was at this conference that the Tenno, after hearing the opinions of the thirteen ministers, ordered the Cabinet to draft an Imperial Rescript which he would broadcast to the nation at noon. At the same time, Japan's acceptance was to be dispatched to the United Nations.

During the final Conference, the A.A.F. were bombing Kure, Hikari Naval Base and Hiroshima with *400 B 29's* while formations of 'Thunderbolts' and 'Lightnings' were plastering Osaka Military Arsenal. And, at intervals, other aircraft dropped millions of leaflets explaining to the Japanese the nature of the Allied reply to Japan's surrender offer.

From time to time, Tokyo Radio warned the people of Japan to stand-by for a vital announcement affecting the future of the 100 million subjects of the Tenno. Then came the special announcement that the Tenno would speak to his people at noon that day. But this did not interfere with the bombing programmes of the A.A.F. From dawn the fighters and the fighter-bombers were in action in the Tokyo-Yokohama area 'shooting-up' the targets: even when the Omori camp-staff and guards were parading in front of the main office for the Tenno's broadcast we were watching a formation dive-bomb the adjacent aerodrome.

Precisely at noon, 14th August, 1945, the recorded voice of Tenno Heika was broadcast over Tokyo radio. The kodoites and the people of the soil listened in silence:

> To our good and loyal subjects: After pondering deeply on the general trend of the world and the actual conditions obtaining in our Empire today, we have decided to effect a settlement of the present situation by resorting to an extraordinary measure. We have ordered our Government to communicate to the Governments of the United States, Britain, China and the Soviet Union that our Empire accepts the provisions of their joint declaration.
>
> To strive for the common prosperity and happiness of all nations as well as for the security and well-being of our subjects is the solemn obligation which has been handed down by our Imperial Ancestors and which lies close to our hearts. Indeed we declared war on America and Britain out of our sincere desire to ensure Japan's self-preservation and the stabilization of East Asia, it being far from our thoughts either to infringe upon the sovereignty of other nations or to embark on territorial agrandisement. But now the war has lasted for nearly four years. In spite of the best that has been done by everyone, the gallant fighting of the military and naval forces, the diligence and assiduity of our servants of the State, and the devoted service of our 100,000,000 people, the war situation has developed not necessarily to Japan's advantage, while the general trends of the world have all turned against her interests.
>
> The enemy, moreover, has begun to employ a new and most cruel bomb, the power of which to do damage is indeed incalculable, taking toll of many innocent lives. Should we continue to fight, it would only result in the ultimate

collapse and obliteration of the Japanese nation and lead to the total extinction of human civilization. Such being the case, how are we to save millions of our subjects, or ourselves atone before the hallowed spirits of our Imperial ancestors?

This is the reason we have ordered the acceptance of the provisions of the joint declaration of the Powers. We cannot but express the deepest sense of regret to our allied nations of East Asia, who have consistently co-operated with the Empire towards the amancipation of East Asia.

The thought of those officers and men, as well as others who have fallen on the field of battle, of those who have died at their posts of duty or those who have met with untimely death, and those bereaved families, pains our heart night and day.

The welfare of the wounded and war sufferers and of those who have lost their homes and livelihood are objects of our profound solicitude. The hardships and sufferings to which our nation is to be subjected hereafter will certainly be great.

We are keenly aware of the innermost feelings of all our subjects. However, it is according to the dictate of time and fate that we have resolved to pave the way for a peace for all generations to come by enduring the unavoidable, and suffering what is insufferable. Having been able to save and maintain the structure of the Imperial state, we are always with you, our good and loyal subjects, relying upon your sincerity and integrity.

Beware most strictly lest any outbursts of emotion, which may engender needless complications, or any fraternal contention and strife, which may cause confusion, lead you astray and cause you to lose the confidence of the world. Let the entire nation continue as one family from generation to generation, ever firm in its faith in the imperishableness of its divine land and mindful of its heavy burden of responsibilities and the long road before it. Devote your united strength to construction for the future. Cultivate ways of rectitude, further nobility of spirit, and work with resolution, so that you may enhance the innate glory of the Imperial State and keep pace with the progress of the world . . .

Then there was silence—except for the rush of aircraft over the camp. Those who had been listening to the voice of the Tenno remained at attention for a few moments. Then Colonel Sakeba left his place in the parade and the next senior officer yelled 'Kei-rei' and those present saluted as if Sakeba was the Emperor in person.

The recording of the Tenno's message was kept in the Palace after it had been made. Some fanatics attempted to seize it before it was taken to the Tokyo broadcasting station. One report stated that Lt.-General Mori, Comandant of the Imperial Guard, was killed because he had allowed the recording to be taken to the radio station, and then the conspirators, led by a son-in-law of General Tojo, rushed there but were too late to stop the broadcast. However, directly the Tenno ceased speaking, Admiral Suzuki resigned with the rest of his Cabinet but received the Imperial Command to remain in office pending new appointments. General Anami, War Minister, lost no time in ending his own life.

The broadcast was full of excuses and explanations for years of aggression in

China, and in Greater East Asia, 'to ensure Japan's self-preservation and the stabilization of East Asia, it being far from our thoughts either to infringe upon the sovereignty of other nations or to embark on territorial agrandisement'.

The chief credit for bringing about the unconditional surrender of Japan goes to the Bomber Command of the A.A.F., to the U.S. Marines, the combined navies and the 'Aussies' who helped the Marines to capture the island bases in the South Pacific.

The Omori camp staff, and the guards, accepted the unconditional surrender calmly. There was only one incident on the night of the Tenno's broadcast. A number of n.c.o.'s and some of the camp staff, got drunk on sake and beer. They held a 'conference' and decided to use their swords on the A.A.F. 'special prisoners' still under guard in the special barracks.

Bubbling with yamato-damashi they advanced on the un-armed captives. Fortunately, one of the sentries gave the alarm and held them off at the point of the bayonet. As 'go-between' I attended, saw what was happening, gave the alert and had all the lights turned out in our barracks, went in to the 'special barrack' to warn them and then returned in time to see three of the guard holding the mob in check. Just then, when things were a bit tricky, 'Gentleman Jim' (Lt. Morigishi) appeared and took over.

One burly Sergeant-Major retired, bleeding profusely from a slash in the neck, a few others were manhandled and then bundled into a spare barrack-room. One by one, Morigishi called them out and disarmed them and received a nasty gash across the palms of his hands from one drunken fanatic. However, it all ended in a few cuts and a little blood-letting.

Next morning, after tenko, a Lieutenant from the Imperial Guard arrived. He came and apologised to me for the incident, emphasising that the culprits were 'camp staff' and not regular soldiers, and that in future an officer, and not an n.c.o., would be in command on the Omori camp guard. But, beyond Morigishi's action, none of the people who ran amok were punished.

The next few days, during the Manila negotiations, it was impossible to obtain a definition of our status under the terms of the cease-fire. Colonel Sakeba declined to discuss the matter and the camp staff continued to act as if they had never stood in silence listening to the Tenno's broadcast. On the other hand there were six-hundred prisoners of war in Omori camp and they had been informed by me of the exact position day by day—some wanted to take charge of the camp but I was against that as quite unnecessary.

On 15th August, Admiral Suzuki's resignation had been accepted. The following day, Prince Higashi Kuni, cousin of the Tenno, member of the Supreme War Council and chief of the Home Defence forces, became Prime Minister. The Tenno's eldest daughter was married to the Prince's son so the appointment was in keeping with the divine traditions.

On 16th August, Higashi Kuni, as Prime Minister and Minister of War, broadcast instructions to the nation, and particularly to the Army, to observe the Imperial Rescript to lay down arms, because 'The decision has been taken to cease fire and return to Peace.'

We had typhoon-weather on Friday 24th August. Our wooden-walls were flattened. Tokyo radio announced that the first landings, of the occupying forces, had been advanced from 28th to 26th owing to the weather conditions, and that General MacArthur would land at Atsugi aerodrome on 31st.

Camp guards had been reinforced, sentries posted at both ends of Omori bridge: Tokyo-Yokohama road was crammed with people moving out of the occupation zones. Inside the camp the 'Special Interrogation Corps' were setting fire to their many lists of questions to be put to the invaders.

On 26th the A.A.F. sent over more bombers. This time, instead of atom bombs, incendiaries and high-explosives they dropped oil-drums packed tight with clothing, medical supplies, sweets, emergency rations and American cigarettes. Plane after plane came in low, skimming the roof-tops, in 'Operation Oil-drum', and there was some indiscriminate bombing which destroyed bits of our barracks so we signalled 'Go slow—or go home'.

Some of the fighter aircraft, from the carriers, dropped packets of chewing gum and cigarettes dangling from parachutes made from their pocket-handkerchiefs—others dropped the latest edition of the *Yorktown News*—'Special Air-mail to Prisoners-of-War-Camps. Western Budget.' So we were kept busy picking up all the good things from the A.A.F., instead of dodging their pellets.

On the third day of 'Operation Oil-drum', Wednesday 29th August, I had just walked out of No. 2 Barracks when a 'hedge-hopper' came whizzing over the bath-house. There was a roar and a crash as a gift from Uncle Sam made a direct-hit on the ledge of my bunk window. It shattered the glass, smashed the table, whizzed through the sliding-door and exploded in the passage between the bunks scattering tins of meat in all directions.

Had that 'packet' arrived a few minutes earlier it would have bashed my head, showered Parker with broken glass and hit Darby and Crossman full in the middle: Parker had been 'bagged' at Hong Kong in December, 1941, Lt.-Commander Crossman, D.S.O., and Lt. Darby (ex H.M.S. *Indefatigable*) had been fished out of the sea on 9th August, 1945.

Soon afterwards I was reading the *Yorktown News* of 28th August, 1945: 'A Berlin woman who wants a hair-do must take to the beauty-shop her own hot water or a brick of pressed coal. Gas is so scarce that beauty shops are not permitted to keep a flame burning all day,' when someone popped his head into the shattered bunk and said, 'You're wanted out in front, sir! I think it's them Red Cross blokes again.'

Red Cross representatives had been in the previous day and I had called the attention of Mr. Junot (Geneva Delegate from the International Red Cross) to the condition of Private Rae's emaciated condition—and his maimed feet—so I took with me a 2,500 word statement, signed by Rae, for his information. But, before I reached the front office, I heard shouts of 'It's the bluddy Yanks with tommy-guns! We're free—we're free!'

By the time I returned, all American PoW's had been taken out of Omori camp—the British contingent and the G.I.'s remained to be dealt with. No boats were due in so I retired to my rather battered bunk. Hardly had I settled down to a quiet smoke with Parker when a sentry wandered in—just to say, sayonara.

I was glad to see him. He was the chap who held off the drunks at the point of his bayonet and threatened to shoot if anyone moved in the direction of the special barracks. We had lots of 'good eats' but he was not interested in food, or smokes, he wanted a few words with me. He was very serious. 'In a few minutes you will be gone. I'll never see you again. All this will be like a dream—but I shall not forget.'

Parker moved out. I told the chap that we all appreciated what he had done that night. He cut me short: 'I did not come to talk about that—I did my duty to Tenno Heika, do not speak about that. I came to ask for a souvenir—something of yours, something to remind me of you, and this camp.'

Luckily, in my holdall, I had an old Northumberland Fusilier great-coat button—my souvenir of World War I. I got it out and handed it to him with an explanation of the motto 'Quo Fata Vocant' (where destiny calls) and the crest of St. George killing the Dragon.

He was pleased. Asked a few more questions about my kami (St. George) and shuku-mei (fate pre-ordained from a former life) wrapped up his kata-mi (souvenir) in a Red Cross handkerchief I gave him, picked up his rifle, stood up and saluted: 'Sayonara-o-daiji-ni'—turned and walked away.

Curious people: 'Sayonara-o-daiji-ni'—if it must be so, take good care of yourself.

In the distance, searchlights were flitting from cloud to cloud or sweeping along the battle-scarred waterfront of Tokyo–as we went down channel and left behind the dying embers of our signal fires. It had been a long day—and a long night. Dawn was breaking as we came to the lee of the U.S. Hospital Ship *Benevolence*, in Tokyo Bay: it was good to breathe sea-air, as free men, after three and a half years ashore in the custody of Japanese who believed in the unification of the ordinary functions of government with the veneration of the divine Imperial ancestors and practised all the tricks of the devil under the name of bushido and sai-sei itchi.

Burn O'Neil, Ian Darby and Jimmy Crossman were surprised to see HMS

Indefatigable *steam into Tokyo Bay and were soon re-united with their shipmates.*

On 11th August, 1946, Okada declared: 'Russian officials knew six months before Russia entered the Pacific War of Japan's desire to yield. Peace could have come many months earlier if Russia had promptly relayed Japanese requests.'

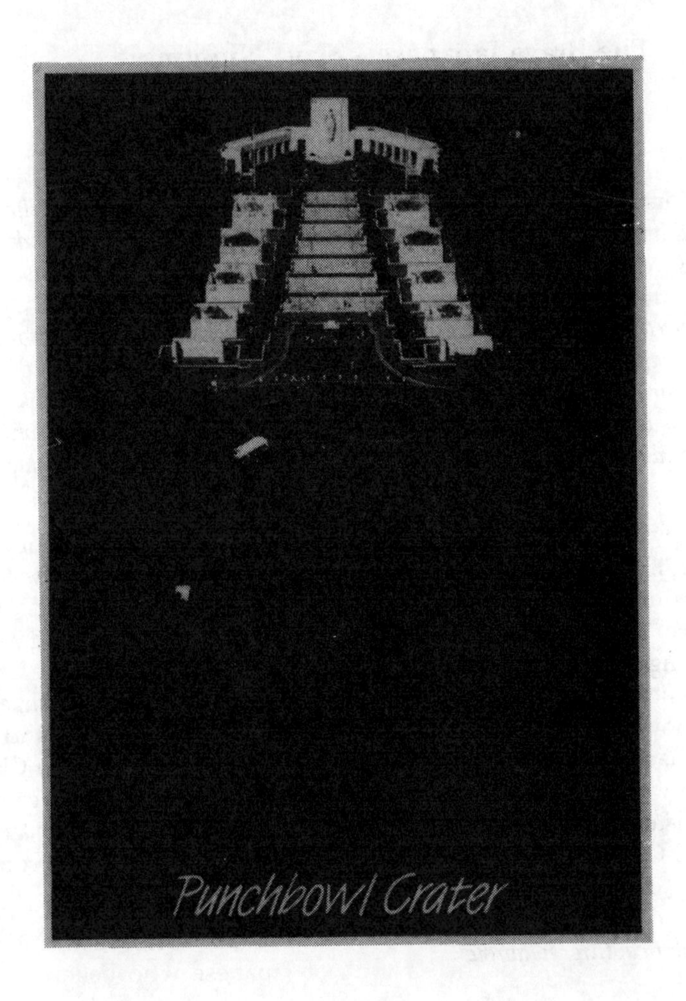

Located within Punchbowl Crater, the statue of Columbia looks down on the over 30,000 graves of the United States War dead. Photo: Loye Guthrie
(See story on page 773.)

CHAPTER THREE

The Brave Japanese — Java Nightmare — The Kamikazes

Kenneth Harrison *was a sergeant in the Fourth Anti-Tank Regiment of the Eighth Australian Division. After fierce action in Malaya and many hair-raising adventures while trying to evade capture, he and his mates reluctantly gave themselves up, hopefully to save their lives.*

They endured atrocious conditions and appalling treatment in Pudu Prison, Kuala Lumpur, Singapore, Changi and Thailand before being taken by sea aboard the Byoki Maru *to Japan. He was, for a time, with Russell Braddon at Pudu.*

Here are a few extracts from his wonderful book, **'The Brave Japanese'** *which may help to illustrate the mentality, character and spirit of the men on both sides of the conflict:-*

. . . In the warmth of the early afternoon our march seemed more like a pleasant stroll through the countryside. We took care, however, always to keep the road on our right. Towards evening we stopped at a Chinese house. We had quickly learnt to distinguish between Chinese and Malay houses, and we were also becoming expert in putting out feelers for food. In this regard the Chinese were magnificent. Not once in all our travels did we meet with a refusal, and no matter how poor or small the house, always we were taken in and given what they had. Sometimes, after seeing the obvious poverty of a Chinese peasant we would feel ashamed and try to withdraw, but always came the anxious insistence that turned into smiles and nods of pleasure as we ate. God bless them. Christ himself could not have wished to meet more complete charity and selflessness . . .

Following their capture, he wrote:

Billy McGlone (brother of Jack McGlone, our gun layer) was almost crazy with pain from repeated bashing and finally got to his feet and charged one of his tormentors. The Jap ran from Bill who, with his hands still tied behind him, returned to the group and sat with his head slumped between his knees. The Jap then returned with others from his tank crew and, coming at Bill from behind, ran him through with a bayonet, savagely, again and again. Ken,

Freddy Turner, and the other anti-tank boys were made to bury his body . . .

. . . Later, when we got to know the Japanese soldier better, we realized that our three officers—fortunately for us and for the Allies—were exceptional. Often small groups that came out of the jungle to surrender, were butchered on the spot.

In fairness it must be added that in our own Army we had the occasional loudmouth who boasted that 'I'll never take any of the yellow bastards as prisoners!' It must also be added that these heroes were invariably useless in action and the first to throw their hands hopefully into the air.

At Batu Pahat we were handed over to the local troops and made our first acquaintance with the stocky little men who were to become so familiar, and so detestable to us in the next three and a half years. At first sight one was inclined to wonder incredulously how these short monkey-like men in the shoddy uniforms had performed so magnificently against us. But closer inspection showed their bow legged frames to be sturdy and powerful, and their equipment—including their split-toed rubber shoes—to be far better fitted for jungle warfare than our own. We were also to learn that, whatever their other faults, their discipline and fighting spirit were completely magnificent . . .

. . . Conditions in the jail proper were completely chaotic, for the Japanese had utilized only a fraction of the available space. During the day more than seven hundred men were crammed into what in peacetime had been an exercise yard for thirty female prisoners. At night we slept on the bare floor of a veranda that ran around the first floor of a cell block, in the few cells themselves, and even on the stairs that led to the tiny court where the latrines were situated.

At night we were far too tightly packed to leave any form of passageway, and, as our rice diet had a high water content and most of us had dysentery in any case, every man was up four or five times a night. This involved stumbling over the packed, sweating bodies on the veranda floor and down the twenty-odd steps to the courtyard, asking permission from the guard, 'Benjo-ka, Okay?' and making for the boxes built over the two shallow holes in the centre of the courtyard. Rainy nights, when water filled the trenches and forced the maggots up on to the seats, were a horror.

As I lay on the floor, my semi-healed ankle was constantly being stepped on, and I came to dread the moonless nights. I tried sleeping with my head to the centre, but the smell of unwashed feet was unbearable. They were unforgettable, hideous, restless nights.

. . . Many a weak and feverish P.O.W. was to die simply because he could not eat his rice. One of our medical officers later coined the phrase, 'Your ticket home is at the bottom of your dixie.' And it was true. While you kept eating there was always a chance. But a man with a temperature that tops the century and who is straining his life away with thirty and forty griping bowel movements a day is not always the most logical of thinkers. And it was hard to convince a man who dry-retches at the mere sight and smell of the rice that he *must* eat, even if he vomits most of it on the spot.

A second spectre that visited us during Pudu days was a complaint known as 'Happy Feet'. For some inexplicable reason only half the men were affected by this searing stabbing in the soles of the feet. Massaging brought only temporary relief, and the touch of even the lightest covering brought a scream of pain. The only sure relief was walking.

Often at night I would stir on my concrete slab and sleepily note the.haggard figures trudging wearily past the cell door, and as I dozed off, hear the never ending clip clop of their wooden clogs on the concrete floor. All night up and down, round and round, with searing pain waiting to stab the moment they stopped.

Ken then relates also his experiences of 'Rice Balls', already described by Russell Braddon.

. . . But if we were short of food and vitamins in Pudu, we were rich in conversation, for Pudu was a paradise of exciting stories. Every man in the jail had been taken behind the enemy lines; some were Malay Volunteers who had stayed behind as guerillas; others were from the Army, the Navy, and the Air Force.

There was the medical orderly who had treated an Englishman who had had the lower half of his face shot away and whose tongue had to be stitched to his shirt with needle and thread to prevent it getting back down his throat and choking him. Mercifully perhaps, he was executed by the Japanese.

Ken tells the same story as Russell Braddon about Jim Wharton, and then continues:

Grim-faced Lieutenant Ben Hackney was the only other survivor of this massacre and his experience had, if anything, been even more hair-raising. Hackney's left leg had been shattered by a mortar shell during the fighting and he too had been left with the wounded at Parit Sulong.

When the massacre commenced, Hackney had shammed dead, and despite being bayoneted eight times by Japanese who doubted his demise, he had been successful in feigning death. Successful in spite of the fact that one of the Japanese had roughly dragged the boots from his feet. What agony this must have caused to his broken leg can well be imagined. And yet in the middle of this nightmare of pain and horror he was still cool enough to observe the arrival of the short stocky commander of the Japanese and to note that the Japanese treated him almost as a god.

When I met Hackney in Pudu he was covered with bayonet marks on his legs and body and his left leg was bent at an odd angle. His horrifying experience, far from breaking his nerve, seemed only to make him grim and unyielding to the guards. Hackney appointed himself as the guardian of poor bewildered Jimmy Wharton and more than once stepped between the boy and the guards to protect him. Grim and implacable was Ben Hackney in those days but what an example of guts he set to us all. I was proud that he was an Australian.

. . . Possibly the most unusual story of all was that of Jan, a handsome and light-hearted Dutchman. Jan had been the pilot of a Wildebeest and in some miraculous fashion had survived without a parachute when his plane had been shot down in flames. He had been forced by the heat on to the tail of the plane and the crash had thrown him clear on to the soft tree tops from which he climbed down unscratched. Knowing his story, one would have been justified in supposing that the gods had other fates in mind for Jan than death. Alas, our charming friend was in the last weeks of his young life.

Also among those unwillingly present were Hugh Moore and his friend, Russell Braddon, who was later to write *The Naked Island*. Hugh, Russ, and several others had been captured by a Japanese patrol who bound them and then dragged them for days through jungle tracks. They were used to find a path through minefields, deprived of food and water most of the time, and systematically beaten up.

. . . The Japanese published newspapers, notably the *Shonan Shinbun*, which for many months was posted on the notice board for our edification. Many of the articles describing 'the kindness of the Imperial Japanese Army to the people of the occupied territories' were laughable, but it was in descriptions of battle scenes that the Japanese journalists really excelled themselves.

One classic related how the pilot of a Zero repeatedly straffed a British battleship until he ran out of ammunition. Undaunted, our gallant friend flew low and upside down over the battleship, and as he zoomed over the bridge he drew his sword and with a mighty swipe beheaded the Captain of the ship!

Possibly the best of these stories concerned another intrepid pilot who engaged an overwhelming force of American planes, and shot down seven, even though he took an awful beating in the process. He finally landed his battered plane, staggered to his Commanding Officer, stood to attention, gasped out his report, and collapsed. When a doctor was summoned from the next room he made a quick examination and reported, 'This man has been dead for two hours.' The article went on to reveal that so invincible was the spirit of this man that it had supported his dead body until his duty had been completed. . . .

. . . The ever-present nightmare to the Australians in those early days was the fear that the Japanese would invade Australia, and to us who knew the country so well it seemed that they had only to attack Sydney and Melbourne to be sure of quick and certain victory. So certain did it seem that Australia must fall to the all-conquering Japanese, that the Pudu guards, many of whom were detailed for the invasion, offered to take letters to Australia for us. Many Puduites, aware that they had almost certainly been posted 'Missing believed killed', and worried at the distress that the uncertainty would bring to their families, did take advantage of this offer, and handed over letters for posting in Australia.

The better we got to know the Japanese, the more clearly we visualized the horrors that would follow an invasion of Australia, and when I saw the torment endured by the married men I felt grateful—not for the last time—that I had left Australia without any close ties. There were relatives and girl friends of course, but only years later when I became a father did I fully realize the despair those who had left wives and children must have felt.

We thanked God from the depths of our being that our fair land was not invaded and we took tremendous pleasure in the thought that possibly the little that we had done—the seventy days it took to conquer Malaya—had delayed the Japanese just long enough to prevent an invasion. And despite the hunger, the work, the sickness, the beatings, and the humiliation, in that thought we were vastly content.

. . . 'The Indians and Malays used to hurl stones and abuse almost every day but now they're starting to wake up and think that perhaps the old order wasn't so bad after all.' It was true; public opinion was rapidly hardening against the arrogant and brutal people who had at first been hailed by many as 'liberators and fellow Asians'.

Minutes later we passed five poles on the side of the main road and on each pole sat a Chinese head. We gazed with fascination at these examples of Nippon culture and were surprised to find that with the blood drained from them, the heads had a waxen peaceful appearance and were not in the least gruesome.

One of the guards, a squat, pudding-faced peasant from Hondo, drew a hand across his throat. 'Mati mati, worku finish, all men sama sama.' We got the scarcely subtle message, 'Wait till the work is finished and you'll end up this way, too.' The guards were always at great pains to impress upon us that we had not been accepted as prisoners of war, and that we would be shot when the work was completed.

. . . With blows from anything handy—a bayonet or a pick handle, perhaps—we were goaded into accomplishing feats of endurance that we had not considered possible. Each day was a nightmare of slavery and heat. For a people who have no swear words in their language, the Japanese managed to sound unbelievably menacing and obscene as they snarled 'speedo speedo', 'bugerro' (fool), and 'damme damme' (no good). We could always rely on returning to Pudu bone-weary, bruised, blood-smeared, and dreading the next day.

Fortunately for our sanity, there was an infinite variety of work at Pudu, and often the Fates were kind and allowed us a glimpse of another side to the Japanese character. . . .

One particular day's duty took a part of us to a Japanese brothel, officers' class, where we were equipped with hammer and nails and set to work with instructions to straighten up some sadly sagging beds and render them free from squeaks. The Japanese women—a race apart from their men—had nothing but kindness for us, and, with much hissing and exclamation over our gaunt figures, insisted on loading us with fruit and rice cakes. Our hapless guards were scolded until their faces were as red as if they had been drinking sake.

. . . If the Japanese despised us for being prisoners, they were at least consistent, for they had proved over and over again that *they* would die rather than surrender.

We could loathe everything they stood for, be disgusted at their cruelty, shake our heads incredulously at their stupidity, be scornful of their duplicity, laugh ourselves sick at the thought of such men believing they descended from the Sun God. But one thing we could not doubt: they were brave. Probably the bravest soldiers in the world. I knew that they had been conditioned to a sort of fanaticism. I knew that it was military weakness that often they stood and died uselessly, when it would have been more effective to fall back and fight again. But to me, as a soldier, they were always—the brave Japanese.

The pity of it was that the honours gained in battle were so tarnished by their callous behaviour as conquerors. Their fierce and savage hatred of us pointed to something beyond the realms of war, to some deep-buried and long-suppressed hatred of one race for another. And yet it was not entirely a question of colour. The Chinese, too, suffered incredible tortures at their hands. They were flogged on the jail whipping triangle; subjected to mock hangings that were stopped at the last minute, just before the trap was sprung; given salt water for days, and then allowed to drink their fill of cold clear water, after which they were jumped on or punched heavily in the stomach so that water gushed from eyes, mouth, and nostrils; or they were suspended by the feet while urine, and sometimes iodine, was poured down the nostrils; or made to kneel for hours on sharp stones. And sometimes it was mental torture. The favourite Japanese trick was to tell the prisoners that one of them was to be executed the next morning. The agony of that night was indescribable for them all.

Little wonder that, in oriental fashion, the next night was filled with their wails of fear and foreboding. Next day the victim would be executed, the survivors would sigh with relief, and we would march past yet another head, peaceful on its pole, and feel a surge of pity and anger that one who had shared our hopes and fears in Pudu was now dead.

. . . As we came to the entrance gate, we saw a Chinese woman tied to a post in front of the guardhouse. She was young and was probably normally quite attractive, but now her face was tear-stained and she wailed with terror. While we were being counted our thickset, bandy-legged little guard found his concentration impaired by her moans and, with eyes flashing with annoyance, he barked a command at her. This only made the girl wail more loudly than ever.

Looking round furiously, our friend spotted me in the front rank and shouted, 'Mota koi, speedo, speedo.' (Come here, quickly.) I came with alacrity, for that red face and swelling neck betokened danger. I was wearing a red spotted bandana round my head, pirate fashion, and the guard grabbed it from my head, rolled it into a ball, and stuffed it into the mouth of the Chinese girl. Like many Japanese expedients, it was highly efficient, and after one startled grunt her wails ceased abruptly.

Twice during the day I went to ask for the bandana in an effort to help the Chinese girl who sagged in her ropes in the hot sun. Twice I was growled away, the second time with a stinging ear for a bonus.

We had a bad day with our evil-tempered friends, and that night when we lined up to be searched there was menace in the air. The First Class Private in charge of the Japs was a diminutive, sadistic man named Tomachi; he was quite good-looking and very vain, and as he strutted importantly in front of us while we were being searched we noted apprehensively that he was carrying his trade mark—a billiard cue.

Obviously disappointed when the search, as usual, uncovered nothing, Tomachi was determined not to be cheated of his finest hour, and mounting a soap-box, he treated us to a stirring oration which might have stung lesser men to shame.

"Englishu soldier no goodera,' said Tomachi with great feeling. 'Very bad worker. Steal all time from Nippon. Benjo benjo all time. Speak bad words like . . . . . . and . . . . all time. Talk jiggy-jig and . . . . all time. Nippon punish one man one!"

None could dispute the truth of his remarks, but the justice of the sentence did not prevent the old hands from immediatelly stuffing anything soft into their hats as a padding. Others, less experienced, stuffed whatever padding they had into the seats of their shorts. Our smiles at their innocence left our faces when the Jap underlings came running up and down the rows, enthusiastically knocking off all headgear. Following them, like the incarnation of Nippon justice, came Tomachi. His task of hitting forty men on the head with his billiard cue was accomplished with an expression of utter dedication.

I was fortunate in being one of the first, for those at the head of the line were treated only to the small end of the cue. Despite Tomachi's size, he was wiry, and when he crashed down the cue with both hands he inflicted stunning pain. We rubbed our bumps and then—human nature being what it is—took a keen and ribald interest in the reaction of our fellow victims as the cue descended on them. However, near the end of the front row, the small end of the cue cracked, and the men in the second row were hit sickeningly with the heavy end and then, abruptly, it ceased to be a joke.

As we came to the guardhouse I rubbed my head, on which there was a most prominent bump, and asked again for the bandana. To my surprise, the little pock-marked guard on duty grinned broadly, rubbing his bullet head in mockery, and said, 'Hei.' I pulled the sodden bandana, greasy with saliva, from the girl's bulging mouth and asked, 'Nippon, mizu Okay-ka?' He looked around and his reply came too fast for me but I caught the words 'Dai ichi' (number one) and then 'Okay.' This was good enough and I held my water bottle to the girl's mouth. She tried desperately to drink, but nine hours of a large gag had stiffened her mouth, so that more water stained her satin jacket than went down her throat.

. . . We left Pudu with its great stone walls, its terrified Asian prisoners, and its memories, and marched through the streets of Kuala Lumpur for the last time. We left behind us, in the cemetery, many of our best and brightest men. We were to leave many more, in many another cemetery, but that lay in the future. For the moment it was enough that we were going to Singapore, to Changi, and to old friends.

. . . The Japanese despised us for surrendering, and had mentally relegated us to the status of work animals. To their surprise and anger we despicable creatures were never humble. In fact we were infuriatingly arrogant. No matter how grim the news and how convincing the Japanese victories, not one prisoner ever doubted that we would eventually win the war, and this conviction showed itself in a hundred ways. I have seen Japanese officers beside themselves with frustration as they tried, with maps and diagrams, to get it into our thick heads that the war was *lost*. But it is always dangerous to become involved in discussion about it, and I always contented myself with murmuring, 'mati, mati' (wait, wait).

Few of us understood the Japanese obsession with 'face', and this fact also caused much friction. Time after time we found the Japanese behaviour inexplicable: they could break promises without shame, and often denied actions that we had seen take place only minutes before.

. . . In spite of their capacity for lying, their strange customs, and their barbarity, the Japanese are in many ways a very polite race, and they were deeply offended when we swore (the Japanese language contains no swear words), or when we—again through ignorance—failed to add the deferential *san* to their names. Another trap for us lay in their different forms of address. Since we learnt all our Japanese from our guards, we naturally spoke to them the way they spoke to us—using the form of address reserved for inferiors. They misconstrued this as just another example of 'the proud British soldier'.

We fiercely resented the Japanese habit of punishing by blows and beatings, but it did not seem quite so bad when we realised that corporal punishment was normal throughout the I.J.A. It was quite normal for officers to beat up N.C.O.s with fists, sticks, or swords, and for N.C.O.s to beat up Privates. It was not uncommon for the unlucky recipient to be left unconscious after such treatment.

. . . The Japanese also had quite a complex about their lack of height, and it was noticeable that when a whole group was involved they invariably selected the tallest men for punishment. They saw nothing incongruous in standing on a stone or a box in order to hit the prisoner about the face and head.

For all their savagery and disregard of human life, they had a sincere love of family life and never failed to show interest in whether you were married and how many children you had. I learnt very early that the Japanese were much more lenient towards family men, and when among a pile of dead men's mementoes I came across a photo of a snowy-haired little boy of about three on a bicycle, I promptly adopted him as my 'son'. Over the years, I showed the photo of Teddy Harrison to hundreds of Japanese, and invariably gained their attention and hisses of admiration. Many replied by producing photos of little black-eyed, round-faced, solemn Japanese children who were quite delightful.

. . .We came to Tarsau camp and saw the first ominous portends of what could be. The high bamboo fence and the working elephants gave the camp an almost romantic air from outside, but within the camp all was dismal and foreboding. Grey beaten scarecrows of men, scruffily bearded and with festering sores on unwashed bodies; men living like troglodytes in dark, bug-ridden huts; smelly foul latrines, hospital huts with living dead staring lacklustre into a twilight world of their own; an air of gloom and depression; never a smile, never, never, a laugh.

An elderly, grey-haired English officer sat holding one of his testicles which was swollen to the size of a boy's football. Tubes led from it into a bowl.

'Good Lord, what on earth had caused that?' we asked the hospital orderly.

'Beriberi, mate,' he replied. 'We all get it in one form or another, but when the fluid gets to the heart or the balls, you've had it. We're draining this chap but he's a goner, take my word for it.'

. . . Ichinoi shouted to a young Englishman to bring a crowbar. The slight, fair-haired boy misunderstood him and picked up a shovel instead. With a snarl of 'Buggero, damme damme,' Ichinoi picked up a crowbar and swung it like a baseball bat. The heavy iron bar hit the boy on the upper arm with a horrid sound and, when he picked himself up, his arm hung twisted in an odd angle.

The bandy-legged horror known as 'The Maggot' hit an Englishman on the ear with his clenched first and burst the ear drum. A lesser man might have been appalled, but the Maggot was made of sterner stuff and walloped hundreds of us on the ear, hoping wistfully to repeat his coup.

Now the men of the Fourth Anti-Tank Regiment began to die. George Atkins, 'Sniper' Emerson, Frank Bryan, Tommy Cahill. From the ration carriers we learnt that Jim Foley, Ted Gamble, and Ernie King had died in near-by camps. Malaria, dysentery, beriberi . . . and malnutrition. Beaten to death. Starved to death.

. . . A gambit that worked occasionally when they were at boiling point was to undertake to give the men a pep talk. On this pretext, work would stop and men would gather round to hear a speech that began, 'Now this is a bloody lot of bullshit, but for Pete's sake try to look impressed. Nippon soldier Ichinoi say speedo speedo, etc.' If one mentioned 'speedo' and 'Nippon soldier Ichinoi' every minute or so, the speech could ramble on until many were almost thankful to return to work.

. . . It was May 1943 and man, as he had since time began, went on killing his brother. On 22 May the monsoon broke on central Thailand and its coming affected every living creature, above or below the earth. The driving rain lashed at us, with only infrequent pause, for sixteen days. It flooded the Menan Kwa Noi which carried in its surging waters the seed of plague. It also washed away the roads and made a quagmire of K3. Drainage was useless in this flat area and the water lay stagnant in great pools. The driving rain poured through our superbly inadequate tents; sometimes in drips of majestic dimension, other times in a penetrating spray.

Our bare feet now slipped and slithered, and we foundered in the mud and tore our feet on the bamboo spikes that we could no longer see. Mud clung obstinately to shovels and found its way into our rice. We lived like automatons. Breakfast was eaten in the dark, with the rain lashing superfluously into our already watery 'pap'. We worked until the light gave out, and then, saturated and muddy, returned in the dark to damp sodden bedding and a tent that leaked and dripped. Only now, there was room for all.

Despite it all, exhaustion brought sleep as soon as we lay down, but often after waking in the night I fought to stay awake and lay savouring every second of the luxury of merely lying quietly, without sight or sound of the cutting and its master of mayhem. I dreaded sleep, for sleep made the hours pass as seconds and swiftly brought the morning and its attendant danger from the mad Ichinoi and the sad-eyed Hazama, squatting like fate on his rock of judgement.

. . . Captain Newton, who was in charge of all P.O.W.s in this area, and who had access to medical records and reports, estimated that sixty-eight men were beaten to death in the cutting. These figures, tragic enough as they were, do not include the many who died in other camps as a consequence of the brutalities experienced at Hellfire Pass. Nor does it include the men who died in the barges *en route* to base camps.

. . . At Hintok River camp there were, for once, guards who were so reasonable that we were allowed to take a short cut through the Japanese tent lines to the river. One afternoon Bob Beaumont, Vic Charlesworth, Dave Wheeler, and Wally Johnston were walking past the Japanese tents on their way to the river. The place seemed to be deserted, so out of curiosity, they cautiously peered into some of the open tents. One tent had dozens of pin-ups on the wall, some cut from magazines, and some actual photographs. Wally Johnson, who had been idly admiring the display, suddenly noticed a photo of a dark-haired lass with a baby on her knee. He stiffened and let out an incredulous shout, 'There's my wife. Look, there she is on the wall!'

'Break it down, Wally,' said Dave Wheeler.

'Come on out of the hot sun,' Bob Beaumont suggested kindly, while Vic Charlesworth observed to the world in general, 'Poor bastard's gone troppo.'

'I tell you it's my wife, Jean.' Wally was vehement, and while the others kept watch he rushed in and grabbed the photo which he had never seen before.

It turned out that mail had arrived at Hintok for the prisoners, and, although the Japanese would not release it, their Bushido code had not prevented them from ransacking the letters for pin-ups.

Which was how Wally Johnston, in the mountains of Hintok, saw for the first time his first-born child.

. . . Once we asked an interpreter what it was the Japanese sang, and he replied proudly, 'It is Umi-yukaba! Japanese warrior sing this song for a thousand years!' Later he wrote down for us the translation:

If the war is on the sea we will die
And be part of the sea.
If the war is on land we will die
And be part of the land.
Our one endeavour is to die
Beside the Emperor's flag
There is no time to look back
Or to think of ourselves.

As we watched them strain and toil to pull their heavy guns and carts through this wild country, and heard their haunting yet menacing song, I felt that here was the soul of Japan. Certainly I could only admire the spirit and courage of this strange and contradictory race.

. . . Again the rains came, and once more we slipped and slithered and slept with mud up to our knees.

The doctors grew more and more concerned at the condition of their worn-out and rusted instruments. At one cholera injection the orderly tried three needles before one penetrated my arm, and even then it was so bell-mouthed that it hurt more coming out than going in. We all suffered from beriberi, and indentations made in our legs remained for hours. There were twenty-five burials in one day at Chungkai—the aftermath of the great Speedo. The extreme lack of vitamins now began to affect our eyes, and there were tragic cases of men becoming blind with agonizing slowness and certainty.

. . . It seemed that this greatest of all wars must come to a climax in Japan and I fancied that the Land of the Cherry Blossom might be a stirring place from which to see out the finish. There was little trouble in getting on the draft as the Japanese idea of what constituted a 'fit' man was not hard to meet and I was helped by the fact that many were trying frantically to get off the Japan party.

We were to embark from Singapore and on 22 June we clambered into the inevitable rice trucks and set our face to the Lion City. My temperature that day was 103 degrees.

We left the wild, beautiful, treacherous land of Siam with few regrets. Many of our friends were to stay and work on the railway until the end of the war and they were to know hard days. We left Bill Morrison, 'Nigger' Miley, Gordon McGrath, and hundreds of other one-legged men behind, but we also said 'sayonara' to Ichinoi, Hazama, Battlegong, the Mad Mongrel, the Storm

Trooper, and many other stout characters.

We travelled for the last time over this futile railway—of no value to the Japanese during the war, and promptly abandoned by the Thais after the war.

Yet, in the final accounting three hundred and four men were to die for every *mile* of track laid . . . One human life with all its hopes, fears, and dreams, for every seventeen feet six inches of track.

. . . We marvelled at the strange quiet of Singapore; there was practically no sign of life anywhere. The Chinese to whom we spoke through the wire said that thousands had been taken to Thailand, and the young men now stayed off the streets lest the Japanese, like the press gangs of old, should swoop down on them and force them into service.

The shops were mostly closed and the few that were open had little to sell and badly needed painting. And over the great city—almost a tangible thing—hung this strange silence. But we slept each night under stars clustered unbelievably thick and beautiful and the palms still swayed, and the frangipani and the flame trees still rioted into colour, to remind us that Nature takes little heed of the foolishness of Man.

On 1 July 1944 we marched through the streets of Singapore for the last time and embarked for Japan. Our ship was a former British freighter that had been captured by the Japanese. She was named the *Potomac Maru*. We took one startled and incredulous look and promptly christened her the *Byoki Maru* (the sick ship), and so perfect was the name that even the Japanese crew adopted it with glee.

The *Byoki Maru* was a very sick ship indeed. She had been bombed in Java, and the entire centre section, including the bridge, had been burnt out. Two long steel building girders ran from stem to stern, one on each side of the ship, and these, welded in slapdash fashion to the deck, served the vital purpose of holding the two halves of the ship together. An emergency steering wheel had been set up in a bamboo structure that stood where the bridge had been and the sum effect was that of a country toilet.

. . . Pop Kennedy, a Catholic Priest, was shortish, sparse of hair, and the good Lord in His wisdom had blessed him with a large and inflamed whisky drinker's nose. He was of the earth, earthy, and he ate with us, marched where we marched, lived by our side, and spoke our own forceful language. But there was a strength and spirit in this rough man with his practical faith, and he spoke not so much of the Kingdom to come, or of texts and dogmas, but of the need for kindness, courage, and cleanliness in our present life. Because he was one of us, seeking no privileges and clearly understanding our problems, his words carried conviction and a strange inspiration.

And when an anti-tank bombadier said, 'I'm grateful that you have restored my faith in God, Father, but I can't come to your Sunday service because I'm an Anglican,' Pop wheeled on him fiercely and said, 'Now you listen to me, you young idiot. God is not the property of any one creed. He made us *all*, Anglicans and Catholics, so you be there, or else.'

. . . The weather became cooler and our tropics-conditioned bodies began to shiver. Then at last we saw green, mountainous land emerge from the sea and the Japanese sailors began to cheer and shout 'Banzai' and we knew that here were the legendary islands of Nippon. We sailed along the coast of Kyushu, and then on 8 September we came to our journey's end and the *Byoki* pulled into the Moji wharf with a splintering crash. Our Captain was true unto the end.

We emerged like troglodytes after exactly seventy days on board the *Byoki Maru*, and as we walked down the gangplank two Japanese medical orderlies sprayed us copiously with DDT powder.

Pross Reid, pulling a ferocious face of distate, grunted, 'Well, you'll never get off *this* island,' but big dark Bob Ansett only laughed and then sang light heartedly, 'One fine day I'll see him, like a cloud of smoke on the horizon.' I smiled back. Bob's rendition was atrocious and I had a suspicion that the words were not quite as Puccini would have preferred, but despite this, Bob was right—it *was* a fine day and we were in the land of Madame Butterfly.

We were still alive and there was adventure in the air.

. . . Our party trudged to the Moji railway station, where the civilians stared at us with a mixture of curiosity and fear. We were still burnt a deep brown from three years of tropical sun, and were long-haired, grimy, and generally unkempt. So anybody seeing us and hearing the whoops of laughter with which we expressed our joy at being once more on dry land, could not be blamed for regarding us as savages.

To our utter incredulity we were ushered into a spotless, well-upholstered passenger train, and, with all blinds drawn so that we might not observe bomb damage, we sped through the night. Eleven hours later we tumbled out on to the platform of the Nagasaki railway station. As we waited on the platform we looked around us entranced.

Nagasaki bustled and teemed with life and colour that were exhilarating after the months at sea. Opposite the station were rows of colourful shops, and behind them flimsy, doll-like houses stretched away to the hills. Electric trams ran busily up and down the street alongside the station, and the air was full of strange, exciting smells, and the sounds of Japanese voices. For the first time we saw the older, kinder faces of the civilians, and were struck by the deep respect in which they obviously held their Army. With much cheering, waving of flags, and singing of the Victory song, a troop train pulled out of the station—the smooth round faces of the Japanese a complete contrast to those of the thin ragged men who watched them with a strange pity . . .

Nagasaki was all life and colour and excitement that morning of 1944.

. . . After a short training course we were accepted as fully fledged shipbuilders. The riveters were given a pair of cheap white cotton gloves to mark their new status, and thus we began our dockyard duties.

Now, the giant American planes were beginning to bomb Japan, and we waited uneasily for the reaction. On the first six or seven occasions that the bombers flew over—before it was realized that Nagasaki possessed a magical immunity from attack—we were herded into the air-raid shelters where, side by side with the Japanese, we listened tensely to the drone of engines overhead.

Never was there a trace of resentment from these strange people and usually the raids were welcomed as a respite from the constant work and dockyard routine. On one occasion we could hear the bombs exploding on a distant town and feel the vibration of the earth, and the Japanese welder sitting next to me—heedless and uncaring of the death and destruction so close—smiled and said, 'Shigoto, shigoto, joto nei. Yasume tucsan joto.' (Work all the time no good. Rest very good.) Similarly, as we marched to work and the silver crucifixes flew overhead, our guards would look up and say with admiration and respect, 'B ni-ju-ku's, number one.' (B29 planes are the best.)

Japanese men and women alike worked at the dockyards and the drab, bow-legged women in the shapeless track suits were given few privileges.

Near by, a young woman stopped sorting nuts and bolts to remove lice from her hair. There was an instant roar from her hancho who leapt at her in a fury and punched and slapped viciously before kicking her back to work.

Watching this sordid scene in some astonishment, I blinked and reminded myself that this was Nagasaki—the setting of Puccini's hauntingly beautiful 'Madame Butterfly'.

Christmas Day was marked by an issue of one Red Cross parcel between six men, and on New Year's Day we received an incredible one parcel per man. This was my first Red Cross issue in almost three years. Men long unfamiliar with any but rice grain coffee drank Nescafé and groped their way to their bunks with swimming heads and slurred speech. American cigarettes made us stagger like drunkards.

1945 came floating into Nagasaki on a snowstorm and I lay awake watching the snow swirl by the window, wondering what the coming year held for us.

Would it be liberation and life? Or would our end come in the camp air-raid shelters when the invasion began?

One thing was certain and the rest was lies . . . The Japanese never bluffed and the air-raid shelters with their surprisingly heavy doors, also had surprisingly large vents on the top. And the drums of gasoline stacked near by held a blood-chilling threat.

The bombers came over consistently—so high that they scarcely seemed to move, and so thrilling that emotion brought a lump to the throat. By now it was accepted that the gods had granted some strange immunity to Nagasaki, and the air-raid sirens were never sounded. The incredible Japanese would look up at the silver planes on the way to slaughter their brothers and say admiringly, 'Americano number one.'

But there was no lack of spirit here, and often we saw the school children drilling with bamboo poles, for even children were to be used to repel the hated invader of the homeland. And we saw little tots of three to six years given sharp bamboo spears and rehearsed in the art of jabbing their spears into the eyes of wounded enemy soldiers. It was cruel and horrible, but there was something magnificently barbaric about it too. Japan was a tiger at bay.

. . . The Japanese in charge of us on that shift, was a savage and powerful man and was said to have lost a brother in an air raid. He drove us unmercifully that night and made us work in suicidal positions in order to clear the fallen rock and rubble. Repeatedly he bashed us and I thought how like a scene from Dante's 'Inferno' it must have been. Our lamps shone eerily through the thick dust and showed his half-naked, sweating figure (for it was always warm and close at this depth) lashing out in a fury. The hazy scene had a nightmare quality about it, but the men who fell and the blood that mingled with the coaldust was real enough, and we who left our blood behind that night, can truly say that somewhere in Japan there is a part forever Australia.

After 'The Bomb', Ken wrote:

On August 14th we did what was to be our last shift at the mine. It was now 15th August—excactly three and a half years since Singapore had surrendered on that black day of 15th February 1942. The Japanese were saying 'Tomorrow, all men yasume.' I knew beyond doubt that we were to live after all.

. . . Life suddenly became absurdly uncomplicated. We lived like oriental despots, and in many ways I wished that it could go on forever. When travelling was necessary, we went to the nearest train and took the best seats. Even if there were no vacant seats, we had no problems, for the Japanese would instantly push their own people off to make room for us. Often a zealous station master would insist on clearing out an entire crowded carriage so that we might ride in comfort. Sometimes we rode in the guard's van—not to hide from hostility, for there was none; but to escape the overwhelming curiosity that followed our every move. When we were hungry, we walked into the nearest restaurant, sat down, and asked for food. There was never a question of payment, and we were showered with service. Money became completely superfluous, although, if we ate at a private house, cigarettes and chocolates were always left as payment.

The complete lack of any sign of resentment or hostility on the part of the Japanese was almost unbelievable, even to us who knew so well their unpredictable qualities. Later we discovered that MacArthur was broadcasting almost daily at this stage, warning the Japanese people not to harm the prisoners of war. What was far more effective and covered us with an invisible umbrella of safety, was that the Emperor had also spoken to his people, asking them to guard our welfare.

. . . Morning dawned crisp and sunny. We joined a carriageful of wide-eyed Japanese on the first through train and by ten o'clock were drawing near to Hiroshima . . . desolate Hiroshima, with its leaning houses and brooding silence.

At the centre of the city we stopped and looked about us, still unable to believe that one bomb had been responsible for this holocaust. But it was not difficult, standing on this hot road in the heart of the dead city, to imagine the great flash that had first dazzled and then incinerated the shocked people of Hiroshima. Nor was it hard to imagine the immense wave of searing air that had followed and blasted down buildings and houses like matchsticks, and that had overturned thousands of hibachis (charcoal burners), so that all over Hiroshima there sprang countless pinpoints of flame that grew with nightmare speed into the roaring furnace that engulfed the living and the dead.

And, as we stood almost ankle deep in ashes, it was not hard to imagine how those who survived the blast must have run screaming up and down this now silent street. Some would have been carrying their crying, clutching children; others half supporting, half tugging, the shocked older people; all frantically seeking to escape from the blistering, searing heat that had turned their peaceful homes into places of horror, and their familiar streets into crematoriums in which perished possessions, hopes, and, in the end, fear . . .

And easy, painfully easy, to visualize the fate that had overtaken them as the countless fires joined hands with glee and danced high in the air, almost as if seeking to touch the evil mushroom cloud above.

But that was imagination.

The reality was the girl with scarred features who passed with averted face. And the listless people who went by so dully; the scarred people; the burnt people; the apathetic people. And the people who even now showed not the slightest sign of hostility or resentment.

Saddened and depressed beyond words at the magnitude of the tragedy, and feeling like ghouls, we decided to leave Hiroshima that same day. There was little to keep us here; nothing to see; no place to rest; nothing to eat; nothing to drink.

Fortunately for our peace of mind we knew nothing of such atomic age refinements as radiation sickness, and although we occasionally picked up a statue or kicked over a strangely fused piece of metal for a closer look, we were never tempted to take a souvenir. One does not rob a tomb . . .

During the last months of the war there had been a small part of our being that, despite our own danger, had felt an odd pity for this strange race.

Now, as we left Hiroshima, our hatred of the Japanese was swept away by the enormity of what we had seen.

All bitterness was shed and left behind forever in the silence, the desolation, the ashes of Hiroshima.

. . . At this stage I was still hopeful of getting hold of the photo the Japanese had taken of me at Nagasaki, for I knew that no one would believe how I looked unless they had this proof. So I spoke with my R.A.F. friends. 'How about going to see our old camp at Nagasaki? It's only a few hundred miles.' They jumped at the idea.

We left Nakarma next day and headed south. Once again our journey was a leisurely one. I had just calculated that we must be getting near our destination when, for no apparent reason, the train stopped at a bare platform in a wilderness of debris and I realized that the tracks must have been too damaged to allow us to go right into the city.

We got out of the train, and looked about us. Curious, I asked a Japanese where we were. Though I live to be a hundred, I shall never forget the tightening of my heart when he answered simply, 'Nagasaki.'

No! It couldn't be! I had stood on Nagasaki station for hours and remembered it well. If this was Nagasaki, where were the station walls with their gaudy advertisements? Where were the colourful rows of shops opposite? And the bright trams that ran alongside? And where were the busy, industrious people?

Then we picked out the street running parallel to the platform, and at intervals through the ashes we noticed the glint of tram lines. Yes, it was Nagasaki all right, but a Nagasaki that was now as featureless as a desert and as heart-wrenching as a blind baby.

Because I had known the city and found it attractive, the tragedy was a more personal one than Hiroshima and in some ways a more shocking one, for the mind's eye could contrast the picturesque past with the tragic reality of the present.

Heavy-hearted, we walked towards the waterfront, but our spirits rose a little to discover that this city had actually been less unfortunate than Hiroshima. For Nagaski is built around a hill, and although one half of the city had been blasted and seared into oblivion, the friendly hill had imposed its vast bulk to shelter and protect those who lived between it and the sea. Indeed, as we sailed across the bay in our ferry, and looked back, Nagasaki seemed as beautiful and untouched as ever. I remembered the people I'd known there, especially the old men with the wooden clappers who had walked the streets at night chanting, 'Hi no yo-jin, hi no yo-jin . . . be careful of fire, be careful of fire . . .'

It was pure luck that we got into the camp at all, for when we hopped off the ferry we found our old friends scouring the island for supplies dropped the day before. Talking animatedly to them we passed into the camp easily enough, but within minutes two grim-faced men wearing MP armbands (the genuine article) had hauled us before six stern officers, who gave us five minutes to leave the camp. They wanted no foot-loose wanderers in this camp, for they were mortally afraid of radiation sickness and of precipitating trouble with the 'angry' Japanese who still controlled the island.

'Fair enough, it's your camp,' I conceded, 'but if you won't feed us, at least give me the photo. After all, I've come over two hundred miles for it.'

'No, Sergeant. These photos are part of camp records and have to be handed over to the Japanese as we leave.'

This was the last straw, and I said angrily, 'Haven't you chaps heard? The war is over and *we* won it—not the Japanese.'

But this was the last straw for the officers, too, and seconds later we were pushed out of Fukuoka 2 and the doors slammed with tremendous finality behind us.

There were still a few men looking for parachutes and supplies, and I stopped one man and asked if he had any news of our dockyard hanchoes. He rattled off a few names and then added, 'We haven't seen Ginty, but old Pop came to the camp gates looking for food last week.'

'Did you fix him up okay?' I asked.

'Not on your bloody life,' he grinned. 'We gave the old bastard a boot up the arse and sent him away faster than he came.'

I felt like shouting, 'What sort of a pack of heartless bastards are you in this camp?' but then I remembered that this man's best friend had been beaten to death in Thailand, and that none of the men here had seen what had been done to Japan. None of them had seen Hiroshima or Nagasaki . . .

But for nearly twenty years I have been haunted by the thought of a fine old man coming to the gates of the camp, seeking Christian charity from his fellow Christians, and being booted away by those who now possessed so much.

We returned to Nakarma just in time to greet the first of the occupation troops. Big, smartly uniformed Americans, armed to the teeth, they came warily into Nakarma with tommy-guns pointed menacingly at the nervous civilians. But although Khaw Kok Teen said, 'Better we tell them that all they have to worry about here is V.D.,' no one laughed, for these were our strong and sturdy brothers who had fought their way to us, while we heaved coal and built ships for the enemy. They were horrified at our condition and appearance.

As the years passed a rather surprising thing happened. I found that I had developed a marked admiration for the Japanese and that, try as I might, I could find no hatred whatever for them. Instead I remembered more and more their basic virtues of loyalty, cleanliness, and courage, and the more I read, the more I became convinced that they were soldiers of tremendous bravery.

I read of Tarawa, where four thousand five hundred Japanese resisted the invasion and only nineteen did not die. Of the nineteen who did not die, most were too badly wounded to resist and the others were captured because they were buried under their own dead. I read of Burma, where after two and a half years of fighting exactly seven Japanese prisoners had been taken. They also, were too badly wounded to resist.

'Ah yes,' said my friends, 'but that was not bravery—they were just fanatical.' I could not agree with this opinion for one moment. The Japanese soldiers were men of flesh and blood—human beings with very human emotions of fear and foreboding. I have seen Japanese afraid on many an occasion, and often we laughed scornfully at their somewhat childish and unreasoning fear of wild animals. But of one thing I had no doubt—a Japanese in a position where he was fighting for his country and his Emperor would fight till he died.

No, it seems to me that it is far too convenient to say that *we* are brave, but that the enemy is merely fanatical. I fancy that I was given the privilege of fighting against possibly the bravest soldiers of all time. One thing I know for certain—if there is ever another war and if I have to fight again, I would like my fellow Australians around me, and a Japanese battalion on my left and a Japanese battalion on my right. Then perhaps, even I might stand firm and give some cheek.

On quite a few occasions my attitude towards the japanese led to strained relationships with those who had lost relatives and friends in the South East Pacific. . . .

He ends by writing of his friends:

. . . My story is their story. We all shared the same hopes and fears. We starved together; we exulted together; and only in the final adventure of all did our paths turn slowly away. They are long dead now in far off lands and I wish them well. Sleep, my comrades, and soft winds bring peace.

Daphne Jackson—Extracts from her wonderful book *Java Nightmare*

Her husband Charles was in Heetjansweg Prison as a P.O.W. She was at: Kleine Lengkong, Bandoeng, Tanah Tinggi, Tangerang, Tjideng Camp, and Kampong Makassar, where she was a worker in the Vegetable Gardens.

I wish I had space to include more.

We again had trouble over the sanitary conditions, as each block had only one lavatory with eight 'stalls' for about four hundred people. Through an iron gate leading to the parade ground, a long line of latrines had been built for the soldiers, but at night this door was locked and a Japanese guard stood on duty there, so it was impossible to get out. After some days on the maize diet even those of the British who till then had not suffered too badly from dysentery were now in a shocking state. Many could not manage to stagger the length of the long corridors to the lavatory, which in any case was quickly blocked up at night, so that the floor became a swimming cess-pool. In the daytime the flies made matters worse, and sickness increased alarmingly.

When the British came to Tangarang, the heads of each room in our block held a meeting to decide what should be done about a hospital, for though the Salvation Army had done their best in Tanah Tinggi, some of us felt it had not been very satisfactory. After some argument it was decided it should be left to the nuns from the big Catholic hospital in Soerabaja—one of the best in Java—since they were now interned with us. They took over, and certainly did their best in shocking circumstances, until all nuns were later concentrated in one Java camp.

The back walls of our ten bungalows, because they lay next to the bamboo stockade, had been broken by the Japanese, so that what had been the servants' lavatory now had a wall through it, with stockade beyond. Obviously this was inadequate owing to dysentery, and we were forced to make use of the filthy sheds down the road.

At last we decided to send two helpers from each house, plus a squad of Dutch boys who were still in Tjideng to clean out the sewage. After an hour only three women and two boys were left hauling the filth in old tin cans attached to bamboo poles, until the pool was empty.

Covered with ulcers—some as large as a fist—on which the flies swarmed, and with little soap and no disinfectant to try to get clean, we could not get the awful smell off ourselves or our clothes.

Many internees had gone down with tuberculosis in various forms, and there were few who did not suffer from beri-beri caused by the perpetual rice diet, oedema brought about by general malnutrition, dysentery or pellagra. This last sickness had attacked many women. It took the form of angry reddish-brown marks like burns over the skin, very often in the form of a butterfly, from which, I think, it got its Italian name. This skin burn, which was also caused by the lack of the right food, very often came first on the face, particularly the nose, as well as attacking hands and feet, and it was of the greatest importance that the sufferer should not expose herself to the sun, which aggravated the burns and could ultimately lead to insanity.

When it suited them, the Japanese disregarded any form of sickness, so they had no scruples in ordering everyone to work in the 'gardens', whether fit or not, and as the internees also had to stand for hours of the day in queues or rollcall, this particular sickness made great strides.

Whilst the sick women and children were either in the punishment house, or lined up in front of the hospital, the doctors once more protested about their cases, particularly one child who, they said, would certainly die if she were moved. They were brutally told to obey orders, and some were beaten, and the internees had to remain where they were.

Sonè was obviously in a mad rage, for as the women passed in front of him, he kicked them with his army boots or hit them over the head. Many fainted from the heat and cruel treatment, but attempts to help them only led to further punishment, and we just had to stand and endure it.

Added to this, the Japanese either could not, or would not, work the sluice gates in the canal which surrounded the camp, so that when the heavy rains fell, we were flooded to a depth of two or three feet. Apart from the horrible job of wading, our legs covered with sores, through knee-deep streams of sewage to get to work, there was always the danger of missing the edge of the road, and drowning in the deep drains on either side.

By December, 1944, it was about eight dead per day, and as there were at times insufficient coffins, boxes had to be used, into which the bodies had to be broken or squeezed as decently as possible. The Japanese provided a bunch of bananas to go on a coffin, which was a temptation to anyone who saw it, and one of the office staff was allowed to go to the cemetery. It was a horrible task, but necessary, as it afforded our only chance to look at the men's plot and see the names of those who had died recently.

Usually in the case of a woman losing a relation, she was called to the office and the Japanese in charge told her that her husband, brother or son was dead, and handed her a small package containing hair and finger nail cuttings. If it was humanly possible, it was wiser to show no emotion, for the Japanese disliked any display of feeling, and were frequently cruel to any woman who cried.

Another cruel trick was to give a man the choice of having such hair and nail cuttings sent to his wife, or be executed as a punishment for some crime. One Dutch woman I knew received such a summons, and many months later found it hard to believe her daughter who, in peeping through the *bilik*, saw her father working on a Bandoeng street-cleaning duty. Only after the war was the poor woman able to establish the fact that her husband was indeed alive after all.

The Japanese played a particularly dirty trick on the men, by allowing them to write their postcards, only to have the cards discovered stacked in a cupboard six months later.

It was difficult to blame those who bargained to get food for their starving children, but many made sales through the *gedek* for sheer bravado and that seemed indefensible when the whole camp would receive punishment if they were caught.

Eventually three girls were caught by the Japanese, or maybe given away by the guards, and they were taken to the punishment cell, which was a beastly place, and thoroughly beaten, then left without food or water for a considerable time. Mrs. Wetter, the head of the camp, at last managed to get food and blankets to them, for they were only wearing tiny brassières and shorts. Each day they were made to parade like that with the Japanese taking rollcall, wearing placards saying why they had been punished. Their heads were shaved, and they were not allowed to cover them. It was a horrible punishment, and they were badly bruised, and though we did not have much sympathy with some of the *gedekkers* we were thankful when the punishment ended.

Many internees, including children, were ill by July, 1945, and though a few of the worst cases were sent off to Batavia hospitals, most were taken to our hospital hut. It was by then packed full, with women and children lying on the usual bamboo platforms each side of the hut, but no beds, so the task of the voluntary nurses was made doubly difficult.

Since it was impossible to reach a patient to lift or wash her as she lay at right-angles to the pathway, when a woman was obviously dying she had to be put sideways along the edge of the platform, so that she could be more easily handled.

Deaths rose sharply once more, and it was at that moment when we were all in a highly overwrought state that we were ordered to remain for punishment and prayer in our barracks for two days without food or water.

We supposed that things were going badly for the Japanese, but did not know then that the bombing of Japan was being carried out.

On the day we were ordered to remain in our huts without food, no adequate reason was given, but we accepted the situation as philosophically as we could, and indeed many of the women were only too thankful to get a rest from the heavy work in the vegetable gardens and elsewhere.

We vaguely knew that the war in Europe had ended, for news of this got through from a hospital, but things had gone on for so long that we felt we had been abandoned, and so long as we could keep going from day to day, we had little thought to spare for what was happening in the outside world, or even for our families. Survival was all that mattered, and we hung on desperately reserving what little strength we had for the daily work.

The Japanese have a name for being kind to children, and it is true that during the three years I was interned I occasionally saw some playing and giving presents to interned children, and teaching them games and wrestling. I also saw them quite unmoved in the hospitals where pitiful sick children lay with arms and legs like little sticks, and bodies and faces swollen out of all recognition by malnutrition. The squads of small children in the vegetable gardens had worked the same as their mothers, and they suffered just the same punishments and starvation as we did, so that many of them died or were sick for years afterwards.

It may be that the orders to starve the internees came from higher up, but the Japanese is a martyr to discipline, and would never question any order given to him, but would obey it whatever his personal feelings.

From Admiral Sir Frank Twiss, KCB, KCVO, DSC, who has kindly written the Foreword for *Kamikaze*.

In 1941 I was Gunnery Officer of HMS *Exeter* and when the Japanese attacked in the Pacific we were sent to Singapore to join the naval force being collected in the Pacific to defend our possessions in the Far East. We reached Singapore the day the *Repulse* and *Prince of Wales* were sunk and remained in that area as the only ship of any size until we joined the ABDA force intended to defend Java. The whole of this force was sunk by the Japanese Fleet in the Battle of the Java Sea in February 1942, the last survivor being *Exeter* sunk on 1st March. On 2nd March I was picked up by a Japanese destroyer and taken to Macasser in Borneo. Later I was taken to Japan and spent some 3½ years in camps there.

At the start of 1945 I was in a camp on Shikoku Island. There were signs that the Japanese were getting rattled and their behaviour became more unpredictable than ever. Raids by B29s were now frequent and planes came over the camp on their way to Osaka and the Inland Sea cities. We were made to dig Air Raid trenches not so much for us as for the guards. Rumours started that prisoners were to be moved and I gathered that my move would be to a place called Hiroshima. It sounded nicer than where we were and thus a move for the better. My wife learnt of this new address shortly before August!

Suddenly early in June we were told we would be moved off Shikoku in 48 hours and frantic speculation and anxiety arose. We were not in a physically fit state to carry much nor to face the likely arduous journey which went with moving camp. But off we set for the railway station for the ferry port of Takumatsu where we boarded a small but already dangerously overloaded ferryboat and forced below decks. Thereafter a short journey brought us to the mainland where we boarded a train and set off for goodness knows where. Not long before midnight we halted in a large city where an air-raid was in progress. It was one hell of a big raid and we began to fear that our years in captivity were to be terminated by American bombs. The noise was tremendous and bits and pieces fell all around. We stayed in that station until after dawn when by some miracle the train moved off through smoking ruins of buildings and every sign of appalling damage. We had survived the biggest raid on Osaka. That evening we stopped at a small junction where fires were also burning and joined another train picking our way through hot ashes and burning rubble. It was an awesome lesson on what Japan was going through which until then we had not appreciated.

Our train slowly made its way upwards into hills finally reaching a tiny station overlooking a broad river and a valley. Here with much roughness and shouting we were pushed out and herded down the hill to the river where we came to a stockaded camp and stumbled in to form up on its parade ground tired, dirty and hungry.

We were not in Hiroshima but Mitsushima, an ex Chinese coolie work camp in the hills some 90 miles from the sea, where a large power station was in the course of construction. As we shambled into the very disagreeable new home we were heartened by the grinning face of an old friend from previous days who had been shipped off to work for Tokyo Rose and having, we heard, declined this honour, was thought to have been decapitated. The friend was a POW with me on Shikoku and a very remarkable person who had been taken on the Gilbert Islands where he was a Colonial Civil Servant. But before we could gather the gen from him we had a most alarming address from a nasty looking Japanese sergeant who made it only too clear that we were not in for a good time, a message he emphasised by knocking down several of our more senior members and lambasting with a club a fair cross section of the others. We finally moved into our living quarters to find that we were in large wooden huts with two tiers of shelves for mattresses, earth floors and a few wood tables. It was not even decent Coolie accommodation. We sought our old friend to question him.

His news was gloomy. This was a punishment camp, hence his presence there. We, it seems, had been labelled un-cooperative and in need of disciplining. For this purpose Sergeant Watanabe the most feared and sadistic man in Japanese prison camps, had been specially selected to look after us. *(I wonder if this was the same Watanabe referred to by Captain James in Chapter 2?—Ed.)*

From then until August we led a miserable and degrading life under the ever watchful eye of Watanabe. Up at dawn, work as coolies carrying stone or cutting and loading wood for nine days at a stretch before one day off to wash your clothing. We started to go down hill fast, partly from fatigue, partly from lack of proper food and partly from the surroundings where the deep valley caused the sun to become obscured about 1600 and did not return until after work started. Nor was our morale enhanced by one day being driven into a dark cellar-like space under the Administration building where we were left in Black Hole of Calcutta conditions for some hours. The only meaning we could ascribe to this was that it must be for bumping us off when the Allies landed. And then one day we heard a rumour. Hiroshima had been flattened in the twinkling of an eye. What, we asked ourselves, was this extraordinary 'Twinkle Bomb'? Whatever it was, the Japanese were very worried and even the poisonous Watanabe remained in his room. Even more unusual, a Colonel turned up and addressed us to the effect that our work routine was to be changed and we would remain in camp for the next few days while new schedules were worked out. By Jingo the war must be over, we said.

But nobody told us so. We stayed in camp and wracked our brains to figure out what was afoot. We then discovered that one person who was afoot was Watanabe. He had disappeared. Only the colonel and a few guards remained. It was imperative to get hold of a Japanese newspaper from which, by a slow and halting method of pooling available linguistic skill, we could make out something of what was going on.

It was several days before we got a man out into the village and captured a paper and for good measure the bearer of the paper said he had been seen by a local who seemed to be indicating surrender by holding his hands up and shouting excitedly. We scanned the paper feverishly and thought it said something about surrender but we could not be sure. What to do? We didn't want to give away our source of news if we were wrong, and if an armistice was imminent surely we would be told. We decided to hold on a bit longer. But to no avail, so we sent our scout back to the village to try for more positive news.

He returned wildly excited and brandishing a paper. On it was a picture of MacArthur landing in Tokyo. Our senior British and Australian Officers marched in to the Colonel's office and demanded an explanation. Yes it was true that the Allies had arrived in Tokyo, but he had not had any orders on what to do with us. He didn't have to wait long. He was thrown out and a new Camp Commandant appointed in the shape of a British Officer.

It took a bit of sorting out. There were the guards who were clearly terrified of what might await them though the two or three who had bad consciences had already gone, and then on opening up of the rice stores we found that there was not much in hand. The really important need was to get in touch with the Allied Command in Tokyo and report our position as we had several very sick people.

We eventually made the necessary contact and were quickly rewarded with the appearance of US Naval aircraft who dropped kitbags filled with goodies. One good thing led to another and within a day or two a train was provided to take us down to the coast where on the first day of September we, from a camp which had never been declared, were taken on board the U.S. Hospital ship *Rescue,* deloused, filled with food and medicines and shipped off to Tokyo for passage to home and Freedom.

Once in Tokyo Bay I was transferred to a British Hospital ship called *Tjitjalengka* (ex Dutch) which was so short of medicines that her Surgeon Captain named Hunt, prescribed a glass of Port three times a day!

My sole contact with the BPF was seeing the ships anchored in Tokyo Bay while I was en route to the *Tjitjalengka,* having been too unfit to travel due to beri-beri. I later flew to the Philippines and was repatriated by the U.S. Navy via Hawaii, Vancouver, Halifax and Portsmouth to reach England on the last day of October 1945.

I think you will find most POWs will mistrust anything the Japanese say, and tell you they constantly boasted in the war that if the Japanese didn't win outright then the war was only the first round in a 100 years or more of conflict. I cannot see that they could do much so long as they are only possessed of the Japanese Islands. If they came to control other lands such as they did in 1940 and so gained raw materials, then watch out. You may of course say they nearly control the world markets today. A lot of exaggeration has plagued the stories of Japanese prison camps. Not that they were anything but brutal and beastly, but that as the years pass more and more so called diaries seem to come to light. For my part I cannot see how anyone kept a diary let alone got it out of a camp. We were searched so often and so often had everything taken off us, that I never had so much as a piece of paper. But the trauma and later effects on prisoners has not diminished with time and you saw this in the reaction at the funeral of Hirohito to the Duke of Edinburgh. Personally I am relaxed about the Japanese; it is all a long time ago and best put to bed.

Having looked at the History of Japan through the eyes of Captain James, Russell Braddon and Admiral Twiss, and those of Ken Harrison and Daphne Jackson sharing their experiences as Prisoners of War, we are still left pondering the philosophy of ***'The Divine Wind—the Kamikaze'.***

Edwin P. Hoyt, Lecturer at the University of Hawaii was a War Correspondent and then a broadcaster and journalist.

His book ***The Kamikazes*** *helps to provide us with what understanding we may muster of how this deliberate sacrifice evolved.*

Before the battle of Saipan, Admiral Takajimo Onishi had said: 'If a pilot, facing a ship or a plane, exhausts all his resources, then he still has one left, the plane as part of himself, a superb weapon. And what greater glory can there be for a warrior than to give his life for Emperor and country?'

'Japan must be realistic. The battleship is no longer the prime line of defence. It costs as much to keep a single battleship in fighting trim as it does to operate a hundred aircraft and provide for casualties. Therefore Japan must now abandon all her concern for major capital ships and concentrate on air power for the national defence.

On 13 October 1944 Rear Admiral Arima was the first pilot to do this voluntarily. His target was the USS Aircraft Carrier *Franklin*. Arima had been to an English Public School and had trained with the Royal Navy. *(Other sources say it was 15 October in position 16°29′ N 123°57′ E, East of Luzon.)*

Admiral Ogawa had lost 3 carriers and 424 aircraft at Saipan therefore there was a shortage of pilots.

As the war drew nearer to Japanese territory, the need for their aircraft carriers diminished, so pilots no longer required the extensive training for operating from them.

Meanwhile, Admiral Togoda had conceived the Sho Plan, which called for the sacrifice of Japan's greatest ships, including the carriers. This called for the use of 3 naval striking forces to attack from 3 directions (except the carriers). The idea was to send out Admiral Ogawa with one force to lure the US Carriers away to allow the fleet to attack the invaders without air opposition. They didn't care if the carriers *were* sunk.

Their own counter attack would be supported by their Army and Navy Air Forces.

It is interesting to note Japanese Army Air-Cadet School Class 518 was due to graduate June 1945. By the time Class 519 was enrolled, the rules and regulations had almost all changed, because the war by that time had adopted an entirely new pattern. Now ex high-school men endured two years of ground training *because of the shortage of fuel! (Thank God for Palembang!)* So, after only 2 months 'in flight' training, they were made corporals and were told they were Fliers.

By October the Japs had lost 5,209 pilots, 42% of their Navy's aircrews. Now, Tokyo realised that the Philippines was to be the scene of the 'Decisive Battle'.

The invasion of Leyte found Admiral Onishi with less than 100 planes. He turned to Japanese history in 1281 when Kubla Khan's forces were repulsed by superhuman efforts and—the Divine Wind—the Kamikaze. He knew that his nation accepted suicide, with no stigma, but more honour for its purity.

Still he had problems with the High Command, so he conceived the idea to make it look as though the idea came from the pilots themselves—a spontaneous reaction.

As fate would have it, he found himself addressing the staff officer and squadron leaders of 26 Air Flotilla and 305 and 306 Fighter Squadrons without his own senior officer who had been delayed by a plane crash. He told them how important it was to immobilise the carriers to effect the Sho Plan and prevent successful invasion of the Philippines. He put the suicide plan to them and asked 'What do you think?'

Some favoured it—others detested it (waste of life). They recalled Admiral Arima's suicide dive.

The decision was put to Cdr. Tama—he consulted Lt. Itusuki, CO 201 Squadron. He agreed. 201st was prepared to go ahead. He called the pilots and put it to them. They were steeped in the legends of 'Bushido' to sacrifice lives for Emperor and country. Everyone volunteered. Lt. Naoshi Kanno 306 Squadron was the leader, but was gloomy. So Tamai selected Lt. Yukio Seki (recently married). Seki—after thought—agreed.

Frustrated Navy pilots had first used the 'taiatori' (ramming attack) in November 1943 at Saipan as a last resort when up against superior training and skill of the US B24 pilots.

Seki wrote: 'My dear Father and my dear Mother . . . At this time the nation stands at the crossroads of defeat; the problem can only be resolved by each individual's repayment of the Imperial Benevolence. In this the man who has chosen a military career has no choice . . . Because Japan is an Imperial Domain, I shall carry out a ramming attack against a carrier to repay the Imperial Benevolence. I am resigned to this. To all of you, obedient to the end.'

Admiral Onishi presented to his staff a scroll:

> Blossoming today, tomorrow scattered
> Life is like a delicate flower
> Could one expect the fragrance to last forever?

Onishi told them that they were already gods—with no further interest in human affairs.

He handed over special bottles of water to take as a final drink. Nobody knows why they didn't go into action on 20th October. Meanwhile on 21 October 1944 at dawn, US forces landed on the east coast, Leyte with only light opposition. The cruiser HMAS *Australia* was hit by the first 'official' kamikaze, killing the captain and 19 Australian seamen. She was not sunk.

On this day Lieut. Seki, with 7 pilots, sang:

> If I go away to sea
> I shall return a corpse awash.

Then, with three other pilots he took off, but couldn't find the target. He had handed a lock of his hair to be given to his widow.

Later, Lieut. Yoshigasu Kuno pleaded for a chance to seek glorious death. He took off and did not return, but no Allied ship had been damaged.

On 24th October, Admiral Fukudome's search planes found the US Fleet, but they didn't have any success because there was no fighter support.

However, 250 Jap planes carried out a traditional attack on Leyte Gulf. Only one succeeded by sinking a fleet tug, the USS *Sonoma*. The mass attack—the

Sho Plan was a failure.

On 25th, Seki led the kamikazes out looking for the carriers, but had no luck.

At 10 a.m. off Samar NE of Leyte Gulf, they stumbled into the Battle of Samar and dived with their 250 kg. bombs. One burst through the deck of the *St. Lo,* their first (escort) carrier success, sank it and damaged 6 other ships.

Admiral Fukudome's Force *(Special Attack Force.—Ed.)* lost 150 planes that day and the Army's Force lost 90 more. But Admiral Ogawa's kamikazes had put up 9 planes and the 6 lost had inflicted much damage.

Thus the suicide mission was adopted as Japanese strategy, especially as the Emperor had said, 'They certainly did a magnificent job.'

On 29th October USS *Intrepid* shot down a kamikaze. It exploded, but didn't hit.

On 30th the USS *Franklin* was hit with 56 killed and also the USS *Bellean Wood,* a light carrier with 92 killed. Both were put out of action SE of Suluan Island.

General Tomonago spoke to the Army Air Force kamikaze pilots:

'When men decide to die like you, they can move to the heart of the Emperor. And I can assure you that the death of every one of you will move the Emperor. It will do more—it will even change the history of the world. I know what you feel now as you put the sorrows and joys of life behind you because the Emperor's fortunes are failing. Do not worry about what happens when you die and what you leave behind you—for you will become gods. Soon I hope to have the privilege of joining you in glorious death.'

By November 1944, B29s were bombing the Japanese mainland, but at 30,000 ft. the ack ack, range 27,000 ft., couldn't reach them. Neither could the fighters until one day a B29 strayed lower in an air current and a Japanese fighter 'kamikazed' into it. The ramming attacks had started.

And so it went on until 9th March 1945 when the B29s started dropping incendiaries on Tokyo.

On 10th March, the US Fleet was attacked while at anchor in Ulithi Atoll. It was 7 p.m. and dark and on the USS *Randolph* the attack interrupted the movies! But the attaekers had run out of fuel and they didn't even explode. They crashed into the sea or were shot down.

Now the Japanese were short of pilots, planes and fuel and on 16th March the Battle of Iwojima was over.

But still the war waged furiously. On 17th the carriers were discovered 175 km south of Kyushu. As the kamikazes flew out, the Allied pilots came in—lower. Even so, the USS *Yorktown* was hit and so was USS *Enterprise.* The USS *Intrepid* was hit, but the bomb didn't go off.

On 19th USS *Franklin* had 1,000 men killed or wounded by a kamikaze, but she didn't sink. Others hit that day were the *Bunker Hill,* nearly 400 casualties, the *Wasp,* over 300 casualties and put out of action until June and the destroyer USS *Halsey Powell.*

The USS *Indianapolis* was hit on 31st March and the battleship *West Virginia* on 1st April along with the Transports *Minsdale, Alpine* and *Achemar.*

The British contingent was operating in the Southern Islands of the Nansei Shoto, largely because the Americans had put them out in left field. But left field had already turned out to be just as dangerous a place as Okinawa. The Japanese had several airfields down there, and kamikazes from those fields and from Kyushu came after the British carriers.

The Ohka (Cherry Blossom) was a small wooden plane carried by a bomber which launched it near to the target. The Americans called them 'Baka' (foolish) because the bombers were sitting targets. With their extra weight, they were very slow.

The first Ohka attack took place on 21 March, led by Lt. Cdr. Nònaka. To evade some 50 Grumman fighters, most jettisoned their ohkas carrying 1800 kgs of explosives. 14 out of the 16 were shot down and all disappeared.

From April 6 to 22 June 'Kikusui' (chrysanthemum) Kamikaze mass attacks were carried out. The first one started with 355 planes and 4 Allied ships were sunk with 24 damaged. Together with the 'normal' Kamikaze attacks, a total of 26 ships were sunk and 164 damaged during this period.

On the morning of April 1st one formation of Japanese planes approached the British force. Four Japanese planes were shot down by British fighters, but the others came in. One fighter strafed the deck of the carrier *Indomitable,* causing several casualties, then zoomed off to strafe the battleship *KGV,* but did no damage. Then a 'K' crashed into the deck of the carrier *Indefatigable.* If the pilot lived, he must have been surprised. The deck of the British carrier was made of steel, and the damage was limited.

The destroyer *Ulster* was also damaged *(A near miss.)* and towed to Leyte. The carrier *Illustrious* took a 'K' but the damage was also limited and it slipped off into the sea.

2nd April USS Transport *Dickerson* hit, also *Goodhue, Chilton, Telfair* and 2 others.

3rd April LST 599—*Pritchett* and *Wake Island* were hit.

Meanwhile, far from the scene of the ordeal of the picket destroyers, lay the main US Invasion fleet. As the sky began to lose its sunny lustre late that afternoon 31 March the shadows on deck darkened.

Just after 5.00 p.m. many little blips began to appear on the radar screens. Something different was happening, something quite unlike the relative quiet of the past five days. Admiral Ugaki's kamikazes were arriving on station.

In a few minutes the American ships began to come under attack. A unit of minesweepers had been assigned that day to work the area between Iheya Retto, a small group of islands, and the Okinawa coast. Coming in from the east, at 3.15 p.m., part of Admiral Ugaki's pinchers passed directly over the minesweepers. The sky was suddenly full of aircraft with the red ball of the rising sun adorning their wingtips.

The destroyer minesweeper *Rodman,* working a channel area, was attacked and hit by three kamikazes. She survived.

When the *Rodman* was first hit, the minesweeper *Emmons* came alongside to assist her. She began circling the other vessel and her gunners shot down six kamikazes. But soon there were more.

Nine of them came tearing down toward the *Emmons,* which was speeding along at twenty-five knots. Four misjudged and splashed nearby, but five were on target and struck her one after the other. The devastation was terrible.

The first hit came on the ship's fantail. The plane struck and exploded, carrying away the ship's sweep gear. Almost immediately the second plane struck on the starboard side of the pilot house. The captain of the ship, Lieutenant Commander Eugene Foss II, was blown over the side.

The third kamikaze came into the port side and hit the vessel where the combat information centre was located. Inside the centre were five officers and ten men who were directing the ship's fire. Four of the officers and the ten men were killed. The fifth officer was Lieutenant John Griffin, Jr., a reservist who was gunnery officer of the ship. He came wandering out, still not quite sure how he had survived.

Griffin heard someone shouting: 'Abandon ship!'

He looked around. Things did not seem that bad. Obviously some seaman had panicked after seeing the captain blown over the side. Some men went over, but six officers and fifty-seven men remained aboard to try to save the ship.

The fourth kamikaze struck the starboard side of the vessel, at the No. 3 five-inch gun, and blew a hole below the waterline. The fifth probably did the most structural damage of all; it came in low and struck at the waterline on the starboard bow.

By this time fires were raging throughout the ship. The entire bridge was destroyed and the ready ammunition on deck was beginning to explode. The captain was overboard. The executive officer was dead. The first lieutenant was wounded. Lieutenant Griffin, now the senior officer present, took charge.

He tried to organise damage-control parties. The fire lines were spread out on deck, but all of them were holed by machine-gun fire, shrapnel and pieces of bursting airplane. The mains were damaged and fires raged. Had it not been for the sprinkler systems in the ammunition rooms, the ship would have blown sky high. All that could be done was get the wounded out, and man the guns as long as possible.

The air was still full of kamikazes. One of them came in strafing, his bullets lacing the deck from bow to stern. An ensign named Elliott saw him coming and threw himself in front of five enlisted men. His body was stitched, but the enlisted men survived.

The gunners shot down another plane, but they were fighting a losing battle against the fires and at 7.30 p.m. Griffin heard a violent explosion from the ammunition-handling room. He knew that the ship was about to go, and ordered her abandoned.

As the men began plunging into the water, or finding places of refuge and waiting for other vessels to approach, the pyrotechnics continued. It was dark now and the exploding ammunition lighted up the sky.

The *PGM-11*, a mine-disposal vessel, stood alongside and took off some of the men in spite of the explosions. Lieutenant Griffin boarded *LCS(L) (3)33* and was saved.

The ordeal had lasted for five hours. Later, that vessel picked up a Japanese suicide pilot who had survived a crash in the water. He was not popular aboard and the crew kept him quiet with a dogging wrench.

At 4.30 p.m. the destroyers *Leutze* and *Newcomb* were battening down for night screen work to protect the fire-support warships off the Okinawa coast. Suddenly the lookouts began to shout. There was nothing on the radar screen, but coming in fast, and very low, in the manner developed by Admiral Onishi, were a dozen enemy planes.

There were seven destroyers in that screen and most of them began to shoot. Hot white traces from 20mm guns and red fireballs from 40mm guns laced the air, and the larger puffs of smoke from the five-inch-shell explosions darkened the sky.

The first kamikaze got inside and crashed on the deck of the *Newcomb*, this time boring down into the bowels of the ship and exploding with a force that knocked out the *Newcomb*'s power and blew the engine room to pieces.

The fourth kamikaze came in and crashed into the forward stack. The splashing gasoline caught fire. Flames raced high above the ship and the smoke so completely concealed her from the vessels around it that it was thought the *Newcomb* had sunk.

The destroyer *Leutze* swung alongside to help her sister ship. The crew were trying to put out the raging fires on the *Newcomb* when another kamikaze came in and hit the *Leutze* on the stern.

Many compartments were flooded and the ship began to settle by the stern. The after ammunition room was in danger of blowing up. The rudder was jammed. The captain, Lieutenant Leon Grabowsky, pulled her away from the *Newcomb* and went to work to save his own ship.

The two ships struggled in the water as the fight went on.

Meanwhile, not far away, the minesweeper *Defense* shot down one kamikaze and then was struck by two more, but luckily they were glancing blows and she did not sink. Indeed, she was able to come to the aid of the *Leutze*, and helped tow her back to Kerama Retto.

The fleet tug *Tekesta* came out and also helped tow the *Newcomb* into Kerama Retto.

Down south, the British experienced some kamikaze activity too, although the Japanese attacks there were not nearly so extensive as those at Okinawa. One kamikaze grazed the deck of the *Illustrious*. All the others were shot down.

The ships of the US fleet congregated in groups around Okinawa, depending on their function. The area outside the island but inside the picket-destroyer circle was occupied by the anti-submarine screen. The Japanese now found these ships too.

The destroyer escort *Witter* was the first ship to come under attack. At 4.12 p.m. a kamikaze crashed into her. Then came a respite of two hours before another kamikaze smashed against the destroyer *Morris*. Large fires started below decks and there was some danger that the ship would go down, until other destroyers closed in and helped put out the fires with their hoses.

Japanese planes seemed to be everywhere. In the transport area, the destroyer *Howarth* dodged two kamikazes and shot them down. Then she was attacked by eight suicide planes. Three were shot down, one grazed a wing against the deck and splashed nearby, and the fifth was shot down at a comfortable distance. The sixth hit the ship and did serious damage. Even so, the ship was still operating and on the way to Kerama Retto for repairs, when her gunners shot down still another kamikaze coming in over the stern.

The destroyer *Hyman* was on her way out of the main fleet area to take up a picket post off Io Shima when she was jumped by kamikazes. Her gunners shot down three planes. The fourth hit on the torpedo tubes and the bomb set off the torpedoes. The explosion was enormous, but the ship could still move, and she started back for Kerama Retto.

Off the east coast the destroyer *Mullaney* was hit hard, began to burn and the skipper abandoned ship. Along came help from several ships. The fires were put out and the captain rejoined his ship and took her back to Kerama Retto.

The kamikazes were literally buzzing like bees around the entire area and arrived at Kerama Retto that afternoon. At 4.30 p.m., *LST-47* was coming out of the harbour when her crew spotted two airplanes low on the water, heading toward the haven. They opened fire. One was hit and began to smoke, then changed direction and headed for the LST. The pilot crashed the plane into the LST two feet above the waterline. The bomb exploded inside and gutted the ship. She was abandoned and burned for twenty-four hours more, then sank.

Kamikazes came into the harbour and hit the Victory ships *Logan V* and *Hobbs V*, which had been converted into ammunition ships. The crews abandoned in a hurry, but the ships floated around the harbour for a whole day. No one dared come near. They burned and their ammunition went off in crackling bursts. Finally they were sunk by naval gunfire.

It was well past dark when the long day of battle finally came to an end. It had been exhausting for both sides. The Americans estimated they had shot down 486 planes. The Japanese escorts who returned reported counting 150 smoke plumes, which Admiral Ugaki immediately translated into burning ships.

So the day ended, but not the battle. It had just begun.

While the Japanese were attacking the American invasion fleet off Okinawa, the American carrier force hit Japan hard to soften up the Kyushu airfields. Consequently Admiral Ugaki had spent a good part of the daylight hours in a cave in the hillside above Kanoya airfield, where he had moved his headquarters.

Watching the planes blow holes in his installations the Admiral grew contemplative.

> . . . We are having our ups and downs in this great final battle. I wonder how it really is, how it would look to Admiral Tojo, or to Admiral Nelson. From a cave it appears that we are going to continue to receive punishment.

The first five days of April were the lull before a storm the like of which the Americans had never before seen.

Admiral Ugaki had invented the wave technique. He would send hundreds of kamikazes against the Americans in waves, accompanied by hundreds of fighters whose job was to divert the Allied fighters. The suicide units were now officially named Kikusui, Floating Chrysanthemum.

On 6 April at noon Admiral Ugaki stood on the airfield and watched as the first wave of 27 fighters passed overhead. These were the decoys, to draw the American fighters away from the kamikaze force. Then came waves two, three and four each consisting of 27 planes bound for Okinawa.

The picket destroyers *Bush* and *Colhoun* were each attacked by about a dozen kamikazes and hit again and again. Both were sunk.

This cost the Japs 14 aircraft and men.

Onishi later committed Hara Kiri.

As for the Holy War on the ships of Okinawa, it languished on this second day, largely because of the weather and because the army air forces were primarily concerned with the B-29 attack on the homeland. Admiral Ugaki sent out about seventy planes to Okinawa. The usual number got lost, and more than the usual number were shot down.

One kamikaze crashed on the battleship *Maryland*, killing and wounding fifty-three men, but not putting the ship out of action. The destroyer *Bennett*, on picket duty, was also a kamikaze victim, as was the destroyer escort *Wesson*. But the bad weather saved many ships that day.

The submarine service did not contribute its share to the operation, through no fault of its own. The *I-58* was sent out to join in the *Yamato*'s foray against the ships southwest of Okinawa. But when Lieutenant Commander Hashimoto arrived, he was informed by radio that the *Yamato* had sunk, and the operation was cancelled. Why that was done has not been satisfactorily explained. The *I-58* could have carried out her mission. But the shock at navy headquarters after it was realized that Japan had absolutely no more surface navy in commission, was too great for common sense to take hold. The *I-58* returned to Japan on a tortuous voyage that involved dozens of American air attacks.

The sinking of the *Yamato* had a euphorious effect on the Americans at Okinawa. Admiral Richmond Kelly Turner, the amphibious commander, sent a jocular message to Admiral Nimitz, suggesting that the Japanese were finished. Nimitz, who sensed what was going to happen, set him straight in a hurry. So did the events of the next few days.

From this point on, until the end of the war, the suicide attacks never ceased.

On April 9 Admiral Ugaki received a message from army headquarters in Tokyo announcing that the planned counterattack by General Ushijima's forces had been delayed until that day. In accordance with the cooperative operations, Ugaki was asked to provide a major suicide attack that evening. He assembled the planes and sent off a wave, but the weather was so bad that the mission was aborted and the planes returned.

The next big attacks occurred on April 12 and 13. Ugaki sent out nearly two hundred planes that first day. The weather was clear at Kanoya and at Okinawa, which was good for the kamikazes but bad for the defenders. The Japanese hit the destroyer *Cassin Young*, sank one LCS and damaged another.

Admiral Ugaki also sent the Okas into action again, and this time the bombers managed to get through to the ships around Okinawa and deliver the rocket-propelled bombs. The destroyer *Mannert L. Abele* was first hit by a kamikaze Zero, then by an Oka, and sank in five minutes.

Another Oka hit the destroyer *Stanley.* The destroyer minelayer *Lindsey* was crashed by two kamikazes. The destroyer escort *Rall* was also hit.

Then the destroyer *Zellers* and the battleship *Tennessee* were hit. So were the destroyer escorts *Whitehurst* and *Riddle.* Near misses were too numerous to be accounted for.

There were more attacks on April 13. By that time the Americans could see the pattern, and it was not a pretty prospect.

The kamikaze attack was hell on ships' personnel, as the counter-attack tactics used by General Ushijima were hell on the soldiers and marines ashore. At the end of the first ten days of the Okinawa operation the shore forces had 3,700 casualties. The forces at sea had 1,200 casualties. The U.S. Navy were taking the greatest pounding of history. To match Admiral Turner's undue optimism, a thread of pessimism was beginning to work its way through the fleet.

When the waves of kamikazes came in, it was impossible for one or two picket destroyers to knock down a dozen planes. Their guns simply could not work that fast. What was needed was more Combat Air Patrol, and even this had proved insufficient.

Still, Admiral Ugaki made one serious error in his planning. Too many kamikazes went after the picket destroyers which covered the perimeter wall outside the area where the transports lay. Destroying the transports would cripple the American army ashore. The destroyers and escorts of the picket force were expendable, and replaceable.

In effect Admiral Ugaki was wasting his fire; creating havoc, no doubt, but still not achieving the utmost in destruction. Even so, the kamikaze attacks were posing the US fleet the most serious problem of the war. And as of mid-April nobody had an answer.

The war continued and so did the waves of *Kikusui*. They came again on April 14 and 15, nearly two hundred of them. The fighters of Task Force Fifty-eight shot down many, and the gunners on the ships shot down more. But the kamikazes damaged a battleship, six destroyers and two other ships.

They were back on April 16 to sink the destroyer *Pringle* and damage the carrier *Intrepid* and the battleship *Missouri*, plus several other ships.

They came on the seventeenth, again on the twenty-second, and then again on the twenty-seventh for a raid that lasted four days. One ship was sunk and twenty-two damaged.

Some officers had predicted that the Japanese must be running out of planes. But the Japanese airplane factories were working overtime, and the waves kept coming and coming.

(What the book does not mention is that all the British Carriers were hit by kamikazes, some twice, and were put out of action for a short time.—Ed.)

May was marked by four big two-day raids which cost the Japanese about six hundred aircraft. The cost to the Allies was five ships sunk and thirty-four damaged. Even on the days when the big flights of *Kikusui* failed to appear, a few kamikazes came in—and did more damage.

Admiral Turner was forced to change his mind completely. 'One of the most effective weapons the Japanese developed, in my opinion, was the use of the suicide bombers,' he said later.

Admiral Nimitz, in his inimitable style, would have said, 'Strike the words "one of".'

By the summer of 1945 concern at the highest levels over the efficacy of the Japanese suicide attacks had reached a peak. In June Admiral King, the Commander-in-Chief of the US Navy, ordered Vice Admiral Willis A. Lee to establish a new Task Force to study the kamikaze problem. Admiral Lee moved up Casco Bay, Maine, with eleven ships and a flock of American fighter planes, Japanese Zeroes and a number of other aircraft, to conduct research into defensive measures.

All that summer the experimenters worked on early warning systems, better control of fighters, better anti-aircraft-gun performance. They tried new weapons, new techniques. They listened to every new idea. And in the end they came up with nothing.

The kamikaze attacks continued in June. More ships were destroyed and hundreds more kamikaze pilots died.

Naha fell to the Americans at the end of May and the fighting grew even more desperate. Every Japanese infantryman was now a kamikaze.

On June 19 General Ushijima paid his last respects to the Emperor and ordered all his men to go out and die. Most of them did. The Americans made much of the fact that at this late date some Japanese surrendered (106 soldiers on June 19), but the truth was that the vast majority of the military men committed suicide or carried out Banzai attacks. Thousands of Okinawans joined them.

When the battle for Okinawa ended, at least a hundred thousand Japanese had died on land, and thousands more had died in the air and at sea.

At Casco Bay, Admiral Lee was still far from solving the kamikaze problem. And now the Allies had to face the prospects of an invasion of Japan, knowing that the enemy would fight even more ferociously on his home turf than anywhere else.

To say that Admiral Nimitz was concerned was a vast understatement.

The army philosophy was chillingly simple: it was better, said the generals, that the entire nation perish rather than become enslaved. They pointed time and again to the unconditional-surrender stipulation of the Allies. The Allies had promised that the army and navy would be disbanded, and the general assumed that the Emperor would be dethroned and probably murdered. They dangled this dread possibility before the Japanese with great success.

And the Holy War went on.

In July Admiral Ugaki's planes continued to attack the Okinawa area, even though it was now occupied by the Allies. The kamikazes came in day after day, and sank more ships and killed more men. Was there never to be an end to it?

Admiral Onishi kept feeding supplies to Admiral Ugaki and urged even greater efforts to destroy the enemy.

On July 1 Admiral Halsey set out from the Philippines with the Third US Fleet. Destination: Tokyo. Object: destroy the airfields and factories.

(Again no mention of the BPF—but we were there!)

For most of the next month and a half the Third Fleet ranged around Honshu and Hokkaido islands, raiding installations. The Japanese air force retreated into their shelters and took punishment. The pilots were under strict orders not to sortie except on orders from Tokyo, and high command ordered few responses to the raids.

Admiral Ugaki's operations were expected, and he was empowered to go after the US fleet with his suicide pilots. But the emphasis had gone from Admiral Ugaki's operations with the fall of Okinawa. Admiral Onishi's and the air armies' main effort was to prepare suicide planes and pilots for the coming battle of Honshu.

As August began even the B-29 raids were barely contested. The presence of the P-51 fighters persuaded the Japanese commanders to keep their planes hidden, saving them for the important battle to the death.

Admiral Halsey was of the private opinion that the Japanese were licked, an attitude that seeped into the dispatches of war correspondents. B-29 pilots began to treat the missions to Japan like a 'milk run'. They were protected by fighters all the way and met little opposition (although plenty of flak). If their planes were hit, and they had to bail out or ditch over the ocean, there seemed to be an American submarine every few miles along the way to pick them up.

The victory attitude also permeated Admiral Nimitz's Pacific Fleet. The submarine captains were bored and disgusted because there were virtually no targets. The captains no longer had to worry about convoys. Some no longer even bothered to zigzag as they moved their ships across the Pacific, so slight seemed the danger from submarines.

Suddenly on August 2, the fleet, at least, was yanked back to reality. A pilot flying a routine mission of the Philippines had discovered a big oil slick and a lot of heads bobbing in the water. Rescue vessels immediately came out. The cruiser *Indianapolis* had been sunk by Commander Hashimoto in the *I-56* on July 29. The war was not quite over yet.

At sea Admiral Halsey was not convinced by a single incident. He was more convinced by the fact that he seemed to be running out of targets. Admiral McCain, the carrier commander, was not of that mind. He knew that somewhere the Japanese must be stacking up hundreds of airplanes, and he wanted to find them. But Halsey insisted on plastering old and battered warships in the harbours and coves because he felt the airfields had already been worked to death.

The naval gunfire would have made very litle difference. The Japanese were now storing their planes underground.

By the end of June the Japanese army air force had organized 340 suicide squadrons. By August, production was back up to two thousand planes a month. Altogether the army had 6,150 aircraft at its disposal, 4,500 of these in the islands of Japan. Standing by were 6,150 pilots with another 2,530 in training. The army had 2,350,000 troops in the home islands. These were real soldiers.

And so, the Divine Wind died down and became a breeze. Weatherwise nothing had changed. Typhoons still continue as they have always done in this area of the Pacific and man has learned to avoid them—as far as possible.

From ACTION PRÉCIS. Oct. '44—The Battle of Leyte Gulf by Stan Smith

It is interesting to view the Japanese attitude at this juncture. How did the young men of Japan feel about orders to sacrifice their lives? And why did they do it? Nakajima, in his excellent works, explains the attitude of the kamikaze pilot and his willingness to die:

'Among the special attackers,' he writes, 'was the young oficer who had graduated from a technical college in Muroran, Hokkaido. He had stayed on at college as assistant professor and he continued with his advanced studies right up to the moment when his application for the Naval Air Corps was accepted. He already had several patents to his credit, and despite his youth showed great promise as an inventor. Some of his inventions were already in production in Japan and doing very well.

I summoned him to the shelter one evening for a chat, knowing that he had volunteered for attack duty at the first opportunity. He responded amiably to questions, but I found him to be less talkative than most of the kamikaze pilots.

'The Special Attack Corps is not the only place to serve our country,' I remarked to him. 'Japan will have need in the future for men with your skills.

Have you considered that your technical ability can be more valuable to our country than anything you can do here?'

He gave careful consideration to my words before answering: 'I have thought many times of the things you say. But my mind is made up. So I hope that you will understand and do nothing to interfere with my decision, because I do not want to change my mind.'

From the tone of his quiet reply our topic of conversation could have been nothing more serious than the weather. Never before had I sought in any way to influence a man's decision about volunteering for special attacks. Now I was suggesting the obvious fact that this man was of far greater value to his country alive than dead, and he responded with casual objectiveness that he wished to die for his country. There was no affectation in his attitude. It was not from fear that his statement omitted any mention of death, but rather death meant nothing to him in the consideration of performing his duty. I said no more and my professor friend left apologetically, as though in fear that he had offended me.

This seemingly unique case was typical of all men devoted to their country. It demonstrated the spirit of loyalty derived from generations of loyal ancenstry. 'A few days later he sortied, leaving four Zero fighters for a crash dive attack on enemy vessels . . . each plane carried a 500-kilogram bomb.

The kamikazes gave us tremendous new strength, their effect on us was obvious in the number of enemy warships and transports, once inviolate from our attacks, safe behind their withering fire power, which now resounded with the roar of flaming gasoline, exploding bombs, the shrieks of men. The kamikazes ripped aircraft carriers from stem to stern, sinking more than all our combined weapons had been able to destroy. They split open cruisers and destroyers, and exacted a terrible toll.

It was determined that five was the optimum number of planes for a sortie, and the pilots' skill of the time dictated that three suiciders with escorts was the best ratio. These numbers, of course, were not rigidly fixed. Depending upon weather conditions, the enemy situation, and the availability of planes, the number in each sortie might be varied.

The two escorting fighters were very important. They had to ward off interceptors until the kamikaze planes could make their plunge at the targets. The fight against interceptors had also to be a defensive one. The escorts could not initiate air duels nor could they seek a point of vantage if engaged. They had to stay at the side of the kamikazes. If attacked from behind, they could not retaliate, if to do so involved altering course. To deviate even briefly from the group's course would put an escort behind, with no chance of catching up. Escort pilots had to be able to dodge adroitly and block the enemy, rather than just shoot him down. An escort pilot's first duty was to shield the suicide planes in his mission, even if it meant the sacrifice of his own life.

It took men of superior skill and ability to fly escorts. And thus the request of our best flyers, like Lieutenant Kanno, to become kamikaze pilots had to be denied. Such men were so urgently needed to guard the suicide planes that they could not be spared to pilot them, despite their strong desire to do so. Many fliers of unit-leader rank flew escort for special attacks, and almost invariably they would volunteer as suiciders.

Kamikaze planes boost their speed as they approach the target area, and the few escorting fighters take position to block enemy interceptors. Kamikaze pilots ready their bombs by removing the fuse safety pin. Enemy fighters rise swiftly to intercept as our formation continues patiently toward the targets. The lead plane banks slightly and signals, 'All planes attack!' The raised arm of the leader is plainly visible and one can almost make out his broad smile. Each pilot selects his target, preferably an aircraft carrier, and plunges to its most vulnerable spot—the flight elevated deck elevator. Into the barrage of shipboard gunfire, into and through the squall of flying steel, each plane makes its hit. Each detonation raises flaring sheets of flame which spew up tall pillars of dense black smoke.'

Darter and *Dace* opened the Battle for Leyte Gulf with the torpedoing of cruiser *Takao*, flagship of Kurita's Centre Force. But it was not until the war ended that a story so secret and so unique in submarine warfare could be told. It was the blow-by-blow account of two of Britain's fleet of daring midget submarines which successfully mined *Takao* and finally sank her at her berthing. The feat characterizes the courage, determination and unalloyed skill of submariners everywhere.

Japan could only offer up the kamikaze fodder which it had so carefully been storing. On October 30, carrier *Franklin* caught one with horrendous damage resulting; *Intrepid* likewise was on the receiving end of a suicide attack. The third attack on *Franklin* punctured her flight deck, making a forty-foot hole, killing 56 men, shattering her Number Three elevator and injuring fourteen. What was it like to be on the receiving end of one of these attacks? We have only the word of a man whose ship was thus attacked, and it is not pretty:

'The dead were littered over the deck (flight deck) and the wounded were moaning for help,' recalls C. V. Killen, Chief Yeoman, attached to the *Franklin*. 'Fires had broken out around the shattered, charred remains of the elevator, and smoke was pouring from the hole caused by the suicider. "Don't try to get in there!" someone yelled. I looked around. An enlisted man was trying to support an officer—I think it was an officer—and both were burned, blackened, and bloody. Behind them, screaming for help, was my division commander with his arm blown off and blood pouring into his pants. He was walking around talking to someone who wasn't there. He dropped dead when several men attempted his rescue, just looked at them and dropped dead. Another man had the piece of a fighter wing's aluminium sticking out of his chest. When we attempted to get him out he just said "Leave me, fellows," and collapsed. Pieces of human flesh stuck to the deck, and the blood lay bubbling from the excessive heat. I grabbed a man who was groaning and staggered out . . .'

Admiral Ohnishi had left the world with a gory legacy. 'It must be said that both the suicide pilots and the men who guided them,' Pineau states, 'were moved by more than merely destructive aims. They realized the fight had to be carried out regardless of personal chances of survival. They fought for an ideal. Their road toward that ideal was *Bushido,* but the goal was "world peace".'

To the men of the United States Navy who had suffered because of the attacks of kamikaze pilots, this was so much unadulterated bunk. If a noble ideal such as 'world peace' was their goal, Japan was taking the long way around.

Extract from *Across the Parallel* by George Odgers, sent by Lt. Cdr. J. Lansdown RN Retd.

The river Nishiki, in southern Honshu, before it enters the Inland Sea, splits and forms a delta. On a flat and featureless island in the delta there is an airfield. It had been built for the Imperial Japanese Navy as a training place for its naval fliers. It had a concrete runway, steel hangars and extensive wooden quarters. If you stand on the slipway at Iwakuni and look northwards you will see, rising mysteriously out of the fogs and rain clouds that so often shroud the Inland Sea in summer-time, the island of Miya Jima. Here the young kamikaze suicide pilots of the Imperial Navy, who exercised and learned to fly at Iwakuni, would go for a last pilgrimage to the Shinto shrine there, and rest for a brief space in the delightful island setting before going off to give their lives in battle for the Emperor.

Miya Jima was the sacred island of eternal life. To ensure its 'divinity' no one was ever born there, and no one was permitted to die there either. If some inconsiderate person showed a tendency towards expiring, they were quickly moved off the island to the mainland of Honshu.

Admiral Fraser inspecting landing parties. Hong Kong.
O/S Bert Crane 4th from right.

Admiral Fraser's Flagship—HMS Duke of York*—19th August 1945. Photo: Ralph Beanland*

PART TWO

WEST PACIFIC ISLANDS

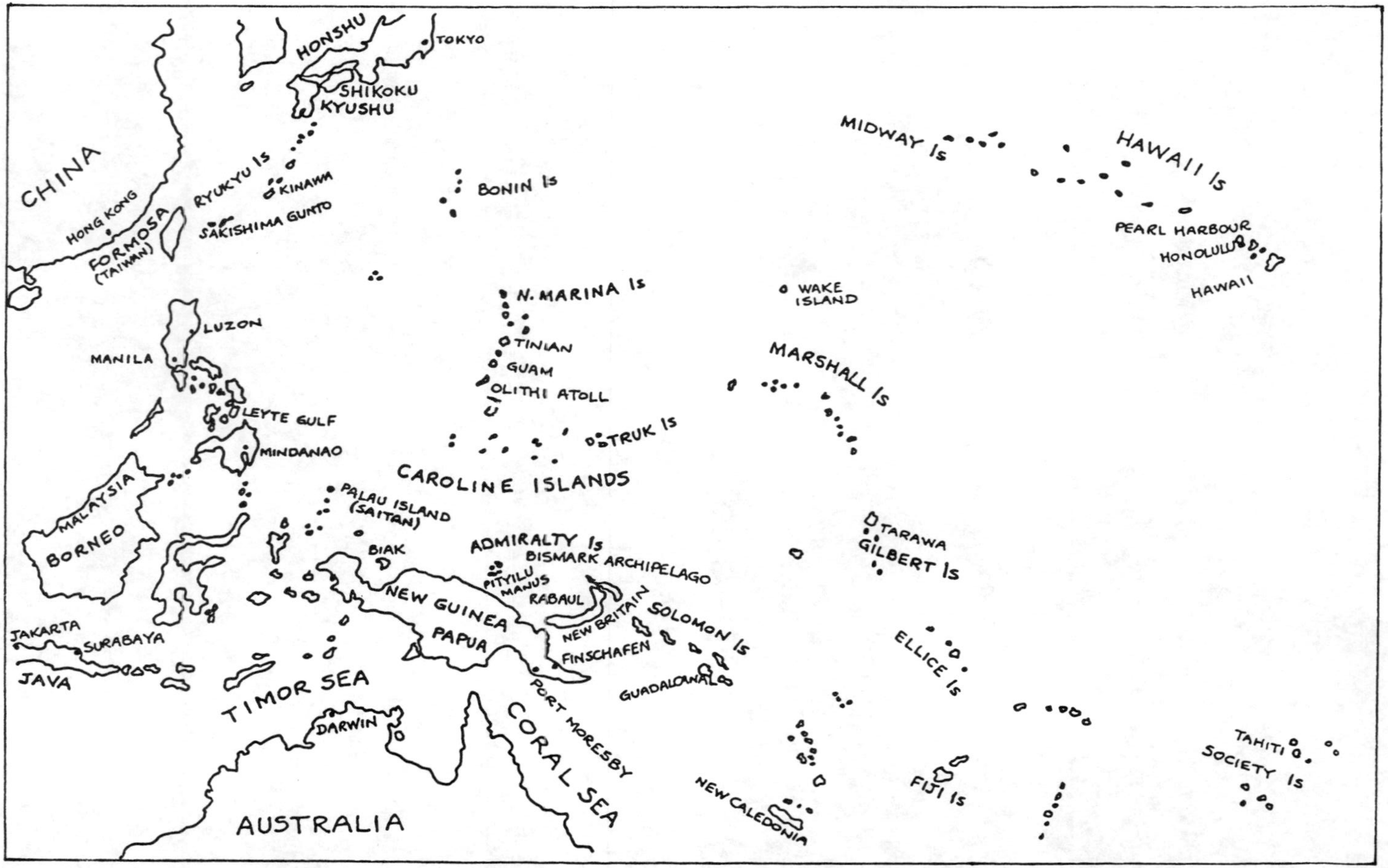

CHAPTER FOUR

The Situation

While the Royal Navy and the Merchant Navy were fully stretched in The Atlantic, the Mediterranean, the Arctic and Home Waters, the Japanese had advanced to the South Pacific. In February 1942 they carried out a bombing attack on Darwin, N. Australia which was to be the prelude to invasion.

At this crucial juncture, a small but vital counter-attack took place on the 800 yard wide airstrip at Tarawa, just 1 degree from the equator. It took 3 days to annihilate and cost 1000 U.S. lives. The Japs lost 6000 dead and only 17 surrendered.

Now the Pacific War was truly on. The Americans advanced and captured Saipan which cost them 3000 lives, but the tide was turning.

By the time they reached Guam, the U.S. aircraft carriers could call upon 900 planes whereas the Japs were down to 430 carrier planes.

From Admiral Sir Frank Twiss

Though I have no means of checking on the facts, I believe that the Japanese lost their big chance by expending effort on securing the minor Island of Rabaul instead of passing it by and going straight for Australia.

The story I had from Australian soldiers in a Prison Camp with me, was that for some time there had been plans to build up a strong position in Papua at Rabaul. Lack of decision, money and men and similar procrastination found the plans still unfulfilled when Pearl Harbour came. It seems likely that the Japanese had obtained a copy of these plans and took them into account in their planning.

Be that as it may, the Australians were caught on the hop and tried to make some amends by sending a force of Infantry to defend Rabaul. But the place was not as well prepared as it was intended to be and so, when the Japanese descended on it, despite valiant efforts, it fell fairly quickly.

But the decision to gain so small a foothold gave the Americans just that extra time to muster a force which caught the Japanese in the Coral Sea and for the first time halted their advance.

The speculation is that had the Japanese followed MacArthur's policy of bye-passing the non vital Islands and throwing everything at the really essential stepping stones, they could have made a bridgehead on the coast of a somewhat demoralized Australia and made a problem for the Allies which might have affected the outcome of the Pacific War.

Rabaul played a fascinating drama later in the war. We had a small band of Naval Telegraphists and others who watched the activities of the Japanese from islands within sight of Rabaul and sent back information which proved invaluable to the Allies. One piece of special interest was that the C-in-C of the Japanese Fleet, Yamamato, was due to visit Rabaul on a certain day. Acting on this an American fighter made a long and speculative flight to Rabaul and by a million to one chance intercepted the plane carrying Yamamoto and shot it down.

So much for the stories I have garnered from what are today called 'well informed sources'!

Extracts from *Wings of War* edited by Laddie Lucas

On 9 April after a gallant fight against overwhelming odds, weary American and Filipino troops on Bataan surrendered to the Japanese. Corregidor, the last American foothold in the Philippines would hold out less than a month more.

American morale was at its lowest ebb.

Then on 18 April 1942, sixteen US Army Air corps B-25 medium bombers struck at the heart of the Japanese Empire. Bombs fell on Tokyo, Yokohama, Nagoya, Osaka and Kobe.

Although the raids caused negligible physical damage (each twin-engined B-25 carried only a ton of bombs), it badly damaged Japanese morale. It was the first successful attack on the home islands of Japan in the history of that ancient and proud nation. An attack that the Japanese people had been told was impossible.

And, military historians have said, the Tokyo raid goaded the Japanese High Command into the face-saving 5—6 June Battle of Midway in which the Imperial Navy was dealt a blow from which it never recovered. It was the turning point of the Pacific War.

. . . The *Hornet* steamed out of San Francisco Bay at 10.18 a.m. 2 April. On 13 April, she and her escort rendezvoused with the carrier *Enterprise* and her escort vessels. Originally the plan was to take off late on 19 April, with Colonel Doolittle dropping incendiaries on Tokyo to guide the other planes for a night raid.

But at 3 a.m. on the 18th the *Enterprise*'s radar picked up two enemy patrol boats, part of an armada of picket vessels stationed 600 to 700 miles off the Japanese mainland. . . .

Messages flashed.

Soon afterwards, another Japanese patrol boat was spotted by a *Hornet* lookout. Then another. Halsey flashed this message from *Enterprise* to Admiral Marc Mitscher on the *Hornet*.

'LAUNCH PLANES. TO COLONEL DOOLITTLE AND GALLANT COMMAND GOOD LUCK AND GOD BLESS YOU.'

Doolittle was first off at 8.20 a.m., easily airborne after a run of only 427 feet. Stiff headwinds helped lift the overloaded bomber. At about the same moment the cruiser *Nashville* was sinking one of the patrol boats with shells—but not before it had relayed a radio warning to another Japanese vessel. . . .

It surprised everyone in Tokyo, when Doolittle's B-25 roared in over their roof-tops, pulled up to 100 to 200 feet and then dropped his bombs at 1.30 p.m.

After Doolittle made the initial run he encountered intense anti-aircraft fire, but the rest of the B-25s, save one, managed to hit either their primary or secondary targets. . . .

The Tokyo raiders were supposed to land at airfields in China. But because of the premature take off (they had planned to launch at about 400 miles and strike by night but lifted off by day at more than 600 miles) and because of headwinds, foul weather and other problems none made it. . . . The survivors went through some incredible ordeals and adventures evading the pursuing Japanese troops. Finally, with aid from Chinese guerillas and civilians, they made their way out of China. Lieutenant Ted Lawson, suffering from head, back and leg injuries, was carried to a Chinese village after crash-landing on a beach. Doc White, who had saved his medical gear, made connections with Lawson and several other injured airmen some time later.

The most remarkable thing about the Pacific war was the huge scale on which everything concerned with it was conducted. . . . Very great distances, many hundreds of ships, thousands of aircraft and astronomical losses by the Japanese.

For example, during the United States' assault and capture of the Marianas and Saipan in June 1944, the Japanese deployed 9 aircraft carriers with about 500 aircraft embarked. The Americans had 15 large carriers, with 5 small ones in support, and nearly 2000 aircraft. They also had 600 other ships.

In the operations, the Japanese lost 3 carriers, and 3 were seriously damaged and put out of action, together with 465 aircraft. Their admiral reported the day after the battle that he had only 35 aircraft left out of his original 500.

The United States lost 23 aircraft shot down, while 4 ships sustained slight damage. The US Navy flyers christened the day the 'Mariana Turkey Shoot'.

The battle of Leyte Gulf on 20 October 1944, was another instance of the sheer magnitude of the Pacific operations.

Here the Japanese had 9 battleships, 2 of which were fitted with a flight deck and could carry a few aircraft, 4 large carriers, 21 cruisers, 40 destroyers—but only 115 aircraft. These were all the aircraft they could muster after their recent heavy losses. The Americans deployed 12 battleships, 46 aircraft carriers, 28 cruisers, 235 destroyers and a total complement of some 1590 aircraft. In addition they had about a further 900 other ships—troop transports, logistics vessels and so on.

The Japanese made a determined effort to prevent the landing on Leyte, but, at the end of the day, they had lost all 4 carriers . . . and, additionally, 3 battleships, 20 cruisers and 11 destroyers. All their carrier aircraft were shot down or lost with the carriers.

For two weeks before the landings on Leyte, the United States' fast Carrier Task Force had delivered heavy air attacks on the fifty-seven airfields in the Philippines and also on airfields in Okinawa, Formosa and Hong Kong. The Task Force consisted of 16 large carriers, with 1110 aircraft embarked plus battleships, cruisers and destroyers in support.

The Americans usually flew 1200 to 1400 sorties a day over shore targets and maintained a permanent combat air patrol of 96 Hellcats over the Task Force all day.

On 15 October, Tokyo Radio announced that Japanese forces had gained 'a glorious victory for the Emperor'. They claimed to have sunk '11 aircraft carriers, 1 battleship, 3 cruisers and 1 destroyer' and to have 'severely damaged a further 8 carriers, 2 battleships and 4 cruisers'. The United States' fleet they said, was now retiring 'helter-skelter'.

All of us in the Task Force heard this announcement direct from Tokyo.

Admiral Nimitz, the Commander-in-Chief, Pacific, replied with a message broadcast on worldwide radio: 'Admiral Halsey reports he is now retiring towards the enemy following the salvage of all the ships of the Third Fleet sunk by Tokyo radio.'

The actual losses sustained by both sides, up to 15 October, i.e. five days before the Battle of Leyte Gulf, were as follows:

United States No ships lost, 2 cruisers damaged and 76 aircraft (out of 1110) lost.

Japan 41 ships—mostly merchant ships—sunk, 525 aircraft either shot down or destroyed on the ground (Japanese figures).

The result of all this was that on D-Day—20 October—there was virtually no Japanese air opposition to the landings on Leyte.

It may be said that it was easy for the Americans, with their great superiority both in quantity and quality of pilots and equipment, to achieve these results. The fact is, however, that they were just as good when the situation was reversed.

For example, the Battle of Midway Island showed how well the Americans could do when the cards were stacked against them.

The Japanese had decided in June 1942 to capture Midway, some 1500 miles northwest of Pearl Harbour, as the first step towards taking the Hawaiin Islands. Their force for the operation consisted of 6 battleships, 4 large aircraft carriers and 1 small one, 15 cruisers, 43 destroyers and a lot of transports. 310 aircraft were embarked.

The United States had no battleships to call on as all had been sunk in the attack on Pearl Harbour. Their force, therefore, consisted of 3 aircraft carriers, one of which had been badly damaged in the Coral Sea and was only partly repaired, 8 cruisers and 17 destroyers. 253 aircraft were embarked in the carriers while a further 53 navy and marine aircraft were available on Midway. At this time the US Grumman F4F fighter was much inferior in performance to the Japanese Zero.

The outcome of this critical battle was that the Americans sank all 4 of Japan's large carriers, 280 aircraft were either shot down or sank with the carriers, while the Japanese lost the cream of their front-line pilots. In the face of these losses, the enemy abandoned the operation and returned home.

The United States' losses were 1 carrier sunk—the previously damaged *Yorktown*, 1 destroyer sunk and 130 aircraft shot down. Of the 48 torpedo bombers involved in the operation, 43 were shot down by the Japanese.

This great victory, the turning point of the Pacific war, was won by naval aircraft inferior in number and performance to those of the enemy. It is a great tribute to the superb courage and excellent training of the USN avaiators.

The typhoon on 18 December 1944 took the US Fleet by surprise and prevented them from inflicting heavy damage on the Japanese at Luzon.

Admiral Halsey was intending to strike at Mindon with his 14 Carriers, 8 Battleships, 15 Cruisers and 50 Destroyers, but none of them had experienced anything like this before.

The Fleet Train consisted of 12 Tankers and 5 Escort Carriers who, after the typhoon had wreaked its havoc, had to replace 146 aircraft.

The trouble was that some of the destroyers were not in ballast, i.e. low on fuel—and consequently suffered more, even though it was not a particularly terrifying typhoon.

Some CAP aircraft could not land on and two pilots had to bale out to be picked up by a destroyer. This was no mean feat as three destroyers were sunk!

Halsey's flagship USS New Jersey *signalled all ships to take independent action to save themselves and the fleet scattered over a distance of more than 50 miles.*

New Jersey *made three attempts at re-fuelling in different areas before finding calmer seas.*

It was a strange irony that caused the typhoon to sweep away super-structures and top-side fixtures enabling some ships to stay afloat.

But as you will see later, this was merely a foretaste of worse to come for both the US 3rd Fleet and the BPF in August 1945.

Meanwhile, having been busy in other theatres of war, the ships of the Royal Navy were gradually diverted to assemble in Ceylon to comply with Churchill's offer to Roosevelt that we 'should be employed in the main operations against Japan'.

Extracts from: *The British Aircraft Carrier* by Paul Beaver

In the spring (1944), *Illustrious,* under Captain R. L. B. Cunlifee, CBE, RN, arrived at Trincomalee to join the temporarily-lent 3,000 tonne US aircraft carrier, *Saratoga,* for a series of operations designed to break in *Illustrious'* new air group—15 Naval Fighter Wing (NFW) and 21 Torpedo-Bomber-Reconnaissance Wing (DTBRW)—and to cause a bit of havoc in Japanese-held Sumatra. The first operation was against Sabang on Apriil 19 1944. A month later both carriers attacked Soerabaya oil refinery in Java—54 aircraft from *Saratoga* and 32 from *Illustrious.* Despite the accidental loss of two Avengers before the attack started, the strike was mildly successful and it marked the beginning of effective support by the RN for the hard pressed ground forces.

The necessity for a 'spare deck' in these waters was becoming apparent, especially if *Illustrious* was going to operate for a while away from land alone, until the arrival of *Victorious* and *Indomitable.* In early June, the escort carrier *Atheling* was used in trials for such a role, but her lack of speed made it impossible to contemplate such operations 'for real'. The need for the two extra armoured fleet carriers in this theatre was even more apparent.

The Eastern Fleet's next sortie was to the Andaman Islands but no worth-while targets were found in the Port Blair area for *Illustrious'* Avengers and Corsairs. The operation was noteworthy, however, for the fact that over 89 per cent of the air group were airborne together—the first time such a high number had been launched by the ship. It is worth recording here, that air-sea rescue services were beginning to be organised in the Eastern Fleet in a very professional way. The need was great because the choice between falling into the hands of the Japanese or into the mouths of sharks had little to choose between them. Initially operational submarines were deployed at pre-arranged locations to pick up the crews of damaged aircraft which could not make it back to the carrier. Later Sea Otter and Walrus amphibians were used to good effect, and some truly gallant pilots managed to land and pick up aircrew from inland lakes in enemy-held territory. In his Autobiography, *Action this Day,* published by Muller (1960), Admiral of the Fleet Sir Philip Vian records his own feelings towards these rescue operations mounted by the amphibian aircraft: 'They were invaluble in smooth water, and, at great risk, made rescues of pilots and observers ditched close inshore.'

It is perhaps a little known fact that squadron COs rarely flew as 'themselves'—the rest of the squadron were given the name of a fictitious officer to quote if captured and if the CO did fly he was known by yet another name. For example, Lieutenant Commander Norman Hanson, CO of 1833 Squadron, flew several missions as a Sub-Lieutenant. The reason for this deception was based on the methods used by the Japanese if the CO was unlucky enough to be shot down and captured. Many pilots did, however, fear more falling into the hands of Bedouin in what was then Trans-Jordan, than into those of the Japanese. In reality, of course, being captured was pretty awful whoever the captors.

The arrival of *Victorious* and later *Indomitable* was not the only change in the Eastern Fleet's carrier force, for *Illustrious* had a change of command in the summer of 1944. Captain Cunliffe was relieved by Captain Charles Lambe (later Admiral of the Fleet Sir Charles Lambe, GCB, CVO). So the first joint work-up of *Illustrious* and *Victorious* was as much for *Illustrious'* benefit as for the newcomers. Sabang was again the target for the new carrier force on July 25 1944, but the operation was mainly to use the big guns of the battleships and the Corsairs would provide forward spotting for the ships off-shore. The airfields ashore were attacked to suppress enemy fighters and for the first time the carriers' fighters were engaged by the enemy in aerial combat, but without casualties to the British. Operation Crimson had been a success and it was cordially received by SEAC's Supremo, Lord Mountbatten, with the words, 'The results will hearten all forces in South-East Asia.'

With *Illustrious* away under refit in South Africa, strikes against the Japanese were kept up by *Victorious* and the newly arrived *Indomitable*; August 24 Padang, Sumatra, Operation Banquet; September 18 Sigli, Sumatra, Operation Light; and October 17 and 19 Nicobar Islands, Operation Millet. During these operations, no counter attacks were mounted against the strike force until October 19 when Corsairs from *Victorious* (1834 Squadron) and Hellcats from *Indomitable* downed eight defending enemy aircraft without loss. *(These strikes were nicknamed 'Moody's Monthlies'—Vice Admiral C. Moody CB was commanding the aircraft carriers of the East Indies Fleet under Admiral Sir Arthur John Power KCB CVO.—Ed.)*

Fly past by 1834 Squadron, CO Lt Cdr Charlton, part of 'Moody's Monthlies', Colombo. Photo: M. Hancock

Despite the professional (and to some extent purely personal) misgivings of Admiral Ernest King, Command-in-Chief of the US Navy, the Allies agreed that Britain should again play a major role in the Far East. Like the armies in Burma, however, the British Pacific Fleet (BPF) was destined to become a forgotten force and it is only almost 40 years later that the public are becoming aware of the effort and success of the BPF. The reasons why the BPF should, in the words of John Winton's classic book, become the *Forgotten Fleet*, are complex and no doubt reflect the distance from the UK of the operations, the somewhat reluctant way in which the USN gave the BPF credit, and the fact that a good proportion of the action took place within months of, and following the end of, the War in Europe (VE-Day).

Captain Duncan Lewin feels that the lack of publicity could have also been due to the fact that there were very few reporters embarked with the BPF. During his time with force H, he recalls 'the warships didn't move without at least half a dozen reporters on board', but in the Pacific the USN provided billets for the press and so the media attention was focused on them and directed at the American public. The BPF was strategic in operational working, rather than being tactical as in the other theatres of the war, so in the latter there were more opportunities to report individual actions.

Columbo was the venue for the disbandment of the Eastern Fleet and for the creation of the British Pacific Fleet. On November 22 1944 Admiral Sir Bruce Fraser (of Battle of North Cape fame) assumed command of the powerful, if small by American standards, fleet. The BPF was centred on *Illustrious, Indefatigable, Indomitable* and *Victorious*, plus attendant battleships, cruisers and destroyers. At the same time as the BPF was created, a smaller fleet was established to fill in the vacuum in the Indian Ocean—the East Indies Fleet centred on the escort carriers, *Ameer, Atheling, Battler, Begum* and *Shah*. Rear Admiral Vian was the centre pin of the fleet as the Flag Officer of the Carrier Force (wearing his flag in *Indefatigable*) later known as the 1st Aircraft Carrier Squadron (1ACS). *(He arrived in* Indefatigable *and transferred to* Indomitable.—*Ed.)*

Several British officers were seconded to the USN during this time, notably the observer who turned pilot, Frank Hopkins (now Admiral Sir Frank Hopkins, KCB, DSO, DSC).

Despite attempts to standardise on the same aircraft types, British Corsairs often differed from their American (usually Marine Corps) counterparts and so the commonality of supply which should have been possible was not achieved. Rather similar, in fact, to the way, 30 years later, that RN Phantoms with Spey engines and British avionics were not compatible with the outwardly similar US Phantoms.

Extracts from an un-named Australian magazine sent to me by J. Haddock, HMS *Anson*

In Trincomalee, an American seaman called to our messman, 'Say Limey, when did you leave the old country in this spud boat?' The messman replied, in a droll voice, 'Yesterday, and by hell, it was raining.'

In the Indian Ocean at the beginning of 1944, the old 'R' class ships had been replaced by *Queen Elizabeth, Valiant* and *Renown*. At last it was possible to take the offensive:

Early in 1944 destroyer reinforcements arrived to join the Eastern Fleet. In March 1944 the American carrier *Saratoga* arrived from the Pacific to join Adm. Somerville's command. The first strike of this force supported by *Illustrious, Valiant* and *Queen Elizabeth* was on the island and port of Sabang in early April 1944. The airfields of nearby Sumatra were bombed and bombarded with 15 in. shells. A good deal of damage was done and the Japanese were attacked for long periods. They were unable to counterattack until late that day when a weak effort was easily warded off without casualties. The fleet returned to Trincomalee.

Some recollect this attack in rather more straightforward terms:

We would operate from Trincomalee in what were known as 'Club Runs'. We would go down with one or two carriers and some cruisers, and we would go and attack Japanese bases in Sumatra in particular. . . . We really started to learn our job against the Japanese for our eventual part in the British Pacific Fleet.

The Eastern Fleet did indeed carry out another 'Club Run' shortly thereafter:

In less than a month after this, the fleet was again on an offensive strike, this time to Surabaya over 2,000 miles away. Aircraft from *Illustrious* and *Saratoga* attacked and damaged the airfields in the early hours. They also succeeded in damaging enemy aircraft and, later in the day, severely damaged oil refineries. Battleships *Valiant, Queen Elizabeth, Richelieu* and the battle-cruiser *Renown* bombarded and left, leaving aircraft destroyed and ships sunk, without any loss to the fleet. These Allied attacks continued at about one per month during the remainder of 1944, and now included the Anderman and Nicobar Islands.

We all took great pride in our wardroom and saw to it that it was kept in good order. We also had a very good ante-room on the port side, as one came in from the quarterdeck. In the Indian Ocean, in the Pacific and in waters around Australia, whilst at sea we wore khaki shorts and sandals plus a khaki cap cover. We hung our shirts up on our pegs in the ante-room lobby and put them on before entering the ante-room and wardroom. We never abused this privilege given to us by the Captain who, I remember, ran *Anson* more like a destroyer when at sea. We had Wardroom Attendants who looked after their own particular officers with regard to laying out uniforms, what to, where and when. There were Royal Marines—full of guile and cunning! They were literally our saviours to us RNRs and RNVRs, who taught us ship's protocol in a battleship. They took a pride in turning out their young charges. We, in turn, learned a great deal from them.

While the BPF was being formed, some of the Australian ships were already in action.

AB R. J. Murray of HMAS *Shropshire* told me:

My first encounter with kamikazes was on the second day of the invasion of

Leyte 21st October 1944. We were protecting the troop transports and closed up at dawn action stations, when two planes came tree top height over the island, thus avoiding our radar. Our 4″ guns, bofors, oerlikons and pom poms opened fire. One plane maintained low height, while the other gained height. The plane that was flying low, I was watching with my binoculars and I was shaken when I saw the after structure and funnels of HMAS *Australia* loom in my sight, with this plane still continuing on and eventually crashing into the foremast and fore control bridge.

That plane was hell-bent on crashing into HMAS *Australia* who was flying the Pennant of Commodore Collins. It is my opinion that the plane that gained height was there as a witness to the deed. I learned at a much later date that the American historians reckon the kamikaze attacks started officially on 25th October 1944. Being an eyewitness, I maintain that this attack was the start of the kamikaze attacks.

During our stay at Leyte I saw several destroyers hit by suicide planes. One in particular, I think it was the USS *Hedley,* was burning and blowing up with dense smoke and the water surrounding the destroyer burning. I saw two sailors make their way to the fo'c'sle and having nowhere to go were trying to force their bodies into the burning sea.

Our next excursion into tiger country was Lingayen Gulf. Kamikaze attacked on the 4th January resulting in the light carrier USS *Ommaney Bay* being hit and subsequently having to be sunk by our destroyers.

On the 5th January, HMAS *Australia* again hit on the funnel and 4″ gun deck, causing many casualties. During these attacks one flew down our starboard side and our short range weapons were literally blowing it to pieces, but what was left of it continued on to smash into battleship USS *New Mexico.* There were a lot of fires, an explosion and the remains fell onto the deck and within minutes the damage control parties had hosed it off the deck. The superstructure of that ship must be two inches thick, there was no damage. Several cruisers and destroyers were hit or near missed including the HMAS *Arunta* which was holed resulting in two deaths, the steering gear was put out of action and the ship went zig-zagging all over the ocean. She was repaired and resumed her station.

Throughout the next four days I was to witness numerous attacks by kamikazes including several more hits on HMAS *Australia*. All told she was to receive five kamikazes inboard. As for my ship HMAS *Shropshire,* we were near missed three times and drove off a number of other planes with our fire power. We had radar control and our 8″ guns with the fuses set to explode at different distances, as well as Bofors, Oerlikons, Pom Poms and 4″ guns. One kamikaze came out of the sun one afternoon and our port pom pom needed only a couple of bursts to blow it up, it also blew the pilot from the plane. He had a parachute on, but by the time he had travelled half way down he slipped the parachute and went free fall for the rest of the way.

My action station was in the Fore control, which explains why I had such a good view. It got to the stage where I could sight a 'bird' at half a mile.

From Sto. George Ashton, HMAS *Warrego*

The landing at Lingayen Gulf was a huge naval manoeuvre, second only to the Normandy landings. There were hundreds of ships involved from battleships down to landing craft. I can remember quite clearly the kamikaze planes and there were quite a few of them.

One morning, it may have been the morning before the bombardment of Lingayen, a kamikaze plane was diving towards the *Warrego,* a sloop. Either the pilot thought we were too small a target or changed his mind, by the time he decided to pull out of his dive, I'm sure I could have hit his plane by throwing a stone, that was how close he was. I am sure it was the same day the HMAS *Australia* was struck by a kamikaze in 'B' turret. A chap I knew who joined up with me was killed in that action.

We were in Manilla Harbour and there were as far as I can remember about 13 ships sunk, some of them only the funnel above the water line, an American cutter (maybe two weeks after we entered the harbour) came alongside our ship and I was on the starboard side on the after deck. In the cutter there was a Japanese sailor, he was as thin as a match. I'll never forget his white eyes as he had been living in the funnel of a sunken ship.

From R. J. Plumb, HMAS *Australia*

I served in HMAS *Australia* and my action station was forward mast head lookout when we were hit five times by the yellow bastards. The crows nest I was in was hit by one a couple of feet below me, wiping out the bridge, killing the skipper at the same time.

From AB QM R. J. Plumb, HMAS *Vampire*

I was an AB QM in HMAS *Vampire* in company with HMS *Thanet*. We engaged a Jap cruiser and three destroyers at Endu, sadly we lost *Thanet*.

I was in *Vampire* in company with HMS *Electra* and *Express* as destroyer escorts to HMS *Prince of Wales* and *Repulse* when they were sunk off Siam. *Electra* and *Express* picked up the survivors from the *Prince of Wales* whilst *Vampire* stood by *Repulse* picking up survivors.

We then took them to Singapore and during this action we were repeatedly attacked by high level torpedo bombers by the score.

When Singapore fell, *Vampire* escorted three Dutch merchantmen to Bombay.

After this HMAS *Vampire* was assigned as escort to the carrier HMS *Hermes* and on the 9.4.42, *Hermes* and *Vampire* were sunk by Jap 'Kazi' bombers in the

Bay of Bengal.

After hours in the drink we were picked up by the Hospital ship *Vita* and taken to Colombo and thence by train to Diatoloa for a couple of weeks rest, then down to Lanka depot Colombo and transit home to Aussie on the *Dominion Monarch*.

After 28 days survivors leave, I was drafted to *The Aussie* and you know the rest.

Vampire picked up the skipper of *Repulse,* Captain Tennant. *(Admiral Sir William Tennant 1890—1963.)*

From P.O. E. E. Fernandez, HMAS *Warramunga*

While we had been on our way to Ceylon, the American and Australian Navies had been hard at it. Petty Officer E. E. Fernandez (deceased 1989) of HMAS Warramunga *wrote:*

The assault on Leyte was under the command of General MacArthur and was to be the first stage in the return to the Philippines for him. *Warramunga* arrived at Hollandia late on the 18th October 1944 and sailed with the Task Force early on the 19th. When all sections of the assault forces took their places there were 6 battleships, 5 heavy cruisers, 18 escorts, 5 H.Q. ships, 46 transports, 1 hospital ship, 17 destroyer transports, 9 landing ships dock, 3 landing ships infantry, 15 sub-chasers, 44 minesweepers, 238 landing craft, 18 miscellaneous craft and 1 seaplane tender. Close fire support was to be provided by Rear Admiral Berkey's Task group, now designated Task Force 77.3 and consisted of *Phoenix, Boise, Australia, Shropshire, Bache, Beale, Hutchins, Daly, Killen, Arunta* and *Warramunga*.

Pre-landing bombardments commenced on the 20th October. At 0300 the assault forces formed up and proceeded between Dinngat and Homonnon Island towards San Pedro Bay, with the minesweepers ahead. During this passage *Shropshire* and one of the transports caught a mine in the paravanes. This was quickly cleared and destroyed. At 0630 enemy aircraft were detected but no attack was forthcoming. At 0710 the first bombardment was commenced by the battleships *West Virginia, Mississippi* and *Maryland*. The cruisers *Australia, Shropshire, Boise* and *Pheonix* then opened fire with devastating effect. It was then the destroyers turn, and at 0900 *Warramunga* opened fire with a barrage bombardment.

Earlier in the day at 0958 it was recorded that General MacArthur had landed on Red Beach thereby honouring his promise to the Philippine people that 'I SHALL RETURN.'

The next day was Trafalgar day and, while patrolling off Samar Island, it was observed at 0600 that enemy aircraft had attacked the major ships of the assault group. *Shropshire* engaged and drove off a dive bomber with a heavy barrage. This plane continued flying westward, suddenly turned east and, although under heavy fire passed the port side of *Australia* and crashed into the foremast at 0605. There was a loud explosion and an intense fire was started on the bridge. The radar hut fell onto the compass platform and the port strut of the foremast was broken. By 0635 the fire was under control and wreckage had been cleared away. Commodore Collins had been wounded and *Warramunga*'s first skipper, Captain Dechaineux, had been killed. General McArthur sent a signal to all R.A.N. ships saying:

'The Australian Navy has played a full and splendid part in the landings at Leyte. It was my great pleasure to see all the ships in action.'

On the 30th December, 1944, *Warramunga* proceeded alongside a tanker to refuel, and at 0800 left for Leyte Gulf which was reached on the 2nd January, 1945 at 1055. She fuelled from the tanker *Carthen* and anchored, prior to leaving on the 3rd January at 10 minutes past midnight.

So the stage was set for the biggest assault of the war . . . the landings at Lingayen Gulf. *(Reportedly equivalent to the D Day landings.—Ed.)* The entire attack force comprised 850 ships. Of these 305 were fighting ships and 11 vessels of the R.A.N. were included. *Warramunga* steamed through the Surigao Strait and into the Mindanoa Sea, part of the Bombardment Force, designated Task Group 77.2, under the command of Admiral Oldendorf U.S.N.

The Japanese Fleet still could muster a formidable force of some 4 battleships, 7 carriers, 9 cruisers, 35 destroyers and 54 submarines, while the air force had control of many airfields on the west coast of Luzon. Opposition was expected to be intense. The distance steamed at the end of December was 129,904.5 miles.

Soon after 1700 on the 4th January, the assault group were attacked by enemy aircraft. *Warramunga* opened fire and several emergency turns were made to avoid being hit. However, a Japanese Naval dive bomber crashed into the USS *Ommaney Bay,* on the flight deck just abaft of the bridge, causing several fires in the ship's hangars. The fires became uncontrollable and the ship had to be abandoned and sunk.

On the 5th it was reported by U.S. planes that an enemy force of destroyers were astern of the convoy. Three ships, HMAS *Gascoyne, Warrego* and USS *Bennton* were ordered to engage. This they did and the Japanese immediately reversed course and retired, making smoke. Several aircraft attacks continued for most of the day.

Dawn broke on the 6th January, and *Warramunga*'s crew went to action stations once again. On this day they stayed at their stations for over ten hours. The sea was a long swell as *Warramunga* made for the gulf to provide protection for the minesweepers.

At 0730, *Warramunga* left the Task Group and was immediately picked out by three enemy aircraft. The first dived at the starboard bow. The 4.7 inch guns opened fire, followed by the 4 inch, and then the short range weapons. It turned away out of control and the second one approached from astern. Instead of continuing on in a suicide mission he released two bombs, one going close to the stern and the other close to the starboard side. U.S. fighter aircraft made for this one and it was shot down. The third decided not to attack but was also shot down by the fighters. *Warramunga* was then recalled to the safety of the Task Group.

At 1145, two enemy planes appeared coming in from the hills at great speed and barely above the water. All ship's guns came to bear and opened fire. One plane came through the bursting shells and appeared almost surely to land on *Warramunga*. At about 1000 yards it suddenly veered and, passing across her bow, crashed into the USS *Brooks*. Fire enveloped the stricken ship. *Warramunga* slowed and turned to render assistance. At 1303 she was alongside the burning ship and the damage control parties got to work on the fires. One fire was close to their 3 inch magazine. It was essential that this fire be contained, so eight hoses were played onto this area. By this time, the sides of the *Brooks* were red hot. Wounded were transferred to *Warramunga*'s sick bay as she prepared to take the ship in tow. It had taken about an hour to have the fires under control, so it was 1345 before the tow could be secured.

At about 1400 the strain was taken up and *Warramunga* departed at 8 knots out of the gulf, leaving them 'sitting ducks' for any other enemy plane that came their way. On her way out *Warramunga* passed the great sight of the battle fleet coming in.

Attacks continued on the fleet by the suicide planes and *Warramunga* was given close support by *Warrego* and *Gascoyne*. At 1545 an attempt was made to pass over the tow to *Gascoyne* but it was not possible, so she continued her slow journey. At 1625 an enemy aircraft attacked again, but the accurate fire of *Warramunga* drove him off and he was seen smoking badly, and then crashing into the sea. At 1629, three more aircraft were seen flying out of the sun and heading her way. They swept astern of the small group and were seen to hit other larger ships. At 1740 it was reported that *Australia* had been hit once again. These suicide attacks continued until 1815. At 1850 it was recorded in the deck log 'Sunset. Thank God for that.' At 1939 Lieut. Commander Alliston ordered 'Secure Action Stations'.

Lingayen Gulf/Leyte Gulf

On the 8th January dawn action stations were called at 0637. At 0730 enemy aircraft were in the vicinity, and *Australia* was again hit at 0735. *Warramunga* went to cover the minesweeping force and, at 0904, closed to *Pennsylvania* to transfer the remainder of the crew of *Brooks*. The transfer was completed at 1022 and *Warramunga* returned to cover the sweepers. Later in the day, when things became a little quiet, *Warramunga* went alongside USS *Colorado* to refuel and take off some several tons of fresh water and a goodly supply of 40 mm ammunition. At 1835 enemy aircraft again attacked with several ships being hit. Action stations were secured at 1943.

On the evening of the 8th January it was reported that the whole outer approaches of the Gulf were filling up with transports, LSF's and Landing ships.

Dawn action stations were called at 0645 on the 9th January, the day allocated for the actual landings. Weather conditions were excellent; little swell and hardly any wind. Pre-landing bombardments commenced at 0745 by Task Force 77.2 comprising 6 US battleships, 8 cruisers, 46 destroyers and other smaller craft, of which *Australia, Shropshire, Arunta* and *Warramunga* were part. The landings were to be made in the San Fabian and Lingayen area. *Warramunga*'s station was on the western flank and she was allocated several targets and also the role of supporting any call from the troops ashore.

Warramunga was about a mile or so from the shore and saw the troops land at 0929. Progress was rapid and there seemed little resistance. Ashore it was recorded 'Devastation caused by the Naval bombardment group was indescribable. Huge craters dotted the ground, trees were either shorn off or riddled with shrapnel. The village of Binmaley presented a dismal sight. Everything had been wrecked.' By noon the town of San Fabian was captured; by 1700 the town of Lingayen was secured; and by dusk the troops had penetrated 6—8000 yards inland.

Late in the day *Warramunga* topped up with fuel from USS *Warhawk* and then anchored. While at anchor *Warramunga* made smoke to give a cover of protection to the ships moored close in to her. At 1905 enemy aircraft were in the vicinity, and she opened fire at several targets.

Action Stations were sounded at 0415 on the morning of the 10th January. It had been reported that enemy Motor Torpedo Boats and suicide swimmers were active in the gulf. *Warramunga* got under way and carried out anti MTB patrols and, while under way, fired on all sorts of garbage which was floating in the gulf just in case a suicide swimmer was underneath. These swimmers carried haversacks of gelignite and floated down stream under provision cases, or other such rubbish, hoping to get close to any ship and activate the explosive. The damage caused was minimal but the reaction to them from all the ship's companies was, to say the least, alarming. On the transports anyone who could fire a gun was firing at objects in the water—bullets whined everywhere. The attack force commander quickly put a stop to this with a brief and sharply worded signal.

At 0645 *Warramunga* proceeded on patrol of the gulf between Tondu Point and Bay Bay. Just before dusk the usual repel aircraft was sounded and at 1943 action stations were secured.

Lingayen Gulf
H.M.A.S. Warramunga
29th January, 1945

CAPTAIN'S NEWS FLASH !!!!!

At 0830 this morning, two divisions of troops were landed at Subic Bay, which adjoins Manila Bay.

Admiral Berkey and close covering groups carried out a bombardment. The landing has ben successful and a landing strip has already been captured. The commodore has made a signal re mail. It is possibly in Leyte now. Another signal has been made in which 'Merkur' has been ordered to arrive in Leyte by the 8th February. Fresh provisions cannot be expected before then.

The question of when Australian ships will go south is not decided. My view, for what it is worth, is that we shall not go to Sydney for at least a month from now.

J. M. Alliston
Lieutenant Commander R.N.

He was about right. Warramunga *left Lingayen Gulf on 26th February, southward bound.*

On the 7th March, in company with *Shropshire, Arunta* and the recently arrived *Hobart*, the force exercised off Manus, leaving at 0745 and returning after practice torpedo runs at 1645.

While exercising with U.S. and R.A.N. ships, the arrival of the British Pacific Fleet was witnessed, making an impressive sight. It was great to see so many other ships flying the 'White Ensign' in Manus.

Foreword to *'Midway'*, written by Professor Michael Lewis CBE, FSA, F.R.Hist.S.

Midway was far more decisive than Leyte, but because Leyte was the last great operation, nobody can ever really forget.

In his Foreword to 'Midway' The Battle that Doomed Japan by Mitsuo Fuchida, former Captain Imperial Japanese Navy and Masatale Okumiya former Cdr. Imperial Japanese Navy, Professor Michael Lewis wrote:

To the student of Naval History in this country the news of Pearl Harbor and of the loss of the *Prince of Wales* and *Repulse* came at once as a profound shock and as the warning of a major revolution in sea-warfare.

But the breakdown of Anglo-American command of the Pacific was a fact, and a very ugly one. It meant, at the very least, a titanic effort to regain it with, in the words of our great war-leader, 'blood and sweat and tears'.

That effort was one which Britain, everywhere committed up to the hilt, was in no position to make just then. Our ally, however, not only could, but did make it. For six months there flowed the full tide of Japan's advance, the immediate product of her new command of the seas concerned, and it swept her irresistibly southwards and south-westwards, until even Australia was threatened. Then it received a half-check—in the Coral Sea—and we almost dared to hope that Japan's highwater mark had been reached. But it was still just a hope; it might be nothing but a daydream.

Then came Midway, and the hope instantly blossomed to near-certainty. For the message of Midway, in terms which no one could misread, was that the tide had actually turned: that the U.S.A., by dint of magnificent perseverance and truly remarkable technical efficiency, had called a halt to Japanese expansion. More, it showed that, having halted it, the States could roll it back—that they had the means to do so, as they certainly had the will. Indeed, the gifted Japanese officers who wrote this book have been at once brave and honest in facing up to this unpalatable fact, and choosing for a sub-title 'The Battle that doomed Japan'. It is exactly what it was. And we in this country, I think, realized the potentially decisive nature of the affair even before the details reached us: for we felt that, while the Japanese war-effort had by now reached its peak, or nearly, that of our allies was only by comparison beginning; and that, now and at an ever-increasing tempo, they could regain the lost command of the Pacific. *Then* where would Japan be, straddled as she was across thousands of miles of sea and island?

Captain Fuchida was an outstanding officer in the Naval Air Force. At the outbreak of war he was senior air wing commander in the Carrier Task Force, which was actually the main striking strength of the Japanese Fleet. In this capacity he led the air assault on Pearl Harbor as well as subsequent air strikes by the same Task Force. In every operation he performed brilliantly and capably. Captain Fuchida was present at the Midway battle from start to finish on board aircraft carrier *Akagi*, flagship of the Nagumo Force.

The Japanese public, of course, was not told the truth about the battle. Instead, Imperial General Headquarters announcements tried to make it appear that both sides had suffered equal losses. The United States, however, promptly announced to the whole world the damage inflicted on the Japanese, accurately naming the ships damaged and sunk. Thus it was clear that our efforts to conceal the truth were aimed at maintaining morale at home rather than at keeping valuable knowledge from the enemy.

When Captain Fuchida and Commander Okumiya brought out the original edition of their book on the Battle of Midway in 1951, the Japanese public learned for the first time the story of the disastrous naval defeat which turned the tide of the Pacific War.

Birth of the BPF

When Admiral Somerville became Commander of the Eastern Fleet in the Spring of 1942, he signalled, 'So this is the Eastern Fleet. Well never mind, there's many a good tune played on an old fiddle.' It summed up the five old 1914—18 war battleships, seven ancient cruisers and the out-of-date carrier Hermes.

True, he had the loan of the fairly modern carriers Indomitable *and* Formidable *and later re-inforcements of two more battleships and a battle-cruiser, the carriers* Illustrious *and the USS* Saratoga, *plus two escort carriers. However this was no match for the might of the Japanese Navy and Air Force. The RN felt the underdogs and were. Soon, the carrier* Hermes, *the cruisers* Dorsetshire *and* Cornwall, *the* Vampire, *a corvette and two tankers had been sunk.*

On 31st August 1943, Lord Louis Mountbatten was appointed Allied Supreme Commander, S.E. Asia Command (SEAC). He was 18 years younger than Admiral Somerville, a Captain and only 44. Churchill wanted Somerville to stay since he had done well through two difficult years with inadequate resources, but thëir lordships advised otherwise, probably due to the obvious personality clash. In any case, who else but Somerville, with his experience, could liaise with the top brass in the U.S.A.?

And so on 23rd August, 1944 Admiral Fraser replaced Somerville as C in C, Eastern Fleet, just as re-inforcements were arriving. Fraser, who had served under Admiral Beatty in the First World War had been a most successful C in C Home Fleet and had thoroughly prepared himself for his new role with contacts in the high places of U.S. Navy, Army and Air Force Commands.

Fraser had 'the common touch'. There was no 'side' to him. He could talk to Dukes and Dustmen and be equally 'at home' with either. And so it was with his relationship with Mountbatten. There was no rivalry. After showing himself to the ships then under his command in Ceylon he set up shop in Sydney. While he was in Ceylon, Rear Admiral Moody led the Carriers Indomitable *and* Victorious *on strikes against Sumatra.*

In September 1944, when Churchill met Roosevelt in Quebec, and offered the services of the Eastern Fleet in the Pacific, the BPF was officially conceived. Resources were split, to provide an E. Indies Fleet under Admiral Power based on Ceylon and the BPF under Fraser to operate from Australia.

Only the Tirpitz *danger could delay these plans and so it was that on 12th November 1944 the Dambuster Squadron of Lancasters was detailed to finish her off—now in Tromsö Fjord, with 6 ton 'Tallboy' bombs.*

On 22nd November, Fraser became C in C BPF, a fleet that was still thousands of miles away and still not a fleet, but a variety of vessels at, or en route for, Ceylon. Although he had once commanded the old carrier Glorious, *Fraser was basically a Gunnery man and had no experience of the latest carriers. Now he was responsible to the U.S. Admiral Chester Nimitz and must have felt inadequate and certainly at a disadvantage in his discussions with the Americans while endeavouring to organise the supply ships which would make up the Fleet Train. He had 'problems' with the Admiralty who were adamant that the RN should not implement USN signalling practice and should not change their white uniforms for khaki. How he overcame these problems, I don't now, but he did.*

He had another problem, in the form of U.S. Fleet Admiral Ernie King, U.S. Chief of Naval Operations who apparently didn't want the British 'helping' him to defeat Japan. However, the rest of the U.S. Command wanted the BPF, and since Nimitz and Fraser respected each other, King didn't stand a chance. In fact the two became good friends, such was Fraser's charisma. He called on General MacArthur and Admiral Kincaid at Leyte and went aboard the USS New Mexico *to witness the bombardment and landings at Lingayen Gulf, North Luzon. During this operation, he experienced the first of the massed kamikazes and was unscathed when the ship was hit on 6th January, but the captain was killed. So were two members of Fraser's staff, Major General Lumsdon and Sub Lt. Morton.*

They were under attack too as they left the ship and his PBY flying boat had been planted with explosives! So the C in C BPF had experience of the kamikazes before his fleet had arrived!

It must have been difficult for Fraser with Admiral Cunningham 'supervising' from the Admiralty. A fine Admiral, but obviously with no experience of the kamikazes or understanding of the vast distances and supply requirements that Fraser had to surmount. He was, like most people in Britain at the time, of the opinion that the Americans had too much of everything for us to try to emulate them, or to get too involved. Fraser knew otherwise from first hand knowledge. Also, he understood the 'lower deck' and knew how to look after them, within his limitations.

What Britain did not have was the 'Seabees', the U.S. Construction crews, so he had to rely on the bases they had created. The nearest, Manus, was 4,000 miles from Sydney.

Les Bancroft P.O. Elect. Artificer, HMS *Indefatigable* wrote to me from New South Wales. *His wonderfully descriptive story would make a fine book. I found it fascinating. From the day he joined the Navy in February 1940—farewells, new friends, technical training, air raids etc. I have only been able to include a few incidents, which help to illustrate what was in the hearts and minds of so many who ultimately served with the BPF, but his character and compassion shine brightly through.*

Here are some recollections of how he came to be there:

As Boy Artificers, at the RN port of Rosyth we were blessed with huge playing fields on which we participated in all types of sport.

One particular day I was in a Boy Artificers hockey team playing against a team from either a frigate or destroyer, I forget which, anchored alonside a jetty in the dockyard basin. My position was half-back and I found my forward opponent to be a tall fair headed Lieutenant; a Prince Philip of Greece. We had a ding-dong battle and I particularly remember in the second half that on one occasion I ran in to tackle Prince Philip just as he cracked an intended fierce through pass up the field. The ball flew from about 5 yards range straight at my face. Fortunately I had time to duck just sufficiently for the ball to literally scrape through my hair; a parting in the middle. Prince Philip looked quite concerned for a moment until realising I was unhurt. Then it was back to the ding-dong battle. It was a good game.

On that day, I believe honours were even. However, I still have a full head of wavy hair.

During my 1941 summer leave, one night when my father was out at work,

I vividly remember, near midnight, standing outside our house back door with my mother and sister Sylvia aged 14 years. We were watching, across the fields to the west, a line of air raid caused fires which appeared to be approaching us. We could also hear a sound like a train approaching; but there was no railway in that direction. The noise rapidly grew louder until, suddenly, a great terrifying shrieking sound enveloped us. Simultaneously, the fields and our back garden, to within 3 yards of where we were standing, abruptly exploded into hundreds of blinding, searing, man-high geysers of flame. Even as the flames erupted I pushed my mother and sister into the house, followed them and slammed the back door. It was instinctive. I went straight through the house, the thought in my mind, although this was my first experience, Molotov Cocktails; the large bombs which blew open some 400 feet above ground level, releasing and scattering a 100 and more incendiary bombs. I shot out the front door and checked for fires to our home. We were lucky, the bombs had jumped us and the house next door. However, the roofs of the corner house one up opposite and many in the adjoining streets, were already burning fiercely. I promptly joined with the local fire fighters in the immediate urgency of pushing and carrying women and children to safety from their beds and under the stairs shelters in their now burning homes.

We then tried to fight the fires; it was hopeless. The local water main had been ruptured by high explosive bombs; we had but a trickle of water to fight what were fast becoming infernos. We saved what little valuables and furniture we could and then watched as the homes were gutted, including one whole block of eight.

The newspapers, I heard, later reported a 125,000 incendiary bomb raid; we had been near the middle of it. No bombs that night landed on the target, Portsmouth.

A year later, whilst on leave again, I was caught in another, much smaller, incendiary bomb raid but this time the incendiaries only landed in the fields below my home. I ran out with a spade to shovel earth onto the flaring magnesium fires. Many other people, mostly women and children, were doing the same. I have a very clear memory of suddenly noticing, next to me, working hurriedly and expertly with little coal shovels, were two small children, a boy and a girl. They were no more than 6 years of age. Amazed, I called to them, 'You two are doing a great job.' Their little faces lit up in smiles, as only a child's can, and without stopping shovelling the boy piped up, and I remember near enough his words, 'Got to put them out quick Mister. So the German's can't see where to drop the big bombs.'

During late 1942 at a dance in the Masonic Hall, Rosyth, I was introduced to a young Scots lass, Christina Ferguson. She looked beautiful to me. We became good friends and for the next year went out together whenever we could. I remember on Sundays we would walk, hand in hand, for up to 10 miles to the beautiful Otterston Loch and Aberdour on the Forth River.

Christina's parents welcomed me to their home. In fact her mother overfed me in true Scottish fashion. Not that I objected.

In December 1943 Christina and I bade farewell with promises to write but with no knowledge when, and if, we would ever meet again. At that time, Perce Raby was also bidding farewell to his Rosyth girl friend, Olive Farnell. The paths of all four of us were to show some unusual coincidences in the future.

One bleak afternoon at Scapa I was conveyed by a small fishing vessel to a colossal, magnificent aircraft carrier at anchor. The climb aboard was up a 20 foot rope ladder in a howling Scapa Flow gale. I was then greeted by a gentleman in all aspects of the word, Chief Electrical Artificer MacKenzie (Mac). That was it, after 7 days travel, HMS *Indefatigable.* A fine ship in which I served until June 1947.

From Lt. Cdr. Colin Mackenzie RN, First Lieutenant, HMS *Indefatigable*

My most vivid recollections seem to be rather trivial. When the brand new ship came to leave John Brown's yard we had a crew many, indeed most of whom, had never been to sea before. With a raw team on the forecastle we were hauling away on a wire to turn the bow down the Clyde when a heavy strain came on. I shouted 'Handsomely, handsomely' and the new cable party, thinking this cry was to congratulate their efforts, pulled all the harder. We were spared a nasty accident by a narrow margin.

Then there were some nightmare weeks during trials at the Tail of the Bank. Nothing went smoothly, the Commander went sick from the strain, and I remember very clearly my relief when his successor Commander Whitfeld stepped aboard.

Next were the months based at Scapa Flow with the bombings of the *Tirpitz*. My most vivid memory of this period is the time when we embarked a batch of very cunning new types of mine to be laid in the Norwegian leads. None of us had seen anything like them before, and the business of getting them ready to lay, without touching the wrong terminal, was an acute worry. In the event the operation was cancelled.

Then, when we went south to Portsmouth and the King came down to wish us well in the Far East. In the preparations for the visit, no-one had thought that what he wanted on arrival was a nice cup of tea. With the staff all dressed up and fallen in for inspection, it took him 20 minutes to get it, and he *was* angry.

Then the long flog to Trincomalee. The visit of Mountbatten being very Mountbatten, and on to Sydney where Admiral Vian, somewhat to my relief, transferred his flag.

Extracts from *Indefatigable* Diary, sent by P.O. Peter Bonney

INDEFAT'S RADIO SHOW

What the station was called I don't know, but it was often worth listening to.

The programme I remember best was, 'Next Port of Call', and I distinctly remember Lt. Lynch-Blosse RNR who was my Divisional Officer, giving a very knowledgable and useful account of the facilities afforded by Port Said, ending on a note of unnecessary caution directed at those of us who might otherwise spend their time researching a bizarre exhibition no longer available.

From PO A/M Jim Dodds, HMS *Victorious*, now living in Australia

The RN truck which had brought me from *Merlin* to Rosyth dockyard pulled up at the main gate so I could report my presence to the dockyard police and receive permission to proceed to the yard below. As I looked downward at the waters of the Firth of Forth and the roadway leading to the basin my eyes caught sight of what I was searching for and what was to be my home from that day until the 29th November 1945, 3 years and 8 months into a dark and uncertain future.

HMS *Victorious* passively lying there tied up alongside the wall was a thing of beauty to me and awesome in size. This then was the culmination, my reason for volunteering for the Navy on my 19th birthday, 30th September 1940 and the realization I was about to board and be a part of the aircraft carrier that had hunted the *Bismark* in 1941 and covered convoys to Russia since then, certainly stirred the emotions from the nether region of my anatomy to the nape of the neck.

Those of us who served in 'happy' ships were always full of praise for and pride in their ship and *Victorious* was no exception. To have sailed in her under such fine captains as H. C. Borell, Lachlan D. Mackintosh and M. M. Denny was a war-time experience I would not have changed for anything else. From Arctic and Malta Convoys to North African landings in 1942, then the vile weather that saw the *Vic.* mid atlantic on Christmas Day 1942 on her way to join the United States Navy in the Pacific, or as Capt. Mackintosh said, 'lease-lend in reverse'.

Norfolk Virginia, Panama Canal, Pearl Harbour, Noumea, followed by sweeps of the seas around Japanese-held islands in the South West Pacific and then the Coral Sea to cover the American landings in New Georgia June—July 1943 in company with USS *Saratoga* and other U.S. Navy units. Then back to the U.K. in September of that year via Pearl Harbour, San Diego, Panama Canal and St. Johns Newfoundland. 1944 saw the operations against Tripitz in Alten Fjiord, followed by attacks on enemy shipping off Norway. Off to join the Eastern Fleet with its subsequent operations on Sabang, Padang, the Nicobars, Medan and Palembang on the way to Australia and the Pacific for the second time.

Victorious had her share of celebrity visitations: Churchill, Stafford Cripps, Montgomery, King George VI, Nimitz, USN; Vian, Mountbatten, Bruce Fraser, Noel Coward, Artie Shaw and his US Navy band etc. etc.

When Capt. Denny assumed command of *Victorious* at the end of 1943 he spoke to the ship's company, 'My name is Denny, M. M. Denny, *not* Make and Mend Denny.' 'In the months that lie ahead I will get you into trouble and its up to you to get us out of it.' 'You will forget all about your wives and sweethearts—your main job will be to keep 50 aircraft in the air.'

Jim sent me this extract from 'Send Her Victorious', which explains the attitude of the FAA while preparing themselves for the action to come:

The domestic arrangements at Grimsetter left something to be desired. We were beset with failures in heating, fuel supply and transport. However, with a diet of baked beans and watery beer we would repair to the squadron dispersal, shut the doors and windows and build up a nice fug with the coal burning stoves.

Most of the squadron had read the famous inscription on a Northern Ireland tombstone. This read:

'Where e'er you be
Let your wind go free.
'Twas holding it in
What kilt me.'

So the atmosphere could have grown a lettuce by lunchtime. Something had to be done. Dougy Yate devised a system of fines. The price list was as follows:

880 Squadron, FART FUND Price List			
Type	*Description*	*Price*	*Remarks*
Peep	Short, musical note	1d	Very small effect
Fizzy Foo	Intermittent	Free	Highly entertaining
Dandy Peep	Longer, with high steady note	2d	Small effect
Fandauzer	More noise, deeper note	3d	Routine
Royal Fandauzer	High pressure version of above, very noisy	4d	Vulgar, Inclined to overshoot
Scotch Mist[1]	Silent	6d	Insidious
'Harry' Clearers[2]	Dreadful	1/-	Mass evacuation of crew room[3]

Notes: 1 Duty Boy to judge, if no one owns up to items starred.

2 Credit is allowed. Please enter fines against your name on list alongside.

3 Patrons are asked not to evacuate the crew room unnecessarily as it cools the place down too much.

Extracts from Dictionary of American Naval Fighting Ships, Volume VIII, Naval Historical Center, Department of the Navy, Washington: 1981, sent by George Colling

Task Force 38 sortied from Ulithi on 10 and 11 December 1944 and proceeded to a position east of Luzon for round-the-clock strikes against air bases on that island from the 14th through the 16th to prevent Japanese fighter planes from endangering landings on the south-west coast of Mindoro scheduled for the 15th. Then, while withdrawing to a fueling rendezvous point east of the Philippines, TF 38 was caught in a terribly destructive typhoon which battered its ships and sank three American destroyers. The carriers spent most of the ensuing week repairing storm damage and returned to Ulithi on Christmas Eve.

On the night after the initial landings on Luzon, Halsey took TF 38 into the South China Sea for a week's rampage in which his ships and planes took a heavy toll of Japanese shipping and aircraft before they retransited Luzon Strait on the 16th and returned to the Philippine Sea. Bad weather prevented Halsey's planes from going aloft for the next few days; but, on the 21st, they bombed Formosa, the Pescadores, and the Sakishimas. The following day, the aircraft returned to the Sakishimas and the Ryukyus for more bombing and reconnaissance. The overworked Fast Carrier Task Force then headed for Ulithi and entered that lagoon on the 25th.

While the flattops were catching their breath at Ulithi, Admiral Spruance relieved Halsey in command of the Fleet, which was thereby transformed from the 3rd to the 5th. The metamorphosis also entailed Mitsher's replacing McCain and Clark's resuming command of TG 58,1—still *Wasp*'s task group.

The next major operation dictated by Allied strategy was the capture of Iwo Jima in the Volcano Islands. Iwo was needed as a base for Army Air force fighter planes which were to protect Mariana-based B 29 bombers during raids against the Japanese home islands and as an emergency landing point for crippled war-planes. Task Force 48 sortied on 10 February, held rehearsals at Tinian, and then headed for Japan.

Extracts from Mamoru Shigemitsu's book *Japan and Her Destiny*

After Saipan, Nimitz moved in to attack Iwojima. This brought home to the Japanese that the war was at their doorstep because the island is administratively part of Greater Tokyo. It proved impossible to send help either by sea or by air but the Tanahashi garrison sold their lives dearly. They had ingeniously turned an inhospitable volcanic island into an armed camp which they defended valiantly. They inflicted great losses on the American forces, struck a chill to the heart of the enemy and died to a man.

Air-raids had been started by B29s as soon as they had captured the airfields on Saipan and Tinian. Aircraft based on Iwojima became a powerful support and the island was an excellent place for an emergency landing. Raids on Japan, therefore, increased in violence.

Bombers from Saipan approached Japan in waves. Fujiyama gave them their bearings so that by night they could bomb industrial areas in Nagoya or the Tokyo-Yokohama district. During the day they flew at a great height and plotted the country.

They also came up the Kishu and Bungo Channels and laid to waste industrial centres in the Osaka district, the islands of Shikoku and Kyushu. They side-stepped to bomb cities in central Japan. Others again struck North-East Japan. Nor were cities and towns on the Sea of Japan overlooked.

Finally, the enemy air forces in China gradually advanced their airfields. They bombed the Anshan Iron Works in Manchuria, inflicting serious damage and causing a panic. They also bombed the Yaewata Steel Works in Kyushu.

The Japanese skies were at the mercy of the American bombers.

The air-raids were the most frightful experience the Japanese people have ever undergone. On the grounds that Japanese production of munitions was parcelled out among home industries, the raiders systematically burnt out the whole of large and small cities and towns. These were mostly built of wood and it was comparatively easy to set them on fire with oil-incendiaries. These were invented by the Americans and, as they improved, were extremely powerful. Their use was perfected to a fine art. The first wave dropped bombs round a town and set up a circle of fire. Nights of strong wind were chosen and bombs dropped to windward in great quantity. The area encompassed by a wall of flame then became the target for the next wave which systematically bombed the whole. The area became a sea of flame. Such was carpet-bombing.

Large cities such as Tokyo and Yokohama were attacked by one formation after another throughtout the night. For small towns, one formation was ample. Picked towns received a baptism of fire; as fire called up wind and wind called up fire, fierce conflagrations arose, in which parks and streams availed nothing as places of refuge. The populace had no means of escape and were burnt to death.

Raids on the low-lying districts of Tokyo in March 1945 killed over 100,000. Sumida River's waters were at one time converted into a Turkish bath covered with burnt corpses. Not even the Great Earthquake could equal the inferno. Over the whole of Japan tens and tens of thousands were burnt to death. Day by day Japan turned into a furnace, from which the voice of a people searching for food rose in anguish. And yet the clarion call was accepted. If the Emperor ordained it, they would lead into the flames. That was the people of Japan.

As though the cup were not already full, the Nagoya industrial district was visited by a great earthquake, which did far greater damage than even the air-raids. Toyohashi *(forty-five miles south-east of Nagoya)* was destroyed; works producing precision instruments were damaged beyond repair. The combination of raids and this earthquake dealt a death-blow to our munitions industry. The Minister of Munitions, the inspectors, managements and hands worked like demons to overcome these calamities. A suggestion was mooted to construct underground aircraft works and a start was made, but it was all too late.

Aircraft, shipping and munitions generally, manufactured with sweat and blood, were despatched from the works but, before they could reach the front, they were sunk at sea or destroyed from the air.

If the people seek a glorious death, what becomes of Japan?

Many a time I turned over in my mind this military concept of death in the hour of glory. Human beings are at one and the same time individuals and members of the state. It rarely happens that death is the only alternative to dishonour but there are occasions when the soul can survive only if the body dies. We Japanese know that well. And, now, here were we in our archipelago in the Pacific Ocean fighting out this battle that could have only one end—death, stage by stage. Devoted men in their storm planes and torpedoes attacked the enemy and died shouting 'Banzai' at the moment they struck home. Living in their mother-country Japan, every Japanese from the Emperor down could have no hesitation when there was no alternative but death if the Japanese people were to preserve their honour and attain everlasting life.

In the summer of 1940, when Germany had rolled up the map of France, I had witnessed the heroic resolution of the British people. At any moment now Japanese soil was to be trodden underfoot by the enemy. Would that we might show the same resolution! And yet! The British resolution was the will to live. Japan today needed that same will. It was for life that the British went on fighting. Japan must now have the will to stop fighting! That conclusion was to be indisputable. I pursued my course, more determined than ever.

Resentment against British and Americans had sprung originally from the 'Manchurian Incident' and mounted as friction between Japan and their countries grew. Japanese susceptibilities were deeply wounded by the anti-Japanese attitude of the U.S. and Britain. At the same time the sudden access of power to the Army and Navy coincided with the growth of a feeling of hostility towards foreigners generally, which newspapers, magazines and books spread among the people. International communism fanned the quarrel.

Naturally this bitter feeling was accentuated by the outbreak of war. Propaganda whipped it up. Reports were current of inhuman handling, and of lynching, of Japanese in the U.S. Specious conversations were retailed imputing malicious treatment of repatriated Japanese when their ship called at British Indian ports. Great indignation was also caused by the Dolittle air-raid, which had no military significance but in which small school-children were killed and wounded.

Presently there appeared reproductions from American magazines showing toys made of human bones, and caricaturing Japanese war heroes, which had a great vogue in the U.S. Pictures were shown of Japanese burned to death by weapons that shot liquid flame in the fighting in the south. Then came the air-raids in which cities and towns were systematically burned to the ground. In this 'carpet-bombing' the inhabitants perished with their homes. The rage of the people boiled over.

Behaviour in battle and treatment of prisoners are two entirely different problems. Under no circumstances whatsoever should the Japanese fail in their humanity. Should they do so, the Japanese would disgrace their traditions and must hide their faces from their ancestos in shame. This was an even greater problem than that of victory or defeat, for I was convinced that, whatever the outcome, the Japanese spirit would rise triumphant, if only we conducted the war magnanimously. Thus would our international relations be restored. After the war with Russia, Japanese travelling in that country were pleasantly surprised by the welcome they received. That was the reward of the spirit of the Japanese shown during the war. Similar results followed the war with Germany.

It is terrible to think that after the Second World War many wrongful acts involving inhumanity were brought to light, so that our good name was lost and an impression was created abroad that the Japanese people are cruel monsters. It behoves the Japanese to study carefully how this came about. None the less, can it be fairly said that it is a common characteristic of the Japanese people to commit atrocities? War conditions were peculiar, food and materials were scarce, communications had broken down and the number of prisoners was greater than there were officials to deal with them. It would indeed be lamentable if instances of misconduct were allowed to overshadow the true spirit of the Japanese people. This unfortunate impression abroad may hinder the restoration of good relations for some time to come and put back Japan's rightful development.

I may add that it became clear at the Tokyo Tribunal that the most thorough investigation failed to show that Government leaders had ever ordered, or planned, any inhuman treatment of prisoners.

It was currently said that when General Matsui, commanding officer at Nanking, learned what had happened there, he was overcome with grief and burst into tears. After the war many instances were recorded of kindly treatment by Japanese in individual cases and a number of letters of thanks were received from ex-prisoners of war and persons who had been in concentration camps.

From April 1943 I was Japan's Foreign Minister. A year and a half had elapsed since the opening of hostilities. Ordinances had been promulgated for the treatment of prisoners of war and of enemy aliens in accordance with the terms of The Hague and Geneva Conventions and the necessary orders had been issued. In accordance with past practice, the Army established a Prisoners' Control Bureau and a Prisoners' Intelligence Section.

The question of the treatment of prisoners and enemy aliens was one of the most serious I had to handle. I think that the conditions will be readily understood by anyone who understands Japanese legislation. The officials directly in charge were Army officers and police; since everything was under the control of the Army, no one else could interfere.

It was the duty of the Foreign Minister to safeguard Japanese subjects who were detained abroad and at the same time to satisfy foreign countries that Japan herself was behaving correctly. Naturally I was most anxious on the point, particularly when I thought of Japan's position after the war. No one could be more concerned than a diplomat that our treatment of prisoners and enemy aliens should leave no cause for complaint, it is his duty to leave no stone unturned to rectify any cause of complaint to which his attention has been drawn.

I myself am convinced that I did all that was possible. The Tokyo Tribunal adjudged me guilty on the point. It is not for me to question their verdict.

I was alarmed by the rancour displayed by the Army authorities. I was, further, disturbed by the popular indignation against the air-raids. This was not merely because I received many protests from the countries with which we were at war. I was dismayed by the gap between my own ideals and the realities of war.

At a Cabinet meeting an influential colleague, who had been formerly a Political Party member, challenged my views. When a brutal enemy murdered non-belligerents, why, he asked, should they receive better rations than the Japanese themselves, who were short of food? When flyers shot down innocent people, why should they not be tried as murderers? But the Minister of War supported my views.

My attitude was assailed in the Diet. It was said that I was half-hearted in my protests against the repeated sinking of hospital ships. Would the Minister explain, I was asked, what was my objection to the term 'American devils' used by his own colleagues? Most of my mail consisted of questions why enemy prisoners, guilty of inhuman conduct, should receive favoured treatment when they burned people to death together with their homes, while those who escaped had nowhere to live and nothing to eat.

In such an atmosphere my task was not easy. Although I had no actual authority in the matter, I did my best to prevail on the Army Chiefs to do their best to ensure correct treatment. Senior officers agreed with my view that it should be beyond reproach. But among the middle-ranking officers as well as the troops at the front were many who were imbued with Nazi ideology. As usual they paid little heed to the orders of their superior officers and appear to have disobeyed them frequently.

To reply to the complaints of enemy countries I had to rely on data supplied to me by the Prisoners' Intelligence Section. The section showed more disposition to second my efforts than did other sections of the Ministry of War. If it failed in its duties, that was because the Army at the front, and the prisoner-of-war camps, withheld the truth.

As the war went on, the flood of enemy protests grew. The Foreign Ministry forwarded them to the Prisoner's Intelligence Section and Ministries concerned and received stereotyped replies. The protests were various—brutal treatment of prisoners employed on the Burma railway, atrocities on Wake Island, wrongful treatment in prisoners-of-war camps, the sinking of hospital ships. Many of the instances were not merely morally wrong, they could not be defended on the score of belligerent law. They were acts of which the Japanese must feel ashamed.

Enemy countries learned of the disgraceful treatment meted out to prisoners from those who escaped, and were stirred to action. In the British House of Commons Foreign Secretary Eden disclosed what was happening and said that when he heard the word *bushido* he felt nauseated. I was filled with anguish at his disclosures, many of which were new to me. I asked the Military Authorities to make strict investigation and was assured that they would do so. I frequently renewed the request but the replies I received usually denied the fact or merely said that any action taken had been quite proper. The Army said that the enemy was inventing incidents to slander Japan. They persisted in declaring that their repeated instructions ruled out the possibility of anything wrong occuring.

I then drafted a plan for a special Commission of Enquiry and put it up to the Military Authorities but they turned it down.

I also brought the matter up in Liaison Conferences *(of the Supreme War Council)*. The Army Chiefs merely replied that treatment was in accordance with the laws but that they would not believe that anything was wrong.

I still felt, however, that I must make one further effort. I thought of an appeal to the Emperor. At the same time I forwarded the whole dossier to Marquis Kido.

At an Audience I explained the serious nature of the subject and begged that the Emperor would issue the necessary order to the Army. H.I.M. was already acquainted with the details. He said that if there was any truth in the reports, it was a serious breach of duty and reflected the shame of Japan. He was deeply concerned and would instruct the Army to put the matter right.

It is within my knowledge that the order, which was duly issued, had an excellent effect.

The shortage of food and materials at the front made the treatment of more prisoners than had been anticipated no light matter. Nor was it easy to make changes in the midst of war. But the Minister of War succeeded in putting through a number of reforms. Conditions disclosed after the war show that they were far from satisfying the requests made by the enemy, who expected the treatment to be in accordance with the terms of the Conventions. The fact that Japan acquired this dishonourable reputation must remain as a slur on her history. That the Japanese Army in the Philippines and the South Seas behaved with an utter disregard of the spirit of the new policy in Greater East Asia is a reproach that cannot be blotted from the memory. In Sugamo Prison Tojo told me again and again that he could not forgive himself for his failure to carry out the Emperor's wishes. The fact is stated in his last testament also.

The requests made by the countries that had taken over charge of enemy interests, that they should be allowed to visit detention camps, was now liberally met. Facilities were given for the distribution of parcels. In particular, Red Cross parcels were sent from designated ports in the Russian Maritime Provinces via Japan and distributed through the whole of the South Seas areas.

I had difficulty in persuading the Army to spare shipping from its supplies, which were woefully short, but I succeeded in extracting a considerable tonnage. One case was that of *Awa Maru* (17,000 tons). This vessel sailed from Japan as far as Singapore. The enemy had granted an unconditional safe passage both for the outward and the return jorney. It successfully discharged its mission and started back, homeward-bound. In the Formosan Straits it was sunk by an enemy submarine. With it perished some 2000 civilians, who went down with the ship. Among them were many whose services would have been invaluable in rebuilding the future Japan. The enemy submarine rescued one single person, in order that he might be interrogated.

This was the last event in my tenure of office. The date was early in April 1945.

Back in Britain in 1940, food rationing meant:

4 oz butter per week per person
12 oz sugar
4 oz Bacon—uncooked—(3½ oz if cooked)

and meat rationing began in March.

Purchase tax raised cigarettes to 8½d per packet of 20 in April.

In May, postage went up from 1½d to 2½d.

and petrol went up by ½d to 1/11 per gallon. *(nearly 10p)*

CHAPTER FIVE

First Operations — Sumatra

On 17th December 1944, the carriers *Illustrious* and *Indomitable,* the cruisers *Argonaut, Black Prince* and *Newcastle* with an escort of five destroyers carried out the first of the OUTFLANK operations on Sumatra.

Codenamed operation ROBSON, the attack was a partial success. Thick cloud caused the strike to divert from the oil refinery at Pangkalan Brandan—although two Corsairs managed to find a break in the clouds and get some oil tanks on fire before they continued to the oil ports of Belawan Deli, Kota Raja and the airfields at Oleelhoe and Sabang. The fleet, now known as Task Force 62, returned to Trincomalee on 22nd December.

As other stories will relate, during the latter months of 1944 and the early months of 1945, ships of all shapes and sizes arrived in Ceylon.

Meanwhile on 1st January, the carriers *Indomitable, Indefatigable* and *Victorious,* the cruisers *Argonaut, Black Prince, Ceylon* and *Suffolk* with an escort of eight destroyers set off on operation LENTIL. This time Pangkalan Brandan was not hidden by cloud and a refinery was set on fire by the Avengers. Seven aircraft were destroyed on the ground at Medan and Tanjong Poesa airfields and two twin-engine bombers—a Dinah and a Sally were shot down. The Fireflies attacked Pangkalan Soe Soe with cannon and rockets. The fleet returned to Trincomalee on 7th January having carried out exercises on the way back.

The main striking force of the British Pacific Fleet left Trincomalee on 16th January 1945, bound for Sydney, which was to be the main fleet base for Pacific operations. En route the carriers undertook strikes on the Sumatran oil refineries around Palembang.

The strike on the Pladjoe refinery was postponed from 22nd to 24th January due to bad weather in the launch area, and 43 Avengers, armed with 172 500 lb bombs, supported by 12 rocket-firing Fireflies and about 50 fighters, attacked the oil installation on the latter day. In order to prevent the enemy fighters from reacting in strength, four Avengers and part of the fighter escort attacked the principal airfields in the target area. The co-ordination of the attack was highly successful, no enemy aircraft being encountered before the strike, while the flak did not open fire until the Avengers and Fireflies were in their dives. An unexpected hazard, however, was the presence of balloons, which caused the loss of no aircraft from this particular strike. The output of the refinery was halved for three months and most of the oil in the storage tanks was burnt out as a result of the attack. The fighter sweep destroyed 34 enemy aircraft on the airfields, but were unable to prevent all the Japanese fighters from getting airborne. The rendezvous and form-up area for the Avengers was in a heavily defended area, and the enemy flak badly damaged several of the strike aircraft, although only two Avengers were lost, the crew of one being rescued. The escort accounted for 14 enemy aircraft, for the loss of a grand total of seven Fleet Air Arm aircraft from all causes.

The Pladjoe strike was followed, on 29th January, by an even more successful attack on the Soengei Gerong refinery, also in the Palembang vincinity. Approximately the same number of striking aircraft was involved, but a revised rendezvous position was briefed and the fighter sweep concentrated on the two major airfields. Although the Fireflies were detailed to strafe the balloons during their rocket dives, two Avengers were lost in this manner. The strike was pressed home, and such was the accuracy of the weapons delivery that all production was stopped for two months, and when deliveries recommenced, they were a mere fraction of the pre-strike output. In addition to 38 enemy aircraft destroyed on the ground by the fighter sweep, over 30 were shot down by the escort, but several Avengers were lost to the enemy fighters. Altogether, 16 Fleet Air Arm aircraft were lost over the target area to enemy action. Enemy reconnaissance aircarft found the fleet, but were driven off by the Combat Air Patrol and A.A. Two G4Ms were shot down by one Hellcat pilot, who in turn was damaged by 'friendly' A.A. from *King George V,* but managed to land back aboard *Indomitable.* No enemy attacks materialised against the Fleet and after recovering the strike the carriers and their consorts headed for Fremantle and Sydney.

At a cost to the Royal Navy of 25 aircraft, the air groups of *Indomitable, Illustrious, Victorious* and *Indefatigable* had cut the aviation gasoline output from Sumatra to 35% of its normal level, at a time when Japan was desperately short of oil in any form. The effects of the resulting shortage on the campaigns in Burma, the Philippines, China and Okinawa are incalculable, but it is probable that the three strikes undertaken in January 1945, against Pangkalan Brandan, Pladjoe and Soengi Gerong, were the British Pacific Fleet's greatest contributions to the ultimate victory. A few merchant ships were attacked in the course of the strikes; at Pladjoe one of Japan's largest surviving tankers was damaged beyond repair. Enemy aircraft losses to the fighter sweeps, close escort, and Fleet CAP amounted to about 140 aircraft of all types.

(First hand eye witness accounts of these strikes are related in ***Sakishima.****)*

Diary extracts from HMS *Indefatigable*, sent by P.O. Peter Bonney

2 Dec. 1944
Proceed down Gulf of Suez. Marvellous weather and very warm. Make and mend. No darken ship. Film on flight deck.

It could have been this one evening, that the sunset inspired Cdr. Whitfeld to broadcast its presence to us all a radiance spread across the sky, to look in wonder, but not to describe. As we continued our way south between the visible coastlines of the Eastern desert and Sinai, the fiery embers faded until its darkness revealed the moonlit dressed flight deck. And we continued to walk. On such occasions the melodious music of those eventful years sometimes filled the night air, providing the heady atmosphere of a peacetime cruise rather than the venture to war. This breath of romance was indeed compensation in kind. Promenading the flight deck or sitting aft watching the receding wake was always a rewarding habit throughout the commission for everyone, time suspending and life relaxed.

11 Jan. 1945
Lord Louis Mountbatten aboard to make speech. As for divisions but Mountbatten says 'Gather around chaps', so we all break ranks. (He used the same technique when I served on aircraft carrier *Albion* many years later in Malta.)

P.O. Peter Bonney also recalls:

WARPING SHIP
I remember how a number of Seafires formed down the flight deck facing inboard, with engines revved up, moved the ship into the jetty. Cannot remember where and why. It may have been due to a dock strike. All the same it is one of the most impressive operations I've ever seen. Normally warping ship is done by pulling on cables attached to the jetty. See any seamanship manual.

From Std. James Paterson, 888 Squadron

Triple eight was on the *Indefat.* in the Pangkalan Brandan operation. It is possible that you may have remembered some of our officers; C.O. Lt. Cdr. Mann, Lt. McCaw, Lt. Godden, Lt. Sahknovsky, Sub Lt. Tomlinson and Sub Lt. Dickson. For our next operation, we were confined to the escort carrier *Empress* which took her place in the photographic operation for the squadron on damage done at Sabang (dock installations) and Palembang (oil refinery). The stupid old *Empress* I seem to remember got in the way of the *Queen Elizabeth*'s guns as she was opening up on Sabang, and only escaped in the nick of time.

It was certainly very crowded on *Indefat.* and very difficult to find a space to sling a hammock. I left my irons (i.e knife, fork and spoon) for one moment and they disappeared, no replacements available, so every time I came up for a meal, I had to borrow someone else's!

A killick gave me a hoover bag, meaning for the contents to be chucked over the side. By error, I threw over the bag, which now lies unceremoniously on the bottom of the Indian Ocean. For this I was placed on Commander's report. The learned gentlemen seemed to be very sympathetic and a few days pay was docked from my wages in consequence.

From Cdr. Eric Back, DSC, RN

The morning we left Colombo (the ship sailed p.m.) Admiral Vian asked Captain Graham to agree to relieving me of my (N) duties for the trip so that I could help the Staff Officer (Operations) in planning the next operation which was a raid on Sumatra. The S.O.O. was ill with a nervous breakdown (not the only one of Admiral Vian's staff to get one!) and was invalided almost immediately.

I took over again early the next morning, about 4 hours before we arrived at Trinco, when the ship's position was very uncertain (we were routed 40 miles off the coast of Ceylon): the trip was not an easy one as there is an adverse current varying from 4 to 8 knots off the S.E. corner of Ceylon in January (caused by N.E. monsoon). We passed close to a merchant vessel (not a coaster) and as she had obviously had a land fix much more recently than ourselves, it was prudent to compare positions.

(This should put paid to the buzz that the Navigator had lost his way.—Ed.)

From Lt. (A) Cliff Miseldine RNVR, 887 Squadron, HMS *Indefatigable*

My first experience of 887 Squadron was when we formed up at Lee-on-Solent prior to joining HMS *Indefatigable*, which was steaming in the Irish Sea. We were to fly first to R.A.F. Mona on Anglesea, then on to the ship.

Two attempts were foiled by bad weather reports, but at the third attempt, 887 and 894 Seafire squadrons took off from Lee in Flight and Squadron formation, which was a truly dicey operation for a bunch of rookie pilots who had never experienced any more than two or possibly four aircraft at a time in formation. Unfortunately, we had only flown as far as the Midlands when thick cloud from the deck up forced the highly dangerous break-up of the formations. Not being able to see anyone but the nearest neighbour the answer seemed to lay in 'Full throttle—stick back—and climb like the clappers'. Eventually, at around 25,000 ft., some of us broke cloud, formed up as best we could and proceeded to our destination, R.A.F. Mona. It was at this time that we suffered our first casualty, Sub. Lt. Johnny Brooks, who hit a Wellington in the cloud (and all were killed). Many pilots of the two Squadrons got thoroughly lost and emergency landings were made at a number of airfields all over England, resulting in a host of frantic telephone calls!

It was a couple of days before all were safely reunited at Mona and we finally took off to fly on to the *Indefatigable,* which was still cruising up and down the Irish Sea. When I say 'we', I mean everyone who took off except yours truly! Every 'Ack' on the airfield was brought into action to try and get my plane started, and it wasn't until late afternoon that I was finally able to take off and attempt to find the ship on my own. Having been given several 'false' headings, the last of which saw me heading towards the Welsh mountains, I decided that prudence was the better part of valour and headed back to Mona, landing in near darkness. Next day I flew back to Lee, as the ship had sailed without me!

There followed my personal 'COOK'S TOUR OF NORTH AFRICA'! With nothing else to wear but the clothes I stood up in, topped by my pilot's 'Goonskin' . . . (all my kit was aboard the ship . . .) I was directed via London to Lynham in Wiltshire where I boarded an R.A.F. Dakota which was ferrying supplies to Gibraltar. I had been assured that the *Indefatigable* was calling in to Gib.—but it didn't—and neither did the Dakota until two days later! Crosswinds had prevented landing, so the R.A.F. pilot, his navigator and I spent a riotous couple of nights in Casablanca.

Eventually, from Gib., I was given passage in an American transport plane which took me, via overnight stops in Algiers and Cairo, to Port Said, where I was reunited with 'Old Greasy'. The overnight stops were 'interesting' to say the least!

I had hardly got aboard, washed and changed (being by that time sorely in need of a change of clothing!) and was starting to recount my experiences to my squadron colleagues, when a 'Pipe' came over the tannoy—'Sub. Lt. Miseldine report to Admiral Vian on the bridge'. At that time, before later transferring his Flag to HMS *Indomitable,* Admiral Vian used the *Indefatigable* as his Flagship.

With a certain amount of trepidation, I sallied forth to meet my fate, but was indeed surprised and relieved when, for the first and only time in my Naval career, I received an apology from an Admiral!

Having asked me how I had caught up with the ship, he explained how the radar and directional equipment had developed a fault at the time I had taken off from Mona, which had resulted in my being given wrong headings—for which . . . 'would I accept his apology?'

So ended an unusual but highly entertaining method of joining ship!

From Ray Durber A/B HMS *Grenville*

'SCRUBBING MY BLOODY HAMMOCK'

In Trincomalee, Ceylon, just prior to an air strike at Sumatra, a visit was paid by Lord Louis Mountbatten to my ship HMS *Grenville* (Capt D 25). He, being an old Destroyerman himself, cleared lower deck and told us of our destiny—first Sumatra then Tokyo and back?? Afterwards he went below with the Capain (for a tot), and as I was crew I returned to the ship's motor-boat.

I was in the motor-boat for about half an hour when I heard a voice say 'What are you doing cox'n?' I nearly said 'Scrubbing my bloody hammock', but on looking up and seeing *more brass than that!!* decided against it and said 'Getting ready for hoisting'—a good job too, it was Mountbatten. He had his barge stop alongside, shook my hand, wished me all the luck in the coming conflict, and said, 'Cox'n, when I said what are you doing, I fully expected to be told "Scrubbing my bloody hammock!"', and with that he laughed very loud, threw me up a salute, and pulled away.

For the next few days I had Sippers!! each day from a different mess re-telling that episode.

HE DESERVED TO SURVIVE THE WAR

We had left Trincomalee for Sumatra to hit the Japanese oil refineries at Palembang. It was during the last dog-watch and about a dozen of us were on the Quarterdeck with the boxing gloves having a gentle spar—or watching the sharks!! Two torpedomen A/B Eric Heyward and A/B Dusty Miller were having a go when, without warning, Eric Heyward was over the side. As the Destroyer's deck is only about six to seven feet from the oggin he didn't have far to fall!!

We called the bridge right away for Man Overboard—A/B Ernie Gingell was the 'phone rating on watch (aft depth charge throwers).

To cut a long story short, by now it was pitch black and the whole fleet was out there. All we could hear was 'I'm bloody well over here'. We had stopped engines and were just drifting astern with the swell, and the next thing we knew Eric Heyward was right under our stern. We got him on board, and he had been in the water for about half an hour. A/B Bill Kelly got him a blanket out of the sick bay, and on board we found that Eric's body was very rough like sand paper. The sharks had rubbed him, and not taken him. The Skipper's remarks were 'Next time I hope he waits till I've finished dinner!!'

P.S. A/B Eric Heyward was given 7 days No. 11s, charge: *Leaving the ship without Capt's permission*!!

(I met Eric and Bill and the lads of the 25th Destroyer Flotilla at their re-union in Blackpool on 1st April (Kamikaze Day) 1990. They were still smiling!—Ed.)

From Eric Heyward, HMS *Grenville*

MY 40-MINUTE SWIM IN THE INDIAN OCEAN

I was still wearing my best shoes from Divisions and morning church service although it was early evening—so it must have happened on a Sunday! I went up on deck and Dusty Miller (who was a professional boxer in Civvy Street) had boxing gloves on and had been sparring with some of the other lads. Seeing me, he called out 'Come on Lofty, what about a couple of rounds?' To which I replied 'No thanks, I have just had double helpings of pot mess,' (tins of vegetables combined with a tin of corned beef all put into the pot as a stew—we all loved it). He then called me 'Windy', and said I was scared to have a go. Naturally I didn't like being called a coward, so I took up his challenge. We sparred about a bit and then I caught him a corker, right on the nose. We got into a clinch, I stepped back from it expecting him to do likewise, but instead he swung a punch to my jaw. Staggering back I went straight over the ship's guardrail into the ocean. In the few seconds it took for me to fall I realised that I was travelling towards the screws which were propelling us at thirty knots, so as I hit the water I kicked out as hard as I could, away from the starboard side of the ship. I was submerged in bubbles and foam, but when I surfaced I was in fact quite a long way behind the ship and on the port quarter in the wash. To complicate matters, the sun had now set and I was in the dark. I managed to remove the boxing gloves, and also my shoes. I remember thinking—Surely I can't die like this, so far from home! Then in the distance I could see the beam of a searchlight, but it was searching the ocean out on the starboard side, and I was at least 90° from that area. I shouted out two or three times as loudly as I could—'Over here you silly b-----ds!' Then, joy of joys, the beam started swinging round in my direction, whereupon I pushed myself as high as I could out of the water and started waving like mad. They had spotted me and the beam stayed on me. The next thing I heard was the Captain on the loud-hailer telling me that they were lowering the Life Boat, and to just keep afloat. However, I ignored this advice and although the light was blinding my vision I swam towards the ship. As I was swimming I could hear voices, and thought ah, good, it must be the Life Boat, but then the light moved away from my eyes and I realised it was the *Grenville* herself coming astern. I swam away to my left—the ship was at a standstill now and I was just off the port side. I looked up and could see them all looking down at me. Somebody called out: 'We are throwing you a lifebelt with a rope attached, get inside it and we will pull you up.' I did that, but as they started to pull me up, instead of leaving the sea behind it suddenly swirled up and thumped me fair and square on the backside! Then I was back on board and blankets were being wrapped around me. I tried to say that I was OK but got taken to the sick bay. My messmates were relaying cups of tea to me, and eventually I was allowed to go back to my mess deck. Then the pipe for 'Action Stations' went, so I put on my anti-flash gear, helmet etc, and manned my action station, which in my case was the Torpedo Tubes. I had been there about three minutes when the Gunner T, spoke to me, saying 'We will be one short here tonight!' I replied, 'No sir, I am here,' and he told me he was the Officer on the Bridge when Man Overboard was called. He asked me how I was, and I said OK. 'That's good,' he replied,

'I suppose you know you are on a charge and that you will be on Defaulters tomorrow?' When I asked what for, he replied, 'Leaving the ship without permission!'

When I saw the Captain next morning, he asked me what I meant by spoiling his pork chop the night before? I replied that I was sorry, which he followed with, 'Bloody good job you could swim. Case dismissed.' On cap. Right turn. Double march.

So, if you are ever holidaying in the Indian Ocean and spot a pair of boxing gloves and one pair of navy shoes size 9—they belong to—Eric Heyward A.B.S.T., ex-Royal Navy.

From Ldg. Seaman Walter Uden of HMS *Grenville*

Leading Seaman Walter Uden who had been sunk on HMS Eagle *in the Med. had already seen action aboard HMS* Grenville. *She had bombarded Albania, Yugoslavia and Anzio beachhead and after a brief refit at Immingham she was now 'D25'. He wrote:*

We arrived in the anchorage at Trincomalee on Christmas Eve and in typical English style the world over, sat down, clad only in shorts and sandals with the sweat pouring off in the unaccustomed heat, on Christmas Day and consumed roast turkey and all the trimmings and Christmas pudding. (We had loaded all that seasonal and unsuitable food into the refrigerated stores at Pompey.) It would have been difficult to think of a more unsuitable menu for such conditions. Lime juice was a daily issue to all personnel; rum tots were still issued to those wishing to draw them, again most unsuitable liquor to consume in the heat.

Christmas afternoon. The ship was at anchor, both motor-boats were down; mine—the Captain's was on the starboard boom—all scrubbed out and tidied up as befitted a Flotilla Leader. The afternoon was very hot and everybody was drowsy; a motor-boat from one of the other destroyers anchored nearby crept stealthily up and, before anyone aboard *Grenville* realised what was happening, they had pinched the 'old man's' boat and it was steaming round the anchorage with a crowd all over it—the singing and cheering arousing the whole fleet. No action was taken—I wondered what sort of a mess it would be in when they brought it back. When their enthusiasm waned they returned my boat to the boom and the matter was allowed to pass as a bit of Christmas fun.

There was not a lot ashore at Trincomalee, but Jolly Jack was glad to get ashore and stretch his legs; if there was native 'ooch' to be tried he was going to try it in spite of warnings from the authorities. There was the native village and a small bazaar and drinking shops. Leave expired at midnight; with my crew I took the motor-boat in to the landing stage at a few minutes to midnight and found most of the liberty men waiting there. I waited a while for the stragglers to appear and we headed back to the ship. It was a beautiful warm night and the troops were oiled and happy; they began to sing and I made no attempt to silence them. By the time we arrived near the ship the Officer of the Day was on the gangway with the Quarter-master and Bosun's Mate. Officer: 'Keep silence in the boat'; effect: nil. Officer: 'Round the ship, coxswain.' A circuit of the ship at about 100 yards range made no effect on the choral efforts. Officer: 'Round again, coxswain—keep silence in the boat.' This performance was repeated twice more before the choir decided that they had had enough on that circuit, the singing stopped and I went alongside the gangway and they went inboard. The time was 01.30. We secured the boats to the boom and went inboard and climbed into our hammocks.

Grenville had an old type Chief Yeoman. He kept his signalmen on their toes the whole time and the flag-deck crew were 'mustered'. The youngest signalman was a bit of a scatterbrain; he was following in his father's footsteps, not entirely by his own choice. He was also handicapped by the fact that his father was chief yeoman aboard one of the other destroyers in the fleet and this same gentleman had asked our chief yeoman to keep an eye on his son. This youngster, who had the same name as the first gospel writer, had a hell of a life from first light until darkness made it impossible to see signal flag hoists. To keep the pressure on, the chief yeoman decided one day to carry out a kit muster of our young bunting tosser. In theory, the whole ship's company should have had such a muster carried out from time to time by Divisional officers, but it was easier to overlook such matters when a tired ship's company wanted all the rest possible when in harbour. As ships were unable to carry sufficient supplies of kit replacement items, we were paid a kit upkeep allowance of threepence per day, but this could only be used when we were alongside a depot ship or shore base. The youngster mustered his kit; socks were supposed to be folded up and turned over in a proper Service manner, so that they resembled small cushions. He was short of the regulation number of pairs of socks so, instead of doing what a more experienced hand would have done and borrowed some pairs from his oppo., he cut his socks in half to double the number, at the same time forgetting that Chief would spot the thinness of his cushions. Chief did just that, holding up a handful of half socks while pouring forth condemnation.

The fleet stayed for a few more days, then we sailed for Sumatra again to give the same targets another pasting. The procedure was much as before, apart from small air attacks on the fleet we saw very little of what was actually going on. Swarms of planes took off from the carriers and swarms returned, but we were too far away to count to see if all had returned or if any were damaged. Each carrier had an attendant destroyer always steaming close on her port or starboard quarter to pick up any crash survivors, but as a flotilla leader *Grenville* was considered above such mean tasks; at least Captain D thought so. About a week of this activity and the fleet left the area for Colombo. Refuelled, we moved the anchorage and leave was granted.

Colombo was a larger and far more interesting place than Trincomalee. We were able to buy duty free miniature chests of tea to send home. In our mail we were not permitted to mention that we were in Ceylon, yet the tea chests were plainly marked 'Produce of Ceylon'. In the bazaars were exquisite wood carvings and hand beaten articles of brass and copper for sale, masses of tropical fruit to buy—something we had not seen since leaving Capri and, of course, Jack's usual temptation—local 'ooch'. With the ship lying at anchor both motor-boats were kept busy running a taxi service back and forth to the jetty. When myself and my crew were on 24 hours duty we had little peace; all leave expired at midnight and both boats were sent in to pick up all the liberty men, including officers. If we had a particularly drunk matelot who was making a nuisance of himself, we sometimes allowed the boat to drift away from the jetty just as the drunk stepped in; as he went under, his white cap would float away and the surfacing matelot would be sobered up. The nights were warm and balmy so little harm was done. With the passengers disembarking, it was intriguing to watch the myriads of small tropical fish which swarmed around the gangway, attracted by the ten-bulb floodlight which was fixed near the bottom of the ladder.

Before leaving Colombo, *Grenville* was moved into the dry-dock for under waterline checks. Destroyers went into the dock two at a time; divers went down to check that the ships settled on the blocks correctly and the timber baulks were in place. The water was pumped out, but, in contrast to Gib., this time it was native labour that was used to clean the filth from the bottom of the dock. There were far more of them than there had been of us at Gib. but they got stuck into the job. When in dry-dock the ship's bathrooms, heads (toilets) and rubbish chutes cannot be used; all such activities must be done in the shore facilities on the adjoining jetty. However, Jolly Jack soon found that a bucket of water 'accidentally' spilt on the upper deck flowed over the side and cascaded onto those working below and brought forth a torrent of abuse in a strange language. About midday the ganger in charge of them, himself a native, called a halt to the work and another native appeared with a large cooking vessel full of some white material—we presumed that it was boiled rice. The workers squatted on the stone steps of the dock, each spread out on the stone a square of cloth about the size of a man's handkerchief and the cook put a ladle full of the presumed rice onto each man's cloth. They all ate their food in the traditional way, using straight fingers, but none bothered to wash before eating. This lack of hygiene horrified me with my memories of the time when we had cleaned out the dry-dock at Gib. They had been down there long enough so that they no longer smelt the stink of their surroundings. From the upper deck we had a bird's eye view of all these proceedings.

Three days rest was all we got, then out to sea again and the Sumatra area for more air attacks, before heading for Fremantle, Western Australia. On the journey to Fremantle we went through the Crossing the Line Ceremony—strictly not on the Line, as we had already crossed it earlier, but now we were in an area where no Jap. interference was possible. It consisted of the usual routine carried out by older hands who had crossed before i.e. sat in the chair, addressed by King Neptune, lathered up by his assistants, shaved with an outsized wooden cut-throat razor and tipped over backwards into a tank of water and ducked by more very willing assistants. In the hot sunshine it was an enjoyable episode for the whole ship's company and being repeated simultaneously aboard every ship in the Task Force. All the newly initiated were later issued with a posh printed King Neptune's certificate for crossing the Line.

From Bill McCullock, P.O. Electrician, HMS *Undine*

HMS *Undine* did not miss a single day of operations undertaken by the British Pacific Fleet from the time of its formation to the end of the Pacific war. *Undine* left England in November, 1944, with HMS *Indefatigable,* and worked up with the newly formed British Pacific Fleet at Ceylon. Her first two operations were against Sumatra. It was then that the *Undine* gained the honour of being the first ship in the newly formed fleet to shoot down a Japanese aircraft.

She was also the first destroyer to take part in the bombardment of Japan. Commissioned on December 6 1943, Undine was commanded by Commander T. C. Robinson DSC R.N. and Commander Brooks R.N.

Passage through the Med. in company with *Indefatigable* and *Urchin* seemed to be one long 'Practice Oil-Store ship' alongside the Carrier so that by the time we reached the Suez Canal we had become quite proficient at this exercise.

Undine, as Flotilla half-leader (*Ursa* also carried the half-leader colours, and this was to cause some 'needle' during the campaign) led into the Canal followed by *Indefatigable* and *Urchin,* after some 10 miles one of our 'Subs' in the Wheelhouse gave an order '15 to port', the Q.M. answered and put enough wheel 'on' to make us climb the port bank. I was on the quarterdeck at the time and we seemed to be at quite an alarming angle, luckily, no damage was done to the ship, only to our pride, it was embarrassing to say the least, but the Sub was to be made to 'pay' when we later crossed the Line. We entered the Indian Ocean and suddenly felt an obstruction on one of our propellers, it was some sort of whale. We informed *Indefatigable* only to receive a rather sarcastic reply. *Undine* was not very popular and had 'lost her medals', temporarily, of course.

Off Sumatra, while our Bombers were hitting the oil fields, our fighters had beaten off Jap attacks on the Fleet but, at around 16.00 hours 6 Sallys and 1 Maku parallel to the Fleet and hugging the water, managed to break through. We opened fire with our first salvo bursting just above the last plane in the line, it immediately turned toward us, very low, and, watching from the forward torpedo tubes, I remember thinking 'I hope it isn't carrying a torpedo'. It wasn't, but suddenly it banked sharply upward , and, as it passed over us, dropped a stick of bombs way off target, it made another run in from ahead dropping another stick but by taking avoiding action the bombs fell nowhere near the ship. He was banking round sharply and firing cannon but he didn't make it, the shells from our twin Bofors studded down one of his wings, cutting it off, the plane rolling over into the water. Captain T. C. Robinson promptly turned the ship and finished the job, thus the *Undine* was the first ship in the BPF to shoot down a Japanese aircraft, we had regained our 'medals' and, I hope, our popularity!

As we were said to be the most 'economical' ship in the Fleet we often had the job of picking up Pilots from rafts and also going inshore as far as possible at certain points along the coast in case Pilots had been able to 'make it' to those coves.

Life in a Fighter Squadron is beautifully described in a letter from Lieut. (A) Mike Davey RNVR, 894 Squadron, Seafire Pilot

All aircrew serving in the Fleet Air Arm were put first through the mill at St. Vincent, Gosport; a training establishment for boy-seamen pre war. As boy-seamen training was abandoned at the outbreak, it was an admirable place to convert to a pre-flight training station. We were put through the mill for two months at all subjects except flying, with a strong accent on matters naval, like boatwork, bends and hitches, pronounced 'benzun itches', how to row a whaler, how to navigate a ship. Many of the Petty Officers were too old to go to sea, and this was their war work. Mostly they used words which are not in the book of common prayer. And their speeches were a concerto in F Major. They mostly bellowed down their nostrils, rarely opening their mouths. However if anyone had any doubts about being in the navy, they were dispelled before leaving St. Vincent. Well done the instructors.

Quite a lot has been written about air training in Canada and the other Dominions, so suffice it to say that we crossed the Atlantic in a massive *Queen Elizabeth* and were spare guns crew, which meant watchkeeping—a very cold job. As she was victualled in New York, the food was what we had forgotten *(UK rations)*. She carried nearly thirty thousand American troops on the return journey and one of them was heard to exclaim that the British ought to have a ship like this! A year in Canada or Florida was a great place to be at the age of 19. No blackout, no rationing, although some food in barracks would have been better rationed. Our course learned to fly on the sides of Lakes Huron and Erie, at the airfields of Aylmer Godrich, and St. Thomas, finishing up with our Wings. By this stage of the war we were producing 5,000 pilots a year, which sounds a lot until you compare it with the 48,000 produced by the American Navy. They were also producing some of ours up to Wings stage. The whole training programme had become like a well organised production line but we both had a large failure rate. There were selection problems and we had to send a proportion of our later intake to Chelsea Polytechnic for further academic schooling, but flying standards weren't lowered. Probably there were 45% failures in the pre-wings courses and another 20% during operational training. Of course the failure rate at pre-joining was quite high too. Whilst at St. Vincent we were shown a film on deck landings which looked a bit hairy, and two of us thought we ought to be confirmed in the Church of England, which we were with several others, by the Bishop of Portsmouth, but it didn't do any good because the other chap had a bad crash on his twelfth landing and never did another. We returned to U.K. in the spring of 1944 to go to Advanced Flying School at Errol in Perthshire on the banks of the Tay. This was to get used to British aircraft and weather. It was a beautiful place but the course only lasted a month, and then we went to what amounted to finishing school. No. 2 Fighter School at Henstridge in Somerset; this course lasted almost three months and finished with only eleven pilots. As part of the course we went to St. Merryn in Cornwall to an air-firing course and finished with deck landings on the escort carrier HMS *Ravager* in the Clyde. . . . October saw the completion of training for about twenty young Sub Lieutenants and two CPOs. We were sent on leave not knowing our destiny or if we should get into the war at all. We needn't have worried on that score, as by a year hence we were all well ready for a rest. Being on leave to me was always a special pleasure, as coming from a long line of farmers, we all had the country pursuits at hand. We had tennis, archery and cricket and areas for hockey and football in the winter. Australian and New Zealand aircrew spent their leaves with my parents whilst I was away. My father, being the local 'Capt. Mainwaring' thought that the bow and arrow could be used as a silent weapon in some circumstances. He himself was a former British Archery Champion, but when the press got hold of the story they gave it the usual bent write up and Lord Haw Haw got hold of it and made sneering references on his 'Germany Calling' programme to the paucity of arms in beleagured Britain!

We were enjoying some pretty good partridge shooting and the telegram which arrived and put a stop to it wasn't too welcome, but when it commanded me to report to Grimsetter in the Orkneys it altered the whole of my attitude. 894 Squadron, Seafires, HMS *Indefatigable,* the largest carrier in Scapa Flow. No Japs yet, but stay in Europe, which was a pious hope. We all rushed up to Grimsetter hoping to be in action, but it took a day to get there. The only one to take part in what was to be our last wartime operation was Don Moir because he was a Scot and got there first. The squadrons of *Indefatigable* flew from her sister ship *Implacable* as she was in Portsmouth for alleged tropicalisation; (it didn't work very well) and so much for the 'No Japs yet' theory. The operations carried out by our squadrons from *Implac.* were mostly against coastal shipping as most of the combat aircraft had been withdrawn to oppose the invasion. We new pilots, there were five of us including Don Moir, kicked our heels until *Implac.* returned. Then we went aboard her, not to fly, but to examine the first large carrier we had seen. We felt that a flight deck of 2.3 acres should be a piece of cake to land on, but weren't so sure, as no carrier looks very big from up there. Our squadrons were ordered to Lee on Solent. The aircraft and pilots were to fly there, but we newly joined party, were to proceed by rail with our 150 ratings and about five tons of stores. This showed us who ran the Navy, the Petty Officers of course.

Occasionally the Chief would ask one of us who looked the senior for permission to 'carry on sir', to which we replied 'Carry on Chief' after which he carried on. Like a lot of junior officers in all the services, we had been in a squadron a week, the chief perhaps ten years. However, as pilots, we could earn their respect if we flew well. Our long journey to Lee on Solent seemed to take an age, for although we had longer journeys in Canada, the trains were faster and the food better. When we arrived at Lee on Solent we found that several of the long serving pilots had left, or were leaving, the squadron. This left only eleven of the old guard with we five new pilots to make up to a full strength of sixteen. This seemed a high ratio of beginners and was to be sixteen pilots in four flights of four. The COs, the Senior Pilots, Sub Lieut. Hayes, Sub Lieut. Heppenstall. It was a great pleasure to fly again, as number two to Jim Hayes, but we had one incident during formation flying when upside down in line astern, the flight leader's engine cut out as Merlins were wont to do, but this one was a dead cut. Fortunately the exhausts blew out black smoke and my reaction to jam on rudder avoided a collision. The other two following took evasive action and we ended up doing a Prince of Wales Feathers involuntarily. One of the exercises we carried out was practice dog-fights. This was done by two aircraft flying to a safe height flying towards one another and then breaking in opposite directions and then trying to get on one another's tail. The older or more experienced pilots could show we new lot a thing or two although we had done it before. The other manoeuvre which needed a lot of practice was battle or finger formation and it was always surprising that we hadn't started it earlier in our curriculum along with aerodrome dummy deck landings, ADDLS. With battle formation we flew in a loose V of four and when turning ninety degrees crossed-over, underneath one another so that the outside aircraft didn't have to fly faster to keep up. We used this formation all the time apart from echelon starboard to break up for landing on. After a week at Lee we were ordered to join *Indefat.* in the Irish Sea, flying first to Mona in Anglesey, but of all the best laid plans of mice and men, this went more 'agley' than most. A solid front of cumulo-nimbus cloud lay across our track with a thunderhead reaching up far too high for us to climb above. Although we were a wing, we flew as two separate squadrons, with Andrew Thompson the wing leader in command of 887 squadron. He decided to bore through with his twenty four Seafires with disastrous results, the turbulence and visibility were so bad that the flights lost touch with one another, that they broke up and landed at several different airfields, some reached Mona, but one piloted by Johnny Brooke collided in mid-cloud with a Wellington bomber killing all the crew and Johnny Brooke. On seeing what was ahead of us, our CO, Jimmy Crossman led us into Yeovilton where we spent the night and flew to Mona next morning, thence to *Indefat.* She was rolling in a grey November sea. My first deck landing on her was quite good and it was to remain that way. Probably because we had a very good deck landing officer. He was like a good professional at golf, didn't try to correct too much at once. We had another loss when Peter Norman of 887 squadron spun in on the approach. Brooke, Norman and myself had all done our training together. Norman took his flying very seriously and had intended to make a career of it.

We set course for Gibraltar, but as the Atlantic, especially the Bay of Biscay, was too rough we didn't fly again until we passed Malta, when we flew on all kinds of exercises. We passed through Suez Canal and then Red Sea and Gulf of Aden. We had our first mishap there, in 894 that is. Don Leighton came in to land too fast and high, finishing up on his back with a barrier cable in the cockpit. We had to lift the aircraft tail to get him out and although he looked an awful mess we were pleased to see him sitting up in bed a few days later, but a fractured skull and broken arm meant he couldn't fly again but became an Air Traffic Controller. We took off one morning long before dawn, but as soon as we got airborne we could see the sun rising in a sheen of gold, we crossed the coast of Ceylon (now Sri Lanka) to land at a beautiful airstrip set in palm trees, Katukurunda. This was to be our home for the next two weeks, when we did more serious working-up as a squadron, as a wing and as an air-group. We juniors had the rough edges knocked off us whilst the seniors learned to tolerate us. Life at Katukurunda was idyllic and although we did a fair amount of flying we had a lot of fun as well. One afternoon three of us were returning to the wardroom on foot after flying, when a lone Seafire took off from the airstrip, when it reached about a thousand feet it streamed out coolant and went into a dive straight for the jungle. It never recovered and crashed without the pilot attempting to bale out. This was Winston Ostergaarde of 887, the third of their pilots to be lost. The following day whilst returning from an exercise, my engine heat clock went over the top, which caused me to do a quick dart for the airstrip, thinking of Winston. The take-off direction was always reversed at noon, and as it was exactly that, my landing was in the opposite direction to an Avenger which met me on take-off; fortunately we both kept to the left and my lower wing passed under his. Jimmy Crossman, the CO was not amused and said 'You'd better have a week's duty boy (squadron duty officer) to cure that Avenger pilot's twitch.' It didn't seem to occur to him that my twitch was just as bad. This in itself produced another incident, for at that time our trolley acs (mobile starter batteries) were having their wheels pinched at night, for sale on the black market. One night the duty petty officer said to me 'If you're flying tomorrow sir, get your head down in the hangar and I'll look after things.' It was a great temptation, as being short of sleep the bunk in the hangar looked very inviting. Only a few minutes and into oblivion, to be rudely awakened by a burst of rifle fire. The two sentries, backed up by the PO, had heard noises in the undergrowth and thinking it to be a wheel pincher had opened fire which was followed by bovine noises from their target—what they had done was shoot a holy cow. There always seemed to be masses of these in Sri Lanka and they had complete freedom to go and do what they pleased. The rest of my guard duty was spent wide awake, but the next day every

Bhuddist monk in the island must have been smoothed over by the Station CO as it was never mentioned again. Sri Lanka has a little advertised coastline, with beautiful sandy beaches and some of the best surf in the world. We surfed in fours or fives with a K type pilot's dinghy which produced a lot of action with bodies in all directions. Whilst on the beach, we came across a trainee albino Buddhist monk. He was of special religious significance and spoke as if he had been educated at Eton; he was the only one we could communicate with.

There were lots of parties, mainly male as the only females were Wrens who were less than ten per cent of the naval population, consequently dances were restricted to Lieut. Commander and above where they still had to queue to dance with a Wren. One night we gate-crashed one of these dances all dressed in shorts when we should have been in formal longs. After whirling round with one or two of the Wrens which they enjoyed because they were with someone of their own age, we were torn a strip off by the Captain of *Tyne,* the depot repair ship and were banished from the hall. Later when waiting without success for a liberty boat back to *Indefat.* the Captain of *Tyne* offered us a lift in his. Some of us were sheepishly holding trees which we had uprooted from the garden. At one of the wild parties in the wardroom at Katukurunda we played the usual mad games and then a rugby match broke out played with an unripe coconut, but this soon palled and our attention became fixed on a large metal tank in the garden, which would have a capacity of several thousand gallons. As one side of the wardroom was completely open it was no problem to slide it along the ground and into the wardroom ante-room. Then the party had another brilliant inspiration, put all the wardroom furniture in the tank, but first inspect the tank. This was done by Stormy Larder, so named because of his far above average wind output, then all the furniture was piled into the tank and everyone stepped back to survey our communal handiwork. Suddenly a shout went up 'Hey Stormy's in there,' so the furniture was removed even more rapidly, and there sure enough was Stormy, fast asleep. Although Sri Lanka is a very beautiful island and the people were always very friendly to us, we didn't mix socially, there was a low Wren density, we could only make our own amusements like British servicemen throughout the world. Most of our amusements were schoolboyish but when you consider that probably eighty per cent of the aircrews were not long away from school, some had left the middle of a degree course, or had left some sort of higher education, we were expected to behave rather wildly, we didn't want to disappoint anyone. The senior officers, on the whole, seemed to view us with good natured tolerance and quite a few, including the Captain joined in when we got out the song books and piano. It was always amusing to see senior officers singing at the top of their voices the most obscene songs that they would never have dreamt of singing in normal life, but if we all had a skinful of gin it was surprising how it let the hair down, and in any case, with gin at 1½d a tot one couldn't afford to be sober. Nevertheless it was strictly taboo to drink on flying days or even the night before, in any case the bar was closed, but the exactitude required when deck landing Seafires called for absolute fitness. When returning to the carrier we broke up from squadrons or flights in timed distances calculated to bring us in a constant stream to make a landing at slightly over one minute intervals. This was spoilt if someone had to do an overshoot or worse stillif there was a crash on deck. We always breathed a sigh of relief as there was a stigma about having a barrier crash, besides it was dangerous, it was commonplace to throw a party when we had completed 50 or 100 deck landings. Of course there were a lot of parties with no excuse. There are those who think that we drank too much and perhaps they have a case, but when a ship is nine weeks at sea with very little in the way of entertainment or relaxation it is difficult to justify criticism. Since most of us were about twenty years old, we had little to do with starting the war as we were fifteen at the time.

M. Davey—894 Squadron

We sailed from Trincomalee for our first operation against the Japs, this was against Pangkalan Brandan in Sumatra. It seemed quite a senseless exercise, as it was not a large operation and didn't do all that much damage, it simply alerted the Japs to our presence and strength and warning them to be prepared for the next strike against Palembang. Pangkalan Brandan was little talked about by the crews who attacked and we Seafires were on fleet patrol duty only. A solitary Dinah flew over the fleet at a great height and dropped a stick of bombs which missed us by several hundred feet. As far as we were concerned that was all, as well as a couple of uneventful patrols. We returned to Trincomalee to pick up the rest of the fleet, to make us up to four carriers and two battleships with attendant cruisers and destroyer screen.

This was to be the Fleet Air Arm's greatest operation of the war as far as damage to the enemy was concerned, although Palembang has never had the same recognition as Taranto, but whereas the attack on Taranto destroyed battleships which were not likely to put to sea anyway, Palembang destroyed huge oil refineries and oil wells which cut off the main Japanese supplies for the rest of the war. Palembang, which took place after Pangkalan Brandan was carried out by four squadrons of Avenger bombers, carrying four, five hundred pound bombs each, a Firefly rocket squadron of twelve, plus six fighter squadrons. We Seafires supplied fleet defence. The whole of the largest oil refinery in South East Asia was bombed and sent up in flames. On the following day our photographic aircraft were flying in thick smoke at twenty-eight thousand feet. The cost to us was very heavy, more than forty aircraft and the twenty-five aircrew who survived the shooting down, were either beheaded or buried alive. We were dealing with a barbaric foe who asked and gave no quarter. We learnt as we went along that it was a matter of honour, if such a word exists in their vocabulary, that they retaliate for any attack on them and Palembang was no exception, for we hadn't long to wait. My place was number two in the CO's flight but my generator packed in on the flight deck, which reduced the flight to three and as the number four Ken Gall lost the other two in the air the flight was reduced to the CO and Ken Ward, who acquitted themselves so well that the other two of us weren't missed, although it has been a question mark in my life, what would have happened if my generator had worked. Jimmy Crossman our CO and Ken Ward were patrolling between the fleet when they spotted the approaching squadron right down on the wave tops, as they were at this height our radar had not picked them up; they both attacked individual aircraft shooting down at least five, whilst Ted Elson also of 894 shared a sixth with a Hellcat, the seventh was credited to the ship's guns. We identified them as Sallys but although author David Brown says they were Lilys, we had the advantage of being there. Jimmy and Ken bored right into our own flak and followed their quarry until none were left for had one of these medium bombers hit a carrier it must have done considerable damage, this was the first intended kamikaze attack on the British fleet and easily the least successful. Jimmy Crossman was awarded a DSO, and Ken Ward a DSC and even Admiral Vian who hated Seafires, had to admit that it wasn't a bad show. *(Ken Ward's running commentary is included in* ***Sakishima****.—Ed.)* Several other decorations were awarded to the Firefly and Avenger squadrons and we all joined in a lively party. To me as spectator on the flight deck it was a great show tinged by regret that my generator had gone U.S., only this and one other during the whole series of operations. On the deck near me was a Paymaster who was hit on the forearm by a small splinter, it just cut his arm enough to draw blood, we decided that he would have been awarded a wound stripe if he'd been an American. It was surprising that with so much metal flying about no-one was hit badly and that no-one took cover, but seven of the enemy were shot down within a few hundred yards of the carriers. Had our radar been able to pick them up in time, say at several miles, as they usually could, they would have been shot down at a much safer distance, for our fighter direction officers Ian Easton, John Paul and Owen Lawrence-Jones were very able, and they were later loaned to the American Navy for a short spell and were very much appreciated.

The only casualties in our Seafires were Jim Hayes who was shot down and recovered by destroyer just before dark. He had not managed to get his dinghy out with him when he ditched and was floating in his Mae West. Jimmy Crossman was hit in the engine, it had a bullet hole right through it and it stopped dead as he caught a wire, but he wasn't worried a bit and as Ken Ward has said since, nothing would have stopped J.C. This had been a Japanese Special Attack Squadron led by an army major and it was obvious that they were aiming at the carriers.

The Japanese and American navies had recognised for years that the Aircraft carrier was the most vital ship in the fleet, in other words the new capital ship, but most of the non-flying RN, the penguins as we called them, still dreamed of Jutland or even Trafalgar. The whole set up on the Fleet Air Arm reflected this, as the R.A.F. had been allowed to take over the flying part with naval observers as captains of the aircraft who conned the aircraft and the R.A.F. pilot as merely helmsman. This resulted in the two-seat fighter, which was often slower than the bomber they were pursuing and having little chance against fighters like M.E.109 or the F.W.190. It took an awful long time before we realised that we needed single seat purpose built fighters and non fighter reconnaissance aircraft, like the American Martlet, Hellcat and Corsair. We hadn't got any so we scrounged a lot of these excellent fighters from America and put hooks for deck landing on our most successful single seaters and called them the Sea Hurricane and the Seafire. As the Sea Hurricane was phased out by 1944, the Seafire became the only single seat fighter in the navy that was both made in Britain and in front line service. The only other fighter, which was a single seater but a bi-plane was the Gloster Gladiator, a good deal slower but highly manoeuvrable. This plane did excellent work in Norway, Malta and on convoys. It was obsolete even at the outbreak of war but much liked by pilots. The theory of naval fighter protection was that the R.A.F. fighters would provide cover for the Fleet flying from land bases. This was one of the non-starters of all time. During the Channel Dash by *Scharnhorst* and *Gniesnau* the promised cover for Esmondeand his squadron never materialised so that all the Swordfish were shot down. During *Repulse* and *Prince of Wales* action up the east coast of Malaya the fighter cover never materialised, with disastrous results; whilst undoubtedly the outstanding example of all was Pearl Harbour, where there were just a handful of Kittyhawks who were overwhelmed. In the early years of the war, carriers were going to sea with perhaps two squadrons of torpedo-bombers and only two flights of fighters. In 1944—45 the ratio was reversed to one squadron of bombers to two of fighters.

The problems with the Seafire, were a weak and narrow undercarriage and, because of a long nose, the forward vision was very restricted, and if flown at only a few knots above stalling speed one could easily miss the wires and end up in the barrier. During the Battle of Britain, Lord Dowding said 'we shall have enough Spitfires if our young pilots learn to land them safely'. However practice makes perfect and by the end of our sojourn in the Pacific our prang rate had been greatly reduced. Having criticised the Seafire it should also be said that when in the air it was the most beautiful aeroplane ever made and had absolutely no vices.

After Palembang we set sail for Sydney around the Australian Bight. We relaxed in a fairly heavy sea and played all the games both in and outdoor. We also had some quite good films with Betty Grable, Dinah Shore all projected on to the island (bridge). We also had good symphony concerts on the quarter deck; you simply took your own chair or camp-bed. We were all issued with light camp-beds and when we were in the tropics slept out on the weather decks. It was here or later that we began to hear disturbing reports of our aircrews at Palembang where we had lost forty aircraft out of which some twenty aircrew escaped. It was rumoured that many of these were beheaded but when the grisly truth came out later, it was much worse. As it was, it gave one a prickly feeling in the back of the neck just to think about it, the best thing was not to. It was about a month before we flew on operations again. During this time we lost our senior pilot, Guy Agard-Butler in collision with his No. two Bob Swart who was lost soon after in action. Bob, or Boekar, was one of the several Dutch East Indians we had in the squadrons. Guy was the only Dartmouth trained officer in the squadron and there was only about one other in all the other squadrons, as second in command he exerted strict discipline over pilots and maintenance staff as well.

From TAG Frank Grainger ex *Indefatigable*

I took part in Meridian Two, and we dropped our bombs on the power house scoring hits, the pilot's words at the time 'the power house is coming up to meet us.' Regrettably only 3 out of the 4 bombs dropped and we had to make two attempts to jettison the remaining offender in the jungle on the way back.

I think there were at best 6 DSMs amongst the TAGs. Its a pity you were not informed for inclusion in **Sakishima** about our CPO (A) TAG Len Barrick, a fine man, quite 'old' too compared with us youngsters, but nothing deterred him, he was severely wounded earlier in the war, awarded the CGM and when recovered insisted on coming back into an operational squadron. He too was awarded the DSM for his part in the Sakishima operation. Sad to say he died last year.

Extracts from 'Avenger from the Sky' by Lt. Cdr. (A) Donald Judd DSC, R.N.V.R. 849 Squadron, HMS *Victorious*

The ramrods took off soon after 0600 while the main strike took off at 0730. Another shake at 0400, after a night of little sleep, and over two hours of jittery, testy feelings and a fear of that dreadful unknown out there. The unwanted breakfast thrust in front of the aircrew, the long and painful wait in the ready room and then all hell let loose on the order to man aircraft. The wind over the deck, the shouts of the deck officers and their handlers and finally the deafening noise of all the engines starting up together. There go the fighters.

A copy of the document carried by Aircrews over Sumatra.

الى كل عربى كريم

السلام عليكم ورحمة الله وبركاته وبعد فحامل هذا الكتاب ضابط بالجيش البريطانى وهو صديق وفى لكافة الشعوب العربية فنرجو أن تعاملونه بالعطف والاكرام .

وأن تحافظوا على حياته من كل طارىء ونأمل عند الاضطرار أن تقدموا له ما يحتاج اليه من طعام وشراب .

وأن ترشدونه الى أقرب معسكر بريطانى

وسنكافئكم ماليا بسخاء على ما تسدونه اليه من خدمات .

والسلام عليكم ورحمة الله وبركاته ؟

القيادة البريطانية العامة فى الشرق

To All Arab Peoples - Greetings and Peace be upon you. The bearer of this letter is an Officer of the English Government and a friend of all Arabs. Treat him well, guard him from harm, give him food and drink, help him to return to the nearest English soldiers and you will be rewarded. Peace and the Mercy of God upon you.

The British High Command in the East.

Useful Words

English	Arabic	English	Arabic
English	Ingleezi.		
English Flying Officer	Za-bit Ingleezi Tye-yar.	Water	Moya.
Friend	Sa-hib, Sa-deek.	Food	A'-kl.

Take me to the English and you will be rewarded.

Hud-nee eind el Ingleez wa ta-hud mu-ka-fa.

PME/1554-9/41

(J. Jenkinson of the SS *San Ambrosio* sent me two cards which were issued to short range gunners.—Ed.)

AIM OFF SPEEDS IN KNOTS ON 20MM CARTWHEEL SIGHTS
FOR VARIOUS PLANE SPEEDS AND APPROACH ANGLES.

PLANE SPEED ↓ / APPROACH ANGLE →	0°	15°	30°	45°	60°-90°
AIM OFF →	NONE	ONE QUARTER	ONE HALF	THREE QUARTER	FULL
300 KNOT FIGHTERS; FIGHTER BOMBERS DIVE BOMBERS	0	75	150	225	300
240 KNOT MEDIUM AND HEAVY BOMBERS	0	60	120	180	240
200 KNOT TORPEDO LAND PLANES	0	50	100	150	200
150 KNOT TORPEDO FLOAT PLANE	0	40	75	115	150

IF SPEED OF PLANE IS UNKNOWN, ASSUME 240 KNOTS.
FOR APPROACH ANGLES OF LESS THAN 15°, REDUCE AIM OFF ACCORDINGLY.

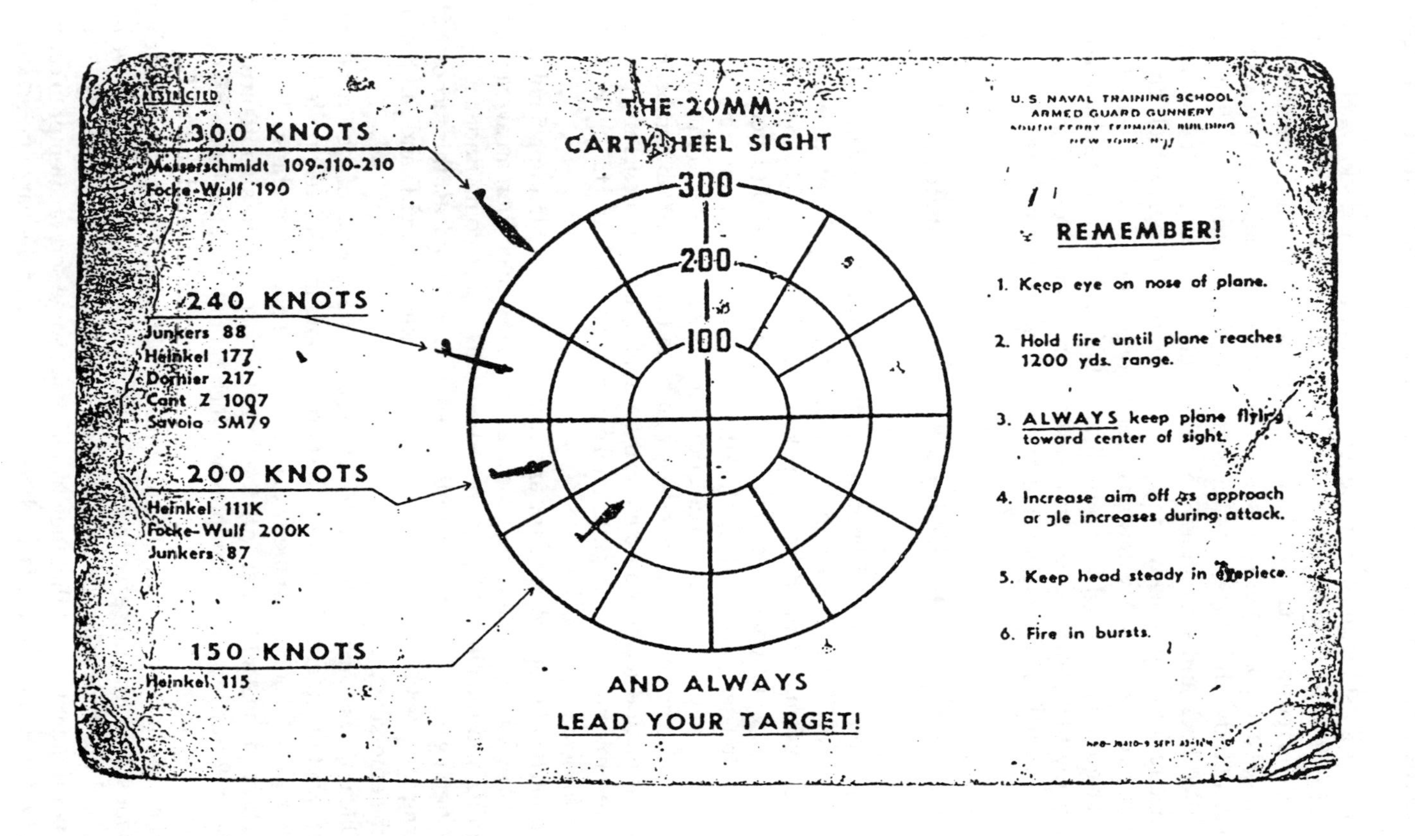
RESTRICTED
300 KNOTS
Messerschmidt 109-110-210
Focke-Wulf 190
240 KNOTS
Junkers 88
Heinkel 177
Dornier 217
Cant Z 1007
Savoia SM79
200 KNOTS
Heinkel 111K
Focke-Wulf 200K
Junkers 87
150 KNOTS
Heinkel 115
THE 20MM.
CARTWHEEL SIGHT
300
200
100
AND ALWAYS
LEAD YOUR TARGET!
U.S. NAVAL TRAINING SCHOOL
ARMED GUARD GUNNERY
SOUTH FERRY TERMINAL BUILDING
NEW YORK
REMEMBER!
1. Keep eye on nose of plane.
2. Hold fire until plane reaches 1200 yds. range.
3. ALWAYS keep plane flying toward center of sight.
4. Increase aim off as approach angle increases during attack.
5. Keep head steady in eyepiece.
6. Fire in bursts.

David Foster is the first Avenger to go. I am seventh with my flight of six behind me.

Here we go, straighten up on the centre line of the flight deck, watch the deck officer who is rotating his arm above his head, a signal for me to jam on my brakes and rev up to maximum. He drops his hand in the direction of the bows, off brakes and go. The old girl sounds OK as we trundle up the deck and just make it off the end of the deck. Then a chase after David and his five. He has throttled back and kept straight ahead of the carrier to give the squadron a chance to form up quickly. He does a gentle turn to port which gives us a chance to cut corners. My new observer, George Graham, tells me that he and the air gunner, Petty Officer Murphy, are OK and then keeps me informed about my flight forming up on me. Apart from my No. 2 on my starboard quarter I can't see the others as they are behind and below me.

Ditching of Avenger 11C.JZ554, 5 miles off coast of Sumatra on 4th January, 1945

Having been airborne for 55 minutes with 849 Squadron from HMS *Victorious* on Operation 'Lentil', my engine cut almost completely. At this time the Strike was about 5 miles inland from Tapakyuan in Sumatra at 5000 feet, heading North East. I immediately pulled out of the formation and turned westward towards the sea and lost height. After 2 minutes it became inevitable that ditching would have to be carried out. I informed my crew to this effect and on crossing the coast, jettisoned my bomb load of 4 × 500 lb bombs. By this time the engine had cut completely; the aircraft was to all intents and purposes on fire, emitting clouds of white smoke from the engine, and filling the cockpit with fumes.

At 100 feet I dropped the flaps and carried out a water landing 5 miles from the coast. The actual landing produced no more shock than an average deck landing and the aircraft floated for 60 seconds before going under.

When I gave the ditching warning the Observer broadcast this fact on VHF giving the position and the Air Gunner broadcast it on H.F. and put the IFF to the emergency stop.

Ditching was carried out at 0805. The Air Gunner got out of the aircraft from the Turret Emergency Escape on the port side and immediately pulled out the dinghy. The Observer climbed out of the Centre Section on the starboard side and helped the Air Gunner with the dinghy. I got out of the aircraft on the port side, collected my jungle equipment which I thought might be useful during a long spell in the dinghy, and my K-type dinghy, and joined the Air Gunner.

Having climbed into the dinghy, our first thought was landwards. It was obvious, from the noise we had made coming down, the smoke trail we had left and our proximity to land, that we had been observed by the Japanese and/or the natives and that they would make some sort of attempt to capture us. Our most immediate task, therefore, was to put the oars into action and make every effort to make more distance between us and the land. This we did by taking turns with the oars in 10 minute shifts, in spite of a current running from our beam and our lack of skill in controlling the dinghy.

After 45 minutes of keeping one eye to landward and the other to seaward and rowing as hard as we could, 5 Hellcats arrived from the westward and just before reaching us, turned south and made for the coast 10 or 15 miles south of us. After 10 minutes they came northwards up the coast and appeared to be searching the beach. Our first reaction was to attract their attention with the various aids but declined from doing this for fear of attracting the Japanese as well. However, one Hellcat flew fairly close to us and we discharged a 'Signal Distress 2-star Mk. I' and he spotted us immediately.

The 5 Hellcats flew around us for some 10 minutes and then disappeared to our sorrow and nothing else was sighted for 30 minutes, during which time we began to give up hope and think that we might be there for some days till the ASR Submarine arrived. Then some Corsairs appeared from westward and repeated the same procedure as the Hellcats. Like the latter, they turned south and appeared to be searching the coast, beach and inland. They were too far away to attract their attention. However, soon one of them flew near us and we directed a Heliograph on to him and he spotted us.

Meanwhile two destroyers had been detached from the Fleet (unknown to us) and were making for a point on the coast some 20 miles south to search for us. Not finding us there, they steamed north and were finally directed on to us by the Corsair and our Heliograph. We were picked up about 10 miles from shore off Tapaktuan at 1125 by HMS *Undine*, whose boats crews did excellent work in double quick time.

What joy it was when we spotted the two destroyers coming up the coast with an escort of fighters. The lead destroyer, HMS *Undine*, came near us, lowered a boat to pick us up and then we scrambled up the netting to the safety of the deck. The ship's medical officer was there to greet us, and took us to a cabin for a thorough inspection. We were all shaking from shock but otherwise fit. Tea and brandy followed and a long long sleep. The ship's captain, Commander T. C. Robinson DSC and his crew were very welcoming and we had a relaxed journey back to Trincomalee. We transferred back to *Victorious* to a wonderful welcome and piss-up. We were grateful to Admiral Vian for his efforts to pick up one aircrew. We heard details of the attack that we had missed. It had been a very successful strike and plenty of damage had been done to the Pangkalan Brandan refinery. There had been little opposition and in fact we were the only casualties of the raid.

In some way or another, word got back to my family in England that I was missing, presumed killed.

Signals went backwards and forwards, eventually confirming that I was safe and well after the ducking off Sumatra.

A. J. McWhinnie, the First Naval Correspondent with the British Pacific Fleet wrote up the incident in the *Daily Herald* of 22nd February 1945 under the headline 'Saved from the Pacific'. He of course meant the Indian Ocean and we did not have to bale out but ditched the aircraft.

Before we left Trincomalee, we took part in a rehearsal attack on Colombo by all four carrier groups. The day after we put to sea on 16th January, Commander Owen, our Commander Operations, called the senior officers of the *Victorious* squadrons to the operations room to tell us about the immediate future.

'Well, boys,' he said, 'we are making for Sydney and up to the Pacific as the British Pacific Fleet. But on the way we will be knocking hell out of two oil refineries at Palembang.' He then described where they were and what they were at the same time removing the dust sheet from the large model of the two refineries and the surrounding land. The model was perfect in every detail. 'Well, there it is—there will be at least one attack on each refinery and if necessary a third to mop up anything that has been left undamaged. Now go along and tell your aircrews and work out a plan. You may come in here to study the model at any time and make sure you know it like the back of your hand. From now on we shall get together every day and all day to perfect plans and ensure that everyone knows his job to the last detail. But I warn you, there will be stiff opposition from ack-ack and fighters. That's all for the moment.'

For the next few days, we talked, dreamt and thought nothing but Palembang. I can't say it was exciting. We all began to get rather tense as the immensity of the task and the likely opposition sank in. We were each given specific targets within the refineries. Mine was one of the cracking plants. The first one at Pladjoe was on a crossroads in the centre of the refinery and was therefore not difficult to pin-point—at least on the model.

'On no account hit the storage tanks. If you do, they will catch fire, belch black smoke and put a blanket over the target.'

This is what happened in fact, except that the smoke fortunately didn't hover low over the target area. The reported opposition filled us with terror.

'There are signs of heavy concentrations of heavy and light ack ack at the target and you must be prepared to be jumped as you approach, in your dive and during the get-away to the rendezvous as well as returning home, but you'll have plenty of fighter cover from the Hellcats and Corsairs.'

Someone asked if there were likely to be any balloons.

'No, aerial reconnaissance doesn't show any balloons.' This was, to our horror, to prove very wrong in the event.

Victorious was to provide twelve Avengers of 849 Squadron to make up No. 1 Bomber Wing with the leading squadron—857 from *Indomitable* led by 'Doc' Stuart. The second Bomber Wing consisted of Avengers of 854 Squadron from *Illustrious* and 820 Squadron from *Indefatigable*. We were all armed with four 500 lb bombs. Top and middle cover was provided by Corsairs and Hellcats and close cover was provided by Fireflies. The Air-Co-ordinator was Major 'Ronnie' Hay from *Victorious*. The whole operation involved 140 aircraft. 849 was to fly in the usual two stepped down formations of six aircraft each; David Foster leading the first and I the second.

We were due to make the first strike against Pladjoe refinery on 22nd January, the flying-off position being between Enggano Island and the coast of South Sumatra. But I for one was pretty tensed up with apprehension for the success of the flight itself with so many aircraft involved and me responsible for five other crews; fear for the opposition we should certainly meet and scared stiff at the thought of falling into the hands of this particular enemy. These emotions were not helped by our meeting appalling weather during the night of 21/22nd which caused a 24 hour delay, that didn't do the nerves any good. Flying was quite out of the question as we met a prolonged tropical storm of high winds and driving rain. Back again the next morning but the weather was no better. Another withdrawal and another run into the flying position of a take-off on the 24th. The wind had dropped and the rain stopped but there was low cloud over the fleet. Would we, wouldn't we? What anxious moments in anxious days those were with that awful fear of the unknown with the inevitability of dangers ahead with frightening results.

Presently, we were put out of our misery. The Tannoy blared 'Stand by to fly off aircraft' and so it was on. This was at 0500 with take-off at 0630. An agonizing 90 minutes to wait.

The take-off was without incident but the form up was a shambles underneath a low cloud ceiling of about 1000 feet. Round and round the fleet we went chasing each other's tails, till I felt like saying, 'For Christ's sake, get on with it.'

Eventually we did and made for the coast underneath the cloud. And then a bit of luck for the cloud dispersed, the coast was clear and the morning bright. We had to climb fast for the coast to clear the 11,000 foot Barisan Range of mountains. No problems this time although I couldn't help thinking of the last time I tried to climb mountains hanging on my prop. We made it to 13,000 feet and there, in other circumstances, was a lovely sight of the lush green of the Sumatran plain and beyond it the misty blue of sea of the Bangka Straits and the South China Sea beyond. Come on, this is no time to enjoy the view. And no sooner thought, but there were the rivers—and Palembang—and the two vast refineries just where the model said they would be. My God, what a size they are.

And then all hell was let loose. Radio silence had been maintained up to that point, but now the ether was filled with shouting. It started with an excited voice bawling, 'Rats, 10 o'clock up,' then the babble became quite unintelligible, like turning on the wireless at full blast with three stations on or near the same wavelength. I saw two of the rats screaming down on us and thought, 'Christ the party has started early.' The bomber wing leader started letting down to increase speed and waving. Another horror of horrors; what were those brown sausage looking things just above the target. There must be a dozen of them and they were climbing. Oh! Lord, they are balloons which aren't supposed to be here. And clearly they are ready for us.

Screaming fighters, theirs and ours were all over the place. Two of theirs got through the cover and were attacking us—my observer, George was giving me a running commentary but they broke away without scoring any hits. Nearing the target now and the heavy ack-ack was opening up. Shell bursts galore just in front and very slightly below us, the brown puffs of smoke passing us in a flash—they can stay there, I thought. There was the target on the starboard side in the angle of the engine cowling and the wing. Come on, let's go, it's getting too hot up here and I feel very naked, good, there we go and the wing leader peels off to starboard and down, followed by his Avengers. OK, there's the cracking plant at Padjoe, no difficulty in seeing it but it looked a small target to hit. There goes David Foster and his flight. Now me and mine. We were in the perfect position for the dive from 10,500 feet. Got through the heavy barrage OK. Now the balloons. Hell, what do I do. The balloons were obvious—big floating innocuous-looking brown sausages with red circles on the side of them. Nobody was shooting them down. But it was the cables that were the worry and I couldn't see any cables. All I knew was that the cables didn't go down to the ground vertically but in a loop. Down to 7,000 feet and they were dashing up to meet us. 250—280—300 knots. Can't do anything about the balloons but just hope. Check bomb doors open, finger on release button on stick. Eyes fixed on damn cracking plant getting bigger by the split second.

Through the balloons and now the light ack-ack opened up. Tracer cut through the sky all around. Up to 320 knots and down to 4000 feet. Will release bombs at 2,500. Didn't have to look at the altimeter as I knew what things looked like at 2,500 ft from long practice. Here we go, press the tit and feel the plane lift as the bombs go. Pull back hard on the stick and nearly black out but the speed of the plane takes us clear over the main river.

George yells out over the inter-com 'You've hit it—a real beauty right on the nail.'

I couldn't see our handiwork but there were things to think of. Kept on three quarters throttle and increased the pitch. Had to get to that rendezvous which meant a left hand turn round the target. God, here comes the tracer again. Hell, it's accurate and intense; weaved and bobbed to shake them off. This was from the neighbourhood of the town of Palembang. Then a strange thing happened.For a split second,I couldn't believe it. I looked out the starboard side and there was a sleek twin-engined Jap fighter—a Nick—sitting on my starboard wing and almost touching me. The two pilots were looking at me with their sickly grin—the bastards. They couldn't shoot at me from there and it was just occurring to me that they were going to ram me or tip my wing, when the Nick burst into flames, keeled over to starboard and made for the ground out of control and blazing. Thank God, two less little bastards.

My emotions were made more frail by the loss of some good friends. Gunn, an observer in 849, died from wounds as his pilot ditched after abortive attempts at landing on *Vic.* Gus Halliday and Pattison ditched too but were picked up by a destroyer. But Ken Burrenston, Lintern, Burns and Roebuck were shot down over the target. They all survived and were taken prisoners but, poor fellows, were not to live. Burrenston and Lintern and at least seven other survivors were taken from the prisoner of war camp after the surrender of Japan on 15th August 1945. They were lined up and brutally murdered by the camp commandant cutting off their heads with a ceremonial sword. The murderers were brought to justice and paid the price with their lives. I was sick when news of these atrocities filtered through after the war. Memories of such things remain always vivid, always bitter.

So, it was with a sense of utmost relief that we left the target area and made for Fremantle, Western Australia, where we arrived on 4th February. In the meantime I had flown over to the *Indomitable* taking with me the Air Co-ordinator, Ronnie Hay, Lieutenant-Commander Tomkinson, the CO of 1836, the Corsair Squadron and Lieutenant-Commander Hopkins, the CO of 1834 Corsair Squadron. We went up to the Admiral's bridge where all the other senior squadron officers from the other carriers were meeting. This was a high powered de-briefing and discussion on the two Palembang operations. What was achieved, what went wrong, lessons to be learnt for future operations in the Pacific were all discussed with candour. Vian encouraged everyone to talk, to air their views and be as critical of the overall plan for which he was responsible as well as the carrying out of it for which the squadron commanders were responsible.

No holds were barred and as a result many faults were examined to see what could be done to improve future operations. There was a long way to go as eventual contact with the American Task Forces was to show but it would be fair to say that the British Pacific Fleet and the Air Group began to grow up into the concept of a fast, efficient and hard hitting Task Force with, if necessary, continuous flying that was a feature of the American naval operations in the Pacific. The idea of the one set piece strike was to give way to constant take-offs and landings by smaller numbers of strike aircraft and continuous streams of fighters as circumstances demanded.

From Ldg. Stoker G. Turner, HMS *Indefatigable*

I remember that on the last attack on Sumatra, whilst under attack I was at my action station, namely the Rocket Magazine, starboard side, a couple of bombs dropped so close that I actually saw the flashes through metal. Captain Graham, in his talk after the attack, stated that he had never witnessed such a poor standard of air attack. Well, Stuart, the pilot who dropped those aforementioned bombs must have been shot down, for he didn't have to show very much improvement to have hit us next time out.

On our joining the BPF my action station was changed to the Hydraulic Pump room, which returned the launcher on the flight deck. It was the most remote station to be allocated, the very bottom of the ship. Even lower than the CO2 room. I took over that station, from the then Ldg. Stoker Lawson, later SPO. Whether he had asked for a change or not, I don't know. I didn't mind, for, I was a bachelor, he was married, with three sprogs.

I also remember, that when in the flight deck control room (machinery) I often rang the Damage Control Party on the Stokers Mess Deck, telling them what was going on, up top, also of every Jap plane I witnessed shot down.

Once, whilst off watch, our E.R.A. and me, were watching activities from a Pom Pom platform ladder, when a shell from a target shooting plane, ricocheted off the sea, struck the ship's side, between us—there was no more than four inches—flipped onto the flight deck, and spun itself out. I did not stay there after that, as I did not want to be hospitalized by our own planes. I had already been wounded at Tobruk in '42 by Jerry Stukas. Whether the Tiffy picked the spent shell up to keep for a souvenir I don't know. Not remembering his name, I do know that he was the shortest Tiffy aboard.

I remember all the pilots that flew from *Indefatigable,* and was quite upset at those who never returned. I also experienced what most of us must have felt at one time or another—excitement, or was it fear?

Lieut. (A) Ray Battison RNVR told me:

Today is 3rd September 1989, 50 years since the outbreak of World War II. Inevitably one's mind goes back—such vivid memories. Whilst it is a statement of the obvious that it was the beginning of probably the greatest catastrophy that the world has ever experienced and which we pray will never recur, it is ironic that for so many, certainly for me, it was also a period of some of the most precious times of my life. Wonderful friendships, tremendous camaraderie (never more so than in the Fleet Air Arm, known to us all as 'The Branch'), and the objective of a job to be done, however awesome. The opening lines of Dickens' 'A Tale of Two Cities' begins to take on a real-life meaning—'It was the best of times, it was the worst of times . . .'. One's memories of the 'best of times' tend to wipe out those of 'the worst of times'.

My first posting to an Operational Squadron—862 Avenger Squadron with one of the Branches characters as C.O.—Bobby Bradshaw and finally joining my last squadron—1772 Fireflies in the Pacific under a C.O. who could only be described as a gentleman in the truest sense of the word—Les Wort.

The Squadronwas aboard HMS *Ruler* in Colombo harbour, on passage to Australia to join the British Pacific Fleet. On boarding *Ruler* I asked to see the C.O. of 1772 and, to my surprise, was taken to Les Wort, a friend of the Norwegian days when he was Senior Pilot of 842's Wildcat flight in *Fencer,* where he had earned the D.S.C. in disposing of a Fokker-Wulf Condor. The squadron had been recently formed in the U.K. and was as yet 'unblooded'. Presumably because of my previous experience Les asked me some few days later to become his Observer. This began for me a very special friendship.

One incident on that voyage from Colombo to Sydney re-inforced my concern at the incredible ignorance of some senior ships officers in carriers of aircraft and their operation. *Ruler* was ferrying aircraft to the Far East, the flight deck one mass of aircraft secured to the deck with wings folded. When the Firefly's wings were folded the 20mm cannon pointed skywards, the barrels being streamlined with a metal casing. Imagine my disbelief whilst carrying out watch-keeping duties when a senior officer came on to the bridge and asked 'What are those things sticking up in the air that look like champagne bottles?'

On reaching Australia we were disembarked to Schofields—a MONAB (Mobile Naval Air Base) in the outer suburbs of Sydney. Squadron 'working-up' was resumed, awaiting the call to join the Fleet during which time, together with a number of other pilots and observers, I was sent on a 'Jungle Survival Course' with the Australian Army at Canungra in Queensland. The object of the exercise to make us fit enough, and sufficiently knowledgeable about living off the land, to survive being shot down over some anonymous Pacific island, to evade the Japanese and 'return to base'. Some hopes! It was probably the toughest, most strenuous two weeks of my life but the laughter overcame the tears!

From CPO Electrician Tom Jeans, HMS *Indefatigable*

In September 1943 along with E. A. Proctor, ex-*Indomitable*, as advance commissioning party, we were billetted ashore in Aussieland with a real dour Scots family. Breakfast was porridge out of a sack, no sugar or milk, only salt.

When *Indefatigable* arrived I was allocated to torpedo duties and was made resonsible for torpedo gyroscopes. She carried 70 by 18″ Whitehead torpedoes and 63 had to be maintained in the ready condition. The air blast gyroscopes which steer the torpedo each had to be 'tabled' every 3 months. To enable this to be carried out I had a workshop on the 'Island' with a port (not a scuttle) on both port and starboard side. It was a rectangular opening about 2 ft. square and enabled me to get a 'fix' on a shore object, when in port to allow the tabling. Everyone envied me the work area, I had the most fantastic view over the flight deck. We never used one; prior to coming out to the Pacific I was sent to Lee-on-Solent to do a course on American torpedoes as *Indefat* was to be equipped with Avengers. Again the torpedoes were not used.

In a re-allocation of duties I was made responsible for the Metadyne control of the 4.5″ guns and also for the Captain's and ADO's sights, that is the power operated binocular mountings on the island which you mention in your book **Sakishima**. The solenoid operated clutch in these mountings was a continuous source of trouble and most of my time in the dog watches was occupied with these instead of relaxing. My boss was Elect. Lt. Clegg, a person I admired greatly.

Article from The Daily Telegraph, sent by Sub Lt. (A) F. R. Stovin-Bradford RNVR

Cmdr. Kenneth Edwards, R.N., *Daily Telegraph* Naval Correspondent reported:

BRITISH PLANES BLAST JAPANESE OIL PLANTS

★ ★ ★ ★

BIGGEST FLEET CARRIER FORCE
LED BY ADML. VIAN

Naval aircraft of the British East Indies Fleet have delivered a series of blows against the Japanese-controlled oil refineries in Sumatra, in the Dutch East Indies. It is estimated that these will cut Japan's supplies of aviation spirit by 75 per cent.

The planes which carried out the operations came from the largest concentration of big fleet carriers used in any series of British operations.

Four carriers—*Illustrious, Indefatigable, Indomitable* and *Victorious*—were used. In support were the battleship *King George V,* the cruisers *Argonaut, Black Prince* and *Euryalus,* and the destroyers *Grenville, Kempenfelt* and *Ursa.*

In command was Rear-Admiral Sir Philip Vian, who has trounced the Germans in the Arctic and the Italians in the Mediterranean. He commanded the British naval task force during the invasion of Normandy and has now transferred his attentions to the Japanese.

ENEMY PLANES DOWN

The text of the communiqué announcing these successes is as follows:

In two successive operations a powerful East Indies Force commanded by Rear-Adml. Sir Philip Vian, KCB, KBE, DSO and including the aircraft carriers *Illustrious, Victorious, Indomitable* and *Indefatigable,* has struck the most damaging blow yet at Japanese oil supplies, which are of major importance to the enemy's war effort in this theatre.

The attacks were made by carrier-borne aircraft on oil refineries at Palembang, in Southern Sumatra.

The first attack against the Pladjoe refinery was carried out on Jan. 24. The importance of the installations to the Japanese was shown by the heavy scale of defence. In this area there are many airfields with defending fighters, an inner and outer ring of A.A. batteries and an extensive balloon barrage.

Our Avengers, with strong fighter escort, including Fireflies, bombing from above and dive-bombing through the balloon barrage, scored direct hits on the oil distilleries and hit or damaged many other buildings.

This attack involved a long flight over enemy-occupied territory. The striking force was intercepted by Japanese fighters some miles short of the target.

In the ensuing fighting, 13 twin and single-engine enemy fighters were shot down and six probables. In addition 34 aircraft were destroyed and some 25 damaged on airfields surrounding the target.

The second attack against Soengei Gerông refinery was made on January 29. Bombing conditions were good and the attack was pressed hard home through the balloon barrage and heavy flak.

Article from an un-named American publication, sent by Sub Lt. (A) F. R. Stovin-Bradford RNVR

TARPON/AVENGER Mk I, II, III
Great Britain

To replace the obsolete Fairly Swordfish and Albacore biplane torpedo bombers in use aboard Royal Navy carriers the British requested that the 1942 Lend-lease program include a number of TBF-1s. Initial early Avengers delivered to the British under Lend-lease were given a special US Navy designation TBF-1B and named Tarpon Mk I by the British. As the program expanded and later models were delivered, the Navy dropped the system of assigning special designations for aircraft supplied to the British.

The Avenger would become one of the most important carrier based aircraft in the Fleet Air Arm and a total of 958 Avengers of all variants would be delivered to the British (402 TBF-1B Tarpon/Avenger Mk 1, 334 TBM-1C Tarpon/Avenger Mk II, and 222 TBM-3 Tarpon/Avenger Mk III) during the Second World War. The TBFs and TBMs in British service retained the Tarpon designation until January of 1944, when all aircraft were re-named Avenger to avoid confusion with operating with American forces in the Pacific.

After delivery to England, the Avengers were modified to meet specific British requirements by Blackburn Aircraft Ltd. British gun sights, radio equipment and oxygen systems were installed replacing American systems. The cockpit was modified to position the navigator immediately behind the pilot, attachment points were installed for rocket assisted take-off equipment, a camera mount for an F-24 aerial camera was fitted in the radioman's station, the radio aerial mast was hinged so that it could be folded over to clear the lower overhead of British carrier hangar bays. To improve visibility from the radioman's station the two oval windows on the fuselage sides were replaced by bulged dome-shaped windows.

The first British squadron to operationally deploy with Tarpon Mk Is was Number 832 Squadron. Initially formed at Naval Air Station, Norfolk, Virginia, Number 832 Squadron with fifteen Tarpon Mk Is sailed with HMS *Victorious* and USS *Saratoga* for operations in the Solomon Islands during the summer of 1943. Later HMS *Victorious* took part in the invasion of New Georgia before returning to England.

In Europe, Fleet Air Arm Avengers were primarily used in the North Atlantic and North Sea areas for both anti-submarine operations, and attacks against German shipping off the Norwegian coast. A number of British Avenger squadrons were land based, flying anti-submarine, mine laying, and anti-shipping patrols over the English Channel. During the summer of 1944 at the height of the German V-1 'Buzz' bomb attacks, Avengers of Number 854 and Number 855 Squadrons were credited with destruction of two V-1s both shot down by gunfire.

In 1945 the Royal Navy selected the Avenger as the principal naval strike aircraft for squadrons being sent to the Pacific. Co-operation between the British and American Fleets was being accelerated for the final assault against Japan in which British Avenger squadrons would play a significant role. Nos. 820, 849, 854 and 857 Squadrons were deployed with a total of eighty-four Avenger Mk IIIs (TBM-3s) aboard four British carriers: HMS *Illustrious, Indefatigable, Indomitable* and *Victorious* as part of the British Pacific Fleet.

On 24 January 1945, Task Force 57 began a series of attacks against the oil refineries at Palembang, on the island of Sumatra (Dutch East Indies). The British attacks almost totally destroyed the refineries adding to the already critical shortage of fuel for the Japanese war machine. Royal Navy Avenger squadrons flew a total of ninety-five sorties against Sumatra losing six Avengers.

Copy from Sub Lt. (A) F. R. Stovin-Bradford RNVR
857 Squadron, aboard HMS *Indomitable*

A few days before I had celebrated my 21st birthday, but I had already logged some 280 hrs. flying the Grumman Avenger—for which, as an aircraft to fly, I held a great affection and respect.

We (USN trained pilots) had been taught to fly using only trimming tabs and rudder, which insofar as I was concerned was to become invaluable.

On January 29th at 0640 hrs., being 'tail-end-Charlie' (WIZ) I sat by the round down behind 11 Avengers and 16 Hellcats—the horrors of Meridian 1 on January 24th were still in the minds of all aircrew.

We eventually took off into atrocious weather, formed up below a low ceiling and flew some 30 miles to the coast of Sumatra, not looking forward to another 150 miles over Jap-held territory to the target—Soengei Gerong Refinery.

Our climb was to 10,000 ft. to clear the Barisan mountain range and our path to the target area was through enemy fighters, heavy anti-aircraft barrages plus the newly discovered (24.1.45) 6,000 ft. high balloon barrage.

50 or so miles from the target my Observer (Sub Lt. (A) Clem Spearman RNVR) reported a personal attack developing from Tojos to port, and my air-gunner, (P.O. Harry Godfrey) opened fire immediately.

A nasty fire started in my port wing bellowing black smoke, and somehow shells entered the fuselage smashing my instrument panel—but missing me. Air was rushing through the aircraft at 10,000 ft.—my throttle was jammed and I noticed a lack of aileron control.

Another attack followed again from port. Harry firing away, the fire had died down—and I actually used my front guns as the Tojo went past my bow.

The rest of my formation had forged ahead and started their dive onto the target. Just then an anti-aircraft shell passed through my port wing without exploding removing my port wheel completely and leaving a large hole through the wing. Harry was still firing away at fighters.

Stability at 10,000 ft. was deteriorating. I remember calling up the C.O. (Lt. Cdr. 'Doc' Stuart DSC, RNVR) and saying 'Give my love to Jackie' (my wife)—before pushing the nose down with bomb bay open and using my trimming tabs to keep a line on the target. We went through the balloons like everyone else, bombs away by manual release at around 3,000 ft. doing some 300 knots. We were then hit again by anti-aircraft fire in the starboard wing. Using rudder, elevator and trimming tabs I turned to starboard away from the target area, keeping to a course from Clem, surprised the engine was still going, feeling light-headed and trying to control the aircraft.

Another Avenger came alongside and called up to tell us the starboard olio leg was hanging down without a wheel . . . I had already lost the port wheel, and my bomb bay was open. No hydraulics.

Clem had realised we could never climb the mountains again, so we flew South-east around the eastern end of Sumatra, all alone at a constant height of around 4,000 ft.

That early training now came into full use as we staggered wobbly-mannered back and approached the Fleet from the East. Last one home.

With one empty olio leg hanging, bomb bay doors open, no flaps—we came towards ditching with distaste. The only way to get into a glide was to turn off the fuel switch. This took a short time and by reeling back the two trim tabs I got the nose up in time to execute a 'two-point' landing. There was a huge swell but we stayed upright.

From our dinghy we were saved by a screen destroyer HMS *Wessex* (Lt. Cdr. Horncastle RN) and spent 5 days aboard en route to Fremantle.

Still shivering in dry clothes from shock, lying on a bunk in the First Lieutenant's cabin (Lt. Mike Parker RN) all of a sudden 'B' turret opened fire above. I got up and witnessed from the deck outside the first kamikaze type attack on the BPF at around 1200 hrs.

Seven enemy bombers approached the Fleet at low level. They were at first broken up by the Seafires but were persistent. Hellcats were launched from *Indomitable* to join the other fighters, and between them all, plus the Fleet barrage, all enemy aircraft were shot down.

The Fleet lost 41 aircraft during Meridian 1 and 2. 30 aircrew were lost including 19 Avenger aircrew.

Meridian 1 and 2 were considered to be the most competent performances of the Fleet Air Arm during WW2—carried out as a direct request of the U.S. Admiral Nimitz to Admiral Fraser when in Pearl Harbour.

Pladjoe Refinery: Output halved for 3 months + oil storage destroyed. Soengei Gerong Refinery: Output stopped.

Cut aviation gas output by 35%.

The BPF's greatest contribution to ultimate victory included destroying 140 enemy aircraft in total + a large tanker + merchant ships.

From Stuart Eadon—temporarily onboard *Indomitable*

The first chairman of The Goldfish Club was a certain Sub. Lieut. (A) Frank Stovin-Bradford RNVR, 857 Squadron. On the back of a scrap of card with a pencil sketch of runways and trees, Frank wrote 'This is my actual target map which I took to Mana. We "did over" the runways and buildings and straffed. Fighters and Hellcats attacked aircraft on the ground, 24th January 1945'.

This was a diversion raid for the main attack on Palembang.

Frank was 'some sort' of artist and sent me this sketch of an Avenger Crew—probably his own—to prove the point.)

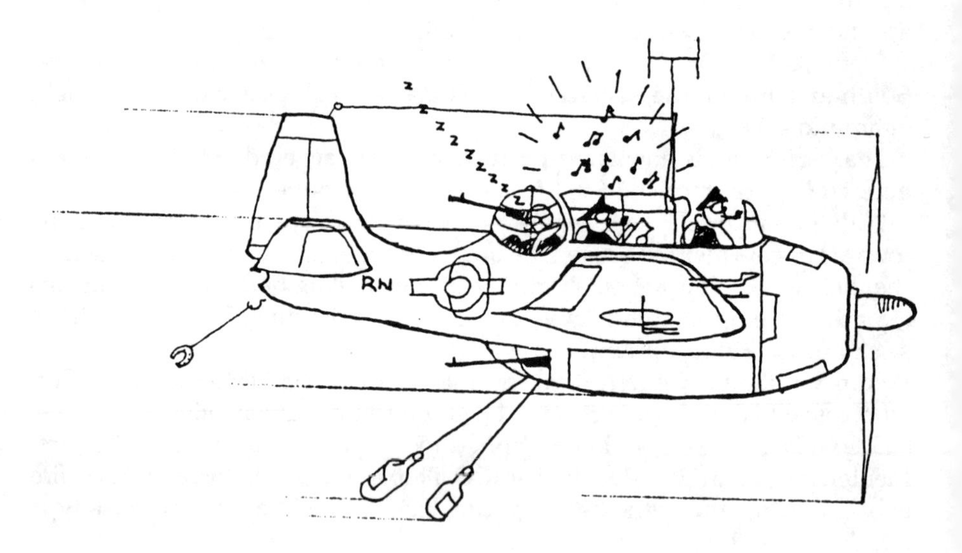

Extracts from 'Action This Day' by Admiral Sir Philip Vian, sent by F. Stovin-Bradford

Admiral Vian wrote of this second strike:

The Force comprised, besides the four carriers *Indomitable, Victorious, Indefatigable* and *Illustrious*, the battleship *King George V*, the cruisers *Argonaut, Black Prince* and *Euryalus*, and ten destroyers. After fuelling at sea on the 20th, we headed through the night of the 21st—22nd for the flying-off position between Enggano Island and the coast of southern Sumatra.

Then the weather took a hand. The inter-tropical front, a belt of high winds and torrential rain, made air operations impossible. I was forced to order a postponement of twenty-four hours. On the following night conditions were no better. Once again we headed out to sea for the day. At last, on the night of the 23rd, the skies cleared. At six-fifteen on the morning of the 24th we were in the launching position, thirty-five miles from the coast, in clear blue weather. Rising over the horizon to the eastward was the mountain range, more than 11,000 feet high, over which the pilots had to fly to reach their target.

The feature of the operation which had been planned was a bombing attack on the refinery at Pladjoe. For this, a striking force of forty-three Avengers, each carrying four 500-lb. bombs, was flown off. We had very little information as to the enemy's fighter strength in the area and did not know his state of preparedness, so, besides a very strong fighter escort, another force of fighters was ordered to neutralize the airfields round Palembang; the principal airfield at Manna was also bombed by four Avengers. Soon after 7 a.m. the striking force and its escort had formed up overhead and taken departure. Beyond the mountain range a further one hundred miles of enemy territory lay ahead, before the aircraft were over their targets. In the crystal-clear weather a protracted running fight might have developed, had the Japanese been thoroughly prepared. As it was, our aircraft were unmolested until they had almost reached their objective.

At twenty miles distance an unexpected hazard was seen, a balloon barrage over the refineries. Then the anti-aircraft defences opened fire. As the Avengers deployed into circular formation before diving to the attack, a number of enemy fighters appeared overhead. The escort went into action at once. While a dog-fight developed above, the Avengers went in, some following the strike leader, Lieut.-Commander W. J. Mainprice, R.N., down through the cables of the barrage, others dropping their bombs just above the balloons.

Their attack completed—and later it was known that the productive capacity of the refinery had been reduced by half—the Avengers made for their rendezvous, fifteen miles to the west of Palembang. This had been unluckily chosen, as our aircraft ran into a heavy concentration of fire. Moreover, they found a number of enemy fighters lying in wait for them.

The fighter sweep over the airfields had been designed to prevent this; but owing to the necessity of flying the fighters off in a second wave, after the striking force was in the air, they were too late to catch all the Japanese fighters on the ground. They did, indeed, destroy thirty-four of them on their airfields, and damaged many others. Nevertheless it was a powerful force which now met the retiring Avengers, several of which were badly hit before the escort were able to drive off the attack, shooting down fourteen Japanese planes, and damaging others. The bombers were then able to make their way back to the carriers without further trouble.

Fighters and bombers were handled cleverly, and there were many examples of exceptional skill and courage. For instance, one of the youngest Avenger pilots was Sub-Lieutenant F. R. Stovin-Bradford, R.N.V.R. His aircraft was one of those attacked and damaged by fighters as they approached the target.

With his instrument panel and aileron control shot away, his engine on fire, his throttle jammed and one wheel hanging down, Stovin-Bradford pressed on indomitably to drop his bombs in the target area. Somehow he managed to reach the rendezvous and struggle back to the Fleet with his squadron, and to make a successful ditching alongside a destroyer which picked up him and his crew.

Frank said that they had been attacked by Betties and Dinahs and that Admiral Vian had given him an immediate 'Mention in Despatches' on his return.

Our losses were not light—six Corsairs, two Avengers and one Hellcat failing to return. Nevertheless it had been a shrewd and successful blow at the Japanese in a vital spot, and we planned to repeat it.

During the 26th and 27th January the force refuelled at sea. We then had sufficient oil for one more attack on Palembang, before proceeding to Sydney. As a result of experience gained in the previous operation, we revised our plans. Fighters to dominate the air above the two main enemy airfields were to proceed in two sections, timed to arrive simultaneously over their targets in the hope of taking both by surprise. The route for the bombers was also changed, to avoid the bad areas of flak which had been discovered.

This time, too, a further precaution was taken. It had to be assumed that the Japanese, by now alive to the presence of a carrier squadron in the vicinity, would react by mounting air attacks on the Fleet. We therefore greatly increased the standing air patrol of fighters over the ships, or, to use an American expression which was soon to be adopted, the Combat Air Patrol (CAP).

Soon after 7.30 a.m. in the morning of 29th January, more than one hundred aircraft of all types were on their way to the target. The fighter sweeps, arriving over the airfields at eight-thirty, discovered that the Japanese were indeed not to be surprised this time. Most of their planes were airborne. Widespread airfights developed, in which the losses on both sides were severe.

Meanwhile, as the Avengers were approaching the target area, Firefly fighters were sent ahead to shoot down the barrage balloons. A number of them were actually going down in flames as the bombers went into their dive. Once again Mainprice led down through the cables, but this time his luck was out. His aircraft, and one other, were caught and destroyed, together with their gallant crews. The remainder caused heavy damage to the Soengei Gerong refinery, which, so we learnt later, stopped all production until the end of March. Even at the end of May, the Japanese had only been able to restore production to half its earlier level. Much of the credit for this must be given to two of the Flight-Commanders, Lieutenant G. J. A. Connolly, R.N.V.R., of

Illustrious and Lieutenant D. M. Judd, R.N.V.R., of *Victorious*. They led their flights on and down, disregarding the daunting sight of their Wing Leader's destruction. Connolly went on to achieve still more notable work.

For although the Corsairs and Hellcats of the escort and the offensive sweep were able to keep most of the enemy fighters occupied, the Avengers came under fighter attack as they withdrew. Seeing one of them badly damaged and unattended by any escort, Connolly assumed this duty. Handling his slow bomber like a fighter, he kept all attacks off the damaged aircraft's tail, shooting down one Japanese with his front guns, and out-manoeuvring the others. As a result, the crippled Avenger was got back to a safe ditching near the Fleet.

Another Avenger, piloted by Sub-Lieutenant W. Coster, R.N.V.R., similarly turned the tables on a Japanese fighter, in a duel at below three hundred feet, he first, by skilful evasion tactics, caused the enemy to expend all his ammunition without scoring a single hit. Then, when the Japanese foolishly broke away ahead of him, he emptied his front guns into him, sending him down in flames. *(Bill Coster's story in* ***Sakishima****.—Ed.)* It was not only the pilots who covered themselves with glory. Avengers carried a crew of three, Pilot, Observer and Telegraphist-Air-Gunner. It was one of these last, Petty Officer A. N. Taylor of *Victorious*, who performed a most notable exploit in this day's operations.

Before reaching the target, Taylor's aircraft was damaged by fighters. The pilot nevertheless went down to dive-bomb, and during his dive the Avenger was hit by flak. Then, as it pulled out, Japanese fighters made repeated attacks, during one of which the Observer was badly wounded. Taylor, in the intervals of driving off the enemy with his turret guns, managed to give the Observer morphia, and to apply a tourniquet to his shattered leg.

Meanwhile the pilot had lost his bearings, and owing to trouble with his compass was, all unknowingly, steering in the wrong direction to get back to the Fleet. Taylor manned his wireless set and got a distress message away with a request for fighter escorts, but these were unable to find the straying aircraft. Taking the Observer's maps, Taylor next managed to pin-point the Avenger's position over the unfamiliar terrain and to give his Pilot a course to steer. Turning then to his high-frequency set, on which he could get a 'homing', he repaired it, and got into communication with his ship, which soon after hove in sight.

After two unsuccessful attempts to get his damaged and barely manoeuvrable plane on to the deck of *Victorious*, the Pilot was forced to go down in the sea. Taylor, heedless of himself, supported the wounded and, alas, dying Observer, until a destroyer arrived to pick them up. It was the end of a most gallant and resourceful action. . . .

The knowledge that prisoners might be threatened with execution or tortured to extract information, not only made casualties particularly hard to bear, but led to our aircrews being kept ignorant of details of all operations other than the particular sortie on which they were engaged. This could not but affect morale to some extent.

At the same time, we naturally took all posible action to rescue any airmen known to be down in areas where we could possibly reach them. For this service, we had, besides our destroyers, two Walrus amphibian aircraft in *Victorious*. The airmen always knew that we would strain every nerve and take risks to rescue them.

From PO TAG Jack Gardiner, HMS *Illustrious*

We were on *Illustrious* at Palembang and through the Pacific. I thought the Palembang raid the equal of a raid like the Dambusters but we never seem to get a mention.

My gun camera took this 'shot' over Palembang.
Photo: Michael Hancock, 1834 Squadron, HMS Victorious

From Captain J. A. Hans Hamilton, HMS *Illustrious*

The Sally which menaced *Illustrious* and was shot down in a timely way, actually flew along the flight deck from aft before finally hitting the drink (pilot probably dead it was thought). KGV's secondary armament failed to take finger off trigger as they swung through the plane's path and hit us twice, once at the island base and into X turret from starboard causing a number of casualties including 3 dead.

(The FAA Museum records this as HMS Euryalus *hitting* Illustrious, *with 12 killed and 21 wounded.—Ed.)*

From Major Cheesman, DSO, MBE, DSC, R.M.

FLEET AIR ARM ATTACKS JAPANESE OIL REFINERY
On January 4th, British carrier-borne aircraft of the Fleet Air Arm delivered a very accurate attack against the enemy oil refinery at Pangkalan Brandan in Sumatra. Weather conditions were excellent and the whole weight of bombs and missiles from the Avengers and Fireflies fell within the target area. The powerhouse and other important plants, together with oil tanks and buildings received direct hits.

I have been asked 'What goes on in a pilot's mind when things go wrong and accident, tragedy, or death raise their ugly head?'

On thinking it over, there have been many occasions when many terrible things could have happened, but I have been lucky, very lucky indeed. Once the occasion is over, I seldom think about it, for if one does too often, one can get twitched up, which is very detrimental to morale.

I am, by nature, an optimist, but one occasion springs to mind when on 6th January 1945, I was flying in 1770 squadron from HMS *Indefatigable* on a Fleet Exercise in the Indian Ocean, in company with 4 of our Fleet Carriers.

Four days previously we had successfully carried out operation LENTIL destroying the Japanese Oil Refinery at Pangkalan Brandan in Sumatra (now Indonesia) and were now rehearsing a possible meeting with a Japanese Carrier Task Force.

Our Fleet was split in two, with 2 carriers on each side—to do a dummy attack. Our squadron role was to do the 'Finding' and I flew off with my observer—Lt. Desmond Wilkey D.S.C.

We found the 'enemy', reported its position, and then returned to our carrier, after flying for 4 hours, 35 minutes and were very low on fuel. All well so far, but alas, the carrier was landing on Seafires, and there had been an accident, so we were told to 'orbit'. We reported fuel showing zero—but we had to wait.

Appreciating that the engine may stop at any moment, I told Desmond to prepare for ditching, and that if it comes to that, then we will do it in a thoroughly disciplined fashion—and all will be well—we hope! As neither of us had ditched before, and no one had *ever* ditched a Firefly we did not know its ditching qualities! However, we had all carried out the drill on several occasions on dry land, but it now looked as if this was going to be the real thing.

And so we were all set—ready for the engine to stop at a height of 300 feet, when, sure enough, a cough, a splutter—and silence! This was a most uncanny experience, for I had never flown an aircraft before on a dead engine, and we had virtually become a very heavy glider.

I must say, I was very fortunate again, as I had flown hundreds of sorties in the Walrus amphibious aircraft, and so many times had landed on the sea in these small flying boats, so the drill would be very similar.

Consequently there was no panic, and I was full of confidence that I would follow the drill and get it right. But I felt Desmond, in the back seat, must be very apprehensive as to what was going on, so I just told him that all was O.K., and as soon as we were in the water, to release his canopy and get out—in other words, just stick to the drill.

I quickly turned into wind and pushed the nose down to retain flying speed, for I must keep that up, to avoid a stall, until the last moment.

I took her down to about 10 ft. and then lifted the nose to lose speed—just above the stall, and try to get the tail wheel into the water first to avoid cartwheeling. This was successfully accomplished, and both being securely strapped in, we came abruptly to a halt.

We climb out of the aircraft and pull the toggles of our Mae Wests, so that they automatically blow up and now we do indeed look like the real thing! Desmond was about to jump into the water when I said 'Hold it, let's see if we can get home without getting our feet wet! I'm going to release the dinghy from the starboard wing,' so I pull the lever, off comes the panel and out comes the dinghy—blowing itself up. We pull it alongside the sinking aircraft and jump in.

We got out the paddles and wonder 'what now?' when we see the destroyer HMS *Wakeful* coming our way and ultimately picks us up. We now envisage a day or two's rest, cruising in the destroyer, but not so, we are to be taken back to the *Indefatigable* forthwith. So off we go to some 20 feet abreast the carrier, which is towering above us—when out swings the starboard crane from which hangs an ammunition tray! We embark into the tray and are left swinging some 15 feet above the swirling torrent of water between the two ships which were making some 10 knots—the most frightening part of the whole day!

Welcome Back
Major V. B. G. Cheesman and Lieut (A) D. Wilkey RNVR return to Indefatigable
Photo: Mjr. Cheesman

The moral of this story is that one should always keep cool, carry out the drill and THINK POSITIVELY—it is all a matter of *discipline* and mind over matter which was instilled into me on the Parade Ground of the Royal Marines many years ago.

The first my wife Elizabeth knew about this was when, as a F.A.N.Y., stationed in Reigate, one of her friends handed her the *Evening Standard* saying 'Look what your husband has been up to now!'

When we arrived in Australia to a rapturous welcome, various leaflets were handed to us. Here are some extracts from two of them:

THE MISSION TO SEAMEN

Flying Angel Club: Cliff and High Streets
Eastern Seamen's Club: 76 Queen Victoria Street

The Mission extends a most cordial invitation to all seafarers to make full use of the facilities available. This little booklet is designed to help you in finding your way around, and its presence aboard your ship is an indication that a Chaplain has been aboard. If you have not met him—meet him at the Mission.

There is a dance every night in the Flying Angel, there is a library and reading and writing rooms—and there is a Chapel too, and we like to think of our Chapel as the heart of the Mission from which all its other activities radiate. At the same time we never ask a man what is his religion or even if he has any religion—but we do try to practise Christianity.

So will you please make full use of the Mission when in port? If you have any problems see us about them. We'll always do everything we can to help. Our job is the welfare of seafarers regardless of race, creed, or colour; and if you feel that there is something we could be doing which we are not doing will you please let us know?

A MESSAGE FROM THE GOVERNOR

Men of the sea wherever you serve, be it in the navy or in the merchant ships of the Allied or neutral countries, we extend a welcome to each one of you, and we thank you for the great service you have rendered to the cause of the United Nations.

Our thanks extend to all who man the ships of the Allied nations the world over.

Transport is life, and to give life to the nations fighting for freedom you have faced untold dangers, endured hardship—you have lived, suffered and died in order that God might exist.

I speak to men of the sea, but I am a countryman and my hope is that when the war ends many of you will become countrymen too. Western Australia is 10 times the area of Britain and Britain's population is 100 times greater than ours—there is room for you in this empty land, a land of great undeveloped resources, and are not the acres of this country as much British acres as are the acres of Kent—well we offer to you a chance of owning some of our acres.

Everything that is fundamental to the life of man can be had from the soil of this State, and in great abundance. I would add there is no better climate anywhere in the world.

All the elements necessary to success are to be found in this country, the one thing lacking is population.

I write not alone as the Lieutenant Governor of this State but also as the Patron of the Mission to Seamen in Western Australia.

WHEN YOU ARRIVE

A special problem in war-time Sydney is accommodation. So, you will be well advised *IMMEDIATELY* following arrival here to make arrangements which will guarantee your freedom from all worry in this connection during your stay, whether it be short or long. There is no need, as was the case, unfortunately, in the past, to bunk in the open. Elsewhere you will find a complete list of hostels which are conducted exclusively for your convenience. Sometimes it happens that these are filled to capacity, but should you experience difficulty in finding a suitable billet, consult one or other of the Information Bureaux named herein which exist only to help you.

It is wise to *set aside so much of your capital as will cover your accommodation expenses,* which will be very small if you use the facilities which have been specially provided for you.

Another first action should be to *make provision for the safe housing of what equipment and gear you will not require* while on leave. This may be left at the Cloak Room at Central Railway or at one or other of the many Hostels.

FOREWORD

This booklet has been produced by the Australian Comforts Fund (N.S.W. Division) and the Amenities Branch of the Australian Military Forces (N.S.W. Area) to provide men and women of the Services on leave with a guide to Sydney in handy and concise, yet comprehensive, form and supplying much special information which is not available in the usual publications.

If it should assist you in the great enjoyment of your furlough in Australia's oldest and greatest city—second only to London, within the Empire, in point of white population (approaching 1,500,000) and extent—it shall have served its purpose.

Sydney, founded in 1788 by Governor Phillip and named after the then British Home Secretary, Lord Sydney, has an area of almost 700 square miles, of which about 140 square miles are parks and reserves. Its harbour and beaches have a world-wide reputation. Its tourist attractions are unrivalled.

Keep on Saving
Printer: Chromoworks Ltd, London
59½" x 39¾"
NSC 5/139

A copy of a War Poster displayed throughout the UK in 1945

CHAPTER SIX

Second Operations. Okinawa

From Ldg Seaman Walter Uden HMS *Grenville*

The BPF arrived at Fremantle soon after breakfast; straight away the queue formed to go alongside the oiler and once again seniority enabled *Grenville* to be one of the first. Once refuelled we moved across to the anchorage. Launches and tugs from the inner harbour began to swarm around us; a ten gallon churn of fresh milk for each mess came aboard—we had not seen fresh milk since leaving Pompey. A pencil, writing pad and envelopes for each man and boxes and boxes of grapes and tropical fruits—common everyday food to Australians—were distributed to all messes. Such sudden generosity and unfamiliar food in large quantities was a recipe for stomach upsets, but it did not happen. Soon after tea, in the first dog watch, the cable was being hauled in and scrubbed and we weighed anchor and were on our way to Sydney.

Ever since we left Immingham, our resident population of cockroaches had been multiplying rapidly. The originals had been all black; now, with the tropical heat, we had three varieties, black, brown and white. They were everywhere; a loaf fresh from the galley was alright, but any of the bread ration kept for breakfast would be full of burrows by the morning. It was possible to place the loaf on the bread board and strike it smartly with the flat of the knife blade and the multi-coloured cockroaches would swarm out onto the table. They infested the personnel kit lockers in the messes; to add to our troubles, our U.K. kit, not being in use, was becoming covered in mould due to the humid conditions in the mess decks.

Five days later the Fleet steamed into Sydney Harbour, passing through the famous Heads and steaming slowly, in line ahead, with the hands fallen in on the upper deck, towards that world famous bridge. The native population greeted us with a carnival spirit, we were escorted by hundreds of small craft of all sorts and the shore was lined by waving crowds. Australia had commercial radio and they made the most of the opportunity. The radios were on in the mess decks and we on the upper deck, fallen in, could hear them. Any listening Japanese radio post got an eye witness account of all that was going on and what ships were present. Sydney was so far from the fighting that the inhabitants had little idea about security. The destroyers turned off to port as we got almost to the bridge and berthed further up river.

Before any boiler clean or repairs were started, *Grenville* was to be sealed and fumigated. Three days and nights of leave were granted to the whole ship's company. The reception was overwhelming, some struck it better than others, but all were made welcome. The contrast between battered Britain in the November blackout, the severe rationing and shortages which we had left in our memories and this land of glorious sunshine, with only a nominal butter ration, no blackout, unlimited cheap fruit and strange licensing laws, crowds of friendly pretty girls and a way of life very different from what most of us had known was overwhelming.

We went to the British Centre, a building specially constructed to deal with the needs of the British Pacific Fleet. Half a dozen of us were given tickets for a church hostel in a Syney suburb and we were made welcome, no charge being made for our accommodation. Crossing the harbour on one of the many ferries, we spent a day in Tarronga Park, an Australian version of Whipsnade, though on a far larger scale. I spent another day on my own—I walked across the famous Sydney Harbour bridge. The approach roads on each side are miles longer than the actual bridge. I did the return journey by tram, thus completing the treble that was my ambition—to walk across, to ride across and to pass under it. In fact it worked out that I went under it many more times than I crossed it. It was strange to come across so many English names; a walk up the hill from Woolloomooloo docks and we were in a park called Hyde Park; a little further along the same road and it was Charing Cross. Everywhere there was a mixture of Austrialian and familiar home names. Further up the coast in Queensland, in the mining areas, Newcastle and many similar names abounded and Geordies and matelots from the north eastern areas of England were swamped with hospitality.

The only real taste of war that the citizens of Sydney had known was when a Japanese submarine had surfaced in the darkness near the harbour entrance and had shelled the city with its gun. In the ensuing panic the authorities had simply thrown all the main switches at the power stations and plunged the whole city into total darkness—not very effective because the Japs already knew exactly where they were. The submarine captain stayed as long as he thought prudent and then made good his escape.

A visit to the renowned Bondi Beach was a bit frightening, at least for me. The surf was awe inspiring and the terrific undertow was scaring for an average swimmer like myself. There were lookout towers with guards on the alert for sharks and there were light aircraft on patrol further out; numerous hair raising tales circulated about shark attacks and the fate of their victims. I did not go to that world famous beach again, preferring to swim in the secluded shark-proof area in Sydney Harbour itself. This was simply an enclosed area of beach and water, guarded by a ballustrade of stout timbers supporting chain link fencing from the harbour's bottom to six feet above the water level. It was always crowded, so we were not cowardly 'Poms' in using it. This was known as Manly Beach.

During this stay in harbour some bright individual in the Wardroom (probably one of the R.N. officers) had the idea of returning to semi-peacetime routine by sounding the ship's bell every half hour of the day watches. Quartermasters were not particularly wrapped up with this idea; it meant that they were tied closely to the gangway and had to keep an eye on the clock all the time. One morning I was working on the upper deck close to the ship's bell, yet out of sight of its mounting. Along came the Quartermaster and struck the bells, then he turned and addressed the atmosphere—"Now some bastard ask me the time."

An Admiralty Instruction was issued that all personnel were to commence to wear chevrons on the left cuff of their uniforms. These were inverted red stripes, about two inches across, similar to those worn by Army corporals and sergeants. One was to be worn for each year of service—we considered that it was simply an attempt to catch up with American servicemen who seemed to be covered with badges and decorations. We had our Good Conduct Badges—which gave a certain amount of standing in the Service and which carried a small amount of extra pay. No one bothered to sew on any chevrons and as we had sympathy in the Wardroom, no action was taken. In the case of the issuing of the 1939-1945 Star, we had been forced to sew on the ribbon—without it we were not allowed on shore leave.

The Australians had strange licensing laws which allowed the bars to be open all day, closing at 6 p.m. This had the effect of turning the drunks out onto the city streets at the height of the evening rush-hour. To Jolly Jack this was confusing to say the least; he entered the 'saloon'—having come ashore at 4 p.m.—the saloon, not the pub, to find a large room with a hollow square bar in the centre and 'Schooners' were the order not the familiar pint. Schooners were larger than pints and, because of the heat, the alcohol percentage was higher. Jack, dealing with an unknown quantity and overwhelmed with generosity, soon became befuddled. I was ashore one evening as Leading Hand in charge of the shore patrol; we were based in an Australian Navy office. The phone rang; we were loaded into Service vehicles and sped to the scene of a fight between British and Australian matelots—the scrap was probably caused by jealousy among the native matelots at the reception that the Poms were getting. We were accompanied by Aussie patrols and sorted out the struggling bodies. Our few were getting the worst of the scuffle—we dragged them to one side and, feeling sorry for them, I told them to get the hell out of it as quickly as possible. In the meantime the Aussie patrol were unceremoneously bundling their matelots into the transport. Their task completed, they looked round to load up our captives only to find that they had disappeared. We returned to the offices where my kindness in allowing ours to scarper, brought me a good blast. In fairness, they had to deal out a good dressing down to their own captives and then let them go. It was just as well that the rest of the evening passed quietly and we returned to the ship sometime after midnight.

The boiler clean was completed, ammunition and stores had been topped up. As a contrast to the European war, not a single depth-charge had been dropped since we had left the U.K. and the heavy job of humping replacements was spared.

Extracts from 'Dry Ginger' by Richard Baker

On 23rd January, 1945, at Ulithi in the Caroline Island, Cdr Le Fanu joined *Indianapolis,* the 9,800-ton cruiser which served as Admiral Spruance's flagship; for four months he saw no Englishmen, and very few thereafter until the fleet moved into Japanese waters. Charged with advising the Americans on the potentialities of the British Fleet, and giving the British some idea of what they might expect in the conduct of joint operations, Michael's job was both responsible and (in spite of the unfailing friendliness of his hosts) lonely. 'The way they fling me out into the cold world with soft words and then leave me to rot is a fair corker' he wrote, commenting on the apparent lack of response to his reports from British Pacific Fleet HQ in Sydney. As a matter of fact his reports were brief and somewhat infrequent. 'I only write', he confessed, 'when I have something to say', and it was only during dull patches that he felt 'hells bells, I must write a report about something'.

But whatever Le Fanu did write was read with close attention—and not only by the British. His impressions of life and methods in the U.S. Navy were considered by the American Chief of Staff to show 'very accurate observation' and were influential in the post-war shape of the Royal Navy. Michael was being less than just to himself when he wrote that his reporting technique was 'to give an account of operations and then discuss higher policy in an elevated tone of voice as it were. This gives the thing a Churchillian air and saves me from delving into details of American ideas and gadgets.' But gadgets were of less importance in the Le Fanu canon than people, and most of his time was spent away from his desk promoting Anglo-US relations in the highly personal—and highly successful—Le Fanu manner.

Ever since the famous 'Order 99' of July 1914, the ships of the US Navy had been officially 'dry', whatever ingenious ways (such as the issue of bourbon by flight surgeons to naval pilots on the orders of Admiral Halsey) were found to modify that state of affairs. Officers and men of the Royal Navy, of course, have always been accustomed to the idea of alcoholic refreshment, whether it took the form (as it did until 1970) of a daily tot of rum for ratings, or a duty-free bar for the officers in the wardroom. As Michael repeatedly had to explain to his new American friends, this did not mean that all British naval officers were permanently drunk; but it did mean that Liaison Officers felt acutely the absence of a reviving draught enjoyed in the sociable atmosphere of a British wardroom.

In the *Indianapolis* there was no wardroom life as Michael had known it. The wardroom—the Admiral's day cabin, in the case of his staff was used for meals, after which people tended to retire to their 'rooms' until required again for duty; and mealtimes were decidedly formal by British standards—officers normally occupied the same places according to their rank, with the same neighbours on either side ('a dreadful prospect if they are nice, and if they are dreary, quite appalling'.) This was not the most receptive setting for Michael's brand of humour, but he decided that the best way to promote good relations was to induce a certain amount of 'letting down of the hair'; and although he felt that 'clowning here is rather like putting on slapstick at the Athenaeum', he embarked without delay on his self-appointed task of cheering everyone up. Privately he felt it a strain to 'come down to supper at six o'clock after a tiresome day with suicide planes and be expected to be the jolly Englishman, when I would have given a lot to have had something under my belt', but he very soon gained a reputation with all ranks as the best of good fellows, which did just what was required for the image of the Royal Navy.

The style was established very soon. 'Diffident charm' and 'a slightly exaggerated English accent' (to use Michael's own phrases) helped break the ice; but the Englishness was soon abandoned, except for a Union Jack on the door of his cabin to declare it 'British territory'.

Not long after Michael joined *Indianapolis* the Chief of Staff informed him that Admiral Spruance had been made a Companion of the Bath and asked when he (Michael) was going to invest him with the Order. Michael explained that in the British forces, junior officers were not encouraged to invest people with Orders—but this did not satisfy the Chief of Staff, so Michael decided he would have to do something about it. 'That evening after supper I rose to my feet, and after dilating on what an honourable Order the Admiral had been awarded, I whipped out from under the table a large ribbon of red bunting with a tin bath tub attached to it. This I hung round the Admiral's neck. Mercifully this was considered to be very droll, and a few days later the Admiral riposted by making a short speech in which he said he was frightened that my shoulder boards and brass hat might get rusty and presented me with an American hat and insignia. I welcomed the opening and wore American uniform from there on in.'

It was not only in the wearing of American uniform that Michael participated in the life of his new ship. He volunteered to take a turn as Staff Duty Officer 'driving the American Fleet round the ocean'; and as he was perhaps less consistently employed than the American members of the staff, he worked hard in his well-studied roll of 'little friend to all the world'. He spent many hours pacing up and down the quarterdeck (the fo'c'sle in a British ship) as the chosen companion of Admiral Spruance, who had a passion for walking and thinking aloud as he did so. This was a testing form of relaxation, for Spruance's thoughts were of a very high order. A quiet, ascetic man who loathed publicity, he had come to be widely regarded as 'the greatest sea-captain of the Pacific'.

Michael was soon to see his qualities demonstrated in the assault of Iwo Jima which began on 19 February after weeks of air attack from the carriers of the fleet.

With no specific duties allotted to him on the flag bridge, Michael adopted a wandering brief in action, and spent much time with the enlisted men in the flag plot. Many a life story was related to him at such times, and many were the small tributes to the confidence he inspired. One day he was approached by a sailor clutching a much-thumbed paperback. 'Good morning, Commander, how are you today?' 'Fine, fine, and how are you?' 'Fine thanks, Say . . . have you read *Call House Madam*, sir?' 'Can't say I have,' 'I have it here, Commander, and I had to talk fast to get it for you. You won't be too long with it, will you?' Michael promised to read this account of life in a brothel, and did, 'The things one does', he wrote in a letter to Prue, his wife, 'for England!'

While the action off Iwo Jima was proceeding—the battle was bitter and tough, and it was a month before the island could be regarded as secure—the British Fleet had made its way to the unhealthy and uncomfortable anchorage at Manus in the Admiralty Islands under the command of Vice-Admiral Sir Bernard Rawlings. There the ships lay waiting uneasily for further orders. Would they be assigned to some minor job, or would they be committed to the main assault, the approach to Japan itself through the chain of islands which lead up to it?

On 15 March the answer came; the British Fleet was assigned to the C-in-C Pacific, Admiral Nimitz, for 'duty in operations connected with Iceberg' '. 'Iceberg' was the code name for the invasion of Okinawa (the main island of the Ryuku archipelago) which was to prove the most costly of all Central Pacific operations.

'Tast Force 57', as Admiral Rawlings' fleet was called, was stationed on the extreme left of the main American battle-line, and although Rawlings had had no chance to meet Spruance before the Okinawa operations began—their knowledge of each other to a great extent depended on impressions conveyed by Michael—he had seized on the vital importance, in his role as British sea commander, of getting on good terms with his American colleagues, and Spruance soon formed the highest opinion of his qualities in action. Spruance also was deeply impressed with the way the British carriers, with their armoured flight decks, stood up to kamikaze attacks. He had special reason to appreciate this because, in the course of the preliminary bombardment of Okinawa, his flagship *Indianapolis* was 'kamikazed' on 31 March, the day the first landing took place. Many casualties were caused—and the incident nearly won Michael a medal.

'I'd just gone from Dawn Action Stations and was having a shower, and there was a rather belated pip-pip-pip of a twenty-millimetre cannon, and I thought 'ah, I know what this is, someone coming out of a cloud' and sure enough there was a bit of a bang. I didn't know whether to dash up on deck because I was frightened or come up in an English way, fully dressed and immaculate. I rather hurried, and cracked my head on the side of the shower; then I went on deck to see what was going on. A bit later in the forenoon a chum of mine, the Flag Secretary, Charles Barber, said 'Hey, Mike, Purple Hearts being given out now." I said, "Oh good, I must see that." He said, "Not see it, you're getting one." Somebody had noticed my little gash from the shower, and had lined up a 'Purple Heart' for me. I managed to get out of it, though.'

Undeserved though Michael's 'Purple Heart' would have been, *Indianapolis* suffered severe damage. The aircraft had gone right through her and blown off two propellers, and Admiral Spruance had to transfer his flag to the battleship *New Mexico.* Six weeks later, on 13 May, she too was struck by a kamikaze, and this time Michael saw the aircraft approach. 'I was scared, of course—one always is scared—but it was very exciting, even though you think the thing is coming at *you*. It hit the five-inch gun deck, and after that I nearly always spent my time in action down there. They were a little bit shaken up—and on the principle that lightning never strikes twice, I thought it a very good place for me to be.'

The battle for Okinawa was long, defended as it was by a garrison of some hundred thousand men and an estimated ten thousand aircraft, of which four thousand were suicide planes. Against them were pitted more than half a million allied troops and an invasion fleet of some one thousand three hundred vessels, and it took three months—until early July—before the islands, three hundred miles from the Japanese mainland island of Kyushu, could be considered conquered. All concerned were under immense strain, which was not helped by a deplorably erratic mail delivery service. Michael helped to lighten the tension with a few lines in doggerel, to be sung to the tune of *Smoke gets in your eyes.*

Extract from 'Escort Carriers in the Second World War' by Kenneth Poolman, sent by Bert Crane HMS *Duke of York*

At this point in the Pacific war it was thought by the American High Command that only a landing on Honshu, the biggest island of Japan itself, where her capital, largest cities and heaviest industry lay, could guarantee her surrender, but there were several more major steps to be taken, more bloody landings to be made, to ease the effort and reduce the butcher's bill of such a giant undertaking. One more large base, from which aircraft and ships could stop all Japanese imports and hit her home defences really effectively before and during an assault on Honshu, was needed, as close to the homeland as possible.

Okinawa, with its good airfield, only 800km (500 miles) from the nearest point of Kyushu, 2,010km (1,250 miles) from Tokyo, was the answer, but first—Iwo Jima. With ships and aircraft working from the Philippines as well as the Marianas, essential oil and avgas supplies, had to run the gauntlet both of aircraft, as in Halsey's strikes, and of the remarkably effective American submarines, but too much was still getting through. The Super-Fortresses in the Marianas could bomb Japanese industry in the home islands, but because of the distance—2,010km (1,250 miles) Saipan to Osaka—could take no escorting fighters and only small bombs. The island of Iwo Jima in the Volcano Islands was small (8 by 3km or five miles by two), but had two good airfields, and its capture as a refuelling point would allow Mustang fighters to accompany the B-29s all the way to Honshu and back. The bombers could thus bomb more accurately, with much bigger bombs, and did so in the pre-invasion bombardment of Okinawa, the taking of which would block all shipping to the homeland, move the Super-Fortresses even closer to it—and perhaps even make an invasion of it unnecessary.

At the end of January Admiral Spruance, having planned the next moves in Hawaii, relieved Admiral Halsey, which made the Third Fleet once again the Fifth Fleet, with Marc Mitscher replacing McCain, who had taken over command of the Fast Carrier Force (now Task Force 58), under Halsey, and Vice-Admiral Turner in charge of the Joint Expeditionary Force. Most of the old battleships, (USS *Arkansas* was the oldest), escort carriers, cruisers and destroyers of the Seventh Fleet were also transferred to the Fifth Fleet and were formed into an Amphibious Support Force under Rear-Admiral Blandy. The CVE force (Task Group 52.2) was under Rear-Admiral Durgin and comprised: *Anzio (ex-Coral Sea), Bismarck Sea, Makin Island, Natoma Bay, Lunga Point, Petrof Bay, Rudyerd Bay, Sergent Bay, Saginaw Bay, Steamer Bay, Tulagi* and *Wake Island.*

D-Day was to be 19 February 1945, when two divisions of US Marines under 'Howling Mad' Smith were to be landed on the south-east coast of Iwo Jima. TF.58 opened the campaign to 16, 17 and 18 February by hitting airfields and aircraft factories in the Tokyo area, to supplement the B-29 attacks and help prevent interference with the Iwo Jima operations.

The main attack started on 16 February with a three-day aerial and gunnery bombardment by Blandy's ships (six old battleships, four heavy cruisers, one light cruiser, the CVEs, destroyers, and small gunboats) and by Army aircraft. The weather was bad, with rain and mist, which camouflaged the heavy fortifications, dampened the fiery ardour of napalm and made many of Cal Durgin's wing tank bombs fizzle out, which rocket attacks, though accurate, were ineffective against the concrete bunkers, gun emplacements and concealed defences which 74 consecutive days of bombing by B-24s from the Marianas had not knocked out.

The next step would be the crunch of the first leather-neck's boot on the sands of Okinawa in Operation 'Iceberg', but Admiral Spruance knew that its big garrison would defend this vitally important prize, so close to the homeland, to the death. The great combined strength of Fifth Fleet carriers and the Far East Air force could not hope to knock out Japanese air power in the home islands by bombardment. Air attacks on the Okinawa invasion fleet from the north, which would certainly include a strong contingent of kamikazes, would have to be defeated in the air.

Enter the BPF

From the south-west, air reinforcements would doubtless be staged in via the Sakishima Gunto islands, particularly Ishigaki and Miyako, and Formosa, where kamikazes were also stationed. These could be kept largely in check by continuous bombing from carriers. Selected for this duty was the newly arrived British Pacific Fleet, under Admiral Sir Bruce Fraser, with Admiral Sir Bernard Rawlings as commander of the Fleet at sea, and Vice Admiral Sir Philip Vian leading four fleet carriers, *Illustrious, Indomitable, Indefatigable* and *Victorious,* the fighting nucleus of the BPF.

The Fast Carriers led off by hitting airfields on Kyushu and Japanese warships in Kure on 18/19 March. On the 19th the Japanese started as they meant to carry on when the CV *Franklin* was bombed as she was launching aircraft and reduced to an almost burned-out hulk. In the holocaust died Captain 'Buster' Isbell, great sailor, aviator, captain and leader, whose taut ship *Card,* CVE-11, had so distinguished herself in the bloody waters of the central Atlantic, and who had seemed destined for the highest rank. Mitscher retaliated throughout the 20th and 21st, left the Japanese air defence much subdued, topped up from his Fleet Train tankers, and took up position for repelling air attacks from the North.

In Ulithi lagoon lay the great fleet, including Task Force 57, which was fuelled from American tankers and sailed on 23 March, its own tanker replenishment group preceding it by 24 hours; on the 26th, on station 160km (100 miles) south of the Sakishima Gunto, it began a series of strikes.

Extracts from: United States Fleet Carriers of World War II by Richard Humble

Kamikaze victims,
Leyte-Luzon campaign
October 1944—January 1945

The first kamikaze attack on an American fleet carrier had taken place before Ohnishi had formally requested Toyoda to agree to the formation of the corps. It happened on 15 October '44 off Luzon, when TG.38.4 was attacking Japanese airfields on the eve of the Leyte landings. Flown by the commander of the Japanese 26th Air Flotilla, Rear-Admiral Arima, a lone 'Judy' dive-bomber had immolated itself and its 500 lb bomb on the flightdeck of *Franklin.* Prompt fire and damage control limited the effects to three men killed and twelve wounded and *Franklin* stayed on station with TF.38, which did not experience its first multiple kamikaze attack until 30 October. It was a sharp awakening to the new menace: *Enterprise* was narrowly missed and both *Franklin* and *Belleau Wood* were now obliged to withdraw for repairs, with the loss of 158 men and 45 aircraft. There were four other casualties before the end of the Leyte campaign: *Lexington* damaged on 5 November and *Cabot, Essex* and *Intrepid* on 25 November, when six bomb-carrying Zeroes and two 'Judies' attacked TGs38.2 and 38.3.

Iwo Jima and Okinawa,
February—June 1945

Iwo Jima was invaded on 19 February 1945 after being bombed and shelled day and night for the previous three weeks, with TF.58 launching carrier strikes against the nearest airfields on the Japanese mainland. As the decision had been made to save the next major kamikaze effort for the American attempt to take Okinawa in the Ryukyus, there was only one sizeable kamikaze attack during the Iwo campaign. This was launched on 21 February by 32 aircraft which broke through the radar picket screens and intensified CAPs. In an unusually effective attack, measured in terms of number of targets hit per number of aircraft attacking, the escort carrier *Bismarck Sea* was sunk, and *Saratoga* and four other ships were badly damaged.

In the slaughter of the campaign on Iwo, which had to be conquered foot by foot, only 216 Japanese prisoners were taken out of a garrison of 22,000. American casualties were 5931 dead and 17,272 wounded. Fighting on Iwo continued until the last week of March, by which time the 5th Fleet had already begun its preliminary strikes for 'Iceberg', the invasion of Okinawa.

The passage from Fremantle to Sydney was far from pleasant, especially through The Bass Straights, one destroyer had a man overboard who was fortunately picked up, and it almost happened to me. I had decided to go for'ard from the quarterdeck along the port side when we probably turned a few degrees and gave a sudden lurch to port, toward me came a huge wave and I tried to hold on to a locker handle but the wave just picked me up and I knew nothing until my legs had straddled a small locker between the depth charge rails. The insides of my legs were skinned and messy but our doctor soon had me walking again! I was very lucky.

From Bill McCullock, P.O. Electrician, HMS *Undine*

We were passing Formosa, it was 0600 Friday 13th April with everything calm and peaceful when suddenly a terrific roar and a Jap plane showing a huge red light underneath dived down on us from the land direction. Watching from the forward torpedo tubes, I saw something leave the plane but whatever it was seemed to float away toward our stern, it could not have been a bomb, it had to be something much lighter, but everything happened so quickly and we will never know.

Extract from 'Carrier Operations in World War II' by J.D. Brown

The main body of the British Pacific Fleet arrived in Sydney on 10th February 1945 and began to prepare for joining the American Fleet, although at that date it was uncertain as to which American Fleet was involved, General MacArthur, whose naval support forces included only CVEs, wanted the BPF for the forthcoming amphibious campaigns in Borneo and Mindanao, while Admiral Nimitz, C-in-C Pacific, regarded the armoured carriers as his 'most flexible reserve' and wished to commit them to the support of the landings on Okinawa. It was not until the beginning of March that the Joint Chiefs of Staff decided that Nimitz had greater need for the four Fleet carriers with their 238 aircraft.

The problems confronting the Royal Navy before it could commence operations with the highly mobile Fast Carrier Striking Force were considerable. The matter of adopting US Navy standard operating procedures in the form of signals, tactical doctrine and carrier operating technique was straightforward, if hard work for the departments concerned. The major impediment both at the outset and to the end of Pacific operations, was the lack of a properly equipped underway replenishment force. The Fleet Train, consisting of oilers, supply and stores ships, repair ships, and the special support ships required to maintain an aircraft carrier squadron at sea for weeks, never reached the strength envisaged by the Admiralty. Those that there were, flew not only the White, Blue and Red Ensigns but also the Merchant Ensigns of many Allied nations, so hard-pressed was the Ministry of War Transport after five and a half years of a war in which some of the heaviest losses had been among vessels of the types most needed by the Fleet Train. The needs of the carriers was largely met by CVEs employed as ferry carriers, repair ships and stores carriers, as well as the few auxiliaries fitted out for these tasks.

When the British Pacific Fleet arrived at Manus, in the Admiralty Islands, at the end of February 1945, there were only 27 out of the 69 ships constituting the Fleet Train awaiting the warships in the anchorage; the remainder had been delayed by Communist-inspired strikes in the Sydney docks. After the decision to incorporate the BPF as Task Force 57 in Admiral Spruance's 5th Fleet, the Fleet replenished and left for Ulithi atoll in the Caroline Islands, arriving on 19th March 1945.

Meanwhile, Task Force 58, the USN Fast Carrier Striking Forces, had been striking at the Bonin Islands, in support of the Iwo Jima landings. The intention was to destroy as many Japanese aircraft as possible prior to the landings on Okinawa; a vast number of enemy aircraft was destroyed, both on their airfields and in air combat, but on 19th March three Attack carriers, corresponding to the Royal Navy's Fleet carriers, were badly damaged off Kyushu. *Intrepid* and *Wasp* were sufficiently damaged to prevent their participation in the early stages of Operation 'Iceberg'—Okinawa, while *Franklin* lost over 700 men killed by bombs and the ensuing fires and was too badly damaged to see further service in the Second World War.

So, after only 3 months from taking command, Admiral Fraser's fleet had arrived in Sydney to the great relief and delight of Australians everywhere. By sheer personality, he had already endeared himself to our cousins 'down under'.

His second in Command was Vice Admiral Sir Bernard Rawlings, who was previously C in C Eastern Mediterranean, with Rear Admiral Sir Philip Vian in charge of the First Aircraft Carrier Squadron (Indomitable, Illustrious, Indefatigable *and* Victorious).

When the American Fleet was commanded by Admiral Raymond Spruance, it was known as the 5th Fleet and when under the command of Admiral William Halsey as the 3rd Fleet.

Although Fraser still hadn't official approval to report his fleet for duty at Manus, that is what he did and the fleet arrived there on 7th March.

Vice Admiral Rawlings sent a signal to Admiral Nimitz, 'I hereby report Task Forces 113 and 112 (BPF and Fleet Train) in accordance with orders received from C in C, BPF. It is with a feeling of great pride and pleasure that the BPF joines the US Naval Forces under your command'.

The reply from Admiral Nimitz read 'The US Pacific Fleet welcomes The British Carrier Task Force and attached units which will greatly add to our power to strike the enemy and will also show our unity of purpose against Japan'.

At the time, I was unaware of these signals, but I was aware of the problem of prickly heat. Open-toed sandals appeared to help, but these could not be worn on the flight deck because the armour plate retained so much heat and blistered the feet, so rope-soled pumps were the only answer in my case.

We remained in the humidity of Manus for ten days, probably while someone, most probably Nimitz, persuaded Admiral King to relent, which he must have done, because we headed for the tiny atoll of Ulithi in the W. Carolines where we re-fuelled.

Now we were designated Task Force 57 and took our station to the S.W. of the U.S. 5th Fleet. So began our part in the battle for Okinawa.

I called my first book **Sakishima** *because that was the BPF's target. This was what we had been training for, although candidly, our 'blooding' at Sumatra had been the biggest and most effective operation of the BPF's war. Sakishima Gunto, a group of islands between Okinawa and Formosa (Taiwan), were being used as staging points for Japanese aircraft. If we could stop them bringing up replenishments, then the US Assault Forces would have an 'easier' time. Here, off Sakishima, we fought from 26th March until 20th April. Ed.*

Lieut. W. H. Procter RNVR, HMS *Argonaut* recalls

It was a thrilling moment, halfway round the world and in Aussie-land. And didn't our Marine Band do us proud. As we entered Sydney harbour they struck up Waltzing Matilda. What a sense of occasion. Not a dry eye in the house. One thing did disappoint me—there was a strike on! I couldn't believe it. What a funny way to win a war.

But the Aussies will always have a firm place in my heart, and I am sure with most others. They were wonderful. They opened their homes, and friendships abounded everywhere. Many of us had Up-Homers. My Aussie friends even sent food parcels to my wife and children in England.

Another memory of Sydney was the ferry which ran from Garden Island to the mainland. Three of us were going ashore and had left it a bit fine to catch the ferry. As we arrived at the ferry-point, the boat began to pull away. We started to run and our Radar Officer who was at the front, leaped for the ferry—and missed. Into the ogging! He got out all right, but we never bothered to go ashore that night.

There was a touch of home about Sydney with such names as Hyde Park, Kings Cross and others. And hadn't we for years spoken of being 'up a gum tree'. Well, now we could see the gum trees, with the lovable koala bear.

But all this didn't last long, although things as tempting as Bondi Beach beckoned. We were off again. It had to be. We had come to do a job down-under. The general feeling was let's get on with it.

From Jack Collins, HMS *Quality*

By March 1944, the 4th Flotilla, now composed of *Quilliam, Quadrant, Quality, Queenborough, Quiberon* and *Quickmatch,* were with the Eastern Fleet in the Indian Ocean. There they participated in the various carrier raids on Japanese-held territory, at Sabang and Soerabaya during 1944, both *Quilliam* and *Quality* being hit by shore batteries off Sabang in July, towards the close of the year, after raids on the Nicobar Islands, the flotilla moved to Australia for duty with the British Pacific Fleet. From early 1945 until the surrender, all the ships of the flotilla saw extensive service in Pacific waters, operating with TF57. *Quilliam,* however, was very badly damaged in collision with *Indomitable* in May 1945. They were still in the Pacific in August 1945 when *Quandrant* was at the re-occupation of Hong Kong and *Quiberon* at Shanghai. In 1945, the three Australian-manned ships, *Quadrant, Quality* and *Queenborough,* were turned over to the RAN permanently, while the only RN survivor, *Quilliam,* went to the Netherlands as *Bankert.*

On December 11th '44 we arrived in Fremantle, but only remained long enough to re-fuel and re-provision. The following day the B.B.C. announced the arrival of the British Pacific Fleet in Australian waters—one battleship and four destroyers. Half way across the Australian Bight, the destroyers left the *Howe* to continue her journey to Sydney unescorted, while they put into Albany, a pleasant sleepy little town that received rather a rude awakening from the sudden influx of 800 thirsty sailors who drank the town dry within a few hours.

On leaving Albany we ran into some very rough weather: during one afternoon we actually made good four miles: all boats received damage to upper deck fittings. We rendezvoused with the escort carriers *Atheling, Fencer,*

Striker and *Battler,* who were transporting aircraft to Australia. We reached Melbourne on December 22nd and docked in Williamstown at midnight, moving over to Fort Melbourne on the Sunday morning—Christmas Eve. Our first sample of Australian hospitality augered well for the future; the Australians were obviously pleased to see the British Navy at long last. Many of us had invitations out for Christmas Day, which alas we were not to enjoy, thanks to the activities of a Japanese Submarine off the New South Wales coast. At 0400 on Christmas morning a general destroyer recall was issued and at 0500 *Quilliam, Quality* and *Quadrant* slipped and proceeded to sea, followed a few hours later by *Quiberon.* Slight recompense was the issue of a bottle of beer per man with Christmas Dinner, a present from the Australian Comforts Fund, with rather devastating results, as seen by the excellent independent zig-zag of the destroyers in line ahead that afternoon. On Boxing Day we rendezvoused with *Quickmatch* who had left Sydney with a scratch crew and rescued the survivors of the merchant ship that had been torpedoed. After a fruitless search for the submarine the flotilla entered Sydney Harbour on the 27th and berthed off Garden Island.

True to form *Quality* was E.M.D. so we had ample opportunity to appreciate the harbour, the sailing boats with their attractive crews on their summer holidays. Signalmen's telescopes and binoculars were in great demand that sunny afternoon! On the Sunday we moved up to Woolloomooloo alongside *Quilliam* and ahead of *Howe.* This was our first opportunity to show visitors around the ship and an excellent chance for 'Jack' to find 'Up-homers'. Between January 4th and 7th our holiday in Sydney was interrupted while *Qulliam* and *Quality* went round to Melbourne to escort *Striker* and *Fencer* back to Sydney. The arrival of the cruiser *Swiftsure* added to the size of the British Pacific Fleet but the Royal Naval organization in Sydney was still in its infancy. On January 13th, *Howe, Swiftsure, Quilliam, Quality* and *Quadrant* sailed for Manus in the Admiralty Islands, one of the main bases of the U.S. Pacific Fleet. When we arrived on the 19th, the harbour was packed with ships of every size and type—a forest of masts in fact—and certainly a masterpiece of organization considering the locality was practically unexplored and uncharted before the war. After a few days liaison with the Americans, the force returned to Sydney where we arrived on January 29th, the same day as the Duke and Duchess of Gloucester arrived to take up duties as Governor General. After a few days holiday at Kurraba jetty, we sailed for New Zealand on February 2nd, in company with *Queenborough, Quadrant,* HMNZS *Achilles* and *Howe* who was flying the flag of Admiral Sir Bruce Fraser, C-in-C BPF. We arrived in Auckland on the morning of the 5th. The following day we moved over to Devonport Dockyard and went into dry-dock for a bottom scrape. On Saturday a party of about 100 ratings went on a conducted tour to Rotorua—the district of Hot springs and Geysers. On Monday and Tuesday, *Howe,* HMNZS *Gambia, Queenborough* and *Quality* carried out various gunnery exercises in Rangitoto Bay, and on the Wednesday we sailed for Sydney after an all too short but very pleasant visit. We arrived back in Sydney on February 17 and what a change had come over the place in our fortnight's absence. The main body of the British Pacific Fleet had arrived; the harbour was full of ships—battleships, cruisers, destroyers and auxiliaries. There was no room for such small fry as us in Woolloomooloo and we anchored alongside *Queenborough* in Farm Cove to carry out our own boiler clean.

On the 27th February the Fleet sailed for the Pacific, having been preceded by the auxiliaries during the previous few days. The Q's formed Task Unit 67.1.9 under Captain D4. The 25th D.F. of U's and the 27th D.F. of W's, were in company. We arrived in Manus on March 7th, having rescued three pilots en route—the first of many. The number of American ships had greatly diminished since our previous visit. After carrying out exercises, we left on the 15th and arrived at Ulithi in the Carolines on March 20th. This group of bush covered coral islands in the midst of the ocean was the advanced base of the U.S. Pacific Fleet—there were no shore facilities at all, but for miles and miles, thousands of ships, big and small, lay at anchor ready for the invasion of Okinawa.

Extracts from 'The War with Japan' by Charles Bateson

As events turned out, the last and largest amphibious operation of the Central Pacific forces was that on Okinawa, which the planners expected to be merely preliminary to the invasion of Japan. This was the biggest island the Central Pacific command assaulted. It was defended by a force of over 100,000 of whom about 70,000 were army troops, under a resolute and able commander, Lieutenant-General Mitsuru Ushijima. The Japanese were well armed and equipped, having adequate artillery, mortars, automatic weapons, anti-aircraft and anti-tank guns and plentiful stocks of ammunition. Ushijima planned his defences skilfully, selecting for his main position difficult terrain that naturally lent itself to defence and then fortifying the entire area in depth.

With Spruance in overall command and Turner as Expeditionary Force commander, the invasion of Okinawa was entrusted to Lieutenant-General Simon B. Buckner's Tenth Army, consisting of Hodge's XXIV Corps (7th and 96th Divisions) and General Geiger's III Amphibious Corps (1st and 6th Marine Divisions), with four other divisions—three army and one marine—available for special tasks or as reserves. The invasion fleet comprised 1,300 vessels of all sizes and the total troops for the assault phases of the operation numbered 183,000. Sixty miles long and varying in width from two to eighteen miles, Okinawa was the largest and most central of the Ryukyu Islands and lay only 350 miles from the Japanese mainland island of Kyushu.

While preliminary operations were being carried out the usual pre-landing softening up was under way. The naval bombardment began on the 25th, but because of the need for extensive minesweeping the bombardment was at long range and largely ineffective until the ships were free to close their targets on the 29th. For the first time a British Force operated with the Fifth Fleet. Its presence was due to Churchill's insistence. He was determined, for reasons of national prestige, that if Japan were to be invaded, the invasion should not be a wholly American operation. The United States Joint Chiefs of Staff did not want British forces present. Technically, they had sound arguments on their side, as British ships, especially carriers, created difficult supply problems owing to their different requirements and their multiplicity of aircraft types, and, tactically, although less vulnerable, they were in some ways ill-suited to Pacific requirements, having too few aircraft. Nevertheless, the Joint Chiefs' primary objection arose from intense nationalism, and it was only the determination of Churchill and the understanding tact of Roosevelt which made possible the presence of a British Force at Okinawa.

Extract from 'Okinawa 1945 Gateway to Japan' by Ian Gow

Overlooked by historians for years, the battle of Okinawa was one of the most fiercely contested and significant conflicts in modern military history. The island was crucial to the Allies' strategy as a key position for launching air attacks, and for the building of a massive force for an actual invasion of Japan itself.

The conquest of Okinawa took an expected three months and was one of the bloodiest and most costly campaigns of the war. The Japanese pulled out all the stops in the last-ditch effort to prevent their homeland from being endangered by invasion. Desperately trying to disrupt American supply lines, Japanese forces sent over 1,900 suicide sorties to attack the U.S. Naval Task Force, plus 4,000 orthodox attacks by the Japanese army and navy planes. On the land the United States suffered 50,000 casualties. It was this enormous human loss and the projection of even more devastating losses during an attack on the mainland that convinced the United States to scrap the invasion plans and instead employ the new tested atom bomb.

S.F. Stan Ward who served on board HMS *Howe* sent me the line book from which I learned:

Battle of the Philippines

Distinguished passengers were always persuaded to speak in the ship over our broadcasting system in the series, 'Fares, please'. The following talk was given by a war correspondent who had landed with the first wave at Leyte:

You men of the Royal Navy, many of you with long and distinguished service in other theatres, have come out to join in a fight across the wider waters of the Pacific against a more outlandish enemy, and the Australian people, I can assure you, have been looking forward with great eagerness to welcoming you.

You are the forerunners of the great naval and military forces which Britain has promised to throw into the Pacific war as soon as possible. You have arrived at an interesting and dramatic stage of this war, when a campaign is being fought out in the Philippine Islands which is both the culmination of the long, arduous and cruel campaigns waged in the humid jungles and fever-ridden swamps of the islands surrounding us at this moment, and the opening of the large scale battles that must be fought on land and sea before the Japanese are finally brought to their knees.

And it is the battle of the Philippines about which I have been asked to talk to you.

The Philippines for more than 300 years were under Spanish domination until the defeat of the Spaniards in the Spanish-American war, after which they came under benevolent American influence. This archipelago of more than 7,000 islands is so important in the strategic picture that its recapture from the Japanese will be the key to the defeat of the Nips. To the south-west of a line drawn from New Guinea to the Philippines lie the rich islands of the Netherlands East Indies, Japan's most coveted prize, and the source from which she draws the oil necessary for her to run her war. But she has to transport that oil over a long sea route that takes her tankers through the comparatively narrow waters lying between the Northern Philippines and the China coast. You can see, therefore, that once we have our bases established in the Northern Philippines our air patrols and naval forces will be able to cut this lifeline, a disaster of the first magnitude for Japan and one that will certainly cause headaches in Tokyo. Apart from this, bases in the Philippines provide possible jumping off places for landing on the coast of China, where it is believed the war against the Japanese will be finally decided, while the Philippines' airfields provide still further bases for the bombing of Japan's industrial cities.

I shall begin my story of the invasion of the Philippines somewhere in the Western Pacific on the night of October 19 last, when with other American and Australian war correspondents I sat in the wardroom of an LST with American Army and Naval officers listening to Tokyo Radio happily telling the world that we were at that moment fleeing back to our base. Five days previously we had turned north from a great American base at Hollandia on the north coast of Dutch New Guinea, a vast convoy of troopships, battleships, cruisers, destroyers, LSTs, LCIs, and the rest of that strange brood of craft designed for amphibious warfare, while squat aircraft carriers were always behind us, sending over their Hellcats on patrol at regular intervals. This great assembly of ships was spread over 450 square miles of ocean, and its size reminded me of a remark made to us by General Walter Kreuger, Commander of the U.S. 6th Army, in his tent at Hollandia, 'We have the stuff to carry this through, and we'll carry it through, come hell or high water.'

An hour or so earlier this evening we had rendezvoused with another great convoy from the Central Pacific, and the whole force of 600 ships had turned west towards Leyte Island, in the centre of the archipelago. It was hot and sweaty, like the nights we have been experiencing. We were wearing full jungle dress and equipment and we lay down to rest on the iron deck with our Yank style tin hats for pillows. Meanwhile, for the past week swarms of aircraft from a strong Task Force commanded by Admiral Halsey had been playing merry hell over the aerodromes of the Philippines from one end of the archipelago to the other. The familiar machine of amphibious warfare had gone into action—the machine perfected in many other landings leading up to this great operation, and always beginning its work with an obliterating air attack. A radio report told us that 1,200 enemy planes had been destroyed in the air and on the ground, and we took some comfort from that.

From the bridge of our LST on the morning of October 23 we watched the most terrific bombardment that had yet been laid down in the Pacific war. The old *Australia,* the *Shropshire,* and the two destroyers *Arunta* and *Warramunga,* which comprised the squadron of the Royal Australian Navy, were not far away from us, taking a full share in the pasting of Japanese positions behind the beach and back in the hills. Dive-bombers from our carrier escorts were hammering away at some enemy concentrations farther down the coast. There were four selected landing places on this part of the east coast of Leyte, and ours was designated in the plans as Red Beach. General MacArthur was going ashore at White Beach, a couple of miles to the north of us. At about 10.30 a.m. the bombardment ceased, and we could see the rockets from the LCIs shooting over the assault craft as they sped into the palm-fringed beach. Our line of LSTs was moving in slowly to keep strictly to its schedule. Then we learned an old lesson once more. In spite of the heavy bombardment, the Japanese opened up with 75s and mortars as the American troops moved into the shore and laid down a screen of shells through which we had to pass. Several of the landing craft were blown out of the water ahead of us. As the LSTs drifted in I saw the two ahead of ours take a number of direct hits and the bridge of one went up in flames. Then we took our first hit, and almost simultaneously we ran aground. We remained fast there for an hour while the Nip plastered us and we shot back with Bofors, and we thought a lot about a load of ammunition beneath us as we sweated out that hour as we have sweated out no hour in HMS *Howe.* When finally we pulled off the sandbar, we were driven out into the bay with several other LSTs, and actually didn't get ashore till next morning. It was while waiting to go ashore that we saw HMAS *Australia* set on fire by a Japanese bomber which hit her bridge.

Although after three days of the Philippines campaign official communiques were saying that the campaign was all over bar the mopping up, it took two months of hard fighting by four divisions to break the last stand made by the Japanese on the western coast of Leyte Island. Landings have since been made on two small islands and now on the main island of Luzon itself, and it is certain that the battle for Luzon will be long and costly. Incidentally, five war correspondents have been killed during the Philippines campaign, and two or three wounded.

Finally there is the interesting question of the Japanese Navy. The whereabouts and intentions of the formidable naval forces Japan is known to possess have been one of the mysteries of the Pacific war, but it now seems clear that she is not prepared to risk its loss in the knockdown drag-out battle until the war reaches the shores of Nippon itself. Japanese naval commanders remember that America has accumulated tremendous naval power in the Pacific, including 100 aircraft carriers and escort carriers, and now that the British Fleet is assembling here also, she will probably be even more cautious. Only four important naval clashes have occurred in the Pacific—in the Coral Sea, north-west of Australia, at Midway, in the Eastern Pacific, in the waters between the Philippines and the Marianas, and off Leyte Island on the third day of the Philippine invasion. Except in the last-named encounter, the Japanese refused to fight their ships, and suffered heavy losses from carrier plane attacks. On Leyte, in the early hours of the morning of the 23rd of October, they narrowly missed getting among our huge fleet of supply vessels and causing untold havoc. Three Task Forces were caught making for Leyte Gulf by Admiral Halsey's fleet and we listened with some anxiety to the thunder of the battle. The Americans suffered the loss of a carrier and damage to two carriers, and lost some destroyers, but crushing losses in battleships, cruisers and destroyers were suffered by the Japanese, and they called off the fight until another day.

There is still plenty of their navy left for the Royal Navy to deal with.

—J.L., War Correspondent, *Melbourne Argus.*

Later, the line book reported:-

When *Howe* took part in a bombardment, Gunner Ward told me that the Captain, H.W.V. McCall DSO, informed them over the Tannoy that they were only doing it because the B.B.C. had announced it had taken place 24 hours before!

14" Salvo Broadside: NZ Herald 2 February 1945

No motion picture ever made, or photograph ever taken, no words spoken or written, can capture the terrific forces which are released when a battleship of today fires her broadside. There is one way and one way only of knowing what they are like, and that is to be on board such a ship when it silently trains its guns on a target, waits for men and instruments that are never seen, to choose their moment, and then explodes with such a crashing thunder of sound, curtain of flame, upheaval of air, great clouds of dirty smoke and reek of cordite that the very world seems to have come to an end.

Extract from United States Fleet Carrier of World War II by Richard Humble

To repel Iceberg, the Japanese had planned a frightening new kamikaze plan: *Kikusui* ('Floating Chrysanthemum'), swamping attacks by a total of 2100 aircraft hoarded for the purpose. There were 300 with the 1st Air Fleet on Formosa, 800 with the 3rd Air Fleet in the Tokyo district, 600 with the 5th Air Fleet on Kyushu and 400 with the 10th Air Fleet on south-west Honshu. The *Kikusui* plan included a one-way seaborne kamikaze mission by the 'Special Sea Attack Force', using the last reserves of fuel oil in what was left of the Japanese Fleet.

The first air attacks hit 5th Fleet when it attacked the Japanese naval bases at Kobe and Kure on 19 March. Bombers damaged *Wasp* and *Franklin*, the latter terribly.

The main weight of the *Kikusui* offensive, however, had yet to fall. The first blow came on 6 April, from no less than 355 kamikazes. Two picket destroyers, two ammunition ships and a tank landing-craft were sunk, and 22 other ships were damaged. On the same day, the doomed 'Special Sea Attack Force' sailed on its one-way mission to the Okinawa beaches. It never stood a chance. Sighted at 0822 on 7 April, 250 miles from Okinawa, *Yamato, Yahagi* and their escorting destroyers came under the hammer of no less than 380 strike aircraft from Mitscher's carriers. The attacks began shortly after noon. *Yahagi* sank at about 1400, *Yamato* 25 minutes later after taking ten torpedo hits—nine of them on the port side, causing damage beyond all control—and six bombs. This brutal execution is usually dignified with the title 'Battle of the East China Sea'. It was the last American attack on an operational Japanese task force at sea, and marks the true closing of the circle begun with the Japanese carrier attack on Pearl Harbor on December 1941. Damage to American carriers on 7 April was limited to the carrier *Hancock*. But the airborne *Kikusui* attacks continued.

On 11 April the kamikazes made a determined effort to attack TF.58, whose carrier fighters were exacting a heavy toll. *Bunker Hill* was badly damaged, and *Enterprise* was damaged again, more heavily, on 13 April and *Intrepid* on the 16th.

By the end of the first week in May, it was clear that the *Kikusui* attacks were losing their edge but there was one more mass attack, on 11 May. For the cost of 72 kamikazes shot down on their way to attack, two got through, sending *Bunker Hill* back for extensive repairs and forcing Mitscher to shift his flag to *Enterprise*. On 12 May, however, while attacking the Kyushu airfields, *Enterprise* was hit again and Mitscher once more shifted his flag, this time to *Randolph*. Never before had the carriers had to take punishment on this scale, but the end was in sight. From 12 May no more *Kikusui* attacks were launched. The last kamikaze attacks of the campaign were launched on 21-22 June, but caused little damage. After an exhausting land battle, Okinawa was finally declared secure on 2 July.

The following are extracts from the line book HMS *Swiftsure*, sent by Captain Ian Garnett, Senior Gunnery Officer to Rear Admiral Destroyers, BPF. *I wish I had room to include all his experiences and adventures. My meetings with him* *confirmed that he should write his own book!—Ed.*

So we came to Manus; at 10.00 on the 18th we passed the boom defences of Seeadler Harbour, and made for an anchorage. Here was our first real Pacific Isle, the first lagoon. At first sight it looked perfect, as beautiful as anything Hollywood had imagined: small islands, surrounded by sparkling yellow sands and snowy surf; coral reefs where the sea laughed loudly, continuously; clear blue water; waving palm trees. Ah, Lord! how we were to grow to loathe the sight of the place; for Hollywood rarely shows the dreadful, sticky, all-enveloping heat (accentuated when everything is battened down, blacked out), the mosquitoes, and the utter boredom of such a place. However, as we anchored, we were still delightfully illusioned, naive; ignorance was bliss!

There was not a great number of American warships in the anchorage, not more than half a dozen all told; but there were some unexpected British ships, ships of Force X, which for some time past had been operating with the Americans. That night the Americans were the hosts, inviting officers and men to their respective clubs and canteens; and there the initial friendship between the Americans and the men of the BPF was formed, a friendship that was to grow daily, as each gradually learned to respect and admire his ally.

Here we stayed until 25th January, landing occasionally on Pitylu Island for a bathe and a bottle of beer, and possibly a coconut if any of us was agile enough to climb the slender palms; swimming from the ship's side in the clean warm water; meeting and fraternising with the Americans; sweating each night. Ashore there was nothing, only an ugly settlement of tin huts., yet the time passed quickly, for we found our own amusement; we challenged *Howe* to a boxing match, and sent a strong team across, under the charge of the P.T.I. In an exciting and blood-thirsty series of duels we were eventually defeated, but by no means disgraced, by 7 matches to 4.

Then everyone became excited upon learning that the ship, in company with two destroyers, was leaving Manus on the 25th for Ulithi. Ulithi! . . . it might have been anywhere. Maps were got out and searched, and the Navigator's yeoman, not to mention the navigator himself, was badgered day and night for information. But whatever our imaginations had conjured up from the magic-sounding name, was as nothing compared to what we saw as we approached the place, on the afternoon of the 27th. Ships, ships—thousands of ships, literally thousands—millions of tons of ships. They stretched in an immense, infinite line, this way, that way. No wonder we had encountered few ships at Manus; here must have been every ship in the U.S. Navy, both merchant and naval. It was unbelievable; we slowly passed down the silent line, passing tankers, cargo ships, battleships, carriers, cruisers, everything, their crews lining the rails to watch us pass, curiously welcomingly. 'Goddam limies, come at last,' we could imagine their thoughts, their jokes, and we all felt vaguely emotional as we looked at our own clean white ensign waving at the gaff. We felt lost in such an ocean of ships. Lights were flashing at us from all sides; we were dazed, bewildered.

For three days we remained there, making friends, all the time marvelling at the ships, their numbers, their cleanliness. We visited them, and in turn entertained them, taking their boasts with a grain of salt and liking them. Their morale was high, for they were shortly leaving to invade Iwo Jima. Yes, that was the answer, it was a vast invasion fleet. On the second night we had an air-raid warning, as a solitary Japanese plane from Yap appeared, on reconnaissance, but nothing developed. And so it was with envy in our hearts, for our allies about to add another page to their country's achievements, that we left the island-dotted lagoon on 30th January, and returned to Manus. Arriving there on 1st February, we learnt that we were about to lose our Commanding Officer, recently promoted Rear Admiral. His relief, according to gossip, was flying from Sydney, and was expected daily. On 4th February he arrived, and at noon on that day, Captain P.V. McLaughlin—now D.S.O.—R.N., became our new Captain. Rear-Admiral Oliver left the ship that same afternoon, to commence his journey to England via Hawaii and America. As his boat drew away from the ship's side, we lined the rails and cheered.

One thought was now present in most of our minds—'Sydney'. And we were not disappointed in our new Captain, for next day we sailed at 21 knots for our 'home from home'. Once again the Jomard Passage was uneventful, and on the morning of 10th February we once again entered the Heads, still smiling in the sun, still full of shrieking gulls (whether they shrieked to warn or to welcome, only those who fell by the wayside can truly say), still the entrance to Sydney Harbour. Forget the Bridge, and surely it is the most beautiful harbour in the world; the crisp wavelets, the eternal sun, the vivacious yachts, the red-roofed houses, the hopeful thoughts. May we not call it **Our** Harbour?

And Woolloomooloo! Dear, dirty, lovely, sordid, desirable Woolloomooloo. We berthed alongside number three wharf for the first time, the first of the all-too-few. And then . . . forty-eight hours leave to each watch. Oh, joys! Through the help of the British Centre, and Miss Marsh in particular (bless her grey hairs!), we all found somewhere to go; Katoomba, Gordon, Killara, Leura, or just plain Sydney; we all found homes; one man even got married. The food, the friends, the entertainment, the fun—how the days sailed past! On the 10th and 11th the remaining units of the BPF arrived, having come straight from their attack upon the Palembang oilfields; the *K.G.V.*, *Black Prince, Indom.*, *Indefat.*, *Euryalus*, cruisers, carriers, battleships, destroyers, all of them had arrived safely. Woolloomooloo was crowded.

Time was growing short now; the sands were steadily running out. We played hard and worked hard, and we began to grow into a united team. We played soccer—alas! we suffered our first defeat ever against a team from *K.G.V.*; we surf-bathed at Bondi and Manly; ten of us became officially engaged; many more came to an understanding—a rapprochement; surely a Rococo of Rococos.

But what about the war? we can hear people asking. No, the war had not been forgotten, not by a long chalk. All this time had been spent preparing for the battle we knew lay ahead, that had to be, must be. The ventilation and living spaces were added to and improved, guns were installed, guns to kill the suicider before he could reach us; the larder was replenished, stocked with sufficient food to last us for three months, ammunition was stowed away in the magazines. Oh, no, we had not forgotten the war!

Neither had the war forgotten us, for on 27th February the fact that the ship was under sailing orders was piped at lunchtime, and the time had come to bid our farewells.

Sakishima Concerto

On 28th February, 1945, that part of the British Pacific Fleet which was to do the actual striking at the enemy and which was known under the American title of Task Force 57—British Fast Carrier Force—sailed from Sydney under the command of Vice-Admiral Sir Bernard Rawlings, flying his flag in *King George V.* Rear-Admiral Sir Philip Vian, in command of the carriers, flew his flag in *Indomitable;* Rear-Admiral Brind, commanding the cruisers, flew his in *Swiftsure,* while Rear-Admiral Edelsten R.A.D., flew his flag in *Euryalus* for the first week of the operations in order to see how his destroyers were getting on before he returned to his more administrative duties in the *Tyne.*

The passage to the Admiralty Islands was occupied with exercises chiefly designed to get us familiar with the American Signal Books, which we were to use throughout the Pacific War, and with manoeuvring the new formations which it was necessary to adopt in a force in which carriers were the end-all and be-all.

The fleet anchored in Seeadler Harbour on 7th March and remained there until the 17th, while other units joined, and employed the time in making final preparations for the forthcoming battle and in waiting for the word 'GO' from Admiral Nimitz. The word came on the 18th and the fleet sailed for Ulithi, where we fuelled on the 21st and 22nd, sailing again the next day. On the 25th the force carried out its first operation of oiling at sea as a fleet, all ships topping up with fuel, and at dawn on 26th March we were in our battle station fifty miles south-east of Sakishima Gunto on the left flank of the U.S. Fifth Fleet, which was about to launch its attack on Okinawa. At 0610 that day the C.A.P. of four Corsairs and twelve Seafires was flown off, and at 0630 twenty Hellcats, 35 Corsairs and two Avengers left the carriers to carry out the first strike.

Thence the routine settled down to two or three days in the operating area flying off continual strikes against the aerodromes and airstrips on the islands with the object of preventing the Japanese staging their aircraft through from Formosa and China to the main battle-front at Okinawa. We would then retire to the southward where, for two days, we would be oiled and replenished by the tankers, ammunition ships, and store ships of the Fleet Train, protected by the sloops and frigates of the Escort Force. On these occasions we would carry out the gunnery practices which the enemy were so reluctant to provide for us, and Admiral Brind frequently transferred to other flagships to attend conferences. Men, mail and provisions were transferred from ship to ship in a bo'sun's chair or bag slung from a jack-stay connecting the two ships—an exciting experience for the individual concerned. Usually an escort vessel came alongside to receive or deliver the goods, but occasionally we went alongside a battleship or aircraft carrier to save time.

It was on Easter Day, 1st April, the day of the initial landings on Okinawa, that we caught our first glimpse of the enemy and fired our first shots in anger, when a kamikaze, or Divine Wind, pilot crashed his plane on to *Indefatigable's* flight deck. The resultant explosion will live for long in our memories, although such explosions were to become distressingly familiar before we were finished. Fortunately *Indefat.'s* casualties were not heavy and the bomb made little impression on her armoured flight deck, so that she was back in action in thirty minutes or so. At the same time another plane scored a near-miss on *Ulster,* flooding her engine room, so that she had to be towed to safety by *Gambia.*

And so it went on. Occasionally the kamikazes got through—much more often they were intercepted miles from the fleet by our fighters and joined their ancestors sooner than they had hoped.

On 11th, 12th and 13th April we shifted our target to the airfields at the northern end of Formosa, which meant that our aircraft had to fly considerable distances over enemy territory before reaching their objectives, but for the remainder of the operation we stuck to Sakishima Gunto.

Swiftsure's job was not wildly exciting, but relaxation was out of the question. The unexpected had always to be expected. For example, at dawn on 13th April there was a grand mix-up. As the first light appeared on the eastern sky the fighter C.A.P. took off and at the same time Air-raid message red was received. Low-flying aircraft could just be seen over the fleet; we opened fire with everything that could see them and were rewarded with a fine blaze in the sky on which several more magazines were expended until someone suggested that the target might be a flare and not a blazing Japanese aircraft. Many swore that both our four-inch and smaller weapons scored hits on an aeroplane, definitely identified by reliable eyewitnesses as either a Judy, a Dinah, an Oscar or any other type and care to think of. The true story appears to be that, as our fighters took off, the Japanese attacked. A Val, which is an aircraft with a fixed undercarriage, came in low and was mistaken for a Hellcat with its wheels down as a sign of distress. It was therefore given a clear run in and rewarded *Indomitable* by dropping a bomb which bounced off the flight deck without exploding and another which did explode but missed the ship. The Hellcat which, attracted by all the gunfire, followed the enemy in, did not have its wheels down and, receiving the full force of the fleet's gunfire, was shot down. No one appears to know for certain whether the Val caught it also. On the whole, our guns had few opportunities of opening fire, but our radar was never late and often first in giving information which enabled the force to carry out its work so successfully.

Although the fleet train had done all and more than was expected of it to keep us fighting fit, it was eventually necessary to retire from the operational area to carry out a major replenishment in harbour. The fleet accordingly spent from 22nd to 30th April in San Pedro Bay, between Samar and Leyte in the Philippines, stocking up with all essentials. The break after so much sea-time was indeed welcome, although there were few leave facilities and the climate was very hot and sticky. A bottle of beer per man per day was, however, available on board.

Empire Salvage *refuelling HMS* Whirlwind *to Starboard and HMS* Illustrious *astern.*
Photo: Frank Manning

The fleet sailed on 1st May, topped up with fuel in the old oiling area on the 3rd, and on the 4th closed Sakishima Gunto once again. But this time, while the carriers and half the cruisers carried out their usual routine, *King George V., Howe, Swiftsure* and *Gambia,* screened by small cruisers and destroyers, closed Myako Shima to knock out the airfields and the radar and wireless stations by gunfire. *Swiftsure,* operating two miles inshore of the battleships and followed by *Gambia,* carried out a very successful bombardment for eight minutes of Notura airstrip, which was clearly visible from the ship and on which all our shells were seen to explode. The other ships were equally successful, and even *Euryalus* and *Black Prince,* on the wing of a screen, managed to get off good shoots. Unfortunately we heard that the carriers, denuded of so much radar and gun protection, had been attacked in our absence by kamikazes and that *Formidable* had been hit and damaged. We accordingly had to finish off the bombardment as quickly as possible and rejoin the remainder of the force at high speed. There we found that *Formidable* was back to full operational efficiency again.

V.E. Day was spent in the oiling area, but, except that the main brace was spliced, it made little difference to our daily round, and our rejoicing had to be confined to very reasonable limits.

From then until the end of the operation we were given a more interesting job, being stationed in daytime twelve miles from the fleet in the direction in which the enemy was liable to appear, with the object of intercepting any very low-flying aircraft. Accompanied by only one destroyer, there can be no denying that we did feel very lonely at first, but we soon got used to it and, strange to relate, not a single attack developed on the fleet while we were there. The Okinawa campaign was drawing to its successful conclusion and the supply of Japanese aircraft was rapidly running out, so that they had none to spare for anything except the main battle. At night we were stationed on the destroyer screen prepared to attack the intefering U-boat with the best of them, but the Japanese submarines foolishly did not play any part in the campaign.

Thus the time wore on until the last strike flew on at sunset on 25th May, and the fleet, with all bombs, provisions, and stores expended, and with prickly heat at its height, left this operational area for the last time. Admiral Nimitz told us in no uncertain terms that we had done our stuff in the highest traditions of the British Navy and that we had played a very important part in the campaign which had brought the war to the very door-step of Japan. Although the credit for our success belonged almost entirely to the carriers, *Indomitable, Victorious, Illustrious, Indefatigable* and *Formidable,* we were proud to be able to say that we had done all we could to help, that we had had a slap at the Jap, and, we hoped, with our guns and radar, assisted in the protection of more valuable ships.

And so the fleet sailed off to Sydney to replenish and give rehabilitation leave, leaving C.S.4 and Swiftsure to hold the fort in the forward area and to introduce the new arrivals to the delights of tropical warfare.

The battles of Truk and Sydney by A.D.H.J. and P.G.R.

On 30th May, 1945, *Swiftsure* arrived in Manus on completion of Operation 'Iceberg'. During the spell in that delightful tropical resort a certain amount of sport was in progress on Pitylu, and hands were employed under 'Pitylu Pete,' alias Lt. Cdr. Mathers, in the construction of better and bigger sports grounds.

The ship celebrated its first birthday on 2nd June. A good time was had by all, and as the soup was placed on the Ward Room tables for the Anniversary Dinner, the Radar got a 'ping' on an unidentified seagull, and Flash Red (no skylark) was piped.

During this period *Implacable* and *Newfoundland* caught up with us pioneers of the British Pacific Fleet, all set to join in the frolic, and so a large-scale exercise was planned. We all thought this was 'a jolly good show, what! . . . ' and the 'buzz-spreaders' duly got to work.

On 12th June, C.S.4 (Rear-Admiral E.J.P. Brind) transferred his flag to *Implacable,* the better to run the operation, and in company with her, *Newfoundland, Achilles, Uganda, Ruler* and the 24th D.F., we sailed under a veil of mystery and excitement. Naturally, the excitement reached fever pitch when it was announced that the Force, *per coelis et per mare,* were to have the single honour of bombarding that Gibraltar of the East, that Scapa Flow of the Pacific, the Truk group of islands situated in the Carolines. Some of the wise old men shook their grey (and/or bald) heads and said that it was too great an endeavour, as it was known by them that there were at least three Coast Defence Batteries to return our fire.

On 14th June the air strikes commenced, with devastating success, and early on the 15th, leaving the 'flat-tops' afar off, we sailed to within two miles of those infamous shores of Truk, which lay basking in the tropical sun. The scenes on board were traditional of the British race—silent men, tight-lipped, with grim determination written on their faces, glided silently about their tasks. In the turrets, the men, in their anti-flash gear, looked like ghosts from some medieval tale.

At about 10.00 the air was rent by a shattering roar as the 6-inch opened fire, soon to be backed up by the crashes of the 4-inch. Our opening broadsides reached the shallow water. (Rumour has it that throughout the island bathers were piped to clear the water). By then the shore batteries were discernible. Some of the shots from some of the ships soon started hitting the shore, and success was rife. There was not a sign of a Nip: the gun-sweepers apparently had a day off, as they did not even 'Uncover Guns'. It was now apparent that our shots were going wide, and it was not till later that it was discovered that a pin had fallen out of the 'speed across' box of tricks in the T.S.!! (Entirely the fault of the makers!).

Having reduced Truk to a state of shambles by this time, the Force withdrew under a smoke screen, which, unfortunately, blew the wrong way, and the general atmosphere quietened down, except for a few friendly shots from the 4-inch guns at the odd Avenger that passed.

(N.B.—It is interesting to note at this juncture that a battleship, not at that time East of Suez, was to have repeated this inimitable operation had she arrived on the station in time. We were, however, delighted that she was in Sydney to celebrate V.J. Day!!!).

And so we said farewell to Truk and sailed peacefully back to Manus for a well-earned rest and to restore shattered tissues. This may seem like 'Line-shooting', but it must be constantly borne in mind that we were about to embark on the biggest, longest and most important operation that *Swiftsure* was ever to know—the 'Seven-weeks Battle of Sydney', otherwise known as 'Operation Beer and Big Eats, etc.'.

It was on 17th June that we arrived in Manus, and on that day C.S.4 rejoined us, only to transfer his flag, on the 19th to *Newfoundland*, as we were to be a private ship for this next great encounter.

Well refreshed by our stay in this atoll, or sleepy lagoon, or whatever you call the place, with bathing under the most romantic conditions, we set sail for the land of Diggers and Kangaroos on the 20th June. The journey down was without incident, and the ship's company was employed mainly in the buffing up of their 'tiddly suits' in preparation for 'H' Hour in 'Our 'arbour'.

It was at 1200 on 26th June that the famous Sydney harbour bridge was sighted, and a very welcome sight it was, too, to the ship's company, thirsting for those amenities which only a large city can provide. Yes, literally thirsting! It seemed that all the watch ashore was crammed into the first liberty boat, which left the ship at 1600, which may have been due to the fact that previous experience had taught us that all the hotel bars closed at the uncivilized hour of 6 p.m.

Extracts from HMNZS *Achilles* by Jack Harker sent to me by Roger Kittering ex HMS *Swiftsure*

Achilles sailed southeast from Colombo on 9 December 1944 in company with the escort carriers *Atheling* and *Battler,* and 1943-built destroyers *Wager* and *Whelp,* joining up at sea next day with Rear Admiral E.J.P. Brind, CB, CBE, aboard his flagship of the 4th CS, *Swiftsure,* with two more escort carriers *Fencer* and *Striker,* and three destroyers. *Achilles'* thirteen years made her their grandmother . . .

HMAS *Shropshire, Hobart* and *Australia* were working as an integral part of the US 7th Fleet in General MacArthur's area; and the British TF.112, with its mass of destroyers, frigates, sloops, minesweepers, and fleet back-up ships of escort carriers etc., made the fleet fairly self-contained.

In a fighter sweep over Ishigaki airfield after the initial surprise, Squadron Leader Lieutenant (A) A.B. MacRae, RNZNVR, reeled with shock when a flak splinter bedded in his right thigh. He recovered quickly and continued leading the attack until his 1839 Squadron resumed its patrol. He then flew the 100-mile return trip alone, encouraged by *Indomitable's* flight-direction officer.

When the British Pacific Fleet arrived in San Pedro Bay, Leyte, on 23 April it had refuelled and stored six times from its fleet train in 31 days at sea. No boats were available in the crowded anchorage for libertymen, so Admiral Rawlings ordered a bottle of beer a day for every man in the fleet.

On returning to the fight, TF.57 found enemy aircraft again using airfields previously devastated, and a considerable flow of planes heading for the battle on Okinawa. At 1205 on 4 May the light cruisers and six destroyers steamed inshore at 24 knots to bombard Miyako Island while being screened by the four carriers' combat patrols. At 1205 on 4 May the light cruisers, *Euryalus* and *Black Prince* shelled A/A batteries at Nobara airfield, while *Howe* and *King George V* stood offshore at 25,000 yards to pummel Hirara runways and installations with 195 rounds of 14". *Swiftsure* and *Gambia* pounded Nobara for almost an hour from 18,000 yards, and *Uganda* concentrated on Sukuma airstrip.

And while the carriers were left without the big ships' concentrated barrages, kamikazes did their best to take advantage of this. Twenty of them approached and then split into groups with some acting as decoys, drawing fighters after them to allow others a chance to penetrate from cloud cover. One dived vertically at *Formidable* through an umbrella of short-barrage, crashed among parked planes and started fierce fires which destroyed a Corsair and 10 Avengers. Its bomb burst and killed eight men, injured 47, and punched a ten-foot wide by two-foot deep depression in the armoured steel flight deck. A large splinter tore a two-foot hole in the centre, ruptured a boiler-room steampipe and finished in a fuel tank in the double-bottom. Barriers on the flight-deck received damaged and radar gear went out of action.

Two more kamikazes tried to follow their leader down, but blew to bits at a safe height when gunned by *Indefatigable's* Seafires. A third diverted towards *Indomitable* who turned hard and shot it into flames; it cannoned off the forward port edge of the flight-deck and exploded while sinking. *Indomitable* now converged all her guns on yet another suicide bomber also being hammered by *Quality*. This one hit the sea as a ball of searing flame 30 feet off *Indomitable's* starboard bow, without doing damage or causing casualties aboard.

By now, fighters required more fuel and the carriers turned upwind to take them on, those from *Formidable* queueing to land on *Indomitable* and *Indefatigable* who flew off covering interceptors which sent two more kamikaze pilots straight to heaven. At 1420 the bombardment force rejoined and stopped firing above *Victorious* while her Corsairs tore the tail assembly off a suicide bomber. Its pilot must have changed his mind about dying for the Emperor. He parachuted (unusual to have one?) down, to be left 100 miles out from Sakishima as the fleet sped by; still under attack. One of his flight spiralled down trailing smoke from 24,000 feet and, moments later, Seafires from *Indefatigable* brought down three out of four others, and Corsairs off *Victorious* bagged the fourth. Fourteen enemy planes went down over the fleet that day for the loss of four British fighters.

Next day's operations proceeded more peacefully for TF.57, and Sub-Lieutenant (A) I.F. Stirling earned the DSC by chasing a Japanese fighter for 300 miles before bringing him down from 30,000 feet, a remarkable achievement according to Admirals Vian and Rawlings who both recommended the award.

Formidable was again in operation, having controlled all fires quickly and filled the hole and depression in her flight-deck with rapid-hardening concrete. Her arresters and barriers were being hard worked, and her radar equipment had been repaired within hours.

The fleet now retired to TF.112, replenishing aircraft, refuelling, completing with ammunition, and transferring 36 wounded from *Formidable* to *Striker*, who took them to Leyte where they were put aboard the New Zealand Hospital Ship *Maunganui*. *Striker* then took aboard more fighters and returned to the Task Force train.

Bad weather and zero visibility near the Sakishimas hampered flying in mid-May while we in *Achilles* were coming up from New Zealand via Sydney and Manus. As soon as it cleared sufficiently for pilots to tell the difference between sea and sky, 71 tons of bombs and 64 rocket projectiles screeched on to Miyako and Ishigaki airfield targets. Fighter and fast-bomber pilots were now devising new tactics for destroying enemy planes discovered to be hidden in caves, and it became hard to tell who was who, with crazy young New Zealanders and other Commonwealth pilots flying with their underbellies mowing grass while racing in to launch rockets at openings in hillsides.

Two days later, with the fleet back at Sakishima operational area, we listened on the TBS American inter-ship radio to our British Fleet manoeuvring by American jargon and codes, heard over my English-manufactured VHF equipment the dry humour of fighter and bomber pilots going in under the squadron leaders' directions to bomb selected targets, the matter-of-fact quiet urgency of Corsair pilots telling Avengers: 'Just keep going as you are Frank, there's one looking up your tail,' Then: 'You can forget that bastard matey, he's gone to see his ancestors'.

'Thanks Alan, my shout tonight'.

And so it went through to the last days of Sakishima Gunto. Five strikes hammered Miyako, several bombed Ishigaki, and the score-board read more favourably yet for the British Pacific Fleet's achievements. We put the canvas muzzles back over our guns and sailed with *Howe*, the carriers, cruisers and most of the destroyers to Manus, while *King George V*, escorted by *Tenacious*, *Troubridge* and *Termagent*, took Admiral Rawlings to Marianas for a conference at Guam with Admiral Nimitz in his C-in-C Pacific Headquarters.

During the Sakishima air raids in support of Okinawa landings and consolidation, TF.57 operated offshore for 62 days, it flew 4852 sorties, dropped 900 tons of bombs and discharged hundreds of rocket-missiles, gulped 87,000 tons of fuel from TF.112, and successfully came through numerous kamikaze and more standard types of Japanese air attacks.

John Short RM on HMS *Swiftsure* wrote:

Captain (later Rear Admiral) R.O. Oliver, CBE, DSC was the first commanding officer. On 4th February 1945 Captain (also later Rear Admiral) P.V. Maclaughlin succeeded him.

On 15th June we bombarded Truk in the Carolines but the shots were falling short due to a dislodged fin in the 'box of tricks' in the T.S. This was a fault due to the makers.

Rear Admiral E.J.P. Brind hoisted his flag on the ship. He was very quiet, having lost his wife at home in an enemy air raid.

I was employed in the wardroom as an attendant but my gunnery station was 4″ guns crew and later I qualified as an anti-aircraft 3rd class rate for close range weapons.

Of the officers I was personally attached to I well remember five US Navy Liaison Officers. I had four in one large cabin originally meant to be the forward wardroom. One of them thought I was a Scotsman. The senior one was not very popular and left little notes in his cabin drawers telling me to keep out.

The first O.C.R.M., Captain F.A.T. Halliday, was son of General Sir Lewis Halliday V.C. His second in command, a Canadian Lieut. Dougie Craig, did have some character and was liked very much. In December 1945 Captain Hathaway Jones succeeded Halliday and was about the tallest officer in the Royal Marines.

Sergeant 'Crash' Naylor, a Lancastrian, had a dry sense of humour and Steve Ledwer was another comical type. Sergeant Alfie Smith from Essex later became an instructor and soccer player for England. He was very popular.

Of the junior N.C.O.s 'Shifty' Tyson very quiet and sombre saying little and yet proved he could be useful to the young lads in the detachment.

The chief Gunners Mate was C.P.O. Reuter D.S.M. very tall, but the real example of efficiency. He was later in the Houses of Parliament as an usher. There was C.P.O. Brown, a driver, never without a pipe in his mouth.

The navigating officer who doubled up as First Lieutenant, Lt. Cdr. P.D.G. Mathers was really a laugh. One morning whilst serving breakfast in the wardroom as I went near him he put his arms above his head and knocked the whole lot across the table and damaged Lt. Cdr. Munford's wristwatch.

Commander Luce (later First Sea Lord) had a good raucous laugh but Ronnie Munford was serious about it. I was on a Brains Trust with Lt. Cdr. P.D.G. Mathers.

Lt. Cdr. I.L.M. McGeoch DSO, DSC was squadron operations officer to Admiral Brind and I looked after him for a time. He was an ex-submariner having Commanded the *Splendid* in the Mediterranean and he had been a prisoner of war but escaped.

I painted his cabin duck egg blue and this caused a few eyebrows to lift but he often asked me to stay in his cabin and talk to him on any subject. As a matter of fact after he left the ship he left behind a blue pullover. I had this for a few years and in 1956 returned it to him when he commanded the depot ship *Adamant*. He invited me and my family to the ship but I was on the move and never did see him again. He later became a NATO commander in the rank of Vice-Admiral.

As regards Admiral Fraser, in the wardroom one evening a film with Ann Ziegler and Webster Booth was being shown. There were some Austrian cavalry present and Admiral Fraser remarked to the O.C.R.M. 'Now beat the retreat like that major'. This raised a few laughs.

On 25th January 1945 Vice Admiral Edelston hoisted his flag on the ship. It was on 15th April 1946 that Admiral Fraser hoisted his flag and we went to Shanghai, Amoy Ching Wang-Tao Kure (2nd May) Yokohama (5th-11th May) and Kobe.

We did get to Nagasaki and saw the destruction by the second atom bomb but I suppose one can never forget the three days in Peking as we were transported everywhere by United States Marines.

There was a National Savings Publicity Parade in Sydney in August 1945 and the Prime Minister of New South Wales was there to inspect us as there were combined R.M. bands including *Colossus* and *Vengeance.*

I shall never forget the rehearsal parade we did for that as we marched up Elizabeth Street and all the windows opened and everyone cheered. They had seen so much of the Americans. Here was a British military band swinging along to a Kenneth Alford tune. It made us feel 10 feet tall!

A lot of what we picked up at Hong Kong was used including blankets but I had some cameras and several wristwatches. The latter never lasted long as they had been repaired with cement.

Many of us caught sandfly fever there and I was laid up for about 10 days. At Shanghai we had a corporal and four marines doing guard duty at the British Consulate. We marched on St. George's day 1946—what a shambles. Kids were all over the place, but we made it to the consulate grounds and an inspection by a Chinese general.

There were some of the detachment at Yokohama—doing guard duty at the British Embassy. The Bosun had a party working in the construction of the White Ensign Club and a good effort it was.

Mr. C.S. Forester, the distinguished naval author was on the ship for a few days in 1945 and was writing one of his 'Hornblower' stories.

Commander W.L.M. Brown DSC relieved Commander Ince on 1st July 1945. We took part in the King's Birthday Parade at Singapore June 1946.

I was in Lt. Commander Maglock's cabin on August 15th 1946, VJ Day at Sydney when all the ships sirens started blowing. The Duke of Gloucester was visiting the battleship *Anson* as we were at Woolloomooloo.

We sailed later laden with everything, but what scenes on the dockside. I was with a sailor from my native home Whitby and some of the young ladies would not let go of their boyfriends. One of the characters and a friend of mine, a marine called Jimmy Price from Liverpool who when photographed with a fez on his head had a bit of King Farouk about him. He was also like him as regards the fair sex! Another called Muggeridge, alias the 'Mole', was sitting round the 4 inch guns with a cigarette dangling from his mouth. Who can ever forget these blokes?

From Lt. (A) RNVR J.F. Shaw, 1770 Sqn., HMS *Indefatigable*

On the 10th February 1945, *Indefatigable* dropped anchor in Sydney harbour. I was directed to repair on board without delay and proceeded to Man-o-War steps in the harbour with my two large trunks and a lot of other clobber, where I waited for some form of transport.

After a while a launch arrived and a gentleman in civvies stepped ashore. He said to me "Where are you going?"

I replied, "To the *Indefatigable*".

Whereupon he turned to the coxswain and said "Take this officer to the *Indefatigable*". On the way to the ship I discovered that the man in civvies was in fact Vice Admiral Sir Philip Vian and I was in the Admiral's Barge!

Lt. Desmond Wilkey, Senior Observer of 1770 Squadron happened to be officer of the watch, and at the approach of the Admiral's Barge he made preparations for the boarding of some person of high rank, possibly the Vice Admiral himself. He didn't realize, until we were close enough in, that all he was about to receive was one Sub. Lt. Jim Shaw.

It was a memorable way to join one's ship and one's squadron.

Rescue Mission

During Operation Iceberg a Corsair pilot was reported to have been seen floating in a narrow stretch of water between two small islands of the Sakishima Gunto.

A section of two Firefly aircraft of 1770 Squadron from *Indefatigable* was detailed to escort a Walrus from *Victorious* and undertake a rescue attempt.

I was the Observer in the leading Firefly and Lt. Ian Martin was my pilot. The second Firefly was piloted by Sandy Sinclair with Bill Croasdell as his Observer. In order not to reveal the position of the Fleet, we were briefed to rendezvous over a submarine before altering course to the islands.

The last minute position of the carrier and wind direction and speed were always displayed on a large board on the superstructure and one had to be quick to make note of these details as we flew past the board on take off. Then as we circled the carrier to form up, came the hasty plotting on my chart of the carrier's latest position and course, and our initial track and course to the submarine.

We had ten tenths cloud below us long before we got anywhere near the Islands. I was feeding Ian Martin with periodical E.T.A.s and when this reduced to just 1.5 minutes he said 'We'll go down through this stuff and see'. We came out below the cloud at about 2000 ft. and there were the two islands directly below us. I remember feeling elated and Bill Croadsdell in the other Firefly saying on the R.T. 'Good Plotting'.

We could see the Corsair pilot in the drink and the Walrus went in to land as close to him as possible. Fire was directed at the Walrus and AA guns opened up at us. The Fireflies attacked the gun positions whilst the Walrus got the pilot on board. The Walrus took off labouriously into wind and in doing so had to fly low over one of the islands, but got away safely.

For security reasons we again 'dog-legged' home, having to rendezvous over one of our cruisers before changing course for the Fleet.

We were all so pre-occupied in those days, I never did discover the name of the pilot we rescued.

From Carrier Operations in World War II by J.D. Brown:

The BPF—*Indomitable, Indefatigable, Victorious* and *Illustrious,* supported by *King George V, Howe, Swiftsure, Gambia, Black Prince, Euryalus, Argonaut* and 11 destroyers, left Ulithi on 23rd March with orders to keep enemy airfields in the Sakishima Gunto group of islands out of action while the Americans secured first the Kerama Retto, some 15 miles from Okinawa, and then Okinawa itself. Sakishima Gunto lies to the south west of the main Ryukuy group, and on the islands of Miyako, Ishigaki and Mihara there were six airfields which were in a favourable position to act as staging posts for aircraft based in Formosa to pass through en route for Okinawa, as well as ideally situated for a positive contribution to the defence of the main target area for 'Iceberg'. The British Pacific Fleet was planned to mount the heaviest possible strikes against the airfields, concentrating on the cratering of the runways, to render them useless. Operations were planned for two-day strike serials alternating with two-day replenishment serials; while the BPF were off-station, the USN CVEs *Santee, Suwanee, Chenango* and *Steamer Bay,* Task Group 52.1.3. took over. With their smaller aircraft complements the CVEs were not so efficient in the suppression role, a fact which became evident as the Japanese counter-attacked in mid-April.

On 26th March 1945, the first strikes were launched from a position some 100 miles to the south of the Sakishima Gunto, attacking the airfields on the two main islands. Avengers were armed with 4 × 500 lb medium capacity bombs for the task of breaking up the runways and destroying 'hard' installations, such as hangars, buildings and fuel dumps, while *Indefatigable's* Fireflies used cannon and rockets against the heavy flak emplacements. Corsairs and Hellcats provided escort and target CAP, strafing targets of opportunity during and after the strikes. Fleet Combat Air Patrol was provided mainly by the Seafires, whose limited endurance detracted from their value as strike escort aircraft. Avenger strikes were flown, on average four times daily, with up to 40 aircraft involved in each. Some squadrons flew sorties by single Avengers, striking at targets of opportunity of the islands and achieving a certain amount of surprise. Additional Corsair and Hellcat dive-bombing sorties were flown, so that the enemy got little respite from dawn to dusk.

Despite the effort, the airfields were unrewarding targets; the runways were constructed out of crushed coral, of which there was an unlimited supply, and they were easily repaired overnight. The flak, of all calibres, was intense and very accurate while there were few aircraft on the airfields, but more in the air, either leaving Okinawa or flying in from Formosa. The result was that after the first serial of two days only about a dozen enemy aircraft had been destroyed on the ground, while the target CAP had shot down 28 Japanese aircraft. 19 Fleet Air Arm were lost to enemy action, principally flak, in this period.

Losses were made good by the replenishment CVEs during the re-fuelling days, the latter giving the aircrew some rest before the next serial. Aircrew losses were lighter than might be expected, thanks to an excellent rescue service provided by USN 'Lifeguard' submarines, destroyers from the Fleet screen and the two Walrus amphibians embarked in *Victorious* for this purpose *(known as Darby and Joan. Ed)*. Fighter cover for the Fleet Train came from the Hellcats of the Assault CVE *Speaker,* but during replenishment periods the fleet carriers provided Avenger A/S patrols, maintaining four fighters at readiness on deck to back up the CAP from the escort carrier.

A typhoon warning resulted in the BPF spending three days over their first RAS (Replenishment At Sea). On 31st March, D-1 for the invasion of Okinawa, the Fleet carriers were back on station and the same round of strikes at the Sakishima airfields was recommenced. On 1st April, D-Day, the Japanese began to react strongly, combining conventional bombing with the first Kamikaze attacks encountered by the BPF. One suicide aircraft broke through the CAP and hit *Indefatigable* at the base of the island; instead of reducing her

07.35 Easter Sunday 1st April 1945.
The first Kamikaze to hit the BPF strikes HMS Indefatigable
Photo: Captain Paddy Vincent

flight and hangar decks to a blazing shambles, the attack resulted in a short inconvenience while the debris was cleared from the armoured deck, the ship being operational within an hour of the attack. *(35 minutes. Ed).* Fleet Air Arm strikes continued on 2nd April, the Fleet withdrawing that evening to replenish. Despite several attacks on the BPF, the only casualty was the destroyer *Ulster,* which had to be towed to Leyte after incurring Kamikaze damage. *(Result of a near miss. Ed).*

A further three-day serial of operations followed, from 5th to 7th April. On 6th, Kamikazes again attacked, but the only damage inflicted was by a glancing blow on *Illustrious'* island, causing no loss in the carrier's efficiency. While the BPF were refuelling on 8th April, the USN Attack carrier *Hancock* was put out of action by a Kamikaze and as it was believed that many of the Kamikaze aircraft were based in N. Formosa, Admiral Spruance requested that Task Force 57 should strike at their bases. The BPF, scheduled for only one more serial off Sakishima, willingly accepted the assignment, which was less harzardous for the armoured Fleet carriers than it would have been for the wooden-decked American carriers.

The carriers were in the launching position at dawn on 11th April, but bad weather caused a delay of 24 hours, and even when the strikes, totalling 48 Avengers supported by 40 Corsairs, did get airborne there was still a considerable amount of low cloud over the airfield targets. A few Corsairs did manage to find and attack the airfields, while the Avengers bombed the port of Kiirun, inflicting severe damage on the docks, shipping, and a chemical plant. Later in the day the Avengers did manage to find an airfield, cratering the runways while the fighters strafed aircraft on the ground and airfield installations. The strikes met with no enemy air opposition on the 12th, but two Fireflies found a formation of five Japanese bombers heading towards Okinawa and shot down four, the fifth escaping damage. *(See **Sakishima** for pilots first hand account.—Ed.)* That evening an enemy attack was detected heading for the Fleet; an efficient Hellcat and Corsair CAP shot down four, damaged half a dozen, and drove off the remainder before they could reach the ships.

The strikes continued in improved weather conditions on 13th April and although the enemy did intercept the Avengers, none was lost, while the escorts destroyed eight more Japanese fighters.

From 'The War with Japan' by Charles Bateson

On April 1, after the heaviest concentration of naval gunfire ever to support a landing—44,825 rounds of 5-in, and larger shells, 32,000 rockets and 22,500 mortar shells—the Americans came ashore on beaches north and south of Hagushi, at the mouth of the Bishi River, on Okinawa's west coast. Simultaneously the 2nd Marine Division made a feint landing, which it repeated next day, against beaches on the south-east coast. Opposition to the main landings, which were made with III Amphibious Corps on the left and

XXIV Corps on the right, was slight, Ushijima making no attempt to defend the beaches. By nightfall the Americans held a beachhead 15,000 yards long and in places 5,000 yards deep, and they had 60,000 men ashore. Next day they had no difficulty in driving through to the east coast, on the shores of Nakagusuku Bay.

Progress in northern Okinawa was rapid. As they advanced northward the marines met only scattered resistance until they reached the rugged hills of Motobu Peninsula, where opposition hardened. Even so, it was quickly overcome after some heavy fighting and by the 18th northern Okinawa was officially considered secured.

The main Japanese defences were in the south, where Ushijima had constructed formidable fortifications amid the steep hills and narrow ravines around Shuri, north-east of Naha. The XXIV Corps, reinforced by the floating reserve, the 27th Division, was bloodily repulsed before these strong, well-defended positions, and it was May 21, after fierce fighting and slow progress before the Americans broke through to the inner ring of Shuri's defensive positions. Then heavy rain—twelve inches fell in the last ten days of May—greatly hampered operations, so that practically no progress was made for some days. On the 31st, however, Shuri, the second town in Okinawa, was captured. It had been relentlessly shelled and bombed and the entire town had been reduced to rubble. The Japanese made an orderly withdrawal to organize another line of defence further south, and another month was required to dispose of them. By July 2 the Okinawa campaign was at an end.

While the operations on land were proceeding slowly to their inevitable conclusion, the Fifth Fleet and the shipping off Okinawa had been under frequent air attack, particularly from kamikaze pilots. Spruance's flagship, the cruiser *Indianapolis* (9,800, 1932), was put out of action on March 31 and, after temporary repairs, had to sail for the United States. On April 6, when 355 kamikazes flew missions, two destroyers acting as picket boats were sunk and others damaged, but the Japanese pilots were unable to get through to Mitscher's carriers. However, 200 reached Okinawa, where they blew up 2 loaded ammunition ships, sank two small vessels and damaged 22 naval ships.

From Jack Collins HMS *Quality*

Quality had developed engine room trouble, we were tansferred to the Oiling Force screen. We had a quiet time back in the fuelling area and our first taste of oiling at sea by buoyant hose method in rough seas. On the 28th the Fleet returned to the fuelling area, having encountered no opposition. *Quality* now rejoined Task Force 57 and on March 31st a series of Air strikes were flown off from the carriers against airfields. Everything was quiet over the Fleet. Air strikes were continued on the following day, but at 0730 we had our first attack from Japanese Aircraft; three were shot down; one made a suicidal crash landing upon the *Indefatigable's* flight deck and burst into flames causing some casualties but only slight damage. *Ulster* suffered 'near miss' bomb damage which caused flooding in her engine and boiler rooms—she had to be taken in tow by *Gambia*. This attack undoubtedly shook everyone into a state of alertness. Strikes were carried out in the following forenoon before returning to the oiling area. This operation had been *Quality's* first experience of an American Cruising Disposition—the main body of battleships and carriers surrounded by an inner circle of cruisers and an outer circular screen of destroyers, giving complete freedom to manoeuvre during flying operations and air or submarine attack.

Air strikes were resumed on the 6th; in the evening enemy aircraft were over the Fleet; one just hit *Illustrious'* Island with its wingtip and crashed into the sea, causing neither damage nor casualties, another plane diving out of the low clouds swept over *Quality* who opened fire with her Pom Pom, so indicating position of enemy aircraft to our fighters who soon shot it down in flames—the plane burned on the water for several minutes. Further air strikes were carried out on the 7th and no attacks were made on the Fleet. The next three days were spent in the fuelling area. On the 12th and 13th our planes objectives were airfields and railways in Northern Formosa. Japanese aircraft made further attacks on the Fleet. On the 14th we oiled again, and parting company with the Fleet, proceeded to Leyte with *Illustrious* and *Urania*. The harbour formed by islands had been made into a temporary advanced fleet base by the arrival of ships of the Fleet Train. On arrival on the 16th *Urania* and *Quality* proceeded alongside the *Tyne* for boiler cleaning. On the 22nd the Fleet arrived in harbour. A run ashore provided few attractions and entailed an hour and a half's boat trip each way. Soap, cigarettes and old clothes could be bartered for grass skirts, straw hats and purses fashioned out of coloured beans; a couple of cans of Yankee beer were the sole refreshment in that humid climate. This week saw the amazing innovation of beer issued on board to the ratings—6 bottles per man per week.

Extracts from *Indefatigable* Diary, sent by P.O. Peter Bonney

20.03 Arrive Ulithi. Massive assembly of American ships and landing craft at anchor filling the entire sea from shore to horizon.

One day the ship's company were mustered at the forward end of the flight deck to be addressed by Admiral Vian, during which he made a despairing gesture when he pointed to the vast American Fleet, evidently referring to the Lilliputian part the British Pacific Fleet had in the Pacific campaign. Continuing at length he said, 'Thank God; there exists today that mutual understanding between officers and men'. Several murmured disaffections could be heard and I wondered why he made the point. Certainly the *Indefat.* was a good ship but whether he meant the BPF or Navy generally was not clear.

It was only after I had attended my first *Indefat.* reunion on 31st March/1st April 1989 that Admiral Vian's proposition of forty five years earlier came clearer to me:

The spirit of the *Indefat.* like so many great ships that had been broken up to face a lonely protracted death, had never really faded, but lingered on in the minds and hearts of all those remaining men who had served in her. Here at last the underlying nature of our wartime association between 2500 officers and men lay revealed, unfettered by the everyday discipline of the ship.

Was this then, the mutual understanding to which Admiral Vian referred? Paradoxically, it could not be, for given the nature of service life, a line of demarcation must always exist between officers and men. That I discern is the mutual understanding between the two; for the effective discharge of executive order and action. Respect and fellowship is not a mutual understanding; it is the knitting grace that only a well run ship might be endowed with. It is probably this that our Admiral Vian really meant so warm heartedly and of that, the *Indefat.* had reason to serve. Commander Whitfeld saw to that and all the men with him.

12.05 Strike, but quiet today. Message to tail destroyer *Quiberon,* 'Keep our tail from heavenly drafts', to which the immediate reply was, 'Yes, we are used to taking blasts'.

From Lt. Cdr. Ivor H.S. Morgan RD RNR (Ret)., at the time a S/Lt.(A) RNVR, pilot in 894 Squadron

The sun shone in a cloudless sky at 0500 on 1st April, 1945, as I climbed the various ladders leading to the bridge. I was not to fly that day, being temporarily grounded by an ear infection. My job that particular morning was that of Duty Pilot, to supervise flight deck movements—including the ranging and striking down of aircraft—noting the number of each as it took off (and, hopefully, as it returned), acting as liaison between Captain and Air Branch and generally assisting Commander (Flying), Cdr. Pat Humphries RN, known universally as 'Wings'. Our control position was a sponson on the side of the main navigating bridge and connected thereto by a sliding, armoured door.

Well, I mused, if one had to perform ground duties as opposed to flying, being 'Duty Boy' was as good as any, for through the doorway one could hear various departments reporting to the bridge and hear the captain's reactions.

"FDO-Bridge" came the voice of Lt.Cdr. Ian Easton, Senior Fighter Direction Officer.

"Bridge."

"Contact bearing 300 deg.—28 miles, closing."

This sort of thing happened day after day. Radar would trace the contact until the range was about 18 miles, when it would vanish from the screen.

'Radar boys with their fingers in again', we would say with some lack of charity, to which those much maligned operators would reply that either the contact had gone down low so as to be below the radar umbrella or perhaps it had been a weather phenomenon—thunder storm, for instance. (Or a rather large seagull perching on the aerial we would add).

'Wings' greeted me affably and nodded to the flight deck below, where aircraft were being ranged for a strike on Ishigaki. Grumman Avengers, heavy TBR's needing maximum take-off run at the stern, Fairey Fireflies next, each armed with cannon and eight rocket projectiles, and Seafires in front. These relatively light fighters could become airborne, at a pinch, in 60 feet, given a 15 knot wind over the deck.

As we waited for the fleet to turn into wind, I was struck by the fact that only the captain was correctly dressed in naval uniform. In order to afford some sort of protection against fire we all wore long trousers and long-sleeved shirts—blue for the ratings, khaki drill for the officers. Dominating the scene was the resplendent figure of Captain Quentin Dick Graham, DSO, Royal Navy, in his high-necked Number Ten tropical white uniform, complete with medal ribbons from 1914 onwards.

'Wings' gave the order to start-up and soon the aircraft were roaring up the deck. Everything went smoothly, not a single machine was U/S and the spare aircraft remained on the deck until such times as they would be taxied forward preparatory to landing-on.

Pat Humphries intimated that he was going in search of some breakfast and departed in the direction of the bridge mess on the deck below, telling me to deal with anything that cropped up in the meantime.

I noticed a most unwarlike sound issuing from an open scuttle in the base of the island. Al Vaughan, Surgeon Lieutenant RCNVR, and a passable clarinetist, kept his instrument in the island sick bay, situated at deck level so that casualties due to enemy action or bad landings could be treated immediately before proceeding to the main sick bay some decks below. The only scuttle was situated above the sink, which afforded a restricted view of the world, so at Action Stations Doc. Vaughan, Graduate of Toronto University Medical School, aviation medical adviser and beloved friend of all, would sit on the draining board, feet in the sink, surveying the outside world to the accompaniment of Mozart whenever things were quiet.

The voice of the FDO interrupted my peace. A Seafire pilot, S/Lt.(A) Bill Gibson RNVR, of 894 Sqdn, was requesting an emergency landing as his Constant Speed Unit (which regulated engine revs, by increasing or decreasing the pitch of the propeller) had gone 'Up the spout' and was stuck in fine pitch. His engine temperature was climbing alarmingly, for this was analgeous to driving a car hard in first gear. It would lead to total engine seizure in a fairly short time. The ship was still into wind, Captain Graham agreed, so I piped 'Hands to Flying Stations' and we prepared to receive the Seafire.

It just wasn't Bill's week. Only a few days earlier he had been unable to lower his undercarriage and, after carrying out various manoeuvres aimed at releasing the oleo legs, had been ordered to bale out.

First he had tried the recommended method of flying inverted and dropping out, but his parachute became stuck on the headrest and he had to regain control, which he did by using his foot on the control column (or stick) and eventually assumed normal flight. He then tried to catapult himself out by crouching on his seat and giving the stick an almighty kick forward. The negative 'G' thus induced should have done the trick but, once again, he stuck. Finally he reduced speed, lowered his flaps and then ran along the port wing. His brolly opened and he was picked up by our 'chummy' destroyer, HMS *Kempenfelt* and returned onboard.

And now this!

Bill landed safely and reported to the bridge—standard drill after any emergency landing—and, 'Wings' still being at breakfast, said he would return in half an hour.

"Meanwhile," he added "I'll go and have a word with Doc. Vaughan—see if I can get a few days off flying—this is the second time in a week that I've had an emergency and quite honestly, Ivor, I'm getting twitched-up."

Unusual, I thought, for Bill, a young man to whom adventure was meat and drink, who never showed any sign of fear and was an extremely sound pilot (he was training to be a steeplejack before he joined up). Still, you never know how the strain of continuous operations over a long period will affect a chap.

'Group of four-plus aircraft—bearing 315—range 26 miles, closing'. As usual, the contacts were followed until, at 16 miles, they disappeared off the screen. We shook our heads sadly. Finger trouble again, we thought. Only this time they had got it terribly right.

The first inkling I had of trouble was the sound of aerial firing and, looking upwards, saw two aircraft in the tail chase about 2,000 feet above the ship. At first I thought they were two of ours and it had only just registered that the leading machine had a radial engine, whereas our Seafires had in-lines, when it turned on its back and I distinctly saw the 'Rising Sun' roundels on its wings as the pilot commenced a power dive directly at the spot where I was standing.

By this time all hell had broken loose. All of our guns, from 5.25's to pom-poms and additions, had opened fire, people were yelling. The Captain gave a helm order, I rushed on to the main bridge, closed the armoured door behind me—and flung myself down full length on the deck, together with everyone else.

We waited. The engine roar got louder and louder. There was no escape. This was it, this was how it was going to end. Pity, I thought, life is so enjoyable on the whole. I felt no fear, only a vague disappointment that the curtains were about to be drawn.

And then another thought struck me. I'd like to be there, as some sort of disembodied spirit, when my father opened the telegram. He was a dogmatic person, who would never entertain any arguments but his own, some of which were quite preposterous, nor would he ever admit to being in the wrong. I suppose to hearten me he would always say, "They couldn't get me at Ypres, they won't get you either". The sheer illogic of this used to annoy me intensely.

Well, at last, he'd be proved wrong. Yes, I did so hope that there was some way in which I could be a fly on the wall when he learned that I had been killed.

Then came the crash, followed immediately by flame and a searing heat. I choked. I could not draw breath. I believe I lost consciousness. I next remember opening my eyes to see all the recumbent forms near me. All immobile. All dead, I thought I must be dead too. I tried to raise my shoulders and found that I was able to move although no one else followed suit. Oh well, if this was being dead it wasn't so bad after all. Interesting to find that there was indeed a life hereafter, a fact in which I had never had much faith.

'Port fifteen'.

The Captain's voice brought us to our senses and we shambled rather sheepishly to our feet. He above all, in his 'ice cream' suit, had remained erect and in command. This was the moment for which he had trained since joining the navy as a thirteen year old cadet in 1914. And he did not fail.

From then on things moved fast. With certain communication lines out of action I was ordered below to assess damage and casualties, for we could now see that the kamikaze had crashed into the bottom of the island at flight deck level. Flames engulfed both forward and after bridge ladders so I swarmed down the thick, knotted manilla rope which had been rigged for just such an emergency.

As I made my descent I saw Lt. Cdr. Pat Chambers, RN, Lt. Cdr. (Flying), staggering aft, his back covered with blood. Someone ran forward and guided him to safety. An Avenger, in the process of being taxied forward, had collided with the superstructure, engine and cockpit blown to smithereens. Of the pilot there was no sign.

The Damage Control Party was already hosing the flames and I could now see a gaping hole where the island sick bay had been. Being of small stature I was able to crawl through the wreckage and there they were, my comrades Al Vaughan and Bill Gibson, showing no sign of injury but both killed by the blast, which had removed most of their clothing. In the passage between the sick bay and the Fighter Ready Room lay Lt. Leonard Teff, RNVR, Air Engineer Officer, also killed by the blast which, miraculously, had left untouched the man on either side of him. Looking upwards I realized that the bridge mess was no more. Oh Lord, what has happened to 'Wings'?

On regaining the bridge I was relieved to see Pat Humphries on the flight deck. A last minute dash to his cabin for some forgotten article had undoubtedly saved his life, in the same way as a faulty CSU had cost Gibson his.

Lt. Cdr. (E) 'Sandy' Sanderson RN, Flight Deck Engineer, and his party were already rigging a replacement for No. 3 barrier which had been destroyed. Twenty minutes later we were landing-on, S/Lt.(A) Dick Reynolds RNVR (894 Sqdn.) holding aloft a gloved hand to indicate two victories.

As soon as I was relieved, I went below to the hangar where maintenance crews were working with every sign of normality. They had thought their last moment had come when, unable to see what was happening, a terrific explosion occurred right above their heads. Flaming petrol ran down the hangar bulkhead, presumably through a fissure in the flight deck, threatening to engulf men and machines alike. Under the leadership of CPO 'Jimmy' Green, Senior Air Artificer, the fire was brought under control without having to resort to sprinklers.

"Right lads. Show's over. Back to work".

The Jimmy Greens of this world are worth their weight in gold.

I proceeded to the sick bay, where the PMO, Surg. Cdr. Yates, RNVR, and his team—Surg. Lt. Cdr. Henry Towers RN, and Surg. Lt. Musgrave RNVR, together with their 'tiffies'—had been working non-stop since the kamikaze struck at 07.30. With over forty casualties dead, dying and/or seriously wounded, accommodation was hopelessly inadequate and the adjoining messdeck had been pressed into service as an auxiliary ward. There, upon mess tables, lay men too badly injured to survive. A steward with a hole in his head the size of a cricket ball, losely plugged with cotton wool, a man with both legs missing. Between them were other casualties—men unrecognizable due to the burn dressings which covered head and body alike—and even as I looked for any of my own chaps, some were quietly slipping away into eternity.

I did find one, however, Able Seaman Gay, 894's squadron messenger, who was well into his forties when he joined up. Quiet, polite, conscientious, he was popular and respected by all. He sat, staring at nothing, in an advanced state of shock. "I'm afraid his mind's gone, Sir," said the Chief SBA, "I've seen them before like this. They never make a complete recovery."

If it had been the captain's moment, so had it been for the PMO. After fifteen hours at the operating table, he was ordered by his superior to take some rest. His reply was to order Captain Graham out of the Sick Bay in which, as a non-medical man, he had no authority. Only when, at 2300, it was obvious that he could do no more, did this 55 year old man consent to turn in. The final toll of eleven dead and thirty-two injured but surviving, was in large measure due to his skill and leadership. The subsequent award to him of the DSC was richly deserved and widely acclaimed.

Tailpieces

In 1949 I found myself in London with time to kill before catching my train and decided to regain contact with Doc Yates, who said that, after the war, he would return to Sloane Street where he had practised as a gyneacologist. An hour's search proving fruitless, I rang a doorbell, at random, hoping that the consultant or his secretary might be able to help.

The dermatologist, who was preparing to go home, suddenly became alert when I mentioned the *Indefatigable.* He did not know Doc Yates, but did I know a certain Lt. Teff—Leonard Teff?

I told him that I knew him well, that I had been the first to find him after the suicide attack. My host offered me a sherry, adding, "His father and I are great friends. He will be here in five minutes to pick me up. They've heard just how he died. Can you wait?"

I was able to give Mr. Teff a full account, stressing that Len was killed instantaneously and knew no pain or anguish.

"I thank you so much," he said, after a pause, "I'll tell his mother when I get home. You've no idea of the weight that has been lifted from our minds."

I eventually made contact with Doc. Yates and maintained the association on and off for several years. In fact he had not resumed practice in London. His wife had died shortly after the war and, being childless and without relatives in this country (you will remember that he was an Australian by birth) he missed the comradeship which he had found in the RN, so he offered his services to Cunard and was soon appointed PMO on *Queen Elizabeth.*

Age and indifferent health, however, took its toll and he died, a sad and lonely man, in the late fifties.

Erratum

I have forgotten two items of interest:

1. The pilot of the Avenger who was taxiing forward at the moment of the attack (I believe it was S/Lt. (A) 'Blackie' Scott RNVR but this needs to be checked with the 820 Sqdn boys) was unhurt. Several pipes were made for him to report to the bridge which he duly did. He explained to me that he heard the noise, assessed the situation, decided that this was no place for Mrs. Stott's son Blackie, so he leapt from the cockpit and fell flat on the deck. He would without a doubt have been killed had he not done so.

2. Souvenirs—Many of the matelots picked up bomb splinters and such like. Rumour had it that one enterprising member of the deck handling party had secured the Jap's third finger of his left hand, complete with a solitaire diamond and gold ring. 'True, Sir," said one of my killicks, "Couldn't get the ring off the 'and what 'ad been blown over the other side of the deck, so 'e takes out 'is knife and 'acks the bugger off."

However, as is often the case with 'buzzes' on the 'Galley Wireless', the perpetrator of this dastardly deed was never identified so I think the incident was apocryphal. I add it here as an example of what men under extreme stress may believe, to which in normal times no credence would be given.

The other souvenir story is, however, perfectly true.

One of my ratings told me that 'a bloke in 820' had found the Jap's cap badge near the scene of the explosion. I said, did it not seem odd to him that a pilot should be flying with a cap on his head or, come to that, in the cockpit? He said well maybe, but that he himself had seen it.

He led me to the 820 rating who, rather reluctantly, was persuaded to display his treasure. Yes, it was an officer's cap badge. No, it was not an RN badge. It was, in fact, that belonging to my Dutch friend, Lt. Le Baron d'Alnis de Bourouill, RNN, 'Foleff' to his many friends.

Finally, 'Guns' (Tony Davis) requested over the Tannoy system that any bomb fragments he brought to him for identification in order that he might have some information on the type of missile being used by the enemy for this sort of attack. Among the pieces which were offered was the nose cone—in fact, that of a Royal Navy 15″ shell, almost certainly captured at Singapore several years earlier!

From Lieut.(A) A.W. 'Brad' Bradley RNZNVR, HMS *Indefatigable*

I joined 894 Squadron CO Jimmy Crossman in *Indefatigable* in Leyte on 26th April 1945 until the BPF returned to Sydney on the 17th June 1945. That day was a very sad occasion for me, as a very young pilot who had on occasion been my wing man, had flown off *Indefatigable* with our squadron, had lost all of the coolant out of his engine and subsequently lost power and height. As all the carriers were still flying off their aircraft, he was not able to even crash land on any deck and had to ditch his Seafire and of course he went with it. I can still remember his screaming for help before the fatal dive.

I am enclosing a copy of my log book which indicates a Zeke was destroyed on the 9th May and I have my camera photo of it before it hit the sea and burst into flames and claimed its destruction. *(Unfortunately its age—like us, prevents it from reproducing well! Ed.)*

Buster Hallett was No. 3 Wing Leader during our 'Normandy' hops and was a well liked leader by everyone. He was a great pilot and gave all of us inspiration to achieve the most out of ourselves and our planes. We had a wonderful back up staff involved with our aircraft and recalling my days with *Indefatigable* had complete confidence in my plane because of the 'boys' looking after it.

You mention Lt. Mike Stretton and his unfortunate death—he was in 894 Squadron with me in *Chaser* with Lt. Cdr. Dennison our C.O. I consider my time with the BPF and *Indefatigable* the most anxious time of my life because of kamikaze attacks on our carriers and not knowing if we still had a deck to land on and even if our aircraft were able to get us down again.

From Ex L/Sto. Den Gregory, HMS *Indefatigable*

In the Indian Ocean and the Pacific, temperatures below decks—i.e. in the AFR Auxiliary Room reached 135°F. The steel ladders going down into same, were so hot that you quickly took your hand onto lower rungs on descending.

Anyone who has kept three watches at sea for a long period will know that sleep is something you get little of. The A.A. room with its Turbo Generators, CO_2 plants and mainly the evaporators (turning out fresh water) were a key part in keeping the ship running smoothly.

The Evaps. turning out six or seven tons of water per hour, were a vital part, as after a time water rationing was in force.

Anyone caught wasting water, was punished by spending a dog watch in the A.A. Room, scrubbing the steel plates. On two occasions, on my watches, I had 3 marines brought down by a Corporal to do just that. But as all plates and brasswork were kept spotless by the various watches, they usually finished up reading what Readers Digests we had down there!

During rough seas the L/Sto of the watch had a full-time job, nipping up and down, to change output of water, from 'MUF.' to 'Ship's Tanks'.

The Co_2 plants making ice cold water were well known to all ship's company. Seamen, cooks etc. would come down with a 'fanny' for a fill up to make their 'Limers', a drink of lime powder to make up for loss of sweat.

If they were 'cooks' a little bartering was done, a tin of corned beef was a good exchange.

Working in this heat, if you had the morning watch when relieved at noon, you wouldn't have an appetite, but after a tot of rum, you could eat a horse!

Off watch we had a stokers island (a catwalk around the funnel) where we could watch aircraft landing on and taking off.

I have ship's photographs of some of the crashes that took place quite often.

Will always have the memory of the Royal Marines band playing us in, or leaving harbour.

The tune was 'The Thin Red Line' which we put our own words to, 'Able Seaman Custard Gun'.

Also, after it was all over and safely back at Portsmouth, my last look round the A.A. Room with all its memories, and of the lump that came to my throat, my age—an old 22.

A.A.R. is After Auxiliary Room (run by a Leading Sto + 1 Sto.) Its function: steam auxiliary machinery—Evaporators for distilling fresh water for ship's tanks (drinking, washing etc.) and for MUF. (Make Up Feed) for use in the main boilers.

This had to be 100% pure and if (during rough seas) salt water splashed into distilled, a quick change of valves, from MUF. to ship's tank was necessary.

The stoker who was singed by the kamikaze blast was as thick as a plank and when told to watch the gauges, the turbo generators for lighting the ship, while I tended the Evaps., fell asleep. I noticed the steam gauge had dropped and just had time to rush up and rectify same, otherwise the generator would have 'tripped' putting most of the ship in darkness and I would have taken the can back!

From R.A. Perry, Artificer Air MR Staff, HMS *Indefatigable*

Since meeting you at the recent *Indefatigable* reunion and then reading your excellent book **Sakishima** it has revived memories of times when comradeship was all-important and the old sweats helped us youngsters to cope with a strange way of life. Apart from the friendship shown by the Australians, particularly the families like Mr. & Mrs. Johnson who adopted me like a son during our visits to Sydney, my memories of my time with the BPF are of the times spent in and out of action. As an artificer on the ship's Air A.Q. staff, I remember the nights spent in hot hangars repairing Seafires which had been damaged by flack or enemy cannon fire and on occasions undercarriages collapsing due to heavy landings. As always our target was to get as many fighters ready as possible for the cover of the fleet next day. Then when action stations were sounded it was a case of trying to get some sleep in the ship's jeep, which was housed in the forward workshops next to the lift.

On one such occasion I was roused from a fitful slumber by an explosion, which felt as if we had been hit. I came to and found that one of the long range petrol tanks which was being welded by an ERA had blown up. It not only started a fire but dented the flight deck which was the roof of the workshops. The fire was soon put out with foam extinguisher but we could not find the ERA. He was located unconscious under the bench on which he had been working and smothered in foam. Unfortunately he was seriously injured and had to be transferred to a depot ship.

I also remember the time we took on aviation fuel from an American tanker and after losing an aircraft found there was water in the fuel. There was much conjecture as to how it got there. It certainly caused the maintenance crews a headache because we had to filter all the fuel through chamois leathers, which was a slow and tedious job and of course slowed down turn round of aircraft. I guess we were lucky, the ship carried a good supply of chamois.

Finally I remember a Firefly engine which had blown up and I had to fit a new engine block. This meant handling a heavy casting on pulley blocks and while the ship tossed and swayed tried to fit pistons and rings in to the close fitting bores.

Needless to say we were praying the ship would keep on an even course. In spite of everything we only had a few trapped fingers.

I feel that like ourselves the squadron personnel worked long hours during these periods and when we came back to refuel we felt envious of some of the ships's company, because we had to work harder to get everything ready for the next visit to the front. Nevertheless we all felt great satisfaction in knowing the flying crews trusted our judgement.

AB Walter Powell, who was the ship's barber on board HMS *Indefatigable* and also Cmdr. Whitfeld's messenger, wrote to me from Australia

My action station was the 279 long range Radar, which was situated on the deck above the flight deck at the top of the first ladder inside the door from the flight deck, so that I was only a few feet from the actual explosion caused by the kamikaze which was about to descend upon us! This morning routine as you know was quite the normal thing, but on this occasion we did not have time to begin operations because the Japs were already overhead. (Had somebody left a tell-tale Radar set switched on with stationary aerials all night, thus giving away our position??).

Almost immediately, the stutter of the Oerlikon guns, let us, in the darkened office, know that the enemy was nearby, and when the pom-poms burst into life, we knew that we were about to be attacked.

Indefatigable began turning hard—was it to port or starboard? *(To port.—Ed.)* I can't remember. She was vibrating as she did at speed. Two members of the 279 crew dived out of the office onto the stairwell to see what was going on—it was the last thing my friends Pete White and Ken Onion ever did.

There was a terrible scraping sound. The kamikaze had missed going down the funnel, but was scraping down its side. It hit the deck near the doorway in the island, but did not penetrate. The blast went straight into the doorway where it blew a huge hole, and up the stairwell causing death and destruction. The 279 office was largely destroyed and did not operate again. I lay on the deck amongst the ruins and not able to see a thing. Where were my colleagues? Pete White had got his head through the porthole overlooking the flight deck when the Jap hit. I shall never forget what I saw of him after the event. Ken Onion died later in Sick Bay. I was there when he died, and his last words to the orderly were, "My name is Onion, *not* Onyon."—Many people thought his name couldn't possible be Onion (as Spanish onion) and politely called him Onyon.

The smell of dead flesh stayed there and in that part of the island till the day I left the ship.

Although we were so close to the explosion, somehow the blast had left us alone and killed many who were much further away. When the smoke cleared, I left the office and although the ladder leading down to flight deck level had gone, I somehow got down below flight deck level and must have wandered around the ship in a daze. I remember some crew members were amazed that some of us had got out of the 279 office in one piece. Having read in **Sakishima** a footnote regarding the steam from the ship's siren preventing a firey death to all in the island, I am even more grateful that I survived!!

I often enjoy the memory of being called upon from time to time to visit

Admiral Vian in his cabin to cut his hair (I am a hairdresser by trade). Although I found the thought of doing this quite unnerving, I was pleased to find that the great man was completely human and made me feel quite at ease, so that I was able to chat away to him with no worries at all. He was interested to know such things as what did the crew think of him, were we a happy ship and so on. He appeared to be a little vain—but weren't we all? You may recall that he had masses of hair growing out from his ears—everyone remarked about it, so I was quite surprised when he asked me to 'get rid of all that growth' in his ears.

I said to him very seriously "Sir, don't you realize that Mr. Churchill is always seen with a cigar. That cigar is Churchill's hallmark, it's part of him. Your whiskers in both ears are well known throughout the ship, and possibly the fleet, you really should keep them Sir!"

Sir Philip looked at me and said "How extraordinary, is that true?" I assured him that it was true, and so the whiskers were spared, and to the best of my knowledge remained with him for ever more!

Commander J. Whitfeld was the finest gentleman and Commander one could wish to meet. I spent many months as his messenger, and it was because of this that I saw so many parts of the ship (like the barber shop). Everywhere the Commander went I went. He would often call me to walk alongside him, as against astern of him and he would chat to me as though we were equals. To illustrate his more human side, I recall on occasion off the coast of New Zealand, when the New Zealand News was on board. They wanted to film for the Newsreel, a man being transferred from *Indefatigable* to the destroyer *Wizard*. The seas were not too friendly. There was a swell, which kept the two ships constantly closing in on each other then drifting apart. However, the lines were sent across to *Wizard* and all was set to go. Commander Whitfeld turned to the little group on the flight deck and said something like 'Who's going?' I think everyone began to realize that if those lines snapped with the ship's rolling as they were, the breeches buoy and its occupant would disappear for ever between the two ships and may be shredded by the propellers! Anyway, I volunteered to my Commander, and as final preparations were being made, he took me aside out of earshot and said to me "Powell, you don't have to go you know." I have always remembered that very fine gesture.

However, I went and appeared on the news in N.Z. cinemas!

From Sub Lieut(A) Bill Coster RNVR, 820 Sqdn. HMS *Indefatigable*

It was about 0735 hrs on Easter Sunday morning April 1st 1945 and I was sitting in 'C' for Charlie my faithful old Avenger waiting to take off on some strike (can't remember where we were supposed to be going) but I remember watching the first Seafire in the range leave the deck. Just as it got airborne something caught my eye above the Bridge and I saw another Aircraft. Probably suffering from a touch of the 'night befores', at first I wondered how the Seafire had got there so quickly only to suddenly realize that it had the wrong markings on it and that it was a Jap. I also remember that this thought came to my mind . . . that I had joined the Navy at almost the same time, 7.30 in the morning at Lee-on-Solent on April 1st three years earlier and that I was 'going out' on the same day. As you know, the next few minutes were pretty hectic and getting quickly out of the plane on reaching the deck I trod on a piece of bound metal which looked as if it could have been a piece of a Jap aircraft. Also close by was a piece of what looked like a white bit of coconut shell but was probably a fragment of skull. Shall never know, but I did keep them for years finally being lost in a 'house move'. What did strike me more than anything else was the strict discipline—no one panicked—but simply got on with what had to be done although there were dead and dying all about. I shall always see in my mind the Jap turning over the bridge and diving into the island watching it all the way down.

Bill Coster

On the 9th April 1945 12 Avengers took off from *Indefat,* to bomb Nobara Airfield on Myako. We were about a mile from the Island at about 10,000 feet and about to deploy to Diving Formation when my engine cut and started to emit a load of black smoke. I left the formation and turned on a reciprocal course and jettisoned my bomb load of 4 × 500 pounders in the minefield which stretched for some distance East of the Island. Closing the bomb doors I trimmed for gliding at the lowest rate of descent hoping that the patrolling American Air sea rescue submarine was in the vicinity. As you will remember we often saw it on the surface and it gave us quite a feeling of confidence in those shark infested waters. Naturally all the time I was doing all I could to revive the engine and had already told the crew, S/Lt. Roy Thomas and A.P.O. Chuck Sage to stand by for ditching. We had got to about 4000 Ft. when the engine started to fire again and we were able to keep going without losing any more height although we were smoking badly and leaving a black trail behind us which did nothing for our state of mind, as we knew that there were enemy fighters in the neighbourhood. The engine continued to mis-fire and when we were close enough we asked the ship by VHF for a priority landing only to be told that the Fleet was being attacked by kamikazes and that we were to fly 50 miles due South and circle until we were recalled. Again this news did not excite us a lot as the engine was getting much worse as we were constantly waiting to ditch. We were also still leaving a trail of smoke in the air and felt that we were sitting ducks if any of the attacking Jap aircraft had spotted us. Then my Gunner Chuck Sage reported an aircraft flying towards us on our Port Quarter and we all thought that this was it, especially as we were powerless to manoeuvre. However we were soon able to identify it as a Yankee Mariner boat plane and it seemed to be bristling with crewmen holding machine guns which seemed to be poking out of just about every porthole in their fuselage. As soon as they identified us the hands that were holding guns soon were holding cameras and we had shots taken of us from every angle. After the war I did advertise in a couple of American flying magazines to try and make contact with any of that crew but had no luck. Anyhow after about an hour we got a C from the ship and staggered on in. How we kept in the air we'll never know, but we aimed for the round down with full throttle and just managed to clear, and as we did so the engine finally stopped and burst into flames. And if my memory serves me correctly, as soon as we got out they pushed the aircraft straight overboard.

Another event which I vaguely remember is on an occasion when we 'lost' the Fleet Tankers and I was one of a search party of five Avengers scrambled to look for them each on a three sided search pattern. The weather I do remember was absolutely foul and visibility was so bad that we could only fly at about 150/200 ft. As we were approaching our second leg of the search my navigator Roy Thomas picked them up on the screen dead ahead and in next to no time we were upon them and it seemed to me that we were so low that I had to pull up to avoid their masts. We flashed the Fleet's position to them and turned for 'home' and when we landed we found out that the rest of the search flight had returned to the ship because of the bad weather. Admiral Vian signalled for our names and when he received them he sent us his thanks and congratulations. I have still got a copy of his signal and although he did not mention this episode in his book 'Action this Day', he did mention the Palembang incident and when his book was published he lived just outside Newbury and there was quite a write up in the local Newbury paper.

From Sto. Dennis Hickman, HMS *Indefatigable*

My Action Station was in the upper hangar and when the flames shot through from the flight deck into the hangar, the asbestos curtains came down and left us shut off to deal with the fire. I remember an officer shouting at me to empty the drip trays of petrol down the scuppers—was I scared?

We served in the two hangars as fire fighters. As we had trained early on as stokers, we became known as Hangar Control Stokers. We also had the duty of getting the fuel up from below for the fleet air arm lads to fuel the planes.

Chief ERA Reg Beaver wrote to me from Aukland and recalled:

The messenger said, 'Chief, you are required at the voice pipe'. On the other end was the Captain, who said, 'Chief ERA, the Japs have just laid an Easter egg on our flight deck. It must have damaged one of the sirens as there's steam and water everywhere. Will you come up and do something about it?'

So Reg was one of the first on the spot to witness the damage to life and ship. On his way back with the damaged part under his arm, he lost his hand-hold and crashed to the deck below. Many years later an X-Ray showed a chipped vertebrae.

From S/Lt(A) John Birtle RNVR, 887 Sqdn. *Indefatigable*

I don't think we'd started up on 1st April when the Tannoy announced bandits approaching range six or seven miles. Blue flight took off and my aircraft was the last, after lifting my flaps and undercart I heard a call over the RT that the ship was under attack, I pulled round to port flicking on my gunsight and switching off the safety on my guns and, in a steep turn to port I saw a silver Zero diving on the ship from forward. At the bottom of his dive he released what I took to be a bomb which splashed into the sea some 10/15 yards off the port bow without exploding. It seemed to me afterwards that if it was a bomb then the arming vanes hadn't turned sufficient times to arm it or, on the other hand it might have been a long range tank. After diving down the flight deck the Zero pulled up into a vertical climb at the top of which he did an immaculate stall turn and commenced another dive onto *Indefatigable.* During this time I was tearing my aircraft round to get into a position to attack, by the time he was into his dive I was coming in at full bore from the port beam and had him in my sights although it was a full (ring and a half) deflection shot. I don't know how long I fired, three or four seconds maybe, but I saw strikes on the Zero and my camera gun film confirmed this and fractionally before he hit, his port wing started breaking away. Discussing this with Erik Govaars (my flight leader) afterwards, we thought that he was trying to dive down the funnel (which the kamikazes were ordered to do if the lift shafts were not open—and fortunately they weren't at the time) and losing control at the last split second the aircraft finished up diving into the base of the island. I hadn't much time to observe a great deal more as every gun in the fleet (it seemed) was blasting away at me fortunately without success. I remember feeling sick as I saw the great orange blast of the explosion as the kamikaze hit and was more than surprised that we were able to land on some 45 minutes later.

From Sub Lieut (A) Mike Davey RNVR, 894 Squadron HMS *Indefatigable*

After Sydney, according to my log book, we were twenty four days in passage from the Coral Sea to commencing operations off Sakishima. We stayed there, with only a short break for repairs until May 25th probably as long an operation carried out by carriers in the whole of the war. Although the whole operation seemed a bit futile, as our Avengers carrying 4 × 500 lb bombs blew holes in the runways by day, the Japs with slave labour filled them in again by night, but the kamikazes still managed to reach us. The duty of our Seafire wing (887 and 894 squadrons) was to prevent the kamikazes from attacking the fleet.

The carrier was not only a vital ship, but usually had a deck park of a good many aircraft which were very combustible when full of hundred octane fuel, they never pentrated our deck though, as they did the Americans for four inches of armour is far better than wooden planks, but not for keeping cool. Our ships were like ovens, which gave us the most severe prickly heat, we never found out how to combat this.

Our Avenger bombers continued to attack the airfields of Sakishima and we continued to patrol the areas off the islands until finally the Americans at considerable loss of life conquered Okinawa. In the aerial fighting we had not had any great bags but they had been made to miss by ourselves and by the carrier captains who had applied full helm when the kamikaze went into his final dive, often this was quite spectacular, if timed right. It was my lot to be close to *Victorious,* when a kamikaze exploded a few feet above the waterline amidships and the explosion showered the whole ship in a cloud of spray.

On April 1st there was an attack by three Zeroes at about dawn. There was some confusion in Orange flight both about who was flying and where. Whatever the correct answer the flight leader Dick Reynolds finished up on his own shooting down the first two and narrowly missing the third, which made a perfect hit on our ship. This did we Seafires a lot of harm, killing on board pilots Bill Gibson, our Air Engineer Officer Len Teff and our Wing Doctor Alan Vaughan as well as several mechanics. Two of us were manning an oerlikon on the quarterdeck which we did when not flying, we first heard a thump and then thick black smoke which was out pretty soon. Everyone was very surprised how quickly damage control had got things damped down. We were landing on again in a little over half an hour. As we went off gun watch to fly, some of the casualties were being stretchered into the starboard medical station, some of them were suffering from blast and burns, not a pretty sight. In 887 they now had quite a few successes. Paddy Kernahan and his flight Alastair Macleod, Ian Bird and Cliff Miseldine all bagged Zeroes except Paddy who got an elusive Dinah. Altogether, including the eight bagged over Tokyo, the total shot down by the pilots of twenty four wing was about twenty five, we ourselves lost fifteen but only four of these were due to enemy action which shows the attrition rate of carrier operations. 894 had quite the worst of the deal, probably because we were the low level squadron flying the Seafire L3, for when operating four carriers in a box the dangers of accidents were greatly increased. We flew our circuits at 150 feet and joined up in very tight circles, with the density of about eight bomber dromes in a square mile, this as well as the hazard of deck landing. The pilot loss in 894 was nine in a sixteen pilot squadron, with three only from enemy action. Of all the casualties in the whole of 24 wing, only one was shot down by an enemy aircraft. The Avenger squadrons had far less casualties even though they bombed at low level and were exposed to a lot of flak, but they were excellent deck landers, as were the Fireflies. We certainly paid the price for the refusal of their Lordships to build a better plane to go to war. After the war there were several excellent fighters and bombers, but the stable door was closed after the horse had bolted. After six weeks of neutralizing the Sakishima Gunto by air attack, with a good deal of success and at the same time absorbing all the kamikaze attacks the Japs could throw at us, on May 4th 1945, it was decided by the Admirals in Command, to detach our battleships, plus half the escorting destroyers and cruisers to bombard the targets ashore by guns. This left the carriers very exposed, a fact immediately recognized by the enemy aerial reconnaissance. There were attacks all throughout the day and hits on the carriers especially *Formidable* and *Victorious.*

After two hours gun crew duty at dawn, (junior pilots manned the oerlikons when not flying) Orange flight led by Dick Reynolds, did a normal C.A.P. but almost at the end of it were vectored onto a single Zero. He was nearest to me and it seemed easy to jump on his tail, but he performed what could best be called a flick-about turn which had been described to us by Jimmy Crossman our CO, the first to experience this turn about. This meant the Zero was facing me and was aiming to hit me without being too worried about it; but I was worried into a steep climbing turn, avoiding him by a few feet and looking at him personally as we passed. It was said rudely that I was never the same again. By the time my turn was completed, Reynolds and Kay had bracketed him and shot him down in a series of yo-yo turns. The best of my efforts could be called was what in ice-hockey is 'an assist'. Soon after this, we returned to the carrier to, hopefully land on sixteen Seafires, fifteen landed on and it was my luck to be the sixteenth, when another kamikaze raid materialized and the batsman gave me the wave off on the final approach, as all the ship's guns were firing. On pulling away to port the fuel guages read four gallons or translated into flying hours, four minutes approximately. Ditching a Seafire was not a recommended pastime as they didn't stay afloat long enough for the pilot to get out and as there appeared to be enough fuel to climb high enough to use a parachute, climb it was. Whilst aiming at the fleet, another kamikaze was diving into *Formidable.* My hopeful turn to intercept him didn't achieve much as he was too far off and too far advanced in his dive and he completed his attack. The flight deck was a mass of smoke and flame, but it was amazing how quickly the fires were under control and the aircraft landing on again. Climbing ahead to just under 3,000 feet when the engine started to splutter; by this time all drills had been done, but it was surprising how long it seemed. Call the ship and tell them Tusco 154 was about to bale out, release Sutton harness, ditch flying helmet and knee-pad, trim to glide at 75 knots, stand on seat, grasp trailing edge of wing and pull hard to go out head first. The parachute worked, but it belonged to Bill Daniel as mine was in for re-pack. Bill was a bigger and wider chap and it needed a double turn round the crutch strap. On pulling the rip-cord it gave me a sharp jerk round the nether regions, which didn't seem to auger well for the future generations, however a quick shout told me that my voice was still bass-baritone. The plane gave me some concern being so well trimmed, that it flew round in a gentle glide, which eventually subsided into the Pacific. It was not my regular and durable 145 Buzzards Crutch, but 283. We flew whatever was serviceable.

On ditching, Bill's parachute collapsed on top of me, and as we were in shark waters it became essential to get in a dinghy as soon as possible. It was some time before a destroyer appeared, long enough for the Pacific Ocean to seem a very large place. When it arrived, everything was done in a great hurry, drop scrambling net, pick up pilot, dinghy and Maé West all at once. Once on board, a short trip to the sick-bay, for a check by the surgeon, some dry clothes, then up on the bridge to see the Captain of the destroyer—HMS *Quality*—Lieut Comm. Viscount Jocelyn RN, who made me his spotting officer for as long as I was on board. This was a pleasant task, meaning being on watch from dawn to dark, with all meals on the bridge (action messing). The comfort of a small ship wardroom with only a handful of officers and an individual cabin, was something that was quite easy to get used to. One incident on the bridge, confirmed how small the world is. A leading seaman came onto the bridge to check the compass. We recognized one another immediately; as young teenagers, we had spent many hours shooting sparrows with air rifle and catapult on our farm at home, where his brother was our chicken lad.

It was a reluctant spotter officer who returned to his carrier two days later. Destroyer life suited very well; it seemed more orderly, more comfortable and definitely less dangerous. *Quality* pulled alongside *Indefatigable*, and a line was shot across by Costain Gun. We all knew the drill; that is the pilots; and I said to the first Lieutenant of *Quality* "It will be best for me to wear my Mae West in the breeches buoy, sir." However he replied, "No, we'll send it in the first load with your other gear." One doesn't answer back to a first Lieutenant. On *Indefatigable* Commander Whitfeld gave the order 'haul taut handsomely'. It often made me wonder what other way you could haul taut; but hey presto, it was back on our own flight deck in a trice, with a welcoming party of pilots. Everyone welcomed me except Comm. Whitfeld, who said "if you'd any sense Davey, you'd have worn your Mae West." Once again you didn't answer back; if you had, you may have walked the plank. It was five days that I had off flying but there were plenty left, at least a month always C.A.P. on the picket cruiser, which kept station about forty miles from the fleet; this enabled returning raids to come on a dog-leg course and be screened by fighters to make sure that no kamikazes were joined on to the bombers. We also had to do normal patrols over the fleet at varying heights. The miles we flew for the number of successes we had, must have been very high indeed, according to a very rough calculation it was 22,400 or about the distance round the world per kamikaze destroyed. However, although we had many long and arduous days, May 4th was the most active day of my life. Early dawn manning the guns on the quarterdeck. Morning flying a patrol with a kamikaze destroyed, later a survivor, finishing the day as a spotter, four jobs in one day without going to the Job Centre.

April 13th was a day to be remembered for Pink Flight. When returning from patrol as number 2 to Hepp Heppenstall we got a wave off on the final approach because the Japs had commenced another attack. Hepp and I pulled away, with Hockley and Taylor a fair way behind, when seemingly the whole fleet opened fire on us with all guns from close range. When I had almost joined Hepp his starboard wing was blown off and his aircraft fell like an autumn leaf into the Pacific from about 400 ft. After a split second of frigid terror, my first reaction was to push the stick forward, open the throttle and dive for the waves as fast as possible. This probably saved my life, although Taylor and Hockley survived, they weren't the targets, but unhappily both were killed later and it became my lot to be the only survivor of Pink Flight. An incident like this was known as a T.F.E. (trouser filling experience).

From Lt.(A) George Carpenter RNVR, 820 Squadron HMS *Indefatigable*

820 pilots had been piped to man aircraft to take these forward, to allow the early morning C.A.P. Seafires to land on. I was sitting in my Avenger, fully bombed up, ready for our own first sortie later on.

I was suddenly aware of our own guns opening up and of other signs of activity around the Task Force when over my left shoulder I saw the Japanese fighter appear, hotly pursued by one of our own fighters—almost immediately, the kamikaze closed over in a dive and to my immediate thought, seemed to be heading directly for me.

From NASEW Alan Rogers HMS *Indefatigable*

Two of the ratings killed when the ship was hit were friends of mine. 'Salty Pepper' one of the ship's photographers, and Vic Buckingham who was married and close to me in London. His wife received the telegram informing her of his death and promptly told my parents that I was most likely killed because we were inseparable friends. I was able to echo the famous writer and let them know that the news of my being killed in action was 'highly exaggerated'.

From John C. Thompson OBE MA, Air Radio Officer HMS *Indefatigable*

The object of an Air Radio Officer (A.R.O.) was to ensure the serviceability of the radio and radar equipment fitted into the embarked aircraft. For this purpose, while on board, the Squadron mechanics were responsible for their 'standards and practice' to the A.R.O. while for their discipline, to the Squadron.

In addition to the squadron mechanics there were four ship's company Air Radio Radar personnel. Squadron mechanics numbered about 50 for the 70 odd aircraft on board.

The aircraft were equipped with a wide variety of equipment, due largely to their country of origin (U.K. or U.S.A.). However all aircraft were fitted with the American V.H.F. R/T equipment (TR5043) infamous for its difficulty in tuning and the lack of spares.

All aircraft carried a homing beacon and an I.F.F. set (forerunner of the present day transponder which could be either U.K. or U.S. made with the appropriate self-destruction explosive used on operations.

T.B.R. aircraft had radar (A.S.V. for U.K., A.S.B. for American built aircraft and some A.S.B. micro-wave 'podded' radar at the end); they also had H.F. equipment.

A major problem—besides the variety of dual type spares—lay in the fact that *Indefatigable* had been designed before the surge of technology in electronic equipment that brought this vastly increased quantity of sets to be installed in Naval aircraft. As a result, the workshop facilities were woefully inadequate comprising initially one small compartment.

One of my first duties on joining as a young and inexperienced Sub-Lieutenant of 20 years old was to try to conjure more space out the Commander who at the time was not very sympathetic to the Air Branch. Eventually we finished up with three work-spaces but even these were not very convenient for hangar or flight deck maintenance, and they were still cramped and lacking in test equipment.

Spares, too, were a problem. I recall I had to make more than one visit to the Central Stores to try to wheedle the appropriate material out of helpful but overworked store keepers. On one occasion at least the spares arrived at the quay-side after the ship had sailed. The maintenance of serviceability of the equipment was at times a nightmare.

So far as I was concerned I was also press-ganged into becoming an assistant flight deck officer, for parking the aircraft after landing. This was simply because there were insufficient bodies available at Action Stations, and it was considered I would not be otherwise engaged if the aircraft were flying. While understanding this point of view, I did not feel friendly towards it with only one A.R.O. on board there were no 'watches', so my day started before dawn and finished when the last aircraft had been serviced—usually after midnight.

Obviously, being ahead of the barrier at 'landing on' there were a number of horrifying or unpleasant incidents. I recall the awful day during working up when not just one, but two Seafires jumped the barrier on landing, causing casualties and damage, with propeller blades flying everywhere.

One incident on 1st April 1945 is perhaps worth recording—though my

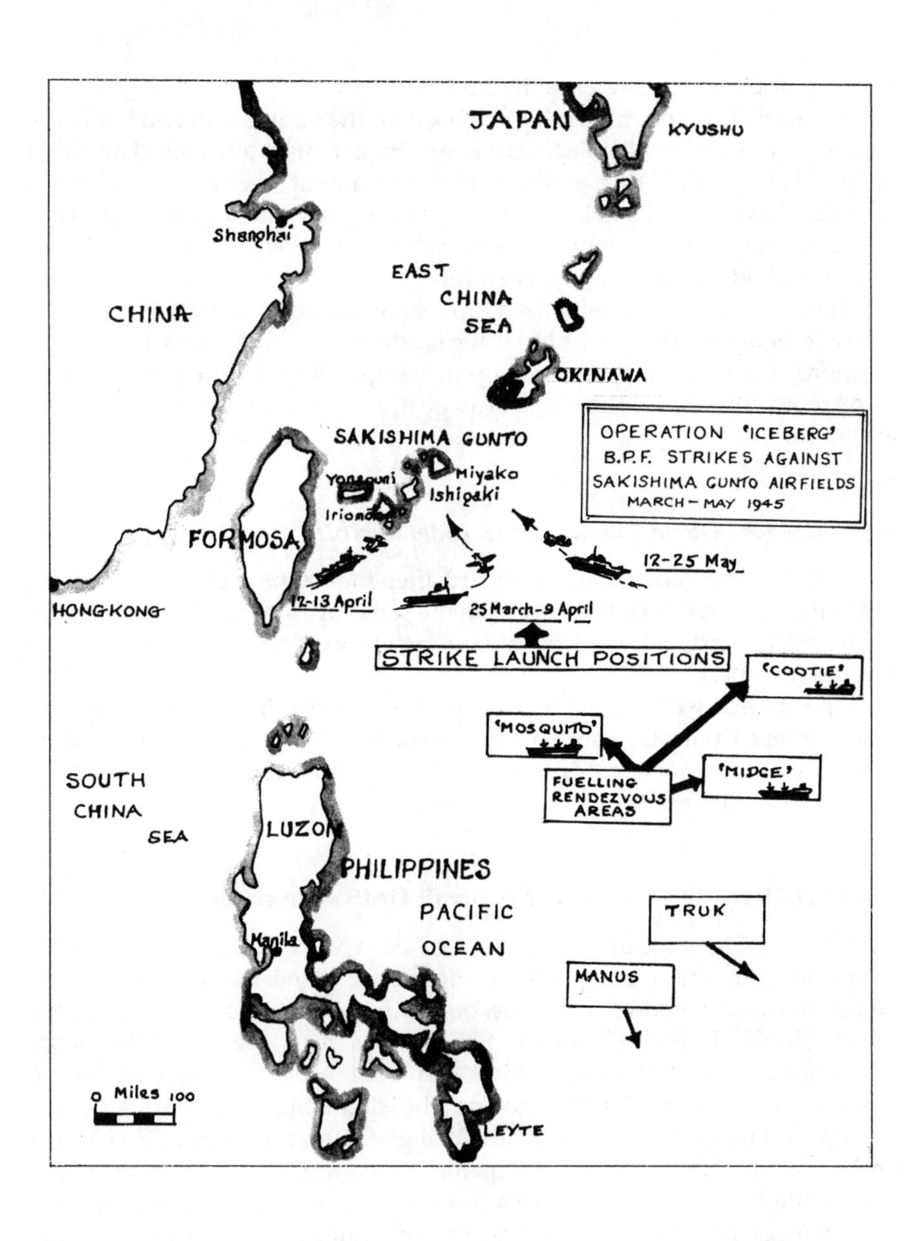
JAPAN
KYUSHU
Shanghai
EAST
CHINA
SEA
CHINA
OKINAWA
OPERATION 'ICEBERG'
B.P.F. STRIKES AGAINST
SAKISHIMA GUNTO AIRFIELDS
MARCH – MAY 1945
SAKISHIMA GUNTO
Yonaguni
Miyako
Ishigaki
FORMOSA
12-25 May
12-13 April
25 March-9 April
HONGKONG
STRIKE LAUNCH POSITIONS
'COOTIE'
'MOSQUITO'
FUELLING
RENDEZVOUS
AREAS
'MIDGE'
SOUTH
CHINA
SEA
LUZON
PHILIPPINES
PACIFIC
OCEAN
TRUK
Manila
MANUS
0 Miles 100
LEYTE

memory of the exact detail is a little hazy.

Apparently a Seafire pilot who had been on the early patrol and landed on satisfactorily after the kamikaze attack, returned to his cabin, to find his cabin-mate still sleeping. He woke him with the comment "we have been hit by a kamikaze"—to which his cabin-mate turned over and said sleepily—"April Fool to you, chum". He had slept right through the crash and the bombardment, and really had no idea we had been hit.

I think all of us were pretty tired, and slept deeply at times.

Beside being on the Flight Deck for landing on, I had two action station positions. One was in the workshop or hangar: the other was in the pilots ready room next door to the F.D. 1st Aid post. Luckily I was at the former when we got hit.

From A/Mech. David Colvan, HMS *Indefatigable*

I was Chief of the Watch in the starboard after engine room and knew the ship had been hit as our fan intakes were on the starboard side just below the pom-poms and we had Guy Fawkes entertainment for a few minutes with smoke and red hot sparks.

As our intakes were on the boat deck I suspected a fire there and reported so to Damage Control. I phoned damage control who seemed to be oblivious to what was going on, but came back later and told us what happened and confirmed no fire existed on the boat deck.

From PO Electrical Artificer Les Bancroft HMS *Indefatigable*

Shortly after 7.00 a.m. on Easter Sunday, 1st April and within seconds of it occurring, our action alarm system reported a kamikaze direct hit on the island. To this day I don't know why, but my immediate thought was, Smithy, C.P.O. Electrical Artificer Smith. Smithy was responsible for the Island electrical equipment, it was also his Action Station. Again, it was instinctive, I turned to Mr. Powley, "Should I go up to the Island, Sir, and check that Smithy is okay (and therefore capable of organizing whatever is required)? I can also find out what help is needed." I remember the thought was in my mind that Smithy might be dead. Mr. Powley did not hesitate, our telephone operator was already failing to receive an answer from Smithy's Action Station phone. "Yes, but get back here as soon as possible. Take one of the seamen with you." A good idea, I turned quickly, "I need a volun . . . " I never finished, they had overheard, they were a wonderful lot, three were already stepping forward. I took the nearest one. I still don't know his name.

We started up the last ladder leading to flight deck level within the Island. We could see that at flight deck level, God, it was a shambles. Fires were burning all round, steam was erupting from burst pipes at the rear end, water was cascading from others. Twisted steel and piles of rubble were everywhere. Four crewmen were trying to manoeuvre through this into an area which I now know to have been the Island Medical Station. They had obviously been removing the injured; the dead remained.

Halfway up the ladder we stopped. I turned to my accompanying seaman and said, "You stay here. If I am not back in five minutes return to Mr. Powley and tell him what you have seen".

There were no heroics in this, it was an instantaneous decision. At that stage, every action, every word, was again instinctive; there was no time to consider.

As I reached the top of the ladder, Commander Whitfeld appeared in the flight deck doorway. I don't remember his exact words but the sense was "Everybody out. On the flight deck quick. We need all hands to clean up. The planes will have to be landed on". They left; Commander Whitfeld looked at me inquisitively, then he was gone.

I started to manoeuvre forward along the passage to reach the ladder leading up to the next deck. Immediately a pile of rubble was practically blocking the passage. Lying atop it, face down, a body, dead; not Smithy. I stepped carefully round and then over other bits, and rubble and jagged steel, pushing aside and trying to avoid projecting ends of electric cables, many still live, some arcing. I reached the ladder, started to ascend it and suddenly, at the top, there was Smithy, coming down; he was unhurt.

We descended to collect the Seaman Torpedoman, a lonely figure, still waiting on the ladder amid the chaos. After a short discussion with Smithy, the Seaman and I returned to our Action Station to report to Mr. Powley.

HMS Indefatigable—*Electrical Power Supply*

Deep below decks it had become hot, appallingly hot. In the engine rooms, the machinery and generator compartments, and especially in the watertight sealed electrical ring main breaker passages which ran, intermittently, full length both sides of the ship. I was responsible, with the able assistance of Seaman Electrician Dixon (Dixie), for the maintenance and repair of the ship's electrical power generation and distribution. This comprised the dynamo ends of seven large turbine generators, three emergency diesel generators, the ship's electrical power Ring Main system with associated switchgear (hundreds of various type breakers) and the Main Switchboard from which the whole system was controlled. The Main Switchboard (the ship's nerve centre) was in its own compartment, some 40 ft. long by 11 ft. wide. Directly alongside it was the ship's Master Gyro compartment. These two rooms were located in what was considered the safest part of the ship from enemy attack, completely amidships, well below the water line and surrounded by watertight compartments.

Here, I should explain, simply if possible, the *Indefatigable's* electrical power distribution system. All at 224 volts Direct Current.

The ship's Ring Main comprised 4″ diameter electrical cables running, continuously, full length both sides of the ship with end connecting cables extreme forward and aft. Fitting into the end connecting cables and at strategic points along each side of the Ring Main were large water sealed Ring Main Breakers. Under action and normal sea conditions all Ring Main Breakers were closed (switched ON) except the end connectors Ring Main Breakers which were open (switched OFF). This meant the ship ran with TWO power supplies. One along the Starboard side fed by numbers 1, 3, 5 and 7 dynamos and one along the Port side fed by numbers 2, 4, and 6 dynamos. The TWO power supplies could be interconnected by the end connectors Ring Main Breakers and other manually fitted inter-connectors. This would never occur except under certain extreme emergency conditions. Sensible, should we be torpedoed one side of the ship, say Starboard, then at maximum, we would lose the Starboard electrical power supply only. The Port side electrical power would still be intact and able to keep the ship running. Further we would isolate the damaged (torpedoed) section of the Ring Main by leaving open (switched OFF), two Ring Main Breakers; one immediately forward and one immediately aft, of the damaged section. The forward and aft end connectors Ring Main Breakers could then be closed (switched ON) to take power from the Port side to the undamaged Starboard sections of the Ring Main. To then restore our TWO sources of power supply it would only be necessary to open (switch OFF) any Ring Main Breakers we chose; probably on the Port side. The ship, once again, would be in a position to sustain a second or even a third torpedo hit without complete electrical power failure.

The Ring Main cables themselves, each side of the ship, passed through many short watertight passages (breaker passages) which were separated from each other by armoured bulkheads. The cables passed through the bulkheads via armoured watertight glands. In these passages were located the sealed Ring Main Breakers and hundreds of various other type breakers.

Excessive Heat Problems

The first indication of heat-caused Ring Main problems was the sudden loss of Main Switchboard control of one of the Ring Main Breakers. I remember first checking the particular breaker control wiring at the rear of the Main Switchboard; no faults there. That meant I now had to check inside the watertight Ring Main Breaker. Dixie drew the small 'Permit' board from Central Damage Control where the watertight passage number and 'Permit' issue time were recorded. We descended the ladders to the passage watertight hatch entrance; the temperature was over 120°F.

Hurriedly remove the bolts of the watertight Ring Main Breaker front steel cover; the cover was some 4′0″ by 2′6″. Cover removed, out of the passage for a five minute breather and cool down, then back in again. I soon located the fault; in the bottom left hand corner of the breaker. The insulation of the four small 6″ long leads which provided Main Switchboard control of the breaker had literally melted away, the wires were exposed and earthing. Tricky, I had to unscrew each lead in turn, sleeve insulate and then reconnect. This, whilst dressed only in a pair of shorts, standing in a pool of my own sweat and the breaker and all leads live at 224 volts. At such times I prayed the Captain to keep the ship steady; to stop it rolling, pitching or both. The Captain seemed seldom to oblige. I received many a mule kick.

Job completed, phone the Main Switchboard and they to operate the Ring Main Breaker OFF and immediately ON again to check the repair effective. I could see and hear the breaker operating; a huge electrical flash and loud bang.

Then it was to re-seal the breaker cover and ensure the passage hatch was tightly reclipped. Dixie returned the 'Permit' board to Damage Control and we re-met in the Main Switchboard to cool down in the steady 110°F temperature under the air louvres.

During April/May 1945 I had to re-sleeve insulate the control leads of all the ship's Ring Main Breakers. Some other type breakers required similar treatment. Loss of Main Switchboard control of the Ring Main Breakers would make the ship extremely vulnerable. We could, if sustaining enemy damage, lose all electrical power.

The extreme excessive heat deep below decks was affecting people as well as equipment. 'Dixie' was particularly affected, physically. He broke out in huge tropical ulcers; first on his arms and legs and then the rest of his body. At the outset he had to be made to report to the Medical Centre for treatment. When told he would be given a job further aloft with more fresh air access, he refused. I believe he felt it was his duty to continue his job. We had an excellent working relationship and, looking back, I think he was conscious that I was eight to ten years his junior, a mere youngster; often he was more concerned for my safety and welfare than his own.

Eventually, just before the end of the Okinawa campaign, Dixie had to be removed from the job. He was a very sick man; I believe he was transferred from the ship.

Dixie was reliable, trustworthy, and brave. He served his country well.

From Ldg. Seaman W.J. Kiddell, HMS *Indefatigable*

I was Leading Seaman of the Flight Deck Handling Party under Lt. Commander Chambers, so I had a great view of all the actions described in your book, **Sakishima**. I have many of the photos used to illustrate it, which I always understood were taken by A.B. Pepper, a 3-badger who unfortunately was killed on April 1st 1945.

On that day I was outside the island and remember the kamikaze pilot in yellow-green (Norwich City's colours). I dived to the deck which seemed to come up and hit me. I felt the heat blast but no bang, and debris fell on me. I looked up and saw a big black cloud of smoke with a very deep red centre.

The next thing I remember was Lt. Roome connecting a fire hose on the port side of the Flight Deck and Lt. Commander Chambers who was obviously injured. I went to help him, but he refused help and as he turned away I could see blood spots seeping through the back of his white overall.

Even today I can hear Lt. Commander Chambers telling our Flight Deck Handling Party that, "Once again Leading Seaman Kiddell has lost the Battle of Sydney"—we had a great working relationship.

In Sydney I sank many a 'schooner' at the Lord Baden Powell in Redfern in the company of the brothers Fred and Bert Ramsbottom from the *Indefat.* and my brother Bert who was now serving on HMS *Teazer.*

From A.B. Fred Piper, HMS *Indefatigable*

I was in the crew of 'X' 4.5 Director and just aft of the island—so not far from the impact of the kamikaze. Ah! the Navy still owes me a breakfast for that morning! We were backing up the flight deck people when the fire was got under control!

But as you said in the book, the ordinary young matelots had mostly boredom to contend with, though I do vividly remember it was always a 'heart stopper' watching Major Cheesman land on—the sharp banking turn—so much closer than anyone else and the quick descent of his Firefly—very flashy! But what a flyer—and what a man!!

Yes, it's all a long time ago, yet curiously it doesn't seem like it. I'm 63 now.

Article in an unknown newspaper re Aircraft Fitter A.C. Groom, from Sub.Lieut(A) 'Bim' Wells RNVR, 1772 Sqdn.

"I got out of the flight deck, but had only been there a few minutes when we were attacked by a Japanese suicide plane. It carried a 500 pound bomb and dived straight for the ship.

"However, this one got it wrong and landed on the flight deck, catching a piece of metal and sending it hurtling along the deck hitting me and breaking both my legs".

The plane then passed over the top of him before going over the side of the ship and exploding, making a wave some 30 feet high, which came crashing down on deck washing him onto the gun deck eight feet below.

He eventually arrived home and only after a long spell in a naval hospital was he discharged.

Ironically the date of his injury was April 1!

(This sounds like HMS Victorious *9th May—Ed).*

From S/Lt. (A) John Birtle RNVR, 887 Sqdn. *Indefatigable*

Bill Gibson was killed, in the island sick bay on April 1st. I noticed in 'The Forgotten Fleet' that he was shown as being killed whilst landing on another carrier—not so. There is some confusion here since it was 'Pop' Quigley who died landing on *Illustrious.* I know this because, as Squadron safety equipment officer Andrew Thompson asked me to borrow a driver from 820 and bring back Pop's parachute and dinghy. I got Geoff Carpenter of 820 to fly me over to *Illustrious* and saw the Safety Equipment officer there. We explained that Pop had landed on whilst the arrestor wires were set for either Corsairs or Hellcats and that when his wheels touched they went under a wire, ripping off the undercart. The hook failed to engage a wire and the Seafire slid under the bottom wire of the barrier which came down over the nose over the windscreen into the cockpit and decapitated him. The parachute and dinghy were bloodsoaked and were ditched, very sad.

So far as the ghost of Sub.Lieut(A) Sam Yarde RNVR is concerned, as I mentioned, I was duty boy in the upper hangar that night and as you know many were the times that maintenance crews had to work through the night. On this occasion I am fairly sure that it was a CPO of 887 who had finished his work and taken his camp bed down to the cable deck, a favourite and somewhat cooler place to sleep. He came dashing back into the upper hangar and asked me to go with him down to the cable deck since, and I quote his words which I remember well, 'I have just seen the ghost of Mr. Yarde sitting on one of the onion lockers, he was laughing and threw onions at me'. I laughed at this, I thought I was having my leg pulled. Sam Yarde had been killed some two or three days before, but the thought of his ghost appearing in an onion locker seemed too silly for words. However I went down with him to the cable deck which was by then deserted, where before, I believe, it had been packed with sleeping bodies and both lockers were securely padlocked, but right enough there were onions scattered about the deck. I went up to the keyboard on the wardroom flat, guarded night and day as you will recall by a RM sentry and asked him if anyone had had the keys for the onion lockers on the cable deck. The answer was in the negative and he showed me the key register which had to be signed when keys were removed which indicated that the keys for the onion locker had not been out for two or three days. I can't now recall whether or not I reported this to anyone. I doubt if I did.

Following on from that, I think it was Joe Halliwell, Eric Cowle and myself who were passing through the upper hangar the following evening when the rating on duty in the control position climbed down his ladder in something of a state to say that the telephones in the entrance lobbies to the upper hangar kept ringing and when he answered all he got was heavy breathing or groaning. So, and we thought this a great lark, we tied down the telephones in every entrance lobby with thread and went up to the control position where we waited. Sure enough the telephones did ring and we heard the heavy breathing or groaning as described, we then dashed down to the appropriate telephone only to find the thing still tied down and apparently not having been disturbed. In any case we were down and into the lobby concerned in a very short time and no-one could have refastened the phone and clipped up the eight dogs (clips) before we arrived. I couldn't explain it then and I can't explain it now. The whole thing could possibly have been a practical joke I suppose, but I can't think *how* it might have been achieved.

From Ldg. Stoker George Turner, HMS *Indefatigable*

My first year aboard *Indefat* was watch keeping on Engine Room, turbo generators, air compressors, motor boat crew (seaplane tender and barge). I was flight deck control room Ldg. Stoker for the remaining eleven months and knew practically all pilots, some of whom we sadly lost. One of whom sticks out most in my mind was Lt. Commander Leggatt, who we lost over Palembang, Sumatra, the one Firefly that did not return. One of his squadron pilots, who had shot down two Japs, saw him chasing a Nip over the island, that was the last he saw of him.

Do you remember the fatal venting of petrol tanks process in Sydney Harbour? More or less as soon as we had moored at Shark Island, which is now where the Opera House has been built, Stoker P.O. Tom Jenner was killed, along with two other stokers, names I have since forgotten.

Do you remember the Avenger going over the side? The crew of that particular kite owe their lives to myself and Ldg. Sto. Robinson, my oppo in the flight deck control room. It was our job to make up the arrester wire shackles on new cables, after the old wires had received their quota of hook ons. We must have done a good job of it, or rather them, for them to hold such a hanging weight, and in the sea that was running at that particular time.

Commander Whitfeld said to me that Ldg. Sto. Robinson and I should be awarded the DSM for our good work and our devotion to it. We weren't! Two more stokers in the flight deck party deserved it too: Pinnock and Vipond. Do you remember their skill and timing, with the crash barriers?

From AB R. Jenkins, HMS *Indefatigable*

May I congratulate you on such an interesting book, which brought back so many memories of my life on the *Indefatigable.*

I am very pleased you have written **Sakishima** and think of it as a tribute to all those who served in the B.P.F.

My action station was 'D' Director of port-side forward 4.5 gun turrets under Sub-Lieutenant Palmer, P.O. Barker on range finder and Leading Seaman Mike Smith on searcher sight. I can remember only too well, the Seafire crashing on top of us, also of helping its pilot extract himself from his plane, safe, but very shaken.

Another memory that sticks vividly in my mind which was very frightening, was an occasion whilst oiling ship from behind a tanker in heavy weather. I was on duty on the cable deck when the ship dipped into a large wave and the sea rushed up the anchor hawse pipes hitting the deckhead above and rushing all over the cable deck. A faint calling was heard for help and on looking down the port hawse pipe was a rating lying spreadeagled on the anchor upside down. Quick action was needed and came with someone with a heaving line, promptly thrown down the pipe and the man clutched it and was hauled to safety before the ship dipped into another large wave. I can't remember the man's name but I'm sure he would never forget this incident.

I recall the time after being hit by the kamikaze. Leading Seaman Mike Smith on the searcher sight suddenly remarking I can't see through my sight. Quickly looking to see what was wrong he discovered his sight clogged up with human flesh which he removed quickly and resumed his position searching for the next target. We assumed when the action was all over that it was part of that Japanese.

Perhaps you may remember, whenever we had breakfast at Defence Stations and if it consisted of sardines in rolls, we always seemed to be attacked afterwards. It seems ridiculous now how small things seem to stay in our memories.

From Lt.(A) Cliff Miseldine RNVR, 887 Squadron, HMS *Indefatigable*

Looking back and reflecting on wartime experiences, one marvels at the naivety of youth. The hair-raising events and actions one took for granted at the time, but which would now, forty-five years later, cause the hair not only to rise but to turn white or fall out—or both!

One such occasion occurred when, having taken off in a Seafire from *Indefatigable* for a routine C.A.P. mission, I went to make the customary 'jink' to starboard in order to clear the deck of the slipstream for the following plane, and found to my horror that the joystick refused to move sideways one iota. Having established it could be moved forward and back, I climbed to a respectable height, thinking the while that my No. 2 who was following, must have had a rather uncomfortable take-off and was probably calling me all the names under the sun.

For several minutes I tried to force the stick sideways with no success so I called up the ship, explained my position, and prepared myself for a first bale-out. Ditching Seafires was a course of action not to be pursued by anyone who had a comfortable old-age in mind! In such an aircraft a pilot, even if he had remembered not to unfasten his harness until after the plane had bounced twice on the sea, had, on average, four seconds to get out before finding himself at least twenty feet below the surface. Seafires didn't float, and Lt. Jimmy Hayes, of 894 Squadron, was one of the lucky few who survived such an option and gained his Goldfish Club badge.

However, at last having managed to get the stick to move about an inch either side, I decided to make a huge circuit back to the ship. Lt. Peter Roome, our intrepid Batsman, had been warned that some idiot Seafire pilot was going to make a stern approach from about two miles out, and the deck-handling crew prepared for an almighty prang.

Because of its lengthy nose, a Seafire normally had to make a tight banking, 'split-arse' approach to land on, only straightening up the last few seconds before touchdown. In this way the pilot had a clear view of the batsman's signals right on to the deck. Dicey, but effective!—although only a non-aviator could have dreamt up the idea of turning a Spitfire into a deck-landing plane.

By undoing my harness and leaning half out of the cockpit—trying to ignore the heat of the exhaust fumes in my face—I could just make out Peter's bats and, more by luck than judgement, caught the second wire and landed in one piece.

When my plane was examined, they found the mechanic had left a spanner inside which had jammed in the aileron yoke—a novel example of the old saying, 'Someone's put a spanner in the works!' Needless to say, some pretty lurid words were passed to the culprit!

One memory that comes to mind was when Buster Hallett finally joined the ship as the Wing Commander towards the end of the Sakishima operation in the Pacific. He brought with him his pet idea in the form of 90 gallon long-range fuel tanks. These had been designed to be fitted under the belly of Seafires enabling them to stay airborne for four hours instead of the normal one and a half hours—or less if full power was needed in combat. The idea was admirable, provided one didn't actually have to stay regularly in the cockpit oneself for four hours! The Seafires of 887 Squadron were programmed to give maximum performance at high altitude and therefore we pilots of 887 were destined to suffer the four hour stints in our C.A.P. (Combat Air Patrol) role, i.e. Fleet Protection . . . and suffer we did!

Anyone who is familiar with the Seafire cockpit, which carried more bulky equipment for radar and communication than its counterpart the Spitfire, will appreciate that even wearing just a flying suit and parachute, a pilot has very little room to manoeuvre. When you add to that equipment other essential items for possible use over sea or in the jungle if one had to bale out, the problem increases. I refer to such extra items as a dinghy, Mae West, water bottle, food rations, revolver, goggles, oxygen mask, lucky charms and photographs of the latest girl friend—there was literally NO room for manoeuvre.

There was a saying in the Squadron that if anyone discovered more than 48 positions in which to relieve one or the other buttock whilst up for the four hours, he could have free drinks for a week!

One of our mechanics nearly failed to return to the bosom of his family when, having taken off for a stint of C.A.P., I discovered (or at least my left buttock did!) that he had put my dinghy on the seat UPSIDE DOWN. To the uninitiated, this meant that I was sitting on the CO_2 bottle used to inflate the dinghy. I have never spent such an uncomfortable four hours in my life!!!

The four-berth cabin right aft and just below *Indefatigable's* steel flight deck, and in which the temperature could rise to 120 degrees in equatorial waters—the cabin shared by Sub. Lts. George Hartland, Alan Gambles, 'Hattie' Hatton and the writer, would at times resound with the voice of Bing Crosby when Sub. Lt. Brad Bradley brought in his collection of records to be played on Alan's old gramophone. It wasn't long before we all knew most of the words!

After dinner, back at Fleet oiling positions after strikes around Sakishima, a Wardroom cry would ring out—"Who's birthday is it?—No?—Well it must be somebody's somewhere . . . Range the piano!!" Then there would be the sound of Sub. Lt. Alan Gambles strumming the keys and the mighty chorus of 'Paper Doll' would resound throughout the ship—followed by other less repeatable ditties!

From O/S George Hunn, HMS *Indefatigable*

I was a very young Ordinary Seaman and my action station was look out.

I did not have a bird's eye view of the explosion as I was at that moment trying to dig a hole with my fingers without success so I had to hope nothing would happen to me, but I can assure you my underpants changed colour.

A fellow lookout had gone to the island toilets prior to the attack and when it was all over he came staggering back with a door knob in his hand and a very small cut on his nose. I said to him he should be awarded a medal for being wounded and then I added what he was doing with a door knob in his hand and his actual reply was, "That's what's left of the island shit house." Of course that broke the tension, and we all laughed.

From Roy Gibbs, TAG 820 Sqdn. HMS *Indefatigable*

Date 4th May 1945, Target Hirara airfield, Miyako Jima. Objective flak-busting.

I was in Avenger 338, Pilot S/Lieut. Alan Ryman, Observer S/Lieut Frank Burgess. As we pulled out of the dive bombing attack, the aircraft was hit in the starboard wing stub, and started a nasty fire. Alan Ryman did a fantastic job of diving, and side slipping the aircraft which extinguished the wing fire. He then flew back to the carrier, and landed on, with no hydraulics and only one wheel down. The incredible thing was that the wing locking bolt had been blown out and it was only the intense heat of the fire which had fused the wing together. Frank Burgess was slightly wounded.

From 'A Matelot at Heart' by Stoker Sam Crook, of HMS *Ulster*

I was now back down in the aft or No. 2 Boiler Room and it was there I had this kind of premonition, I got all claustrophobic, my inner self told me to get out as something was going to happen in that Boiler Room that had been so kind to me on D-Day and down in the Med. Tomorrow 1 April 1945 we were invading Okinawa, I came off watch and sat in the mess deck talking when the Chief Stoker came in and said he wanted a messman for the officers aft. My hand shot up like magic, some unknown force put my hand up, I heard the Chief talking to me it seemed like miles way, to change all duties there and then which I duly obeyed. Then I thought I am out of the Boiler Room and the fear and thoughts in my head had stopped; I was relieved and now a messman for the officers aft, duties were damage control and ammo carrier when in action. Next morning with the bombing of the island the fleet opened up with all guns, while all this was happening the suicide planes started their attack. Whilst running back for more ammo I felt *Ulster* roll to starboard and looking up saw our 'present' on its way down, yes it was a kami and the pilot had selected us for his target. He came hurtling down as we rolled one way and another I thought Dear God but it was not to be, this time He couldn't help us, as the kami' came between No. 2 Boiler and Engine Room. All those below were killed.

They say you cannot look into the future—I did!

From AB J. Slade HMS *Ulster* and HMS *Grenville*

I joined HMS *Ulster* from *Tyne* in Manus March 1945 and left her in Leyte April 1945, by which time I had travelled some 14,000 miles to be in a war—never fired a shot—saw my ship crippled by a kamikaze—lost 5 shipmates—attended a burial at sea, and received a hero's 'Cock-a-doodle-doo' welcome. I was 18!

As an 'Asdic' rating, my hearing had to be safeguarded at all times, so I was not allowed near a gun. Dawn action stations on Easter Sunday 1945 found me in the forward P.O.'s mess on *Ulster* as 'A' Gun supply party—about 8 feet behind 'A' gun, and above my head was 'B' Gun—4.7s that could go off bang! We couldn't see what was happening outside, and when a big bang materialized, we thought 'B' gun had fired. It wasn't until we were stood down from action stations that we were told that we had been in imminent danger of sinking. We were set to ditching top-weight, and the first things over the side were the 'wash-deck' lockers. The 'tin fish' went (£2,000 each), depth charges, shattered boats and davits, anything that could be unshipped went over the side until she appeared to stop settling in the water.

When *Gambia* took us in tow we had time to assess the situation. A huge hole in the starboard side, 4 lads killed below and one who got topside but didn't survive. We had no power, we couldn't make fresh water, so what water we had was rationed to one cup per day per man, to be taken as tea. *Gambia* trailed water barrels astern which we tried to pick up with grappling irons with no success. We rigged awnings slackly forward and aft to catch rainwater, but it didn't rain for the whole week of the tow to Leyte. Ironically, when we tied up alongside *Tyne* in Leyte, and were invited to an evening film show on her upper deck a tropical rainstorm washed the show out.

During the tow we tried boiling dried potatoes, cabbage, onions, etc. in sea-water—inedible!

When we spotted a rain-cloud a few miles ahead, we stripped naked and stood on the iron deck in the sun, holding bars of soap, and we waited for it to rain, but at our speed the rain-cloud was faster than us and we missed it—frustrating!

We didn't carry salt-water soap, but the messdeck think-tank came up with the idea that Libby's evaporated milk would mix with Lux soap flakes, and would lather and wash off with salt-water. April fools like me tried it—disastrous!

For some reason, a forward locker held a large supply of tins of Libby's milk and tins of gooseberries. These were dished out at tea-times. Very nice at the time of consumption but the after effects were an even more pronounced thirst, and much freedom of bowel movement.

We had large sharks swimming close alongside by the shattered plates, and an attempt to catch one, using a ham bone on a meat hook, lashed to a heaving line resulted in the shark taking bait and hook and snapping the line.

Evenings on the upper deck were quite eerie. The turbulence caused by the shattered plates caused a strange fluorescent effect. It looked as if a bright light was shining out of the flooded boiler room, and the shifting water made strange noises which at times seemed to sound like a muffled bell.

The lad who died topside was buried at sea—a very moving experience for me—a boy of 18 on my first fighting ship. The other four lads were recovered by divers at Leyte and a burial party took them to sea to lay them at rest. By this time I was back aboard *Tyne* as spare crew, but I attended the 'sale of dead man's effects', yet another moving experience, where the lad's kit etc, was auctioned, even down to a penny box of matches which raised a bid of half a crown and was put back in to be auctioned again.

I joined *Grenville* when the BPF returned from Sakishima to Leyte and went with her on the next series of strikes, where, besides providing anti-submarine cover etc, we carried out duties as crash boats which involved steaming astern of the carriers when aircraft were flying on, with the intention of picking up pilots from aircraft, who dropped short or ditched, some suffered this fate, but we never rescued anyone.

The kamikaze attacks on the carriers caused a few butterflies when I recalled the near sinking of *Ulster* because although I didn't see the one that got her, I was now seeing what the lads who were topside on *Ulster* saw—Jap pilots flying deliberately to their deaths.

Re-fuelling and receiving supplies at sea from the Fleet Train was a tricky and skilful operation. All our requirements passed from ship to ship whilst under way. We even had a British Pacific Fleet Newspaper—Pacific Post.

On V.E. day, we spliced the mainbrace—I got a cup of lime juice—and I think a lot of folk back home thought the war had ended on that day and that the Pacific war was an all-American affair—not so. The B.P.F. was an awesome fleet and the grand entry into Sydney after the war was as fine a spectacle as Sydney had ever seen.

From H. Johnson, ABST, HMS *Black Prince*

'Action Stations'—thinks—more bloody D.C. exercises. No, it's the real thing, 0900, aircraft carrier sending off strikes on Myako and Ishigaki. I hope they give the yellow B's hell, I want to go home.

A typhoon warning hits us on 11th April. It's really rough out there, never thought waves could be so high. I've lost everything but my ring. It's quiet now, spoke too soon, Japs attacking the fleet, I can't see a bloody thing—battened down in the forward messdesk. There's a lot of banging going on up top, what's happening? It's the same thing day in day out. Action Stations, exercise, duty. When will it all end?

Now we've another duty. HMS *Quilliam* hits carrier in fog, we are to tow her to a tug, out of the area, she's badly damaged and it's a terrible job towing her. Her bows acting as a rudder. Fleet tug takes over, and we can't get the tow wire in as the capstan's fallen over (packed up). We are a sitting duck.

HMAS *Norman* and HMS *Black Prince* were detailed off to tow the *Quilliam* away from the area, *Norman* could not tow her, so *Black Prince* took over, when the ocean tug came to us to take her in tow.

From AB D.C. High, HMS *Black Prince*

My action station was starboard look out, so in some respect you could say that I had the opportunity to see everything that went on. One of my most vivid recollections was the period when our carrier force was attacked by suicide aircraft on the 4th May 1945. HMS *Formidable* was hit, but the most amazing sight was when the second plane hit the deck of HMS *Indomitable* and literally bounced along the deck and then slid off into the sea and a third narrowly missed the *Indomitable*.

From Ex. Lieut W.H. Procter RNVR, HMS *Argonaut*

As we left for northern waters, I recall a piece of irony. Some of the seamen had not been on their best behaviour ashore in Sydney and detention was the inevitable punishment. But it was rough justice that these defaulters were put ashore at New Guinea detention quarters, whilst the rest of us proceeded further north to face—well we weren't sure what it would be, but it was operational.

At this point I would like to say that our Sin Bosun, The Reverend John Roberts took a most human feeling for our lads who had misbehaved. His line was what can you expect when the lads have been at sea for some weeks. John was a most likeable fellow.

In an unbelievable way, I have to confess I was not at the time cognisant of the whole plan. I've learnt more about the BPF strategy in later years than I knew at the time. I suppose that sounds silly, but one's concern at the time was your own patch as an escort cruiser, rather than what those carrier lads were up to. We, of course, could see the planes take off and land, sadly not always getting airborne, just flipping off the deck of the carrier. But the exactness of it all was vague. We were having a go and doing our own thing. A single-mindedness and eagerness in the belief of why we were there.

The Fleet Air Arm pilots were my pin-ups: I had the greatest admiration for them. They were at the sharp end. But of course we were all part of a grand plan. We were all needed.

The battleships and cruisers were shelling shore installations and, I suppose, we had submarines around. And how could we have remained at sea for such long periods without the RFA and tankers.

The *Argonaut* occasionally had a special role as guard-cum-picket ship for the planes. Stationed some 30 miles nearer the enemy coast than the main Fleet, our job was to assist with any of our planes which had ditched, and to alert the main Fleet if any enemy planes were filtering back with our lads to attack the Fleet. I'm not sure why we were selected for this task. It could be that we had the latest radar fitted at the Philadelphia yard. What I do remember was that it was a dawn to dusk operation. It was tiring, but were we really aware of this at the time? I don't know, which is another example of how the passing years dim one's memory.

For me, our guard/picket role was a feeling of isolation. There was an accompanying destroyer, but the strength and might of the main Fleet which was always a comfort, wasn't with us.

We, of course, rejoined the main Fleet at dusk when we all cruised up and down in the darkness until dawn when it all started again. I recall one incident which could have been disastrous for the *Argonaut*. It was nightfall and the Fleet was cruising up and down and the *Argonaut* was at the rear—Tail-end Charlie. All ships were darkened, no navigation lights. Suddenly the rest of the Fleet were bearing down on us! We were on a collision course. I was not on the bridge at the time but learned later that the Fleet had been given a 180° turn by the command ship, but we had not received the signal! I'm told that navigation lights were turned on and we managed to weave our way through our own ships.

From Sto. Arnold Swift, HMS *Urania*

Jan. 1st 1945 Fleet left Trincomalee for Sumatra raids returning to Colombo *Jan. 9th*. Left Colombo for Fremantle Australia with the destroyer *Ulster* and cruiser *Suffolk* escorting the troopship *Rimutaka* taking the Duke and Duchess of Gloucester and children on board.

Jan. 21st At dinner time our escort to the *Rimutaka* was relieved by two New Zealand destroyers and the cruiser *Achilles*. We steamed past in line ahead giving cheers as they steamed on to Sydney. We left for Fremantle.

Jan. 22nd Arrived Fremantle at dinner time. All the crew received an Xmas present from the Australian Comforts Fund. Leave given to starboard watch from 12 p.m. till 11 a.m. next day.

Jan. 23rd Went ashore at dinner to Perth. Had a walk round a lovely city had a drink till 6 p.m. when bars close, then saw a film before turning in at the Services Club.

Jan. 26th & 27th On leave in Perth enjoying ourselves. Returning on board about 4 p.m. in Fremantle.

Jan. 31st Left Fremantle at night with *Ulster* for sea and did a shoot, after went to relieve two sloops escorting the maintenance carrier *Unicorn* and cruiser *Suffolk*. Relieved the sloops on Feb. 4th and returned to Fremantle arriving Feb. 8th leaving at night for Sydney with *Ulster* and *Unicorn*.

Feb. 12th Arrived in the afternoon and joined up with the British Pacific Fleet. Went under Sydney harbour bridge after oiling ship and tied up alongside another destroyer.

Feb. 13th Went to see Mr. & Mrs. Woods of Cammary with my mate. Walked over Sydney Bridge, we met the Woods' son who was a soldier in Perth. They made us very welcome.

Feb. 14th Boiler cleaning party came aboard. I met Soker Coley from Matlock.

Feb. 16th Visited Luna Park at night.

Feb. 18th Left the ship at 8 a.m. with my mate to visit the Woods at Cammary, who took us out for the day into the country and coast. Stayed the night at Woods' house.

Feb. 20th Was alongside in Vaucluse. Ship's company dance night given by our Captain's father Harold Gardiner.

Feb. 28th Left Vaucluse in the afternoon and joined up with the British Pacific Fleet bound for Manus.

March 2nd Left the Fleet and returned to Sydney in the morning on our own, arriving March 3rd in Woolloomooloo. Went ashore in the afternoon, met a young lady who took me to Epping, met the family, very nice people. Arrived back on board 1 a.m.

March 6th Left Sydney at night for sea with the destroyer *Undaunted* and the carrier *Illustrious* on the way to Manus.

March 12th Still on the way to Manus with the destroyer and carrier at night off New Guinea was searching for a man who fell overboard from the carrier, but we had no results. Arrived Manus March 13th.

March 18th Left Manus with the British Fleet for an advanced Pacific base arriving on March 20th at Ulithi.

March 23rd Left Ulithi with the Fleet for raids on Sakishima Islands.

March 26th At action stations most of the time.

March 28th Moved back to the fleet train for supplies.

March 20th Left the fleet train for further raids on the Sakishima Islands, on the radio today stating British Pacific Fleet operating near Japan.

April 1st Jap suicide planes raided Fleet.

April 7th In the afternoon we left the fleet to pick up one of the carrier plane pilots who had crashed 80 miles away near the Sakishima coast. We had air cover, but when we recovered the pilot he was dead. We buried him at sea.

April 12th & 13th Our planes still raiding and we had raids by the Japs on the Fleet.

April 14th Arrived oiling area, we left the fleet for Leyte with a destroyer and the carrier *Illustrious,* who was relieved by the carrier *Formidable.* Arrived Leyte April 16th for boiler cleaning alongside the depot ship *Tyne.* British Fleet joined us in Leyte April 23rd.

April 26th Still in Leyte. Every man on board had the privilege of one pint bottle of beer, price 1/3. Just the job.

May 1st The Fleet left Leyte for more raids on Sakishima.

May 2nd Hitler reported dead on the radio.

May 4th At dinner time we and other destroyers screened the battleships *KGV* and *Howe* and cruisers shelling the coast, enemy aircraft raiding the fleet all day.

May 8th Heard over the radio the war with Germany is over. Everybody happy to hear it. Only wish it was here.

May 9th Fleet raided at teatime. A carrier hit by suicide bomber.

May 10th Fleet arrived oiling area and oiled ships. We were taking wounded pilots and ratings off the damaged carrier and transferring them to Woolworth escort carriers all day. At night we spliced the mainbrace.

May 12th—14th Return with the Fleet to do more raids. I have got prickly heat rash very bad. Our raids on Sakishima broadcast over the radio today and the strikes still go on. Oh! for a run ashore in Aussie.

May 25th & 26th Last day of strikes with our carrier planes on Sakishima and arrived oiling area after sailed for Manus. *KGV* and three destroyers went to Guam. We were told during the fleet's operations we had done 25,000 miles of sea time in two months.

May 28th Still on the way to Manus with the fleet at night we did a practice shoot and shot off the galley funnel. Arrived Manus May 30th.

June 1st Passing through the islands on our way to Sydney. Carriers flying off aircraft in the afternoon.

June 5th Arrived in Sydney about 10 a.m. and we went into Cockatoo dry dock. I caught a ferry to Sydney and went to Epping to meet my friend. Came back on board at midnight, it was grand to get ashore again after being at sea so long.

June 6th Went to Epping at night and slept in the new British Centre at Hyde Park, a lovely place for the British serviceman.

June 7th—11th Went on four days leave to Epping. Went to the La Park Zoo. Bought a boomerang. Pictures of the British Fleet in action on at Epping pictures.

June 19th Ship's company dance given by captain's father.

June 22nd Our Captain, Lieut-Commander Denis Gardiner D.S.C. RN, left the ship. He will be missed. A damn good skipper.

From AB J.M. Montgomery, HMS *Indomitable*

On the 1st April 1945, Flying Stations was at 0500 hrs., then we flew off strikes. Later on we were attacked by Zekes, they straffed the flightdeck and I was trying to take cover behind some rivets and arrester wires, my adrenalin was spouting like mad, as I scrabbled for cover. My lucky day, as we had 3 killed and some injured. Our deck officer was wounded and later transferred by Bailey stretcher to another ship.

From A.B. Ronald Fidler, HMS *Indomitable*

As an A.B. my job was the after lift driver, and when the aircraft were landing I was talker for the batsman, I had a pair of binoculars, and as the aircraft approached the stern I would inform the Batsman that the hook, wheels and flaps were down for landing.

One day we were to make a bombing attack. I had taken the lift to the lower hangar (we had 2) and was waiting for the first aircraft to be pushed on to take to the flight deck, when without warning the armoured doors closed. Not quite certain what to do and not knowing what was happening I decided to take the lift to the flight deck, as my head came level with the flight deck, not a soul was to be seen, by this time all guns were firing and I could see what they were firing at, within about a minute of crashing onto the deck. I did not wait for the lift to reach the top, but jumped up to the deck (in the meantime the lift would reach the deck level and stop itself). I ran across the deck, to the starboard side, the twin 4.5 guns were pointing over the deck fired, I felt the blast of the shells as they went over my head, I managed to reach the manhole by the side of the ship, about 6 yards away and jump down the hatchway. My feet did not touch one step on the way down. In the meantime the kamikaze had hit the deck, slid along it and over the side. Another kamikaze was following and was hit by our gunners, was set alight and finally shot down before it could reach the ship.

During the first attack on the fleet I witnessed an attack on HMS *Indefatigable.* Her planes were fully loaded with bombs, lined up on deck for take off. A kamikaze hit right in the middle of them, in seconds the deck was a mass of flames and smoke from stem to stern. I could see the flight crew manhandling the burning planes and pushing them over the side, the heat must have been terrible, 100's of burn casualties besides those that died on the day. While *Indefatigable* was ablaze, through all the fire and smoke, every gun on board continued to fire. On that day I learnt first hand why the British Royal Navy can boast such a proud record. I feel privileged to have served in this service with such men.

From George Milcoy, HMS *Indomitable*

My thoughts go back to the occasion when the seamen refused to 'turn to' one afternoon.

This all took place at the advanced base of Ulithi atoll—a vast natural harbour.

I can only put this action down to discontent over the food and the way the ship was being worked. I would say that it was some of the worst food I ever had whilst serving on the *Indomitable* (especially remembering we stored ship in Sydney a week or so before and had seen a good variety and plenty of it being taken aboard).

We were also working normal routine as opposed to other ships who were working tropical routine.

The trouble started just before 'Cooks to the galley' sounded off. Someone came into the Mess and said 'You want to see what's being dished up for dinner. It's curry. Looks like a lot of spew'. In the meantime more men came into the Mess and after a few minutes of shouting, the men whose turn it was to collect the food from the galley were told to go and if what we were told was true, refuse the curry. The men returned from the galley empty handed. Now the men had nearly an hour before falling in at 13.15. This all took place in my Mess. The men from the starboard mess opposite joined us. These two Messes were used by the Forward 4.5 Gun crews. Also more seamen from other parts of the ship joined in. I cannot say for sure if the stokers joined in. In the meantime a member of my Mess—an old three badger AB, made a short speech. He said he agreed with what we were doing and supported us but didn't want to get involved because he had been involved in the Invergordon mutiny and would be picked on as a ringleader and asked us to understand his feelings.

13.15. The first G had sounded, no one moved out of the Messes. Just before the second G sounded the GI came to the Messes and told us to get fell in. He was told in no uncertain terms to clear off. So it went on.

Lt. of the Focastle and Jimmy the One the Commander all came to the Mess one after the other. The Commander was told we wanted to see the Captain. So Clear Lower deck was sounded.

We all crowded round the island on the Flight Deck. Captain Eccles appeared, his first words were 'I don't know what's going on. I've been called away from my lunch'.

A voice from the crowded Flight Deck shouted 'you're effing lucky. We haven't had any'. The Captain then said he could have us all shot for Mutiny in wartime. What will our American allies think of us. After a lot of shouting of questions to the Captain, he said he would set up an investigation.

Needless to say we got better food after that incident. Then came the retributions. Two men from my Mess were court-martialled and sentenced to serve their punishment in the cells of other ships in the BPF—*King George V* and the *Howe,* while the ships were in the operational area.

The rest of us got a warning and a dressing down.

After the war at a Reunion, several of us were talking to Captain Eccles about the mutiny and he said it gave him nightmares.

From March 1945 until the end of 'Operation Iceberg' being a member of the 4.5 Gun crew meant that we spent a lot of time in the Gun turret Cruising, Defence and Action Stations. In fact most of us at night slept on the deck in the turret to make sure we weren't late to go on watch. Being in the Gun turret we didn't see what was going on outside but were kept informed by the Director. For instance on 4 May, Japanese aircraft attacked the Fleet. One crashed on the *Formidable* and one hit the *Indomitable,* bounced off B Group 4.5 Gun turret into the sea and blew up. I was in the turret at the time, but we didn't know a thing about it until we were told.

I didn't mind while the 4.5 guns were firing at the Japs but got apprehensive when the close range weapons—Bofors Pom-Poms and Oerlikons opened up.

From Stoker Frederick D. Clark, HMS *Indomitable*

My first recollection of this period was the heat, the stifling heat which caused so much misery. The massive armoured flight deck soaked up all the heat and so turned the ship into an oven in which we had to live and work. Prickly heat and sweat rash from which most of us suffered, brought on itching which went on for 24 hours a day seven days a week, for week after dreary week and even worse during action stations when overalls and anti-flash gear had to be worn.

In a carrier the ratings' living quarters take second place to machinery space. The more aircraft carried, the more F.A.A. personnel have to be accommodated. Every inch of hangar space was taken up with aircraft plus a large deck park so the messdecks were very much over-crowded and poorly ventilated, even more so when the ship was battened down for action which made it very uncomfortable indeed.

The long hours at Action Stations, from dawn until dusk in the combat area, meant very little sleep as after standing down, messdeck cleaning still had to be done and night watches kept, so a full night's sleep was a very rare luxury. Another thing we had to put up with was the cockroaches. Of other ships I have served in, none had a cockroach population as great as *Indomitable's*. They thrived in the hot conditions and bred in their thousands, but it was rare to see anybody killing them, so I suppose it could be said that they were accepted as part as the ship's company.

Regarding food, I believe most ratings preferred the sandwiches which were brought round to us when the ship was closed up for action. The normal meals were not too bad, but this was only due to action taken earlier by the ratings.

Referring to the near mutiny over food (while in Ceylon) Fred noted:-

Probably this sort of thing could have been avoided, but in those days officers were unapproachable and ratings were not allowed to speak to them unless spoken to first, especially on the big ships where discipline was rigid. It is ironic that today people will queue at their local Tandoori clamouring for the stuff that caused a mutiny.

In your book **Sakishima** you stated that you were given shore leave at Manus, Ulithi and Leyte. This may have been an officer's privilege, but the impression was given that everybody got it. This was not so. Speaking for *Indomitable* nobody from the lower deck was granted shore leave from the day we left Sydney in early March until we returned in June, over 100 days later.

I have not mentioned the attacks on the fleet or the collision with *Quilliam.* These are best left to those more suited to do so, as most of the ship's company did not know what was going on outside unless their duties took them within vision. The Major R.M. gave us some idea over the ship's Tannoy system.

This is just an outline of what life was like on the *Indomitable,* conditions which in those days were endured as our lot but would not be tolerated today. Water was severely rationed and was only turned on for short periods during the day.

Whether or not the Pacific operations were worthwhile is debatable taking into account the number who lost their lives and those who were wounded or suffered broken health, and bearing in mind that today the Japanese have got all they ever wanted and more including 'colonies' in the U.K.

When the war ended the Australians and New Zealanders did us proud, as they did all the time we were in their countries which is more than can be said of our own who hardly knew the BPF existed.

The books I have read about the BPF have all been written by officers who knew little or nothing about life on the lower deck. The Fleet carriers were huge and the impression would be that they were comfortable ships to live in. In fact they were overcrowded and one slept where one could, be it in a hammock or on or under the mess table. Some ratings even slept in the hangars among the aircraft. A room not much larger than the average living room served as a wash room for some 200 stokers. Add to this a top-heavy heaving mass in a typhoon and a truer picture comes to life.

Soon after my release from the service it was found that I had T.B. from which I took 3 years to recover and a further 21 years of hospital visits. When diagnosed, my doctor's first words were 'Another one from the Pacific Fleet I suppose'. Perhaps those few words sum it all up.

One event which I have never seen in print, but which I think deserves a mention is the day Task Force 57 stopped while at sea. I am of course referring to the day of President Roosevelt's funeral. It is very unusual for H.M. ships to stop in wartime but unique for a fleet to stop (or very nearly, the engines were just turning over) near enemy waters. Divisions and a service were held on *Indomitable's* flight deck. I remember that the sea was calm and all was quiet and still, except for the buzzing of our fighter planes overhead circling the fleet. After the service, the Royal Marines band played 'The Star Spangled Banner'. This was a very moving experience and I think most of us were glad when the ship got on the move again.

Kamikaze on fire dives on HMS Indomitable, *11.34 on 4th May 1945. 'Deck landed' and crashed over port side (see Sakishima p.198). Photo: J. R. Northeast*

On 4th May 1945 *Indomitable* was struck by a kamikaze. The ship was turning to starboard as it hit the deck so it careered along the sloping deck and exploded as it went over the port bow. The following morning, attached to the ship's daily orders was a piece from Captain Eccles *(later to become C in C Home Fleet.—Ed)*. I cannot remember the exact words but went something like:

'Yesterday's attack could have resulted in serious consequences but the outcome had nothing to do with good luck or God's will, but was due to *my* orders being promptly obeyed by the cox'n'.

Then followed a few paragraphs on the merits of being alert at all times.

I remember one evening after dark we were outside the Sakishima combat zone and we were granted a film show, the first for many weeks. The after lift well was used as a cinema. This lift served both upper and lower hangars. When used as a cinema, the fire curtain to the entrance of the lower hangar was dropped and used as a screen. The lift was brought to the bottom and the audience settled on it to enjoy the show. This made an ideal open air cinema. On this occasion, due to black-out regulations the lift had to remain at flight deck level so the men had to sit in the lift well which was about 3 ft. lower than the hangar deck. The film showing at the time was I believe, Van Johnson in 'Three Girls and a Sailor'. About half way through, the bells started to ring and the lift descend. Of course there was near panic below with the men trying to negotiate the 3 ft. deep well to get out. It turned out that the lift was needed at the upper hangar to take an aircraft to the flight deck and that is as far as it went. If only somebody had told us. The lift could have been stopped from below by turning a lever but I doubt if this could be reached as we were below deck level, with bodies everywhere. Those were a few seconds I would not like to experience again.

We left dry dock with an ice cream making machine on board. It was said that this was provided by the Australian people. I do not know if this was so but one thing is almost certain, it wasn't supplied by the Admiralty. The ice cream was issued every evening after an arduous day but by the time it reached the messes it was in liquid form. I cannot remember if we had to pay for it but it was offered and accepted as a dog would a bone after a hard day in the fields. This is just to point out how today's values differ from then. The ice cream really was appreciated judging by all the grumbling that went on each time the machine broke down!

From Lieut. Denis Moore, RNVR HMS *Indomitable*

Indom. had been at sea for 62 days when we arrived at Leyte: (no shore leave) 26 of which were operational.

She steamed 27,000 miles.

Her aircraft made 1,200 deck landings (only 3 prangs).

Dropped 900 bombs, fired 250,000 rounds of .5 ammunition, shot down 20 and damaged 18 enemy aircraft.

Indomitable *Avengers over Ishigaki, bombs bursting on runway, 9th May 1945.*
Photo: J. R. Northeast

From Lt. (A) K. E. Ward DSC, RNVR, 894 Squadron, HMS *Indefatigable*

*(Although the following incident was told in **Sakishima**, I have received this other recollection from a different viewpoint.—Ed.)*

May 3, 1945—N.E. of Luzon heading north.
The shady quarterdeck was a popular place for relaxing on those hot afternoons spent taking on oil. Our speed was reduced to about 8 knots and the sea had a long gentle swell, reflecting the beautiful blue of a cloudless sky. On the quarterdeck next to the railings and stretching around the stern of *Indefat.* was a line of folding camp beds—perhaps twenty or so—brought there by squadron types wanting to kip or read. I was perched on one bed with a book when somewhere a heavy machine gun opened up. It was unexpected and startling. Several heads looked up—including mine—alert for possible danger from an attacking Jap plane. But there was nothing—no activity at all in the air or on the sea. Yet the gun was still firing and it seemed very close. The hammering racket it made went on and on relentlessly, getting nearer and much louder. The guys around were as disturbed as I was, fearing impending danger. But we also felt helpless for we could see nothing. The hammering noise was now like a pneumatic drill reverberating through the ship. It concentrated unbelievingly overhead, where there was solid steel—several decks in fact. The adrenalin was beginning to flow now in everyone listening

and waiting. Then one man moved; quickly away from his bed to the centre of the quarterdeck, and squatted on his heels, still listening. Seconds later he leapt to his feet and tore into the safety of the starboard gangway. As if on a signal several other men got up and ran forrard. By this time I was standing by the rail wondering what to do—was I in danger? Where was it coming from? Another five or six men leapt to their feet and ran to the rear of the deck and flung themselves down between ammunition lockers—then another two men—and now the hammering was all around us and deafening. I felt very alarmed now, so I fled—to the rear—and leapt on top of the other men. By now there must have been ten or twelve of us in a heap, like a collapsed rugby scrum.

Then came the shock of heavy bullets or shells bursting through the bulkhead above us. They seemed to crush and burst their way downwards for ever—and then suddenly all was still! Nobody could move at first, for there was smoke and dust and the smell of cordite with hot metal. Eventually we disentangled ourselves and with relief we stood up and looked forrard. There in the bulkhead above were jagged holes in a twenty-five foot spread, and by our feet, many, many large metal tears. The shells or bullets had passed right through the ship—or almost—from top to bottom. I stood there and looked in disbelief at the jagged holes above and below, and then I wondered what lay below us. So I bent down and looked through one of the holes. Immediately beneath me was a cabin and a bunk, and lying there was S/Lt. (A) J. A. R. Mackintyre RNVR—on his bunk bleeding and dying from two large bullet wounds in his body.

(Caused by an Avenger with folded wings on the flight deck accidentally opening fire.—Ed.)

Extracts from 'Alarm Starboard' by Lieut. Cmdr. G. Brooke RN

I am grateful to Geoffrey Brooke for permission to quote the following from his marvellous book 'Alarm Starboard'. Before the events described here, he had been present at the sinking of the Hood *while fighting the* Bismark *in HMS* Prince of Wales. *He was on board her when she too was sunk with the* Repulse. *There followed a series of amazing adventures escaping across the Indian Ocean in a native boat, the* Sederhana Djoharis.

In HMS Bermuda *he was at the landings in Africa and the Arctic run to Russia. After a brief respite, he volunteered for the BPF and served aboard the carriers* Indomitable *and* Formidable. *At his own request, he retired in 1958 as Lieut. Cdr. DSC, RN.*

When HMS *Formidable* approached the jetty at Woolloomooloo on March 10th I stood looking up at her great grey bulk with understandably mixed feelings. She looked much like the *Indomitable,* but in fact as a sister of *Illustrious* and *Victorious* was a couple of years older.

Having said my traditional joining piece to the Officer of the Watch I repaired to the spacious Wardroom and was musing on the last occasion of being there—bearded and somewhat lighter in weight from *Sederhana Djohanis*—when a large hand descended on my shoulder and a pleasant Canadian voice said 'My relief I believe?' I turned to find an immensely tall Lieutenant—he made my six feet look diminutive—who introduced himself as McPhee. After a few pleasantries, 'What's the job?' I asked. 'You're Fire and Crash officer and Chief Flight Deck Director.' 'I'm *what*?' He laughed. 'Yes, it's a bit unusual; you are part of the flying organisation when at sea, not allowed below the flight deck in fact. In harbour, you're the Commander's Assistant.' 'But what on earth is a Flight Deck Director?' He explained that, when taxiing, the nose of an aircraft stuck up in the air so that the pilot could not see his way ahead and relied on hand signals from a Director to one side. The half dozen Flight Deck Directors were all 'fish-heads'—seamen officers—including the Captain of Marines.

Some time back the Fleet Air Arm officers so employed had indulged in a number of prangs until the Captain, fuming, had said, 'Bring on the seamen officers, it's only common sense!' The 'A' boys had stood back and waited for the inevitable smash-ups, but there weren't any and to their chagrin the system had become permanent. 'It's an excellent idea anyway,' said McPhee (who I soon learnt was called 'Moose'; with a large proboscis and equally prominent adam's apple, he did look rather like one), 'because it gives the ship's company a stake in the flightdeck. There's none of the "them and us" you so often get and she runs like clockwork.'

Responsible for action at all flight-deck fires and crashes, I would have a large specialist fire party and live entirely in the island at sea.

The fire-fighting equipment of this near 800-foot expanse was headed by eight red machines, strategically placed around the perimeter just below deck level. They looked basic but were apparently efficient enough, big open coffers into which were poured the contents of adjacent drums of a stinking glutinous liquid, 'I believe its mainly blood from slaughter houses', said my mentor. 'Terrible stuff, you mustn't get it on your clothes.' A fire hose extended from one end with a special five foot nozzle and usual handwheel. On switching on, the water sucked the liquid up a pipe from the coffer and on passing through the nozzle the mixture became foam much like the top of a glass of Guinness; this settled on the flames from burning oil or petrol and put them out. Looking at the contraption with some interest I wished I could remember more of my Midshipman's fire-fighting course; something told me I was going to need it.

There were a number of hand 'foamites', water-spraying versions, an asbestos suit which allowed a man to go right into a fire and various gadgets (including a CO_2 machine, a cylinder on wheels with a long rubber pipe) for fighting fires in confined spaces such as the cockpit of an aircraft.

The CO of the Avenger squadron proved to be 'Pablo' Percy, a prematurely balding two-and-half whom I remembered from Dartmouth, but most of the other aviators, including both Corsair squadron COs (Lieutenant Commanders A. M. 'Judy' Garland and R. L. Bigg-Wither) were RNVRs whom I had never met before. One of the Fighter Direction Officers—Philip O'Rorke—had been at Dartmouth with me and I had been shipmates with a Lieutenant Berger before, but that was the sum of known faces. Joining a new ship, especially a big one, is always something of a trial and doing it twice in two months a bit hard. However, the spirit of this particular one was almost tangible and the good luck of dropping into such an unusual and challenging job too good to be true. In any case being up to the eyes learning the ways of the Commander's Office (mainly planning the next day's routine under his aegis), making the most of Moose before he left, and keeping the Battle of Sydney boiling out of working hours, hardly left time for consecutive thought.

The few days before we sailed for the forward area were crammed with last minute preparations, mostly topping up with minor stores that had been overlooked or hearsay suggested would be needed. In the latter connection I was most fortunate.

We were shown a US Navy film called *Fighting Lady*, a magnificent record—several cameramen died in the making—of a carrier's recent experiences in the Pacific (though actually made up from several different ships). Kamikazes screamed down to crash yards away, blow up just beyond the muzzles of belching guns or plummet on to the next ship. Appalling fires raged, aircraft landed on to skirt smoking holes in the deck and all in all we were very impressed. I noted in particular the plethora of excellent fire-fighting equipment deployed, some of it unfamiliar.

Of 23,000 tons, *Formidable* was 740 feet long, capable of 32 knots and had the same gun armament as the *Indomitable*. Some 20 Avengers were carried (848 Squadron) and 36 Corsairs (1841 and 1842), four night fighters being added later.

We put to sea for concentrated flying exercises on March 21. Moose having left, I was on my own with a vengeance, rather self-conscious and hot in a yellow jacket and red skull cap on top of overalls (the standard khaki shorts and short-sleeved shirt being no rig for fire-fighting) as I waited at the foot of the island with the remainder of the fire party—including an unfortunate in the heavy asbestos suit—for a dash into action. My first duty would be to get the pilot out before the aircraft went up in flames, to which end there was the standard aircrew knife with blunt end for cutting free if necessary. I went over the various connections for the umpteenth time (it was best to assume that the pilot would be knocked out or at least dazed)—parachute harness (twist to the right and bang in), safety harness (a variety of methods of release), r/t lead, oxygen tube—cravenly hoping I would not be called upon too soon.

Seen properly for the first time, the dark blue Corsairs did nothing to slow the adrenalin. 'Jolie laide', they were beautiful and brutish at the same time with incredibly long snouts that had the pilot sitting near the base of the very large tail, with kinked gull wings that combined to give a curiously reptilian air. I have read that one pilot on first introduction went straight off and made his will and can quite believe it. *(Carrier Pilot, by Norman Hanson.—Ed.)* The view forward was even worse than usual and enforced a method of landing on that kept my heart in my mouth to begin with. They came skidding in at a sharp angle with nose up and flaps down but seemingly pretty fast, until straightening up at the last moment. At first I found it difficult to tell whether they were making a good or bad approach, except that the 'batman', a lonely figure right aft on the port side, would in the latter case be gesticulating frantically with his two circular red bats.In a hopeless case he would wave the pilot round for another go, 18-cylinder engine roaring with the sudden full throttle. After a satisfactory approach the batsman would cross the bats in front of him to signify 'Cut!' at which the pilot would cut the engine to sink—or virtually drop in the case of a Corsair—on to the deck.

There were eight wires lying across it, about ten yards apart, the object being to catch an early one with the special hook lowered for the purpose. The wire went round revolving sheaves at the sides and disappeared into hydraulic systems below. When a wire had been caught it gave enough to halt the aircraft in a few yards and then went limp, at which two aircraft handlers would run out and disengage the hook. The pilot would then taxi forward, folding his wings as he went (Avengers' were folded manually) to take instructions from a flight deck director waiting for'ard; these included a beckoning 'come on' with both hands held high, clenched fists for stop, or one hand pointing to the side the pilot was to alter direction by pivoting on that wheel. When he came abreast you pointed at the next director and so passed the aircraft up the deck.

Both Corsairs and Avengers were very heavy and strong. Sometimes, coming in a little too high but still catching a late wire, they would be clawed down to land with bone-shaking force, but none the worse. Beyond the wires were two vertical barriers, made of three heavy wires slung between large steel uprights and held apart by vertical pieces. These, one just abaft the island and the other a few yards forward, were to prevent aircraft that had missed all the wires from crashing into others manoeuvring or already parked forward. On an aircraft catching a wire the barriers were lowered for taxiing over and then raised again for the next customer.

After oiling at Manus, a very large anchorage bounded by distant grey hills, we left again for Leyte in the Philippines, anchoring in the even larger San Pedro harbour four days later. Leyte had only recently been wrested from the Japanese, in fact fighting was still going on in the north.

We sailed from Leyte on April 10, those in the open air thankful for a breeze in exchange for the indescribably uncomfortable heat of this tropical Scapa Flow. The BPF's oiling force was joined two days later and, turning out on 14th, I saw that the BPF had arrived; two battleships, four carriers, five cruisers and a dozen destroyers. After they had fuelled, *Illustrious* left for home and *Formidable* took her place, Admiral Vian flying over from *Indom.* to have a quick look at us and brief the Captain. The BPF, under Admiral Nimitz as his Task

Force T F 57, was now operating in parallel (but not in close contact) with the American 58, both coming immediately under Nimitz's second in command, Admiral Spruance.

Our ships had not come off unscathed, as one could see from a glance at *Indefatigable's* blackened island. A kamikaze had come vertically down on her flight deck, four officers and ten ratings being killed and 16 wounded. Equipment was damaged but her flight deck only dented—a matter of great satisfaction all round—and she was soon operating aircraft. *Illustrious* and *Victorious* were very near-missed, in fact both were touched and suffered bomb explosions, the former losing two Corsairs and both being deluged with impedimenta and bits of Jap pilot (eyeballs and skull fragments were found on *Illustrious'* flight deck and a sliver of burnt flesh hanging from a gunsight; *Indefat.* had a finger to show for hers). There were casualties in *Indomitable* from machine-gunning by a Jap fighter and the destroyer *Ulster* had a near-miss bomb that did so much damage that she had to be towed to Leyte. Eight Avengers had been lost and nearly double that number of fighters, though the crews were saved in several cases. Tragic incidents had been the shooting down of a Hellcat and a Seafire (unfortunately not the first, or indeed to be the last occasion) and the blowing up of a Corsair—the petrol tank had ignited—on board *Illustrious*. It had crashed on landing and a number of people who were swarming over it trying to free the pilot were killed with him.

Each one- or two-day strike period was numbered so that, when at about 03.30 on April 15 the strains of Flying Stations banished sleep, it was *Iceberg 5* on which our boys were about to embark. The object was to keep up a rain of bombs and machine-gun attacks on the runways and nearby installations of the same two islands from 06.00 almost without a break until dark. *Formidable's* contribution was 12 Avengers for both the first and third strikes, two strikes of eight Corsairs, each armed with two 500-lb bombs, and more Corsairs for the CAPs over the fleet and targets ashore.

It is cold, dark and hostile and I step out on the hard steel deck and not for the first time feel the unfairness of things that keeps most of us safely on board while a select few roar away to an even chance of death. I test my special want torch used for signalling to the pilots; its perspex finger, projecting from the metal cylinder, glows satisfactorily. Corsairs are coming up the lift and being manhandled, wings still folded, on to spots right aft; then the 12 Avengers in front of them, the leader on the centre line, a little in advance and wings spread. The pilots, observers and tags (telegraphist-air gunners) emerge from their island briefings to disperse among the forest of angular shapes among which the odd shaded torch flickers like a firefly. It is getting lighter. Little F, with two flags that one can just see are red and green, materialises abreast the leading Avenger, in which Pablo Percy and his aircrew are now ready. One can just make out 'Wings' (Commander Flying in an island sponson. We Flight Deck Directors, in yellow waistcoats and skull caps, who have been conversing in a group, distribute ourselves down the deck park, in a line behind Little F.

Suddenly a voice comes over the loudspeakers: 'Start up, start up, start up!' The engines cough angry spouts of flame and then roar into steady life. The air reverberates and one would like to cover one's ears. Then the flight deck heels a little—we are altering into wind; in fact the whole fleet is altering into wind as, elsewhere in the vast circular formation, the scene is mirrored in three other carriers. There is a slight movement on the island at which Litle F waves the two chockmen away, raises his green flag and revolves it round his head. The leading Avenger thunders as it strains against the brakes, shaking violently; Percy raises his thumb, the flag drops and the aircraft, heavy with bombs—*Formidable*'s first Pacific flight in anger—moves forward. It accelerates and is soon trundling down the deck at surprising speed—off the end, a slight dip, then up into the air and away to starboard. The next is already on the spot and roaring. Off it goes. Soon all 12 are away, formating on the leaders who are flying round. The first snarling Corsair is following them, its raven-like companions unfolding their wings and crowding forward in their turn. Each fairly rockets up the deck. They fly round too, in formation, and then suddenly all are gone and there is comparative quiet.

But no respite. The big barriers go up with a clang and the bells of the forward lift scream as it descends for the next lot of aircraft. The flight deck aft has to be clear for landing on—though everyone got away without trouble—so the newcomers will be bunched forward and then brought back to take off, towed tail first by the dodgems, as soon as the first strike is back and out of the way below. All at once it is 'Standby to receive aircraft' and here they are. No-one requests an emergency landing and a quick count shows that they are all there. They land on, taxi forward, and—pilots handing over to their fitters—the aircrews walk back to the island for debriefing, sweating, laughing and ribbing each other about some incident. After waiting its turn (aircraft land on quicker than the lift can cope) each machine is struck down, pushed to its corner of the hangar and attacked by fitters, mechanics and armourers; they work until it is either ready or pronounced u/s (unserviceable), in which case they work even harder. Meanwhile, debriefed, dehydrated and temporarily drained of energy, the pilots and observers have only a warm shower and a hot, vibrating cabin to unwind in, the tags even less.

When the last aircraft of the first strike had disappeared below, *Howe* made to *Formidable*: 'To our now very critical eye your chaps made that land-on look very easy'. The Avengers had bombed Ishigaki airfield, scoring, in the strike leader's opinion, 90 per cent hits on the runway; the Corsairs had bombed opportunity targets including flak positions and aircraft on the ground at both Ishigaki and Miyako.

Then it was 'Start up, start up' . . . and the whole process was repeated. A few enemy aircraft were detected by radar but the only hostile act was the approach of a flying bomb, radio-controlled from a parent aircraft, that came within eight miles and then dived into the sea (probably out of fuel). A decidedly unfriendly act, though not enemy inspired, followed the failure of a

Corsair to release one of its two 500-lb bombs. No amount of aerobatics would shake it off and so there was no alternative but to land on and hope for the best. We watched with bated breath. The bomb came off with the shock of landing and cartwheeled down the deck towards us. Everyone dived for what cover there was but it rolled to a stop in a corner and was pounced upon. Exactly the same thing happened with another Corsair a few minutes later and the Captain, never at a loss for a pithy comment, spoke for all concerned when he signalled to Admiral Vian 'It's nice to know they don't go off.'

We were beginning to think this was an auspicious first day's operating when in the late afternoon word went round the flight deck that pitched us all into gloom—'Judy' Garland, CO of 1842 Corsair Squadron, had been shot down by flak over Ishigaki. Of course, I hardly knew him but apart from the fact that to lose a squadron CO on the very first day was bad, to many this was a great personal blow. Apparently he had dived from some height, the hard-earned experience of other ships being that one should come and go at the lowest possible level.

Except that different airfields were the targets, the next day's operating was a carbon copy of the first. Getting into the routine, I was not so tense and even able to take an interest, at odd moments when there was no flying, in other things that were going on. Intrigued by the extraordinary snatches of apparent conversation (in the most matter of fact tones except on the odd occasion of high drama) that were sometimes broadcast round the ship, with talk of angels, bogies, bandits and such like, I squeezed into the ADR. This was where Philip O'Rorke or one of the other FDOs (Fighter Direction Officers) with a highly trained team of ten officers and 15 ratings, sitting in semi-darkness, watched the big perspex and other displays, listened to reports from pilots and their own staff, assessed the constantly evolving situation, as often as not projected their minds several minutes ahead and having decided what to do, instructed pilots accordingly.

Though several enemy aircraft were reported no attack developed; but there was another sharp reminder that Japanese AA fire was very accurate. One of our Avengers was shot down; the pilot and air gunner were killed but the observer, Sub-Lieutenant Gass, baled out. He came down in the sea only two miles offshore and was rescued under rifle fire by an intrepid Walrus from *Victorious*.

The fleet retired to refuel in the evening and Admiral Vian signalled 'All airfields unserviceable—Iceberg 5 completed'. which was satisfactory. The next two days were spent refuelling and replenishing from the Fleet Train. A ceaseless stream of unfortunate maid-of-all-work destroyers acted as go-betweens, from whom we hoisted in stores of all kinds. Of course 1,800 men use up a lot of everything. *Formidable* took her turn to provide Avenger anti-submarine patrols and so there were several interruptions for flying. Meanwhile feverish work was going on in the hot hangar servicing aircraft and all in all this was the reverse of a rest period.

At 06.00 on the 20th flying off started again. One of our Avengers ditched on the return journey and four others were detailed to search for it. They found nothing—it must have put out an inaccurate position—and returned disconsolate. However, 24 hours later an American Mariner flying boat on rescue patrol sighted the three men and picked them up ten miles from the coast. No wonder many airmen were superstitious! Life so often hung on a few gallons of petrol, a word heard on the r/t, a glance in the right direction . . .

By this time the fleet was on its way back to Leyte, *Formidable* having received the signal from Admiral Vian 'As good a three-days operating as I have seen'. This was confirmation of what most of us had already sensed—HMS *Formiable* had no reason to have an inferiority complex about being the new girl. The ship was fighting fit, morale was sky high and to be fair on the others, we were fresh.

Return to Leyte and expected let-up proved but a repeat of the hectic storing and making good of the days with the Fleet Train, plus even worse heat thrown in. Sitting in a pool of sweat in the Commander's Office as I wrestled with applications for special working parties, the next day's boat trips to distant store-ships, routine inspections of this and that, one could only marvel at how the poor devils in the various machinery spaces kept going at all. Of course carriers were, as already described, particular heat gatherers. Another annoyance special to the breed (and the great Pacific distances) was the necessity to fill up—apt description—with drop tanks. These were the lozenge shaped, discardable aircraft petrol tanks that, carrying 176 extra gallons, provided greatly extended range. We had to stow large numbers—awkward to handle—wherever we possibly could.

The new CO of 1842 Squadron, Lieutenant Commander D. G. Parker, joined and on May 1 the fleet sailed for the same hunting ground, now becoming very familiar to our aircrews and presumably like the backs of their hands to those of *Indom, Indefat* and *Vic*.

I had expected to find it a new experience, for once having nothing to do with guns, but this was not the case. The Gunnery Officr (Lieutenant Commander Dan Duff, a most likeable fair-haired giant with a puckish sense of humour—'hands to the pumps, guns I mean' was his stock phrase in an emergency) required me to supervise a pair of 20mm Oerlikons when aircraft were not being operated. These were on the port side abreast the island, about eight feet below the flight deck. *(Same as me Geoff, in* Indefat.*—Ed.)*

A good start to Iceberg 7 on May 5 was provided by the news that Hitler and his dreadful little hunchback henchman Goebbels were dead; the end in Europe could not be far off. There was one difference between this day's attack and all those going before: *KGV, Howe,* the four cruisers and some destroyers detached before first light to bombard various targets on Miyako Island—simultaneously with the bombing—leaving but one cruiser and six destroyers. We thought little of this; the poor devils had done nothing but steam about for weeks and it was time they had some employment; in fact it was more for morale purposes than anything else that Admiral Rawlings had decided on the move. He underestimated the enemy, however, who appreciated at once that the carriers were for the first time without the gun protection of the remainder.

Action stations were sounded off at 05.15. Corsairs were in front this time, then Avengers and more Corsairs which were not going off until later. As ever, they looked sinister, dark against the greenish sky. The order came to start up, drowned in staccato reports as a score of whirling propellers flickered among blue exhaust flames. The steady roar took over and we resigned ourselves to wait, the wind tugging at our trouser legs as the minutes ticked by to zero hour. To the east crimson streaks were already silhouetting the jagged black fretwork of massed planes, when a flag dropped from the yardarm and at once the stern began to slide as the rudder bit. I was aware of an avenue of faces, ghostly pale in their anti-flash gear, peering intently from each side and down from the island structure. The leading Corsair—prima ballerina of this scene that never failed to grip—was already responding to the conductor's baton. The ship steadied on her course into the wind, which was strong (how useful this was soon to prove!). By now Harry Hawke's flag was vertical. The pilot, animal-like in his weird get-up, watched it from his shuddering cockpit with gross pentagonal eyes. His chockmen were gone, but those at the machines behind crouched as low as they could to shield their streaming faces. The audience craned forward. Down came the flag and the goofers and gun's crews ducked away from the shower of grit that whirled aft to start another operating day.

As usual the first trio of Corsairs was flying past in formation as the early Avengers started off. One of the latter lost height, banked to the right and fell into the sea, to come past our starboard side. Few saw this and we were surprised to hear the action commentator say that the crew had joined the Goldfish Club (of those who had ditched) and been picked up by *Ursa*.

Once the strike was away we moved the remaining aircraft forward and bunched them in the bows. The sun came out and hands went to breakfast leaving only the duty defence watch closed up. The various preparations had been made and there was nothing much to do until the strike returned and the next Combat Air Patrol took off.

The Avengers got back safely, although some were well shot up. Then—it was just before 10.00—came reports from the ADR that they had a bogey at long range. *Victorious*'s fighters were sent off to intercept and we went to repel aircraft stations. On arrival at the Oerlikons I found that Midshipman (S) Basedon, recently joined from *Illustrious*, had been detailed to help spot targets. He listened politely to an account of his duties and then let it pass in the course of conversation that the wing of a kamikaze had grazed *Illustrious*'s funnel about ten feet from his head when employed on the same job; at which we had a good laugh.

The loudspeakers announced that *Victorious*'s fighters had shot down a 'Zeke' fighter 70 miles from the fleet. This almost certainly meant others somewhere and we spent an anxious time looking all over the sky, but particularly up-sun. All at once I heard, above the guns' electric motors, the sound of our own aircraft engines on the flight deck behind. Three Avengers were being moved forward. As there were enough directors there to cope I nearly did not bother but in the end hoisted myself on to the flight-deck and signed a couple past. In doing so I moved up a few yards to a position a little forward of the island on the port side.

Suddenly, without any warning, there was the fierce 'whoosh' of an aircraft passing very fast and low overhead and I looked up in time to see a fighter plane climbing away on the starboard side, having crossed the deck from aft at 50 feet. I was thinking casually what a stupid thing to do and that he was lucky not to get shot at, with a scare on, when the starboard bow Oerlikons opened up a stream of tracer at the retreating enemy. He banked steeply, showing the Japanese red blob markings, and flew down our starboard side, the focus of a huge cone of converging yellow balls as every close range weapon on that side began to hammer away. I thought he was certain to buy it and stood watching until he passed behind the island.

I remember PO Lambe at this moment standing with his hands up as a sign to the Avenger he was directing to stop, about 30 feet from me.

The the Jap came into view again from behind the island, banking hard to come in towards the ship from the starboard quarter, apparently unharmed and by now the target of fewer guns. His silhouette changed to a thin line with a lump in the middle, and he seemed to hang in the air as he dived for the ship.

I waited for no more but sprinted to a hatchway some 20 yards forward on the port side. Expecting to be blown to bits at each stride, I arrived at the hatch just after a tubby leading seaman of the AHP, so I launched myself at his back and we fell in a heap to the bottom. At the same moment there was a flash and a great crash shook the ship. I gave it a second or two to subside, during which the light from the rectangle of sky above turned to deep orange, and ran back up the ladder.

It was a grim sight. At first I thought the kamikaze had hit the island and those on the bridge must be killed. Fires were blazing among several piles of wreckage on deck a little aft of the bridge, flames reached right up the side of the island, and clouds of dense black smoke billowed far above the ship. Much of the smoke came from the fires on deck but as much seemed to be issuing from the funnel and this gave the impression of damage deep below decks. The bridge windows gaped like eye sockets and most of the superstructure was burnt black. The flight deck was littered with debris, much of it on fire, and there was not a soul to be seen.

I grabbed a foam generator nozzle from its stowage nearby and ran out the hose, indicating to a rather shaken turret-safety number who was lying down between the turrets of B group, to switch on the machine. Men began to pour up from the sides of the flight deck and I pushed the foam-erupting nozzle into someone else's hands, to go round the crews of the other machines who were getting to grips with the main fire. It was very fierce with occasional machine-gun bullets 'cooking off'. Smaller fires in the tow-motor park, fire-fighter headquarters and odd bits of aircraft scattered around were attacked with hand extinguishers. The AHP were pushing unburnt aircraft clear and carrying casualties below. Some enthusiast appeared from the boat deck to cause initial confusion by playing water hoses from there on to burning oil and petrol; both float and so the fires merely spread, but this was dealt with. Generally speaking the foam machines—both old and new—did good work, some blistering and almost too hot to touch. Soon there were pools and mounds of foam all over the place and the pungent smell everywhere. Large reserves of manpower materialised which did sterling work under the Commander, dragging heavy lumps of scrap iron that had been aircraft to the cranes, bringing up fresh drums of foam compound, refilling hand appliances, and generally helping to clear up. With reserves in the Fleet Train we could not tie up hangar space unprofitably and whole though badly damaged aircraft were ditched without ceremony (except for a rush for the clock!). A boat deck crane would be trained over the flight deck to collect the load on a tripping hook; the crane would be swung over the sea and the hook tripped for a fine splash.

In the middle of this there was another kamikaze alarm and we all took cover while two attacked the *Indomitable*. One blew up, disintegrated by pom-poms, about a hundred yards off the ship, and the other hit at such a low angle that he merely skated down the fortunately clear deck and over the side.

The kamikaze which hit us carried a 500 lb bomb and it was thought (there were no living witnesses) that the pilot released it just before he struck. By bad luck the bomb had caught the point of intersection of four armour plates, a very persistent slice about one foot by nine inches going down through several decks to come to rest in a fuel tank. On its way it wrecked the barrier operating machinery, bucked the hangar fire curtain and cut a steam pipe which filled the centre boiler room with steam. One or two valves had to be turned very quickly before the area was left to scalding steam. This one splinter had reduced our speed temporarily to 18 knots and been responsible for much of the smoke that had towered above the ship. Shipwrights were soon at work filling the hole (about two feet square with an 18-inch depression over 16 feet) with rapid hardening cement and steel plate, engineers were getting one barrier operable by hand (turret crews from the two forward groups were to haul it up and down with large tackles) and work on radar and communications damage was under way.

Considering the appearance of the deck immediately after the incident, our casualties seemed comparatively light: two officers and six men killed and 45 wounded. The Air Engineer Officer (Lieutenant Commaner Knox) lost an eye and sadly the stalwart Petty Officer Lambe of the Aircraft Handling Party later died of wounds. Lieutenant Berger was killed in the Operations room, and a steward in the Bridge Mess, which was punctured by shrapnel. A pilot was killed in an Avenger on deck. Another Avenger (the one Lambe had been directing) and the kamikaze himself were blown to smithereens, and seven more aircraft on deck burnt right out.

The Jap pilot had started his initial dive at the ship, but finding that he was overshooting the bridge decided to pull out (luckily for most of us originally on deck) and, after firing a cannon burst, had come round again. His coolness and audacity, to say nothing of skilful handing of the machine, were indicative that high class pilots were being used on suicide missions. Several bits of Jap pilot and aircraft were found. I collected a piece of tyre, cannon shell, and part of his bomb-release mechanism; someone found his hand with wristwatch still on it (though not going!); a yellow silk jacket was discovered for'ard and Guns was to be seen during the general clean-up poking bits of Jap off the funnel with a long pole.

When things had quietened down I remembered, with grim amusement, an extraordinary feeling I had experienced when running for the hatch. It was that my knees were made of water, my feet of lead and that my real self was yards ahead of my body, left floundering along behind! Actually I was probably running as fast as I ever had. (This was quite forgotten until reading Sir Roger Bannister's account of his epic four minute mile, when he described the same sensaton; presumably something to do with willpower.)

Though she could do 24 knots by 13.00, we could not fly off any more strikes that day (the 16 Corsairs aloft when we were hit roosted temporarily elsewhere). However, life continued potentially eventful. Though *Indom*'s main radar had been put out of action her fleet fighter direction team under Captain E. D. G. Lewin functioned with great skill so that eight Jap aircraft were shot down in four different attacks. All the carriers had a hand and no enemy aircraft got through. Admiral Rawlings returned with the bombardment force some time before the last and highly successful sortie, when Seafires from *Indefat* 'splashed' three out of a group of four attackers and Corsairs from *Victorious* shot down their 'Gestapo' aircraft (whose job was to instruct his evil brood about which ship to dive on to). All this meant several calls to repel aircraft.

On the first occasion I found my guns deserted, no Midshipman and no guns' crews. There was a certain amount of blood about and tin hats on the deck. The nasty realisation that they were casualties and the nearness of my own escape were confirmed from the pom-pom crew nearby who said that the seamen were wounded and they thought the midshipman was dead. (He and one other turned out to be badly wounded and the third just slightly. The latter, A B Fowler, continued for months to spit out bits of shrapnel as they worked into his mouth from his jaw and throat.)

I strapped myself into one of the vacated Oerlikons, and proceeded to shoot down an aircraft with my own fair hands. During a stand-to a lone fighter came in sight on the port beam, almost out of the sun, and made for us in a shallow dive. I gave him a long burst and had the immense satisfaction of seeing him dip suddenly and splash into the sea. Easing the leather straps off my shoulders I locked the gun stationary and stepped down from its platform with a sense of deep satisfaction. Not only was it a good effort but I had almost certainly saved the ship considerable damage.

The Gunnery Officers' broadcast system clicked on to introduce its usual background hum, and I stopped to listen. Five words in Dan Duff's driest tone drained the colour from my face—'That was one of ours.' I have had some shocks in my Naval life, but for unmitigated horror, this was probably the worst, only eased when *Undaunted,* creaming to the scene to stop with a convulsion of astern power, signalled that she had picked up the pilot more or less unhurt. He proved to have been coming back for an emergency landing, on what must have been *Indomitable,* and may not have been in full control of his aircraft. I was exonerated—in fact nothing was ever said—as friendly aircraft never approached like this and in such circumstances shoot first and enquire afterwards was the thing. I resolved to go over and apologise to a pilot for the second time in my career but the opportunity did not occur until it was all rather ancient history. However, it is one of many things I wish I had done.

The Captain was able to report by 17.00 that his ship was operational and soon afterwards all but four of our absent Corsairs landed on. We felt rather pleased with ourselves as each one bumped over the 12-inch depression in the deck, followed by a roar from the Captain of Marines to his Royals to haul the battered barrier up again.

Corsairs from *Victorious* shot down a last enemy aircraft at supper time, lowering the curtain on an eventful day. Throughout it, the enemy, though not too successful with three hits and a near miss, had shown considerable ingenuity. It appeared that the kamikaze which got us had achieved surprise by flying very low (and so indetectable by radar) until quite close. But it did look as if they had shot their bolt for the time; next day, a repeat from the BPF's point of view, there was little retaliation. Our four Corsairs, still in *Victorious,* distinguished themselves when directed on to a very high 'Zeke' snooper, to splash it before returning home. The Admiral congratulated *Victorious* but she replied that those responsible were 'paying guests from *Formidable*' and added 'Nice work your flight; 40 minutes from the deck to 28,000 feet at 70 miles!' No flak came from Ishigaki, so it was presumed that the bombardment had proved effective; yet again all runways were believed unserviceable and in the evening the fleet withdrew to refuel.

It was a very busy two days for *Formidable;* improving the deck depression, plugging splinter holes, repairing equipment of all sorts, scrubbing and painting the island, in addition to replenishing ammuntion, foam compound and the usual provisions. Not least was the transferring by crane, in large rigid cots, of over 30 wounded.

Operations were supposed to be resumed on May 8 but heavy rain storms and ten-tenths cloud dictated a postponement of 24 hours.

There was nothing to do now but watch and wait. As a terror weapon these kamikazes were unsurpassed. It was a sensation of 'the full twitch' as Air Branch slang had it, especially on a cloudy day, after perhaps ten minutes of a broadcast running commentary on the steady approach of a formation to hear the dry announcement, 'They have split up now and are too close for radar detection'. Everyone who has to stay in the open searches the sky with his neck on a swivel, light weapons traversing back and forth, up and down, in amplification of the Gunner's nerves. There is not a man, streaming with sweat under his protective clothing (flame-proof balaclava, gloves, goggles and overall suit with stocking, not to mention tin hat) whose hands have not discovered some piece of equipment that needs last minute adjustment. When at last you see him and all the guns are blazing it's not so bad, but there is still something unearthly about an approaching aircraft whose pilot is bent on diving himelf right on to the ship. Wherever you are he seems to be aiming straight for you personally, and in the case of those in or near the island, that's just what he is doing.

We had been searching the sky for some minutes when gunfire broke out to port. *Victorious* was firing and even as I looked there was an explosion on her flight deck. Moments later she opened up again and there was another attacker coming in from astern. It was streaming flames but kept going and also crashed on her flight deck. More gunfire from the same direction. Both *Victorious* and *Howe,* ahead of her, were firing now and I could make out two aircraft in the distance, fairly low, flying so as to pass astern. The blue sky was full of little black puffs marking their passage towards us and tracer criss-crossed as each ship came within range. Our port after batttery opened fire and then most of the port close-range guns although the distance was really too great. Both aircraft passed astern about a mile and a half away. One began to shallow dive on to *Howe* and was shot down in flames alongside her; the other, to our intense interest, banked to its left and headed straight for us, fine on the starboard quarter.

It dipped its nose and came tearing down. The air was shuddering with gunfire and again I thought it could not get through.

It was a large machine carrying either two bombs or two drop tanks and liable to make a big mess. I watched it long enough to see bits fly off its starboard wing and then retired to a prone position in the walk behind my guns, which being on the disengaged side could do nothing. At the after end of the walk was an eight-barelled pom-pom whose size made a recess in the flight deck necessary. This gun could not bear either and the loading numbers were on their stomachs. Being plumb abreast the aiming point we could all expect 'the full'. It was a long four or five seconds.

Then a terrific detonation and a wall of flame curled down from the deck above and seemed to encircle the pom-pom mounting. I got up to run as it looked like coming my way, but a lot of smoke took its place. At the same time the sea, for perhaps hundreds of yards from the ship, was a mass of splashes, big and small, from descending objects.

With the thought that the pom-pom's crew must all be burnt I climbed on to the flight deck to much the same sight as before. Several furiously burning piles of wreckage that had been aircraft, the island all black, smouldering debris everywhere and clouds of thick smoke welling upwards.

The kamikaze seemed to have exploded close to the pom-pom mounting at the after end of the island because the area was in considerable disarray. The gun itself was surrounded by a protective steel wall about six feet high; I ran and looked over this at a sight that stamped itself on my inner eye from that moment. The blackened body of the Gunlayer, headless, sat rigid in his elevated seat, crouched forward in the aiming attitude with hands still grasping the 'bicycle pedal' control in front. There was an aeroplane wheel on the deck beside and the brave man must have continued to fire his gun until the very last moment. The rest of the crew, who had probably ducked down in time, seemed to be all right.

Looking round I saw that, among several flaming aircraft, the immediate danger was a Corsair fitted with a drop tank in the middle of the flight deck just abaft the island, on fire and standing in a large pool of burning petrol. Nobody was doing anything about it and I noted to my fury the red skull caps of some of the fire party just showing above the flight deck each side as they awaited events with some prudence. The quickest thing to do was to shame them into action, so I ran for the mobile CO_2 machine which was housed at the fore end of the island and trundled it up to the Corsair. The latter's machine-gun bullets were cooking off with the heat, whether up the barrels or not I was unsure but took the seamanlike precaution of advancing in line with the engine. As expected the CO_2 machine was no use—being designed for confined spaces—but it had the desired effect. One or two men appeared and then we were joined by the rest, all bringing equipment to bear, mostly the new knapsack foam throwers. The fire was intense and for some time we did not seem to be making any impression. Though mostly directed aft by the wind over the deck, the flames from the burning petrol rose up every so often to envelop the drop tank and it was evident that should the wind come up from the side, or worse still astern, that would be it. The Captain was probably otherwise concerned so I sent a man up to ask him not to alter course if he could help it. Eventually, as the number of appliances increased we got the upper hand; even so, as the petrol pool was extinguished in one place it would flare up in another.

My lungs filled with smoke and I had moved out of the way for air when there was a tap on my back and 'The Captain wants to see you, Sir.' The fire was not out, the petrol under a thick blanket of creamy foam, the firefighting had eventually gone rather well and I thought 'What the hell does the old blighter want to criticise now?' A senior air officer who had been watching circumspectly from the island doorway said something rather nice as I passed but I was quite unprepared when the Captain was congratulatory fit to take my breath away. I descended to the flight deck in a rosy haze—one is only human—but behind it was a cautionary voice saying that if I had not acted at once I would have been in line for a court-martial, or at any rate had to live with a personal stigma for the rest of my life.

Meanwhile, and quite unknown to me, another kamikaze had dived on the ship but been shot down. The rest of the flight deck was brought fairly quickly under control. Our recent experience had enabled me to improve parts of the fire-fighting organisation and at least no one sprayed water about. There were more fires because there were more aircraft to provide the fuel; the kamikaze had crashed through a deck-park of 11 Corsairs out of which we lost eight. As fires were extinguished unburnt aircraft were hauled clear. It did not help that the concussion had burst all their tyres; nor that the towing tractors had previously been destroyed, though two jeeps that must have been procured from the Fleet Train stood in quite well. Once, when busy in a corner with a hand-extinguisher, I looked up to find the whole flight deck deserted. The take-cover klaxon had gone again as another attack was expected and I had not heard it. Reaching the boat-deck down a vertical ladder in record time I knocked into Commaner (Ops) who was running for a good cubby hole (presumably he had been caught like me) where I joined him. Nothing happened so we cautiously made our way up again.

All fires were out about 20 minutes after the incident. The bomb had exploded ten yards further aft than the first, without penetraton, except that a rivet had been blown out, allowing burning petrol to fall through the hole to the hangar below; a nasty fire had ensued resulting in damage by flame and water spray to four Avengers and eight Corsairs. On the flight-deck we lost one Avenger as well as the eight Corsairs, with one Corsair damaged. Apart from the loss of aircraft and doubling the shrapnel holes in the island, which now resembled a giant black pepper-pot, not much harm had been done. Casualties, thanks to the new warning system, were only one killed and eight wounded. (Evidence of our second Japanese casualty was one eye, picked up by a rating with a strange sense of humour; it was put in a match-box which he would suddenly push open in front of unsuspecting messmates.) We landed on a strike shortly afterwards—they had taken temporary refuge in *Victorious*—and continued much as if nothing had happened.

Admiral Vian signalled 'Well extinguished. Any foamite left?' and it was gratifying to get from *Uganda* 'Our sincerest admiration'. I hope that Moose would have approved too.

It was surprising to find that the crew of the pom-pom that had been engulfed in flames were quite all right; anti-flash gear was made of uncomfortably hot material but it was good to have such evidence of its efficiency. Not so reassuring was the plain fact that our pom-poms and Oerlikons simply did not have sufficient physical stopping power. Both our opponents were hard hit but came on, possibly aided by the freezing of control surfaces at high speed. The new *Implacable* had a quadruple Bofors gun of large calibre and we hoped for something similar when next in Sydney.

An event that had gone quite unnoticed on the 9th was VE-Day, the end of the war in Europe; however we spliced the mainbrace on the 10th. At home there was naturally wild rejoicing. From my mother:

Hart's Gorse
9/5/45
VE-Day

This is VE-Day at last! We have just been listening to the King broadcasting—and then Eisenhower—Tedder (bad)—Montgomery, etc . . . One can hardly believe it has at last really come . . . when we hear the Japs have thrown their hand in too, then we shall have a real V day! However, it is a wonderful thing that it's over in Europe, and at the end that it went so quickly . . . Hitler disappeared—bumped off I expect. Goebbels poisoned, Goering disappeared . . . no word of our having located that arch-swine Himmler. Lewes was festooned with flags—out of every window and across the streets and everyone wearing red, white and blue rosettes—and the girls with their hair tied up in red, white and blue ribbons! There is a procession and bonfire at Firle tonight.

De Valera has finished himself and Ireland by sending condolences to the Germans on Hitler's death.

Thursday 11th

Lewes went mad in the evening and had a torchlight procession and bonfire. Everyone got drunk and you could hear the noise from here at midnight!

They have found Goering, decked out in gold lace and with many rings on his fingers, one a huge sapphire! The Pacific news say that our fleet is bombarding and bombing again—I wonder so much if you are among that lot?

'That lot' learnt at dusk on 10th that the fleet was 'retiring to lick its wounds' since *Victorious* could only operate a few aircraft at a time due to damage to her forward lift and we had only four Avengers and 11 Corsairs serviceable. So the next morning saw us back in the fuelling area for a repeat of the last occasion. One satisfacory difference was the smaller casualty list due to the Anti-Hawk scheme. *Ursa* came alongside for transferring this and that.

Arrival at Manus marked a month at sea. When they desisted four days after we left, the remainder of the BPF had done two months, divided by eight days at Leyte. This way of operating had not been experienced in the Royal Navy since Nelson's blockade of Toulon and, all things considered, had been a success. 203 aircraft had been lost from all causes out of an original complement of 218, 93 per cent losses for 57 enemy aircraft destroyed was not a victory by that count but the object had been denial of the Sakishima airfields to the Japanese at a time when the conquest of Okinawa was proving most difficult. Eleven strike days had been completed (2,449 sorties) and all five carriers taking part had been hit by kamikazes at least once. CTF 57 (Admiral Spruance) sent Admiral Rawlings a most appreciative signal and reported to Nimitz that the BPF was experienced enough to operate closely in future operations with the American Fast Carrier Task Force.

The girls were there all right when we arrived at Woollomooloo but almost outnumberd by dockyard mateys who swarmed on board to tackle our various defects, including the welding of bigger and better plates over the hole. This became quite famous. HRH the Duke of Gloucester, Governor General of Australia, was our first visitor and Admiral Fraser the second. Aircrews were given 14 days' leave and the rest of us four to six.

From Royal Marine Norman Coombs in Australia, HMS *Formidable*

I trained first as a soldier and then trained in Naval gunnery and seamanship and although I served at sea I was never allowed to forget that I was a soldier. Regular landing exercises were part of our life. During my service aboard the *Formidable* my action and cruising stations was turret trainer of Y2 turret.

The Marines aboard the *Formidable* manned Y1, Y2, X1 and X2 4.5" turrets also the close range weapons on the stern of the ship just below the flight deck. During cruising stations, we often assisted the aircraft handling parties, especially chockmen.

I remember one day in the Pacific during a lull in the attacks against us, we were at cruising stations and my turret Y2 was not closed up. I was with a group of other marines on the after close range weapons sponson watching our aircraft returning from a strike, some badly shot up.

One Corsair was approaching the ship to land and on touching down on the flight deck his wheels hit the rounded down part of the flight deck and was unable to roll forward, it tipped backwards and sank into the ocean tail first. We all watched the pilot, who was slumped forward in his cockpit, disappear.

We felt so helpless, he was so close to home and we could do nothing to help him. To this day I remember with sadness the loss of a gallant man, like ourselves at the time, so very young.

On another occasion I remember a Corsair landing with a 500 lb bomb which he couldn't release, on hitting the deck the bomb bounced loose and rolled across the deck. It was the greatest scattering match of all time, fortunately the Lt.Cdr Deck Officer raced out and defused it much to the admiration of all present.

I also remember the times when the seas were so rough we had to tie the aircraft down with extra canvas bands around the fuselage as well as anchoring them with the usual steel stays to the eye bolts in the deck. We didn't need an enemy on those occasions, the sea was enemy enough.

Also vivid in my mind are the many times when we joined up with the fleet train and took supplies aboard, bags of spuds, shells, bombs and of course transferring pilots to destroyers to take them to the Auxiliary carriers to get new aircraft. There never seemed to be enough men to man the running end of the jack stay line. To the pilots it must have been like the big dipper in a fun fair. They very often went close to being dunked in the ocean. In fact I think some did get wet feet.

I often think of my old shipmates whose names have disappeared into the past and the times when we felt so frightened. None of us wanted to let our mates know that we felt fear, although I suppose we all did. We were so well trained and disciplined that under attack we were too occupied to think of anything other than our job, it was after the attacks that I found the shakes set in.

I am still in touch with Ken Watts (Watty) in Sydney and Ron English here in neighbouring Logan City. *(Met Ron* Formidable *Re-Union '90.—Ed.)*

After being repaired in Captain Cook dock for damage by two kamikaze attacks and one fire, we were lined up on the flight deck for leaving harbour. One of the Marines close by said, 'I wonder if we will ever see Sydney again.'

The first time out of Sydney we didn't know what we were going into and we were in a much more jovial mood. But on this occasion we were more serious knowing what to expect and thinking there were better places to be.

Who could forget the delicious 'Tiddy Oggies' the cooks made for our lunches, served at our action stations on the many days when we were unable to go to our mess decks to eat. They were a good meal in themselves. I loved them. I began to feel part of Y2 turret. During our stay in Sydney for repairs after the kamikaze damage, all the barrels of the 4.5″ guns were changed and the twin oerlikons on the power mountings were changed to single bofors.

From Lt. Cdr. (A) R. Bigg-Wither CO 1841 Sqdn, HMS *Formidable*

Kamikaze No. 1. Sub. Lieuts Maitland and Crosland were resting in their shared cabin, after a ramrod, when it struck. They felt the ship shudder but since the guns had been firing for minutes, they thought nothing of it. Then came the pipe 'All hands on deck'. Maitland (the diary keeper and writer, shot down on August 10th) said to Crosland 'Don't you think we ought to comply.' Answer from C (who does not wish to be named!!!) 'We are not *hands*, we are *officers*.'

You asked me what it was like to be C.O. of a FAA Squadron—well I think most C.O.s (I was 26) would say the same, having been catapulted from being 'just one of the boys' into that position with 18—24 young pilots (19—20 years old) and some 150 ratings under your command—a daunting experience particularly if one had very little knowledge of KR and AIs. *(Kings Regulations and Admiralty Instructions.—Ed.)* Fortunately, my training period in Brunswick, Maine, U.S.A. I had a wonderful disciplinarian, Regulating P.O. Draper to assist me with defaulters. I was inclined to let ratings off for minor misdemeanors—rather to his disgust—but soon, when the defaulter repeated his offence, I realised that I had to be much tougher or else the whole discipline of the squadron would suffer. Result I think was a happy squadron.

From the start I tried to know every rating's name and where he came from and something about his family—very difficult—and I made some mistakes, but better than saying 'You there, old so and so'. They were truly a wonderful crowd of young men who took enormous pride in their squadron. Riggers, fitters and armourers looked after their pilots' aircraft with loving care and the latter were always delighted when all ammunition had been expended! I cannot praise them too highly! It was most distressing for all of us when we had to push all those beautiful Corsairs over the side under lease/lend (not before having unscrewed the clocks!).

The striking force—the pilots—mine mostly came from basic training and Pensacola USA aged 19 or 20 with one exception who was 6 months older than me, and turned out to be a marvellous band of warriors. I had to keep myself rather at arms length from the beginning—a lonely job but I was able to confide in my senior pilot and 3rd in command which helped a great deal.

We had an early baptism of fire with the July and August 1944 *Tirpitz* raids where everyone performed with great courage and that knitted us all together so to speak.

We had put up a dismal performance in our deck landing trials at Norfolk V.A.—about 5 barrier prangs! but directly we joined *Formid.* we hardly had another one due to pilot error until the end of the war.

Having done 2 years flying a Walrus in *Manchester* and *Queen Elizabeth* and later shore based with 805 Martlet squadron in the desert, I had never been 'on the deck'. I kept this very dark from my boys telling them it was a piece of cake and luckily I never had an accident myself. I think, in fact, it took more skill to land in the 'slick' of a battleship than on the deck of a carrier. Cheesman would undoubtedly agree with this.

It was a great shock to me when Judy Garland, C.O. of 1842 was shot down the first day of our Sakishima ops. followed a few days later by my dear friend 'Gammy' Godson RN, C.O. of 1835 Corsairs from *Indom.*—both made the fatal 2 runs. I determined that nonc of my squadron would go the same way and also that we should attack airfields in fours line abreast, with other flights coming in from different angles to confuse the Jap gunners as they invariably concentrated on the leader. We suffered no further losses on the Iceberg ops.

Extracts from 1841 Squadron Diary, loaned to me by the C.O. Lt. Cdr. (A) R. Bigg-Wither, HMS *Formidable*

Sunday April 15th

The Squadron provided pilots in readiness state 11 and state 12 during the early morning and late afternoon. The highlight was the visit of Vice Admiral Sir Philip Vian K.C.B. D.S.O. during the forenoon. He was flown on in an Avenger and met first the Captain and heads of departments. He spoke for a little time to the aircrews confirming the target as the Sakishima Gunto—neutralisation of—since the airfields are being used as staging posts to the island of Formosa. He then broadcast to ship's company.

The C.O. gave a talk after lunch to all pilots passing on general hints and guidance for the next two days, stressing the necessity for aircraft to stay in pairs and the crimes of leaving an escort flight to knock down the odd Jap. Modifications possible in take off and landing on procedure were dicussed, and pilots were reminded of the absolute necessity of giving accurate fixes for any of our planes which may have to ditch.

It was noted that among those who did not look forward to long spells of C.A.P. was Sub. Lt. McLisky but may be he will have an opportunity of getting his first kill soon. What is worrying most pilots is how hard the parachute is going to seem after four hours.

Sub. Lt. Glading suffered the torments of Tantalus at the film show last night—watching Americans eating ice cream and drinking sodas—now he is wondering about his twelve hours sleep!

Later

Ruling from Cmdr. Flying to the effect that watch duties are scrubbed for the time being! On the flight deck the troops are busy arming up,cleaning cockpit covers, fitting belly tanks, and doing the last minute odd jobs. Rumour has it that 'H' is 0600 tomorrow, and our first flight is to be off at H–½ which puts briefing about 0430!—Time we were all in bed!

Friday May 4th

Iceberg 7

The first two flights took off at 0530 to carry out C.A.P. over the fleet; they were Sub. Lts. Ferguson, Harrison, Blade and Abbott, and Lt. Gray heading the flight with Crosland, Maitland and Reeve.SubLt. Wood was duty boy. These patrolling a/c were not fortunate enough to see an enemy plane though at one time Ferguson's flight was hot on the trail. Owing to the difficulty our F.D.O. experiences in accurately estimating heights—due probably to the fact that our radar sets are not as modern as they might be, it is thought that the bogey was about 5000′ above our fighters. *Indomitable* confirmed this suspicion.

The ship sent out only one strike of Avengers to the islands, to bomb runways and these all returned safely.

Owing to the abortive chase by Sub. Lt. Ferguson's flight they had to get rid of belly tanks, all successful except the flight leader, and when he came on the deck away went the tank, the propeller cutting off the end as it did so. However, it was almost dry and no fire resulted.

At about 1045 the next two flights went up, the C.O. leading Blaikie, Geordie and Hawthorne and Sub Lt. Morten leading Humphries, Broom and Anderson.

Whilst in the air we could hear the C.O.'s flight being vectored out, though we learned subsequently that they had no luck: we in Morten's flight were soon vectored out, after climbing to 20,000 ft on a westerly heading to intercept a bogey at about 40 miles range.

It must have been at that time—around 1145 that the ship was attacked by two suicide bombers, because for a long time we received no further vector and were steadily flying towards China! Ultimately we were taken over by *Limbo* who vectored us back. We were unaware that the ship had been hit, and it was not until the two flights were ordered to land on other carriers that we realized something was wrong. Sub. Lt.'s Brown, Anderson, Humphries and Blaikie landed on the *Victorious*, and the C.O., Sub. Lt. Morten and Glading went to the *Indomitable.*

Upon their return to the ship in the evening the superficial damage appeared great. The flight deck had a big circular depression, fairly shallow however, just opposite the island and slightly to port; the centre of the saucer-like hollow was covered over by a steel plate. The island was burnt and blackened; punctured by heavy shrapnel holes and the heavy glass lights were mostly blown away. The bridge had escaped with only a few broken windows, the A.L.O.'s office and the next office were in a state of chaos—full of debris. The for'd barrier was smashed up and apparently all our little dodgem cars used for towing, had been badly burned. The belly tanks which had adorned the bridge had all disappeared from the port side.

We learned the story which had been pieced together. After a fly off, the deckpark consisting mainly of Avengers was being taxied for'd. When the ship, being on the outside of the formation and astern was attacked by two Japanese suicide bombers which came in so low over the water that practically no armament was able to engage them. They were travelling extremely quickly and pulled up over the deck into a high stalled turn. One gave way to the other which dived onto the flight deck, exploded and burst into flames. The other was shot down between ourselves and the *Indomitable.* Everything happened very quickly and it was unfortunate that at the moment the deck park was moving which meant that pilots and directors were exposed to shrapnel and blast.

About 50 officers and men were wounded, eight were killed outright including Sub. Lt. (A) John Bell RNVR of 1842 Squadron, and Lt. Burgess RNVR of A.O.R. Lt. Cmdr. Knox A.E.O., was badly hurt in the face and two of 848 pilots Lt. 'Gillie Potter and Sub. Lt. D. Judd D.S.C. were wounded. Amongst the men hurt were P.O. Lamb of the A.H.P., P.O. Merritt and many others. Of our squadron, the duty officer Sub. Lt. (A) D. Wood RNVR was peppered by shrapnel and splinters, hurt in the legs, chest and face.

According to all reports everyone worked hard to do what they could, the foremost being the doctors upon whom fell the greatest blood.

848 Squadron lost most of their Avengers only one remaining serviceable, at least two taxied themselves over the side, and about seven were disposed of in the same way since the extent of the damage was such that repairs were out of the question.

1841 Squadron lost number 118—the engine charger which was almost complete. It received the full blast and had to be ditched.

In the late afternoon, when the flight deck was made serviceable again for landing on, most of the pilots returned with their aircraft, from the *Vic.* or *Indom.* where they had been spending some of their time doing state 11. Sub.

Lt.'s Hawthorne, of 1841, Stirling and Ewing and Lt. Clarke of 1842 did not come back until the next day.

So far as the one strike in which our Avengers participated during the forenoon was concerned reports from AC1 said that it was moderately successful. In the morning while the carriers stood off to the south east of the islands, the two battleships, accompanied by 'all the cruisers and some destroyers—about 6 and 5 respectively steamed to within bombardment range and opened fire on the aerodromes and gun emplacements. The spotting was done by Lt. Cmdr. Parker and Lt. Loudon of 1842, and recent signals state that the firing was good but generally, pilots reports were not very complimentary.

It was during this time, when the carriers were left with only eight destroyers to screen them, that the *Formidable* was attacked and hit. Soon afterwards the striking force returned and the whole fleet was together again.

The second strike of the day by Avengers was carried out; gun emplacements and air strips were bombed fairly effectively.

During the afternoon pilots of the *Vic.* and *Formidable* on the quarter deck of the *Vic.* saw a Hellcat come in from up-sun and get shot down by gunners from these two carriers and the *Howe* It was not a pleasant sight especially as the aircraft was so obviously a Hellcat, though his approach was highly suspicious. He made a controlled ditching but owing to his belly tank nosed downwards into the water. A destroyer went over but I do not know if he was picked up.

The Task Force retired during the afternoon.

Wednesday May 9th
Iceberg 8
At 0515 the fleet was back again in the operational area—about 120 miles from the islands, to continue the attack by sending in Avengers and Corsairs to bomb and patrol.

First flight off from this ship was Sub. Lt. Morten's with Humphries, Brown and Anderson at 0545; the clouds were fairly solid from 8,000′ down to about 2500′, and their patrol was uneventful, apart from the fact that Lt. Anderson's belly tank would not work and he was obliged to return before 0900 which was when they were to finish.

Sub. Lt. (A) Ferguson with Harrison, Blade and Abbott relieved the 'dawn patrol' who let down from 10,000′ and pancaked. His radio (Fergy's) was u/s so Blade took over, though their hop too was fruitless.

1842 took over part of the C.A.P.—they had sent 8 Corsairs to bomb the island airfields earlier in the day—and another flight went to state 11.

Panic stations around 1250 resulted in Morten's flight being hurriedly briefed and stood by for possible immediate fly-off, but the emergency faded and the normal patrol took their place at 1330—consisting of Lt. Clarke's flight 1842 with Ewing, Martin and Wakeling. They were flown off at the rush, slightly before their time and the performance of 115 and 128 on take-off—Morten and

Wakeling—was enough to give anyone twitch, the engines backfired and sounded very rough.

Still Morten's flight did not feel released—Lt. Gray seemed to think that it was still state 11. Eventually however, Lt. Gray himself flew off with Crosland, Maitland and Asbridge in Sub. Lt. Reeve's place who had the duty. At the same time the C.O. with his regular 2, 3 & 4 Blaikie, Glading and Hawthorne went off to 10,000 ft. They were not flying all 1841 cabs, since '42 were just about to bring four back and others were in the barges, either u/s or inaccessible.

At the same time—1545 approx. other Corsairs and Hellcats went up as fleet C.A.P. together with a flight of four Seafires.

All day the Jap had been lying low, the main activities had been the bombing and strafing by 1842 who found one Judy in a cave which they set on fire, and the gallant work by our friends in 848—with their few remaining Avengers.

But around 1615 the storm was let loose. We were ranging 8 F4U's for a state 11 provided by '42 pilots, the a/c were mixed. Unfortunately the kamikazes struck too soon and we were unable to get the a/c off, since the big ref flag was displayed from the bridge, and that meant 'Everyone on the flight deck—TAKE COVER!'

Everyone did! The guns opened up on enemy a/c which were closing rapidly; at one time there were three being engaged. The action commentator gave a pretty good account stating that our guns had shot down one would be suicide and that another had crashed into the side of the *Indomitable*. This was later proved incorrect—the *Victorious* had been hit but the fire was not serious.

Quite suddenly—with no more than 'Oh my God!' from the action commentator and a long silence came our turn. The general opinion was that it was a Betty which came in low from the stern and struck the flight deck at a fairly shallow angle, just abaft S3 pompom and almost in the centre of the deck, in front of the first Corsair on state 11 (by this time minus a pilot!). Apparently the plane which had been repeatedly hit and was on fire—may not have been carrying bombs.

The fire parties worked almost unceasingly on the burning Corsairs—little was found of the Betty—a few bits of Jap—they had to run once or twice when the red flag was displayed. An Avenger in C hangar caught fire and that section was sprayed, the ammunition boxes in the planes and on deck went up and .5 calibre was everywhere, the flames and smoke were easily visible from a great height and the boys thought we had more or less had it.

Down in the ante-room and wardroom were most of the types not flying, clearing space for possible casualties: we were fortunate to have one man only killed—the captain of S3 pompom—and four injured.

We smoked and conjectured until the flight deck was declared clear of fire, and most people went up to help clear away debris.

The two fighter squadrons suffered equally. Six Corsairs went quickly over the side; we lost 112 (Blaikie's), 116 (Crosland's) and 122 (Harrison's). 848 lost another Avenger.

Below, the hangar was in a sad state and so were many aircraft, for the salt water spray had done much damage and many immediately became 'flyable duds'. The number is still to be confirmed; the ratings were swabbing down with fresh water but this can only postpone corrosion.

Number 1 barrier had been blown away—only the wires this time, the hydraulics were serviceable and, the deck being reasonably clear again, the eight Corsairs were landed on. We learned that the Seafires had been given the interception and we already knew that one enemy was sparked by them. They—the Corsairs—were rather cheesed at not making a contact.

We now have a flight deck with a gentle undulating motion going for'd from abaft S3 pompom, not to mention a square patch which breaks this movement and causes 'premature flight', a number 2 barrier which is 'getting tired' to quote the Captain's telegram and many foamites which need replenishing. Our new towing cars have had their time and so have the special elevators. Only Jumbo remains! They may yet find shrapnel in his insides. The island needs painting again though there is little fresh damage. The radar is beginning to look like a set of rusty pipes!

But! The captain was pleased with the performance of all ship's company and congratulated them later, the *Uganda* signalled her sincere admiration.

But—A.O.O.W. comes into force again this evening at 2000!!!

From Royal Marine Joseph Jones, HMS *Formidable*

During the actual engagement I was closed up in X2 4.5 inch turret, which was the after turret, starboard side. The guns crew were ordered from the turret to help with fire fighting and clearing debris from the flight deck.

During the dog watches of that day a number of marines were sent to clean the officers ante-room where the casualties were being attended to, this was a rather traumatic experience as we were about 18 and 19 years old at the time.

I remember I did not draw my tot until after the war had finished, two days after to be precise. We spliced the mainbrace in 'Limers'.

From ex Ordinance Artificer Ron English, HMS *Formidable*

I can still recall one incident when the first Kamikaze hit us (4th May 1945). My action station was 'A' turret, we had stood down and Ordinance 'Tiffie' Norm Healey came into our turret with the words, 'Our Mess has been hit.' This was as serious matter, as I had an H.P. Sauce bottle full of 'neaters'. On reaching our Mess, it was intact. The 'Chicago Piano' aft of our mess had been knocked around. Norm said 'What do we do?' Without hesitation my reply was, 'We drink the lot in case another b . . . . . d hits us.'

HMS Formidable*—clearing up the mess. Photo: S. Chatterton*

Alwyn Doyle, TAG 848 Squadron recalled:

A typical strike consisted of two, perhaps three, squadrons of fighters and usually a higher proportion of bombers. The fighters formed up and flew in advance to 'soften up' the target, an act which drew considerable enemy fire as our Corsairs swept in at low level. The Avenger bombers would select their targets and dive bomb. I remember the clear view of the grass, and what seemed a gigantic pattern of runways, and the surrounding mosaic of fields. And during the dive as I watched our bombs clear the bomb-bay I saw immense clouds of dust form as the bombs burst. This was the culmination of our training and our long journey to the North Pacific Ocean. I experienced fear at my vulnerability and a thrill at delivering a blow at the enemy. After the dive 'G' force glued me to the cabin floor as we climbed; levelling out, I climbed into the turrret to keep vigil for enemy fighters. It was well known that the Japanese war effort was in serious trouble and that pilots and aircraft were in short supply. Nevertheless I was always aware that we might just be 'jumped' by a stray Jap., and I did not relax until we had landed. Landing was an art and I was fortunate in having in Sub Lt. Peter McClintock, and subsequently, Lt. Hughes, pilots who had mastered the art. And without detracting from my pilots' skill, the Corsair and Avenger proved extremely well designed, robust aircraft.

Personal contact between officers and men of both fleets was very limited and confined to the periods of re-supplying the fleets at Manus or Leyte, in the Philippines. Such occasions gave rise to friendly rivalry and banter, and an opportunity to sample American drinks. We aboard the *Formidable* would swim in the bright blue Pacific ocean below the towering grey hull. A lookout would be posted for sharks! From an open section outside their mess TAGs would plunge from the gunwhale thirty or so feet out to sea. I joined in the fun and thought my lungs would burst.

An eye witness of the kamikaze explosion on my ship described it as 'The light from above changing to bright orange', and up on deck he saw 'The bridge windows seeming to gape like eye sockets, and much of the island was blackened.' It was the 4th May, 1945 at 11.31 hours when this disaster struck *Formidable* and I was in the TAG mess, which surprisingly served as our action station during an attack. Following the boom and rattle of our own guns there was a devastating explosion, which shook the entire main ship, all loose objects around us rattled. After the immediate danger had passed we were allowed to move about and I had to steel myself to go on deck to look on the carnage and damage. What seemed to be the kamikaze was a tangled skeleton dripping in white foam sprayed by fire-fighters, and fires in our own aircraft were being extinguished. The protective shield encircling a bofors gun was completely perforated. To my surprise I felt strengthened by a disaster we had clearly survived. The following day it was business as usual, although one could never forget the cost. We were to learn later that two officers and six men of other rank were killed, whilst six officers and forty-one men of other rank were wounded. One officer was dragged from his burning plane a minute before it blew up. Several aircraft were burnt out. The Japanese lost eleven aircraft.

I took part in 15 strikes on the islands and Japan. Seven of these were with Peter McClintock. The remaining eight strikes were with Lt. Hughes, Red Flight Leader. In all I completed 52 sorties with 848 Squadron.

I can give you my version of the attack on *Formidable.*

Fortunately for the TAGs their role when 'Action Stations' was piped was to muster in their mess below the island on the starboard side. Above was the armoured deck to protect the ship below.

The sound of gunfire from the ship heralded a devastating explosion from the bomb slung under the Zeke kamikaze. Loose objects in our mess shook and rattled as the ship shuddered under a massive blow, then quietness before orders were given over the Tannoy for rescue and fire-fighting parties to close up.

We TAGs were given to speculation as to what was happening above. Individual TAGs no doubt reacted differently to the sudden reality of war as it affected the ship, our home, and hitherto, a haven to our crews and aircraft following operations. My feelings were tinged with apprehension of the unknown. Eventually we were allowed on deck and were met with a scene of unfamiliar activity. Men wearing anti-flash helmets were everywhere hosing out fires started in our aircraft and clearing debris; fragments of metal strewed the deck. Holes peppered the island and gun positions. There was a hole in the deck approximately 2′ in diameter and a surrounding dent where the explosion occurred. It was a salutary lesson that on occasion the enemy could hit back.

I spent my twenty-first birthday at sea and, miraculously, I received a magnificent cake sent by the very hospitable Mullins family who had adopted me in Australia. Birthdays were celebrated by sippers all round and that day I imbibed more rum than my body could reasonably contain. I slept peacefully and unobtrusively on the anchor deck for the rest of the day watched occasionally by fellow TAGs, hopefully to prevent another disaster of 'Man Overboard'.

My eldest sister, Dora, kept a number of my letters to her. I told her about life on board. We were able to study a variety of subjects in the evenings during lulls in action. 'Make and Mend' sessions were well occupied, and although we had a ship's laundry one had to do one's own dhobiing. Letter writing and reading had become part of the weekly routine. I took walks on deck with friends for two hours at a time on most days. The heat in the Pacific was intense, above and below decks, precipitating us to take numerous showers (the Navy had come a long way since Nelson's day.)

I attended music-on-record sessions held in the church on board and not a little time was spent on radio and gun maintenance; cleaning the radio cabin, gun turret and perspex windows was part of the routine.

It was Peter McClintock's idea to name our aircraft 'Hassen Ben Sober' after our training period at Dekheila and we decided on a fez with wings as a motif. This was the beginning of a vogue and pilots queued up for a painting job too. I developed an art in scrounging paint and brushes. And such was the state of the latter that I made a joke of substituting them for a poker.

Article from an un-named, undated newspaper cutting
***Formidable*—Victim of a Kamikaze**

Dawn on May 4, 1945, found the aircraft carriers, *Indomitable, Victorious, Formidable* and *Indefatigable* with escorting destroyers in Japanese home waters ready to take part in supporting operations for Operation Iceberg, the assault on Okinawa, the last enemy-held outpost before the mainland of Japan itself.

One man with a particular reason for remembering the day is Lieut. Commander Rex Baseden, a young midshipman at the time who had the unnerving experience of almost being mistaken for a kamikaze pilot.

He recalls: The battleships *King George V* and *Howe* with cruisers and destroyers had left us earlier to bombard nearby airfields, and their supporting anti-aircraft fire was to be missed later in the day.

From my position on the midships port pom pom I could see the radar aerials revolving, searching the skies for enemy aircraft and the lookouts anxiously scanning the heavens waiting for the kamikaze to arrive, the aircraft of the Divine Wind whose pilots would commit suicide by crashing their planes on to their targets.

I had joined *Formidable* only four days before when the ships had sailed from Leyte Gulf but before this I had served for several months in the *Illustrious,* which in the previous month had had a near miss from a kamikaze aircraft which grazed the island structure before crashing into the sea. It was estimated that on that day 700 Japanese aircraft and kamikazes had attacked the Allied ships, inflicting considerable damage.

In *Illustrious* I had been below decks in the Action Plot and had seen little of the action but here as Fire Direction Officer on an anti-aircraft weapon I was well placed to see the action that was bound to take place as the Japanese desperately tried to repel the invaders.

As a teenaged Paymaster Midshipman I felt quite elated at the prospect of action, elation no doubt inspired by the sight of four large carriers and their escorts with flags flying in the breeze, signal lamps winking and dozens of gun muzzles pointing skywards, ships of the Royal Navy, cleared and ready for action. The hard-nosed Rear-Admiral Vian commanded the carriers, flying his flag in *Indomitable,* and he was just the man to inspire confidence in his crews.

My duties on the eight-barrelled pom pom were quite simple, to point out the best targets to the gun's crew. It was difficult for the layer and trainer to shift targets once they had started firing and were concentrating on ranges and deflections, and shooting at an aircraft diving on the ship was more important than firing at a passing aircraft, however close.

The communications number on the gun alerted us to the fact that the Japanese were on their way and he constantly shouted out bearings and decreasing ranges. In a flash the aircraft was upon us and the shooting started. The noise and smoke from guns and aircraft hurtling past all made up a mad kaleidescope of war and I found it very exhilarating.

I was quite surprised to see that Japanese aircraft actually had a red circle painted on their fuselages. I pointed out an aircraft diving on us and the pom pom started its chattering with all the oerlikons and machine guns joining in. I was thinking to myself that this was just like the movies when there was a tremendous explosion and everything went black.

I woke up to find a hostile circle of sailors glowering down at me and from their language I gathered that they thought I was the pilot of the plane that had hit us. I was very sunburnt, and unknown to them having just joined this large ship and like other midshipmen, had no shoulder straps to indicate rank. I managed to croak out a few words which convinced them that no Japanese officer would have such a command of profanity and I was carried to the sick bay and not, as I expected, to be given a swimming lesson.

Being waist high above the flight deck I had been wounded by shrapnel when a Zeke aircraft dived on the ship from a high altitude and crashed near the island structure. My wounds did not appear to be too serious and I turned in to the sick bay. Fortunately for me, Surgeon Lieutenant Commander Steele-Perkins, who had joined from *Illustrious* with me and knew me, looked at my wounds again and found a small wound which would have proved fatal if left unattended.

Wilf Gillard, a TAG with 848 Squadron told me:

I had the runs very badly and whilst warming up on the flight deck I had to keep on getting out of the aircraft and crawling under other aircraft to go to the heads. After the last one it was nearly take off time so I took some newspapers with me. On the way to Ishigaki, every time my tummy rumbled, I had to leave my turret, drop my trousers and get on with the business. Eventually the papers were all used up so I had to use my blue American cotton underpants. I opened my small window and making the remark of 'Share this amongst you you bastards' I let go. At this moment my pilot Bob Eatock said over the intercom 'Here we go' and immediately dived for the target. I, with my trousers down bounced about the aircraft like a man in space. When we formed up and things were back to normal Bob asked me what I had been up to and had the biggest laugh of his life, especially when the story was repeated at his wedding which I was happy to attend.

From Sto. PO Arthur Camfield DSM, HMS *Formidable*

I was sent to the *Formidable* to take charge of the firefighting in the hangar. I had been through a special course of firefighting. At that time I was Stoker P.O. I had to report to Mr. Charlcraft a Sub-Lieutenant and he just said, 'Well, it's all yours.' I had a fire party of 12 and we used to keep the equipment in good working order and four were always on duty. On this day in May we were going back to Sydney for repairs, stand easy had just finished that morning I was walking through 'B' hangar when I heard what sounded like shooting and then a flash and a shout of 'Fire!' I turned round and there in 'B' hangar was a plane on fire. I grabbed the first fire extinguisher and started to fight the plane on fire. Five of my firefighters came and helped and we almost got the fire out but someone opened the big sprinkler wheel in the hangar access and sent tons of water down on us—we had to evacuate the hangar wet through, but the fire was out. Our lungs were full of smoke and we went out on the weather deck to get some fresh air but were ordered back into the hangar by the upper deck Commander to investigate what had happened. We found that a m/m had been renewing batteries in a fighter plane and had set off the guns and the bullets had pierced the petrol tank of an Avenger and set it alight. We returned to Sydney where the Duke of Gloucester came on board and the fire parties were introduced to him. I remember what he said: 'You started the fire yourselves and you put it out yourselves. Good.'

About my D.S.M., the citation arrived on the ship November 1945. Till I actually got the Medal in the post with the ordinary mail took 16 months, yet a brother-in-law won one a week before me on another ship and he went home and the King presented his. All I got with mine was a typed notice saying the King was sorry but too busy. Surely the Captain should have given it to me. I was disappointed, but when I opened the letter with the medal two of the men in my mess cried and started to say it was not fair, but there it was.

From D. Nash, A/B ST., HMS *Formidable*

Having been watchkeeping for some time I thought I had everything well organised, even to the lashing and stowing of my hammock after I had started my watch. As it was extremely warm I was sleeping on the forecastle and was on the morning watch. I reported for my duty and forgot to return to stow my hammock so when the hands fell in in the morning so did my hammock.

Somebody was very upset and I was invited to fall in outside the Jaunties Office and I was put on a charge and given the pleasure of having to attend at the Captain's Table.

The fatal morning arrived and I fell in on a freshly scrubbed quarter deck with rather a lot of surplus water around. I was called to attend at the Captain's defaulters table at the double and I responded coming to an abrupt halt in front of his table with a salute suspended in mid air only to disappear completely under the table flat on my back, my wet shoes being the cause of this unfortunate position. When I came above the level of the table and returned myself to an upright position and completed the salute I am sure Capt Ruck-Keene had just that slight start of a grin.

My performance made no difference—it was a one and one job—hard times.

When I first joined the *Formidable* as an Ordinary Seaman straight out of training I was given as my Action Station a position in 'B' Gun Transmitting Station as an operator of a Roll Corrector.

I stood in the corner of this room along with a small 'magic box' feeling quite a dunce. I was told that my job was the correction of the pitch and roll of the ship in final directional readings to the Gun Turret.

The piece of equipment consisted of a small square box on a pedestal and on the outside two handles and two spirit levels. Have you ever had to determine which way the bubble will go when you have been doing that DIY job at home with a spirit level? I still haven't mastered it. In the noise of gun fire in action I was always in difficulties in turning the handles in the right directions to keep the bubble between the lines. This worried me as I felt the guns would not be pointing in the right direction! I was sure that the war would be lost due to my bubbles being in the wrong place.

If ever I need to make thanks to my maker I think of the man that I feel died for me. Over the years I had forgotten his name but reading the Roll of Honour at the Reunion it all came flooding back.

As an A/B S.T. my Cruising Station was a watchkeeper in a compartment just forward of the main entrance to the island at flight deck level. When not actively engaged I sat in a chair whose back was against the baulkhead facing the flight deck. Action Stations sounded and my duties changed to a damage control position in the torpedo flat. I was relieved by a stoker who was involved in flight deck arrester gear during Action Stations.

Within a very short time of leaving my seat the first kamikaze landed on and the shrapnel from the bomb load pierced the island baulkhead and killed the stoker. His name was Stoker Williams.

From L. G. Banks, HMS *Formidable*

Stoker 'Brummie' Williams, on flight deck duty, was killed during the first attack.

Chief Stoker 'Tiddley' Ball was on watch in the boiler room when the bomb crashed through, missed his back by inches, he is reported to have said 'I'll have to dhobi these overalls.'

A bomb or shrapnel came down the torpedo lift, creating small fire. The engineering officer and myself were very close by, we both ran forward, I picked up a nearby bucket and threw its contents over it. By then a fire squad arrived and completed the action as required.

From P.O. George Bullamore, HMS *Formidable*

The aircraft were returning from the strike, landing on, then 'spotted' for refuelling and rearming. Everyone was getting on with the job when we realized Anti Hawk Stations had been sounded and the gun's crews already in action. I sprinted down the flight deck, down the after access ladder without touching the treads following the one in front, landing at the bottom and dived right for cover when this almighty crash and judder rocked the ship. Then back up on deck again with the gang. L/AM Dackombe responsible for the rope hooked on to a piece of burning wreckage and pulled it away from what looked like an overload tank. At the same time being swamped by one lot spraying foam and another lot with water. And the ammunition cooking off. In the middle of this P.O. Harvey who was in charge of a fire party came rushing up to me and said the spare Avenger was on fire in the Hangar. A rivet from the flight deck armour had been blown down and smashed into the turret of the aircraft we had worked on the previous night. I left L/AM Dackombe in charge and made my way to the port side after access to the hangar, as the armoured doors were across and the access doors dogged on.

There was the 'Stoker Damage Control' by the door I had to convince him quickly to let me in as the aircraft still had the bombs on. The hangar sprayer was working but the fire curtain was buckled and would not operate (from the impact of the kamikaze). There was smoke but I couldn't see any fire. As quickly as I could, I removed the detonators from the 4 x 500 lb bombs thus making them fairly safe. Also the arming pistols. Taking the detonators and the phosphorous bomb from the pilot's cockpit (this was to be activated by the pilot should he land in enemy territory). With this lot he managed to get damage control to let me out of the hangar and promptly rushed to the weather deck and tossed them over the side. Seemed a good idea. By this time Mr. Branch W.O. arrived (I/C ships and H.Q. Armoury) to see what the situation was as he was concerned about a number of semi armour piercing bombs which were also stowed in hangar ready for the next strike. These also had detonators in ready. I got one of my armourers, a lad named Peers, to bring me a detonator extractor from our deck-head office and any spare tins of det. holders. (These bombs were prepared in readiness to be loaded on the Corsairs.) Anyway I removed all the detonators and safely stowed, as they had all to be accounted for at some time later. I then collected the other four armourers and we removed the 500 lbs from the Avenger and secured them to the bulkhead in the hangar. I wonder if the captain ever knew how close it was should I have slipped up and punctured a detonator while removing it from the bombs?

During one forenoon we were closed up with the fleet train having transferred supplies and ammunition. We were all engaged in daily tasks required to keep aircraft serviceable, when a clatter of machine-gun fire ripped through the wing of an Avenger injuring one of the lads in the leg. One other air mechanic on a Corsair had unfortunately pressed the firing button. this caused a fire which eventually became a disaster as the hanger became filled with smoke and the fire curtains would not operate because of previous damage from the first kamikaze. Again I was involved because of the bombs stored in the hangar which were to be taken up to the flight deck later for the strike aircraft. Earlier in the service I had been at Rosyth Dockyard and completed the damage control fire fighting course in the mock-up of ships compartments. So this training stood me in very good stead giving me the confidence to get to grips with the situation. Anyway much later, covered in grime, soot, oil, etc., wet through I eventually made my way back to our P.O.'s mess to find that they had a mess muster and I was still missing, which fortunately was not true. This damage really had made a mess of things almost wiping out most of the aircraft.

George Bullamore P.O. 848 Squadron. HMS *Formidable* sent me some pages of Instructions which are some indication of the unseen planning required on the carrier:

AMENDMENT NO. 1 to MEMO NO. 447 HMS *FORMIDABLE*'19th April, 1945

Foamites are stowed as follows and are to be taken to the scene of the fire by:

1 by each Flight Deck Foam Generator	A.H.P. Fire Party (8)
8 by after door of Island	No. 5 Squadron Gang
5 in main lobby of Island	No. 9 Squadron Gang
8 in each Flight Deck Access Lobby (To be taken up under the supervision of section officers at 1st Action Stations and returned to correct stowage when ship leaves operational area.)	Nos. 1 & 2, and 6 & 7 Squadron Gangs

2. A Foamite Re-loading Gang will be stationed by the Pilots and Observers Waiting Room in the Island, expended foamites are to be turned over to this party as quickly as possible.

3. *Cranes.* Tripping wires are to be rigged on both cranes at 'Prepare for Action' and two Crane Drivers are to close up at each crane at the order 'Fire in the deck park' for ditching aircraft.

4. Lt. (E) Gardham and/or Lt. (E) Boyle are to assist the Flight Deck Firefighting Officer.

5. *Striking Down.* If the fire is reasonably well under control, Cdr. (F) is to arrange to strike down aircraft using the lift furthest from the fire.

6. *Hook Ropes* marked 'For Anti Hawk only' are stowed in the access lobbies, each squadron gang is to take one to the Flight Deck for towing aircraft. Turret Action Gangs are to take their own hook rope with them.

(Sgd). Donald Fuller
Commander

From AB Ron Tovey, HMS *Formidable*

AIRCRAFT DIRECTION ROOM (ADR)
The ADR in *Formidable* was situated half way up the island, and, being air conditioned was a popular place to visit.

All *Formidable*'s aircraft, when airborne, were subject to flying control from the ADR. When flying was taking place, the ADR was fully manned, which meant, at times long hours closed up for the crew.

The ADR was manned by Radar Plot Ratings and Fighter Direction Officers, under the control of the senior FDO.

When fully operating although much was happening the dimly lit room was very quiet with only the hum of machinery and low voices.

Dominating the room was the vertical plot, a large perspex compass rose the centre of which represented the ship, with intersecting lines representing distances from the ship. Behind the plot sat the ratings each of whom was connected by internal phones to the various Radar sets around the ship. These ratings, who had been trained to write backwards in special symbols and words, plotted the reports on to the plot each one being responsible for different echoes being received.

The senior FDO's task was to interpret the various tracks, to decide whether they represented friend or foe. He was in communication with our own aircraft by Radio Telephone (RT) to establish their positions.

If he decided that the plot represented a possible foe the interception was handed to one of the other FDOs who had the use of a horizontal plot, lit from below, on which again was etched the compass rose. The rating manning this plot sat opposite the FDO and marked the plot with upside down writing and symbols. The FDO using RT directed the appropriate fighter patrol to the target, which would then be confirmed as either friend or foe.

Seated around the room were further members of the crew manning the Low and High Frequency RT sets, their task being to listen out for messages and to log all incoming and outgoing calls in a special RT shorthand. These log books could be called for in the event of any questions arising over incidents that may occur.

Possibly one of the most notable interceptions was made off the Japanese coast with a dusk patrol of four Hellcats. A possible group of enemy aircraft was detected at about a range of 94 miles and in spite of the disbelief of the American FDOs the Hellcats intercepted them at 20,000 feet. Angels 20, 30 miles from the fleet. They were four torpedo bombers and three were shot down and the fourth damaged. As a result of this the Americans were convinced and put their own patrols up and intercepted further groups of bombers.

On the 4th May, the day before my 20th birthday, we were at action stations, in full action gear and exposed to the Pacific sun.

The battleships and cruisers had departed on a bombarding mission leaving just the four carriers together with their attendant destroyers. Our aircraft were away on a strike and preparations were being made to receive them back by moving the deck park forward.

There had been mutterings about possible bogeys in the area, but nothing in sight. One of the look-outs below us reported a Seafire approaching from astern. Looking aft all I could see was a brown blob in the heat haze from the funnel. I then became aware of a plane tracking along the Flight Deck and thought to myself what a bloody silly thing to do, and then looking down I realised that I was looking at the top of a Zero with its Red Circles. The three of us then watched helplessly as it banked off the starboard bow, climbed, and flew astern, by which time all the close range weapons were in operation. We watched it as it reached astern of the island and put its nose down, which gave us the feeling that it was aimed at us. As it dived at us, by now I think on fire, we three also dived for the deck. As I went down I was aware of a tremendous explosion and a sheet of smoke and flame passing overhead as the deck came up and hit me under the chin. When we 'came to' we were very aware of the narrow squeak we had had as the canvas dodger on the inboard side was totally shredded, and all of our equipment had disappeared.

Five days later we were again operating, this time with the other Capital ships, and again mutterings of bogeys were heard. Suddenly the portside 4.5's opened up and the starboard guns of the *KGV* also commenced firing. The target then came into view, this time a twin engined plane, flying between us. I must admit that I did hope that it would go for the *KGV,* but was aware that it had turned towards us, and again as its nose went down so did we. This time the strike was further aft and so we did not have quite so much local damage.

I think that my abiding memories will be of the disgusting smell of the fire fighting foam, the ammunition cooking off and the smell of the boiled oil that we had to use to clean down the island superstructure before repainting on both occasions.

From P. D. Evans, HMS *Formidable*

My action station was on S2 pom pom where Petty Officer George Hinkins was killed during the second kamikaze attack on *Formidable.* My job with the gun's crew was to pull open when ordered, two ejector levers which controlled two magazines which I had to keep fed with ammunition. On this occasion, George shouted to open ejector levers and then to take cover which I did. I went behind the funnel of the ship which was adjacent to the gun, where I remained with others until after the kamikaze hit. During this time S2 pom pom had kept firing. After the explosion I very cautiously went back to the gun with the Leading Seaman, who was second-in-command of the gun. There were bits of fabric burning on top of a ready use ammunition locker which we attended to. There was also an eerie feeling which is difficult to describe. I'm sure we both suspected that George was dead or badly wounded. It took me a couple of seconds to pluck up enough courage to climb onto the gun and look towards the position where George was. I can clearly recall that a small part of the knee of his overall was smouldering but there did not appear to be any injury. At this time Buffer appeared and shouted for a sick berth attendant who was quickly on the scene. He examined George and conveyed to us that he was dead. I can assure you that this is a true account—and I can also assure you that George Hinkins was the only one on the gun when the kamikaze hit *Formidable.* I hope that this will help you with your book and hopefully bring some recognition to what George gave his life for. (*A baby son he had never seen.—Ed.*)

From H. Chapman, HMS *Undaunted*

Leaving Sydney we went to Manus, worked all night alongside the HMS *Tyne* getting the evaporator coils cleaned—was it hot!

I remember going to Leyte, where we were invited on one of the carriers for a film show. We had just sat down, when the air raid siren went. We never did see the film.

One incident I remember was a pilot we had to pick up. He came alongside in his dinghy, looked up and said, 'Which way to Australia?'

HMS Undaunted. *Photo: H. Chapman*

From an unnamed Australian Magazine

The suicide bombers certainly attacked us. There was one particular day that I well remember when the *Howe* and *KGV* were called over to attack an island with some particular airfields and this we did, and we left the carriers and the cruisers. We took some destroyers with us. We did the job and, as we sailed back in the later afternoon, it was an incredible sight that met our eyes. The carriers. . . . some of them were alight . . . wreckage was strewn all over the flight decks. They had been attacked by suicide bombers . . . It wasn't over by any means. They went hell for leather for us and we were absolutely delighted to be able to shoot one down, which was actually aimed at the bridge, but which went between the foremast and the mainmast, below the radio aerials, and came down off the starboard quarter.

From RM R. Putland, *KGV*

When we were at action stations during a kamikaze attack (our action station was on the quadruple Bofors on the Port After gundeck of the *KGV* we had a full view of the intense fire power that was sent up from the entire BPF and I still can't think some did make it to the carriers. Was it courage or something else!

Hit by kamikaze off Sakishima Gunto, 1945. (Hit deck and bounced off!)
Photo: J. M. Montgomery, HMS Indomitable

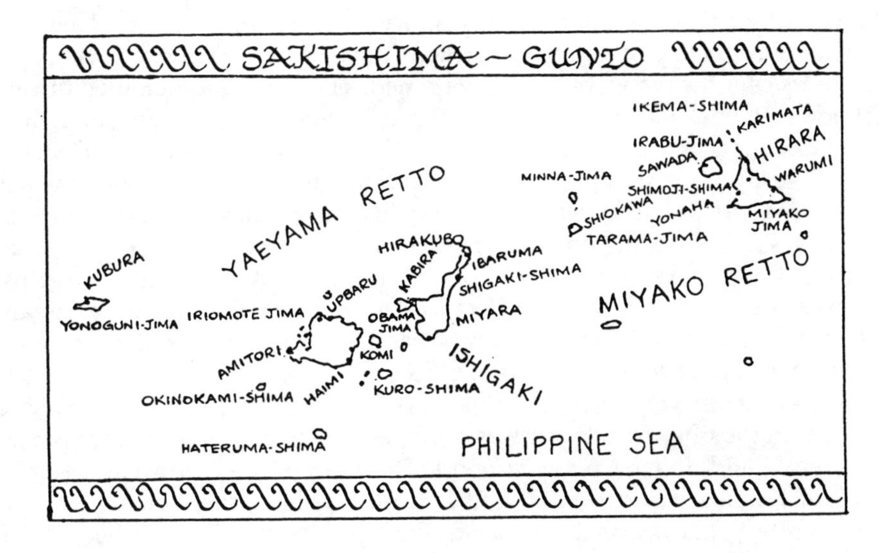

From Lieut. (S) W. H. Procter, HMS *Argonaut*

After Sakishima it was on to the Philippines. Again the US Fleet had it all tied up. Stores in abundance. It was amazing. Whatever you wanted, it was there. For us? All we wanted was a set of coffee brewing machines. Modest, yes. But highly rated by the American officers we had aboard. They were communiction experts and their job was to familiarise our telegraphists on the American jargon. The concern of the two officers was the absence of coffee-on-tap in the wardroom. It was the American way of life to drink coffee just about any and every time of day. No trouble at Leyte. A set of coffee brewing machines was installed in the wardroom and we all soon caught the habit.

From Jack Collins, HMS *Quality*

On May 1st, we left Leyte for good, in company with the Fleet, and having fuelled at sea, recommenced air strikes against the Sakishima Islands on the 4th. On that day also the battleships and cruisers successfully bombarded airfields without opposition. This entailed splitting the force and the 4th flotilla remained behind with the carreirs. About noon a number of Japanese suicide planes attacked us; one landed full in the middle of *Formidable*'s flight deck causing a fairly big fire—we were alarmed to say the least at the clouds of black smoke which rose from her, but everything was under control within an hour. Another plane dived at *Indomitable*, astern of whom *Quality* was at that time stationed; our Pom Pom and Oerlikons registered hits on this plane, as also did *Indomitable*'s after Oerlikons, with the result that the plane was practically shot to pieces and only struck the carrier a glancing blow. A couple of hours later the bombarding force rejoined. The Japanese attempted further attacks but their aircraft did not succeed in breaking through our fighter patrols. Our planes bag for the day was 25. Air strikes were resumed on the 5th. One Jap plane snooping over the Fleet was shot down; otherwise the day passed quietly. The next two days were spent in the fuelling area. May 8th was VE day. We were in the operational area but the weather was too bad for air strikes. On the evening of the 9th, after a day of successful strikes against Kiyake and Hirara airfields, the Fleet was again attacked by Japanese aircraft. *Victorious* and *Formidable* were both hit by suicide planes, but the fires were quickly got under control and the carriers were operating aircraft the next day. This was the final and most sustained attack made by the Japanese kamikaze planes on the BPF. A destroyer was stationed two cables astern of each carrier to provide additional AA gun support. The 'Q's now became known as 'KK' or 'Anti Kamikaze Destroyers'. Needless to say we had grave qualms over this honour, but amazing as it may seem, the Japs attempted no further suicide attacks, so we never had the chance of proving our valour. Further air strikes were carried out on May 12th and 13th against runways, hangars, barracks and barges. During the next oiling period *Quality* was busily employed on D.S.B. transferring stores and casualties to and from the Dutch hospital ship *Tjitjalengka*, better known as H.S.3. Our captain proved so efficient at going alongside other ships that we were detailed off the D.S.B. duties very frequently from now on. Strikes were continued on the 16th and 17th; we picked up the crew of three from an Avenger that crashed after taking off from *Formidable*. The duties of Air Sea Rescue boat was also to be one of our specialities. After fuelling again on the 18th and 19th, we returned to the operational area on the morning of the 20th. A heavy fog came down suddenly as the 'Q's were taking up their appointed stations astern of the carriers and *Quilliam* collided with *Indomitable*; her bows were stove in and she was taken in tow. Our flotilla leader was out of the fray for good and she subsequently returned to U.K. Later in the day, we picked up yet another pilot from a fighter that failed to get sufficient lift as it took off from *Formidable*. Again no Jap air opposition was encountered. After fuelling on the 22nd and 23rd, the final air strikes of operation 'Iceberg' were successfully carried out on the 24th and 25th. On the 26th *KG5, Troubridge, Tenacious* and *Termagent* parted company in the fuelling area and proceeded to Guam. *Quality* and the rest of the fleet set off for Manus.

57 Japanese aircraft had been shot down for a loss of 54 of our own. Royal Naval records had been created . . . 4852 sorties were flown off: the mileage steamed in two months at sea was 25000. Special commendation was made of the engine room, elecrical, radar and communication staffs, who had worked in heat or discomfort.

On May 30th we arrived in Manus, fuelled and left the following day in company with the carriers, for a replenishment period in Australia. We arrived back in Sydney on June 5th after an absence of over 3 months. *Quality* berthed at Fort's Dock where we enjoyed a fortnight's well-earned rest. Each watch had four day's leave; many of us were rather disillusioned about 'Sunny Australia'; the weather was very wet and quite cold. Nevertheless it was good to enjoy the amenities of a modern civilised city.

The 4th flotilla was now reduced to 4 boats—*Queenborough* was not attached to the escort force as she was running on one boiler, the other having burnt out. June 26th saw the departure of *Quality, Quiberon, Quadrant* and *Quickmatch* for Brisbane where we arrived on the following day. This was but a brief visit and we left on the 29th to rendezvous with the Fleet en route for Manus where we arrived on July 4th. While at Manus, our Captain, Viscount Jocelyn received news of his promotion to Commander. He also cleared lower deck on the evening of the 5th and quietly informed us that our next operation would be off Japan itself.

From PO A/M Jim Dodds, HMS *Victorious*

My diary for Sunday 1st April 1945 baldly states: Attack kept up today, more aircraft destroyed on the ground and in the air. Jap suicide bombers attack at dawn one hitting *Indefat.*. 5 destroyed. One gets through at dusk making for *Vic.*, but the skipper slews and the Jap glances off the flight deck and explodes in the sea.

Wednesday 9 May: Weather OK today. The island airstrips well bombed. Jap suicide bombers from Formosa attack the fleet. Two hit us, one for'ard and one aft, the one for'ard penetrating the deck into 'B' turret killing 3, the one aft smashing up a couple of Corsairs. One suicider hits *Formid.* again, destroying 6 planes on deck.

Operations against Japan from July 6th to August 18th. We did 44 days at sea and 42 days out of sight of land. *Victorious* was always nearest to Japan (including US Forces). Since leaving Ceylon we have steamed 65,000 miles. Out of 214 days since leaving Ceylon we have spent 163 days at sea.

Since leaving Liverpool we have steamed 117,000 miles and since commissioning in March 1941 she has steamed 268,000 miles which is equal to 30 years peacetime steaming.

Victorious has operated in every ocean except Antarctic and is the only ship in the world to sail from Coral Sea to Coral Sea. She has taken part in every operation in the Eastern Fleet and Pacific Fleet except for two days.

Distances: Manus to Sydney—2,300 miles
Manus to Tokyo—2,300 miles
Manus to UK, via Pearl Harbour—12,000 miles
Manus to UK, via Sydney—14,500 miles

Victorious under Capt. Denny was a happy and efficient ship, overcrowded at sea and affectionately named 'Denny's dungeon'. She had a ship's newspaper called 'Dungeon Dust', an in-house radio programme with talks and record playing and Perfidia as its signature tune. Her CDA mess was normally occupied to varying degrees depending on where the ship had been and the cheery disposition of its inmates showed out at Christmas time with their decorations and banner hanging from the deck head—'A MERRY SYPHILIS AND A HAPPY NEW YEAR'.

. . . The bang as it hit and then exploded over the port side For'ard was an ear shattering experience. We weren't at action stations at the time as the Jap came from nowhere, swung round the island as the ship did a tight starboard turn and SWOOSH-BANG. To us on the flight deck for'ard, reaction was instantaneous but even at that too late—the attack was over. I'm not sure what the record is for the number of people able to squeeze into a VW and close the doors but the *Vic.* had a ready use locker at the front end of the island with access at flight deck level and you should have seen the scramble to get in there and close the door—there must have been dozens (including me). Bits and pieces from the Jap plane littered the flight deck after it exploded on going over the side and I souvenired a small portion of the fuselage or wing with some red markings on it—I kept this safely until the end of the war when on re-packing my gear prior to demob., at Waxwing on 11.12.45 I left it lying on the mess table along with my 'housewife'.

May, Wed 9th: Weather OK today. The island air-strips well bombed. Jap suicide bombers from Formosa attack the fleet. Two hit us, one for'ard and one aft. The one for'ard penetrating the deck into 'B' turret killing 3 the one aft smashing up a couple of Corsairs. 1 suicider hits *Formid.* again, destroying 6 planes on deck.

The bald fact written in a diary shows how callous we all had become after more than 5 years of war, death and injury were all around us, fatal accidents in the air and on board were the norm and yet we continued to carry out our duties in the manner that the RN expects. Of course options were limited—it was them or us.

May 9th was a busy day in a hectic month so far and having as an action station 'Action crash party', I was on the flight deck more often than not. The small area of deck space between the after end of the island and S4 pom-pom was our domain along with the fire-fighters with little protection against wind and weather and even less against kamikaze attacks. Petty Officer Jock Foster from Dumfries was responsible for my having this action station—he was our HQ divisional officers' regulating P.O. (Jock was regular navy and had worked himself into a nice little office number) and to get out of the action station I had on joining the *Vic.*, in 1942, the 4.5 magazines in which I *heard* the *Eagle* sinking during the Malta convoy of August that year was worth sippers, gulpers and sandy bottoms. Jock was a chocolate addict with little given away and his

9th May—HMS Victorious*—close encounter—last seconds. Photo: Ted Tisdale*

HMS Victorious*, a glancing blow. 9th May 1945.*
Photo: Captain Hans Hamilton RN Ret'd

'Nutty drawer open, nutty drawer closed, mind your fingers', was one of his classic outbursts when satisfying his sweet tooth.

Funny how details of the first kamikaze attack on the *Vic.*, that day, the 9th, are rather sketchy and yet the second is still vividly etched into my mind.

The attack was on, the pom-poms S3 and S4 were blazing away and the 20mm's along the starboard side of the island were doing likewise and there was I, not game enough to make a dash for the comparative safety of the innards of the island but cowering down behind the steel plated guard rail that ran along the outside of S4 pom-pom. Amidst the noise and confusion the first kamikaze must have hit the flight deck port side for'ard, the explosion punching a hole through into 'B' 4.5 turret and as well as the resultant fire, putting the catapult and forward lift out of action. I didn't see it hit the deck yet I suppose I was only about 300′ or so from the spot but partly obscured by the after end of the island and I'm sure my concern at that time was self preservation and little else and looking aft to where every possible gun was now firing another Jap had us in his sights and coming fast fine on the starboard quarter. Not only did the kamikaze plane have the *Vic.* in its sights but it had *me* too—this bloody thing was coming straight for me and there was nothing I could do other than get down again behind the guard rail at S4 pom-pom—I waited a few seconds and then had a quick glance round in the open end of the rail and there it was, still on course, still in a shallow dive, much closer and no way that it was going to miss me, S4 pom-pom and the after end of the island and though the guns were now hitting it at point blank range the plane had 'DODDS written all over it and as I made myself as small a target as possible, eyes squeezed tightly shut, I awaited the final bang and explosion—this was it then, no panic, surprisingly calm as a matter of fact amidst the din that I hardly heard and with flashes of by-gone life chasing each other through my mind (it's true) the seconds ticked away. I was convinced that the inevitable should have occurred by this time so I opened my eyes for another quick look and sure enough the kamikaze was still there but no longer pointing in my direction, Capt. Denny had the *Vic.* in a tight starboard turn which brought the Jap at right angles across the after end of the flight deck where it ploughed its way on fire through a deck park of Corsairs writing off a number of them before it itself in a ball of flame shot over the port side leaving a good fire going amongst the planes on deck. There was an incident in this attack that was different and worth repeating. When I had raised my head to have a look at the oncoming kamikaze and ascertain that its dive was still toward S4 pom-pom (and me) there was also a parachute floating sea-ward which appeared to have come from the kamikaze plane. As the plane didn't have any great altitude by this time the parachute soon hit the water and our escorting anti-aircraft cruiser coming up astern at speed altered course ever so slightly to cut through the water where the parachute had touched down—a sort of involuntary action as much as to say 'I'll get you—you bastard'. Now I've never seen any report of this incident anywhere and I've always assumed that it was the pilot who had baled out whilst in his final dive and that's what probably saved my life—the suicide plane couldn't follow the tight turn of the *Victorious* to starboard and so crashed on the after end of the flight deck. It was only on reading The Forgotten Fleet by John Winton that I came upon the following mention of a parachute on page 148 when the author was relating the action of May 9th and the two kamikaze hits on *Victorious*. Quote:

> The suicider was taken under fire and hit but dived over the starboard quarter and crashed on the flight deck forward, abreast 'B' 4.5 inch turrets: the Zeke appeared to release a small white parachute when about 300 yards from the ship . . .

Winton was talking about the first hit when mentioning the small parachute and was possibly relying on someone else's memory for his book but I can assure you that *my* parachute was bigger than the small parachute and came from the second suicide plane to hit *Victorious* that day—I know, I had a front row view.

Whenever a Walrus waddled across the round down to return on board the duty flight deck party were lined up ready to give chase up the flight deck, grab her by the wings, tail or whatever and pull her to a stop. Not having an arrester hook there was always the chance that either Darby or Joan would gracefully float too far forward before touch-down and continue on over the bows.

Without being 100% positive, the rescue as shown on the photograph *(not included)* could be that of Sub/Lt. J. B. Gass observer in one of *Formidable*'s Avengers shot down on 17.4.45 and rescued by the Walrus less than two miles off the coast. Both the pilot and air gunner were killed. Sorry, have nothing on the pilot or observer of the Walrus that day but the following were on board: Pilots: Flight Lt. D. R. Howard and Flying Officer B. L. Ada, RAAF. Observers: Sub/Lt. J. Wilson, R. Humphries and A. Braithwaite, RNVR.

Quote from 'Send Her Victorious':

> S.A.R. Two Walrus. Embarked in *Victorious* in November 1944 and remained with the ship until the end of the war. On 10th August 1945, W3085 ditched and as it couldn't take off, the Walrus was eventually sunk by gunfire.

HQ squadron (or for'ard workshop as it was also known) was a good part of ship to be, we had our own workshop just ahead of the forward lift at hangar deck level and with our equipment were capable of carrying out aircraft maintenance work and repair beyond the scope of squadron personnel working in the hangar or on the flight deck. We were also responsible for the stowage of spare aircraft engines (bolted onto hangar bulkheads at deck-head height), spare mainplanes, long range fuel tanks and any other odd shaped bulky items that had to be securely lashed to the hangar deck-head or deck-head stowages, all hauled up by block and tackle or 2 ton purchase—sweat, blood, toil and prickly heat. Being conversant with timber and the joinery trade I was often in demand for aircraft chocks, picture frames, packing cases for drafting offices, scale model of *Victorious*—'things' for divisional officers and 'rabbits' for others. All essential for the war effort.

HQ division was also responsible for flight deck duties—action crash party and disposal of aircraft, jumbo mobile crane, aircraft towing vehicles, officer to the flight deck officer when receiving aircraft and other duties too numerous to mention including storing ship. The beauty of it was that we were 'ship's company' and unlike the aircraft squadrons we were not continually embarking to proceed to sea and disembarking on returning to harbour. We certainly had our hectic moments but to be truthful I've often wondered since what I did achieve on board *Victorious* for 3 years and 8 months where I rose from a humble AM 1/C(A) to the dizzy heights of A/PO.AM(A) (TY). Maybe the old joke of 'as long as you have a few sheets of paper in your hand and walking pretty smartly nobody will ever ask you what your'e doing' was in some instances quite true. But I jest—I was never caught skulking on the mess deck and my time on the *Vic.* was exciting and certainly character building and I mourn the loss of those whom I knew in that period of time.

From Tony Britton of Brentwood. Extracts from The War Illustrated, No. 215, Sept. 14, 1945

Darby & Joan

TWO 'GRAND OLD CABS' WITH THE PACIFIC FLEET

> For the two months April May 1945 the fleet maintained constant operations against the Sakishima Group, a vital link in the Formosa-Kyushu defence chain. This involved over 4,000 sorties, the destruction of over 100 Jap planes, and the hazardous task of refuelling and transferring stores at sea. This account, by Sub.-Lt. (A) D. Ash, R.N.V.R. who flew on one of the strikes, was written specially for 'The War Illustrated'.

After many months waiting, our crew ('Abe' the pilot, and 'Fozz' the air-gunner) joined a fleet carrier. During March, as one of several reserve Avenger crews, we followed the fleet in an escort ship. Many miles from land, she had come out from operations to refuel and take on supplies. Rocket lines were fired between ships, followed by thick cables, and soon, 'all hands on deck' were having them taut, as large canvas bags went back and forth with supplies. Abe was almost the first of these 'supplies' over to a destroyer and then to the carrier. Fozz and I were luckier; we were flown over.

Next day the fleet, with battleships in the centre and carriers on each side, ringed by escort destroyers, steamed back to the operational area. Ahead, two Avengers kept an anti-sub patrol, and fighters maintained an all-day air defence against possible kamikazes. The planes that got through were put out of operation. The fleet's task was to bomb the island runways and prevent their use by any reinforcement aircraft coming up from the south to attack the Americans on Okinawa. Avengers and Corsairs were responsible for keeping the Japs busy night and day filling in bomb craters. Towards mid-May the Japs 'threw in the towel'.

This was the climax of the amazing growth of the Fleet Air Arm during the war. The Swordfish, which did such great work at Taranto—with other biplanes—has now been superseded, and the performance of modern carrier planes is not far behind those which are land-based. That is, all but two—Darby and Joan. In the 1930's the Supermarine Walrus was the king-pin of the Fleet Air Arm, and still she chugs bravely on. Many Allied aircrews have cause to thank her for air-sea rescue; she played a valuable part in saving four out of every five American airmen who came down in the Channel. Though laughed at, *Darby* and *Joan*, the two Walrus on this carrier, are viewed with affection. Two grand old cabs, we call them.

On April 19, aircraft from another ship were returning from a raid. As they passed over the enemy coast, one shuddered and caught fire—hit underneath by Ack-Ack. Unfortunately, only the observer managed to bale out. Landing in the sea from oly 500 feet, he found himself less than a mile from the coast. He had slight burns, and though his Mae West would not inflate he managed to keep afloat for nearly two hours.

In the meantime, *Darby* was sent to the recue. We all turned out to watch P.O. Bruce Ada of the R.A.A.F., totter him down the deck and soar off the end like a prehistoric bird, racing towards the island at 85 knots. The waiting Japs must have been amazed, probably thinking it to be a new British 'suicide' weapon! *Darby* had to land in shallow water, quite half a mile from the survivor, and then weave slowly up to him, avoiding jagged coral beds. Sub. Lt. (A) R. Marshall, R.N., the observer, had great difficulty hauling the survivor aboard, but the Japs encouraged him to hurry by firing their A.A. guns. Fortunately these wouldn't depress sufficiently, and shells whistled overhead. Chugging speedily out to sea again *Darby* took off, and returned safely home.

Modern planes have so increased their landing speeds that it becomes very necessary to control them. Hooks, fitted to the tail of the aircraft, engage arrester-wires stretched across the deck and quickly haul the planes up. Not so *Darby*; as he came slowly over the stern of the ship many hands seemed to grab him and haul him safely on to the deck. This is the second time *Darby* had made a rescue in this way, earning himself a bouquet from the Admiral. 'Understand,' the Admiral had said in a signal, '*Darby* bombarded Japanese with his machine-guns.' 'No,' replied *Darby*, 'we threw coral at them instead!'

Extract from: *Victorious* news sheet 'The Buzz', sent by Ern Crimp

THE COMMANDER'S TELESCOPE by Buck Rogers
We were storing ship, a group of us were way down below storing the cases

as they were sent down, a hot, sticky job. During the operation we had a surprise visit from Commander Surtees. Complete with telescope tucked under his arm, he stood watching. Then a huge rat suddenly darted behind the stack of cases . . . We were ordered to lift and shift . . . keeping our opinions to ourselves we did just that, the stack was shifted from one side to the other. The rat also decided to make a move scuttling behind the new stack! Lift and shift . . . We began stacking them back once again . . . Suddenly we had the rat cornered against the baulkhead. What now, we thought? A quick move by an agile Commander, a flash of his Telescope, Thump! The rat was dead, and several seamen in that store room found out why a Commander carries a telescope!! (Well, no one had ever seen him looking through it!)

From A.M. (O) S. Porter, 1834 Squadron HMS *Victorious*

My oppo Arthur Groome and myself were working re-arming a Corsair on the sharp end of the flight deck, so, intent on getting the job done, we were oblivious to the knowledge that there was a flash red on, and that we were being attacked by kamikazes. I just happened to look over my shoulder and saw everyone running in all directions. Realising that something was happening, I gave my mate a shout, 'Come on Arthur there's a flash red on.' We both scrambled down off the plane and made a dash for the nearest hatchway which was the port side. I got there first, Arthur just behind me. I'd barely got to the bottom step, when there was a hell of an explosion and I heard my mate cry out, 'My legs have gone.' He had caught the full blast of an exploding kamikaze which could only have been four or five yards away. I looked up and saw his hands hanging over the hatchway, before I fully recovered from being knocked on my backside and wet through from the water that came down after the K had hit the sea. They got my mate away to sick bay. I visited him the same night, had a chat and from that day to this not seen or heard of him since. We've tried every avenue possible, the 'Navy News', local newspapers, the M.O.D., you name it we've tried it. But no luck.

From Leading Seaman Radar P. J. Davis, HMS *Victorious*

When we were off Tokyo, it was during the middle watch and suddenly up popped an echo at about ninety miles; within about nine seconds that echo closed to about seven miles and then disappeared, so you can see it was too fast for aircraft and it was reported to the bridge. It was a definite echo and now I wonder if it was a missile? The reason I write my few words is that I know a real echo from a ghost echo.

I have two humourous stories. One was from a mate of mine, a P.O. Ordnance who was responsible for the cannon on the starboard side of the island, a kamikaze was hurtling in and one of the lads called out, 'I've run out of ammo.' The P.O. called out, 'Fling your bloody helmet at it!'

My story was the same kamikaze, I believe. I was stationed on top of the island, my job was height finding, estimating the height of the enemy aircraft, which was done by a series of graphs of each radar set, and the height of the echoes on their way in. We were working away with guns going and one of my blokes opened the door and I remember looking round and seeing this Jap framed in the door. I said, 'Shut that bloody door.' I turned back and saw the same kamikaze go by (through a porthole) and that was the one that hit port side forward. I believe the European war had just finished.

I was taught the height finding by a Radar Officer Lt. Maynard, a Canadian, who was great! Trouble was that by teaching me this business it stopped my promotion, I had five radar officers and they all said when you have taught someone your job you can go! That was said to me right up to the day I left for demob, which was arranged by a Fighter Direction Officer.

We were very successful with estimating the height, but I can remember first detection was a good indication of height, and I estimated a height of 'Angels Two'. Then I could see things weren't going right, luckily we sorted it out pretty well because what had happened was that the Japs had flown over the main or first lobe of the radar, struck the second lobe and it turned out they were at 'Angels Twenty'. We found out by the fades (when the planes flew in the blind spots). That was my worst experience doing the job, but we got away with it.

Another little story, when we were in the Pacific, I was suffering with skin disease. I had a real whack, ringworm, dhoby itch from my knees to my navel. I remember a doctor shining his torch on me and saying, 'The best whack of dhoby itch in the Navy!' It was getting me down, I was sitting up by the 293 radar with a radar officer and I saw the surgeon commander walking the flight deck. I said to our officer, 'I bet that old bugger hasn't got dhoby itch.' He replied, 'He has!' I felt a bit better after that!

From: 'Avenger from the Sky' by L.t Cdr. (A) Donald Judd DSC, 849 Squadron, HMS *Victorious*

For me the month or two up to the end of the first series of operations at Sakishima Gunto were pretty miserable. I shared of course the dislike of the area and the type of operations we were called upon to undertake, as well as the sadness at what I regarded as unnecessary losses and accidents. But by then, there were other factors having a bearing on my morale. Of course, fear was ever present but I began to get twitchy and a feeling of premonition that something was going to happen (an imagination that, thank God, didn't materialise). Fear is normal and perhaps necessary like, in a different sphere and different degree, pre-concert nerves. But twitchiness and an over active imagination is dangerous and can lead to mistakes, bad judgement and poor leadership. I think I must have begun to get tired after nearly four years continuously in operational squadrons. Perhaps it was the reaction of the ditching at Pankalan Brandan followed immediately by the costly attacks at Palembang and the loss of so many friends.

It was made worse by a personal sadness. After we left Manus, I began to hear news that my father was ill. But there were four letters from home which didn't reach me till weeks later. And I was ten thousand miles away and couldn't just phone up from mid Pacific. By the time we got to Sakishima it appeared that his illness was more serious than I had at first thought and I started worrying. Finally, a letter telling me that he had died—weeks before. The news shattered me coming relatively soon after my mother's death and catching me when I was at a low ebb anyway. After the last operation on 20th April when I attacked Nobara airfield on Miyako for the last time, we finally withdrew to Leyte for a rest to everyone's relief. On the way Captain Denny called for me to see him on the bridge. 'Ah, Judd,' he said, taking me on one side. 'I am going to send you home; I think you've done enough. I want to thank you for all you have done in *Victorious. Illustrious* is leaving the Task Force at Leyte and I am arranging for you to take passage in her to Sydney. Good luck . . . Oh, and I am so sorry to hear about your father.'

I began packing up with much relief. I felt I just couldn't face another spell off the Sakishima Gunto and whatever was to follow. A farewell party in the wardroom at Leyte and a picnic on the beach and a final goodbye to that happy ship *Victorious* and all my friends in 849 Squadron as I was taken over by boat to *Illustrious*. There I joined Norman Hanson and his Corsair boys and 854 Avenger crews who were going home with the ship. I was to disembark at Sydney to fly back to the UK.

From: 'The Pacific' 1942—an Australian newspaper—sent by Jim Dodds

A British plane swooped low over a U.S. aircraft carrier in the Pacific. It dropped this S.O.S.:

> 'We've boiled 'em, stewed 'em, fried 'em. Now how the hell do you prepare 'em for eating?'

The note referred to potatoes—lend-lease dehydrated (dried) variety. They had been flown to the British aircraft carrier *Victorious* when her food ran low while she was working with American carriers during the drive against New Georgia in the Solomons.

In response to the S.O.S. a torpedo-bomber flew to the *Victorious* with 1,100 pounds of dehydrated potatoes—and Chief Commissary Steward Harvard Byron Price of Los Angeles. Price investigated the dehydrated potatoes in the *Victorious* and reported that they had been neither soaked for eight hours nor boiled for four. No tinned milk or butter had been added to the potatoes, and 'the British mess steward had used Epsom salts to swell the potatoes in volume—with telling results'.

From Ldg. Air Mechanic (E) B. M. Evans, HMS *Victorious*

I served in *Victorious* from early 1944 to October 1945 as a Ldg. Air Mechanic E., 1834 Corsair Squadron. My tour of duties mirrors yours, Norway, Ceylon, B.P.F., so I could relate to your experiences in **Sakishima**.

As the years pass by one remembers the laughs more readily than the unpleasant aspects of war, but to this day, two tragic incidents on the *Victorious* are always present and I can visualise them in great detail.

The first is that of a Corsair, in trouble, landing on at a great rate of knots, missing all but the last but one arrester wire. This was torn out of its socket together with the last wire which slewed it to port, demolishing the barriers and bursting into flames enveloping our Deck Officer Lt. Banning and his Petty Officer and I witnessed instant cremation. I supoose the whole incident took only seconds but I seemed to watch it all in slow motion, knowing what the outcome would be, and yet I calmly, even coldly, proceeded to assist with the clearing up. In no time at all the deck was cleared, a Jury Barrier erected and the remaining aircraft accepted. Later that day however an Avenger demolished the Jury Barrier and twenty Corsairs were accommodated on other carriers.

Lt. Banning was respected and liked by the Lower Deck. Apart from being a good D.O he was an excellent Fairy Queen in our pantomime and I have a photograph of him in costume.

The chapel was too small that night.

At the auction of P.O. Groves' effects, the items were sold over and over. I doubt if anyone actually took possession of them.

The second incident refers to a Seafire. I do not know its parent carrier, but it was obviously out of action and we were to land a few on. I was standing on the mainplane of a Corsair parked up front at the time, keeping one eye on what was landing. The Seafire appeared to approach rather high and fast, and when it touched down the undercarriage disintegrated. Our barrier was set for Corsairs, and the Seafire's cockpit hood and pilot's head were removed by the lower wire. At that moment all the guns fired, and I have no recollection whatever of moving, but I know I was pushing my nose through the deck thinking how ridiculous it was to have jumped after the guns had fired.

To be honest, whilst the Seafire appeared to be good in the air, it left a lot to be desired as a carrier borne plane. We dreaded receiving them, and I cannot recall a successful landing.

On the lighter side, one of the kamikazes exploded on our catapult rail piercing four decks just aft of our mess. When matters had calmed down, I was absolutely amazed to see the lift ascending loaded with a wheelbarrow, sand, gravel, cement, shovels and shuttering. In no time at all the hole was filled with concrete which soon hardened in that climate, and we were operational once more, albeit minus a catapult for the remainder of the war. Consider what the results would have been on a U.S. carrier. Whilst we envied them all their mod cons and home comforts, we did have well built ships with reasonable security.

Our last day of operation, the 15th August, coincided with my 22nd birthday, and though we were to start the long journey back to Sydney we all felt cheated. Having been involved in the entire campaign and given all that was asked of us and more, we felt we had earned the right to be in Tokyo Bay at the end. Realistically, the entire fleet could not have been accommodatd and someone had to decide who stayed and went, but it hurt at the time, and still does.

Our shadow, the destroyer *Wager,* in foul weather, nudged our stern. Signal from *Victorious* to *Wager,* 'Touch me there again and I'll scream.'

Again in atrocious rain, dawn take off, and a deckhand manning the chocks was waved away. Hanging on to the chocks with one hand, he lost his grip on the wet deck, and caught in the slipstream, he slid under one propeller and was en route to the stern. Voice over, 'Stop that man deserting.' Fortunately, he was able to grab an arrester cable, but all credit to him, he did maintain hold of the chocks.

Awaiting the return of our aircraft on a glorious day, a deckhand sat on an arrester pulley housing, reading a novel. He did not realise we were about to receive the first plane until the arrester cable tensioned and he pushed the book into the pulley housing. After landing on, the book vanished with the retracting cable and the next plane had a disastrous landing due to the seized mechanism. We were unable to accept any further aircraft for four hours. That night, 'Captain Speaking'. He related the incident to the entire ship's company and concluded with the words, 'If any man commits a similar offence he will be shot.' We all knew he meant just that and it was only then we realised he had the authority to carry it out.

I am glad you have written **Sakishima**. It has filled in so much background. For most of the time we had no idea where we were or what was going on. Now I know. Communication between decks was rather sparse, probably with good reason. The exception was Admiral Mountbatten. The moment he stepped on board he had all the men in the palm of his hand ready to do whatever he bid of us. The manner of his death saddened and sickened me. He was a wonderful leader.

Tape from P.O. Radio Mech. George Parkinson, 1836 Corsairs, HMS *Victorious* *(Now aged 80 and blind.—Ed.)*

There were some wonderful chaps amongst those pilots and one comes to mind on 1836 squadron: Johnny Apted. He was such a nice fellow—a gentleman. He often used to come down without firing a shot, where the other pilots had used all their ammunition, and his armourers used to say Johnny hasn't the heart to fire on anybody—he wouldn't do that. He was so considerate, and his cabin-mate used to dread being taken away from the cabin. He said, 'Johnny looks after me like a mother. He has my laundry all fixed up and he does everything for me.' He added: 'He's a wonderful man.'

Johnny was like that and I remember while we were in Ceylon, I was on duty one day and I had to muster the squadron at dawn. They were going off at about five in the morning and I had arranged for a shake at half past four. I hurriedly got dressed in the dark and got my duty roster list of all the blokes. I'd already arranged for somebody to shake them and they were all scrambling out onto the tarmac and I got my list. I could hardly see it and I was saying 'As your names are called out, fall in on the left'. All of a sudden a little pencil torch came from behind me onto my reading material and I could see every line and every bloke's name clearly and I just happened to look behind—it was Johnny Apted, he was the duty officer—and he just sneaked up behind me without saying a word!

Wonderful bloke he was, and he used to come down onto the messdeck, and he'd day to the boys there 'How are you going on—alright? How long is it since you wrote to your mother?—Now look that's not good enough! You haven't written to your mother for a month, you sit down and write to her—tonight—of course she'll be worried about you.'

One time—during Operation Iceberg—we were always eagerly looking out for the return of the aircraft coming back and here they were, coming into circuit, ready to land on. The fleet had turned into wind, and we landed the squadron on. We knew Johnny Apted's plane and we could see it flying round and round but not offering to land on and he hadn't got his undercart down. Now on a Corsair there are three methods of dropping your undercarriage. The first one is by pressing on an electrical switch which operates the main hydraulics and forces it down. If that fails you had a CO_2 bottle which you could turn on and it would force the undercarriage down and if that failed there was an emergency hand pump—you could hand pump it down. And evidently Johnny had tried all these and the last resort was to climb up to about 3,000 feet, take a steep dive at about 45° and then flatten out and the inertia of the 3 Gs flattening out plus pressing everything and pumping everything would sort of—if you're lucky—bring your undercarriage down. He tried all this and we said 'Ah, poor old Johnny Apted.' And he had been shot up too, but he was O.K. himself.

Anyhow he was sent a signal by Aldis to ditch at the duty destroyer. But where Johnny ditched he was probably half a mile from the destroyer. Now a Corsair will usually stay afloat for about 2 minutes before it sinks—and gives plenty of time for the pilot to get out. As the aircraft was sinking there was no sign of Johnny Apted. Suddenly everybody was on the deck, there was almost a list to starboard. And the aircraft was under water and we thought 'Well, poor old Johnny's had it.' Suddenly the Mae West bobbed up and the destroyer came alongside him and picked him up.

During the dog watches after we had secured from Action Stations and

Flying Stations, the duty destroyer came alongside and everybody was there waiting, and one of the blokes said to Johnny: 'How are you Johnny, we thought you'd had it?' 'No,' he said, 'I'd always wanted one of the clocks from the dash and I was screwing it out'—while his aircraft was going down he had screwed out the clock, the lovely Waltham clock, and it was so easy to take out—you just need a little Philip's screwdriver which Johnny always carried with him for that purpose!

We were discussing the canned food. The buzz got round the ship that a chef officer from the American fleet was to fly on board *Victorious* specially to show us how this stuff should be prepared. We weren't cooking it right, and he would fly on board—which he did—to give us the good oil. While we were all agog the buzz went round that the chef was in charge of the kitchen and we would be assured of a good meal that evening. Do you want to know the worst? It was worse! When we ate it it was worse than if our own cooks had done it. So we gave up in despair at this dehydrated food, but it wasn't very nice, was it?

M. M. Denny, our skipper used to give us a little talk every night on what was going on with the fleet. He was very good and everybody looked forward to it. This particular day had been a pretty heavy day during Operation Iceberg. Something had gone wrong with the arrester wire mechanism and we could not land on aircraft. So here is M. M. Denny making his nightly talk to the ship's company—'Today I had to send a signal to the Admiral of the Fleet that *Victorious*, as a carrier, was u/s. Why?—all because some stupid rating had got a novel fast in the arrester wire mechanism. I repeat NOVEL—N O V E L. If I eventually find out who that rating was, I will make such an example of him that it will horrify the ship's company.'

I suppose the bloke by this time was shaking in his boots! But they never did find out who it was. I suppose it must have been an awful thing for the Captain—in the middle of an operation—to have to send a signal that *Victorious* was u/s.

Another character who comes to mind was Sub Lieut. Rhodes. We always called him Dusty Rhodes. I never knew his Christian name. He was a New Zealander and he was the senior pilot. He was next to the CO of the squadron. If the CO got knocked off, and this happened, I remember, three times within a month, that the leader of the squadron did not return, then the No. 2 would take over, but Dusty Rhodes would never accept the position. He let the next man in line take it—he declined. He would come down onto the messdeck and chat with you and just forget about protocol or his station and talk to you about your family and ask you all about yourself. Lovely fellow, a great pilot. Everybody respected him and I recall when the pilots went into a briefing before going on a sortie that they would all come out to get into their aircraft and another pilot would say to Dusty 'What was that about so-and-so, in case of so-and-so?' And Dusty Rhodes would just pause and he would say word for word exactly what he had been told. He was really a born pilot. He was wonderful, every other pilot respected him, and if you remember Stuart, when the Fleet returned to Sydney after the war, there was an AFO that said that all Australian serving men with the Fleet and New Zealanders had to leave the ship, because the ship would be going back to the U.K. So that we had to lose Dusty Rhodes. Everybody in the squadron looked him up to shake his hand and say how glad they were to have been connected with him. And so when we left Sydney we realised we had seen the last of Dusty Rhodes. Not to be . . . Half way to Colombo, which was our next stop after leaving Fremantle, on the deck, doing some exercises was Dusty Rhodes and it turned out that he had stowed away on the *Victorious* and was not found out by the Captain until the ship had left Fremantle for three days. His reason was that he wanted to get back to England to finish his education. He had a chance of going to Oxford to finish his education and so he sort of stowed away on the ship! And the skipper just put a blind eye to it, so Dusty Rhodes came back to the U.K.

When we arrived at Manus, some of the American pilots came aboard to have a look round. And here's Dusty Rhodes walking along the flight deck with the U.S. Marine pilot who turned round to Dusty and he said: 'Say, Limey, you gotta have a job landing these Corsairs on steel decks?' and Dusty said, 'Well, I've made 730 landings on the steel deck and I haven't found them too bad.' This Marine's mate said, 'Ah, listen to him, I'd like to see his log book.' And Dusty said, 'Well, I've got two, I've filled one up already!' The Yanks couldn't believe that he had made so many landings on the carrier's deck.

From AM(E) 1st Class Roy Wood, HMS *Illustrious*

Roy Wood A.M.(E) 1st Class, FX 561695
Bill Vince A.M.(E) 1st Class FX 585607
Charlie Gould A.M.(E) 1st Class FX 110074

Young men with little or no knowledge of the foe except what we had read in newspapers or heard on the radio.

These three young men were part of 854 Squadron, which consisted of Avenger torpedo/bombers on board HMS *Illustrious*. The Squadron's C.O. was Lt. Commander Charlie Mainprice who sadly was lost during the strikes on Palembang when his aircraft hit a balloon cable.

One occasion that still stands out. A group of Avengers assembled on the flightdeck loaded with torpedoes ready for a sortie. Having the final checks made air mechanics sat in the cockpits, feet firmly on brake pedals owing to the heavy weather we were experiencing at that time. One of the leading aircraft had an inquisitive mechanic in the cockpit. He was evidently fiddling with various controls for the next minute the torpedo slung in the belly of the aircraft dropped through the open bomb doors onto the flight deck *and its motor started up!*

One minute there were scores of personnel around, ten seconds later no-one except the guy still in the cockpit unaware of what he had done. There were people dropping into gun emplacements along the sides of the carrier, diving down gangways and various other ways of making yourself scarce on the flight deck. Later we were informed by an ordnance Petty Officer that no explosion would have taken place because of the lack of pressure on the nose of the torpedo.

But clearly that day nobody waited to find that out!

From Capt. (E) J. A. Hans Hamilton RN, HMS *Illustrious*

A point which I feel very strongly and which in other books about the 'Forgotten Fleet' has not received attention is the absolutely appalling living conditions in our Fleet Carriers which both the ship's company and the aircrews had to suffer. You must have experienced this. Talking with Ronnie Hay, the totally inadequate ventilation and disgraceful disregard of tropical conditions by the naval constructors and ship design team had a deleterious effect to efficiency and flying capability. The resulting decimation of our pilot strength through the resulting accidents was proof of these awful blunders by those responsible for the construction of our ships.

At one stage, we in *Illustrious* were so short of Engineer Officers that our watchkeeping roster at sea was one watch in the machinery control room followed immediately by another in Damage Control HQ, then to sleep in temperatures of 105°F for four hours only—thence 2 more watches. We had a hell of a lot of sickness. Clothing became so sweat ridden, and fresh water so short, that one remained permanently swathed in prickly heat and acne.

Action stations meant full clothing and anti-flash which became insufferable. One tends to forget the bad bits, and not want to recall them. After all these years I really wonder how the hell we managed to do a job in such an impossible environment. The engine and boiler rooms, electrical spaces and galleys were the worst. The over-crowded messdecks accentuated the permanent sweat shop existence.

Charles Lambe, Captain in *Illustrious* was punctilious about seeing that we saw plenty of daylight during suitable breaks, and I know that my skin was in such a shocking state, that when Dick Sear the Flight Deck Engineer Officer had to be transferred to the Hospital ship with a bad injury after a Flight Deck fire, I replaced him. This helped a great deal and I was told that my transfer was the best that could be done for me after the PMO put the boot in and threatened to have me transferred to the *Tjitjalengka* as well as Dick. It is only one example of our poor physical condition and mine was not the only case. My stokers and ERA's fared no better, in particular my part of ship was looking after the distilling machinery where the compartment was regularly 120°F.

Distilled water was used the moment it had been made, so domestic cold taps exuded hot whenever the system was turned on. Rationing of fresh water was restricted to 10 hours per day at specified periods. The boiler tubes and other steam leaks in our clapped out under maintained machinery used up

60% of the distilling capacity, and this capacity had already dropped to about 70% of its designed output. To add to our problems before we left Sydney to join the CTF our centre propulsion unit was emasculated by the removal of our centre propeller and our maximum speed reduced to 25 knots. Our turning circle was considerably increased because the propeller wash no longer played against the rudder. All this due to the weakening of the hull aft during the Malta convoy landings earlier in the war.

Illustrious was never intended to join the Pacific Fleet and was due to refit in U.K. in 1944. Because of gearbox failure in *Formidable* and lateness of completion of *Implacable,* we had to do a makeshift refit in Durban and press on as the lame duck until mercifully we were relieved by *Formidable* and withdrew to Sydney after waiting at Leyte in reserve whilst the Fleet carried out a further mission at Sakishima.

I hope you won't mind an old plumber having a real good drip!

We were an extremely happy ship. The Commander, A. J. Wallis (Baldy) encouraged all of us to support and include aviators within the fold. As a result I inherited a totally novel attitude for the rest of my full R.N. career from all my R.N.R. and R.N.V.R. shipmates which stood me in very good stead for the future with a dedicated devotion to Naval airborne attack and a loathing of the big gun philosophy. When *Illustrious* returned to Sydney finally in May before she went home, out of 135 Wardroom officers including the aviators I was one of just 19 R.N. regulars, 8 of whom were plumbers. Our Task Group was a monument to what can be done by volunteers?

I can tell of a supreme P.U. at Manus U.S. canteen organised in watches during that all too short stop off. Also the two jeeps acquired by our batsman (Lt. Cdr. Cunningham) for two bottles of scotch. He had to decline the offer of a Dakota aircraft by the same U.S. Officer in exchange for a whole crate!

I have a photo of *Victorious* near miss, also one of Heppenstall under fire.The Judy was riddled by the forward Bofors on the island superstructure just in the nick of time when the junior seaman leapt in to the layer's position and opened fire after the layer had deserted his post. He shot off the port wing resulting in the Judy corkscrewing to port just clipping the glass of the beacon and plunging over the side to explode there. There was plenty of debris. The PMO (Mackenzie) had a piece of the pilot's skull cured and mounted. I have a piece of the main wing frame. The explosion so close to the ship's side fractured one of the twin oil fuel tanks which we did not discover till later when we next replenished. The junior seaman was awarded the DSM and the gunlayer court martialled. At a recent *Illustrious* reunion on board the current ship, I was shown part of the pilot's scarf collected by an A.B. on the ADP at the time.

From Captain R. E. Hartley, RN, Watchkeeping Engineer Officer in HMS *Illustrious*

My departmental duties consisted of being in charge of the Boiler Rooms, and my action station was in the Centre Boiler Room. I, therefore, had very little personal knowledge of what was going on in the 'outer world' during the various operations. We had 15 officers in the Marine Engineering Department—just enough for a Rugger team—the Commander (E), Senior Engineer, Flight Deck Engineer and 12 watchkeeping Lieutenants and Commissioned/Warrant Engineers. At sea, we were normally in 4 straight watches, a Senior and Junior Engineer Officer of the Watch and a Damage Control Officer of the Watch who kept his watch in Damage Control Headquarters. I was in the Senior E.O.W. union, and usually kept watch with a Warrant Engineer. The *Illustrious* had a primitive Machinery Control Room—nothing like a modern warship's set-up—merely a monitoring position with repeat gauges from the various machinery compartments, and we kept our watch from there. To visit all the numerous machinery compartments in a Fleet Carrier during one watch in the tròpics was really too much for one man, so rounds were shared between the two watchkeepers. My visits were sometimes influenced by what culinary delights were available—particularly in the Middle Watch. Certain Boiler rooms and Engine Rooms had a reputation for a variety of refreshments—baked potatoes, soup, tiddy oggies (Cornish pasties), as well as the usual lime juice and kai (cocoa). Actually conditions in the main machinery compartments were not too unpleasant, due to the large amount of forced ventilation, but it was very exhausting visiting the more remote spaces, such as the Stern Glands and Plummer Block Compartments. I found that I could keep going provided I had an adequate intake of salt, either through tablets or dissolved in water.

After the operations against Palembang in January 1945, we developed severe vibration in the centre propeller shaft while we were south of Australia. On arrival in Sydney we had to dock in the new Captain Cook dry dock, before it was officially opened by the Duke of Gloucester, then Governor General of Australia, to have our centre propeller removed. This meant that, while we were part of the 1st Aircraft Carrier Squadron during the initial operations off Sakishima, the speed of the Fleet was effectively reduced to 25 knots. During this period, the Centre Engine Room main engines were not in use. As the ship steamed in units, with each boiler room providing its own engine room, the centre boiler room was not providing main steam. The two boilers were kept steaming with full pressure at low power, ready to connect to the outer units in the event of damage or defects. This meant that an Action Stations life was fairly quiet and peaceful. On 6th April 1945, peace was disturbed when a Japanese kamikaze aircraft touched the island of *Illustrious* and then exploded alongside.

In the centre boiler room we seemed to leap many feet into the air, but no machinery damage was done. No doubt a lot of soot was cleared from the

HMS Illustrious, *near miss, 6th April 1945.*
Photo: Captain R. E. Hartley RN Ret'd

boilers and funnel! A certain amount of structural damage was done, so that with only two available propeller shafts *Illustrious* was becoming a bit of a lame duck. On the 14th April 1945 we were relieved by *Formidable* in the operational area and we made our way back to Sydney. Here, a lot of equipment was removed as spares for the remaining carriers. We then steamed to Rosyth were we arrived by the end of June.

One poignant moment was when the ship stopped for 'Hands to bathe' in the Eastern Mediterranean, the European War then being over.

Shortly after the ship arrived at Rosyth, the ship's company was inspected by His Majesty King George VI and Queen Elizabeth. After refit we were due to go out to the Pacific again, but this, of course, was overtaken by events. I will always remember my time in *Illustrious* with great affection. She was undoubtedly a happy ship, for which Captain Charles Lambe deserves much credit. The Engineroom Department formed a good team, and although the ship was tired after a very busy war, we kept her going with a lot of hard work and not a few laughs.

Not all the excitement came from enemy action. During the Palembang operation, one of our cruisers—the *Euryalus*—put a couple of 2.25″ shells into our island, while firing at a Japanese aircraft flying over our flightdeck. This caused a number of casualties, including some killed.

From 'Escort Carriers in the Second World War' by Kenneth Poolman

Hellcats gave meaning to the Allied nickname of Baka (Foolish) bomb of the MXYs, by shooting down 18 Bettys and their unlaunched 'Bakas'. *(The only Baka attack on the BPF was 16 April. It was not a success—fortunately.—Ed.)* Some 200 suiciders hit and damaged their targets, which included the big carriers of TF.58 and TF.57, as well as smaller craft. The outriding destroyer fighter-direction pickets suffered badly. On 16 April the CV *Intrepid* was badly damaged, and on 4 May HMS *Formidable* was hit off the Sakishimas, followed by *Indomitable*, and on the 9th *Victorious*, and *Formidable* again. None of the tough British carriers was out of action for more than a few hours, but they lost aircraft and sometimes speed of handling was reduced. On 11 May Mitscher's flagship *Bunker Hill* was struck by two planes practically simultaneously and almost burned out, with 400 men dead. Three days later the *Enterprise* was hit. On the night of 11—12 March 24 Francis PIY navy *Ginga* (Milky Way) bombers made a 2,250 km (1,400 mile) one-way trip from Kanoya. Twelve got through to the Ulithi anchorage. One hit an islet in mistake for a carrier, one hit the carrier *Randolph* while she was ammunitioning, and the others were destroyed.

Having contributed to CAP cover and support of the landing on Kerama Retto, *Sangamon* returned to TV.52.1.3 and throughout 8th April launched supporting strikes and patrols over the Hagushi beaches of Okinawa from an area some 80 km (50 miles) south of the island. On the 9th she moved with her unit into an area 112 km (70 miles) east of Sakishima Gunto and relieved the British TF.57, raiding the airfields on Ishigaki and Miyako while the British group sailed for replenishment area Cootie for two days of refuelling, storing and shipping replacement aircraft from *Striker*. As CAP carrier, *Speaker* had to have four aircraft in the air, and one spare on the deck, from dawn to dusk in two-hour sorties when replenishment was taking place.

'Carrier Operations in World War II' by J. D. Brown

On completion of these operations, TF.57 withdrew to replenish prior to proceeding to San Pedro Bay, Leyte, for a week's rest and recuperation. Again their assistance was requested by Admiral Spruance; the USN CVEs had been unable to maintain the same pressure against the airfields in the Sakishima Gunto, and there had been increased enemy air activity in the area. While the Royal Navy had been operating against the Formosan airfields, which were not as active as had been thought, the USN had been suffering heavily from the kamikazes. Two carriers had been put out of action, three battleships were damaged, seven destroyers sunk, and another 13 damaged; enemy losses were high, but at this stage the Japanese showed no sign of easing the considerable pressure.

Formidable replaced *Illustrious* in the 1st Aircraft Carrier Squadron, the latter beginning to show signs of wear: she had not had a full refit for nearly two years, her centre shaft was giving trouble and causing a reduction in speed to 26 knots, and her No. 15 Fighter Wing, 1830 and 1833 Squadrons had done rather more than a full tour of operations. *Formidable*'s arrival had been delayed by shaft trouble, both ships still suffering the after-effects of bomb damage received in the Mediterranean in 1941.

Strikes against Ishigakijima and Miyakojima were flown on 16th, 17th and 20th April. Another 50,000 lb of bombs were unloaded on the airfields during the three days, while enemy landing craft also suffered from the Avenger strikes. At dusk on 20th the BPF and Fleet Train left their operational area for Leyte, the tankers almost dry and the ammunition and stores ships empty. San Pedro Bay was reached on 23rd April, the Fleet having spent 32 days at sea on operations and RAS. During the week that followed the ships were stored and replacement aircraft and aircrew transferred to the carriers. These last ships were particularly in need of rest. Fully extended at all times to keep up with the American standards of operating, the carriers were hampered by lack of handling crews, maintenance personnel and armourers: the entire ships' companies were exhausted. The climate in the Philippines was humid and the ships not air-conditioned, so that the return to sea on 1st May was welcomed by many.

While the Fleet had been at its anchorage in San Pedro Bay there had been renewed pressure for its employment off Borneo, but in view of further USN losses off Okinawa, Admiral Nimitz was again allocated the BPF for covering operations off Sakishima. The air strikes were resumed on 4th May, against Ishigaki. Miyako was subjected to a bombardment by *King George V* and *Howe*, in the course of which much damage was inflicted by the 14" guns. The absence of the large calibre A.A. and considerable volume of close-range A.A. was inopportune however; the return of TF.57 coincided with a renewed kamikaze offensive, and during the forenoon of 4th May a force of about 20 suicide aircraft attacked the Fleet. Eight were shot down, one by the A.A. after it had penetrated the screen, the others by the CAP, and of the remainder only two reached the carriers. The first hit *Indomitable* aft on the flight deck, slid diagonally across the deck and went over the side; the other hit *Formidable* fair and square abeam the island, the favoured aiming point for the kamikazes. The damage was not serious, fires were soon extinguished, and although a splinter put the centre boiler-room out of action temporarily, the ship's speed did not fall below 18 knots. The damage had been inflicted at the join of four armour plates, but the two-foot dent was swiftly patched with quick-drying cement and she was operational before dusk. As strikes were airborne at the time of the attack, only 11 aircraft were lost on deck; of 18 Corsairs airborne 14 were recovered on the following morning from three other carriers. A total of 12 Japanese aircraft were shot down by the Fleet fighters on that day.

The success of the bombardment of Miyako was evident on the following day when the striking aircraft found that the flak was less intense, and again the runways were cratered by the Avengers. *Formidable's* losses were made good during the replenishment on 6th and 7th May, while her wounded were transferred to a hospital ship. Bad weather hampered strikes on 8th, but on 9th the weather was good enough, not only for Fleet Air Arm strikes, but also for another kamikaze attack on TF.57. At about 1700, a small group of enemy aircraft broke through the CAP and A.A. screen and again *Formidable* was hit. On this occasion, her strike aircraft had been recovered after the pm strikes, and 18 Avengers and Corsairs were destroyed, but, as the flight deck was not holed by this attack, she was operational again in 50 minutes, albeit with only 15 aircraft serviceable. Another Kamikaze hit *Victorious* near the forward lift, setting fire to the ship and damaging the lift. While firefighting was in progress a second suicide aircraft hit her, but bounced off the flight deck, destroying another four Corsairs.

These were the last kamikaze attacks on the BPF although two more USN Attack carriers, *Enterprise* and *Bunker Hill*, were sufficiently badly damaged to prevent their further employment in the War. Seven USN Attack and Escort carriers were hit by kamikazes between 1st April and 15th May, all being rendered unfit for further service in the Okinawa campaign. Four Royal Navy carriers were hit squarely by suicide aircraft, two on two occasions; apart from reduction in aircraft strengths the carriers were all fully operational within a matter of hours.

After RAS on 10th and 11th May, two more two-day serials were flown against the island airfields and small craft in the group. Enemy air activity had slackened off after the large scale raids of 4th to 19th May, while TF.58 was again striking at airfields in Kyushu, land-based Marine fighters having taken the main weight of air support for the American forces ashore on Okinawa. Shipping strikes around Sakishima were stepped-up, with gratifying results.

As if *Formidable* had not suffered sufficient punishment, while she was replenishing on 18th May an accident in the hangar resulted in the destruction by fire of 30 aircraft in the hangar, as well as damage to the ship herself. Despite the accident, she was ready for action by night-fall, although very short on aircraft. When operations were resumed on 20th May *Formidable* could only provide Corsairs for Fleet and target CAP. She refuelled and left on 22nd May for Manus and Sydney, to repair her damage in time for the next series of operations. The remaining three carriers carried out another serial off Sakishima before they too left the area at dusk on 25th May 1945, with Okinawa firmly in the hands of the Americans.

The British Pacific Fleet had spent 62 days at sea, with only a break of eight days for storing ships at Leyte. Sorties over the Sakishima Gunto and Formosa had been flown on 23 days. Exactly 5,335 sorties had been flown from the five Fleet carriers, in the course of which nearly one thousand tons of bombs had been dropped, half a million rounds of ammunition fired and 950 rockets released. Ninety-eight enemy aircraft were destroyed in combat, and about the same number on the airfields. The Fleet Air Arm suffered quite heavy losses—26 aircraft were lost in the air, mainly to flak, 61 in accidents (deck landings, take-off, 'friendly' A.A., etc.), while no fewer than 73 were destroyed in the kamikaze attacks and in *Formid.*'s hangar fire. 41 aircrew lost their lives and 44 personnel were killed aboard the ships, mainly in the kamikaze damage. By contrast, *Bunker Hill* lost 387 dead in the kamikaze attack on 11th May. While the armoured deck cut the number of aircraft aboard a British Fleet carrier to half that of an American carrier of similar size, its value was made apparent in dramatic fashion on 4th and 9th May 1945.

Throughout the time at sea, the principal hindrance to operations had been the inadequate Fleet Train, Task Force 112; the tankers were slow and small and re-fuelling equipment obsolete. On several occasions the Fleet was ready for the next serial only because there had been cancellations or postponements due to bad weather, either in the target area or at sea. Aircraft replenishment presented a more cheerful picture with ferry CVEs providing replacements to keep the Fleet carriers complemented. However, this was possible only by virtue of the extremely hard work of the Air Stations in Australia, modifying aircraft on delivery from the United Kingdom, 12,000 miles away, and United States, 6,000 miles in the other direction. Spares remained a problem as did modification kits: the American types in Fleet Air Arm service did not have the same degree of interchangeability with their opposite numbers in the USN as might be supposed.

The British Pacific Fleet arrived at Sydney at the beginning of June, to re-arm the squadrons and rest the ships' complements prior to the next round, strikes on the Japanese home islands themselves.

From: 'HMS *Tenacious*', a book loaned to me by Admiral G. C. Crowley DSC, 2 Bars

We reached Leyte, in the Philippine Islands, on 11th May, and we went straight alongside an American oiler. The Americans had established Leyte as a very large advanced base, although it had not long been liberated from the Japanese, and there were still quite a few of the enemy in the surrounding hills who had yet to be rounded up. This did not affect us, as no leave was granted to the ship's company; in fact we were anchored several miles from the shore, amongst the impressive fleet of American ships which dotted the vast expanse of San Pedro Bay. Rear-Admiral Edelston, who commanded the destroyers of the British Pacific Fleet, inspected the ship during our stay. He made a short speech to us, and we were grateful for his clear picture of what life with the Fleet would be like. After travelling many thousands of miles, the time had come to start the job for which we had been sent. On the 14th May we left Leyte to join the fleet, which had been operating since Easter off the Sakishima Group.

By this time it was common knowledge that the Pacific War was being waged primarily at sea, and many hundreds of miles from our nearest bases. In order to maintain a large fleet at sea, it was necessary to keep a continual train of tankers and supply ships running backwards and forwards from the operating area to the forward bases. A force called the 'Fleet Train' was allotted this duty, a separate and independent unit of ships on which the task force entirely relied for the necessary continual supply of oil, food, ammunition, and last, but not least, our mail.

After a 'strike' the Fleet would rendezvous with the 'Train' about a hundred miles to the east of the striking area, and replenish. It was during one of these replenishing periods that we met and joined the Fleet.

The first job which fell to us on joining the Fleet was to transfer mail and light stores to almost every ship present. A rather nerve-wracking, yet very necessary operation was the transferring of men from one ship to another. This was achieved by means of a steel wire jackstay stretched between the ships, along which ran a metal pulley supporting a small breeches buoy. In this manner the man was hauled over the twenty or so yards between ships—a simple device which was frequently used without any accidents occuring. Mail, of course, was always the most highly prized of the commodities transferred, and to see the look of eager anticipation on the faces of the men in the larger ships, was thought by us in the destroyers as being worth every pound of the energy expended in loading and unloading it. Late in the evening of our first day's work we took up station as part of the destroyer screen covering the Fleet.

So the days passed, each one much the same as the last: planes taking off from the carriers to go on 'strikes', returning, refuelling and striking again. One of the most important jobs for destroyers was rescuing pilots who might be forced to 'ditch' their planes in the vicinity of the fleet. On our second day we were initiated in this duty when we picked up a Corsair pilot whose aircraft developed engine trouble. Apart from this and other minor incidents, the operation continued without any very exceptional excitement. Although the much-vaunted 'kamikaze' suicide planes had previously attacked the carriers and had also badly damaged the destroyer *Ulster,* the air raids for which we constantly waited never materialised.

The Sakishima operation ended on the 25th May, and when the order to retire came we were all pleased that a rest was in sight. We were surprised when, in the evening, we were detached from the Fleet, and in company with the battleship *King George V* and the two other 'T's', set course to the south-east for the island of Guam.

The reason for the trip was so that Vice-Admiral Rawlings could talk with Admiral Nimitz and make plans for future operations. Earlier in the Pacific War Guam had been much in the news, as well remembered for the magnificent struggle which the island defenders put up when invaded by the Japs. Now once again it was in American hands and had been converted into the Headquarters of the U.S. Pacific Fleet.

When we steamed into the harbour on the 28th May we were the first British warships to have visited the island since its recapture, and an Autogyro overhead appeared to be making a film record of the event. No sooner had we come to anchor than there arrived on board printed pamphlets bearing the words 'Welcome to Guam', with the name of each of the British ships on the cover. Everything concerning our visit was highly organised. Trips round the island, showing us all the battle scenes, visits to the airfields, and, what intrigued most of us more than anything, free beer at the canteen. Our stay lasted two days, and it is unlikely that any of us regretted the time we spent there, then on the way out the Americans supplied us with sleeve targets for A.A. firing practices. Fine, big red drogues they were, and as might be expected, the Americans were very slick at streaming them. But British gunnery was no less efficient. It was with some satisfaction that we saw three targets shot down as fast as our Allies could stream them. And it was with even greater satisfaction that we proceeded to shoot down more ourselves.

From Tel. George Lancaster, HMS *Termagant*

My vivid memories are of the very poor conditions aboard HMS *Termagant* as a telegraphist. Poor, and insufficient food.

Bread which was scarce was, after being in the bread locker overnight, literally covered with cockroaches on opening the locker next morning—of course, it was eat it or do without.

On two occasions fights among the lads in the mess took place—which resulted in the hot meal cooked in the galley thrown all over the mess. Result no meal and no action at all taken from higher up.

Never even at any time was the ship's company addressed by the C.O. to inform us where we were going to next.

The only time I had the 'wind up' was while in the Plotting Room. The radar screen showed a huge fleet approaching the area the 27th Flotilla was in and for about two hours everyone in the lower deck said this was our fatal end in sight as the buzz quoted the whole Jap fleet coming out to meet us. However luckily the fleet turned out to be a shoal of whales!

Thank God—we are still here.

Even after being at sea for 6½ days the only beer was one bottle per man, before the final attack on Japan.

On one occasion I had the unfortunate position to report to the Doc at morning sick parade with severe toothache. Instructed to report back at 5 p.m. for extraction.

I was sat on the after deck on an ordinary metal canvas chair, with a rating on each side holding my head in a firm grip, ready for the needle to be thrust into my gum, which it was and yes it snapped, so while the M.O. went back to the sick bay for another needle, I was stuck there with my mouth wide open with half a needle in my gum which eventually was removed thank goodness and the affected tooth pulled out with great force.

I remembered quite vividly while under attack by the Japs from the Air, at action stations I had to man the emergency C/T office aft. Even though it was hot in this small area where I was closed up, I fell sound asleep for about 35 minutes. Luckily I was not noticed and what woke me was the hysterical screaming from the bridge by one of the officers 'Fire! Fire! Fire!' at the gun crews as they were being heavily attacked by the Japs. Luckily we received no damage at all but many many misses, and of course lots of cheers from the crew when the Japs were either shot down or 'Baled out' not to surface again.

From Ldg. Seaman Walter Uden of HMS *Grenville*

We steamed north through the Coral Sea, on past New Guinea, well to the west of the Philippines and into the combat zone to the east of Formosa and the Sakishima Group. From now on we were steaming at about 30 knots all the time that we were in the combat zone; at 16 knots the strain on the asdic dome became too much and it was withdrawn into its housing in the lower hull of the ship. The asdic ratings had a rest from listening to the eternal pinging of their sets and we relied entirely on our speed to avoid submarine attacks. This once again substantiated the stoker's claim that our engines were the ship's main armament! All day long during the hours of daylight the Fleet carriers were launching strikes against Japanese installations ashore; Seafires provided fighter cover around the fleet, while Avengers carried out the bombing attacks. As Avengers are American built, it may not have occurred to the Japs that the British were the attackers. *Grenville,* along with the other destroyers of the screen, carried 900 tons of fuel oil and this would only last for three days at high speeds. We had already steamed north from Sydney and so it was necessary after two days to withdraw from the combat zone and retire south to meet the fleet supply train and begin a novel new operation of refuelling, storing, replacing lost aircraft and, most important of all, receiving mail whilst under way at sea.

The Fleet Train, as it was known, did a first class, if unspectacular, job. Becuse of the fuel limitations of the destroyers, only two or three days at a time were spent in the actual combat zone; even with reduced speeds at night the ship was beginning to ride high in the water at the end of three days. The fleet became highly skilled at refuelling three ships at a time from one oiler—a destroyer and a destroyer or cruiser on each side, while a capital ship was refuelled astern, fed through a floating pipeline. Stores were transferred too, sometimes with disastrous results if the two ships swung close together during the actual transfer. On one occasion we were transferring 5 cwts. of Demerera sugar (always used in the RN in preference to white sugar) from the supply ship to *Grenville* when the two ships swung towards one another and the sling containing the sugar was immersed in the sea as the supporting wires between the two ships went slack. All we succeeded in hauling inboard were five wet and sticky sacks. A rating suffering from toothache was likewise transferred to a carrier for a visit to her dentist and collected an hour later. As destroyers were replenished, they went out onto the anti-submarine screen to relieve other ships; the whole fleet was topped up in about five hours in decent weather. Life was made more difficult in rough weather; ships swinging apart in heavy seas, stretched and sometimes broke oil pipes and the sticky black stuff was sprayed all over the ship before the pumps could be stopped. The thankless task of clearing up that mess fell to the stokers—but the stains on the paintwork had to be erased by the seamen. Most important of all for the morale of the fleet was the arrival of mail of all sorts. Converted Lancaster bombers were flying the mail out from the U.K. to Sydney and from there it was flown north and brought the last stage of the journey by the fleet train. On one delivery, I received a letter posted in Ongar, Essex. We were in an area to the east of the Philippines and that letter reached me in three days; the cost was one threepenny Forces Mail stamp.

Thus we carried on operations for six weeks, by which time the destroyers were due for boiler-cleans—most had run over their 1,000 hours steaming time. We spent all our time at defence stations i.e. 4 hours on watch and 4 hours off watch—the 4 hours off watch had to be used to clean ship, prepare and eat meals and to sleep. The two hour dog-watches ensured that midnight watches were equally shared. Of course there was no guarantee that the alarm bells would not start ringing when you were off watch or as you sat down to the frugal meals that were the norm. As with bombing, a couple of suicide attacks and the ship's company could be at action stations and ready to open fire almost within seconds rather than minutes.

I had just completed the middle watch (midnight to 4 a.m.) and the humidity in the blacked out mess-deck was almost unbearable, so I took the camp-bed which I shared with my opposite number in the mess and decided to sleep on the upper deck, next to the funnel on the port side. We were at sea so there was no need to undress, just fold up a coat for a pillow and crash down and get to sleep as soon as possible. I had been sound asleep only for a few minutes when I was jolted violently and soaked in warm water. A stoker had just been relieved off his watch. Coming out of the brightly lit engine-room into the darkness his eyes had not had time to become accustomed to the change and so he had not been able to see me as he walked forrard to his mess-deck. A perk of being a stoker in time of water rationing was that they could 'pinch' a bucket of freshly distilled water as they came off watch and could do their dhobying and bathing in the peace of a deserted bathroom—bathroom which they had to share with the seaman branch. There was a bout of mutual cursing—I was soaking wet and he had lost his bucket of precious water. It did not take long to change into the dry scanty wear necessary in the warm air; I had propped my bed against the funnel while I was away and the heat had dried it by my return. By the time the Bosun's mate came round to call the hands just after 6.30 a.m. all my clothing was also dry.

Task Force 57 withdrew to the shelter of Manus, the American base in the

Philippines. There the destroyers took turns to go alongside depot ships to clean boilers and ancillary equipment and carry out any necessary repairs. A gaze at the shore line was enough to tell the ferocity of the battles which had been fought over the islands to evict the enemy. Blackened tree stumps, shell and bomb holes and smashed equipment all told their own tales. There was no point in asking for shore leave—there was nothing there and the only exercise available was swimming over the ship's side. Film shows were arranged in the forward mess-deck and an epoch making change was allowed. The Australian Government had sent up a quart sized bottle of beer for every man in the fleet. Now alcohol on the lower-deck was a totally unknown institution—apart from the rum ration; only the Wardroom was allowed duty-free alcohol at any time. To his eternal credit Jack accepted this gift with surprise and appreciation and without any abuse. *Grenville* spent a couple of days in a small American floating dock for below water-line repairs; this gave an opportunity to get off the ship and sit on the dock's upper-deck during the cool of the evening. At the same time we came into close contact with Yankee matelots and in conversaion I found that they were much the same as ourselves, fed up with being away from home, domestic troubles and the fact that Yankee Land was not anything like that shown on the films. We came once again to compare our food with that of the Americans. Every yankee escort vessel and destroyer with which we had had contact had an ice-cream making machine attached to the winch on the Fo'c'le; when 'Hands to Chow' was piped the upper-deck seamen were heard to express the hope that it would not be turkey *again*. Darkey seamen did all the washing up after meals and manned the ship's laundry. We surveyed our food—it looked a mess of pottage.

This rest period was over, no more full nights of undisturbed sleep for the foreseeable future. Getting back out to sea meant that as soon as we were a few miles out we were free of the plague of insects and the ship's movement reduced the temperature and the humidity dropped. Ever since we had left Suez, water had been rationed. The boiler rooms could not produce enough water to meet the enlarged demand, so rationing was introduced and enforced by the simple means of turning off the supply except at specific times. Unlimited supplies of salt water were available through the fire mains, but at the best this was only suitable for rinsing and could lead to skin rashes and such problems with the amount of sweating that we were doing. When we first entered tropical waters and began to sweat heavily, it was possible to run one's thumb down one's abdomen and the dirt would come rolling off in sausage shaped lengths—the very effect which the wealthy paid to have happen to them in Turkish Baths. Lime juice was also issued daily to everybody as a protection against scurvy. The skipper's cabin was the only place on board where there was a real bath, one day the unfortunate duty stoker turned off the water supply to this bath as well as cutting off our supply. The resulting explosion when the skipper—a big man who sweated profusely—slipped down from the bridge for a quick bath and found no water, shook the engineering department. Ways and means to get round this water problem had to be found by us lesser mortals. The skipper insisted that everybody shaved daily except those who had requested to grow 'sets' or beards. He insisted that smartness would maintain morale and he would not have a ship's company which resembled a load of pirates. Thus one small amount of our water ration was gone; because of the sweating, clothing needed to be dhobied daily and almost everyone had his own personal bucket. So the routine that we worked out was to use the bucket of water to dhoby our gear first, then bath in that same bucket of water. The same procedure applied with the rinsing water—and all the time we had to keep a weather eye open in case the alarm bells began to ring. We were allowed to wear any sort of comfortable tropical gear that we liked; some had bought native gear ashore, especially leather sandals. These were excellent, they ventilated the feet and this helped to keep at bay the toe-rot or athlete's foot which is a common scurge among seamen who have to use a communal bathroom, the fungus spores being spread on the tiled decks. It should be remembered that in all theatres of war ships' companies slept fully clothed and booted; hammocks were never slung, Jack slept on the mess tables, on mess stools, on camp beds and even on the deck. If the alarm bells began to ring during the night, everyone was on their feet and ready to run in a flash. These conditions (luxurious compared with what the troops ashore were suffering) demanded strict personal hygiene. Early in the commission we had a young seaman, a native of East London, living in our mess. A likeable enough youngster and good natured, but not a great saop and water fan; in spite of hints, he did not bother to wash himself too often and so to teach him a lesson, three of us took him to the bathroom and, armed with the mess scrubbing brush and a bar of Pusser's hard soap, we scrubbed him all over. He looked like a fresh boiled lobster when we had finished, but he never needed a second dose.

When *Grenville* had been lying in Colombo, the skipper had had a cushion and canvas cover made ashore, at his own expense, for his seat in the stern-sheets of the motor-boat. The first that I knew about this was when he presented it to me. We were at sea and I had used some of my precious water ration to wash out the cover and I hung it to dry in our usual drying area, the forward boiler-room. Imagine my horror when I went to collect it and found that someone had half-hitched it. The matter was reported to the Coxswain and to the 1st Lieutenant and, though we hunted high and low, it was never found. It could be that someone had a grudge to settle and slung it over the side. It fell to my lot to report the matter to the 'old man' and to suffer the blast of his wrath. He did not buy a replacement; our boat had to look a little less tiddly.

For the next six weeks we continued the aerial bombardment; suicide pilots continued to carry out attacks on the carriers. The duty of the screen destroyers in these attacks was to close the main body of the task force and assist in putting up an anti-aircraft barrage. Though spectacular, these barrages were not 100% effective against the determined suicide bombers; in turn all five carriers were hit by the kamikazes—the armoured flightdecks saving the terrible losses which were suffered by the American wooden flightdecked carriers. These types of attack have an unnerving effect on all ships' companies; to fight a normal enemy who will retreat when the battle becomes too hot (in the hope of fighting another day) as would be the case of most European navies is entirely different from fighting a man who is going to die in a few minutes anyway. It is impossible for anyone who has not experienced such a situation to understand. The routine for this warfare was as follows: the aircraft used were usually Zeros, fitted with a long range petrol tank under one wing and a five hundred pound bomb under the other wing. The pilots, indoctrinated into the belief that they were doing a patriotic deed and that they would at once go to their equivalent of heaven, were given an exotic two weeks of wine, women and song before their sorties. At take-off, the group would be escorted by a leader in a twin-engined aircraft who would do the necessary navigating and, having found the target, would circle at a safe distance to ensure that all pilots carried out their missions. For us the recipients, it meant that the ship was hit by an aircraft weighing about three tons, travelling at high speed in a dive, with a bomb exploding on impact and the whole engulfed in flaming petrol from the long range tank. Small wonder that such attacks had a spine chilling effect on all concerned; it was more frightening than Malta convoys where three types of air attack were carried out simultaneously. An example of how trigger happy the fleet became happened after tea one evening. I was off watch and enjoying the sunshine down on the quarter-deck; *Grenville* was on the destroyer screen, near the *King George V,* when the signal came for the whole fleet to turn about and steam into the wind as the carriers wished to change Seafire patrols. Thus the *KGV* was following *Grenville* on her starboard quarter when a lone Seafire approached the fleet, flying at little more than a thousand feet. Without any warning, *KGV*'s anti-aircraft opened up and their shooting was good enough to make the Spit. pilot take violent evasive action and waggle his wings to show his identity. The pilot was at fault in that all pilots had been instructed to approach the fleet high up and in an unthreatening manner. These same pilots had also been told to circle the fleet in one direction only, yet in a clear sunny sky, one managed to do the opposite and two Seafires collided head-on; two aircraft and two valuable trained pilots disappeared in a cloud of black smoke and falling debris.

The weather was not always sunny and warm; there were days when life-lines had to be rigged along the upper-deck aft of the break in the fo'c'sle to allow safe passage from the forward living quarters of the ship to the after quarters. There were some nights when the sheet lightning ran round the horizon all night long, yet we did not hear any thunder. Other nights, looking over the side at the bow wave, the phosphorous in the water showed up as great green blobs moving about in the disturbed water. As daybreak came in some areas, the morning watch-keepers were able to watch the flying fish skimming the surface of the sea. Those that came inboard were quickly gathered up, cleaned and taken to the galley to be cooked and to provide a pleasant variation for breakfast. These fish resemble a herring in size and flavour; they have an elongated lower tail fin with which they give themselves extra glide over the sea surface after having shot through the surface to escape their enemy. The enlarged front fins provide 'wings' to enable them to glide. I attempted to dry and preserve some of these fins to bring home as curios, but the cockroaches soon found them and consumed same. Dolphins kept us company, sometimes for days on end and standing up on the bridge it was possible to see them swimming under the ship while we were under way. In one period of rough weather five of us were hurt enough to put us in the midget sick-bay. In my case, it was mid-morning, no work was possible on the upper-deck and we had cleaned up on the mess-decks. I had the afternoon watch, so I decided to have a wash and shave while things were quiet. That job completed, I was returning to the for'd mess-deck; my shaving gear I kept in an enamel jug (Service issue)—this I was carrying in my right hand; in my left hand I had my towel and soap. I was on one leg as I stepped through the watertight door into our mess-deck when the ship was hit by a big wave—a wave which flung her bows upwards and sideways. Completely off balance and with both hands full, I was flung in a nose-dive onto an ammunition manhole mid-ships—the next I knew was as I came to in the mess on the starboard side and heard someone saying 'He's hurt himself'. I was bleeding from the nose and mouth, having broken the bridge of my nose. I had assistance to reach the Sick Bay; following treatment, I was put in one of the top bunks. The deckhead above me was a quarter inch thick steel plate that also formed the deck surround of X gun, a 4.7 inch gun. The rest of the day passed peacefully—it was an ideal opportunity to catch up on some sleep. Next morning after some food (breakfast aboard a destroyer can hardly be called a meal), the surgeon lieutenant gave us his attention. I was feeling better, but the two ringer said stay in the bunk for the time being. Dinnertime came and went and the weather had changed to clear sunshine, with a swell running. The alarm bells were ringing—standby for kamikaze attacks; I leapt from the bunk, grabbed my gear and ran forward to my action station in the T.S. I had no intention of lying there during a suicide attack, nor did I want to be in such close proximity to X gun when she ws firing. In the T.S. the crash of firing guns was music in our ears—it would have been almost the opposite in that bunk. I did not return to the sick-bay when things quietened down again, the tiffy just had a look at my injuries the following morning and said 'You'll be alright.'

The frequent gun-fire meant that mess-deck damage was a regular occurrence; lights fell down and smashed, crockery, though stored in specially designed racks which functioned perfectly in normal conditions, was thrown to the deck and smashed by the crash of A gun firing just up above. Cups and/or containers from which to drink became an increasing problem; I had bought myself a cup ashore and someone borrowed it to use while I was on watch and that person managed to break same cup while washing up. There was a daily issue of 1 lb. of butter to my mess; this had to be shared equally between 26 men, split into two watches. This works out at a fraction under one third of an ounce per man for each of the two meals, i.e. tea and breakfast; to strictly enforce this ration was a problem in itself. The Admiralty issued enamel butter dishes which strongly resembled a dog's bowl. There was in the mess a young Active Service able seaman, married with a son, a likeable bloke with whom I had run ashore on more than one occasion, who on this particular afternoon insisted on using our butter-dish to drink his tea, there being by that time about a 50% shortage of cups. I asked him to desist and allow the mess to use the butter-dish for its proper purpose. His repeated defiance in front of half the mess which was not on watch gave me no option but to take him to the Coxswain's office and from there to the Officer of the Day's presence on a charge of wilfully disobeying a lawful command. The subsequent apearance in front of the Captain meant the reading of a Warrant, the loss of his Good Conduct Badge and threepence in daily pay. The Central Stores then managed to find a few cups to issue to messes to provide temporary relief; the officer responsible being unaware of the difficulties. The Admiralty always issued china cups and plates in preference to the Army issue of enamel ware.

After three months, the fleet steamed into Sydney harbour to a slightly less rapturous welcome than we had received last time.

Leave was granted on a normal basis this time, i.e. liberty men returned to the ship each night. Those with relatives ashore or who had invitations to revisit homes where they had been last time, were allowed longer periods ashore. For the majority of us it was a time of cleaning up, storing, boiler-cleaning and painting ship. The rust streaks and caked salt on the funnel all told of a long time at sea.

The ship had to be painted from the top of the mast to the water-line; under our first skipper painting ship had involved everybody, except officers' stewards and engine-room staff. Piratical rig was allowed and the W.T. department rigged up loudspeakers on the upper-deck to provide musical accompaniment. Both motor-boats were lowered and circled the ship to pick up anybody who fell in and to collect each pair of painters as they and their stage reached the water-line. Several 'fell' in the water and swam round to the gangway as a cooler. This carnival atmosphere enabled the job to go with a swing and everybody enjoyed themselves. However, not this time, with this skipper. He had slept ashore and came swinging down the hill to the ship in the mid-morning in a towering rage. 'Stop all that. I won't have my ship like a bloody funfare.' Thus the job which usually got done in one day was not completed by the time that 'Hands secure' was piped; the next morning normal routine was resumed and the side party were left to struggle on and finish the job as best they could.

An engine-room party from HMS *Golden Hind*—the shore base establishment on the outskirts of Sydney—came longside *Grenville's* starboard side in a thirty five foot pinnace soon after breakfast one morning, the coxswain putting his bows level with the for'd depth-charge thrower rack. An engine-room artificer's hand was on the gunwale of the pinnace and as the boat rose with the swell the gunwale hit the depth-charge rack and the artificer's four fingers of his right hand were guillotined and fell on the deck. He looked at his hand and promptly passed out; as this happened right outside the sick-bay port-holes the limp body had only a short distance to be carried once it had been hauled inboard. I was hosing down the deck and the four fingers still lay where they had fallen. I put my head through the open port-hole and asked the Tiffy what he wanted done with the aforesaid and he told me to hose them over the side. With modern-day techniques those fingers could have been sewn back on, but in those days their only destiny was the bottom of Sydney Harbour.

After nearly a fortnight in harbour, the boilers were flashed up and we were once again ready for sea. A few of the seamen had formed attachments ashore, some had fallen in love with the country itself while others had found girl friends and had been accepted by their families.

From AB Eddie Mosling, HMS *Howe*

(VE Day was when a Zeke suicider attacked the Howe.—Ed.)

As a gunnery rate I was at Action Stations in the 14″ turret, but for repel aircraft stations 14″ personnel were on other duties. I was on Q Deck Fire Party and as soon as Repel Aircraft was piped I had to rush to the Q Deck and connect up hoses to the hydrants and wash down the Q deck and then remain there until the All-Clear.

We went to Repel Aircraft Stations at about 16.45 and as usual there was some activity around the carriers, over the past weeks I had witnessed all the attacks on the carriers as the suiciders came at them, and of course saw several of them hit and others shot down. It was indeed an experience.

However this day after a short while all the after short range guns started to let go and all hell let loose as the Pom Poms, Oerlikons and Bofors sent out thousands of shells of death astern of the *Howe*. I then was able to see this Zeke coming, in a long shallow dive straight for the *Howe*. As she got closer the shells from the Pom Poms etc. started to hit the target but she still bore down on the *Howe* until only a few hundred yards away she veered under the tremendous fire power of the close range weapons and crashed into the sea just a few dozen yards from the *Howe*'s port quarter, and to this day I think that if she hadn't been hit she would have crashed with her bomb either on Y Turret 14″ or the after superstructure. As she was so close, the pilot was visible before he crashed.

From AB Tony Jenner, HMS *KGV*

I was an A/B Q.O. My main job being assisting the ordnance articifers with the maintenance of the guns etc. Action Stations were as ammunition loader on top of 'B' turret, and in the working chamber of the same turret.

I recall the incident you mention on page 153 of your book **Sakishima** very well, as I was one of the gun crew on the pom-pom that hit the Jap plane, and can remember seing the faces of the plane's crew as we steamed past it on our port bow before it sank. It certainly was a spectacle with all the planes and gunfire around, and being on top of 'B' turret we had a grandstand view of all that was going on, and I must confess that at the age of 19, being somewhat frightened.

Cutting from The Sydney Daily Mirror of 9th July 1945, sent by R. M. Bob Putland, *KGV*

SUICIDE PLANES BOUNCED OFF DECKS OF OUR CARRIERS

Japanese suicide planes, power-diving at 600 miles an hour through a hail of A.A. fire, attacked three of the newest and most powerful carriers of the Royal Navy in one of the fiercest attacks of the Pacific War.

The carriers were the *Indefatigable, Victorious* and another, the name of which has not been disclosed.

The planes touched the decks in two instances but they cannoned into the sea with the force of their terrific momentum and exploded harmlessly alongside. Admiral Nimitz's H.Q. have withheld the exact time and place of the attacks, but it is evident that in the series of Allied strikes.at the Sakishima Islands, about 120 miles east of Formosa, the Japanese have done their best to send major British units to the bottom.

Decks were ablaze

Their decks scarred and ablaze, and strewn with the wreckage of shattered planes, the carriers kept on fighting while damage control crews worked heroically to extinguish fires, take the wounded to safety and restore the flight decks to operation.

Seventy men were killed and thirty-four seriously wounded.

In no instance were the carriers' operations impeded for more than a very short time, nor was any British carrier withdrawn from action.

The sturdy construction of the British carrier force withstood the blows by which the Japanese tried to knock the Royal Navy out of the Pacific war—blows as concentrated and punishing as those that left the American carriers *Franklin* and *Bunker Hill* shattered and fire-blackened says Reuter.

The destroyer *Ulster* was the only vessel of the Task Force whose replacement was made necessary throughout the two months during which the attacks on the Sakishimas continued.

Official sources have not disclosed whether the *Ulster* was the victim of a suicide plane or of a bomb.

Throughout the raids the task force, commanded by Admiral Sir Bernard

Rawlings, remained at full strength.

From Boy Seaman H. V. Heal, *KGV*

The combined BPF and US fleets were at anchor at Leyte. During the stay, each member of the ship's company—including the Boys (Young Seamen Division) had a ration of two, quite large, bottles of beer per day, issued on the upper deck during the evenings. This had to be consumed before going below, and the bottles disposed of.

Soon the sea was dotted with thousands of bobbing bottles, not only from *KGV* but from all the accompanying ships of BPF steaming downtide through the ships of the U.S. Fleet. Then there was a small armada of boats from that fleet following the trail of bottles back to this source, and much disappointment among their crews when they found out that they were too late to participate in some British drunken binge!

Lower deck 'buzzes' the following day were of a flurry of signals between the two fleets, with Americans complaining that the Brits had done more damage to their morale in one evening than the Japs in 3½ years. How much truth there is in the rumours I don't know—but that evening everyone had orders to break all bottles before throwing them overboard.

The captain decided that the ship would be painted *in one day*. To do this the entire ship's company, officers included, had to 'turn to' before dawn in order to commence painting as soon as it was light. Everything went very well, and as the evening drew near it was clear that our efforts had been very successful, and very little remained to be painted. As everyone relaxed to enjoy the cool of the evening, our attention was drawn to what appeared to be a hazy cloud moving out from the shore towards us. This turned out to be a swarm of large black flies, and *KGV* soon became the largest 'fly-paper' in history, and our three-tone BPF paintwork took on a distinctly darker tone! The outlines of these insects remained on the paintwork for many months later.

When I think back on those days, the harder times are forgotten, and memories are of the comradeship and humour. We even found humour in Action Messing, and it occurs to me that, if by any chance you should happen to be contacted by one of our ship's cooks, please tell him that I humbly apologise for what I said at the time—and could I please have the recipe for Sakishima Pie!

Leading Seaman Walter Uden continues his memories of HMS *Grenville*

When Task Force 57 once again steamed down the harbour, there was a feeling of sadness and of being 'chocker' in the mess deck. We steamed north outside the Reef, the gulls and insects had deserted us but the Albatrosses still kept us company as they skimmed the wave tops.

The Gunner's Mate, who as well as looking after the gunnery side of the ship also had the task of making out watch-keeping schedules and duties, was shifting round the leading seamen in their departmental duties. Leading Seamen, when working on the upper deck, were always allocated to a different part of the ship from the one in which they lived, i.e. in all my time aboard I had lived in the forecastle and had worked on the Iron Deck (midships) and on the Quarter Deck. He thought that I deserved a break, having been on the upper deck continuously since commissioning; accordingly, he gave me the seamen's mess decks, flats (passages) and bathrooms and 'heads' of the whole ship. There was a small office/store in A gun support on our mess deck; it was a quiet job so long as the ship was kept clean and no cause was given to any trouble maker in the Wardroom to go looking for dirt. I was reasonably happy, life consisted mainly of dishing out cleaning materials and chivvying up cleaners to see that they completed their work properly and on time. This state of affairs only lasted a fortnight; one morning the Gunner's Mate came to me and apologised and told me that I had to go back on the upper deck, on the Quarter deck and I was relieved by an Admiralty made Killick i.e. a rating made up to Leading Hand by Admiralty decree without having passed the necessary exams. So I went back into the sunshine—no explanation was ever given as to who gave the order or why.

Once back in the combat zone, we settled down to the usual routine of screening the carriers whilst almost continuous air strikes went on during the hours of daylight. These attacks brought the inevitable retaliatory suicide attacks. The bombing of Japanese airfields became an almost daily milk run; but the Japs simply adopted the same tactics as used by Western nations by filling in the runway craters almost as soon as they were made. They had an almost inexhaustible supply of slave labour to do the job for them. A reconnaissance Seafire pilot had the courage to fly past one Jap airfield at almost ground level and his photos. showed that the Japs had their aircraft hangared in caves hewn out of the cliffs skirting the airfield, totally safe from the high level bombing of the carriers' Avengers. Next morning the battleship *King George V,* with heavy cruisers and a screen of destroyers (including *Grenville*) detached from the Task Force and headed in the direction of the island airfield. The time was soon after 8 a.m. when the executive signal was hauled down from the yard-arm of the *KGV.* The bombardment lasted about one and a half hours in the middle of the morning, the targets were out of sight and completely out of the range of the destroyer's guns. Our job was simply to provide anti-submarine screening. The ton shells crashing down on the airfields should have destroyed both the aircraft and the caves housing them. The heavy ships and their escorts turned away and headed back to join the rest of the Task Force, arriving in the area soon after noon. Long before the ships themselves appeared over the horizon, we were able to see a pall of black smoke rising high into the sunny sky. During our absence the kamikaze pilots had been busy—the carriers had been hit and were dealing with flightdeck fires. It took most of the rest of the day to clear up the mess aboard the carriers. Next morning the remaining aircraft were off again on their attack missions. Reprisal attacks came in reply, but the damage was minimal with the extra fire power from the ships which had been away bombarding added to the barrage. That was how we carried on for about seven weeks, withdrawing every three days from the combat zone to meet the ships of the Fleet Train to replenish and, most important to us, to receive mail. The mail service really was first class—putting modern day services to shame. Even gift parcels which we had despatched from Sydney were getting home safely and quickly. This more than anything helped to keep up the Fleet's morale when three months at sea at a time were becoming the norm.

The destroyers were once again over their 1,000 hours steaming time and in need of boiler cleans. This time the force withdrew to Manus Island, reputed to have the largest natural harbour in the world. Again the shore line showed the ferocity of the fighting which had taken place during the overcoming of the Japs. It was reputed that Japanese stragglers were still at large in the hinterland, there were tales of American despatch riders being decapitated by wires stretched across their routes, and the more blood-thirsty spoke of cannibalism. Rightly or wrongly, there was nothing to go ashore for—the only means of exercise was walking up and down the upper deck of an evening or organised swimming over the ship's side. This later meant that the 'heads' or toilets had to be closed an hour before swimming began on whichever side of the ship was designated and a motor boat had to be on patrol on the outskirts of the swimming area.

With the ship at anchor or tied up alongside the depot ship and with only signalmen, gangway staff and some engine room staff on watch, the mess decks were crowded during the evening and night. The high humidity meant that sweat just poured off anybody without any exertion; numbers of us took to sleeping on the upper deck, using camp beds which had been issued or laying hammocks flat on the deck. We were fortunate that the insect population did not come off shore to bother us, but there were stampedes and much cursing when tropical storms suddenly deluged us. This was one of the occasions when the carriers' crews had a laugh on us, their flightdeck overhang provided all the shelter that they needed on their upper decks.

This stay in harbour was used as an opportunity to Court Martial some poor devil. We never found out who was charged, what his offence or what was the sentence, but the R.N. element used the occasion to have a full scale peacetime C.M. this involved a lot of extra work for myself and my crew. We had to paint the boat inside and out, all bright-work to be 'unpainted' and polished, both ensign masts to be sandpapered and varnished (we had never used these before, although they were stowed in the boat), a Union flag and boat size White Ensign to be obtained from the Chief Yoeman. A little before 9 a.m. on the morning of the trial we were called away and came alongside the after gangway (normally officers only)—both flags flying and boat and crew looking really tidy. The skipper, Captain D. 25th Flotilla, was piped over the side and we headed for the Flag ship, on the way joining Captains' boats from other ships. We went alongside their gangway, the skipper went aboard having given me instructions to return to the ship and await a signal. It was well into the afternoon before the signal came; no doubt the occasion was used to consume large quantities of Plymouth gin in the Flagship's Wardroom. In correspondence with old shipmates many years after the war, I learned this Court Martial was of an Engineer Commander who was alleged to have struck our Captain D. in the course of a row. Such behaviour amongst higher ranking officers indicated the stress and tension that existed.

As Captain's boat crew we were kept busy, day and night. Once, returning to the officers' gangway, aft on the starboard side, I noticed a square box floating and jammed under the metal work at the bottom of the ladder. As soon as the officers were gone out of the boat, I moved her forward until I was able to hook my boat-hook onto the wire handles of what was obviously some sort of ammunition box. I dragged it to me and heaved it into the boat; the marking plainly identified it as an American box of twenty hand grenades, probably dropped overboard from one of the Yankee Liberty ships unloading stores in the harbour and, with the usual American could-not-care-less attitude, had been allowed to drift away. Circling round and returning to the gangway, the gangway messenger was at the bottom of the ladder to collect the box from me and it was handed into the safe keeping of Gunner T. 'Pusser' as he was about explosives, it would be treated far less casually than would have been in the case of U.S. hands. In fact, the grenades were used later as 'Mini' depth charges while we were exercising with one of our submarines.

During one afternoon of this stay in harbour the Captain sent for me and told me that he would be dining aboard a certain ship at 7.30 p.m. I went up to the bridge and enquired of the duty signalman up there where this ship was anchored. He pointed her out to me; I took a bearing on her as she lay at anchor, well up this huge anchorage. Down into the boat to ensure that I had sufficient oil in the compass lamp and to make sure all was ready for this long trip in the darkness of the blacked-out harbour. We set out in style before 19.00 hours; the skipper was standing beside me in the stern-sheets as we sped through the warm night. He was always sociable when we were alone in the boat—in fact, whenever he kept us out late at nights his last words as he left the boat and climbed inboard were always 'See my steward in the morning and get a bottle of beer each for the three of you.' This was quite a gesture as the mess decks were strictly 'dry' apart from the rum ration. This was a very different side of the man who would sometimes order me to steam slowly round the anchored ship at about a couple of hundred yards range; the unfortunate First Lieutenant would be with him—faults in paintwork and anything else that he could spot would be forcibly pointed out before we returned to the gangway. But now we steamed on, no challenges came from the merchant ships that we passed, but R.N. ships' challenges—'Boat Ahoy'—

came across the water. I answered in the proper Service manner, but I was becoming increasing worried as we were passing close to where our destination should have been hoving in sight and there was nothing but darkness. The old man must have sensed my concern; he casually remarked that the ship was not where it should have been. Actually he had hit the nail on the head, she had shifted her billet after I had taken my bearing and even if the signalman had noticed her movement, Bunts had not bothered to inform me. We went alongside several merchant ships and enquired the whereabouts of our ship, but none was able to help us. Finally a British warship was able to give us precise bearings and we found our ship—the time was coming up to 22.00 hrs., we were only two and a half hours late in arriving. I had had one spell of deafness when we had been in Sydney and I was again having trouble, so I did not properly catch the order which the skipper gave me as he climbed out of the boat. In fact he told me to wait alongside the gangway; his intention was to see his host and arrange refreshment and accommodation for us while he was being entertained. However, the Officer of the Day on the gangway told me to lay off, probably because he was expecting more boats coming alongside. We lay stopped for a short time when a call from the Officer of the Day told me to return to our own ship and I headed for *Grenville,* finding her without any difficulty. Next morning I received a summons to the Captain's cabin and an explanation was demanded as to why I returned to *Grenville.* My explanation was accepted—the unfortunte coxswain of the host ship had the trip to bring the old man back in the small hours. Considering how the Captain had wiped the deck with some officers in my hearing on a number of occasions, I was lucky to get away with a mild rebuke for this night's work.

Our stay at Manus Island came to an end and we headed back to the combat zone, usual routine was resumed; swarms of aircraft took off from the carriers and disappeared from our sight, returning an hour or so later. These operations involved manoeuvres for the Task Force to turn into the wind; sometimes we heeled hard over as we altered course, other times the alteration was only noticed by the change in direction of the funnel fumes. The worst times were when there were only light winds from stern—anyone on watch in the vicinity of the bridge was choked by the funnel fumes. Things soon warmed up when the Jap retaliation came. Five men were killed aboard one of the carriers in one attack—a sickening day for us. Officially 'Pipe Down' was at 22.00 hours, duty watch were at their stations, the remainder of us had got our heads down early ready to go on watch at midnight and the mess decks were in darkeness by 9.30. Somewhere on the telegraphists' mess deck below ours a wireless was switched on and the transmissions came up to us through the open hatch. It was a broadcast from London of the crowds celebrating VE Day and the end of the war in Europe. For them it was joy and relief at the end of their suffering—what of those five who had died that day? *Cynically we remarked among ourselves that the celebrators had forgotten that we even existed.*

The Task Force continued its attacks; American losses on Okinawa were reported to be enormous without any apparent great progress. Rumour had it that the Yanks were losing a destroyer a day to the kamikaze attacks on their beachheads. Certainly filmed reports showed American reinforcements going ashore and running over the wreckage of previously landed equipment as they left the tide-line. All were fully aware of the fact that the struggle would become more and more bloody and bitter as the Allies approached closer to the central islands of the Japanese homeland.

During all these operations no Asdic contact were made with any enemy submarines, the air attacks occurred intermittently every day that we were in the combat zones.

Another six weeks of operations and the destroyers were again over their steaming hours and the Task Force headed for Sydney. We arrived in about a week and entered Sydney Harbour, steaming in line ahead with the seamen fallen in on the upper deck; each ship proceeding to its usual berth as in previous visits. We were beginning to know our way about Sydney and streamed ashore, glad to be on dry land again and able to stretch our legs. Jack lapped up the chance to buy large quantities of fruit at what was to us ridiculously low prices, to swim in warm waters, to visit Tarronga Park and to link up again with families ashore. Some matelots had found girl friends ashore, others had been adopted by families who had befriended them, often because matelot and family had the same 'home town' roots back in the U.K. The day-to-day routine of cleaning, repairing and painting the ship went on. Stores were humped aboard, boilers and engine room equipment were cleaned and overhauled.

The ship had been lying alongside the wall at Woolloomoolloo for about a week when I was shocked at being told that my relief had arrived on board.

From Fred Fallows CPO Coxswain (Senior Rating) of HMS *Ulysses*

It was a great pleasure to welcome Fred Fallows to my home. He epitomized all that is honourable in the Royal Navy. He served in the BPF as CPO Coxswain (Senior Rating) on board HMS Ulysses.

His commanding officer said of him:

'His path was not easy, but by virtue of his integrity, character, understanding of human nature and good organising powers, he played a big part in raising the morale of the ship' company to a high pitch. His unselfish work for them and his all-round co-operation reaped a rich reward.'

The following are extracts from 'The Story of HMS Ulysses*' which he kindly loaned me.*

Sydney's reaction to VE Day was much the same as ours: the thankfulness was there but not the wild jubilation. That would come when Japan was defeated. Till then there were too many Australians in prison camps, and for us there were, for all we knew, months, perhaps years, of fighting. On May 9th, which was a public holiday, most of the cinemas, cafés and shops were closed, and natives of Sydney used the occasion as just an ordinary day off. It was lovely autumn weather, ideal for walking or sitting in the parks, and consequently ideal for our first sight-seeing tour of the city. Our meals were provided in the British Centre or the Anzac Buffet, where, for very small expense, we ate food which would have seemed like a dream in war-time England.

Most people walked or rode over the bridge. I shall never forget the sight of Sydney and the harbour seen at night from the bridge; the whole city lit up, ships lying peacefully at anchor with all their lights burning, the sky a rich dark blue with stars as clear and bright as sunlight glinting on a stream, and over the whole there seemed to be an atmosphere of tranquility. This strong sensation was enhanced by the height of the bridge, where we seemed strangely detached from the life below, like watchers from another world. In the main squares, such as Martin Place, there were attempts at revelry, but the feeling of unsettledness, of a job only half done, was too acute to allow any really spontaneous outbursts. In a way, it was a relief when all the official celebrations were over and life resumed its normal course, and we were able again to concentrate on the future.

The carrier *Illustrious* arrived while we were still at Woolloomooloo, very rusty and with damage from attacks off Sakishima. From members of her crew we heard something of what to expect.

While undergoing several minor readjustments, we were visited by Admiral Sir Bruce Fraser, our C.-in-C., who, very unobtrusively and with no ceremony, walked around the ship.

A strange way of judging position at sea is by the various radio programmes. After only about twenty-four hours we were out of range of the Sydney commercial stations, with their constant advertising and stock phrases which had gradually become jokes with the ship's company. Then, as we proceeded up the Queensland coast, we were entertained by Brisbane until that faded too, and then we received a mixture of B.B.C. programmes, Australian National and Radio Madang.

We were told the unbelievably good news that we were only to be in Manus for a few days and then to go back to Sydney with the fleet, which was returning from its long task off Okinawa and Sakishima. So it was Manus where we were to rejoin the 25th Flotilla. We felt confident that we would be able to hold our own in competition with any of our sister ships.

On May 30th we watched the finest ships of the Royal Navy steam proudly and slowly into this tropical base—the carriers *Indomitable, Victorious, Formidable, Indefatigable,* the flagship *Howe* (*King George V* was at Guam, where she was visited by Admiral Nimitz), the cruisers *Black Prince, Newfoundland, Euryalus, Gambia, Uganda, Achilles,* and the many destroyers—including the 25th Destroyer Flotilla: *Grenville, Ursa, Undine, Urania, Urchin, Undaunted.* These, with *Ulysses,* made up a complete flotilla. (*Ulster,* bombed off Okinawa, was on her way to the U.K.)

First to anchor were the carriers, like a line of triumphant kings, scarred in battle but victors. This was their first rest for months.

Before she had been in long, *Grenville* came alongside and Captain (D) came on board to, as he put it, 'say Hullo' and tell us what he knew of the future. Referring to Australia, he said: 'I hope you enjoyed Sydney. We did—it nearly killed us.' He told us we would be returning there for a replenishment period before the next operation, which he thought would be more exciting from the destroyer point of view than the Sakishima strikes had been. It was hard not to contrast our own newly-painted, clean and tidy ship, untried in the Pacific warfare, to the rusted, sea-stained weather-beaten *Grenville*. In three months' time there was to be no contrast!

On May 31st we sailed with the fleet from Manus. This was our first experience of working in a big task force, and we found there was plenty to do. We were part of the destroyer screen, and every day there were shoots and exercises with aircraft. Our gunners put up a very good show and we soon lost a slight inferiority complex, due to being the 'new boy' of the fleet. The weather was calm and we soon became experts at distinguishing individual ships among the carriers and cruisers. We were to have plenty of time in the future for that same job. The days soon passed, and at last, on June 5th, we heard the familiar voices of Sydney's radio. Instead of going straight in, we sailed further south to Jervis Bay, where the carriers flew off their aircraft. It was arranged that, as junior ship, we were to lead the fleet into Sydney Harbour. We very nearly lost this honour as the result of lagging behind to pick up one of *Indefatigable*'s pilots who had crashed into the sea. When we received the signal to 'hurry up' if we wanted to go in first, we really showed our turn of speed and, doing over 30 knots, passed the rest of the fleet and steamed through the Heads and into the harbour to our buoy in Farm Cove, where we were in sight of the beautiful Botanical Gardens and almost within the shadow of the bridge. It was good to be back. Already many of us were losing our hearts, if not to Australia at any rate temporarily to certain of its inhabitants.

The King's Speech, VE Day

King George VI in his Victory Day broadcast to the Nation and the Empire warned the British people that they still had to deal with the Japanese, a determined and cruel foe. 'And to this, we shall turn with the utmost resolve and with all our resources.'

The King said:

Today we give thanks to God for the great deliverance. Speaking from our empire's Oldest Capital City, war battered, never for one moment daunted or dismayed, speaking from London, I ask you to join me in that act of thanksgiving.

Germany, who drove all Europe into war is being finally overcome. In the Far

East we have yet to deal with the Japanese a determined and cruel foe. To this we shall turn with the utmost resolve and with all our resources; but, at this hour, when the dreadful shadow of war has passed far from our hearts and homes in these Islands, we may at last make one pause for thanksgiving, and then we must turn our thoughts to the tasks all over the world which peace in Europe brings with it.

First let us remember those who will not come back; their constancy and courage in battle, their sacrifices and endurance in the face of a merciless enemy; let us remember the men in the Services who have laid down their lives. We have come to the end of our tribulation, and they are not with us at the moment of our rejoicing.

Next, let us salute in proud gratitude the great host of the living who have brought us to victory. We cannot praise them to the measure of each one's service for in total war, their efforts all rise to the same noble height and all devoted to the common purpose. Armed or unarmed, man and woman, you have fought and striven and have endured your utmost. None knows better than I, and as your King I thank with a full heart those who bore arms so valianty on land, sea and in the air, and all civilians, who, shouldering their heavy burdens carried them unflinchingly and without complaint.

With those memories in our minds let us think what it was that upheld us through nearly six years of suffering and peril. The knowledge that everything was at stake: our freedom, our independence, our very existence as a people. But knowledge also that, in defending ourselves, we were defending the liberties of the whole world: that our cause, was the cause, not of this nation only, not of this Empire, and Commonwealth only, but every land where freedom is cherished and law and liberty go hand in hand. In the darkest hours we knew that the enslaved and isolated peoples of Europe looked to us, their hopes were our hopes, their confidence confirmed our faith. We knew, that if we failed or faltered the last remaining hope against world wide tyranny would have fallen in ruins but we did not falter, and we did not fail. We kept faith with ourselves, and with one another. We kept faith and unity with our great allies. That faith and unity have carried us to victory through dangers, which at times seemed overwhelming.

So let us resolve to bring to the tasks which lie ahead, the same high confidence in our mission. Much hard work awaits; both in the restoration of our own Country after the ravages of war and in helping to restore peace and sanity to a shattered world. This comes upon us at a time when we have all given of our best for five long years and more, heart and brain nerve and muscle have been directed upon the overthrow of Nazi tyranny. Now we turn, fortified by our success, to deal with our last remaining foe. The Queen and I know the ordeals which you have endured throughout the Commonwealth and the Empire. We are proud to have shared some of them with you, and we know that we shall all face the future together, with a stern resolve and to prove that our reserves of will power and vitality are inexhaustible.

There is great comfort in the thought that the years of darkness and danger, in which the children of our country have grown up are, please God, over for ever. We shall have failed and the blood of our dearest will have been in vain, if the victory for which they died to win does not lead to a lasting peace, founded on justice and established in good will. To that then, let us turn our thoughts, triumph and proud sorrow, and tomorrow take up our work again, resolved as people to do nothing unworthy of those who died for us, and make the world such a world as they would have desired for their children.

From Dick Douglas-Boyd 820 Sqdn, ex Lieut. RNVR

I left *Indefat.* after the Sakishima strikes and stayed in Australia firstly as CO Station Flight at Jervis Bay MONAB and then to NOWRA where I rejoined a few shipmates including 'Joybells' Virgin. I can vouch for the story of the latter's victory celebrations in the steam roller which he drove around the airfield at midnight without realising that he had lowered the digging spike at the rear. I saw him four weeks afterwards thumping fresh tarmac into the runway and the peri' track!

A collection of Signals sent by Captain Ian Garnett DSC RN, HMS *Swiftsure*
(As you will see, they are not in chronological order.—Ed.)

H 5264 SECRET IN L.T.G. 270948Z May 45
To: CTF 57 Date 28/5/45
Infor: C. IN C. B.P.F. CINCPAC (ADV)
FIFTH FLEET
W/T HOW FOX CCM GR 125 PRIORITY TORCO 280430/KING
On the completion of your two months operations as a TASK FORCE of the FIFTH FLEET in support of the capture of OKINAWA, I wish to express to you and to the officers and men under your Command my appreciation of the fine work you have done and the splendid spirit of co-operation with which you have done it. To the American portion of the FIFTH FLEET, TASK FORCE 57 has typified its great traditions of the Royal Navy.—SPRUANCE.

D.T.G. 270948Z May 45

DIST: Sec.A.Sec(2) Staff Log(2) S.C.O. S.O.O. NS.N.O. S.O.A. RAD File Capt. Sec(2)

To: B. S. 1. R.A.F.T.
(R) V.A.(Q) FONAS (A)
From: C In C.
BRITISH PACIFIC FLEET

BASEGRAM

Following is an extract from 'NEW YORK TIMES' and was reprinted in

'LONDON DAILY TELEGRAPH'. Begins:
'American Naval Observers with the BRITISH PACIFIC FLEET agree that the spirit and aggressiveness of the Men is unsurpassed in any Navy. No one is more anxious to get into Battle than these Men.
Their morale is immense.' Ends.
The report which came from ROBERT TRUMBRILL is headlined:

BRITISH NAVY UNSURPASSED

08 0807 Z May 45

To: BPF. P119, RESTRICTED ROUTINE From:CINC BPF

Following signal has been received from ADMTY begins . . .
THEIR LORDSHIPS wish to congratulate the BRITISH PACIFIC FLEET on successful completion of their first major operation with UNITED STATES PACIFIC FLEET in the Pacific. The great administrative difficulties that have been overcome in the preparation of the Fleet for this operation and the sustained effort required by all Officers and men during the prolonged operations of this nature are fully appreciated by THEIR LORDSHIPS. It is evident that the task of (reinforcements??) (to the ??) B.P.F. in this operation was efficiently executed.

ENDS . . .270721Z

HAND PL TOR.1010'I' A.HOLT . . 1.5.45
GRAY. C. CROSS

(The brackets and question marks etc. are copied from the signal pad.—Ed.)

R.153 RESTRICTED BASEGRAM

B.S.1. R.A.F.T. (R) A.C.1. FRO C.IN.C. B.P.F.

On the return of the FLEET after its first period of co-operation with UNITED STATES FORCES I express to you my great appreciation of the work done by the FLEET and FLEET TRAIN. You have materially assisted in the operations against JAPAN and carried on in spite of the difficulties of supply over these vast distances. The work that you are doing will help to shorten the war in the EAST and as the EUROPEAN WAR moves to its conclusion the additional resources we shall obtain will go far to lighten the strain (which) is thrown upon the FLEET. My best wishes to you all.

(R 125)

T.F. 57. (R) C.E.F. C.T.F. 112. R.A.D. C.T.F.

(1). The enemy continues at great cost to himself his all out effort to save Okinawa.

(2). We have returned to fuel and rest aircrews and will proceed tomorrow 19th April for a final knock against our target on 20th April, and then withdraw to arrive Leyte about 23rd April.

(3). When A.C.1. informed me that the carriers could just manage one more strike with the aircraft and aircrews available I informed commander 5th Fleet. CIN C Pacific in his signal to me noted the change of plan with gratification and states 'It is characteristic of your force to repeatedly put forth extra efforts whenever there is a chance to do added damage to the enemy. You have my appreciation for an offer so in keeping with the tradition of the British Navy.'

(4). The last two days added 4 aircraft splashed on the ground making a total of 72 destroyed for certain plus a good number destroyed on the ground by bombing and many damaged.

NAVAL MESSAGE

To: B.P.F. From: C. IN C. B.P.F.

NR WO 327

Thank you for your kind message. The close co-operation and support that has been proved by units of the B.P.F. have been of great assistance in defeating Japan. Your own personal support and loyalty have been a source of great satisfaction to me.

FLEET ADMIRAL C. W. NIMITZ

NAVAL MESSAGE

To: ALL SHIPS From: C.T.F.37

Following has been received addressed C.T.F.37 from C.T.F.38.
It is fitting that our great allies in many a previous hard fought battle should have helped us in the last campaign.

Good fortune to those who are departed and my humble respect to all your gallant airmen.

120107

Back in the U.K., the headlines read:

Daily Express—Tuesday 8th May 1945

THIS IS VE DAY: THE KING AND THE PREMIER WILL SPEAK

WAIT FOR IT—TILL 3
BUT THE WEST END STARTED VE FUN LAST NIGHT

The official statement had to be co-ordinated with Moscow and Washington

Evening Standard—Tuesday 8th May 1945

Eden speaks for Britain on the morning of VE Day
A MAJESTIC AND TRIUMPHANT HOUR

Daily Express—Wednesday 9th May 1945

THIS WAS THEIR FINEST DAY
Churchill in the midst of the people

Extracts from 'The Other Hundred Years War 1941—2041' by Russell Braddon

OKINAWA
From ashore, the sea and the air, they were hopelessly outgunned. Despite their valour, their kamikazes and their ruthlessness, the campaign lasted only eleven weeks, and killed only 12,500 Americans. As against that, 110,000 Japanese soldiers and 75,000 Okinawans lost their lives, not all of them to the Americans.

Civilians in caves, taking refuge from shellfire, were ordered to vacate them in favour of the Imperial Japanese Army. They died in the open, under the American bombardment.

Whole families fled from the American advance, wondering how best to kill themselves. One family used a hoe, another a baseball bat, a third a pen knife, many others a boulder.

'I'll start with mother,' said the head of the family whose weapon was the pen knife, and severed her jugular. Then killed each of his children, and finally himself.

To kill one's family with a baseball bat, a hoe or a boulder is easy, but to kill oneself with a baseball bat, a hoe or a boulder is extremely difficult. The father of such families, his responsibility to them fulfilled, usually had to hang himself.

Other families, whom some envied, had been issued with a hand grenade. But grenades are capricious; and even though they sat close together, there was often a badly wounded survivor. Such survivors were usually clubbed to death by the nearest Japanese soldier, who would shout, 'Here's another,' as he wielded the butt of his rifle.

Schoolgirls were conscripted as nurses, and died in caves with the soldiers. Fathers scavenging for food for their families were seized by the Army and asked, 'Who is more important, your family or the Emperor?' Whichever the answer, they were executed.

Only the very fortunate found themselves in caves where they were offered milk laced with cyanide. They were the wounded. Upon drinking their potion, they were listed as killed in action and their souls became eligible for a better life at the Yasukuni Shrine in Tokyo.

Amid this inferno of fire and shell, the pain of hunger and the anguish of obligatory death, the Okinawans can be excused if they failed to notice Hitler's suicide on 30 April, and the surrender of Germany eight days later.

Okinawa fell.

Supplement to The London Gazette of 1st June 1948 announced:

THE CONTRIBUTION OF THE BRITISH PACIFIC FLEET TO THE ASSAULT ON OKINAWA, 1945

The following Despatch was submitted to the Lords Commissioners of the Admiralty on the 7th June 1945, by Admiral Sir Bruce A. Fraser, G.C.B., K.B.E., Commander-in-Chief, British Pacific Fleet.

Office of the Commander-in-Chief
British Pacific Fleet
7th June, 1945

'ICEBERG'—REPORT

Be pleased to lay before Their Lordships a report on the actions fought by the British Pacific Fleet during the first phases of Opertion 'Iceberg'.

2. It is impossible yet to judge the effect of these operations on the conquest of Okinawa, but I consider that we have successfully carried out our undertakings, employing a method of sea warfare with which we were previously unfamiliar.

3. It is not less than was expected, since all had turned their minds to it, but the credit must go to Vice-Admiral Sir Bernard Rawlings, K.C.B., O.B.E., whose inspiring leadership, resolution and fine judgement were responsible.

4. Doubt as to our ability to operate in the Pacific manner was somewhat naturally in American minds. This, however, was soon changed. The toll taken by the suicide bombers of the more lightly armoured American carriers led to an incease in the proportionate effort provided by our carriers, and the evidence of American eyes that we could support ourselves logistically, relieved their anxieties on that score. We have now, I am sure, become not only

welcome but necessary in Central Pacific operations.

5. Despite their doubts, the Americans put their trust in us unstintedly, and the generosity and help of all were invaluable to our success, a result which I know is most satisfactory to them.

6. We shall not, however, be able to play our full part until sufficient forces are available to form a second task group, since the effort of one, alternatively striking and re-fuelling, must necessarily be discontinuous and uneconomical of force.

7. The British Pacific Fleet have been making British naval history by operating off the enemy coast for periods up to 30 days each, but it is well to remember that similar American task groups are doing the same thing for twice as long. When we have mastered the technique of ammunitioning and storing at sea, we shall also be able to do this. These are matters receiving close attention.

8. In this connection, I wish to commend most whole-heartedly the work of Rear-Admiral D. B. Fisher, C.B., C.B.E., whose successful servicing of the Fleet at sea and in harbour has been the admiration of all.

(Signed) BRUCE FRASER,
Admiral

Admiral Sir Bruce Fraser's Report to the Admiralty dated 7th June 1945 included a Report from Vice Admiral Sir Bernard Rawlings extracts of which appear below:

17th March

8. In order to have the Tanker Group in position for the Fleet to top up with fuel at the last prudent moment, Task Unit 112.2.1 and Task Unit 112.2.5* were sailed on 17th March. The former consisted of H.M. Ships *Striker* (with replacement aircraft), *Crane, Findhorn, Whirlwind* and the Tankers *San Ambrosio, Cedardale* and *San Adolpho*; the latter consisted of H.M. Ships *Pheasant, Speaker* (for CAP** duties) and *Kempenfelt*.

12. The British Pacific Fleet, until then Task Force 113, sailed from Ulithi at 0630 on 23rd March, 1945, as Task Force 57.

Composition of TF 57 on sailing from Ulithi on 23rd March, 1945.

1st Battle Squadron TU** 1
King George V (Flag of CTF 57),
Howe

1st Aircraft Carrier Squadron TU 2
Indomitable (Flag of A.C.1 and Second-in-Command TF 57)
Victorious
Illustrious
Indefatigable;

4th Cruiser Squadron TU 5
Swiftsure (Flag of C.S.4)
Gambia

Black Prince
Argonaut;

Destroyers—TU 8
25th Destroyer Flotilla
Euryalus (Flag of R.A.(D) temporarily)
Grenville (Capt. D.25)
Ulster,
Undine,
Urania,
Undaunted;
(Note: *Ursa* was docking at Manus.)

4th Destroyer Flotilla
Quickmatch (Capt. D.4)
Quiberon
Queenborough
Quality;

27th Destroyer Flotilla
Whelp,
Wager.
(Note: *Kempenfelt* (Capt. D.27) was attached to TU 112.2.5, the group remaining in the replenishing area.
Whirlwind and *Wessex* were attached to TU 122.2.1 and TU 122.2.2 respectively, the Tanker Groups proceeding between Leyte and the replensihing area.)

25th March
At 0310 with H.M. Ships *Euryalus, Black Prince* and *Argonaut* spread 8 miles apart, 8 miles ahead of the Fleet, radar and Task Group 112.2.1. Rendezvous was made by 0600 and the above ships with destroyers detached in turn to fuel. The Rear Admiral Commanding Destroyers, in HMS *Euryalus,* was made Senior Officer of the oiling force and oiling arrangements.

It had been hoped to complete this fuelling (from three tankers) by 1100, but a strong north easterly wind and swell and hose troubles soon ruled out that desire. To enable the Fleet to keep to this, its first appointment, on time, both battleships and *Striker* were ordered to fuel destroyers. In spite of this, of leaving one destroyer to follow later, and accepting other destroyers up to 30 per cent. short, the operation had to be stopped at 1450.

CAPs were flown by *Speaker* and *ASPS by the carriers while fuelling was in progress and aircraft carriers took on replenishment aircraft from HMS Striker.*

At 1530 the Fleet, formed in Cruising Disposition 5B, proceeded at 23½ knots, this speed being then necessary to reach the operating area by dawn the next day. A.C.1 assumed tactical command.

HM Ships *Quality* and *Whelp* had to be left with the Tanker Group, HMS

Whelp, who had bearing trouble, was replaced by HMS *Whirlwind* from Task Unit 112.2.1, HMS *Quality,* also with defects, was replaced by HMS *Kempenfelt* from Task Unit 112.2.5, HMS *Wager* was left to continue fuelling but was able to rejoin the Fleet the following morning.

At 1820 HMS *Indefatigable* was observed to be on fire on the starboard side under the island structure. The fire, which had originated in Carley floats, was soon extinguished and no damage to the ship occurred.

27th March

At 0245 a bogey to the eastward was contacted by radar. As it seemed that the Fleet was being shadowed, course was altered in an attempt to shake off the aircraft. At 0307 HMS *Euryalus* was ordered to open out from the screen and fire on the enemy aircraft which then remained at a respectful distance for a time. A Hellcat was then flown off from HMS *Indomitable* to intercept, but the moon became obscured by a cloud when the pilot was about to open fire and the enemy made good his escape. At 0305 Japanese ASV (radar equipment in aircraft) transmissions on 152'MC5s were reported and the Fleet was ordered to commence jamming.

It is of interest to note that the fighter flown off was called by an aircraft which claimed itself to be a U.S. aircraft and warned the fighter of his approach from the south. Although there is no substantial evidence, this may have been a ruse by the Japanese aircraft to avoid inspection while closing the Fleet.

At sunrise a fighter sweep was sent in to Ishigaki only from a flying-off position 100 miles 180° inland from Miyako Jima. No increased activity was reported.

Two bomber strikes were directed against radio stations, barracks and airfields not covered the previous day. Coasters off the islands were also attacked. The final strike was a small fighter bomber strike. Withdrawal was begun at dusk.

At 1130 HMS *Undine* escorted by fighters was despatched to the rescue of an aircraft which had ditched 56 miles from the flying-off position. At 1750 she rejoined the Fleet having picked up the Avenger crew and also a United States Corsair pilot who was discovered after having been adrift for 48 hours.

The American Rescue Submarine USS *Kingfish* was requested to keep good lookout for any of our ditched aircrews, but apparently she had not been fully instructed by the American authorities as she replied that 'she would have to ask her boss first'. The situation was soon clarified when the Commander-in-Chief, Pacific informed the submarine that Task Force 57 was operating in her vicinity and that she was to act as rescue submarine when required. At 1805 American Rescue Submarine USS *Kingfish* reported that she had rescued the pilot of one of HMS *Illustrious*'s Avengers.

31st March

It may be assumed in this narrative henceforward that CAPs and ASPs were part of the normal daily flying programme. At 0530 HM Ships *Argonaut* and

Wager were detached to a position 300°, 30 miles from the Fleet centre to act as pickets to prevent enemy aircraft returning with our own strikes. HMS *Argonaut* was chosen for this purpose as having the most suitable radar. At 0630 a fighter sweep was sent in from a flying-off position 23° 10′N 125° 23′E and thereafter fighter patrols were maintained over Ishigaki and Miyako. There appeared to be little activity in either island. Two bomber strikes were sent against Ishigaki airfield, installations and barracks.

USS *Kingfish* again did useful service and rescued the crew of an Avenger which had ditched.

At dusk the Fleet disengaged to the south westward and CTF 57 assumed tactical command. Two fighters were kept at readiness from moonrise but the Fleet was not shadowed.

1st April

A.C.1 assumed tactical command; HM Ships *Argonaut* and *Wager* opened out to their picket positions before the fighter sweep was sent in at 0640 from a flying-off position 23° 26′N 125° 25′E.

At 0650 bogeys were detected by radar to the westward, height 8,000 feet, closing at 210 knots. The fighter sweep was recalled to intercept and additional fighters were flown off.

The raid split up more than 40 miles from the Fleet. The first interception was by Corsairs from HMS *Victorious* which shot down one enemy. Seafires shot down two more close to the Fleet and a fourth was destroyed by Hellcats recalled from the fighter sweep. At 0705 the Fleet had been alerted to 'Flash Red' and a few minutes later the enemy planes commenced their attacks.

One enemy single-engined aircraft machine-gunned HMS *Indomitable* in a low attack killing one rating and wounding two officers and four ratings. Still flying very low it made a similar attack on HMS *King George V* but without causing casualties. Considerable difficulty was experienced in identifying enemy from our own planes who were hard on the enemy heels.

At 0727 an enemy plane dived into the base of HMS *Indefatigable*'s island. Four officers and ten ratings were killed, and sixteen of her complement wounded. The flight deck was put temporarily out of action, but within a remarkably short time, and in a most creditable manner, aircraft were again being operated from this ship, although that day on a reduced scale.

At about 0755 HMS *Ulster* was near missed by what apeared to be a 500 lb bomb from an aircraft then being chased by one of our fighters. They reported that the bulkhead between the engine-room and the after boiler-room had blown, flooding both compartments, but that the ship was floating well. Casualties were two killed and one seriously wounded. *(5 killed.—Ed.)* She was unable to steam but her armament remained effective. HMAS *Quiberon* was ordered to stand by her and as soon as the raid was over HMNZS *Gambia* was ordered to tow her to Leyte.

At 1215 a bombing strike was sent in against Ishigaki to bomb airfields and runways. No activity was noted. At 1430 reports were received from combat patrols over the islands that more aircraft had been sighted at Hirara and Ishigaki airfields. These were attacked by the fighter patrols and were followed by a fighter sweep. It was estimated that about 14 enemy aircraft were destroyed on the ground during this attack and others damaged.

At 1730 a low flying bogey was detected by radar to the north westward. Hellcats were sent to intercept this raid which developed into 2 plus but the enemy avoided them in cloud. Soon afterwards the Fleet sighted the enemy and opened fire, sometimes, it is regretted, at friendly fighters. One enemy aircraft dived on HMS *Victorious*; her swing under full helm was successful and the plane touched its wing only on the flight deck edge spinning harmlessly into the sea where its bomb exploded clear of the ship.

The manuscript instructions to the pilot were blown on board HMS *Victorious*; this interesting document, denoting priority of targets for suicide planes, has been translated and the contents forwarded to intelligence centre. It seems certain that *Victorious*'s guns hit this aircraft during its dive.

This matter of differentiating between our own aircraft and the enemy becomes daily of more importance. With the suicide attack and, as is inevitable, with our own fighters pursuing the enemy right on to the Fleet's guns there is only a matter of seconds in which to act. Presented at certain angles there is very little difference between the suicide-equipped Japanese single-engined aircraft and some of our own fighters. On the other hand the means of controlling, particularly of stopping, the fire of the innumerable small guns that are now scattered about ships, often with poor communications, makes the problem difficult.

At dusk the Fleet disengaged to the south eastward and CTF 57 assumed tactical command.

At 1450 HMS *Illustrious* reported man overboard. Fighters of the CAP and destroyers were sent to search and the Fleet was turned 360° for a period. Unfortunately the man was not recovered.

6th April

At about 1700 bogeys were detected on the screen. Fighters intercepted them and splashed one Judy. One enemy aircraft out of an estimated raid of four broke through in cloud and later dived on HMS *Illustrious*, who took radical avoiding action. The suicider's wingtip hit the island, spinning the aircraft into the sea where the bomb exploded. Only slight damage and no casualties were caused. Ship probably hit aircraft in dive.

One Judy and another unidentified enemy plane flying low were engaged by destroyers of 4th Destroyer Flotilla on the screen, one being hit after it had jettisoned its bomb. The other plane was seen in flames on the horizon about five minutes later and is considered to have been destroyed by the 4th Destroyer Flotilla. A second Judy orbiting the Fleet at about 10 miles range was intercepted by Corsairs and Hellcats and splashed.

Most regrettably one Seafire was shot down by gunfire of the Fleet during the raid: the pilot was not recovered.

7th April

In the afternoon HMS *Urania* escorted by 2 fighters was despatched to the rescue of a Corsair pilot who had lost his way and landed in the sea about 70 miles from the Fleet. An American Privateer, having reported him, dropped dinghies and remained in the vicinity until relieved by Fireflies. HMS *Urania* recovered the pilot, but he was unfortunately found to be dead. The afternoon strike destroyed one and damaged other aircraft found on the ground at Nobára.

8th April

American Task Group 52 was instructed to cover Sakishima during the day in the absence of Task Force 57.

0600. Met Task Unit 112.2.5 and Task Unit 112.2.1 in position Cootie One 21° 12′N 128° 44′E and commenced to refuel the Fleet in excellent weather conditions. By dusk all ships except one battleship and one carrier had fuelled from the 5 tankers. HMCS *Uganda*, HM Ships *Urchin* and *Ursa*, reinforcements together with HMNZS *Gambia* rejoining after towing the damaged HMS *Ulster* to Leyte, joined TF 57.

9th April

0630. Recommenced fuelling, which was completed by 1500. HMS *Undaunted* from Leyte rejoined TU 122.2.5. HMS *Whirwind* joined Task Force 57 from TU 11.2.5. HMS *Whelp* with A/S defects was despatched to Leyte.

14th April

06.30. Made contact with Task Unit 112.2.5 and Tanker Group consisting of 5 tankers in position Cootie One 21° 12′N 128° 44′E.

HM Ships *Formidable, Kempenfelt* and *Wessex* were also met and joined Task Force 57.

Fuelling was commenced in fine weather and proceeded with less delays than usual.

HMS *Illustrious* was sailed for Leyte at 1755 screened by HM Ships *Urania* and *Quality.*

16th April

In the afternoon a Seafire landing on *Indefatigable* bounced, cleared the barriers and crashed. The pilot was unhurt, but the plane wrecked an Avenger, damaged a Firefly, and knocked two ratings over the side. *Quiberon* picked up one, but the other man was unfortunately not recovered.

18th April

0630. Commenced fuelling from Tanker Group of 5 tankers in area Mosquito. Also met Captain D.7 in *Napier* with *Norman* and *Nepal*, all of whom joined Task Force 57, and *Undaunted* who rejoined her Flotilla. Mail, stores, and correspondence were transferred but no replenishment aircraft were available; owing to the extension of operation programme none had been expected. By dusk the Fleet had completed fuelling and disengaged from the Tanker Group for the night.

Three of the five tankers, with Captain Escort Forces in *Pheasant*, were detached and sailed for Leyte.

21st April
HMS *Crane* was despatched to overtake the Tanker Group who were on their way to Leyte, to relieve HMS *Kempenfelt*, who was ordered to proceed at best speed to Leyte.

22nd April
During the day, and taking advantage of the presence of Chief Staff Officer to C.-in-C., BPF on board HMS *King George V*, Rear Admiral E. J. P. Brind, C.B., C.B.E. (Flag Officer Commanding 4th Cruiser Squadron), and Captain J. P. Wright, D.S.O. (C.S.O. to A.C.1), were transferred by destroyer to the Fleet Flagship for conferences. C.S.4 in HMS *Swiftsure* was detached at 2000 with HM Ships *Gambia, Uganda* and *Euryalus* to proceed ahead to Leyte. Paravanes were streamed at 1700.

Rear Admiral Sir Philip Vian's Report in the C in C's Despatch included the following:

3. *Fighter Direction*. Whilst the number of aircraft shot down by the fighters is small, it represents, I think, a high proportion of those available for this treatment. Fighter direction, under the control and inspiration of Acting Commander E. D. G. Lewin, D.S.O., D.S.C., Royal Navy, making use of experienced teams in HM Ships *Indomitable* and *Victorious*, has been of the highest order; the Staff Fighter Direction Officer, Fifth Fleet, Lieutenant-Commander H. A. Rowe, United States Navy, loaned for the operation, informs me that it has been as good as or better than the Fifth Fleet standard.

4. *Hellcats*. The operational efficiency of No. 5 Wing, trained and led by Acting Lieutenant-Commander (A) T. W. Harrington, R.N., has, throughout the whole course of the operation, been remarkable. 5. *Corsairs*. The Corsair Squadrons have done all that was asked of them and more.

In leading their squadrons the work of Temporary Acting Lieutenant-Commander (A) A. M. Tritton, R.N.V.R., No. 1830 Squadron, HMS *Illustrious*, and Temporary Acting Lieutenant-Commander (A) C. C. Tomkinson, R.N.V.R. (since killed), No. 1836 Squadron, HMS *Victorious*, has been outstanding.

6. *Seafires*. The Seafires have been used for CAP over the Fleet. Owing to their short endurance they have not been suitable for accompanying offensive strikes to the range at which these operations have been carried out.

7. *Fireflies*. It had been intended to use Fireflies against enemy coasters and coastal vessels, but these have been painfully few. On the only occasion on which the chance of air combat presented itself, they lost no time at all; four

Sonias out of five to the guns of two Fireflies.

Acting Major V. B. G. Cheesman, D.S.O., M.B.E., D.S.C., R.M., continues to lead this Squadron with distinction and address.

8. *Avengers.* Avengers have been employed throughout as bombers and have executed this task with success; their losses to flak have been relatively high; this I attribute firstly to the determination of their leaders in coming through cloud, which has frequently been at 2,000 feet, to discharge their load, and secondly to the invisibility of the enemy flak. Four hundred tons of high explosive bombs have been unloaded on enemy airfields and installations.

The service of Acting Lieutenant-Commander (A) D. R. Foster, R.N.V.R., HMS *Victorious*, 849 Squadron has been outstanding.

13. *Performance of Carriers.* The carriers have, I think, stood up well to, what is for us, so extended a period of operational duty in the course of which 2,429 operational sorties have been flown. The maintenance crews, whom it has never been possible to stand down on any day throughout the operation, have done their work well; the carriers, but for shortage of pilots, bombs and stores, would be good to continue operating; that this should be so reflects credit on their Commanding Officers:

Captain M. M. Denny, C.B., C.B.E., R.N.—HMS *Victorious*
Captain Q. D. Graham, C.B.E., D.S.O., R.N.—HMS *Indefatigable*
Captain C. E. Lambe, C.B., C.V.O., R.N.—HMS *Illustrious*
Captain J. A. S. Eccles, R.N.—HMS *Indomitable*
Captain P. Ruck-Keene, C.B.E., R.N.—HMS *Formidable**

(*This ship was brought forward from Leyte at short notice to relieve HMS *Illustrious* and has operated in an admirable manner in spite of having joined the Fleet without previous experience of existing practice.)

In his reports Admiral Rawlings mentioned:

On arrival at Leyte I waited upon Admiral Kincaid, Commander 7th fleet, and with him met Vice Admiral J. L. Kauffman, Commander Philippine Sea Frontier and Rear Admiral R. O. Davis, Commander Amphibious Group 13. They all lunched on board my Flagship. Commodore E. M. Evans-Lombe, Captain (S) J. R. Allfrey, Chief of Staff and Secretary to C.-in-C., BPF, after most useful discussions with Flag Officers of the Task Force, left Leyte by air for Guam: Captain E. C. Ewen, U.S.N. Liaison Officer with TF 57, travelled with them.

By the evening of 30th April the replenishment of the Fleet was completed, thanks to the energy and foresight of the Rear Admiral commanding Fleet Train, and those under him, the arrangements made by the Rear Admiral Commanding Destroyers greatly contributing. The Tanker Group, to top up the Fleet on their passage north, sailed from Leyte at 0700 on 30th April. HMS

Quilliam from Australia joined TF 57 on 29th April.

The 7th Destroyer Flotilla, consisting of HM Ships *Napier* (Capt. D.7), *Nepal, Norman* and *Nizam*, were, for the initial stages of the operation, assigned to Task Force 112 for duty as escorts with the Tanker Groups.

HM Ships *Illustrious, Argonaut, Wager* and *Whelp* remained at Leyte to sail on 4th May for Sydney and refit. HMS *Argonaut* was left with orders to put into Lae, New Guinea, on her way south.

HMS *Ulster* with bomb damage remained at Leyte having damage made good sufficient for her to proceed to another port for major repairs.

3rd May

At 0600 made rendezvous in position Mosquito (1) with the Commander, Logistic Support Group in HMS *Crane,* HM Ships *Avon* and *Whimbrel* and RFAs *San Ambrosio, San Adolpho* and *Cedardale.*

Uganda, whilst casting off from her tanker, inadvertently lay back on one oil hose, which parted and fouled a propeller. This she was able to clear by the use of shallow water divers. By 1530 fuelling was completed.

4th May

At 0827 an enemy aircraft approached the Force at a great height. Our fighters could not get high enough to intercept through lack of oxygen, and the enemy was never seen and retired to the westward.

Before deciding to disengage from the carriers for bombardment I weighed up the following considerations:

(a) The need for bombardment in an endeavour to reduce A.A. fire ashore.

(b) Conditions for bombardment near the target had been reported as excellent.

(c) The effect of morale of ships of the bombarding force would be most beneficial.

To be balanced against this I took into consideration the fact that the Fleet had been sighted. That in itself was nothing strange, and had happened several times before without being followed by any attack on the Fleet.

After discussing the situation with A.C.1., I detached with the bombarding force at 1000 in position 23° 54′N 125° 10′E and closed Miyako at 24 knots. The carriers provided an additional CAP for this force as well as aircraft for spotting.

At 1155 the bombarding force passed through position 24° 33,5′N 125° 10′E on the bombarding course of 070° at 15 knots. HM Ships *King George V* and *Howe* were in open order line ahead and screened by 25th Destroyer flotilla and HM Ships *Euryalus* and *Black Prince* who occupied the two port, i.e. inshore, positions on the screen. HMS *Swiftsure,* HMNZS *Gambia* and HMCS *Uganda* in open order line ahead were stationed 27° 3 miles, i.e. fire off port quarter of the Fleet Flagship. Conditions were ideal.

At 1205 fire was opened. HM Ships *Euryalus* and *Black Prince* carried out a simultaneous 'air burst' shoot on the A.A. defence area of Nobara airfield. HM Ships *King George V* and *Howe* bombarded Hirara airfield and the A.A. defence area to the north of the airfield, respectively. On completion of the 'air burst' shot HM Ships *Swiftsure* and HMNZS *Gambia* bombarded Nobara airfield, and HMCS *Uganda* Sukhama air strip.

In spite of comparatively close ranges, no form of opposition from the shore was encountered. Fire was ceased at 1250.

A few minutes after bombardment was commenced I received a signal from A.C.1 to say that HMS *Formidable* had been hit and was reduced to 18 knots. I accordingly informed the Bombarding Force and instructed ships to speed up the bombardment. As signals were corrupt and the situation not quite clear I ordered the cease fire a little earlier than planned and at 1247 turned the force to the southward and closed the carriers at 25 knots.

At about 1100 three small groups of bogeys were detected to the westward, and were soon followed up by a fourth. Probably 16 to 20 enemy aircraft were employed with some acting as decoys. Fighters engaged one group working round to the southward, but one kamikaze group penetrated to the carriers and was first detected when a plane was seen diving on the Force. Analysis shows that this group escaped detection either because, in the absence of the Bombarding Force, too many of the reduced number of radar sets were fully engaged tracking the diversionary planes and too few acting as warning sets, or else because they made a very low approach followed by a very high climb at about 15 miles range.

There were no bandits on the screen within 20 miles when at 1131 a Zeke was seen diving from a great height on the HMS *Formidable* and engaged by gunfire. A.C.1 there-upon manoeuvred his Force under wheel at high speed by successive emergency turns. Though reported hit by close range weapons from his target, the kamikaze crashed into the flight deck of HMS *Formidable* near the island structure and started a large fire in the deck park of aircraft. A.C.1 manoeuvred the formation to keep in close touch with the damaged ship, whose speed was temporarily reduced to 18 knots.

The kamikaze appeared to release his bomb just before the aircraft hit the deck, causing the following damage: casualties 8 killed and 47 wounded; 1 Corsair and 10 Avengers damaged, beyond repair; all radar except one set put out of action; both barriers damaged,the forward one irreparable; flight deck holed 2 feet square, indentation 10 feet square and 2 feet deep at the centre; armoured deck splinter passed through hangar deck, horizontal partition between down takes, escape hatch which was shut, and so to the centre boiler room where it caused slight damage and loss of steam, and finally pierced the inner bottom.

Two minutes later, at 1133, 2 enemy aircraft crashed in flames ten miles to the southward, the result of our fighters.

At 1134 a Zeke flying from forward to aft off the starboard bow of HMS *Indomitable* was engaged by 4.5 in. guns and temporarily disappeared in cloud.

It soon reappeared diving at the ship steeply at about 60° from the starboard beam. The Force was turning to starboard at the time and HMS *Indomitable*'s wheel was increased to hard over. As the plane approached it was heavily engaged by close range weapons from the ship and set on fire; it flattened out at the last moment, deck landed on the flight deck, and bounded over the side, taking the radar arrays of the port midships directors with it. The bomb appeared to explode shortly after the plane submerged.

At 1142 another Zeke dived steeply on HMS *Indomitable* whose close range weapons and those of HMS *Quality* hit him hard and often. The aircraft burst into flames and crashed into the sea about 10 yards off the starboard bow of the ship.

No damage or casualties were sustained in either of these two attacks, apart from that caused to the radar arrays.

At 1220 a Jill was shot down by fighters from HMS *Indomitable* and half an hour later a Val met the same fate by Seafires from HMS*Indefatigable*. By 1420 the Bombarding Force was being manoeuvred close to the Carrier Force, and the Fleet reformed in Cruising Disposition at 1450.

At about 1515 Corsairs from HMS *Victorious* intercepted and shot down a Judy to the northward.

Although at various times during the afternoon there were enemy aircraft in the vicinity, it was not until 1720 that the developments of another attack became evident. This was however broken up very satisfactorily by our fighters. At 1721 a Judy, believed to be the Gestapo of the Group, was shot down from 24,000 feet to the eastward by fighters. A few minutes later Seafires from HMS *Indefatigable* intercepted 4 Zekes to the southward and shot down 3 before the other escaped to the northward.

At 1732 a Hellcat returning for an emergency landing was fired on by HMS *Formidable* and hit. The aircraft crashed but the pilot was rescued unhurt by HMS *Undaunted*.

At 1820 Corsairs from HMS *Victorious* were sent to intercept a bogey to the northward. They found and shot down the Zeke.

6th May

At 0630 met in area Cootie, HM and HMA Ships *Crane, Ruler, Striker, Napier, Norman, Nepal, Avon, Whimbrel, Pheasant,* and RFAs *Wave King, Wave Monarch, San Ambrosio, San Adolpho, Cedardale.*

HMAS *Napier* joined TF 57 vice HMS *Kempenfelt* with defects.

Casualties from HMS *Formidable* were transferred to HMS *Striker*, who in company with HMS *Kempenfelt*, took departure at 1915 for Leyte. The need for a hospital ship in the vicinity was considered and CTF 112 was requested to sail one as soon as ready if Admiralty instructions could by now be complied with.

9th May

At 1145 the Fleet was sighted by a bogey which approached within 30 miles, fighters drove it off but were unable to catch it.

At 1645 bogeys were detected very low 22 miles to the westward, coming in fast. Four Seafires intercepted at 15 miles, but allowed themselves to be all decoyed away by one aircraft which they shot down. Meanwhile four other enemy planes evaded another division of Seafires, and after climbing to about 3,000 feet penetrated to the Fleet.

From 1650 onwards the Fleet was radically manoeuvred by emergency turns at 22 knots. One minute after such a turn of 60° to starboard was executed, a suicider made a 10° angle dive onto HMS *Victorious* from her starboard quarter. The enemy was well hit by close range weapons but crashed onto the fight deck near the forward lift. The resulting fire was quickly brought under control, but the bomb explosion holed the flight deck, put the accelerator out of action, rendered one 4.5 in. gun unserviceable, and damaged one lift hoisting motor.

At 1656 another kamikaze made a shallow power glide from astern on HMS *Victorious*. Though hit hard by gunfire, and well on fire, it hit the flight deck aft a glancing blow, and burning furiously passed over the side. Damage to the ship was confined to one arrester unit out of action, a 40 mm. gun director destroyed, and four Corsairs on deck damaged beyond repair.

Casualties from both these attacks were three killed, four seriously injured, and 15 wounded.

At 1657 a third suicider made a pass at HMS *Victorious* but then shifted target to HMS *Howe* further ahead, and approached her from the starboard quarter in a long shallow dive. This time the attacker was hit at a more reasonable range, and continued to be so until he crashed in flames 100 yards from HMS *Howe* after passing over the quarterdeck.

At 1705 a fourth kamikaze approached HMS *Formidable* and then HMS *Indomitable*, being engaged by both ships without apparent result. It then turned and dived into the after deck park of HMS *Formidable*.

There was a large explosion and fire and a great deal of smoke. Speed was reduced to 15 knots to aid control of the fire which was extinguished at 1720. Six Corsairs and one Avenger were destroyed by fire on deck. The explosion blew out a flight deck rivet and thus allowed burning petrol to fall into the hangar which had to be sprayed. As a result a further three Avengers and eight Corsairs were damaged. The total replacements required were therefore four Avengers and 14 Corsairs, of which three Avengers and seven Corsairs were flyable duds.

Casualties were fortunately light—one killed and a few injured.

At 1755 HMS *Formidable* reported being fit to land on aircrat and that during the engagement she had definitely shot down one enemy by gunfire.

10th May

At 0610 in position Cootie (1) met and formed on Tanker Group consisting of HM Ships *Speaker, Ruler, Nepal, Crane, Pheasant, Whyalla, Ballarat, Woodcock, Weasel* (Tug) and RFAs *Arndale, Aase Maersk, Dingledale, San Amado.* The usual fuelling, exchange of mail correspondence and stores, and the replenishment of aircraft continued throughout the day.

A.C.1 visited HM Ships *Victorious* and *Formidable* to inspect damage, and found that temporary repairs being carried out showed that both ships would be sufficiently operational to continue the programme of strikes.

A.C.1 and C.S.4 then visited me to discuss measures to give better protection to the carriers, and in the light of the enemy's apparent change of tactics in attacks on this Force. The enemy appeared to have abandoned his previous practice of a high approach in favour of a low one, thereby greatly reducing the length of warning and making interception by fighters much more difficult.

To combat this, it was decided:

(a) To station two radar pickets, each consisting of a 6 in. cruiser and a destroyer, 12 miles to the north west and south westward of the Fleet so as to increase the range of detection. Two fighters would be allocated to each picket, and at first contact with the enemy, other fighters would be sent to the threatened sector.

(b) To bring in the 5.25 in. cruisers from the screen and to station them with the main body of the fleet to increase A.A. protection for the carriers whenever in the operation area.

(c) To station a destroyer astern of each carrier to afford more gun protection in what appears to be the enemy's favourite position for attacking carriers.

(d) To increase mutual gun support when attack threatened by bringing in the carriers to the 2,000 yards circle, and the battleships and cruisers of the main body until their distance from adjacent carriers is 2,000 yards. This new disposition was to be given a trial during the next strike period.

16th May

Five bomber strikes were sent to the islands during the day, three to Miyako and two to Ishigaki. As a result of these and the efforts of the CAPs, all runways were made unserviceable; four new aircraft which appeared operational were straffed but did not burn, 3 others were damaged; 10 small craft of various classes were damaged and four of them left in a sinking condition; 4 lorry loads of Japanese troops were exterminated; a large explosion was caused in Ohama town; 5 direct hits with S.A.P. bombs were made on a large cave shelter.

Several of our planes were damaged by flak.

One Avenger taking off from HMS *Formidable* ditched; HMS *Quality* rescued the crew one of whom was injured. A Corsair from HMS *Victorious* developed engine trouble at 20,000 feet and was forced to ditch near the Fleet; HMS *Tenacious* rescued the pilot.

At 1735 a Corsair from HMS *Victorious* ditched 3 miles from Miyako; the Lifeguard submarine USS *Bluefish* was informed and made another skilful rescue by picking up this pilot during the night. The Dumbo aircraft from Kerama Retto, unaware of the rescue, as was A.C.1 at the time, carried out a search the following morning. These fine efforts by the American rescue sumbarines and aircraft have been greatly appreciated.

17th May

At 1200 a Hellcat from HMS *Indomitable* was ordered to bale out just ahead of the Fleet as the pilot was unble to release an armed bomb. The pilot was picked up by HMS *Troubridge.*

18th May

At 0545 met in area Cootie HM Ships *Crane, Ruler, Grenville, Chaser, Norman, Whimbrel, Bendigo, Parret, Weasel* and RFAs *San Ambrosio, San Adolpho, Cedardale.* The Fleet formed on the Tanker Group and fuelling and exchange of aircraft and stores commenced.

HMS *Black Prince* transferred bombs from HMS *Formidable* to HMS *Indefatigable.*

At 1103 HMS *Formidable* was observed to be on fire, caused by a Corsair in the hangar accidentally firing her guns into an Avenger: the latter exploded. Fighting this serious fire was made difficult by the fact that the fire curtains were out of action due to earlier enemy suicide attacks. It was extinguished by drenching the hangar, but at a cost of 7 Avengers and 21 Corsairs in conditions varying from complete loss to flyable duds. By the evening the Commanding Officer reported that he considered his ship capable of operating with jury lighting in the hangar. Arrangements were therefore made to replace her damaged aircraft as far as possible, and for the ship to continue operations at any rate for the next strike period. As the repaired barriers in HMS *Victorious* could not be guaranteed to stand up to further barrier crashes or enemy damage the availability of HMS *Formidable*'s flight deck was an important factor, and in any case, it would only lower her morale were she unable to continue in the Fleet.

19th May

At 0645 the Fleet again formed on the Tanker Group, which now included the *Robert Maersk* with supplies of bombs, and HMS *Cairns*. The transfer of bombs, fuel and stores was continued. HMS *Victorious* and later HMS *Indomitable* went alongside *Robert Maersk* and embarked bombs by whip and inhaul method, the rate of transfer being about 75 bombs per hour.

Continuous rain and low visibility in the afternoon prevented flying and seriously upset the numbers of replenishment aircraft to be flown in to HMS *Formidable* and the flyable duds which were to be flown from her to HMS *Chaser*.

Hospital ship *Tjitjalengka* was contacted by aircraft and directed to the Fleet: she embarked a few sick and casualties.

HMAS *Norman* joined TF 57 replacing HMAS *Nepal*. Captain D.27 in HMS *Kempenfelt* assumed Senior Officer Destroyers for experience, vice Captain D.4 in *Quilliam* who remained with the Force.

At 1800 detached HM Ships *Bendigo* and *Cairns* with RFAs *San Abrosio, San Adolpho* and *Cedardale* to Manus. HMS *Parrett* acted as additional escort to them until dusk on 21st May, with orders to detach and proceed to Leyte at that time. AT 1930 HMAS *Nepal* was detached to Leyte to augment the escorts available to CTF 112 for the forthcoming move south of the Fleet Train.

22nd May

At 1800 HMS *Formidable* was detached with orders to proceed to Manus and then Sydney to expedite repair of battle damage. She was escorted by HM Ships *Kempenfelt* and *Whirlwind*, both of whom were due for refit.

23rd May
At 0745 the Fleet reformed on the Tanker Group, and fuelling and exchange of stores were continued.

HMNZS *Achilles* joined TF 57.

During the day 2 Hellcats from HMS *Chaser* crashed into the sea: neither pilot was recovered.

At 1800 HM and HMA Ships *Chaser, Speaker* and *Napier* were detached for Manus.

25th May
CTF 57 in HMS *King George V* with HM Ships *Troubridge, Tenacious* and *Termagent* detached at 2200 and set course for Guam.

From A/B Ern Crimp, HMS *Victorious*

'TAKING STEPS' IN SYDNEY
HMS *Victorious* had returned to Sydney from a series of raids on Sakishima Gunto, and my flight deck duties were now swopped to harbour routine, that of sternsheetsman of the Captain's motor boat. We had just taken Captain Denny ashore and on return to the ship had been instructed to take a party of officers ashore. Our boatload of immaculately clad gentlemen shone in whiter than white tropical uniforms as we sped towards Circular Quay. All then disembarked except one, he demanded to be taken to another part of the harbour not used by us. The coxswain on querying was angrily and loudly told to 'obey his order'. The motor boat then sped across the harbour again. When we reached the spot, the boat slowed and the coxswain was pointing out something to the lieutenant who was angrily banging on the cabin canopy and pointing inshore. As we made our approach I saw the reason for our coxswain's query, a flight of steps that was covered with green slimy weed. The lower steps washing in the waves created by our approach, rather slowly and cautiously the boat then closed in, just as we were preparing to hook on somehow and being two or three feet out, to our amazement the impatient officer made a flying leap . . . up . . . out . . . and down, arms and legs flying as he bounced on his back and head first into the mucky flotsom laden water at the bottom, a spluttering green slimy officer was hauled aboard the Captain's boat. His cap fished out with my boathook, without waiting for an order the coxswain sped back to the ship in the distance, both the coxswain and bowman hidden up forward must have been in fits of laughter, I was in agony trying to hide my feelings as I stood within sight of 'Neptune's Reject' dripping and smelling strongly of seaweed etc. in our spotless boat. . . . It was a long journey back as I tried to look concerned when all I really wanted to do was howl with laughter. At last the after gangway with a shocked unbelieving gangways

staff peering down at us. As I hooked on to the boatrope I kept my eyes glued to the boathook not daring to look at them. He raced up the ladder and away inboard. We were told to secure to the boom and report at once to the officer of the watch. We three were laughing like idiots as we climbed to the boom and came back aboard, pausing to control ourselves we then returned to the officer of the watch, as the coxswain was telling the full story I stood this time with eyes glued to an overhead rivet, determined to keep a straight face, until . . . the coxswain said 'and then he fell in sir' . . . I saw it all so clearly again, my control went, I burst, I shrieked with laughter setting off my mates. The quartermaster and the marine bugler, the officer of the watch must have been a credit to Dartmouth training, a brief smile, and as we fought for control again he said in those well known words of an officer, 'I see, carry on please' . . . Words which had me howling again as we doubled away through the hangar. If visits to Sydney eased the tension of action in the Pacific with the BPF, then we must have been ready for anything the Japs could throw at us including themselves after that afternoon. Sydney to this day means 'slimy steps' to me, pride before a fall indeed.

It goes without saying that any ships' boats crews would always try to prove how good they were especially when coming alongside another ship fully aware that critical eyes were watching you, in the Captain's motor boat our boathook drill was naturally perfection. Our leading seaman coxswain matched our drill with his handling of the boat, he would head for the after gangway of a ship flat out and as we neared the ship both the bowman's and sternsheetsman's boathooks would go through the drill as one, sheer perfection to watch. Then a last second change to neutral flashing into reverse and the boat stopped dead at the gangway, our boathooks catching on the respective boat ropes hanging over the ship's side. The Captain simply taking an easy step on to the gangway. That's how it worked . . . until . . . we had a relief coxswain this day. We had to go to HMS *KGV,* flagship to pick up our Captain. The flagship, critical eyes indeed, we hoped our 'relief driver' was up to our coxswain's standard. We couldn't ask him if he was any good but we hoped. Well, on the way he seemed to know what he was doing, we arrived at the flagship and received a haughty wave off from the officer of the watch, then we saw our Captain on the quarterdeck with the Admiral, eyes everywhere, a raised arm signalled us in, bosun's party standing ready at the head of the spotless gangway, marine sentry at attention looking like a carved figure, we stood ready as the relief coxswain headed flat out for the gangway, we both went through our drill with the boathooks knowing this was even more vital to put on a perfect display. We'd show them, flagship watch this in envy, here we are, change gear now, both our hooks flashed towards the ropes and then . . . he missed the bloody gears and we crashed full speed into the bottom of the gangway and bounced off . . . leaving my boathook swinging on the flagship's side. If I hadn't let go I'd have been swinging on the end of the damned thing. Horror struck me, if the fool does get alongside how the hell would I hold the boat's stern in the gangway? The gangway was being examined. Oh! all eyes were on us, no doubt about that now, in disgrace we crawled back, my eyes looking straight ahead, I did not dare lift them to deck level. My boathook was about two foot out of reach of my hands when fully stretched up. My brain frantically trying to find a solution. Then the final humiliation, a grinning marine lowered the boatrope until I could reach up and retrieve my lost boathook, pipes shrilled and our very red-faced Captain came down the gangway, as we left the side of the flagship I saw many laughing sailors' faces, so too must our Captain have seen. My thoughts were that at the least I was due for a change of job. After the obvious inquest our 'relief driver' was relieved of his leading seaman rank on the spot. It was decided that my boathook had been torn out of my hands. For months we dreaded getting an order to proceed to *KGV.* We felt sorry for our coxswain for you see no perfection could ever wipe out 'our suicide attack' on the flagship's gangway, and the navy is very slow to forget such episodes. No doubt we were the main topic over many gins in a few wardrooms after that day, and without a doubt laughed at on a few messdecks too.

It was some time at the end of 1945. We were back in Sydney for a welcome break. *Victorious,* in common with other ships of the British Pacific Fleet had been made very welcome by our Australian friends. My mate and I were at our 'home' and our hosts had laid on a party for us. Now I must say here I was a most anti-social blighter. I detested parties and especially the silly games that were played at the time, all very childlike in my opinion. I groaned when it was suggested 'Let's have some games'. During the next ten minutes or so I was a reluctant participant. Then came the moment I had dreaded, I had to pay a forfeit. 'Show us all how to do a Hula Dance'. Clever boy replied only if I can do it properly dressed only in a grass skirt (that's got them). I remember this girl picking up a grass skirt and passing it to me with a charming smile. I could have crowned her! To loud cheers I was led out of the room to change and led back to the strains of Hawaiian guitars (to think that up to then I had loved that sound). Well I had to perform my dance, hastily glossing over that performance that ended to rousing cheers I went back to dress again, then I heard another loud cheer and on returning to the room found my mate had had to pay a forfeit. When I was told what it had been I knew that luck was not with me! He, poor fellow had been told 'To pick out the nicest girl in the room and take her out in the garden to look at the moon for ten minutes.' Now it's just possible that I could have managed that! Actually the good Aussies as usual had unwound us from the tension of war in the Pacific on a carrier for a week or so. Believe me it was a strain, yet even today I groan at the mention of a 'party', the Hula Dance? That took some living down, I remember cursing my mate when some Hawaiian music was being played on the radio and chaps in the mess said, 'Listen Ern, they're playing your tune!'

'SLOPS' STORE SURPRISE SALE

The clothing store was open for business. Clothing was known as 'Slops' to Jack. I joined the queue that vanished down the ladders of a couple of decks, casually chatting to my mates. Gradually we got nearer to the store issue window. Commotion, then sounds of laughter floated up to us, when the next man came up, we asked what was going on. Still chuckling he asked what we were getting. When one of us said some underwear, he said with another laugh 'I bet you do!' We found later there had been a mess up when the clothing allocation had been made to the ship and instead of an issue of cotton underpants we only had a choice of WRENS knickers. There was white, navy blue and black available. Strange to say they were sold out by the time the store closed. A sort of morale booster perhaps?

WHERE IS THE CAPTAIN'S MOTOR BOAT THEN?

As we were in harbour my flight deck party job had been once again suspended and I was working normal duties as a seaman. Now at this particular point in time I was one of the three man crew of the Captain's motor boat. We were in a large harbour out east which had a fast running powerful tide. It was a job I liked and weather conditions were perfect. I was the sternsheetsman in the boat. Another seaman as bowman and a Leading Seaman as Coxswain. This day we had taken the Captain ashore and returned to the ship. Secured to the quarterdeck boom and one by one climbed up the rope ladder, walked along the boom, over the guardrails and went forward below to our messdeck. As we reached there the ship's Tannoy was loudly calling, 'Away Captain's motor boats crew at the double.' Also, 'Away motor cutter crew at the double.' Cursing ourselves we raced up and back along the passageways aft, burst out on the quarterdeck and were about to climb over the guardrails onto the boom when we stopped in confusion. The boat had vanished. We then rushed to the starboard after gangway and the Officer of the Watch, reported our presence. He glared at us and barked, 'Where is the captain's motor boat then?' We mumbled that we did not know, noting at the same time the grinning faces of the Marine Bugler and Duty Quartermaster who were standing behind him. He then screamed 'I'll tell you where it is, out there,' pointing to a distant motor boat that was bobbing about en route to the harbour entrance. 'Get it back and then report to me.' Now we knew why the motor cutter had been called out. They took us out and I dare not repeat their comments here. Later the motor boat safely retrieved and correctly secured this time to the boom we very sheepishly faced the Officer of the Watch again. As expected we were truly for it. Unheard of! No-one loses a boat in harbour! A disgrace! We progressed up the line, Commander's report. Captain's report. Defaulter, off caps. We stood in line facing the Big Man. We all admitted blame. Records checked. Strong lecture on not taking things for granted. Check, even if you know your mate has just carried out the work. Finally no punishment. The Captain realised our messmates would never let us forget 'Losing my Boat'. Incidentally, neither did he. On leaving the boat for a long time after that episode, he would say, 'Carry on thank you . . . make sure she's secured lads.'

From: 'The War with Japan' by Charles Bateson

Towards the end of May, because of the strain on commanders of continuous action, especially under kamikaze attack, Halsey relieved Spruance and McCain took over from Mitscher, the fleet again becoming Third Fleet. By June 10 there was no need for Third Fleet to remain in Okinawan waters. Kamikaze attacks had declined sharply in the face of improved methods of meeting them and the reduced supply of suicide pilots, air power on Okinawa had been built up substantially, and the airfields of Kyushu were being neutralized by superfortresses bombing from bases in China and the Marianas.

Okinawa was the costliest operation in the Central Pacific. American losses were 12,520 killed—army 4,675, marines 2,938 and navy 4,907—and 36,631 wounded—army 18,099, marines 13,708 and navy 4,824. Non-battle casualties among the marines and army troops totalled 16,211. Thirty-six ships were sunk and 368 damaged, the majority by air action and 763 American aircraft were lost in the three months from April 1 to July 1. About 110,000 Japanese were killed in the land fighting and 7,400 were taken prisoners.

From: 'Okinawa 1945' by Ian Gow

The participation of the British Pacific Fleet in Iceberg was, despite all the concern beforehand, a model of co-operative relations and a resounding success which did much to improve the sometimes strained relations between the British Empire and the United States.

From J. C. Thompson, OBE, MA

Memory says there was a moan that the U.S. Authorities gave every combatant at Okinawa a white medal ribbon to be worn on the right breast—and better still, 50 bucks.

Rumour said that the Admiralty had turned the offer down for the British Fleet.

CHAPTER SEVEN

The Third Operation — Japan

From 'Carrier Operations in World War II' by J. D. Brown

The only Fleet carrier of the British Pacific Fleet to see action during June 1945 was *Implacable,* which had arrived early in the month from Europe, sailing for Manus almost immediately. In order to complete her air group's work-up with some operational experience she sailed from Manus on 10th June in company with the CVE *Ruler,* which had replaced *Speaker* in the Fleet Train in May, and five cruisers to strike at Truk, in the Caroline Islands. This once-important Japanese naval stronghold had been reduced to impotence by the repeated carrier air strikes from TF 58 and by the American strategy of isolation. There were therefore few worthwhile targets for the Avengers, Fireflies and dive-bombing Seafires, but the two days of operations, 14th and 15th June, brought the ships up to a fully operational status by the standards of the remainder of the fleet.

On return to Manus *Implacable* was joined by the main body of the BPF, reduced by defects and refit requirements to *Formidable, Victorious* and *King George V. Indefatigable* was delayed at Sydney with machinery defects and although she rejoined the Fleet at Manus she was unable to sail with them for Japanese waters, rejoining after the first series of strikes. *Indomitable* was refitting and took no further part in major operations before the end of the war, although six of her Hellcats were transferred to *Formidable,* providing the Fleet with its only night-fighter defence.

The BPF sailed from Manus on 9th July to join Admiral J. S. McCain's Fast Carrier Force, TF 38, off Japan. On turnover and re-designation of the US Pacific Fleet, the Fifth under Admiral Spruance to the Third under Admiral Halsey, the former told his relief that he considered the British Pacific Fleet to be sufficiently experienced to join TF 38 as an autonomous group. Accordingly, TF 37 became virtually the fourth group of TF 38, adding its 180-odd aircraft to the 1,200 embarked in 16 American carriers. After the arrival of *Indefatigable* there were 255 Fleet Air Arm aircraft aboard the carriers of 1st ACS.

From: Sub. Lt. (A) D. R. Wells, RNVR, HMS *Implacable*

The first incident happened on the night of June 4, 1945 when the ship was practising prior to carrying out strikes on the Truk Islands on our way from Manus to join the BPF.

The C.O. Alan Swanton and I were to be catapulted off the ship on some night exercise, with the C.O. first to go. As we were preparing the aircraft, the C.O.'s observer, a Lieut. Matthews RN, came to me and said the C.O.'s radio was on the blink and would I swap aircraft with him. The ground crew duly attached the aircraft to the steam catapult (it was a dark night). I revved up the engine and flashed the green light to indicate I was ready for launch and braced myself for the kick. Instead of being catapulted into the air, the aircraft swung round on the deck, tottered on the edge of the flight deck near the 4.5″ guns and fell backwards into the sea. The first thing I remembered was water rushing into the open cockpit and me thinking it was time I got the hell out of there.

It took some time to disentangle myself from safety straps, parachute and wireless connectors and when I finally broke surface, I was very pleased to see my observer, Tony Younger and TAG Durnell were already out, but were beginning to think the worst had happened to me.

We were picked up by our attendant destroyer which I believe was HMS *Terpsichore*. We had not been aboard very long when I was asked to go and see the skipper who informed me they had a message from *Implacable* who wanted to know what had happened. I replied, 'So would I!'

As they could not make use of the catapult again until they knew, I was asked to return to *Implacable* that night. This involved stopping the two ships, lowering a boat and rowing across—I vaguely remember someone shouting 'slip the grips' and off we went. I had not heard that term since I did a bit of boat drill at St. Vincent. When we reached *Implacable*, they lowered a Jacobs ladder and there was quite a swell. The bosun said, 'When I say jump, you bloody well jump.' When the order came, I lunged and caught hold of the ladder and climbed what seemed a hell of a way to the quarter deck. The following day they held a form of court of enquiry and eventually came to the conclusion one of the restraining bolts had come off the aircraft.

The ironic thing was that my own aircraft, U for Uncle, was being flown by my best friend Phil Meakin, later on the same night. He did not get sufficient speed along the flight deck and went off the bows straight into the drink. Fortunately he and his crew also got out safely although his observer Andy Moseley was injured in the process.

The second incident which is a little more light-hearted happened on the night of July 11th after we had joined the main force of the BPF.

I was doing an exercise called a SHADEX, which involved dropping flares for some Grumman Hellcats from HMS *Formidable*.

Again it was a pretty dark night and our Commander Air, Charles Evans (who later went on to become a Vice-Admiral), believed in the minimum of deck lighting for night landings (just two rows of cats' eyes). I managed to find the fleet after carrying out the exercise and suddenly the whole flight deck lit up and they flashed a green 'C' with an aldis lamp to join the landing circuit. I thought the old sod has taken pity on me as I'm the only aircraft flying and given me some more light.

The batsman picked me up and I made what must have been my best night deck landing—only one problem—it was the wrong ship!

As they disengaged the arrester hook, I looked out and saw a crane on the starboard side which I knew we had not got on *Implac.* I called up my observer, a Sub Lieut. Ray Milton-Hine, and TAG Durnell and said, 'I've got some good news and some bad news. The bad news is we're on the wrong ship, the good news is, it's one of ours.'

They took me up to the bridge and the captain welcomed me aboard and congratulated me on my good landing. It turned out to be HMS *Formidable,* the flagship of Admiral Vian.

The following morning, the whole of the BPF, consisting of the *KGV,* four fleet carriers, and cruisers and destroyers had to turn into wind to allow me to fly from *Formidable* to *Implacable.*

As you can imagine all the boys in the squadron were there to cheer when I landed on. The frivolity was silenced when Charles Evans' voice came over the loud speaker: 'Send that pilot up to me!!' He asked me what the hell I thought I had been doing. When I tried to explain, he told me not to talk such rubbish and to report back to him at 10.00 hrs. with my C.O. I briefed Alan Swanton on what had happened, and he had a word with Charles Evans—I never heard any more about it.

From: 'HMS *Tenacious*', loaned to me by Admiral G. C. Cowley DSC 2 Bars

The first day of June found us back in Manus, whilst *KGV* had continued down to Sydney, where most of the Fleet had gone. How much we envied them, and how little we relished the prospect of several weeks in the Admiralty Islands! Anyway, we did at least spend some nights in harbour, between excursions to sea for exercises. Three or more of our flotilla arrived—*Terpsichore, Teazer,* and *Tumult,* although the latter touched a shoal on the way in and was sent back to Sydney for repairs. Night life in Manus depended entirely on our ship's cinema, which, thanks to Leading Seaman Ward and the Americans, gave us a different film almost every evening. Frequently air-raid alarms, or, as they were called, 'Flash Reds', occurred—always in the middle of the Ch. & P.O.'s cinema shows, but no aerial attacks developed. Then HMS *Implacable,* a new Fleet carrier recently out from England, came to Manus to work up. Many of our days were spent in escorting her on exercises, and some nights. One of these nights we were called upon to rescue some airmen who had landed in the drink instead of on the flight deck. We did this promptly, and the men were rescued within a few minutes, only one of them being injured. It made us feel our presence fully justified.

In order to break the monotony, perhaps, and to give the Japanese a reminder of our presence, a small task group left Manus as soon as these exercises were successfully completed, to strike the Japanese base of Truk. Besides the destroyers of the 24th Flotilla and the aircraft carriers, there were four cruisers—*Newfoundland, Swiftsure, Uganda,* from Canada, and *Achilles,* from New Zealand. The first part of the operation was one day's 'softening up' of the defences by aircraft from *Implacable.* Then on the second day the cruisers, screened by the 'T's', went in to bombard the shore batteries and the Radar installations. Creaming through the glittering blue seas beneath the tropic sun, the freshly painted ships made a proud sight with their battle ensigns streaming in the breeze. Boldly the force steamed up to the coral atoll which surrounds the islands themselves. Away to port we could see the *Achilles,* with her great New Zealand Blue Ensign, pumping shells into one island. To starboard the Canadians were plastering another. Further up, the *Troubridge* and *Swiftsure* were making a retreat under cover of smoke. Our particular target was a coastal gun sited on a coral islet some two miles to the west of us, and into this, the water, and the palm trees behind we poured no fewer than 140 rounds of H.E. shell. The cruisers fired more. And though Truk had been called the 'Gibraltar of the Pacific', the only resistance we saw were some shell-bursts near the spotting planes. Nevertheless we were wondering all the time when the little yellow men were going to bare their fangs.

At length ammunition was expended and the force rejoined the carriers. We could afford to (and did) feel more confident, and contemptuous of the enemy for such a poor display. On the way back to Manus we had a submarine alarm. Closing up at Action Stations, we waited anxiously and hopefully while the Asdics pinged, and when depth-charges were dropped our hopes rose still further, but, to our extreme disappointment, no evidence of a 'kill' came to the surface. The echo was later classified as 'Non-sub., probably fish', and we returned to normal duties. Every day the carrier was flying-off planes, and destroyers took turns to stand-by in case of accident. We greatly admired the courage and skill of those pilots, and watching them performing the art and intricacies of their trade was a sight of which we never tired.

In Manus again we settled down to a period of harbour drills and training. Each day a party of A.A. ratings would leave the ship and spend a day on the range ashore. Learning the difference between Allied and enemy aircraft was an essential in those days, and we learnt why a 'Val' couldn't possibly be mistaken for a Seafire. During Pacific air-sea operations it wasn't policy to shoot first and identify afterwards. Too many of our own planes had been lost in that way.

For some time it had been known that our Captain was to be relieved, and on return to the ship we discovered that his relief had joined. The departure of Lieut.-Cmdr. Townsend filled us with regret, for he had commanded *Tenacious* since she first commissioned, and he felt the parting as keenly as we did. Our new Captain was Lieut.-Cmdr. G. C. Crowley, D.S.C. and Bar, R.N.—stockily built, and looking very young for a destroyer Commander, although the job was not new to him, as he had previously been in command of HMS *Walpole*.

From Tony Britton of Brentwood. Vol. 9 The War Illustrated No. 211, July 20 1945—HMS *Implacable*

I FLEW TO TRUK WITH FIRST WAVE OF AVENGERS

From dawn on June 15, 1945, to late evening of June 16, Seafires, Fireflies and Avengers from British Pacific Fleet aircraft carriers pounded the Jap bases in the Truk islands. The story is told by Arthur la Bern, Evening Standard reporter with the Pacific Fleet.

My pilot was a 23-year-old Londoner, Sub-lieutenant Walter Davis RNVR. The tail-gunner was Petty-Officer 'Shorty' Elliott, of Romford. I was in the observer's seat. Pilot Wally Davis and Air Gunner Shorty Elliott helped me buckle on my parachute harness and Mae West. Shorty showed me how to work the Browning machine-gun in case of emergency. We climbed into the airplane, and it seemed an eternity while we sat there waiting our turn to take off.

Suddenly, the pilot's voice came over the inter-com: 'Hell, the Boss is in the Oggin!' In Fleet Air Arm slang this meant that the commander of our flight, his crew and airplane had fallen in the sea. I looked down and saw three heads and a yellow dinghy bobbing up and down in the rain-pitted blue of the Pacific.

Their Avenger was sinking some yards away. Their engine had cut out just as they were taking off, and although the pilot put the brake on, it was too late, and they slithered into the sea. All three were picked up, but we had no time to watch the rescue. We were next off, and got away to a clean start. The only thing dirty was the weather.

Our target in the Truk group was the important airfield at Moen. As we approached Truk the sun began to break through the clouds. I looked down and saw huge coral and basaltic reefs circling the lagoon in which we had to pinpoint our target. When we did spot the target I was disappointed. Ten thousand feet below us it looked not more than a heart-shape clot of green jungle. The intercom whistled and Wally Davis said: 'Bomb doors open!'

We were diving down now and bumping with every thousand feet drop. I got the sensation that the target was rushing up at us at something over 300 m.p.h. Every second it seemed to swell in size, and then it seemed to be tilted up at us at an angle of 30 degrees. Then, on the fringe of the steaming mangrove swamps, I saw the airstrip and four parked aircraft like motionless ants. As we dived down there was no sign of life on the target.

We did not see the flak coming up at us, because the Japs were not using tracers. How accurate it was we were in no position to judge. We just could not see it. Even crews of aircraft that got back to the carrier with holes in the wings and fuselage reported that they did not see flak. One pilot did not realize there was any until he got back and found a piece embedded in his Mae West.

We were flying in close formation. I saw the first two Avengers peel off and bomb, and then we bombed at 1,500 ft. The airplane jumped as the bombs were released. We kept going down, while Shorty blazed away in the gun turret. We went down so low that a 300 ft. hill was towering above when we began to climb up again. Then for the first time in my life, I was violently air-sick. Wally Davis happened to glance round just as I put my head down, and his voice came urgently over the inter-com. 'Shorty, has la Bern been hit?' 'No, just being sick as a dog,' said Shorty.

Throughout the whole strike of two days and nights, the Japs put up no fighter opposition, much to the disappointment of the Naval Air Arm boys. One aircraft was lost by enemy action; others were damaged taking off and landing on the carrier, a factor always to be reckoned with in this type of warfare. Whenever an aircraft went down 'in the Oggin', destroyers were on the scene in a matter of minutes to pick up the crews.

In a later flight I took off in another Avenger. We flew into more dirty tropical weather and for ninety minutes were completely lost in a raging Pacific rainstorm. As the Naval Air Arm boys might say, it was touch and go whether this story went down in the Oggin.

The anticipated climax of the Pacific war was approaching—the invasion of Japan. For the landings on Kyushu and the invasion of Honshu which was to follow in 1946, the command structure was rationalised, with all Army forces to be under General MacArthur, all Air Force planes under Spatz, all naval units to be commanded by Admiral Nimitz, and for the first time Admirals Halsey and Spruance were to be in active command simultaneously, Spruance to be responsible for the direct support of all amphibious operations, and Bull Halsey to wield the magnificent weapon of the Fast Carrier Force, in conjunction with the Twentieth Air Force, to bomb the heart out of Japan, with principal attention given to the air force and aircraft industry in Honshu.

After three weeks in Leyte Gulf, the Fast Carriers, with Halsey flying his flag in the battleship Missouri, put to sea in early July.

The 'softening up' strikes on the Japanese mainland were to be the start of the invasion and Operation Olympic. This was to be planned for early November, although at this stage, there was no sign or even awareness of an atom bomb—let alone two!

The Australian people loved Fraser—and his fleet. The feeling was mutual. The only sour note was caused by the Australian Prime Minister, John Curtis who was suffering dire ill health. Probably due to this, co-operation with supplies and dockyard requirements was sadly lacking and many ships had to go into action badly in need of repairs.

When Deputy/Acting Prime Minister Joseph Chifley took control, he complained to the British Government about Fraser, but the latter explained the facts more forcibly and things began to move.

At home, in June the country was in the throes of General Election fever, due to the fact that the Labour Party, under Clem Atlee, refused to continue in a Coalition Government until the end of the war with Japan.

In this political atmosphere, Fraser found himself more and more in the role of British Ambassador or Minister for Trade and Industry or even Foreign Secretary! No one, it seemed, wanted to know.

Thus were nurtured, at the 'sharp end' of operations, the growing feelings of 'The Forgotten Fleet'. Indeed, the same conditions applied in the case of 'The Forgotten Army' in S.E. Asia Command, but that is another story.

Nevertheless, the magnificent efforts of the BPF in the Tokyo area, which commenced on 17th July, continued under Fraser's guidance. What a man! In the Churchill mould.

In an article from The Sydney Morning Herald, Saturday, June 23 1945, Correspondent Harry L. Watts writes:

To R.N. from the A.I.F.

In recent issues of the 'Herald' have appeared several letters from men of the Royal Navy full of praise of the hospitality of this State. But if there is a debt, it is ours.

A letter from the captain of H.M. aircraft-carrier *Illustrious* ended with these words: 'We want to thank our many hosts and friends and to express our regret that we have been unable to do much to reciprocate their kindness.'

Masters of understatement these Britishers undoubtedly are, but we of the A.I.F. cannot let the Royal Navy get away with that. For the boot is on the other foot. Not only our soldiers, but the whole of the civilian population too, owe to the men of the R.N. more than can be repaid.

The navy meanwhile was fighting for its life in cold northern waters; running the dangerous 'beef and spud' run to Tobruk; fighting for the Atlantic lifelines; struggling successfully, though with bitter losses, to get convoys through to Russia.

Its small ships were busy on arduous and dangerous jobs—minesweeping, convoy work, commando jobs, and the hundred and one tasks performed by these policemen of the seas, each task being carried out with the stark efficiency and lack of swank as is the wont of the R.N.

And now Sydney's streets are swarming with quiet, well-mannered men of the R.N.—men who have already shown their mettle to the Japanese.

Wherever they sail, in whatever actions they may fight, they will always live up to the proud traditions of their service.

Men of the Royal Navy, the debt is ours.

From an un-named Australian magazine:

The Australians in those days were so keen to have anything as a souvenir, the sailors and ourselves had to guard all our personal items. I well remember when, as Officer of the Watch in harbour at Wooloomooloo, Sydney, having inspected libertymen for shore leave, some 10 minutes later one rating came back on board, literally wearing only his underpants! The 'Welcome Australia' folk had cleaned him of all his uniform as keepsakes.

The Admiral *(probably Rawlings.—Ed.)* must have been a very lonely man. Most evenings he would appear on the quarterdeck for his evening constitutional, walking slowly up and down, his head bowed in thought. Occasionally when I was Bosun's Mate, he would ask the OOW if he could spare me for a while to join him. We would talk of life at home—mine and his—my aspirations, all those little things that men talk about without the vast differences in rank interfering. 'Leave out the sirs,' he told me. 'I just want to chat.' I would be dismissed with a quiet 'Thank you, Bosun's Mate, back to your duties,' and his slow pacing would continue.

From: P.O. Electrical Artificer Les Bancroft, HMS *Indefatigable*

AUSTRALIAN ADVENTURE

After a few drinks, the Trocadero dance hall in Sydney was a favourite haunt for several of us Artificers. One particular night after dancing with a girl, she accepted that I should take her home.

We caught a train at Central Station for Parramatta. Then a bus, the last one for the night, which drove us some four miles into the bush (countryside). I saw the girl home, we dallied and I then commenced the return journey. Four miles on foot, mostly along a track, through the Australian moonlit bush. The bush sounds were many, not alarming, and blast, I had a fresh packet of cigarettes but had run out of matches. Parramatta railway station, at 2.30 a.m. on a June winter morning, was much too cold for sleeping on a bench. The Hotel opposite the station was closed, the streets deserted, but there was a lighted phone booth. The phone number was in the book; I rang the local police and explained my predicament. The answer, with a genial chuckle, 'Come out of the phone booth, face left, up the hill, the Police Station is on the right.' A few minutes later, I was there. The two duty policemen, after a friendly chat, showed me to a bed. A mattress cover, straw filled to 15″ high, lying on the floor in a small cell. It was marvellous, I was asleep immediately.

6.30 a.m. I was awakened to a plate of hot steak, eggs and bacon followed by steaming coffee. A wash and clean up and one policemen then escorted me to a tram; the quickest way back to Sydney. Repay them, they would have been insulted. I had thanked them and left my packet of cigarettes; that pleased them.

From: Lt. (A) Mike Davey RNVR, 894 Sqd., HMS *Indefatigable*

Before returning to attack the Japanese mainland, we were inspected by

Admiral Sir Bruce Fraser. The night before this event we had a good dinner preceded by several gins, but my cabin companion Randal Kay was still hungry at bedtime and we had suggested worm tablets. However on passing the wardroom galley he nipped in and pinched a loaf of bread, not to eat, but something far cleverer than that. He undressed and climbed into his bunk with the bread loaf and the largest hook and line from his escape kit. He hung the hook, baited with the loaf, out of the porthole and lay there waiting for a bite, of course the gin sent him to sleep with the line still tied hopefully to his bunk rail. Next morning early, a bright young messenger knocked on the cabin door, looked in and tapped Kay on the shoulder and said, 'The Commander wishes to see you in his cabin sir,' the reason being that the Admiral had come alongside the after gangway and, ten feet above it on a line, hung a loaf of bread. Although he was a genial man, Commander Whitfeld was also a strict disciplinarian, so that Kay would leave the Commander's cabin feeling rather small.

Eric Cowle of 887 had been determined to fly under Sydney Harbour bridge, but it had reached epidemic proportions with first a Lancaster then a flight of four Corsairs in line abreast. This had forced the authorities to ground anyone who attempted it.

From 'Carrier Operations in World War II' by J. D. Brown

Operations commenced on 17th July 1945, at the height of the typhoon season. The USN re-called their first strikes, but the Royal Navy Corsairs and Fireflies managed to find and attack airfields and railway yards on the north coast of Honshu. That night *KGV* joined American battleships in bombarding the Hitachi industrial complex, in the Tokyo area.

On 18th July, the USN attacked the largest Japanese naval base—Yokosuka, in what was regarded as retribution for Pearl Harbour. For political reasons the BPF was excluded from the strikes and were allocated targets to the northeast of Tokyo, the reason given by the American Command being that the Fireflies and Seafires did not have the endurance for covering their attack aircraft. As on the previous day, adverse weather prevented all but the Corsairs from reaching the briefed objectives, and this type, flying with only two fighter wings, dropped 13½ tons of bombs during the two days.

Replenishment was scheduled for only two days, but the recurrent typhoon warnings and heavy weather in the RAS areas delayed the beginning of the next serial until 24th July, by which time *Indefatigable* had rejoined the Fleet. Again the USN undertook 'private' strikes, on Kure, while the Fleet Air Arm concentrated on airfields on Shikoku and struck at shipping in the Inland Sea. Light flak was intense around the airfields and losses began to mount, particularly in the Corsair squadrons. The low cloud base hampered the shipping strikes, but on 24th six Avengers, two Corsairs and two Fireflies found and struck the Japanese escort carrier *Kaiyo,* leaving her on fire and with her back broken for American aircraft to finish off at a later date. This strike was significant in that it was the only attack on an aircraft carrier by Royal Navy aircraft. While the USN sank a Fleet carrier and three battleships at Kure on 24th, the Fleet Air Arm had to make do with plainer fare, and apart from the damage inflicted on *Kaiyo*, they sank destroyers, small escorts and many small coasters. Altogether 416 offensive sorties were flown by the four carriers on this day, in addition to over 100 CAP details.

Bad weather again curtailed flying on the following day but again much damage was inflicted on the enemy around the Inland Sea. That evening, just after dusk, *Formidable's* Hellcat detachment intercepted a group of Japanese Navy torpedo bombers heading for TF 37; two Hellcats shot down three B7As and damaged a fourth, the remainder being driven off without their attempting an attack.

Japanese Carrier Kaiyo *hit by aircraft from* Indefatigable *and* Victorious *24th July 1945. Light area is escaping fuel oil*

Two days of replenishment were followed by more shipping strikes on 28th, 29th and 30th July. On 28th, the Inland Sea was again the principal target, the important dockyard at Harima being bombed in a dawn strike by 20 Avengers. The naval base at Maizuru, on the north coast of Honshu, was attacked by Corsairs, four destroyer escorts being sunk or damaged badly during the day. A few Japanese aircraft were shot down; air combats were rare at this stage as the Japanese had done an extremely efficient job of dispersing their aircraft in an attempt to husband their resources for the inevitable amphibious landings

Hira. Inland Sea, 28th July 1945. Taken by Cliff Miseldine in a Photo Reconnaissance Seafire from HMS Indefatigable. *Strike on docks. Bombs on target centre left*

which the Allies would attempt at a later date. Unfortunately for the enemy the dispersal was so effective that they found it almost impossible to gather sufficient fighters to meet a threat to any one target. As a result the Allied fighters were rarely called upon to protect the strike aircraft from interference, although the flak remained intense to the end.

On 30th July, the airfields in the Tokyo plain were fogbound and the strikes had to seek alternate targets, again on the coast. At the end of the day the Fleet withdrew for replenishment, but instead of just two days in the RAS area, the combined Fleet eventually spent nine days off operations. Initially the delay was occasioned by the succession of typhoons but when refuelling was complete at the end of 3rd August, further strikes were delayed until the first atomic bomb had been dropped on Hiroshima, on 6th August.

The next serial was intended to begin on 8th August, but yet again a typhoon warning postponed operations. On 9th the weather was much improved and the Fleet Air Arm enjoyed further success against shipping south of Tokyo and off northern Honshu. Corsairs alternated with Avengers in strikes which kept up continuous pressure against the enemy's dwindling navy and merchant fleet. Small craft suffered most heavily, but in Onagawa Wan all the shipping remaining afloat was sunk by the concerted air attacks mounted by Task Forces 37 and 38. Lieutenant R. Hampton Gray, DSC, RCNVR led a Corsair 'Ramrod' (bomb-armed strike) from *Formidable*'s 1841 Squadron to sink the escort sloop

Amakusa; despite being hit and set on fire by the flak, Lt. Gray pressed home the attack but lost his life when his Corsair crashed near the escort. This courageous officer, who had diistinguished himself in operations since the strikes on *Tirpitz* a year before, was awarded a posthumous Victoria Cross, only the second to be awarded to a naval aviator in World War II.

Sweeps over the enemy airfields on 9th August, resulted in the destruction of over 50 Japanese aircraft by the RN aircraft, the latter losing seven aircraft and five pilots.

The 10th August had been scheduled as the last full day of operations and the carrier aircraft roamed at will over Honshu, destroying what remained to the enemy of his aircraft, shipping and railway system. TF 37's share was over 50 enemy aircraft destroyed on the ground, three destroyers sunk and three more seriously damaged at Maizuru and in the Inland Sea, damage to factories shipyards and barracks. Altogether the enemy lost over 700 aircraft to the strikes of the Fast Carrier Force on 9th and 10th August 1945, and the Royal Navy aircraft losses for the two days were 13 aircraft and nine crews. The kamikazes made their only appearances during these two days; improved defensive techniques denied them any success bar the damaging of a picket destroyer, while the CAP, usually over 100 strong, shot down the majority of the enemy aircraft venturing out.

On 13th August the air attacks were directed at the Tokyo area once more, only targets of opportunity remaining, so effective had been the strikes during the preceding month. In the course of the last large-scale attacks on the carrier forces, the CAP shot down another 21 Japanese aircraft, the Seafires destroying five of these. Aware that surrender was near, Task Force 38 withdrew to refuel, but in the absence of notification of the cease-fire further operations were laid on for 15th. The dawn strikes were launched, and *Indefatigable's* Avengers were intercepted by a dozen A6Ms and in the last fighter combat of World War II the Seafires of No. 24 Naval Fighter Wing shot down eight of the enemy for the loss of just one Seafire. Most of the remainder of the enemy fighters were damaged in the encounter.

All further strikes were cancelled at 0700 on 15th August, and only a few die-hard Japanese attempted to attack the Fleet, *Indefatigable* being near-missed. The Royal Navy contingent remained with the Fifth Fleet, replenished by the USN Fleet Train, until the signing of the instrument of surrender in Tokyo Bay on 2nd September 1945.

Extracts from 'Alarm Starboard' by Lieut. Cdr. G. Brooke, DSC, RN

HMS *Formidable*

The ship duly received some single Bofors guns instead of the Oerlikons and six Hellcats from *Indomitable*—four night fighters and two photographic—but these additions paled into insignificance alongside the big one. This was AC1—Admiral Vian—for we were to fly his flag during the next tour of operations. In practical terms the vacating of cabins and offices to make room for the staff was the biggest bore and this, of course, occurred, but I think we were all pleased to have Vian. It was an undoubted honour that he had chosen *Formidable* (*Indom.* just relieved by *Implacable,* had retired for a refit) and, though it would sometimes be uncomfortable to have big brother right on top of us, we felt equal to anything he might require (the first thing he required was a bathroom alongside his bridge, not easy to implement). Lastly, Vian's mode of operation was stimulating, similar to the Captain's, and no doubt we felt 'in for a penny, in for a pound'. In the event there were no dramas that I remember and four weeks after arrival we were twisting out of Sydney harbour again, proudly sporting his flag.

Under Nimitz and Vian

Manus came and went unlamented and, on July 16, we were treated to a memorable sight the American Third Fleet provisioning from their Fleet Train: nine heavy and six light carriers, seven battleships, 15 cruisers and 60 destroyers! Though there were more carriers but fewer battleships it reminded me of our combined Home and Med fleets congregated at Gib before the war. They filled the horizon over a wide arc, a numerical concentration of naval power that has not been matched since.

The BPF was to operate as one of the four Task Forces (TF 37 this time) of the Third Fleet, which had just begun the preliminary softening up of Japan itself, prior to invasion. In the late afternoon the whole armada moved off towards the flying off position, four groups in line abreast (the BPF, on the right, the most northerly) advancing over a 45-mile front. *Formidable* launched 16 Corsairs. Joining up with seven Fireflies from *Implacable* that flew off north-west about 200 miles to carry out 'Ramrod' attacks (bombing and strafing airfields) at Sendai, Masuda and Matshushima. Tokyo was about the same distance south-west and for the first time I felt great satisfaction, though heaven knows it was secondhand. Those two ships at the bottom of the sea off Malaya with their Midshipmen in captivity, Richard Onslow and his *Hermes*, Anthony Terry and those men at the Malay School in Padang—seldom out of my thoughts—it had been good in May to feel we were doing something about them, but to be actually bombing Japan, that hitherto had seemed so far away . . .

Three of our Corsairs were shot down or had to ditch but all the pilots were rescued, one by an American and two by our destroyers. The next two Ramrods, provided by *Victorious* and *Implacable,* were aborted because of bad weather, but ten Corsairs from *Formidable* and 12 from *Victorious* got through successfully and attacked installations on the far coast of Japan. South of us the Americans had flown off two strikes which had been aborted and Admiral McCain, our immediate superior, cancelled further strikes for the day to leave, we felt, a feather in the British cap. This was the season of typhoons, with unsettled weather of extraordinary local variation. Strikes took off in bright sunshine to find the target shrouded in low cloud and driving rain, or the reverse applied, and sudden dense fog patches made life hazardous for aircraft returning low on fuel.

After dark we flew off our night fighters in sheeting rain to provide CAP over a bombardment force which included *KGV.* This went to within 14 miles of the coast and bombarded industrial establishments, one of *KGV*'s targets being the Hitachi engineering works which received 91 rounds. Landing-on aircraft at night in pouring rain is an unpleasant business and never was I more sure that my services were going to be required. Dim lights along the edge of the flight deck provided an uncertain avenue for the pilots to aim at and Joyce's bats were illuminated. Apart from reflections in the streaming, swaying deck, this was about all the pilots could see. My admiration for them knew no bounds. All got on without trouble and when they had disappeared into the welcoming if muted glow of the hangar I turned in, thankful and tired. It had been a long 21 hours.

The next few days followed an irritating on-off pattern with bouts of bad weather allowing CAPs and an occasional strike to be fitted in. On July 24 when we were about 200 miles east of Kyushu—the southernmost of Japan's main islands—848's Avengers bombed Tokushima, one of them being lost, and all four British carriers went for a *Kaiyo* Class carrier, leaving it with a broken back and on fire. (A photograph taken showed a clean break, with the two halves sagging.) Japanese fighters claimed four victims, though none from *Formidable.* Two Ramrods followed, the second of which got lost due to the weather closing in. By the time they sighted the fleet their tanks were practically empty, one Corsair coming down in the sea before it could land and another taking the first carrier it saw and just making it. I think it was a member of this party who found himself over an American carrier and quickly obtained permission to land. Unfortunately the American landing-on signals were diametrically opposed to our own. At the first approach the pilot was waved round again; the second was as bad but he landed on somehow to heap invective on the batsman for giving him the wrong signals. The batsman defended himself stoutly and then they both realised that the pilot had been reading the signals as American while the former had been doing his best to provide the British version! It must be added that on subsequently reaching *Formidable* this Corsair finished up half over the port side, with me thankful that the pilot climbed out under his own steam and stomped off cursing.

Much the same happened to an Avenger the next day; the only one to find the allocated target, it returned with only ten gallons left. The collapsing of one wheel occurred several times. The sea had been calm for so long that perhaps it was the swell that caught some new pilots unawares (there had been some very young replacements at Sydney). The result was not particularly frightening so long as the aircraft, scraping to a halt on one wheel and the opposite wingtip, did not slew too much. One such pranger scooped up an arrestor wire with its bent propeller, the wire coming down just forward of the perspex cockpit which was probably fortunate.

Strikes continued against shipping in the Inland Sea and against Tokushima airfield. The weather worsened yet again and course was set for the next replenishment area. Enemy air activity was now increasing. A high-speed reconnaissance plane was shot down by the Americans to crash in flames inside our screen and yield two Japanese bodies to *Tenacious*. There were reports of balloons and 'window' *(aluminium foil dropped to clutter radar screens.—Ed.)* over the fleet and just before landing on at 19.00 one of *Formidable*'s Hellcats shot down a parachute with a black box dangling from it, thought to have been a radio homing beacon. All this spelt danger, and in fact it was only averted by the efficiency of our fighter direction team. The fighter cover of four Corsairs and four Hellcats were landing on *Formidable* when three groups of bogeys were detected and the Americans reported splashing a 'Myrt' bomber. Landing-on was accordingly stopped with two Hellcats still aloft.

The perspex display in the ADR was full of aircraft, amongst which was a group at 94 miles which Captain Lewin was sure were hostile. The American Group CIC (Combat Information Centre) officer in overall fighter direction command was sceptical but Philip O'Rorke was instructed to intercept and directed the two Hellcats onto these bogeys. Shortly after 20.00 there was a excited 'Tally ho!' from Lieutenant Atkinson who, with Sub-Lieutenant McKie, was at 20,000 feet, 30 miles from the fleet. They tore into the formation, shooting down the leader and two others and damaging a fourth. American fighters from the night fighter carrier *Bonhomme Richard* then arrived and dealt with the remainder. There were 30 Japanese 'Grace' torpedo bombers in all, none of which carried out an attack. Torpedo bombers have the advantage at night—*vide* the 'Torch' attack on *Bermuda* and *Sheffield*—it was now bright moonlight and many ships would undoubtedly have suffered if the Lewin/*Formidable* team had not lived up to their name. As can be imagined the two gladiators returned to considerable acclamation.

After two days' fuelling the BPF was back with attacks on airfields and shipyards with the usual outlandish names, and on shipping in the Inland Sea. Opposition was strong, both in the air and from flak, the fleet losing eight aircraft. Two Corsair pilots of our 1842 Squadron were forced to ditch in a harbour mouth. All dreaded falling into Japanese hands with good reason (they were briefed only on their part in any operation so as not to give much away under torture) and the two pilots must have felt that this was it. Their delight can be imagined when an American submarine came right in and picked them up. The American rescue service of submarines and flying boats was excellent.

The pattern continued with replenishment periods every few days. One of these was greatly complicated by a tremendous typhoon-bred swell. To keep a safe distance between the ships, the jackstay along which we were receiving 500 lb bombs was 300 feet long, tended by a large body of men who continually hauled or rendered so as to keep it taught.

We were to have returned to the attack on August 3, the BPF's targets being in the Hiroshima area. The day dawned bright and clear but a mysterious signal cancelled operations and to the perplexity of all there was no further development for four days. Then, on August 7 the reason was made plain. A monster bomb had been dropped by the US Air Force on Hiroshima. Few if any of us knew what an atomic bomb might be, but it was obviously something pretty special and the first wonderings stirred as to whether the war might end sooner than we had dared hope. The enemy's reaction was unknown and to help them make up their minds Admiral Halsey intended continued attacks.

(At the start of this book I mention the Enola Gay, the name of the aircraft which dropped the first Atomic Bomb. The second aircraft, for communications, was Great Artiste; the third was for photographic purposes and all flew from the island of Tinian.—Ed.)

August 9 proved to be a full and for HMS *Formidable* a tragically memorable day. Conditions, unfortunately, were good and an Avenger strike plus three Corsair Ramrods were flown. The first Ramrod and the Avenger strike caused much destruction, especially to airfields in the north of Honshu. The second, led by Hammy Gray, sank a destroyer and damaged other naval vessels; but they returned with the news that he had been shot down. With the war probably in its closing stages the Captain had told the squadron COs not to take unnecessary risks. This was duly passed on to Gray, but true to form he must have taken little note of it. Leading the others, he came in low over some hills in a high speed dive but was met by intense fire, both from the shore and five ships. Gray dropped his bombs on the destroyer *Amakusa* and was beginning his getaway run to seaward at 40 feet when his port wing erupted in flames. The aircraft banked steeply to starboard and then, both wings now ablaze, turned on its back and plunged at full power into the sea. (The others re-formed under Sub-Lieutenant Mackinnon, the next senior pilot, circled round and repeated the attack. The *Amakusa* had already been sunk but two other ships were damaged.)

One of his pilots, Sub-Lieutenant A. Hughes wrote: 'It was my first raid over Japan, but Lieutenant Gray was so cheerful and inspired such confidence as a leader that my nervousness was allayed before it started . . . he was liked and respected by all and his death cast a shadow not only on the pilots but on the whole ship.' This was true; his gallant end after five years of war and within days of peace put a lasting damper on us all, which not even the eventual award of a posthumous VC (the only one earned by the Royal Navy in the Pacific Campaign) did much to lighten.

Nor was this the only blow. When Gray's men returned, one—with no hydraulics—carried out a successful belly landing but another, almost out of fuel, requested permission for an immediate landing. He was approaching normally when his engine stopped about 50 yards off the stern. The Corsair, descending fast, hit the very top of the rundown, where the flight deck curved down towards the stern. It remained there for a second and then began to run back. The batsman, powerless to do anything, took a couple of agonised steps forward as if to will it to stop. The plane gathered speed, slewed round, pointed one wing in the air as the other dropped over space, and disappeared.

Moments later it could be seen in the wake, almost submerged, and then was gone. There was no sign of the pilot. It was thought he might have been knocked out by the original shock as the brakes should have held the plane until help arrived. Another five seconds of fuel would have saved him. Also a Canadian, he was due to go home, whether or not the war went on, and this second tragedy all but extinguished such euphoria as we had left on that subject.

However, two other Corsairs on CAP shot down a 'Grace' bomber over an American Task Group and the day ended with another atom bomb, this time on Nagasaki. Presumably there was an adequate supply of these astonishing weapons and the least optimistic felt that even the Japanese could hardly go on while city after city was obliterated. This appeared to be the case when next day the enemy agreed to the terms of the Potsdam agreement (unconditional surrender) except that they stipulated that the Emperor should be left on his throne. Presumably this had to be discussed by the Allies (Russia had declared war on Japan the day before) for there was no further development. In fact both sides went at it as hard as ever. All day BPF aircraft ranged far and wide; not without cost as six aircraft did not return. One was Sub-Lieutenant Maitland's, one of the best pilots of 1841. In the spirit of Hammy Gray he was making a second strafing pass over an airfield. Though we did not know it, this was the last attack to be made by *Formidable* in the war. The enemy in their turn, as a last defiant gesture, tried all day on the 9th and 10th to get through to the ships—both kamikazes and conventional bombers—but not in massed attacks and the CAPs shot most of them down.

And then came an announcement that, foreshadowed but still unbelievable, put the sighting of land from *Djohanis* in the shade and set us slapping each other on the back.

HMS *Formidable*
14/8/45

We have just spliced the mainbrace in honour of VJ-Day, the Japs having packed in this morning. Well, it's all over now and with luck we shall be home soon, though we still don't know when. It really is incredible that it is all finished when two weeks ago it might have lasted two years. I'm glad I got out here and saw it finished I must say and rather hope we get to Singapore, though that will come under the Indies fleet I expect. We lost three pilots on the very last strikes which was very sad.

I must say it seems a long time ago when I was 19 and a Midshipman in the *Nelson*.

So the war was over. My immediate reaction was one of thankfulness that I had escaped whole. I had been prepared for sudden death but it was the idea of being badly wounded that appalled. I suppose this feeling was natural, if selfish in view of the thousands—such as those in Japanese prison camps—who should have been uppermost in one's mind.

From Admiral G. C. Crowley DSC, HMS *Tenacious*

'Buzzes' had been increasing in strength throughout the month concerning our future movements, and every indication pointed to something big on the way. On 5th July the Fleet came back from Australia, and hurried preparations were completed for our next job. The next afternoon we left Manus and proceeded on a northerly course. The force consisted of one battleship, three carriers, six cruisers and eighteen destroyers, and out of the ship's companies none but the very privileged knew our ultimate destination. The Quartermasters were steering 040° and the engine-room gave 15 knots. They were the only clues we had.

On the way north we went alongside *Achilles* to top up with fuel. The method of fuelling at sea was by then a well-known evolution, requiring good seamanship and handling of the ship to keep perfect station on the ship supplying the oil. Unfortunately on this occasion our Gyro chose to fail, and caused us to sheer towards the cruiser close abeam. However, a clear head and immediate action averted what seemed a certain collision. Apart from severing the oil pipe-line, no other damage was caused. Still the secrecy continued, and one could hear from the messdecks the old refrain 'We don't know where we're going 'til we're there'. In this case the words were aggravatingly applicable.

Then the wireless announced that the American 3rd Fleet had commenced operations against the Japanese mainland, and shortly afterwards the Captain spoke over the S.R.E. The British Pacific Fleet, he said, was proceeding north to join with the Americans under Admiral Halsey, in the attack against Japan. 'So it will be our duty to attack, withdraw to replenishing area, re-fuel and back to the attack again . . . and so on until the Powers that Be decree otherwise.' Yes, what we had been waiting for had arrived, and there was no small task before us. On 16th July we rendezvoused with the U.S. 3rd Fleet, and became the 4th Task Group of the largest array of warships which had ever operated together. As we took up position that morning, ships covered the sea in every direction as far as the eye could see. It was a thrilling and imposing display of Allied Naval strength.

With all fuelling completed the huge Fleet moved into attack the next day. The first flight of Corsairs took off from *Formidable* at 0400, and thereafter a continuous stream of planes flew overhead towards Japan. Over a thousand planes took part on that day alone, and at the same time B 29s from the U.S. Army Air bases commenced their destructive attacks.

The air strikes continued throughout the month of July and on into August. Each new strike brought us a little closer to the enemy's mainland. The spirit in which Admiral Halsey took every conceivable risk in order to hurt the enemy more is best shown in a signal he made to all ships on 23rd July: 'Under punishment from this next foray the enemy will probably retaliate. Let's go.' In spite of all the tempting targets presented to them, the Japanese aircraft found it almost impossible to penetrate the defensive air patrols which covered us, and those which did get through were soon put into the sea by gunfire from our ships. Every day 'Bogies' *(codeword for unidentified aircraft—Ed.)* would be reported approaching the Fleet, only to be followed shortly afterwards by the victorious cry from one of our fighters, 'One bandit splashed'. The Fleet Air Arm was doing a grand job.

So strike after strike was completed, with a short respite between each as we retired to replenish from the Fleet Train. This was the part we liked best, for it meant receiving our mail. Another advantage of the refuelling area was that we were able to revert to four watches instead of the two-watch defence system worked when striking. Other things, too, made life in the rear area easier; our film projector, for instance, was more appreciated than it had been in Manus, and we swopped films with other ships which came alongside. Action rig could be discarded for the time being to enjoy the hot sun, and many opportunities occurred to see friends in the other ships. Although this was called the Rest Area, some wag amongst us renamed it the Unrest Area, for on a busy day nothing was thought of closing twenty ships or so in turn and transferring anything from pilots to petrol tanks.

Days lengthened into weeks, and still we persisted in our efforts against the enemy. Then one day came a pleasant change. We were detailed with *Terpsichore, Termagent, Newfoundland* and *Gambia* to take part in the first daylight naval bombardment of the Japanese coast. Our target was the industrial centre of Kamaishi and included in the bombarding force were the U.S. battleships *Missouri* and *South Dakota*. It was a tense moment as we approached the shores of the Japanese homeland on the morning of 9th August, particularly as *Tenacious* was the leading ship of the line. As the coast came nearer and nearer we expected the shore batteries to open fire at any moment. At last at 1240 the order came: 'Ships to be in position to open fire by 1245', and all ships turned together, forming a long line parallel to the coast at a distance of about two miles, though it seemed much less. The *South Dakota* opened fire exactly on the appointed time, and then right down the line could be heard the thunderous crump of heavy gunfire. The concussion from their guns was terrific, and the whine of projectiles passing overhead sounded like a thousand express trains. We could not see the results of our exploding shells, for the target was screened by a range of hills, but rising volumes of smoke and a reddish glow in the sky soon began to tell the tale. The battleships did not have all the fun either, for a little later we were ordered to open fire on a mountain road leading to the town. Much amusement was caused later when reading in the preliminary reports that '*Tenacious* shelled a road, causing a cyclist to swerve and fall off his machine.'

The bombardment had lasted two hours, causing us to partake of our first 'action meal', comprising an excellent brew of soup and an issue of small tins of action ration handed round by Stores P.O. Griffin in person. Without meeting opposition of any kind, save for spasmodic A.A. fire at the American spotting aircraft, we retired at 1445 and headed back towards the main Fleet. Later reports of reconnaissance planes confirmed the success and accuracy of the engagement, but the failure on the part of the Japanese to oppose such a bold sortie still remained a mystery. By dusk we were back in station on the Fleet Screen, and settled down into normal routine again. By then we had been at sea for thirty-four days, and we all were feeling weary. Early every morning we would go to Action Stations, on the alert for surprise dawn attacks, and the same procedure again just before dusk. Only once was a concerted attack made by enemy planes and five of these were shot down in the vicinity of the Fleet.

The news that the Japanese were suing for peace came as a great surprise to us all. No one had expected such an early collapse, and this news was so good that, like the atomic bomb, it was beyond full comprehension. The operation was due to end about that time, and we had been looking forward to a second visit to Sydney. Now plans had to be changed, as obviously a fleet would be required for occupational duties. So there followed a rapid reorganisation whereby some ships were sent south in readines to occupy Singapore, Hong Kong, and the East Indies, whilst the remainder stayed in the Tokyo area. *Tenacious* was detailed to remain off Japan, and whilst rumours were numerous and all news vague about surrender negotiations, we continued the air strikes. On 15th August at six o'clock in the morning, whilst our carrier planes were on their way to bomb Kobe, official word came through that the Japanese had agreed to surrender unconditionally. The aircraft were therefore recalled, and we withdrew to await developments to a position some 200 miles from Tokyo.

At 1100, the time of the official 'Cease Fire', Admiral Halsey broadcast to the Fleet from his flagship, the *Missouri*. No sooner had he started, however, than 'Flash Red' was ordered, and in the middle of his speech a Japanese aircraft was seen to fall vertically down onto the *Indefatigable*. Luckily it missed astern of the carrier, but this incident served to put us on our guard against similar acts of treachery.

Although we at first had visions of immediately sailing into Tokyo, this was not to be the case, and there followed a period of waiting which seemed all the longer for our impatience. It was during this period that we ran into a typhoon.

To describe that awful day by mere words on paper is indeed a hard task. Those who have been at sea in a typhoon will readily understand this paragraph. Those who have been to sea, but not experienced one, may understand half the horrors. But to those who have never traversed the oceans, it will be impossible to convey an impression of what is now stamped so vividly on our minds.

The day of 25th August broke calmly enough, although there was a certain stillness in the air which one had learnt to distrust and associate with the beginnings of a storm at sea. When the forenoon watchmen came on deck the wind was already increasing in violence, and the sea was becoming choppy. The sky looked menacingly black. By midday the storm was upon us. The wind reached an almost unbelievable degree of violence, and it seemed hardly possible that it could ever blow any harder. The sea was whipped into a white confusion of flying spray, through which one could only see the mountainous waves, which at times appeared to tower many feet above the masthead. We began to roll to an extent beyond any previous experience. Life on the mess deck was by this time just a question of hanging on to the nearest immovable object. It was quite impossible to consider anything else—even being seasick or eating were quite beyond our physical scope. Owing to the seas, passage along the upper deck would have been madness, so we stayed in our reeling corners. Those whose duty kept them on the bridge could see nothing of the other ships in company, although they knew that but a few cables away, aircraft carriers and other destroyers were suffering the same discomforts as we were. By evening the worst had passed and it could be seen that wind and sea were moderating fast. Later on it was possible to take stock of the damage sustained, and apart from smashed boats and bent rails, this was surprisingly light. Other ships had been less fortunate, life having been lost and serious structural damage sustained. The typhoon had lasted only a few hours, and we had missed the centre of it—for these mercies we were truly thankful. We sincerely hoped that we should never hit such a gale again.

It was with great relief that at the end of August we did our 'rounds' of the ships present collecting mails and were then detached and sent into Tokyo Bay. The main portion of the Fleet had entered the Bay two days before, but the surrender had not yet been signed, and we were pleased to arrive in time for the historic event. We also looked forward to relief from sea watches and getting a decent night's sleep for a change. Thus early on the 1st September, we anchored in Sagami Bay. There was certain speculation as to whether Lieut. Noakes would remember what to do, for it was so long since the anchors had last been used. But, in spite of this, amidst clouds of red dust the anchor rushed from the hawse-pipe down onto the bed and the cable emerged once more from the cable locker where it had been lying for fifty-seven days. We had been at sea for all that time, and of such a feat we were justly proud.

The signing of the surrender took place in the U.S. battleship *Missouri* on the following day. Although the American flagship was lying only about a mile from us, it was difficult to see much of the important historical events taking place, but the white uniforms of the sailors crowding every viewpoint were clearly visible, and we could not but envy them a little as we listened to a broadcast commentary of the ceremony. It seemed almost unbelievable that such a short distance away a long and terrible series of wars was finally being brought to a victorious conclusion.

It was a pity that this otherwise completely happy event meant that we should lose the U.S. Liaison team headed by Lieut. Bill Conyngham, which had been with us throughout our period with the Pacific Fleet. Much might be said of the valuable assistance this team rendered in helping us to grasp the intricacies of American procedure and manoeuvring. However, perhaps it is sufficient to say that we found the 'Yanks' grand shipmates, and knew that we should miss their happy comradeship now that the time had come for them to leave.

Our next job was to go down the coast to Hammamatsu and bring back Allied prisoners of war from a large camp there. Now we were to see the fruits of our labours, or, more accurately, of our sea time and attendant discomforts. Early the next morning more than a hundred ex-prisoners arrived on board, with close-cropped hair and new American clothing, and there were few amongst us who were not shocked by their pitiful condition. Ill treated and starved by their captors, they ate ravenously of the breakfast we set before them. After drinking what was their first cup of tea for many months, they sought those who came from their home towns and asked for news of their homes and families. Naturally there could only be a few such happy meetings, but all were overjoyed to see us and to regain their lost freedom. We returned to Tokyo at full speed, and took our passengers through the cheering Fleet to a hospital ship at Yokohama, and so set them on their way home.

Admiral Crowley recently wrote to me:

With regard to the typhoon, Admiral Halsey instructed the American Admiral to patrol up and down a line, and this he was determined to do. As the weather got worse, I decided to move to the safe quadrant, and this I did. Later on, when we rejoined I was not asked where I had been, but I learnt that 3 American Destroyers had been sunk, and there was considerable damage to the Flight Deck of a carrier. *(USS* Wasp*—Ed.)*

We were instructed to collect a large number of Internees from North China and take them to Hong Kong—including the Bishop of Shantung—they were all in a terribly emaciated state.

I had two cousins, who were interned in Shanghai—Bernard and Joyce Crowley—who I contacted as soon as I got in, and had them on board several times. Their main complaint was boredom and terrible food—but their Chinese servants saved their lives by smuggling in food.

The part in the HMS *Tenacious* book about Shanghai does not say how hard the Navy worked repairing the British Clubs and Institutions.

From Ray Durber, A/B, HMS *Grenville*

We had returned to Melbourne after a few months up the islands. I was Duty Quarter-master and the ship's company was on shore leave, just the duty part of watch on board. Everything was quiet and it was just about eleven a.m. (up spirits).

I was gazing ashore (meditating according to the gospel of Saint John) when I heard a voice say 'Your First Lieutenant is expecting me Quartermaster, I'll go forward—I know the way.' With that I said 'Sorry Sir, I'll have the Bosun's mate take you. I don't like to have unknown officers wandering around on board during my watch.'

He smiled, and went off with the Bosun's Mate. About an hour (and a few pink gins) later, our First Lieutenant, Lieutenant Jones, came to the gangway with this other Lieutenant (RN) who then said his farewell and went to the

Destroyer tied up about five hundred yards astern of us. It was HMS *Whelp*. The visitor was Lieutenant Philip Mountbatten, RN.

From: Jack Collins, HMS *Quality*

The fleet sailed from Manus on July 6th. For the next ten days we steamed northwards, fuelling or exercising daily. Stanley Maxted the BBC Commentator was on board *Quality*, and gave us several interesting talks on his previous experience. On July 10th we rendezvoused with the American Third Fleet which was now known as Task Force 37, under the command of Admiral Halsey, whose avowed ambition was to ride into Tokyo on the Emperor's white horse. Dawn on the 17th saw the carriers of the combined fleets flying off their planes to attack the Japanese mainland just north of Tokyo. *Quality* was now permanently stationed astern of *Formidable* as air-sea rescue boat, and that morning we picked up one pilot unhurt. In the afternoon *King George V*, *Quality* and *Quiberon* parted company with Task Force 37 and joined up with an American force comprised of 6 battleships, 2 cruisers and 11 destroyers. Our objective was to bombard the Japanese mainland. It was a pitch black night, wet and foggy, as the force approached within 12 miles of the coast; at 2315 the big guns opened up—the night was rent with deafening roars; the skies were torn with curtains of red and white flame; the air was full of the smell of burnt cordite. *Quality* was last in the line stationed astern of *King George V* so we had a magnificent view of the whole firework display. The show finished at midnight and the force returned unmolested to rejoin the main body of the fleet about 8 o'clock the next morning. Air strikes were flown off throughout the day. In the evening the fleet withdrew owing to the approach of a typhoon: the next four days were spent refuelling and reprovisioning the fleet from ships of the Fleet Train. On the 24th and 25th air strikes were again carried out against Honshu: *Quality* picked up another two airmen. *Terpsichore* picked up 2 Japanese pilots who crashed in torpedo bombers when attempting to attack the Fleet. The 24th saw the creating of an R.N. aviation record—418 sorties flown off—100 tons of bombs dropped. After fuelling again on the 26th and 27th strikes were resumed on the 28th. On the 29th the battleships carried out another bombardment of the mainland.

Air strikes were continued on the 30th. Arriving back in the fuelling area on the 31st, we were busily engaged for the next few days in transferring mail and stores between various ships. On the 2nd August *Quality* acted as D.S.B. between Task Force 37 and 38, and transferred despatches to U.S.S. *Missouri*, flagship of Commander Third Fleet, and to the aircraft carrier *Bennington*. Our force was not short of tankers so we fuelled from *KGV* on the 3rd. Receipt of a typhoon warning postponed further air strikes. Eventually air strikes were resumed on the 9th. Japanese aircraft were in the vicinity of the fleet but did not attack. One Corsair attempting to land on the *Formidable*, crashed into her stern, folded up and dropped into the sea. We searched for the pilot, but in vain. Air strikes were continued on the 10th and we rescued another of *Formidable's* pilots. News was also received of the Japanese acceptance of the United Nations surrender terms: it looked as if our job was nearly complete.

We withdrew to the fuelling area on the 11th. *Quality* and *Quadrant* escorted *King George V* to the Yankee Fleet where she fuelled from a U.S. oiler while we took station on Task Force 38's screen. We also transferred Vice Admiral Rawlings and other high ranking officers between *KGV* and *Missouri*. In the evening we returned to our own force. At 1300 on Sunday the 12th August, the BPF divided its forces: *KGV, Indefatigable, Gambia, Newfoundland* and the 'N's and 'T's were to remain off Japan to await developments. *Achilles, Euryalus, Argonaut,* and the 'Q's and 'U's set off southwards for Manus. Vice Admiral Rawlings made a general signal congratulating all concerned and wishing everyone the best of luck.

HMS Quality

We of the *Quality* will remember those months in the Pacific for the part we played as air-sea rescue boat and D.S.B. for the fleet during fuelling and storing periods. 35 pilots owe their lives to the *Quality*—the top 'scoring' destroyer. Those who were on the bridge will never forget the way the Captain carefully made chalk marks of the number of planes taking off and landing on *Formidable,* watching like a cat watches a mouse, ready to spring into action, should a plane falter in its flight—how many times were we awakened into action by his stentorian shouts '240 revs., Port 30, standby with heaving lines.' *Quality* also captured the destroyer record for the number of times going alongside other ships—96 times between July 7th and August 12th, for fuel, stores, mail and passengers. During the previous operation *Quality* had been the 200th ship alongside *KGV*. The memory will live long of the way we dashed round the fleet from ship to ship, of the 1st Lieutenant, splashed with oil, hauling away on the foc'sle with the rest of the hands, of the Jackstay on 'B' gun deck, of the Captain on the bridge irately cursing everyone but soon forgetting our faults, of his orders while alongside—'Up two turns, I'll take 400 lbs. Can you give me more pressure? I'd like some apples.' Well at least we fed well in spite of being at sea for weeks on end, helping to create records for the Royal Navy.

We went alongside *Formidable* almost daily, sometimes transferring ratings for dental treatment, and one occasion we took Vice Adl Vian on a visit of the carriers. The news of the Japanese ultimate surrender was received on the morning of the 15th. I think our main interest in the auspicious occasion was in the splicing of the mainbrace. A far bigger cheer went up on the messdecks a few days later when we heard *Quality*'s name mentioned on the radio as having taken part in the recent Pacific operations. We arrived in Manus on the 16th and went alongside the *Montclare* for boiler clean. It was not the luck of the 'Q's to return to Sydney yet. The carriers and 25th Flotilla of 'U's continued on southward to enjoy the victorious return of the BPF to its rear base. *Quality* had missed the celebrations for both VE and VJ days.

CPO Fred Fallows of HMS *Ulysses* continues his story:

On June 28th, the British Pacific Fleet sailed north, whither bound it did not know, but its strength showed that its purpose was anything but a pleasure cruise.

Here, then, is the composition of Task Force 37 of the British Pacific Fleet in June and July, 1945. It was commanded by Vice-Admiral Sir Bernard Rawlings, flying his flag in HMS *King George V*; and the carriers were under the command of Rear-Admiral (now Vice-Admiral) Sir Philip Vian, flying his flag in HMS *Formidable*.

Battleship
HMS *King George V*

Aircraft Carriers
HMS *Formidable*
HMS *Victorious*
HMS *Indefatigable*
HMS *Implacable*

Cruisers
HMS *Newfoundland*
(Flying the flag of the Admiral Commanding
4th Cruiser Squadron—Vice Admiral Brind.)
HMS*Black Prince*

HMS *Euryalus*	HMCS *Uganda*
HMNZS *Gambia*	HMNZS *Achilles*

(For the last few weeks of the operations
HMS *Argonaut* was present.)

Destroyers
HMS *Barfleur*
(Flying the flag of the Rear-Admiral Destroyers,
British Pacific Fleet—Rear-Admiral Edelsen.)

HMS *Troubridge*	HMS *Quadrant*	MHS *Undine*
HMS *Terpsichore*	HMS *Quality*	HMS *Urania*
HMS *Termagant*	HMAS *Quiberon*	HMS *Urchin*
HMS *Tenacious*	HMAS *Quickmatch*	HMS *Ulysses*
HMS *Teazer*	HMS *Grenville*	HMS *Undaunted*

We sailed north, following the same route as a month before. This time we were on the outer screen, which consisted of the destroyers and two cruisers. This screen was thrown round the fleet like an armed wheel. In our care and charge were the mighty carriers, the cruisers and the majestic *King George V,* symbol of Britain's naval power. As we steamed slowly north, gradually becoming hotter (with the attendant miseries), every branch continued exercising. Radar pickets ahead of the fleet were detailed, aircraft launched dummy attacks, there were several shoots and the communications branch were kept busy: the signalmen keeping watch on the bridge for signals from whichever of the numerous ships might be flashing, and the telegraphists and coders manning the T.B.S., a very modern and efficient wireless set on which every ship kept constant watch and by which all manoeuvres and orders were passed by voice. In the engine-room and boiler-rooms, the stokers, working in appalling heat, were playing their vital part, rising to every occasion and answering every demand made on their resources. The ship was working as a team.

We again passed close to the New Guinea coast, and fuelled in Manus, where we stopped for only a day and a night before continuing on our journey. On leaving Manus, the Captain broadcast to the ship's company and told us what we were going to do.

The operations were to be among the most daring of the Pacific war. The BPF Task Force was to rendezvous with a very powerful American force, and the combined fleets were to launch air attacks, from the carriers, against Tokyo and surrounding areas. We were then to sail southwest to Southern Honshu and Kyushu, to attack targets in the inland sea and naval bases in the area, and finally go north to Hokkaido and attack up there. Besides all this, there were to be several bombardments, and throughout the six or seven weeks the fleet was to be continually in Japanese waters. There was every prospect of a very exciting time, and we were given talks by the Engineer Officer on damage control, arrangements for dealing with casualties were posted on the notice board and we all began to wear our lifebelts half inflated.

In hot weather, the force steamed north through calm seas. From our position on the outer screen we had a magnificent view of the powerful fleet. Many years ago Winston Churchill said something to the effect that Britain's warships were the rock on which the Empire was built. Certainly the British Pacific Fleet, sailing relentlessly towards Tokyo, in July, 1945, was an inspiring sight. It will be a long time before we forget how impressive it looked: the sun setting over the untroubled waters, the opposite side of the screen just visible on the horizon, and, in the centre, protected by the destroyers, the grey carriers, line upon line of planes on their decks, and further ahead, *King George V*, her massive guns reflecting the rays of the dying sun. Interspersed amongst these mighty warriors of the seas were the sleek cruisers, streamlined and efficient, their bow waves and wakes showing pure white against the dark ocean. Then, in a huge circle around all this majesty, whose safety depended on their speed and alertness, were the seventeen destroyers, rolling slightly even in such a calm sea, and conscious that, though the smallest members of the fleet, they were a vital part of its fighting efficiency; and, conscious, too, that they endured the most discomforts for the least share of the glory. Perhaps, too, they felt more smug than disappointed that, although they ran the same risks, their names were never mentioned in the Press or radio. There is a peculiar satisfaction in anonymity.

On July 13th we met the Fleet Train and oiled. This was our first experience with this motley collection of merchantmen and warships. All over the ocean could be seen ships linked to ships by oil pipes, while others waited astern 'in the queue' to go alongside. Each day a destroyer acted as duty steamboat, distributing messages around the fleet, taking mails or tranferring ratings. This last was a spectacle which never failed to be good 'box office value', if that can be judged from the crowd of spectators on the upper deck. Lines were fired from one ship to the other and, by means of pulleys and seated precariously in a 'bosun's chair', the officer or rating journeyed slowly across the 30 yards of angry water which, compressed by the nearness of the ships, swished roughly against their sides or whipped across the destroyer's deck. The passenger's safe arrival was always greeted by vociferous cheers from both sides.

The 'train' brought us fresh provisions and mail, and being with it was also relaxation from the 'keyed up' mental state of fleet work.

The organisation of the Fleet Train was one of the miracles of the BPF, and it was obvious that a master-mind in logistics was behind its organisation.

We left the oilers and, on the 16th, joined up with the United States Task Force. It was of greater size than ours—it boasted five battleships—and together we were a powerful array of naval might. We steamed slowly throughout the day and night, headed for Tokyo.

At dawn on the 17th we went to 'Action Stations' and the first planes flew off the carriers on their mission. The sky was filled with bombers and fighters and we were all prepared for quick retaliation from the enemy, but nothing happened and soon we were able to relax Action stations. All that day we screened the great fleet, ever watchful for enemy planes, particularly the deadly 'Kamikaze' suicide planes. The fleet had experienced this typically Japanese form of attack off Sakishima and knew that the carriers would be the targets. But the only planes which ever came were our own Fleet Air Airm aircraft returning. Before they touched down another strike would fly off, and so it went on throughout the day. As night came on, reports of damage inflicted on the enemy began to be passed over T.B.S. That night we retired and cruised slowly around. At dawn the next day we again went to Action Stations and the first planes flew off once more. Again there was no sign of any opposition and we began to wonder if the enemy was on his last legs or keeping something up his sleeve. At any rate we were at constant readiness for any emergency.

With the return of the planes that evening, the first series of strikes came to an end, and we retired, all that night and the next day, to our rendezvous with the fleet train. On the afternoon of the 20th we joined up with the oilers and provision ships, and throughout that day, and the next two, the business of refuelling went on. The 'train' had brought us some mail, which we were delighted to receive as expectations of receiving any during the operational period had been rather small. During fuelling time we went alongside *King George V*, the first of many such occasions, so that all interested ships were able to get close-up views of her. Many enthusiastic photographers received golden opportunities, as we went close to nearly all the big ships: all the carriers, *Achilles* (the famous New Zealand ship, one of the loveliest to look at in the fleet, graceful and beautifully designed), *Gambia* and *Newfoundland*.

Late on the 22nd we said au revoir to the Train and sailed towards Japan once more. On the 24th, once again at dawn, the Avengers, Fireflies and Seafires, etc., took off, this time to attack naval bases in Southern Japan such as Kure and Kobe. We were screening the fleet all day, but no enemy planes showed themselves. At 0230 on the 25th we were roused from sleep by the alarm bells warning of an impending attack. Everybody rushed to their Action Stations, guns' crews waited eagerly for the chance to fire, but nothing happened, and at dawn the aircraft flew off again to accomplish their missions of destruction. Four times that day the alarm bells called us to Action Stations—the only day on which the enemy showed any signs of reaction to our presence on his doorstep. Three Japanese planes were shot down over the fleet, one of the dead pilots being picked up by our friend *Terpsichore*. The attack was abortive.

The next day we returned to the Fleet Train, and the 27th found us all oiling again. We casually talk and write of oiling at sea, but do not forget what a complicated operation it is and what a wonderful organisation it was that kept this battle fleet at sea for weeks just off the enemy's homeland. The fact that we took its work so much for granted, is the finest tribute which can be paid to the Fleet Train.

For the next two days we were back in the forward operational area, while the planes created havoc with shipping in the Inland Sea of Japan, sinking, among other craft, a Japanese escort carrier. On the afternoon of the 29th the fleet retired, but a bombardment force stayed behind to join up with a similar American force. The British ships were HMS *King George V*, escorted by HMS *Undine, Urania* and *Ulysses*. There were three of the Americans' largest battleships, and three cruisers, as well as many destroyers, present. As night came on we made our way towards Hammamatsu, and industrial town in Honshu, which the big ships were to bombard. The sea was calm and soon a full moon rose. Standing on the upper deck, one could feel the expectancy in the atmosphere, the calm before the storm, the thrill of knowing that shortly we would be taking destruction to a Japanese city.

To describe what happened next will require the reader knowing some details. The British force was known as Task Group 37.2, with Commander Task Group 37.2 in *King George V.* In signal, early in the afternoon, the destroyers were told that after the order to deploy had been given, they were to execute all manoeuvres made by the American Task Unit Commander. At 9.40 p.m. the Force was enveloped in a fog blanket which reduced visibility to about 100 yards. Fog at sea is the sailor's most deadly enemy, and even though the sky this night was clear, with a moon, that did not in any way lessen the potential menace. At 10.05 p.m. we were ordered to deploy on a certain course at a speed of 12 knots. Later, speed was increased to 20 knots. At 10.20 p.m. the first manoeuvring signal to all ships present—a right-angled turn—was made by the American commander.

One of the leading characters in the drama that follows was the P.P.I., a wonderful radar device on which all ships or land, within a certain area, appear as light smudges on a darker background of sea. That is a layman's description, but it will give a rough idea of this marvellous instrument. It is kept in the plot, which in *Ulysses* is situated under the bridge. By a special viewing device the captain on the bridge is able to see the P.P.I. in the plot below and thus keep himself well informed as to the exact range and bearing of the ships in company and judge how accurate is his own station-keeping.

While the turn was being made, our captain was constantly using the viewing device, relaying his orders to the wheel-house via the navigator. He noticed that *Urania* was not far from us and realised that she might have made a mistake and not executed the turn ordered by the American commander, since this was his first signal to the combined force. Sensing danger, he reduced speed to 15 knots and ordered that a good look-out be kept ahead. A little later he looked at the P.P.I. again and saw that *Urania* must be within 600 yards of us. Even had she not executed the turn, we estimated that we would pass astern of her. The captain looked up and ahead and saw a dark shape going left at right angles to our course, on our starboard bow. The next minutes were dramatic. 'Port Thirty,' 'Stop Both,' 'Full Astern Together' were ordered in quick succession. Due to one of these cruel strokes of fate which are unaccountable and for which nobody can be blamed, the last order was received in the wheel-house as 'Slow Astern Together'. This was partly offset by the engine-room artificer on watch in the engine-room who felt there was something wrong, so gave revolutions for about 10 knots astern. However, this was not enough to pull us up and we hit *Urania* while we still had way on. The time was 10.22 p.m. Those on the bridge realised what had happened. Signalmen say they heard shouts from the men on *Urania* as we went towards her. But to men working in offices or positions below decks the sudden jolt and shudder of the whole ship, after which she heeled over to port, came as a shock, and naturally they wondered what had happened. However, the lights remained on and the ship righted herself almost immediately.

Urania disappeared into the fog and reported the collision to *King George V.* At 10.30 p.m. we told the British commander that all our damage was above the waterline. *Urania* was ordered to stand by us and proceed to a rendezvous, but at 10.55 p.m. the captain reported that we were fully combatant, able to maintain 27 knots, and asked that we might remain on the operation. This permission was granted and the force sailed on. We had made a hole in our bows, and temporary shoring was carried out there and then by Able Seaman Doyle.

At ten minutes past eleven the bombardment began, the first shots being fired by *King George V.* Her first salvos landed on the target and she held this throughout—a truly fine piece of gunnery. We were in position a little stern and to starboard of her, and those who were on the upper deck obtained a magnificent view of her in action. As the American battleship to her port fired we saw her lit up by a flash, her guns pointed high—a magnificent and powerful ship. Then she would fire. First a great flash, followed by the angry report of the charge, then across the sky a trail of light marking its path. Before the bombardment had been in progress for long, a red glow on the mainland showed that the shells were finding their mark. About half-way through, *Undine* reported contact with some small Japanese craft and drove them off with her gun-fire. At twenty-eight minutes past midnight the order to cease fire was given and we began to retire, leaving a blazing Hammamatsu behind us. As we went back to the fuelling area we began to feel the results of our collision. Our damage consisted of a hole in the forepeak six feet above the waterline. This caused the forepeak to be flooded and water was leaking into the cable locker at about one half-ton per hour. Our stem was bent to port at a point six feet above the waterline, causing the fo'c'sle deck right for'ard to sag slightly to starboard. In addition a bulkhead on the starboard side was distorted. We discovered that it was far more serious than we had imagined. If we struck any really rough seas our speed would have to be greatly reduced so as to avoid further damage.

On August 2nd we topped up. We left the train and began our slow, rather tedious journey south in boiling hot weather, to Manus.

D. C. High, ex AB HMS* Black Prince *sent me a copy of the front page of the first issue of the BPF's own Daily Newspaper. Here are the lead stories:

AIR STRIKE AT JAPS' HIDDEN FLEET

250 Planes Blast Base

Guam. Thursday—Continuing the non-stop blasting of Japan, Allied planes yesterday swept down over Tokyo Bay and attacked the remnants of the Jap Fleet hiding in Yokosuka naval base.

These ships had remained in hiding under camouflage since their defeat in the Philippines last October. Tokyo Radio said 250 planes took part in the attack.

In all, five hundred planes took part in this and repeated attacks on Tokyo airfields and military establishments. Last night the attacks were continued. Admiral Nimitz confirmed the raids, but said that accurate reconnaissance of damage was prevented by adverse weather.

The latest raids were bringing to a close the blackest week in Japan's history. They followed two, fifteen hundred plane sweeps by aircraft from the combined Anglo-American Fleets and four poundings in as many days from the heavy guns of both Navies.

100 Shelling Victims

While east coast areas of Honshu north of Tokyo, and parts of Hokkaido were still aflame from the rocket strafing and shelling of the past few days, Tokyo Radio admitted that one thousand civilians were killed and wounded in the Hokkaido shelling.

The great majority of Tokyo residents are now living in underground shelters, preferring to stay there rather than move elsewhere.

British aircraft taking part in the sweeps have destroyed thirteen enemy planes on the ground and blasted out of existence hangars, airfield buildings, three locomotives, a railway station and barracks.

'Expect More'—Tokyo

Japanese comments on the pounding of the homeland state that it does not necessarily mean an immediate invasion, but admitted the possibility of a surprise landing.

Domei Agency said, 'We must expect further naval bombardments, but the homeland must be defended without fear now that the Allied task forces can attack us at any chosen time and place.

B.P.F. ACTION NEWS GETS HOME AS OPERATION CONTINUES

When the British Pacific Fleet Task Force joined the United States Third Fleet in this week's heavy air and sea bombardment of the Tokyo area, British War Correspondents were able to send home their action stories even while the attack was in progress.

Breaking of radio silence in the operational area made this possible for the first time in the history of the Royal Navy. Naval listening posts picked up the messages, which were cabled to newspapers in the United Kingdom, America, Australia and New Zealand.

People at home never before had been able to read of a naval action while the ships still were hammering the enemy.

Among the correspondents who put through stories of the bombardment were Reuter's Astley Hawkins in HMS *King George V*, John Ridley of the London 'Daily Telegraph' in HMS *Black Prince*, A. D. Divine of Kemsley Newspapers, Graham Stanford of the London 'Daily Mail', and John Loughlin, Melbourne 'Argus'.

All Sydney newspapers featured the British Fleet's part in the attack. The 'Daily Mirror' devoted the whole of its front page to the story on the evening of July 17, and gave pictures of *King George V* and *Formidable* and of Admiral Halsey and Vice Admiral Rawlings. The 'Sun' also front-paged the story that evening.

Sydney's 'Daily Mirror' reported:

'The arrival of the British Pacific Fleet to take part in attacks against Japan has been headlined in the American Press.'

From: Sto. A. Swift, HMS *Urania*

June 23rd New skipper came aboard
June 24th Did asdic exercises in Jervis Bay all day with other destroyers.
June 30th On our way to Manus with the fleet arriving July 4th. We left Manus *July 6th*. New captain gave the ship's company a speech at dinner. Rumour going round the ship that we are going to strike at the Jap mainland.
July 16th Arrival off the Japanese mainland and joined up with the large American 3rd fleet.
July 17th We had dawn action stations 4 a.m. our carrier planes along with the Americans started strikes on the Toyko area.
July 18th At night *KGV* was shelling the Jap mainland near Tokyo.
July 24th Raids on Kobe. The Fleet caught the tail end of a typhoon.
July 25th More air strikes at Kobe. We had alarms all day.
July 26th Arrived in oiling area. We were the mail boat today.
July 29th We oiled off a cruiser in the morning and joined up with the American 3rd Fleet leaving some of the British Fleet behind. At night we joined *KGV* the U.S. Battleship *Massachusetts* and heavy cruiser *Quincy*. 1,000 tons of shells into Hamamatsu on the south coast of Honshu, the shelling took part from a distance of 4½ to 6 miles off the Japanese mainland lasting 72 minutes and setting the coast ablaze. No opposition was encountered. While this

HMS Urania. *Sydney Harbour 1946*

shelling was going on our carrier planes of both fleets were attacking other targets in the Tokyo area. Also during the shelling one our our destroyers, the *Ulysses* collided with us making a large hole in the side of the after mess deck, this damage had to be plugged with hammocks etc.
July 30th Left the American 3rd Fleet in the morning and joined up with the rest of the British Pacific Fleet carriers raiding Kobe all day.
August 2nd Typhoon in strike area, raids cancelled.
August 8th Russia at war with Japan.
August 10th Air strikes on Northern Honshu. Japan put out a peace proposal to the Allies today.
August 18th Fleet arrived in Manus.
August 19th Left Manus for Sydney, arriving at teatime to crowds of people lining the shore cheering ships and sirens and whistles, a sight to remember.
August 31st Victory march through Sydney. Now for leave at Epping and Bondi Beach, Manly, Blue Mountains, Katoomba. The Aussies did give us great time.
Oct. 6th Left Sydney for Manus. Then on to Guam October 14th with the *Grenville.*
Oct. 17th Arrived Guam, oiled ship and left for Kagoshima, Japan, with *Grenville.*
Oct. 20th Arrived Kagoshima.

Oct. 21st Left Kagoshima with *Grenville* and the cruiser *Swiftsure* for Wakayama arriving October 22nd.
Oct. 23rd Left for Tokyo Bay. Had newsreel photos taken of us doing full speed.
Oct. 26th Arrived Tokyo Bay, oiled ship and anchored in Yokohama Harbour. Most of our flotilla joined up today.
Oct. 27th Went ashore to a RN canteen in Yokohama, had 3 bottles of Jap beer. Bought some chopsticks and photos.
Oct. 30th Had a letter from home saying my father was ill in Derby's Royal Infirmary. Still in Yokohama Harbour.
Nov. 6th Left Yokohama for Ominato, northern Japan with *Grenville* and *Undine*, arriving Ominato November 8th. Weather very cold.
Nov. 10th Left Ominato for Otaru, across from Vladivostok, on the coast of Russia. Snowing and hailing all the time arriving November 11th. Shore leave cancelled owing to gale.
Nov. 13th Left Otaru arriving Hakodate with *Grenville* and *Undine.*
Nov. 14th Heard today my father was very ill and saw the engineer officer about compassionate leave and a naval telegram signal was sent home by the Captain.
Nov. 17th Left Hakodate for Yokohama with *Grenville* and *Undaunted* and we exploded 2 large Jap mines by rifle fire. Arrived Yokohama November 19th and oiled ship.
Nov. 20th We had a Japanese working party on board.
Nov. 21st Was told I could go on two day's leave to Nikko, a Japanese holiday resort about 4 miles from Tokyo with other members of ship's company.
Nov. 22nd We left the ship 6 a.m. for Nikko, had a reserved train compartment and a Jap guide. Stayed at a lovely hotel taking our own food with us. Spent the rest of day sight-seeing, turned in sleeping on mats on floor.
Nov. 23rd Got up about 9 a.m. and four of us hired a Jap taxi to a temple and shrine on top of a mountain. Signed the visitors' book and had our photo taken with a party of Japanese school children. Went shopping in Nikko in the afternoon, afterwards took the train back to Tokyo arriving on board about 10 p.m.
Nov. 25th Still in Yokohama. Just lately I had been having bouts of toothache and in the afternoon I went aboard the Aussie cruiser *Hobart* and had one tooth out and one filled. Received a signal from home today to say my father had not long to live. I was told to pack my kit and await orders.
Nov. 26th & 27th Feeling rotten with sore gums and was told I was to fly home tomorrow on compassionate leave.
Nov. 28th Left HMS *Urania* today maybe with some regrets, having gone round the ship saying cheerio and filled with sips of rum and leaving most of my kit on board I was allowed 19 lb. of gear to take with me. I went to the British Consul in Yokohama and then on to the British Embassy in Tokyo and stayed the night with members of the Aussie Navy.

Nov. 29th Still all the day at the British Embassy waiting for a plane. I was taken pretty well round Tokyo in jeeps to one office and another.
Nov. 30th Left the British Embassy Tokyo at dinner time for Kugi airfield and joined a R.A.A.F. Dakota mail plane and flew to another airfield a short distance away. My first trip in a plane. It certainly was strange but exciting. I stayed with the Yanks and made very welcome at the airfield.
Dec. 1st Left Tokyo in the morning by R.A.A.F. mail plane and flew over the volcano Fujiyama and then over Hiroshima—a sight I shall never forget—and this was a small bomb to what they are using today. Pathé newsmen were on board the plane filming. We arrived at an airfield in Kyushu staying at a Yank transit camp at night. I and some of the Aussie crew joined some Yank pilots drinking ale (Jap) and strange enough they had all kinds of Scotch whiskey, we were all stoned blind drunk. The Yank pilots started to play Russian roulette with the revolvers (mad devils).
Dec. 2nd Left Kyushu feeling pretty rough with hangovers we arrived at a Yank airfield in Okinawa at dinner time and stayed the rest of the day. My word the Yanks certainly lived well in food and drink and we enjoyed it.
Dec. 3rd Left Okinawa in the morning still with the R.A.A.F. plane and weather getting warmer, arriving at Luzon, then after a break we went on to Leyte staying with the Yanks again. They gave us many boxes of cigs. I was wondering how I was going to get through customs at Sydney.
Dec. 4th Left Leyte in the morning, arriving at Morotai at dinner time, after saying cheerio to my Aussie airmen friends, I was taken to a R.A.N. barracks for rest of day and night. It was very hot, my weight 140 lb.
Dec. 5th & 6th Still in Morotai R.A.N. camp waiting for an R.A.F. plane coming from Hong Kong.
Dec. 7th Left Morotai by R.A.F. plane in the morning. It was nice to see and hear British lads again and arrived at Darwin at teatime, leaving again at night, flying through a bad thunderstorm for Glencurry, Queensland. (Flying is strange when you hit air pockets. Keep going down and down, whereas in the Navy rough sailing you go down and come up again.)
Dec. 8th Arrived Glencurry in the morning and left again for Mascot Sydney arriving at dinner time in another bad thunderstorm. I got through customs O.K. with my cigs without being searched and reported to HMS *Golden Hind* officers at Woolloomooloo. Then went up to Epping to see my friends. Left Epping at night by train for R.N. Barracks *Golden Hind* at Warwick Farm. (I think I did well with Sydney Harbour Bridge, having flown over it, sailed under it, walked over and rode it by tram, is this a record?)
Dec. 9th Joined HMS *Golden Hind* barrack joining routine in the messing (barrack life not for me) but was sent to join the liner *Aquitania* at dinner time at No. 6 Wharf, Woolloomooloo. No shore leave given, my hopes of saying goodbye to friends at Epping gone.
Dec. 10th Left Sydney at 8 a.m. in the liner *Aquitania* for Southampton and we had a big send-off by people and ships around the harbour. It was the

largest departure of passengers (4,650) since the war finished, including 4,000 naval personnel. We had boat drill 11 a.m., rest of the day was spent getting to know the ship. I had duties in the naval regulating office.
Dec. 14th Arrived Fremantle and a lot of Aussie servicemen left the ship.
Dec. 15th Left Fremantle at night for Cape Town. It seemed strange being on a large ship after life on a destroyer. Food not too bad. Plenty of film shows etc. and the weather rough at times.
Dec. 24th Nearing Cape Town, we had Xmas dinner on board ship today instead of tomorrow with arriving in Cape Town. For dinner we had soup, turkey, potatoes, peas, Xmas pudding and custard, ice cream, oranges and one bottle of beer.
Dec. 25th Went alongside in Cape Town and shore leave given. We went to the Union Jack Club and a tour round and into the out of bounds native quarters trying some kind of drinks they produce. Arrived back on board around midnight. Still we had a good time.
Dec. 26th Left Cape Town for Freetown in the afternoon. Sea very rough and the journey still the same duties, film and altering clock every day. Weather getting warmer.
Dec. 31st Still on the way to Freetown in *Aquitania*. Crossed the line 1745, saw the new year in drinking brandy.
Jan. 1st—9th 1946 Still duties etc. and weather getting colder after leaving Freetown.
Jan. 10th Went alongside in Southampton. Large crowds and bands greeted us, in the afternoon passengers started to go ashore. The first being Japanese prisoners of war. We stayed on board the night.
Jan. 11th In the morning Plymouth ratings got ready to leave *Aquitania*, customs etc. and had a special train to Devonport barracks arriving midnight.
Jan. 12th Went through barrack joining routine in the morning and was paid then left for home. Arrived Matlock and home around midnight, tired but happy to find dad still alive but ill. I had not received any news of him since leaving Australia. Sorry to say he died soon, after I was demobbed.

Ingli C. Morgan, L/S AAI, HMS *Black Prince*, told me:

I remember we tied up alongside a Yanky Cruiser. I couldn't help comparing it with ours, as about half a dozen American cooks were lined up all in whites being inspected by their Officer of the watch, their hands held out while he looked over them.

I was sitting on a Fan Shaft with my dhobi bucket and standing by the guard rail was our cook. He had on a pair of marine boots which hadn't seen polish since they left Guss (Devonport), a pair of shorts one would never call sparkling white, his body was covered in heat rash, and he was holding a Gash Bin on his shoulders gazing down at the inspection. 'Christ Taff,' he said, 'They are fussy . . .'

We were being attacked by the Jap planes and during a lull in action, the communication boy said, 'It's coming through on the phones that Roosevelt is dead.' Walking around the Ack-Acks I saw a rating sitting on a bollard with his head in his arms. I told him Roosevelt was dead. 'Carry on like this we will all be effing dead,' he replied. I somehow saw the humourous side of the statement and managed a smile.

Having repairs in Sydney, the dockyard mateys were on strike—'not safe to work in dry dock'. My side party was working with no quibble and I told one of the Aussie dockers, 'The thing I notice with you lot is that the only things that don't strike are your matches.' We got on well with them.

About a dozen of us were walking down the street in King's Cross and a woman's voice shouted: 'Go back up to the islands, you Pommy Kippers.' Looking up, we shouted back: 'What do you mean calling us Pommy Kippers?' She replied, 'All eyes and not enough guts.' We had a good laugh.

They opened a large house as a canteen for the fleet to have beers and you were queueing up for hours before it opened and as the glasses were in short supply, if you were lucky enough to have one you held on to it like glue. While in the queue waiting for opening time, a Salvation Army band would be playing popular hymns, and there would be a mass choir singing away. Once the doors opened, only the band were left.

From: AB Doug High, HMS *Black Prince*:

Apart from the stress and strain of being at Action Stations for long periods, there are two vivid pictures that come to mind. The first concerns our baker aboard *Black Prince*. I know most men really like good food, my favourite was when we were at Action Stations sometimes it would be hot soup with 'corned dog' *(corned beef—Ed.)* sandwiches, but to top it all were the 'oggies that our baker could produce, there is only one way to describe them—superb. They were a sight to behold and the taste was out of this world. To this day, I have never seen or tasted 'oggies to compare. My wife is an excellent cook, but even hers do not match the ones on board *Black Prince*, that picture will be with me to the end of my days every time I see a Cornish pasty.

The second vivid picture is one that is very near to my heart, it was when the war with Japan was almost at an end, we were anchored at Manus when our Captain D. M. Lees left the ship to return to the U.K. It was one of the most moving periods of our life together, the boat taking him ashore circled the ship amid cheers and I must confess tears, it felt as though we had lost a limb, he was a father to us all. To say that I was proud to have been one of his men goes without saying, we would have gone to hell and back under his command. We had what we thought the happiest ship in the Navy. On reflection, the biggest mistake that I ever made was being demobbed. I should have signed on and made a career of the Navy. All I have left is memories, revived by your book.

To you I say thank you, God Bless and may your next book be as successful as **Sakishima**.

From: LSA J. Banks, HMS *Urchin*

The flotilla, all freshly painted, sailed out of Sydney Harbour, in line ahead, all together for the first time.

Out in the open sea, somehow, the Tanky, A/B Stan Mills, who was coming up out of the aft storeroom flat, was washed overboard. The hooter was sounded for 'man overboard'. The ship immediately turned to starboard, located the rating, and rescued him.

I went to see Tanky in the sick bay to ask him what happened, he said that all he could remember was that he was taken over the side, as soon as he surfaced he was hauled on board.

He sustained a broken leg.

From: S/Lt. (A) M. J. Brown, RNVR—887 Squadron, *Indefatigable*

It was 7th July 1945 when the Seafire wing left Schofield to rejoin dear old *Indefat*. We had now obtained 90 gallon drop tanks which increased our range considerably and allowed us to carry out escort cover from our Avengers, strikes on Japanese targets and photographic missions as well as the familiar CAPs.

On the 27th July the fleet was off the Japanese mainland, and included in air strikes for 30th July was a briefing for two flights of Seafires to carry out a strike against a Japanese airfield and shipping in the Nagoya area. The attack was to be led by Lt. (A) Doug Alexander RNZNVR and his flight consisted of Ian Hepworth, myself and Eric Cowle, the other flight was led by Lt.(A) 'Mac' Macleod RNZNVR.

I remember the day well—on the morning of the 30th July we climbed into our Seafires and awaited the 'start up' signal, the excitement mounted, and we watched *Indefat*.'s bows swinging into wind, chocks were waved away from Doug's aircraft and he was given the 'wind up' signal and then the green flag dropped and Doug was away down the deck followed by the remaining seven Seafires. We quickly formed up and set course for the Japanese mainland. There had been a warning of possible poor weather near the enemy coast which proved correct, we quickly ran into low cloud and fog. It was a hopeless task in these conditions, but Doug decided to fly along the coast in the hope of better weather conditions and an alternative target.

We were flying in a loose four finger formation with the weather improving a little but still very low cloud. Suddenly Doug spotted what I remember to be an inlet with shipping and shore installations, and he gave the order to attack. We opened our throttles, switched on gun sights, gun buttons to fire and peeled off towards our targets. It all happened very quickly with little time to select a target.

It was soon obvious the Japs were ready to receive us, I watched Doug's aircraft go down into a shallow dive and quickly followed suit. I picked out what I thought to be an armed coastal vessel and centred the gun sight on the wheelhouse area. Light flak came up from a number of sources but I was too intent watching the target grow rapidly in size—I pressed the gun button and watched my shells streaking into the ship, pieces of superstructure flew in all directions and the bellhouse started to smoke. As I pulled up over the ship I hosed the harbour installtions, finally pulling up and climbing over the approaching hillside.

I watched Doug climbing away but he was trailing white smoke, obviously hit and losing glycol, he appeared to be in control of the aircraft but did not respond to my call 'Are you O.K. Doug?' He disappeared into the low cloud and that was the last time I saw Doug's aircraft.

As I climbed up the hillside and over the other side, there in front of me was another river inlet with a small craft chugging along. I remember the moment so well, I was full of anger at losing Doug and I pushed the stick forward until the small craft filled my gun sight. The crew were running in all directions trying to escape my attack, my thumb hovered on the gun button—it would have been so easy to blast them away but something stopped me and I passed overhead and away out to sea.

As we left the target area Eric Cowle called me up and asked me to look over his aircraft for suspected flak damage. I slid underneath and peered upwards, sure enough there was a hole through his starboard wing. Eric and I returned safely.

I have never discovered what actually happened to Doug, or the exact location, but will always remember him as that quiet, good-humoured, kind-hearted New Zealander who never made it home.

From: AB J. Slade, HMS *Grenville*

Grenville went up for the bombardment of the Japanese mainland and one of the most impressive sights was when we were steaming ahead of *KGV* when she was firing broadsides. A few weeks later, after the war, we were ahead of her again, doing speed trials. We were clocking upwards of 37 knots and *KGV* came up from astern and passed us!

When we heard that the war was over, *Grenville* was at cruising stations. We had an asdic contact which was identified as a possible midget submarine. Not having received orders to cease fire it was decided to drop a single depth charge as a warning, and we blew to the surface—an enormous palm tree! The splash had hardly died down before the pipe came: 'Cease Fire—Splice the Mainbrace!' I got a cup of lime juice.

From: Sub. Ltd. (A) Roger McCahey, RNVR—HMS *Indefatigable*

I joined *Indefatigable* in Sydney in February 1945 and I was the replacement pilot for Lt. Agard Butler who was killed in a mid-air collision. He was the senior pilot of 894 Squadron and Jimmy Hayes became the new senior pilot. I became No. 4 in Jimmy's flight, flying wing to Ivor Morgan. When Ivor was hurt in deck landing I moved up to fly wingman to Jimmy Hayes. The mid air collision of Sam Yarde and our No. 2, Sam Cooper, on March 27th 1945, took place a few feet in front of my eyes and bits of their planes flew past my windscreen. I can still remember the silhouettes of their heads in the cockpits as they spiralled down to crash in the sea a few feet apart. The role of flying No. 4 in a flight had no regard to rank. No's 2 and 4 were the wing men respectively of the No. 1 and No. 3. It was a highly successful flying pattern that had been learned from the Germans and was called finger formation. The exact flying pattern was based on the four finger nails of the hand. The only problem with it was that in cloud it was necessary to fly line astern. For the leading pair, 1 and 2, it was easy. It was more difficult for No. 3, and for No. 4 in bad weather it as a nightmare. By the time the bumps and swerves of the leading three had been repeated down to No. 4 it was like flying on a roller-coaster. Every time I saw black clouds rolling towards us and heard Jimmy say, 'Line Astern,' my heart sank. In the cloud the tail of the plane in front would be swaying up and down left to right and worse, start to get fainter as the cloud thickened. This meant increasing revs to catch up and THEN! the tail of the plane completely filled your windscreen. It was only inches from your prop! Put the nose down and chop throttle! Missed. Relief. Yes but where the hell is he now? Increase revs and try to catch up in the cloud. Sometimes it thinned and there he was a few feet away. Sometimes it stayed black. The only thing to do was maintain course and keep climbing. As the cloud broke and the blazing sun appeared one looked for one's flight. With a bit of luck they were not too far away.

On July 25th 1945 Jimmy led us on a strike to Shikoku in some very bad weather. When I saw the massive black clouds ahead of us I prayed that Jimmy would decide it was too rough for Seafires and turn back, but no—'Line astern' came the order. Gently I slid behind my No. 3 (on this day I was back to No. 4 behind Don Moir) and he led us behind the No. 2 and Jimmy. Within a few minutes the wisps of cloud began to flash past the wings and soon we were within the white mist. The mists slowly began to get darker and then within seconds it was like night. I glared at the tail plane in front slowly disappearing into the blackness. In a flash I realised several things. This was no ordinary cloud, it must go up to at least 15,000 ft. and if I lost my leader there would be precious little chance of finding him again. Furthermore we had been flying for an hour. We must be near the coast of Japan and it was no place to be wandering around like a lost sheep. I clutched the control column and increased revs to get closer. With a sickening lurch the fin of the cab in front swooped towards me. To this day and until the day I die, I will always be able to see that fin, the tail, all the rivets and struts. I can recall my surprise at not feeling the shuddering crashes as my prop chewed into the metal. I slammed the throttle shut and stuffed the nose down. The fin disappeared into the blackness of the cloud.

I kept the throttle shut and the nose down and wallowed in the sheer luxury and abandon of just flying to suit myself. Slowly my heart stopped pounding. I thought of Don Moir cheerfully flying ahead not realising how close he had been to suddenly being sent spinning down into the dark sea.

I kept on descending. I might just as well find out what the cloud base was and what the sea was like. Who knows I might find a friendly cab down there? At 1,000 feet I was still in cloud. I made up my mind to stick at it down to 500 feet. Below that it would be likely that the base was completely clamped down to sea level and I would probably go straight into the oggin. At 600 feet I could see my wing tips and at 500 feet the sea appeared below me. It was grey and sullen with white horses all over it. Uninviting was the way to describe it.

The sight of the sea concentrated my mind on the next problem. Where the hell was I and what to do next? I tried a tentative call on the R/T. I did not expect any reply at sea level and 100 miles away from the Fleet and I did not get any. What were my choices now? Fly West toward Japan and hope to pick up a friendly plane. Very unlikely. Get to Japan and bale out? Sod that. Alright, head East into the Pacific and hope for something to turn up.

I set the revs and pointed the nose at the black clouds above me and climbed into them. After ten minutes I had to grit my teeth and stick to my purpose. Lightly built fighters are poor handlers in cloud and bounce all over the sky, and fighter pilots are by temperament and training unsuited to prolonged cloud flying. At 14,000 feet and still in blackness I had to recall all my training to keep going. I remembered the instrument training instructor in Canada. 'Lower the seat, put your nose up to the instruments and DO NOT LOOK OUT.'

At 15,000 feet the darkness eased and at 16,000 I caught a glimpse of the sun. Within minutes I was out of the cloud and in the enormous blue vault of a cloudless Pacific sky. Well now that's alright, but what the hell to do now? I tried again in the R/T, calling up the *Indefatigable.* I listened to the crackle on the R/T and now at last I began to feel a different sort of fear. Up to now the fear had been counteracted by the pumping adrenalin. As the R/T stayed silent with no comforting voice acknowledging my call I realised that I was completely alone, just the blue sky above, dense clouds below and not the faintest idea where to go. I felt very lonely.

I checked the fuel. About another 40 minutes left. Should I press on hoping to bump into the Fleet? No, I decided to circle where I was but keep climbing higher and higher. It would use more fuel but hopefully I would get high enough to pick up someone's transmitting beacon.

Round and round I went, the Seafire's nose just above the horizon, pulling up ever upwards! Every few minutes I would call up the *Indefatigable.* 'Are you receiving me? Over' and each time I listened to the crackle and hiss of the radio but no answering call came.

At 20,000 feet I was down to about 30 minutes fuel. Should I try something else? At least try the *Indefatigable* once more. I listened hard for the reply. Was there someone's voice through the crackle? Try again. Yes! I could just make out a voice giving my call sign and saying 'What's your problem?'

'I'm lost, running out of fuel and I must get a vector back to base.' 'Hang on. I'm on high level CAP over the fleet and I'll pass your request down.'

A few minutes later and back he came.

'Yes they've got you now on the plot. Steer North.'

I was still a long way from home, but at least I was going in the right direction. After a few more mintues I picked up the *Indefatigable*'s homing beacon. Straight ahead. Below me the cloud began to break up and the blue sea showed through.

I called the *Indefatigable.*

'Can you hear me? I must land at once. I've got about ten minutes fuel left.'

'O.K. We're turning into wind. Come in with the others.'

I wasn't going to hang around waiting for my turn. How to get priority? My eye fell on the Verey pistol, already loaded in its container. I pulled it loose. There right ahead of me was the Fleet. I spotted the *Indefatigable* and putting the nose down I roared down her starboard side. I pulled the pistol out, loosened the canopy and fired the gun. The flare made a graceful crimson arc over the ship. An irascible voice came over the R/T, 'Alright you've made your point. Come on in.' I checked the fuel. Empty now, it could cut at any time. I pulled hard across the bows of the ship, a few seconds on the down wind leg then port again into the approach, undercart and full flap down, prop in fine pitch, nose up and pour on the revs. This was what would gobble up the last few drops of fuel. The round-down flew under the engine, bats gave the cut and half a second later came the lurch and leap as the arrestor wire pulled the plane down.

The deck handlers leapt forward, released the hook and a handler beckoned me forward. I opened the throttle and then . . . the engine cut out.

I looked to the left to tell the deck handlers to give me a push. I saw 'Little Wings' sprinting towards me. He leapt onto the wing and thrust his head into the cockpit.

'You daft sod. Why have you cut your engine. We've a bloody great gaggle of cabs stacked up behind you.'

I pushed my face straight at him. 'Little Wings' was a Lt. Commander Bryce-Buchanon known as B.B. in less stressful moments, but I had had enough. 'Because I've run out of effing petrol.'

B.B. jumped off rolling his eyes upwards as though nothing better could be expected of young pilots.

That evening after Commander Whitfeld had given his usual little chat always starting: 'Well, it's getting dark now . . .' I went to the Fighter Direction Office and Radar Room. I asked the Fighter Direction Officer Lt. Easton how they had managed to get me back. He said 'You are a very lucky pilot. Our radar screens only go out to 120 miles and they are not much good at that distance either. We had seen you disappearing off the plot when we got this call from a plane doing CAP just above us at 20,000 feet. He said he could hear you bleating for help and could we give you a course for home. We guessed it was you and we gave him the course and sure enough back you came on the plot a few minutes later.'

I said that the CAP plane had never given his call sign so I couldn't buy him the customary noggin.

'In that case,' said Lt. Easton, 'there will be all the more for me to drink. Let's go.'

Lieut. (A) Ray Battison RNVR, 1772 Squadron picks up his story:

The American Fleet comprised three other Task Forces and I shall never forget my initial feelings of disbelief on seeing such a massive concentration of sea-power. When flying at 2000 feet it was as if there was nothing but ships round 360 degrees to the horizon!

The Firefly was a two-seat fighter-ground attack aircraft but, with a plethora of Corsairs, Hellcats and Seafires to fulfil the fighter escort role, our main task was ground attack with 20mm cannon. The target for this vast fleet was Japan itself, ostensibly the softening-up process prior to a full-scale invasion later that year.

The sorties carried out by the squadron were so many and varied that many of the details escape me, although one or two stand out. An attack on a Japanese airfield at Sendai. We arrived over the airfield just as an American strike was being completed. If I ever had any doubts about the efficiency of the U.S. Naval Air Service they were dispelled then and there! The attack had been so ruthlessly efficient I wondered what there was left for us to do! We carried out numerous attacks on Japanese shipping in the Inland Sea. (I particularly remember one on Harima because my squadron colleague and fine artist Val Bennett, subsequently presented me with one of his water-colours of the attack, which I now gaze at with nostalgia on my study wall.)

I well remember that whenever we carried out an attack on the Inland Sea we were invariably briefed not to attack Hiroshima. This puzzled me until August 7th when we heard that Enola Gay had dropped the first atomic bomb on Hiroshima. I can only assume that the U.S., in a subsequent survey, wished to be certain of the bomb's effect.

Another sortie I remember for many reasons was a raid on Takamatsu airfield. Avengers were to bomb the airfield from 7000 feet whilst our role was to go in at 100 feet, just prior to the Avenger attack, to destroy the anti-aircraft defences. This we did, only to find that, besides the Japanese shells whizzing past our ears, bombs were exploding all around us. Unfortunately the Avengers were slightly out in their timing!

It was on returning from this attack that one of our wing-men had to ditch in the sea short of the fleet. The pilot, Maurice Goodsell, sadly went down with the aircraft but the observer, Don Banks—one of our many prized Kiwi squadron members, managed to climb into the aircraft dinghy. That was the beginning of a very traumatic experience for Don. He was fortunate not to be spotted by a Japanese plane which passed overhead, circled by a Japanese destroyer which then departed, but, at the beginning of the third day of being adrift in his dinghy, he was in a very bad state. He felt that his condition was hopeless and prepared to end it all when he was sighted by an American submarine and taken aboard.

The submarine then proceeded with its mission to bombard the Japanese coast. *Sterlet* subsequently withstood attacks from bombs and depth charges before returning to its base in the Marianas. Don was eventually flown back from Guam, to rejoin us before *Indefatigable* entered Tokyo Bay and the signing of the Japanese surrender. In recounting his ordeal to us he said he wasn't scared—just bloody terrified!

Re-fuelling was a period of rest and relaxation for the aircrews, my fondest memory is of being stretched out on the quarter deck of *Indefatigable* on a camp bed listening to a selection of classical music played over the ship's loudspeakers. I think that experience brought home to me the serenity that can be induced by such music after a period of nervous tension. I particularly remember Rimsky Korsakov's Scheherazade, which remains one of my favourite pieces to this day.

Shortly after the dropping of the second atom bomb, the majority of the BPF left the Task Force and set sail for Australia. The fleet was now desperately short of fuel and spares and surrender by Japan appeared imminent, indeed it came three days later.

Indefatigable remained with the Task Force and I vividly recall standing on the flight deck looking at the flag signal flown from the yard-arm: 'Cease hostilities with Japan' when a Japanese Judy bomber appeared and dropped two bombs uncomfortably close. American Corsairs shot the Judy down but further attacks continued for another hour or so. One Japanese pilot baled out and I was horrified to see one American fighter firing at the pilot hanging on the end of his parachute. Few people have greater hatred of the Japanese and their actions than I have, but I thought this was totally pointless.

Our task was now two-fold—to carry out armed reconnaissance over Japan to ensure that the terms of the surrender were being complied with and to pin-point POW camps to enable teams to be sent in to free the prisoners. Before this was fully underway however, more drama awaited us. On 25th August this still massive fleet was hit by a typhoon to end all typhoons! I recall standing on the bridge of *Indefatigable* looking *upwards* at the top of the waves! The U.S. Admiral signalled the fleet to act independently. When the storm finally abated and the fleet was rejoined, we could see that our own 'independent action' had been more effective than the Americans.

We had suffered damage to our forward lift and I recall that the quarter deck ladder was splintered like matchwood. The U.S. fleet however, was in a far worse plight. The forward 30ft. of the U.S. carrier Wasp was bent downwards at a right-angle, whilst their cruisers cranes for hoisting aircraft aboard had been ripped out of the deck, either lying as tangled metal or missing altogether.

During the last days of August our armed reconnaissance flights began. The terms of the surrender required all aircraft to be lined up on airfields and the engines to be removed and placed on the ground. We had noticed earlier when attacking Japan that their fighters were conspicuous by their absence unless the attacks were in the Tokyo/Yokohama area. I had assumed that Japan was running out of Zeros, but, on seeing these airfields now, nothing could have been further from the truth! The airfields were covered with line upon line of Zeros. They were obviously being conserved for the final invasion of their homeland which must have appeared inevitable. When I hear so many well-meaning but misguided people to-day decrying the action of the Americans in dropping the atom bomb I wonder if they had bothered to think of the much greater carnage that would have been wrought on both sides if it had not.

Our other task of locating POW camps was highly emotional to me. I particularly recall one camp which we found, on the roof of which the prisoners had daubed in white paint: Prisoners from Bataan and Corregidor. The roofs and the compound were alive with American prisoners, waving their arms, dancing and going completely mad with relief from an ordeal which they by then may have thought would never arrive. We dropped naval kitbags into the camps full of food and other comforts, to sustain them until release came.

This was now the end of what had been, for me at least, the longest and most concentrated period of action against the enemy that I had known, not surprisingly it had its cost. 1772 had lost four of its twelve aircraft in action. In addition to Maurice Goodsell and Don Banks mentioned earlier, we had lost our Senior Pilot 'Steve' (C.P. Stevens, a Canadian) Mike le Grange (S. Africa) Glen McBride (New Zealand) and Glynn Roberts. The last two are known to have been beheaded by the Japanese after capture and I subsequently heard that Steve's father had investigated an enquiry after the war which seemed to indicate that the same fate had befallen Steve and Mike. People talk of 'forgive and forget'—for me—never!

The other crew shot down were Burn O'Neill and Ian Darby, also New Zealanders. They managed to bale out and landed in a rice field. They suffered countless beatings, kickings and other indignities and at one time were led out at dawn ostensibly to be shot, but were relieved when a Japanese official ordered that they be put on a train to Tokyo. They were eventually returned to us aboard *Indefatigable* in Tokyo Bay amidst unbelievable rejoicing all round. Ian, a big man by any standards, had lost 2½ stone in his short time in Japanese hands. He recounted to us how their POW camp had been located by American planes who, like us, dropped supplies for the prisoners. Predictably these included a number of baseball bats which he and Burn put to good use by chasing one particularly brutal guard round the camp compound. *(See Ian Darby's own story in* ***Sakishima*** *Ed.)*

Whilst in Tokyo Bay we invited a number of naval fliers aboard from USS *Ticonderoza.* They spent a pleasant afternoon inspecting a British carrier, their particular thrill was sitting in the cockpit of the legendary Spitfire. (Naval version—Seafire). After a typically 'English tea' in the wardroom they returned to *Ticonderoza,* promising to come back that evening to join our celebrations in the wardroom. This they did, although we were initially puzzled to see that they were accompanied by a large number of others in Warrant officers uniform, all carrying a diverse collection of musical instruments! It turned out to be the ship's band who had been rigged out as W.O.'s in order to be allowed to play in the wardroom! Sufficient to say that a good time was had by all!

After the signing of the surrender we set sail for Sydney, cruising down the Japanese coast. I had heard the legend that if on leaving Japan you can see the top of Fujiyama you will return one day. The weather was fine and visibility crystal clear as I stood on the flight deck. I solved the problem by facing the other way.

On arrival at Sydney the squadron flew off to the MONAB at Schofields, preparatory to returning to the U.K. There a most incredible thing happened as far as I was concerned. I had originally left U.K. for Ceylon, together with two other 852 colleagues (Frank 'Ginger' Bromilow and Bruce Armstrong) aboard the *Durban Castle,* converted to a troop-carrier. We spent Christmas 1945 on board and, being a 'trooper', no alcohol was allowed. We therefore pledged to celebrate on arrival in Ceylon. The day after arrival there, two of us went into Colombo to find a bottle of genuine Scotch on the black market. After acquiring it, we thought it best to check that it was the real stuff and repaired to the Gaulle Face Hotel to sample same. The inevitable happened, one 'sample' followed another, an hour later the bottle was empty and, rather the worse for wear, we hailed an open-topped taxi and returned to the mess. En route my cap blew off and, what with the darkness and our rather inebriated state, was never found. I had been wearing my working cap, the top of which under the white cap cover was in a rather disgusting state from oil stains caused by walking under aircraft etc. Now, some nine months later, on walking into the wardroom at Schofields, I was greeted by my old C.O. of 852 days, Bobby Bradshaw, who had also come to Sydney via Ceylon some time after me. We repaired to his cabin for a drink and a chat where he told me that he had received a parcel from Wren officers in Columbo who had found a Naval officer's cap in the street and, upon examination, decided that the only naval officer who would wear such a filthy cap was Bobby Bradshaw—'The cap is enclosed herewith'. Bobby then produced the offensive article and my cap and I were re-united.

I look back now and think how it all began for me when I met up again with Les Wort in the wardroom of *Ruler* in Colombo Harbour. How fortunate I was to have such a first-class pilot—how fortunate we all were to have an absolutely super C.O. Les was a mild-mannered, but very single-minded chap, whose prime objective was to weld together an efficient and, above all, happy squadron. A happy squadron it most certainly was, as to our efficiency, we must leave that judgement to others. I am certain that not one man in either aircrew or ground crew, would have failed to follow Les to the end of the earth if that was what was wanted. There was no 'pulling of rank', just simple honesty and sincerity.

As a pilot he was perfection for me! Deck take-off and landing is not exactly the safest pastime in the world and we certainly made enough. During the whole of this we had one prang when landing on *Indefatigable.* Les was given a 'Wave off' by the batsmen just before touch-down, but unfortunately, our hook had already caught an arrester wire. The engine was pulling us skywards at full throttle and the wire was dragging us down on the deck. The inevitable happened, when at bridge height we dropped like a stone, hitting the bridge superstructure with our starboard wing. The aircraft was a write-off but neither of us suffered so much as a scratch! The sequel to this happened just a few years ago when Les sadly died. Dorothy, his wife, gave me our aircraft clock, beautifully mounted on a piece of the aircraft's wooden propeller. Members of our ground crew had obviously done this for their C.O. and it sits here on my desk as I write.

In 1980 after Les and I had finally retired, we decided, with our wives, to go to New Zealand to meet up again with so many super Kiwis for whom the Branch was renowned. I was delighted to meet up with Kiwis from my old Avenger squadron, in particular, Ian Davis who had been my pilot in 852 squadron — also a pilot 'par excellence'—what a lucky chap I was! Come to think of it, I never failed to get Ian or Les back to our carrier so I guess honours are even!

We, of course, met up with Don Banks, Ian Darby, Burn O'Neill and Pete Kingston of 1772—it was if August 1945 had been yesterday!

When Les died in the mid 80's, Dorothy suggested donations to the Fleet Air Arm Museum instead of flowers. I therefore wrote to old 1772 members suggesting that, if cheques were sent to me rather than the Museum, we could place some specific memento in the museum. After consultation with the then Director of the Museum, Denis White (another old comrade of Les, having been one of his Wildcat pilots in 842 squadron), we commissioned a large oil painting by Brian Witham of that raid on Takamatsu Airfield, with the Avengers bombs falling all around! The legend beneath is 'In memory of 'The Boss' Lt. Cdr. Les Wort D.S.C. R.N.V.R. from the officers of 1772 Squadron'.

Even that is not the end of the story because, in 1987 my wife Edith and I paid another visit to New Zealand and I was able to pass on to our Kiwis a lithograph print of the painting. It meant a lot to them, particularly Don Banks who went into the drink about thirty minutes after the action depicted took place.

The submarine then proceeded with its mission to bombard the Japanese coast. *Sterlet* subsequently withstood attacks from bombs and depth charges before returning to its base in the Marianas. Don was eventually flown back trom Guam, to rejoin us before *Indefatigable* entered Tokyo Bay and the signing of the Japanese surrender. In recounting his ordeal to us he said he wasn't scared—just bloody terrified!

The following is an extract from the log of the submarine USS *Sterlet*, commanded by Lieut. Cdr. Lewis.

26th July (1945)
1446 received report of a downed flier in raft about 30 miles from us. Report, sent via 4475 Kcs, was from orbiting Privateer.
1447 sent ETA 1630 king and headed towards making full power.
1633 picked up Sub. Lieut. D.W. Banks, RNZNVR of HMS *Indefatigable*. Position Lat. 32-58N, Long. 136.33E. He had been in water for two and one half days, was slightly bruised and sunburned, but in very good condition. Communications were excellent; the position reported was extremely accurate and when we reached the position not one but three planes (two Privateers and a B17) were orbiting the downed man.
1830 sent *Sterlet* first to IFO Liaison Officer reporting pick-up.
1925 sent *Sterlet* second to COMSUBPAC reporting pick-up.

Don's own brief account of the incident:

When I was hauled onto the deck of *Sterlet* the executive officer, Lieut. 'Buck' Benny called to the conning tower—'Hey Captain he's a goddam Limey—shall we throw him back!!??—much laughter from the crew!!

From Lieut. (A) Mike Davey RNVR, 894 Squadron, HMS *Indefatigable*

Wing Leader, Buster Hallett, had organized some 90-gallon slipper tanks, which were double the size of our previous ones, and would increase our endurance from two and a half to three and a quarter hours. We had always been short of fuel in the past and, as we said, we'd no longer be quite as short. Soon after we got back to sea we had to test the new tanks as they had an attachment problem. The first two pilots to test them were the senior pilot of 894 Jim Hayes and myself. We were making passage between New Guinea and New Britain in the Solomons Sea. Jim Hayes took off with no problems. Before take-off all my checks seemed to be clear, they were fairly complicated, but ended up with me taking off on main tank before switching to slipper tank which we should use first when airborne, then the rest of the flight would be on main, but my tank refused to function at all and cut out when switched on. After this, the drill was something like this: try again to use tank several times, after which ship says 'drop tank', try this but tank won't drop, so try negative G, try steep turn, so report to ship tank won't budge. Next radio message from ship was: 'Tusco to 154 steer 280 for about 100 miles, when you hit the coast of New Guinea turn south and the first airstrip you will see will be Finschafen, land there and they will see you alright'. The fighter direction officer who gave me these instructions was Ian Easton, later Admiral Sir Ian Easton and his instructions were, as usual, spot-on. The airstrip took no finding, but Jim Hayes for some reason best known to himself had dropped his arrester hook which meant he couldn't land on the Summerfield tracking of the airfield so he stayed in the air, and my landing was unheralded with no fire tender or crash wagon. There was a fair chance of the tank dropping off and exploding on the runway, which happened on the deck with poor Mike Stretton, senior pilot of 887. However in this case the tank stayed on as this was a gentler landing than a deck landing. Apart from this, 24 Wing had no other problems with the 90-gallon slipper tank, not only that, but we flew with them in combat when empty.

On landing at Finschafen, my first confrontation was with an American sergeant who greeted me 'Hiya Mac, what can we do for you?' Not being partial to being addressed as Mac, my reply was an acerbic, 'Good morning sergeant, Lieutenant Davey, Royal Navy, can you drain my reserve and re-fill my main tank?' He replied, 'Sure thing Lootenant', and did it very promptly. Take-off was less than half an hour after this with an empty drop-tank and a safe land on. The mechanics were able to find out what the attachments were, and apart from Mike Stretton's horrendous episode *(See **Sakishima.** Ed.)* we never had another. In fact Buster even complimented me on my handling of the whole show.

After abandoning aircraft or having an accident it was the custom of pilots to fill in their A25 accident report form, this usually included all flying gear which could be written off or kept, as it had been on loan. When the CO, Jimmy Crossman read my A25, he said with a wry grin, 'O.K. I'll perjure myself to say you were flying in a temperature in the eighties in an Irvine Jacket and fur-lined trousers and fur-lined boots, as long as I can have your beacon watch'. This was a small chronometer which we no longer used but kept in our cabins. My reply was equally wry, 'Never mind sir, we could soon be getting a new CO and he'll sign it'. Imagine my horror when in a few days we did get a new CO because Jimmy was shot down, but fortunately he was taken prisoner and survived, we picked him up in Tokyo when we went into the harbour. The Navy are not usually given to displays of emotion, but the decks were lined with cheering ship's company and squadron personnel as he walked up the after gangway and it must have surprised everyone, especially Jimmy himself, how popular he was. He was worth a book of his own, for on one of the early courses like No. 10 course at St. Vincent he was posted to C.A.M. ships, this meant sitting on a catapult in a Hawker Hurricane carried by a merchant ship, hence Catapult Aircraft Merchantmen. Jimmy did this for some time and was launched several times; this was to drive off or shoot down Fokker-Wulf Condors which were attacking or shadowing the convoy. To the pilot of the Hurricane after his launch and successful sortie or otherwise, there were three alternatives; bale out and hope to be picked up, ditch and ditto or make for the coast of Ireland. Jimmy did this on all his sorties; there were two big advantages to this, firstly the pilot didn't get wet and it saved an aircraft, at a time when they were very scarce. Having had a fair spell of this, he was posted to the Western Desert and for a spell fought against the Vichy French, being shot down by them and taken prisoner, but he didn't like them and escaped, picking up a bottle or two of wine in the process. He was back in England on a Hurricane squadron in 1943, followed by instructing at Henstridge and then at last as CO of 894 *(and 24 Wing Leader. Ed.)*, where he distinguished himself even more.

During these last strikes, Jimmy Crossman told the rest of his flights to stay above whilst he dived with the Avengers firing his guns to make the ack-ack keep their heads down, eventually he paid the penalty and was hit in the engine again, but this time it stopped when he was still in a dive. He pulled up to about 1,500 feet with what speed he had left, rolled his plane on its back and dropped out head first by parachute, we had all seen him practice this manoeuvre when on training flights, without baling out of course. He was taken prisoner, not by the Japanese army, which would have been fatal, but by a civilian organization who treated him quite well. *(He was taken to Omori POW Camp, where he met up with Ian Darby, Burn O'Neil and Vic Spencer. Ed.)*. After we picked him up he took passage to U.K. and was de-mobbed, he was next seen by Ken Ward and said he was deep-sea diving, but he must have tired of that for he went back to flying, this time with the R.A.F. as a Flight Lieut. No-one knows of his later life, but he died in 1984 when he would be perhaps 68. A truly remarkable man of great modesty and charm.

We continued to attack the Japanese mainland for some time, July 24th to August 12th. During that time my log book shows fourteen patrols or strikes and then it was all over—or nearly—for even after the armistice the Japs refused to surrender and we had to carry on patrolling for sixteen more days. The final day of the war had been, for 24 Wing, our greatest success, when eight Seafires had escorted twelve Avengers on a daylight raid over Tokyo, on one of the few times they saw the enemy fighters, they were bounced by twelve Zeroes. Our Seafires shot down eight of the enemy and another was shot down by an Avenger for the loss of Freddie Hockley who baled out, but was brutally beheaded by his captors.

Our new CO, after the loss of Jimmy Crossman, was Alastair Mcleod, who was promoted from 887 Squadron, a New Zealander and of the best quality. He had come through his part of the war with Doug Alexander who had just been killed in an attack.

We flew on patrol over Japan when my position was number 2 to our new CO, Mac as he insisted on being known. In fact when we saluted him on the flight deck and said, 'Good morning sir', he said, 'What's all this mucking sir business?'; yet he himself was very polite to his seniors. On this particular morning we took off for what was to be a long patrol of about three hours plus, and some twenty minutes after take-off he signalled to me that my take-off flaps were still down, which played havoc with petrol consumption. At the end of an unventful patrol with no war, my tank would just have lasted, but the ship ran into a storm and was obliterated and my tanks would soon be empty. Looking round for somewhere to land, there appeared in the clear weather a large American carrier landing on Helldivers. One of them must have been surprised to see a Seafire cut into the circuit ahead of him. As American signals were the reverse of ours, and we were in such good practice it seemed prudent to ignore them. It was obvious that the landing was as near perfect as could be, for the tension on the wires was for Helldivers or about double that for Seafires. It would have broken her back, but it didn't and we taxied forward *(Notice how Mike uses 'we' for himself and his Seafire! Ed.)*, and were immediately surrounded by curious Americans who wanted to see the famous Spitfire at first hand. A young Ensign led me to see the Captain through a multi-labyrinth of gangways and companionways. The Captain of this massive carrier, which carried 100 aircraft, was dressed in a sort of siren suit and on his head was a baseball cap, he poured me out a cup of coffee with his own hands, greeted me in a friendly manner, and talked of aviation like the pilot he was. This was the difference, owing to the period when our pilots were all R.A.F., we had nobody with pilot's wings and enough seniority to be Captain of a carrier. This carrier was the USS *Hancock*. My cabin was a large one, probably usually occupied by a Commander. In a dry ship the doctor found me some 'medicinal' whisky and put me at the Commander's table for dinner; this was a bit embarrassing as they were dressed for dinner and my only clothes were my flying overalls which were distinctly gamey. Although they were very friendly no-one talked much and the upper echelons of the US Navy are quite top-drawer with a fair smattering of southerners, which precludes the word Yank. Next morning, all those not engaged in not operating aircraft plus the non duty watch paraded on the flight deck for P.E., which is an anathema to the Royal Navy. However we had a long spell, after which my Seafire was ranged. We had to arrange two batteries in series to start her, but she struck up magnificently and it was an easy take-off from such a long run. After a modest beat-up on her island a return to *Indefat*. Here the reception was similar, for the timekeeper jumped on my wing and said, 'The Captain wishes to see you on the bridge sir'. The contrast between the American and British Captains was very marked. Captain Graham asked me about the whole of my treatment by the Americans, he was resplendent in white shorts, epaulettes, uniform cap with braid. He finally dismissed me but as I was walking away he called after me, 'Davey, did you pay your mess bill?' to which I replied 'No Sir!' He knew full well that I had no money with me, especially not dollars. This was the Captain's sense of humour at all times. When, after the war, we met in a restaurant in Piccadilly, he left himself open to leg-pull by saying he was going into farming after his long naval career. My quip to this was, 'Have you any idea sir?' The Captain replied, 'Of course I have', to which my reply was 'If you are as big an amateur at farming as we were at flying, heaven help you'. The delightful Mrs. Graham laughed and encouraged me to say more. Not everyone appreciated that the Captain was an inveterate leg-puller, but Mrs. Graham also said he was very upset when he lost any of his boys and felt he was losing his own sons. Certainly he introduced two of us to his wife as 'My boys'. He was heard to say to his successor when showing him round the hangar 'Now these are the Harry Seafires, McIntyre'. 'The what Graham?' 'Well you'll find that everything the boys refer to is preceded by 'Harry' ', and we never realized he'd noticed. On rare occasions the Captain left his 'flat' where he lived in Nelsonian isolation and came to drink in the wardroom ante-room. He always drank with the young aircrews and managed to get a bit pie-eyed, but we never knew if this was put on for our benefit. On one occasion he made a loud statement; 'I have been in the navy 45 years,' to which one of the juniors replied 'Well sir, if you'd done 45 deck landings you'd know something about running a f . . . . ng aircraft carrier. The Captain turned round a said, 'Who is this cheeky young sub?' to which someone replied 'His name is Gall sir'. The Captain replied, 'Remind me to clap him in irons in the morning'. Then he went on singing 'The Harlot of Jerusalem', or something equally obscene, with his shirt hanging out and a bowler hat on the back of his head. He was back at work next morning with no trouble. We had to make our own amusements for we had no radio and certainly no television; this left us with ludo or uckers, bridge, shove ha'penny and draughts. It was a long time to be at sea. If you imagine the average hotel lounge and then put up to two hundred men into it, it will be pretty cramped. There was no provision for swimming, but when we were in anchorage we swam over the side. We tried to spend as much time as possible on the flight deck to exercise and also to combat prickly heat which was the scourge of that and several other latitudes. The combination of heat and humidity meant that a very large proportion of the ship's company were suffering from it. The poor engine fitters probably suffered from it most, as grease and oil got on the rash and the whole lot festered.

My last operation of the war on Japan was an attack on coastal shipping, which was way up north. We Seafires went down and strafed, but there were only some barges which didn't appear to be armed and when we arrived back on board we learnt that 'The Bomb' had been dropped and words of Henry V came to mind 'We few, we happy few, we band of brothers, for he that sheds his blood this day with me shall be my brother'. So we all went home and didn't meet again for forty-four years. In my family we had a sequence, my grandfather was discharged, permanently disabled in 1898, my father was discharged in 1916 also permanently disabled and both incurable, it had been my lot to break the sequence.

Mike Davey concludes:

When we sailed into Tokyo Bay the tensions seemed to have gone out of life, and as the aircraft were no longer used at all until we got back to Sydney, life went a bit flat. However we had sailed and flown a great many miles in the last year, since we had left Lee on Solent. We had left behind quite a lot of pilots:

Guy Agard-Butler, Boeker Swart, Norman Heppenstall, Bill Gibson, Sam Cooper, Ken Gall, Freddie Hockley, Pop Quigley and Jack Taylor, all these from a sixteen-pilot squadron, plus one grounded by injury and the C.O. a prisoner, plus 2 time expired, meant that 4 of those who started were still around, this was in 894, whereas in 887 they had lost six pilots in a squadron of 24. We had also lost our mutual surgeon Lieutenant Doc Vaughan and our Air Engineer Officer Len Teff both killed by the Kamikaze on 1st April.

From Sub Lieut (A) Teddy Key, RNVR 1772 Sqdn. HMS *Indefatigable*

During those last days of flying-off *Indefatigable* we searched for, and found, a POW camp at Yokkaichi. Thus the limited life of 1772 as a front-line squadron came to an end on a constructive note rather than a destructive one. Perhaps those medical supplies pushed down the Firefly flare shute by my excellent 'Looker' Sammy Samuelson saved a life, or at least did a little good for our less fortunate fellow-men, bursting out of those prison walls below us. Sometimes I feel that I was lucky in my cleaner war! We did our fighting and then went back to a wardroom. Thinking about Freddie Hockley and Glen McBride—I then think again!

You mentioned the Hellcat incident when the American pilot did quite a lot of damage to parked aircraft. He also did much damage to arrester gear and crash barrier mechanism in the carrier. As far as my memory will permit, he put the *Indefatigable* out of commission! We did not fly after that and from Tokyo Bay we sailed back in comparative style to Sydney, albeit short of decent food, as you stated. I sensed that our gratitude to that pilot knew no bounds. To quote Val Bennett in **Sakishima**: 'I would have been very happy not to have to risk my neck, unnecessarily at this stage . . . ' The American from the 'dry ship' (I think, *Shangri-la*) left the 'wet *Indefatigable*' via breeches buoy in a softened state—no doubt heading for a monumental bollicking! I remember this comment in the wardroom, during 'the session', when asked why he didn't go round again, as indicated by the batsman. 'Well', he drolled, 'I've been in that little 'ole drink before, so I kept my little 'ole head down and came straight in'. That Hellcat must have landed on—nay—crashed on—after August 30th.

The hoisting of the cease-fire signal on the ship's island was a joyous sight. So eventually no war and no more flying seemed to add up to 'Home James'! But as in much of life, happiness and sadness are fellow travellers. Freddie Hockley died—I found out much later—a horrible death, just about the same time those flags were hoisted *(As reported elsewhere, he baled out and was beheaded. Ed.)* I met Freddie Hockley on Peterborough station on the way to join the Navy at Royal Arthur (remember the sign over the entrance: 'Our true intent is all for your delight'—thank you Mr. Billy Butlin). Freddie and I went through to Canada on 75 course in Kingston, Ontario. We were the last Hurricane course at Yeovilton but from there we parted company: he to convert to Seafires and me to wait for a Firefly squadron after a short while with the Fleet Requirement

Unit at RNAS Twatt in the Orkneys—a wonderful opportunity to fly a wider range of aircraft.

Freddie and Glen McBride had one thing in common other than that they met similar deaths (though even here perhaps there is some doubt, and perhaps Roberts and McBride were shot). They both had premonitions of death! For the most part, the FAA aircrew seemed to be a philosophical, extrovert lot rather than fatalistic. I know about Freddie's depression at the end of the war from my mother. He called on her in Cambridge on his last home leave—he had an arm in plaster. He told my mother on that day that he would never see her again. I never told her how he died: he was one of her favourites.

One evening on *Indefatigable* I remember listening to Glen McBride's deeply-felt feelings of gloom and doom. I remember telling him that on my last leave I had set about preliminaries of arranging a place at Oxford as soon as I had a chance to take it up. I had decided to become a teacher: keep my feet firmly placed on a flat classroom floor! Our evening talk was one of much contrast—but I remember it vividly: a time of loneliness when you pour things out. I wonder how much those who helped you to put **Sakishima** together—a story of courage, laced with great humour—also had a story of fear to tell you?

On the morning of my first operational flight over Japan I sat next to the Boss (Lt.Cdr(A) Les Wort RNVR) in the wardroom, trying very hard to eat breakfast. He looked at me and quietly said, 'Nervous?' 'Yes', I answered, 'Very!' 'So am I', this man, sporting a DSC flash, replied. His answer was typical of the pragmatic, tolerant, uncompromising competent and efficient but very human fellow he was. A most able, yet friendly, leader: Les Wort made us into a very respectable, hard-working unit. Goodness knows how good or how bad we really were as a squadron. I will leave that for others to decide and judge. He *was* uncompromising when it came to the standards he required of us and the standards he expected of himself as a commanding officer. He was in fact just a thoroughly nice, caring man and I for one am grateful for his life and the privilege of serving under him. Looking back over nearly 40 years of teaching I pay him a high tribute in believing that he would make the sort of headmaster that is badly needed now. I despair of what is happening in some schools now at that level of management, particularly state schools. But Les Wort was a really great fellow. He restored our respectabilities and confidence: he took us over when the 1772 morale must have been at its lowest and things were not going at all well. At Schofields, Sydney we had further problems with such seeming trivia as wheels. Hot tarmacadam runway and ADDL's (Aerodrome Dummy-Deck Landings) caused much havoc and we were desperately short on aircraft supplies. Two sections of 1772 were hived off to join 1770 and 1771 for Sakishima 'do'. If things had gone a little better perhaps the whole of 1772 would have relieved 1770 on the *Indefatigable,* much earlier than we did, instead of being so fragmented. But then, I suppose, many of our lives might have been very different. 'Que Sera, Sera', as the delectable Doris Day would have said.

Val Bennett's description of the prevailing feelings and sentiments at the end of the Japanese hostilities brought back stark memories of one's own feelings at that difficult time. I quote him again, 'Our part in the raid was not particularly distinguished . . .' Perhaps that sums up 1772's overall contribution, but even so, it cost *us* quite a lot and just about played the biggest part in my education, as a young man. It was a way of growing up fast: the influence of 1772 is indelible. Some of our colleagues are no longer with us to enjoy the mellower years of retirement and some very good memories among the bad stuff.

In **Sakishima** you mention Glyn Roberts only in the context of his and McBride's death. In life Glyn was the essence of the more than courageous fearless FAA pilot. The incident when he kept his Firefly in the air, mixture weakened, pitch coarsened to 'hover' around a downed pilot in the sea may have been forgotten but I bet he must hold the record for the time a Firefly ever stayed airborne on a tank of petrol. Glyn McBride I think, found his fearlessness difficult to fly with. I hated flying as a passenger!

Rod (Steve) Stevens, our Canadian Senior pilot *(and an aerial photographer.—Ed.)* in whose section I flew most of the time is not mentioned in your book. Steve (or Rod as he was known to his wife and family) Stevens, became senior pilot of 1772 Squadron in succession to Lieut. Wright RN. I remember that just before we left the UK, he wanted to see his very new daughter in Dundee. He took an enormous chance of being caught (sic) marshalled, because our departure was imminent. He made it—just, but he never saw his wife, or daughter again. His wife Agnes was in the WRNS from June 1940. Steve, like Les Wort our new CO, became the other senior officer to bring about a rebuilding of the squadron. Steve was a Canadian, trained in a Canadian military school at Kingston, Ontario, I believe. He came from a family with a strong military background. His father, Colonel Stevens, became a distinguished military historian in Canada. Steve did not bear outwardly the characteristics of such a background for in his outward manner he was scruffy, relaxed—very casual. Again another very easy fellow with whom to work. He was 'laid back' I think is the modern term. He was supremely confident and very able both as a senior officer and a pilot, eminently dependable and trustworthy. In many ways he seemed such a contradictory character. Here was a man you could trust with your estate; behind his craggy rugged 'out-backer' appearance was the gentle, retiring family man. Steve was in every way 'hostilities only' officer material. As a pilot and leader I found him quite outstanding and so in my opinion 1772 had found two very fine officers. There was never any doubt about Steve's discipline in the context of flying. He was skilled without being foolhardy and he suffered little those of us who were guilty of foolish errors—and sometimes those errors did seem to accumulate in 1772. He was a courageous fearless man in a very different way to Glyn Roberts. Glyn seemed to have no fear but neither did he have the instincts of survival. Steve did and we could talk about what we'd do after the war. We discussed the possibility of a year, roughing it in the wilds of Canadian lakes.

On a raid on shipping in the Inland Sea, Steve and Mike LeGrange just disappeared! Our section of four Fireflies dived, let go of everything and pulled up to rendezvous point after the usual very low level exit from the target. There we found 'one of our chickens was missing'.

He and Mike LeGrange, a South African with remarkable rugby skills, were lost over the Inland Sea on 28 th July 1945. To quote the Admiral Halsey signal after this raid, 'For the great flying fighters who fought it out over Japan to a smashing victory, I have no words that can add to the glory of the record with their courage, their blood and their lives.' Well that was Steve—I did not know Mike nearly so well—a brilliant pilot and a very close friend. I remember with everlasting gratitude how the day before he died, he got Sammy and I back to the carrier on sheer flying skills and that remarkable core style of his. We were on the edge of one of those typhoons which lurked around the fleet before the 'big one' which you described in **Sakishima** and had enough power to bend down the whole forward end of an American Carrier's flight deck *(USS Wasp—Ed.)*. I had lost some electrics in my Firefly and the homing beacon was almost inaudible. I just could not lose the sight of Steve's wing tip in that wet turbulent heap of cloud and with canopy open a bit I hung on to him. We got back by the shortest course possible in that terrible weather. I landed on early with unfriendly red lights (or whatever) telling me all was not well. Maurice Goodsell was not so lucky on that day: *he* didn't have a Rod Stevens, but Don Banks his observer (God, how I admired the courage of men who did not control situations, but just had to sit there—and trust—and pray! I still wonder if it was a compliment to my flying that Sammy spent his gratuity learning to fly! Or was he trying to prove something else?)—after a long time in a dinghy, was picked up by an American sub. Maurice G. was like many FAA pilots, probably not totally cut out to do this job, but 'hostilities' offered an exciting choice. Maurice was a quiet, droll, dry-humoured academic type with whom I enjoyed talking about the cinema. There were many more naturally talented pilots of considerable genius—such as Dickie Reynolds.

Your book is alive with old memories for me; thoughts have been set in train. I was especially interested in Major Cheeseman's *(CO 1770 Sqdn—Ed.)* comments about the Hiroshima Bomb. As a geography teacher after the war I included geopolitik in some of my grammar school sixth form work. Those eighteen-year-old young people registered the expected cynicism about war, but I too pointed out the truth that without 'the bomb', an invasion of Japan from Okinawa and the Aleutians would have brought an awful carnage. I still believe that the bomb *saved* many lives—and not the least mine! Whilst we enjoyed the role of 'policing' POW camps, we were also expected to patrol aerodromes. Japanese aircraft had to be brought into the open, the airscrews removed and the canopy covers in place. Where, on attacking runs before the end of the war, we strafed amid the real aircraft (very few, I remember at that time because Japan was starved of aviation fuel)—old or damaged or dummy aircraft propped up on say, old oil drums, we now saw aerodromes covered with aircraft. These aircraft, no doubt hidden in nearby woods and the like, would have been taken out and used in one final slam at the American and British Fleet. The kamikaze approach to such a finale would I think have made the Sakishima battles look like a picnic. All this against not only the carriers but the troop carriers with thousands of men on board.

Well, for what it has been worth, just a few random jottings which your book brought vividly to life. I hadn't given a great deal of thought I suppose, to those days in the FAA; very formative years, but often sad, sometimes dangerous and always awash with great comradeship. A combination of your book, telephone calls 'from the distant past', one which began 'Hello yellow 3, this is yellow 4 here,' stirred up one's thoughts over this winter period. I'd even forgotten that old colour call-sign. I have I suppose rejected much of that period of my life which took place over 40 years ago. I have been too occupied with the 'today', with my family and my school career. Now in retirement there has been a little more time to think back.

From Charles Birch, Canada re S/Lt (A) Glyn Roberts DSC (see Sakishima)

The last time I saw Glyn was at Jervis Bay when some of 1772 came into practise deck landings before rejoining the *Indefat*. Nothing had changed and when he put on his flying helmet to depart, I noticed that someone had sewn on two little red horns just like the devil!

And so, it seems, he ended his life in typical fashion. Talking to some of his squadron buddies upon their return to Sydney I recall one of them saying that Glyn made one pass over the target and then, for some reason, made a second run which proved to be fatal. I don't know if you are aware of it, Stuart, but for this action Glyn was awarded the DSC.

Glyn's father is still alive and celebrated his 102nd birthday earlier this year. (1990)

From S/Lt. (A) C. Golightly, DSC, RNVR, 820 Squadron, HMS *Indefatigable*

The Last Raid
Indefatigable *to Tokyo*

Evening of 14 August 1945—the atmosphere was tense.

The wardroom was packed, everybody was there. We were still in active service and sat listening to the wireless. New York and London were celebrating! The Announcer was jubilantly indicating peace was at hand, the War was over—but not for us. 820 Squadron Avengers, Squadron Fireflies and Squadron Seafires were to raid Kizarazu on the outskirts of Tokyo, a fighter base with an estimate of 70 fighters.

Lt. Woodroofe, our Senior Pilot, a fine New Zealander, suggested to the Captain in the wardroom that we cancel the raid. His reply was, 'We must fly the flag to the end.'

Dawn of 15 August arrived and at the Tannoy announcement, 'Pilots, man your aircraft' we tramped out and climbed in to our still dark planes that were covered in early morning Pacific spray. 'Start engines'—we were now committed. As usual, there was orderly turmoil, but soon we began to fly off—4 Seafires, 6 Fireflies and 6 Avengers—each to knock hell out of a 70 fighter airbase.

As usual, after approximately 1 hour of flying time, the sacred mountain of Fujiyama appeared, at which point guns were tested. We were ready.

We arrived at our target at 10,000 ft.—the Fireflies had gone to 'soften up' the Ack Ack. Unfortunately, to no avail, as we were unable to see the target. Clouds were at approximately 1,000 ft. at which height we pulled out.

The Commanding Officer in the lead plane turned to look for a fresh target, the cry 'Bandits' came on the air, at the same time I felt canon shells hitting my aircraft and what looked like stitching appeared on my starboard wing, leaving gaping holes.

Two Zeros flew over me and knowing there would be no 'next time' I hit the clouds to escape. After a 360° turn, I appeared to see some of the squadron going home and on the order 'Jettison bombs' I decided to hang on to mine.

A few minutes later the clouds suddenly opened up, and there below was a large camouflaged complex. Without hesitation, I opened my bomb doors and bombed at low height, scoring 4 direct hits. The whole complex blew, the force was such that it tossed me all over, however, it was soon over. I guessed it must have been a chemical plant, so great were the explosions.

Arriving back at the ship the 'Cease Fire' signal was flying.

Len Baldwin, my wing man, had been hit by the Zeros, his aircraft had been damaged considerably more than mine, as a result of which he had to ditch his aircraft at the destroyers guarding the ship. Johnny Bonass, his observer, had been badly hit, the cockpit was full of blood. He had bailed out over the mountains—we never heard from Johnny again.

Japanese aircraft constantly attacked *Indefatigable* and were shot down 'in a friendly way'.

The war was over.

Oscar Ash, an observer flying with the Squadron that day, witnessed my successful attack.

Incidentally, I was awarded the DSC for which the citation read 'For Gallantry in Air Attacks over Tokyo'.

From TAG Bill Jones, 820 Sqdn

I was a TAG aboard HMS *Indefatigable* with 820 squadron, pilot Sub. Lieut. Dave Thomas and observer Sub. Lieut. Johnny Walker until part way through Operation Iceberg when we had a number of notorious landings. One of them is most likely the one you outline on page 191 of **Sakishima**, not that we found it too amusing at the time. Certainly we ended up between the barriers with flames belching from the engine, reaching way past the gun turret. My pal Chuck Sage, Bill Coster's TAG, described it all later in graphic detail having watched it from 'Goofing Stations' up on the island. Apparently I disappeared from the turret rapidly, only to reappear seconds later having forgotten to unplug my headset. Even so I caught up with the others before they reached the island!

The last bad landing took us over the side in similar fashion to the photographs on page 212 except that having hit the round down we missed all the arrester wires and took one of the gunners with us. He must have had exceptionally sharp reflexes. Fortunately we were all picked up by HMS *Quiberon* and returned to the *Indefat.* a few days later by breeches buoy. Some of the *Quiberon*'s ratings recognised me while we were on leave when the fleet returned to Sydney and insisted on taking me and my friends for a drink—an embarrassing experience.

After this, Dave Thomas left the ship and Johnny and I were joined by Sub. Lieut. Roy Hawkes whose deck landings were superb.

I have often wondered if that same gunner went overboard again when Sub. Lieut. Baldwin followed Dave Thomas' act!

However, the real reason I am writing to you concerns the dropping of supplies on Yokkaichi POW camp. I have a copy of a letter from a POW at the camp which, if you haven't already seen, I am sure you will find interesting. Even today typing it out for you, my eyes have filled with tears just as they have each time I've read it.

It was given to me by Johnny while we were anchored in Tokyo Bay. My understanding is that Johnny, like so many others, added his own personal message to the official one and received this reply. Certainly it is addressed to 'Dear John' but as I have not been in touch with him since 1947 and more recent efforts to trace him have been unsuccessful I cannot confirm this.

I expect that my copy is a typewritten copy of the original handwritten letter but nevertheless I have tried to copy it exactly except for the line spacing.

It occurred to me that if L/Cpl. G. Rochester of the Northumberland Fusiliers could be traced it would be marvellous to have him as a special guest at our April 1st reunion.

FROM EX-POW
YOKKAICHI
L/Cpl. G. Rochester
Northumberland Fusiliers

1st September 1945

Dear John, *(Sub Lieut. (A) John Walker—Ed.)*

I wish to thank you and all on board for everything you have done for us in the past few days, the first day we saw the British Navy overhead we went absolutely mad, and we were scared in case you missed us. You men have no idea how we felt when we knew the Navy was here, because we have been looking for you every-day for the past three and a half years, but we always knew that someday you would win this war.

The food you gave us has done wonders for everyone, we are all looking much better so we shall be fit and well by the time we reach 'Good Old England' which, we hope, will be very soon.

You sure made the Yanks look with your fine air-display, they sure got a big kick out of it, we have 200 in this camp against 25 British so we have had a hard time of it keeping the old flag flying but we won through the day you men arrived.

I wish you could have seen the men get mobile on the cigs and all the other food, everybody was talking between big mouthfuls of peaches and crackers and cheese, and it did not take long to finish off the lot. I hope that you did not run short in the messes but we thank you from the bottom of our hearts.

We looked for you all day yesterday but you never came and we were very disappointed, I hope that you have not moved as we want to see you again as often as possible. We had food, cigs and clothing dropped by a B29 yesterday and he promised to come again today, it is a big day for the camp as we have a lot to square up with these heathens.

We are all at a dead loss as to how to send these letters but we are expecting Red Cross Delegates today so hope to send them through to you.

I have more letters to write so I will close wishing you and the ship all the best.

G. Rochester

P.S. The Japs have left us alone.
P.P.S. Cheerio: Good Luck: and a Happy Reunion soon!

From CPO (S) Jack Smith, HMS *Indefatigable* *(Died 1989. A true gentleman—Ed.)*

Wednesday, 15th August 1945 . . . Aboard HMS *Indefatigable*

Suddenly a racket and chaps come piling down off weather-deck. Something has just crashed into the sea, port-side and astern. Guesses, torpedo, kamikaze, bomb? Commander tells us later a Jap plane 'shot-up' by CAP at 20,000 ft. In Mess late that night hear from gunners on light armament who saw whole scene. 'They first saw a Jap plane, flaming, being chased down by Corsairs (USA). Seemed trying to hit us which could have been original object. Another burst spread pieces of "kite" around, the pilot jumped but although his primary 'chute opened the secondary one did not. He landed in the water and was not seen again. His bomb had already been ditched on our starboard side. Therefore, wrecked plane had landed in sea *port-side* 150 yds from us.

Plane not kamikaze because pilot had parachute (of a sort).

(I witnessed this too from port side, midships bofors. The pilot was unconscious or dead before he hit the water as his body hung limply. See ***Sakishima.****—Ed.)*

From PO Electrical Artificer, Les Bancroft, HMS *Indeftigable*

TYPHOON—25th August
During the early hours of this day the seas rose and the wind increased to alarming proportions. We were being caught by a typhoon, a bad one.

About 7.00 a.m. Chief E. A. Mackenzie (Mac) informed me that Electrical Lieutenant Clegg had telephoned and ordered that I proceed immediately down to the Main Switchboard. I was to relieve the duty watch EA. The ship, at that stage, was rolling and pitching considerably as would be expected in exceptionally bad weather.

At 0730 I visually checked the 24 ft. long Main Switchboard (running fore and aft) with its hundreds of illuminated, coloured Control buttons each controlling an electricity power supply to some section of the ship; there were no visual problems. I then checked the 7 ft. long Dynamo Control board running athwartships at the far aft end of the Main Switchboard. We were running on five of our seven turbo dynamos; normal for sea travel under non-action conditions. The voltmeter gauges, one for each dynamo were flickering at 224 volts each (normal) except for No. 3 dynamo; it was showing 221 volts. I adjusted on No. 3 Voltage Control lever until the dynamo output increased to 224 volts. The ammeter gauges (electrical load indication), again one for each dynamo were nicely balanced at about 2,000 amps. each if I remember correctly. The ship was consuming some 2,200 kilowatts per hour; similar to that used by a small city.

Meantime, the Switchboard Watchkeeper had been checking that all circuits of his special Telephone Exchange board were functioning correctly. The board gave us a direct telephone link to all priority services, emergency centres, the Bridge etc.

The ship was ready, electrically, to face even a typhoon; or so we thought. Occasionally, nature serves up a special typhoon of devastating proportions; this we were to meet. Already, the ship's movements, rolling, pitching, shuddering, in the wildly churning seas, were far beyond any that I had previously experienced.

At 0800 my Switchboard Watchkeeper had completed his watch and was relieved. The new watchkeeper, Bert, would now serve the morning watch 0800 to 1200 (noon).

From about 0815 I lost all track of time. I found myself permanently standing, facing the Dynamo Control Board, my legs well splayed for balance against the ship's vicious shuddering rolling movement. Fortunately, a horizontal handrail ran full length front of the board.

The dynamo voltages were wildly fluctuating as the excessive movements of the ship affected the steam supply to the turbine engines which drove the dynamos. I was busy; rapidly operating the dynamo control levers, attempting to keep a reasonably steady 224 volts on each dynamo.

The roll movements of the ship increased. Suddenly, a dynamo stalled and dropped out; a turbine failure or overheating. Immediately, I adjusted to share the load (amps) of the stalled dynamo equally between the four remaining dynamos. Then, the ship rolled again and another dynamo dropped out; I adjusted frantically with the control levers. Behind me I could hear phone bells ringing and then Bert's voice, 'Engine Room phoning, they are putting No. 6 dynamo on.' I replied 'Good' although I already knew; I had seen the needle of No. 6 voltmeter rising. The dynamo still had to be put into the Ring Main circuit however. I watched the needle rise to 220 volts; now I could help, my voltage adjustment would assist the Engine Room final turbine speed adjustment. 'Stand by,' I called. Bert knew the procedure, he still had the Engine Room connected on the phone, he would relay my commands. I heard him repeat, 'Stand by.' The needle crept up slowly; 'Now!' I called and simultaneously pressed the Control Button to bring the dynamo into Ring Main circuit. Bert's repeat 'Now!' sounded in my ears as the dynamo immediately took up load (amps) which made it tend to stall. We were ready for it, the Engine Room personnel and I, working in unison, the ERAs immediately increasing the steam turbine speed and I adjusting the voltage control. We were back to four dynamos. But, another was now stalling. I had to reduce the electrical load.

The phones; many of them were ringing, Bert trying to answer. I called to him over my shoulder, 'Don't answer any more phone calls. Keep the lines open to the Engine Rooms, Machinery and Dynamo compartments. Ignore the rest.' His reply 'But, the Captain's cabin is ringing.' Again, over my shoulder, 'Ignore it.' I then added, 'We have to reduce the load. Go along the Switchboard and open (switch OFF) all the red coloured breakers and the white coloured ones.' I watched the load on the three remaining dynamos; it was reducing, not enough. Bert's quiet voice, 'All red and white breakers open.' The red breakers controlled all gunnery and armoury services; I had disarmed the ship. The white breakers were lighting and ancilliary, small appliances, services. I had no fears for the lighting, the ship's emergency battery operated lighting although dimmer would immediately and effectively take over.

Then, the Engineers gave us another dynamo, the ship rolled again, and we lost it; and again and again. So it went on until we were down to two dynamos only, fortunately, one Port and one Starboard side; we still had, although inadequate, a source of power supply along each side of the ship. But, one of those dynamos was threatening to stall.

Bert's voice came again, 'The Captain's cabin, it keeps ringing on and off.' Worriedly, almost absent-mindedly, my reply, 'Ignore it.'

We had already reduced load to the minimum. In addition to the red and white coloured breakers, we had also opened (switched OFF) many yellow and blue breakers. The only colour remaining, the green breakers, we had to maintain; they supplied all the ship's navigational aids which included the big steering motors. Even for a short time, we could not afford to lose steering in this typhoon.

One good dynamo, one threatening to stall. I called to Bert, 'Close (switch ON) numbers 1 and 2 Ring Main breakers.' These were the forward end interconnector breakers. Bert's voice came back, 'Numbers 1 and 2 Ring Main breakers closed.'

I had completed the Ring Main. Instead of TWO electrical sources of power supply, one each side of the ship, we now had only ONE power supply completely encircling the ship. I operated a procedure only to be adopted in the event of Extreme Emergency. My decision; what the hell else was this except Extreme Emergency?

Some time later the engineering department gave us one or two other dynamos and as we put the first one into the Ring Main, it blew out the one that had been threatening to stall. It didn't matter, we still had two good dynamos and then subsequently three. I ordered Bert to open (switch OFF) numbers 1 and 2 ring main breakers; we were again back to TWO electrical power supplies, one along each side of the ship. We were winning, at last.

Eventually, the seas and ship's roll subsided slightly. Sometime during the afternoon we were again running on five dynamos and had restored electrical services throughout the ship. Bert missed our full restoration of the ship's electrical services; he had been relieved at 1200 (noon) by a new switchboard operator.

Bert had done a good job. So too had the engineers who had managed, under appalling conditions, to always keep at least two turbine dynamos running.

Three Musketeers
Perce Raby, Les Bancroft, Tom Jeans. Photo: L. Bancroft

At 3.30 p.m. Lieutenant Clegg came down to the Switchboard. 'Any problems?' he asked. I replied, 'We did have, but not now, Sir.' I did not enlighten him further. He too would have been busy all day. He told me to stay until 4.00 p.m. when the normal duty watchkeeper EA would take over.

The phone calls from the Captain's cabin? We heard no more about it. Was it the Captain? Or would he have been on the bridge? We shall never know. Later that evening, I heard many stories of typhoon-caused incidents.

Whilst writing this I have just remembered. I believe I was given no blasted lunch that day. Starved as well.

Extracts from Dictionary of American Naval Fighting Ships, Volume VIII, Naval Historical Center, Department of the Navy, Washington: 1981, sent by George Colling

On 25th August 1945, a severe typhoon, with winds reaching 78 knots, engulfed *Wasp* and stove in about 30 feet of her bow. The carrier, despite the hazardous job of flying from such a shortened deck, continued to launch her planes on missions of mercy or patrol as they carried food, medicine, and long-deserved luxuries to American prisoners of war at Narumi, near Nagoya.

From Lt. (A) Cliff Miseldine RNVR, 887 Squadron, HMS *Indefatigble*

I remember vividly the typhoon that struck the fleet off Japan. We pilots hated being confined below when there was action about. Having survived kit, crockery and other non-lashable items that were being thrown about our cabin and Wardroom, Alan Gambles, Freddy Hurlock and I made our way to the Admiral's Bridge which, being enclosed and glass-fronted, kept the elements at bay, but at the same time enabled us to witness the terrifying scene outside.

Sad to say, Alan, who had emigrated with his family to Canada, died there of a heart attack seven years ago, whilst Freddy was killed in action serving as a Batsman aboard HMS *Ocean* in the Korean war.

Looking out from the bridge into the darkness, we could still see the white plumes and spray of the huge waves towering sixty feet high as the bows of 'Old Greasy' dipped into troughs, shuddered, then struggled up, only to meet the next wall of water.

The three of us watched transfixed; it was a truly terrifying sight to witness the wrath of nature, and wondered how on earth even the mighty 33,000 tons of *Indefatigable* could survive the battering. She did—but only just—because the force of one huge wave broke the mechanism of the forward lift and drove it down to hangar level. This fact has been mentioned briefly in **Sakishima** but perhaps deserves further reference. There was the knowledge that the equivalent of only three inches of sea water over the entire hangar deck would, if the ship heeled over to 45° be sufficient to turn it turtle. This gave a great deal of extra urgency to all available members of the Ship's crew when we were ordered to man brooms, squeegees and anything else suitable and get down to the hangar deck to help clear the water away into the scuppers.

Although it was a combined effort organised by Taffy Griffiths, for which he received a commendation, perhaps the prize for greatest effort went to the team of men who, because the electrical system had been broken, took it in turns to manually raise the lift back to deck level whilst being continually soaked to the skin by more sea water. Altogether a magnificent effort!

I can also confirm the story about the messages that were relayed when the fleets finally emerged from the typhoon—the British Fleet still in formation—the American Fleet scattered to the four winds! I was duty officer on the bridge that day and, as I recall, the message came from the American Admiral (Halsey?): 'Congratulations on weathering typhoon.' Captain Graham's reply was: 'Many thanks. What typhoon?' *(I believe the US Admiral was McCain.—Ed.)*

When the *Indefatigable* arrived back at Sydney, after the conclusion of the war with Japan, we were given three weeks' leave and I decided that driving a car would make a nice change from aircraft.

Only having a provisional British driving licence, I was told by a local car hire firm that I would have to pass a test in Australia. With no other option available, I therefore boldly presented myself at a Police Station in the centre of Sydney, from where tests were carried out.

A burly, grizzled Police Sergeant took me outside in the Square to a battered old Austin 10 and we did a couple of circuits (without bumps, fortunately!) of nearby streets. Not only had I not driven at all regularly before, but I was totally ignorant of the double-declutching required by this old banger!

'You're a bit out of practice, lad,' remarked the sergeant as we returned to base. 'Been more used to a pair of wings lately,' I replied. 'If you can't do better than that, *you'll* probably end up with a pair,' came the quick response.

However, I still have the licence with which I was presented—more or less under false pretences . . .

It was then back to the car hire firm. After being relieved of a ridiculously small amount of cash (by today's standards), I found myself in charge of a gleaming bright red Ford open-top roadster. After a spot of well needed practice which scared the pants of a few back-street locals, I drove to where the *Indefatigable* was berthed at Wooloomooloo. I wanted to change into civvies, having failed miserably to impress the Constabulary with my uniform!

As I parked near the ship—or rather slid to a halt in a cloud of dust—and stepped out nonchalantly, who should approach riding a bicycle but Commander Whitfeld, RN—Commander of the *Indefatigable*! Having whipped off a hurried salute to him, he stopped, looked at my then single gold stripe, stared at the car and said 'Subbies! Cars! Can only afford a bike myself. By the way Sub, only the Yanks have the temerity to salute without their caps on!' He then turned and cycled off in the direction of Sydney!

The idiotic licensing laws in Australia when, between 12.00 and 14.00 hours and 16.00 and 18.00 hours, gallons of booze were rapidly consumed in and around the Pitt Street area of Sydney, so that when the local folk were starting to leave work for their homes, they had to circumnavigate the numerous drunks laying in doorways of shops and offices (not too many in Navy Blue fortunately!).

The hotels and bars of Sydney when, on entering, one was faced with long counters stacked with trays of glasses. The barmen would first take large small-spouted glass jugs filled with their 'own' brand of chemically brewed beer and, starting at one end of the counter, would proceed to fill each glass with 'froth'! Having completed one row, they would then return to the first lot to find that the froth had settled enough to allow them to filter in a bit more beer into each glass—and so on. After what seemed hours, the waiting matelots and locals could actually buy a pint! (schooner)—or, as we soon found out, two or three rounds at once if one wanted to beat closing time and come out reasonably refreshed.

The sight of *KGV* steaming through the fleet off Japan flying the 'Cease Fire' flag to signal the end of the war, and the *Indefatigble's* flight deck which as a result, became thronged with hundreds of celebrating matelots and airmen—until one solitary Jap pilot, who obviously couldn't understand British Flag Signals, decided to bomb us. Fortunately, due to Captain Graham's smart 90° turn which tested 'Old Greasy's' construction to the limit, the missile dropped 100 yards or so astern. *(See photograph in* ***Sakishima****.—Ed.)* Never in my life have I seen such a huge number of bodies disappear from sight in such a short space of time—one minute the flight deck was crowded, the next minute all one could see was the odd head poking out from gun positions!

From Lt. Cdr. Colin Mackenzie, RN, HMS *Indefatigable*

The night of the typhoon found us in close company with US and our own ships. These typhoons mostly follow a northerly course and in these latitudes curve eastward. Our captain all through the previous day was longing for the US Admiral to turn the fleet south and west, but, clearly relying on the curve, which did not happen, held on until he was getting squeezed between the China coast and the typhoon. He belatedly turned us south and through the middle of the storm.

I had the middle watch that night which was dark, blowing like stink and pouring with rain. Even the nearest ships in the formation were invisible either by eye or, owing to clutter, on the radar. About 2 a.m. a greenish light appeared on our port bow; it looked close and remained on a steady bearing, so I put the wheel hard over. The ship swung but the light swung too; I reversed the wheel but it took a long time to reverse the swing, and the danger of hitting one of our invisible neighbours was a horrific fear. We clawed back into place eventually and few, except our unruffled captain knew much about it.

What had happened was that St. Elmo's Fire, which neither I nor anyone else on the bridge had ever seen before, had settled on the foremost of the wireless masts. An awful five minutes and we were certainly in close company formation.

From Rear Adl. A. Davies, HMS *Indefatigable*

After nearly six years of war the following signal was received in *Indefatigable* in which ship I was serving as a Lieutenant Commander.

'From C-in-C Fifth Fleet
'The war with Japan will end at 1200 on 15th August. It is likely that kamikazes will attack the fleet after this time as a final fling. Any ex-enemy aircraft attacking the fleet is to be shot down in a friendly manner.'

Three further signals were also received each instructing ships to 'Splice the mainbrace'—one was from C-in-C Fifth Fleet, one from C-in-C British Pacific Fleet (Bruce Fraser) and one from His Majesty the King.

We could not loyally ignore such authoritative instructions. Accordingly our wise Commander decided that one additional tot would be issued at midday and the other two with supper in the evening. And so it was done with some surprising but connected results.

I remained sober as I had the middle watch in company with a junior RNVR Lieutenant. Most of our first peace-time night watch for six years passed uneventfully enough. I had no hesitation in lighting my pipe openly on the bridge instead of inside the chart table.

Towards the end of the watch, about the time we were wondering whether our reliefs had been called I said to the other watch keeper, 'This is the moment when the unexpected happens. Let us exercise our minds. What would you do if a man fell overboard?' He went through the drill: Lifebuoy Alarm, Stop Both Engines, Hard a Port or Starboard, Siren Signals, Away Lifeboat crew, tell the Captain.

This mental drill had just been completed when the Lifebuoy Sentry's alarm bell did ring. 'Man Overboard from the Quarter Deck'. It would have been too late either to stop or to alter course. It would be unnecessary to man a lifeboat as several destroyers were in company on a circular screen. But we did tell the nearest destroyer and we informed the Captain.

Even before our reliefs had arrived on the bridge the destroyer had sighted the lifebuoy, then the man in the water, and recovered him quickly, wet but unharmed. We kept the Captain informed of this succession of events. He seemed to take the whole affair calmly and never appeared on the bridge. We also informed the Commander, so that he would be aware that a jackstay transfer would be required in due course.

Later when the Commander went up to the bridge some time after daylight he said to the Captain: 'Lucky that man was picked up last night. When are we going to get him back? I can't understand how he managed to fall over the side in the middle watch?' The Captain's reply was surprising: 'What do you mean? What man overboard?'

The answers to these questions took some unravelling. They lie in the juxtaposition of three apparently disconnected events but connected to a common cause—'Splicing the mainbrace'.

The man overboard was a young air fitter who had enjoyed his double tot at supper and felt he needed some fresh air. It was a fine and pacific summer evening. He strolled aft on the flight deck and decided to enjoy the view of ships and the sea. So he sat down, leaning back against the wheel of an aircrft parked at the after end of the ship, his legs dangling over the edge of the flight deck. Before long he dozed off. Later he awoke. It was dark. He stretched his arms above his head and his legs outboard with the inevitable result of dropping over the side.

Five minutes or so earlier the messenger who was calling our reliefs walked across the quarter deck and inadvertently stumbled over one of the pilots who was asleep on a camp bed. The disturbed pilot decided it was an opportunity to visit the heads to relieve himself of some of the beer he had drunk to complete the splendid evening which had started with splicing the mainbrace. As he was turning in again he saw, to his astonishment, a body descending from above and falling into the sea. He called the lifebuoy sentry, who was looking elsewhere. The Lifebuoy Alarm was rung 'Man Overboard'.

But what about the Captain's apparent ignorance of these events? He was a splendid Captain, who had been in command at sea for most of the war. He had always slept well, but not heavily, at sea with the help of a thimbleful of whiskey. A double tot of rum in peace time seems to have had a different effect.

From PO Radar Mech. Bob Bowie, HMS *Indefatigable*

As far as I know, I was the only New Zealander in the ship's company (apart from FAA) from that date until I was sent home for discharge after we returned from Tokyo Bay. There was a buzz going around that the ship was going to NZ before heading back to the UK so I asked the Captain's secretary if he could substantiate the rumour as I wanted to leave the ship in NZ and not in Sydney, but he came back to say that the *Indefat.* was NOT going to NZ and if I remained aboard I would have to find my own way back from England at some future date.

So I left the ship in Sydney and arrived at Devonport (Auckland) by the *Dominion Monarch*, was sent home on discharge leave on November 20th. The *Indefatigable* turned up at Wellington on the 27th. What hurt me most of all was the fact that the only money I had been advanced was earmarked for civvie clothing which I had bought, and I didn't even have enough dough for the fare to Wellington in order to see my old ship and shipmates for the last time. I still bemoan the money shortage.

My memories are only insignificant things like a Lieut. Commander, who, when annoyed, would throw his cap on the deck and jump on it. His next in line, a Canadian Lieutenant, who used to send for a certain Radar handbook when a set had a break down so as to work out the fault, and remedy theoretically, and by the time the book arrived, we had the fault rectified and the set operating again.

Tokyo Bay, where I was one of the volunteers waiting at the gangway to be taken ashore to locate prisoner of war camps, and at the last moment we were told that it was all off because the Yanks wanted to do the whole show themselves.

The 'Illegal' radio which two of us Radar mechs had constructed from an ex-US Army base and modified to take English components on which we were the first to hear the US President's statement that Japan had capitulated, and which was 'blackmailed' from us by a Gunnery Officer who purloined it for himself. I wonder if he ever got it home as it was a fair size.

We, the Radar mechanics, didn't get a chance to see all that went on above decks, as our action station was in our own workshop where we were on call in any breakdown emergency, and even during normal cruising stations we were usually too busy doing routine maintenance to observe the world around us.

One of my worse memories is of climbing the main mast whilst at sea to clean the dipoles on the 281 Radar aerials of salt and sulphur deposits, being almost suffocated by the fumes from the funnel and swaying madly about so that one moment we'd be hanging well out over the starboard side and the next practically over the port side of the flight deck. We did have one of the most effective Radar systems in both our, and the Yank fleet.

From Sub Lieut. (A) Cecil Golightly DSC RNVR, HMS *Indefatigable*

Ref: **Sakishima**. Page 235. One night, I was on duty and had to do rounds with Commander Flying and a Yankee Liaison Officer. He had a revolver and I remarked on it. He suggested he had put it on because he sensed mutiny—another saveloy sausage story—TRUE.

Page 245 Dickie Bird, one night in the dark was feeling his way past an Avenger—the outboard Avenger with wings folded protruded over the side—naturally he went overboard. Len Baldwin in our cabin woke us all up, rushed to the telephone and informed the bridge 'Man Overboard'. He had heard the yell from Dickie Bird as he flashed past our open cabin porthole.

An escorting Destroyer switched on his searchlight and picked up Dickie Bird—good job war was over!

The Avenger going overboard was piloted by Len Baldwin, who was flung out into the sea and saved by a sailor from the escort Destroyer. He was actually drowning—he said his equipment—'revolver, machete etc' was making him sink.

His gunner PO Simpson climbed back on board up the arrester wire.

From Rear Ad. Ridley CB OBE, Chief Engineer Officer, HMS *Indefatigable*

The occasion when, on the way down from Tokyo Bay, offered to take John Ridley (Daily Telegraph Naval Correspondent) round the Engineering Department on my evening rounds. He enthusiastically agreed, and a day or two later we set off. Started with the refrigeration machinery up forard which if you remember was down 4 vertical ladders—all hatches open as it was peace time! He blanched a bit but kept going through 2 boiler rooms and 4 engine rooms—my intention being to do the others later. At last we got to our shaft passage—more vertical ladders; and he said 'I think I feel a bit faint—do you mind if I go and have a breather on the Quarter Deck?' I called on him on the QD on my way forard and said 'Come on we've got 2 more engine rooms and 2 more boiler rooms to do yet.' He muttered something about having rather a lot of work too, and that was that. The sequel was a letter from my father some weeks later enclosing a Daily Telegraph cutting by John Ridley, in which he wrote of 'The Engineers, sweating down below in indescribable conditions' etc. It made me laugh! My father had no idea I was the cause of it.

Fuelling at sea during the '2 days oil' periods, when Colin Mackenzie and I shared the fo'c'sle, and Colin would literally be jumping up and down while some poor unhappy stoker (or was it an AB?) was fishing for the line with a grapnel to haul the oil box on board.

From S.Lt. RNVR—Lt. Cdr. RN Roy Hawkes, 820 Squadron, HMS *Indefatigable*

By my calculations, the ship was no less than forty-eight days out of Sydney. In those circumstances, the quantity of goodies which was supplied to POWs by the ship's company was remarkable. The flight was the first to be made over Japan by aircraft of 820 Squadron since the cease fire. We were relieved to find that the erstwhile hostile gunners had received the message and did not extend their usual welcome. Otherwise we would not have enjoyed swanning around, low and slow, near a sensitive area.

The complement of the camp was written in the sand—'YANKS 196, BR 25, DU 75'. The enthusiasm and excitement which erupted on the ground was something which can never be forgotten.

In addition to the parachuted supplies some aircrews left their own messages. My observer, S/Lt. John Walker wrote a newsletter which was placed in an emptied Verey cartridge case suspended from a parachute which was improvised from my Pusser's pyjama material. Eventually, he had a reply from a Lance Corporal of the Northumberland Fusiliers. That POW was pleased to relate how much *Indefatigable*'s effort had enhanced the status of the British prisoners who were in a small minority at that camp.

The supplies were dropped on 24th August. The US camp CO's letter was pinned on *Indefatigable*'s notice boards on 2nd November. By then, most, if not all aircrew involved had already dispersed. I found and obtained a copy of the letter only because I had to revisit the ship on other business. Regretfully, I cannot remember the names of the other aircrew, but some years ago, hoping that the message might reach a wider readership, I did leave it at the Museum for copying. I do not know if anyone responded to Major Thompson's invitation:

'The following letter has been received from Major Donald G. Thompson, US Army, who was senior officer at Yokkaichi POW Camp which was discovered in August by *Indefatigable* aircraft and on which the Avengers of 820 squadron dropped supplies.

Dear Sir,

First of all I wish to make myself known to you. My name is Donald G. Thompson, Major, US Army Reserve and I was the Senior Officer present at Yokkaichi, Japan, POW Camp which your men found first after the Japs quit fighting.

It is beyond my ability as a writer to express the heartfelt thanks which my men and myself feel toward the men aboard your ship. The wonderful spirit which they showed in gathering up all the many food, clothing and tobacco items from their own personal supplies and messes is what makes life really worthwhile. Especially after having spent three and a half years under the Japs!

There were many, many tears shed that first day when your 'Avengers' came over our camp and dropped the food bags—I know when I read your note I dropped a tear or so too from nothing more than happiness!

Everything which you and your men dropped to us was recovered, even those which dropped in the Bay—we saved all—the personal items which the men sent were truly wonderful and all of us there were mighty thankful for everything.

I wish too, to thank your medical men especially for getting the sulpha drugs to us—we had an American Staff Sergeant who had been hit July 30th with a 50 cal. explosive bullet in the legs. Both feet had to be amputated. By the time your men arrived over the camp, there was much infection forming on both legs, but thanks to the good old HMS *Indefatigable* and her men, my American Sergeant went aboard the USS Rescue Hospital ship with no infection at all, and in good physical condition, everything considered!

The camp strength was 297—195 Americans, 75 Dutch and 25 British. I had one Sub. Lieutenant Dutch Infantry and one Navy Lieutenant (Dutch Doctor) with me at Yokkaichi.

If, by chance, any of your men took pictures of the camp there in Yokkaichi the day they flew over us, I should certainly like to receive one or several of them. That is, if at all possible, for, needless to say the Japs wouldn't let nor did they have cameras to take pictures with anyway.

It is my deepest desire that you will convey to all your flyers and men my heartfelt thanks to them all for their fine spirit and gifts. It was just like 'Gifts from Heaven'.

I should enjoy hearing from you or any of your officers or men at some future date if you have the time—my home address is Donald G. Thompson, Major, C/o J. Thompson, Chappell, Nebraska, USA.

Hope to be able to meet you and your menpersonally some day—but until then, thanks again.

Signed. Donald G. Thompson. Major, US Army'

(Gerry Purnell, Secretary and Instigator of the Indefatigable *Association, wrote to Major Thompson and invited him to the '89 Re-union. He was delighted to hear from us, but could not attend due to ill health. He died shortly afterwards, but we hope to welcome his two sons one day.—Ed.)*

Various signals and Diary extracts from HMS *Indefatigable*, sent by PO Peter Bonney

TO: T.G. 38.5 FROM: C.T.G. 38.5

The following has been read from C.T.F. 38 to all T.G.C.'s this circuit(R) T.F. 38:

Enemy planes smartly handled today. Performance of control and CAP truly magnificent. C.T.G. 38.4 maintained a difficult and irritating option, other task groups excellent position.
(2) Incidentally give the tomcat a saucer of cream and the watchdog not a bone but a stick. Action smart throughout. A hearty well done to all hands.

(D.T.G. 13 1121)

124.02 P/L TOR.0528 R.C. 14/8/45

TO: C.T.G. 38.1 (R) C.T.G. 38.5 FROM: *Indefatigable*

At 1122 yesterday, a Judy diving on me was exploded by one of your Corsairs. Please thank the pilots for their timely assistance and tell them we greatly admired the neat and skilful manner in which they splashed it.

(D.T.G.)

Light P/L TOD 0841/16/8

TO: *Indefatigable* (R) C.T.G. 38.5 FROM: C.T.G. 38.1
C IN C BPF

Your kind message has just been received and will be passed with pride to the pilots concerned. I consider their kill a partial payment on our debt to you people for the skilful protection of my northern flank on a number of occasions.

(D.T.G. 16 0118)

Light P/L TOR.1147 16/08/45

Japanese Midget Submarine: Kure Dockyard. Photo: George Burton

20.08 Storing from *Fort Wrangler* but no defence watches. Film, 'Bathing Beauty'.

21.08 Joined up with Americans at 0830. Oiling from one of their tankers.

22.08 Flying exercises with Americans. About 1000 carrier borne aircraft in the air. An impressive sight.

25.08 Action stations at 0415. Terrible weather. Fall out and go to defence stations. Enter typhoon. Waves appeared above flight deck level. Forward lift knocked down by force of water from one wave. Boats smashed up. Minor injuries. Carley floats washed away. Died down about 1800 and saw that the American carrier *Wasp* had about 30 feet of flight deck hanging at right angles over its bows. A few decks were flooded and the ship rolled 20 to 25 degrees, somewhat short of the 35 degree danger mark. All flight deck secured aircraft held O.K.

29.08 Captain Graham spoke and said this was the 47th day at sea and we were getting short of food and that our meals would get even worse. An Avenger went over a POW camp sighted yesterday and many items contributed by all *Indefat.* messes. (See letter of thanks by an American Major Donald G. Thompson published in the Pacific Post.)

2.09 Captain announced that the war is officially over.

LT CDR JIMMY CROSSMAN RETURNS

5.09 Enter Tokyo (Yokohama) Bay at 1630. Lt. Cdr. Crossman comes back on board about a month after he had baled out over the sea and was picked up by the Jap navy.

I believe it was the 2nd motor cutter which brought him back from another ship that day. I was the bowman of that boat and remember picking up some scruffy individual with tied up ditty bag in what looked like a poor No. 8 rig. When we got back to the *Indefat.*, there were a number of officers on the quarterdeck obviously waiting for him to hurl their jokey abuse of his holiday with the Japs. Also I believe it was Lt. Cdr. Crossman who gave a talk of his experiences over our ship radio show and indicated his desire to be allowed ashore in order to return favours received.

2nd motor cutter went to escort carrier *Ruler* to pick up 350 ratings to make room for unexpected POWs to be taken back home. Wrote letter to my uncle Fred who is an RAF POW in Tokyo (he never did get my letter).

6.09 Mail on board.

From Royal Marine Joe Sharp (ex Cpl.) in *KGV*

We were very incensed at Admiral Bruce Fraser coming in to take over from Vice Admiral Rawlings who had done all the operations. In fact we had on board a special wireless unit for Rawlings to talk to his fleet and Fraser requested he transferred this unit to *Duke of York*. Admiral Rawlings was so mad he ordered us not to listen to Bruce Fraser's broadcasts. Another thing upset us was that we couldn't have the Pacific Star Medal because we had been in the Burma Star area first, so had to have that with a Pacific clasp. Rawlings wrote to the King about it but they wouldn't change the rules so, the Flagship of the BPF couldn't have its own medal.

Most of the Royal Marines on the *KGV* were transferred to American frigates or similar ships prior to our entering Tokyo Bay and were eventually landed on Azumi Island. But I can't tell you anything about this operation as I didn't go. I was left behind with a few Marines to man our 5.25 turret and being a qualified gunner I was captain of the turret. This was in case shore batteries fired at us as we entered Tokyo Bay. Do you remember entering? And what a fantastic sight, a thousand aircraft overhead, and the first sight of the Sacred Mountain Fujiama was something I will never forget. All the shore batteries had to display white flags and there were hundreds of them. I was particularly pleased I remained on board as beside the entering of Tokyo Bay, those put on the ships for landing had a pretty rough time with typhoons about. Beside the turret duties, I had to provide colour guards with my small band of men and I was proud to have to form a guard of honour for Admiral Nimitz when he came aboard. As we didn't go on the initial landings we had to go to the British Consulate in Yokohama and I remember the senior NCO being Colour Sgt. Moore but I don't remember if there was an officer or not. When we arrived we billetted in the gatekeeper's lodge. Presumably it was manned by Japanese, the bamboo floors were a foot thick as the Japs took their shoes off to go indoors. We ripped this all up and had a good scrub out and laid our hammocks out on the floor. I don't remember how we ate. Must have brought rations from the ship but that part is blank. We stayed about a fortnight and besides guarding the place we interrogated people who wanted to see the Consul and arranged it if we thought they had a reason. I remember one Chinese woman wanting help as she said she was married to a British soldier in Hong Kong and had travelled round with Japanese soldiers for you know what and was stranded in Yokohama. The Consulate was in good shape and was partly occupied by the Swiss Consulate during the war, that's why the Japs never plundered, and at the top of the building there was a Japanese caretaker and family in residence. The British coat of arms was still over the front door covered in sacking which we took off. In a cupboard inside the front entrance there was a Union Jack; I formed a guard and the bugler sounded off as I had the U.J. raised on the mast at the roof of the building. I also saw that the Consul's desk was just as he had left it in 1941/42. There was a newsreel taken of the Union Jack raising; the cameraman took our names and addresses and when I saw him later he said he had to destroy the newsreel so that Admiral Fraser could raise the first Union Jack over the British Embassy there!

I always remember with shock that we landed in a country we had been at war with and we didn't have a round of ammunition between us. It was amazing that the Japs didn't use this building as there was devastation all round. The other interesting fact was that in the porch were stacked Japanese newspapers for every day of the war, printed in English. I brought home some with some astonishing stories of the so-called destruction of the British and American fleets, but somehow I lost them.

From Lieut. (S) W. H. Procter, MBE, RNVR, HMS *Argonaut*

From Leyte, it was off to the really Big One—Tokyo. The routine was the same. From dawn to dusk the FAA flew off bombing missions, the *Argonaut* was on its guard/picket duty, at night pulling back to refuel. It may sound rather boring as I'm writing this, but I do recall an incident worth telling—Man Overboard! We were refuelling cruising at slow knots with the tanker alongside. One of our lads fell in, between us and the tanker. The danger was the possibility of being sucked in by the ship's propellors. It didn't happen, because both ships were only cruising at a few knots. The seaman was picked up by a destroyer and later transferred to our ship by breeches buoy.

Boring? Certainly not. We all had a feeling of purpose and just got on with it, until suddenly and unexpectedly we were told to stand off. We couldn't understand it. We weren't even in sight of Japan. Why, we wondered? The Bomb. We didn't see it. We didn't hear it, not even the much published mushroom dust cloud. Hiroshima and Nagasaki were of course much further south than Tokyo. Little wonder we knew nothing about it.

But that was it. All over. We could now go home.

From PO George Bullamore, HMS *Formidable*

I did try to locate Pityilu even at the local library as a matter of interest, but it must be only on the Admiralty charts. Luckily I still have my original sketches for the stencils with the name Pityilu in Old English style, so it wasn't a myth.

As is usual with the Americans it was exceptionally well run and stocked up. There was a well-equipped hospital and quite a few American forces convalescent. The hospital gave us a good check over and advised us to take a daily Mepacrine pill which would be given out in the dining hall each morning. Whatever else they did, we all developed the yellowish tinge, even the whites of the eyes. The cook house was first class, run by diesel electric generators for cooking plenty of choice meals. The first morning after landing there I remember going in for breakfast 0700, joining the queue with one of those partitioned trays moving along the counter with the servers passing out the food. All the bacon sizzling on the hot plate. Also eggs. My eyes almost out of their sockets, looking at the layout. No ration. You had to move quickly or they just kept piling it onto the tray—1 lb mashed potato, 4 or 5 slices of bacon, 2, 3 or 4 eggs as required, beans, marmalade, gravy for the spuds. Sauces. You had to fend off most of this and just get what one required in the right partition on the tray. It was the same for every meal—a choice of meats cold, or chicken, pork chops, they had it.

Tumbler, put in handful of ice and fill up with fresh water(we never had an ice cold drink on the *Formid.*), coffee (no tea). They did put some tea on specially for us one morning, but it was in a large galvanized tub, with ice blocks floating in it. By the time we left we would have liked a slice of the old

Desert Chicken—corned beef—for a change!

From Sub. Lieut. (A) John Blade, RNVR, HMS *Formidable*

As you know, aircrews were especially discouraged from keeping diaries, in case information of significance should pass into the hands of the enemy. And as memories fade, one tends to remember the silly things which happened to oneself personally: as when landing a Stearman (N25 trainer) on my first solo I finished up with my wing on a barbed wire fence—because I had failed to unlock the tail wheel!

Flying strikes over Japan, there was always concern over the fuel consumption of the aircraft, even with the use of drop tanks. With the fleet steaming up to 100 miles off the coast, sorties over 3 hours' duration were common, and at over 4 hours, safe return to the fleet became a worry—especially if there had been some active engagement at full throttle. Add to that the possible hazard of having to find one's own way back to the fleet—as I had to on at least one occasion—after being separated from one's Flight Leader. In theory, of course, everyone was capable of keeping a check on the mission's navigation; but in practice, having to take account of several changes of course and speed, not to mention wind drift, the absence of landmarks over 100 miles of ocean was not comforting.

The greatest worry, though, was undoubtedly the high casualty rate among aircrews. I calculated that, in the squadrons in which I served, by August 1945 I had stood a 1 in 3 chance of not returning. So the odds were becoming pretty steep, and we were all thankful when the atomic bombs put an end to it all: but not in time to save Hammy Gray, alas. About which, I think, all has been told that there is to tell.

In Stuart Soward's 'A Formidable Hero' is a copy of the letter John Blade wrote to Hammy Gray's Mother

My log book reads:

Aug. 9 RAMROD; strafed and bombed combatant shipping in Onagawa Wan; sank enemy destroyer.

Our briefing had been very much as usual—there was thought to be merchant shipping worth attacking in Matsushima Bay, a few miles S.W. from the airfield along the coast. Of course, if we saw any aircraft on the ground or in the air, those would be primary targets. And alternative targets were left to the discretion of the flight leaders.

As Senior Pilot, Hammy (as we used to call him) was in command of two flights; I was flying as Section Leader in the second flight led by S/Lt MacKinnon. We crossed the coast ten or fifteen miles N. of Kinkasan To, and turned southward towards our assigned objective. We were flying at a safe height of just over 10,000', and about 5 miles inland, I think we all noticed the ships in Onagawa Wan, but for the benefit of the Japs we pretended not to see, and marked them out for future attention after we had inspected our original targets.

A few puffs of heavy AA appeared from the direction of Minato, but they were well below us. As we had half expected, there was very little at Matsushima. So on the way back Hammy told us what we were going for. There was a destroyer, a destroyer escort, and a boom defender vessel lying at anchor; and we each had a couple of 500 lb bombs in addition to our normal machine gun ammunition.

We split up slightly, and made a normal converging attack from the N.W., and Hammy of course was leading in. We were in a fairly shallow dive to make use of our cover afforded by the hills, and then to make our getaway out to sea. But we must have had well over 300 knots when we reached the target. We strafed on the way in and dropped one of our bombs. I must have been using a little more throttle than the rest of my flight because I seemed to arrive first of my flight of four, in fact even before the laggards ofHammy's flight; we all went down low to make our exit at water level; I flew through the smoke billowing from the destroyer, at mast head height. Someone (we never exactly knew who) must have scored a direct hit. As the smoke cleared I saw two planes ahead of me.

Suddenly one of them, 300 yards ahead of and slightly to starboard of me, seemed to flame from the port wing root, probably the oil cooler was hit. Then almost immediately the plane went into a steep bank to the right, but the wings continued to turn until it was on its back, and it plunged into the water from a height of only twenty or thirty feet. It must have gone straight to the bottom, and there was hardly even a trace of oil left.

Someone else had seen it, and yelled a warning. We all 'jinked' even more furiously than before. I remember thinking (as I still think) that the pilot must have been killed instantly by a shot from behind as he was making his escape, because the plane was obviously out of control before it hit the water, and it is unlikely that all the control cables were severed. It was only when we rendezvoused over Itzu Shima that we found that it was Hammy who was missing.

Mack of course took over, and we made a second attack. The destroyer was already sunk, but we had still to make a job of the rest. Even after a third attack, however, the destroyer escort was only sinking by the stern and the BDV was only smoking.

During the second attack my hydraulics had given up, and my wheels came down, so I returned home with my wingman right away. As we approached the fleet I sent a 'flash report', and my undercarriage folded up when I touched down on the deck. I went up to see Vian on the Admiral's bridge and told him what had happened. I think perhaps I succeeded in convincing him that the results we had achieved were not worth the cost.

I don't know whether I should congratulate you on the honour your son has won; at any rate I know that we in his squadron are very proud of him.

But I think the best thing I can say is that although I have only been with the squadron three months, I would have done more for Hammy than for any other Senior P I have served under. He had an unfailing joviality, and a sense of proportion which gave me, at least, the greatest confidence in his judgement.

From Nobby Clarke, HMS *Formidable*

The ship was overcrowded with officer flying personnel. This meant that officer accommodation had to be doubled up with 2 in a cabin. Only officers of equal rank were allowed to share. As there was only one telephone in each cabin the Torpedo Officer decided that one ring from the telephone exchange would be for the permanent occupant and 2 rings would be for the temporary occupant. On the second day out of Sydney in the first dog watch it was decided to have a dummy-run and test out the new system. Telephone operator A/B Whitley carried out the test and in one cabin occupied by 2 Lieutenant Commanders, in answer to one ring the usual occupant a ship's officer answered and was told of the proposed calling arrangements whilst the cabin was jointly occupied. When the operator gave the 2 rings for the temporary occupant, also a Lieutenant Commander, he answered giving his rank and name. The operator A/B Whitley said, 'That's right sir—you have 2 rings!' The Lieut Cdr. misunderstood the operator and obviously felt deflated and bellowed at the operator, 'No you fool!' and carried on a diatribe re the importance of the extra half ring. When the operator eventually was able to explain the object of the exercise, the officer smartly hung up.

We were at Manus—it was Sunday morning and the call to Divisions had just sounded and the hands were jostling for position and taking their dressing from the 'Markers' with most eyes heavenwards following the track of a heavy dark patch of cloud heralding the imminence of a sharp tropical storm when another bugle call range out across the Flight deck. Divisional officers and their petty officers exchanged glances and questions till the Chief Bosun's Mate reminded them that it was 'The Disperse' but there was still some confusion re procedure—did we just dismiss or march off? in divisions? The situation was promptly resolved when the captain's head appeared over the port wing bridge yelling—*'Clear the floody Flight deck.'* We did, and the rains came tumbling down!

From Sub. Lieut. (S) Stanley Chatterton RNVR, HMS *Formidable*

When they took off the POWs (Aussies, Brits and Indians) the Indians insisted on bringing on board all their confiscated goats, cows, fowl etc. to be consumed on voyage to Sydney then onto Bombay. They were not allowed below decks and luckily the weather stayed good for weeks, but the smell got worse—they killed and cooked it all on the flight deck, and it still stank entering Pompey even after hosing and scrubbing down the deck.

Signals, sent by Ldg Seaman Radar Tom Roxby, HMS *Newfoundland*

A) FROM: CTF 38 TO: TF 38

The following message has been received from Com. Third Fleet:
'A Well Done to the fighting Blue Team on today's operations. Your pick up and go on short notice this morning as the situation developed left nothing to be desired. A special congratulations to the Tom Cats, Watchdogs, all FDOs, Radar Operators and CAP for a perfect performance.

1416 13/8/45

B) FROM: *KING GEORGE V* TO: CS 4

Your 211125. Noticeable improvement in Radar reporting and Height finding generally. Heights from *Uganda* and *Newfoundland* especially good.

212354

0923/22/7/45

Here are some extracts from a diary sent to me by E/A Peter Daly of HMS *Newfoundland*

1945

Tue May 8	*VE DAY* Arrive Manus (Admiralty Islands)—Spliced Mainbrace.
Wed May 9	Depart Manus—Joined HMAS *Hobart*
Thur May 10	Bombarded Wewak (New Guinea) with *Hobart* and two Destroyers
Fri May 11	Covered Aussies landing at Wewak
Sat May 12	Arrived Hollandia (Dutch New Guinea)
Tue June 12	Depart Manus with *Implacable, Swiftsure, Uganda, Achilles* Destroyers and small aircraft carrier.
Thur June 14	Aircraft attacked Truk (Caroline Islands)
Fri June 15	Bombardment of Truk (Airfields and Gun Batteries) by 4th Cruiser squad
Tue June 19	Hoisted flag of Rear Adm. Brind i/c 4th Cruiser Squadron
Mon July 16	Joined US 3rd Fleet of 15 Carriers—8 Battleships—17 Cruisers—60 Destroyers. Total of 129 Ships including BPF
Tue July 17	Moved into Strike Area—FAA Planes joined with Yanks at hitting Japan—*KGV* and Yank Battleships bombarding factories and foundaries 75 miles NE of Tokyo
Wed July 18	Air Strikes continued—Withdrew from strike area pm
Fri July 20	Replenishment area about 500 miles from Jap coast. Received mail

Tue July 24 Arrive strike area south of Honshu—Carrier planes started striking 0400 Mercantile and Naval ships etc.

Wed July 25 Continued strike successfully, Jap carriers and cruisers and smaller ships and shore installations hit by bombs—departed strike area Wed night

Thur July 26 Arrived replenishment area—stored ship

Thur Aug 9 Joined Yank force of battleships, cruisers and destroyers along with HMNZS *Gambia* destroyers *Terpsichore, Tenacious* and *Termagant* in bombardment of Kamaishi on Honshu at 0345—withdrew at 1900—2nd Atomic bomb dropped on Nagasaki

Wed Aug 15 *VJ DAY*—Strike day—1st strike of planes hit target—2nd strike called back—'CEASE FIRE' Signal at 1120—Suicide plane shot down at 1122—'REPEL AIRCRAFT STATIONS' 1125 FOR 2 HOURS—5 Japs downed—US Admiral Halsey spoke to fleet—Spliced Mainbrace

Mon Aug 27 Put landing party ashore at Yokasuka Naval Base. Entered Tokyo Bay with *KGV, Duke of York, Gambia* Destroyers and US Fleet—Anchor down for the first time for 52 days. Anchored in Sagami Wan in shadow of 12,300′ sacred volcano Fuji-yama

Fri Aug 31 Entered inner bay—Laid off Yokohama

Mon Sept 3 Escort Carrier *Speaker* leaves Tokyo Bay with 473 Commonwealth POW's on board

Wed Sept 5 Our landing party returned to the ship after 10 days in Yokasuka

Tue Sept 12 Changed billet and moved close inshore off Yokahama

Sun Sept 16 Went ashore for few hours at Yokahama—place ¾ flat and nothing to buy—first time ashore for 106 days

Mon Sept 17 Attended hoisting of colours ceremony at British Embassy, Tokyo. Went up to Tokyo in destroyer and in trucks to Embassy—Had bottle of beer

Tue Sept 18 Typhoon hits bay

Sun Sept 23 Visited USS *St Paul*

Tue Sept 25 Depart Tokyo Bay—Civilian released internees on board—Also taking caskets with ashes of 22 POW's down south

Wed Sept 26 Met *Wizard* coming up and received mail.

From Bill McCullock, PO Electrician, HMS *Undine*

The 'Mail Ship' was sending over mail in nets which suddenly split and it was awful to see the long awaited letters finish up in the sea, it happened more than once.

The few days 'Rest' periods at Manus or Ulithi were mainly taken up with maintenance or repairs. We heard that one of the Ulithi Islands must, in a certain kind of light have looked something like a carrier from the air as a few kamikaze planes had hit it and not all had exploded. Our doctor and his colleagues decided to take a trip to the island, they found out quite a lot about kamikaze pilots and even brought back a few 'samples'—some in jars!

During a quiet period a raft had been spotted some miles from the Fleet so away we went to investigate. It was an American pilot in pretty poor shape with a huge shark swimming round keeping him company, we went alongside and he shouted, 'What flag is that?' Someone shouted, 'The Rising Sun' and he was only just prevented from jumping into the sea, obviously preferring the company of the 'friendly' shark to the Japs. We received a nice letter of thanks from him later.

The bombardment of Hammamatsu was a great success with the coastline ablaze for as far as the eye could see, although I would have been much happier if we could have torpedoed some shipping in shore as we had hoped, but there were just no ships round. A few days later we received a message saying that we had ousted Winston Churchill from the headlines. The Daily Express headline read: '*KGV* and *Undine* bombard Japan'. I would love to get a copy of that paper.

We were in Manus when the atom bombs were dropped. Later, anchored off Osaka, having set foot on Japanese soil that afternoon for the first time, in pouring rain, the typhoon hit us suddenly at approximately 03.00. How we managed to weigh anchor I'll never know, but we did, and headed into the storm at full speed and rode it for three hours. Then, as suddenly as it began, the wind dropped. It had been an experience that one would want to forget but our accompanying destroyer hadn't fared so well, she was unable to weigh anchor in time and was beached, but she was lucky, no damage was done when she was hauled off.

When we entered Tokyo Harbour it was sheer coincidence that we tied up quite close to the house occupied by Commander Brooks' father when he was there in the Diplomatic Service. During our stay alongside I was given the task of taking a party to board HMS *Thracian*, one of our destroyers captured by the Japs, she had been equipped as an experimental torpedo ship, she was a mass of radars and scanners, with rail lines running for about a third of the length of the ship with sets of points leading to a massive set of torpedo tubes—the two outer tubes were 30″ and the inner 21″—we spent hours inspecting the equipment which, of course, had been rendered inoperative, most of it with hammers. We spent the night on board accompanied by rats, and as the ship was touching bottom and half full of water we were glad to get back to the *Undine* next day.

When we left Tokyo bound for Sydney we saw an amazing thing during our passage through the Coral Sea. It was almost dusk and a huge 'V' sign had appeared in the sky, very appropriate but it had to be seen to be believed and was very much a mystery. On arrival at Sydney we loaded a consignment of gold to take back to the UK. It arrived guarded by one policeman, whereas in Harwich about twenty arrived. We took three months to get home, Showing the Flag everywhere.

CPO Fred Fallows, HMS *Ulysses*, remembers:

Then, on 15th August, came the wonderful news. The War was over. A good proportion of the ship's company was at a cinema show on the fo'c'sle, and the rest were sitting quietly on the mess decks, listening to the wireless or reading. The film was 'Stage Door Canteen'. About two thirds of the way through, the bosun's mate rushed excitedly into the audience and 'piped' something. He was told by most people to keep quiet, but a few who had half-heard what he said and could not believe their ears asked him to repeat it. 'The Japs have packed in.' Immediately the word spread, there was a great cheer, and the film was forgotten as men dashed excitedly down to their messes to get confirmation of the report. They were told by those who had heard the announcement on the wireless that Japan had offered to surrender, under the terms of the Potsdam Declaration, provided she could keep the Emperor. Although, therefore, the war was not over, the excitement was great, and what followed was never quite as thrilling as that first hour, when we realized that peace was nearly ours and our return home, therefore, much nearer. The suspense of the next days, while negotiations proceeded, was almost unbearable.

From AB N. J. Taylor, HMNZS *Gambia*

Life on board was great, the Kiwis were very friendly, there were just fifty poms aboard and everyone fitted in to make a very happy ship.

We were very near to the *Victorious* when she was hit, also the destroyer *Ulster* was crippled and we took her in tow, eight days into Leyte, Philippines, while floating barrels of water to her, also provisions—the sharks were numerous.

Later we bombarded Kamaishi and I have a certificate which says the *Gambia* actually fired the last shot of the war against the Japs.

From R. Merry, HMS *Implacable*

A Jap plane came over the ship, dropped a radio on parachute. Seafire went up, the crew jumped out without parachutes, dead when picked up by our escort.

An Avenger landed on, opened bomb doors, bomb dropped out, everyone on deck disappeared with a bellow from bridge, and it rolled into the sea.

Firefly coming in to land. Rocket came off its rack, sliding up flight deck with everyone diving out of way. That went into sea.

Seafire, Firefly had a race to be first over Japan. Firefly won. We had the distinction of flying the first British plane over Japan.

The Marine band assembled on the flight deck for retreat (lowering the ensign). The lift man took it down two decks with half the band on, with a snarl and comments. The band appeared still playing. He got put on jankers.

On 21st July 1989, ex-Sub Lieut. (A) Vic Spencer RNVR of 828 Squadron, Avengers, who had flown off *Implacable* in 1945, visited me and I recorded our conversation.

Why do you reckon Japan bombed Pearl Harbour?

Well the US had cut off their oil supplies and raw materials because they had allied themselves to the Germans. In any case Roosevelt had a pretty good idea what they would do. There were no Aircraft Carriers at Pearl were there? Only old battleships. It was a good excuse for Roosevelt to get into the war.

Well, Vic, I won't muck about, I'll come straight to the point and ask you to tell me all you can recall of the day you were shot down over Japan. But before I do, how many of you were in the Avenger, was it three?

No, after Truk only the Flight Leaders carried Observers for daylight ops. They were mostly coastal targets anyway and there was a YG Beacon on the parent carrier. Jack Royasson was my TAG (Telegraphist Air Gunner). On 10th August the target was Koriama some 40 to 50 miles inland and the AM Strike was airfields and storage tanks at Yokkaichi. If I remember correctly it was easy to spot because there was an Ox Bow in the river.

When we started down, the target was slightly to the right and I saw what I thought was a drop tank falling—then I realised that it was the plan form of the wing of a Firefly rotating as it went down and into the ground. There were two Fireflies, one Corsair and one Avenger—us—shot down. The one that I saw come down was the one that Burn O'Neil and Ian Darby off *Indefatigable* had parachuted out of. The others were executed. I was Number 6 of the COs Flight. My target was a hangar, but as I got lower I saw it had great holes in the roof. I thought it was a long way to come to drop bombs through holes so I shallowed out a bit and went for some aircraft in dispersal along the side of the airfield. We were trying to take out anything they could use for kamikazes. Got a bit lower than intended, about 1,500 ft. At that stage it's better to go over the grass.

The Air Gunner told me afterwards that there was a hole under the turret on the left hand side of the airplane about the size of a dinner plate and we were certainly hit forrard.

As I pulled away and opened up I realised I hadn't got full power. I thought the throttle had slipped, then realised it was wide open, but I hadn't got the boost I should have. All happened within a few seconds. The TAG called me, 'We are leaving thick black smoke behind.' I looked at the instrument panel and saw I had no oil pressure at all and the cylinder head temperature was climbing off the clock. Oil all over the port wing. It was coming back over the wing and in through the hole behind the trailing edge and in through the fuselage back aft.

Instead of making for the rendezvous, I thought I would see if I could get back to the coast. 'Call the CO and tell him' I asked the TAG. Alan Swanson got the message and detached a couple of fighters to see us out of the target area—but I didn't see them. In the letter he wrote to my parents, he said that his observer had last seen us losing height with WHITE smoke. He must have been looking at someone else because we were leaving thick black oily smoke.

The engine was getting rougher and Jack said, 'Shall we jump?' I said, 'No, stay where you are,' you see it wasn't easy for a TAG to get out of an Avenger. He couldn't wear his parachute in the turret, it was too small, so he'd have to get down into the belly and get out through the door, during which time you couldn't talk to him.

I had great faith in the Avenger to hold together. It was a big heavy rugged aeroplane. I could see the sea at one point, but there were hills between us. Losing height, I realised we weren't going to make it. Although it was heavily wooded, I saw a few terraced paddy fields off to the left. We just made it on the last few kicks of the engine. We still had hydraulics and I'd got my flaps down as we slid in and hit the ground with my tail coming up. It turned half left, bouncing along and a great sheet of flame came out of the top of the gills. The prop wrapped itself around the cowling. If there was a fire it was now out and we had landed in mud.

There was a village at the end of the clearing and I got out on the left, but Jack got out on the right and we circled the plane a couple of times before we met up. Neither of us was hurt. We could see people in the distance and as nobody expected to survive in Japan, we more or less expected to be bumped off. It seemed a futile gesture to try and run for the coast—but when you've no alternative well . . . It must have been a triumph of hope over reason when I said to Jack, 'Keep your Mae West.'

We set off for some trees, but we weren't making it fast enough, so I said 'O.K. Throw away your Mae West,' and we made our way into a small wood. This is where our training came in useful. We used to do a thing called 'Operation B' Training for Survival Escape and Evasion. If you can't get clear away, it's sometimes not a bad idea to go to earth near the aircraft and let the search spread out around you. We could hear voices and people shouting so we dived into a thicket and pulled undergrowth over us. Then we heard dogs, but they gradually died away; we waited until dark and then moved on. Our intention was to reach the coast and get a boat of some sort. We kept going all the time on the night of 10th and then feeling depressed we stopped and made a fire to cheer us up. There were special matches in our emergency kit and a plastic bottle of bouillon. You take off the tape, add water and heat it up. Although it was August, the nights were very cool.

We decided to move on in daylight and came across a mountain stream where we stripped off and washed. Further on we spied one of those Japanese Arches which only served to drive home our situation.

We lay up on the night of the 11th and moved on in the morning with the use of our compass. Going down a track in the heavily wooded mountains, we met a Jap civilian and walked past him nonchalantly. Obviously he was going to blow the gaff. That afternoon while we were resting, Jack was looking over my shoulder when he said, 'There's a soldier.' I looked round and there was a cordon all round the area. A Jap Officer came up to us, but we didn't get roughed up too much at that time.

We learned later that Burn O'Neil and Ian Darby got banged about and that the two in the other Firefly were executed. We may have been saved by the fact that we were obviously the objects of a search. Not so easy to bump somebody off out of hand if you've been sent out to bring 'em in. They marched us quite a way, put us in a truck and took us some distance. We had a mild interrogation and were told we should have stayed with the plane. They spoke English.

There was a moderate amount of violence—pushing and shoving with a rifle butt—but not torture. Next day we were imprisoned in a school with a wall round it. If they moved you they blindfolded you (not very effectively) and you were manacled. I had marks on my wrists for months.

They took us out into a courtyard where we saw there were two posts with sacks stuffed with straw on them. They had been used for bayonet practice as there were holes in them. To the side there was a row of about a dozen infantry men. At this point I was sure we were going to be shot. Our blindfolds had been removed. The guards 'eased springs' on their Arasaka rifles—you know the rattle they make—so it could have been a change of guard routine. Sometimes I wonder if it was done to scare us. Then we were blindfolded again and taken away. Once you've survived that experience, your morale goes right up. If you think you are going to die and you don't, your morale is restored considerably. After one more night in a small place, we were taken to Sendai where we were thoroughly interrogated. That was the only real unpleasantness. They were bloody rough, not torture but really banged us about. It's hard to take over a period of some 14 hours. The officers were changed after a while. They were always so immaculate and of course wore their swords. Their English was good—sometimes with an American accent—but they were repetitive. They didn't seem to mind what we said, they just seemed to be filling up the paper.

We had been told to forget the 'Name, Rank and Number' thing, but when he asked the name of ship I said, 'Sorry I can't tell you that.' He nodded to the soldier behind me who then knocked me off my chair. It's very difficult sitting manacled. I was hit around the ears and kicked on the thigh. Occasionally he would come this 'officer and gentleman' stuff, 'You have done your duty as a Naval Officer—now you are a POW—now you are entitled to save yourself.' In some ways I think they did have some respect for us. You see a lot of the ill treatment that some of our soldiers suffered was contempt because they couldn't understand anyone surrendering. We hadn't surrendered, we had been shot down and captured.

They didn't mention the Atom Bombs.

Although I didn't tell them the name of the ship, their Intelligence would know that the big 'N' on the plane's tail fin was *Implacable. Indefatigable* was 'S'. I didn't tell them the Squadron Number, but they seemed more concerned with the movement of merchant and troop ships. I said I was only a Sub Lieutenant so wouldn't know things like that. Senior officers kept their rank secret. For instance, I didn't know that Jimmy Crossman was a Lieutenant Commander until we were released.

They wanted to know Captains' names, but if we didn't know we got clobbered. They wanted to know our plans for the future and couldn't understand why we didn't know.

Implacable's Fireflies 1771 Squadron were the first British to attack the Jap mainland. It's strange that their first target was Sendai!

Here we were in cells the size of a telephone kiosk with a bench across one side. You could sit with your back against the wall and your feet on the other wall—and I'm only 5′7″. The cells were in a row with a grille in the front. If you wanted the loo, you shouted 'Bengo' and if you wanted water, 'Mesu'. The days were hot and the nights cold. Mosquitoes were a menace. There was an iron water pipe on the wall about 1″ diameter, so we started tapping morse to each other. Ian Darby was next to me and I tapped, 'It's bloody cramped in here.' He answered, 'You should worry, I'm 6′4″.'

They never did find the hacksaw blade which was stitched into the seam of my trousers. I've still got it. It stayed there until we got to Omori Prison Camp and I used it for making some chopsticks.

Jack was beyond Ian and it was depressing not knowing how long we would be there. After a few days we were taken to Sendai Railway Station and I was sitting on the floor blindfolded and manacled when a Jap damn near crippled me with a rifle butt in the thigh. I was limping for weeks. We took a train to Tokyo and thence to Omori which is on a sort of isthmus. It was like a slum surrounded by barbed wire.

You remember the funniest things. In the huts were benches with mats on them for sleeping. Each hut had a room at both ends. Captain James was in one of those. That was the officer whose book you are quoting from.

Well there were some RN Petty Officers there and they seemed like old men. One of them said, 'Would you like a cup of tea?' 'Come off it,' I replied. 'Sugar and milk?' he continued. At the back of the sleeping space they had got panels they could take out. The spaces behind were full of stuff that they had pinched on working parties. There was condensed milk, sugar and tea. I can't remember how they boiled the water.

Some of the American B29 crews were there. I remember Captain Mansfield, Major 'Pappy' Boynton USM who was a famous fighter pilot. He wrote a couple of books afterwards. One was named after his squadron who were known as 'The Black Sheep'. Then there was Cdr. Waters of the USS *Houston* which was sunk early on and Lt. Cameron, a Corsair pilot shot down earlier. The Japs were supposed to pay those in Working Parties. Suddenly there was a rush to heed the Geneva Convention and we were paid some money just before release. I've still got it. It's Yen paper money. Then we heard rumours that the war was over and that some of the Jap officers were going to kill an Englishman before the surrender.

They began to relax a little. I noticed that the hut where our Guard slept was empty, the windows were open and on the bed was a bayonet and belt. I pinched it so that I would not be entirely defenceless. Captain James wasn't too happy with me. Still, he gave me a stick of rough chocolate. God I was hungry.

They seemed to get our officers to deliberately do the dirty jobs. We had to empty the urine pits—buckets on sticks. They allowed us one bath. You wash yourself, then all get into the bath together.

When we saw the US Naval aircraft fly over unmolested, we knew it was over. They threw out anything they had with them like bars of chocolate. Then came the boxes. One case came hurtling through the roof. Some landed in the sea, so I got a pair of salt water washed trousers.

On 31 August the Americans came up the beach in landing craft.

We heard the US officer said to the Jap CO, 'I've come to take the prisoners.' The Jap replied 'I have no authority to release the prisoners.' Whereupon the Yank said, 'You have NO authority,' and laid his .45 on the desk.

You know, that place was lousy. As soon as the light went out, the bed bugs would come out in their thousands.

How do you feel about them now Vic?

It's difficult now to remember how I felt then, how bitter I was. It's hard for me to believe I felt this way, but if someone handed me a rifle at that time and said, 'Go and shoot a Jap,' I could have done it with as little compunction as I would shoot a rabbit. We didn't think of them as a human enemy and I absolutely hated them.

As a young man of 20 or so you are not used to being knocked about. Suddenly to find yourself at the mercy of a bunch of guys who just punch you about for the fun of it—that's what used to get to me. I know the Germans did it, but you had the feeling with them it was done for a reason. The Japs knocked you about because they enjoyed it. They liked showing you that they were on top and you were underneath.

I admired their personal courage and the original Aircrews were among the best in the business, but they got 'used up'. They were not prepared for a long war.

People who lived in Japan know them better than I do, but unless you've been in a situation where he is completely in control, you don't know them in their true colours.

They are different people altogether from us. They think differently and given a free hand, they act differently.

What do you think their motive is now?

The same as it was in 1941. They're just using a different method. Domination is the ultimate. I don't have any hatred any more and I find it difficult to look back and remember how I felt. I think of some of the other FAA pilots who never made it to a POW Camp 'cos they got their heads chopped off.

They were still executing pilots right to the end. Some of the chaps in Changi were executed on the beach when the war was officially over. It's these chaps I think about.

I can understand the Germans. I can even feel a certain affinity with German pilots. I can never feel that way about the Japs—they're DIFFERENT—and they still worry me. It's difficult to see ourselves at war with the Germans again, but I can see that Far East thing blowing up again. You see, they don't feel we beat them.

Although religion is not a big part of my life, I try to live by the Christian ethic.

There was a long silence and he saw me looking at the tape recorder to see how much longer we had got.

Yes, well, we were taken onto the Hospital ship *Benevolence,* and had a medical examination, bathed, were issued with US clothing and then went on board HMS *Speaker* when the *Indefatigable* steamed in.

Yes, and I was on the Quarterdeck when the boat brought you back. I remember Jimmy Crossman telling us all briefly what had happened as you stood in a group by the Port After Gangway. You were ushered inside and I didn't see you again until today.

I remember someone coming out onto the Quarterdeck that evening as I took a last stroll before turning in. 'There's a helluva party going on with those chaps who've come back,' he said. 'Yes I know,' I can clearly remember saying. 'It can't be good for them with what they've been through.'

Free Again. Sept. '45
Burn O'Neil, Ian Darby and Jimmy Crossman being interviewed by Canadian reporter, Stanley Maxted (wearing beret)

From Leading Telegraphist Albert A. Scott, HMS *Wakeful*

I took down the message that the Japanese had surrendered. We then went into Tokyo Bay. After two days we were sent 400 miles up the coast to a large POW camp at Sendai, we brought out 350 of our POWs and took them back to Tokyo Bay, ready to be flown home.

AB Joe Mole and Sto. G. Postlethwaite kindly loaned me the 'Pacific Commission 1944—1946, HMS *Barfleur*' from which I obtained the following:

Adpoted by the city of Darlington, Durham.

Fourth ship of her name in the British Navy, built by Swan Hunter, Wallsend, she was the first of a class of revolutionary design, laid down 28th October 1942, launched 1st November 1943—finally completed 20th January 1945.

The very latest gunnery control system, the Mark 6 Director (teething troubles at Vickers delayed completion 12 months).

Largest destroyer in the world at the time and first to meet her French namesake (April 1945 Gibraltar).

Barfleur's first strikes were 24th/25th—Inland Sea—Kure Naval Base.

The Rear Adl. left by jackstay on 31st to *Speaker* for passage to his flagship HMS *Tyne*. In the history of the war he was the only RA Destroyers to fly his flag in a destroyer at sea during an operation.

Typhoons first week August

On the 22nd August *Barfleur* joined forces with Task Group 38.3, and American Fast Carrier Group. Only two British Destroyers, *Wakeful* and *Wrangler* were in company. The duty assigned to this group was to provide air cover for the Fleet in Sagami Wan, and for the occupational forces in the Tokyo area, until sufficiently powerful air forces had been established in Japan. Operating about 100 miles from the main islands, continuous day air cover was provided over these areas. There was still a possibility, even at this eleventh hour, of Japanese treachery. Our US Liaison Officer was transferred to an American Carrier towards the end of August.

We continued to operate with this Group until we were detached on the 3rd September. It was not until we anchored in Tokyo Wan on 5th that the war really seemed to be over, and our first landing in Yokohama convinced us that we had nothing to fear from the Japanese for some considerable time to come. The policy of American bombing had left undamaged the railways and commercial docks as these lines of communication would have proved invaluable in the occupation, but practically everything else was flat except for a few concrete buildings which remained standing—burnt-out skeletons—monuments to futility.

Of paramount importance amongst the duties of the Fleet at this stage was the rehabilitation of prisoners of war. On the 7th September we sailed, under the orders of the US Destroyer *Bronson* for Ominato, in the Matsu Kaiwan at the northern tip of Honshu, arriving without incident on the 9th. *Barfleur* was the first British vessel to enter Ominato since the Japanese capitulation.

Extracts from a letter dated August 9 1945 from Ian Garnett, Senior Gunnery Officer to Rear Admiral Destroyers BPF, to Commander Dickson, Whale Island Gunnery School

Fitting of Bofors
Since February, 53 Single Army Bofors have been fitted in destroyers. The 'Q's and 'N's are losing their after set of tubes to make way for single bofors. The 'Boffin' conversion (i.e. displacement of the Oerlikon barrels in the Twin V Mtg. by a bofors barrel) is going ahead fast.

Wakeful is our first all-bofors destroyer—7 barrels altogether including the Hazemeyer. *Barfleur* had a trip to the next door American Task Group the other day. We went close to *Missouri* and one of their latest DD's. *Missouri* mounted 18 Bofors Quads. The destroyer's armament consisted of:

3 Twin 5″ Turrets
2 Bofors Quads
2 Bofors Twins
11 Single Oerlikons
10 Torpedo Tubes (2 Pentads)

4.5″ Guns and Ammunition At the beginning of this operation the ship contracted a particularly nasty disease in the form of prematures with 4.5″ HE fuzed 211, caused by two bulged barrels. Mercifully no one was injured though the foc'sle was peppered by shell fragments. As yet the INO Dept. have provided no solution to the problem of why the barrels bulged. A tentative opinion is that trouble may be traced to the 4.5″ VIICT shell which are fitted for No. 16 Tracer. The hole in the shell base to take this tracer extends through into the shell filling and at present is plugged. If perchance a plug was loose then flash entry might cause a partial disruption of the shell body in the bore. The lives of all the guns at this time was no more than an average of 400 EFC's.

Playing safe, all her guns were changed at Manus.

The Pacific situation could hardly have changed more quickly than it has during the last fortnight. After the departure of RAD from *Barfleur* there was a nine day blank period during which there were no strikes. The reason for this interruption in the programme was a typhoon. Eventually it was possible to commence operations again on August the 9th and 10th—with strikes in the Sendai area. A day bombardment was arranged and took place at the same time as the strikes, the target being Kamaishi—it was a combined party, *Newfoundland, Gambia* and three of the T's represented our side. Again no opposition.

On the evening of the 10th, the first news was received of the surrender. On Sunday the 12th the major part of the British Force comprising three carriers, three cruisers and eight destroyers all under AC One, were ordered south to Manus. *KGV* and the token force remained with the 3rd Fleet, to play their part in the occupation of Japanese ports. *Barfleur* stayed up and so, very reluctantly, I transferred to *Achilles* for the passage south.

The position at the moment is that:

1. C in C is afloat in the *Duke of York*, keeping in close touch with Nimitz.
2. *KGV* and our 'token force' under Rawlings is lying off Tokyo with Halsey.
3. A force under AC II in the *Indomitable* is heading for Hong Kong.
4. A force under CS2 in *Bermuda* is heading for Sh'ai.

Already the BPF Destroyer Command is being whittled down. The Q's being relieved by the 19th DF (Battles) and we're not getting the 'Caesars'. I have a feeling that the post of RAD out here will lapse in the not too distant future.

From A. Moss, RM, HMS *Duke of York*

The fact that we were the C in C's ship, Admiral Bruce Fraser in command, in my opinion, made it seem like a 'Cook's Tour'.

Upon arriving through Sydney heads we were on the Newsreel, and described as being 'battle-scarred'. I thought that the commentator must have been supping plonk the night before.

A few weeks later, a ship's dance was held. A limited number of tickets were available. A proviso was that you had to take a female companion with you and you were only allowed two bottles of beer.

The Admiral, Captain, Commander and Jimmy the One, arrived accompanied by their guests, the Lord Mayor and Lady Mayoress.

The Admiral started off the dance, his partner being the Lady Mayoress. After a couple of minutes had gone by, a stoker went on to the floor, and excused the Admiral, and finished the dance with the Lady Mayoress! This stoker returned his partner to the Admiral, thanked him and said he hadn't had a drink, and Admiral Fraser signed a 'chit' for two bottles of beer from the bar.

When the dance ended a big black Rolls Royce, driven by two Royal Marine corporals, arrived to take the Admiral, Captain, Commander and Jimmy back. This very same stoker went up to the car and said 'Are you going anywhere near the Dockyard, and could you give me a lift?!' Needless to say, he got a lift, by those two corporals—right into the arms of a Naval Patrol.

After a ten-day trip to Hobart, Tasmania, we proceeded to join the main British Pacific Fleet, which was on operations.

First calling in at Guam, our two destroyer escorts were *Whelp* and *Wager*. Prince Philip was aboard the former.

The two atom bombs had been dropped and the Japanese had surrendered.

A Japanese destroyer came alongside and delivered to our ship, two emmissaries representing their government.

One was a very small elderly man, with a very long white pointed beard, the other was a tall man about thirty-five years of age, and a very smart appearance. They were both in civilian clothes.

The elderly man was a professor who I believe used to translate English classics into Japanese. The younger man was a Naval Officer.

They were given accommodation up top in the Captain's sea cabin and guarded by eight Marines, I myself being one of them.

It was ironic that they were served some beautiful meals, all on silver trays, whilst one morning on our mess, we were having herrings in tomato sauce, bread with no butter, tea with no sugar. I wouldn't have minded a chip buttie from their tray!

One day, whilst giving them some fresh air, I was in conversation with the young chap. He asked me what part of England I came from and I replied 'Manchester.' He surprised me with his knowledge of Trafford Park and where Metropolitan Vickers was. He asked how long I had been a Marine. Had I seen any action, especially against the Japs, which on my previous ship, I had.

The other point I remember which I thought was funny at the time, was the custom of bowing, head high, from the older gentleman.

Whilst the fleet was anchored in Tokyo Bay, there were two British prisoners of war, one from the Manchester Regiments, and the other being a Royal Marine, who had escaped.

The ships were that far out, the Marine could not recognise their outline, and class, and thought it was the Japanese Fleet and in dismay thought they would be in trouble for escaping.

They spotted a Gold Flake packet, and a Wrigleys gum wrapper, washed up on the water's edge. They ran into the water, and were picked up by an American craft and taken back to their ship.

For the couple of hours they were aboard the American ship, with all the good food they were given to eat, we were told they would be ill for many, many months to come. They were eventually brought to the *Duke of York*, and placed in the sick bay in intensive care until they were sent to a better facility.

As we all know, a lot of prisoners were taken to aircraft carriers, as makeshift hospitals. They say one of our matelots helped one individual prisoner up his carrier's gangway and carrying the POW's bits of belongings the officer of the day said to the matelot, 'Don't worry my man, after a few weeks on here, we'll soon fatten you up!' The matelot replied, 'I'm one of the ship's company, *he's* the POW!'

On board HMS *Duke of York* the Royal Marine detachment were all kitted up, and ready to land ashore. I could never understand when our Sergeant Major Hanson gave us orders to stand down, saying 'the Yanks don't effing want us.'

After the Armistice was signed, on the *Missouri*, we sailed for Hong Kong, where about sixty Marines were put ashore, to help in the formation of the civilian police till my demob in 1946, having served five and a half years, from age seventeen and a half to nearly twenty three.

From AB/ST Bob Boon, HMS *Duke of York*

Entering Tokyo Bay we were met by a Japanese Destroyer which guided us in. The *Duke of York* and the USS *Missouri* led the Fleets into the Bay with over

1000 aircraft flying overhead.

After about two days at anchor a signalman spotted two men waving at us from the beach and the Captain ordered a motorboat to investigate. It turned out to be two POWs who had escaped from a camp and were living in the bushes along the beach. They couldn't see whose ships we were until they spotted some cigarette packets washed ashore.

When the boat brought them back, we learned that one was a Royal Marine and the other a RAF pilot, both in very poor condition. They were in the ship's hospital for quite a few weeks. *(As previous story—almost. Ed.)*

While we were there and after the surrender we had a day-trip to Hiroshima.

Returning to Sydney, we suffered a sad loss. We encountered a very heavy swell and the ship started to roll. The anchors were crashing against the side of the ship making a terrible noise. I had started the Middle Watch and about 02.00 the Chief Duty Officer and 'Jimmy the One' went to check the anchors as it seemed to be getting worse. They were standing near the hawser holes when a huge gush of sea water came up through the holes. The CDO was washed up against the breakwater and knocked clean out with injuries to his head, but 'Jimmy the One' was never seen again. His wife had arrived in Sydney waiting for him.

I thought when we got back to Sydney that it was a bit unfair really that we should be getting all the publicity. After all *KGV* had been out there well before us and had taken a battering from the Japs, but very little was mentioned about her in the Aussie papers.

From Bert Crane, HMS *Duke of York*

Extracts from 'United States Fleet Carriers of World War II' by Richard Humble

The worst enemy was the weather, which restricted air operations to thirteen American and eight British strike days. There was no opposition at sea and very little in the air; the *Kikusui* attacks of April and May did not rematerialise, with the last reserves of Japanese aircraft being hoarded for mass attacks as soon as the invasion of the homeland began. Halsey and McCain, however, took no chances, and maintained TF.38's three-group deployment adopted by Spruance during the Okinawa campaign. This permitted a stronger picket line of destroyers and cruisers to be deployed to protect the carriers, and concentrated the fighter strength of CAPs.

In those last thirteen days of air operations, however, the carriers of 3rd Fleet achieved the mission which had become of supreme propaganda value, and from which the British were still jealously excluded: the final destruction of the Japanese Fleet. This was achieved in three days of attacks on naval bases, on the 24, 25 and 28 July, which sank the carrier *Amagi*, battleship-carriers *Ise* and *Hyuga*, battleships *Haruna* and *Nagato*, five cruisers, and many smaller warships.

The last carrier strike by 3rd Fleet was carried out at dawn on 15 August, Nimitz cancelling all further attacks at 0700; but there were a few attempted kamikaze attacks, all of them shot down. The closest call was at 1120 on 15 August, when two bombs fell close to the British carrier *Indomitable. (Incorrect, it was* Indefatigable—*Ed.)*. The last massed carrier operation of 3rd Fleet was Operation 'Tintype' on 22 August 1945; a victory flypast over the fleet by over 1000 aircraft. The long voyage from Pearl Harbour was over.

Extract from an Australian Magazine

King George V had the honour of being in Tokyo Bay for the formal surrender of Japan on 2 September 1945. She had also been the last British battleship to fire her guns in anger when she had bombarded Hammamatsu, south of Tokyo, on 29 July.

We sank 3 frigates and damaged an escort carrier, while bombing airfields and industrial targets. Meanwhile, at Singapore, our X-craft had got in to sink the cruiser Takao *and also cut submarine cables between Singapore, Hong Kong and Saigon. The Royal Navy had not been idle while the politicans fought for power!*

There was a story, no doubt based on truth, which I heard, that while the BPF withdrew for the Hiroshima bomb, Admiral Fraser called on Admiral Nimitz at Guam in Duke of York, *he invested Nimitz with the Order of the Bath. Thereafter, he took him to witness and sample 'up spirits'. He then led him to the wardroom, the gunroom and Warrant Officer's Mess to enjoy their hospitality too. Although Nimitz, it was said, never forgave him, they remained firm friends.*

With the Russian invasion of Manchuria on 8th August, and the second atom bomb on 9th, at Nagasaki, the BPF were scheduled to return to Australia on 10th.

Fraser came up from Guam in Duke of York *on 16th and ordered the flagship* KGV, *the carrier* Indefatigable, *the cruisers* Gambia *and* Newfoundland *and the destroyers* Barfleur, Napier, Nizam, Troubridge, Termagent, Tenacious, Terpsichore, Teaser, Wakeful *and* Wrangler *to stay behind to enter Tokyo Bay as a token BPF Force representing The British Empire. This was designated Task Force 38.5. During this time we continued to strike under the overall command of US Vice Admiral J. S. McCain on the US Carrier* Shangri La.

Fraser called on Halsey on board the USS Missouri *and invested him with the KBE. They steamed into Tokyo Bay on 27th August with* Duke of York *anchoring astern of* KGV.

On the 2nd September 1945, Fraser signed the Surrender Document for Great Britain—using chairs from the Duke of York.

The BPF's aircrews, now represented by only HMS Indefatigable *took part in what was known as the 'Fraser Sunset' parade. Senior US officers, as well as our own, were in tears.*

Charismatic, as ever, Fraser turned a Nelson blind eye when General MacArthur tried to retrieve the pens used for The Surrender. He sent his to Churchill who replied by special cypher: 'I am most grateful to you for your very kind letter of September 5th written on the date and with the pen of the unconditional surrender of Japan. Your work during the war has always commanded my highest respect and admiration. Not once or twice in our rough island story the path of duty was the path of glory.'

From Jim Dodds, HMS *Victorious*

JIM'S DIARY OF FINAL WAR DAYS

Frid. 10 August 1945 Another full day's attack on Japan similar to yesterday's but less opposition. No air raid scares today at all where yesterday ten to a dozen aircraft were shot down close to the fleet. What with 'atomic bombs' and Russia declaring war, Japan is getting into a sorry state. Skipper gives it another month (unless they've gone mad).

Sat 11 August Back to the oiling area again—intend to strike again tomorrow.

Sun 12 August Today's strike 'off' owing to weather. The Japs are asking for peace (Friday), stating that the Emperor remains. Allies considering terms and reply that the Emperor may remain but must take orders from Allies, so it's up to the Japs again. Some ships of the British Pacific Fleet join up with the American Task Force to strike in the Tokyo area tomorrow. The remainder—*Victorious, Formidable, Implacable,* 3 cruisers and 8 destroyers steaming south to Manus to completely store ship and stand by to occupy Japanese ports.

Mon 13 Aug Steaming south—managing to keep on the outskirts of a typhoon.

Tues 14 August Rumours today that the Japs have capitulated. Much excitement throughout the ship. The defeat of Japan means more to us than the defeat of Germany. The atomic bomb has been the means of bringing this war to such a quick finish—it might have dragged on for another year or more.

Wed 15 August Official confirmation today of Japan's surrender. A great day for us. Make and mend—splice the mainbrace, service held on flight deck. It's hard to believe that it's all over, but knowing that there will be no more 'action stations', no more suicide attacks etc. makes us all very jubilant. Great night in the mess.

Copy of a Signal

TO *KGV* FROM—C T F 37.

Having seen the photographs of your target it is evident that your bombardment was highly successful and reflects credit on all concerned.

020917 AUGUST.

TO C T F 31. FROM — C T G 38 PT 5.

Your 160305

(A) Royal Marine Battalion 250 strong organised and ready.
(B) Bluejacket Battalion 200 strong from *KGV*
Newfoundland and *Gambia* also ready.

Ships boats only available for landing either party.

170044 AUG.

To . . . BRITISH PACIFIC FLEET From . . . C IN C BPF

(FULL DIST—NBs)
On conclusion of hostilities I wish to congratulate and to thank the British Pacific Fleet, the Fleet Train and all those on land and sea and in the air that supported us, for a job very well done.

2. We have further tasks ahead in re-establishing authorities, rescuing POW and internees and ensuring a proper surrender of the Japanese which I hope we will carry out equally as well.

3. Release of age and service groups will continue as speedily as can be arranged.

D.T.G. . . . 150430 AUGUST

From 'The Other Hundred Years War' by Russell Braddon

The Allies met at Potsdam and formally demanded Japan's unconditional surrender. Russia, to Japan's consternation, denounced the neutrality pact of 1941. Japan's new Prime Minister, the octogenarian Admiral Suzuki, broadcast an apparently contemptuous rejection of the Allies' Potsdam Declaration. And fleets of B-29s ranged the skies over the Japanese homeland, putting one city after another to its ordeal by fire.

While still a POW Russell Braddon recalls:
August 15, 1945, I remember because that was the day the maddest and most skilful thief in our midst announced his intention of slipping away from the tunnel to steal a radio. So we covered for him, and when we returned to camp that evening he returned with us, having deposited his stolen radio just outside the perimeter fence.

He had walked brazenly along the road to the Japanese Headquarters in Johore Bahru, bowing en route to all passing Japanese (who had bowed back), had found the radio in an unoccupied officer's bedroom, bowed to the sentry as he left with the radio, and walked brazenly back to our camp, confident that any Japanese soldiers who saw him would take him for just another Australian electrician repairing a radio for the Imperial Japanese Army.

That night he crawled through the wire, plugged his radio into the power lines that ran between the telephone posts outside, took it into the latrine, switched on and tuned in.

Some quarter of an hour later someone near the guard house called out a soft 'Red Light', which was passed down the line to the latrine, whence emerged our thieving friend. 'I've just heard the King,' he told us incredulously. 'The war's over. We've won.'

The monarchy! There was the crux of unconditional surrender—which would leave the Allies free to depose the Emperor, thereby abolishing the whole imperial concept, which the Japanese called the National Polity. It could even result in the prosecution of the Emperor as a war criminal. Rather than that, his 'hundred million' subjects would fight till not one survived. Meantime, their government had sought Moscow's good offices, and Washington was awaiting its response to the Potsdam Declaration.

Which began: 'The time has come for Japan to decide whether she will continue to be controlled by those self-willed militarist advisers whose unintelligent calculations have brought its Empire to the threshold of annihilation, or whether she will follow the path of reason.'

Had those who formulated the Declaration been determined to *prolong* the war, they could have used no more effective language. Not only were the people of Japan powerless in the hands of the militarists, but the militarists—dubbed self-willed and unintelligent for waging war—would lose face to an even greater extent if they accepted the insult and stopped the fighting. What came next, though was worse:

'Following are our terms. We will not deviate from them. There are no alternatives. We shall brook no delay.

'There must be eliminated for all time the authority and influence of those who have deceived and misled the people of Japan . . . Stern justice shall be meted out to all war criminals . . . We call upon the government of Japan to proclaim now the unconditional surrender of all Japanese forces . . . The alternative for Japan is prompt and utter destruction.'

Neither Japan's Foreign Minister nor her Prime Minister chose to oblige those who had issued the Potsdam Declaration, for three reasons. First, they knew that the Army was determined to fight on; second, to have consented to the Potsdam demands would have been to invite their own instant assassination, and the Army's reversal of their decision; and third, they still hoped for Moscow's intercession on Japan's behalf.

Suzuki, therefore, stalled; but in the process let slip a word much stronger (because it was ambiguous) than either he or his advisers can ever have intended. Declaring that the government would 'maintain a discreet silence' on the subject of the Potsdam Declaration, he was quoted by the Tokyo Press as having said that the government would 'treat it with contempt'.

President Truman, in the words of Stimson, his Secretary of State for War, thereupon decided that the United States, 'could only proceed to demonstrate that the ultimatum had meant exactly what it said.' A less magisterial version of this turning point in history is that Admiral Leahy warned Truman that the policy of unconditional surrender would make the invasion of Japan inevitable, and inflict huge American casualties. Truman then proved himself to be made of sterner stuff than Roosevelt and General Eisenhower, who had succumbed, in the war against Germany, to the impulse to spare American lives.

General Anami said: 'We cannot pretend that victory is certain, but it is far too early to say that the war is lost.' The difficult part of his argument thus blithely disposed of, he proceeded less tortuously to more serious matters. 'Furthermore,' he said, 'our army will not submit to demobilization. Our men simply will not lay down their arms. And since they know they are not permitted to surrender, since they know that a fighting man who surrenders is liable to extremely heavy punishment, there is really no alternative for us but to continue the war.'

It was the kind of illogic to which only the Japanese could have subscribed; but an entire race had come to accept it as irrefutable. Then, as now, they believed that nothing unacceptable to Japan would be allowed by the fates to come to pass: or, conversely, that Japan was entitled to anything the Japanese wanted. Being divine, they had divine rights.

With his cabinet evenly divided, and unable to agree a compromise on a matter of such national importance, it would have been in keeping with precedent for Suzuki to resign and bequeath the problem to a successor. He declined to do so.

Unable to put forward any agreed policy for the Emperor's approval, he took the unprecedented step of asking the Emperor to act as arbitrator. Accordingly, at ten minutes to midnight on 9 August, Suzuki and ten others sat at two tables on either side of the Emperor's stuffy air raid shelter while the Emperor sat at the head of the room. Behind the uniformed Emperor was a silver screen; in front of him a small table covered with a cloth of gold. His eleven subjects wore either morning clothes or uniforms.

Suzuki read the Potsdam Declaration; confessed the cabinet deadlocked; apologised for requesting the Emperor's presence; and called upon each of his ministers in turn to argue for or against surrendering in view of the fact that the Allies had declined to give assurances that the National Polity would be preserved.

Togo, the Foreign Minister, and Admiral Yonai were in favour of accepting the terms of the Potsdam Declaration, as of course, was Suzuki, Generals Anami and Umezu, and Admiral Toyoda opposed acceptance unless their conditions about the National Polity, war criminals, a small occupation force and disarming of Japanese troops by Japanese officers were incorporated. Closely questioned by Baron Hiranuma, a Privy Councillor, each remained adamant.

'Your Imperial Majesty's decision is requested as to which proposal should be adopted,' Suzuki then begged. 'The Foreign Minister's, or the one with the four conditions.'

At two o'clock on the morning of 10 August, the Emperor gave his answer. With his first quietly spoken words he dashed the hopes of Anami, Umezu and Toyoda. Not only did he declare that to continue the war would mean the annihilation of the Japanese people, he also made it clear that he no longer believed in the boasts of the militarists.

'Since the beginning of the Pacific War there has been a tremendous disparity between our calculations and the realities. Now I hear that the Army and Navy are preparing for a battle in the homeland. One of the main defensive positions is Kujukuri-hama. But there is a great differenne between the advice of the Chief of Staff about the state of the defences at Kujukuri-hama and the observations of our chamberlains. They tell me that they are only one tenth completed. Also the production of aircraft is quite inadequae.

'In these conditions, how can we prevail, even in the homeland? If the entire population is killed, we can hardly hope to perpetuate the nation! It is my opinion that we must end the war, although that is an unbearable thing.'

Finally a statement was cobbled together for release on the afternoon news broadcast. It suggested that, although the enemy was employing a new and barbarous bomb, the Army would doubtless repel any invasion. 'But,' it continued, 'we must accept that the situation has become very bad. Nevertheless, the government is exerting itself to the utmost to ensure that our last line of defence is held, and to protect both the National Polity and the honour of our race. The government expects that the nation will surmount the present difficult situation and preserve the polity of the Empire.'

There was no mention of the Potsdam Declaration, nor of the government's conditional acceptance of it; but there was the sort of hint that the populace, accustomed as it was to tortuous metaphors and an unusually ambiguous language, should have been able to interpret.

Doubtless the Japanese would have done so (particularly since they had already been appraised of Russia's entry into the war against them) had not the Army, with the War Minister's consent, deliberately muddied the waters of comprehension with a communiqué of its own that was blatantly bellicose.

'The Soviet Union,' the Army declared, 'had directed its armed might against the wrong enemy by invading Japan.'

In fact, the Soviet armed forces had merely begun to round up the hopelessly outnumbered Japanese forces in Manchuria; but the Army, like the Navy, had never hesitated to lie, for all that its samurai code proclaimed that a soldier always spoke the truth; and if its words were taken to mean that Russian soldiers had actually invaded the northern islands of Japan, so much the better for its plan to prevent the government from surrendering.

'Nothing remains to us,' the statement continued, 'but to see through to its conclusion this war for the defence of the Land of the Gods. Chewing grass, eating stones and living in the fields, we shall fight on, for in our death lies our country's one chance of survival.'

Desperate to counter the adverse effect this news statement would have on Truman, Togo's Foreign Office at once authorized the Domei News Agency to transmit, in morse, the text of its own note to America. Its concentration lapsing yet again, the Army, which normally censored all tranmsmissions abroad, failed to block this vital message—which spread to the desk of every newspaper editor in the world.

Though unaware, in fact, of the Japanese Army's belligerence the American State Department replied firmly to Japan's equivocal note. From the moment of surrender, it advised, the authority and future of both the Emperor and the Japanese Government would be decided by the Supreme Commander of the Allied Powers, General MacArthur, alone.

It was by now mid-morning, Saturday, 11 August. As the Emperor summoned War Minister Anami to his presence, to reprimand him for allowing the Army to issue its inflammatory proclamation, fifteen junior officers met in the War Office bomb shelter to brand Suzuki, Togo and Marquis Kido traitors fit only for assassination, and to discuss plans for the occupation of the Imperial Palace and the protection of the Emperor from further 'bad advice'. Confident that they would have the support of both Anami and General Mori, who commanded the Imperial Guards, they expected their proposed coup d'état to transfer the reins of power into their hands. Washington's insistence that the Emperor's fate would depend on the whim of General MacArthur further inflamed their passion.

A group of B-29 crewmen held prisoners at Fukuoda were about to learn just how inflamed their passions were. Eight of them had already been executed: now eight more were taken to a field near Aburayama, stripped and, one after the other, butchered. Where the sword was used, it was used clumsily; but those were the fortunate victims. Others were treated like bulls in a corrida manned by a team of callous but clumsy toreadors. They were slowly beaten, stabbed and hacked to death. Though there were few fliers left in Japanese hands, there were still some 350,000 prisoners of war in the hands of the Imperial Japanese Army: Fukuoda boded ill for them all.

Thus Sunday 12 August, was marked by intrigues and confusion. Togo wanted to comply with Washington's demands; the Emperor concurred; Anami reminded Suzuki of his promise to continue the war in the absence of an Allied assurance that would preserve the national polity; Suzuki agreed to insist upon such an assurance; the Imperial princes (suspecting that the Army might ask one of them to supplant Hirohito) pledged their support to the Emperor; the cabinet met, and fell into instant disarray.

Extracts from 'Dry Ginger', by Richard Baker

For Spruance and the majority of his staff there came relief towards the end of May. At midnight on the twenty-seventh, Admiral Halsey took over command, and the Fifth Fleet thereupon became the Third again. But there was no relief for Michael; with the two suitcases which constituted his only luggage throughout the assignment, he transferred on the twenty-sixth with the Japanese-speaking Intelligence Officer Gil Slonim to Halsey's staff, the battleship *Missouri* ('The Mighty Mo').

The prospect of getting to know a whole new staff appalled him—a staff twice as big as Spruance's, with the result that he had to share a room. This he found a real problem. 'I absolutely crave a soupcon of privacy sometimes. Like most people who live by their wits—i.e. who can put the switch to charm, intelligent appreciation, or pseudo-man-of-action at will, I definitely must drop the facade from time to time.'

The change in the style of management also took some getting used to. Far from riding in 'some old and inexpensive craft' like Spruance, here was Halsey running round in 'a large and expensive ship with considerable fanfare'; and in place of the withdrawn, publicity-shy Spruance, here was a gutsy extrovert, a colourful, flamboyant man and a born leader, only too anxious to let the world know (through his Public Relations man, Jim Bassett) how effectively the Third Fleet, and he, Halsey, were 'clobbering those yellow bastards'. At supper the first night with the Admiral, Michael—whose convivial reputation was already known—found he had to parry 'massive shafts of wit from the top end.'

Just before Halsey's arrival, the British Fleet, after sixty-two days continuously at sea (broken only by eight days at Leyte Gulf in the Philippines) had withdrawn to Sydney for a more extended period of repair and replenishment. Michael was offered a passage, but decided he would be better employed getting to know the new boss and his staff, even though this involved such apparently unwarlike activities as playing medicine ball and deck tennis and watching endless movies—'Ninety-nine per cent of American Naval Officers never dream of missing a movie—it is the only relaxation available.'

But in mid-June, when Halsey withdrew for a spell to Leyte, he did decide to go to Sydney for a four-day meeting of Liaison Officers. It was a trip, as Michael later said, 'Ostensibly to see my boss—actually to have a drink'; his British colleagues found him incredibly American and could hardly believe it when they saw him approach Admiral Fraser with a Yankee-type salute and the unheard of greeting: 'Good morning, Admiral!'

Everyone knew that the final stage of the Japanese war was now imminent. Michael rejoined Halsey's staff at Leyte on 28 June, the day the Pacific Fleet left Sydney. Three days later Halsey sailed with the Third Fleet to attack the enemy's home islands and on 16 July, Michael in *Missouri* had the great joy of seeing the British ships join the American Fleet off the north-east coast of the Japanese home island of Honshu. 'It was,' he wrote, 'the high spot of one man's Pacific war, the end and the beginning.' After meeting Admirals Rawlings and Vian on board *Missouri* Admiral Halsey told 'Lef' how confident he felt at the prospect of working with the British. Some of that confidence was no doubt due to patient salesmanship over the previous few weeks on the part of Michael, who, now that the two fleets were together, worked hard to promote co-operation, particularly in the area where the British most needed help—that of fuel supplies.

One of the American anxieties about the presence of a British Fleet in the Pacific had been the question of keeping it replenished, and the US Commanders were officially forbidden to give any assistance, for they had enough problems in keeping massive numbers of their own ships at sea. By assembling in record time a motley collection of transports, the British had managed to set up a fleet train which functioned amazingly well by and large, but difficulties none the less remained. However, Halsey, like Spruance, was capable of turning a blind eye. One day there arrived from the British Fleet a Biblical signal which read: 'And the foolish virgin said unto the wise virgin, give us of your oil, for our lamps are gone out', and Michael devised the reply, 'Foolish—no. Wise—maybe. Virgins—no comment.'

It was not long after this that Halsey visited the *King George V* and after talks with Rawlings, Michael took him to the wardroom where he was invited to consider himself an honorary member of the mess. On the way back Michael explained what the title meant, so the next time Halsey visited the British flagship's wardroom, he marched—well briefed by Le Fanu—straight past the welcoming party and up to the bar, banged on it and demanded in a loud voice, 'Six gins please!' Fortunately for Michael, the state of total prohibition had slightly eased under the Halsey regime; for one thing Michael himself had managed to bring back a few bottles of whisky from Sydney which had found their way on board '*Missouri* as 'electronic spares' (the brand was VAT 69 which the Chief of Staff insisted was the Pope's telephone number) and for another the Admiral had, in Michael's words, 'his own ideas on what was medicinal'; the 'fruit cocktails' which were served at supper in Halsey's mess were often mysteriously potent affairs.

At this stage in the war, although there was a good deal of action, with constant air strikes and bombardments of the Japanese main islands as a preliminary to the projected invasion of Japan, there was some chance of relaxation, and time for Michael to reconsider the course of his life thus far, and his plans for the future. As his letters to Prue reveal, he had no illusions about his ability to handle men—American or British; he felt that perhaps the most worthy of ambitions was 'to make everyone you meet feel good—I daresay it would be more useful than anything we could achieve in the Navy or politics or anything else. You should know, seeing as how you have rung the above-mentioned bell in all cases of which I am cognizant. If I put my mind to it, I am reasonably confident that I could do likewise . . . indeed to some extent it has been my professional stock in trade. The only people who present any problems are those I love, because you are the only people with whom I can "let down", as the Americans say. So there you are, you can look forward to thirty years with a husband who is perpetually morose and fretful because he's ever so busy spreading sweetness and light.'

At this time Michael was entertaining serious doubts about the Navy as a career. 'I cannot believe it is morally right to be no more than a hired assassin, no matter how much I talk to myself about the values of waving a flag and keeping the peace; secondly, I don't think it is a full enough existence. On the other hand as a Commander or better, one exerts quite an influence on the men under one, an influence I would not exert were I to manage a pub, take holy orders or do welfare work in a slum. In the event I daresay I shall soldier on in the Navy; but if I do, it will be to some extent through laziness and I shall always have a lingering doubt about "that one talent which is death to hide".'

As July turned to August, there was less time for personal philosophising, for in the first fortnight of that month the final defeat of Japan was achieved. At noon (local time) on 7 August Michael learned of the dropping of the first atomic bomb on Hiroshima. The full horror of the event was not yet clear, but Michael at once realised, 'It was the pay-off as far as war is concerned, and made certain what was already probable that any future war will be the end of this reputed civilisation.' Such broad issues apart, hopes at once rose for a quick end to the war, and on the tenth—the day after the second atomic bomb on Nagasaki, the Japanese opened peace negotiations. Michael thought nothing less than a complete surrender should be accepted. Meanwhile he had engineered a lunch for Sir Bernard Rawlings in the *Mighty Mo* with Admiral Halsey and had taken good care to have them filmed together afterwards against a background of White Ensigns and American flags. Michael himself was invited to appear in some of the shots 'wearing my baseball cap, which I am afraid may look rather silly'. A pleasant interlude during four days of 'hanging around off Japan and not knowing whether to hit them a crack or get ready for the hurrah party'.

On 15 August, it was all over. Peace was heralded in the American fleet with the hoisting of battle flags and long blasts on the ships' sirens. 'Then we hoisted the flag signal "Well done" to the fleet. And that was all—it was queer to think of the people in America going wild, about ten o'clock in the evening in the middle states. After lunch Admiral Halsey made a very good and deeply felt speech to the fleet. He really is a fine old boy—64 years of age, and he has been at sea practically the whole war. Now we have a vast problem on our hands—the end has come so quickly and one doubts if we are anything like ready for it. People have been pretty busy winning the war without thinking of the peace.'

Meanwhile if ever there was an event which called for celebration it was this. At about 4 pm on 16 August, the British C-in-C, Sir Bruce Fraser, came on board the *Mo* to meet Halsey with the words, 'Well, Admiral, I *have* looked forward to this', and to present him with a KBE. At Michael's suggestion, on the same day, Admiral Halsey made the time-honoured British signal to the fleet, 'Splice the Mainbrace'. Since the American ships were 'dry' the signal of course had to read 'negative groups 38.1, 38.2' etc.—the American groups of ships. However, in the meantime Michael had done a little quiet fixing with Sir Bernard Rawlings (referred to by Halsey in his autobiography as 'Bert') in *King George V.*

That same afternoon, at about 4.45, Rawlings and his staff were transferred by jackstay from a destroyer to the *Missouri*, and after Rawlings had made a prearranged broadcast to 'the fighting Third', he joined Fraser and Halsey with their staffs in the Admiral's day cabin. 'Now Admiral,' said Rawlings to Halsey, 'I have been studying with great care your "Splice the Mainbrace" signal and I see you've exempted all the American groups except 38.0—your own group in *Missouri*.' Upon which two jars of 'Pusser's' rum were produced and, in Michael's words: 'we proceeded to splice the mainbrace aboard the good old USS *Missouri* in a big way. This really made the party go—everyone loved everybody else madly—and I glowed a stinker as they say! Later on we had a victory dinner for Admiral Halsey (a family affair—the Limeys had left). Lots of speeches. I am quite a cynical old thing, but I have been much drawn to this team who are very closely bound and very sincere in their loyalty towards one another and towards the Admiral.'

As for Halsey himself, Michael described for Prue one incident in particular which showed him as a 'marvellous, very loveable chap'. Among the Admiral's wilder threats had been tht he would ride the Emperor's white horse through the streets of Tokyo when the war was over. 'Poor man,' wrote Michael, 'he is really worried about it now; just an idle word to a press conference months and months ago and now here he is with a terrific build-up about it. Two beautiful sets of spurs arrived some time ago, but the saddle and bridle that arrived today (25 August) really were something. I've never seen a more massive or luxurious bit of work. Beautiful leather with chased silver all over it, and an enormous built-in rug. We set it all up over the backs of a couple of chairs this morning. Then when the Admiral walked in, we proceeded to sing *Home on the Range*. Great laughter.' The story, as told in Halsey's autobiography, relates that he then pretended to ride but caught himself in the crutch. After letting out a yelp he said, 'Why can't I remember I'm just a poor clapped-out old bastard and keep my big mouth shut goddamit!'

Extracts from 'The War with Japan' by Charles Bateson

Ohnishi, the originator of Kamikaze, committed hara-kiri *before dawn on August 16 1945, the day after Japan's decision to surrender was publicly announced. 'I wish to express my deep appreciation to the souls of the brave Special Attackers,' he wrote, in a farewell message. 'They fought and died valiantly with faith in our ultimate victory. In death I wish to atone for my part in the failure to achieve that victory and I apologize to the souls of these dead fliers and their bereaved families.'*

Charles Bateson wrote:

As early as February or March the Japanese had put out peace-feelers to the Russians. They would have been better advised to have made a more direct approach to Britain and the United States through a neutral power, but although many high-ranking officers and officials in Japan were convinced by early 1945 that Japan was doomed, Japanese psychology was such that steps to bring the war to an end could not be taken. At all cost, if the approach for peace were to be initiated by the Japanese, there had to be some face-saving formula. The Russians appreciated this and since the seeds of the cold war with the western world were already being sown they refused to furnish the face-saving pretext. The Japanese approaches thus came to nought. On the Emperor's insistence they were renewed in July but were completely ignored by the Russians. Although the necessity for peace and its inevitability were appreciated by influential Japanese, the need to preserve face precluded immedite unconditional surrender.

Then, on August 6 an atomic bomb was dropped on Hiroshima. It destroyed 40,653 of the 50,160 buildings in the city proper and severely damaged a further 8,396. Casualties were estimated at 71,379 killed and 68,023 injured, without taking into account those resulting from the latent effects of radiation. The bomb destroyed 4.7 square miles. Thus, the first atomic bomb ever dropped neither caused as much destruction nor as many casualties as the March fire raid on Tokyo, but its psychological effects were probably much greater. Three days later, on the 9th, a second bomb was dropped on Nagasaki. On this occasion there was no wind to fan the flames and destruction was not as complete as at Hiroshima. An area of 1.45 square miles out of 3.84 square miles was destroyed. The Japanese estimated that 25,680 people were killed and 23,345 injured, but post-war American investigators considered these figures too low and raised them to about 40,000 killed and 60,000 injured.

The Russians, who had been transferring divisions to Manchuria for nearly six months, declared war on Japan on the 8th and next day attacked. There is no doubt their action was precipitated, firstly, by the dropping of the atom bomb and, secondly, by the knowledge that Japan was anxious to surrender. Stalin was determined the Soviet Union would be engaged in the war against Japan before peace came. The Russian operations were well planned and caried out with overwhelming superiority in numbers and weapons. They at once invaded Manchuria, Korea and southern Sakhalin, using airborne troops.

Extract from 'Carrier Operations in World War II' by J. D. Brown

On VJ-Day there were four light fleet carriers at Sydney, with nearly 160 Barracudas and Corsairs embarked, preparing for operations in the East Indies and Philippines. These four ships, the 11th Aircraft Carrier Squadron, were given the task of re-occupation of British territories. *Venerable* accompanied *Indomitable* at Hong Kong, Rear Admiral C. H. J. Harcourt, RN, flying his flag in the latter, where the two ships launched the last offensive sorties against Japanese forces. On 31st August and 1st September, Corsairs, Hellcats,

Avengers and Barracudas dive-bombed and straffed suicide boats sortieing for a last attack, and went on to destroy those that remained hidden in the bays on the north of Hong Kong Island.

Glory took General B. A. H. Sturdee of the Australian Army to Rabaul to accept the surrender of the Japanese in New Britain in early September, meeting no opposition.

After the last shots and final operations, the British Pacific Fleet was soon dispersed. The Socialist Government had given undertakings that personnel would be returned for demobilisation as soon as possible, and the operational strength of the fleet as a whole diminished as the most experienced men left. Two important tasks were left for the carriers. The vast available space of a carrier's hangar and flight deck were eminently suitable for the evacuation of ex-prisoners of war, and hundreds of thousnds of these unfortunates were repatriated by the carriers of the BPF, 11th ACS, and CVE Service Squadron.

The other, rather sad, task of the carriers was the dumping of Lend-Lease aircraft at sea off Sydney. With thousands of Corsairs, Hellcats, Avengers, Wildcats and secondline types in the Naval Air Stations and Repair yards, this process took many months, but under the terms of the Lend-Lease Agreement, which stipulated that aircraft retained had to be paid for; as the United States Navy did not wish the aircraft to be returned, the waste was inevitable. A few Hellcats and Corsairs were retained until the autumn of 1946, embarked in the Light Fleet carriers. The majority of the Fleet carriers were in home waters by the end of 1945, together with the CVEs which were returned to the United States during the succeeding months.

Article from The Daily Telegraph . . . August, 1985—'40 years on'

MILLION LEAFLETS ORDERED THE FIGHTING TO STOP
By Maj.--Gen. Edward Fursdon

The Japanese surrender was a complex and lengthy process. Fighting had gone on in wide and disparate areas and more than a million leaflets telling the Japanese troops how to surrender were dropped by air on known positions. In one instance instructions were put on a railway wagon and shunted down the line to a Japanese-held area.

Even so, the war went on in some places for weeks after the signing of the surrender documents. In isolated places the guns did not finally fall silent until well into October.

It was on August 19—ten days after the dropping on Nagasaki of the second atomic bomb and five days after the unconditional surrender on Aug. 14—that a team of Japanese envoys left Tokyo to discuss the surrender arrangements.

Led by Lt-Gen. Kalabi Takashima, vice-chief of the Japanese Imperial Staff, they went to Gen. MacArthur's headquarters in Manila. As the Tokyo team set off to see Gen. MacArthur, a personal representative of the Emperor left to instruct Gen. Hyotaro Kimura to surrender his forces in Burma.

CEASEFIRE ORDER IN BURMA

Plans were soon being made, too, covering the surrender of Japanese forces in Java, New Guinea and the Solomons; and opposing Gen. Chiang Kai-Shek's Chinese forces in Western Hunan Province. Gen. MacArthur decreed that the Japanese in Hong Kong would surrender to Rear Admiral C. H. F. Harcourt of the Royal Navy.

On August 20, Lt-Gen. Sir Montagu Stopford, GOC 12th Army, ordered the Commander of the Japanese Burma Army Area, Gen. Kimura to cease hostilities immediately and make arrangements to surrender.

Following the order of Admiral Lord Louis Mountbatten, Supreme Allied Commander, South East Asia, to Field Marshal Count Hisaichi Terauchi, Supreme Commander of the Imperial Japanese Forces Southern Regions, a Japanese delegation from his headquarters in Saigon, led by his Chief of Staff Lt-Gen. Tokazo Numata, arrived at Mingladon Airfield, Rangoon, on August 26 for talks before the signing of a preliminary surrender agreement.

Six Spitfires and a L5 light spotter plane escorted the two silver-painted Japanese 'Topsy' aircraft in to land, both bearing the specially-agreed green cross code-markings on their underwings.

Gen. Numata, short and wearing black-rimmed glasses, Admiral Kaigyo Chudo, Deputy Chief of Staff, and Lt-Col. Moro Tomuria were all dressed in drab khaki uniforms. The collars of their open white shirts were worn outside their tunics, their high field boots were immacuately polished, and all carried swords. They did not salute.

While the 22-strong Japanese team were being taken to a nearby tent to be searched for poison and weapons, a security team of Flight Lieutenant Carr of Shrewsbury, Flight Sergeant Durrant of Luton, Armament Warrant Officer Rice of Gosport and Sergeant Wattens of Glasgow searched their aircraft.

The delegation was then marched across to where Maj.-Gen. W. S. Symes, GOC Southern Burma, was waiting to receive them. Their escorts from the Royal West Kent Regiment, were Prvts J. Dutton of Stoke-on-Trent, F. Fisher of Bow, London, G. Dickson of Bromley, Kent and J. Howell of Southend.

After a brief introduction, the Japanese were then driven off under Military Police control in three station wagons, with blinds drawn down, to their accommodation. They were followed by an Army 3-tonner carrying their kit and the rations they had brought with them of corned beef, rice, cucumber and raisins.

Capt. Brian Selwyn and his men from the Durham Light Infantry were the guards on the two houses which were enclosed with barbed wire and floodlit by night.

As the final talks began in the Throne Room of Government House it soon became clear that the Japanese team had come in a mood to bargain over and comment on Mountbatten's terms of surrender.

Lt-Gen. Sir Frederick ('Boy') Browning, Mountbatten's Chief of Staff who led the Allied team, acted quickly and firmly. He allowed no discussion whatsoever of the actual terms laid down and permitted only genuine questions of clarification and amplification.

The preliminary agreement, originally to have been signed at 6 p.m. on August 27, was eventually signed at 1 a.m. on August 28. Instructions were then sent through Field Marshal Count Terauchi to all his senior Japanese field commanders that they would forthwith obey and assist the British commanders of the re-occupying forces.

Peter Eastwood, then a reporter with the Forces' newspaper, SEAC, and now Managing Editor of the Daily Telegraph, was present at the signing ceremony. He introduced Lord Mountbatten by writing at the time that the Throne Room of Government House with the Union flag, the Stars and Stripes and the Chinese, Dutch and French flags draped from its balconies, and specially fitted out with 12,000 candlepower floodlights 'looked like a Hollywood film set'.

Mountbatten complained mildly to SEAC's Editor-in-Chief Frank Owen that all his life he had tried to live down his play-boy image; and even now, when as a sailor on horseback he had defeated the Japanese Army in Burma, he was still stuck with it—with 'a Hollywood style' surrender.

For the signing ceremony, a small lonely table with three hard-backed chairs was set out for the Japanese—facing a long table for the Allies. Both had ink wells, pens and pencils but—perhaps significantly—only the Allies had rubbers.

The three Japanese, Lt-Gen. Numata, Rear Admiral Chudo and Lt-Col. Tomuria, marched with dignity to their table, took off their caps and stood stiffly to attention whilst the Press photographed them. The Allied delegates then entered under a large Union flag.

Gen. Browning, dressed in a jungle-green bush shirt, came in last and sat down at the centre of the long table. Rear Admiral W. B. Patterson, from the East Indies Fleet, was on his right. After Gen. Browning had briefly explained the terms of the agreement, Brig. J. G. Nicholson of the Intelligence Staff took the papers over to the Japanese.

Gen. Numata took off his black-rimmed glasses before looking them through—then quickly dipped a pen into the inkwell and signed. Beside him Admiral Chudo and Col. Tomuria sat to attention looking straight ahead with faces devoid of expression. The papers were returned to Gen. Browning, who signed them with his fountain pen, and then back to Gen. Numata again for the affixing of F. M. Count Terauchi's seal. The ceremony was over.

Massive air cover from carriers

Typhoons raging over Japan forced a delay in the planned date of Gen. MacArthur's arrival in Japan to take the overall Japanese surrender. But on August 26 a massive air cover from its carriers sailed into Sagami Bay, just outside Tokyo Bay, ready for the first landings on Japanese soil.

On August 29 the British battleship HMS *Duke of York* and the American

Missouri anchored off Yokohama in Tokyo Bay.

1000 Carrier aircraft of the US 3rd Fleet and BPF off Japan. 22nd August 1945.
Photo: Bert Crane, HMS Duke of York

After hurried preparation by engineers and communication specialists Gen. MacArthur finally landed at Atsugi Airfield on August 30, together with the leading elements of the American 11th Airborne Division. Of the 10,000 men in the landing force, 540 were British. There was a simultaneous landing by 400 Royal Marines and 1,800 American Marines at Yokosuka naval base.

The formal Instrument of Surrender of the Japanese Emperor, his Government and his people was signed on a mess table on board the American battleship *Missouri* at 10.30 a.m. on Sunday, September 2, 1945. Mr Shigemitsu, Japanese Foreign Minister, signed first. Then Gen. MacArthur, flanked by Lt-Gen. J. M. Wainwright of Corregidor fame and Lt-Gen. Sir Archibald Percival, who as former British C-in-C Malaya had surrendered to the Japanese in Singapore, signed the document himself and called upon the representatives of China, Britain, the Soviet Union, Australia, Canada, France, the Netherlands and New Zealand to sign in that order.

The Daily Telegraph article continued:

Singapore is re-occupied

Before the British re-occupation of Singapore Island, a preliminary local agreement had been signed on board HMS *Sussex* by Rear Admiral C. S. Holland and Lt-Gen. Sir Philip Christison, Commander 15th Corps, on behalf of Lord Mountbatten; and by Gen. Seishiro Itagaki, Commander of the Japanese Seventh Army Area, and Vice Admiral Fukudome, Commander of the Tenth Fleet Area, for the Japanese. More than 85,000 Japanese troops, including 85 generals, were involved.

On September 10 came the surrender of one-fifth of all Japan's Armed Forces—those in China and Korea. One million Japanese troops serving in China, Formosa and French Indo-China were surrendered by the Japanese Chief of Staff, Gen. Okamura, at a ceremony in Nanking.

A further 360,000 were surrendered at the Governor-General's Palace at Keijo Korea, by Gen. Mobuyuk Abe.

Lord Mountbatten summoned Field Marshal Count Terauchi to appear in Singapore on September 12 formally to surrender his forces in the entire South-East Asia theatre of operations. But pleading ill-health, the Field Marshal asked to be excused from attending.

Mountbatten therefore permitted the Field Marshal to delegate responsibility as Supreme Commander to Gen. Itagaki, the 'Tiger of Singapore' and the local Seventh Army Commander, for the official surrender. But at the same time he warned that the Field Marshal would be expected to make his own surrender in person as soon as he was fit enough to do so.

So, on September 12, in Singapore's Municipal Building, the Supreme Commander South-East Asia, Lord Louis Mountbatten took the surrender of the Japanese Expeditionary Forces of the Southern Region, a total of 738,400 men of all Services. Later in Saigon on November 30, the ailing F. M. Terauchi finally completed the bargain in person when he surrendered his sword to Lord Louis. Terauchi died in 1946.

In fact there were two swords. One, Lord Louis presented to King George VI, and one he kept to add to his own collection at Broadlands.

From Lt. Cdr. (A) R. Bigg-Wither, CO 1841 Squadron, HMS *Formidable*

When we sailed for Sydney on 28th June 1945 for what turned out to be the final assault on the Jap mainland we had only 2 months to go before completing our 15 months 'first line' service and being relieved. Up to then we had lost 3 pilots in accidents, 3 in action and 2 shot down or lost in Norway—both POWs.

We were expecting a much better reception when striking at the heart of Japan and I wondered how many of us would survive these last few weeks. In fact they never came up against us in the air.

The desire to stay alive was very strong, but at the same time we were keen to inflict as much damage as we could on Jap ground aircraft and shipping, which was our duty. The spectre of being shot down and captured was never far away as we knew what that would mean.

My inner conflict between these two objectives was a continual battle particularly after the first atom bomb was dropped on the 6th August. I remember telling Cmdr. Dick Sweeton (later Admiral Sir Richard) on Vian's staff, that I thought it quite crazy to risk further lives and why did we not retire until the results were known? He replied that the Yanks required us to keep up the pressure.

During those last 2 days August 9/10, we lost Hammy Gray, Alan Maitland (the diary writer) and Anderson RCNVR. Morten and Storheill my Norwegian pilot were severely damaged and ditched—Morten, quite near land, picked up by a US Submarine whilst under small arms fire from shore and Storheill near one of the US picket destroyers. All this after orders not to press home our attacks! I believe that *Indefat.* went on operations and losing pilots until August 15th—surrender day. I have always resented this quite unnecessary loss of lives.

I felt completely shattered by our own losses which I suffered so deeply and spent a miserable return to Sydney writing letters to their families. At least more of us were alive than I expected and it has been an absolute joy to meet many of the brave survivors since the war.

At our dinner at Yeovilton on May 12th 1990, the enclosed letter was read out to my complete surprise. It was sent to one of my boys by Bob Glading NZ who usually flew with me. He was a teetotaler—just as well to have *one* in a squadron! 'Alcohol has no effect on me, so I don't drink it,' was his maxim. I was most embarrassed at the time and said he must have consumed too many milk shakes! I felt very proud and rather humble that they thought of me in those terms when I read it later:

R. H. Glading
8—25 Saltburn Road
Milford, Auckland 9
New Zealand

April 1990

Dear Biggy and the 1841 Squadron chaps,

How much I should have enjoyed being with you for the 1990 reunion, however, perhaps one more gathering may be organised before we all become too ancient and doddery to travel to far away (and near) places!

The last one in 1983 was certainly a happy and memorable occasion which provided untold pleasure for both Margaret and myself.

While I had through the years since 1945 met up with your dear self Biggy, together with Eric Humphries, Johnny Crosland and 'Blue Smoke Blaikie', it was a particular pleasure to see others who I had not seen since *Formidable* left Sydney. I shall certainly never forget the shock of finding Matt present, as I was under the impression that he was under 100 feet of snow on some Norwegian mountain, or up in FAA Pilots heaven singing clean versions of his bawdy songs!

Throughout my lifetime (dear me, 70 in March!) I have always counted myself more than fortunate in serving in the Fleet Air Arm and in particular my good fortune to be appointed to 1841 squadron and as a result to be associated with such a band of fine fellows and above all our CO who in my opinion, was the bravest and most un-flappable man one could ever imagine in the air. We were probably too young at the time to fully appreciate his outstanding leadership, but we certainly loved and respected him and for those of us still here, we largely have Biggy to thank for that situation.

Finally may I wish you all a happy occasion—my greetings and I hope that we shall meet again,

Most sincerely yours,
Bob
(The milk shake king of 1841 squadron)

Last entry in Vic Spencer's flying log book and extracts from the English Language version of the Nippon Times

This is the last war-time entry in Vic Spencer's flying log book.

August 9—Avenger JZ448—Strike on Matsushima airfield. Four 500 lb. M.C.s. Target—Twin engined A/C in revetment. (OP)

August 10—Avenger JZ135—Strike on Koriyama Airfield—Last seen heading for coast. (OP)

Note to Entry date Aug. 10—Attacked A/C dispersed in S.W. corner of airfield—four 500 lb M.C.s. A/C hit twice by flak, in engine and fuselage. Resultant engine failure necessitated forced landing in paddy field approx. 10 miles east of target. Evaded capture until Aug. 12, when T.A.G. and self apprehended by Japanese military. Imprisoned Sendai Aug. 13. Imprisoned Omori, Tokyo, Aug. 14—Aug 31. Released Aug 31.

Among his souvenirs ex POW Vic Spencer found a copy of the English language version of the 'Nippon Times' dated Wednesday 8th August 1945.

It shows the Tokyo office as Itchome, Uchisaiwai-cho, Kojimachiku and the Osaka office as Dojima Bldg. The publisher and printer was Shoichi Kawamura.

Here are some extracts, beginning with the start of the leader article:

Tokyo, Wednesday, August 8, 1945

THE INCALCULABLE RESERVE

The enemy attacks with a meticulous precision awesome to behold. He brings into effective play his slide rule and his compass, his charts and instruments. He apparently knows through photography and a vast and well-laid espionage network the locations and nature of the vital organs which are necessary to the conduct of this war. Even of the things that he does not know, he seems to have the technical craft and equipment with which to calculate the greater part of the same. There is only one thing which completely defies his diabolical calculations and that is the spiritual reserve of the Japanese people.

Such a reserve has been noted elsewhere, in the recent past. Surely Leningrad, Stalingrad and Moscow could not have been held with guns alone. If material weight alone had been the final criterion in the conflict, Yiojima and Okinawa should have fallen weeks sooner at a far cheaper cost to the enemy. In the Japanese eye the Special Attack Force is not a 'suicide' squad, as our materialistic enemy sees it; it is one of the incalculables in its most concrete expression.

IMPERIAL RESCRIPT OBSERVANCE DAY

Imperial Rescript

We, by grace of heaven, Emperor of Japan, seated on the Throne of a line unbroken for ages eternal, enjoin upon ye, Our loyal and brave subjects: We hereby declare war on the United States of American and the British Empire. The men and officers of Our Army and Navy shall do their utmost in prosecuting the war, Our public servants of various departments shall perform faithfully and diligently their appointed tasks, and all other subjects of Ours shall pursue their respective duties; the entire nation with a united will shall mobilize their total strength so that nothing will miscarry in the attainment of Our war aims.

To insure the stability of East Asia and to contribute to world peace is the far-sighted policy which was formulated by Our Great Illustrious Imperial Grandsire and Our Great Imperial Sire succeeding Him, and which We lay constantly to heart. To cultivate friendship among nations and to enjoy prosperity in common with all nations has always been the guiding principle of Our Empire's foreign policy. It has been truly unavoidable and far from Our wishes that Our Empire has now been brought to cross swords with America and Britain. More than four years have passed since China, failing to comprehend the true intentions of Our Empire, and recklessly courting trouble, disturbed the peace of East Asia and compelled Our Empire to take up arms. Although there has been re-established the National Government of China, with which Japan has effected neighborly intercourse and cooperation, the regime which has survived at Chungking, relying upon American and British protection, still continued its fratricidal opposition. Eager for the realization of their inordinate ambition to dominate the Orient, both America and Britain, giving support to the Chungking regime, have aggravated the disturbances in East Asia. Moreover, these two Powers, inducing others to follow suit, increased military preparations on all sides of Our Empire to challenge us. They have obstructed by every means Our peaceful commerce, and finally resorted to a direct severance of economic relations, menacing gravely the existence of Our Empire. Patiently have We waited and long have We endured, in the hope that Our Government might retrieve the situation in peace. But our adversaries, showing not the least spirit of conciliation, have unduly delayed a settlement; and in the meantime, they have intensified the economic and political pressure to compel thereby Our Empire to submission. This trend of affairs would, if left unchecked, not only nullify Our Empire's efforts of many years for the sake of the stabilization of East Asia, but also endanger the very existence of Our nation. The situation being such as it is, Our Empire for its existence and self-defense has no other recourse but to appeal to arms and to crush every obstacle in its path.

The hallowed spirits of our Imperial Ancestors guarding Us from above, We rely upon the loyalty and courage of Our subjects in Our confident expectation that the task bequeathed by Our forefathers will be carried forward, and that the sources of evil will be speedily eradicated and an enduring peace immutably established in East Asia, preserving thereby the glory of Our Empire.

(Imperial Sign Manual)
(Imperial Seal)

The 8th day of the 12th month of the 16th year of Showa.

AMERICA DIGS HER OWN GRAVE

High Time for Our Enemies to Repent

by Jun Matsumiya
Former Ambassador

The Anglo American nations are fanatical believers of force and material power. They think that the world is ruled by the strong and that the weak should bow and be subservient to the strong. For the Anglo-Americans, force decides everything and thus neither justice, humanity nor reason has any voice before force. They believe that might is right. They will overcome and oppress any claim others may make though it contains much justice or truth, as long as it is against their own interests. On the other hand, they will bow before any nation that happens to be stronger than they regardless of justice. Thus, here is the possibility of hundreds of thousands of troops submitting themselves to their enemy. They do not regard such capitulation before their more powerful enemy as an act of humiliation. When a once powerful nation is overcome by a newcomer who is more formidable and who takes away from her her sway, she bends her knee before her rival as if she were doing a right thing. They never realize that the principle of common prosperity is the immutable common highway of heaven and earth but consider the grim struggle for existence as a law of nature. Thus, they pay their supreme attention to force. They even think that a person without power has no right to exist in this world. This faith is manifested in the field of politics, economy and diplomacy as the phenomenon of a beastly struggle for existence. If their opponent is found to be weak, they are likely to crush him without mercy and threaten him with intimidation or a display of armed power. Thus, the enemy has been announcing as their war aim the destruction of Japan's armaments and industrial power, to turn Japan into an agricultural nation, to limit the territory of Japan to the restricted area that existed before the time of the Meji Restoration.

The Anglo-American nations attained their present position by overcoming the more advanced nations by force and this experience makes them ever watchful of a similar fate for them; they fear that they may be overcome by some newcomers. Their minds are full of scepticism and uneasiness.

They say that there will always be all conceivable methods in keeping what they once acquired by predatory practices. It is only natural that demands should be made for a revision or that there should arise movements for breaking up such a condition.

What gives rise to their idea of mutual opposition in everything also gives rise to the struggles between capital and labor at home and war in international relations. So intense is their sense of opposition that they desire to destroy their enemy so that there arises the beastly struggle of existence among the nations of the world. As the results of all this, there persists a rankling resentment and antipathy deeply implanted in their hearts so that there will be no real and hearty peace in the world however long we may wait for it.

Such, indeed, is the character of the Anglo-American nations. This perverse enemy is about to make his invasion of our mainland in the immediate future. It will be inevitable that once we are defeated, we shall be mercilessly trampled upon and placed in a condition of permanent slavery.

The only way for Japan to live at present is to repulse this enemy, destroy and annihilate him. The only question is whether or not our national power will be able to accomplish this.

This is a war in which we should never be defeated. If material power should decide the outcome of the contest, it must have been clear from the very outset. Here lies the main strategy of our fighting in contriving the method of overcoming the enemy's superior material power.

Being materialists, the Anglo-Americans believe that a man's happiness depends on whether or not he is blessed by material things. Not knowing what contentment is they cause sufferings and privations to others: and their ideal consists of having more territory and resources than others and in leading a materially rich existence, even though they have to exploit others for their private purposes. As the result of such ideas and ideals, there arises the unbalanced existence of lands, resources or wealth and social or international discontent and dissatisfaction. Attempts to remedy such discontent or dissatisfaction are manifested in the movements of socialism, communism and in the attempts to break up the status quo by armed force. It is because of this that the capitalistic countries with the Anglo-American nations as their leaders consider communism and militarism as their dreadful enemy, but they ignore the fact that these two are the offsprings of capitalism itself. Although the condition in which a small financial group or nations monopolize the world's wealth while a large mass of people or nations are very poorly endowed is intolerable from the standpoint of justice and humanity.

Again, the Anglo-American nations have frequently attempted to prevent the dangers of war by disarmament, but their armament reduction was intended only as a means to keep Japan down. Instead of assuming the attitude of friendliness the Anglo-American nations closed their doors tightly against Japan and imposed terms convenient to themselves. As the result of this selfish attitude, the disarmament treaties were repudiated and finally resulted in the outbreak of the War of Greater East Asia.

All these facts show that the so-called peace of the Anglo-American nations is not justly conceived. Since their community is based on individualism, everything takes the form of opposition or rivalry.

YANKEES FIND HOMESICKNESS UNBEARABLE IN FAR-FLUNG BASES IN PACIFIC WAR FRONT

The July number of British journal Vogue reveals the intense nostalgia which the American soldiers are suffering from in the Pacific islands, the name of which they cannot pronounce' and for which they had risked their existence so foolishly, says a Stockholm dispatch of August 6 to Mainichi.

The article which describes their lonely life on the occupied islands is entitled 'The American Soldiers on the Pacific Front and Nostalgia'. The article is to the following effect:

'Their illness, namely, nostalgia has become the main topic of their daily conversations. They wish to have their people at home know the realities of their difficult fighting in the far-flung islands of the Pacific Ocean. Their private letters indicate that they have absolutely no interest in their lives on the islands—the name of which they cannot pronounce and in the life of which they find no source of humor or jokes. Some of their comrades fought and died in order to capture these islands.

'The newspapers in their home country are reporting with much care the celebration in Europe over the termintion of the European battle. The papers also report of the reconversion of American industries from the war to peace basis. These reports and private letters which the American soldiers on the Pacific front receive from their folks at home give them the conviction that the victory of the Allies in Europe will directly influence the Pacific War situation. However, the American soldiers know better. It is not difficult for them to calculate that it will be a matter of stupendous difficulty to transpose the armed forces and munitions from the European to Pacific fronts and that it will take a considerable time to do so. The American soldiers are praying that their folks at home will understand the realities in the Pacific fighting.

'Their nostalgia is like a jungle fever. Their loneliness grows limitlessly. When they receive letters from home complaining about the bad ration of food and other provisions, they doubt as if they are still living in this world: and such letters further increase their unbearable loneliness. Some of the soldiers fear their return to that separate world—their home land. Others become despaired of life itself saying that they would not care for anything.

'At first, the soldiers tried to describe their life on the islands in their letters to the folks at home but found it impossible to give even a semblance of its realities and gave up their attempt. This is only too natural because it is impossible to describe their lives adequately even by war correspondents on the front. The newspaper men know the facts and figures of the war situation and can write about them, but they themselves become a prey of nostalgia which is beyond their control and are unable to describe their moods, sentiments and souls. They cannot control the movement of their minds, and their loneliness increases steadily.

'The movie stars come to the fronts in order to console the soldiers but the latter find no consolation from their visit. On the contrary, their talks only annoy the soldiers. The soldiers find the heavy wall which separates their present life from the home front and realize that this wall can be penetrated only by means of death and bloodshed. Thus, their loneliness and nostalgia further increase."

TOBACCO RATION IS CUT

Three Cigarettes a Day Per Person Is New Standard

On August 1, the cigarette ration was reduced from five to three cigarettes per person a day throughout the country.

The Tobacco Bureau of the Finance Ministry assures that the present standard of three cigarettes per person a day will be maintained however intense the enemy's air raids may become.

Officials of the Tobacco Bureau say that it may happen sometime that the production of cigarettes sich as 'Kinshi', 'Hikari' and 'Hoyoku' may become impossible, but in such a case cut tobacco will be supplied, the amount of which will equal three cigarettes.

From Std. James Paterson, 888 Squadron (Initially in *Indefatigable* for the Sumatra Operations—the first BPF Strikes)

Indian Ocean. Our last operation consisted of boarding three escort carriers in one day (no wonder they called them Woolworth carriers!) from the shore establishment at Bombard Trincomalee. First of all we boarded *Emperor,* but only a few miles out of Trinco, she broke down completely. Barracudas circled the vessel, and she was towed into harbour by the cruiser HMS *Royalist*. We then awaited the arrival of HMS *Shah*, fresh from the refit at Simonstown, South Africa. She hit a buoy with her props coming into the harbour. We boarded, disembarked and then embarked on HMS *Ameer*. The *Emperor* later joined her sistership and we seemed to be stooging around the Andaman Islands, Sumatra, Java and entered the Malacca Straits. We were not allowed to go to sleep that night, but others and myself kept dozing off. We were told we'd be put on a charge, but nothing seemed to come of it! We had our only casualty on this operation. The nicest chap on the squadron, doesn't it always happen! Sub Lt. Tomlinson was flying a Hellcat normally flown by Lt. Godden, it had previously been troublesome and on this rec. flight, problems arose. He had to ditch off Port Swettenham. He got ashore in the rubber dinghy, lay low for several days, but alas the Japs found him and he was beheaded. A sad loss indeed. After this we then sailed on HMS *Smiter* to Singapore (RNAS Sembwang), where we arrived just before Christmas 1945, the war had now ended and we sailed for home in P & O Trooper *Maloja* in June 1946.

From Captain R. Laird RASC, ex-POW, Changi

For those of us who were 'in the bag' in the Far East, you were certainly not the Forgotten Fleet'. I finished up in Changi after a spell on 'The Railway': in Changi we had a very regular 'News Service' and I was one of the links in the chain for the distribution of News, so that I was very well aware of the operations of the British Pacific Fleet—aided by the fact that I grew up on Merseyside in close contact with the ship-building world.

One incident from 'The Forgotten Fleet' which you recount on Page 157 of your book, is news to me, re the execution at Changi beach on August 18th/20th 1945 of FAA survivors from the Palembang raid. Although I was in Changi at the time and in touch with most things that were going on, news of this incident did not leak out at the time. It does not, however, surprise me as Itagaki, the Japanese GOC in Singapore, was known to be a 'hard-liner' who refused to accept the Surrender until he had got it straight from 'the horse's mouth' in the form of a personal representative of the Emperor, i.e. one Prince Terauchi who was flown down specially from Japan—in a white-painted plane with green crosses on the wings and fuselage. This plane arrived at Singapore round about August 25th and a day or two before that, some of our planes from the Cocos Islands came over and the Nips let fly at them with everything they had got. So I think it highly probable that the FAA lads were executed on August 18th/20th on the direct orders of General Itagaki. I rather think that he was later tried as a War Criminal and executed, but I cannot quote chapter and verse.

You can imagine that until the Surrender was accepted officially, we were very conscious that things were very touchy for us: it is greatly to the credit of the 7,000 or so POWs in Changi at the time, who knew exactly what was going on in the outside world, that no one gave the show away by being over-cocky with the Nips and working parties continued going out to the aerodrome as usual.

Extracts from 'The Other Hundred Years War 1941—2041' by Russell Braddon

15 August was a broiling day, and all over the country Hirohito's subjects were wondering what they would hear when their Emperor spoke to them.

At 11.30 a.m. the recording for which the conspirators had searched half the previous night was delivered to Studio 8 of the NHK building. Just before noon, Hirohito sat down by a radio to listen to his own voice. General Tojo and his wife knelt before their radio. In every street people knelt beneath loudspeakers attached to lamp posts. At every factory and back street workshop, in every house and office and barrack, all work stopped and all traffic halted as the people of Japan knelt and waited.

'A broadcast of the greatest importance is about to commence,' radios and loudspeakers warned them. 'All listeners will please rise.' Of the whole nation, apart from the sick and disabled, only Hirohito remained seated.

'His Majesty the Emperor will now read the Imperial Rescript to the people of Japan,' said the announcer. 'We respectfully transmit his voice.'

'To Our good and loyal subjects,' it said. 'After pondering deeply the general trends of the world and the conditions actually obtaining in our Empire today, we have decided to effect a settlement of the present situation by resorting to an extraordinary measure.

'We have ordered Our Government to communicate to the Governments of the United States, Great Britain, China and the Soviet Union that Our Empire accepts the provisions of their joint Declaration.'

Which meant nothing especially ominous to the people of Japan who had been told nothing of the Potsdam Declaration and none of the details of the Notes cabled between Tokyo and Washington over the past six days.

'To strive for the common prosperity and happiness of all nations, as well as the security and well being of Our subjects, is the solemn duty which has been handed down by Our Imperial Ancestors and which lies close to Our heart.'

Whatever followed, it was not understood, was not merely for the well-being of Japan, but of all nations.

'Indeed, We declared war on America and Britain out of Our sincere desire to ensure Japan's self-preservation and the stabilization of East Asia, it being far from Our thoughts either to infringe upon the sovereignty of other nations or to emabrk upon territorial aggrandisement.'

Which may well have been true of Hirohito himself, but was a bare-faced lie by those who had written the Rescript for him.

'But now,' the thin, deliberately high-pitched voice went on, 'the war has lasted for nearly four years, and despite the best that has been done by everyone—the gallant fighting of the military and naval forces, the diligence and assiduity of Our Servants of the State and the devoted service of Our hundred million people—the war situation has developed not necessarily to our advantage, while the general trends of the world have all turned against Our Empire's interests.

'Moreover, the enemy has begun to employ a new and most cruel bomb, the power of which to do damage is indeed incalculable as it takes its toll of so many innocent lives. Should we continue to fight, not only would that lead to the ultimate collapse and obliteration of the Japanese nation, but it would also lead to the extinction of human civilization.'

For the second time it was being made clear that it was not of the Japanese alone that the Emperor was thinking, but of all mankind; not even Hirohito can have believed that.

'Such being the case,' the voice proceeded inexorably, 'how are We to save the millions of Our subjects or to atone to Ourselves before the hallowed spirits of Our Imperial Ancestors? It is to that end that We have ordered the acceptance of the provisions of the joint Declaration of the Allied Powers.

'We cannot but express the deepest sense of regret to Our allied nations of East Asia, who have consistently co-operated with the Empire to secure the emancipation of East Asia,' the Imperial voice asserted.

Comparatively few of those listening to it appreciated that Japan's allied nations had never been willing allies and were all now rejoicing in her defeat; but that was not the real import of Hirohito's words—which were an oblique invitation to the colonies of East Asia to seek emancipation from their masters, Britain, France and Holland.'

Hirohito had doubtless felt more sincere, and no one can doubt his sincerity, as he recorded the words that followed.

'The thought of those officers and men, as well as others, who have fallen on the battlefield, of those who died at their posts of duty, or of those who met with untimely death, and of all their bereaved families, pains Our heart night and day.

'The welfare of the wounded and the war sufferers, and of those who have lost their homes and livelihood, are the objects of Our profound solicitude.'

Then came the crunch, and the exhortation.

'The hardships and sufferings to which Our nation is to be subjected hereafter will certainly be great. We are keenly aware of the innermost feelings of you all. However, it is in accordance with the dictates of time and fate that We have resolved to pave the way for a grand peace for all the generations to come by enduring the unendurable and suffering what is insufferable.

'Having been able to safeguard and maintain the structure of the Imperial State'—a generous lie aimed at averting any position to the coming occupation—'We are always with you, Our good and loyal subjects, and We are relying upon your sincerity and integrity.

'Beware most strictly any outbursts of emotion which may cause needless complications, or any fraternal contention and strife which may create confusion and lead you astray and cause you to lose the confidence of the outside world.

'Let the entire nation continue as one family from generation to generation, ever firm in its faith in the imperishability of its sacred land, and ever mindful of its heavy responsibilities and of the long road ahead.

'Unite your total strength and devote it to rebuilding for your future. Cultivate the ways of rectitude; foster nobility of spirit; and work with resolution so that you may enhance the innate glory of the world.'

As he sat in his Palace, head bowed, and listened to his own words, Hirohito must have known that he alone of the Heads of State of the three defeated Axis powers had spoken to his people as a leader should; that he had touched the heart of every one of his subjects; that he had given them hope even as he prepared them for the worst; and, above all, that he had never once mentioned the word surrender. In short, that he had laid down the guide lines for their spectacular future.

Switching off his radio, Tojo turned to his wife and said, 'Well, up till now it's been our life for our country. Now things have changed, and reconstruction may be more difficult than giving our lives. But, if that is the Emperor's will, we must do everything we can to bring it about as long as we live.'

At that moment the telephone rang and Tojo was told of his son-in-law's suicide. He warned his daughter that her husband's body was being brought home. Completely composed, his daugher observed that in death her husband would remain forever a Major.

All over Japan, but particularly in Tokyo, there were suicides; and outside the Palace people were kneeling, foreheads touching the ground, murmuring, 'Forgive us, oh Emperor, our efforts were not enough.'

Doubtless, Hirohito's generals overseas heard his broadcast, but if one is to judge by the reaction of those who guarded in Johore, the rank and file of the Imperial Japanese Army did not. While their comrades in Japan wept, mutinied and killed themselves, they behaved as they always had done.

The likelihood is that they were also told nothing of Anami's last order cabled to all Headquarters under his name the day before the Imperial Broadcasts. 'The Emperor has made his decision,' it began. 'The Army expects you to obey that decision and make no unauthorized moves that would disgrace the glorious traditions of the Imperial Army and its many distinguished achievements. You must so behave as never to incur the judgement of posterity. It is expected of you that your conduct will enhance the honour and glory of the Imperial Japanese Forces in the eyes of the world.'

Yet mere hours after the war had been terminated, those American fliers who had survived Fukuoda's first and second massacres were taken down the same road to the same field outside Aburayama, stripped, driven into the nearby woods and cut to ribbons in a carnival of swordsmanship.

Knowing none of this in Malaya, we nevertheless knew our Imperial Japanese Army; and when our guards ordered us out to work as usual, we behaved as usual, carefully concealing from them the fact that they had lost the war; until someone came and disarmed them, none of us was safe.

For those Japanese in detention in Australia, the situation was very different. 'Gentlemen,' their Australian commandant told them, 'the war is over—and with it the life you have had to endure as prisoners of war. No doubt you will be able to return home within a few months.'

They were appalled. In his broadcast the Emperor had specifically exonerated everyone except those who had allowed themselves to become prisoners of the enemy. They found the prospect of going home frightening.

For the moment though, it was we who should have been frightened, because Itagaki, now standing in as Commander in Chief in South East Asia for Field Marshal Terauchi, who was ill, was on the point of disobeying Hirohito. Speaking of and to his hitherto undefeated forces, he broadcast from Singapore that they had 'an unchallenged dignity' and were eager to 'crush the foe'. Although the ashes of war were two days old, its embers still glowed wickedly in the Philippines, Indo-China, Thailand, Burma and Malaya.

Japan's press and radio were already taking up the Emperor's plea of mitigation. The war had been lost, they insisted, because of the Allies' 'scientific offensive'. Defeat was only temporary. The sooner the Allies were convinced that the Japanese had submitted to their terms, by accepting occupation, the prosecution of war criminals and a change of government—the sooner they would be gone.

Nor was General Tanaka prepared to fail his Emperor a third time. When a group of students threatened further rebellion, he told them, 'All you men have bright futures. It is you who must lead Japan from now on. The Atom bomb has changed the state of the war completely. It is the will of God that we abandon the long history of the Japanese Army. New generations will come. Please concentrate on the construction of a new nation.' On the ninth day of Japan's defeat, he shot himself.

But we were as yet enjoying only the third day of a decidedly muted victory, working in our tunnel and suddenly examining every green pit prop with acute mistrust. There was no news, because our enterprising thief, upon hearing the whispered *Red Light*, had thrown his radio down a thirty foot borehole from which, since boreholes were used as latrines, no one had felt inclined to retrieve it.

It was either that morning or the next that we were called out of our tunnel to be confronted by a Japanese colonel. His jack-boots were glossy, his sword too long, and his face wreathed in a strangely avuncular smile. He saluted us and bowed. Warily we bowed back.

'War finish,' he said. 'All men go home'—and bowed again. We remained vertical.

'If you insist upon this form of surrender,' Slim's advisers assured him in the days of Itagaki's sullen procrastination, 'all the Japanese senior officers will commit hara kiri.'

'Offer them every facility,' Slim had retorted—and it was Itagaki who had compromised. But he and the rest of the Imperial Japanese Army had elected to live not because Slim had made it obvious that he was quite happy for them to die, but because Suzuki had recorded a message (which was broadcast on the hour every hour, from 6 p.m. till midnight) saying 'So far as the preservation of our national structure is concerned, I have a positive plan. You must all behave with the utmost calm, maintaining a dispassionate attitude.'

And dispassionate they were; and almost relaxed—because at that time they believed that the Emperor had 'terminated the war', not surrendered. It was ten years, in fact, before the Japanese admitted that their armies had surrendered rather than stopped fighting. *Shusen* was the word they used until 1955; but then they changed it to *haisen*.

In Changi we ignored the Imperial Japanese Army, lay in the sun, ate regular meals (of rice, which suddenly was available in abundance) and waited for someone to take us home.

Eventually, Mountbatten's fleet and soldiers arrived—so big and fit we were unable to believe that we had ever been their equals—and looked fierce when they saw what the Japanese had done to us. Lord Mountbatten (whom we had dubbed Linger Longer Louis when he failed to release us in 1944) arrived the following day. Standing on a wooden box in our gaol courtyard he told us that he knew what we had called him, and said, 'So now I'll tell you why I lingered so long!' The delay had been caused by the people planning the invasion of Normandy and southern France. 'Every time I was ready to invade Malaya,' he said, 'they pinched my landing craft.' We forgave him instantly. And when he said that he had come to Singapore to accept Itagaki's surrender, we roared our enthusiasm. We had waited a long time to witness the Imperial Japanese Army's surrender.

But our senior Australian officer indulged himself in one last officious flight and ordered us *not* to go into the city. I suppose he thought we might get lost. A number of us ignored him. Watching Itagaki hand his sword to Mountbatten was a perfect way of celebrting the war's end—and a marvellous moment of theatre.

Great theatrical experiences suspend all disbelief in their audiences, and we who watched Itagaki submit to Mountbatten were no exception. There were huge gaps in the drama we had witnessed, yet it never occurred to us even to ask how the intransigent Imperial Japanese Army, in a matter only of days, had been transformed from fanaticism to compliance. Satiated with the drama we had merely *seen,* we were incurious about the Japanese, and asked no questions. We just waited for ships to come and take us home, serenely uninterested in the details of Japan's formal surrender to MacArthur on the decks of the *Missouri* in Tokyo Bay, and completely unenthused by the prospect of the promised War Trials. Not because we disapproved of them: simply because we had won the war and thought nothing Japanese any longer mattered.

The day of departure—and of partings—came abruptly. As I walked toward the convoy of jeeps that would transport us to the docks, I passed one of the Imperial Japanese Army's few English-speaking officers who was being escorted into the gaol. In a spirit half of elation and half of spite, I turned and shouted, 'This war last one hundred years?'

'Ninety-six years to go,' he called back; and neither of us bothered to bow.

INSTRUMENT OF SURRENDER

We acting by command of and on behalf of the Emperor of Japan, the Japanese Government and the Japanese Imperial General Headquarters, hereby accept the provisions set forth in the declaration issued by the heads of the Governments of the United States, China and Great Britain on 26 July 1945 at Potsdam, and subsequently adhered to by the Union of Soviet Socialist Republics, which four powers are hereafter referred to as the Allied Powers.

We hereby proclaim the unconditional surrender to the Allied Powers of the Japanese Imperial General Headquarters and of all Japanese armed forces and all armed forces under Japanese control wherever situated.

We hereby command all Japanese forces wherever situated and the Japanese people to cease hostilities forthwith, to preserve and save from damage all ships, aircraft, and military and civil property and to comply with all requirements which may be imposed by the Supreme Commander for the Allied Powers or by agencies of the Japanese Government at his direction.

We hereby command the Japanese Imperial General Headquarters to issue at once orders to the Commanders of all Japanese forces and all forces under Japanese control wherever situated to surrender unconditionally themselves and all forces under their control.

We hereby command all civil, military and naval officials to obey and enforce all proclamations, orders and directives deemed by the Supreme Commander for the Allied Powers to be proper to effectuate this surrender and issued by him or under his authority and so direct all such officials to remain at their posts and to continue to perform their non-combatant duties unless specifically relieved by him or under his authority.

We hereby undertake for the Emperor, the Japanese Government and their successors to carry out the provisions of the Potsdam Declaration in good faith, and to issue whatever orders and take whatever action may be required by the Supreme Commander for the Allied Powers or by any other designated representative of the Allied Powers for the purpose of giving effect to that Declaration.

We hereby command the Japanese Imperial Government and the Japanese Imperial General Headquarters at once to liberate all allied prisoners of war and civilian internees now under Japanese control and to provide for their protection, care, maintenance and immediate transportation to places as directed.

The authority of the Emperor and the Japanese Government to rule the state shall be subject to the Supreme Commander for the Allied Powers who will take such steps as he deems proper to effectuate these terms of surrender.

Signed at TOKYO BAY, JAPAN at ____________

on the SECOND day of SEPTEMBER, 1945

By Command and on behalf of the Emperor of Japan and the Japanese Government

Mamoru Shigemitsu, Foreign Minister

By Command and on behalf of the Japanese Imperial General Headquarters *Yoshikiro Umezu, General*

Accepted at TOKYO BAY, JAPAN at 0908

on the SECOND day of SEPTEMBER, 1945,

for the United States, Republic of China, United Kingdom and the Union of Soviet Socialist, and in the Interests of the other United Nations at war with Japan:

General Douglas MacArthur

Supreme Commander for the Allied Powers

United States Representative

Admiral Nimitz

Republic of China Representative

General Hsu Ung Chang

United Kingdom Representative

Admiral Sir Bruce Fraser

Union of Soviet Socialist Republics Representative

Lt. General K. N. Deevyanko

Commonwealth of Australia Representative

General Blamey

Dominion of Canada Representative

Col. L. M. Cosgrove

Provisional Government of the French Republic Representative

General P. le Clerc

Kingdom of the Netherlands Representative

Admiral C. E. L. Helfrich

Dominion of New Zealand Representative *Air Vice Marshall Isitt, LM*

Translation

HIROHITO

By the Grace of Heaven, Emperor of Japan, seated on the Throne occupied by the same Dynasty changeless through ages eternal,

To all to whom these Presents shall come, Greeting!

We do hereby authorise Yoshijiro Umezu, Zyosanmi, First Class of the Imperial Order of the Rising Sun, Second Class of the Imperial Military Order of the Golden Kite, to attach his signature by command and on behalf of Ourselves and Our Imperial General Headquarters unto the Instrument of Surrender which is required by the Supreme Commander for the Allied Powers to be signed.

In witness whereof, We have hereunto set Our signature and caused the Great Seal of the Empire to be affixed.

Given at our Palace in Tokyo, this first day of the ninth month of the twentieth year of Syowa, being the two thousand six hundred and fifth year from the Accession of the Emperor Zinsu.

Seal of the Empire	Signed: HIROHITO.

Countersigned: Yoshijiro Umezu
Chief of the General Staff
of the Imperial Japanese . . .

CHAPTER EIGHT

'The Fleet Train'

Admiral Fraser had not only to adjust his training, experience and thinking from a conflict of capital ships to carriers, but had to do it with the largest Fleet and the longest Fleet Train Britain had ever known or required.

This he had to do, while resources were employed in other theatres of war. At this point in time he only had about a quarter of the ships that were to become available to him by V.J. Day.

His main cause of concern was Supply Ships. During Operation Iceberg 1, this included only 10 tankers. However, on VJ Day he could call on 24 tankers, but only 4 of which could do 15 knots. Most of the rest of the Supply Ships could only raise 11 knots. No match for the highly organised Americans.

Those of us who served in the BPF are only learning now that Fraser also had RAF Transport under his command which was flying men and materials from all over the world.

To the civilian, a job in the Supply and Secretariat Branch of the RN meant you had a non-combatant 'cushy number'. Not so, these men not only saw to all stores and pay, but manned the short range weapons too. Many of them were killed in action, and that includes Writers, Supply Assistants and Stewards.

There were few who thought as Admiral King. Most of the U.S. Navy were truly grateful for us being there and aware of the fact that although the Pacific War was their war, they did fully appreciate that the Royal Navy had been protecting their freedom in the North and South Atlantic, the Arctic, the Mediterranean and Indian Ocean before they had commenced operations in the Pacific.

At grass-roots level, there were of course petty jealousies over pay and conditions, but by and large, we both respected each other a great deal. We were on the same side and were full of praise for each other.

Fraser's decision to adopt US Signalling—and the khaki clothing—had played their part in fostering close relations too.

John Winton's excellent book 'The Forgotten Fleet' includes a comprehensive account of the Fleet Train. I understand that it is now available in paperback.

Here is a collection of stories from some of the men who were there, plus a few quotations from other sources to set the scene:

Extract from Escort Carrier in the Second World War by Kenneth Poolman

In the early stages, US Navy tankers provided the fuel, but in future a British Fleet Train on the very successful American model would replenish the BPF. From an advanced base, Logistic Support Group would sail to replenish the Fleet at intervals when it was operating in the forward areas. Without the American resources, the British Fleet Train had taken and would continue to take, a long time to create. For the early replenishment operations there was a shortage of supply ships, and tankers carried extra stores, from fresh vegetables to depth-charges. The equally important supply of replacement aircraft (and the removal of damaged duds) was provided by escort carriers of the 30th Aircraft Carrier Squadron, at first comprising only 'Bogue' Class *Striker* and 'Rulers' *Slinger* and *Speaker*, with *Striker*'s erstwhile commander Captain R. P. Carne promoted Commodore of the Squadron, and *Speaker* (the only escort carrier to be completely 'RN-manned', with no men under T124 articles) flying CAP over the replenishment.

After a month of duty, 14 out of *Speaker*'s original 16 Hellcats were still serviceable. One of them, the CO's personal aircraft, consisted of the engine of one damaged plane buttoned on to the undamaged fuselage of another. 1840's Hellcats had performed consistently well, and towards the end of April were all transferred, with pilots, to *Indomitable* to replace losses, while *Speaker* was switched to replenishment duties, loaded up with Avengers, Hellcats, Corsairs, Seafires and Fireflies, and the newly arrived *Ruler* became CAP carrier, for which she retained 16 of her less experienced pilots for working up before transfer to the Fleet carriers.

HMS *Slinger*. Ruler Class Escort Carrier

HMS Slinger. *Photo: J. Lawson*

Rough notes based on personal recollections of John Lawson, John Dunn, Jack Hill, Gordon Showell, Richard Brooke, John Howse, Clive Oakes, and Richard Rowell

My first sight of *Slinger* was on joining Woolwich Basin on 15.8.44 and the ship looked massive, even though it was only an Escort Carrier and nothing like as large as a Fleet Carrier. The Signals Office was on the portside forward, just below the aircraft catapult, which made a tremendous noise when it was in use. During our stay at Woolwich we had plenty of chances to visit London and have a good time on Liberty runs. It was at this time that the 'doodle bugs' started coming in. One day when we were all doing PT on the Flight Deck under the eyes of the Commander, we were very apprehensive and continually looking over our shoulders. 'Get on with it,' roared the Commander, 'I'll tell you when to take cover.' The next minute we saw the Commander flat out on the deck as a 'doodle-bug' appeared to be coming in to land on. Fortunately, it plunged into the Thames about 200 yards astern of us.

We sailed round the South Coast and up to Greenock. Then we sailed to Belfast to pick up our Squadron of Corsair aircraft to augment our Avengers and Seafires. We then spent several weeks on Deck Landing trials up and down the Clyde, putting in each night at Rothesay or Greenock. There were some hairy moments when new pilots could not get the pitch and roll of the ship correct and crashed their planes into the barriers or flight deck. Sailed to Gibraltar on 11th January, 1945, in company with the Escort Carriers *Speaker* and *Khedive*. Our destroyer escorts were *Eskimo, Volage, Venus, Wolverine* and *Whitehall*. Arrived at Gibraltar on 16th January then Malta, Alexandria, Suez Canal, Aden (28th January). On 1st February, one of the aircraft handling party fell overboard and was picked up by *Eskimo*. Unfortunately he died later that day.

We arrived in Colombo on 4th February and left on 6th February. We 'crossed the line' on 7th February and of course we all had to go through the ritual of shaving and ducking in the pool. We entered Sydney Harbour on 26th February 1945 and tied up at Circular Quay, just near the Harbour Bridge.

We all had a wonderful time while we were in Sydney. The population were very hospitable and the British Centre was an eye opener to us matelots, who had experienced rationing and shortages in England. The Centre had a wonderful restaurant, reading room, library and plenty more. They also arranged for us to visit families in and around Sydney. We called these people 'Uphomers', since they made their homes a 'home from home' for us. My 'Uphomers' were the Camerons. Mr. Cameron was a retired Teacher at the Kings School, Parramatta (one of the top Public Schools in Australia) and they were of Scottish origin. Their son was in the Australian army in the Islands, so they looked on me as a second son. It was one of the happiest times of my life and we kept in touch even after the war, though not for long, as they were both quite elderly and passed away soon after the war finished. It was almost like being in Civvy Street for me, since when I transferred to C in C's staff in

William Street, I was working 48 hours on and 48 hours off. After my last watch, I was on the train at Wynyard Station for the journey to Harris Park, just outside Sydney, where the Camerons lived.

While on board *Slinger* we made several trips up to the Admiralty Islands and back, before taking charge of Task Group 112.2 which consisted of oilers and stores ships to replenish the BPF on station off the Okinawa islands. It was during one of these visits that we witnessed the kamikaze attacks on the Fleet, though we were not targetted at all. Although we did not appreciate it at the time, we were having the opportunity of a South Sea Islands cruise, for which we would have to pay a fortune nowadays. On one occasion we passed close to the island of Krakatoa in the Straits of Sunda. This was the volcanic island which blew itself out of the sea in 1883, killing 36,000 people with an explosion heard 3000 miles away in Australia.

We sailed from Sydney on 11th March 1945 and arrived at Manus, Admiralty Islands, on 17th March. The whole of the BPF was there including battleships *King George V, Howe,* and Fleet Carriers *Indefatigable, Illustrious, Indomitable, Victorious,* together with Cruisers *Gambia* and *Euryalus. Slinger* became leader of Task Group 112.2, part of Task Force 57 which took part in the Iceberg operation to take Okinawa. The Fleet Train left Manus in the Admiralty Islands on 19th March 1945, the main fleet having sailed the day before. The other ships in the Task Group were oil tankers of the Maersk line. Some of the ships of the Fleet Train were: *Lothian* (Rear Admiral D. B. Fisher—Commanding the Fleet Train), *Empire Spearhead, Artifex, Bacchus, Wave King, Wave Monarch, Arndale, Dingledale, Fort Colville, Aase Maersk, Robert Maersk, Denbighshire, Thyra S., Hermelin* and *Tyne*. This convoy was an impressive sight and the Ships Companies were glad to be on the move and away from Manus, which was not very popular with the sailors.

At 7.30 pm, the loudspeaker announced that there was to be a cinema show in the aircraft hangar later in the evening and immediately the seamen started rigging up the cinema, pushing the parked planes towards the stern to make room for the seats and screen. Many men had missed their suppers in order to secure a seat overlooking the big aircraft lift, which for climatic reasons had been lowered. The film 'Bathing Beauty' with Esther Williams was just what the matelots liked and by the time the film was over, everyone had enjoyed it. So, after a long day 'storing ship' and making ready for sea, everyone but the watch on deck retired to their bunks for a good night's sleep.

All through the next day *Slinger* and her convoy of ships made their way through placid, unruffled seas with the sun beating down on the half naked bodies of the crew. Hoses were laid along the decks and used to cool down the burning wood and metal. During the evening, as dusk gradually obliterated the other ships, the watch off duty assembled at the forward end of the flight deck for a sing-song, led by a trio of instrumentalists who were lounging on the foc'sle.

The convoy reached Leyte, which was around 800 miles from Iceberg operation zone, on 26th March, 1945, anchoring in the large San Pedro Bay. *Slinger* and *Striker* ferried 56 aircraft to replace the damaged ones to the Fleet Carriers, and took off 19 repairable aircraft to be returned to Leyte. They also took on board severely damaged aircraft which they later ditched over the side.

Next day at 9.30 pm the pipe was 'Fleet has been sighted on the port quarter'. In *Slinger,* everything stopped. Men rushed to the upper deck to see this full force of the Royal Navy in the Pacific. First came the two battleships *King George V* and *Howe,* hull down on the horizon, followed by five cruisers and four fleet aircraft carriers. Dashing in and out of this convoy were the fussy little destroyers, the Navy's 'maid of all work'. By 3 pm, the fleet had been oiled, re-armed and restored while all the ships taking part were still under way. At 3.15 pm, a destroyer came alongside *Slinger* and passed a line over. Very soon a breeches buoy was attached and boxes containing wounded men were winched across to *Slinger* for urgent passage to the sick bay.

By noon the next day the fleet had left the rendezvous ready to make another raid on the Sakishima Islands.

At 6 pm the whole of the Ship's Company were all feeling melancholy owing to the recent death of one of the wounded men from the carrier *Indefatigable,* P.O. Mitchell. As darkness drew near he was buried. The ceremony, as is always the case at sea, was very simple. To the strains of the Last Post and a three volley rifle salute, the wooden coffin was allowed to slip over the side of the flight deck and went to rest on the sea bed. There was no cinema or sing-song that evening.

Slinger returned to Leyte on 8th April and next day sailed for Brisbane arriving there via Manus on 19th April. We went into dry dock at Brisbane for repairs. Left Brisbane 27th May and arrived in Sydney on 29th May. Another trip to Brisbane before returning to Sydney on 8th June. While at Brisbane, some of the Ship's Company were drafted and travelled over 600 miles by rail (nearly 24 hours of boring bush and desert), the most horrible rail journey of my life. On 18th June, I was transferred to HMS *Golden Hind,* the shore base at Warwick Farm Racecourse in Sydney.

After a few days, I was drafted from *Golden Hind* to C in C's Staff and was billeted at HMS *Cairo,* a large house in Macleay Street, Wooloomooloo. I did not spend much time in this billet, since at every opportunity I became a civilian and stayed with my 'uphomer' at Harris Park. Recollections of life in Sydney are that there were many excellent theatres and Cinemas and the Sydney Symphony Orchestra under Eugene Ormandy played regularly at the Town Hall. There were plenty of things available in the shops, particularly sweets, which had been on ration in the UK. There was however no sign of milk chocolate.

From CPO (S) A. L. Davies—HMS *Golden Hind*

HMS *Golden Hind* was the RN Barracks at Sydney for the BPF. Its main function was to act as an accommodation base for naval personnel arriving from the U.K. and awaiting passage to join the BPF at Manus or elsewhere, and for personnel from the fleet awaiting passage home.

I served there as a Supply Chief Petty Officer for about 18 months. There was a constant flow of people in both directions and at the end of hostilities with Japan there were, of course, many hundreds of men—'hostilities only' ratings awaiting passage home for demobilization and also RN ratings on regular engagements who had completed time for pension—all most anxious to return home as quickly as possible. At peak times there were about 1,000 in the barracks—probably the largest RN base in the world.

Troopships arrived at Sydney with reliefs and then filled up with officers and ratings for the passage home. Fleet aircraft carriers, such as *Victorious, Indomitable* and *Indefatigable,* no longer required to fulfil their FAA role also acted as troopers—double tiered bunks taking the place of aircraft in the hangars!

Key personnel had been flown out to prepare the base in October 1944. The barracks had not been built, indeed I believe construction had barely commenced, so tented accommodation was provided at Warwick Farm Racecourse, situated about 15 miles west of Sydney and on the electric railway line from Sydney to Liverpool, a few miles beyond Warwick Farm.

The main draft, of which I was a member, sailed from Liverpool (UK!) in November 1944 in *Empress of Scotland* which prior to hostilities was *Empress of Japan*—Canadian Pacific's flagship on their North Pacific service. We sailed on a Saturday afternoon, independently but with cruiser and destroyer escort. Because of our high speed capability and rough weather we were soon on our own and in about 7 days arrived at the Caribbean end of the Panama Canal—after bunkering we transitted the canal and after a good and uneventful passage across the Pacific, arrived in Sydney harbour 4 weeks out from Liverpool. We anchored in the harbour after dark, and what a sight—a blaze of lights. No black-out in Sydney. For the youngsters—or many them—it was their first sight of a large city in peace-time conditions—and for the 'older hands', memories of pre-war days.

The next morning we docked at Wooloomooloo and disembarked. I would also mention that our trooping voyage was code named J1—the first of a huge build-up to emphasise the British presence in the Pacific, alongside the Americans. On board we also carried medical staff for the RN hospital at Herne Bay, Sydney, including a large contingent of QARNNS and also MONAB 1 (Mobile Operational Naval Air Base 1) which would be based at Nowra, south of Sydney on Jervis Bay.

It was rather hot and dusty out at Warwick Farm—but we had the Australian summer, Christmas was not far ahead and we had the Sydney beaches to discover and above all the Australians gave us a wonderful welcome and extended most generous hospitality to all.

The barracks (wooden huts) were completed in the early part of 1945 on the opposite side of the railway line to Warwick Farm.

When the war ended there was a rush for home. The BPF dispersed and the British Centre in Sydney, which did so much to make our stay there so enjoyable, became deserted. There was by this time no need for the fleet to have an operational base as far south as Sydney.

I left for HMS *Gould*, outside Colombo where I remained for six months before returning to the UK.

Supply officers included: Captain (S) Law, RN, Commander (S) Harold, RN, Mr. P. Bendle RN and Mr. J. Bienvenue RN—Warrant Supply Officers and Lieut. (S) Cash RNR.

Extracts from 'Escort Carrier in the Second World War' by Kenneth Poolman

Meanwhile the 'cast-iron carriers' of TF.57 carried on digging holes in the Ryuku runways and the Japanese kept filling them in. There were excursions, first an uncomfortable one to Leyte, known as 'Heat Rash Bay', from 23 April to 1 May, and after that to one or other of the replenishment areas Cootie, Midge or Mosquito on the 10th, 14th, 18th and 22nd May, with *Striker, Speaker, Arbiter* and *Chaser* supplying, two at a time, replacement aircraft and crew, who also had the chance while aboard the carriers to brush up their carrier operating procedures. *Ruler* remained CAP carrier.

Arbiter, formerly USS *St. Simon* AVE-51, whose motto 'Jus a caelo' (Justice from the skies) spoke for all the CVEs fighting in this just war, had come out from the Clyde with a squadron of Corsairs. The sound of F4Us starting up aft on the flight deck was impressive, something like the sudden racket of Formula One cars bursting into song in the paddock before a race, but *Arbiter*'s squadron had some spectacular prangs on passage. For some time after the failure of the Vought Corsair F4U-1 in its carrier qualification trials with the *Sangamon* in September 1942, the 'U-bird' with its bent wing and cyranoic nose was allocated only to the US Marines for shore duty, and to the Royal Navy, which received 95 Corsair F4U-1s as Corsair 1s. Their first deck landings, aboard HMS *Illustrious,* were traumatic. The CO of 1830 Squadron skidded over the side to his death, and many more of 1830 and 1833, the second Corsair squadron, finished pranged and prostrated. Modifications were made by Vought's Emergency Programme Dog and were all incorporated after the 688th machine, but the Corsair did not fly from US carriers until 1944.

By 17 July Halsey was back off Tokyo, and was joined there by Admiral Rawlings and the BPF, which now assumed its proper relationship to its parent Task Force 38 as a task group, bringing four Fleet carriers to add to the American 16 as well as three battleships and the cruisers and destroyers. There had been a big increase in the size and in variety of supplies offered by the British Fleet Train, ships of all nationalities within the British Commonwealth. There were tankers and colliers; ammunition and aircraft replenishment ships (escort carriers); repair and maintenance ships for escorts, aircraft (the carrier

Unicorn) and armaments, torpedoes, mines, hulls, radar and aero-engines; a floating dock; victualling ships, with much frozen meat and fruit from Australia and New Zealand, water-distilling and accommodation ships. The Americans, who had created the Fleet Train feature of modern naval war, were amazed at the variety of goods and services on offer by this jewel of logistics, which would not, however, have been possible without their earlier, and continued, generosity. One flaw in this array was the slowness of the British tankers, but when the BPF got into difficulties of supply, the US Navy never said 'No' to requests for help, provided they were made realistically through sympathetic channels—which meant well outside the orbit of Admiral King. In this way Charles Evans, Commander (Air) of *Implacable*, obtained six new Avengers from American stores (having only asked for three)—for a bottle of Scotch.

Another feature of the British Fleet Train was the hospital ship, which had not originally been specified, but perhaps the most outstanding vessel of the Train was the exclusively British Amenities Ship, the converted Blue Funnel Liner *Menestheus*, which contained a 400-seat combined theatre/cinema, where its own *Pacific Showboat* revue was staged; canteen, NAAFI shop and restaurant; library, reading/writing rooms; tailor's, barber's and boot repair shops; ice cream parlour, soda fountain and, most welcome of all to thirsty matelots, a brewery with a production capacity of 6,8101 (1,800 gal.) a day. Unfortunately the *Menestheus* did not reach a Logistics Support Group before the war ended, but immediately afterwards she made a cruise comprising five days in Yokohama, ten in Kure, six in Shanghai, and three weeks in Hong Kong, entertaining 40,000 men, before urgent demands by the Blue Funnel Line forced her return to England and peacetime service, though she visited Allied Servicemen at Singapore, Trincomalee, Aden and Malta en route. She astounded the Americans, who tried to buy her in vain. A part-completed sister ship *Agamemnon* was never finished. At its peak the Train (TF.112) comprised 125 ships (712,000tons) and 26,200 men. It was often said that there was only one creature comfort not available in the Train—and there was plenty of that in Sydney.

At the British base on Manus, a derelict airstrip became a busy airport, with satellite strips at Lorengan, Moberang and Pityilu. Later the Mobile Operational Naval Air Base (MONAB) *Nabaron*, one of seven such establishments, was set up, six of them in Australia, with an eighth at Hong Kong after the war, for the assembly and flight testing of replacement aircraft, which mostly arrived in crates, before they were loaded aboard replenishment escort carriers.

The aircraft replacement cycle, Fleet-Manus-Fleet—carried out by a CVE making an average speed of 14 knots took about three weeks, and sometimes the right aircraft were not at the replenishment area when wanted, especially with TF.57's losses so high in Iceberg (a disproportionate 98 lost to 57 enemy planes destroyed, which rises to a staggering 301 if the 203 aircraft rendered non-operational and requiring replacement are added, a reversal of statistics for comparable US Navy operations). In fact the British assault on the Sakishima Gunto, if confined to these statistics, looks very much like a Pyrrhic victory, as the destruction of only 57 enemy aircraft cannot be considered a sizeable contribution to the victory at Okinawa. Between them, HMS *Slinger* and *Striker* ferried 56 aircraft to the replenishment area, 43 of them to Fleet carriers, in three replacement trips, returning to Leyte with 19 'flyable duds'. 'Non-flyable duds' had their engines removed and were ditched over the side. Admiral Fraser thought it 'a pity to reduce such fine fighting ships to the role of mere ferries'.

The BPF/TF.37 had left Sydney on 28 June and rendezvoued with its Logistic Supply Group early on 20 July. Rawlings' ships were required by Halsey to refuel in one day. The BPF found this almost impossible, with its comparatively few, small, slow tankers, and by the end of the day was 94,601 (2,500 gal.) short. Rawlings had to ask Halsey for help, and was topped up by the US Logistics Group, TG.30.8. The arrival of a typhoon helped out, as Halsey was forced to postpone the date of action, but the situation would almost certainly arise again.

American and British battleships bombarded coastal positions, and there were further air strikes in the Tokyo area, particularly against the remnants of the Japanese Fleet. Immobilised in Yokosuka without fuel, *Nagato* was damaged beyond repair, the attack was shifted to the Inland Sea and in the days 24—28 July, the remaining Japanese big carriers were knocked out of action and the last three battleships sunk in the main naval base at Kure. TF.37 was not allowed to take part in this act of retribution for Pearl Harbour, and was given subsidiary targets of airfields in north-east Shikoku, ships in the Inland Sea and at Osaka. The escort carrier *Kaiyo* in Shido Wan Bay was sunk.

A sudden change in the schedule of operations put the next refuelling point 1,125 km (700 miles) beyond the original. Admiral Fisher's BPF Logistics Group just got there in time. The oiling problem had got so acute for the British that the CVEs *Arbiter* and *Ruler* had been converted to Auxiliary Oilers, but the difficulty was not resolved, and again the US oiling group supplied the deficit. Refuelling took place on 31 July and was made more difficult by a typhoon swell which made the tankers as they emptied roll and pitch more and more violently, the replete warships ride more comfortably. *Chaser* and *Speaker* transferred replacement aircraft, *Ruler* flew CAP, Rawlings just completed fuelling in time, on 2 August, but felt sure that next time he would have to miss a day's strike. Then, mysteriously, Halsey was ordered to withdraw for a 'Special Operation'. The Fleet was then struck by another typhoon but was refuelling again on 6/7 August. Just as the British tankers ran dry, with many bunkers still half-full, the force was told via the BBC and Sydney Radio of the dropping of the atomic bomb on Hiroshima. On the 9th the second bomb was dropped on Nagasaki, and the Japanese began negotiations for surrender. The savage duel the Japanese had called 'Taiheiyo-no-Pacific' ('Cancer of the Pacific') was over.

HMS Chaser, *Sydney 1945. Photo: Lt. (A) Geoffrey St. Leger-Chambers, RN, Air Engineer Officer*

From Regulating Chief Stoker, Bill Cardew on *City of Edinburgh*, later renamed HMS *Lothian* and used as a wireless headquarter ship for tank landing craft, carrying an Admiral

We would be formed up with four or five other ex-Merchant ships all fitted out with Marine Commandos and their tank landing craft and we would be known as Force X.

We got through the canal alright and tied up alongside the wall in Panama City. What did not help matters then was that before leaving England the fresh water tanks had been treated inside with a lining called Rosmanite to keep the tanks clean, what the people didn't realise was that once we arrived in the tropics the warm sea water would affect the Rosmanite inside the tanks, which it did and the Rosmanite softened and ran down to the bottom of the tanks which in time choked the suctions on the pumps and then we had no fresh water, only from tanks that were above the water line and this was strictly rationed. This made the crew very angry and one afternoon as we were getting ready to sail for Australia the seamen mutinied and left the ship and gathered on the jetty, the Captain asked the men to come back aboard and that the ship would sail even if he had to cast off the ropes himself; no one moved on the jetty so the Captain turned to the Army Sergeant and said 'Arm your men with pick axe handles and take them on to the jetty and bring the mutineers on board.' When the army got out there the seamen took away the trenching tools and threw them in the sea, so the Captain said 'Right Sergeant, bring your men in board,' and turning to the Sergant Major Royal Marine Commandos he said 'Get your men together with fixed bayonets and bring the men in. The marines surrounded the seamen on the jetty and like sheep the seamen came in board. We sailed that night and of course the rest of Force X had gone on, we arrived in New Guinea after a few days and dropped anchor in Port Moresby. After refuelling we steamed on to Brisbane. On arrival there we had a court marshal of the mutineers and a lot of the senior Petty Officers and Chiefs were demoted. I, as the regulating Chief Stoker, had to attend the three day hearing although our branch had nothing to do with the mutiny.

From Brisbane we sailed to Sydney and joined up with the main BPF, also the remainder of Force X. After Xmas '44 which we all had at Manus Island, we carried out several sorties among the Pacific Islands and with the Americans started to push the Japs back. For some reason or other the *Lothian* wasn't to the standard the Americans expected of us and so we were detached from the rest of the fleet and sent back to Manus Island where the ex-Liner *Montclare* was waiting and had been fitted out as a wireless headquarter ship for tank landing craft. We went alongside her and transferred all the top officers, also the Royal Marine Commandos and army and air force ranks.

We were then sent back to Sydney and our job then was turned into Fleet Train Floating Post Office and would go to sea with a destroyer escort and supply the Fleet with the mail. We did this job until the bomb was dropped on Japan and eventually arrived back in the UK in 1946.

One of the Naval Stores Assistants was named Caroll, an Irishman, and is now Danny la Rue, the famous female impersonator.

From Fred Brown, HMS *Empire Spearhead*

She was a Liberty ship which carried Landing Craft and was taken over from the Merchant Navy towards the end of July 1944, when a party of us were sent up to Glasgow from Devonport to commission her.

As far as I am aware the only photograph of her is the one I took myself when we were in New Guinea. You will probably not even have heard of her, for although I have read numerous naval books she was only mentioned in one and that was 'Task Force 57' Appendices 'The Fleet Train. May 1945—The British Pacific Fleet 1944—45', by Peter C. Smith.

Our first port of call was New York where the *Queen Mary* and *Ile de France* were berthed. We picked up about 900 white and 200 coloured American troops.

It was my first visit to America and it was strange to find the shops and cinemas open all night. We visited the Stage Door Canteen—no well-known actors or actresses about. We were able to send home parcels as there did not appear to be any shortages.

We made several trips to the various Islands, Philippines, New Guinea,

Society and Admiralty, carrying troops for exercises in landings. No towns to visit and only recreational leave—swimming, so it was quite a relief when after a few months we called in at Cairns and were allowed ashore.

On one occasion in the Philippines permission was given for swimming over the side but a few of us saw sharks nearby and reported this to the Officer of the Day and the sharks went hungry! One of the cooks while fishing over the side caught a shark and it had to be shot before he brought it aboard.

On the 2nd January we sighted land at 7.00 a.m., and the mountains reminded me of the Pyramids. This was Brisbane. We were allowed ashore at 5.00 p.m., and went to the cinema at the Winter Gardens, at the end of which we were given a lift back to the ship at 12.30 a.m.

We met up with a person who had emigrated from Sheffield and had a taxi business in Brisbane. He took us home to see his wife and two children and then drove us for a trip in the car.

I was duty watch next day but the day after was up at 5.00 a.m., unloading clothing stores, but went ashore at 1.00 p.m. This must have been a Sunday, for after visiting the Botanical Gardens and listening to the Band, we had tea in Toc H, then a walk around town, and then attended a service in the Methodist Church near the Town Hall where the congregation must have been going on for a thousand.

When we came outside we were given a car ride around the town and then caught a tram back to the ship at midnight.

The following day we left at 6.00 p.m., with troops. We stopped to pick up an escort, which as far as I can remember, was the only time we had one, from the time we left New York and through all our visits to the Islands.

We reached Finchaven two days later and the troops were disembarked and another lot embarked and we sailed at 3.00 p.m., arriving in Leyte just over a week later.

After just over a week we took on board more troops and four days later dropped them at Lingayen.

We arrived in Hollandia and spent the next few days between the different islands and eventually arrived in Manus where we met up with the fleet.

I think by this time we had our own projector on board. At the beginning of April we were visited by a concert party from the *Tyne*.

One day I had a dental appointment on board *Resource* and left the ship by LCA, at 7.30 a.m. This happened again a week later. Two more days and the Fleet returned off operations on Formosa etc.

Another week at sea and we entered Sydney at 7.30 a.m., and were ashore at 2.30 p.m. We spent a week there and were fortunate enough to see Gracie Fields in person at the Centre, Hyde Park.

Among the coloured troops we picked up in New York, were several Golden Gloves champions and they used to give exhibitions on the upper deck, but I cannot recollect them being opposed by any of the whites.

On one occasion crates were being unloaded with 'Comforts for the troops' stencilled on them. I was on the upper deck among a crowd of Americans when the crates came aboard, and a bunch of the fellows grabbed hold of one crate, dashed the corner on the iron deck and the contents (bars of chocolate) disappeared in a matter of seconds!

On one recreational leave we were taken in a LCA, and when the ramp was lowered we had quite a distance to go before reaching the beach. One of the officers who for some reason was all dressed up although there was no town or village near, appeared dubious of getting in the water so another officer offered him a pick-a-back and 'accidentally' slipped and both went under.

Things were not as peaceful as may have been gathered, for on the way out, the troops appeared to be restless at night and roamed about the deck. Whether this was the heat or the probability of action I cannot say. Out in the Islands we had action stations many times but nothing developed. We had no radar or asdic but managed to evade subs and aircraft.

From the above, it may appear to have been a holiday cruise we were on, but this was not so, as, for the first few months we had no mail, and no entertainment apart from the odd film show on the deck of another ship. Our trips to Australia were the only breaks we had as there were no towns or places of interest up in the Islands.

I wrote to Tommy Trinder last year, as one of my Mess mates was friendly with him and, in fact when we returned from the Far East, Tommy Trinder and Elisabeth Welch were on at the Palladium and my shipmate went up from Portsmouth to see them backstage. Another shipmate was corresponding with Ann Shelton.

From Telegraphist John Gillis, HMS *Pheasant*

HMS *Pheasant* was a sloop (Bird Class) and operated as Captain, Escort Forces in the BPF supervising the Fleet Train of supply ships, oilers etc. Our Captain was Cdr. J. B. Palmer.

Having spent most of 1944 in the Mediterranean, escorting convoys from Gibraltar to Alexandria and back again, we went home for a refit and leave. On 18 Decemer 1944 we sailed from the Clyde for Gibraltar and onwards through the Mediterranean, Suez Canal, Red Sea, across the Indian Ocean for a brief call at Colombo, Ceylon. Crossing the equator on 11 February 1945 we sailed through the Timor Sea to Darwin, North Australia. Then round New Guinea to the island of Manus in the Admiralty Islands, which was to be our forward base during our stay in the Pacific.

Mon. 5 March: Arrived at Manus Island in the Admiralty Islands. Palm trees on sandy beaches, waves breaking on the reef—and a lagoon!

Tues 6 March: Two American radiomen came aboard this evening as liaison staff. Don Hill and Ron Weissman.

Sun. 18 March: Captain, Escort Forces, Captain P. Frend, who was on board, spoke to us today and said we shall be operating NE of Formosa and will be at sea 5 weeks.

Mon. 2 April: *Slinger, Pirie, Bendigo, Parret, Woodcock, Arndale, Dingledale, Aase Maersk* joined us this morning.

Sun. 15 April: *Woodcock* joined with some more oilers.

Wed. 18 April: Left the oiling fields for Leyte with 3 oilers and *Wimbrel* at 1830.

Wed. 25 April: Paid today—I got £19 (Australian)—put £12 sterling in bank. Also got 2 bottles of beer!

Mon. 7 May: Transferred a casualty from the *Formidable* to an oiler. Fleet moves off again at 1400.

Sat. 12 May: We got a couple of buoys wrapped round one of the screws and had to stop for 4 hours to get them off.

Mon. 14 May: Fleet arrived back to fuel. *Parret* and *Striker* and *Nizam* arrive from Leyte with mail for every ship—except *Pheasant*!

Tues. 15 May: We leave Fleet this evening for Leyte with 2 empties and *Woodcock, Troubridge* and *Tenacious* join Fleet with mail—still none for us.

Mon. 28 May: Arrived at Manus this forenoon, mail came aboard. We refuel and leave for Brisbane during afternoon.

Tuesd. 29 May: In company with *Woodcock* and, later, *Whimbrel* we dash along at 15 knots!

Sat. 2 June: Arrived at Brisbane, Queensland, Australia. Went ashore this evening and drank plenty of lovely cold fresh milk and milk shakes.

Mon. 4 June: Went ashore with Roy Creffield—saw film 'A Song to Remember'.

Tues. 5 June: Started on six days leave—travelled up to Toowoomba and stayed night in an hotel.

Wed. 6 June: Spent forenoon in Toowoomba and then went on the Crows Nest in afternoon to stay with Mr. and Mrs. Ben Fitch.

Thur. 7 June: Our hostess is an ex-Londoner—knows Lambeth Walk and all! Lovely and quiet here.

From J. Jenkinson, DEMS Gunner on *San Ambrosio*

I had the privilege of serving on the tanker *San Ambrosio,* as a DEMS Gunner and point out with pride The Fleet Train, against all odds, managed to keep the Fleet supplied to help them fight on.

I still remember the long weeks at sea. Shore leave was non-existent, we just sailed from Manus and Leyte back and forward to the fleet as they pulled back from ops. filled them up and then the long haul back for more fuel.

There was no glory, just endless weeks of being crowded together, food was so-so, and water limited, at times most of us suffered skin disorders. The only female voice we sometimes heard was that of Tokyo Rose.

Most of the DEMS Gunners were like myself, no more than teenagers, but on the most part we got on well even though we were a bit envious of the Fleet, at least to us at the time they were the action men.

When the war ended I remember it as though it was yesterday, we all thought 'Australia here we come', but it was not to be at that stage. Our next stop was Hong Kong.

Had the kamikazes found us, the history of the British Pacific Fleet would have been changed. Very few people today know how thinly stretched the supply line was.

From F. Manning, Engineer SS *City of Dieppe*

*Extracts from **The Fleet Train in the Pacific War** by Vice-Admiral Sir Douglas B. Fisher, KCB, KBE*

The war against Japan called for an entirely new conception of naval warfare, wherein our naval forces were called upon to take the offensive not only tens of thousands of miles from the United Kingdom, but thousands of miles from their nearest base.

It was thus impossible, during the operations, for HM ships to replenish with fuel and stores from their bases, and all sheltered harbours within reasonable distance of the operational area were in enemy hands, so it was essential to replenish the fleet periodically at sea, and for this requirement the Fleet Train was formed.

The fact should not be lost sight of, that we were about to engage the Japanese on two fronts, i.e. from the Indian Ocean, and also from the Pacific, but as in the latter area the distances involved were considerably greater, the problem of supply was correspondingly more complicated.

As far back as 1936, a committee was set up in the Admiralty to consider the methods to be adopted for supporting a fleet at sea far in advance of its nearest base, and by 1939 we knew what we wanted.

But in the early years of the war no immediate need arose for a Fleet Train, and as every ship, both afloat and building, was needed to replace sinkings, it was only with the greatest difficulty that, after the entry of Japan into the war, a very modest start was made to build up the nucleus for the Fleet Train which would eventually and inevitably be required for an ocean war.

The first serious step was taken early in 1942 when five liners were taken up for conversion as repair ships, or as depot ships for destroyers and submarines.

At that time we had lost Hong Kong and Singapore, and the Japanese who had virtual command of the Western Pacific, had emerged into the Indian Ocean, and were threatening Ceylon and Australia. Our Eastern Fleet based in Ceylon, but prepared to withdraw temporarily to the West, was then on the defensive.

By the middle of 1943 we had a nucleus of auxiliaries capable of replenishing and repairing a small fleet in an advanced base in the Eastern Theatre without shore assistance, and towards the end of that year a new branch of the Naval Staff was formed at the Admiralty to deal solely with administrative planning, thereby leaving the Plans Division free to concentrate on operational and strategic planning.

Thus prime responsibility, from then onwards, for the composition and formation of the Fleet Train in the planning stage, fell on the Director of Plans (Q).

In the autumn of 1943 the Quebec Conference decided on the broad scale of operations to be undertaken by the Royal Navy in the Pacific, and it was then possible for the Admiralty to make a firmer forecast than hitherto possible of the size and shape of the Fleet train needed to support our fleet in that area.

The requirements were put before, and approved by, the Defence Committee, who invited the Minister of War Transport to provide the ships.

In general, the types of ships asked for included:

(a) *Maintenance and Repair*
Repair ships to deal with major and subsidiary repairs
Floating docks
Depot ships for destroyers and submarines
Maintenance ships for escorts, coastal forces, minesweepers, naval service craft, armament, instruments and radar.

(b) *Supply*
Tankers for oil and water
Store issuing ships for naval, victualling, armament and air stores
Vegetable carriers
Store carriers

(c) *Administration*
Headquarters ships
Accommodation ships
Amenity ships
Naval servicing craft and carriers
Tugs, lighters and harbour craft
Hospital ships

(d) *Defence*
Seaward defence ships
Boom and net laying and operating ships

(e) *Air*
Replenishment carriers
Aircraft transports.

It at once became clear that the labour and shipyard facilities required to convert ships for the above purposes, was the key to the situation.

The outcome of the many discussions which followed was that as many ships as possible would be converted in the United Kingdom, preferably during initial construction. It was also decided that Canada should be asked to convert suitable ships under construction there, especially where a number of each type was required, and the United States were asked to provide available types already under construction in that country.

These requirements for a Fleet Train were, of course, in direct competition with our vast demands for import of foods into the country and for the world-wide transportation of men and material.

During the spring of 1944 many discussions took place as to the number of ships which could be made available from UK, Canadian, and US resources for the Pacific Fleet Train—and at the same time it was accepted that the size of our combatant force in the Pacific depended directly on the size of the Fleet Train available to support it.

And it must be remembered that all of this was proceeding at a time of dire requirement for shipping for the Normandy landings, and for the maintenance of our ever increasing forces in Europe, in addition to the increasing activity in the Indian Ocean.

In September 1944 a further Anglo-American conference was held in Quebec at which the Prime Minister specifically offered a British Main Fleet to take part, under US Supreme Command, in operations against Japan, and restated that support for that fleet would be provided by a Fleet Train, which would render the fleet independent of shore bases for a considerable time.

This offer was accepted.

It was then possible for the Naval Staff to work on more definite premises, since it was known when the various ships allocated to the Fleet Train would become available, the consequent size of the fleet which the Train would support could be worked out, and the approximate state of affairs forecast when our forces would arrive in the Pacific.

In January 1945 the first units of the combatant force began to arrive in Australian waters and consisted of battleships, aircraft carriers, cruisers and destroyers.

Sydney became the main point of assembly for the fleet and Fleet Train and was the scene of much naval activity.

In regard to air matters affecting the Fleet Train it was apparent from the start that they were too large to be handled entirely by the then nucleus of staff of the RAFT.

Responsibility for these was therefore delegated to the Commanding Officer of HMS *Unicorn*, an aircraft repair ship in the Fleet Train.

It had first been expected that the British Pacific Fleet would be required to begin operations in June of 1945, but by January the United States Forces were pushing the Japanese back with increasing speed, and it was apparent that we must take our part at a much earlier date. It was therefore decided that the first British naval operation on a large scale would be begun in March, and planning was progressed accordingly.

At that time the southern part of the Philippines had been recaptured by the Americans who were using Leyte harbour as a defended anchorage.

At the end of February the first units of the Fleet Train left Australian waters, and arrived at Manus in the Admiralty Islands in the first week in March.

Manus had by then been in United States naval hands for some time, and a vast organization had been set up ashore there which was capable of supplying, maintaining, and repairing a large fleet.

The situation there, in so far as our forces were concerned, was curious, as the islands were Australian but were occupied and administered by the US Navy, with a Commodore USN in charge. We were therefore in the role of visitors or lodgers in an American port.

But such was the co-operation between the two navies that at no time either at Manus or at the other American bases which we subsequently used was there the slightest friction or lack of harmony.

Shortly after the Fleet Tain arrived at Manus, the fleet itself assembled there, and after a week spent in filling up with fuel and stores from the supply ships, sailed for the first operation.

The Fleet Train then proceeded to Leyte in the Philippines, which was to be an advanced base in the initial stages of the British operations.

At that time the Fleet Train consisted of only the following ships: headquarters ship and flagship of RAFT; 1 destroyer depot ship; 1 escort aircraft carrier; 2 repair ships (*Resource* and*Artifex*); 2 accommodation ships for Fleet Train working parties and drafting pool; 1 aircraft repair ship; 1 netlayer; 9 tankers; 4 naval or victualling store issuing ships; 6 armament store issuing ships; in addition to several sloops and escort vessels required for convoying.

Before the operations off Okinawa started, detailed plans had to be made for refuelling the fleet in certain refuelling areas in the vicinity of the operations.

The available tankers of the Fleet Train were therefore organized into groups, it being arranged that each group should be sailed from the advanced base in use (Manus, Leyte, etc.) so as to reach the refuelling area on a pre-determined date.

The fleet would withdraw from its attack on or before that date, meet the fuelling group, refuel, and then return to the attack area.

A typical tanker group at this early stage of the operations consisted of 3 tankers, 1 replenishment aircraft carrier, 2 or 3 escort vessels, and 2 destroyers. Owing to the shortage of repair and store ships, it was not then possible to send any forward of the advanced base, so the oilers each carried about 5 tons of fresh vegetables, survivor kits, aircraft de-icing fluid, lubricating oil, depth charges and some close-range ammunition—these stores being intended principally for the destroyers in the forward area.

Originally, too, passengers (e.g. reliefs), mails and urgently required naval and air stores were carried in the oilers, but it was found preferable to use the escort vessels for this duty in order to save double handling in the fuelling area, and also to save the already overworked and undermanned tankers.

A medical officer and sick berth rating took passage in one tanker of each group in order to look after any small number of casualties sent to the rear.

It was thus of the utmost importance, in order to enable the fleet to carry out its operations to a fixed programme, that the tanker groups should arrive in the correct place on the correct day, and that the fuelling should proceed day and night with the utmost speed.

Considerable organization was therefore necessary in the fuelling area, and a Captain RN was permanently stationed there in a sloop to take charge of each tanker group as it arrived, and to send it back to the advanced base on completion.

The first series of refuellings brought out our weaknesses, and our lack of realistic practice in peace time was at once apparent.

To start with, all our heavy ships oiled from astern of the tankers and difficulty was experienced in picking up the trailing hoses, in connecting up, and in keeping station.

The tankers themselves also suffered from the following disabilities:

(a) Insufficient pumping capacity when under way.
(b) Insufficient derricks and winches for fuelling ships abeam.
(c) Inability to ballast empty tanks while pumping to maintain trim and manoeuvrability without risk of contaminating the fuel.

With the very bad weather conditions, great delays took place and hoses were continuually being parted. Thus the crews of HM ships and particularly tankers who were still only manned for freighting duties, got insufficient rest, and the stock of hoses dwindled to an alarming extent.

In fact the situation nearly arose when it would have been necessary to delay the operations due to these difficulties. But new hoses were flown out from Australia, broken ones were repaired, ships became better at station keeping and handling hoses, and the weather improved. The fleet's operations therefore continued, but it was a near thing, and the long time spent in refuelling, added to the shortage of tankers, meant that on their return to harbour to replenish they had to turn around and sail in 24 hours, often without having time properly to repair main and pumping machinery and fittings.

At the end of the first series of operations the fleet came down to Leyte to fill up with ammunition, stores, and provisions, and the Fleet Train repair staffs were most actively employed in repairing the deck and superstructure of an aircraft carrier which had been hit by a suicide bomber. *(Indefatigable—Ed.)*

In the six days available, repairs were effected enabling the fleet to sail for its next series of operations which roughly followed the previous pattern.

Both of these anchorages are subject to a considerble swell, and the greatest difficulty was found in berthing tankers and supply ships safely alongside the warships. This was particularly the case with aircraft carriers, as the large overhang of their flight decks broke the masts and upperworks of the merchant vessels alongside when any movement of either ship occurred.

In fact on some occasions at Manus the only safe way to fuel aircraft carriers was to anchor the tankers ahead of them, and to fuel as for the 'astern' method at sea—a laborious business especially when the wind changed in the middle, as then the fuelling had to be stopped, the tanker had to weigh anchor, and anchor in the new position and hoses run across again.

During these operations the organization for the supply and repair of aircraft was being built up.

Replacement aircraft were freighted from UK in their 'boxed' state to Australia, where they were trans-shipped to 'ferry carriers' for transport to Manus. (Ferry carriers were standard escort carriers but packed tight with boxed aircraft on deck and in the hangar, and therefore not operational while so employed.)

On arrival at Manus as many aircraft as she would take were sent to HMS *Unicorn* for assembly and to be made fit for flying, after which they embarked in 'replacement carriers' (escort carriers loaded operationally). Those aircraft for which there was no room in *Unicorn* were landed direct on the air strip and assembled there.

From there, the replacement carriers brought the aircraft on to Leyte, where they joined up with the tanker groups sailing for the refuelling area.

On arrival in the refuelling area, the new aircraft would be flown over to the aircraft carriers of the striking force. 'Flyable duds' were flown from the striking force carriers to the replenishment carriers and taken back to the base for repairs.

'Non-flyable duds' had their engines removed and were then thrown overboard as no means existed for transferring them at sea.

When the war ended, the following vessels comprised the maintenance facilities (excluding Air Train) actually in the forward area in the Fleet Train:

HMS *Montclare,* fleet train flagship and destroyer repair ship
HMS *Artifex,* heavy duty repair ship with her associated accommodation ship *Lancashire*
HMS *Tyne,* destroyer depot and repair ship
HMS *Resource,* fleet repair ship
HMS *Assistance,* auxiliary repair ship
HMS *Flamborough Head,* escort vessel maintenance ship
HMS *Kelantan,* minesweeping maintenance ship
Admiralty Floating Dock—No. 20
HMS *Springdale,* deperming ship.

These represented a small proportion of the planned repair resources.

Battle Damage
The only battle damage which was repaired at the forward base was:

(a) *Indefatigable.* Damage consequent upon a hit by a suicide bomber at the base of the island was repaired in one week by *Artifex* during a replenishment period at Leyte Gulf, allowing the ship to continue operations with the fleet as planned, and

(b) *Ulster* (destroyer) had a large hole blown in her side by a near-miss bomb, flooding the engine-room, and the after boiler-room. Our own docks had not arrived at this time and to our disappointment hull repair work and docking had to be undertaken by the Americans at Leyte Gulf, although the job was well within the capabilities of our repair ships. Machinery repairs sufficient to enable the vessel to steam to Australia on one shaft were carried out by *Tyne* (destroyer depot ship).

Defects Undertaken
(a) *Formidable* (aircraft carrier). Developed cracks in the bulkhead carrying the stern tube of the centre shaft while on passage from Australia to the operational area. This resulted in flooding of the stern tube compartment, and to enable repairs to be carried out, the stern tube was made nearly watertight by jamming oakum between the shaft and the outboard end of the shaft tube. This work was done by the ship's own divers at Leyte Gulf, and repairs to the bulkhead were carried out by HMS *Artifex*, allowing the ship to join in the operations as planned.

(d) *Achilles* (cruiser). Cracks which developed in the outer bottom plating were repaired by *Resource* in a US dock at Manus. 'A' bracket bushes were re-wooded at the same time.

(e) *Tumult* (destroyer). Grounded entering harbour at Manus and broke two blades of the port propeller. The propeller was removed in a US dock to allow the ship to steam to Australia on one shaft.

(f) *Glenearn* (transport). Modifications were carried out at Leyte to petrol and ventilation systems by *Artifex* after a petrol explosion.

(g) *Gerusalemme* (hospital ship). Was partly repaired at Manus by *Artifex* after damage by fire.

(h) *Aorangi* (submarine spare crew ship). Was converted to Commodore Fleet Train flagship by *Artifex* the necessary offices, telephones, furniture, etc, being installed. This vessel was also fitted out as a fleet chart depot and fleet medical store issuing depot.

(i) *Eaglesdale* and *Brown Ranger* (tankers). Were docked at Manus in an American Dock for periodical bottom painting and minor defects. Work was carried out by Fleet Train staff.

(j) Admiralty Floating Dock No. 20 at Manus docked her first vessel (destroyer *Nepal*) on August 20th, 1945, the associated repair work being carried out by HMS *Artifex*. Subsequently eight dockings were completed in two months. This dock was shortly afterwards moved to Singapore as her usefulness at Manus had come to an end.

It is worthy of note that at the end of the war, the repair facilities and staff had built up to only about 30 per cent of their planned strength.

In the narrative of events, it will be remembered that after the first series of operations off Okinawa, the fleet came to Leyte for a week to replenish with stores, etc., and after a week there the fleet sailed for a second and similar series of attacks on the islands south of Japan.

The pattern of these second operations largely followed the first in so far as the Fleet Train was concerned, and at the end of about three weeks the fleet and Fleet Train returned to Australian waters for major replenishment and repairs.

This would not have been necessary had the Fleet Train been completed by then to its planned strength. But this was far from being the case, with the result that the supply ships were emptied, and the tankers needed time off to repair their main and pumping machinery and equipment.

Opportunity was taken during this period to carry out considerable work on ships of the Fleet Train.

In addition to running repairs to the tankers, most of them had to be altered to allow for fuelling ships abeam which method was in use by the Americans and was proved far quicker in any but very bad weather.

During this time, too, certain victualling store and armament store issuing ships were fitted to allow them to transfer stores at sea, and a corvette was fitted out as a radio and radar first-aid ship.

However, after a few weeks' absence, the Fleet and Fleet Train came forward again and a new series of operations was begun with the mainland of Japan as the target.

For many reasons (including the prevalence of typhoons in that season) it was decided not to use Leyte as the advanced base for this operation. The Fleet Train therefore used Manus as its base, which, however, had the disadvantage of a great distance (2,300 miles) from the refuelling area off Japan.

This meant that the round trip for the tanker groups took about three weeks from Manus back to Manus, and with our still woefully inadequate number of tankers and their low speed, the most careful planning was necessary in order that the fleet could operate against Japan and withdraw to fuel on pre-selected dates.

To shorten the distance from the advanced base to the refuelling area, some of our tankers used Eniwetok in the Marshall Islands to replenish cargoes, which reduced their double journey by some 1,500 miles.

During this third series of operations the service which the Fleet Train was capable of giving to the fleet became progressively better consequent on the improvement in the resources available.

As a result of alterations during the replenishment period in Australia and to practice at sea afterwards, a victualling store issuing ship was kept in the refuelling area, being joined later by an armament store issuing ship—these ships being relieved when nearing exhaustion.

It should be mentioned that although the armament store issuing ship carried replacements for every nature of ammunition likely to be used, the only requirements they were called upon to supply were AA ammunition and 500 lb bombs.

The radio and radar repair ship was also sent forward, in addition to the only tug available, the latter in case any small ship needed assisting back to harbour. (Unfortunately the tug was too small and unsuitable for ocean work and in fact had herself to be towed back to Manus by a destroyer.)

During the third series of operations, the weather was infinitely better than it had been at the outset, and this, combined with the practice obtained by both HM ships, tankers, and supply ships, enabled the operations of refuelling and transferring stores at sea to proceed on each occasion without delay or damage.

In mid-August 1945 the Japanese surrendered and the work of the Fleet Train as such came to an end.

The conditions were entirely novel; moreover, we were using bases of which we had but little information, and our resources were of the slenderest.

It was, however, somewhat of a surprise that, in an area of extremely heavy rainfall, our first really major difficulty was lack of fresh water.

HM ships are capable of self-maintenance in that respect as long as they have fuel, and as this was abundant no problem arose in their case. But the merchant vessels forming the Fleet Train were in a very different state, and many of them having no distilling plant needed water at frequent intervals. It is true that this had been foreseen to some extent, and distilling ships were included in the requirements for the Fleet Train—but at first we had none.

We did have some small water carriers, and while we were at Manus we were able to make use of the American facilities and ferry it off from their pipe line ashore, though this was slow, as the Americans needed water themselves and a lot of queuing for it was necessary.

But at Leyte, no water supply was accessible and improvization had very hurriedly to be made. So we were forced to clean out and convert a couple of our precious tankers; a 10,000-ton one was used to ferry water from Manus, 1,200 miles away, and the smaller one of 1,500 tons fetched water from a waterfall about 60 miles from the base.

This just, and only just, kept us going, and we eagerly awaited the first distilling ship. She arrived during the second series of operations, but our hopes were dimmed when it was found that, with the high sea-water temperature and some recurring defects in the plant, she could only supply a very small proportion of our needs. She used coal at an alarming rate when distilling (being the only coal burner in the Fleet Train), so our only collier was berthed alongside her, and a small party of sailors was employed fairly continuously on transferring coal from one to the other. But the collier (oil-fired) used a prolific amount of fresh water as her boiler leaked badly, so the result was that these two ships spent most of their time furiously maintaining each other. The incident was not amusing at the time.

It was apparent that the air side alone called for a separate organization of its own, so a Commodore Air Train and staff were formed with headquarters in HMS *Pioneer.* The Commodore Air Train (COMAT) was given the responsibility, within RAFT's command, for the supply of replacement aircraft and spares from the rear base to the fleet, for aircraft repairs, for replacement of personnel, administration of the aircraft repair—and store ships—in fact, for all matters between the rear base and the fleet.

In the first month or two of operations, the tanker groups in the fuelling area consisted of only three or four tankers, the same number of escorts, and a replacement aircraft carrier. These tanker groups grew both in size and complexity—more tankers were used—store issuing ships, rescue tugs, and a radar repair ship were included—repair ships were about to be included also but for the end of the war—and the number of escorts of these groups had to be strengthened correspondingly. Thus the necessity for Captain Logistic Support Group (CLSG), who from the very beginning was stationed in an escort vessel permanently in the fuelling area was continually felt, and in fact this officer and his staff had one of the busiest jobs in the British Pacific Fleet.

No account of the operations of the British Pacific Fleet would be complete without mention of the amenity ship for this area. This was planned with the object of providing those units of the fleet which had perforce to remain for long periods continuously in and around the Pacific Islands with at least some of the creature comforts which are normally available, even in the more remote shore bases.

This amenity ship was provided with a stage (complete with concert party) and cinema, buffets and recreation space, barbers, tailors and shoe repair shops, library, and last but not least, a brewery whose endeavour was to brew the best of British beers from distilled water. The amenity ship did not arrive on the station until the war was over, but even then she provided welcome relief to the naval (and other) forces, particularly those on Japanese stations. Unfortunately, demands for shipping at home were such that she had to be withdrawn after a short tour of duty, but not before proof had been given of her value in sustaining morale in the forward areas had the duration of war been extended.

One of thecharacteristicsof the Fleet Train was the variety of the types of naval personnel, and the number of races and nationalities among the merchant seamen—a mixture which presented many problems of administration.

Among the naval personnel were included representatives of the Dominion Navies and Reserves, uniformed civilian officers, DEMS and Maritime Royal Artillery for manning the guns of merchant vessels, SRR(D)'s etc.

The merchant ships of the Fleet Train included ships registered in and manned by officers and men of the United Kingdom, Australia, New Zealand, Holland, Denmark, Norway, and Belgium—and many of the crews included Lascars, Goanese, and Chinese, while one ship was manned by Papuans.

Thus a variety of charter parties, articles of agreement, customs and habits, and food, had to be dealt with—the greatest complication occurring of course when several races were serving in one ship.

It is doubtful whether the Royal and Merchant Navies have ever before been actively employed so closely together in one administrative and operational body, and it is impossible to overstress the spirit and goodwill with which they pulled together and, in extremely trying climatic conditions and absence of shore amenities, they overcame the difficulties and hardships confronting them.

Those of us who served in the Fleet Train in the Pacific War were essentially in the position of 'middlemen' between the fleet as customers and the Admiralty and their representatives in Australia as producers and wholesalers. It was inevitable therefore that we should bear the brunt of the fleet's demands for supply and maintenance, and feel acutely the lack of facilities to remedy these. Moreover, as we could not be in full possession of the knowledge of events at home or in other parts of the world, it was not at the time apparent to us why our insistent demands for more and more ships, stores, and general facilities could not be met at the rate we hoped for.

It is easy, too, to be critical after the event. But in the light of knowledge now available, it is abundantly clear that taking everything into consideration, especially the extreme shortage of men and shipping needed to meet our urgent requirements in every part of the world, the vast losses we experienced, especially in tankers, and the fact that our operations were taking place the other side of the world, everything possible was done to provide adequate and timely support for our fleet in the Pacific.

In addition, what were virtually novel conditions to us throughout the 'pipe line' from the United Kingdom to the fleet at sea off Japan, were met by all service and civilian personnel with the resource and efficiency characteristic of our race. Lessons have been learned and the invaluable experience gained in every aspect of that great adventure has been carefully preserved.

Thus it rests with those at present in power and their successors to ensure that plans are adequately made in time to ensure our preparedness should the need for a similar undertaking ever, unfortunately arise.

NSIS City of Dieppe, *July 1945, Sydney. Photo: F. Manning*

Engineer Frank Manning and 2nd Radio Officer Bill Nutton, City of Dieppe

Also from Frank Manning

The SS *City of Dieppe* was stationed in the Far East from 1943 until the end of hostilities serving as a combined Naval Store, Victualling Store and NAAFI Issuing Ship.

This ship was managed by the Ellerman and Brucknall Steamship Company on behalf of the British Admiralty and sailed under the Blue Ensign.

On-board management of the cargo issuing service was in the hands of UK Civil Servants and NAAFI personnel all holding temporary RNVR ranks and ratings.

Defence of the ship was provided by about 20 DEMS gunners under the command of Petty Officer G. Hardy who in turn was accountable to Second Officer K. Dobson.

All ship's officers, cadets and quartermasters were UK Merchant Seamen, and the catering personnel were domiciled in the Portuguese colony of Goa.

Engine-room and seamen ratings who numbered over 60 were all Indian nationals.

Considerable modification was made to the ship to accommodate its wartime role and the extra personnel needed to carry out the distribution of a very large number of products.

To give some idea of the quantities of food carried on board; when fully stored, the ship carried sufficient food for a balanced diet to feed 15,000 men for a month.

During service in the Indian Ocean it was the general rule that stores were transferred by lighters (small scale landing craft) or by ship's motor boats during periods in port. Exceptionally, say in an emergency, equipment was transferred in mid-ocean. One such occasion occurred in January 1945 when the *City of Dieppe* was en route from Colombo to Fremantle to join the newly-formed Pacific Fleet Train. At mid-voyage the escorting warship's sonar equipment became defective and new components were needed to supply ship. The *City of Dieppe* was not yet equipped with the means for transfer of stores whilst under way. Both ships hove to about 200 yards apart and then followed a nail-biting half hour when the warship insisted on lowering its whaler into the ocean and rowing across the gap to collect the spare parts, and then rowing back again. To us on the *City of Dieppe* which was equipped with powerful motor boats especially provided for rapid transfer of stores in such a situation as this, it seemed criminal to risk the lives and loss of two crews and ships by such a demonstration of independence. Fortunately no Japanese submarines seemed to be in the vicinity and this time no harm was done.

Parting company with our escort upon arrival in Fremantle and after 2 to 3 days in port, the *City of Dieppe* resumed passage to Sydney alone and unescorted. This part of the voyage was uneventful and we entered Sydney Harbour where the headquarters of the Fleet Train had been established.

For the next month or so the ship's cargo stock was replenished, minor repairs were carried out to machinery and deck equipment. One interesting addition to the engine-room was the attachment of an explosive scuttling charge contained in a steel box welded on to the starboard ship side plate about eight to ten feet above the double bottom rank. At this level the charge was situated below the waterline but in full view, and from that day onward its presence in the engine-room was a constant reminder that there was a war in progress and we were in a serious business.

For a merchant ship the *City of Dieppe* was better defensively armed than most others of its type. In addition to the 4.7 inch gun aft there was a 3.7 inch at the bow. Against aircraft attack there were four 20mm Oerlikon guns on the boat deck plus a multi-rocket projectile assembly. On each bridge wing there was a twin-barrel Browning machine gun of small bore probably 0.303". Whenever the ship was at sea, firing practice would be carried out usually once a month. In view of the sometime lengthy stays in port or at anchor, off-duty gunners were offered the unusual perk of paid work, helping with the cargo handling.

By today's standards, on-board amenities for the crew could be described as primitive. The Admiralty had provided a fully equipped sailing whaler and dinghy. These were in great demand by the younger set for rowing, and for sailing by the not-so-young. A small library of books was provided plus a record player with many Bing Crosby and Andrews Sisters records which were played to death. To keep fit at sea there was a medicine ball and deck tennis facilities.

Many friendships were made with Australian families through the Missions to Seamen and other organisations that provided hospitality such as the Victoria League. It is worth recording that not a single member of the crew of the *City of Dieppe* deserted in Australia. The temptation was certainly there, as in 1946/47 when an amnesty was declared for those seafarers who had 'jumped ship' in Australia, a very large number surrendered. I was then Fourth Engineer on another supply ship, VISS *Fort Constantine* whose task was to carry 30 of these 'ex-sailors' from Sydney to Singapore to complete broken service. I had not previously encountered any deserters.

The stay in Australia throughout February 1945 seemed to produce a magic cure for all the tropical ailments acquired in and around Ceylon. Prickly heat and other rashes vanished never to return. Australian fresh food, milk and fruit appeared unbelievable after years of austerity. To have a beer when desired instead of eking out the two bottles a week ration, required a certain amount of self control.

Sailing through Sydney Heads and then north to the Admiralty Islands brought everyone back to earth with a bump.

The anchorage at Manus was crammed with units of the Pacific Fleet, many of which were old customers from Trincomalee. There was no resemblance to our former base in Ceylon as the only place were were allowed ashore was a bleak uninhabited island called Pityilu.Memories of the place are hazy—I recall some sort of swimming facility was there and a canteen with warm beer. I collected some interesting sea-shells and one called a cat's-eye which was rumoured to be used by the locals as money. However there were no local inhabitants to be seen.

Remaining on station at Manus for a week or so we provided shopping facilities for the Naval Customers. Transport of goods was similar to that provided in 'Trinco'. Either we delivered in our own barges, or the 'customer' carried out his own collection with the ship's launch. The *City of Dieppe* beer was now unrationed, which maintained morale at a high level throughout the stay. Various competitive events associated with rowing and sailing skills took place between ship's companies.

As was the custom in port in Ceylon, daytime working hours in Manus were from 6 a.m. to 12.30 with a 45 minute break at 8 a.m. for breakfast.

One unpleasant fact emerged when carrying out a lifeboat check; it was found that the emergency food stores had been taken from one of the lockers. There was not much doubt that it must have occurred in Sydney when either cargo was being loaded or ship repairs were being undertaken by the Australian workforce. Had the Australians been short of foodstuffs or poorly paid there may have been a semblance of excuse for such an action. Food in the Sydney shops was cheap and plentiful and dock workers were well paid, so the reason must lie elsewhere.

At Manus, the *City of Dieppe* received invitations to film shows on nearby warships all of which were gratefully accepted. Our ship's officers who were equal in number to the RNVR officers on board and sharing all dining and recreational facilities with them, soon found themselves adopting common standards.

As an anchorage, Manus was very hot with little or no breeze and we were all very pleased when the orders to sail were received. The *City of Dieppe* was to be behind the Commodore Ship of a convoy of a dozen or so assorted supply ships, tankers, plus an ammunition carrier and a repair ship. The convoy destination was Leyte Gulf in the Philippines and this time would have a full escort group for protection. During the voyage we always seemed to be in close proximity to the American short-wave radio stations set up on the chain of recaptured Pacific Islands. The various military radio announcers always commenced by saying typically, 'This is WVTK the Voice of America' giving then the Island name and then playing the latest of the popular records—Bing Crosby and the Andrews Sisters! These programmes were relayed over the *City of Dieppe* loudspeaker for the whole ship's company to hear. It was so loud that the whole convoy must have heard it.

Ships in the convoy were called to action stations once only during the voyage. A suspected submarine contact was made by the northernmost escorting warship at about 3 p.m. one day. A flurry of activity followed with no definite result, and an hour later all ships stood down from action stations.

It must have taken a week or more to get to Leyte Gulf with a convoy speed of 10 knots. At this speed it was very difficult to get any cool air into the engine-room as only one of the engine-room ventilator air shafts was fitted with a fan. Engine-room watchkeeping was a very hot and sweaty time for all concerned.

On arrival at the anchorage, the ships of the convoy dispersed to their duty positions and commenced their various businesses. The *City of Dieppe* was anchored about a mile away from the nearest shoreline which was part of Takloban Island. The facilities provided for the US Navy for their own warships included floating docks and every conceivable support function needed to make Leyte an efficient repair base. I do not think that I have ever seen so many allied naval ships gathered together in one place, either before or since that time in the spring of 1945. During this time President Roosevelt had not long died and all ships' flags were still being flown at half mast for up to 30 days.

Units of the British Carrier Fleet which had been in action north of the Philippines were arriving for repair and replenishment of stores and ammunition. HMS *Artifex,* the principal repair ship was equipped with special dockyard staff and greatly in demand. Invitations to film shows on the *Artifex* were sent to the *Dieppe,* but it was my misfortune always to be on duty on such occasions.

The water on Leyte Gulf was very inviting for swimming and for the first week we were on station, swimming parties were all the rage. This came to an abrupt halt when our Indian seamen who were fishing over the ship's stern caught two nasty looking barracudas with very sharp teeth!

So it was back to sailing! Five of us, Engineers Dahl, Williams, Taylor, DEMS Gunner Burlingham and I were out in the whaler, sailing very close to the Takloban shore, when we decided that as the beach was sandy and gently shelving we would take the whaler up on to the beach, picnic and bathe at the water's edge. The beach area appeared deserted up to the jungle area fifty yards away. As we dried ourselves back at the boat an armed American sergeant came out of the bush and enquired our business there. We told him and learned he was with the 13th Army Air Force stationed locally, I think his name was Schulz or Schwarz. He took all of us up a few hundred yards along the beach where a small wooden jetty projected out to sea. Standing at the end of the jetty and looking down into the clear water a large 5 to 6 foot shark was seen swimming in the direction where twenty minutes earlier we had been reckless enough to bathe.

After recovering from that shock, a cutter from one of the US Transport ships in the bay tied up at the jetty. Then a group of armed American troops from the shore marched onto the jetty with ten or more Japanese prisoners who were herded on to the cutter with their guards. They were no further than ten feet from our group and this was the one and only time I and my companions saw any Japanese troops in World War Two. I have no idea what army unit they belonged to but to me they looked well fed and showed no visible signs of ill-treatment from their captors. The cutter departed from the jetty, we thanked the sergeant, returned to our whaler and sailed back to the ship with an unusual story to tell.

We remained in Leyte harbour for many weeks dispensing our stock of goods to the Royal Navy ships until provisions were running low and it was time to return to base to fill up again. The return journey was hot and uneventful calling in at Manus for a few days before returning to Sydney. It was now June and the cooler weather demanded navy uniforms instead of shirt and shorts which had been worn exclusively for almost a year.

Arriving in Sydney we tied up at the dolphins opposite Tarronga Park Zoo for an overnight stay until a dockside berth was available in Darling Harbour. The following morning at about 7 a.m. just as the first movement of the engine was requested by the bridge there was a nasty banging noise in the engine-room and the main engine LP cylinder valve chest cover fractured. In consequence our departure from the dolphin was delayed to allow a temporary repair to be effected and then the vessel moved at a very slow pace to the loading berth which was adjacent to the Pyrmont Power Station and close to Pyrmont Bridge. The *City of Dieppe* remained at this berth for 4 to 5 weeks allowing a permanent repair to the engine. I had the job of making the drawings of the broken components for the Ellerman Lines' official record!

Off-duty hours were spent on a round of on-board parties, occasional cinema and theatre going and enjoying the very generous hospitality offered by the Australian people. Our DVSO Lt. Cmdr. Legge became engaged to a local Sydney socialite and many other romances blossomed. Sub Lt. Peter Barnett tried his hand at horse-riding, fell off and broke and arm needing a day or two in hospital. Peter Barnett unfortunately did not survive 1945 and was lost in a missing aircraft over the South China Sea in November or December 1945. I was taking presents for his mother in Sidcup and was greeted sadly on my return to the UK with a letter from her containing the news of his disappearance.

Included in the chilled cargo that was being loaded was about 5 tons of green stick beans. During the loading period it rained and the Australian dockers refused to work in the rain, so half of the cargo was left on the quayside for an hour until the rain stopped and the workers returned. The temperature of the beans must have exceeded the safe loading temperture as subsequent events revealed. Industrial action by the Australian dockworkers further complicated the loading which forced us to use Service Personnel to complete the job to enable the ship to sail on time.

At that particular time, it was my turn to be the assistant refrigeration cargo engineer and a regular duty was to measure all cold chamber temperatures twice daily and log the results. During the first week after loading the beans, the temeperature of the air in the bean cold room started to rise slowly every day. The vessel was now back at sea on its way to Manus with a stop for a couple of days in Brisbane. Two out from Brisbane and the bean temperature was high enough to warrant a visual inspection of the inside of the cold chamber. This meant removal of other cargo to facilitate access. The result in a nutshell was five tons of a manure equivalent in soggy sacks all of which had to be dumped into the sea and the chamber then hosed down to remove all trace of the cargo contamination.

Arriving in Manus in July we had the honour of being invited to a film show on the Fleet Train Flagship HMS *Lothian* which was formerly the SS *City of Edinburgh*. The ship was well known to a number of *Dieppe* officers who had served in her in peacetime, and this made the evening all the more pleasant.

After a week or so in Manus we set sail to a secret destination in a north-westerly direction. Two or three days out from Manus news was received that the atomic bomb had been dropped and the *City of Dieppe* was ordered back to Manus.

Shortly after returning to Manus, Japan surrendered and the *City of Dieppe* crew held a celebration party on board inviting a number of Americans from a nearby warship. Signal rockets were fired into the air, a special meal was provided and I still have a faded menu, signed by many of my shipmates, in my possession today.

We were still in business as a storeship and on the day before the surrender, a barge was secured to the side of the ship loaded with a valuable cargo of radar spares. At first light on the morning after VJ day, I looked over the side of the ship and saw the barge barely afloat. Those packing cases that had not sunk were floating in the water and drifting away from the *Dieppe*. Was it an act of God or of merry American sailors in a landing craft leaving the ship in the early hours of the morning hitting the barge a glancing blow? There was only one witness, the war was over and the witness has remained silent—until now!

This was a waiting time while the Allied Command decided what to do. The second engineer, Jack Dahl left the ship to become Chief Engineer to fill a vacancy caused by death. There were various promotions on the *Dieppe*, but we were now short of one engineer and extra work was required from all. Eventually we sailed from Manus to Tokyo Bay arriving there precisely as the Japanese formal surrender took place on the USS *Missouri*. The *City of Dieppe* berthed at the dockside close to the hospital ship *Tjitjalengka*.

Contrary to Fleet Orders of which we were unaware, a number of our personnel paid a visit ashore venturing a mile or so away from the ship. Quartermaster J. Wiseman claimed that he persuaded an American soldier to drive him to Hiroshima to see the devastation from the bomb. I went ashore with acting Second Engineer Norman Williams with one pistol between us and we obtained a lift to Yokohama for a brief visit and returned on foot. We encountered many US armed troops, a lot of Japanese civilians as well as seeing much bomb damage. No trouble of any sort was encountered. Returning to the ship we were told that we were not entitled to go ashore but no more was said about the matter. From the decks however we were able to see the British and Australian prisoners embarking on board the hospital ship some of whom looked to us in very bad condition.

We remained in Tokyo Bay for ten days providing stores to the many British warships present. Our enterprising radio officer, Bill Nutton a Yorkshireman and former sub-postmaster at Toler Lane Post Office near Bradford, who dealt with the ship's mail decided to record the unusual events of those days by making special place name and date franking marks on all mail passing through his hands. My scrapbook contains two such airletters, one stamped Tokyo Bay dated 9 September 1945 and the other Shanghai dated 21 September 1945.

The ship sailed for the Yangtze Estuary with a 24 hour stop at Sasebo in Japan. My notes at the time dated 19 September at sea near Saddle Islands states that we had been 4 days at the Yangtze Entrance in company with a Cruiser Squadron, Rear Admiral Cervaes, flag officer in HMS *Belfast* plus *Bermuda, Argonaut, Colossus, Tyrian, Tuscan, Tumult, Plym* and *Quiberon*. Log sheets from HMS *Belfast* dated 15 and 16 September 1945 confirm that the *City of Dieppe* transferred stores at sea to *Belfast,Bermuda* and *Argonaut* on those days when steaming at 10 knots. The *Belfast* log did not state that it was the very first time that the *City of Dieppe* had performed this task with its newly fitted equipment and untrained crew.

HMS *Belfast* was provisioned on the 15 September 1945. A supply officer was transferred across to the *City of Dieppe* to supervise and sign for the stores. The method of transfer was by the cargo wire with the victim secured in a dining-room chair. Shortly afterwards due to alleged erratic steering by us, the cargo line parted. Upon reconnection and completion of the transfer of stores, the gentleman was returned intact to the *Belfast* to his great relief as the vessels were still proceeding at 10 knots. On 16 September HMS *Bermuda* and HMS *Argonaut* were similarly successfully supplied with stores.

One problem on that particular occasion not officially recorded was the consternation in the cargo hold when the Indian seamen discovered they were handling frozen pork and promptly withdrew their labour. All convenient personnel regardless of rank had to lend a hand to complete the job.

Orders were received on or about 20/21 September 1945 to enter Shanghai and the *City of Dieppe* in company with *Belfast* and *Argonaut* sailed up the Whangpoo River becoming the first British ships to return since the Japanese occupation. The *City of Dieppe* occupied the British concession Buoy in mid-river immediately astern of an American cruiser berthing at a jetty at the Pootung side of the city. No restriction to going ashore was in force and a frequent liberty boat service to the Bund was in operation when the ship was berthed in the river. Money was a problem in Shanghai as local currency was unsafe due to the astronomical rise of inflation. Cigarettes were the most stable currency or Australian cash for those lucky enough to possess it. On 21 September 1945 the Chinese Yuan was available at about 20,000 per Australian pound. Within ten days the going rate exceeded 1 million Yuan to the pound and 10 cents notes were available in the currency. When the *City of Dieppe* left Shanghai at the beginning of October 1945 the current Yuan was declared worthless and the Central Reserve Bank of China introduced a new currency at 3,000 New Yuan to the pound.

Last year I telephoned Mr. H. W. Carter OBE now living in Paignton who was for many years Managing Director of Shanghai Waterworks up to 1949 and a former internee in Shar-Pai internment camp. He confirmed the super-inflation that I have described and vividly remembers paying his servants during the week in question by the carrier bag full of banknotes.

During our stay in Shanghai, former inmates from the nearby internment camp (Pootung) which I believe was the former Anglo-American Tobacco Company factory, became frequent visitors to the ship. A Mr. Blackwood with his wife and baby in arms were our most frequent visitors together with two Australian girls in their early twenties. Their physical and mental conditions were surprisingly good seeing that when we had been in Tokyo Bay two weeks before we observed the Allied Prisoners of War there being shipped home and many of them in very bad shape. Mr. Blackwood was fit enough to take me and two of my colleagues to see some of the sights of the city including a visit to the notorious Fats Bar in Blood Alley. I still possess some photographs taken that day which amply illustrate Mr. Blackwood's good physical condition. Visiting the city almost daily, I did not see any Japanese troops. There were however armed Chinese nationalist soldiers supposedly from Chungking very much in evidence in the Shanghai streets.

One final comment about our stay in Shanghai and that concerns the feeding of allied civilian internees in the immediate period following the end of the war. The *City of Dieppe* was a near-full grocery shop in September 1945 and I personally saw none of the cargo delivered to any of the former captives. Those of us who had private stocks of sweets, chocolate and tinned fruit made gifts of these to our ex-internee visitors. I suppose food supplies could have been flown into Shanghai by the Red Cross or other aid agencies, but we were the first and only British cargo ship in the port during our short stay and our supplies went to HMS *Belfast* and HMS *Argonaut*.

Orders to sail to Hong Kong were received about 1 October 1945. Engines were prepared for movement and at the agreed time of departure from Pootung Wharf, the *City of Dieppe* was firmly stuck in mud and refused to move. When the next tide was due and the river was at maximum depth, aided by tugs the ship broke free of the mud and we were on the last leg of our commission. Advice was received by the Captain that a relief crew for all those of us who had been away over twelve months were on HMS *Arbiter* due at Hong Kong in the coming week. Rumours had been rife concerning this matter of repatriation and we were all pleased at the thought of going home. Some of the crew had been away for over two years without any leave whatsoever.

The *City of Dieppe* arrived in Hong Kong on 4/5 October 1945 to drop anchor for the last time as far as I was concerned. Since leaving Japan the process of resuming a peacetime ship role commenced. All ammunition was dumped into the sea. Hundreds of rounds of 20mm Oerlikon bullets plopped into the water with the shells for our 4.5 inch and 3.5 inch guns. The engine-room blackout—a curse for years in the tropics—was completely dismantled. All wooden shields and barriers at the boat deck level were chopped down and all skylights were fully opened.

On 5 October 1945 I and many of my shipmates were discharged from the ship. The new crew came on board and after a short briefing session the ex-members were transported to the floating transit camp, MV *Aorangi*, a former New Zealand passenger ship and submarine depot ship to await repatriation to UK. *Aorangi* was one of the earliest quadruple-screw diesel-engined passenger ships and was built in 1925 and should not be confused with the Dutch MV *Oranje* pronounced the same.

The week or so spent on board the *Aorangi* in Hong Kong was very comfortable and relaxing. A strong naval presence was at anchor in the bay including HMS *Howe* and many other warships. While in Hong Kong we were surprised to learn that Norman Padwick (Admiralty Staff *City of Dieppe*) was reunited with his father who had been a civilian prisoner of the Japanese in Hong Kong.

First leg of the journey home was arranged to be on HMS *Arbiter* to Sydney. *Arbiter* was an American built escort carrier and would be carrying as many ex-prisoners, ex-internees and service personnel for repatriation as could be squeezed in. Accommodation was all camp beds and blankets in partitioned off hangar areas and the like.

Shortly after boarding the vessel I was in conversation with an ex-RNVR Sub Lieutenant (E) from a salvage tug. He was a man in his early 50s and was worried that he was going to be called upon to assist on watch in *Arbiter* and he felt that having no steam plant experience he was not up to the job. I was young, keen, bored and at that time a bit big-headed I think, because I told him that I would be quite happy to take his place if it was OK with the Chief Engineer. One hour later, after seeing Lt. Cmdr. (E) Edwards RNR (ex-Cunard) my offer was accepted, my kit was transferred to a cabin shared by two Irish T124X Sub. Lieuts. (E) RNVR Bullick and Terry. I was assigned as an Assistant Watch-keeping Engineer to the Second Engineer Lt. (E) Waite RNR partnering Sub Lieut. Bullick for the journey to Sydney.

HMS *Arbiter* was under the command of Captain D. H. Everett from 1944, who later in December 1945 became Commodore Hong Kong, retiring finally in 1952 as Rear Admiral. I often wonder if he knew that he had a Merchant Navy Engineer on watch in his engine-room for the two weeks ending 26 October 1945.

Arbiter entered Sydney Harbour on 26 October 1945 with the band playing and the crew lining the flight deck. After securing the ship alongside the quay, we transit passengers bid our new-found friends farewell, and were then whisked away to another transit billet—this time it was a hotel in Sydney's King's Cross area where we remained for about two weeks.

There was considerable demand for shipping berths to the UK in the autumn of 1945 now that the war was over. Early in November most of the *City of Dieppe* ex-crew members joined the Blue Funnel Line vessel MV *Empire Rawlinson* as part of a complement of 36 passengers—destination Liverpool. Stops for cargo en route were made at Melbourne, Durban and Cape Town, the ship finally arriving in Liverpool one cold foggy day, 29 December 1945. Two months leave at home soon went by and I was promoted Fourth Engineer and appointed to the VSIS *Fort Constantine*. This was a one year old fleet supply ship based in the Far East. Joining her in Hong Kong I remained on the China Coast for 18 months which is another chapter of my life at sea.

Allied Sea Forces Return to Shanghai—1945

On the 19th and 20th September 1945, the British Task Group 111.3 headed by HMS *Belfast* flagship of Rear Admiral Servaes sailed up the Whangpoo River to Shanghai. In this group were HM ships *Argonaut, Ursa, Tumult, Tyrian, Quiberon* and *Plym* plus the fleet supply ship SS *City of Dieppe*.

In company with this British group, was a similar American Unit headed by the light cruiser *Nashville* and comprising destroyers *Waller, Radford, Robinson, Saufley* and *Micka* together with a hospital ship *Refuge* and HQ Communications ship *Rocky Mount*.

The *Nashville* saw much action in the Pacific War at the West Aleutians, New Guinea and Leyte where, on 13 December 1944, she was struck by a kamikaze raider port side aft. One hundred and thirty-three men were killed and one hundred and ninety wounded from this single attack.

Article in Bulletin January 1990

A POPULAR SHIP IN THE BLACK MARKET TRADE

Built by Burrard Drydock Company of Canada, SS *Fort Constantine* was a 7221gt purpose-built victualling store-issuing ship for HM Service in the Far East in 1945.

I served as Fourth Engineer on the ship from Spring 1946 until October 1947. The luxury of a bed-sized bunk, hot and cold running water in all cabins and air-conditioned accommodation throughout the ship, seemed unbelievable after my previous two years in the merchant navy as Junior Engineer on a fleet supply ship converted from a 1929 cargo ship.

Fort Constantine, managed by Ellerman and Bucknall Steamship Co., had a crew of British officers and Hong Kong Chinese ratings. UK civil servants and NAAFI staff managed the cargo under the direction of the British Admiralty. Duties varied: from taking part in fleet manoeuvres and storing at sea, transporting service personnel from Hong Kong for demob, to even transporting a group of former UK service deserters in Australia who had surrendered in the 1947 amnesty. Part of the cargo space was allocated to

NAAFI stores for issue of wines and spirits to fleet personnel, thus in the Orient, *Fort Constantine* became both a popular and notorious ship on the China Coast.

Financed by wealthy Hong Kong merchants, the Chinese crew traded sugar with Japanese mushroom growers on a pound for pound basis—dried mushrooms were in short supply and a much valued delicacy in Hong Kong. In 1946 Kure Harbour was under the control of New Zealand military personnel, who fortunately had no orders regarding the import of sugar, etc. The first time the crew carried their 40 lb bags of sugar out of the dock area they were detained by the military police who phoned the ship's master (Capt. Chapman) as to the ownership of the sugar. Once the crew's ownership was confirmed they were released, later returning to the ship with sacks of mushrooms which were then legitimately landed in Hong Kong.

A few months later a repeat performance was attempted. This time however the sugar was confiscated by the military police as black market activity was now illegal. However, when the crew returned to the ship they were again seen carrying sacks of mushrooms, which were delivered to Shanghai. Payment was made in diamonds, which were then delivered to the Hong Kong backers. How the crew acquired the Japanese mushrooms was that each member carried a small pack of saccharine of equivalent value to the sugar confiscated, and as the trading profit was high, the sugar loss was acceptable to the backer in Hong Kong. Until a stop was put to this activity, we were the only supply ship to have our own new jeep and an American base had a mysterious supply of Scotch whisky.

On a visit to Shanghai in 1947, the black market price of branded cigarettes on *Fort Constantine*'s arrival was £20/1000—duty free. It was rumoured that up to 3M cigarettes had been put on the black market from *Fort Constantine*'s cargo.

The ship was in Hong Kong when the SS *Sai On*, laying alongside the harbour wall, caught fire on 4 February 1947 with a loss of 149 lives. The ship was also in Hong Kong when the British Army Engineers blew up the partially complete Japanese war memorial, built by the Allied prisoners.

Fort Constantine's endurance was proven when it successfully rode out a severe typhoon in Hong Kong in 1947 when more than ten ships were sunk or forced aground. I remember well the typhoon warning received by the Captain. I was senior engineer on board at the time, and was asked how long it would take to prepare the engines for sailing to safer anchorage. Power was limited as one of the two main boilers was empty of water, awaiting examination. Fortunately, there were sufficient Chinese engine room ratings on board, so we prepared to depart immediately. Ten minutes before sailing, Second Engineer Bob Fairley rushed to the ship having seen smoke rising from the ship's funnel—the cold boiler, now filled with water, had its first oil burner ignited. Once he realised what the problem was, we agreed to two watches of two engineers per watch, four hours on and four hours off, until the storm abated. The ferocity of the storm was such that with the anchor dropped and the main engines operating between quarter- and half-speed ahead, we just held our position safely for nearly 30 hours until the winds and waves subsided.

After returning to the UK in October 1947, *Fort Constantine* was laid up in South Wales, first at Cardiff and then in Barry Docks. The ship remained there until 1950 when it became a permanent Royal Fleet Auxiliary vessel, remaining so to the end of its life.

'Give it me $100 . . . make you $1000'

Frank Manning's account (January Bulletin) of his sojourn in the Far East brought back happy memories for Mr. W. R. Anderson, who has contributed this month's photograph and memories:

"I joined the NSIS *Fort Sandusky* just before VJ Day which we celebrated in Montreal.

As a first tripper, I thought all ships had air conditioning and h&c in all cabins, only to discover this was not true.

After arrival in the Far East, our first trip to Yokohama gave us an opportunity to see the damage in Hiroshima after the bomb, something we will never forget. Back in Hong Kong, we met up with *Fort Dunvegan* and *Constantine* plus one other *Fort* (possibly *Rosalie*).

Like the *Constantine,* we were also involved in sugar, saccharine, dried mushrooms and dried fish. I recall one greaser on the middle watch being signed on becuse he was fluent in Japanese and not for his talents on triple expansion engines. I remember the No. 1 Fireman coming to me saying 'lumber 5 give it me $100, come back Hong Kong, make you $1000', but I reneged on that one seeing as my monthly salary was £28.15, so I lost out.

I made up for it in Shanghai by trading in a 9d razor with blades, 200 ships' Woodbines, a bottle of Black & White and two pairs of engine room socks, for a Japanese Leica camera which served me for 15 years. Total outlay 12/-.

Another lucrative incident was during a trip to Kure where four of us paid a visit at midnight to the tunnels where the Japanese had built the midget submarines. You can imagine the time we had in the tool rooms. Two lathes with 14 in. swings and 24 in. between centres found their way back to Hong Kong, together with various hand tools, the profit being shared.

I also remember Mr. Manning's account of that typhoon in 1947, because we also rode it out at half ahead whilst the *City of Hereford* lost part of her bridge and two lifeboats.

Being repatriated in 1947 for leave study, I have no idea what happened to NSIS *Fort Sadusky*."

From John Lawson (Coder)

I recall coming out of a cinema in Sydney and seeing a placard: 'New Bomb dropped on Japan' and not thinking much of it. However, it soon changed my life. Within a few weeks, the C in C (Sir Bruce Fraser) was leaving Sydney for passage to Hong Kong, so we went with him. He flew his flag in *Duke of York*, which was one of the biggest battleships in the Fleet and a far cry from *Slinger*. On arrival at Hong Kong, we were billeted at HMS *Tamar* (Wellington Barracks) just below the Peak. Our offices were halfway up the Peak which could be reached by a funicular railway or, when wet, by trudging through the underground passages (constructed I think by the Japanese) which led from our offices right down to a point almost opposite our barracks. Life in Hong Kong was different from Sydney, but was quite good with several cinemas and a good Fleet canteen. We made some visits to Kowloon on the Star ferry.

Clay Maxwell was a LSA on a LST! That means he was a Leading Supply Assistant on a Landing Ship, Tank. Otherwise known as LST(3) 3029 (nearly 5,000 ton. Steam driven. 14 Officers, 90 Men)

He wrote to me:

With the Japanese occupied Territories in mind, towards the end of 1944, British and Canadian shipyards were launching a new type of ship—a Landing Ship, Tank, Mark 3. It was steam driven and larger and heavier than the previous American LST 2s.

So, from Scottish, Irish and Canadian waters came the new LST3s on their way to the other side of the world.

Their deck cargoes were LCTs (Landing Craft Tank), tugs and Bailey Bridges and their Tank Decks were loaded with tanks and vehicles of every description—in short, everything required for the Invasion of Malaya, Java and whoever knows where.

But the end came suddenly and the role of the LST(3) changed to that of carrying soldiers, POWs, sacks of rice and even railway rolling stock, at one time acting as a train ferry from Chittagong to Jahore.

Reading about the war at sea, Clay feels that the LSTs played an inglorious part, but this is not so. It was the luck of the draw or Drafting Office as to where one was appointed and all work was important to the success of the whole.—Ed.

Extracts from a Magazine on HMS *Maidstone* from William Capseed, ex-Ldg. Sto.

There must be very few ships in the Royal Navy which mirror history as vividly as *Maidstone*—her attached submarines were in it from the start. There was no let up from September 3rd, 1939.

She had her part to play in the defence of Britain, her submarines struck hard and often at German sea supplies. As the war moved on so did *Maidstone*—to Freetown, to Gibraltar, Algiers and Alexandria.

With victory in Africa, with the southern invasion of Europe an accomplished fact, *Maidstone* moved on to the Far East through the Suez Canal, Massawa, Aden and Trincomalee. As the eastern war moved onward to its triumph, so *Maidstone* moved with it, to Fremantle, Sydney and Subic Bay, until that grand hour when she was in the vanguard of the liberating fleet at Hong Kong. It was a *Maidstone* party which hauled down the Japanese flag from headquarters in Hong Kong, a flag which to-day is one of Captain Shadwell's proudest possessions.

TO THE GLORY OF GOD

AND IN PROUD MEMORY OF THOSE WHO LAID DOWN THEIR LIVES IN SUBMARINES OF THE 8th FLOTILLA ATTACHED TO HMS *MAIDSTONE* DURING THE WAR 1939—45.

HMS *Olympus*
HMS *Talisman*
HMS *P.222*
HMS *Tigris*
HMS *Thunderbolt*
HMS *Turbulent*
HMS *Sahib*
HMS *Splendid*
HMS *Saracen*
HMS *Usurper*

I have fought the good fight. I have finished my course.
I have kept the Faith. —II Timothy iv.7

Maidstone will be remembered for being the first ship of the relieving fleet to enter Hong Kong waters, thereby adding to the special affection the colony has long borne towards the submarine service.

The impression of one of the Stanley internees of that historic event:

Ever since the beginning of June, the Nips had closed down on the entry of the local newspaper into the camp, and of course wireless was forbidden—six of the internees had been shot in 1943 for running a wireless news service. This in itself was an indication of their jitteriness, and as the local Chinese newspapers kept on being smuggled into the camp, and we got the news of Okinawa and the sea and air bombardments of the Japanese islands, we grew more and more confident of an early end to our troubles. This was increased by the fact that in July they started giving us meat or fish one day a week (the first time for over eighteen months) and even so far as to issue us with a roll of 'bumf' each.

As the days went past, the demeanour of the Formosan guards made it more and more obvious that they too thought the end was very near. As far back as July, 1942, I had been appointed by Mr. Grimson, the Colonial Secretary, to sit on a committee with five others to prepare plans for the taking over of the government of Hong Kong when the Japs were kicked out. Alternative plans had been made for various eventualities—the one we did not foresee was the manner in which the end in fact happened.

As bits of information kept coming in, we revised and altered our plans, arranging exactly what each department was to do, and who was to do it—billeting, catering, police, sanitary services, medical services, food control, harbour regulation, electric light and power, wireless communication broadcasting, post office, etc., were all arranged for and men detailed individually for their respective jobs. These plans were rather shaken on August 10th, when the Japs suddenly took about 100 of our engineers and technicians and removed them to a camp in Kowloon. A Jap officer later told them that it was intended to take them to Canton and shoot the lot, but Hirohito's surrender had just come in time to save them. Mr. Adams, of Butterfield and Swire, who is a passenger on board, was one of this party.

Finally came the news of the atomic bomb and VJ Day. You can imagine our delight and our hope of seeing the White Ensign any day. The Japs soon withdrew the guards at Stanley, and told us we must stay in the camp and look after ourselves. Day after day went past and still no sign—we hoped and prayed it would be the White Ensign and not another flag, until finally Mr. Gimson got the Japs to let a few of us into the town 'to prepare for the orderly handing over'. He and six others went into town on Sunday, 26th August and some thirty of us followed him on the next day. We took up our quarters in the French Mission. Then I found that my wireless engineers from the Kowloon camp had already been over the Kowloon transmitting station and the broadcasting station and found the gear in workable order. We got busy at once, and we were able to arrange for Mr. Gimson to broadcast twice on the evening of the 28th.

Other departments were equally busy, and though we still insisted on the Japs being responsible for our protection and food supply, we rapidly took over all the other essential sources. By this time we had heard of the arrival of Admiral Harcourt's fleet outside the Liwa Islands and that arrangements were in hand for their entry and the Jap surrender. I was in our headquarters, the French Mission, when *Swiftsure* and *Prince Robert*, followed by *Maidstone* came up the harbour from Subic. Soon after we heard a series of crackles from the naval yard—some said Chinese crackers, but being an ex-machine gunner, I thought not. However, that excitement soon died down, and very soon afterwards whom should I see coming up the steps of the building but your Captain, whom I had last met some twenty years ago when he was a young submarine officer on the China Station.

You all know what happened afterwards, but none of you can realize what

August 30th meant to us who will in future say with great sincerity and more gratitude than ever before 'Thank God for the Royal Navy.'

E. Wynne Jones

THE CAPTURE OF THE JAPANESE HQ

On arrival in Hong Kong several duties were assigned to the various ships. HMS *Maidstone* was ordered alongside the dockyard wall, an operation which was neatly executed in view of the sniping that was taking place in the vicinity of the dockyard.

As per normal, *Maidstone* had plenty of extra lookouts all down the starboard side, namely, out-of-work tiffies and lower deck critics, scrutinising the results of our occupation against the Japanese. Much to the surprise of the ship's company, the Japanese Imperial Ensign and Admiral's Flag was still flying over General Headquarters; by this time *Maidstone*'s 'Commandos' were well into the dockyard clearing out suspicious characters. After a few days everything was well in hand, but the surrender terms had not been carried out and the Jap flags were still flying boldly over Headquarters.

On Saturday morning, 5th September, a signal was sent that the Japanese flag will be hauled down at 12.00 hours and all armed Japanese would be disarmed. By 08.30 excitement in the Gunnery Office was tense; in came the Gunnery Officer, armed to the teeth and ready for the kill, and told us in the language of the modern navy that we had got to take the Japanese HQ and disarm the troops holding out. After a hurried conference in the Gunnery Office it was decided that thirty-three men would be sufficient to cope with the 500 Japanese that were still in the vicinity of Headquarters. Zero hour for landing was 09.00, and to the delight of the Gunnery Officer, on appearing on the upper deck, the *Maidstone*'s Commandos were all ready on the jetty all top and primed for action. It was suggested that a short prayer be said, but the QM refused to pipe for the Padre. It was now time for the Gunnery Officer to give a speech, and a short briefing took place, an emphasis on *those two Jap flags are to be taken at all costs.*

Owing to the uncertainty of which buildings were held by the Japanese, a bus was chartered to take the Commandos to the scene of action; after a short ride in the bus the Commandos were rudely shaken when to the surprise of all, the back wheel fell off, thus causing a delay in the programme, but owing to the alertness of the driver and a Commando, the bus soon made headway through the dockyard gate the forward lookouts reported pillboxes and machine gun nests ready to serve out shrieking shrapnel; however, the course was resumed along East Street. So far there was no opposition, except by Chinks looting.

On reaching the entrance to Headquarters, it was decided to debus and march in battle order to the scene of action. On a blast of a whistle by the Gunner's Mate the unit soon took up their stations ready for the advance. It was a remarkable sight to see the bayonets glistening in the sun, as we marched towards the main gate, which was well guarded by Japanese machine gunners. To the surprise of the Japs, not one of the men batted an eyelid, but continued up the roadway which led to HQ. By now it was quite warm and boys were perspiring a little as the going was pretty heavy. After marching for two miles the unit was halted and a conference was held by the Gunnery Officer and staff, and it was decided to deploy No. 1 Section to the rear of the building without making themselves conspicuous to the Japanese. No. 1 Section under the command of Lt. Brislee, RN and the Gunner's mate commenced to stalk towards our first objective, which was the scaling of a fifteen-foot wall. To do this a twenty-foot stream had to be crossed.

The Gunner's Mate was the first one to try the crossing, and succeeded after jumping into three feet of slimy mud, he being followed by Lt. Brislee and the remainder of the section. By now the objective was clearly in view, and it was decided to take cover in the undergrowth but still advancing towards the wall. Lt. Brislee, being nimble, was the first to attempt to scale the wall, whilst the remainder took cover in the shrub. All of a sudden a shriek filled the air and Lt. Brislee fell down from the wall. A drone could be heard, and at first an attack from the air was thought to be imminent, but on close observation a swarm of bees had attacked two stokers and one seaman, and they were stung in the most awkward of places. After a few minutes all was quiet and the wall was scaled.

By now the alarm had been spread around the Japanese HQ, and the sentries were on the lookout for us. This, however, did not worry two men from No. 1 Section as they were advancing towards the roof of the building, but two stokers taking cover behind a small bush observed two Japanese machine gunners about to sight a gun on the leading section. However, they turned out to be quite friendly as all they wanted was an English cigarette.

In our briefing, the Jap flags were to be hauled down at 12.00, but somehow two men from No. 1 Section had anticipated this and were well on their way towards the flag masts on top of the building. Whilst this was in progress, 2 and 3 Sections were advancing towards the front of the building, from which the Japanese were evacuating all their personal belongings. By 11.40 the building was now completely surrounded by the *Maidstone*'s Commandos, and all were waiting for the lowering of the two Jap flags.

Two scouts from No. 1 Section were now in position to cross the bridge leading to the flagstaff. At the foot of the flagstaff was a Jap signalman about to unbend the halliards, but as he turned round he was confronted by two of the *Maidstone*'s Commandos all ready to carry out a bayonet attack. Discretion being the better part of valour, the Jap turned round and nipped like hell along the roof and disappeared down a ladder. In the meantime the Jap flags had been hauled down and the White Ensign and RA's flag hoisted in their place.

As soon as this was observed, the whole of the platoon converged on the building ready to deal with any suicidal Jap. By now all signs of resistance had ceased, and much to the surprise of the party, one of *Maidstone*'s jeeps tore round the lawn with an urgent meessage sent by Commander Junor: 'Hold the fort, food and water is being sent; the surrender will take place at 16.00.' Quite a large number of the boys were feeling the strains of thirst, and one stoker was heard to remark 'I couldnt arf go my tot'; but like most things in life he had to wait.

The Gunnery Officer and the Gunner's Mate had now moved over to the main entrance with tommy guns and revolvers at the ready, when the Japanese General strolled out to greet them, but this was no time for handshakes. A few minutes after, the whole staff appeared complete with suitcases and Samurai swords and ready to be taken away. Although the Japs were keen to get away they insisted that they should keep their personal weapons, so to avoid any altercations all of the staff were placed in a car and driven to the pier where a boat was waiting for them. The object was now to carry out a thorough search of the buildings in case of booby traps and time bombs. By now all the platoon had fallen in in front of the building waiting for the next orders.

As it was a three-storey building each section was given the task of searching one floor each. Lt. Brislee with AB Done decided to search the officers' dining room. Complete silence reigned throughout, except for a ticking noise which sounded very much like a time bomb. However, this did not stop them from carrying out their duty, but curiosity was deep in their minds and this bomb must be found or else the whole building may blow up. After a thorough search the time bomb was found to be a domestic refrigerator, full up with Jap beer! By 13.10 the building had been searched completely and the food from the ship had arrived, but alas, it was too late: the boys had filled up at the expense of the Japs.

The next job to be done was placing of sentries around HQ to prevent looting, as the Chinese are masters at pinching from under the nose of any one. Several of the roads were absolutely chock-a-block with wardrobes and grand pianos with a Chink underneath struggling towards the town. The Chinks must have been desperate, as cold pussers steel and a burst of tommy gun fire would not drive them away, but after seeing several of the *Maidstone*'s Commandos, they realised that they meant business (and chow!), so after a few more short bursts they eventually dispersed.

The time was approximately 16.00, and several brass hats and flag officers had walked around HQ, including a couple of press photographers, but they were too late for any good pictures. All was quiet now, and the routine of sentries was being carried out, while the men off watch were searching for souvenirs. This turned out to be a rather heavy job as by the time every one had completed their search a three-ton truck was required to take it away.

It was now time for the *Maidstone*'s Commandos to be relieved, and after all the work was done, a platoon from the aircraft carrier arrived. After a long blast on the whistle by the Gunner's Mate (a general recall to all the Commandos) a converted lorry in the shape of an armoured car was parked in front of the building, chauffeured by the Gunnery Officer, whose knowledge of car driving was quite good, so after a brief meeting it was decided to return to the ship with it. *Maidstone*'s Commandos had completed their task, the total number of casualties was five, thanks to the bees, and so all embussed in the armoured car and a course was steered for HMS *Maidstone* in the dockyard. On arrival at the ship the sight of an armoured car caused much mirth amongst the lookouts still closed up along the starboard side.

After debussing, arms were inspected, and the weary thirty-three returned on board tired, thirsty and hungry, and all were ready for their ration of spirit, which was well earned. And so ends another episode that will go down in the annals of naval history!

Copy of a page from 'Pacific Stars and Stripes' Features dated Sunday March 17, 1946, sent to me by Lt. Cdr. John Haddock RN

BRITISH HOSPITALITY SHIP BRINGS ENGLAND TO EMPIRE FORCES ABROAD
By SGT. ANDREW HEADLAND, Staff Writer

YOKOHAMA—Aboard His Majesty's vessel *Menestheus* they have a saying 'Helen's face launched a thousand ships, but the *Menestheus* launched a thousand slips.'

That's because the *Menestheus,* strictly an oddity ship of the first water, is the only vessel in the King's navy equipped with a sea-going brewery. The brewery, which imbibers refer to as 'Davey Jones Brewery', has a daily output of 1,800 gallons of fine, English beer.

The brewery, however, is just one unusual feature in a shipload. For the 11,000-ton craft, formerly a minelayer, was converted into an 'amenities' or entertainment ship by order of the British Admiralty in 1945. As such, unique among sea going vessels, it pokes its saucy prow into the seven seas bringing a cargo of pleasure to the amusement of starved enlisted personnel and officers of the British Merchant Marine and Navy.

Now on its first Far Eastern tour, the *Menestheus* made Yokohama its first port of call in Japanese waters. A visit to the vessel at Yokohama revealed the following amenities: A 350 seat concert hall (with full theatrical stage settings), and a cafeteria also capable of seating 350 people; a cinema; a soda fountain; buffets; large library; smartly furnished reading and writing rooms with festive colour schemes throughout, tailoring and pressing rooms; various shops; glass and chromium bars; and a city style chapel, which ship Chaplain John Nickels stated was the best in the British Navy, with one exception.

This exception, he pointed out, was due solely to the fact that pipes from the brewery on a deck below the chapel run up and behind the chapel's altar. The result is that sometimes during services brew gurgling through the pipes vies with notes from the organ's pipes for the audience's rapt attention.

Radio equipment throughout the night-clubish vessel is American made. The ship can accommodate 1,000 men daily in two shifts, one in the afternoon, another by night.

The ship's complement numbers 324, including 21 members of a Royal Marine Band, and 27 members of an all male revue company for entertaining visitors.

Started as a morale boosting, war time enterprise, the *Menestheus* is continuing her peacetime activities under joint control of Captain P. Purkis, Merchant Navy, and Commander J. M. D. Hunter, Royal Navy. From Yokohama it sailed to Kure, and from there it will go to Hong Kong.

From Lt. Cdr. John Haddock RN, (then a Lieutenant), HMS *Anson*

Hong Kong was a mess and the people had suffered a terrible time under the Japanese.

I happened to be amongst one of the first of the armed landing parties ashore, when we landed 3 companies of seamen. Our Royal Marines had landed the first evening on arrival and faced the Japanese on the Kowloon side. As second in command of 'B' Company Kennedy Force, we stayed ashore for some three months or more, releasing POWs and rounding up surly Japanese.

As dear old *Anson* was returning home to the UK, in January 1945, I requested to remain in Australian and Far East waters and subsequently was in HMS *Bonaventure* (Midget Submarine Depot ship), taking QARNNS and VAD's up to Hong Kong to staff the hospitals and tend the population medically, plus a variety of stores, mainly medical.

In 1946, I joined TSMV *Menestheus* as 1st Lieutenant of the RN Party.

A fully integrated modern day floating leisure centre! The idea being that the Pacific War was going to be a long hard slog with an estimate that over 1 million servicemen would be lost!

What an incredible spirit prevailed throughout that wonderful British Pacific Fleet—the like of which we shall never see again—especially will I never forget seeing all those hundreds of ships at anchor at Manus!

From Gerald Barcock, *Empire Salvage*

EXTRACT FROM 'THE ROYAL FLEET AUXILIARY'

Empire Salvage (ex *Lotharingen*, ex *Papendrecht*). 10,476 tons gross.

This ship was built in 1940 by the Rotterdam Dry Dock Co. Ltd., for Phillips van Ommeren of that port. Commandeered by the Germans on the invasion of Holland, they renamed her *Lotharingen* and set her to sea as one of the *Bismarck*'s supply ships, having altered her decks and fittings considerably for replenishment at sea.

She was captured by HMS *Ark Royal*, having been slightly damaged by one of her aircraft.

Altered by the Admiralty for use as an RFA tanker being entirely manned by the RFA personnel for some years, she provided an insight into the German methods of replenishment at sea.

They, having no bases, had been forced to experiment and had evolved the rubber hoses which have now become the only type of hose in use by the Navy, after further experiment and modification by us.

Another German tanker captured about the same time also provided information on their equipment.

In Admiralty service at Halifax, Nova Scotia, and later with the Eastern Fleet, she participated in the Burma landings and then proceeded to Chinese and Japanese waters until 1946.

Returned to her owners at Bombay in April 1946, and reverted to her original name of *Papendrecht*.

She had an eight-cylinder stork diesel, with a speed of about 12.5 knots, and dimensions of 496 x 73 x 35 feet.

Her name was somewhat unhappily chosen by, presumably, the Ministry of War Transport, as with its salvage connotaton, it constantly gave rise to confusion when she arrived at war damaged ports such as Bizerita, where salvage ships were urgently needed when she turned up shortly after its recapture by the Allies as an oiler!

Also at Trinco was HMS *Adamant* which was Supply and Depot ship. Our task was to rendezvous with the Fleet prior to an attack on bases in Sumatra. The Captain was a Geordie, RN retired. His rank on board the oiler was Capt. G. Williams RNR.

The Ship's Company

There were 16 RN DEMS Gunners, 1 Petty Officer, 1 Leading Hand, 1 Wireless Operator, 1 Radar Rating and 6 Maritime Gunners, in charge of them was a sergeant, also the MN crew.

Armament on board

1 4.7 gun sliding breech astern, 1 12 pounder on the bow, 2 twin Brownings on the bridge, 6 oerlikons in various places.

Routine on board ship

It was much the same as on RN ships. Discipline was very strict as you can imagine, having an ex-RN Captain. If we passed any RN ships on leaving or entering harbour it was rig of the day and dress ship.

Refuelling the tanker

We would leave Trinco under orders, travel to Abadan in the Persian Gulf, refuel, return to Trinco to await orders, no escorts.

When we were refuelling we had to have hosepipes running on deck to help the tanks cool as the decks and handrails were red hot. The cargo consisted of diesel oil, fuel oil and 1,000 tons of high octane for the aircraft aboard the carriers. When under way we would have to open the valves on various tanks to get the fumes away, several times a day.

Refuelling at sea
We would leave Trinco probably 2 days prior to the Task Force with a destroyer as escort, or sometimes a cruiser: HMS *Ceylon*, for a rendezvous 'somewhere at sea'. Those that wanted refuelling would come alsongside, refuel, go in and bombard off Sumatra then return to Trinco.

Preparing for oiling
The hardest part was for the RN ships to synchronise their engines to our speed which would be about 7 knots, 2 destroyers on each beam. The procedure was for an RN rating to fire the lanyard across for pulling the 5″ pipes across, it was all hands on deck on the tanker for about eight or twelve hours, connecting and disconnecting the pipes. Many a time the RN engineer made a bad connection and got covered in fuel oil when pumping commenced.

When we were running on our own, the watch keeping would vary owing to the mood of the Captain. Sometimes it was 4 on 4 off; or 8 on, 8 off. When with the Fleet he would cancel all watches.

Entertainment on board
For us it was mostly bingo. When we had the Monopoly board out it was 8 hour sessions, very good. The skipper would have a dance for the officers. He would signal for part of the RM band to come on board then he would invite the nurses and Wrens on board, with us in rig of the day on the gangway.

From Peter Longhurst, ex-signalman HMS *Barle*

April 1st 1945
In company with HMS *Usk*, we were escorting 4 troopships *Highland Prince, Highland Monarch, Esperance Bay* and *Largs Bay* who were carrying Australian troops returning from the Middle East. On April 6th 1945, one soldier on board *Highland Prince* died and was buried at sea. Another week and he would have been home.

On arrival at Fremantle (April 12th) I received a letter from home, my mother informed me that she had just bought apples from Australia, the first for many years, (mental telepathy . . . that I should arrive in Australia on the same day).

May 8th 1945
We are told that it is VE Day, the war in Europe is over. For the past few weeks we have been bottling our daily grog, with sultanas, etc., with a celebration in mind. When the news came through, I was on watch, the middle I think, however, I went down to the messdeck and woke everyone with the news, and then the bottles came out. The entry in my diary reads: 'Today is VE Day, we have waited for this almost six years, and here we are at sea in the Pacific.'

13th June 1945
Darwin Australia. Awaiting departure of AFD 20, under tow by tugs *Spritely, Empire Sam* and *Destiny.* Cinema show; we are sitting on a hillside looking at the screen below us in a valley. The film Laurel and Hardy in 'Always in Trouble', there are hundreds of viewers sitting on the hillside.

We were also entertained by an RAF Spitfire squadron who were stationed at Darwin. Darwin appears to be one big aerodrome, the roads are used as runways. We spent the afternoon wandering around the many US Air Force bombers and fighters, just looking at the colourful mascots painted on the planes.

10th August 1945
Barle was ordered to leave the fleet and contact the Dutch hospital ship *Tjitjalengka*. I remember at dawn, during the morning watch, I was the signalman on duty on the bridge, when a plane from one of the carriers arrived and circled around us, sending by light an alteration of course and position of the fleet. I dashed from one side of the bridge to the other in order to read the signal, the First. Lieut. writing the signal down as I read it. After rendezvousing with the hospital ship, we made our way to the new position of the fleet, steaming for some hours. We had not made contact with the fleet, and it seemed possible that I had misread the signal, but to my relief we finally sighted them at about noon.

16th August 1945
Back at Eniwetok, crowded with US vessels. That night, searchlights swept the sky and pyrotechnics were fired from ships anchored around us. The end of the war with Japan was being celebrated.

Note on the 31st August
Since leaving the UK, January 1st 1945, *Barle* has steamed 33,459 miles and since leaving Sydney May 7th 1945 has steamed 21,170 miles.

8th September
Arrived Kiirun, Formosa. That night, after the Japanese had posted guards alongside the ship on the jetty, we slept peacefully, almost like peacetime, but on the 10th, HMS *Belfast, Bermuda, Argonaut* and the destroyers *Tyrian, Tuscan, Tumult, Quiberon* and *Quadrant* with carrier *Colossus* arrived, and we were ordered to keep normal sea-going watches with all guns manned at night and to sweep the hills around the harbour with searchlights.

In mid September the US ceased the Lend/Lease and we had problems acquiring stores, including food. On the 18th, we arrived at Subic Bay, hoping to find stores, but after going from ship to ship, without success, we finally went alongside USS *Comfort* (hospital ship) from whom we managed to get boxes of K rations (a few biscuits, toilet paper, bottle of liquid to make water drinkable).

Regarding signals . . . The following was received by light at 1836 on 10.7.45:

To *Barle* from HMAS *Gawler* (SOE)
To V/S staff. All the best. Your flag hoisting was pretty slick.

The following signal was received by TBS by myself at 1125 on 15.8.45 while escorting oilers from the fleet off Tokyo to Eniwetok:

To *Barle. Findhorn. Wave Emperor.* From *Olan.*

The following was read on Australian Radio:

Both British Prime Minister and American President say that Japan has accepted our peace terms. Time of origin: 1115.

(I have the original signals, but as they are written with pencil, both are beginning to fade.)

The Editor
'British Pacific Fleet Post'

HMS *Barle*
August 10th 1945

Sir,
In a recent copy of your paper it stated that comment from some of the ships of the BPF would be welcome, here therefore, are some comments from the ship's company of a river class frigate.

After ten days in Sydney we sailed, before VE Day to take up our duties with the Fleet Train, since then we have covered some 25,000 miles mostly in the forward area, and at the time of writing are still at sea. Our few short stays in harbour—if we may so designate Pacific Atolls—have been spent at Leyte, Manus and Eniwetok, where most amenities have been conspicuous by their absence.

During this period we have received most of our fuel, food and entertainment from ships. The latter have been however, picture-shows provided by the Americans. (We are too small (150 souls) to be allotted a cinema of our own.)

We have noticed that the columns of your paper give recognition to all the larger ships of the fleet, few of whom, if any, can approach our record of sea time. Particularly we have in mind the account of the gallant action fought in Sydney Harbour on VJ Day by one of our ships when single handed she beat two harbour tugs in a battle of hoses.

We feel that some measure of recognition is due to the smaller and so far apparently forgotten ships of the BPF escort force, amongst whom may be found the real veterans of this campaign.

We mention the above not because we want to boast, but because we have worked hard in the Atlantic, Mediterranean and now the Pacific and so feel that some mention may help the Ship's Company to bear the period of waiting before returning to civilian life.

We remain,
Yours faithfully,

GFVD DMNG DHLT ADB WJW BGS BM KB
Wardroom Officers of HMS *Barle* on behalf of Ship's Company.

From G. Luscombe CPO Tel., HMS *Ruler*

About two weeks after arrival in Australia, I was drafted to the aircraft carrier HMS *Ruler*—a converted merchant ship operating several thousand miles to the north in the vicinity of the Ryukyu Islands south of Japan. I took passage in HMS *Tenacious*, a destroyer on its way to join the fleet. The commander asked me if I would double-bank the operator practising on the typewriter, with a pencil copy of the broadcasts. Whilst in Australian waters we read Australian broadcasts, for which I was thankful because messages were sent at 25 wpm. We put into Leyte on May 8th—VE Day. I was listening to press reports from San Francisco and heard an item which went—'Yo Ho Ho—British Navy splices mainbrace'. The captain issued a double ration of rum that day but few took up the ration because many were suffering from the heat. Besides—it was Australian rum and tasted like oil fuel!

I joined *Ruler* somewhere in the Pacific and we proceeded to make a strike on Truk Island in the Carolines where there was a Japanese garrison. Since the American navy had smashed Jap sea power, the garrisons on the Pacific Islands had been isolated and allied aircraft, both carrier and land based, periodically bombed them to keep them subdued. As a consequence Jap troops without fresh supplies and near to starvation had turned to cannibalism with their prisoners and any allied airmen shot down in air strikes, their victims. To prevent Allied airmen who were shot down being captured, a rescue service, consisting of flying boats and named DUMBO aircraft, was organised to pick up airmen shot down in the sea. We didn't carry any, but it was possible ships in company did.

The primitive nature of 'Woolworth' type carriers, of which *Ruler* was one, meant there was no other means of launching aircraft other than by working up speed over the length of the deck. The deck was short by fleet carrier standards and the tar in the deck seams acted as a brake. Add to this the fact that the ship could manage no more than 20 knots with little or no wind to turn into to give our Avengers and Corsairs lift, it was no wonder we lost more aircraft from failure to take off than from enemy action!

After about a month on *Ruler*, a colleague was made Chief Sparker and as he had been with the ship for some time, the commander asked me if I would mind transferring to *Arbiter*—another Woolworth carrier located with the Fleet Train off the coast of Japan.

Inevitably *Arbiter* ran out of planes and set off on the long journey back to the 'forward' base at Manus Island in the Admiralty Islands. Whilst still on our way, news was received of the atom bombs dropped on Hiroshima and Nagasaki which was quickly followed by the Japanese surrender.

I had to include this extract from a handbook available to the BPF sent to me by E. J. Foster of HMS *Golden Hind* (Stone Frigate, Sydney). *(How times have changed.—Ed.)*

During 1944 as a telegraphist aboard the battleship HMS *Rodney*, a fleet order was issued asking ex-GPO employees to volunteer for service with the Writer branch for Fleet Mail Office duties.

After initial acceptance and promotion to Leading Writer, I received a draft to HMS *Golden Hind*, Sydney, Australia, for service with the British Pacific Fleet and on the surrender of the Japanese received a further draft to HMS *Tamar*, Hong Kong, where a Fleet Mail Office was established in the dockyard.

The staff was a mixture of naval personnel and Chinese civilians, always very busy dealing with Naval and Merchant Navy shipping, also making dispatches to the UK and other countries, by air and sea.

We slept under mosquito nets, swallowed Nepecrine tablets which after a while made your skin as yellow as the locals, and off duty went swimming to cool down, always watching for sharks.

Promotion later made my duties very varied, with every aspect of dealing with a sailor's mail, this all came to an end with my demob. in 1946.

Handbook issued in 1945

The following are the postal rates in the United Kingdom for correspondence addressed to HM Forces serving overseas:

Letters .... 1½d for the first ounce and 1d for each additional ounce

NOTE: All letters under 1 oz. are sent by air where air services are available. Letters over 1 oz will also be sent by air if prepaid at the rate of 6d. for 1½ oz. and 6d. for each additional half ounce.

Postcards .... 1d each
Printed Papers (including newspaper) .... ½d per 2 oz

Parcels—
Not exceeding 3 lbs 9d
7 lbs 1/6
11 lbs 2/-
22 lbs 3/6

Postal Regulations in British Pacific Fleet

(a) All letters written by naval personnel serving in HM (seagoing) ships should normally be posted on board, and included in the ship's mails. These are sent to the nearest Fleet Mail Office for sorting and despatch to destination. Shore-based personnel may, if they so desire, use the facilities of the Civil Post Office like ordinary civilians instead of the Fleet Mail Office. In that event the civil postage rates and regulations will apply.

As a general rule, letters for addresses overseas and the HM ships have cheaper postage and quicker delivery if posted through Naval channels.

Naval Active Service Postcards

A supply of specially printed Naval Active Service Postcards, which contain set phrases, as 'I am quite well', 'I have been admitted to hospital', etc., have been supplied to all Depot Ships, Hospital Ships, base hospitals and Fleet Mail Offices for issue as required. These postcards are primarily intended for use when the normal writing facilities are not available or practicable, i.e. during operations or by casualties. They are not suitable for ordinary private correspondence.

When you are on Leave in Australia

To assist personnel of the Royal Navy who are on leave in Australia, or are attached to an isolated unit, i.e., a training post, etc., to enjoy the postal concession rates for HM Forces even when they are not near a Fleet Mail Office, arrangements have been made with the Australian GPO for correspondence addressed to the UK to be accepted as follows:

Correspondence should be addressed in the usual way and prepaid where necessary in British postage stamps.

There is just one more hint. This time to those Salts who prefer to write with a Marlin spike dipped in cocoa instead of with pen and ink—if they would only PRINT the address, the rest would be forgiven. It is equally important in telling other people your address, to make sure that they get it right the first time, as afterwards anything can happen. Believe it or not, 'HMS *Sameasbefore*' sails in an out of Fleet Mail Offices with great regularity in company with other vessels camouflaged out of all hopes of recognition even by expert mails staff.

The moral is always make sure that the letters YOU post are properly addressed, i.e., clear and complete, and that your correspondents know your correct address. When you change your address make certain that your new address is officially approved before broadcasting it—don't just take the opinion of the first person you meet.

In all Fleet Mail Offices are to be found expert ex-GPO or GPO-trained officers and ratings who are able and anxious to answer all your postal and telegraph inquiries. Questions asked 'over the counter' are both numerous and varied and it is gratifying to observe that there is a keen interest by both officers and ratings in the 'whys' and 'wherefors' of the Fleet Mail business.

From Ex PO.LR.1 Lawrence A. Curtis, HMS *Glenearn*

HMS *Golden Hind*, at Warwick Farm, Sydney, Australia, was an encampment where replacements of men for the BPF were 'barracked'. I left this encampment on 27.3.45 and joined HMS *Glenearn* for passage to the Pacific Islands, as one of many replacements for men serving in BPF—I had no particular ship to go to, I was therefore employed in the Forward Drafting Pool office (FDP), *Glenearn* was a Glen Line merchantman, equipped as an Infantry Landing Ship (LSI) carrying a large number of LCA's (Landing Craft Assault). The holds of the ship were used for carrying service personnel for Fleet replacements, also stores for the Fleet.

The ship was just off Fremantle, when the LCA fuel tank, located beneath the RM's messdeck for'ard, blew up killing a few men and injuring many others. We thought that we would return to Sydney, or at least Fremantle, but we continued towards the Islands, leaving the casualties in Hollandia, in the care of the US Military.

I replaced one of the Petty Officers who was killed, and joined the ships company of *Glenearn*. The ship wandered around the Islands, Manus (in the Admiralty Group) and Leyte in the Philippines, dropping off men and stores. We were at Leyte when VE Day was celebrated in Europe—which did not please us too much. After VJ Day we became very active picking up Dutch, Indian, British and Australian POWs—both civilian and service, from Hainan Island in the South China sea off Vietnam, I believe that we also picked up some from Hong Kong and Shanghai, dropping them at Singapore. I think that there were other ships performing this task obviously—I know that we made a couple of trips to and from Singapore.

This task having been completed the ship sailed for Kure, Japan, and became the Headquarters Ship for the British Commonwealth Occupation Forces. Kure was a shambles and had been knocked out as a Japanese Naval Base. It was rather a miserable existence, we couldn't buy very much—everything was by barter—cigarettes and chocolate. The Occupation currency bought was shown in the pay book—so there wasn't much point in amassing millions of Yen—we couldn't change it back again!

Newspaper articles from the 'Sydney Sun', October 1945, sent by Ex-telegraphist J. R. Murphy, HMS *Speaker*

With the arrival of the British Aircraft carrier *Speaker* with 659 Diggers from Manila today, Australian prisoners of war so far repatriated number nearly 7000.

The *Speaker*, which was the first British aircraft carrier to go into Japan for prisoners of war, and the last one to come out, *(Incorrect—she was the first.—Ed.)* made several trips to Manila before it came here.

The men, who lined the flight deck, were given a full-throated reception by ships and launches.

The hangar of the carrier was a vast dormitory, and was crammed with camp stretchers.

'Hospitality has been warm' said Able-Seaman F. G. Skeels of Perth, one of the 12 HMAS Perth men repatriated by the ship. 'We were released by the British and have been with them right through. This voyage just tops it off.'

Three musketeers, who enlisted together and were rarely separated, are brothers Sid Goodfellow and William Goodfellow of Mt. Lofty near Adelaide and Lance-Corporal NormanLawson, Grange (South Australia).

Lawson went through a dreadful ordeal on the Burma-Thailand railway. The Jap guards, to punish an alleged breach of rules, made him stand on a large burning log.

'My mates were ordered to heap piles of wood around the log to make the fire blaze up and scorch me. It was as hot as hell, but the boys were cunning. They heaped on all the green boughs they could find to make a lot of smoke, and not much fire.'

After nearly an hour, when Lawson was scorched almost red, the guards permitted him to leave the log. He was not seriously burnt, but he was sick for more than a week.

Although the Government policy has been to give the returning Australians as big a welcome as possible, on several ships, through Army and Navy confusion, Pressmen and photographers assigned to record the arrival of the men have been hampered.

Today an Army officer blocked a party of Pressmen and photographers at the foot of the gangway when the *Speaker* arrived. They had passes issued by Victoria Barracks to cover these arrivals. Only through the intervention of a Royal Navy officer did the Press party get aboard.

Carrier Sails it with Music

HMS *Speaker,* a new escort carrier, delivered from America under Lease-lend some time ago (she was formerly the USS *Delgada*) will have music wherever she goes.

Besides a nine-piece band she has more than 1,000 gramophone records on board. Five hundred of the records were presented through the American Red Cross by a wealthy New York woman, and another New York woman supplied the instruments.

Lieut. Allan Milne, RNVR of Dundee, whose home is now at Liverpool, runs the dance band.

A string bass

'We found two or three musicians among the ship's company,' he said, 'but the others have learnt to play since they've been in the ship.

'One man was so keen he made his lip sore with practising the trumpet. I had to stand him off for a few days to recover.

'The only instrument we haven't got is a string bass. If anyone has one to spare we would be very grateful for it.'

Atom Bomb Kills 20,000 Christians

When the second atomic bomb was dropped on Nagasaki it wiped out practically the whole of the city's Christian community of 20,000 while the rest of the population was left unharmed. *(This is what the Sydney Sun reported, so I have included it!—Ed.)*

The story was brought to Sydney yesterday by men in the aircraft carrier HMS *Speaker,* which was the only British ship to enter Nagasaki Harbour after the Japanese surrender.

Lieut. Commander L. G. Hudson RNVR, said he was told by a few surviving Franciscan nuns that they thought the sun had burst. The sky became a sea

HMS Victorious *alongside VSIS* Fort Wrangell, *re-fuelling area. Photo: R. C. Hill*

VSIS Fort Wrangell *alongside wharf, Mosman, Sydney. Photo: R. C. Hill*

of flame and they believed they were seeing the end of the world. The nuns told him that they were strangely protected from the atomic rays by their white habits. Others in the same convent wearing black robes were severely burnt.

Lieut. Commander Hudson said that, despite the terrific devastation, Nagaskai had still escaped comparatively 'lightly'. If the bomb had fallen at the opposite end of the city the blast would have been unobstructed by cloud masses, and might have obliterated everything.

HMS *Speaker* brought from Manila more than 600 former prisoners.

From R. C. Hill, VSIS *Fort Wrangell*

On arrival at Canadian Naval Depot we were informed the ship would not be ready for six weeks, so were found private accommodation. The VSIS *Fort Wrangell* sailed late December 1944, we called at San Pedro, and then Sydney, before the BPF arrived.

I believe there were 4 or 8 store ships, *Fort Wrangell, Fort Alabama, Fort Dunuegan, Fort Beauharrais*, I'm afraid that's all I can remember! as you know our job was to keep the Fleet at sea.

We flew the Blue Ensign and always berthed at Musgrove Street Wharf.

The *Fort Wrangell* visited Manus, Eniwetok, Hong Kong, Shanghai plus some other places.

We arrived in Tokyo Bay about August 27th and remained for the Surrender, after which we sailed for Sydney, with a dozen or so POWs on board.

Extract from a Hong Kong Newspaper

ONE OF NAVY'S FLOATING SHOPS HERE

In Hong Kong on her first call here is the VSIS *Fort Wrangell* from Sydney and Manus en route to Shanghai and Japan. As a member of the Fleet Train the *Fort Wrangell* may be described as a floating shop. One of the eight ships of a similar type, she is one of sixteen victualling stores issue ships operating in the Indian Ocean since mid-1944 and supplying the Pacific Fleet throughout the operations.

When peace was signed, the *Fort Wrangell* was the first supply vessel in Tokyo Bay and replenished all the ships there with stores, including the escort carriers *Ruler* and *Speaker* which she specially equipped with bedding, cigarettes, tobacco, food and clothing so that they could immediately embark released prisoners of war for Australia.

The *Fort Wrangell* has 'delivery vans'. These are small motor craft carried on her upper deck which can take ten tons of cargo

Orders from ships, however, are usually supplied by sliding them across a wire rope (jack-stay). The record for a single jack-stay is nine tons, supplied to the *Newfoundland* in one hour while at the same time another jack-stay was working on the other side of the ship at the rate of five tons and hour.

At Sydney, the *Fort Wrangell* performed the unique feat of signing on a ship's doctor who is feminine, believed to be the only one in the British Fleet. Dr. Hotchkinson, who is an Australian, is described as efficient and meticulous on the point of hygiene. Approached by our reporter for more information on herself, she said that now that she had been found there was no escaping the fact being reported, but she was personally publicity shy.

Fully Equipped Hospital

The *Fort Wrangell* carries a fully equipped hospital, and in Fleet Train operations she carried additional X-ray equipment and clinical gear in order to supply any ship which might have had its own damaged in action. Frozen blood, plasma and penicillin were also available.

The ship carries a Merchant Navy Captain, Capt. A. Stanley, and a crew of about 150. In the good old days, she had a whole deck devoted to rum, in order to keep the Fleet supplied. She carries personnel with duties out of the ordinary line and as many as eight engineers. Three are required on the refrigerating system.

While employed as one of the Navy's floating shops, she has often had to make issues in operational areas while all ships were on the move. Occasionally a ship's telephone would be passed across by firing a line, and the 'shopkeeper' would be asked if he had any pickles or brown bootlaces.

Ships other than those borne on the Admiralty's books at home paid cash for their goods. The money was passed over the jack-stay in a tin can—and the receipt was returned in the same way.

Eight Before Breakfast

After peace was signed in the Pacific, the victualling ships eventually returned to Australia with stacks of unissued goods in their holds. Everything on board is stowed for quick and easy access, all clearly marked in shelves and special drawers. It is just like a well-stocked wholesale shop.

The *Fort Wrangell*'s records include one supplying eight destroyers with all their requirements before breakfast one morning. The biggest single sea issue to one ship took about five hours from the time she came alongside to the time she left. Eight tons of goods were supplied.

She was built in Vancouver, Canada, to Admiralty specifications for duties with the Fleet Train, and these have included supplying any type of vessel from a hospital ship to a motor fishing boat. Supplies carried included anything from a pair of pyjamas to a box of cornflakes or a bar of soap to a packet of herbs.

In his letter, J. Jenkinson of SS* Ambrosio *enclosed a menu from The Trocadero Cafe, Sydney, which I was fascinated to see:

'Our Motto—Civility and Promptness'

Grilled Rump Steak—1/9d Roast Lamb 1/6d (!)

He added:

I hope you make a point of how us young kids handled the conditions and those long, seemingly endless days at sea.

I was transported to the BPF in HMS *Pioneer* to Sydney, a few days under canvas in *Golden Hind*. A plane ride to Brisbane which I would not recommend. I was sick all the way, much to the amusement of some Aussie WRAFS who travelled with us. We joined the *San Ambrosio* there and sailed for the Islands. Little did we know then the next time we stepped on dry land would be in Hong Kong many months later after the war had finished.

I left the *San Ambrosio* there, after a month or so and was transported down to Sydney on HMS *Slinger*. By that time I had, like a lot of the lads, contracted skin trouble, so instead of the bright lights of Sydney, it was hospital for a week or two. From there we joined HMS *Formidable* and home round the Cape. I was better by that time, so we did get a few days in Cape Town.

My second son was born with skin trouble 15 years later and suffers from it to this day. Was he another casualty of a war that ended 15 years before he was born? I have often wondered.

I had a pal on the ship but only got to know him well after. Like a lot of lads you only knew them in the terms Paddy, Jock, Yorkie, Geordie, etc.

We never saw any action on board *San Ambrosio* so there are no glory tales to tell and I think after it was all over we looked back on the fighting ships with some kind of envy. But on listening to some of the *Formidable* lads one night on our way home, one of them pointed to the lads and said they could not have done it without us—meaning the Fleet Train. That made our day.

Article by Mrs. G. M. Schofield from the magazine of RN Museum Portsmouth, sent by Paddy Vincent, HMS *Swiftsure*

On 23 April 1945, the 56,000 ton *Nieuw Amsterdam*, the pride of Holland, sailed from Greenock with 6,000 service personnel and crew on board. With overnight stops at Suez and Fremantle, she arrived in Sydney, Australia, on 23 May. The Japanese War was at that time estimated to continue for another two years.

On board were 16 WRNS officers and 200 ratings for various posts on the staff of Admiral Sir Bruce Fraser, C-in-C British Pacific Fleet, all of whom had either been called up or had answered the call years before to 'Join the Wrens and free a man for the Fleet'.

On arrival in Sydney the WRNS were distributed between Sydney and Melbourne, where they served in numerous capacities, among which were the following—Secretarial (PAs), Intelligence, WRNS Administration, WRNS Quarters, Press, Cinema, and Plotting.

In Melbourne, signals were received relating to the movements of RN ships, the Fleet Train and some merchant ships. This information was all recorded by WRNS ratings on a card index filing system so that at any time details of a particular ship were available. From this information officers kept a huge wall chart showing the positions of all ships in the operational area—Manus, the naval base north of Australia in the Admiralty Islands, and beyond.

I had good shorthand and typing speeds, and so had been selected by the late Captain Anthony Kimmins RN to serve on his staff of NILDIV in Sydney. Within a few weeks of our arrival, eight reporters and photographers representing various newspapers and I were sent to Fremantle, 2,000 miles away to interview Commander A. R. Hezlet RN and his crew who had just arrived in Fremantle. Their submarine *Trenchant* had recently sunk the Japanese heavy cruiser *Ashigara* in the Banka Strait off Sumatra, thus reducing the Japanese naval forces in SE Asia to no more than a sorry remnant.

From LSBA(O) Norman J Burt

HMHS Tjitjalengka *steaming alongside VSIS* Fort Wrangell. *Photo: R. C. Hill*

HMHS *Tjitjalengka* was a modern and fully equipped Hospital Ship of the Royal Navy and at 14,000 tons was large enough to carry at least 500 casualties, having been converted from a Dutch liner of the 'Java, China, Japan Line', which escaped from Holland just before the German occupation. The crew was made up of the original Dutch Captain and Officers and Chinese crew and Medical staff headed by the Senior Medical Officer, Surgeon Captain Campbell, together with the Medical Officers and about 90 ratings from the RN Sick Berth branch and 6 nursing sisters of Queen Alexandra RN Nursing Service.

Commissioned in October 1942 the ship was based with the Fleet at Freetown, Mombassa and at Trincomalee and finally joined the British Pacific Fleet arriving at the Rendezvous area on 13th May 1945, 3 days sailing north of Leyte. We maintained station in this 5 mile square area where the fleet could contact us immediately we were needed. A plane would be sent from an aircraft carrier and it would circle round us using a lamp to flash directions as to how to find the fleet. During the day we could be seen for miles away in our distinctive all white colour, and of course at night time, the ship was fully lit with flood lights illuminating all the red crosses on the sides and deck. On reaching the Fleet we would be escorted through the destroyer screen by a cruiser, which would then follow us in, dropping depth charges behind us in case any Japanese submarine should try to come in under cover of our propellers. The casualties had previously been collected from the other ships by a destroyer which then came alongside on a parallel course to our Hospital Ship transferring the casualties in a cot using the same technique as with a Bosun's chair. Once casualties had been transferred the Hospital ship would then return to the rendezvous area.

The Fleet Train

After re-patriation of POWs:

HMS *Archer* became SS *Empire Logan*
HMS *Attacker* became SS *Costel Forte*
HMS *Chaser* became SS *Aagte Kerk*
HMS *Fencer* became SS *Sydney*
HMS *Stalker* became SS *Pioneer*
HMS *Activity* became SS *Breconshire*
HMS *Campania* became SS *Festival of Britain Ship*
HMS *Vindex* became SS *Port Vindex.*

From PO SM Fred Caffery, HMS *Berwick* and HMS *Royalist*

We entered Singapore with *KGV, Victorious,* yes and even French battlewagon *Richeliue* and on arrival (we were going in to engage) the *Suffolk* had been alongside 5 days. I had the pleasure of seeing soldiers of the 14th army with rifles and bayonets prodding Jap arses whilst sweeping the streets of Singapore with bundles of twigs.

Royalist became flagship of NZ Navy, so I was told.

From Geoffrey Tomlinson, HMS *Chaser* 1943—1946

HMS *Chaser* was an AVG hull, built at Ingalls shipyard, Passagoula, USA and transferred to the Royal Navy on 9th April 1943 when she was converted into an Escort Carrier.

In the new year 1945 Captain R. G. Poole took over from Captain McClintock; and after collecting her squadron (399) of Seafires from Belfast, *Chaser* worked up in the Firth of Clyde and then sailed to Australia.

Chaser was ready to join the Pacific Fleet in time to celebrate VE Day. The following weeks were largely uneventful as far as any action was concerned, until the build up to the final assault on Japan saw the assembly of a vast fleet of British and American warships, stretching from horizon to horizon. Then the atom bombs—and VJ Day—and the dispersal of the fleet, with *Chaser* ordered to Hong Kong for the official surrender of the island by the Japanese. She was soon sent back to Sydney, with a considerable number of civilians who had been interned since the capture by the Japanese. For the next few months, as part of the fleet Train, *Chaser* made regular trips to Hong Kong and back to Sydney carrying personnel and cargo in each direction.

In February 1946, *Chaser* was ordered to return to UK, again with a considerable number of passengers. After home leave, a much reduced ship's company sailed her back to the USA with several hundred passengers and returned her to the US Navy on 12th May. She was later converted back to a cargo ship, and renamed *Aagte Kerk*.

Tokyo Bay. Article from an un-named magazine

Broadcasting from the *Duke of York* last Saturday night, BBC correspondent Stanley Maxted referred to the British Pacific Fleet's Logistic Support Group as the Service Force which had none of the glory and plenty of hard work.

'I have just been talking to Captain Love who is in command of the Logistic Support Group,' he proceeded, 'and he names them for me as they lie at anchor. There are the two escort carriers who carry spare aircraft and pilots, HMS *Speaker* and HMS *Ruler*. There is the Hospital Ship *Tjitjalengka*, whose crew is Dutch and whose doctors and nursing sisters are from the Royal Navy. Then there is the Victualling and Store Ship SS *Fort Wrangell*, who sends us everything over life-line and jackstay.

Then there are the escort sloops: HMS *Pheasant* who gets most of the dirty work, because, says Captain Love she has me and my staff on board her to worry about; and HMS *Crane* who claims she is the first of the group to drop anchor off Japan; HMS *Woodcock* whose Captain is the youngest commanding officer in escort vessels; HMS *Derg* who spent a long time in the East Indies escorting slow convoys in the Indian Ocean. And then there are the four Australian minesweepers *Ballarat, Ipswich, Pire* and *Cessnock*.

They are all a husky bunch of workmen, and without them the Fleet could not have operated, so it is only right that they should be riding out here at anchor, and be on hand when the signing on the dotted line puts an end to the additional hazards of their work that war always imposes.'

From CPO R. Scott, HMS *Tyrian*

When VJ Day arrived, the *Tyrian,* three other British destroyers, two British cruisers and two Hospital Ships were quickly formed into Task Force 28, with orders to proceed to Keelung in Formosa and get the allied prisoners of war out. We were then ordered to Woosung outside Shanghai to wait for the Americans. We opened up Shanghai. Then on to Hong Kong and opened up the Port. The captain then called lower deck and told us he was ordered to take the ship back to Sydney taking the passage between the Aussie mainland and the Great Barrier Reef which we were surprised to find was 1260 miles long.

Some recollections of TSMV *Menestheus* (RN Amenity Ship), December 1945—May 1946 by Dr. A. J. A. Ferguson, Medical Officer

TSNV Menestheus*—Shanghai 1946. Photo: J. Haddock*

The Blue Funnel Line cargo/passenger ship *Menestheus* had already been converted to serve as a mine-layer and her conversion from this to an amenity ship was to be her third rôle since she first came into service in 1929.

I have always believed that the thinking behind the conversion of *Menestheus* to an amenity ship was as follows: If the Pacific Fleet Train's purpose was to fuel, victual and repair the fleet at sea there why not provide the fleet with all (or nearly all) the amenities which were available ashore but which the huge distances involved in the Pacific war precluded. Assuming that the idea originated from their Lordships then they should be congratulated on its originality and the superb final result.

The original plan was to convert two sister ships, *Menestheus* and *Agamemnon*, in Vancouver but with the sudden and unpredicted end to the Pacific war the conversion of *Agamemnon* was abandoned and, disappointingly, so was the idea of allowing a detachment of Wrens in both ships! However the conversion and manning of *Menestheus* had reached the stage that there was no point in abandoning the project and it was, in the opinion of many, as nice a piece of one-upmanship over our American allies as could be imagined. Whatever they may have thought of they had never known of anything like this!

Menestheus sailed under the Red Ensign, the watch-keeping officers, Engineer officers and wireless operators were all Merchant Navy and were under the command of Captain Percy Purkis MN. They were all very experienced, the more senior ones in peace time service as well as war time service. The Chief Engineer, whose name I forget, had a DSC. I found them all very friendly although I believe there was an occasional niggle of rivalry between the two services.

The RN party was under the command of Commander J. M. D. Hunter RN and consisted of about 125 ratings, PO's, CPO's and a Master-at-Arms. They came from various branches of the service—seamen, signallers, electricians, SBA's and so on. A large number were canteen assistants and stewards. The Royal Navy officers (all RNVR at that time except Commander Hunter) could be divided into two groups—those associated with the theatrical company and the other amenities of the ship such as the brewery and the bars, the buffets, cafeterias, shops, etc. and those who were not. Among the latter were Lieut. Commander (S) Frank Ballard RNVR, Lieut. John Haddock RNVR (First Lieutenant), the Padre, the Rev. John Nickels RNVR and myself.

PART THREE

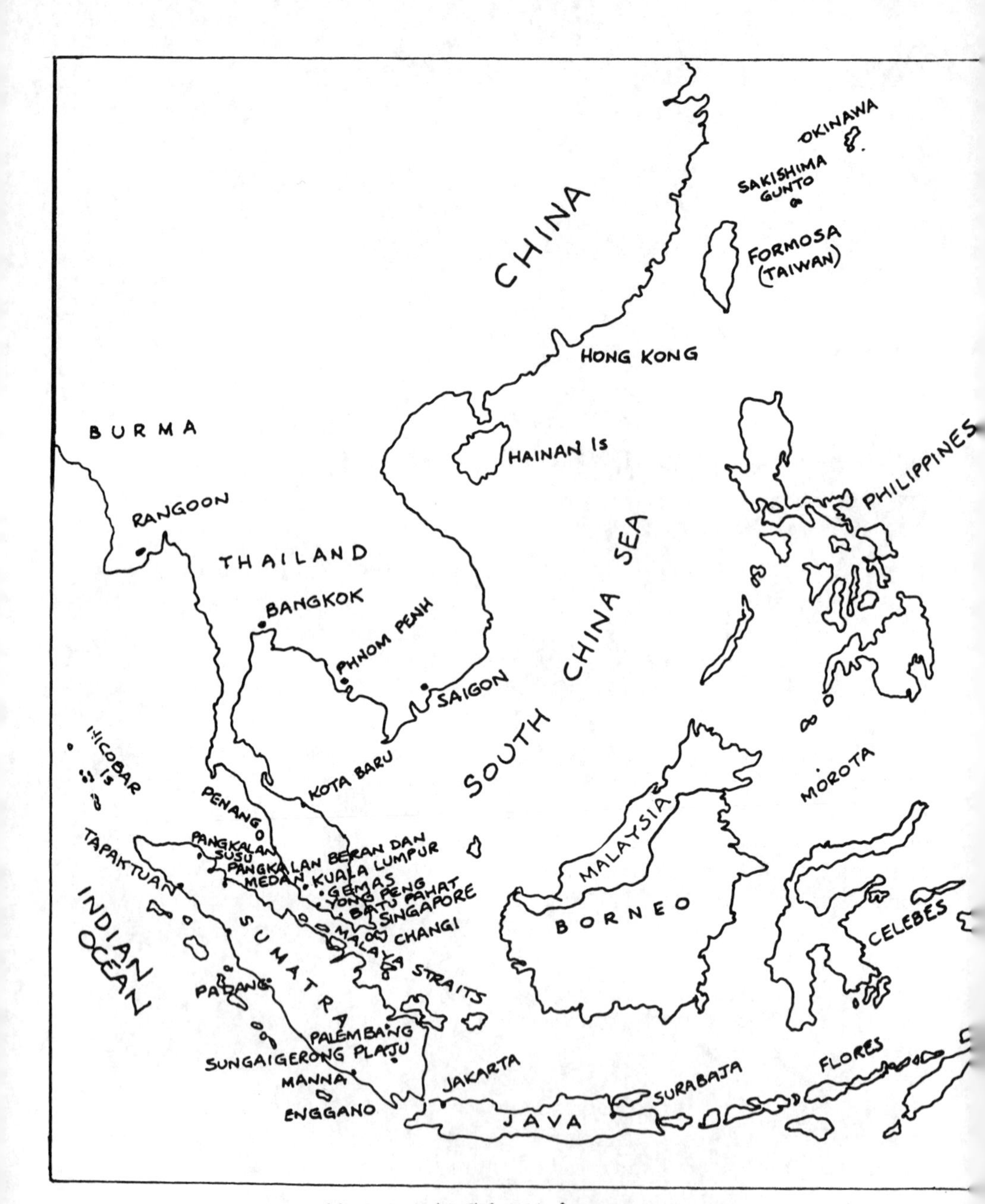

WESTERN INDONESIA

CHAPTER NINE

The Aftermath

From Royal Marine Bob Putland, HMS *KGV*

MESSAGE OF ADMIRAL WILLIAM F. HALSEY, COMMANDER THIRD FLEET TO THE OFFICERS AND MEN OF THE THIRD FLEET 15th AUGUST 1945

The war is ended. You in conjunction with your brothers in arms of all services have contributed inestimably to this final result. Our fighting men have brought an implacable, treacherous and barbaric foe to his knees in abject surrender. This is the first time in the recorded history of the misbegotten Japanese race that they as a nation have been forced to submit to this humiliation.

I said in 1942 the Nips were no supermen. You have helped write *finis* on that estimate in 1945. Your names are written in golden letters on the pages of history, your fame is and shall be immortal. Wherever you have met the foe, on the sea, on the land or in the air, you have been supreme. From early days of fighting with a very frayed shoestring to the finish of fighting with the mightiest combined fleet the world has ever seen, the results have been the same, victory has crowned your efforts, the forces of righteousness and decency have triumphed.

At this moment our thoughts go out to our happy and fortunate homeland, to our loved ones. Deeply rooted in each and every heart is a desire, now that the tumult of war has ceased and victory, absolute and unconditional victory, has crowned our efforts, to return to our homes.

A simple process of thinking will demonstrate how impossible this is at the moment. The boredom, the homesickness, the periods of fear, the tragedy, the sweat, the blood we have shed so freely, these have been endured by all with fortitude and brotherly comradeship and gladly. This a common and proud possession of each and every rank and rating. We are and shall always remain a band of brothers tried in the fire of the greatest holocaust this world has ever experienced and because of this, indissoluble. That which we fought and bled and died for has become a reality. That reality cannot be—must not be—transient, it must rest on firm foundations. The structure that we build must be so firm that the storms of all ages to come cannot touch the surface. Because of your fighting qualities and the fighting qualities of our brothers in arms of all services, our beloved land has not known the ravages of war, our dear ones at home have not been endangered.

Give praise to the God Almighty for this and give humble thanks that he saw fit to use us as his instruments.

Victory is not the end. Rather it is but the beginning. We must establish a peace, a firm, a just and enduring peace; a peace that will enable all decent nations to live without fear and in prosperity; a peace that will glorify the inherent dignity and nobility of mankind. Never again should we permit the enslavement of decent human beings—never again should tyrants be permitted to rise in a civilised world. To attain this requires unremitting toil over a period of years. The enemy over the entire world is conquered and has been forced to bow his collected knee to us the victors. He is unregenerate. It is our cross, our duty to make him regenerate. This cannot be done in a day. It may take decades and generations. The present and immediate duty of the Third Fleet is crystal clear. We must in conjunction with all Allied Forces so employed reduce Nippon to military impotency. We must keep him militarily impotent. Following this it is imperative that instrumentalities be set up to educate them and divorce the Japanese from their barbaric traditions, teachings and thoughts. This is a matter of common sense, good judgement, policy and tenacity of purpose and will require military might for implementation and very wisest understanding statesmanship.

From Captain P. M. C. Vincent, CBE, RN: *BBC Broadcast to the nation by Commander Anthony Kimmins RN*, August Bank Holiday 1945

THE FORGOTTEN FLEET

British Carriers and the Fleet Air Arm reached a glorious peak in the Pacific during 1945. Yet, in Britain, following the end of the war in Europe (VE Day), the British press literally ignored the existence of a vast Royal Naval Fleet still at war with Japan. Men of the Fleet bitterly complained (with justification) that they were the Forgotten Fleet. Strikes against the islands of Japan were all credited to the American Navy, until the day that Commander Anthony Kimmins RN made the following broadcast to the Nation over all BBC wavelengths.

Only a few days ago I was in the Pacific, and in a few more days I shall be back there again. I flew here from Australia in exactly two days almost to the minute, and yet, d'you know, the moment I stepped out of my aeroplane and found myself amongst the lovely green English countryside, Australia and the Pacific suddenly seemed just as far off as if I'd been about six weeks on the journey.

Now why is that? It is largely, I suppose, because—however fast one may have covered the distance—one is still very conscious of the fact that the Pacific lies on almost the opposite side of the world, and that while it is mid-winter in Australia it is mid-summer over here.

But there's another factor even more telling, I think, which makes it so awfully difficult to come to real grips in one's thoughts with what is going on on the opposite side of the world—the difference in our daily time, the difference in our watches. Here, now, in London, it is late evening, and we shall shortly be thinking of going to bed, but for the men of the British Pacific Fleet the day has only just started. And that is all very confusing, isn't it?

When, during the European war, someone who was very dear to you was fighting close by in the North Sea or in the Channel, and you knew that he was sharing the same time of day, the same sun, moon or rain, it was very easy—as you looked out of your window—to build up a real picture of him in your mind and so be able to feel very close to him in your good wishes and in your prayers.

But, today, when that same man is fighting in the Pacific on the opposite side of the world, that full moon, instead of being a helpful link, is just the opposite, for its cool caressing beams remind you instinctively that he is probably sweltering under a fierce tropical sun.

I know that for our part, our there, on such days as VE Day and Election Day, we all found it very difficult to think about what was going on at home except in the most general terms.

When, for instance, I tried to imagine what my wife and family were doing at some particular moment, and wrestled in my mind as to whether I ought to add or subtract ten hours to our local time, and finally decided that she was having a bath tomorrow morning, it all became too confusing and unreal and I gave it up.

And so, when I hear complaints that people here at home aren't taking sufficient interest in the Pacific War, I sympathize because I realise all too well how difficult it is for you here at home to concentrate your thoughts on your friends or relations in the British Pacific Fleet. Nature and circumstances have very unkindly intervened, rather like a fog which suddenly shuts out your favourite view. But somehow we have got to try and see through that fog, for if ever any men deserved your thoughts and your good wishes at this moment, it is those men who are fighting that grim and dangerous war out there.

So let's try and break down that barrier. Let's think of them for a moment now. Don't worry whether it is night or day, for actually it doesn't make much difference, because they are almost continuously at action stations throughout the twenty-four hours. They are off the coast of Japan at this moment—very close—impertinently close. They have been there for several weeks and will be for many weeks more.

Our British Task Force, under the command of Admiral Sir Bernard Rawlings, is, at the moment, fighting alongside the American Task Forces and the whole vast fleet is under the command of Admiral Halsey, that great character and fearless fighter. I was sitting with him in his cabin a few weeks back, discussing the present operations. It was a sweltering hot day and Admiral Halsey was stripped to the waist and wearing only a pair of shorts and an old pair of sandals. But 'Bull' Halsey is one of those unmistakable admirals who doesn't need gold braid and decorations to remind you of his position. There is a glint in his eyes and a direct approach in his colourful speech which tells you immediately that here is a real sea dog with wide experience and tremendous powers of leadership, and how he hates the Japs!

'This time,' he said, 'we are going right in to hit those little yellow so-and-so's just where it hurts most, and I am mighty proud to have a British Task Force with me.' And so that is what our British Task Force is doing at this moment. Getting into the ring whenever possible, taking the fight right into the enemy's corner, and hitting the Japanese just where it hurts most. Our Task Force is letting fly continuous rights with bombs from its naval aircraft, and in betweenwhiles lashing out with shattering lefts, the heavy guns of the battleships and cruisers. But this is no wild 'free-for-all'. It is a carefully thought out plan of rights and lefts and occasional feints, with the main object of uncovering and dealing a knock-out blow on the enemy's solar plexus—his communications.

Now Japan happens to be very vulnerable as regards her communications. Her islands being long and thin, there is nothing like the network of rail communications that we had to deal with on the Continent. In Japan the main railway lines run down the length of the islands and, as in the southern half, most of the railways are single track, a well-placed load of bombs can do devastating damage. But at the same time the Japs are experts at effecting repairs, so the destruction has to be kept up continuously.

Super Forts and Mustangs, based on the Marianas and Okinawa, and naval aircraft from our carriers, have been concentrating on the Jap aerodromes to keep down their air power and then letting fly at those vital internal lines of communication, so as to force the Jap to forsake his roads and railways and use sea traffic. Then more naval aircraft and the big guns of our ships plaster his ports and sea communications until finally—under cover of darkness—he has to resort to using junks, sampans, schooners, and any old craft he can find to slip through the inland sea between Honshu and Kyushu in a desperate effort to maintain contact with his rapidly diminishing production plants on the mainland.

But even at night those junks and sampans aren't safe, because our destroyers sneak in beneath the shore batteries and play havoc with them.

And so it goes on—day after day and night after night—the gradual but intensive wearing down. It's like a boxing match on a huge scale, except that here it's a fight to the finish with no gloves on—where there are no timekeepers, and the main idea is to keep in the ring for as long as possible and reduce the time out with your seconds to a minimum.

And—there's another great difference. In European waters our seconds, without whom the fighting man and his ships couldn't possibly keep going in the ring, were well established dockyards with every conceivable modern device for repairing ships, and precious shore-leave to revive the men. But out in the Pacific there's nothing like that. In fact, our nearest docking facilities for big ships are down in Australia, 4,000 miles from the actual scene of action.

Just try and imagine what that means. It's as if we were based on Portsmouth and trying to fight the enemy off Brazil. Now, obviously, it would be impossible to return all the way to Portsmouth every time the fleet had to replenish with oil fuel, stores and ammunition. The enemy would be left unmolested for far too long. But that was the problem which faced Sir Bruce Fraser when his fleet arrived in the Pacific. There was only one possible solution. As the fleet couldn't return to its seconds, those seconds—the repair and supply ships known as the Fleet Train—must be afloat and waiting handy for the fleet the moment it comes out of the striking area.

Try and imagine the scene. The Task Force arriving over the horizon, their guns scorched from hours of bombardment. The huge aircraft carriers, men frantically repairing the aircraft down in the hangars—some too badly damaged must be ditched over the side.

The Fleet Train steaming round in circles at the rendezvous. No ship must stop for a moment or they would be at the mercy of Jap submarines.

And then by a series of manoeuvres the Task Force and the Fleet Train split up and in a few moments oilers and supply ships are approaching the battleship or aircraft carrier they have to replenish. Coston guns are fired and heaving lines fly across between the ships; a few seconds later hose pipe and jack stays are hauled across between the gap and the precious oil fuel, ammunition, supplies and mails pour in to top them up for the next round.

And all the while they steam on looking rather like a giant three-legged race while the ever faithful destroyers screen them against any Jap submarine who may dare to interfere. And all this at a time of year when typhoons and heavy seas are a constant menace. If ever there was an expression of the value of sea power, this is it.

Now what is the Jap doing to counteract these tremendous blows our Task Forces are dealing out on his homeland? During the present operations he is so far doing remarkably little. Whether this is entirely due to the tremendous damage that has already been done to his aircraft factories and petrol installations or whether he is reserving his aircraft for the invasion remains to be seen. But make no mistake, when that invasion eventually takes place it is going to be a most costly and hazardous affair. Distances and the supply problem will make it far more difficult than that on D Day in Normandy.

Up till now, of course, his main countermeasure had lain in suicide attacks by members of the Kamikaze Corps. I have seen several of these attacks and, believe me, they are a strange form of warfare to have to compete with. I have watched Hun divebombers come screaming down at our ships, and have frankly admired their guts. I have watched buzz bombs spluttering towards our cities and despised the use of such a diabolical weapon. But, when the suiciders come down out of the skies, it is neither one thing nor the other. It is something strange and unreal. Something almost beyond one's comprehension. What, one cannot help wondering, is going on in his mind as he starts that last desperate dive to certain death with his feet padlocked to the rudder bars. Is he drunk with saki, is he doped, or is he just fanatically obsessed? I don't know, but I do know that each time as I have watched that final dive, watched the tracer racing up to meet him, I felt instinctively that here was something inhuman coming at you, a sort of robot bomb with a strange ability to twist and turn.

On one occasion I got a very close view of one. Much too close. He was coming straight at us and although he must have been hit several times before, he didn't start to flame until he was about 500 feet off. No doubt the pilot was already dead by now, but on came his aircraft, plunging drunkenly towards us until it eventually crashed across the flying deck, only a few yards away from me. At that moment I caught a fleeting glimpse of a figure in what looked like a green hood hunched up over the controls. A fraction of a second later it had crashed through a pom-pom and exploded as it went over the side. As it blew up, a lot of pieces were thrown back on to the flying deck—bits of joss, a lucky bracelet, a broken statuette with a head missing, and other things which I won't describe, but which had once been flesh and blood. It feels odd saying it now, but at the time the sudden reminder that a living person had been in that aircraft came as quite a shock.

Often, of course, the attacks are more effective. I saw one aircraft carrier hit amidships, and, with the first flash as the bomb exploded, great clouds of smoke started pouring up from her flying deck. From where I watched, horrified, it looked as if everyone on that deck must have been killed or suffocated. But another Kamikaze was on the way and to my amazement, tracer went racing up through the pall of smoke as strong as ever. Those gun crews were going to fight for their ship to the bitter end.

I was standing alongside Admiral Vian, commanding our aircraft carriers at the time. He was watching anxiously, but refused to send any signal asking the extent of the damage. He knew those men on board were all too busy saving their ship; at last a light flickered from her bridge 'Little Yellow Basket'. Within two hours that light flickered again—'All ready to continue operation'.

Yes, it is a strange and tough war out there. A war in which the men of the British Pacific Fleet and their seconds, the Fleet Train, are enduring a strain unequalled in Naval history. For weeks and months on end they remain at sea. There are no week-ends, no Bank Holidays for them.

They have few distractions except the thrill of battle and the ever longed for mails. Beyond that it's the same constant throb of the engines, the interminable blue of the Pacific, the identical flying fish scudding out the way, and the same incessant strain.

But each one of those ships, whether a great battleship, an aircraft carrier or one of the ever faithful destroyers, is a little piece of our homeland. It may be much hotter than here. It may be far more dangerous. But in between his heat of battle you'll hear the same voices, the same jokes and laughter as you'd find in any group here at home.

So do give those men a thought during this August Bank Holiday.

There will be no time off for them. They'll be far too busy risking their lives in their determination to defeat the Japs, so that you and I may enjoy the fruits of peace. Give them a thought as you take a well earned rest—the gun-crews at action stations; the pilots waiting to take off on the next raid; the men sweltering down in the boiler and engine rooms. Your men of the British Pacific Fleet.

An Australian War Correspondent's report of his experiences are worth including, especially as he was not influenced by loyalty to a 'unit' other than his own country.

WITH THE BRITISH PACIFIC FLEET
FAST CARRIER FORCE
(Aboard HMAS Napier*)*

ESCORT DUTY FOR
RAN DESTROYERS

Our turn had come to join the British Pacific Fleet Fast Carrier force, which, to us, was the most important assignment any fleet destroyer could be given. Working with a task group is a wonderful experience. The group leaves the refuelling area and goes to a position from where planes are flown off the four carriers, *Formidable, Victorious, Indomitable* and *Indefatigable,* to strafe and bomb Japan. The British Fleet worked under direct order of American 3rd Fleet, and each strike day was given a specific area and targets to attack. . . .

If their own radar equipment does not pick up approaching enemy aircraft they are warned in advance by the carriers, which carry larger radar equipment. If an enemy plane comes in low enough, the destroyers open fire with anti-aircraft weapons. If the attacking plane passes through their defence, the cruisers open up, and if the plane is once again successful, the carriers defend themselves with the terrific fire power they possess.

Strike day starts at first possible light, and does not finish until darkness falls. For the whole time crews on all ships are at action stations. Almost all are on their feet the whole time. At dawn on the day of attack, one of the carriers flies off a patrol to report the general situation in the target area. This includes visibility for bombing and amount of air or anti-aircraft opposition.

On its return, the first strike of bombers—usually about 12 or 20—leave their carriers. Strikes are taking off and coming back all through the day, while the carriers and their escorts continually sweep around in circles, turning and twisting within a small area. . . .

All ships' crews wear special clothing in case of enemy attack. Rig of the day is a shirt, long trousers tucked into socks, boots or shoes, a type of balaclava which comes down over the head with enough length to be tucked into the shirt and with only the eyes and nose protruding, thick gloves which reach almost to the elbow, steel helmet and cotton wool. On a hot day the dress is most uncomfortable, but affords everyone protection from bomb-blast, fire or flying pieces of hot metal or acid. *(White Anti-Flash gear.—Ed.)*

When enemy planes are picked up on radar, the whole fleet receives the signal by voice in plain language 'Flash blue'. Our radar information was so good that it was possible for every ship in the Task Force to know within seconds how many planes there were, in what direction they were flying, their altitude, their speed, often the type of plane, and from what direction they would be likely to attack.

On receipt of this information, according to their position on the screen, cruisers and destroyers warned their gun crews and trained their guns in pre-arranged directions. Quite often we had warning of possible enemy planes approaching 20 minutes' flying time away.

GOOD WORK BY INTERCEPTORS

Simultaneous with notification of enemy planes going to ships it is despatched to our own aircraft patrols, which form an umbrella over the Task Group. *(CAP—Combat Air Patrol.—Ed.)* They break into sections and what we call 'Interceptors'—there might be four of them—fly fast toward the enemy planes, which our radar operators are tracking in and providing information of, about every half-minute. Three American Task Groups always operated closely to us and information any Task Group had from its radar operators concerning the approach of enemy aircraft was distributed by voice to all others. All the Task Groups were about the same size.

During the Sakishimas operation some months before, the British Fleet was attacked constantly by Japanese aircraft and when members of the Fleet returned to Sydney for refit before we came away with them, they were equipped with additional anti-aircraft weapons. *(40mm Bofors had replaced many 20mm Oerlikons.—Ed.)*

No praise is high enough for our interceptors. With the help of radar one day, they found an on-coming enemy plane when conditions were just like pea soup. You feel so useless on the bridge of a destroyer knowing that a 'bogey' is on its way, and all you can do is to sit and wait, while reports come in of its bearing and height.

But if you're lucky, your air information centre on the ship, which is in constant touch with carriers, will shout through the public address system 'tally ho, one bogey', which indicates that the interceptors have done their work well.

Many officers' meals are taken to them on the bridge or at their action stations, which many do not leave, except for calls of nature. . . .

Throughout the strike day, 'Flashes' are wirelessed from either the Task Force Commander or the carriers independently. These give the results of the various strikes, and an officer broadcasts them to the crews. Captain Buchanan usually did this himself, and on one occasion broadcast a description of one of our planes coming in to land. The plane made several attempts, but apparently did not have the speed or height, and it made five dummy runs before it pancaked on to the flight deck. What remained of the undercarriage was torn apart, but the pilot was uninjured.

A bad crash by a returning plane on its flight deck is as much a nuisance as it is dangerous. If a strike is returning, and one plane crashes on the deck it may burst into flames. If the fire spreads, it holds up the landing of the remaining planes. Apart from a delay in schedule, the planes coming in may be short of fuel, because they carry no excessive weight, which means no more fuel than is essential to get there and get back with a minimum of unnecessary manoeuvring.

During one of the air searches, one of our carrier planes landed too fast on the deck of the carrier and smashed into the island or bridge situated half-way along the carrier on the starboard side. The plane and the carrier burst into flames, but a damage control party was on the job within seconds. From the *Napier*'s bridge, we were near enough to see the fight they made.

The carrier's captain turned the ship around so that the breeze blew the flames away from inflammable sections as yet untouched. The control parties closed in on the flames with the wind behind them, and covered the area with foam, which has saved many Allied carriers in this war from destruction.

The *Napier* closed in on the carrier in case the fire spread.

We had our hoses on deck with fire-fighting parties ready to pour seawater on the blaze if help was needed. The pilot of the plane, although badly shaken, was able to release himself from the cockpit before the flames took control of his craft. He dragged himself along the wing, and was carried out of the way by members of the flight deck crew.

Our help was not required, and in 20 minutes the fire was extinguished. What remained of the plane was dumped in the ocean.

Sometimes it is impossible for returning aircraft, which have been hit by flak, to land with any degree of control and the pilot will signal his intention of crashing into the sea. Following each carrier at a few hundred yards interval is one destroyer. The pilot of the doomed plane attempts to pancake it on the water near his carrier and in advance of the destroyer, which makes full speed to the spot to pick up the crew. Australian destroyers *Quickmatch* and *Quiberon* have saved pilots in this manner.

Landing on a carrier is not easy, and planes have done some amazing things. One day an Avenger (a bomber with a crew of 3) which had been badly hit over the target area, hit the edge of the flight deck, careered a few hundred yards out to sea, and crashed. A destroyer rushed to the spot, and was astonished to find four men in the water. When the plane had hit the edge of the flight deck it had picked up a member of the ground staff, and taken him out to sea with it. . . .

RN DESTROYERS
MANNED BY RAN

Quickmatch and *Quiberon* escorted the British Pacific Fleet Fast Carrier Force for longer than any other Australian ships. Originally these two ships were in the Royal Navy, but were given to Australia for manning. Through most of its career *Quickmatch* has been commanded by Commander Humphrey Becher, DSO and Bar, of Sydney, but he was relieved in July, 1945, by Commander Walton, of Western Australia, who was commanding a Corvette Flotilla and succeeded Becher while *Quickmatch* was in the operational area.

Some identities were in *Quiberon*'s crew, for it boasted the fattest man in the RAN and also the slowest. The fat man was Chief Stoker Lynch, of New South Wales, who was awarded a BEM while on the *Warramunga* in 1944. He weighs nearly 25 stone and has been 22 years in the RAN. An Englishman, he joined an Essex regiment in the last war at 15, and was overseas at 16.

The slow character was the captain's servant. His nickname because of his 'speed', was 'Bow Wave'. Many stories are told of him. Here is one. One night he was on duty in the wheelhouse, guiding the ship. The officer of the watch noticed his course astray, and shouted down the voicepipe what sounded like 'Who the hell is on the wheel?' 'Bow Wave', who, like a Dickens' character, 'kept falling asleep', straightened with a start, and looking quickly at the Quartermaster, whose name was Beswick, shouted back, 'AB Wheel on harbor, Sir, 10 deg. Beswick on.' I believe this story now has almost reached the Australian Naval Board.

I wrote in my diary:

August 20th—

August 19 had been a big night. In the wardroom of the *Napier* we had been playing dice until very late and 'splicing the main brace'. During the late evening a signal arrived, putting the landing party on eight hours' notice. 'Buck' had selected 34 officers and men from the *Napier* and about 15 from the *Nizam* to form Australia's representation as part of the British Fleet Occupation Force.

We laughed. We had seen those signals before. The landing party would be lucky if it moved out within three days we figured. Everyone was disgruntled by the already long delay in any movement of the occupation force that it looked as though we would be lucky to get to Japan at all. So we went to bed late, in anticipation of no hurry in the next eight hours.

On the *Napier* I lived in the First Lieutenant's day cabin, while he occupied a bunk under the bridge. His name was John Crabb, a permanent RAN officer. I climbed into my bunk. The next thing I remembered was a sharp flash of light, and I saw young Crabb standing before the mirror shaving in a hurry, while his cabin hand (good old Fogarty) was buzzing about.

I decided it was time to get up, so silently I half dressed, and went into the wardroom, yawning my head off, for a glass of cold water. And did I want it cold. My mouth felt like the inside of a bird cage. Then, for the first time, I looked at the clock. 4.45 a.m.! What is this? I made a quick rush to the cabin, to be told that the party had to be ready to disembark by 7 a.m.

So this was it.

For days we had been waiting for the word to go. The *Napier* and *Nizam* were the only two Australian vessels whose crews were included in the British Pacific Fleet Landing Party which consisted of more than 500 British marines and sailors, and sailors representing South Africa, New Zealand and Australia. The marines were equipped with heavy weapons, including mortars, in case there were Japanese who believed they should continue to oppose the Allies.

August 22nd
A conference was held today aboard the senior transport ship—one of some 50 or 60 with which we were moving slowly toward Japan. It was the first time that the *Sims* had transferred personnel at sea, and one of our officers was dumped into the 'drink' and a Major of the Marines came extremely close to it.

The Major is 'a character', and sports a moustache cultivated over years and which, I think, has never been trimmed. It is a sandy moustache sprouting out at the sides like a thick bush, and it is so big that it dwarfs the little Major's face. But he takes our chaffing with good humour. He has quite a family background to his career, and his presence here is almost historical.

His grandfather landed in Japan as a Lieutenant of Marines in 1858, when the British Government was asked by the Japanese to show the flag there, help to quell rebel risings, and, if possible, help to organise the Japanese Army.

His grandfather carried his regimental colours with him, and later the colours were returned to England, where they were placed in the regimental mess. Years later they were transferred to the regimental chapel at Plymouth, where they became more and more threadbare through age. One night a German plane bombed the chapel, and the colours were destroyed.

Our Major decided to take ashore with him a small replica of the regimental colours, which he intended to return to England to replace the lost ones (and I believe he did).

Another conference was held today, and we heard more of our operational plans, but we also had news of another delay. We would not land until the 28th, which means yet another week of stooging around the ocean. . . .

The Radio also announced that on Tuesday troops would land all around Tokyo Bay. The Japanese were warned not to fraternise with the occupation forces, but that the Government was prepared to supply the occupation forces with food and quarters, if required.

We gathered from the broadcast that all civilian transport had been cancelled and that Japanese troops were being withdrawn rapidly from the areas we are to occupy. We are all happy about this, because none of us wants to buy trouble.

There is never any friction between the Americans and the British boys. They constantly gibe each other, and this often leads to an exchange of some excellent stories.

Today I heard an Englishman told this story by a US seaman: 'Two Englishmen, two Australians and two Americans set up a bookmakers' ring, but the Englishmen did nothing because they hadn't been introduced.'

VIGIL OF THE PATROL BOATS

August 28th—

Commanded to place white flags over all their shore batteries, the Japanese carried out these orders late yesterday afternoon and this morning. There were scores of them, which gave us an indication of how stiff a fight it might have been had the Allies landed in Japan under wartime conditions.

Today we noticed that a lot of Japanese had come back to their homes, and were showing themselves more openly. Apparently they are satisfied that the Allies are not going to fire on them, provided they start no trouble, some of them even came down on to the rocks today to fish. Our fellows were not allowed fish, because it was considered by medical authorities that the fish would have been bad to eat.

Sagami Wan had been converted into a veritable fairyland—lights from scores of ships twinkled over the water. The lifting of the blackout must have surprised the Japanese ashore considerably, and there is no doubt many of them crept down to the cliff's edge to view this fairyland.

The first film we were shown was a Donald Duck, 'In the Army', which Japanese watching it, probably thought was a military training film. Everyone's spirits were high, and all laughed uproariously. Seeing thousands of lights around us was the first conclusive proof we have had that the war is over. It could easily have been a gala night on Sydney Harbour. Right around the harbour and under the shadow of Fujiyama, a ring of lights from the ships showed that every possible porthole had been opened. The ships were cooler than they had been since war began, and it was the first time films had been shown on decks of warships outside Allied harbours since before the war.

But security had not been lifted entirely. Patrol boats still kept a sharp lookout for possible visitors. Last night, one of these patrol boats picked up two prisoners of war—British Marines captured three years ago. They had escaped from their camp after hearing that the Allied Fleet was in Sagami Wan. They found it hard to believe, but when they reached the water's edge they found a Chesterfield cigarette carton, which had been washed to the shore from one of the ships. They began swimming towards the closest ship, and were picked up.

During the late afternoon today, the Japanese took the covers from their six-inch guns which surrounded the Bay. The Allies have not yet secured these, and the guns from the warships are trained on them in case any 'accidentally' opened fire. All types of Allied planes, both land-based and carrier-based, gave us a protective umbrella from early dawn.

We had enough planes to bomb the areas before we landed, but most of the coastal guns are set in deep caves, and the only way they could be neutralised would be by a direct hit from a bomb or a shell. The caves are set in the sides of sheer cliffs, and the war in the Philippines taught us that the Japanese were past masters in the art of caved artillery.

From here the Fleet in the harbour presents a mighty spectacle. There is enough there to give any enemy food for thought. This probably accounted for the almost complete absence of sight-seers on the day of our arrival. But the information must soon have passed around that we were not firing our guns, and that our sailors were not rushing ashore looting and raping.

Today quite a few townspeople could be seen walking up and down the promenade. One Japanese, riding a bicycle, suddenly saw our landing craft approaching, and beat a hasty retreat, leaving his bicycle in the middle of the roadway. But others barely gave us a glance, apparently satisfied that we had no designs of personal retribution.

Some beautiful two-storied homes stand behind the cottages further up the hill. My eye was taken by two modern fishing launches which lay on the sand. A few people were fishing from the rocks, and some others were swimming. The factories were closed.

No smoke came from their chimney stacks, and small railway trucks used to transport material were stationary. The country was remarkably green, and looked very beautiful but for all we knew the quality of the soil must have been very poor. Obviously almost all the villagers were of fishing stock. The small fences bordering their homes from the promenade were covered today with drying fishing nets.

CAPTAIN BUCHANAN ACCEPTS SURRENDER

August 30th—

After breakfast we saw the steep blue shores of Tokyo Bay. Our three APD's were travelling in line with our ship in front. As we came to the head of the harbour which had already been cleared of numerous mines by the Japanese and our own minesweepers, the party of New Zealanders who were to secure the island fortresses, began their journey in their landing craft.

They landed around 9.30 a.m., and were quickly well implanted on them. They met no opposition. On the contrary, in each case, Japanese officers came down to the shore to meet them, carrying pages of information which the force might need.

About 9.45 a.m., the marines landed at Azuma Peninsula, and at 10.40, the New Zealanders and Australians landed on the Japanese mainland at the Yokosuka base. Correspondents landed with Captain Buchanan. We left the APD in the usual type of landing craft, and after a few minutes' travel, entered a small basin.

At the end of it, and waiting under a verandah, which was joined to the roof of a store-house, stood three Japanese. As the landing craft sidled up to the small jetty, Captain Buchanan jumped ashore (making him the first Australian to land in Japan), and, with a guard behind him, went straight to where the three nervous Japanese were standing. They saluted Buchanan, who returned the compliment.

Then a Japanese standing in the centre of the group bowed low, and handed over a large ring of keys, which opened every door in the area. This Japanese was a Naval Commander, who had been in charge of the stores depots of the base. The men on each side of him were interpreters. A guard of Australian sailors quickly formed up beside the Japanese.

Instead of wearing the usual jungle-green battledress, which we associate with all Pacific landings, the sailors, who were part of the British Pacific Fleet occupational force, went ashore in freshly-laundered khaki shirts and shorts, highly polished boots, shining brasswork, and steel helmet.

A table was erected quickly, and on it were placed the plans of the area which Buchanan studied in conjunction with the Japanese. The interpreters were good, and information was gathered quickly.

Although the landing was British, it might well have been Australian, judging from the scene around the table. The guard was Australian, and the whole of Captain Buchanan's headquarters was composed of Australian naval officers, who had been taken from the destroyers *Napier* and *Nizam*.

WHAT THE BRITISH LANDING FORCE FOUND IN YOKOSUKA NAVAL BASE

The Japanese smell badly anywhere, but they smell worse in Japan than anywhere else. The same musty stench which pervades their battlefields and the dwellings they occupied in their Pacific tour is more noticeable in their own country. The area we have occupied is filthy. Rats are prevalent, and the place is bug-ridden. Fortunately everyone who went ashore was innoculated many times against diseases.

The Japanese Commander told us that almost all the office records had been burnt on the orders of higher authority.

During our initial tour we saw Japanese policemen for the first time. As we expected, they were dressed in black, and carried swords. The Japanese policemen seem a better class than the general run of Japanese, and certainly demand much respect from civilians. They were courteous without being patronising, and helped the occupation forces everywhere.

Throughout the tour of the area almost all Japanese we saw were perceptibly shaken, and I don't think any of them would have been surprised had we suddenly shot or bayoneted them. They took us through the caves which had been burrowed in the hillsides beside the naval base.

One of these was a complete block of offices, with telephone communication and steel files, where the headquarters moved as a body when our planes were overhead.

The vehicles we saw had mostly been captured during the retreats of early 1942. One car was a Buick 8 sedan, which had been brought to Japan from the Philippines for the use of the Admiral who commanded the base.

We found English Corona typewriters, which had not been taken from their cases since the fall of Singapore, and Japanese Admirals' dirks, which were silver inlaid and stood beside a case of Samurai swords.

It was a strange feeling to be walking round this great store, which only a week before had been a hive of activity and whose asphalt streets today were dead.

A BOOK ABOUT AUSTRALIA

The guides at Azumas offered interesting information. As an excuse for the way in which the Japanese public had been kept in the dark about their position in the war they said that the Government itself was not sure of what was going on. The commanders of outposts like New Guinea did not admit all their defeats, for fear they would be classified at home as failures and that their families would be in disgrace.

Instead they preferred to fight on until they lost general communications with the homeland. None of them had heard so far of any high government or military officials committing hara-kiri, although we had reports of this happening outside the Emperor's palace.

Those guides had also been told, as had the people of Japan, of the dreadful atrocities the Allies had committed against the Japanese everywhere they met in action. One officer said he understood the Americans ran over wounded Japanese with tanks and bulldozers.

None would tell us where the nearest prisoner-of-war camps were, and we were all sure they did not know. Even the Japanese commander, who met Captain Buchanan at the landing, did not know that a large midget submarine base existed only a few miles from his office, and there was no reason for us to doubt his word.

We knew, however, that the prisoner-of-war camps in Japan are clustered together, and it seemed strange to us today that after four years these officers did not know where even one was.

We are satisfied that they knew more about our prisoners than they cared to admit, and would not admit anything for fear we might blame them for treatment we have heard that our prisoners have received from Japanese guards. Like their compatriots this morning, these Japanese also would not admit the hopeless and utter defeat of their country.

We boarded a Japanese destroyer, and found a large navigation text-book dealing extensively and comprehensively with the south coast of Australia. Its information was as full as our own text-books which could be bought before the war at most bookstalls. This should be a lesson to us.

About the Surrender, he wrote:

About 8.45 a.m., the Japanese delegation arrived, headed by the Foreign Minister, Namoru Shigemitsu, who has a wooden leg, apparently jointed at the hip. They were all made to stand for several minutes before anything happened.

The only greeting they received was by an officer at the gangway, who frisked them for weapons when they came aboard. They all looked very uncomfortable, and Shigemitsu acted as though his leg was giving trouble. His colleagues lacked bearing and demeanour.

None stood to attention, despite the fact that most of them were senior service officers. And their uniforms were untidy and creased. No one could have looked as though they were representing a defeated nation better than these men did.

Those not in uniform wore formal cut-away coats and striped trousers. Shigemitsu wore a great silk top hat, which seemed many sizes too large for him.

MacArthur came to the microphone with a prepared speech in his hand, and told the world on one of the greatest radio hook-ups in history.

> 'We are gathered here as representatives of the major warring powers to conclude a solemn agreement whereby peace may be restored. The issues involving the divergent ideals and ideologies have been determined on the world's battlefield. Hence it is not for our discussion or debate.
>
> 'Nor is it for us to meet here, representing as we do the majority of the earth's peoples, in a spirit of distrust, malice or hatred, but rather it is for us, victors and vanquished, to rise to that higher dignity which alone befits the sacred purposes we are about to serve, committing all our people unreservedly to the faithful compliance with the undertakings they are here formally to assume.

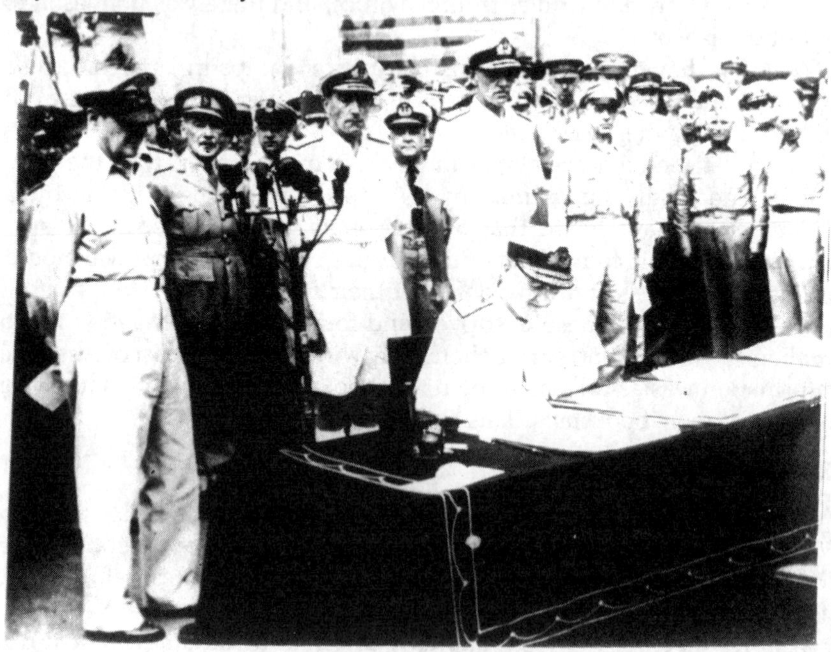

Admiral Sir Bruce Fraser signs for Great Britain. USS Missouri, *2nd September 1945. General MacArthur standing left*

> 'As Supreme Commander for the Allied powers, I announce it is my firm purpose in the traditions of the countries I represent to proceed in discharge of my responsibilities with justice and tolerance while taking

all necessary dispositions to ensure that the terms of the surrender are fully, promptly and faithfully complied with.

'I now invite the representatives of Japan, the Japanese Government and the Japanese to sign the instrument of surrender at places indicated. It is my earnest hope, and indeed all mankind's that from this solemn occasion a better world shall emerge from the blood and carnage of the past—a world founded on faith and understanding dedicated to the dignity of man and the fulfilment of his most cherished wish for freedom, tolerance and justice.'

Shigemitsu then limped forward to the table shortly after 9 o'clock. He wore a troubled frown. He took off his top hat, removed his gloves, tinkered with his pen, and seemed to delay his signing by consulting, at regularly short intervals, two watches. This surprised everyone.

From Jack Tindall

LIBERATION OF PRISONERS OF WAR AND INTERNEES
SIGNAL SENT TO ADMIRALTY ON 14th SEPTEMBER 1945

1. The liberation and evacuation of prisoners of war during this last few days has witnessed scenes which will live long in the memory of those of the British Pacific Fleet who are here in Tokyo Bay. In the absence of any representative of the British press the following account is sent in order that the public at home may have some idea of how British Commonwealth prisoners of war are being repatriated from the Japanese mainland.

2. This is an American theatre and the American Forces are responsible for the collection and evacuation of all Allied prisoners of war. The White Ensign however has offered all available ships to assist in the evacuation and, which matters most, is doing everything within its power to ensure that contact with British prisoners of war with their fellow countrymen shall be established as early as possible and maintained.

3. The British Task Force which was operating as part of the American Third Fleet at the time when hostilities ceased is now spread about the coasts of Japan and China, including Hongkong, Shanghai and Formosa, and only a part is available to assist in the repatriation from the Japanese homeland.

4. Among the ships in Tokyo Bay off Yokohama which have lent a hand in the evacuation are HM Ships *King George V, Duke of York, Indefatigable, Speaker, Ruler, Newfoundland, Ariadne, Apollo, Troubridge, Termagant, Tenacious, Wrangler, Wakeful, Wizard, Wager, Whelp, Wessex, Quality, Teazer, Terpsichore, Erne,* HMA Ships *Shropshire, Hobart, Napier, Nizam, Nepal, Quickmatch, Warramunga, Bataan,* HMNZS *Gambia,* Hospital Ships *Tjitjalengka, Vasna,* Storeships *City of Dieppe, Fort Wrangell,* Oilers *Dingledale, Carelia, Serbol* and *Wave King.*

5. The first stage has been the identification of prisoner of war camps. Much was known from information given by the International Red Cross and the Japanese themselves. Further searches by aircraft from the Third Fleet carriers (including *Indefatigable*) and of the United States Army have not only revealed additional prisoner of war camps, but have enabled them to be supplied from the air during the early stages. To-day in the hospital ships there are unfortunately some former prisoners of war suffering from broken limbs because, in their enthusiasm, they allowed the food containers falling by parachute, to strike them.

6. When the Allied Fleet anchored outside Tokyo Bay the first Allied prisoners of war to be repatriated were a Royal Marine and a British soldier who escaped and attempted to swim out to the Fleet and were picked up by an American patrol boat. When units of the Fleet entered Tokyo Bay and advanced landing parties of American sailors and British sailors and Royal Marines were landed to occupy strategic advanced posts, they were in many instances met by prisoners of war who had broken camp and received them enthusiastically on the beaches.

7. Naturally, those men came off in the landing craft which had taken the landing parties ashore. Before the British and American Navies had even anchored the evacuation of former prisoners of war had, in fact, started.

8. Wherever camps were known to exist parties of American, British and Australian soldiers and sailors were sent off as 'contact teams'. These teams have gone into the depths of Japan, have found the camps, and with the assistance of the Allied Commanders of those camps have organised the initial journey to Yokohama.

9. That journey was, in the case of camps close by, made on foot or by motor car, while in the more distant cases trains have been arranged, or, where near the coast, destroyers have been sent out to fetch the parties in.

10. Naval Hospital ships were rushed into Yokohama and into Tokyo itself and all former prisoners are first received on board these Hospital ships, where they are examined medically, given baths and clothes, fed, and particulars taken of every man. Telegrams are sent to next of kin.

11. Those who, owing to malnutrition or other causes, are seriously sick are retained on board. Those who are reasonably fit are sent to ships for immediate evacuation. What has been perhaps more noticeable than anything else is the longing of every man to shake off the dust of Japan once and for all at the very earliest opportunity.

12. HMS *Speaker* was quickly converted into an evacuation ship and within 12 hours of being warned for this duty she was filled to capacity with over 450 British Commonwealth men whose imprisonment in many cases dated from the fall of Singapore, or the sinking of HMS *Exeter*.

13. Next day she sailed for the south and as she steamed through the British anchorage the ship's companies of all the British ships gave her a send off which those who saw it will never forget. The sight of this small aircraft carrier with her ship's company fallen in for leaving harbour in accordance with naval custom, but with, in addition, these hundreds of ex prisoners of war ranged on the flight deck cheering like mad and being cheered, brought tears to the eyes and the realisation what the presence of the great Fleet in Tokyo Bay meant to these men.

14. As the camps in the immediate neighbourhood of Tokyo Bay were cleared, ships went further afield. The *Tenacious* to Hamamatsu, where the *King George V* in company with American battleships had carried out a naval bombardment only a few weeks before; *Wizard* to Hamamatsu and later to Sendai. *Barfleur* to Hokkaido, *Wakeful* to Sendai, *Gambia* and *Nizam* further west.

15. The resources of the Fleet, limited as they are after two months away from any base, have been used to fill each of these ships with blankets, beds, cigarettes, chocolates and other stores necessary for a sea passage.

16. Lately, each evening, one or more of these destroyers has come back, arriving at Yokohama just as, seen from the British ships at anchor, the sun has set over the Mountain of Fujiyama. But it is a different picture from the usual Japanese drawings. It has been a scene which in some ways has reminded one of Dunkirk. Destroyers carrying many hundreds of passengers, in all sorts of clothing, crowding all over the upper decks, and receiving the tumultuous cheers of all HM Ships as they went by into the inner harbour of Yokohama where the hospital ships are lying.

17. The United States air evacuation is now in full swing and over a thousand men are being evacuated daily from the Tokyo airport. A number continue to be sent by sea in order to maintain the maximum flow of evacuation.

18. Tomorrow, HMS *Ruler*, another escort carrier, leaves with over four hundred officers and men, including on this occasion a number of civilians and children. They include the citizens of all the nations of the British Commonwealth and of many of the Colonies. The ship is very changed from the warship she was. The flight deck has been marked out for every kind of game, and this evening a Royal Marine dance band was playing outside the island structure. Forward and aft a few rather disconsolate aircraft are made fast and serve as a reminder of what naval air power has done in achieving that for which the Navy stands.

19. Down below, the ship has been transformed as far as possible into a passenger liner and as the Captain remarked, 'I have never before heard the hangar called a fairyland.' The change may perhaps best be summed up in the 'pipe' which was broadcast at 1800 'Children to supper'.

20. The hospital ship *Tjitjalengka* with her American sister ships, the US

Benevolence and *Marigold*, has been doing magnificent work in looking after the really sick, and in strengthening those who would soon be fit for air or sea travel. There is however always a certain number who have to be kept behind and on Sunday next the *Tjitjalengka* will be sailing for Australia with over four hundred cot cases.

21. Every effort has been made to enable men of HM Ships to mix with and help those returning victims of the war who have not seen a new white face for years, and to whom, in many cases, the events at home since 1942 are a closed book. Many, too, are anxious to tell of their experiences and so ease their minds. As may be expected they have found a very sympathetic audience in the British sailor.

22. And so the repatriation goes on. It is estimated that already a third of the total number of Allied prisoners of war on the Japanese mainland have left Japan, and it will only be a matter of days before the evacuation of Northern Honshu, including Tokyo, has been completed. It will be as much the privilege of some of the harbours of the British Commonwealth to welcome these men as it has been of the White Ensign to start them on their journey home.

Extracts from *Dry Ginger* by Richard Baker

The days following the surrender were busy ones for Michael Le Fanu—'organising a peace is quite a job and I have to try and cut the British in on all the info.' In addition, he had another report to complete. For this he got the draughtsmen's office to make a cover using the photograph of him wearing a baseball cap and standing between Admirals Halsey and Rawlings—'Fraser will laugh (I hope) but their Lordships will be furious; I shall probably be slung out!' Then on 27 August came the memorable and uncanny experience of entering the harbour of Sagami Wan near Tokyo. 'It was a lovely sunny day as we led up harbour, with Fujiyama loud and clear on our port beam. Rather an over-rated eminence I'd say. No snow and rather a dull shape. We anchored at 1330 and Fraser in the *Duke of York* was close after us.'

Thus the British presence in Japan was firmly established and the cause was furthered with Michael and Bill Kitchell, Halsey's Flag Secretary, were together charged with making the arrangements for the surrender ceremony, fixed for 2 September on board the *Missouri*; it seemed the ideal location since President Truman of the United States was Senator for the State of Missouri. 'Hey,' Halsey had said one day, 'I hear from the President we've gotta fix this surrender. You two had better go and do it. The General (McArthur) will be coming on board.'

'You know, it was rather amusing,' recalled Michael later, 'for one young Commander and one young Lieutenant-Commander, formerly of Du Ponts, to be told to go and fix the surrender of the Japanese Empire. So we just sat down and I said: "Well, the first thing we want is a table and some chairs."

I provided the chairs which came from the *King George V*—nice wooden ones instead of these American metal ones.' The table, too, was to come from the British battleship—and Michael took good care the Press knew about it (they didn't cotton on to the fact that at the last moment the table proved to be too small and a larger American one had to be substituted). The Press, in fact proved the biggest problem. 'You know the kind of thing,' Michael confided to Prue. ' "Give me all the facilities I want or I will blackguard you in the papers"'. The three hundred and twenty Press representatives arrayed in 'various natural and artificial grandstands' outnumbered the two hundred or so people involved in the actual ceremony on the superstructure deck.

Michael greatly enjoyed it all, not least seeing a Russian reporter (the Russians had declared war on the Japanese six days before the surrender) almost knocked off his perch by an American. The arrangements he and Kitchell had made seemed to work well; Michael had a grandstand view 'only twelve feet from Uncle Doug' (McArthur) and he relished the contrast (in the run-up to the actual ceremony, which took place at 9 am local time so as to catch the US papers) between exchanging good-humoured banter with his friends among the enlisted men, while greeting each new grand arrival as a long lost buddy.

One of these was Admiral McCain, commander of the famous Carrier Task Forces, who pleased the newly anglicised Commander Le Fanu by putting his arm around his shoulder and exclaiming, 'Mike you old rascal, you've gone British on us again.' And there was the gratification that evening ('I detected a slight post-wedding atmosphere') of organising a party in HMS *Duke of York*, Fraser's flagship, which was a great success, with Halsey repeating to tremendous applause (after being made an hon. member of the *Duke*'s wardroom) the 'six gins' trick he'd worked so successfully in the *King George V*.

Two days after the signing ceremony, Michael had the 'odd sensation' of attending a 'conventional matter-of-fact party' ashore at the Yokosuka Officers Club, an all-male affair which he found civilised, but which made Halsey and his staff 'really angry and upset' owing to the absence of nurses from the hospital ship—an omission rectified at a repeat performance a few days later 'with everybody rather tipsy and cutting in on everyone else'. More to Michael's liking was the party given by Sir Bruce Fraser for some of the junior officers of the American Fleet. 'What shook them was there being a party at all. Though the Americans are excellent on mass production items such as ice cream and movies, they do not make a habit of dealing with their juniors as individuals.'

As for Commander Le Fanu's own relationship with his Admiral, it was close enough for him to be able to tell Sir Bruce that, other things being equal, he would like to go home soon; but he could hardly refuse when the Admiral asked him to stay on for a while 'if he was not too tired'.

Seven days after the surrender ceremony Michael travelled through the streets of Tokyo with Jim Bassett, in a borrowed jeep. 'It was an extraordinary sensation driving along there, just two unarmed Commanders and a driver, when only a few weeks ago we were at each other's throats. Going into Tokyo we went for mile after mile and met nothing but devastation . . . except for the centre of the city, Tokyo is quite flat. I have no brief for the Japs but all the same it really shocked me—what a reflection of our civilisation. At the British Embassy we found the caretaker, a queer shrivelled old man who was delighted to see us; he wasn't at all popular during the war and his only relaxation was to take the tram once a week and go down to compare notes with his opposite number at the American Embassy. Luckily it seemed that everybody had got the word about the war being over, and though we excited a good deal of curiosity, nobody bothered us. One party of girls, great strapping wenches who could have seen us off easily, fled like the wind as we approached their door. I suppose they had been listening to Tokyo Rose!'

Tokyo Rose (the Japanese equivalent of Lord Haw Haw, the Germans' English language propaganda broadcaster) was the subject of one of the most successful of the Le Fanu doggerel verses, entitled *Oh to be in Nippon*..

In the days following the surrender ceremony, Michael was kept extremely busy on his liaison duties and became increasingly involved in the repatriation of prisoners of war, many of them in a pathetic state of health. But he also found time—in response to numerous requests—to put together some of his best verses in a 'volume-ette' entitled *Limey Rhymes*. It was printed on board USS *South Dakota* (now the flagship) in early September and produced in a second edition in USS *New Jersey* in November, after the return of Admiral Spruance to the fleet. The little book bears the dedication: 'To my friends of the United States Navy: I have learned many things from you, not least that you have an abiding passion for souvenirs. So I have collected these doggerels that you may have a keepsake from me. For the rhymes themselves, I offer no excuse beyond saying that nearly all were written in haste, to meet a special occasion and to be forgotten.'

Limey Rhymes, however, was not forgotten. Many a sailor in the Third/Fifth Fleet has it to this day, a reminder of the extraordinary Englishman who served with them in the last days of the Japanese war.

Now that the war was over, Michael began to feel increasingly weary of his assignment. When he rejoined Spruance's staff in the *New Jersey* on 19 September, however, he masked any reluctance he might have felt with a welcoming rhyme called *All Yours, Fifth*, addressed to Admiral Spruance.

Life on board Spruance's flagship was not quite so stark as it had been formerly; one or two congenial spirits managed to secrete 'medicinal supplies' in their rooms, though Michael grew tired of the eternal movies and American-style parties in officers' clubs ashore with the inevitable contingent of nurses and the fixed determination of all hands to get drunk before six o'clock. He became involved with diplomatic comings and goings of various kinds, and managed to organise some fascinating runs ashore for himself and sundry friends, American and British. One of the most entertaining involved 'two arch clowns' from the cruiser *Swiftsure*—Charles Bennett and David Jones, Captain of Marines, who were requested to assemble 'wines and spirits for a week (courtesy of RN)' and come aboard 'a jeep with Rations' (courtesy of US Govt.) on 'a safari to meet our Japanese cousins'.

'The only thing we had in common,' recalled Charles Bennett later, 'was a sense of the ridiculous. When we stopped in villages, Mike was a master in communicating goodwill whether English was spoken or not; but the inn-keepers at our palatial rest-houses were absolutely terrified. Fortunately we found the local policeman—nicknamed "Rushing Water" for reasons I will not go into—and he restored order. The next three days were pure farce and we were almost sorry to start the trip back. When nearing the port we met head-on a truck of armed US soldiery who took up a very threatening attitude. "Leave the talking to me," said Michael as the Colossus of a Sergeant approached. Passes were demanded. The first pass was rejected—"never heard of the guy"; second pass "no dice"; a third pass was offered with deliberate care. This pass staggered the Sergeant, who waved his men back into the truck and waved us on. I asked whose signature was on the third pass. "McArthur," said Mike with a grin—"no one bucks that." Asked why he had not produced this pass at once he replied "When you hold a good hand don't lead with your main trump." I only hope that somewhere in today's Navy there is another "rogue" in the pack who will develop into another Le Fanu.'

Fun and games apart, Michael interested himself that autumn in writing a document addressed to the C-in-C British Pacific Fleet which incorporated many of his impressions of the US Navy and which was, in spite of the deceptively light tone of voice, a prophetic glimpse of the future Royal Navy. Realising that 'the Americans have all the aces' and that England has exhausted herself' he felt that 'all our energy should be devoted to making a Navy of the highest quality and to hell with the number of ships'. His 'What Shall We Do with the Post-war Sailor?' emphasised the many fields in which the Royal Navy needed to learn from the Americans—in such matters as ship design, organisation of watches and more civilised living facilities for ship's companies. 'The food in British ships,' wrote Michael, 'would in many cases be eyed distastefully by a performing seal.' He advocated a total revolution in lower-deck life with its hammocks and individual messing arrangements ('shamefully squalid'), in favour of bunks and cafeteria feeding, employing the advice of successful civilian restauranteurs'. Above all, Michael recommended rates of pay comparable with those paid for work of similar quantity ashore.

'What Shall We Do with the Post-war Sailor?' incorporates recommendations by a relatively junior officer which have now come one hundred per cent to fruition in the Royal Navy; in 1974 the document was deposited at Spruance Hall in the Naval War College in Newport Rhode Island, together with other memorabilia of one who gave unique service to the cause of Anglo-American naval co-operation.

On 8 November, 1945 Admiral Spruance was relieved by Admiral Towers. As a four-star Admiral, Spruance was entitled to a farewell party of eight sideboys and Michael made the suggestion ('ever so dashing for an American ship') that the eight should in fact all be members of his staff. 'I need hardly tell you,' Michael wrote to Prue, 'that the British Liaison Officer was one of the eight.'

After this farewell Michael had to wait with increasing impatience for several more weeks for news of his own future movements and the arrival of a relief. There was time for some serious reading, of Blake and Walt Whitman among others, and time for some depressing reflections on the way the American Press, in the immediate aftermath of war, was misrepresenting the British contribution to victory. 'They cannot get the idea that anyone had anything to do with the war except themselves. The men I talk to are fully aware that Britain bore much of the heat and burden of the day, but in the public pronouncements, even the Service people—big wigs—are so busy proving that the Air Force did the job as opposed to the Navy or vice-versa, that they quite forget to state that Russia and Britain may have had something to do with the final result. I dislike seeing so much popular goodwill being dissipated. In any case I reckon our worries should be directed at the really important things. There seems to be no urgency in the deliberations of the great, and the great are ultimately only the spokesmen of the people's will. I suppose that sometime the masses will rise and say in a loud voice: "Now look here! Stop all this nonsense and let's set about organising world peace—otherwise we have batted".'

At last, on 3 December, Michael's relief arrived, and he was free to go home 'with two suitcases I brought with me in January'. In due course he was to be awarded the American Legion of Merit for his work with the Third/Fifth Fleet, work which bore valuable fruit in the years ahead; and he was deeply disgusted when he was told that not long after his departure, his relief had informed the Admiralty that there was nothing for him to do—no one seemed to want him—and he asked to be recalled. Their Lordships complied.

'To think,' Michael told a friend much later, 'that we actually *had* a permanent place with the afloat staff of the US Fleet which *they* wanted us to keep, and it was thrown away. What a lack of imagination. The Liaison Officer's job was to "be there on the spot, when needed; out of sight if not wanted; unobtrusive yet helpful; eventually essential at all levels . . ." not sitting in an office writing reports or issuing orders. We have thrown away something which will never be offered again.'

Perhaps the job could only be done by someone of the Le Fanu stamp. As for him, in his last letter home before setting off via the States for the UK, he said flatly, in spite of a year's exhausting endeavour, 'I have not made as much of this job as I might have.'

From Marine Norman Coombs, HMS *Formidable*

I sometimes think of all the men, with action stations below decks, listening to the banging and crashing and smell of cordite fumes, the vibration of the ship at full speed and wondering what was happening. I am sure many had to fight the fear of claustrophobia which I feel is inherent in most people to a degree.

You mentioned chockmen in your book **Sakishima**. This is a job I will never forget, having performed it many times.

When a full deck park was set out prior to flying off there never seemed to be enough aircraft handling party men to man all the chocks. It was usual to call on the crews of one or two of the after turrets and of course we always copped the tail end of the deck park. It was a most uncomfortable job, copping all the slip streams and paint chippings blown off the flight deck.

On the termination of hostilities we, like many other carriers, put our aircraft ashore and went around the islands picking up POWs. We did two trips to Sydney and one trip to Bombay. This is an unforgettable period, it is one of happiness and great sadness. Happy to be able to help and make friends with men who had suffered so much. And sad when told of the privation and torture they suffered at the hands of an inhuman enemy. Most of the men were just skin and bone and many suffered beri-beri, leg and body ulcers.

It just hurt to look at them and try to realise what they had been through. I would think that some would never properly recover.

Bringing these men home made us feel that we were doing something worthwhile instead of so many futile things.

HMS Formidable. *Hanger Deck rigged as a dormitory for POWs. Facing Forard. 'Hospital' aft. Photo: N. Coombs*

You also mentioned in your book the kindness and hospitality extended to men of the fleet. To me and I suppose many others Sydney was a haven of peace in a troubled world. I always looked forward to my up-homers—the Crawford family of 216 Auburn Road, Wally and Elva (Ma) Crawford and their teenage children, Jean, Nan, Elsie and Bob. They always made us welcome with a nice meal and a place to stay, it was just like home. Ma Crawford was my Australian 'mum', and when I migrated to Australia in 1953, I was able to take my wife Peggy and daughter Brenda, who was 6 years old at the time, to see the Crawford family, it was a very happy meeting.

We are still in touch with the family although Wally and Elva have been at rest for quite a number of years. I loved them so much.

From Nobby Clarke, HMS *Formidable*

Admiral Vian and staff had been put ashore in the morning. The dockyard staff were quickly aboard to convert the ship into a 'trooper' to ferry Aussie POWs from Manila to Sydney. The hands fell in after dinner. The Captain addressed us and expressed the congratulations on behalf of Admiral Vian for our successful and efficient spell as his flagship, during the final operations against the 'Nips'. However it was with regret that the Admiral's wine and spirit store had been burgled. As an admiral receives a hospitality allowance to provide a wine and spirit store for guests and visitors, Admiral Vian was almost TT, but would have to replenish the stock at his personal expense. The Captain was so sure that none of his ship's company should be held responsible and qualified this claim by stating that 'The Sydney waterfront was full of vice,' and the hands were dismissed. By 'stand easy' we were all aware that the dockies were not at work and noted that they were all ashore and huddled in groups on the jetty conversing or playing cards. 'Where's all the dockies?' we enquired, to be informed that they had taken umbrage at the captain's reference to the vice on the Sydney waterfront and had 'downed tools' until an apology was received. As they constituted part of the waterfront personnel, I have to assume that the captain conceded, for the ship was alive with dockies carrying out their duties the next day.

I have since heard that the contents of the wine and spirit store were available that evening at Kings Cross!

From Roy Forrest, HMS *Formidable*

I feel sometimes, 'It's time for my watch on deck. Get the planes ready for a strike. Meantime have a squat on the chocks.' I used to get a bit nervous at times behind the chocks when the planes started to rev up.

Once the war at home was over people did not realise that another war was still on thousands of miles away. I think the only people who knew and thought, were those who still had someone away fighting.

I had people say to me when I finally finished, 'Where have you been then? The war has been over for ages.' I told them 'You had better think again.'

From an anonymous ex FAA Pilot RNVR

In writing of one's experiences of war it is easy to fall into the trap of thinking that personal experiences and feelings are shared by all. One often reads, 'We hated the Japs, we disliked the top brass,' when really it should read 'I' not 'We'. So I ask forgiveness of my erstwhile colleagues if inadvertently I foist off on them feelings that were in truth only mine.

In starting down memory lane I am convinced that one little known, yet extraordinary achievement of the second war, was the Empire Flying Training Scheme. To imagine that a country like Britain, in 1940, financially bankrupt, bombed by the Luftwaffe and surrounded by U Boats would be able to train and equip aircrew the equal of the best in the world would appear to be a dream. Yet the dream became reality and all over the Empire, Canada, Rhodesia and South Africa, aerodromes and hangars were built. Aircrew were seconded from operations to man the schools. Recruiting of boys of above average physical fitness and good intelligence commenced. By 1944 thousands of these young men had passed through the scheme.

It started with three months basic training by the old sweats of the Service which you had joined and for the Fleet Air Arm it was HMS *St. Vincent* at Gosport. The first thing that hit you, literally, was a sign hanging from a door lintle which announced 'Join the Fleet Air Arm—but be a sailor first'.

For three months, hard-bitten Petty Officers bullied and shouted at us and demonstrated a discipline that would mark us for the rest of our Service careers. But an ever enduring memory for me is the girls of the WRNS drill squad. They were magnificent. Their Petty Officer drill instructor took a delight in parading them in front of new entrants, hardly any of whom could co-ordinate arms and legs, and carrying out the most complicated drill manoeuvres with the ease and precision of a platoon of Guards. I met one of them at a dance in Southsea. I did not spend the evening whispering sweet nothings. I wanted to know why they were so good at drill. I realised I was out of my depth when she described one of their manoeuvres, the command of which was: 'On the right, to the half, half form SQUAD'.

But there is another memory. I am well into my sixties now and erotic thoughts are brief and far between. Across all the years I still get a warm glow at the memory of a warm June afternoon and those black silk clad legs moving in unison, those thighs and bottoms thrusting against blue serge, those high bosoms straining against cotton shirts as their arms swung out together. The hussies knew that it was not only their drill precision that held us spell bound. Wherever you are now girls—thank you!

Then on to flying training—and what magnificent training it was, progressing from school to school and ever more powerful aircraft. Firstly Elementary Flying School then Service Flying School, on to Advanced Flying School and finally THE ONE—OPERATIONAL TRAINING UNIT. At this school the instructors were just back from occupational flying and knew all the wrinkles of survival in action. They were marvellous instructors. Never once did they portray any of the gut rending fear that they had only too recently experienced. Always they inspried you with confidence: 'Do it this way and you'll be alright.'

Throughout the whole of the training period, the weeding out process had been taking place, with checks and cross checks to seek out those pupils who were not going to acquire the necessary degree of flying skill. The final hurdle for naval fliers was deck landing. Eight successful landings had to be done, generally on one of the smallest carriers available, acting on the principle that if one can get down into a postage stamp one should be able to do it on one of the massive Fleet Carriers coming into service.

Finally the posting came to a front line squadron. One departed from practice and training and flew with men to whom you would be trusting your life and they theirs to you. Now for the first time one experienced reality. One aspect of this reality was in fact a strange type of cynicism that pervaded the fliers in operational squadrons. Up to now all one's training had been in controlled aggression with the result that after two years we were bursting to get into action. This boyish enthusiasm suddenly appeared very out of place ina front line squadron.It was simply not done to show such keenness. Line shooting was one of the most heineous of wardroom gaffes. Anxiety to have a crack at the Hun was very bad form. English understatement and reserve was what was required of young pilots. Not that this affected operations. These were undertaken with a grim determination that came from the knowledge that operational flying was not a boyish prank as shewn in some films—hack down the Hun and home for tea. As I got to know these men and indeed became one of them, I realised we were all very frightened indeed. In retrospect I think one's fear came in three stages. The first and early stage was pure adrenalin pumping away and one is buoyed up in the day time and rocked to sleep at night with the death defying thoughts of youth—it won't happen to me. To all my friends—yes, but not me. During this phase one eagerly looks forward to the operation hoping to see some real action.

As the days and months wear on and slowly one's friends disappear from the wardroom or die horribly in front of one's eyes, the fear enters its second stage. It is the realisation that death can happen to you and on the then current laws of average it undoubedly will, within days if not hours.

It was now that whatever depths of character one possessed, whatever impact two years of training had made, would play their part. The ability to keep going, to obey orders, to give orders and to act out the normal life of a ship's officer. We may have looked normal to others but our state could be detected by experienced men who had seen prolonged action. It was apparent in several ways, possibly most of all in simply doing what one had to do—no more—no less. One did not seek out dangerous tasks, one avoided them. One did not go round for a second attack unless actually ordered to do so. At this stage in my life I remembered the old adage 'He who fights and runs away lives to fight another day.' I thought as a child that this was the punishment for cowardice. I realised during the war that it was good advice for survival—there will always be another operation tomorrow—don't be a dead hero today.

This then was the significance of the cynicism of operational fliers that so distressed young sprogs joining front line squadrons. It became a matter of interest to me when talking to my cousin after the war and he told me exactly the same thing. He served in tanks and he came from battle school and training to join a regiment just returned from the Mediterranean, who were to spearhead the invasion of Europe. Our leaders in Westminster might have thought that they were battle hardened warriors steadily going forward to thrash the Hun. My cousin told me they were indeed battle hardened. Their object after three years in North Africa was to survive the next six months. They would indeed fight the Hun but only when it had to be, and when there was a reasonable chance of success. My cousin said that twelve weeks later after the Battle of Caen his attitude was the same as his colleagues. Taking fear beyond this, to its third stage, produces two types. If one is kept in stage two for too long without a break, mental breakdown can occur.

Hopefully this is seen and understood by one's seniors and one is relieved from flying for a few months. Sometimes a flier will give off danger signals without knowing it. I recall a colleague whom I knew to be near breaking point. His personal pride would not allow him to report his fears. However his flying abilities became more and more atrocious and his carrier landings were a byword for exciting crashes, which were highly dangerous not least for him. He was taken off flying, not only for his own sake, he was slowly wrecking the operational capability of the squadron by running out of aircraft. In my opinion his subconscious mind was rejecting the thought of being airborne.

Personally I know of only one occasion when the strain became too much for a pilot. For some time we had suspected he had a 'twitch' problem. Every time he took off he immediately swung round and landed on again, reporting a fault which on inspection was not there. One day, early in the morning, he would not get out of his bunk to take an early flight. The C.O. was sent for and it seemed as though a court martial might ensue. At last another pilot bravely stepped in and said, 'It's OK, I'll go in his place.'

The other pilot is alive today. The flier who refused, was dead within minutes, killed by a kamikaze.

Whilst these are but two examples of pilots in the second stage of stress there are many fliers who went through this period and seemed to be fearless. I have read two phrases that seem to sum up their attitudes. One by Roosevelt during the Depression: 'We have nothing to fear but fear itself', and another by the Long Range Desert Group commander 'Popski'—'When one has realised and accepted that death is the worst that can happen—the rest is easy.'

There are other examples of such ice cold courage, yet for me the finest examples I ever saw of calm courage was demonstrated by Fleet Air Arm Squadron Commanders. Due to the lack of pilots and overwork, most CO's had to fly the same amount of hours and number of ops, as their juniors. However, because of who they were, they always had to lead the squadron on the most dangerous raids. At the end of the day they had to check all the squadron reports, work out the flying duties for the next day's operation (and allotting themselves yet another hair-raising role) see ground crew chiefs and serviceability of aircraft, have a jar in the wardroom with the aircrew to check morale, visit the sick bay, and finally pay a visit to the Commander and probably the Captain. At the end of such a day, their nerves must have been wound up to screaming pitch, but I hardly ever saw a drunken CO and certainly never at sea. Their final nightmare must have been the knowledge that if captured and identified as a CO they would have had the most appalling treatment from the Japanese.

How did we regard the Japs? Certainly by 1944 we had a high regard for their skills. Why shouldn't we? In the first six months of the war they had wiped out most of the USA and RN Eastern and Pacific Fleets! I still possess secret briefing notes from a fighter pilot school I attended in India in 1944. 'All the stories of Jap pilots being poor shots and having poor eyesight are untrue. They are good pilots, good shots and there is nothing wrong with their eyesight.'

But even so, in our view, our training for war lacked nothing. We knew we were as good as, if not better than, any other aircrew in the world. By 1944 we knew of Japanese atrocities. This did not make us fear them in combat. It induced, anyway, a high degree of contempt for such a race. The advent of the kamikaze confirmed my contempt. To deliberately throw away one's life was a complete negation of everything in which I believed. Our whole concept of war was based on survival. Keep going even in defeat. Live to fight another day. Whilst the prospect of swarms of kamikazes descending on us was not pleasant, it did have a cheerful side. A nation reduced to such idiocy was obviously not running out of men and material.

One's introduction to operational service was somewhat like seduction, not rape. A little light flirtation to start with, then a few days later ending up with the grand bedroom scene. The days of inexperienced Battle of Britain pilots being brought straight from Training Units and flung into action against fifty plus German fighters were long gone. Even so, the thrill of flying close to one's wingman, hearing the R/T crackle and then his voice: 'Enemy coast ahead. Sharpen up' is a memory for me that will never fade.

On my first flight over enemy territory, I heard his voice and a few minutes later looked down. We were approaching a small harbour with surrounding houses. We swung over and hurtled down. A building looked in my gun sight. My finger hovered over the gun button. Then my thoughts. 'Oh Christ, is it a school?' I roared over the roof not firing and swung out over the bay. I spotted a large boat. 'That wasn't a school!' I pressed the button and the aircraft bucked and kicked with the recoil and bits of the boat flew off into the air. My R/T crackled: 'You bloody fool, form up on me.'

I had committed the crime of leaving my wingman alone to go off on a jolly on my own. I cruised up beside him and he shook his fist at me. But anyway I had fired in anger at last.

What then was this relationship with one's colleagues, one's wingman? I had to watch his tail and he mine. Not for formation flying, but simply to save our lives. Neglect of this task could mean death and as a result over the weeks one came to trust the man you guarded and indeed all one's colleagues. They were all with you, watching the grim reaper stalking through the squadron day by day. We never achieved the closeness or bonding of front line infantry or indeed seamen. To be like them, one not only had to fight beside a colleague, one had to live, sleep, eat and even excrete beside them. For us fliers it was a lonely life, stuck in a tiny cockpit with the engine droning on and on. Whatever closeness one felt in the air to a friend, once back onboard ship, one resumed the normal life of civilised eating and private showers. However, aircrew were a cliqué lot, often bunching together and excluding non-fliers. This sometimes led to bad feeling particularly in a large carrier. All aircrew tended to be boisterous, noisy, often drunk and generally acting as though the ship was there for their personal use which, to some extent it was. On one ship the feeling between aircrew and ship's officers became so bad that a senior ship's officer, a non-flier, called us all together for a talk. As I recall, he said, 'The purpose of this ship being here is for our aircrew. Without them and their planes we have no purpose and I would ask all my non-flying colleagues to remember that and to make allowances and give encouragement to these brave young men. I would ask the aircrews to remember that their lives, their machines, their food and their comfort depend on us, the ordinary men of this ship, often working long hours without ceasing in conditions of dreadful discomfort. We also have a part to play.'

Relations improved from that day onwards. The same happy state of affairs rarely occurred on a shore base at an aerodrome. Here the aircrew would fly in for a few days to be replaced a few days later by another squadron. Each squadron acted as though they were the first and only fliers to arrive, roaring across the airfield a few feet off the ground, peeling off in split-arse turns to do tight landings and then bouncing into the wardroom bar to drink and sing far into the night. After a few visits like that, it was no wonder that the permanent shore based staff (the shiny arse brigade) looked upon all fliers, no matter how heroic, with a jaundiced eye.

Finally I must recall how the young men could respond to good leadership. The end of the war came with surprising suddenness at a time when the casualty rate among aircrew was high. The immediate reaction of fliers was, 'Thank God—I've survived. There's no need to fly any more.'

To our annoyance, a full day's flying was laid on and there was a lot of discontented muttering amongst the aircrew. Even the standard of flying deteriorated, with poor formation and slow landing-on. Two days later a secret meeting of all aircrew was held. The senior flier got up and said: 'We have now come to the victorious end of six years of war. Many better men than us have died in getting us to this point. This ship and you are now the sole representatives of the British Empire in action. We are searching for Prisoner of War camps. It is a poor thing if we can't get a few aircraft into the air to show our POW friends that we still care for them. I don't want to hear any more binding. It's not worthy of you and you let yourselves down.'

From that minute onwards not another complaint was heard and we flew as often as wanted and as well as possible.

An American Forces paper included the following:

'Atrocity', Tokyo Says

SAN FRANCISCO—(UP) *(United Press. Ed.)*—Tokyo radio last night broadcast without comment the criticism of the atomic bomb by a Vatican spokesman.

The enemy broadcast recorded by United Press stressed the statement that the bomb was 'regarded as marking a further step in the direction of indiscriminate employment of means of destruction.'

The Japanese continued to avoid direct mention that an atomic bomb had been dropped against Japan, according to Tokyo radio.

The broadcast, recorded by United Press, said the use of the 'new type of bomb' in the Hiroshima attack was 'another manifestation of the enemy's diabolic nature of having no scruples and massacring civilians in order to attain his end.'

Comments of the newspapers included:

The Asahi—'The enemy's new type bomb is a 'new atomic weapon' invented and employed in flagrant violation of the code of humanity.'

The Mainichi—'The enemy's new type bomb has a destructive power that cannot be minimized. The enemy will lavishy resort to the new measure without the least of scruples.'

Tokyo, said Mainichi, promised that it would work out 'effective counter measures to protect civilians.'

The *Yomiuri Hochi* added the comment that the US was the 'eternal enemy of humanity' and asserted that use of the atomic bomb 'clearly shows that Japan has already won a significant victory in war in the cause of justice and humanity.'

Prince Killed

SAN FRANCISCO—(UP)—The Japanese Imperial Home Ministry announced Wednesday that Prince Rigu died Tuesday of wounds suffered Monday in the atomic bombing of Hiroshima, Tokyo radio announced.

The Japanese radio broadcast, recorded by United Press, said the Prince, who held the military rank of Lieutenant Colonel in the Imperial Army, was wounded 'while fulfilling his official duties as a result of the enemy's air raid on Hiroshima on Monday.'

From Ex-POW W/O Fred Parsons RAF, sent by PO Peter Bonney

PO Peter Bonney's uncle was W/O Fred Parsons RAF who, after many adventures, was taking passage on the SS Harauki *from Melbourne to India, in June 1942 when they sailed into a Japanese Fleet. They were diverted to Penang and then Singapore before being put aboard the* Tokio Maru *bound for Yokohama.*

From their POW Camp at Ohua, some were put to work in the Mitsubishi factory (electrical, rivetting etc.). Here are a few extracts from his diary:

During the early part of the voyage the Japs supplemented their rations with cakes and other edibles that were taken from parcels that had been sent to British servicemen by their loved ones. Several sacks of these parcels had been taken on board and distributed around.

The toilet facilities consisted of two small huts perched over the water at the stern of the ship each of which was supported by two thick planks. A hole in the floor was the method of disposal and an aid to evacuation could be obtained by taking advantage of the rise and fall of the stern of the ship. This was of benefit, as I found that the rice diet tended to induce constipation. There was a never ending queue waiting to take advantage of this amenity and they were apt to become impatient if one dilly-dallied over one's toilet.

On the 8th October we were told to have a dysentery test. We never heard the result of the test and assumed that it was put on as an entertainment for the Jap troops. The test took place in a hold and the layout was reminiscent of a theatre. The open hatchway of the hold taking the place of the gallery and situated immediately above the stage. The 'orchestral stalls and the pit' surrounded the stage—the missing items being 'boxes' for VIPs and an 'orchestra'. Soon after making our entrance to the 'stage' the hatchway was lined with eager Japs and the lower vantage points were soon occupied. When all was ready a Jap medical officer and his followers arrived, one of whom carried a case which on being opened disclosed a number of glass rods. (*Note:* the dysentery test provided for the insertion of a glass rod with the object of collecting a sample.) We were instructed to drop our trousers and touch our toes. The MO took one of the rods and advanced on the first recipient. This went according to plan until he tried the fourth man in the line who unfortunately sufferes from a stomach disorder. The insertion caused him to lose the key of his back door and consequently the MO received a sample in a place which was not intended, much to his displeasure. Further sordid details have been omitted in order not to offend the susceptibilities of readers.

. . . In the afternoon we were all lined up on parade and told that as a prisoner had not answered questions satisfactorily he was to be punished.

He was made to stand in front of us with legs astride and arms in the air while two guards, one on each side, laid into him alternately with thick sticks. They carried on until he dropped. It was very distressing to hear him cry out in agony and, of course, wondering who was next on the list for similar treatment. The following day the prisoner, who occupied the next cell, was very depressed and expressed doubts of survival.

We could not foresee when our captivity would end and therefore lived for the present. The constant brutality and mental torture together with an absolute lack of medical supplies was a major factor in the heavy death rate among the prisoners. The standard reply to any request for medicine was that Japanese water was the best in the world and was good medicine for any ailment. There is no doubt that captivity under these conditions brought out the best and the worst in the prisoners sometimes with surprising results. Some who seemed poor specimens, became a source of strength whilst others could stoop so low as to steal another prisoner's rations.

At work, one of the American prisoners was reported for not working hard enough. On our return to camp all the guards took it in turn to bash the POW about the head until they were tired. The POW's face swelled up like a balloon and hid his eyes. His ears, nose and lips were in a mess.

We have a visit by a representative of the Swedish Red Cross. We are told to put on our best clothes. These clothes are specially issued for occasions such as this and are collected as soon as the visitors go. We are warned not to discuss conditions in the camp. The Red Cross tell us that they will send bedding and money to buy necessities for the sick.

My turn has come to help transport the bodies of deceased prisoners to the crematorium. The cortège consists of a handcart pulled by two prisoners at the front manning the shafts and pushed by two prisoners at the rear. The bodies are kept in the wash-house until four are awaiting transport. These are individually placed in roughly assembled crates and piled in the back of the cart. The procession sets off under the watchful eyes of the guard. We proceed down the main street passing the communal baths. Everybody has a bath here irrespective of sex or age. We traverse the shopping centre. We call a halt here in order for the guard to go in a shop for a drink and chat with a friend. We leave the town and follow the road through the countryside for about a mile to the crematorium. We unload the coffins and dump them on the ground. After a delay while the necessary forms are completed to account for the delivery of four prisoners we retrace our steps and eventually the ashes arrive at the camp to join the already impressive pile of boxes.

The toilets are overflowing. In order to avoid walking on the noxious mess, bricks are used as stepping stones. The Japs say we must wait for the tanks to be emptied. The British MO says he fears an epidemic.

At the end of the month we are paraded for a prize giving ceremony. Prisoners who have worked hard during the month are rewarded with four sheets of toilet paper and four cigarettes. Those prisoners who did not work hard were given a slap across the face.

The Japs are tightening up and are insisting on a greater number of prisoners going to work at Mitsubishi. This meant that some of the sick had to go. All the sick who could walk or even stagger were paraded for selection. The guard corporal made the selection as to their fitness for work. One of the prisoners selected for work had acute appendicitis and, with the aid of a fellow prisoner and rifle butt from a guard, joined the working party. His condition deteriorated at work, but he was not allowed to return to camp. When work finished and we returned to camp, he was conveyed there in a cart as he was unable to walk. He had a burst appendix and died the next day.

Christmas Day once again and we wonder how many more we will see in captivity. We are told that the Emperor is letting us have the day off. We have to bow towards the palace to express our thanks. In the evening we have a visit from the Chief Electrical Engineer of Mitsubishi. He wishes us a Happy Christmas and, when no Japs were about, gave me a small parcel containing a Christmas card, two eggs and some butter.

14th July 1945
The first bombardment of Kamichi was carried out by an American Task Force under the command of Rear Admiral Shaproth. The Task Force comprised the following units:.

Battleships *Dakota, Indiana* and *Massachusetts*
Cruisers *Quincey* and *Chicago*
Nine destroyers.

The fleet opened fire from a range of 29,000 yards and the shelling lasted for two hours.

9th and 10th August 1945
The second bombardment of Kamichi was carried out by the same Task Force that carried out the bombardment on 14th July plus the following British contingent under the command of Rear Admiral Brind RN.

Cruisers: HMS *Newfoundland* and HMNZS *Gambia*
Three destroyers.

We take over the camp under the command of the senior officer—the MO. The MO sees the commandant and relieves him of his sword and I collect from the guard two bayonets as souvenirs. We demand an immediate withdrawal of guards from our quarters and an immediate increase in rations. Both demands are conceded. We relish our new found freedom and make excursions into the surrounding countryside.

15th August
At work this morning the Hancho (Jap foreman) tells us that all Japs have to assemble midday and listen to a speech that the Emperor is giving on the radio. When they return the Hancho is crying and so are other Japs. We are told that

the war is over. The speech said a new and cruel bomb had been dropped—killing many people and so, to avoid further loss of life, the Emperor was asking for peace.

24th August
Another ex prisoner dies from burns and two others are in a critical condition.

25th August
A US fighter aircraft flies over the school and drops some cigarettes together with a note which says that he is Ensign W. F. Harrah and that supplies will shortly be arriving by air. Later the same day a squadron of US aircraft flew over the camp with more cigarettes and a message saying that we will be taken off in a few days.

August 30th
An aircraft drops tinned goods and the Commandant makes us an unwanted gift of cigarettes. The Japs are getting worried. They are now bowing to us and conversation is punctuated by hissing (sucking air through gaps in the teeth). This is a Japanese indication of pleasure and goodwill. In the past we were the recipients of bellows and grunts denoting displeasure and often leading to a slapping session. Later today we are invited to dinner by the Commandant. We are waited on by our ex guards. The Commandant said as we had been treated with every consideration he would like us to give a good report about him to the Americans when they arrive.

15th September
A hospital ship arrives together with cruisers and destroyers. We are taken off by a landing craft and put aboard the hospital ship. We are de-loused and then, except for those ex prisoners too ill to move, we are transferred to an APD (Amphibian Personnel Destroyer). This ship was the US *Wantuk* commanded by Commander Simpson, the ex husband of Mrs. Simpson who married King Edward VIII.

16th September
We leave Kamichi with no regrets. We are now having civilised meals and we have our first film show for some years.

From Lt. Cdr. Colin Mackenzie RN, HMS Indefatigable

Then there was the night when our U.S.A.Admiral took the fleet through the middle of a typhoon. I remember well the middle watch that night. I had never before seen the phenomena of St. Elmo's Fires and when this affected a wireless mast on the starboard bow it appeared to be a light approaching, close to, on a steady bearing; I put the wheel hard over to the utter confusion of the formation but mercifully no collision.

From Jack Hibberd—Article in 'John Bull', September 1st 1945

HAVE THE JAPS SOMETHING UP THEIR SLEEVES?

After spending many years in the Far East before the war, I have come to know the Japanese fairly well. I have had my doubts about their surrender ever since it was first made. Why did they stall the negotiations until MacArthur got tough? Why were their speeches those of a defiant, not a beaten, nation? Why did they continually emphasise reconstruction for the future? Future what? I want answers to these and many other questions.

Are the Japs merely playing for time? Have they got something up their sleeves? Don't forget that they developed planes as good as ours. Can it be that they are well advanced in atom research, and, given six months or so of 'negotiating' during which they can complete their experiemnts will drop atom bombs on San Francisco and our Pacific island bases with as much warning as they gave of the Pearl Harbour attack?

Or perhaps it is that as the Oriental mind takes a different view of time, Japan is cunningly preparing a long term plan. This time she has failed through trying to ride too quickly on Germany's band-wagon. Does she now intend to behave outwardly as a 'good nation' for as long as 30 or even 50 years until the Western nations trust her—and then suddenly to strike again for the domination that has never been out of her mind since she started to build an empire?

We should forever be on our guard against Japanese soft words and duplicity. We should keep in Japan an occupation force twice as strong and twice as efficient as the one we placed to keep Germany under control.

THESE ARE THE JAPANESE

Seen through the eyes of a Japanese woman writer
by the Lady Murasaki*

(*The Lady Murasaki—the non-de-plume under which she writes, conceals the identity of a Japanese woman who knows England almost as well as she knows her own country. She has spent the past five years in active war work for Britain. Her opinions neither defend nor attack—they are merely given in the hope of making her country more intelligible to us.)

So you would like to know what a Japanese thinks about the recent conquest, and hear what sort of situation your son may find and what sort of people will greet him if he goes there to occupy my country?

I cannot promise you a very pretty story. Please remember that this is the first defeat that Japan has had for 2,600 years. Our official history begins in 660 BC when the 'divine born Emperor Jimmu ascended the throne'.

Remember also that freedom as you understand it here in Britain, has little meaning to the Japanese. We have an inborn and profound respect for authority and decree. For that reason if you go to occupy our country we shall bow to your power even if we hate you in our hearts. We are far too well disciplined to give you much trouble in that way.

Lastly, remember that though Confucius gave us our religion it seems to have taken a Christian civilisation to invent the atom bomb.

But if you would really understand the people you have beaten to submission, you must hear a little of our back history. To most Englishmen our country is only a mental picture—the land of cherry-blossom, poetry, and exquisite women in kimonos, or a land of murderers, suicide pilots, and fanatical Emperor worshippers.

The Emperor's Divinity

The militarists who seized power during the 1930's exploited this legend to their own evil ends. To-day nobody who values his life would be so silly as to question the matter in public.

Whatever the people may have been drilled to believe, the Imperial Family certainly do not consider themselves as divine! If that were so they would not dare to mix openly with mere generals. I used to play golf with the emperor's brother-in-law at Hakone, not far from Tokyo, and he behaved in an extremely 'mortal' manner to the waiters if he were over-charged for ice-cream.

Our Emperor, as supreme head of the State, is accorded great respect by all classes of Japanese. Whether they believe he is god or mortal in no way alters their deep reverence. You will perhaps understand this reverence for a family when you realise that it has reigned without interruption for at least 1,600 years.

Even when the first Japanese history was written in the eighth century (before England and France had become States at all) the myth of the Japanese who die for their king and country (as you say here in England) lay down their lives for the same reasons that the British or any other nation might have.

This attitude to the emperor is the result of our religious outlook. Like the religions of the ancient Jews, Greeks and Romans, our ancient religion was at first a tribal one. God, the supreme ancestor, was worshipped by the emperor alone, as chief of the senior family. Lesser families had their own ancestors for patron saints. Thus ancestor-worship has made the family more important than the individual, and the nation—as a family of families—the most important of all.

The modern Japanese do not usually believe in life after death, but they still regard it as quite natural to sacrifice themselves unhesitatingly for the sake of their parents or for the Emperor. This is why a daughter will voluntarily enter the 'Red Light District' to support her impoverished father, and a young pilot dives to certain death for the sake of the Emperor.

Whether one regards such behaviour as barbaric and fanatical, or unselfish and heroic, depends entirely upon one's upbringing and the side on which one happens to be fighting.

During the sixth century (about the time that England was converted to Christianity) Japan welcomed the disciples of Confucius and Buddha and the arts and literature which they brought with them from the mainland. Confucius taught us that the State was more important than the family, and that the family was more important than the individual.

Modern Army of Peasants

Until AD 1600 there were constant civil wars between the different feudal rulers, all of whom had armies of armed retainers—the 'Samurai'. These wars were conducted according to a strict code of honour, sometimes referred to as Bushido.

Bushido involves the obligation to fight according to certain rules and to show mercy towards one's defeated enemies. The modern Japanese army is composed mainly of ignorant peasants. Like the old Samurai, these peasants are ready to die for their country, but they have lost all the requirements of Samurai honour.

The modern Japanese soldier has indelibly stained the name of Japan by his behaviour in this war in Nanking, Hong-Kong and elsewhere.

But do not forget that most of them certainly believed the stories that the Chinese roast their prisoners alive and the Americans kill theirs under steam rollers.

Japan's first contact with the West was in the sixteenth century. At first the Japanese welcomed the foreigners with open arms, just as they had welcomed the scholars, monks and artists, from China a thousand years before. Soon, however, they discovered that Spain was planning to turn Japan into a colony, and they decided that the only course was to expel all foreigners except the Protestant Dutch and the Chinese. Japan enjoyed 200 years of peace.

In 1853 this was rudely shattered by the American Commodore Perry, who sailed his squadron of warships into Japanese home waters and demanded at the point of the gun that Americans be allowed to live and trade in Japan.

The Japanese Government was then too weak to resist the heavily armed Americans, so it gave way. This action caused Japan to set about turning itself into a modern State. By 1895 we were strong enough to defeat the Chinese Empire, and in 1904 Czarist Russia.

How 'modern' Japan was just before the war, can be seen from the fact that in 1939 there were twice as many telephone calls in Japan as in the whole of Great Britain.

Bert Crane has always felt that HMS *KGV* should have continued as Flagship to steam into Tokyo Bay for the surrender. He wrote:

US Admiral Halsey was a battleship man, that's why he was aboard USS *Missouri*. Some say because President Truman's home state was Missouri and that was why it was chosen for the Surrender Ceremony.

Likewise, Admiral Sir Bruce Fraser had an affection for *Duke of York*. After all, he was a battleship man too and had been involved with the sinking of the *Scharnhorst* and many of the crew had been on her since 1939.

Bert sent me copies of some pages from a book of unknown title, in which it says:

The suddenness of the onset of peace made major changes in war plans impossible. We in *Implacable*, therefore continued on our planned journey south to Sydney as if we were still preparing for 'Olympic II'. Only at the very top could the plan be altered, so that our C-in-C, Bruce Fraser, could now leave Sydney in his Flagship—*Duke of York*—to add his presence to the proposed peace signing ceremony in Tokyo Bay.

The *Duke* was an extraordinary choice of Flagship. Whereas the Americans in the Pacific had heard of *Formidable, Victorious, Indefatigable,* and perhaps *King George V*, they had never heard of the *Duke of York*. She had the signal honour of catching the *Scharnhorst* on a dark night in the Arctic winter of 1942. She had taken advantage of 'Ultra', her possession of radar and an inexplicable error by the Germans, to sink her with her guns and with 50 or so torpedoes from her accompanying cruisers. This irrelevant feat was not appreciated in the Pacific either by the Americans or by the Fleet Air Arm. It was not therefore in the least surprising for us to hear that the *Duke* had been pelted with potatoes by the carriers as she had steamed into Guam on her way north to the peace-signing with Admiral Fraser on board.

I am again indebted to Boy Seaman First Class A. C. W. 'Bert' Crane for providing the following memories of HMS *Duke of York*

The Sydney Daily Telegraph of Wednesday 4th July 1945 carried a large photograph of Admiral Sir Bruce Fraser saluting the arrival of the great ship and reported:

BATTLESHIP ARRIVES TO JOIN FLEET

The British battleship *Duke of York* (35,000 tons) has arrived in Sydney Harbor to join the British Pacific Fleet. *Duke of York* is one of England's latest battleships, having been completed in 1941. She is a sister ship to *King George V.*

On Boxing Day, 1942, *Duke of York* sank the German battleship *Scharnhorst* (26,000 tons), after the battle of North Cape, Norway.

The Commander-in-Chief of the British Pacific Fleet, Admiral Sir Bruce Fraser, was on board *Duke of York* during the action as Admiral commanding the British Home Fleet in Arctic waters. Sir Bruce was the first official visitor on board the battleship on her arrival at Sydney. Accompanied by Captain A. D. Nichol, RN, and Commander M. Hodges, RN, of *Duke of York*, Sir Bruce visited most parts of the ship.

Battle Reminder

On the Admiral's bridge, he paused a few seconds and rested his arm on the Admiral's chair. It was from this chair he saw the *Scharnhorst* go down in flames.

During his visit, Sir Bruce renewed the acquaintance of men who were on board during the North Cape battle.

R. Harrison, AB, of Milford Haven, South Wales, said he was staff officers' messenger at the time of the North Cape battle. 'Admiral Fraser kept me running about most of the afternoon, but it was worth it,' he added.

F. Clements, of Plymouth, Chief Yeoman, was yeoman of the watch on the Admiral's bridge during the action. 'The Admiral was cool throughout the action,' he said. 'He walked up and down the bridge. When he saw *Scharnhorst* go down in flames, he smiled and said, "That's that." '

Manus, in the Admiralty Islands was her next destination. Here Admiral Fraser once again hoisted his Flag in HMS *Duke of York*, after which she sailed for Guam, the Advanced headquarters of the United States Pacific Fleet. Admiral Fraser, acting on behalf of his Majesty the King, invested Fleet Admiral Nimitz with the GCB. The ceremony took place on the Quarterdeck.

On August 11th, the rumours of the Japanese peace overtures reached us, after the Russian declaration of war and the dropping of the first Atomic Bomb. Our departure was delayed and we sailed from Guam on August 13th and joined the American 3rd Fleet south of Japan. We then steamed around, dodging a typhoon which was in the vicinity and finally anchored in Sagami Wan (close to Mount Fujiyama). Here the first two escaped British ex-prisoners of war were brought off to the ship—Pivate Edgar Campbell RASC of Fifeshire and Marine John Wynne of Manchester. *(This version appears correct.—Ed.)*

It sounded like an invitation to a Party, but it wasn't *Duke of York*'s fault that this particular party was almost over, and after all she did carry our C in C.

Everyone on board received this leaflet:

WELCOME
to
GUAM

The officers and men of the United States Pacific Fleet and shore activities on Guam take pleasure in extending a hearty welcome to the officers and ships' companies of HMS *Duke of York*, HMS *Whelp*, and HMS *Wager*.

It is our desire that your stay in Guam may afford the fullest opportunity for rest and recreation, and the facilities of the Island are at your disposal. It is our further hope that your visit will provide opportunities for friendly companionship between personnel of the two navies, so closely linked in the common cause.

Fleet Admiral, United States Navy
Commander in Chief, US Pacific Fleet and
Pacific Ocean Area
9 August 1945

Reprint of VJ Message from the Commander-in-Chief, British Pacific Fleet

If anyone had asked me one year ago where I would wish to be one year hence I might have told them: 'Flying my Flag in the *Duke of York* on VJ Day in Tokyo Bay.' But at that time few things could have seemed less likely. To begin with there was no British Pacific Fleet. The invasion of Europe was only two months old and, while things were going well, there was still much to be done before the Germans were beaten. In the Pacific the Americans were performing miracles, but the first few milestones on the way to Tokyo had only just been passed. Guam, finally cleared of Japanese resistance on August 10th 1944, had yet to be developed into the amazing base we have all seen it to be.

The Japanese held the whole of the Philippines, the whole of Borneo and were fighting fiercely in New Guinea. Iwo Jima and Okinawa were formidable and far distant Japanese fortresses. No heavy bombing or shelling of the Japanese mainland had taken place. Further to the west the Japanese held the whole of Burma with their forward troops inside the frontiers of India itself. The British Eastern Fleet, though dominant in the Indian Ocean, was by no means in undisputed control of the western seaboard of the Malayan peninsula.

When I was appointed to be Commander-in-Chief of the British Pacific Fleet in November 1944, the picture was a little happier, though even then the Americans were predicting that the war might last for another two years, and now, only 14 weeks after victory in Europe we find ourselves celebrating victory in Asia. It is an astonishing change of situation in so short a time, and let us give full credit to those great leaders General MacArthur and Admiral Nimitz for their far-sighted and valiant leadership. But we must not, in our friendship and admiration, forget the courageous part played by the men of the British Pacific Fleet and by our cousins from the dominions of Australia and New Zealand who at sea and on land and in the air have contribued a most worthy share in the destruction of the Japanese. We acknowledge, too, the determination and valour of those gigantic forces under the command of Admiral Mountbatten in South East Asia.

But to particularise, let us recall that since last March, when the British Pacific Fleet Task Force first went into action under Admiral Rawlings, they have accounted for nearly 600 Japanese planes and have sunk or damaged more than 250 Japanese ships. We have, during these nine short months that the British Pacific Fleet has been in being, supported and maintained in action a powerful and offensive Task Force that has not only struck at the heart of

Japan from the air, but has also bombarded the Japanese mainland with many hundreds of tons of destructive shells from the sea. Japan has felt and suffered the power of Britain's naval might.

Men of the British Pacific Fleet, you have every reason to be proud of the part you have played in the defeat of Japan. You have reason too, to recall those fine words from one of the prayers which we use in the Service which say 'That we may return in safety to enjoy the blessings of the land and the fruits of our labours.'

ADMIRAL

HMS *Duke of York*
15th August, 1945

Reprint of VJ Message from the Captain of HMS *Duke of York*

When the first news of Japan's peace overture came through on August 11th, I feel pretty sure that we all had the same immediate feeling of slight disappointment; not that the fighting was over—no-one would wish to delay that for a single second—but because we had not had just one crack at them before the end.

This was a very natural reaction, and we should be no good as a fighting ship if we were not keen to show the enemy what we can do. Apart from that, however, we were all delighted, particularly as our dear ones at home need have no further anxiety for our safety.

Since we left Liverpool in April we have had plenty of hard work, much variety of scene, and a good deal of luck. We have been especially lucky in being able to mention the ship's whereabouts so often, contrary to the usual run of censorship, first at Malta, then at Sydney, then at Guam and now at Tokyo. This has been a great help in our letter-writing, and the mention of the ship's name so often in the Press or on the wireless must have been of great interest to our families.

It is a crowning piece of good fortune that we should be in at the Japanese Surrender as Admiral Fraser's Flagship. I feel myself that it comes as a reward for your drive and determination and patient hard slogging during the work-up period. Of course we *would* like to have had that one crack as well; but, after all, many of us have seen action and we have all been bombed in this war, so we will let that be.

When the ship sailed out of Scapa in September, 1944 on her way to Liverpool for the refit, the *King George V* made us the following signal: 'Goodbye, and good luck. Hope to see you in Tokyo.' It is interesting and highly satisfactory that *Duke of York* and *King George V* have met again in Tokyo.

When we have got the Japs where we want them, my dearest wish will be to sail with this ship and this company into Plymouth Sound.

CAPTAIN
HMS *Duke of York*
A. O. Nicholl CBE, DSO, RN

NAVAL AIR MIGHT DISPLAY OFF JAPAN
By our Own Correspondent
(In HMS *Duke of York*)

Off Japan, August 22—Sam Goldwyn would have turned technicolour green with envy to-day if he could have seen the massed flying display given by planes of the Third Fleet, including representative Seafires and Fireflies from British carriers. It gave us an advanced display of what the Japanese are likely to see when we move into Tokyo.

Between 950 and 1,000 planes packed in tight like spectators at a football match, soared little more than mast high over the *Duke of York*, whose decks were lined with spectators. One officer standing next to me said: 'I have seen nothing like this since I ran into a plague of locusts in North Africa.'

Roared up the Line

The planes flew so far ahead, then turned to go astern on the starboard side. Then they banked and roared up the line, in which steamed Admiral Halsey's flagship.

All were most disappointed when an impersonal voice from the loud-speaker announced that it required 50,000 gallons of petrol an hour to keep this force in the air—a remark which prompted many to reflect what that amount of petrol would do for their cars after their demobilisation in England.

Radar officers agreed that the display was the most spectacular they had ever witnessed. Finally a rainstorm arrived just in time to make the landings a tricky procedure.

Believe it or not

During a recent test of wireless telephone communication between the Ship and London a call was put through to a certain Air Vice Marshal. Owing to an error at the London end, the Ship was given a wrong number—the number of a Mental Home—and the following conversation took place:

Ship: 'This is the *Duke of York* in the Red Sea. Will you ask Air Vice Marshal so-and-so to come to the phone please?'

Reply: (without the faintest trace of surprise) 'Sorry; we have a Duke of Wellington, three Napoleons and a couple of Henry VIII's but, at the moment, no Air Vice Marshals.'

'Yorker' Office
HMS *Duke of York*

In 1988, I had the good fortune to meet Captain John Q. Edwards US Navy retired. We discovered that we had both served in the 5th and 3rd Fleets!

Here are two newspaper cuttings which he sent to me. The Brotherhood of the Sea is a powerful comradeship—perhaps as powerful as the element which nurtured it! It is one of integrity and respect and is indifferent to class, colour or creed.

'The Washington Post', 30th August 1980

Retired US Ship Sinks Off Coast

London, Aug. 29 (AP)—The mothballed American Cruiser *St. Louis,* nick-named *Lucky Lou* when it escaped the Japanese attack on Pearl Harbour in 1941, went down in heavy seas off the coast of South Africa, Lloyd's Register of Shipping said today.

Lucky Lou sank Aug. 24, Lloyds said, while being towed to the Taiwanese port of Kaohsiung to be broken up for scrap. The vessel began listing heavily in the rough seas and finally capsized and sank, Lloyds said.

Lucky Lou served throughout World War II with the US Navy and later was transferred to the Brazilian Navy and renamed the *Almirante.*

The cruiser was finally sold to a firm in Hong Kong for scrap and renamed the *Tamandare* just for the tow to Taiwan. Lloyds did not know the name of the Hong Kong purchasers.

'The Washington Post', Saturday September 6, 1980

A Final Salute to the *Lucky Lou*

The Aug. 30 AP story on the sinking of the *Lucky Lou* (USS *St. Louis*) off the coast of South America brought back many memories of the gallant ship that was my 'home away from home' during World War II. She was the first major warship to get under way and escape the holocaust of Pearl Harbor. *Lucky Lou* seemed an appropriate nickname, since the torpedoes fired at her by Japanese submarines as she reached the open sea exploded harmlessly on an intervening coral reef. Her skipper at the time was Capt. George A. Rood, a Washingtonian, and one of the very best.

Lucky Lou had a proud war record indeed. After Pearl Harbor, she fought in most of the major actions in the Pacific, from the Aleutians to Guadalcanal, through the Gilberts and Marshalls to the Philippines by way of the Marianas, and finally to Okinawa and Japan. At the end, her captain had the honour of accepting the Japenese surrender of Formosa (Taiwan).

So it was only fitting that her last act was to refuse to go to the ship-breakers yard in Taiwan, but, rather, to choose an honourable end with burial at sea—thereby joining those who gave their lives while serving in her during some of the great naval battles of World War II.

The story contains an error with respect to her name while in Brazilian navy. She was rechristened *Almirante Tamandare,* after a famous admiral in the Brazilian navy.

John Q. Edwards,
Captain, US Navy (Ret.)

Springfield, VA

(Thanks John, and Happy Landfall.—Ed.)

Now on 13th August, Fraser was instructed by the Admiralty to re-occupy Hong Kong. While Chiang Kai-Shek's approval was awaited, Fraser ordered Rear Admiral C. H. J. Harcourt on 27th August to steam from Australia to Hong Kong with Euryalus, Prince Robert and escorts. This they did on 30th August and the surrender was signed on 16th September with Fraser 'in attendance'.

At the request of the Australian Government to provide 'a ship', Fraser ordered the light fleet carrier Glory and two sloops to allow General Sturdee to accept the surrender of the Australian dependencies, New Guinea, Solomons, Bismarks, at Rabaul on 6th September.

The British Merchant Navy, as everyone should be told, had experienced, perhaps the hardest and most important battle of all during the Second World War. Their convoys through treacherous seas and conditions, particularly in the Atlantic and the Arctic, inadequately protected most of the time, to bring supplies of food and munitions to Britain and Russia, demanded men of the highest calibre. Like the Forgotten Fleet, their efforts did not receive the public acclaim they deserved, but they know in their own hearts what they did—and we who served in the Royal Navy know also. We will never forget them. They have our highest admiration.

Thus it was that Fraser, aware of the tremendous loss of merchant vessels, turned to the carriers to solve his problem of re-patriation.

In SE Asia, there were 127,000 ex Prisoners of War to re-patriate and Fraser was responsible for them. He urged the Admiralty to retain the very close co-operation between the RN and the USN which he had fought so hard to establish, but the plea was ignored. He went some way to retrieve the situation when he became First Sea Lord in 1948, but the real opportunity which he saw had been lost.

A few ex BPF men have reported an incident of potatoes being thrown at Fraser's flagship Duke of York, but I have not received any letters from actual witnesses. It must be one of those happenings which have been blown up out of all proportion. Just as there was friendly rivalry between the carriers, so there was between the battleships KGV and Duke of York and the KGVs must have wished that Fraser had flown his flag from their ship in Tokyo Bay, because they had been Rawling's—the Fleet's—flagship for all the action. However Duke of York had seen plenty of action too and had been Fraser's home for many months and perhaps he didn't wish to overshadow Rawlings?

Duke of York was booed by a group on Euryalus while entering Hong Kong and Fraser did wonder whether they were booing him. It couldn't have been The Royal Marines because they were on duty ashore. Fraser was too big a man to let it worry him.

As I said in **Sakishima**, the potato story, if true, couldn't have happened in Tokyo Bay, because we hadn't any potatoes—only de-hydrated—so maybe someone threw one—or two—at Duke of York in Hong Kong. Though unimportant, this does illustrate the feelings of some of the ship's companies who knew nothing of the great man's responsibilities.

Fraser also had a problem with his two BPF admirals. Rawlings and Vian didn't 'hit it off'. From my small knowledge of Vian, I didn't either, and neither did our Captain, Q. D. Graham. It was generally agreed by all who knew him, that Vian was a difficult *man, but a great Admiral and very pleasant when you really go to know him and off duty—whenever that was. I didn't like his manner, but I'm glad he was on our side.* (See Appendices.—Ed.)

In due course, the three were, from what I can gather, all very friendly with each other. C'est la guerre.

When Fraser finally left Sydney on 16th November 1945 the Institute of Journalists wrote to him:

We are most anxious, before you leave Sydney, for an opportunity to express to you our feelings after this, the most notable visit ever paid by the Royal Navy to Australia. To let you know our appreciation of the attitude of yourself and of all under you, while in our country, but especially to tell you publicly that though in wealth, material force and military power, the old country comes out of this war no longer first among the nations, yet in admiration, affection and pride of her daughter nations, she has never stood so high at any time in our history.

It was kind too for the British Centre—the home from home for the BPF—to write:

It has been a pleasure to work for the men under your command. They have been a credit, first to you as their Commander, and to the Country they represent.

Even the Sydney Commissioner of Police wrote, about 'The splendid bearing and orderly conduct of the men under your command.'

Perhaps the letter which will bring lumps to our throats because it came from those closest to our hearts was from the Australian Comfort Fund who wrote:

The presence of the navy in our waters gave us all new heart. The boys at all times conducted themselves in such a manner as to receive approbation of all members of the community. We have all taken them into our homes and by this means have created friendships which we think will last for all time. The presence of the Fleet in these waters has created a feeling of friendship and understanding, the result of which can never be truly measured.

Fraser's final message to the Australian people read:

In a few days I shall be leaving Australia for Hong Kong. Many of my ships will be coming back to Australia at intervals, but for many of us it is farewell for the time being.

In Naval life one should get accustomed to farewells, but in my experience from a Midshipman, aged 15, to an Admiral it is always a very sad occasion when parting with friends whom one has grown to know so well.

One stands on the ship's deck watching the hawsers cast off, the waving handkerchiefs growing smaller and smaller and then at last ship and shore fade in the distance, but just the sky and sea with us. The memories will not fade, we hope it will be the same with you.

We sailors may be happy-go-lucky people by reputation and to a point it is probably true. The long periods at sea battling with the elements, and the somewhat brief spells on shore all make for a natural inclination to get the best out of life when opportunity offers. But deep down, sailors are the most sentimental people on earth, and they will always have the deepest appreciation for the little things which count, the friendships, the kindnesses, the laughs, and in these ways how wonderfully Australia has shown the genuineness of her welcome . . .

As Commander-in-Chief, much of one's time is taken up with official duties and functions where, under the scrutiny of many thousands of eyes, one's personal fancies must be sacrificed for what one represents. One's uniform inevitably makes one conspicuous and one cannot wander freely about. But in Australia I have occasionally managed to slip into a civilian suit and mix for a time unknown amongst you and see some of your character.

In such a manner I walked to a little Newsreel Theatre in Kings Cross and took my place in the queue. A long one, and it seemed doubtful if I should get in. Presently I was joined by a young Australian pilot and we started talking about Australia; then we talked of England—I suppose he had discovered by that time that I was a 'Pommie', although I don't know how! Then he started to look at me rather intently and I knew my number was up. For he said, 'I believe you are Admiral Fraser,' and I said, 'Yes.' He then said, 'But sir, you should not be standing here, let me take you straight in past the queue.' I said, 'I don't think I can do that. They might take me for an arrogant Englishman!' He thought for a moment and said, 'Sir, I would like to pay for your seat.' The value of the gift was a shilling, the value of the thought and deed was, to me, infinite. Then he said, 'Could you help me to join the Fleet Air Arm?' which thrilled me even more. Today there are 20 Australian pilots serving in my carriers, and there would have been many more if the war had not ceased . . .

This has been a year of much anxiety to me. I knew that the Fleet would distinguish itself in whatever activity it was engaged, but with the vast distances involved, should we be able to supply them, give them the provisions, replace casualties, get up the mail to them—and it is these human things which are so important. With the co-operation of the Australian people and the Americans, we just managed it with the barest margin. We got through with very few casualties, but let no one forget that for the men at sea it was a tough war, and I am very proud of them.

Since the peace, the human side becomes even more complicted, the compassionate cases to deal with, the demobilisation, the resettling in civil life. At the same time the work of the Navy, which never ceases, must go on. In these difficulties, in a world still unsettled with many internal conflicts, let us remain cool, calm and collected, whatever disappointments or setbacks we may have the stabilising influence of the British Commonwealth of Nations is very great—we must keep strife and suspicion away from our doors, and preserve that integrity on which the world so much relies . . .

And now the year draws to a close. I feel more and more convinced, as time goes by, that the ties which have been cemented in Australia between you and us, will never be severed however many thousands of miles we are away.

For our part we are deeply conscious of the great work of the Australian Navy, and of the gallantry of the Australian Army and Air Force. From the days of ANZAC, we shall always remember them. We are sincerely grateful to you for the homes you have thrown open to us, and in which you have made us feel one of the family.

There is a favourite tune of mine, of which many of us will be wistfully thinking, should we again head towards Australia—'I'll be seeing you in all the old familiar places'; and finally we shall ever remember what you have done for us, the Voluntary Workers who have given their services for so long, the Australian Comforts and Red Cross organisations, the British Centre and Anzac Buffet, the food gifts for Britain, and many others.

For all these things, for all you good wishes, for all your kindnesses, thank you so much Australia.

I cannot help but wonder if the British tabloid press of today would ever be able to print such deep felt occasions, or whether our football followers abroad could even now deserve such an accolade. One lives in hope.

In spite of his enormous success in control of the BPF, Fraser chose as his title for the peerage which Atlee offered him, 'Baron Fraser of North Cape' but that is another story.

Someone told me a true tale about Fraser in Hong Kong on Christmas Day 1945. Two ratings from the destroyer HMS Moon *went to the Fleet Club where they saw Fraser at the bar with some staff officers. One plucked up courage to approach him and enquire whether he might be allowed to buy him a drink. He was delighted and asked if he might have a small beer. The lads asked if they could make it a large Scotch. He agreed and then bought them a drink and chatted with them. In my estimation these recollections are the sign of a great man. What a pity that at the time we were not aware of his greatness. Perhaps that too is an indication of the man!*

He ended his term as C in C BPF in Singapore on 11th June 1946 when he handed over to Admiral Sir Denis Boyd.

Prior to this he had visited Shanghai, Nanking, Peking and Chinwangtao then on to Kure, Yokohama and Tokyo flying his flag in Swiftsure *and then* Newfoundland.

An interesting story is told of a large reception he held in Shanghai at Easter 1946 to entertain American, Chinese, French and Russian dignitaries on board the amenities ship Menestheus.

Apparently the Admiralty refused to pay the bill, but so did Fraser! The Americans were so impressed with Menestheus *that they offered to buy her for £1,000,000, but the Admiralty refused that too and brought her home to be scrapped. Now, I'm not in possession of all the facts and they must have had very good reasons for these decisions. It's just that nobody seems to know them.*

However, the Admiralty did send him a signal in July 1946 which read:

PERSONAL FOR ADMIRAL LORD FRASER
On the occasion of your return to the United Kingdom and hauling down your flag, the Board of Admiralty wish to express to you their high appreciation of your services as Commander-in-Chief of the Eastern Fleet and British Pacific Fleet.

My Lords recall that you assumed command of the Eastern Fleet at a time when it was building up in order to strike in increasing strength against the enemy. Upon the formation of the British Fleet to operate in the Pacific you were selected for the high responsibility of commanding it, and My Lords appreciate the fine spirit, high standard of efficiency and eager desire to come to close grips with the enemy which under your outstanding leadership pervaded the whole Fleet.

They know how much your personal example and inspiration contributed to the success of the many and gallant operations conducted by the ships and aircraft under your command.

They recognise that there were great technical and strategical problems to be solved before the success which was achieved could be guaranteed and in this connection your great experience was of outstanding value.

The Board are happy to feel that your services to the Royal Navy continue.

That's how we all felt.

Extracts from the line book HMS *Swiftsure*, sent by Captain Ian Garnett

On 1st July Commander Luce was promoted to Captain and left *Swiftsure* to take up an appointment on the staff of C-in-C BPF, and we welcomed Commander W. L. M. Brown, DSC, as his successor.

One of the highlights of this visit was the fact that five days' leave was granted to each watch. The British Centre at Sydney provided a list of town and country hosts and hostesses willing to have members of the ship's company as guests, and all tastes were catered for.

That all *Swiftsure*'s efforts on this visit were not entirely social is shown by the fact that the RM Band 'Beat the Retreat' to an appreciative Australian audience on no fewer than five occasions in co-operation with bands from ships in company, the grand climax arriving on 3rd August, when the RM detachment, commanded by Captain Hathway Jones, RM, and the massed bands of *Swiftsure, Colossus* and *Vengeance*, under the baton of BMI P. G. Renn, marched through the centre of Sydney to Martin Place, where the RM detachment formed a Guard of Honour to receive Admiral Sir Bruce Fraser. Then followed the ceremony of Beating the Retreat by the massed bands, and a speech by Sgt. Rattey, VC, AIF, the detachment, headed by the band, then marched through the crowds to the Public Library and dispersed.

The above ceremony was in aid of the Australian Comforts Fund; thus in a small way we repaid them for the hospitality rendered.

At this period (31st July to 7th August) *Swiftsure* carried out a small self-refit at Cockatoo Island and then proceeded back to our billet at Woolloomooloo Docks.

Two dances were held by the ship's company at Mark Foy's ballroom, the second being graced by the presence of the C-in-C, BPF. Both were a huge success, and judging by the number of ladies present, the ship's company had not been idle during the visit. The Chiefs and PO's also held a dance at Paddington Town Hall, which was up to the usual *Swiftsure* standard, music at these functions being provided by *Swiftsure*'s own dance band. The RM detachment and RM band decided to keep the party spirit going, so each gave a social evening, the former at the State Ballroom, and the latter at Sergeant's Hotel. Sydney folk will remember both for many years to come.

On Friday, 9th August *Swiftsure* sailed for Jervis Bay for seven days' working up. About this time rumours began to filter through of Japan's impending surrender, on Sunday, 12th August, we were recalled to Sydney to load up with Red Cross stores in anticipation of a dash to Hong Kong to relieve Allied prisoners of war at Stanley Prison Camp.

A feeling of expectancy hovered over all Australia at this time, and many anticipatory revels took place at King's Cross and other lively spots, the RN contributing their share. At 10 a.m. Wednesday, 15th August, everyone downed tools as the official surrender of Japan was announced, and rejoicing became the order of the day, the ships in harbour contributing to the din with their sirens. *Swiftsure* was due to sail for Hong Kong at 1400 on that day, but rumours were rife that the sailing would be delayed so that we could rejoice with the populace. However, officialdom ruled otherwise, and at 1400 we set sail, in company with the carriers *Indomitable, Vengeance, Venerable* and *Colossus*, the cruiser *Bermuda*, and seven destroyers, amidst unparalleled scenes. The whole populace of Sydney seemed to have come to wish us farewell and Godspeed. They lined the Botanical Gardens, Woolloomooloo Docks and other vantage points, waving flags, singing national airs and cheering. We felt sad, leaving such a people on such a day, but this feeling was tempered by the fact that all of us knew that speed was essential to the well-being of Allied prisoners of war. We raised speed to 25 knots, and 'Our Bridge' faded in the distance.

So ended *Swiftsure*'s visit to Australia's premier port.

RECONSTRUCTION
by J.G.W.

During the forenoon of 15th August, we heard the voice of Mr. Attlee, broadcast from every loudspeaker in Sydney, announcing the end of the war. The city went wild with jubilation, an infection that soon caught on in Woolloomooloo Creek, where ships abandoned work and let off steam intermittently for the remainder of the day. It was no easy task to sail *Swiftsure* at 1400, because the girls persisted in holding hands with the ship's company after the hawsers had been cast off. A touch of irony was provided by *Anson*, who remained in harbour to celebrate in a dry city. (It was rumoured that she had engine-room defects, but we know better!) On our quarterdeck, two harbour launches nestled against 'Y' turret guns—a sure sign of victory—and amidships were stowed two jeeps, six motor cycles, four bicycles, a large quantity of victualling and medical stores, all sorts of ammunition and many small arms. It was certainly an odd departure. In a few hours, however, we settled down once more and the Captain explained the nature of our next job. With Admiral Harcourt in *Indomitable*, and in company with *Venerable, Ursa, Kempenfelt* and *Whirlwind*, we were to take the surrender of the Japanese at some place unknown and then rescue our prisoners of war and internees. Precautions had to be taken against submarine attack, and the routine was anything but peaceful. One very welcome signal abolished censoring, and the Sydney Mail doubled in size.

On the 21st August we fuelled at Manus, and then sailed for Leyte. By this time we had got down to the task of organising a landing party on a big scale, training officers and men in shooting to kill and getting some idea of what was to come. At Subic Bay we found the US Seventh Fleet and took the opportunity of exercising boats' crews in taking men ashore. We waited another two days before Admiral Harcourt decided to proceed to—HONG KONG! The buzz had been correct for a change. Another 24 hours' delay ensued while bad weather held up the Jap envoy, who eventually flew on board *Indomitable* with the redoubtable Commander Craven. Terms for our entry were settled, and on the forenoon of 30th August, Admiral Harcourt and his staff transferred to *Swiftsure*. At 1145 we entered the Lie Mun Pass astern of Captain D.27 in *Kempenfelt*, with everyone at Action Stations and wondering what life was left in the shore batteries. Scores of fighters roared overhead, but no trouble was experienced, and we anchored off the battered dockyard in company with *Euryalus* to disgorge a total of 500 seamen and marines. The boats made for the dockyard, and Operation Lion started. Commander W. L. M. Brown, DSC was in charge of the combined landing party, later to be known as 'Brownforce', and he met a Japanese officer with ideas about surrender at the top of the jetty steps—rather an anti-climax and disappointment for the blood-thirsty Royals who followed up. Our job was to ensure an orderly exodus of Japanese troops from Hong Kong, take over from the Japs the security of the food and ammunition dumps, and generally to police the island.

The Japanese were cleared out of the dockyard by sunset, a few unfortunates being caught by the Chinese mob outside the gates. We picketed and patrolled the dockyard during the night and welcomed a number of POWs from the Sham Suipo camp. The next day *Anson* and *Indomitable* landed their troops, and 'Brownforce' established their HQ at the Cecil Hotel with outlying platoons at Aberdeen, Taiko and Stanley camp. A relief party was sent out to Stanley with food and cigarettes for the internees, and it was amazing to see their reactions to fresh bread, English cigarettes and chocolates. Some of us

HMS Swiftsure *enters Hong Kong—30th August 1945. Photo: Captain Paddy Vincent*

HMS Kempenfelt *at 38 knots. Mirs Bay, N. Hong Kong, having visited HMS* Anson *in quarantine with smallpox! Photo: R. F. Parton*

sampled their daily bread made of rice and linseed oil. It tasted like sawdust, but they thought it a great delicacy. They were genuinely pleased to talk to any visitors, and we made a point of running a regular service to the camp with a bus that had severe wheel wobble, but an ample capacity for passengers.

The *Anson*'s 'Kennedy Force' established itself at the Police Station, which housed a number of Jap officer prisoners. Guarded by Marines, they looked an evil bunch of scoundrels. A fat, bellicose major turned on his guards one evening and the Royals took down his pants and beat his backside with bayonet scabbards. He certainly lost 'face' over that incident.

The Hong Kong Police Force and Naval Volunteers were a broken reed. Three years in an internment camp had left them so weak that they were only fit for interpreters for our patrols, who very soon got to know their own way around the town. Our men had a way of dealing with the Chinese that was never bettered by any soldier, and there was remarkably little trouble. Liberty-men from ships were a different matter, and the scheme of 'walking parties' very soon had to be dropped.

Although the island was fairly quiet, there was never a dull moment for 'Brownforce'. For instance, ex-Japanese junks had to be searched and guarded, whilst escaping Japanese and 'Quisling' Chinese were frequently brought to the 'Cecil' for protection and custody. Our enterprising Torpedo-gunner's Mate forced his way nefariously into a petrol dump and supplied all the 25 'Brownforce' vehicles with fuel. A/B Marshall injured himself fatally with an automatic pistol and was buried on 4th September at Happy Valley. Innumerable ammunition dumps were discovered all over the island, which the Chinese persisted in looting at the risk of their lives in order to secure charges for fishing. We saw the late Jap High Executioner caught in the act of escaping to Kowloon, and his end was not pleasant.

The strain of patrolling and sentry duties soon began to tell, and platoons were relieved weekly. A few cases of malaria occurred at Taikoo, and sandfly fever broke out at the Cecil Hotel. But everyone enjoyed his spell ashore, even if it was hard work.

Gradually other ships arrived to lend a hand and finally General Festing came with 300 Commando troops who eventually relieved 'Brownforce' of their duties. Admiral Bruce Fraser arrived in *Duke of York*, toured the positions occupied by the Navy, and seemed very satisfied with the organisation. The Signing of the Surrender ceremony was postponed no less than seven times, and the last act of the *Swiftsure*'s landing parties was to line the route near the Queen's pier through which Admirals, Generals and Japanese passed on their way to and from Government House. *Swiftsure* fired a 21-gun salute of 'Forty Special' charges, and the results nearly sank Side Party Jenny. Laden with her trophies, our troops returned aboard on Sunday, 16th September.

While our landing parties were busy on shore, those left on board were by no means idle. The primary duty of the ship was to keep the shore supplied with everything they needed, a task in which all departments co-operated with

Colonel Takunada, Commandant of Hong Kong POW Camps being taken into custody. 'We removed his braces to prevent his escape! Hence his hands in pockets.' Reg Parton. Photo: R. F. Parton

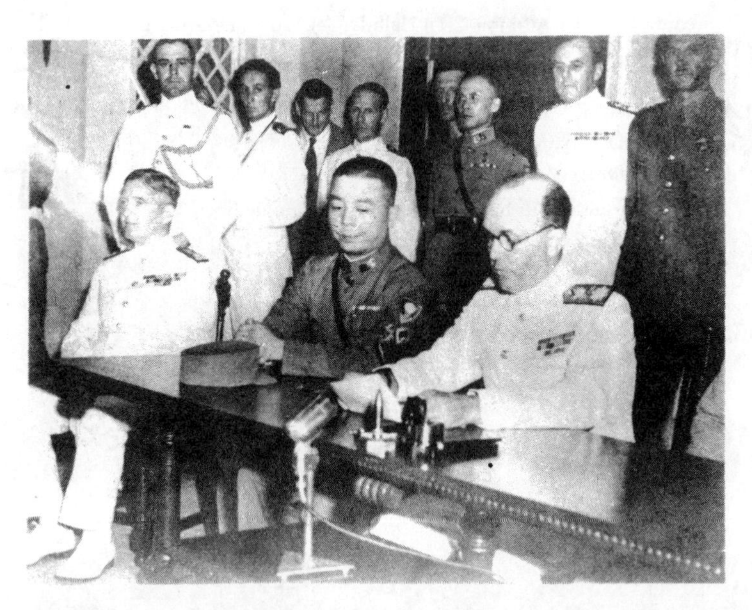

Surrender Ceremony. Rear Admiral C. H. J. Harcourt C in C Hong Kong signs for Britain. Admiral Sir Bruce Fraser sitting extreme left. Photo: R. F. Parton

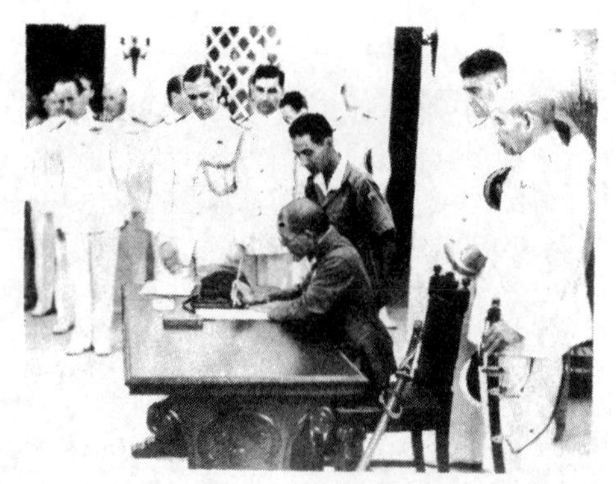

Hong Kong Surrender 16th September 1945. Major General Umekichi signs for Japan. Captain Eccles HMS Indomitable *second right. Commander Stokes HMS* Vengeance *extreme left. Photo: R. F. Parton*

INSTRUMENT OF SURRENDER

We, Major General Unekichi Okada and Vice Admiral Ruitaro Fuhita, in virtue of the unconditional surrender to the Allied Powers of all Japanese Armed Forces and all forces under Japanese control wherever situated, as proclaimed in Article Two of the Instrument of Surrender signed in Tokio Bay on 2nd September, 1945, on behalf of the Emperor of Japan and the Japanese Imperial Headquarters, do hereby unconditionally surrender ourselves and all forces under our control to Rear Admiral Cecil Halliday Jepson Harcourt, CB, CBE, and undertake to carry out all such instructions as may be given by him or under his authority, and to issue all necessary orders for the purpose of giving effect to all his instructions.

Given under our hands this 16th day of September, 1945, at Government House, Hong Kong.

海軍中将 藤田類太郎

陸軍少将 岡田梅吉

In the presence of

On behalf of the Government of the United Kingdom

On behalf of the Commander-in-Chief China Theatre

Copy of original document of surrender. Hong Kong.
Photo: J. M. Montgomery, HMS Indomitable

pursers so successfully that not one twitter of complaint was heard. It was on the ship, also, that the rehabilitation of the ex-prisoners of war and internees fell, and a vast amount of entertaining of men and women, of soldiers and sailors had to be done. At the beginning they were introduced to the luxury of white bread and butter, but by the time we left, most of them had renewed their acquaintance with the best that we could provide. Although we were doing a job which we were only too glad to be able to do, their gratitude knew no bounds, and in that we received rewards far in excess of our deserts.

One day the Chaplain arrived by bus from Stanley camp, accompanied by all the children in the 9 to 11 age group, who, after looking round the ship—during which no one fell off the mast or wrecked too many valuable fittings—they settled down to tea in the wardroom. Never had so much been eaten by so many in so short a time. Before taking them to see a cinema show consisting of two 'Mickey Mouses', the first lieutenant, as senior father on board, carried out the duties of 'Uncle Potty' in a most efficient manner. One small boy was sick on the Padre on the way home—as he had foolishly eaten the whole of his chocolate ration!

Towards the end of our stay, the officers, getting impatient at the continual delays in the signing of the surrender, decided to hold it themselves. A Japanese general, in the form of a torpedo officer, was captured, the captain was hurriedly promoted to the rank of Governor-General, and, in front of an admiring audience and representatives of the press (who thought they were coming to the real thing), and accompanied by a fourteen-gun salute, the Japanese envoy signed a complete, unconditional surrender—without trousers!

And so we left Hong Kong. It was a wonderful experience for all who took part in its liberation and the subsequent endeavours to clear up the mess. The Chinese had suffered terrible losses: their pre-war population of one and a half million was more then halved by starvation and cruelty, and their trade had come to a standstill. But, in spite of it all, John Chinaman had started to smile away his difficulties and use his great sense of humour and limitless energy to recover the prosperity that was Hong Kong. In *Swiftsure*, we felt it was a job well done and yet another feather in our cap.

JAPAN
by P.M.C.V.

It can hardly be said that Tokyo itself merited the fifteen months of hard work that it had taken us to get there, but we felt justifiably proud to be the forerunners of the Commonwealth Forces of Occupation in Japan, who were not to arrive until four months later. The ship arrived in Tokyo Bay on the 23rd September in what afterwards proved to be typical Tokyo weather—windy and raining, and with a typhoon warning on the signal files. Steaming to our berth we passed through the enormous fleet of United States ships lying in the bay, and anchored well out off Yokohama harbour, where the other British cruisers were lying. The first view of Japan was uninspiring; the land on either side of the bay was low and monotonous, and for a lot of the time was barely discernible through the rain and the mist. Fujiyama, which we had all looked forward to seeing, was nowhere in sight, and it was generally presumed that the GI's had already taken it.

Soon after our arrival, we once again became the flagship of Rear-Admiral Brind, and HMS *Newfoundland* left, none too regretfully, for the lesser glories of Sydney, turning over to us the few odd duties required. Unlike Hong Kong, there was no call for landing parties on any large scale, and for the majority of the ship's company the period spent in Tokyo Bay was one of extreme monotony.

The ship did, however, man the British Consulate at Yokohama with an officer in charge as the British Naval Representative and a staff of two officers and some fifteen seamen. The duties of the British Naval Representative were to act as a liaison officer between the Royal Navy and the US forces ashore, as well as to carry out what really amounted to the British Consul's duties in Yokohama.

A party of twenty Royal Marines also landed during this period and took over the guard duties at the British Embassy in Tokyo from the *Newfoundland*. This party constituted the entire British occupation force in Japan for ten weeks, and although the guard was of varying strengths and composition, Royal Marines from the *Swiftsure* were in Tokyo continually until we eventually left the area in December. This Guard made a great impression upon the Japanese and upon the United States occupation forces, both on account of the smartness of their drill and bearing and on account of their calm efficiency. They soon became one of the sights of Tokyo, together with the Diet and General MacArthur, and they had to withstand a veritable daily barrage from cameras of all sizes. One GI, having asked a Royal Marine what the idea of having Generals on sentry-go might be, received the reply, 'Oh, we work downwards in our army!' Later on this Guard provided a Guard of Honour for the Chief of the Imperial General Staff, Lord Alanbrooke, when he visited the Embassy, as well as giving a ceremonial beating of the retreat with the Royal Marine Band for the benefit of many senior Allied officers.

Another duty undertaken by the ship was the cleaning and repair of the old British destroyer *Thracian*, which was lying in the Yokosuka naval base. This destroyer had been captured by the Japanese in Hong Kong in 1941 and used as a radar experimental ship during the war. Chief Petty Officer Brown was installed as Captain with Petty Officer Taylor as his executive officer with an able-bodied ship's company of ten to clean and prepare the ship for her journey back to Hong Kong. From their comments afterwards, it did not appear as though Japanese standards of ship cleanliness were quite up to our own!

In effect, *Swiftsure* was also acting as general depot ship to all destroyers of the Tokyo force, as she had to supply them with bread, men and many other items of provisions and clothing, as well as helping them out with any repair work required.

One of the duties of the British Naval Representative ashore was the most important task of organising a supply of beer from the Japanese breweries to the ships lying in the bay, but it was quite obvious that one bottle of beer a day would not be sufficient to compensate for the monotony of several weeks in Tokyo. Work was therefore, started as early as possible to convert the Yokohama Yacht Club into a beer canteen. Working parties under the bosun, using stores from the ship, got the job done in double-quick time, and the canteen was officially opened by Rear-Admiral Brind as the 'White Ensign Club' on the 5th of October.

Most of the ship's company visited Tokyo once during her time in the Bay, but few cared to make the trip twice. For the first week a destroyer came alongside daily and took the libertymen direct to Tokyo, but when this scheme was discontinued, the visitors had to face the three-quarter-hour train journey from Yokohama. A special carriage for military personnel only was supposed to run with each train, but few managed to find it; the remainder obtaining first-class opportunities to study the Japanese at extremely close quarters. As there were no recreational facilities for British personnel in the capital, the visits to Tokyo looked something like a glorified hiking picnic, and at midday numbers of the ship's company could be seen sitting in Tokyo's parks eating pusser's sandwiches. There was little to buy in Tokyo, and all prices were very high; but strangely enough, most of the Tokyo libertymen brought back large numbers of souvenirs with them. One remarkable point was that the pay office had more yen returned to it than it had issued during this period, and it was noticed that the sales of tickler tobacco for the month showed a marked increase!

During our first week in Tokyo Bay the distinguished British author, Mr. C. S. Forester, visited the ship for two days and gave an interesting talk on some of his war service in Hollywood. He also stated that he intended to finish off the last chapter of 'Lord Hornblower', the last book in his famous 'Captain Hornblower' series, whilst he was on board the ship that night.

The ship left Tokyo for a short cruise with the destroyer *Wessex* on the 12th of October, calling first at the naval base of Sasebo on north-western Kyushu, and although the town itself was devastated and uninteresting, we were given our first opportunity to see something of the nearby Japanese countryside. A party from the ship also visited and inspected the new and undamaged Japanese cruiser *Sakawa* which was lying in Sasebo, and which has since been sunk by atomic bomb at Bikini Atoll.

We moved south to Nagasaki early on the 18th, and thanks to the co-operation of the United States marines, everybody got the opportunity to visit what was left of the city. Pictures and articles in the newspapers had taught us what to expect, but nevertheless the sight of such complete devastation came as an unpleasant shock to many of us. The newspapers had in no way exaggerated the damage; only a few twisted buildings stood amongst the acres of rubble, and although a few roads had been cleared, the rest was as it had fallen, with charred bones, and even skulls, amongst the rubble. Here and there amongst the wrecked buildings could be seen torpedo-warheads and other evidences of smashed war-plants, but the presence of so many small, unbroken ornaments and chinaware amongst the rubble showed only too clearly that most of the rubble had been small Japanese homes. Most of us returned on board from our visit in an extremely depressed state of mind, and nobody was sorry when we sailed again for Kagoshima that same evening.

The countryside around Kagoshima is most attractive, and our two visits there were enjoyed by nearly everybody. The bay is surrounded by high, tree-covered hills, and the two-cratered volcano of Sakurashima rises straight out of the harbour opposite the town itself, which was devastated, but Sakurashima island proved popular with the more energetic members of the ship's company. There are several Japanese villages on the island, attractive to sight if not to smell, and tangerines were to be had almost for the asking. One of the most noticeable points about the place was the complete absence of United States forces.

The fact that the volcano was gently smoking did not deter one group of climbing enthusiasts who managed to reach the 4,000 ft. crater after a somewhat arduous day's climb across the lava. Contrary to the usual practice, these pioneers failed to leave the customary Union Jack flying from the summit, but in order that their achievement should not go unrecognised the volcano has been referred to ever since as 'Dougalyama' after the well-known leader of the expedition.

Whilst in Kagoshima, the first party from the ship to strike inland went for forty-eight hours' leave to Kirishima-Hayashida, a place famous for its hot springs, and their glowing accounts made us all eager to do the same, when opportunity occurred.

We were joined in Kagoshima on the 20th by the destroyers *Grenville* and *Urania*, who brought some very welcome mail with them, and on the next day we sailed in company for Wakayama on the eastern end of the Inland Sea. There were the usual number of United States ships in the port, and, as with everywhere else, the rare sight of a 'limey' cruiser aroused a fair amount of interest amongst them. There was little of interest in the small town of Wakayama, but for those who had the Yen there was a fair amount of lacquer-ware on sale.

The 26th October—one year after leaving the United Kingdom—found us back off Yokohama. The weather, always windy and raining, was now getting cold into the bargain, and the arrival of sheepskin coats and other gift clothing from South Africa in HMS *Ariadne* was opportune. The arrival of these minelayers was always very welcome as there was no airmail service to Japan, and all our mail was brought from Hong Kong in these fast minelayers and destroyers. Meanwhile, the gradual change-over in the ship's company was taking place; the minelayers brought reliefs for the men with high age and service groups, who went back in them to Hong Kong for passage back to the United Kingdom. The occasional arrival of store ships was also very welcome, as their fresh fruit and vegetables brought a change from the dehydrated spuds and cabbage which had to suffice for a lot of the time.

During the beginning of November it was thought that the ship might be able to pay a visit to Wei Hai Wei in North China, and in company with HMS *Ulysses* we once again sailed down to Kagoshima in readiness. Owing to the complicated diplomatic situation prevailing in North China at the time, however, the proposed visit never materialised, and we spent a further very pleasant week in Kagoshima instead.

On this occasion *Swiftsure*'s mountaineers were out in force. One large party followed the route taken by the pioneers of the previous month, whilst an even larger party of about thirty, headed by the Commander, overcame all difficulties of language and terrain and climbed to the southern and active crater of the volcano, which had fine large patches of sulphur inside it and was steaming well. The main pastime of the climbers at the top was rolling huge boulders down into the crater, but it is reported to be only a coincidence that the volcano erupted in a most damaging manner four months later.

The ship returned to Tokyo after a week, and on leaving Kagoshima-wan, yet another abortive anti-fish depth-charge attack was carried out. Only one somewhat bloated fish came to the surface, and even the supply department admitted that it was insufficient for the whole ship's company.

The monotony of the last three weeks in Tokyo Bay was considerably relieved by the organisation of forty-eight hour leave parties to Nikko and Myanoshita in the mountains near Fujiyama. Each party went by train, looking more like a complete expeditionary force than a forty-eight hour leave party with their crates of food and sacks of bread. The parties stayed for the most part in small Japanese hotels, and living Japanese-fashion was an experience in itself-eating cross-legged; sleeping between kimono-mattresses, and living between paper walls, to say nothing of the communal baths! The Japanese staffs of the hotels were most co-operative, to say the least, and for most of us the two days went by all too quickly. For hiking, the country was unsurpassed with its unexpected views of Fujiyama, its lakes, its gorges and its sulphur springs. Luckily also it was not too late for the famous Japanese maple tints, and the mountains covered with so many different shades of red made an unforgettable sight for many of the ship's company.

Throughout our time in Tokyo, the ship's concert party really came into its own, and besides one show for the RN in the Octagon Theatre, Yokohama, it gave no less than eight performances for the United States forces in the Tokyo and Yokohama areas, as well as giving a number of shows in destroyers and store ships. These shows were extremely popular, especially with the Americans, and they always drew large audiences.

We eventually turned over all our shore duties to HMAS *Hobart* at the beginning of December, and left for Manus on the 6th, where we met and commiserated with HMS *Tyne* northward bound for Tokyo, where it had snowed on the day after we left. Although it always appears less unpleasant when one is southward bound, none of us was sorry to see the last of Manus, but when we sailed on the 14th December we little realised that we were destined never to visit the BPF's own tropical isle again.

Extract from 'South China Morning Post', dated 27.2.1983, sent by Captain P. Vincent CBE RN

THE DAY JAPAN GAVE UP HONGKONG

As the fleet approached Hongkong, one of the vessels was picked to be vanguard ship to enter the harbour and spy out the lay of the land.

'We came in at battle stations,' remembers Phil Grout, who in those days was a young gunnery officer aboard the cruiser HMS *Swiftsure*. 'Admiral Harcourt was taking no chances. Nobody was sure if the Japanese would surrender or if there were fanatics who would fight to the bitter end as the Japanese soldiers had fought so bravely and stubbornly right through the Pacific.'

For days previously the fighter planes from the aircraft carriers accompanying the fleet had made low level reconnaissance flights over the island. They had told the fleet that all looked quiet in the Colony.

'Quiet was right,' Phil Grout remembers. He looks out over the concrete spires of Causeway Bay and the skyscrapers on the hills above North Point. 'It was certainly nothing like this,' he says. 'Those on board *Swiftsure* who had been to Hongkong before the war, were shocked at the state of the Colony. They couldn't believe how battered and rundown it looked.'

The slow passage of the *Swiftsure* down the harbour, guns on either side of the ship levelled at the shore ready to open fire at any hostile move, ended off the Royal Hongkong Yacht Club at Kellett Island where she dropped anchor.

There had been no firing at the cruiser so landing parties were put ashore, first Royal Marines and then parties of sailors. One of the first parties of sailors put ashore was under the command of Lieutenant Grout.

The 25 tars, armed with rifles and sub-machine guns, cautiously fanned out through the streets and rounded up members of the Japanese garrison. The sight of the British uniforms brought warm welcomes from those few hungry and lean Hongkong residents who were on the streets.

The worry about Japanese resistance in Hongkong—and the secret fear that the defeated garrison might massacre the prisoners of war and internees—was laid and put to rest. Although the soldiers of the Imperial Japanese Army had long proven their willingness to die, they were now following the orders of Emperor Hirohito and were quietly laying down their arms.

But not all of them were able to surrender.

'We rounded up the enemy garrison and held them in the old naval dockyard,' Phil Grout recalls today. 'There was a big crowd of Chinese at the gates seeking revenge. Those Japanese who had taken to the hills were hunted down and killed by the crowds. From a distance, the dockyards must have looked peaceful but when stragglers from the Japanese garrison tried to join their comrades, they were attacked and killed by the crowd.

'I saw one Japanese grabbed and used as a battering ram, his head smashed against the steel gates of the naval base. And when the long line of prisoners was marched away, armed troops and sailors had to protect the column.

'There were some cases of Japanese hiding in buildings making a dash to try to join the column, but if the crowd caught them before they could get past the protective ring of British troops, the Japanese met a grisly end.'

The people of Hongkong, the 600,000 of them who were left in the Colony, were taking their revenge for three years and eight months of brutal occupation, starvation, rape, murder, torture and humiliation.

But as the rest of Admiral Harcourt's fleet entered the harbour and troops and sailors established the core of a British military government, order was swiftly restored.

From Sub Lt. (A) R. F. Parton, RNVR

LIFE IN HONG KONG IMMEDIATELY AFTER
JAPANESE SURRENDER

5th September 1945

Light Fleet Carrier HMS *Vengeance* slipped quietly along the Li-Moon pass toward Hong Kong Harbour in grey mist and pouring rain.

The quiet, broken only by the constant low pitched hum, that always seems to emanate from a vessel under way, was eerie. We did not know what to expect around the corner.

What was around that corner was HK Harbour alive with shipping including men-of-war, merchant men and junks. We had followed Rear Admiral Sir Cecil Harcourt (flying his flag in HMS *Venerable*) C in C 14th CAG to become Military Governor of Hong Kong following the Surrender of the Japanese.

Flying was suspended and the pool of Officers and men thus created from 812 squadron (CO Lt. Cdr. Cedric Coxon—Barracudas) and 1850 squadron (CO Lt. Cdr. Wilf Waller—Corsairs) became work horses in the task of rehabilitating Hong Kong Island and the New Territories.

My memory of the next six weeks is of hard, dirty work, heat, happiness and camaraderie. Everyone pitched in with a will—the cheerfulness of the Chinese being matched by the matelots now the terror of war was passing. There is *no doubt* that the H-bombs on Japan saved millions of lives—amongst them I am sure were our own.

With a gang of 20 Chinese coolies my task was to clear up HM dockyard. Sorting out the good from the scrap. All the various stores were sorted in turn—I cannot remember if we got all the correct Requisition Forms squared off, but the Chippies Shop was a marvellous place for 'Rabbits'. This describes 'the day job'.

The 'night job' was i/c the St. Francis Hotel in Victoria, shared this chore with 'Stormy' Fairweather.

The hotel had been requisitioned as Servicemen's shore billets. During the occupation it had been used as a Japanese Brothel, for which they had fitted it out with sub-floors of rice straw, two feet above the originals, with partitions, to the cubicles, of bamboo. There was a large main hall and sweeping staircase to a balcony, all around at first and second floor levels.

My abiding memory is of dozens of ratings clad only in shorts, tearing out this fragile, dirty dusty cladding, with bare hands and primitive tools. Then with whoops of glee, hurling it off the balconies into the hall below. I can close my eyes now and recall the scene akin to a *hot* pre-war London fog.

We brought two submarines alongside the dockyard wall, and coupled them into the city power supply. This enabled some of our colleagues to put the city transport back into operation, including tram-cars. It seems this problem necessitated the commandeering of flashy cars, i.e. Mercury coupés and the like—presumbly to visit the terminal points of the transport systems? 'Bert' Burman from Birmingham—Corsairs to Mercury. J. F. K. (Bill) Williams, a looker on 812 landed the job? of restoring!! liberating!!? Mr. Chung's warehouse—Kowloon Side. What Mr. Chung had done to, or for, the Japs remains a mystery. But whenever we saw 'Bill' and that was not too often, he would only talk in riddles and hint of mysterious arrangements.

'Stormy' Fairweather's 'day job' involved the notorious Stanley Prison Camp. As a direct result of his experiences there, he persuaded the majority of the ship's company to give anything they could to relieve the privations of the newly released prisoners, who had been incarcerated in that vile place. We all queued at 'Slops' and almost emptied it, to this end.

The recipients insisted on some form of payment for these presents—often small trinkets that they had salvaged after nearly four years. They were unbroken, proud and still independent, and so insistent that many of us have a small item today that, looked at in 1990, tells of analloyed British Grit.

The Port Party arrived in *Fencer* early in October—we returned to flying from Kai-Tek. The Chinese were removing a small hill on the approach to the main runway from the West. They used only yokes (similar to yesteryear's dairymaids) and two wicker baskets. Talk about ants!!

My log book records mine searches in the mouth of the river; chasing pirates in their junks around the numerous small islands; supporting Marines landing on these islands to flush them out. Border Patrol—keeping watch on Chang-Kai-Chek's army coming down the mountain passes to embark for Japan.

Light relief—as the only light aircraft available we flew VIPs up to Canton. I remember one smashing man, the Swiss Consul, rotund, about 5′2″, a small gentleman of the old school who had the greatest difficulty in gaining access to the observer's cockpit in the Barra. Never mind, he took me to a super reception at the British Embassy in Canton.

Not perhaps the most glamorous war—but we contributed at least four months of our lives to see Hong Kong begin to rise again. To what heady pinnacles in the world's economy—and soon 1997!

From Stoker Frederick D. Clark, HMS *Indomitable*

Another unusual event was when we reclaimed Hong Kong from the Japanese. On this occasion the minesweepers entered harbour first, followed later by the rest of the Task Force except *Indomitable* and *Venerable*, both staying outside to provide air cover. We in *Indomitable* had been on full alert for some time, so when it was our turn to go in we did not know what to expect as our aircraft *(857 Sqdn Avengers.—Ed.)* had already warded off one attack by explosive suicide boats on 31 August so were surprised to hear the order 'Hands to Clear' shortly followed by 'Clear Lower Deck, Hands fall in to enter harbour'. And so it was that *Indomitable* with ship's company lining the deck proudly entered enemy held Hong Kong as though she was entering her home base in Portsmouth. The formal surrender was signed about two weeks later on 16th September 1945 and the Victory March was held in early October. Before we left Hong Kong we embarked two suicide boats which were secured in the upper hangar.

After *Indom.* left for home I took a few days leave with friends in a small town in the Australian outback. On my last day there on my way to the station I was approached by a very thin Australian who said he had seen me on *Indom.* I didn't recognise him but he said he was a prisoner who had returned on that ship. He more or less offered me the moon for 'helping to bring him back from Hell' as he called it. Naturally I declined his offer but settled for a drink. We had a very pleasant drink in the short time I had before departing for my train. This small instance multiplied for each prisoner proves that the BPF was needed after all.

All these bits and pieces are from memory only, I kept no diary and all my photographs were stolen. While serving in *Amethyst* in Hong Kong, the stokers mess deck was raided one night by Chinese who took all our personal gear including over 100 of my photos amassed during my service years. But that is another story.

From Leading Seaman Radar Tom Roxby, HMS *Newfoundland*

Shortly after the surrender I took a small party up to Tokyo from Yokosuka where the *Newfoundland* was berthed. We were in resplendent whites and well stocked with corned-beef sandwiches. On the way we secured a lift on the back of a lorry which turned out to be carrying coal!

Looking for a place to clean up we entered a tea-house. The staff ran away

Hiroshima.
22nd March 1946.
Photo: Bert Crane

Hiroshima Station
still stands
March 1946.
Photo: Bob Boon

Nagasaki,
14th March 1946.
Photo: Bert Crane

only to return carrying cups of green tea. The language barrier was total and, as a gesture of goodwill, we offered them our corned-beef sandwiches. They cowered away and refused to take them ostensibly because the foreign devils would have poisoned them. We decided to eat a piece from each sandwich and proferred the remainder; immediately the sandwiches were taken and wolfed down. The green tea was not to our taste and indeed previously unknown to us. But manfully we took our share, and left the tea-house with a warm glow of humanity.

From H. Johnson, Ex AB ST, HMS *Black Prince*

Our worst accident happened on July 13th, Friday. Firing some acoustic shells, one explodes in left gun in 'A' Turret, I'm underneath in the messdeck, the gunlayer was badly injured, he never recovered (it was my first burial at sea and I hope and pray I never see one again).

We have been ordered back to Sydney for a new gun barrel, sailing down we stop at Guam, then that god-forsaken Manus.

0300, August 15th 'Japs finished' over Tannoy. Thank God we'll soon be going home. That's a laugh—we finish up in China, Hong Kong, Shanghai, four rotten months!

Had a news flash we're going to New Zealand, Oh blast, aren't we ever going home! Eventually we did, on July 17th, 1946, almost two years away, but we did not bring back our wonderful ship HMS *Black Prince*, she was sold to the NZ Navy. She ended her days in a scrap yard in May 1962 and, would you believe, in Osaki in Japan with several other great ships of the once proud British Pacific Fleet?

From O/Tel H. W. Lemming, HMS *Black Prince*

HMS *Black Prince*, a modified DIDO class cruiser, was one of the first ships to form a part of the British Pacific Fleet.

I was a wireless operator, and remember a message coming through telling us to steam out of the area as a bomb was about to be dropped that was 100,000 times greater than an ordinary TNT bomb—this was the first atom bomb that was dropped on the Japanese.

The whole fleet was on its way to Tokyo Bay to bombard and carry out strikes when the second bomb was dropped and the Japs surrendered.

On the way we had a gun turret blown up and were considered to be at risk to defend ourselves against attack, and were ordered back to our base at Sydney harbour—and therefore were the first ship to return to Sydney after the surrender—this having taken place while we were on our way back.

HMS *Black Prince* was then sent to Hong Kong where she helped release the prisoners at Kowloon, and carried out anti-piracy patrols in the Celina Sea.

She was then sent up to Shanghai which meant sailing up the Yangtse river at night with all lights out as the Communist troops were still at war with the Nationalist troops on the other side.

At the end of our time in this area, we were given a six-week cruise, covering the North and South Islands of New Zealand—as our Captain at the time was a New Zealander.

HMS *Black Prince* was paid off in New Zealand and transferred to the Royal NZ Navy.

This very happy and efficient gunnery cruiser was eventually towed to the Japanese shipyards and sold as scrap metal. Probably ended up in some Datsun/Toyota cars.

From Lt. (A) Gordon Aitken RNVR, HMS *Illustrious*

I was in 1833 squadron, CO Monk, until he was replaced by Norman Hanson. Unless we were old or very young it was normal to do two and a half years as a sub and eight years at Lt. I became Lt. (A) RNVR shortly before leaving the Pacific.

Once I had to land on *Victorious* because of a fire on our deck. Before I could take off again, an old friend in an Avenger damaged my wing and prop. resulting in three days holidays while repairs were carried out. An old school friend was a pilot in the Avenger squadron, Arbuthnot a very small person. I had to laugh when I heard his mechanics discussing him while he was climbing up into his plane, saying he was too small to be sent to war. His father was a well-decorated General and he is now a Marquis with a DSC.

We started off as a 10 plane squadron and ended up I think at 18. Baxter (NZ) and Reggie Shaw were taken out of Changi and executed after the war was over. The perpetrator committed suicide. Baxter suffered a lot with skin trouble in *Illustrious* in the tropics. I hate to think what life was like for them with the Japs.

Vian did very well for himself and his signals sounded terrific, but he had the knack of upsetting us when he talked to us en masse. On our way to Australia after Palembang, *Euryalus* put three anti-tank shells into *Illustrious*, firing at a Jap flying over our deck. I felt he credited us with no understanding. Mike Crosley was in a similar gathering.

Illustrious had a lovely old Pay Commander called Tottenham. Unwisely we used to allow the squadron writer to type any official letters we had to write. This invariably ended in long lectures from Tottenham about putting the 'Sir' in the wrong place. I never did understand. Of course we were at fault due to our light-hearted attitudes. Ian Savel, our Commander Flying, once caught me on deck in harbour without my hat and asked me where it was. Teasingly I said, 'Downstairs in my cabin.' I wish I had thought more quickly and said, 'Downstairs in my room.'

You mentioned Major Cheesman on a number of occasions. I have not met him, but I have read about and of him a lot. I think of him always with a smile.

There were times when his squadron was given the job of doing a low level patrol to try to foil kamikazes. Every now and again he would pop up to see if the fleet was still in sight, bringing a blip to the radar. On one occasion my flight was sent down to investigate. Camouflage had the effect of making it difficult to make out the shape of a plane against the sea until one was pretty close. Cheesman, when he saw a flight coming at him would say over the radio, 'Go away, silly boy.'

Your book has brought back all sorts of memories, for instance, instead of 'cheers' when drinking, 'Up your Sakishima Gunto', or, 'Up your Ishigaki Jima', became popular. And do you remember those odd loos at Manus at the end of those little piers?

From George Burton, Leading Wireman, HMS *Welcome*

George Burton explained how there were two types of mine in which he was trained to deal, magnetic and acoustic. Those ships where percussion is used for rivetting etc. have a magnetic field induced into the metal because of the earth's magnetic field. In the Northern Hemisphere this points downwards.

Sweeping for magnetic mines—known as LL or Double L sweeping—two ships or more used to discharge a heavy electrical current into the sea between two cables trailed astern, the first 50 yards or so of which were insulated to keep the charge away from the minesweeper.

This charge of magnetic field would actuate the trip mechanism in the mine.

Acoustic mines were actuated by sound waves of the ship's machinery so minesweepers created artificial sound waves to discharge the mines at a distance.

Some minesweepers carried Oropesa gear using a towed steel cable to bring moored mines to the surface.

At the cessation of hostilities there remained the huge task of mine clearance in sea lanes all over the world and being attached to the British Pacific Fleet, HMS *Welcome* worked her way into the Pacific, eventually sweeping between the islands of Japan where the Americans were already active. The presence of a minesweeping flotilla together with other British naval units in these waters also played a part in a 'Fly the Flag' exercise and among places visited were Hiroshima and Nagasaki.

On 9th August 1985, The Worcester Evening News carried the following story:

THE DAY I SAILED INTO HELL

It was the sight of the little children that turned George Burton's stomach over. He'd been through the war and was used to death, but this was something different.

'Most were swathed in bandages, they had been terribly burned and many had lost limbs. They were hobbling about in splints and they looked at you

HMS Welcome *enters Hiroshima. Photo: George Burton (taken by ship's Photographer)*

with such pleading eyes.

'I had a camera with me but I just couldn't bring myself to take any pictures. I thought to myself "Have we really done this?" It made you want to cry.'

As a crewman aboard HMS *Welcome,* George had been in the seas around Japan in the late summer of 1945 assisting the American Navy. He was one of the first British people to visit both the stricken cities of Hiroshima and Nagasaki and see at first hand the carnage the atomic bombs had caused.

It was a cold, overcast morning when his minesweeper sailed slowly into the harbour at Hiroshima. 'We had heard what had happened but nothing could prepare us for what we saw,' he said. 'Our first overriding impression was one of utter desolation—everything seemed to have been flattened, razed to the ground—but then amazingly we saw several tall chimneys still standing. I couldn't understand how those chimneys, which seemed so vulnerable, had survived. They were just like long blades of grass sticking out of a lawn that you've just cut.'

The ship docked and the crew were allowed to go into the town—or what remained of it.

'There was debris everywhere. You couldn't see where the streets had been, everything was covered over and strewn about. Trees had been stripped bare and flattened in lines like matchsticks.

'The Japanese were walking about with masks over their faces to keep out

Hong Kong, September 1945. HMS Vengeance, *812 Squadron Barracudas. 1850 Squadron Corsairs. Moored on port quarter are HMS* Venerable, *HMS* Montclare *and HMS* Artifex. *Photo R. F. Parton*

the dust and the stench of rotting bodies. You were afraid to move incase you uncovered a body. It was like a nightmare.

Through the city ran a large canal and this had been choked with rotting bodies. The dust had made people very thirsty and they had crawled to the water to try and drink. Many, being too weak, had fallen in and drowned.

The 'ultimate area' was within a half-mile radius of the centre of the blast. Everything in that mile circle had gone, blown to smithereens. But worse than that, the terrible radiation and shock waves had spread out for many more miles.

'Strangely we never thought that we might be affected by the radiation at that time,' George added. 'It was something new and I suppose no one really recognised the danger.'

The British sailors had to put handkerchiefs over their mouths but even these soon became caked with the dust which blew off the rubble.

From Hiroshima, George—who is now a keen military historian and lives in Malvern—brought a cup with a piece of glass fused to it by the atomic blast. From Nagasaki he brought part of the huge bell which crashed into a thousand pieces as the Roman Catholic church collapsed.

'Having seen the results at first hand I wish there was some way that nuclear weapons could be outlawed,' he said. 'No-one wins. They are terrible devices. But I can't see it happening. Once you invent something you're stuck with it.

If Hitler or Japan had had the Bomb they would have used it, so what were we to do?'

Alongside, a second article appeared. It read:

BOY WHO SAW THE ATOM AGE DAWN

Hiroshi Nakashima remembers no noise, just a blinding flash of light and then crawling from the wreckage of what had been his home in down-town Hiroshima.

In a split second his world and that of thousands of others in that Japanese city changed forever. People were running, screaming, their flesh hanging off them like torn clothes. Solid buildings crumbled like matchwood, acrid dust filled the air like fog and everywhere there was panic.

It had been a lovely summer's morning and Hiroshi, then a student of 17, was looking forward to another day of his college vacation. He was at home with his 14-year-old brother and grandfather when The Bomb dropped out of the sky. Their house was about a mile from the centre of the blast.

'There was no heat,' he said, 'just a sudden blinding light that seemed to go on forever.'

It was the luck of the draw whether you survived. Hiroshi did, so did his brother, but his grandfather died in the rubble. His parents, who had already left home, survived but his elder sister who was in another part of town did not.

He clambered from the remains of the once neat home and ran. He didn't know where, just anywhere to be away from the nightmare. But all the landscape was the same. As far as the eye could see was rubble, destruction and panic.

He ran nearly 40 miles before he reached an army building where he thought he could get treatment for the pain he felt, although then he didn't know what his wounds were.

But more and more people arrived and as the crush increased and Hiroshi could see many more with worse wounds than his, he slipped away.

It was three days later before he eventually managed to get medical treatment. There were 80 wounds in his body, caused by flying glass and debris and whole pebbles had been embedded in his skin. It was six months before he was sufficiently recovered to return to school and after graduating he spent his time working for a fertiliser company.

Hiroshi is now in Britain with several other British survivors to mark the 40th anniversary of the horrendous blast. Tonight he will be in Worcester to take part in a peace procession. Paper cranes, the symbol of peace, are to be launched on the Severn.

'I used to have bad feelings about the United States, but not now,' he said. 'But I think nuclear weapons should be outlawed. There are so many of them that if there was another war the world would be destroyed.'

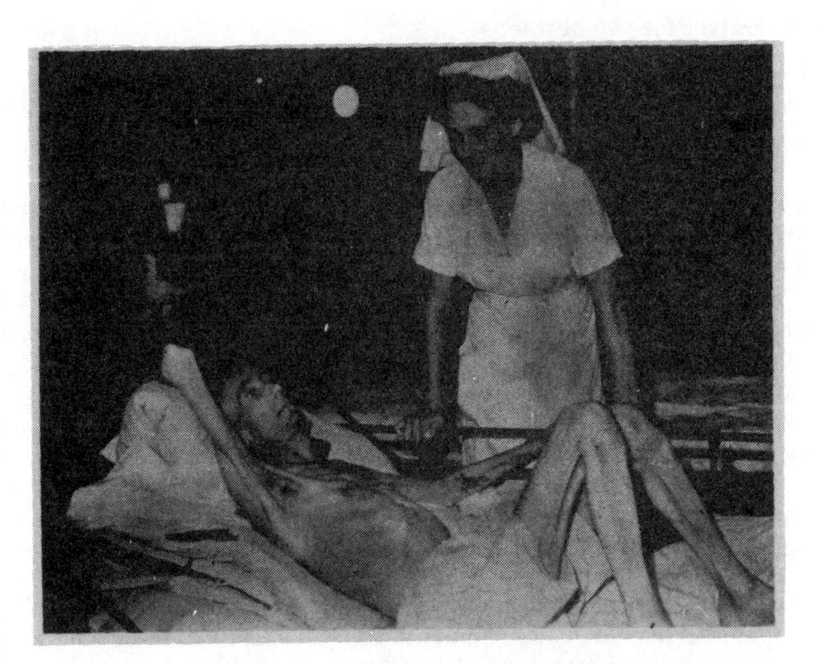

British ex-POW on board HMHS Oxfordshire, *Hong Kong. Photo: R. F. Parton*

Japanese Envoy Makemura aboard HMS Indomitable *to discuss surrender of Hong Kong.*

From L. Hurst SBA, *Menestheus*

Menestheus was in distress in the Pacific shortly after leaving Vancouver BC on her maiden voyage as an Entertainment Ship. With her engines breaking down, she was out of control and at the mercy of the seas.

At one stage, after the wheel had been lashed—which caused quite a few injuries in the frequent attempts to do so—a course was set for the Hawaiian Islands. However, the mechanics, who must have gone through hell as the ship tossed and pitched, were successful in making a repair, and *Menestheus* was able to resume its voyage.

On reaching the UK on June 29th 1946 she ran aground on a shingle bank at the Needles, Isle of Wight. The Yarmouth Lifeboat stood by for 2 hours and HMS *Rochester* stood by, plus 5 tugs, and a passenger tender from Southampton. She remained all day stranded high and dry until evening when she was refloated.

'The War with Japan' by Charles Bateson reads

The war in the Pacific certainly should have ended at least six months before it did. Japan had been defeated when the Tojo Cabinet fell on July 18th 1944, and its successor, the Cabinet led jointly by General Kuniaki Koiso and Admiral Mitsumasa Yonai, could scarcely have had any illusions as to the war's outcome. Even if the loss of the Battle of the Philippine Sea, the American capture of Saipan and the first bombing of the Japanese mainland since the Doolittle raid of 1942, did not convince them that victory could no longer be won, they could have been under no delusions once Leyte was lost and Luzon invaded. The fire blitz, at least after the disastrous March holocaust in Tokyo, underlined the inevitability of early defeat.

There was no peace, however, because of the intransigent decision of Roosevelt and Churchill that only unconditional surrender was acceptable. This applied both to Germany and to Japan and it prolonged the fighting both in Europe and the Pacific, at the cost of thousands of Allied and enemy lives and untold misery and suffering. Asian psychology, with its extreme sensitivity to loss of face, prevented any overtures from Japan with an acceptable excuse for ending the war, such as Hiroshima and Nagasaki eventually furnished. Despite all the reverses, the military and naval junta was still firmly in the saddle in Japan and was not prepared to admit that it had failed. The military leaders would not suggest unconditional surrender to the nation, and no civilian statesman, no matter how influential or how convinced he may have been privately that the war was lost and should be ended, could gird himself to oppose the militarists and advocate such a course—but the peace-feelers to the Russians show clearly enough that the Japanese were looking for a way out of the war they had so wantonly begun.

Perhaps no overture by the Allies would have succeeded, but at least the effort was worth making and should have been made. Only an approach direct to the Emperor, possibly ignoring normal diplomatic channels and protocol, would have produced results, and it may have been necessary to accompany it with a guarantee of the continued sanctity of the Emperor's sacred person. There certainly is some evidence for thinking that if the future position of the Emperor had been clarified at the time of the Potsdam Declaration, peace might have come sooner than it did. The question is intricate and involved, and cannot be determined with certainty. Yet a genuine and determined effort to bring home to the Japanese leaders the consequences of continued resistance—the devastation of their cities, the destruction of their shipping and the starving of the civilian population—and to provide an acceptable explanation for surrender might have ended the war in March.

President Harry S. Truman's decision to drop the atom bomb is a second question of paramount concern. Since it introduced nuclear warfare, the decision has been closely analysed and has provoked much controversy. When Hiroshima and Nagasaki were bombed Japan was already defeated, a fact which, as we have seen, her leaders knew but would not publicly admit. The fire blitz took heavier toll of life and property than the destruction wrought by the atom bombs, and the blockade, the dismemberment of her conquests and the sinking of her merchant ships were combining to bring Japan to the brink of starvation. At a time when the whole nation was organizing to resist an expected invasion, the bombing of Hiroshima and Nagasaki provided an immediate face-saving excuse for surrender. As the United States Strategic Bombing Survey stresses, the atom bombs 'permitted the Prime Minister to bring the Emperor overtly . . . into a position . . . to override the remaining objectors'.

The alternatives to atomic bombing were not confined to a full-scale invasion of Japan or a continuation of the blockade and of orthodox bombing. The true alternative was the creation of conditions which would have made it possible for the Japanese to surrender before Hiroshima and Nagasaki were laid waste. If this could have been achieved, if the Japanese leaders could have been given a face-saving formula, then the decision to drop the atom bombs was morally indefensible. It is the fact that no attempt was made to induce Japan's surrender that justifies moral criticism of Truman's decision. This writer believes that if the Allies had shown an awareness of Japanese susceptibilities in respect of the sanctity of the Emperor's person, had guaranteed that his status would not be altered and that he would not be tried as a war criminal, but that these guarantees would not operate if resistance continued, an earlier peace might have been secured and a decision to drop the atom bombs rendered unnecessary.

If this premise is wrong, if no undertakings by the Allies would have prompted early surrender, Hiroshima and Nagasaki were justified. Truman's decision, however much humanitarians may deplore it, was correct, the result of a realistic appraisal of the situation. Invasion would have brought the war to an end, but despite Japan's parlous plight it would have been a frighteningly costly operation to the Allies and, more particularly, to the Americans. United States casualties in capturing small islands in the Central Pacific drive sufficiently indicate that the Japanese defence of their mainland would have been dogged and fanatical, and losses among the invaders, even with crushing superiority in the air and in *matériel*, undoubtedly would have been heavy. It is probable but not certain that reliance upon a continuation of the blockade and orthodox bombing would ultimately have resulted in surrender, but the process would have been slow and might have been prolonged, and would have caused the Japanese heavier casualties and greater suffering among civilians than the use of the atom bomb. From the Allied point of view, Hiroshima and Nagasaki were a more economical, effective and quicker way of bringing the war to an end than either invasion or reliance upon the blockade and orthodox bombing.

It was not known for certain until July that an atom bomb had been successfully contrived, and it was believed that an invasion of Japan would have to be carried out to bring the Japanese to surrender. In these circumstances, the assaults on Iwo Jima and Okinawa were necessary preliminaries. In the event, though the planners could not be expected to foresee this, both were unnecessary. Neither was used by the air force to the extent expected in the bombing of the Japanese mainland, and each contributed very little to the fire blitz on Japanese cities. This was the tragedy of these two costly operations; their contribution to ultimate victory was not commensurate with the casualties suffered in their capture. But if capitulation had not come, if it had been necessary to invade Japan, the capture of both islands would have been amply justified.

The 'War with Japan' concluded

Victory in the Pacific was not, as, for example, MacArthur's propagandist communiques made it appear at the time, and as many American writers have made it appear since the war's end, a wholly American victory. It was an Allied victory, although the United States played the predominant role, with its principal and decisive advance, not MacArthur's drive to the Philippines but Nimitz' sweep across the central Pacific. Indeed, the first successes against Japanese troops were won by the Australians in the South-West Pacific; they held the arena after the fall of Malaya and the Indies as in Europe Britain had held the arena after the fall of France. However, the role played by the Australians was not solely a defensive one. They defeated determined Japanese offensives in Papua, and in both Papua and New Guinea, seizing the initiative, they followed up their successful defence by swinging over to the offensive. Although United States forces participated in certain phases of these offensives, they were essentially Australian victories and shattered a Japanese army. More than 100,000 Japanese died in Australian New Guinea. In Burma the British and Indians secured no parallel results until the closing months of the war.

Throughout the war in the Pacific, Japan had the Chinese war on her hands and she had also to guard her Manchurian frontier. These commitments absorbed never fewer than half her combat divisions, athough as the war continued these were increasingly new and raw. Most of her veteran, battle-tried divisions fought, and fought well, in the Pacific.

Putting the facts in their true perspective, however, does not minimize America's contribution to victory. India, Australia, Britain, New Zealand and her other Allies put into the field almost as many as the twenty-seven divisions which the United States had in the Pacific when the war ended, but after 1943 these played relatively minor roles. The war with Japan could only have been won by the United States Navy and Army. America's immense man-power, enormous industrial resources, unrivalled flair for logistical organization, originality and imaginative thinking in solving the peculiar military, naval and air problems encountered in the Pacific—these were decisive factors leading to victory. From mid-1943 the Americans bore the brunt of the fighting, especially in the Central Pacific. They defeated the Japanese by superior numbers, superior equipment, and superior fire power. Their policy of saturation, of overwhelming the defence by sheer weight of numbers and *matériel,* were skilfully applied.

The Japanese soldier was hardy and courageous, skilled and obedient, willing, even eager, to die for his country. The quality of the Japanese command and administrative systems was inferior to that of the soldiers it directed and administered. Japanese military and naval planning was tortuous and rigid, without flexibility or originality. Once a plan was made it was seldom changed, no matter how circumstances varied. Supply services were rudimentary and often almost non-existent. These were defects which the heroism of the rank and file could not retrieve and they, along with the inadequacy of Japan's industrial resources for modern war on a great scale, were important contributing factors to Japan's defeat.

From AB Joe Higham, HMS *Queenborough*

My job during the BPF episode was a Gun Layer on B Gun 4.7. My part of ship job was assistant gunner's mate. My fondest memory of course was when they announced that the war was over; along with the rest of the fleet we were laying off not far out from Japan, and the rumour was that we may go into Tokyo Harbour, however we were detailed off to pick up POWs from the small island of Hainan. Prior to our arrival at Hainan the Japanese had been told to provide transport to the POW camp and guide our ship through the minefields. The gunners yeomen and myself were selected to go ashore on the lighters provided by the Japanese, one to each lighter. Before leaving our ship we were armed with a Browning Automatic, and revolver; of course the humorous side to it was the ship's crew saying farewell; after serving through the war we might cop it during the peace, shaking hands and bidding farewell. We arrived quite safely at the POW camp and the emotional reception was something that will live in my memory forever. I must mention the few sandwiches we packed for our lunch were shared by the POWs. How many tasted the white bread and bully beef, I couldn't count. The speeches and farewells brought tears to our eyes.

For 3½ years they had been held captive. English, Australian, Dutch and Indians, we took 90 of them back to Hong Kong. Another incident was an Australian who had been living with the guerillas, hiding in the hills, came down to the POW camp after reading the leaflets, which had been dropped informing the Japanese that the war was over. He asked what type of gun we were armed with, during his inspection I thought he was going to start WW III with his remarks as to what he would like to do, we soon retrieved it. I must also mention about the rum ration which had been bottled for several weeks, in anticipation of the war ending, was a great treat on the trip to Hong Kong for quite a few of the POWs. The POWs told us many stories, how the camp was overrun with rats when they went there, and after a while not one could be seen and dogs were also eaten when caught. The cases of beri beri were pitiful.

The carriers were the main targets, and on one occasion we were quite close to HMS *Victorious* which copped 2 or 3, one hitting the gun turret in which my brother operated, fortunately he was uninjured.

During a lecture by the Captain of our ship, describing these Dive Bombing Planes, he assured us that it wasn't the intention of every pilot to commit Hara Kiri as one recently picked up out of the sea had several condoms in his flying suit.

Ldg Wtr George Chere told me

My job in the Pacific was 'Typist' on Admiral Vian's staff, and I did in fact type every Top Secret operational order issued to the BPF from 15 November 1944 up to the end of the war.

Extracts from 'Japan and Her Destiny' by Mamoru Shigemitsu

HUNT FOR WAR CRIMINALS

The war pursued its course relentlessly to its end. Life itself, which had been considered man's most valuable asset, was of no more consequence than a blade of grass. Air-raids became ever more violent. Finally, atom-bombs were dropped on Hiroshima and Nagasaki to test out their efficiency and at one blow more than 200,000 non-combatants were sacrificed. At that moment Japan had already decided to surrender and was taking preliminary steps.

The United States, Britain, China, the Philippines, the Netherlands, France and Russia, sometimes in union and sometimes separately, punished those guilty of atrocities. The trials reflected the characteristics of each nation. I have no desire to record them in detail. Each displayed only too completely the characteristics of a court martial by the victor. Some indeed were mediaeval in their outlook.

Even the American Tribunal awarded heavy sentences on the basis of written statements by prisoners and detained persons, which were accepted as they stood without further question, no opportunity of cross-examination being afforded.

Up to date (June 1949) more than 4000 persons have been sentenced, of whom more than 700 have been condemned to death. Not only that. Though some four years have elapsed, Japanese, not only prisoners of war but also civilians, are still detained by the conquerors and are employed in hard labour. The number published amounts to many tens of thousands.

It has hitherto been generally accepted that acts of war end with the Armistice. Many years have elapsed since the end of the Second World War and yet today the relations are still those of a vendetta. The slaughter of an opponent after the war has ceased may be cloaked by a legal procedure but religion condemns it. On September 2nd, 1945, on board the *Missouri*, I attached my signature to a document that witnessed the end of the war. For the sake of a restoration of amicable relations in future, in the cause of humanity I trust that the victors will now cease punishing the conquered and will re-establish peace and goodwill on a foundation of liberty and equality.

(It should be remembered that the book was published in 1952. The author recorded such facts as were available to him at the time.—Ed.)

THE EMPEROR PROMOTES PEACE

The Prime Minister now admitted that the war situation was far worse than he had thought. Okinawa left little room for doubt as to the outcome of the war.

On June 13th Marquis Kido called on Yonai, Minister of the Navy, and asked him if he had given thought to a termination of the war. Yoni replied: 'What can I do? Suzuki is very set in his views.' Kido, therefore, called on Suzuki and enquired, 'Have you any ideas as to the restoration of peace?' To his utter amazement he got the answer: 'What can I do? Yonai is very stubborn.' He suggested that they should get together and thrash it out. A similar enquiry made to Togo elicited the reply, 'What do you expect me to do when the Council before the Throne only the other day came to the decision to continue the war?'

It was Kido's alarm at this decision (June 8th) that had aroused him to action. It was worded: 'The war must be prosecuted to the end. Thus only can we hope to preserve Japan's integrity, defend her Imperial soil and attain the object of this "Sacred War".' A further clause read: 'In the sudden changes that are taking place in world conditions it behoves us to seize any opportunity that may occur of conducting the war under more favourable circumstances. Suitable measures should be devised that can be actually pursued, for instance in China or in Russia.' Kido, therefore, obtained Imperial assent to his embarking on the project to bring the war to an end. Anami, the War Minister, had maintained a stalwart attitude but, at a conference of the Supreme War Council on June 18th, he went so far as to speak of making a study as to which country should be asked to conduct peace negotiations.

Shortly afterwards the Emperor gave fresh instructions to the Prime Minister to prepare plans for terminating the war. On June 22nd His Imperial Majesty summoned the members of the War Council to a tea-party and made his views known to them. Time passed and little was done. Then again on July 7th the Emperor urged the need for haste.

The fact was that only Japan's surrender would end the war. And that the Army would not countenance. It maintained that the war must be fought out on the homeland before there was talk of peace. Both the Chief of the General Staff and the War Minister, therefore, opposed peace. The Navy, under Yonai's guidance, did not oppose it. Suzuki ran from one to the other, and finally, on a suggestion from the Army which accorded with the Supreme War Council decision, decided to send a Special Envoy to Moscow armed with a letter from the Emperor requesting Russia to mediate; Konoye was to be the envoy.

Prince Konoye was received in Audience and was entrusted with the Imperial instructions. He was affected to tears by the Emperor's words and vowed to lay down his life in this great mission. But when Ambassador Sato spoke of the visit to the Russian Government and on being pressed explained its purpose, Molotov said that his reply would have to be postponed, since he was on the eve of a journey.

On July 17th Molotov left Moscow in company with Stalin, who was proceeding to the Potsdam Conference.

The terms of the Potsdam Declaration were that, in the first place, Japanese troops must surrender unconditionally at once. Politically the terms of the Cairo Declaration were to be followed: Japanese territories were to revert to those held before the war with China; Korea was to be independent; Formosa and the Pescadores were to be restored to China; the mandatory Islands in the Pacific were to be withdrawn from her administration. Further, references were made to reparations; ban on the munitions industry; rejection of military government; adoption of democracy; punishment of war criminals, etc. In one respect the terms differed from those imposed on Germany—the continued existence of the Japanese Government was allowed and Japan was guaranteed a viable economy with access to sources of supply.

In Japan first reactions were divided between acceptance and refusal of the terms, but before any decision could be taken Prime Minister Suzuki came out with a statement that the Potsdam Declaration should be treated with silent contempt. The Public Relations Section echoed his view in the newspapers. His attitude was, however, simply that of the Army. Foreign Minister Togo heard the statement with indigation.

While Japan was still debating what response to make to the Potsdam Declaration and was torn with anxiety as to Russia's reply to her appeal,

August 6th came with the news that a strange bomb had fallen on Hiroshima, the Western Army Headquarters, that the city was wiped out, that Governor Otsuka had perished with the citizens, but that Hata, the C-in-C, had escaped unhurt. Declaration of war by Russia followed and her Army began to pour into Manchuria.

On August 8th Molotov interviewed Ambassador Sato and handed him Russia's reply to the suggestion of Konoye's special mission—a declaration of war. Since Japan had rejected the Potsdam peace proposals (he used Suzuki's statement as a pretext for this announcement), it would be impossible for Russia to mediate. Since Japan was so intractable, therefore, Russia declared war in the interests of world peace and joined forces with the US and Britain.

The US announced that the missile dropped on Hiroshima was an atom bomb, that an area of some ten square miles was destroyed, within which no human being could live. The Army *communiqué* endeavoured to minimize the disaster: the bomb was of a special nature but its effects had been exaggerated, in fact there was no need for alarm. The US Government, however, knew quite well the nature of the bomb and travellers from the West brought news of the tragedy that had occurred; the city had been entirely destroyed at the moment of explosion and over a large area scarcely a living thing survived.

POTSDAM DECLARATION: THE EMPEROR AGREES TO INTERVENE

For a long time past the Emperor had decided that the war must stop and had instructed the Supreme Command and the Government to take steps. Knowing this, the Army could not openly oppose the Emperor's wishes. They had, therefore, agreed to Konoye's mission and they now agreed to accept the Potsdam Declaration on the following conditions: (1) the position of the Emperor must be retained as a national institution; (2) the enemy must not land in Japan or attempt to occupy it; (3) Japanese forces abroad should be withdrawn by Japan on her own initiative; (4) war criminals were to be tried and punished by Japan herself.

In their nature these 'conditions' were far from consistent with the aims of the Potsdam Declaration. Even if presented, they could scarcely call for a reply. The enemy was in a position to invade at any moment now. The populace, watching recruits drilling with wooden cannon and rifles, were filled with apprehension. On the 9th the second atom bomb was dropped on Nagasaki and, in effect, a breach was made in the defence of Kyushu.

At the Supreme War Council conference (August 7th) the four conditions aroused little argument. Prince Konoye was filled with gloom. If the Government adopted the Army's conditions as they stood and the enemy rejected them, then a war of extermination was likely. He asked me for my views. I replied that the presentation of such conditions would merely stiffen the enemy demand for unconditional surrender, if indeed they did not impose still stiffer terms. Since, sooner or later, we had to accept them, the longer we delayed, the worse it would be for us; meanwhile it was our people who were paying the price.

It had come to Konoye's ears that the Government lacked the strength to stand up to the Army. Only an Imperial decision would meet the situation. But I gathered that Kido was hesitating. Accordingly I went once more to call on him.

Marquis Kido was not in the best of humours. He had already taken it upon himself to induce the Emperor to order that the war should be brought to an end; he hesitated to worry HIM a second time in order to ensure that his wishes were carried out.

I exerted myself to persuade him. One false step and there would be a struggle between the Army and those who opposed it. Who but the enemy would benefit? We were hovering on the verge of an irretrievable disaster: rather than leave matters in the hands of a Government that was too weak to restrain the Army, it was right and proper to invoke an Imperial decision. Finally, Kido agreed with me. Meanwhile Russia was overrunning Manchuria, was invading Southern Saghalin and the Kuriles, and showed every sign of crossing into Hokkaido.

The Emperor accepted Kido's recommendation and signified his readiness to issue an Imperial order as soon as the Government desired him to do so. HIM so informed the Prime Minister in person. The problem had now narrowed down to a draft, prepared by the Foreign Ministry, dropping the four conditions and accepting the Potsdam Declaration, provided only that the 'Imperial Prerogative' institution be retained.

The Army representatives had displayed no special objection to the Imperial Decision at the time but in military circles alarming passions were aroused. In the morning of that same day no one had voiced opposition to the four conditions. And yet that evening a Council before the Throne had been convened on the spur of the moment, at which the morning's decisions had been overthrown. The malcontents decided that it must have been a plot and they suspected that the Cabinet were the culprits.

The air-raids went on day after day. News from Manchuria and Saghalin was confused. The people wandered about aimlessly, a prey to despair.

Meanwhile the enemy dropped leaflets explaining the Potsdam Declaration in the hope of winning over public opinion. The situation did not brook delay. Finally the question was left to an Imperial Decision.

The last Council before the Throne was convened on August 14th. In addition to the Supreme War Council the entire Cabinet attended. The Prime Minister recounted in detail the progress of this question of acceptance of the Potsdam Declaration, which he said had resulted in a difference of opinion between the Army and other parties concerned. The meeting was then open to discussion. Army representatives contented themselves with a brief statement of their views, but there was no general debate.

The Emperor then gave his decision. HIM adopted the view of the Minister for Foreign Affairs and announced that the American reply should be accepted.

The final decision was taken to accept the Potsdam Declaration. On the following day, August 15th, the Emperor himself broadcast to the nation that the war was at an end.

The Suzuki Cabinet then tendered its resignation. In the concluding stages there had been complete disagreement between Suzuki, the aged Prime Minister, and Togo, the Minister for Foreign Affairs.

The *Coup d'état* That Failed

OPPOSITION FROM THE SENIOR STAFF OFFICERS

Extremists in the Army and Navy, who had always contended that the war must be decided on the Main Island, were extremely dissatisfied with the decision to stop fighting. Their pride would not allow them to acquiesce. Anami, the War Minister, had raised no particular objections to the Council before the Throne and had attached his signature to the Imperial Decree, but, in the stormy atmosphere prevailing, found the task of restraining the senior staff officers more than he could manage. These were in fact the men who had exercised the real power in the Army throughout the 'Showa upheaval'.

The plan of these staff officers was to carry out a *coup d'état* by a military operation; to set aside the Emperor's advisers and Government officials who had advocated the termination of the war; to take the Emperor under their protection and to continue the war. Then they would oppose the enemy landing and decide the issue—victory or defeat. If by any chance they were defeated, then the nation must go down fighting. In any case they would not consider peace before that. Had they not already prepared a refuge for the Imperial Family, and made arrangements for the transfer of Government to Nagano Prefecture?

ATTITUDE OF ARMY CHIEF

On his way home from the Council on the 14th, the War Minister, Anami, called on Umezu, the Chief of the General Staff, with a face registering indignation. Here was a pretty pass, he said; there was nothing for it but for the Army to take the Emperor under its protection by a *coup d'état*, to establish military government in order to continue the war. He asked Umezu to take part.

Umezu had had a shrewd suspicion what was toward. When he had heard out Anami's request, made at the instigation of his Staff, he quietly pointed out the duty of a loyal soldier. Once the Emperor had given his Imperial Decision in Council before the Throne, a loyal servant obeyed. He urged the Minister of War to control his unruly staff.

Anami made no comment and left in silence.

During the morning of that day, and before the Council meeting, the

Emperor had summoned the top-ranking officers—Fleet Admiral Nagano and Marshals Hata and Sugiyama—had announced that the war must be ended and invoked their best efforts. That day arrangements had been made for the Army Chiefs to lunch together at the War Ministry. Umezu, Chief of General Staff, proposed that those present (viz. himself; Anami, War Minister; Doihara, Inspector General of Military Education; Marshal Sugiyama, C-in-C Eastern Headquarters; Marshal Hata, C-in-C Western Headquarters) should sign a covenant swearing to carry out the Emperor's wishes. All had agreed and had signed. Anami had then moved heaven and earth to persuade his staff officers to agree but had failed.

He expiated his failure by committing suicide (disembowelment) at the Ministry of War before daylight on August 15th.

THE *COUP D'ÉTAT* FAILS

The revolt was set in motion at once. Major Hatanaka and other officers from the Bureau of Military Administration formed the vanguard. It was their idea to attack the Palace. In company with staff officers from the Imperial Guards Division, they proposed as a first step to prevent the Emperor's broadcast to the nation on the ending of the war.

They called on Mori, Commander of the Guards Division, and tried to talk him over but, finding that they could not do so, dispatched him on the spot, together with his Chief of Staff. They then forged an order in his name, armed with which they led out a detachment from the Division and attacked the Palace. They proposed to put the Emperor's advisers under restraint, take the Emperor under protective custody and proceed to direct action to attain their object.

The private residences of the Prime Minister and of the President of the Privy Council were burned at the same time.

But, though they searched the Department of the Imperial Household from top to bottom, they could not lay their hands on the record on which the Emperor's broadcast had been taken nor yet on the Keeper of the Privy Seal. One detachment, therefore, seized Radio Broadcasting House. But the record was duly broadcast from a station that they failed to discover.

General Tanaka, Commander in charge of Tokyo Defences, had by now arrived at the Palace. He harangued the staff officers leading the revolt. His voice broken with emotion, he reproached them for their outrageous behaviour and adjured them to desist. Realizing that they had shot their bolt, the rebel leaders committed suicide.

That was the end of the *coup d'état*.

Tanaka assumed responsibility and, having satisfied himself that all was in order, himself committed suicide with his own sword.

It will be noted that this theme of *coups d'état* runs through the whole of the 'Showa upheaval'.

The whole nation listened respectfully to the Emperor's Broadcast. Troops at the front and people abroad also heard it. Thinking people were prepared for it. To the masses, however, who had no means of knowing the inner workings of government but had simply been told that they must fight to the death, it came as a bolt from the blue. But when it dawned on them that their Emperor had graciously decided that this tragic war must cease, their hearts were filled with gratitude. It seemed too good to be true.

Nevertheless many people could not bring themselves to acquiesce. Many Army and Naval officers signalized their opposition by committing suicide: Onishi, vice-Chief of the Naval General Staff, was one such. Among the people, also, those who had put their faith in that divine wind that had once routed the Mongol invaders accounted surrender a national shame. Fanatics crowded the Niju-bashi *(the bridge forming the approach to the main entrance of the Palace compound)* and addressed their lamentations to the Palace; many indeed in their frenzy committed suicide.

Taken in conjunction with Army resentment, the situation looked extremely threatening.

It is reported that one group, belonging to a right-wing organization, gathered on the Yoyogi Parade Ground *(to the north-west of Tokyo)*. There they prostrated themselves before the Rising Sun and ten or more young men ceremoniously registered their protest by disembowelment. Rioters assembled on Atago-yama *(a small hill north of Shiba Park. Atago is an avatar of Izanami, the consort of Izanagi. By their union they created Japan)*.

In the midst of this alarming depression, the Cabinet of Prince Higashi-Kuni was formed to carry out measures for ending the war.

The Instrument of Surrender was much what had been expected but the complete closure of munition works under Directive No. 1 created a serious problem because, in the way munitions were made in Japan, it meant the closing down of nearly every factory in the country. Nonetheless, in its determination to abide by the terms to which it had agreed, the Government complied with this as with other clauses of the Directive.

Since the surrender the people had lapsed into inertia. But disquiet lingered; there was no knowing what further trouble the extremists might be planning.

Signature of the Instrument of Surrender

ARRIVAL OF THE ARMY OF OCCUPATION

It had been announced that the Instrument of Surrender was to be signed at the end of August but the date was changed to September 2nd and the ceremony was to take place on the deck of the *Missouri* off Yokohama. The Americans had their own delicate questions of protocol between the Army and the Navy. As Supreme Commander, MacArthur represented the Navy as well as the Army, but the designation of the flagship *Missouri* as the venue represented a graceful recognition of the tremendous sacrifices made by the Navy in the Pacific War. The *Missouri* is named after the state from which President Truman came.

American (Allied) Forces were brought by air to Atsugi on August 28th as the forerunners of the Army of Occupation. MacArthur arrived by the same route a few days later and set up his headquarters at Yokohama. At the same time the American Fleet occupied Yokosuka. Tokyo Bay had been designated as the first stage in the occupation with Yokohama as the centre.

Atsugi had been only lately the home of the Special Task Squadron. Accordingly the Japanese Navy were hard put to it to get it ready in time to hand over at one or two days' notice.

In my interviews with the Press I was forced to reiterate time and again that the only way to put Japan on her feet was first to realize that we had lost the war and then to study where our previous actions had been wrong.

It came hard to the Japanese to use the word 'surrender'. Military circles contend that in translation it should be rendered *Kyusen* (suspension of hostilities, armistice or truce). But whatever you call it, 'surrender' is 'surrender'. Japan's rebirth depended on her realization that she had surrendered as a result of defeat. The Ministry of Foreign Affairs insisted that she must give up glossing over unpleasant realities.

ARREST OF WAR CRIMINALS

There was no particular reason why the Army of Occupation should show mercy towards Japan. General MacArthur certainly displayed the magnanimous attitude of a statesman, though most of the persons benefited were sycophants begging for favours. But the American attitude was based on a calm, enlightened self-interest; it was not particularly concerned with altruism. That was only natural.

Before occupation was fully established, American Military Police arrested General Tojo in his residence and, having foiled his attempt to commit suicide, took him to Yokohama. The next day they arrested Admiral Shimada. I at once called on SCAP and pointed out this action ran counter to the promise given me that the Occupation policy would be conducted through the agency of the Japanese Government and it was arranged that in future 'persons wanted' would be arrested and handed over by the Government.

Article in 'The Australian Women's Weekly', September 8, 1945

'BRITISH CARRIERS BACK IN PORT, SEA-STAINED AND TRIUMPHANT'

By Betty Nesbit

The boys who flew the first British planes over Japan and her home islands have come back to Sydney with all flags flying.

In the huge aircraft carriers HMS *Formidable, Implacable* and *Victorious*,they sailed into port last week. Commanders of two squadrons on *Formidable* tossed to see which would go into action first in the first attack.

Vice-Admiral Sir Philip Vian, fiery, blue-eyed personality of the Royal Navy, who directed the RN aircraft operations against Japan, led the ships down the harbour on board his flagship *Formidable*.

The rust-marked funnels and sides and the thick green line at the waterline of the carriers and their escort destroyers told of their long sea time.

Although aircraft carriers have been coming in and out of the harbour since the British Pacific Fleet was based in Sydney early in the year, it was the first time that their arrival had been publicly announced. For the first time the people of Sydney could look at these warships without pretending they weren't there.

In the guest wardroom of HMS *Formidable*, just after the carrier had berthed, I talked to some of these men who had flown their planes to make the final attacks on Japan which with the atomic bomb spelt the end of the war.

There were Sub-Lieutenant Alan Ewins, 21 of Staffordshire, who's been in the Fleet Air Arm since he was 19, Sub-Lieutenant Peter Stapleton, 22, of Northampton, bomber pilot and Sub-Lieutenant Gordon Smith, 21 of Leeds.

Over their 10 a.m. mug of orange juice (an old ship's custom) they told me how the commanding officers of the two squadrons of Corsair fighter-bombers Lieut. Commander Douglas Parker, DSC and Lieut. Commander Dickie Bigg-Wither, had tossed to see which squadron would go first on the first British attack on Japan.

'Lieut. Commander Parker won,' said Sub-Lieutenant Ewins, who is in his squadron, 'and we were pretty proud of the fact that we were the first British planes to fly over Japan.'

'Certainly not the last,' interrupted a bomber pilot, Sub-Lieut. Stapleton.

'Stapleton was getting practice for his postwar job,' the other two told me. 'He's planning to be a pest exterminator.'

They weren't kidding, anyhow. When he was training in Florida he met some English people there who have a large business in that line, and he hopes to join them when the war is over.

I liked the story of US and British co-operation that Sub-Lieut. Robert Mullard, of Bath, told me.

A Corsair had been shot up pretty badly, and the plane was taken in escort by an American Hellcat. This was the message that came over the RT in a drawled southern accent. 'I'se found a lone Limey. He ain't got no electrics, no radio, no gas, no nothing. I'se seein' him home.'

Pilots met with little enemy fighter opposition.

One of the gunners, Petty-Officer Frank Smeeton, of Manchester, said he hardly fired his gun, except in strafing.

The atomic bomb was discussed aboard for days.

One of the pilots told me that they had been instructed not to bomb Hiroshima. They realised later that this meant the full extent of the damage could be gauged.

Losses of both planes and men were fairly light. This was due mostly to Air Sea Rescue which, say the boys, did a great job. Air Sea Rescue worked in co-operation with Allied submarines and aircraft. When a plane was shot down, either the pilot or the pilot in an accompanying plane notified the position. Air Sea Rescue would then send out a message to either a submarine, destroyer, or amphibious aircraft.

On one occasion two survivors were picked up by an American submarine only a mile and a half from the Japanese shore.

Sub-Lieutenant James Turner of Dunfermline, Scotland, attached to ASR, said that when planes were hit over the target pilots immediately made for the sea, preferring to land on the water and hope to be rescued rather than bail out or make a forced landing and be taken prisoner by the Japanese.

An Australian on board *Formidable* is Captain David Fitzhardinge, AIF of Perth, formerly of Manly, NSW. He is the anti-aircraft intelligence officer, seconded to the RAAF and lent to the Fleet Air Arm.

'Looks like I'll be getting three discharges,' he said.

To the Fleet Air Arm boys he is known as 'Fritz Flak'.

'He gives us the duff-gen on flak,' explained one of the pilots.

'He means the dinkum oil,' explained Captain Fitzhardinge.

Fully interpreted, it meant that he instructed the pilots as to the areas in which they could expect the heaviest ack-ack fire.

'And when the flak is heavier than was expected and the boys get twitched up, do I hear about it,' he said.

My interviews in the cheery little guest wardroom came to a somewhat abrupt end at lunch time. The other journalists and photographers had gone into the officers' mess for lunch. I was waiting to be asked, too.

The helpful young lieutenant in charge of the Press party, blushing madly, explained that as a woman I could not dine in the wardroom as the Commander did not approve of women in that very masculine domain.

'I could give you a few sandwiches in a cabin,' he said placatingly.

It sounded a bit too middle-watchish to me, so I declined and went ashore. Certainly a man's ship is HMS *Formidable*.

HMS *Argonaut*

Adopted by the City of Coventry—HMS Argonaut *(5000 tons)—had been on the long hauls to Murmansk and back and then the ship had been hit by a 'spread of fish' (torpedoes) in the Med. and her bows and stern blown off. On two propellors, she made it to Philadelphia where the missing one third of her was replaced (complete with some US Navy bedspreads).*

After numerous 'adventures' at the D Day landings and at Salonika she joined the BPF for the strikes on Sumatra. One of her longest serving crew members was a female! Her name was Minnie and she produced a total of 33 kittens.

Captain W. P. McCarthy—who wore his wings above his medals—took command on 10th February in Sydney.

After the war she liberated POWs from Formosa and Shanghai where she was the first British ship to enter.

On Friday 14th June 1946, the Coventry Evening Telegraph told how the Mayor had been presented on board the Argonaut *in Portsmouth with an ancient Samurai sword forged in 1600 and bearing the emblem of the Japanese Imperial Family. It was obtained for this purpose from Lieut. Gnl. Seize Arrisue, formerly chief of the 2nd section of the Japanese Imperial General Staff.—Ed.*

From Lieut. (S) W. H. Procter MBE, RNVR, HMS *Argonaut*

The *Argonaut* was despatched to Formosa (now Taiwan) to help repatriate our POWs. What a sight it was. They were so emaciated. They came aboard for a meal and general bonhomie. It fetches tears to my eyes even now to think of it.

From Formosa, we went up the river Yangtse with other ships to help with the re-occupation. My memory of this was that it was the first time I had seen canned beer. Not Chinese, but American. An American Landing Craft downstream had signalled us asking if an American Officer could wear a British war medal or ribbon. The Captain deputed me to look into this strange request. The best way to do this was to invite the fellow aboard for dinner. He came with a crate of canned beer. It was great. But don't get me wrong, we did get down to the nitty-gritty. The American officer had volunteered for the British forces before America came into the war. But I never did find out if he was entitled to wear one of our war ribbons.

Come in number 49, your time is up. Yes, the Admiralty had announced my Age and Service Group Number for discharge. I could go home. But who wants to leave one's ship, my other home, after all that had happened. I didn't want to hitch-hike half way across the world on a tramp steamer. I decided to stay with the *Argonaut* until she was due for recall to the UK.

But it was the end of the BPF for us, which is what all this is about. We looked in again at Manus and Sydney and Fremantle. We also showed the flag at Port Adelaide and went again to Hong Kong and, of course, Singapore.

Oh yes, we also went to Hiroshima. It was now 4/5 months after the bomb. The devastation was horrific. Just rubble with the occasional remains of a concrete building.

I sensed a certain arrogance with the Japanese. A cockiness. But my lasting memory of it all is with a snapshot I have in my photograph album. It shows a group of Japanese school children gathered around me and peering through my binoculars. There is excitement in their eyes and on their faces as they look into the distance—or was it the future of what their life held for them?

Looking to the Future. Photo: Bill Procter, HMS Argonaut

From Harry Lock, A/B Gunlayer on HMS *Quadrant*

Here is a copy of a signal sent by my 'Skipper' to the C in C Hong Kong:

FROM : THE COMMANDING OFFICER HMS *QUADRANT*
DATE : 15 SEPTEMBER 1945
TO : THE COMMANDER TASK FORCE 111.2 (THROUGH CAPT. D 27th DES FLOTILLA)

It has been noted with regret that no mention has been made in the local press of HMS *Quadrant*'s presence at Hong Kong. The SOUTH CHINA MORNING POST and THE HONG KONG TELEGRAPH for Saturday 15th September contain a summary of the Re-Occupation in Hong Kong by the Naval Task Force. This summary contains no mention of the part played either by HMS *Venerable* or HMS *Quadrant* IN THE BIG JOB.

HMS *Quadrant* arrived off Hong Kong with TASK GROUP 111.2 on the 30th August and remained outside the harbour in attendance on HMS *Venerable* until the 2nd of September. On this date she proceeded in company with HMS *Whirlwind* to PICNIC BAY. The two ships brought back to Hong Kong some 250 Japanese Suicide Troops who were a potential threat to our forces, having in their possession approximately some 70 suicide motor boats which might have been used against us. On 3rd September *Quadrant* landed a fully armed platoon and demolition party on Hong Kong island, these formed part of Kennedy Force and had their HQ in St. Josephs College. This landing party was relieved on the 7th of September so that *Quadrant* could take over duty as duty Destroyer. The ship went alongside HMS *Vindex* on Saturday 8th September and embarked 50 tons of Red Cross Stores for the use of Prisoners of War and sailed to Kiirun in Formosa 13th September. *Quadrant* returned from this duty with over 1500 hours steaming time on both boilers and is now enjoying a well earned boiler clean.

Since leaving Sydney on 22nd June to take part in operations off the coast of Japan, the ship's company have had NO shore leave with the exception of two nights in Brisbane on the way North. After leaving Manus on the 6th July the ship spent 43 days at sea operating with Task Force 37 and the US Third Fleet. During this time we oiled at sea 13 times and went alongside 69 ships of the combined fleets doing DSB duties and transferring personnel etc. After returning to Manus, *Quadrant* was immediately sailed to join Task Force 111.2 for the present operation.

After such a record of sea time and hard work I think it is natural for all of us in *Quadrant* to feel that we should receive the same amount of publicity as other ships of the original Task Group which came to relieve Hong Kong, almost all of which have now been mentioned by name in the local press or in the BBC general news. I consider that to see the ship's name in the press always gives a boost to the ship's company's morale and when morale is naturally somewhat low I think it is aggravating to find that other ships, including all the other ships who have not achieved any more than our own ship have been mentioned by name.

(Sgd) P. C. Hopkins
Lt. Commander RN

From Mrs. R. Gibson, Mona Vale, NSW, Australia, 1990

Dear Mr. Eadon,

I would like to offer a small contribution, with the following story.

The experience took place in 1945, and is very clear, in my mind. What is unclear, is the day on which it occurred. It was probably on Easter Saturday morning, or on Easter Monday morning. I seem to recall, that both were working days, during the war years. The time would be approximately 7.30 a.m. I had just arrived at work, and I was in the 'Ladies Rest Room', combing my hair, before a mirror. Suddenly the mirror took on the appearance of shimmering water, and waves, and all seemed to be dark. At the same time, I 'heard' my fiancé's voice cry out, as he called my name, 'Agnes'.

I experienced great fear, and I backed away from the mirror, and so my back touched the wall, I slid down it, and into a faint. Other women in the room gave me assistance, and a glass of water.

That night, I wrote to my fiancé, telling him of my experience. In due course,

I received a letter from him, written to me, at approximately the same time. The censor's scissors had been at work. There was very little of the letter left. However, one sentence had been left in, quite complete. It read, 'Yes, it certainly was, "April Fools Day"'.

This indicated to me that something had happened that day, which he could not discuss with me, openly. Later, it became clear, when news reached me, of the Kamikaze Attack, on April 1st, 1945, on HMS *Indefatigable.*

My fiancé, Roy Gibson, aged 22 years, was serving on board the *Indefat.* as an Engine Room Artificer.

Roy and I both wish you 'Good Luck' with your book, 'Kamikaze'.

I remain,
Yours sincerely,
Agnes Gibson

Notes: I was 20 years of age, at the time of the experience. Roy and I married, in March 1946, when the *Indefat.* arrived home, in England.
My maiden name was Hall.

*(It was Easter Sunday and the time was 'spot on'. My fiancée and I experienced a similar 'event'—see **Sakishima**—Ed.)*

From a member of the *Indefatigable* Association in Australia

Another episode concerns John Bywater and his fiancée Faye who states she was combing her hair when the mirror went blood red and Faye immediately sensed that John was in trouble—something terrible had happened but she didn't know what. Here again taking the time difference into consideration, this premonition of something happening, coincided with the time *Indefat.* was hit.

From Jack Collins, HMS *Quality*

On August 25th our boiler clean was finished; we slipped and steamed northwards at 25 knots, loaded with mail for the BPF who were still waiting off Japan. We refuelled at Guam on the 27th. The 30th was a very busy day for us all. At 0400 we transferred mail to our oiling force lying off the Japanese coast; at 0900 we entered Sagami Bay where ships of the British and US fleets lay at anchor; at 1200 *KGV, Quality, Napier* and *Norman* sailed into Tokyo in line ahead, battle ensigns flying at the masthead, and for the first time 'Jacks' at the peak. Who would have imagined when we left Sydney 2 months earlier, that we should sail into Tokyo Bay before we sailed into Sydney Harbour again? *Duke of York* flying the flag of C-in-C BPF had entered the day before with the *Missouri* and the first of the US ships. We tied up alongside *KGV* and transferred our mail. At 1600 we slipped to rendezvous with *Indefatigable* and the 'T's who were patrolling with an American carrier force some miles down the coast. We remained on this monotonous patrol for some days, before returning to Tokyo Bay on September 5th. Here we remained for 3 weeks. On the 11th we were Duty Destroyer which entailed several trips into Yokohama Harbour. On the 14th an excellent concert by members of the ship's company was given on the Iron Deck. On the 15th we were Duty Destroyer again and did a trip around Kokasuka Naval base, passing the damaged Japanese battleship *Nagato,* midget submarines, large submarines which house an aircraft in the conning tower superstructure and our own old Destroyer *Thracian* which had been captured when the Japs invaded Hong Kong. On the 16th we tied up to a buoy alongside *Nepal* in Yokohama Harbour; two and a half hours leave was given to 25 ratings at a time. The bomb damage in Yokohama was enormous; only a few large buildings remained standing; there were acres of burnt out rubble which Yankee bulldozers were flattening. There were no shops left, what few goods the Japs had to sell were laid out on the pavements. Inflation was terrific—a Yen, valued at 48 to the pound, was practically worthless, yet a bar of chocolate, packet of cigarettes, chewing gum or sweets, would buy almost anything. A few members of the ship's company were lucky enough to obtain Japanese kimonos (probably they smuggled an extra lot of chocolate or cigarettes ashore) others returned on board with silk handkerchiefs, trays, slippers, postcards and various knick-knacks. On the 17th we collected a party of 300 ratings from *KGV* and *Newfoundland* and proceeded up river to Tokyo, followed by *Nepal,* who was carrying Vice-Admiral Rawlings and other 'Brass Hats'. They were attending the ceremony of the re-opening of the British Embassy. The Jap pilot who accompanied us on the trip up river said we were the first British warship ever to berth in Tokyo. The ship's company were allowed ashore within the 'Dockyard' area for an hour or so, and returned on board with such trophies as Japanese coins, cap badges, tiles and other junk as souvenirs of our historic visit. On the 18th, the outer area of a typhoon raged across Tokyo Bay: landing craft were blown adrift, ships had steam up to get under way at a moment's notice, but by 5 p.m. it had practically blown itself out. On the 22nd we again tied up inside Yokohama breakwater, and leave was given to the rest of the ship's company.

On September 24th *Quality* slipped and proceeded southwards in company with *Barfleur.* The top of Fujiyama gleamed through the clouds as we sailed out of Tokyo Bay. This was the start of our long journey home. The long awaited news had at last been broken to us. Our skipper was now Lieutenant Commander Graves. Commander Jocelyn had taken passage in the *Duke of York* to join the *Anson.* At night we steamed along with all lights burning and pictures on the Iron Deck. This was our first experience of no blackout. On September 30th the 'crossing the line ceremony' was held on board *Quality,* and homage was paid to 'King Neptune' by the Captain, 1st Lieutenant, all officers and most of the ship's company. In the afternoon we arrived in Manus, now an almost deserted harbour, fuelled and continued on our way to Sydney where we arrived on October 6th. After anchoring off Garden Island, we subsequently berthed at Woolloomooloo the same procedure for our first and last entry into Sydney. The following day the bombshell came. Alas we were not to take our own beloved *Qual* home after all. The *Q*s were being handed over to the RAN and the crews were to take the *N*s home. The next week was our last in Sydney. We said goodbye to all the friends we had made and all the places with which we had become so familiar—George Street, Hyde Park, Circular Quay, the 'Criterion', the British Centre, the Tivoli, Luna Park, Manly, Bondi, Mosman, 'Maggie's' Plonk shop at Balmain, the ferry boats, 'Our Bridge' and 'Our Harbour'. They would just be happy memories which we shall always cherish and recall whenever we hear those tunes 'Advance Australia Fair' and 'Lili Marlene'. On October 12th we sailed down Woolloomooloo dock playing 'I'll Be Home for Christmas' on the loud hailer to *KGV, Formidable, Indomitable* and other ships of the BPF berthed there. Passing through Sydney Heads we took a last long glimpse at the fair city that had opened its arms to us for the past 12 months. We arrived at Melbourne 2 days later and tied up alongside *Napier* at Williamstown. That afternoon the ship was opened to visitors for the first time since January. On the 17th we went to sea for the last time in *Quality,* to do full power trials in Port Phillip Bay. On the 20th *Quiberon* arrived and tied up alongside *Quality;* the chummy ships were together again. Probably they would be together again often in the future under the RAN.

At 0900 on October 25th the ships' companies of HMAS *Napier* and HMS *Quality* were mustered on the forecastles; pipes sounded the 'still', the Union Jack was lowered on the *Quality* and the navy blue Australian Jack hoisted in its place. A simple but impessive ceremony, she was now HMAS *Quality.* Wherever she steams we wish her the best of luck; whenever we see her name in print, we shall remember.

On 19th November 1985 a newspaper cutting from the Daily Telegraph reported

DEFECTIVE SHELLS COULD HAVE COST BRITISH LIVES

by Our Naval Correspondent

Defective ammunition would have cost the ships and men of the British Pacific and Eastern Fleets appalling losses from Japanese air attacks if the war had not ended in August 1945.

According to private papers of the late Capt. F. T. Boswell, the Pacific Fleet's Chief Inspector of Naval Ordnance at the time, a new design of anti-aircraft gun ammunition was first discovered to be defective in the new destroyer *Barfleur.*

There was a partial detonation of a 4.5 inch shell within the gun barrel shortly after her arrival in Leyte 1945 at Manus Island, the fleet's forward base off New Guinea.

Captain I. G. H. Garnet, DSC, replied to the Editor

As the Destroyer Staff Gunnery Officer I was embarked in *Barfleur* at the time of her 4.5″ shell trouble.

Captain Boswell and I investigated this problem together and we agreed that the prematures were probably due to HE shell fitted to take tracer but with weak bases.

Barfleur's outfit of this type of ammunition was changed at Manus and there were no more prematures. *Barfleur* was the only Battle Class destroyer to take part in war operations.

December 5th '85

From: Capt. I. G. H. Garnett

To: Naval Correspondent,
The Daily Telegraph.

Ref. your letter to me dated 26th November about *Barfleur* and defective ammunition.

Dear Mr. Wettern,

Thank you for your reply to my letter to the Editor.

No further action—but thank you for your offer to put me in touch with Dr. Boswell.

Two points

1. I thought that your 'would have cost 600 ships . . . appalling losses . . .' was overdoing it a bit.

On VJ day the BPF totalled 387 ships of all sorts, but as I pointed out in my letter only 29 warships were in the front line with the US Pacific Fleet Carrier Strike Force. I do not know the Eastern Fleet numbers at this time; they were considerably less than the BPF.

2. *The Battles*—A further 3 were due to join the BPF if operations against mainland Japan had continued.

Yours sincerely,

Ian Garnett

Extracts from 'Avenger from the Sky' by Lt. Cdr. (A) Donald Judd DSC, 849 Squadron, HMS *Victorious*

Soon after returning to the UK, I reported to Queen Anne's Mansions which housed the Department dealing with the postings of FAA aircrew. I met one of the officers in charge of postings whom I knew from former days.

'You are going to be promoted to Lieutenant-Commander and given 711

Squadron at Crail in Scotland. Although the war is over in Europe, there is, as you know, a lot to do in the Far East and Pacific to lead up to the invasion of Japan. We want you to use your experience out there to train up the young Avenger pilots who will be going to the Far East at the end of their training. You'll be taking over from the present CO at the end of July but before you go to Crail we want you to do a lecture tour in Yorkshire.

Off we went to a local factory making aircraft components. I was met by the board of the company who told me about the work and personnel of the factory. What I was not prepared for was that I had to give the lecture in the canteen in the lunch hour. I was introduced by the manager and then the mike was handed over to me and I was on my own. I was quickly aware that I had to compete with the din of lunch in the huge canteen including the clatter of plates and cutlery. I never did quite know whether I came across—after all, Japan and the Pacific were a long way away and the war that these people knew about was over and peace was restored. How could I get over to them that there was an even bloodier war going on in the Pacific with big casualties in men and ships and planes with torture and murder thrown in for good measure. I think they were more interested in their steak and kidney puddings. Different factories but similar scenes followed during the week ending up with the biggest audience of all at the Blackburn Aircraft Works at Brough. A huge canteen with up to 2,000 people eating while I was talking. But by then, I had got my lecture to the stage where I didn't need notes and stories of the atrocities, bloodshed and horrific prangs rolled off the tongue to accompany their plum pudding. Whether anything I said had any effect on production was another matter—I doubt it.

Selection of signals from various sources

To: ALL SHIPS — From: AC 1

So, if there be no further treachery from the enemy, victory, final and complete, is ours and peace in our time has come at last.

2. For this we thank God in his mercy in the proud knowledge that every man here has played his part to the end in the defeat of the last enemy.

3. As a man is proven in battle so will he show, if it falls his way, in the inevitable aftermath of war, the patience and endurance required to affect the release of tens of thousands of our countrymen still in Japanese hands and the restoration of allied territories despoiled by the myriad of Japs who still inhabit them.

To: BRITISH PACIFIC FLEET — From: C IN C BPF

On the conclusion of hostilities I wish to congratulate and to thank the British Pacific Fleet, the Fleet Train and all those on land and sea and in the air that supported us, for a job very well done.

Para 2 . . . We have further tasks ahead in re-establishing authorities rescuing prisoners of war and internees and ensuring a proper surrender of the Japanese which I know we will carry out equally well.

Para 3 . . . Release of age and service groups will continue as speedily as it can be arranged.

150430

Dist..CAPT*..COMDR*..RMO*..SCO*..RMB*..WONB*..MAA*..LOG*..

NAVAL MESSAGE

To: TF 37 From: CTF 37

Following received. Begins:- on the occasion of parting company with some units of TF37 I want all hands in your outfit to know that during this last month the fine co-operative attitude and fighting spirit of the British force have made as many friends and admirers as there are officers and men in the American section of the team.

Halsey. COM THIRD FLEET SENDS ACTION CTF37DTG111331.ENDS

NAVAL MESSAGE

To: CTG 37.1 (R) ALL SHIPS From: CTF 37

On parting company I can speak for the whole fleet in saying how much we have admired the gallantry and persistence and the stout hearted work of the carriers and air crews. You have written a new chapter in naval flying which has been the reward to write 'finis' to Japan and her fleet not less valuable for our future are the links you have helped to forge between us and the US Fleets.

120325

To: TASK GROUP 37.1 From: KING GEORGE FIFTH

The following has been received from San Francisco: The Allied Leaders have agreed to accept the surrender terms provided that the Emperor takes orders from the Supreme Allied Commander, and a reply has been sent back to the Japanese Government via the Swiss Government.

= K

TBS P/L TOR 0207/12/8/45 Snowden

1.2.3.17.LOG.WRL

MONDAY 3rd SEPTEMBER 1945

JAPAN

Japan signed the surrender terms at 1030 a.m. today on board the quarter deck of the USS *Missouri*. At the same time Emperor Hirohito issued a short proclamation commanding all his people forthwith to cease hostilities and lay down their arms and to carry out the conditions of the surrender terms. The scene was broadcast to the world and witnessed by the mightiest array of Allied warships.

General MacArthur said 'it is to be hoped of all mankind that from this solemn occasion, a better world will emerge out of the blood and carnage.'

Admiral Nimitz said he proposed to bring Japan in to the world of nations.

From the White House in Washington, President Truman said American thoughts are centred on that piece of American soil in Tokyo Bay, USS *Missouri* and also on that other small piece of American soil—Pearl Harbour, which America will never forget as likewise Japan will never forget USS *Missouri* in Tokyo Bay.

Japanese foreign minister Shigemitsu and Chief of General Staff, General Umezu stepped forward and signed two copies of the surrender document. General MacArthur was next to sign on behalf of the Allied Nations. Lieutenant-General Wainwright and Lieutenant Percival witnessed the signature followed by Admiral Nimitz for the United States, General Hsu Ung Chang for China, Admiral Fraser for Britain and representatives for Canada, France, Netherlands, and New Zealand. *(And Australia.—Ed.)*

American Airborne and Seaborne troops continue landings. Occupation goes on in Tokyo Bay area, and first units of US 8th Army land at Yokohama.

Red Army and Navy Forces complete occupation of Kuriles Islands.

Hong Kong radio reports Rear Admiral Harcourt Commanding Military Administration in Hong Kong.

Units of British East Indies Fleet are waiting North of Penang to take over Georgetown.

First contingent of French troops for Indo-China sailed from France this week.

British ninth army in France to be disbanded.

Field Marshal Sir Bernard Montgomery received a rousing reception after luncheon tended by the Netherland Government.

Mr. Stettenius who is in London discussing whether the secret of the Atomic Bomb was to be turned over to the United Nations.

US 7th Fleet of which Australian ships are part is on its way to Korea for Korea's surrender.

Troops in Hong Kong, over which the White Ensign now flies will soon be joined by troops from South East Asia.

ENDS

From A/E Ray Durber, HMS *Grenville*

On our way home to the UK in early 1946, we, HMS *Grenville* (Capt D 25), were diverted to Bombay to pick up eleven million pounds worth of diamonds and six million pounds worth of gold, gifts of the Aga Khan. Before the war he used to make a gift of his weight in gold and diamonds to the UK.

On arrival in Bombay, being Duty Quartermaster, I had to see that there were a couple of scrambling nets under the gangway in case a porter should drop a box. The OOD (Mr. Brooks), the First Lieutenant (Lt. Jones) and the Flotilla Gunnery Officer (Lt. Aldis) were all armed.

I too was given side arms (but no ammo), and was told in the strictest confidence about the diamonds—although I had known at least three days earlier. Expecting an MP lorry with Red Caps, everyone was very surprised when a pre-model T Ford open truck pulled up alongside the gangway and out jumped a lone 'Gunga Din' type chap who shouted: 'I have your diamonds here, where do you want them?' The look on the officers' faces was something to behold!!

Extracts from 'The Other Hundred Years War 1941—2041' by Russell Braddon

In Burma, Slim's XIV army had killed tens of thousands of those who had sought to invade India via Imphal and Kohima. In the retreat that followed, starvation, disease, and the monsoons had killed tens of thousands more. Our captors knew it. They also knew that, though relentlessly harried and shockingly emaciated, their comrades in Burma fought on, the wounded being told to commit suicide, and shot if they refused, the feeblest of the non-wounded being drowned in raging torrents, and the last 65,000 of them being re-grouped and, at the instigation of the ubiquitous Colonel Tsuji, ordered to defend Rangoon to the death.

On the island of Biak—stepping stone to a dozen other islands—10,000 Japanese had retreated into caves. Using flame throwers, the Americans had cremated them.

On Saipan—a German colony Japan was awarded after World War I—30,000 soldiers, outnumbered two to one, had died; and 15,000 civilians had elected to die with them. Of the civilians, more than 10,000, at Tokyo's behest, had withdrawn to the northernmost tip of the island and brained their babies before hurling themselves—mothers, fathers and older children—from the high cliff tops into the rock-strewn sea.

At Guam, 18,500 of the 20,000 Japanese defenders had been wiped out by 55,000 US Marines; and at Tinian, 8748 Japanese had been killed by almost twice that number of US Marines.

On the Philippines, and in the seas around them, 200,000 of Hirohito's soldiers, pilots and sailors had been ordered to achieve a strategic victory by destroying Nimitz's enormous fleet of 840 vessels and killing more Americans than Washington would be prepared to continue sacrificing. Roosevelt, the theory was, would then forget his doctrine of Unconditional Surrender and agree to a negotiated peace.

By the end of 1944, 65,000 Japanese had been killed on Leyte; and, despite all the skills of 'Tiger' Yamashita—recalled from the oblivion to which Tsuji's malicious intrigues had consigned him in 1942—much worse was to come on Luzon and the remaining Philippine Islands.

In one year, then, some 300,000 of Hirohito's servicemen had died, and 2,000,000 more (occupying Korea, China, Indo-China, Thailand, a corner of Burma, Malaya, Singapore and the Dutch East Indies) awaited the same fate.

It was against this background that Japanese soldiers and airmen who had sought no quarter, and been ordered to kill prisoners rather than allow their liberation, had sent thousands of them on death marches and executed almost every flier who fell into their hands.

Conversely, after the starving survivors of Saipan's main garrison had staged a final suicide attack, and after 10,000 civilians had killed themselves, more than 900 Japanese soldiers had surrendered, and 10,000 civilians as well. Similarly, 1250 out of 20,000 defenders had been taken alive on Guam; and another 250 out of 900 on Tinian.

In Section B of the Federal Detention Camp on the outskirts of Cowra, in Australia, there were 1104 of them, who decided in 1944 that their lost self-respect could only be repurchased with their lives.

They learnt the fearful fate of Saipan's defenders and civilians; and new prisoners from New Guinea told them that the last of Japan's troops there (upon whom the camp had been relying to invade Australia) were trapped and starving.

They therefore rioted, attempting either to scale the high barbed wire barricades and escape, or be shot. One hundred and thirty-one were killed. Those who escaped hanged themselves, or threw themselves under trains. The death toll passed two hundred. But four hundred rioters survived, and another five hundred had neither escaped nor rioted.

'The way of the samurai is the way of death', the more fanatical now began to remind those who had hesitated the first time. An atmosphere of near frenzy affected everyone, even the sentries—who, in the words of the official history, became 'alert and tense'.

Some of the sick lined up beneath a convenient rafter and, encouraged by their friends, hanged themselves, one after the other. Others said, 'We apologize for our inability to join you,' and facing north, where the Palace lay, gave three banzais before accepting a razor blade and slicing open their carotid arteries.

While the unfit killed themselves, their comrades collected baseball gloves, blankets and strips of cloth, to help them scale the barbed wire, and improvised weapons with which to kill Australians.

That night, they set fire to their huts; a bugle sounded; they charged the wire; the searchlights came on and the sirens wailed; the Australians fired high at first, and then, when their warning was ignored, more purposefully; the attack was checked; and an Australian interpreter urged them to desist over the Public Address System.

A Hundred Year War
Never has Great Nippon known defeat
The present difficulty is but a stepping stone to
the future.
Rally round the Imperial Throne and fight on,
for this is a HUNDRED YEAR WAR

'In this hour of her peril,' wrote Marmoru Shigemitsu, the Foreign Minister, 'Japan must tread the path of honour. If we do not stray from that path, Japan may fall, but she will rise again.' The seeds were being sown for what, by 1967, *The Economist* would describe as 'the world's most intelligent system of planned economy'.

Why, Shigemitsu was challenged, did he object to the term 'American devils'? And why should enemy prisoners be better housed and fed than the Japanese, of whom the American B-29s had just burned to death hundreds of thousands? And anyway, the Army snarled, there was no truth in the enemy's claim of atrocities. Such claims were lies, invented to slander Japan.

As to which Shigemitsu would subsequently lament, 'The Army at the front withheld the truth'; but Hirohito's response was both more immediate and robust. The mistreatment of prisoners of war was, he said, 'a serious breach of duty that reflected shame on the Army'—whom he thereupon instructed, 'to put the matter right'.

As was its wont, the Army took no notice at all of the Foreign Minister's words, and not much more of the Emperor's—which were attributed (as always when he said anything not entirely to the Army's liking) to bad advice.

That the Army 'withheld the truth' is now as well known to the world as eventually it became to Shigemitsu; but the extent to which it denied what it knew to be the truth is breathtaking.

Of the 235,473 British and American prisoners of war in Axis hands in Europe, **four** out of every 100 died. Of the 95,134 British, Australian, Canadian, New Zealand and American prisoners of war in Japanese hands in South East Asia (the rest were Indian Dutch, Indonesian and Filipino) **28.65** out of every 100 died—an unforgivable proportion of them on marches they were never intended to survive, as targets for bayonet practice, as the victims of capricious but elaborately staged executions, or like garbage in an incinerator (which was the fate of the Americans imprisoned on Palewau. They were herded into three air-raid shelters into which buckets of kerosene and lighted torches were also thrown. Those who attempted to escape were machine-gunned and bayonetted as they burst through the flames).

The Emperor having spoken, the Army allowed us a distribution of a few of the Red Cross parcels which had been regularly despatched to us since February 1942, but delivered, in my experience, only thrice. In some camps there may have been a few more deliveries, but nowhere more than half a dozen. One parcel a month was despatched from home for each of us in captivity. Most of us received one fortieth of one parcel on three separate occasions over a period of three and a half years.

'We found ourselves living in huts like pig sties,' snarls Yuji Aida of the accommodation provided for them by the British—quite disregarding the fact that those same huts had hitherto been the accommodation provided by his Army for us.

Even worse was the invisible havoc that had been wrought by the war at sea. As well as her entire navy, Japan had lost 8,600,000 tons of merchant vessels. Indeed, Aida and his comrades had spent up to two years in captivity simply because there were no Japanese vessels on which to repatriate them whilst the first priority of Allied vessels was to feed Europe and repatriate Allied armies.

All too long, then, 500,000 Japanese soldiers had languished in captivity. Yet time after time, as they caught their first glimpse of the sacred homeland from the decks of ships belatedly repatriating them, they had killed themselves rather than inflict on their families the shame of their 'surrender'.

These, then, were the subjects, civilian as well as military, to whom Hirohito would direct his words a second time when he addressed their Diet a few days after the surrender.

'It is our desire,' he declared 'that Our People will surmount the manifold hardships and trials attending the termination of the war and, making manifest the innate glory of Japan's national polity, win the confidence of the world and contribute to the progress of mankind.'

If Churchill was the architect of the Allies' victory in World War II, Hirohito must be said to have been the architect of Japan's industrial counter-offensive against its former conquerors; but no one in Japan ever says so.

At the war's end, however, his ex-enemies had been much less reticent. The governments of Holland and Australia had wanted him deposed at least, as had a lobby of Republicans in Washington who considered monarchies no less reprehensible than empires. There were even those in MacArthur's entourage who presumed to suggest to him that Hirohito be tried as a war criminal—or at least summoned to the general's headquarters like a common criminal.

But MacArthur had declined. Thanks to the discipline of the Japanese, and the easy-going generosity of the American forces under his command, the occupation had been achieved without incident. True to their traditions, the Japanese had almost unthinkingly transferred their allegience to the dominant power in their land, which was now an army of occupation comprised almost entirely of Americans.

Who, far from gouging out Japanese eyes and cutting off Japanese noses, seemed anxious only to spend large sums of money, share their gum and get themselves laid. Finding them infinitely more congenial than their own militarists had ever been, the Japanese unlocked their daughters, set up a chain of brothels, provided anybody who wanted one with a charming mistress, and forgot their terror. Life would remain 'very hard', but at least there were no longer any Thought Police to monitor their every word, no Kempeitai to torture them, and no generals to demand that they die for their Emperor.

It was MacArthur, in fact, who now ruled Japan; and he ruled it not even as the great Shoguns of the Toshugawa family had thought to rule it. Half amused, half incredulous, his subordinates said that he was often to be observed walking on the waters of the Palace moat, and called him Our Father Which Art in Tokyo. The Japanese called him the Blue-eyed Shogun. Nevertheless, he frequently displayed an understanding of his subjects that no foreign statesman has since matched. Thus, far from summoning Hirohito to his presence (which, as he said, 'would be to outrage the feelings of the Japanese people and make a martyr of the Emperor'), he waited for Hirohito to solicit an interview with him. And quite soon the appointment was made, and Hirohito, small, bespectacled and nervous arrived. 'I come to you, General MacArthur,' said the man who only weeks before had been deemed a god by all in his land, 'to offer myself to the judgement of the Powers you represent as the one to bear sole responsibility for every political and military decision made, and action taken, by my people in the conduct of the war.'

Before the surrender, he had told those assembled in his palace bomb shelter, 'I am not concerned with what may happen to me: I want to preserve the lives of my people.' Now he had come to MacArthur to prove that he had been indulging in no mere rhetoric.

It has been argued, of course, that the sole responsibility *was* his. But the truth is something that only he knows; and he, with monumental impassivity, declined until 1971 ever to elaborate on those few words he spoke to General MacArthur.

In 1971, however, on a State Visit to Britain, where an unforgiving public virtually ignored him, he broke his silence at a banquet at Buckingham Palace. 'We cannot pretend,' he said, 'that the relations between our two peoples have always been peaceful and friendly.' But added, 'It is precisely this experience which should make us all determined never to let it happen again.'

Unmoved, the British continued to ignore him; and, when he went to Holland the Dutch responded with overt hostility. Noting that everywhere on his tour the speeches of welcome were 'perfunctory', the Japanese press began to carp that the tour was 'ill advised'. Undeterred, Hirohito plodded on. His task was to re-establish his nation's credentials in the eyes of a still contemptuous world: he was 'not concerned' with what might happen to him.

Worse, though, was to come when David Bergamini's massively researched book, *Japan's Imperial Conspiracy*, charged him with personal responsibility for starting and conducting the Pacific War, and for condoning all the atrocities perpetrated by his forces during it. In November 1971, he submitted himself to his first press conference and, denying Bergamini's accusations, insisted that he had acted throughout the years of Japan's aggression only 'as a constitutional monarch'.

If, in fact, he was guilty, his refusal in 1945 to stay silent until the likes of

General Togo could cover up for him, as they planned to do at their trials, was the act of a man whose integrity could not be denied. If, however, he was innocent, his 1945 attempt to offer himself to MacArthur's judgement, thereby to expiate thousands of crimes, to save the lives of thousands of war criminals, and to exculpate an entire nation, was a huge sacrifice for so small a man.

Beyond doubt, the crimes of which some would still accuse him sprang originally from the militarist adventures upon which his army embarked in 1931. In March of that year the Army assassinated its most prominent opponents in Tokyo. The only excuse it gave was that it was 'purging' Hirohito of those influences that made him unsympathetic to the Army's intentions. He could hardly have been a party to the militarist's plot if he was at the same time so unsympathetic to it that he needed 'purging'.

Extracts from 'Alarm Starbord' by Lieut. Cdr. G. Brooke

It was given out that except for *KGV, Indefatigable,* two cruisers and ten destroyers, the BPF under Admiral Vian would be returning to Australia. This caused general but not universal rejoicing. Personally I would have liked to have stayed and seen something of the Japanese surrender—even from afar—but then I had not been away from home as long as most and had a vested interest in this occurrence anyway. A fortnight later *Formidable* as flagship led in through Sydney Heads to a tremendous reception that ended with a thousand individual crescendoes as we went ashore to ecstatic friends. On the 31st there was a victory march through the streets, with most ships represented and then, heavily engaged in paint ship, we fell to wondering 'what next?'

Our part in this was soon foreshadowed by the receipt of a thousand camp beds, a thousand deck chairs, mountains of relevant stores—incuding 6,000 bottles of beer—and, to the astonishment of all except Ruckers who had organised it, 21 attractive nurses and four ditto female Red Cross workers. To cope with the sick, these were accommodated right aft in the Admiral's quarters under the aegis of Philip O'Rorke (officially Liaison Officer with the Female Staff, but soon shortened to The Chief Eunuch).

HMS *Formidable*
10/10/45

We are just getting into Sydney having been up to Manila to collect 1,000 Australian and 100 British prisoners of war. We didn't get ashore at Manila. We have no aircraft on board and are doing a sort of pleasure cruise which has gone very well though quite hard work. I am in charge of the 100-odd officers and their arrangements, which has kept me busy. They are in better shape than we expected though treatment seems to have varied to extremes from one camp to another. Some of them are fit and others almost skeletons. Only a few lucky ones who could pinch food have had anything but boiled rice for four years. I heard that the POW Midshipmen (ex-*Prince of Wales*) from the *Exeter* were

OK, also Colonel Warren (up to a year back), but no news of any of the people in Sumatra with me, although we are not by any means the only ship doing this.

One little man came up to me and said wasn't I the officer in charge of the ferry boat from Penang to Port Swettenham after the evacuation of Penang? We had a long talk. He was a Corporal in the RAOC. Apparently the Japs were absolutely down and out, the POWs got no less food than the civilian population, and the civilians were kind to the POWs when they could be and were very glad when the war ended. On the whole the chances of Japan being reformed seem good. I did my chair act at two concerts. The Aussies loved Uncle Atty's 'Once before death and twice afterwards' story!

When the last man had eventually disappeared ashore we felt both emotionally drained and glad to have known them; what we found both noble and surprising was a lack of bitterness against the Japanese. This was an attitude which I myself found impossible to adopt when there was news of daring raids which had been carried out on Japanese shipping in Singapore harbour, secret until now.

From CPO Fred Fallows, HMS *Ulysses*

Sailing south, this time, there was a holiday atmosphere about the ship. We could smoke on the upper deck at night, scuttles were left undarkened, and we knew that there would be some leave and good times awaiting us in Sydney. We were not disappointed. After a day or two at Woolloomooloo we moved to Cockatoo Island, where our bows were stripped and replated. Each watch had a week's glorious leave, and many visited places far from Sydney and saw something of Australian country life. Some went to stay on sheep stations. The 'Butcher' chatted with the Australian Prime Minister at Canberra, others visited Melbourne, and the rest stayed with friends and were entertained in marvellous style. We heard the broadcast of the surrender ceremony in Tokyo Bay—so soon to become all too familiar—and were perhaps a little disappointed that not one of our flotilla was present.

On September 21st we left Sydney, this time knowing our final destination—Tokyo. As we sailed under the great bridge and out through the Heads, many eyes were turned longingly towards shore and earnestly hoped that they would gaze on Sydney again.

And so, on October 4th, we steamed through the mists into vast Tokyo Bay, under the shadow of Fujiyama, where the terrible second World War ended.

There was a great array of shipping, mostly American, but including the British and Australian squadrons. We felt proud that our flag flew in the harbours of our defeated enemies.

In Yokohama we soon began to catch the 'disease', which kept its grip on us throughout our stay and for which many families must be very thankful—the collection of gifts to take home. Revealing no secrets, it can be stated that every

Mount Fujiyama—The Sacred Mountain. Photo: Ron Dovey, HMS Swiftsure

The Imperial Palace. Photo: Ron Dovey, HMS Swiftsure

British and Australian sailor in Force 'T' (the name given to the naval force in Tokyo Bay) was always paid in Australian money; there was no exchange, and yet each man, during his stay, probably had hundreds or even thousands of yen pass through his hands. It was soon discovered that the Japanese liking for cigarettes far exceeded his respect for money, and everybody took mutual advantage of this, both sides being satisfied. Soon silks and all manner of strange garments began to appear in the ship, not to mention table-cloths and other useful household commodities. We had just become acclimatised to Yokohama and turned ourselves into experts at barter when we were sent on our first cruise. Our orders were to accompany *Swiftsure* to Wei-Hei-Wei, the peace-time exercise base of the China Fleet or, as some would have it, the 'Scapa of the Eastern Fleet'. From the start, there were some doubts as to whether we would be allowed to proceed there. Our first stop was to be Kagoshima, on the southernmost tip of Kyushu. There we were to await orders to carry on to China.

Among certain members of the ship's company you will find fairly general agreement that, apart from Australia, our stay in Kagoshima was the pleasantest part of the commission. On our way there we found an abandoned US Army tug, which we took in tow, and then had to proceed very slowly along the coast. At that speed we were able to admire the splendid rugged coast-line. Warm and green in places, as one goes further south, the mountains become volcanic and the scenery takes on a fiercer, more aggressive aspect. We passed a volcanic island smouldering still from its 1934 eruption; at the entrance to Kagoshima Kaiwan we saw the extinct Kaimon-Dake, whose steep sides run down into the sea, where years ago lava had poured in a burning stream. Surrounded on all sides by Nature's awesome splendour, made less forbidding by the kind sunlight, we entered Kagoshima Bay, a very lovely natural anchorage. There, too, we found a volcano, Sakurazima, 'our volcano', which last erupted in 1914 and from which smoke now winds lazily upwards. Sakura being Japanese for cherry, this then, was Mount Cherry. We never went ashore in Kagoshima itself. Only a small town, it was used as a supply base for Okinawa, and a visit by super-Fortresses had razed it. All the interest lay on the volcano side of the bay, where little fishing villages had sprung up among the lava beds. Leave was given from early morning and, clad in overalls or any rig we liked, we set off in groups to climb Sakurazima, to walk through the villages, to sail the whalers or to go on 'banyan' parties. Outdoor exercise was the order of the day, and this was the ideal place for it. Most people reached the crater of the volcano and saw the steam rising from sulphur-surrounded holes. To stand on the summit and see how far boulders and lava had been flung in 1914, was enough to convince most of us of Nature's power, besides which even atomic bombs appear futile. Speaking for myself, I have seen few lovelier views than that of the quiet waters of Kagoshima Kaiwan, like a mirror in the sunshine with the mountains as a frame.

The fisher-folk lived in very primitive fashion and at first were terrified of the invaders, who strolled slowly through their orchards, picking dozens of delicious tangerines. Yet, soon, they became accustomed to us and were friendly, making us gifts of fruit and trying to understand what we said. Their very simplicity may have been a hoax, yet it was hard to imagine that these friendly people were the 'Yellow Peril' of whom the world must always beware. And yet even at Kagoshima we saw evidence of very unfriendly preparations to meet a less peaceful type of invader.

In Kagoshima, too, we made many friends with Americans on board the depot ship *Markal* and received many kindnesses at their hands.

For nearly three weeks we spent our time in these delightful surroundings, enjoying our last bathes before the winter and astounding the Japanese, for whom the bathing season had ended weeks previously. *Swiftsure* returned to Tokyo, the trip to Wei-Hei-Wei was cancelled and, after a week or so on our own, we met the New Zealand cruiser *Achilles*, with whom we went on to Nagasaki. This visit was of very great interest to us, as we were able to see just what effect on a town an atomic bomb really has. The Americans provided lorries for us and we were driven round the ruins. It is difficult to describe the devastation to be found there. It was as if a tornado had swept over the land, leaving in its trail a few twisted factories and heaps of rubble. Great as the havoc at Nagasaki is, it would undoubtedly have been greater but for the protection afforded by the hills which hem the city into the sea.

From Nagasaki we continued to Sasebo. Nobody really knows very much about this port, as an epidemic of dysentery was raging ashore and nobody was at all anxious to come into close contact with it. We took great precautions and were very fortunate in only having one case. A few days before, the US cruiser *Boston* had a great percentage of her crew out of action with the disease. We were thankful to leave Sasebo astern as we started on our way back to Yokohama.

We were lucky to be often alongside *Hobart* and *Arunta*, who both showed good, up-to-date films, especially *Arunta*, who had a different film each night—provided the audience was prepared to weather the cold on the upper deck. On both Australian ships we were always treated very kindly and shown many favours. For radio entertainment we had the local American station, WVTR, from Tokyo. For those who like US entertainment this was a godsend and, as befits all thing American, slickness. For those less fond of our friends' brand of entertainment it was not always the boon which others found it. Most of us, however, can drowse nostalgically over titles like 'Make Believe Ballroom', 'Tokyo Mose', 'It Pays to be Ignorant', 'GI Jill' and 'Mystery Playhouse'.

Winter came and with it the snow. Fuji became whiter and whiter. We got colder and colder. A spell of 'rest' at Takeshiba Dock, Tokyo, just before Christmas, enabled us to see the capital at close quarters and also to obtain far more entertainment ashore. The excellent Red Cross Club and the cinemas, not to mention the 'Oasis of Ginza' were all very well run and provided relaxation and interest. One of the main attractions of Tokyo was the PX Store, an

American-controlled souvenir shop, where the very best quality goods were obainable at a sensible price. There was always a long queue, but the waiting was well worth while, for some beautiful gifts were obainable. Above the main store was another smaller store, where sweets, biscuits, stationery, toilet gear and even watch repairs were available at fantastically low prices—the whole store was an example of that wonderful genius for organisation which the Americans demonstrated everywhere, but nowhere more clearly than in the Pacific.

Tokyo suffered terribly from raids. The Ginza is hardly recognisable as one of the world's famous streets. Once it glittered with lights and life: now it is a shabby avenue of death. On its scarred pavements, street-sellers offer their cheap wares, the poor beg alms, and only the pathetic brightness of women's clothing relieves the air of despondency and defeat which haunts the great thoroughfare. As I mentioned earlier, the area round the Imperial Palace is by far the most attractive section of the city. The great Marunouchi business firms had flourished here, and their impressive buildings, housing American Occupation HQ, are as pleasing to the eye as many Western products. Nearby is Hibiya Park, only a few minutes' walk from the Diet, a noble building completed in 1936; and all those who saw the interior of the Houses of Peers and Representatives must have marvelled at their splendour and appreciated the excellent acoustics, so essential for intimate debate. Not far from the Diet is the British Embassy, a set of white buildings which overlook the palace moat and are situated in one of the pleasantest parts of Tokyo. We encountered no unpleasantness from the Japanese, many of whom seemed anxious to show us their city. I wonder how many others felt as I did, that it was fantastic to think of ourselves, our roots firmly in English soil, walking round this strange city as though we had lived there always. There are certain cities which we can never visualise, except as a word on a printed page, or a photograph in a travel book. Tokyo is one of them, and writing at a distance of some months, I find it hard to recapture the atmosphere of those days when time did not count and so much seemed uncertain and improbable.

While in Japan, one of the most popular methods of recreation was the 'Hotel Party', when groups of ratings went for forty-eight hours to stay at Japanese hotels in places inland or further along the coast. In this way we saw many interesting features of 'small-town life' in Japan, and came to admire the special beauty of Japan's countryside. A disadvantage was the question of food. We always had to supply our own, usually out of tins, and if entrusted to Japanese cooks it was liable to be prepared in somewhat unorthodox fashion. Among places visited in this way were Nikko, Odawara, Ito, Atami and Kamekura. Photographic records of these visits exist with most of the crew, and as cameras were quite easy to obtain, a craze for photography soon swept the ship.

It was now time to think about Christmas and decorating the ship with the gay trimmings which were so plentiful ashore. Rather than submit to baleful gloom, the ship's company decided to make December 25th as bright and gay as was possible under the circumstances. Every mess had turkey and many provided themselves with plum puddings. There was beer, rum and a feeling of happiness, for it was at this time, I believe, that the ship reached its highest peak of comradeship and good spirit. The feeling between officers and ratings was one of understanding of each other's difficulties and could well serve as an example to less happy ships. Much hard work had gone into the production of this fellowship, but *Ulysses* had certainly proved herself a first-class ship in every way, and if anyone had a smile of self-satisfaction on his face during those days then he was entitled to it.

As soon as Christmas festivities were over, we sailed with *Urania* and *Hobart* to join *Arunta* at Kure, which was to become the base for the British Commonwealth occupation forces. We stayed in this very much battered port over the New Year, which passed with less excitement than Christmas and was heralded by 'Land of Hope and Glory' *ad nauseam*, as many will remember. Kure is not far from Hiroshima, where the first atomic bomb was dropped, and sight-seeing parties were able to compare the damage there with what they had seen at Nagasaki. If we have any civilised feelings left, we must admit that even on such a people as the Japanese the right to use such a weapon is questionable. A view of the bleak horror which had been created, where once a thriving city stood, was sufficient to convince many people that mankind has very little of which to be proud, and that 'a last chance' for civilisation is most certainly all we deserve. While at Kure, searchlights were kept on in the harbour all night because the Japs had developed an unpleasant habit of rowing out to ships and lobbing grenades through the scuttles.

From Kure we went back towards Tokyo, but stayed a few days in a very attractive anchorage called Shimizu, about 60 miles west of Tokyo Bay. Reminiscent in some respects of beautiful Kagoshima, the crowning feature of the landscape was snow-capped Fujiyama which out-topped the other mountains and, calm, remote, impersonal, and very, very lovely, overlooked the harbour and sea.

When, eventually, we returned to Yokohama we found that *Ursa* and *Undaunted* had sailed for Sydney on their way home. This immediately began a number of 'buzzes' about when we were leaving. No two reports agreed, and the restlessness which was already making itself felt was increased. *Cossack* was expected to relieve *Grenville* very shortly, and *Undine* and *Urania* were said to be leaving before January was over.

The torpedo destroyer *Thracian*, which we had brought from Yokosuka, had been partially refitted alongside *Tyne*, and we were supposed to be taking her to Hong Kong and, said some, proceeding homewards without visiting Australia. This alternately depressed or elated people. Our relief was HMS *Contest*, and a map of her progress from UK was pinned on the notice board and eagerly watched in case she broke down. We would naturally be last to depart and we thought we could expect to leave Japan in early March.

We paid another visit to Tokyo for recreation leave, of which everyone was badly in need. Constant unrest, as a result of spending too long in one place, the unsettling effect of watching other ships come and go, with no mention of our leaving, was beginning to have a bad effect on the crew, and the captain did all he could to provide entertainment and relief from monotony. We spent ten days alongside *Tyne* for a boiler-clean, *Thracian* went to Hong Kong with an Indian sloop, *Grenville* and *Undine* sailed for Sydney, *Urchin* arrived from Australia and New Zealand, where she had been extensively refitted, and *Urania* and *Ulysses* remained at No. 8 Buoy, Yokohama, under orders to proceed shortly to Eno Ura, a small anchorage not far from the bay. Suddenly the cruise was cancelled. Meanwhile, depressing rumours had begun that *Urchin*'s relief had been delayed and *Contest* was to relieve her and not us. Our mood at that time was not the happiest—going home seemed to be tantalisingly near and yet so far away.

Then the news changed and all the waiting was over. The captain cleared lower deck and announced that the Rear-Admiral Destroyers had decided to send *Urania* to Sydney on February 10th, *Ulysses* on February 13th, and *Urchin* on February 19th. From Sydney we were to sail for UK. This grand news was well received by the ship's company, most of whom had seen enough of Japan.

Urania left, and three days later, wearing our paying-off pennant, we steamed joyfully past *Tyne* and the other ships, and out of Tokyo Bay for the last time. On board we carried a lot of Australians from the cruiser *Hobart* who were due for release. They shared our messes, and all the way down we had the opportunity to discuss their country with them. This led to some heated debates, but both parties argued in a healthy fashion and without malice, and the trip probably cleared up many misunderstandings on both sides.

We called in at Manus for a few hours to take on stores and passengers, and looked for the last time on this tropical base which a few months before had seen the BPF and the Fleet Train in the full flower of their strength and was now practically deserted. The heat was as great as ever and we had begun to regain the tan which we had lost in the Japanese winter.

The next day we put in at Dregar Harbour, in New Guinea, not far from the base at Finschhafen. Here we took on some RAAF personnel and saw at close quarters the dense green jungle through which the Australians had fought. There was a small air strip and some wooden huts as signs of civilisation, but otherwise the small harbour might have been exactly as it looked to the first ship ever to enter.

The next stop was to be Sydney, and the excitement of the Australians at seeing their country again was rivalled by our own enthusiasm, mingled with fear that our stay might be prolonged by the drafting officer! We looked forward to the stay in Sydney, but were almost afraid to think about home, in case we had to leave the ship. At last February 26th dawned, and in summer heat we entered the lovely harbour once again.

For ten happy days we savoured the pleasure of Sydney for the last time, each watch having four days' leave. There was great activity while in Woolloomooloo, where we loaded the 2,700 boxes of food which we were taking home as part of the Lord Mayor of Sydney's Appeal Fund for aid to Britain. Ashore, most of us bought presents for our families and friends at home, and the messes were soon filled with big suitcases and bulky parcels. The weather was perfect for our stay and we sampled a little of the Australian summer. The short visit passed too soon and the day came when we had to say a sad farewell to the many kind friends we had made. Though we were sailing for home, we were also leaving a home. Quite a crowd of people gathered on the jetty to watch us go and we gave them a heartfelt cheer of thanks as we slowly moved out into the stream and down the harbour. Clouds obscured the sun, which until then had shone so brilliantly, and it became quite cold. We watched the bridge, Manly Ferries, and other familiar sights, disappear and, after anchoring for a short time inside the Heads to repair a small mishap, we went out into the open sea and left the lights of Sydney twinkling in the darkness.

The joy of our home-coming was marred by the tragic loss at sea, in the Bay of Biscay, of *Urania*'s First Lieutenant. His disappearance was not noticed till nine hours later, when all hopes of finding him in the heavy swell had to be abandoned.

On April 18th, bright, sunny morning, full of the freshness of English spring, we saw the Cornish coast gradually draw nearer until we were in Plymouth Sound and steaming up the river to Devonport, where we berthed alongside at Flagstaff Steps.

The rest is fresh in all our minds—the gladness of reunion, the happiness of demobilisation for some, leave for the others, Britain once more for all of us. This is the time to end this narrative, for the fellowship of *Ulysses* ended then and all our ways diverged. That day was our day, the day we had longed for and which had seemed, at times, so distant. Yet there it was—a reality.

This may well have been the story of many ships who served in the British Pacific Fleet.

As the years go on and memories recede, we shall find that only the happy times remain clear in our minds. That is as it should be; but let us not forget the reasons why we had to go to war, and let us be sure that in the happy days of peace, in the pleasure of civilian life, we do not forget the price paid for our happiness, in other ships and in other seas.

From H. Chapman, HMS *Undaunted*

After the action we went back to Sydney, and what a welcome, we entered the harbour flying a very large Jap flag on the starboard side, and Union Jack port side, all the ferries and small boats gave us a rousing welcome, next day the Sydney Herald had on the front page 'Rusty Battleship returns'.

Then to Auckland New Zealand for a refit. We had fourteen days leave, went on a sheep farm with a Mr. and Mrs. Taff, they just couldn't do enough for us, when I say we, I mean my oppo Jim Goodwin. We would go round the sheep on horseback, went to see a small church—it would only hold 12 people, this was a place called Ngarawahice. One morning I saw four children on one horse, going to school.

After New Zealand, back to Sydney and on to Japan, Yokohama. As we arrived off the coast we just missed two mines. The *KGV* blew them up. We went to a place called Hokkodute. We went to the post office, for some stamps, and the man invited us in. We sat on the floor, there was a charcoal stove in the middle of the room and we had some tea, it was awful. He invited his two daughters in, and they were dressed in kimonos. As it was Xmas we started to sing carols, and they joined in, in Japanese. I was motor boat driver and I had the job of bringing the young Japs to work on the ship. They would bow to us, and would have one smoke and pass it round. We used to have warnings not to drink certain drinks, as a lot of Yanks had been poisoned. We had a leave, and went to a place called Niko. It's where all the shrines and temples are. We stayed in a hotel but had to take our own food. We slept on the floor and had a bean bag for a pillow.

Three Undaunteds at Niko. Photo: H. Chapman

Had a bit of fun, took over the tram down the main street. I can remember the toilets, they had two footprints and a hole in the floor. Went ashore in a place called Atami, and we had some soap to barter with and in no time the women were fighting for it. Also we got a lift in a Yank's lorry. I was the last in, he shot off, and I went straight out of the back, looking up I saw a lorry with three Japs in it, but I had the sense to roll over off the road. Well now it's back to Sydney. While there we met some Australian soldiers who had been prisoners, they told us they had received bad treatment, and they could not speak properly.

When we arrived back in good old 'Guss' (Devonport) there was not a soul to meet us.

From LSA J. Banks, HMS *Urchin*

HMS Urchin *was alongside* Swiftsure *in Wooloomooloo, Sydney, Christmas 1945 and LSA J. Banks wrote:*

I (Jack Dusty) was in my naval store late on Christmas night, when signalman Farthing came in. He told me that he had just taken a signal, ordering the ship to sea, to the Duty Officer.

Of course, one watch was ashore on leave, and this was due to cause a problem. Duty Stokers starting 'flashing up'. I went up to the gangway to watch what was happening on the deck as crewmen came back on board, after being ordered back by the shore patrol.

Some of the crew came down the ladder off the *Swiftsure*, asked what was going on, they dodged back up another ladder and back ashore. Of course, they had been drinking.

It seemed that a ship was in difficulties outside Sydney Heads. We never sailed, I believe another ship did the job.

I cannot remember the exact location, but according to A/B Howard, we were sailing through the Bass Straits, when a freak wave washed the Gunnery Officer (J. F. Barker) overboard. He was on the port side, by the break of the Fo'castle. He washed back on board and wrapped around the depth charge racks toward the aft of the ship.

He sustained injuries to his face and leg. The doctor on board (Lt. Arblaster) was a surgeon, so he stitched him up. He was later put ashore to hospital and he returned to *Urchin* some weeks later.

From Kenneth Peberdy, HMS *Jamaica*

On 4th January 1946, HMS *Jamaica* sailed from Singapore with HMS *Cavalier* and rendezvoused with HMS *Norfolk* and *Carron* to arrive at Sourabaya on 8th. Having fought a guerilla war against the Japanese throughout the occupation of Java, the Indonesians were now fiercely resisting the return of Dutch and Allied forces. On 12th January, the ships carried out a bombardment of Indonesian concentrations at Semerang. The bombardment was mainly blind firing over the surrounding hills, controlled by a spotter team on the summit. Strangely, it was in support of a very mixed bag of ground troops, Dutch, Indian and Ghurkas, as well as considerable numbers of Japanese troops, who had been re-armed to enable them to protect themselves from the Indonesian rebel forces. *Norfolk* spoilt the show by shooting off the barrel of the right gun of 'A' turret, the second time she had shot herself 'in the foot', having done it earlier in the war. It was a peculiar time altogether—we were allowed a run ashore in Sourabaya, with the shore patrol armed with Lanchesters, and the Dutch Government gave all the ship's company a spending allowance. Unfortunately, it was in Japanese occupation money and totally valueless—I think mine just bought a pair of chopsticks! Supposedly the Dutch were going to issue a medal to all who were involved in the fighting, but our government refused to accept it.

From PO A/M Jim Dodds, HMS *Victorious*

Victorious had been having rudder trouble since 1942 caused by an aircraft going over the side and getting tangled up aft. This trouble persisted until the end of the war but before this the *Vic.* used to do a hurried docking in Bombay then back down to Colombo before re-joining the fleet at Trinco'. My diary for 1944 shows that we did this docking in September and November much to the delight of a crafty CPO from for'ard workshops who was buying wrist watches in Bombay and re-selling them at Colombo at a very, very good profit. When rudder trouble used to strike *Victorious* it was pretty sudden and the *Vic.* with two black balls at the mast head would be left going nowhere fast in circles and the rest of the fleet disappearing over the horizon. A new rudder had been chasing us around the world but didn't catch up with us until we reached Sydney in August 1945 and again I quote my diary—'September, It is now confirmed that instead of doing a refit in Sydney we are going home soon. We get four days leave. All the aircraft stores and spares are disembarked and instead of taking back our own planes we are returning to UK with Seafires which aren't required so much now and also about 500 extra personnel whose time has expired out here.

Our new rudder which has been the main hope for a decent docking period since leaving home arrived in Sydney some time ago but we are taking it back home again *on our flight deck*!'

Victorious was in Sydney from Friday 24th August until Tuesday 25th September. Captain Denny having been promoted Rear Admiral on July 7th and now about to leave the ship gave us a farewell speech on August 26th. He was full of praise for the work done during the time under his command. He told Admiral Vian it was the best ship's company in the fleet. Captain Annesley is his relief. Nice to have diaries to refer to—nobody can dispute what you say.

Tuesday 25th September. Leave expired at 0800 hrs. and we cast off at 10.30. A big crowd of civilians (mainly young ladies) came down to the jetty to see us off and to the strains of 'Now is the Hour' we slip out to sea where our squadrons who have been left ashore to a most impressive flypast. The weather is rough and cold a few hours out and even the thought of going home cannot cure my sorrow at leaving such a fine place and all the friends I've made there.

From Stuart Eadon—*Indefatigable*

Indefatigable had fired half a million rounds of ammunition and dropped 450 tons of bombs, used 102,000 tons of fuel oil. Her aircraft had used over 720,000 tons of aviation spirit.

Admiral Lord Fraser related to a Daily Mail reporter: 'The Americans doubted whether we could support ourselves logistically, and Nimitz himself wondered whether our presence would clog his own supply line. Our government however, had promised that the BPF would be self-supporting, and in December 1944 I spent three days at Honolulu with Admiral Nimitz. I said "You realise all the difficulties—I hope it will work." Nimitz replied: "Admiral, you and I together will make it work. We will have a private line which neither Washington nor London can intercept." Thus started the partnership which brought the Pacific war to a triumphant conclusion. 'Once the Americans are convinced,' Lord Fraser said, 'they don't do things by halves. The difficulty there was not that we were unwanted—as some people suggested—on the contrary both General MacArthur and Admiral Nimitz were competing for our support.

'The apparent delay in bringing the British Fleet into action against the Japanese is explained by the fact that a high-level decision had to be taken in Washington as to where the Fleet should operate.

'The right course, in my view, was to help Admiral Nimitz in the assault on Japan, rather than support landing operations in Borneo or elsewhere.

'Early in March, with the fleet waiting in Sydney we were still waiting orders from Washington. I decided to move the fleet up to Manus in the Bismark Archipelago so as to be nearer the scene of action.

'The long awaited signal came on 15th March from Admiral King, US Commander in Chief in Washington. The British Fleet, Task Force 113, later Task Force 57—together with Task Force 112, the Fleet Train and escort vessels—was directed to report for duty in the "Iceberg" operations under the command of C in C Pacific—Admiral Nimitz.

"Iceberg" was the assault on Okinawa, where lightly armoured American carriers were taking heavy punishment from Japanese kamikaze and other aircraft based on Kyushu and Formosa. These aircraft had, however, to refuel at Sakishima Gunto, between Okinawa and Formosa. Task Force 57 had to neutralise these airfields.'

Vice Admiral Rawlings, who commanded the Force, tells how TF 57 was at sea for 62 days, broken by 8 days at Leyte. During this time they flew 4,852 sorties, dropped 875 tons of bombs and rocket projectiles, destroyed 100 enemy aircraft and damaged 70 others. Our own losses were 33 aircraft from enemy action: in addition, 92 were lost operationally.

He paid tribute to the Fleet Train under Rear-Admiral Fisher and the spearhead of the Force, the 1st Aircraft Carrier Squadron under Vice-Admiral Vian.

The latter—later Fifth Sea Lord—said of the airmen, 'They were wonderful, for they must have known that they were for it if they landed in Japanese territory. Actually of 30 or so pilots lost from my squadron, all but two were murdered by the Japanese.'

Vian praised American co-operation, emphasising, 'The air-sea rescue service by lifeguard submarines and Dumbo aircraft was simply splendid. Of course,' he added, 'the operation showed that a British carrier task force could do as well as the Americans—in a game they had been playing far longer.'

From Telegraphist John Gillis, HMS *Pheasant*

Fri. 3 Aug: Still heading NE—next fuelling with be 350 miles east of Tokyo!!

Sat. 4 Aug: We actually blew up a mine today—at least, the navigating officer did, with a rifle. Also dropped charges for exercise.

Sun. 5 Aug: *Chaser* and *Nizam* join, and bring mail.

Wed. 15 Aug: JAPAN ACCEPTS TERMS OF SURRENDER
CEASE FIRE

Thurs. 16 Aug: 'Splice the Mainbrace' today.

Fri. 17 Aug: We proceed to rendezvous with Fleet tomorrow. *Odzani* and two tankers join.

Sat. 25 Aug: Eight weeks at sea today—and still no sign of going anywhere. Sea getting very rough.

Mon. 27 Aug: The US and British Pacific Fleets entered Tokyo Bay.

Thur. 30 Aug: Ordered to join the Fleet in Tokyo Bay—on our way.

Fri. 31 Aug: The *Pheasant* entered Tokyo Bay this forenoon!!

Wed. 5 Sept: Left Tokyo Bay with *Crane, Woodcock, Whimbrel, Cessnock, Pirie* and *Ballarat* on way to Hong Kong via Subic Bay.

Tues. 16 Oct: Arrived in Brisbane this forenoon.

Once back in Australia the disintegration of the British Pacific Fleet, and the ship's company of HMS *Pheasant*, commenced as men were repatriated home in the order of their demob seniority. Our war was over, and we could look back over 2½ years of service, much of it at sea on the type of boring, dangerous, but vital work for which we and our sister ships had been built—convoy escort.

We had sailed the dark and stormy waters of the Atlantic, the sparkling blue, but no less dangerous, of the Mediterranean, and finally the unbelievably beautiful Pacific, all of which had been stained with blood during the six years of war. But the *Pheasant*, a lucky ship if ever there was one, had come through unscathed, a fact for which we were all sincerely grateful.

Article from 'The China Mail', 1946

HONG KONG TO LOSE KENNEDY FORCE

Hong Kong is about to bid farewell to that fine body of servicemen known as The Kennedy Force who, from the first day of the re-occupation, have played such an important and vital part in the re-habilitation and reconstruction of the Colony.

Many will be genuinely sorry when they leave and many are deeply grateful to them for the excellent manner they have, during the short stay here, contributed to the maintenance and preservation of law and order.

Kennedy Force, named after Commander A. R. Kennedy OBE, RN of HMS *Anson*, who with Captain A. C. Madden of HMS *Anson* was the first to land at the Central Police station where they found the Japanese still in occupation. At first the force was composed from men from HMS *Anson* and later from HMS *Bermuda* and HMS *Euryalus*.

THE OCCUPATION

The force is now composed of men from HMS *Duke of York* and a great proportion are due for Home and demobilisation.

The present commander is Commander P. A. Roche, DSC, RN of HMS *Duke of York*.

From the very start the force undertook patrol and street duties and co-operated with the local Police. When the force first arrived Hong Kong was in a turmoil but the members of the force have assisted in making it a safe place to live in.

Captain A. B. Nicholls of HMS *Duke of York* said that the men liked the work. It was a change from their usual work on board. They were pleased that they were doing valuable work.

Members of the Kennedy Force will always look back on their work and will be able to say with pride that they had helped Hong Kong to maintain order and helped Hong Kong on its feet.

TATTOO

As a finale to their work ashore Kennedy Force staged a tattoo, on a small scale at the St. Joseph's College compound last night. The programme which took just over an hour, was gone through without a hitch and afforded excellent entertainment for the large number present. Of the force of 400 men about 250 men took part.

Letters re Doc Vaughan, Surgeon Lieut. HMS *Indefatigable*

Received from Alan 'Doc' Vaughan's brother Bryan in Toronto, to their father.

April 5th 1945

Dear Mr Vaughan,

It is with a profound feeling of personal loss that I write offering you my deep and sincere sympathy in your bereavement.

I can honestly say that the whole ship's company, and especially, of course, the aircrews, were devoted to Alan, genial, kindly, most sympathetic, and able.

He devoted most of his time and energy to the flying personnel, in fact he was in every sense, their 'champion'. He was always ready to be spokesman for them, knowing them all intimately with their troubles and difficulties. He was 'Doc' to them, and he had pet names for almost every one of them. It has been my privilege to be shipmates with him since the ship commissioned, and although we disagreed heartily on many subjects we invariably finished as good friends.

He was killed instantaneously, or least he did not regain consciousness during the few minutes before he died, and he had no pain nor were his features marred. I helped to get him to the sick bay, but he had no chance of living.

A remark I have heard several times is that if Alan could have chosen a way to die in war-time he would have chosen this way; at his post on duty, with some of his friends, in action.

Surgeon Cdr. Yates has lost a valiant colleague, and all of us have lost a kind and noble friend.

Alan's gear is being packed by Surg. Lt. Cardew, one of his brother doctors, and Kenneth Leigh-Smith, Alan's countryman and special friend on board. I expect it will be some long time in being forwarded, owing to our present situation and our future movements.

As is inevitable in this sort of warfare, one does in a way become resigned to losing one's shipmates suddenly, but the loss of our 'Canadian Doctor' is a blow from which we shall not easily recover.

When I was ill some weeks ago, Alan lent me a book to read, and on its flyleaf was written 'Vaughan, Easter '35'. He asked me to pass it on to Leigh-Smith when I had read it, which I did. I feel sure you will agree with me in letting Leigh-Smith keep the book as a memorial of his friend who was killed, whilst doing his duty, on Easter Day 1945.

I buried Alan at sea, with several of his shipmates the same day.

More information I am not able to give you at present.

Be sure, Sir, that you have our deepest sympathy, and I do assure you of our personal prayers. At our next church service we shall remember Alan with proud thanksgiving before God, and we shall pray that you may know God's peace in your heart.

Yours very sincerely,
Fred Hadfield, Chaplain

Lieut. (E) C. F. Jackson RN
HMS *Indefatigable*
C/o British Fleet Mail
San Francisco
Calif.
April 29th, 1945

Dear Mr. & Mrs. Vaughan,

It is a hard fate, indeed, that makes my first letter to you an expression of sympathy for your loss of Alan. Words are so inept, but I would like to say that I am thinking of you and sorrowing with you, with all those whom Alan knew and has now left.

We here, on this ship, all feel the loss; above all others Alan seems irreplaceable. The stoker, steward and the seaman, and I'm sure almost everyone aboard has lost a grand friend who did so much to help when one was in need. He always acted with a courage, frankness and truth which was an inspiration to all.

To me as my friend and my family's friend, his passing is a horrid blow. Our little Lyn would have loved her godfather, I know, but she will learn of him, and, I hope, grow up in life as a citizen with some of those great qualities of Alan.

Forgive me if this letter should arouse your wound: I did want you to know that he meant a great deal to us also, I have always been proud to know your son.

Sincerely,
Claude Jackson

HMS *Indefatigable*
C/o GPO London
6th May 1945

Dear Mr. Vaughan,

I postponed writing this letter until things had quietened down. I would like Alan's mother and yourself to know how proud I was to be a friend and messmate of his. He had high ideals and lived up to them; no-one, seaman or officer came to him in vain and in this little world on board the loss that you have sustained has been felt by one and all of us. He was so alive and active that even now I feel it difficult to believe that he shall not come along with a laugh and a joke to cheer us all.

It is seldom that one sees a man who had the courage of his convictions and yet had such a happy way of making them known and carrying them out.

He was a good man and therefore could not help being a good doctor; and his influence, amongst the people who were fortunate enough to know him, will be something that will endure. I felt I had to let his mother and you know these things.

Yours most sincerely,
Charles J. W. Towers
Surgeon Lt. Commander RN

HMS *Indefatigable*, British Fleet
C/o Chief mail Office
San Francisco
California
16.7.45

The Secretary
Timothy Eaton Memorial Church
230 St. Clair Avenue
W. Toronto, Ontario, Canada

Dear Sir

We have received for Surgeon Lt. Vaughan your gift of 300 cigarettes. You will perhaps have heard already of Dr. Vaughan's death in action, if not it is sad news to break to any of his friends as he was so loved by everybody.

May I suggest, that as tobacco is dutiable and cannot be returned to sender, and as it would probably have been his wish, that I give these cigarettes to the sick men on board and to those at action-stations during battle. We are just about to enter danger zones and you can probably appreciate what a cigarette or two means, especially when we are rationed, even if they could get away from their stations to reach supplies at the time.

Trusting that you approve of my suggestion, and thanking you on behalf of the men, whom I shall tell where the cigarettes came from,

Sincerely yours,
Lieut. V. Longden
Chaplain RNVR

HMS *Indefatigable*
C/o BFMO San Francisco
April 26th 1945

Dear Mr. & Mrs. Vaughan,

This is just another of Alan's many friends on board this ship trying to put into words his sorrow and sympathy with you at this time. I am 'Ken' from Montreal and got to know and like Alan more and more through our common bond of being Canadians.

Please forgive the late date at which this letter is being written. It was done purposely to make certain the official notification would reach you first. We were not more than fifty feet away from each other when the tragedy occurred and I can assure you he was joking and happy right at the end. This loss was felt very keenly throughout the ship as he had won a very special place in our hearts.

There is little I can say of comfort except that he was doing the job he loved, and had seen and enjoyed more of life than many are privileged to do. It is my sincere hope that I shall one day be able to visit you in Toronto and meet the parents of whom Alan was so proud.

Sincerely,
Kenneth Leigh-Smith

HMS Indefatigable
British Fleet Mail
April 29th

Dear Mr. Vaughan,

Please accept my deepest sympathy in your tragic loss. It was a great shock to all in this ship and no one could be more missed than Alan. To the aircrews whom he looked after his loss is irreplaceable. To me, in the fifteen months we served together, he was a great personal friend and an invaluable colleague.

I should just like to say that Alan died at his action station and instantaneously. He more than paid a dividend to this ship and the Navy.

The medical profession is much the poorer for his untimely loss.

Yours sincerely,
A. C. K. Yates
Surg. Cmdr. RNVR

Article in The Toronto Star, Monday May 29 1989

Canadian hero's former foes welcome plans for memorial
by Gerald Utting Toronto Star

Tokyo—The Battle of Onagawa Bay is not likely to go down in the history books as a turning point of World War II. In fact, Japan was already beaten. Yet a lot of men died on that day of conflict, August 9, 1945, and they have not been forgotten, either by comrades or families and friends.

One of those who died was a Canadian, a 26-year-old from Nelson, BC, Robert Hampton (Hammy) Gray. Piloting a Corsair fighter from the British carrier *Formidable,* Gray bombed the destroyer escort *Amakusa* of the Imperial Japanese Navy, sinking the vessel with 71 hands aboard. In pressing home the attack with incredible determination, he lost his life. Gray was posthumously awarded the Victoria Cross, the highest award in the British Commonwealth for bravery in action.

Last Canadian killed in war
Hammy Gray is believed to have been the last Canadian killed in action in World War II.

One place where the battle remains in people's minds is the city of Onagawa, whose residents—among them survivors of the sunken destroyer *Amakusa*—enthusiastically welcome a plan to erect a memorial to the Canadian pilot, and who remember him as a hero. The monument is being completed on a headland at the mouth of Onagawa Bay, overlooking the spot where Gray's Corsair crashed into the water. A service of dedication and remembrance will be held there Aug. 9, the day before the annual remembrance service is held for the Japanese dead of that battle.

The man who negotiated with Onagawa authorities over the Canadian memorial is Ottawa's military attache in Tokyo, naval captain Terrence Milne. In 1986, he said, a retired Canadian carrier pilot, Stuart Soward, wrote a book, *Formidable Hero,* about Gray's life and death. The National War Museum in Ottawa then asked him to find out what had happened to Gray's aircraft and whether there might be any chance of recovering it, or parts of it, for a display. Milne talked with Onagawa mayor Eichiro Suda, citizens, and with Japanese naval veterans who took part in the battle. 'The people were remarkably helpful,' said Milne, 'harboring no resentment.'

Later, one veteran told me that for a long time he had been unable to bring himself to talk about events of that day. Now he realized those on both sides had done their duty. As an old man, he wished to overcome the bitterness of the past. Milne asked the mayor if it would be possible to raise some form of monument to Gray, close to where his plane came down. The mayor wrote to him after consulting with citizens:

'Over 40 years have elapsed since the war. We are now being called upon to join our efforts for eternal peace and prosperity. By forgetting our past sentiments and feelings of rivalry, we must make our best efforts to enhance our ties of goodwill and friendship between Canada and Japan, and to deepen exchanges and understandings between our two peoples. Paying our respects to the great Canadian hero, Lt. Gray, for his bravery and erecting a monument to his memory, is, I trust, the most relevant and really excellent thing for us to do.'

Bay surrounded by high mountains

Onagawa was a naval port when eight aircraft from the *Formidable* carried out the attack. Many of the seamen on the ill-fated vessel lived there. The bay is surrounded by high mountains, and on the day of the raid there were about half a dozen warships anchored in the area. The wing of planes from *Formidable* was made up of experienced British and Canadian pilots and some Norwegians.

Gray, who had left the University of British Columbia to enlist as an ordinary seaman, was an experienced and determined pilot in low level attacks. He had taken part in a 1944 raid on the German battleship *Tirpitz* in a Norwegian fjord, and in a number of other raids in the Pacific. He already had the Distinguished Service Cross. Gray came on to the bay over a mountain behind the city, then headed straight for *Amakusa*. The destroyer and all the ships and flak batteries immediately opened up. His Corsair was carrying two 500-pound bombs under its wings, but when he reached the point where an attacking plane launched its weapons, one bomb had been blown off the wing by the ship's guns. His engine was hit and caught fire. This was the time for Gray to pull out and try to bail out, but he pressed grimly on. The veterans who had served on *Amakusa* told Milne they remembered how Gray's plane kept coming right at them.

'I could see his face,' one former gunner told Milne. Only after he released his bomb did Gray move his Corsair up and over the *Amakusa*. His aircraft then plunged, hit the water, turned over and sank near the mouth of the bay.

Search begun for lost Corsair

The single bomb penetrated to *Amakusa*'s engine room and exploded. The survivors told Milne how the destroyer rolled over and sank within five minutes.

Further attacks by other carrier planes in that battle lifted the total number of Japanese dead to 157. Today, a monument to them stands near where the monument to Gray will be dedicated Aug. 9. The people of Onagawa have donated the site for the Gray memorial, overlooking one of Japan's most beautiful coastal areas. The government of British Columbia donated a three-ton block of granite. The English language plaque on the monument includes these words: 'May the dedication of this memorial be an eternal symbol of peace and friendship between our two nations.' A Japanese translation of the inscription, in calligraphy, will be provided on a bronze plaque. It was donated by the chairman of the giant Marubeni Corp., himself an anti-aircraft gunner during the battle in which Gray perished.

A special fund has been set up to raise money to search for the lost Corsair. A US Navy diving team will join the search with electronic gear, while a local diving club and a British Columbian diving firm have volunteered their services. The Corsair may have been destroyed by a postwar tidal wave, but is probably buried under silt. Milne said the chances of finding it are about 50—50.

From CPO TAG Dick Sweet, who was the last person to speak to Lieut. (A) Hammy Gray VC, 1841 Squadron HMS *Formidable*

I first visited Japan in June 1935 when I was a Boy Seaman 1st Class on a First World War Light Cruiser HMS *Capetown*.

We made our courtesy visit to Kobe and being boys on pay of 7/6 a week and liberty leave ending at 1800, we were not involved in any night life. As was usual in those days, visits to places of interest—shrines etc.—were laid on and we saw a lot of the countryside. I was most impressed with the cleanliness and beauty of the country, the city and even the dockyard. I found the no personal touch custom fascinating and marvelled at how people in a crowd never bumped into each other. My impression of them as a race was that they were ultra polite, clean and considerate. Nobody stared or was embarrassed if a mother in a full tram bared her breast to feed a babe, in fact they appeared very civilised and certainly in better social status and superior to the Chinese, but—and I have no answer to this—despite their clasping of palms and bowing, their impassive faces—no apparent emotional light in their eyes—left me with a gut feeling that they could just as well stab you in the back and still show no emotion. I knew of the Samurai and their fighting qualities, but accepted the fact that this was history. I enjoyed my visit and left with what every sailor visiting Japan leaves, 'a full Japanese Tea Set', pieces of which I still have and which survived the 4½ years of German occupation of my home in Guernsey, CI.

In 1938/39 I volunteered for Rating pilot but got press ganged into air gunner (in the eyes of the RN I had volunteered for flying and would get it as an AG). In 1940 I formed 827 Albacore Squadron at Yeovilton (their 1st) and stayed with the squadron for 2 years, 3 months and left the squadron the last of the originals who formed. We operated initially from the *Victorious* having done 6 months with coastal command.

The squadron reformed at Hatston and embarked on HMS *Indomitable* (a new carrier). With 831 squadron on board the ship ran aground at Kingston, Jamaica and history now acclaims that that catastrophy spelt the doom of the *Repulse* and *Prince of Wales*, the fall of Singapore and allowing the Japanese to surge west—sinking the *Hermes, Dorsetshire* and *Cornwall* on the way.

During this time the *Indomitable* had ferried two lots of fighters to Singapore and Ceylon, the Albacores and Fulmers being left at Cormaksa, Aden. Our next action was the invasion of Madagascar—no casualties.

After foreign service leave I was appointed to No. 1 Observer School at RNAS Arbroath and during the next 18 months qualified TAG2 and eventually TAG1. During this time also I qualified for the new Warrant Air Officer (Air Gunner). The first course for it forecast for January 1945 but in October 1944 the bombshell fell. I received a Pier Head Jump (emergency drafting) to HMS *Formidable*—within 24 hours (no foreign draft leave—usually 2 weeks) I was on my way to a transit camp west of Glasgow and 24 hours after that I joined HMS *Tyne* the Destroyer Repair Ship at the Tail-of-the-Bank and sailed for the Far East. As we went through the straits of Gibraltar I little realised that the *Formidable* was in dry dock there with a broken centre engine main bearing. At Port Said I was put ashore and eventually I arrived at Dakheila Air Station (Alexandria) and met up with Cdr. Elliott, the *Formidable*'s Cdr. Operations, half of 1841 Corsair Squadron and 848 Avenger Squadron. In December 1944 I flew by SAAF Dakota all the way along the N coast of Africa back to Gib. and the *Formidable* where we spent Xmas.

In January 1945—after successful sea trials—*Formidable* set sail obviously for the British Pacific Fleet—at Ceylon we picked up the other half of 1841. Via Sydney, *Formidable* relieved *Illustrious* on 14th April 1945 on Operation Iceberg

One. On the 4th May 1945 Operation Iceberg Two, *Formidable* was hit by a kamikaze Zeke. Like most people who volunteered for flying duties without any heroics—scared as I am sure we all were, whether pilot, observer or TAG—at least you had the vehicle—your own expertise and the drills of Pilot Observer and AG and guns to fight with. I never liked being part of the ship and grovelling on the deck and trying to crawl into a screwhole during a kamikaze attack. One felt so frustrated, you couldn't fight back and the mere thought that there was a human diving at you with the one intent to kill himself, was very demoralising. Unfortunately it wasn't possible to do that with an Avenger turret.

At this stage after the second kamikaze on VE Day I indulged in a little self pity. The overseas BBC had said that the Channel Islands had been liberated. I was abroad in 819 squadron on the *Illustrious* when they were invaded and captured and now that they were free, here was I on the other side of the world still fighting and at that time there seemed no end in sight, what with the fanatical kamikaze, ground fighting going on and the known Japanerse threat that the moment any Allied troops set foot on Japanese soil all Allied POWs would be executed, which meant 300,000 men would be butchered plus the loss of life to invade Japanese soil and pursue the war to a finish. But somehow this seemed to spur the BPF to greater effort—the tempo on *Formidable* certainly increased. With no Lt. Burger who had been killed by the kamikaze on 4th May, I found my daily duties much increased, finishing at about 2300. A special position was reserved for me in the CPOs mess so that at 0300 the quarter-master's mate could give me a shake and the next day's programme would commence.

Formidable carried 'Y' staff (they were an officer and ratings specially trained to monitor enemy transmissions). They were located on the starboard side of the island directly underneath and liaising with the Fighter Direction Officer who was next to the AOR Operations room.

Cdr. 'Ops'—W. Elliott obviously spent a lot of time with the FDO and if you read 'The Forgotten Fleet'—having spoken to some of the Jap survivors through an interpreter—the Y boys obviously intercepted the activity in Onagawa which led to my being directed to convey a message to Lieut. Gray as the force was turning into wind.

Then came the day when a list of Japanese cities was made available with no explanation attached other than when notified the Task Force would retire from the operational area and no air strikes or ops would take place against the target names. The rest is history but it is a fact no one in my knowledge or contact were aware of an atomic bomb—super bomb—yes.

That the war ended as it did I have no quarrel. The fact that 300,000 POWs who had suffered so much brutality, degradation, starvation and bestiality warranted the action taken, my feelings personally were of relief and when the signal from Admiralty arrived (which I still have) directing CPO(A) TAG1 A. E. Sweet to be discharged to UK for WAO (AG) Course I was overjoyed. But on return to Lee-on-Solent it was to find that someone else (probably with friends in the right places) had been put in my place—this was the last straw—the pier head jump to the *Formidable* and the BPF had won—so I withdrew from the WAO course when the Admiralty said they couldn't create a precedent and allow back-dating of seniority—so I took my 12 and joined civil airways.

I am indeed grateful to Dick Sweet for obtaining permission from author of 'A Formidable Hero', Stuart Soward, to reproduce the following which he wrote for the Canadian Veterans' organisations:

REMEMBRANCE AT ONAGAWA

On August 9, 1989, forty four years after the event, whilst overlooking the placid waters of Onagawa Bay, a final honour was accorded to Lt. Hampton Gray, VC, DSC, RCNVR.

Sited in beautiful Sakiyama Peace Park and with a dominant view of the crash location in the bay where Hampton Gray died, a gathering of two hundred Japanese and forty Canadians paid tribute to a fallen warrior who has no known grave.

This occasion was unique in many respects, but one fact stood out over the others, namely, it is the first time that a foreign combatant has ever been accorded the honour of a hero's recognition in Japan. Among the many individuals who attended the ceremony were several survivors of the Japanese ships that went down fighting, as they were vanquished by overpowering carrier aircraft attacks. Others, were men such as Charles Butterworth a friend of Hammy, who, on that same day flew the next attacking strike to Onagawa Bay; Bill Atkinson, who strapped Hammy into his aircraft that fateful day and Dick Sweet (travelling all the way from England) who was the last person to directly speak to Hammy, clambering up on the Corsair's wing to brief him on the amended shipping targets at Onagawa. Others were boyhood friends, a university and fraternity brother, Hammy's sister Phyllis Gautschi and her family, and the officiating Reverend, and only surviving Chaplain of the Fleet, eighty year old retired Captain C. H. Maclean.

There were many wreaths laid at the foot of the granite memorial, from Japanese dignitaries such as Mayor Suda of the city of Onagawa, who eloquently spoke at the ceremony and who was the prime driving force from Onagawa to support the memorial *(it was he who in his speech referred to Lieut. Gray as 'Canadian Hero of the Sky' and said his motto is 'Shed sweat for your family, shed tears for your friends; shed blood for your nation.'—Ed.)*; Mr. Kanda, head of the Onagawa veterans; Bill Atkinson, and Charles Butterworth who each spoke briefly and jointly laid a wreath from the Naval Officers' Association; Mary Collins, the Associate Minister of National Defence, who also gave a graceful address; Dick Sweet who placed a floral wreath in the form of the *Formidable*'s crest from the *Formidable* Association; Mr. Stephen Heeney the acting Canadian Ambassador, who gave an address and presented a wreath, as did Mrs. Phyllis Gautschi who also unveiled the monument to her brother.

It is important to record that the site preparation for the granite memorial was financed by donations totalling in excess of $30,000 from over thirty Canadian and Japanese members of the Canadian Embassy and twenty five Canadian and Japanese corporations and institutions, virtually all in Tokyo. Contributions from Canada to the Hampton Gray fund totalled $275.00. Logistic support however from Air Command (General Larry Ashley) consisted of the essential transport of the granite to Japan from Victoria with local assistance from the staff of the Maritime Commander, Pacific (Admiral Bob George).

The design of the site approximately 20'x20' was beautifully constructed by local Japanese craftsmen and consisted of granite-walled planters decorated on each side with engraved Doves of Peace, the tiled floor was in decorative colours with a large maple leaf superimposed in the centre. On the seaward side of the square were splanted two maple trees, one on each side of the monument. Beneath the two bronze plaques with English inscriptions on the upper faces of the granite monument, was a translation in Japanese on an identical bronze plaque. This particular plaque was a gift from Mr. Haruna, Chairman of the Marubeni Corporation, one of the largest Japanese trading companies. Mr. Haruna was a Sub-Lt. at Onagawa during the battle and manned a gunnery observation post ashore.

It is interesting to note that the Japanese national television and CNN United States Television coverage was extensive with the CNN video subsequently being shown world wide. The entire proceedings were a particularly moving experience for us all, and fully justified for me, the considerable work and expense that I incurred in developing the project.

On the following day, the 10th August, the Canadian members of the group (approximately 18 in number) including Attaché Capt. Terry Milne and his relief Capt. Ron Richards were all invited to attend the annual Japanese Memorial Service for their dead comrades. This took place at their memorial site not far from the Gray memorial and was quite an emotional event attended by veterans and bereaved family groups. The faded battle flag of the *Amakusa* (Ocean Escort sunk by Hammy) was raised, then lowered to half mast, and the religious aspect of the ceremony began. As foreigners, we were all invited to participate in the incense burning part of the ceremony which was indeed considered an honour. After the religious aspects were completed the ensign was raised and the Japanese veterans, many of whom were survivors of the battle, sang some of their wartime songs, including a stirring rendition of the Kamikaze march, which was most moving. Following the ceremony, we were invited to the home of Mr. Kanada, the Custodian of the Onagawa Veterans Association. Kanada in his seventies, gave a remarkably eloquent and compassionate speech welcoming us all to his home and paying his great respects to the valour of Hammy Gray. This was followed by a typical Japanese banquet with plenty of beer, sake and rye. It is a particular honour to be invited to a private Japanese home, which again made us feel very welcome. An additional, unusual event was the signing of names by us all, on the Japanese flag, which will then be used by the veterans group at their subsequent annual Remembrance ceremony. A rather remarkable camaraderie developed during the party with Bill Atkinson, myself and Charlie Butterworth discussing the Onagawa battle details with some of the Japanese survivors through the aid of our interpreter. One amusing comment came from one of the surviving gunners of the battle when he said, 'We wouldn't have tried so hard to shoot you down if we had known you were Canadians.' Perhaps a bit of bar talk but we all enjoyed it.

To summarize, I think it was a most memorable event for us all and the sincere Japanese welcome and friendliness was apparent throughout our entire visit. Without doubt, the Embassy organization, courtesy and exclusive and generous assignment of a bus and their driver, (Mr. Doi, an ex Kamikaze pilot) together with our own interpreter and all Embassy facilities made the entire trip not only pleasant but indeed possible. It should also be noted that it was the exceptional efforts of Terry Milne who persevered, and skilfully organized the entire Japanese phase of the trip, in spite of an initial lukewarm reaction from the Embassy. This changed to wholeheartedsupport,however, when it was established that this project was 'going to fly'. Strangely, support for the project on the part of the Canadian Federal Government remained non-existent, throughout, other than the very brief appearance of the Associate Minister of National Defence, which was primarily intended for political and public relations purposes.

Also present were: Stuart Soward, author of 'A Formidable Hero', Bill Atkinson, SP of 1844 Squadron, *Indomitable,* Charlie Butterworth, 1842 Squadron, *Formidable,* Mrs. Gautschi, Hammy's sister and the Rev. Chas Maclean, former Captain RCN and Chaplain of the Fleet.

Dick Sweet ends his letter:

I could not understand how a person bowing and walking backwards all polite and proper could a short while later—in uniform—bayonet pregnant women or parade POWs naked and insultingly in front of people forced to watch.

Capt. T. Milne (N) the Naval Attaché for the last 4 years in Tokyo Canadian Embassy assures me there is a change in culture throughout the land and who am I to argue? Everyone was very polite, I marvelled once again at their kindness, the no-personal contact, their patience and their acceptance of ex-enemies on an equal level. It was an historic occasion and I was thankful for being invited. It could be the first breakdown of the East and West barrier and Hammy Gray in some peculiar way opened the door.

From Lieut. (A) Alex Appleton RNVR, HMS *Formidable*

Yesterday, at the HMS *Formidable* Reunion, you asked me to write what I could of the time when 'Hammy' Gray and I flew together. I have no tangible records of those times—after the war I ditched everything, even my flying log book. I had lost too many friends and colleagues to wish to retain any mementoes. I have regretted getting rid of them in more recent years, but the action fitted my mood at the time.

Alex then goes on to describe how he was Hammy's Observer, flying Fairey Fulmars mainly on long range reconnaissance missions with 803 Squadron in Formidable *and* Illustrious, *and from Mombasa under CO Lt. Cdr. (A) B. F. Cox. When Alex contracted malaria the partnershp ceased and shortly afterwards the Squadron disbanded towards the end of 1943. He concludes:*

What do I remember of Hammy as a person? Well, we were good friends away from our aircraft but, as was normal, not intimate in the sense of talking much about our innermost beliefs. He was fairly extrovert, more so than I, cheerful and calm. I cannot recall him ever being angry, in fact he smiled a lot. Also, unlike some of our pilots, if he was pining for a single seater fighter, he never showed it. In a word, just the sort of pilot I would have picked to fly with, and to have off-duty time with. I must say that when circumstances permitted,he liked his drink, I put him to bed a few times! One final comment about the operations we were undertaking. A danger during those long flights at quite low altitudes in tropical latitudes was that one or both of us might fall asleep. Our only contact was through the voice pipe so, would you believe, from time to time we sang to each other. Those old Bing Crosby songs got a hammering over the Indian Ocean!

If you have visited the Hiroshima Peace Memorial Museum, you will have read the leaflet which is available there. If not, there here is what it says:

HIROSHIMA UNDER A-BOMB ATTACK

8.15 a.m., Monday, Aug. 6 1945. Weather fine and cloudless.

Three US B-29 had approached the city of Hiroshima from the north-eastern direction, maintaining an altitude of approximately 8,500 metres (about 27,800 feet) as observed by an anti-air artillery unit. One of them glided over the central part of the city, and dropped one Atomic Bomb, and making an abrupt right-angled turn, departed away at full speed. At the time of the bomb explosion, it had flown 16 kilometres (about 10 miles) to the northwest.

The bomb fell rapidly with a trail of thick red column of flames in its wake and 43 seconds later at the height of 580 metres (about 1,900 feet) above the ground level, exploded with a terrific detonation. According to some of the eye-witness' account, it was an unimaginable big fireball, bluish-white or white-pink.

Soon after the explosion, an enormous pillar of smoke rose up and immediately reached 9,000 metres (about 29,700 feet), in the shape of a mushroom cloud. By blasting wind a vast amount of dust covered all over the city and most houses were destructed or heavily damaged. Fire started raging at numerous places, and almost all the areas were turned into ashes. The air-raid alarm was cleared off in the morning lending a sense of relief but inviting unpreparedness and human damage of over 200 thousands.

GENERAL INFORMATION

The yield of the Hiroshima A-bomb is equivalent to about 13 kilotons of TNT explosive (1.3 x 10^{13} calories of energy). Three factors are considered to have worked concurrently at the instant of the atomic bomb explosion. They are thermal radiation, blast, and radiation.

1. *Thermal radiation*

The temperature of the fireball that developed in the air with the explosion is estimated to have been 300,000°C, 1/100,000 of a second after detonation. 0.3 second later, the fireball attained a surface temperature of 7,000°C and 1 second later, a maximum diameter of about 280 metres and a surface temperature of about 5,000°C.

The intense thermal radiation released from this fireball caused burns on the human body of those who were within 3.5 kilometres from the hypocenter. Not to mention clothings and wooden houses, the surface of granite stones within 1 kilometre from the hypocenter was melted to exfoliate and the roof tiles formed glassy bubbles on its surface within 600 metres from the hypocenter.

2. *Blast*

The blast pressure at the ground zero is estimated to have been approximately 35t/m^2, and even at the point 1.3 kilometres from the hypocenter a maximum blast pressure and velocity are estimated to have been approximately 7t/m^2, 120m/sec respectively.

The effect upon the human body can be observed by the rupture and protrusion of intestines and other internal organs; at the same time stripping off clothes, tearing away the burnt skins, even blowing some off several metres.

Wooden houses within the radius of 2.3 kilometres were almost all totally destroyed, and within 3.2 kilometres half-destroyed. The outer structure of most large concrete buildings endured the blast, but ceilings fell in and windows and doors were shattered away leaving the interior to the menace of conflagration.

3. *Radiation*

Among the initial radiation emitted within 1 minute after the explosion, gamma rays and neutrons played a primary role in causing somatic disturbances, which differs from the case of conventional bombs, and the effect extended to the point 2.3 kilometres from the hypocenter. In particular, the area within a radius of 1 kilometre from the hypocenter was seriously affected by a great dose of radioactivity.

Residual radiation was present on the ground for a long time from 1 minute after the explosion. Anyone entering the area within 1 kilometre from the hypocenter for the relief of the victims or in search of his family members within 100 hours of the explosion was considerably affected by the external exposure to gamma rays of induced radiation. For half to two hours after the explosion, 'Black Rain' fell in the city, containing a great dose of radioactivity to bring about a great deal of damage.

Many have died in the years to follow due to the late disturbances of radiation, namely leukemia, malignant tumours. And some are still in bed today contracted with the disease.

It includes photographs of an Atomic Cloud, the impressive approach to the Museum, the burnt-out area showing just 7 or 8 buildings standing, a bridge blow up(wards) by the pressure wave, and a human shadow imprinted on the stone step in front of Sumitomo Bank.

This is the English language version.

Articles from the Radio Times, 2—8 Sept. 1989

LEST WE FORGET

For servicemen and women separated from their loved ones, Vera Lynn's words 'we'll meet again' helped them to keep smiling through. Now, she says, it's vital we remember those who died to keep Britain free.

'The only time it gets a bit desolate,' says Dame Vera Lynn, whose eyes could not have been less blue or less bright than when she sang to the boys in Burma, 'is when people come up to you, old people, and their eyes swell with tears, and you think, what can have happened to them to make them so sad?'

Otherwise Dame Vera, the East End girl who made her debut at the Coventry Hippodrome in 1939, has kept smiling through—through tropical heat, through sandstorms, through jungle journeys with only an armed pianist for protection and through 50 years of being a living legend, which may be the toughest thing of all.

"I didn't think of the responsibility then,' says Dame Vera, Sue Lawley's castaway on Sunday. 'You don't; you just get on with it.'

But even though she is now 72, fans still expect to see the glowing girl who used to assure them in her inimitable voice that their loved ones were waiting, and that they'd soon be home again.

'They still expect me to look and sound the same,' says Dame Vera, 'Which can be tricky. But any time I do feel a little sorry for myself, I think back, to the things I saw, to what the boys went through and I put on a cheerful face.'

Putting on a cheerful face, as she calls it, was Vera Lynn's job in the jungle; since then, it has become her life's work. 'It's true that the war has dominated my life,' she says, 'but in a positive way. It brought me a public I'd never have reached otherwise. My only ambition had been to be a good band singer.'

It was as a singer with the Ambrose band that she met Harry Lewis—'small, dark, handsome Harry' who married her and worried incessantly during the war. Invalided out of the RAF, he had to make do with the odd message from Burma.

Vera Lynn was 24 when she went to Burma. She started her journey in a flying boat and ended up reeling with migraine, soaked with sweat, battered by insects, but singing like that nightingale in Berkeley Square.

Girls of 24 then were like 18-year-olds now and nothing but her stalwart spirit had prepared her for the sounds and smells of death. Nothing had prepared her for meeting people one day who were dead the next. 'No contact can be that close. Today I meet the Burma boys, and they won't ever forget.'

(Dame Vera—no wonder you were The Forces Sweetheart!—Ed.) Not forgetting, or put more positively, remembering is something that Dame Vera is passionate about. 'I don't think the horrors of war should be re-created, but children should be reminded that the sacrifices made were for *them*. I go over to Holland every year for their Liberation Day, and I see the children standing in front of the little slabs in the British Cemetery, reading the names and the ages, 18, 19, and pausing and thinking. We don't do anything like that here—but we should—so that every child in this country could stand and pause and think: "There but for the boys go I".'

Eithne Power

Extracts from an Article in The New Zealand Observer, Weds. December 12 1945

Big Flat-Top Draws NZ Crowds

Wellington went for the *Indefatigable* in a big way. Thousands watched her berth, thousands more strolled along Aotea Quay every lunch-hour to gaze at the ship and her attendant destroyers, and, on a wet Saturday afternoon, thousands endured drenching rain as they stood in a queue for an hour-and-a-half waiting patiently to get on board.

The Fleet Air Arm pilots, of whom about 200 came from New Zealand, and most of those from the South Island, were trained with a thoroughness unsurpassed in any other branch of the fighting services. Throughout their service, the necessity of keeping them in constant practice for the ticklish job of making deck landings was recognised, and, whenever they had an enforced spell (at sea) exercises were conducted at the earliest possible moment. On one occasion, when the *Illustrious* was exercising pilots who had not flown for several weeks, four of the boys were killed in crashes within an hour.

From H. Chapman, HMS *Undaunted*, Extracts from The Argus, Capetown

Headline: *Indefatigable* in Cape Town
South Africans return from Pacific
Ships exploits off Japan

The aircraft carrier HMS *Indefatigable* and the destroyer HMS *Undaunted* arrived in Capetown from Australia at 6 a.m. today. The Ships left Fremantle on February 8th. Eight SANF officers and 59 ratings came home in the *Indefatigable*. There were two passengers in the *Undaunted*—a midshipman from Rhodesia and a Johannesburg civilian who visited Australia on official business. Relatives and friends were waiting for them and the ships berthed in the Duncan Basin.

On Monday the two ships put into Algoa Bay and 24 Seafires from the *Indefatigable* carried out exercises . . . one of the Seafires developed engine trouble and had to land at Port Elizabeth.

. . . Another Seafire crashed over the side of the carrier and was lost.

The Seafire which was piloted by Sub Lieut. I. G. Hatton RNVR made a low approach to the carrier, drifted to port and lost sight of the control officer. It landed with the port wheel over the side of the flightdeck, caught fire and dived into the sea. A crashboat from Port Elizabeth which was standing by during the exercises at the request of the *Indefatigable* and fishing boats in the vicinity carried out a search, but no trace was found of the aircraft or pilot.

A South African seaman, Jansen, was blown off the flightdeck. The crashboat rescued him and he was pulled aboard.

Algoa Bay—off Port Elizabeth. Sub. Lt.d (A) Ian G. Hatton, lost sight of batsman, caught fire and dived into sea. Sank leaving no trace. Photo from: R. D. Pankhurst—18/2/46

The Portsmouth Evening News of 16th March 1946 carried the following story

Royal Marine policemen on duty at the Main Gate of Portsmouth Dockyard at 4 a.m., to-day, were surprised to see a small 'invasion' force of women approaching down the Hard. They were the advance guard of several thousand of relatives of the crew of the 23,000 ton aircraft carrier *Indefatigable*, which berthed at 11.30 to-day.

Portsmouth has welcomed so many famous ships back from the Far East in the past few months that the homecoming scenes have become familiar, but they will never be mundane, for the look of joy on the faces of women and children who are welcoming home their menfolk is one that observers can never forget.

At Southsea

The 4 a.m. arrivals were advised by the police to go away to obtain food, and many others who arrived at frequent intervals from Midland and Northern trains were told to go to Southsea, where they could see the carrier anchored at Spithead. She arrived in the Solent at dusk last evening, after flying off some of her aeroplanes to Gosport during the day. A large notice was exhibited outside the Dockyard gate stating that visitors to the ship would not be allowed in until 11.30. By 11 the waiting queue extended from the gate along the pavement to the road leading to the Harbour Station. People in it came from many districts, and a large number of them had travelled overnight. In a chat to the waiting womenfolk an Evening News representative had to accustom himself to several different dialects. From Rhosllanerchrugog in North Wales came Miss J. Parry, of 64, Cyngurorfam Road. She was there to meet her fiance, Supply Assistant Mabon Milton, and started her long journey at 7 o'clock last night.

Brides-To-Be

Able Seaman Ronald Ollier, of 26, Townsend Road, Rugby was met by his sister, mother, father, and fiancee, and another bride-to-be was Miss P. Wilkins, fiancee of AB Leslie Johnson Clarke of 45 Burrard Road, Customs House, London.

A Worthing family was led by Mrs. R. Miles, of 2, Edinburgh Cottages, Western Road, the mother of Stoker Edward Miles, who had been away 1½ years. With her were the stoker's two sisters.

There were large crowds at all vantage points at Sally Port. As the *Indefatigable* came up harbour flying her paying-off pennant, the crowd was allowed into the Dockyard, where they swarmed over the cobbly roads and caissons to the middle slip jetty, where the carrier was berthed.

Article in Sunday Times, January 12, 1947

NAVY LOSES ITS BIG CARRIERS from A Naval Correspondent

Although fully one-third of the new personnel of the Royal Navy is now concerned with the air, it is understood that all six of our fast fleet carriers are to be laid up in reserve on account of the manning situation.

The *Implacable* has been given a brief respite in the Home Fleet, and the *Illustrious* is at present acting as trials carrier, but the *Indefatigable* and *Indomitable* have already been withdrawn from service, and the *Victorious* and *Formidable* will follow them into retirement when they return from their last trooping trips on January 14 and February 3, respectively.

When they are withdrawn from service, British naval air operations will devolve upon our six light fleet aircraft carriers (capacity about 40 aircraft), which are much smaller and slower.

Sonny Hogben ex Warrant Officer RAF has died, but I have had the privilege of reading the manuscript of his experiences. He called it 'Tomorrow does Come'

The Folkestone & Hythe Herald of Saturday 2nd August 1980 said, 'The fighting spirit of the British soldier has never been in doubt and it was this courage and determination that helped Sonny and the other POWs pull through. But despite the suffering he endured, the book contains no bitterness towards his captors.'

He was imprisoned at Sham-Shui-Po near Hong Kong and later, on the Japanese mainland for nearly 4 years. It is a similar story to the others—no blankets even in the snow, sleeping on concrete, only rice to eat resulting in beri-beri, 'strawberry balls', diptheria, 'electric feet', diarrhoea etc.

His tremendous courage and hope made me weep with admiration for the spirit of this gentle man. 'Man's inhumanity to man' is enough to make anyone weep, but the spirit to overcome that is an inspiration.

He wrote:

At the outbreak of hostilities in the Far East on December 8th 1941, I had been in the RAF Station at Kai-Tak since December 1938, but on that day December 8th 1941, I was in a hospital bed at the Royal Naval Hospital in Hong Kong, and had been there since the end of August that year suffering with rheumatic fever, and was discharged that day, as all the beds were required for casualties, and I remember the Medical Officer telling me to take things very easy, as the illness had affected my heart.

How could I take things easy with a war going on around me. Within two days I was back in Hong Kong. Not as a hospital patient, but with a rifle and ammunition, and on the hills of Hong Kong, sleeping rough, and moving from hill to hill. All our aircraft, all five of them had been destroyed on the ground by the Japanese Air Force in the first half hour of war being declared. So there was nothing else left to do but be a soldier. We knew how to fire a rifle, but that was the extent of our training as soldiers.

We had no idea of camouflage or bayonet fighting, or any aspect of a soldier's training. But we did what we could, and we did our very best too.

(They were ordered to lay down their arms and were then taken to Sham-Shui-Po POW Camp.—Ed.)

I was beginning to find it very difficult to get around. I felt so weak, that a walk of a few yards would tire me out. The toilets were about a hunded yards from the huts, and it would take me quite a time to get there, and sometimes I didn't just make it.

Nothing much was changed on the camp as we enter the year 1943. One year completed, will it be this month, this year? or when will our great tomorrow come? Come it must, but when? We wandered around the camp in small groups, and each group would have the same topic of conversation, food, food, and more food, wine, women and song were not mentioned much. Our bellies were the rulers of our head. Dirty and lousy, but our spirits were good. Don't ever give up, that is the main thing, and the only hope of keeping alive. Think of the good things to come.

Little did some of us know, that within a matter of eight months we would be in another part of the Far East, or what lay in store for us. It was at that time a foregone conclusion that we would remain here, and possibly until the end of the war. I was getting into my fifth year overseas, and the only place I wanted, was to go home. But in the meantime we must keep our spirits up and wish, and wait for that great tomorrow. It will come, it *must* come.

We were still living or existing on two bowls of rice a day, and an occasional drink of rice coffee, but most of the time we were drinking just cold water. Apart from the two eggs at Christmas, and my special diet of a little milk, there was no other addition to our diet. No Red Cross parcels, and no mail had been received by anybody, and no mail had been sent by anybody. We used to call ourselves the forgotten army, but it was only the Japs who were to blame for the conditions in which they kept us. I never knew that the human body could take so much punishment before giving up.

(Sonny was then taken aboard a small ship bound for Japan.—Ed.)

We had no food that day, but hungry as we were I think at that moment we were more concerned about our future. Such things as 'how long will this last', 'what arrangements are they going to make for feeding us' went through our minds. We were soon to find out. That night I don't think many of us slept at all. We were all lousy and dirty. There were no facilities for the call of nature. In no time at all the stench in that hold was unbearable. Words fail to describe fully the conditions under which we were subjected and yet, not one man died or was seriously ill. I am convinced that it was sheer guts and will-power that saw us through.

After three or four days we arrived in Formosa. When we docked there we were not allowed on deck or ashore. There was another swab taken for dysentery and remained there for three or four days.

At last we set sail again. By our reckoning it would take another four or five days to reach Japan, but where in Japan were we bound for—Nagasaki, Osaka, Tokyo or Yokohama. Well! as it turned out we arrived at Osaka on 3rd September 1943 and we all were thankful indeed to get off that Japanese tub.

JAPAN

As a schoolboy, one of my greatest ambitions was to go to Japan. Why that should be, I don't really know. Maybe I had seen something at the cinema, or read a book, or perhaps it was a sense of adventure. But there it was, my first glimpse of Japan, on September 3rd, 1943. Another month and I would be reaching my thirty-second birthday so it had taken me a few years to fulfil my ambition. I never thought then, under what conditions I would ever get to Japan. Perhaps I should have wished for something different, but that is fate.

We were all disembarked from the Tub, and taken by tram to a small empty building not very far away but near the railway station. We still did not know our final destination or whether we were going to stay in Osaka. We were given a meal—a bowl of rice—and bedded down for the night. Although we had no blankets or sheets, or even a bed we slept on the concrete floor, but to us it was a posh hotel after the experience and conditions on the Tub. We had slept on the concrete floor all the time at Sham-Shui-Po, so this was no great hardship to us. And it smelt a bit sweeter too, although we were all ragged, dirty and lousy.

The next morning we were all taken to the railway station, but they seemed to keep us well away from the civilian population. They just stood at a distance and stared. I wonder what went through their minds? To see such a sight would have made many a person want to throw up, and we noticed many a handkerchief came out to cover their nose. But still we hope to clean up when we finally get to our destination.

What the actual time was, I do not know, but it was about mid-morning. The train arrived and we could see it was a 'Special' laid on for us. We clambered aboard. What luxury it seemed to actually sit down on a seat. Our morale was beginning to get still higher, and were as excited as children going on a Sunday School outing, and at last we were moving out of the city to open land. It seemed that the train was avoiding any large towns, and the surrounding countryside that we saw was very beautiful. Quite a contrast to the hills surrounding Kowloon, which we had been staring at for so long. It was appreciated by all concerned.

On arrival at the camp, he wrote:

Just outside the huts were the toilets. Another hut with a small platform about two feet wide with a gap of 6″ running full length and underneath a trench which was our latrine. This trench was about 6 feet deep and had to be emptied every so often by means of a ladle on a long pole, emptied into buckets and carried out to the Japanese gardens at the rear of the camp. This was a duty for sick personnel unable to go to work with the normal working party. Not very hygienic I can tell you, and that alone must have contributed to much of the disease.

Towards the end of September the winter started. Snow, snow and more snow. And the temperature falling fast. This did not stop the working parties. Working on the hillside, knee deep in snow, and often in a raging blizzard. No protection at all, snow covered, cold and hungry. The only time in the winter we took our clothes off, was at night when we tried to de-louse ourselves, and immediately put the clothes on again, and they would be wet and damp. The other times were when we were allowed the luxury of a bath. That would be about once a month. The bath consisted of a square about 9 foot x 9 foot and a wall around about eighteen inches high. The water in the bath was about a foot deep. Into that went about 150 men not counting the sick. Soap was non-existent. Even a simple wash in the morning was with a handful of snow. And our clothes were never washed during the winter. No wonder we were all lousy. They must have been the best fed lice in the Far East. It was during this time that we started losing men. By the time the winter was over we had lost about a quarter of the original 200. It was nothing to find a man had died during the night. You may have been working with him the day before. Many times I have heard a man say, 'I am finished, I cannot carry on.' And to be sure, that man would die in a couple of days . . . Such was the state of that camp. How we had all looked forward to this trip to Japan. Of all the dreams and hopes we had. How much longer will this last? Surely our bodies cannot take much more. As I said before, if we had known we were to spend two winters in Japan, nobody would have survived.

We had no idea of how things were going, and had as our motto 'Maybe tomorrow'. Spring into summer and what a contrast. The summer months were very hot. Soon we found out about the landings in France. This was quite by accident. One of the prisoners happened to find a Japanese newspaper, and this had a map of the southern coastline of England with arrows pointing to the northern coast of France. That's it, we were really thrilled over that. But how can we confirm that. The Japs will not tell us, even if we ask them. But there must be some way. And we soon found the answer to that. Whilst out on the work party, we were guarded by the most hated and detested sentry on the camp. A Jap we called 'Shavex'. He always appeared to look as if he needed a shave and a good wash. We made him understand that we knew the invasion had begun. He was not having any, and strongly denied that it was true. But we persevered with him, and at last one of the prisoners made a rough diagram on the earth with England and France and he marked 'Paris' on the French side, and then drew a half circle from Paris to the coast and said to 'Shavex' 'England'. Well he wasn't having that. He drew a line just inside the French coast, and thanks very much 'Shavex' you have just confirmed the landings.

Now that the summer is here we can do a bit of washing. I say washing, dipping your clothes in cold water, and laying them out to dry. Even then you had to sit there until they were dry, because if you didn't then someone would pinch them, and leave their ragged and dirty clothes behind. Nothing was sacred in that camp. But I honestly think that the experience we were all going through brought the true character out of every man.

During the time here in Japan, we were in receipt of a monthly bonus in rice. A monthly check of the rice store was made by the Japs. After their inspection and check a prisoner was detailed to sweep the place out. Several sacks would have a hole in them where the rats had been, and of course there remained quite a bit of rice on the floor. When that was swept up, that was a bit of perks for us. The next job would be sorting out the rice from the rats droppings. I can tell you there was no waste and no swill bin on that camp. The only swill bin was us. A human swill bin. Occasionally a bucket of blood from a slaughtered horse and the intestines would be sent to the camp. It all went into the pot, and made a change from Dicon Soup. Or perhaps a snake would be caught whilst out working, and a rare dish was frogs' legs. We would go frogging behind the huts on the camp, kill them and take the legs off. It tasted like chicken to us at that time. If we saw a piece of orange peel or an apple core on the road while going to work, this was soon picked up and eaten. We were hungry men.

Our hopes for the war to end that summer were gradually fading. What had happened to the invasion, we had no news at all. We were just ekeing out an existence on that camp. Try as we might there was absolutely no news at all, and we were resigning ourselves for another winter here. And in no time the winter was upon us. More snow, and just as bad as the previous winter. But this winter they had given us a different job. No more working on the hillside and quite away from camp. This time they have put us at the factory to work. Our job this time was to load tip-up trucks with coal or rather with coal dust. Great mounds of this were laying about five to six hundred yards from the factory proper. These trucks were loaded by us and taken up to the factory by a small engine. This was driven by a Royal Navy seaman—naturally nick-named 'Barny'. Our first job in the morning was to clear the track of snow. When you are up to your knees or further in snow, this was not a very good start to the day's work, but work we had to do. No slacking off in those days, and to finish the day's work we looked like one piece of black soot. Cold, hungry and dirtier still.

So we managed to exist through the long winter months, and the winter of 1944/45 was harder than the previous one. How much longer have we to endure this life? How much more can our bodies take? To let go of hope was a sure way of dying. The months dragged on. Please God let us see England and our loved ones once again. It was nearly seven years since I had left England and almost four years since I had any news from home.

(Then, on 15th August they realised that the Japs were behaving differently. Ed.)

Everybody was busy thinking and talking about home. When are we leaving for home? Is anybody coming to fetch us? What will be our first meal? Soon the Americans who had landed in Japan were in touch with us by 'phone. Instructions were given to us to remain in camp and await further orders, and in the meantime we were told to paint the letters P O W on the roof of the huts. The paint was supplied by the Japs, and the job was done in quick time. We knew that this meant spotting us from the air, but we did not know exactly what it was for, so imagine our surprise about two or three days later when we heard the drone of heavy aircraft. And there they were, coming over the hill tops. They circled the camp, and everybody was laughing, cheering and waving. They were B29 bombers, and as we looked up at their long huge bellies, we could see the bomb doors open. I don't think anyone of us were prepared for what happened next. The whole camp was out on the square watching and waiting for the next move. Suddenly from the bomb doors several objects came tumbling down to earth. They were fifty gallon drums. They were filled with all kinds of goodies. Sweets, chocolate, cigarettes, chewing tobacco, gum, underclothing and medical supplies. And in quite a few of them tinned peaches. A party or several parties were soon organised to collect all the goods as some of them fell outside the camp. When all were collected a party was organised to share everything except the medical supplies among us prisoners, and the medical supplies to the sick quarters. It did not take long to share everything out, and soon I was in possession of my share. What riches—cigarettes by the hundred,sweets and chocolate. Now these were bars of vitamin chocolate, and were marked off in about five sections. Instructions were given on the wrapping that one section was to be eaten at so many hours between. Perhaps I couldn't read, or perhaps I didn't want, I ate the whole bar. I was ill after that. I really thought I was going to die, but I did enjoy the chocolate. It was a good job the Americans dropped medical supplies as well. They certainly saved the day for me.

A few days after we were paid a visit by American fighter bombers, and for several days afterwards they made a delivery of freshly baked bread. Over the cookhouse door we had painted in large letters 'Hell's Kitchen', and those pilots had the reputation of delivering the bread right through the open door into the kitchen. They would make their run in dead line with the door and drop the bread which was in sacks, in such a position that nine times out of ten the sacks would enter the door. We used to look forward to their visits. Good entertainment and something different to eat.

After so long being brow-beaten, down-trodden and ill-treated, it is a wonder a few killings did not take place. But I never saw a finger laid on any Jap. The reaction of the end of the war was one of relief, not revenge. We were happy men, and nobody knows the feeling of relief that is felt if they have not experienced what we all went through.

Into September and still no news when we were leaving. A few more weeks and the winter will be here again. My God, let us get out before that happens.

At last we had the message through from the Americans. Get ready to leave on September 9th. A train will be waiting at the station and you will leave at 18.00 hrs. for Yokohama. What joy that message brought to us.

Just before the train pulled out, the Jap commandant came aboard to wish us 'God Speed', and a happy journey. What cheek! but we all thought the same, that he came aboard to get what he could from us, in the way of cigarettes and chocolate. But he was completely ignored, and I think very lucky to get away without some sort of damage to his person.

When we arrived at the docks, we were all taken into a warehouse which was fitted out with tables and forms. A delicious smell of cooking was noticed, but we could not think what it was, but another delightful smell was noticed and that was the smell of coffee, and not the burnt rice coffee which we had in Sham-Shui-Po.

We were told to form a queue at the end of the warehouse and we would be supplied with a meal. To our great surprise we were given pancakes and syrup, and a most delicious coffee to wash it down. Knives and forks, and spoons were on the table. And to be able to sit down and eat with a knife and fork, and drink out of a cup was out of this world. We had hardly finished that meal, when one of the cooks called out, 'Does anybody want—' he never had time to finish the sentence and we were all down there for a second helping. We would have been down again for a third helping, but we were told another draft of POWs was expected and they had to prepare for their arrival. We were so hungry that we would have eaten them out of supplies.

After the meal we were all ushered into another warehouse, this was partitioned off in various sections, and the first section they put us in was a shower room. And a shower with real soap. I laughed under that shower, and thought, this is the first time my lice have tasted soap. I wonder how they like that. I had never been covered with so much soap in all my life. This was the first of many, many delights we were to encounter for some time to come. After the shower we were all sprayed with delicious powder and given new underwear, and an American Army uniform, or rather a shirt, trousers, socks and shoes. Although they fitted where they touched, it was much better than my old rags, and I felt quite smart and clean for a change. From there we were processed by American Service Women. These women were sitting at a table with a chair in front, and there must have been about twenty or more sitting there. We had to go up to them and sit facing them. And to see them and to be so near to them was quite a new experience. It was the first woman I had spoken to in nearly four years, and what a sight it was for us. I don't think it was an attraction for the opposite sex, but rather more as a mother figure. I do believe that had they put their arms around us we would have cried like babies. They asked us various questions, where we were taken prisoner, what camps we had been on, what illnesses we had, and finally they took our pulse rate. Needless to say all of us had high pulse rates. That was to be expected. These girls were certainly a tonic to us all, and very nice and homely to us. But I knew at that moment it would take some time to adjust ourselves to the opposite sex. One of the many many things to adjust ourselves to.

From there we went to another section, where we were examined by American doctors. The very sick personnel were taken off to hospital, but the remainder were ushered into another section. And what a surprise awaited us. As we entered we could see several tables laid out, and on these were all kinds of toilet items. Soap, toothpaste, face flannels, combs, scissors, hair cream. Every item you could think of. It looked just like a Woolworths store. These were for us, and we were told to help ourselves.

Not many combs or hair cream were taken, as just prior to leaving camp we had our hair, what there was of it, close cropped all over with clippers, but it certainly was a beautiful sight to see so much laid out, and all for our taking. After our selection of the toilet items, we were all told to assemble outside the warehouse. And it was there a mate of mine produced a small tin of milk powder. The instinct of eating anything edible was still with us, and we did no more, but sit right down and eat as much of that milk powder as we could. At the time it tasted very good but I don't think I would like to try it now. Although we had been given a meal of pancakes we were still very hungry.

(They were then taken on board an American transport ship to Manila.—Ed.)

At night there was always a cinema show on. This was in the open air and we would sit on wooden planks, and would make sure we had some sort of covering, as it rained every evening for a short period. We were also given a concert by 'Our Gracie' (Gracie Fields) and believe me there was many a wet eye that night. We stopped on the camp about four days, and then one morning we were told to get ready to leave in the afternoon. The Royal Navy were going to take us over. At that time the news dampened our spirits. What discipline are they going to impose on us. Up to now we had been treated like VIP's and the thought of coming under the RN did not go down very well with us, but that turned out to be unfounded, and many, many thanks to the RN for their marvellous effort.

The first thing we asked was what kind of ship are we sailing on, and where are we going. We were told you are going on the aircraft carrier HMS *Implacable,* and your destination is Vancouver via Honolulu. What a surprise. Nobody had ever thought that one up for rumours. And that means we are sailing right across the Pacific Ocean. And that means we would have gone around the world. But it has only taken seven years to do it.

Once again we boarded landing craft and out to the *Implacable.* She looked enormous, and looked as if she would topple over. But once aboard it was marvellous. The crew were there to help us, and we were soon shown to our quarters. All the aircraft had been left in Australia, so all the hangars down below had been made into a dormitory, and camp beds had been placed for our use. We were given the run of the ship, and to save climbing up ladders to either go below, or come up on to the flight deck, the aircraft lift was put at our disposal. This was operated by one of the sailors, and even if only one man wanted to go up or down, then that was operated. During wet weather the lift was taken up, and a cinema show would be held in the well. And at night a cinema show would be held on the flight deck. During the day we would sit or walk about the flight deck, always in groups and talking and laughing with each other. Every day a ration of either fruit, soft drinks or cigarettes would be made. We would line up in an orderly fashion, and no rank was pulled on these occasions, no such thing as officers, warrant officers, NCOs and men. And the food that was supplied at meal times, was excellent, nicely cooked, nicely served, and well eaten. The RN certainly did us proud.

Via Honolulu, Implacable *took them to Vancouver from where they entrained for Halifax and on to the* Ile de France *and so to England and Southampton. His final recollections are most poignant:*

As I sat on the train speeding towards Folkestone, I thought then, this is the last 70 miles of a journey half way round the world, and I sat there looking out of the window all through that journey. Strangely enough I did not feel happy or elated. I felt very depressed and sad. I was going to my home town, but what would I find. I felt so alone, and missing the boys I had been with all those years. Nobody spoke to me on that train, and I did not feel like conversing with anybody. Anyway what could I talk about. I was simply lost.

At last we pulled into Folkestone Central Station. It was about five o'clock in the evening and a very dismal day at the end of October 1945. I jumped out of the carriage and then I remembered I had three kit bags in the guards' van. And they were full to the top with clothing, cigarettes and cigars. I soon got those out on to the platform, and asked a woman porter if she could take them to a taxi for me, to which she replied 'There's a truck over there, you can take them down yourself.' That's it, I thought, this must be Folkestone.

Into the taxi I bundled and on my way to home. Now I will soon know, one way or the other. Passing the Church near my home, I noticed all the railings were gone. I wonder why they have done that I thought, it looked so bare. But the Church was still there; and just past the church to No. 5 the taxi stopped, but no sign of life either in the street or at No. 5. I told the driver to wait, and went up the steps to the front door. I had only got half way up, when the door opened. There they were, my Uncle and Aunt, both in their seventies. They really cried when they saw me, and I felt ashamed afterwards that I could not produce even a tear. I was soon inside the house, and gathering all information I could. My sisters and their families were OK.

On the first Sunday at home, I carried out a promise we all made whilst we were in the camp. And that was, if ever we got out of that camp alive, we would all go to church on the first Sunday at home. I am not a religious man, but I attended church that morning, as soon as I heard the Church bells. I walked into that church and was surrounded by young children. After the service the parson spoke to me and enquired why I had attended a children's service but I had done what I had promised myself I would. My tomorrow had come.

CHAPTER TEN

Half Way There

Article in a Sydney newspaper, Nov. 1973, sent by PO J. Dodds, HMS *Victorious*

Memorial to British Wartime Fleet

A memorial to Britain's World War II Pacific Fleet will be unveiled at the RAN Headquarters, Potts Point, on December 2.

When it entered Sydney in February 1945, the 336 ships made up the largest fleet to enter an Australian port or the Pacific Ocean.

Despite successful action in the waters off Sumatra,Okinawa and Japan, the achievements of the British fleet were over-shadowed by those of the US 5th and 7th fleets.

The memorial, which will be unveiled by members of the Naval Historical Society of Australia, will stand a short distance from the site of the fleet's wartime headquarters.

Former members of the fleet are invited to attend the unveiling of the memorial—tread plate from the gangway of the flagship, the HMS *Duke of York*.

Details may be obtained from the society, PO Box 3, Garden Island, NSW 2000.

The BPF Memorial Order of Service

The Naval Historical Society of Australia

Unveiling Ceremony

THE BRITISH PACIFIC FLEET MEMORIAL
ORDER OF SERVICE
Sunday, 2nd December 1973

A British Pacific Fleet operated in the broad waters of the Pacific from the first day of World War II until the final surrender in Tokyo Bay in August, 1945. It fought under a variety of names such as Force Z, ABDA Command and the

Eastern Fleet and suffered losses which at times could be ill-afforded.

The BPF for which this memorial was erected was born on 13th September, 1944 at the Quebec Conference when Prime Minister Churchill offered a new British Fleet to operate in the Pacific. Roosevelt's acceptance was immediate 'No sooner offered than accepted'.

Fourteen days later Churchill announced in the House of Commons: 'We have offered the fine modern British Fleet and asked that it should be employed in the main operations against Japan.'

The fleet offered was no empty token. At its greatest strength it numbered 300 ships and 255 aircraft. It consisted of 4 battleships, 5 fleet aircraft carriers, 4 light fleet aircraft carriers, 9 escort aircraft carriers, 10 cruisers, 40 destroyers, 18 sloops, 13 frigates, 29 submarines, 33 minesweepers and a host of support vessels. Represented in this fleet were such battle honoured names as *Duke of York, King George V, Anson, Howe, Victorious, Formidable, Indefatigable, Indomitable, Implacable, Achilles, Euryalus, Troubridge, Camperdown, Undaunted, Kempenfelt, Black Swan*, and many more of equal renown. *(No* Illustrious?! *Jim—Ed.)*

It was a five navy fleet with ships of the Royal Navy, the Royal Australian Navy, the Royal Canadian Navy, the Royal Indian Navy and the Royal New Zealand Navy. The 24 Australian ships in the fleet were: *Quiberon, Quickmatch, Napier, Nepal, Nizam, Norman, Ballarat, Bendigo, Burnie, Goulburn, Maryborough, Toowoomba, Whyalla, Cessnock, Gawler, Geraldton, Ipswich, Launceston, Pirie, Tamorth, Wollongong, Kalgoorlie, Lismore* and *Cairns*. Five others were commanded by Royal Australian Navy Officers.

The Commander-in-Chief was Admiral Sir Bruce Fraser, GCB, CBE, and under his command were many of the great names of the British navies in World War II.

Admiral Fraser hoisted his flag in HMS *Howe* on 22nd November, 1944, at Colombo. The BPF suffered its first loss on the same day, the submarine *Strategem*.

Within a month the fleet struck its first blow at Pangkalan Brandan in Sumatra. Then followed a series of blows which continued until Japan was out of the war. The battle honours read Palembang, Arakan, Okinawa, Formosa, Sakishima Gunto, Truk and Japan.

The BPF arrived in Sydney on 10th February, 1945 and received a tumultuous welcome. The fleet's headquarters was HMS *Golden Hind* and its base was located at Woolloomooloo. A public appeal launched by the Lord Mayor of Sydney raised $400,000 in two weeks and within a month a British Centre was established in the City to cater for the fleet's recreation needs.

Despite its abundance of anchorages and berths, Sydney Harbour was taxed to the limit to accommodate the greatest fleet ever to enter its placid waters.

The British Pacific Fleet was overshadowed in the Pacific by the massive US 5th and 7th Fleets and history has named it the Forgotten Fleet. However, its contribution, and the spirit of that contribution, given after five cruel years of war, will never be forgotten.

The Memorial

This memorial is dedicated to the Royal Navy—Royal Australian Navy relationship forged under the stresses of war. It was proposed by a former officer of the British Pacific Fleet, Lieutenant-Commander T. Ferrers-Walker to the Naval Historical Society of Australia in 1971. The relics which embellish the memorial, the badge and tread-plate of the last flag ship of the BPF, HMS *Duke of York* were presented by Lieutenant-Commander Ferrers-Walker and flown to Australia in the aircraft bearing the British Minister for Defence, Lord Carrington.

The eminent site which it graces was made available by the then Flag Officer Commanding, East Australia Area, Rear Admiral W. Graham CBE. The design and manufacture of the memorial was arranged at the expense of The Naval Historical Society of Australia. The unveiling ceremony was arranged by kind permission of the present Flag Officer Commanding, East Australia Area, Rear Admiral W. Dovers, CBE, DSC.

Rear Admiral G. D. Moore, CBE, who will unveil the memorial was Acting First Naval Member at the conclusion of hostilities with Japan. As Commander South West Pacific Sea Frontiers he issued the instructions to 'Cease offensive action'.

The memorial will be a reminder to future generations of Australians of a British Fleet which sailed the waters of the Pacific to keep Australia free.

From S/Lt. (A) Ian Darby RNZNVR

I have written in **Sakishima**, trying to explain what happened to us, Burn O'Neill and me, when we were shot down by AA fire whilst strafing the airfield at Koriyama, Japan in August 1945.

I was never conscious of 'knee shaking' fear and do believe that nature protects us in difficult circumstances by shutting down the brain processes involved, and indeed I can't recall having been physically scared of the Japs at all, although I had my doubts about getting out of Japan alive, especially after one occasion whilst being moved from Sendai to Tokyo at dawn we were lined up against a wall to the accompaniment of clicking rifle breeches, and I remember being very cold—probably that was fear.

Fortunately we were prisoners for only three weeks—any longer, things could have been different.

During my interrogations, I was made aware of the Japanese attitude towards we 'special' prisoners. They hated us with fervour, as we had dared to attack their country. As far as I could see, all aircrew were hated bitterly. Also I was told with some glee what the Japs would do to we New Zealanders and Australians when the invasions took place. In addition they would take over Australia and New Zealand, rape the women and kill the men, leaving some as permanent slaves. So even at this stage of the war, some hadn't given up hope of victory. We were, as special prisoners, not given any of the 'luxuries' of the other prisoners i.e. the chance to wash with soap—that didn't come until the surrender was made known to us in Omori POW camp sometime after the 25th August 1945. Until arriving at Omori, we had no knowledge that the war was over. We were taken by rail from Sendai to Tokyo and thence, blindfolded, by open truck from Tokyo to Omori. We managed to slip the blindfolds and saw what was left of Tokyo—a vast plain of rubble. I then knew there was no hope for Japan, but couldn't imagine when they would surrender, as we had heard tales of the 'Divine Wind' and Jap proclivity for hurling themselves against invaders.

During the rail trip my interrogator accompanied us and I had quite an interesting discussion with him. He postulated that 'the Japanese would take over the world even if it took one hundred years, and not necessarily by warlike means'. To men now, this prophecy is well on the way to becoming fact. In 44 years the Japs have virtually cornered the electronic industries of the world, also the car manufacturing industries, photographic and many more. The Japanese are also destroying the fishing grounds of the Pacific including whales, seals and dolphins. They are quite ruthless in their quest for seafood, having no regard for the natural food chain, or the ecology generally. This will spell disaster for the Pacific Ocean in particular, and when the supply here runs out, the Japs will pillage the rest of the world's food stocks from the oceans and seas of the world including the Arctic and Antarctic. The Americans and Canadians are losing their salmon fishing to the Japs this year (an estimated $30 million) and New Zealand and Australia have entered into fishing ventures with the Japs (and also Korean and Taiwanese vessels) and are proceeding to wipe out our traditional fishing grounds. These countries pay the NZ Government royalties for the fish caught and of course rackets have evolved and our stocks are now critically low.

A relative of mine owns a fishing boat and he has licences to fish for orange roughy, a very acceptable fish and very popular. Several times he has been driven out of the area whilst fishing by these big joint fishing vessels—they home onto his schools and take the lot. He has identified the vessels and reported the offenders to the authorities—but nothing has been done to stop the intimidation or the rape of the fishing grounds—which leads me to think that the politicians are money hungry but lamentably they can't see the damage these vessels are doing. Why we don't just cancel these fishing venture contracts and let them out to smaller local vessels I don't know.

I rather think that strong action is required. We are at the moment toying with the idea of buying 4 deep water frigates for our NZ Navy. I am in full agreement with purchasing these as we desperately need an extended defence line and also to show the flag in the South Pacific. Unfortunately there seems to be a vocal lobby which advocates a 'belly up' approach to defence needs. Apparently a lot of people are of this opinion, never having heard of the quotation 'eternal vigiliance is the price of safety'. Neither can they be great students of human history. Our land is too precious to us to allow this approach to continue.

Australia has the same fear, strangely not through the memory of Japan, but of Indonesia, its near neighbour to the north. So I am sure in my own mind that these frigates are vitally necessary for our own protection and also to show these pillagers of the sea that we mean business.

This brings me back to the Japanese proclivity for the piracy or plundering of the planet's natural resources. The latest method of fishing involves the use of a huge monofilament nylon net which is invisible to the fish. The nets have been dubbed the 'wall of death'. One has just been found (August 15 1989) close to the coast of NZ. The length of the net is 60 kilometres (37 miles), the depth 15 metres. The fish have no chance of escape. It is easy to imagine hundreds of Jap trawlers shutting off vast tracts of ocean to the passing fish and mammals. Unfortunately when storms occur it is possible, in fact likely, that numbers of these nets will dangle down indefinitely, catching fish for up to 200 years which I understand is the estimated life of the nets in seawater. Of course the fish will eventually rot and be of no use. I am in favour of a world authority making it quite clear that this method in particular should be outlawed and the Japs and the rest should be sent back to the respective lands to fish only in their territorial waters (at the moment a 200 mile zone as in NZ is envisaged). Adequate policing should be undertaken to enforce this.

Now of course we have the spectre of Japanese military resurgence. This principle has gained much ground of late. I do hope that the politicians of our various countries recognise the threat and try to prevent another confrontation.

Despite protestations to the contrary there is a tremendous military lobby in Japan which is active in seeking its own authority to re-arm and equip the Japanese military forces with the ultimate view of military take-overs of countries starting in the Pacific. The Japanese have always believed that they are indirectly descended from the Sun God and they regard their emperor as the direct link between them. All other races thereby are subservient to them and are automatically regarded as inferior and should be treated as slaves.

I don't believe that the Japanese race has altered much in the years since WW II except for the visible signs of prosperity, which I might add, to be fair, they so richly deserve.

Mind you, a tremendous amount of credit must be given to a far-seeing US government in helping these people to a full and peaceful recovery. I think that the American decision to allow Hirohito to survive and lead his country was probably the correct one in view of the fact that Japan was totally dependent upon the US for its military security and therefore of that region's security as well.

Most POWs hated the thought of Hirohito still being alive when so many of their friends died whilst POWs. A lot were also upset that Prince Philip attended the funeral ceremony in Tokyo, but I feel that he was obliged to go.

One cannot help but admire the Japs for their single-mindedness and devotion to their country in the pursuit of their goals. If only we had had the same attitude we may well have been better off today!

25th July 1989

Have just heard that the Japanese have dangled a very large sum of money in front of the noses of the Samoan Government to enable them to fish in their waters. Maybe the temptation of easy money will be too great for the Samoans to resist, if so it will be the death knell for the fishing grounds and even for life itself in Samoa.

I was disappointed to say the least to find out partly the extent of the Japanese financial empire in Britain, and whilst we were in your country (March—May 1989) the newspapers were cock-a-hoop with the news that another Japanese car manufacturing plant was to be built and eventually 5,000 jobs would be created! I don't understand.

On the 7th May 1989 we flew from Heathrow to Los Angeles in the USA. I had previously written to an American fellow POW in Omori telling him that we would be visiting him.

Freddie had been blown out of a Superfort (B29) by a huge explosion whilst they were on a high level bombing mission and he was one of four out of 11 souls to land in Japan as prisoners. Of those four, two died in POW camp and one died in America not too long ago—and Freddie is the last. He was envious of me being able to attend the reunion in the UK—he said he had never heard of a squadron reunion in the States. We had a marvellous time together and I'm so glad we spent time with him. We are both worried as to what is going to happen to the world eventually if the Japanese manage to achieve their ambitions. Even in America the Japs are building car assembly plants all over—while we were there two more vast factories were being planned and the Americans seemed pleased that more people would be employed, never mind that the Japanese are gradually taking over the car business, not only in the USA but also worldwide. Also in the pipeline are insurance companies, electronic factories, e.g. Silicon Valley to name but a few.

We flew by Delta airlines on 20 occasions and on almost every flight there were at least 2 or 3 Japanese business men and on one occasion we had the privilege of flying with 30 of them.

Whilst travelling in the US we heard somewhere on the radio that in May 1989, the US Government had a huge deficit in the balance of payments entirely due to the Japanese not allowing full two-way trade.

Closer to home, the Australian Government for some time, has allowed Japanese to purchase land and buildings, businesses and residences, on rather a large scale, and now the NZ Government is following the Australian example.

An approach was made by the Japs to the Australian Government to allow the building of 'retirement complexes' for hundreds of thousands of Japanese retirees, as Japan was running out of room. Fortunately there was a great cry of rage led by the Australian Returned Services League. No doubt the Japs will keep trying after the current RSL members die off. An unofficial approach by the Japs to some property developers in Auckland (NZ) was made subsequent to the Australian approach, the initial figures quoted I believe, were 250,000 retirees to be housed near Henderson (a western suburb of Auckland). When one considers that the population of the entire Greater Auckland area is approximately 800,000 people, one can gauge the impact this would have on us, of course it would also be the thin edge of the wedge.

We appreciate that Japan has an over-population problem, but after all, this problem is planet-wide. An approximation of densities may help picture the problem.

COUNTRY	SQ. MILES	POPULATION	DENSITY SQ. MILE
Japan	142,719	132,000,000	925
China	3,759,000	1,000,000,000	266
UK	94,207	56,000,000	594
USA	3,615,212	250,000,000	69
Australia	2,971,081	15,000,000	5
NZ	103,736	3,200,000	31

In this day and age it is so easy to get into strife by appearing to favour one race as opposed to others and the cry would go up quickly 'RACISTS'! Obviously the politicians of the world do not recognise the fragile balances of race and culture in multi-racial societies.

Both China and India have made attempts to restrict the population growth.

Ian and Ngaire *(pronounced Niree—Ed.)* wish to express their sincere thanks for wonderful hospitality, while in the UK, to former members of 1772 squadron and their wives. These in order of staying with were: G. Trollopes, S. Jobbings, A. Rowlinsons, V. Bennets, R. Bettissons, J. O'Driscolls and G. Trollopes again. Also of course, but not of the squadron, were the V. Spencers, Stuart Eadon, Doris and Harry Pybus and Freddie in Chicago.

We noticed that in all these places visited that there was a continuous haze present which in Norfolk was called a Fret but elsewhere a heat haze! This occurred during a complete lack of heat! I might add that we left the UK on 7th May 1989, so it was unlikely to be heat.

So to the USA to the reunion in Chicago with Freddie and then to Dayton Ohio to see through the fabulous a *huge* aircraft museum at Wright Patterson airfield. Has to be seen to be believed. From Dayton to Orlando—Florida for 3—4 days, Epcot centre there was tremendous, and thence to San Antonio and Tucson where we stayed for a few days and contacted a distant nuptial relation Russell Robinson, who showed us around everywhere including the living desert museum, and a huge aircraft museum. Near to this was the greatest collection of aircraft I could ever imagine.

(Ian commented on the hazy atmosphere in the UK and the USA and noticed the 'clear clear air' on return to NZ. But he didn't go to Scotland—on a clear day!—Ed.)

From an article in Radio Times by William Greaves

HIROSHIMA: NO REGRETS

The men who dropped the first A-bomb have come to terms with their terrible past. But have the Japanese? 'Inside Story' follows the original nuclear warriors on a second—more peaceful—mission:

When the biggest man-made explosion in the history of the world blew his hospital—and the greater part of Hiroshima—apart, Dr. Kaoru Shima escaped death because he was tending patients on the far side of town.

Now, nearly 45 years later, the rebuilt hospital is run by his son. Dr. Shima Jr. was on duty a few months ago when a party, including five elderly Americans, asked if he had time to show them around. He was busy, but too polite to refuse.

'Do you know,' someone asked, apparently by way of casual conversation, 'what happened to the men who dropped the bomb?' 'I think they are all dead,' said Dr. Shima Jr. 'No they are not,' came the reply. 'They are standing in front of you now.'

General Charles Sweeney and fellow airmen Richard Nelson, Frederick Bock, George Marquardt and Don Albury were also standing under the very point where the A-bomb had detonated—to such horrible effect—at 8.15 a.m. on 6 August 1945. The dramatic scene was captured in the first of a new *Inside Story* series, *Return to Hiroshima*.

As in 1945, there was no warning of their arrival. For a few anguished moments the Second World War's most poignant reunion was locked in a state of suspended animation. Gradually, Shima's eyes filled with tears. A voice from the back broke the silence. 'What do you really think of us?' With massive dignity, Shima replied: 'I say, as my father would have said, I forgive you.'

Not even the necessary presence of an interpreter could insulate against so much emotional electricity. Cameraman Ian Stone recorded every flickering eyelid.

The most remarkable revelation to emerge from *Return to Hiroshima* is that Dr. Shima, entirely understandably, had missed the point. Whatever mixed motives led the five men to return to the country, remorse was not among them.

Back home in Massachusets, General Sweeney, captain of *Great Artiste*, the B-29 Superfortress which dropped scientific measuring equipment into the mushroom at Hiroshima and three days later dropped the second atom bomb on Nagasaki, seemed almost bemused by my suggestion that the main purpose of his Oriental odyssey was to say sorry to his victims' descendants.

'Apologise? No, there was no question of that. The Japanese had done terrible, terrible things in China and south-east Asia. Ten times as many people had died in Tokyo than were incinerated at Hiroshima. The only dramatic thing about our raid was that one bomb did what it would have taken thousands of fire bombs to do. And, by ending the war in this way, we were saving millions of lives—Japanese as well as American.'

Yet the massively-built 6ft 4in New Englander took time off from the rest of his itinerary to visit the Hiroshima orphanage to which he had for years sent private donations. Was this not a conscience payment?

'Not at all. Because of my role in the mission, I had a large number of speaking engagements over the years and it didn't seem right to profit from them,' says Sweeney.

It was the end of November last year that producer Michael Latham and his crew Gordon Thomas—author of a book about the men who dropped the bomb—and the five Americans assembled at Columbus, Ohio. And from there they retraced the route of the original mission across the Pacific to Tinian, one of the Mariana Islands, from which the three Superfortresses took off on their two fateful assaults.

It was Sweeney's idea to make the return journey to see how the city had risen from the ashes. The men admitted they were frightened of what the Japanese reaction to them would be, but all five saw it as a way of coming to terms with their past.

However much present-day critics might disagree, the men of 509th Composite Group, 20th Air Force, who flew those devastating missions, have no doubt where they belong in the theatre of modern warfare. They were the act that stopped the show.

Article from the Sunday Express, December 3 1989

A-BOMB AIRMEN RETURN TO SEE ORPHANS OF HIROSHIMA

Five of the US aircrew who dropped the atomic bombs on Japan have visited Hiroshima for the first time. They brought £5,000 for the 67 children at the Hokari-No-Sono orphanage in the city they destroyed on August 6, 1945.

Run by the Sisters of the Sacred Heart, it was one of the first buildings to be rebuilt. Many children have been orphaned as a result of radiation sickness.

Led by their former squadron commander, retired US Air Force General Charles Sweeney, who led the raid on Nagasaki, the crew were close to tears as they played with the children. Father-of-ten Sweeney said: 'I love these children of the ashes as if they are my own.'

Millionaire Richard Nelson, 64, radio operator on Enola Gay, the plane that dropped the A-bomb on Hiroshima, confessed: 'I had been reluctant to come but the joy of these children makes it all worthwhile.'

Sweeney, 69, a Boston banker, began to fund the orphanage in 1945. 'I kept it secret because I did not want anyone to think I was doing it out of guilt. I feel no guilt. It was war.'

But his sureness faltered in the Memorial Museum, as the crew came face-to-face with their past. Everywhere there was horror.

Nelson and Don Albury, 70, Sweeney's co-pilot, finally turned away with trembling lips from gruesome models of a mother and child emerging from the inferno. 'My God, my God,' murmured Albury. 'I just don't want to see this.' Sweeney, who had visited Hiroshima as part of his mission days after the raid, stood, tall and silent. He had vowed then never to return. Now he limped on, shaking his head.

Japanese stared silently at him. Miko Tada—a former Imperial Army officer—finally spoke. 'We want to understand because we did terrible things as well.'

Then they saw the Atomic Bomb survivors' hospital and the 'living dead'—cubicle after cubicle of old people dying of radiation-produced cancer. 'War is just terrible,' Sweeney kept repeating.

Later, they talked to Josie Katana, a Japanese grandmother. She had survived being only 1,000 yards from the centre of the explosion—and now has six children 'all radiation-free'.

She looked at each of them and said 'I forgive all of you. You were right when you say it was war.'

Sweeney, now not bothering to wipe his eyes, murmured: 'Amen—and God bless you.'

From Norman Coombs, Article in The Vancouver Sun, Friday January 27 1989

MEMORIAL TO FLYER WILL RESIDE IN JAPAN

Canadian Press

VICTORIA—A two-tonne stone memorial to the last Canadian serviceman killed in the Second World War left Victoria for Japan on Thursday.

The stone, a tribute to naval Lieut. Robert Gray, of Nelson, is to be placed beside a Japanese war memorial in Onagawa, 200 kilometres north of Tokyo, where Gray's Corsair fighter-bomber was shot down.

Gray was killed Aug. 9, six days before the Japanese surrender, while on a mission from the British aircraft carrier HMS *Formidable*. He was awarded the Victoria Cross posthumously for his last mission, which resulted in the sinking of 15 Japanese vessels and 200 enemy dead. Gray already held the Distinguished Service Cross.

The marble memorial was paid for by the provincial government and will be placed in Onagawa Park on the 44th anniversary of Gray's death, said his sister Phyllis Gautschi.

'I have no bitterness about the Japanese people,' Gautschi said in a telephone interview from Nelson.

Robert Gray's plane, holding his remains, is believed to be still at the bottom of Onagawa Bay, said Stuart Soward, who wrote a book about Gray's exploits. Soward said 150 Japanese divers have volunteered to help raise the plane and the project may go ahead this year.

Plans for the memorial were made well before the controversy over Japan's war record, revived in the wake of the death of Emperor Hirohito. Canadian veterans who were prisoners of the Japanese urged Canada not to send a delegation to his funeral, arguing he was an unprosecuted war criminal.

'I can sympathize with those who were there,' said Soward, but added he hoped the two surviving Canadian pilots who flew from the *Formidable* would attend the two-day memorial ceremony planned for August. 'It's nothing to do with animosity,' he said. 'It's two nations paying respect to a war hero.'

Extract from the Journal of the Royal British Legion, Sept/Oct. 1989

JAPANESE HONOUR LAST VC OF WORLD WAR II

In Sakayima Park overlooking Onagawa Bay on Japan's Honshu coast there now stands the only known memorial erected by the Japanese to a member of the Allied Forces.

Unveiled on 9th August 1989, 44 years to the day since he lost his life in the bay below, it commemorates the courage of Lt. Hampton Gray VC of the Royal Canadian Navy Volunteer Reserve. Among those invited to attend were Canada's Associate Defence Minister, Mary Collins and Lt. Gray's sister, Mrs. Phyllis Gautschi.

Nearby stands a memorial to the 157 Japanese sailors sent to the bottom by the attack Gray led.

At dawn on the morning of August 9th 1945, Hampton Gray and his flight of Corsair fighter bombers lifted off the deck of the fleet Carrier HMS *Formidable* on a 200-mile mission to attack Japanese warships at anchor in Onagawa Bay. Gray led the attack and was hit almost at once, but he held his course to release his bombs at the last possible second to sink the Ocean Escort *Amakuse* before crashing to his death in the water. Lt. Hampton Gray was posthumously awarded the Victoria Cross, the last Canadian so honoured.

Later that same 9th of August an atomic bomb dropped by an American B29 bomber destroyed Nagasaki, and five days later the Second World War ended with Japan's surrender.

Gray's parents and his sister Phyllis were looking forward to his return to join their victory celebrations when they received the news of his death, the last Canadian to die in the war. They had already lost his elder brother, RCAF Flt. Sgt. Jack Gray, an air gunner killed in 1942 when his plane crashed in England on return from a mine-laying mission.

Hampton Gray was highly regarded by the Captain and ship's company of HMS *Formidable*. Only a fortnight before his death he had been recommended for the DSC after sinking a Japanese destroyer with two direct hits. In a letter to Gray's parents Captain Ruck-Keene said their son was '. . . the best and bravest fighter pilot in the ship, and everybody loved him.'

When HMS *Formidable* was broken up in 1953/4, somebody remembered the fame Hampton Gray's gallantry had brought her—and sent the ship's wheel anonymously to Mr. and Mrs. Gray in Nelson, British Columbia. They have both died, and Phyllis Gautschi now has the wheel.

Legion is indebted for the outline of this news story to Dennis Smith, Branch Secretary, Syston RBL, himself a *Formidable* man, who visited Phyllis Gautschi while on holiday in Vancouver earlier this year.

Golf Crazy—Article from Sunday Express, 1989

WENTWORTH

Property developers Chelsfield are investing more than £55 million to turn Wentworth in Virginia Water, Surrey into one of the most luxurious golf centres in the world. The Savoy Hotel has already snapped up three of the 40 £800,000 corporate memberships, enabling them to offer guests free access to the club—but it is likely that most of them will be bought by the Japanese, who are buying up golf clubs all around the world.

OLD THORNS

Since the Japanese company Kosaido took over the Kenwood club at Liphook, Hants in 1984 and renamed it Old Thorns, you can have sukiyaki washed down with sake after your round instead of a pie and a pint. Kosaido now owns 12 clubs around the world—everywhere from China to Chicago. 'Executives from the top Japanese companies in London come down here to play,' says Old Thorns' PR, Jean Palmer.

The Japanese takeover of British clubs is another aspect of the current golf boom.

The Nitto Kogyo group now own Turnberry; Sanyo Oil paid £5 million for the Rolls of Monmouth golf and country club; the Matsushita Investment and Development Corporation bought Camberley Heath; and the Kosaido Development company had had Old Thorns in Hampshire since 1984.

Although Old Thorns does not boast a Japanese restaurant, Japanese bath house and facilities for shiatsu massage, fears about the wholesale introduction of sushi bars into the hallowed halls of British golf have not been justified.

'Hitoshi Matsuura and the rest of them of Nitto Kogyo are purists who are very aware of the traditions and history of a Scottish golf course,' says Chris Rouse, general manager of Turnberry. 'They regard themselves as custodians whose only desire is to enhance the place.'

Tony Mills, golf director at Camberley Heath since the takeover, says: 'People's attitude seems to depend on how old they are. If you came through the war and you were out in the Far East or had friends and relatives who were there, you are obviously more likely to have deep feelings, and some members left. But we needed the investment, the club was put for sale and these people came in first. They paid £7.3 million and are going to invest another £5.5 million on improving the clubhouse and the course.'

He has little sympathy for other clubs who suddenly find themselves vulnerable to takeover, not only by the Japanese but by developers who are keen to cash in on the golf boom. 'Golf is beginning to show its commercial teeth,' he says.

There are a lot of unpalatable truths to be faced. Many clubs date back to the 20s and have been run for years by a bunch of amateurs who are quite good on committees but know little about the business end of running a golf club. And members who do run successful businesses seem to leave their brains behind in the car park. 'The result is a lot of threadbare golf clubs. No provision has been made for a rainy day—and now that rainy day's nearly here.'

From A/M (E) Roy Wood, 854 Squadron, HMS *Illustrious*

At the conclusion of the World War II Pacific action against the Japanese, I sailed back home with thoughts that Australia had been spared from the Japanese agressor and that our side had won the war!

How wrong can you be? Recently I spent three months in Australia (April—June 1990) to hear and see how the Japanese have infiltrated the commercial and business side of Australia's affairs!

Numerous top hotels from Cairns on the NE Coast to Brisbane on the Gold Coast—large building organisations and much of the wood-chip process which is exported to Japan are controlled by Japanese consortia.

I am only an onlooker now, but I wonder how the natives feel?

From PO Jim (Jock) Dodds, HMS *Victorious*

The first immigrants to Australia after the Second World War would undoubtedly have been sailors from the British Pacific Fleet. Many of them took their discharge in Australia without going back to the UK. Others transferred to the Royal Australian Navy and continued serving under the Australian White Ensign whilst others returned with their ships to Britain to complete their service and demobilization before going back to Australia as civilians, many with wives and families in the latter half of the 1940s.

> *'The reason I write is to just say, ''G'day''*
> *to those I came here with and lost down the way,*
> *Jock McLachlan, Ted Weekes, Jack Howell and Jan Baxter,*
> *George Parkinson, Ted Wearn, Jock Hydê and Roy Manchester,*
> *other names I forget . . . there were so many more of us*
> *All shipmates of old on the carrier Victorious.'*

From John Northeast, Sub. Lt. (A) RNVR, 1844 Squadron (CO Lt. Cdr. M. S. Godsen RN) HMS *Indomitable*

Drop-tank or Boomerang?

Tokyo airport was quiet. Japan Airlines' Boeing 747—12 hours across China and Siberia non-stop to London—took off on time with 350 passengers on board, mostly Japanese businessmen. A conventional enough picture in 1989 with only one challenge to the mind, 'What will they give us for lunch?' Now we were at about 3000 metres, still climbing and I gazed idly out of the cabin to the West and saw the Rising Sun Roundel on the port mainplane and, further to the West as we left Tsushima behind us, the waters of the East China sea in the far distance. Tsushima, a name to turn over in the mind. The first evidence of Japanese superiority over Western military technology. Suddenly, I remembered that I had been here before, 45 years ago, but then the aeroplane carried only one passenger, me!

That flight had also started as routine but was destined to finish otherwise. Aircrew in the British Pacific Fleet's carrier force were accustomed to the 3.30 am. call to anticipate that day's dawn strike or Combat Air Patrol. Operation 'Iceberg' was into its second month, its objective being to cripple all the Japanese airfields in the Nansei Shoto, stretching from Japan down to Formosa, thereby disallowing the enemy any chance to move supplies, aircraft and aircrew, while the US Fleet moved inexorably closer to the mainland for the final onslaught.

So many dawn patrols and strikes had been done that the programme was etched into our brains. Four hours of CAP without a single sighting of enemy aircraft was not always conducive to high concentration. The Sumatra operations had been characterised by heavy action always at the target and intervention on the fleet. Iceberg was the opposite. The strikes on the islands were not quite so hectic, but the fleet found itself an immediate, frequent target for the kamikaze squadrons which sometimes caused heavy damage and also some miraculous escapes from total disaster.

On April 6th 1945 it had been another flight without incident when, just as we were turning for base, I spotted a twin-engined aircraft in the distance, heading for the north. Presumably a 'Helen' or 'Frances', too far to tell. I went in chase and found myself slowly overhauling the target. It took a long time and being so excited after the relative inactivity, I opened fire too far away for any hope of success. In fact, I have to admit that I used all my ammunition. Being now somewhat lighter, my closing speed increased. Right on his tail, part elated by my 'catch' and part bemused at having no fire-power, I decided on the only available course of action. I flew close above the 'Frances' and released my drop-tank on top of it. A quick, climbing turn and below me I saw a large patch of disturbed water. I fired the empty guns at it, hoping that the wing camera would collect the evidence. Then, back to base.

On the lengthy return journey, I mused. Chuffed to think that I had made my first, personal score, I pondered on possible comments on my technique. A gong? No, no. Perhaps a Mention? Calm down, you were just doing your job.

After landing on, I was told to report to Commander (F) and the CO. Hopes rising, I presented myself. No time was wasted by these two senior gentlemen, but a lot of words were used, all in my lexicon, many not in the dictionary. I was given a first-class slating and told, forcibly, that I had

a. gone off on my own, i.e. without cover,
b. thereby possibly hazarded the rest of my group,
c. engaged in a likely, futile undertaking (my choice of words)
d. thrown away government property, viz. 1 drop-tank!

Being then not much over 20, I have to suppose that my cognitive was prey to my emotive on the day.

Back in the Boeing in 1989, I reflected. I had perhaps consigned some men to a watery grave with no thought of the outcome. But then it was war and, Rules of Engagement or not, the moral climate was unquestionably different and many principles of ethics had been put on ice for the duration.

Now, several of my peers regularly queried my interest in the USSR and Japan. Why did I go there so often? Why did I have friends there?

Difficult questions for some, but not for me. As an Old Age Pensioner in retirement, I have a little more time both to think back and to think over. My concluded position is simple. The war is long over. The view must be to the future and to the well-being of my own species, mankind. If I can make a small contribution at all, it is to hold the past in my memory, but not to use it as a crucible for regenerating dead animosities, and to move on to new ground. What better than to tackle this head-on in the former enemy's homeland and mix with them to discover how they, too, see the time ahead, and can they, too, put past behind them for an optimistic future?

Besides that, I AM nosey!

From Ldg. Seaman Walter Uden HMS *Grenville*

We were spending a week's holiday at Southsea, our son was now three and a half years old and beginning to take an interest in his surroundings. It was 1950. We were aboard a ferry to Ryde on the Isle of Wight and leaving that same jetty at the Harbour Station, we steamed—or rather—paddled out of the harbour and round the Gosport head and headed for Ryde. Almost immediately the bulk of an aircraft carrier loomed up and I straight away recognised her as *Formidable.* She was the only one that I knew that had that great old-type gramophone horn sticking out of the curved section of the Fo'r'd flightdeck. She lay there at anchor—a dead, cold ship just waiting for the tugs to come and tow her to the breaker's yard. She just disappeared quietly, none of the bally-hoo that accompanied the *Ark Royal*'s departure from Plymouth; *Formidable* had served the navy well through five years of battle from the time that she had joined the Fleet. It seemed a poor ending, having survived all that the two different types of enemy had thrown at her.

My wife and I were staying the night at an hotel on the Esplanade at Weymouth, having travelled down from Wales. It was a bright sunny morning as we sat having our breakfast, looking out over Weymouth Bay—the time must have been about 8.30. A grey ship appeared as she passed through the gate in Portland's stone breakwater—I recognised her as *Grenville.* She turned to starboard and headed out to the exercising area in the English Channel—those very same waters that she had sailed in the twilight before D-day. It was several years later that we were again on holiday in the Weymouth area, this time we had our married son, his wife, two step-sons and our little grand-daughter with us. It was 1972. I knew from news reports some years previously that *Grenville* had been involved with an Italian merchant ship in a collision in the Channel; five boy seamen had died in that accident. Close to the Channel Island Terminal in Weymouth harbour the fishermen were advertising trips round Portland harbour; the youngsters wanted to go, so we went aboard. I had made that trip out to the breakwater many times before, so there was not a lot of interest until we entered the harbour itself. Only the training squadron was based at Portland at that time and one ship was tied up alongside the outer wall. Our coxswain took us across to have a closer look at this converted Emergency class destroyer. It was only when we were stopped a few yards from her and drifted down to opposite the gangway down aft and I was able to read her name on the ornamental life-belt that I realised with a shock that I was looking at *Grenville* and did not recognise her. How many times I had gone alongside that gangway in the motor-boat was beyond remembering—yet everything looked so strange. My wife asked our fisherman if he would go close enough alongside so that she could touch her hull and he willingly obliged. Thus she laid a hand on the ship to which she had addressed so many letters. Some twelve years later my son and his family were on holiday on the Isle of Wight and they too decided to take an advertised boat trip round Pompey harbour. Of course, the main attraction of such a trip was the Dockyard and its contents. At the far end, near Porchester Creek, was a forlorn *Grenville;* cold, dead and with a white line painted all round her water-line, she was awaiting her final tow. Forty years old, the Navy's oldest, no one had responded to offers to sell.

Various cuttings from newspapers re Prince Philip's attendance at Hirohito's funeral—sent by Jack Hibberd

HIROHITO FUNERAL

Sir, It had been my intention to stay silent and not express my feelings at the news that Prince Philip and Sir Geoffrey Howe were going to Hirohito's funeral. However, as the time begins to draw near,, I find myself becoming tense, and I feel I must express my feelings.

Whatever Japan has done since the war, whatever trade they may or may not have with us, whatever factories they build here, nothing can undo the untold damage, both physical and mental, they have caused us, or bring back the thousands who died out there through torture, brutality, starvation and disease, simply because they would not supply medical supplies. All this was done under the name of Hirohito.

It is also ironic that Prince Philip is going to Japan to pay his respects to a man who denied us the privilege of paying our respects to our King by forbidding us singing the National Anthem. We rebelled against this order and all stood and sang the National Anthem. The results of this were fast and brutal. I do not wish to say more, except to say we suffered very greatly for our token of respect to our King.

He is also the man who refused to pass through a list of names, so that we could be posted 'POW'. Instead we had to be posted as 'Missing'.

My poor old mum lost two brothers in the First War and as time went on she could see herself losing her only son in the Second War. These sentiments applied of course to all my loved ones.

These are another group of people who should not be forgotten, for I personally have not been easy to live with. I have my nightmares. I have my bouts of depression, and I feel very angry at times. But through all this, my mum, when she was alive, my wife, daughter and all my loved ones have helped me through, without complaint, for they, more than anyone, know what a tragic time I had been through.

There are my workmates who, when I was able to work, saved me from getting into very serious trouble.

There is my doctor and his staff, who have cared for me through all these years since the war, and will have to do so throughout my life.

There are also my sister and brother-in-law who have helped me a lot.

My health was reduced to this state under the direction of Hirohito, who was obeyed by his troops, etc., without exception.

This is the man Prince Philip is going to Japan to pay his last respects to. It hurts me very much indeed.

Yours etc.

J. GUYATT

(Address supplied)

Article in 'The Sun', Thursday, January 12 1989

King George VI wrote a letter to POWs on their return home

The widow of one prisoner, who was forced to work on the Burma Railway and who died at 53, has sent us the letter he received.

'The Queen and I bid you a very warm welcome home.

Through all the great trials and sufferings which you have undergone at the hands of the Japanese, you and your comrades have been constantly in our thoughts.

We know from the accounts we have already received how heavy those sufferings have been.

We know also that these have been endured by you with the highest courage.

We mourn with you the deaths of so many of your gallant comrades.

With all our hearts, we hope that your return from captivity will bring you and your families a full measure of happiness, which you may long enjoy together.'

Buckingham Palace
September 1945

The News Editor
Southern Evening Echo

Dear Sir,

I would like to register my disgust with regard to Prince Philip's decision to represent the Queen at the Funeral of Hirohito on the 24th February 1989, for the following reasons:

Having been actively engaged in the repatriation of mostly stretcher cases of the Japanese Prisoners of War from Changi in 1945, I shall never Forget or Forgive the Japanese for the Brutality to our Forces, the unnecessary suffering was unforgivable. Arms brutally amputated from the shoulder joints, legs amputated from the thighs, so that artificial limbs could not be fitted.

Men blinded, suffering from malnutrition, beri-beri etc., caused by the brutality and starvation.

Having served under Admiral Lord Mountbatten, on many occasions, particularly the S.E. Asia Command, holder of the Burma Star, I was saddened to hear that his nephew, Prince Philip was chosen to represent the Queen, he after all being the Patron of the 'Burma Star' Association.

If as has been suggested the younger generation of Japanese are not as barbaric, would it not have been more fitting (if at all) to have sent a much younger representative of Royalty and Government?

In conclusion I shall not send back my medals, but keep them in the role of Yesterday's Witness, carry on with my Welfare Work still needed by those who to this day, suffer from those atrocities.

W. R. Gumma
Service/Welfare Secretary Royal British Legion

WE OPPOSED DUKE'S GOING

I am incensed by the misinformation being published by the media regarding Prince Philip's attendance at the funeral of Hirohito.

It has been stated recently that the Duke's visit has the support of the 17,500 members of the Burma Star Association. This is not so.

At a meeting of the South East Area Committee in London on January 27, the delegates of this, the largest area of the association with over 60 branches and so very representative of the whole membership made a strong and unanimous protest against the Duke going. This view was presented to the two members of the National Council there to relay to the council's meeting on February 1.

To our utter dismay and disbelief we read in the Press and saw on TV that the opposite was true.

I was present at the area meeting as delegate of the Southampton branch of the Burma Star Association and that information given to the media is totally the reverse of that of the majority of the members.

A statement made by Sir Geoffrey Howe stated that the Japan of today is not as it was 40-odd years ago, but a recent TV documentary showed prominent and respected members of Japanese universities who had admitted the most horrendous war crimes against their prisoners.

Some of the now senior Japanese military personages in this funeral would have been among those very ones who perpetrated this treatment and have never been called to account in the cause of political expediency—small comfort to those who suffered and the kin of those who never returned.

The overwhelming majority of our members are royalists and regret that this government has placed our royal family in this position.

J. E. Hibberd, Delegate of
SE Area Burma Star Association
Southampton

(I agree with the aforegoing, but with our type of constitution, a member of our Royal Family was required to attend. Quite apart from protocol, had I been in Prince Philip's situation, I too would have gone on my own, in order to keep my sons free of contact, which could have had long lasting repercussions. I believe that he deserves our thanks and admiration for the perfunctory manner in which he undertook this onerous duty. He served in the BPF on board HMS Whelp.*—Ed.)*

In reply to a letter which Dennis Edwards sent to Foreign Secretary Sir Geoffrey Howe in February '89 expressing his displeasure at the Duke of Edinburgh's attendance at the funeral, the Foreign and Commonwealth Office said in conclusion:

The fact is that Japan now is a very different country from the Japan of the 1930s and 40s. All of this owes much to the sacrifices made during the war by people like you and your fellow members of the Royal British Legion.

Dennis who was Lieut. (E) D. Edwards RN in HMS Formidable *sent me a selection of relevant paper cuttings from which I quote the following extracts:*

FURY AS FOREIGN HEADS ATTEND SHINTO WORSHIP
. . . The Grand Funeral Committee, chaired by Mr. Takeshita, Prime Minister, cleverly devised a schedule which drew Prince Philip, President Bush and the other invited mourners into a Shinto rite.

This ceremony was bitterly criticised by opposition parties as a threat to Japanese democracy. Critics said it violated the post-war constitutional separation of religion and state.

'Without knowing it, world leaders joined in an act of Shinto worship which violates Japan's democratic constitution,' said Mr. Masaaki Nakajima, general secretary of the United Church of Christ . . .

Of the Hirohito funeral, one National Daily said:

. . . The mix of Shinto ceremony and public occasion comes close to violating Japan's constitution. It is also unsettling that Japanese schoolbooks wilfully distort the past, speaking of Japan's 'advance' into China, rather than its unprovoked invasion of the country, and describing the barbarous murder of 200,000 Chinese in Nanking in 1937 as an 'incident'. Japanese children are told little or nothing of their nation's institutionalised barbarity towards Allied prisoners of war. Worse still, the Prime Minister, Mr. Noboru Takeshita, recently told Parliament that 'there are various arguments on whether the past war was a war by accident or for self-defence'. This misrepresentation of a record that was awesomely clear to the Chinese victims of Japanese invasion, the Americans at Pearl Harbour and the British in Singapore and Burma, is grotesque.

Modern Japanese attitudes to the 1939—45 War appear to be dominated, therefore, not by shame for the manner in which they conducted it, but by mere sorrow that they lost it.

MERRIMENT RULED OUT IN WEEK OF HIROHITO FUNERAL
Gangsters will refrain from brawling, and prostitutes will withdraw their services, in gestures of respect on Friday, the day of Emperor Hirohito's funeral. Tokyo faces a total clampdown on normal life this week, with all merriment strongly discouraged, as police tighten their grip on the city.

In the OBITUARIES of a national newspaper:
General Minoru Genda—August 17 1989
Gen. Minoru Genda, who has died in Tokyo aged 84, was the brilliantly resourceful young Japanese naval commander whose feasibility study for an attack on Pearl Harbour resulted in the 'Day of Infamy' which brought America into the 1939—45 War.

On the afternoon of Sunday, December 7, 1941, 360 Japanese aeroplanes of the 1st Air Fleet caught the United States Fleet unawares at its home base in Hawaii and in the course of two hours sank or seriously damaged five battleships, 14 smaller ships and numerous aircraft, as well as killing more than 2,000 people. Genda's audacious plan to devastate the Pacific Fleet in the security of Pearl Harbour had its roots in a Japanese concept dating back to 1937. In 1940 it germinated when, on the night of November 11, Swordfish biplane torpedo-bombers from the British Carrier *Illustrious* crippled the Italian fleet at Taranto.

This naval air victory greatly impressed Genda, who was then in London as Japanese naval attache. His talents, especially as a torpedo specialist, were already highly regarded.

Also in this period he and fellow 'young Turks' in a conservative Imperial Navy had been particularly intrigued by an American film of carriers steaming as a combined force. Why not, mused Genda, consider using as many as four carriers in a major assault?

. . . Throughout the summer he experimented on the Inland Sea, making short, shallow torpedo runs to prepare for the 45ft depth at Pearl Harbour. His attention to detail was such that when the torpedoes began to stick in the muddy bottom of the shallows he had wooden stabilisers fitted to their fins.

. . . He remained unrepentant about Pearl Harbour and in 1961 on a visit to Britain for the Farnborough Air Show he publicly regretted that Japan had failed to follow up the attack 'again and again'.

In 1962 Genda entered the Japanese Parliament as a member of the ruling Liberal Democratic Party and remained there until his retirement in 1986.

He was awarded the United States Legion of Merit in 1962.

Why this tyrant got such a massive Obituary in preference to others that day, is a mystery . . . D.W.E.

A further extract sent by D. W. Edwards

. . . Japan's formidable military build-up, the visit to the Yasukuni Shinto Shrine by Mr. Nakasone when Prime Minister; censorship of textbooks so that young Japanese learn nothing about wartime atrocities, or Hirohito's role in them; the government order last year to schools to pay respect to the Red Sun flag and sing an anthem once played as part of Emperor worship—all these show the determination of Japan's conservative government to efface the 1945—1952 Allied occupation, and that abiding reminder of defeat, the constitution—an 'artificial flower imposed by foreigners'—in the words of Mr. Nakasone.

Right-wing idealogues like Hideaki Kase insist the Emperor Hirohito's renunciation of divinity, made 'at gunpoint' in the ashes of defeat, has no validity today. For them the *daijosai* marks the triumphant reversal of Hirohito's 'I am not a god' declaration—a major advance in the subversion of the Occupation legacy.

The *daijosai* has far-reaching implications that few outside Japan appear to have grasped. The Japanese claim to 'uniqueness', or superiority, is based on a belief in their divine descent, sensed vaguely even by the most 'westernised' young people . . .

PEACE OF MIND ON THE RIVER KWAI

For forty five years, Trevor Dakin was haunted by a nightmare—a terrible legacy from his experiences as a Japanese prisoner of war. He would wake up in a sweat after seeing a vision of an old comrade who died beside him as they toiled in the steaming heat, building the infamous death railway from Burma to Siam.

As Lance Corporal Dakin, 519302, of the 5th Battalion, the Bedfordshire and Hertfordshire Regiment, he served two years on the Japanese slave labour gangs building the railway over the River Kwai. It left him a bitter man. He kept reliving his memories and developed an aversion to all things Japanese.

Finally his son told him: 'Go back, Dad. Purge it out of your system.' Mr. Dakin, now 70, took the advice.

He has set up home in Thailand, renting a small two-bedroom house in the Thamakarn district of Kanchanaburi, 500 yards from the notorious bridge which featured in the film, The Bridge On The River Kwai.

'It has worked,' he said. 'My nightmares have gone and I now have more peace of mind. I won't forgive or forget, but I no longer harbour the hate I held for so long.'

He was captured when Singapore fell and, in October 1942, was taken to a camp near Kanchanaburi. 'We were put to work on the railway where most of my friends died,' he said. 'They caught beri-beri, dysentery, malaria or cholera—and were severely beaten by the Japanese. On one stretch of the railway, where we were cutting rock, 10 men died for every yard. We often had to exist on half a cup of rice a day and buried our dead where they collapsed at the side of the railway.

'Shortly after my arrival, I revisited a place called Devil's Gorge—where the most deaths occured—and met an elderly Thai woman. She was the same woman who used to risk her life by giving us water and small pieces of fruit as we worked under the noses of the Japanese guards. I used to see her being beaten by them for helping us. This place has healed old wounds for me. I can now hold my head up high and be proud.'

Mr. Dakin, who comes from Duffield, Derbyshire, now spends his time as a part-time guide for tourists visiting the site of the famous bridge.

The enterprising Japanese have designed the first tourist hotel in space. But it could take another 30 years before the order to 'beam me up Scottie' becomes reality.

The Shimizu Corporation of Tokyo plans to offer the extra-terrestrial trips after Australia's first commercial spaceport, on the remote Cape York Peninsular, opens up around the turn of the century.

From Bert Crane—Article in Australian Newspaper 1989

JAPAN OVERTAKE AMERICA
AS WORLD'S RICHEST NATION

Kevin Sullivan in Tokyo.
'Japan has overtaken the United States as the world's richest country,' the Economic Planning Agency in Tokyo announced yesterday.

The rapid appreciation of the yen since 1985 has boosted Japanese spending power abroad and fuelled a boom at home, according to the report from one of three ministries in charge of the economy. Japan's assets rose from $28.3 trillion (thousands of billion) at the end of 1986 to $43.7 trillion at the end of 1987 while American assets grew only from $34 trillion to $36.2 trillion over the same period.

The report confirms what most Japanese have believed for a long time: that economic strength, achieved through four decades of industrial expansion based on manufacturing know-how and entrepreneurial expertise, has made Japan the senior partner in the trans-Pacific economic relationship.

Underlying trends in the economy, however, suggest that many of the fruits of economic success have not yet trickled down to the population. The Japanese do not enjoy the same high standard of living as Americans or Western Europeans, and their economic pre-eminence may well succumb to the growing demands of a rapidly ageing population and a declining industrial base.

But economic performance remains impressive. Last week, the Nikkei average of 225 stocks on the Tokyo Stock Exchange reached its highest ever. Strong manufacturing sales, low inflation and a sustained boom in consumer spending point to underlying stability. The economy is in its 33rd month of expansion, the longest growth period since the war.

However, low interest rates and easy credit are emerging as early symptoms of an over-heating economy. The vast outflow of capital, some economists believe, will have a debilitating effect over the long term. Last month, Japanese investors bought 40 per cent of US Government bonds and Treasury notes.

Disenchantment with the Liberal Democratic Party, which has had a share of power for four decades, and the new cabinet of the Prime Minister, Mr. Toshiki Kaifu, have led to political instability.

The growing gap between the small number of people who own property or shares, and those who do not, has also fuelled resentment.

In a shift of policy aimed at bringing other opposition parties into a coalition, the Japan Socialist Party has accepted a continuation of Japan's military force and the security treaty with the US.

Mr. Tsuruo Yamaguchi, Secretary-General of Japan's largest opposition party, said the party also would not seek any drastic changes in economic policy. But the party would aim for a gradual reduction of US bases in Japan.—Reuter.

The Weekend Australian on 19—20th August 1989 reported

'Japan's new vision of history'

Hardline MPs and revisionists are enjoying a new-found favour in Japan with the belief that the country must shake off any sense of national guilt left by the war by rewriting history and denying reports of wartime atrocities, writes PETER WILSON from Tokyo.

Japanese atrocities against prisoners, including Australians, in World War II were not really as bad as they are portrayed . . . and the infamous Rape of Nanking was also a matter of gross exaggeration by the Chinese.

These are the controversial findings of a small but growing group of government MPs in Tokyo who are working hard to draw Japan's past actions in a more favourable light. Their campaign is perhaps the most disturbing contribution to a period of national soul-searching as Japan tries to adjust its self-image to accommodate the new international clout that has been created by its remarkable economic success.

Japanese society is certainly not ready to plunge back into militarism or facism but with right-wingers hoping to shift the nation's direction towards a more aggressively confident nationalism the hardline MPs and other revisionists are making their presence felt with a growing vigour and impact.

This view of the war is an outrage to Japan's neighbours and war victims, and is certainly not supported by the majority of the Japanese public nor the official policies of the Japanese Government. But the revisionist push does tap into several common themes in Japan, including the tendency of the recent Hiroshima Day ceremonies to focus on the horrific bombings and their victims without ever mentioning the Japanese aggression and bloodshed that preceded the bombing.

The revisionists have been at work for some time but they have recently been spurred on by Japan's new international stature and the national navel-gazing prompted by Emperor Hirohito's death earlier this year.

An education minister, Mr. Fujio, stated several times that Japan's 1910 invasion of Korea was justified, and that the Rape of Nanking should be considered an act of war rather than an atrocity. The Education Ministry is well known for its controversial attempts to water down text-book accounts of Japanese war activities.

Historian Mr. Saburo Ienaga, who is suing the Education Ministry for its censoring of his high school history texts, said in court recently that the ministry had asked him to change the term 'Japan's invasion of Asia' into 'Japan's advance into Asia' and to change sections referring to the Rape of Nanking, Japanese germ warfare experiments and the *bloody Battle of Okinawa*.

The Education Ministry argued that 'It is reasonable for the Government to give adequate instructions on matters concerning education.'

The most recent schoolbook row centred on an English text which contained a report on Japanese soldiers bayoneting Malaysian babies during the war. The publisher dropped the report after Mr. Kamei's group of Diet men said it was a fictitious incident. An independent scholar, Professor Horishi Hayashi of Kantogakuin University then visited Malaysia and found witnesses to the March 4, 1942 incident. Mr. Kamei argues that it is still 'dangerous' to accept the Malaysian incident as fact and wrong to highlight it as typical of Japanese military behaviour.

'If you are talking about historical fact I do not know whether the incident in Malaysia was fact but I am sure of established facts like the bombing of Hiroshima and Nagaski. The Americans did drop those bombs and I also know of many rapes of Japanese women by US occupation forces. Those are facts.'

Revisionists spurred by economic success

He insists that atrocities committed by the allies have been brushed over by conventional history while Japanese and German crimes have been harped on as a 'result of the exaggerated propaganda by the winners to justify what they have done themselves.

'Any war gets human beings into crazy situations,' he says when pressed about specific, well-documented atrocities. 'We can't allow people to believe that the Japanese are the most cruel people in the world. We have to wipe out the notoriety which darkens the name of our ancestors. There could have been some incidents but it would not have been massive organised atrocities like the Nazis killing the Jews.'

Mr. Kamei cites details of alleged Allied atrocities, but has selective amnesia when asked about Japanese crimes. He dismisses the Rape of Nanking as 'an example of the Chinese tradition of exaggerating things' saying he had seen no proof of the Chinese claims of 300,000 dead.

Asked about the treatment of Allied POWs he says he is not sure that the atrocities really happened 'but in any historical warfare there would have been cruel acts in the process on the parts of both the winners and losers'.

In December, more than 350 Japanese historians, MPs and businessmen gathered in Tokyo on the 47th anniversary of Japan's attack on Pearl Harbour to 're-evaluate the causes and results of the Great East Asian War'—a re-evaluation aimed at shifting blame away from Japan and crediting Imperial Japan for liberating Asia from Western colonialism.

The symposium was organised by a group of scholars and public figures including Mr. Seisuke Okuno, a former Cabinet minister who resigned in a storm of controversy last year after claiming that Japan was not the aggressor in the war.

Mr. Natsuo Sakomoto, a former history professor at Kogakukan University told the meeting that the attack on Pearl Harbour was 'provoked by the American government in spite of efforts by the Japanese government to avoid war.'

Mr. Shiro Sakama, a spokesman for the organisers said that 'our basic position is to insist that despite the thrust of popular education since the war, it was not a war of aggression but one to liberate Asian countries from colonialism by European and US powers.'

This attempt to justify Japan's actions is based on a popular slogan of imperial Japan—that Tokyo was only trying to free Asia from the white man's rule.

Mr. Sakama refuses to comment further when it is pointed out that Asian nations actually gained their independence as a result of Japan's defeat rather than its victories, and that it is extremely unlikely that a victorious Japan would have granted that independence.

Symposium organiser Mr. Sakama acknowledges that 'it will take some time to change the popular view (of history) into a more confident and independent one'.

'It is true that economically the Japanese have regained power and confidence but they still maintain the common view of the war—that Japan was the aggressor as it was defined at the Tokyo International Tribunal Court.'

Mr. Ikuhiko Hara, a historian who supports that conventional interpretation of Japan's war role, agrees that the revisionists are still in the minority but says that *they are gaining ground*.

The problem, he says, is that while the Germans are still going through a painful examination of the Nazi era, Japan has preferred to virtually ignore the war experience as part of a national tendency to hide uncomfortable truths.

Many war criminals were quickly re-habilitated after the war and allowed to regain prominent positions in Japanese public life, largely as a result of the American desire to use those rightists to battle communism.

Young Japanese in particular are largely unfamiliar with the history of the war.

When 'The Last Emperor' was shown in Tokyo last year distributors censored the film, claiming that the public would be offended by scenes such as the Rape of Nanking, in which tens of thousands of civilians were raped and slaughtered by Japanese troops. But when I spoke to young viewers leaving a Tokyo screening, most confessed that they had *never even heard of the incident* before seeing the film.

(Japanese women became entitled to vote during General MacArthur's leadership of the country.—Ed.)

From a newspaper cutting 1990

ATOM-BOMB ISLAND HITS THE JACKPOT
by Gordon Thomas

This historic 'spit in the ocean', just 20 miles by three, is to challenge Las Vegas as the world's big gambling capital.

Work has begun of the first of five gigantic casinos which will rival anything Nevada's city of glitter has to offer. Ironically, part of the estimated £600 million funding is coming from developers in Hiroshima and Nagasaki—the two Japanese cities devastated by the American B-29 planes which flew from Tinian in August, 1945, with the atomic bombs.

One year ago, Tinian farmer Pete Osaka's 20 acres were each worth about £1,500—if he could find a buyer. The Japanese consortium has just paid him £900,000 an acre.

Pilot Jerry Lampton gave me a tree-skimming flying tour of where the casinos will rise above the jungle. One will be near Suicide Cliff—a corner of the island where scores of Japanese soldiers leapt to their deaths rather than surrender to the Americans.

The developers expect the project to be completed by 1992. They estimate that more than half a million gamblers will fly from the United States—and even more from Japan.

The runway from which Japanese Zero fighters flew missions against US bombers is being refurbished to take jumbo jets.

One veteran who viewed these developments with mixed feelings was retired US General Charles Sweeney. In 1945 he flew the B-29 which dropped the bomb on Nagasaki. Last week he revisited the island.

He said 'There are a lot of ghosts down there. Somehow it doesn't seem quite right that their resting places will be disturbed so that a lot of gamblers, who probably have no idea what happened here, can play blackjack.'

But Sweeney, a Boston banker, is not averse to doing business with his old enemies. On Tinian he held several meetings with Japanese contacts to see if they would be willing to buy a Boston bank, US Trust, that Sweeney has been instructed by his board of directors to sell for £300 million.

Extract from ICI Magazine, from Tom Roxby

Insight into Japanese business philosophies from Shoichi Saba, ICI non-executive director and former chief executive of the Toshiba Corporation.

THE DIFFERENCE BETWEEN JAPANESE AND WESTERN COMPANIES

As a Japanese, who has only participated in the management of ICI for four years, it gives me great pleasure to speak to a group of senior managers of the Company whose career backgrounds are brilliant and diverse.

Speaking honestly, before joining the ICI Board, I was not alone among Japanese who believed that British industry was on the decline. However, frequent visits to the UK and contacts with many British friends, have furnished me with a very encouraging discovery that there are still several big, first-class world industrial firms like ICI, which have real competitiveness in the international arena.

Now, my talk is about my experience and views on manufacturing industries in the East and West. All of you are probably familiar, or have become familiar through this course programme, with the general state of comtemporary Japanese industry. However, some of you may not realize that the concepts of capitalism and modern industry were introduced into Japan just about 120 years ago, following the restoration of the Meiji Emperor to power in 1868.

These concepts were taken, mainly, from the West . . . Western cultures are generally characterized by belief in individualism, and these cultures generally welcome the guidance of strong leaders. In contrast, Japanese find it difficult to accept strong individuals and Japan has a group-orientated society that prefers working through an equality-based concensus.

If you ask an American or a European what he does for a living, he will name a job. Ask a Japanese, and he will name a company. For decades, Westerners have hoped that their careers could be developed through the selection of their jobs. In contrast, and until recently, Japanese workers have preferred to build their careers within a single industrial group.

Tom Roxby comments:

This is interesting. The Japanese group identity is on a par with the British Army's philosophy of regiment identification. There is nothing comparable with the Royal Navy or RAF. The Group Identification may explain in part the 'loyalty to death' of the Japanese fighting man. In accordance with their individualist philosophies, members of Western corporations orientate their lives around themselves, their families and their communities, while their work is primarily a means of receiving financial remuneration. As everyone accepts this, it is not considered traitor-like behaviour to leave one's company when better remuneration is available. In Japan, however, one's company is on a par with other important group affilitions and thus represents one of the basic social group situations in life. Capitalistic economic activities are engaged in, with the prime goal of sustaining and developing the corporation as a group and as a social unit. Within the lifetime employment system, one's job represents a life-long affiliation, and as management is promoted from within the ranks, there is an unconscious concensus, regardless of what shareholders may think, behind the idea that the employees are the true owners of corporations. In major Japanese companies, employers remain tied to their companies throughout their working lives, and because all corporate members perceive their respective fates as being closely linked, this is a natural basis for enthusiastic co-operation.

From Sub Lt. (A) R.F.Parton, RNVR

The cold, clinical efficiency of the Japanese nation is clearly illustrated by my experience in the Republic of South Africa as General Manager of a new company involved in Power Station and Industrial, design and construction.

I was sent to the Republic by British Steel, to initiate a joint venture with a major South African company committed to construction of steelwork in power generation, industrial, gold, diamond and coal mining projects.

The South African construction scene then was almost opposite that of its British counterpart with its interminable delays and increases of cost. Quotations had to be highly competitive, covering price, discounts, delivery, engineering standards, and company capabilities. You may say the same as UK! except that the South Africans meant it!

Failure to perform, having been awarded a project, resulted in the customer *exacting* stringent penalties, agreed in the pre-contract conditions.

It was in this scenario, that in order to obtain work for my company, I found it necessary to buy Japanese. Their sales force (located in all major cities) would visit, to talk and meet your demands and queries, backed up by a never diminishing flow of experts who would come from Japan on demand. They were formidable opposition to their competitors from UK (including my own British Steel), Germany, Switzerland, Italy and the United States.

Not only were their financial packages excellent, if you gave them an order it was with spine chilling competence that your goods would arrive almost to the hour, within the agreed standards and quality. This experience was shared with numerous business colleagues out there, and in spite of our exhortations—it took UK companies many decades to emulate.

Prince Charles's 83-year old friend Sir Laurens van der Post, who is Prince William's godfather, is a remarkable man. Born in South Africa and widely travelled, he has been quoted as saying:

'The secret of living a good life lies in the unconscious, in listening to your dreams, following your intuition and accepting that coincidence is more than random chance.'

Some extracts from: 'A Walk with a White Bushman', Laurens van der Post in conversation with Jean-Marc Potting.

Do you remember, the first time I wrote to you, I said that only the African like you could understand the Japanese? Because of their special relationship with nature, and their special kind of sensitivity. You give a good example of this in the The Night of the New Moon *when you show how strangely the Japanese behaved with the new moon. How do you explain such behaviour?*

Of course, I had known from my reading and from my visit to Japan that the role that the moon and the moonrise play in the Japanese character. But here suddenly I was in this prison where the whole of life was under a microscope—it was super life sized. Everything was enlarged, really. And it seemed to me that, unconsciously, their link with the moon was far greater and far more immediate, more accessible, in terms of mood and feeling than it was to us. It was a little more remote to us, more in our background, whereas, because I was an African, what was a very important part of my life was the sunset. The Japanese would go to certain places to celebrate the moonrise, they would go to Arashiyama and watch the moon come up—and you know how lovely it is to see the full moon come up there. But we would say in Africa, 'It's going to be a lovely sunset now—I think we'll go there, that will be the best place to watch it from . . .' We were very much sunset-conscious. And our moods were influenced by it.

So I was predisposed to notice in prison a strange kind of longing among the Japanese for the moon; and out of this longing a kind of frustration and a kind of rage over the frustration which added to the power of this very deep longing. It was just like a tide in the sea being pulled up in their characters. And this seemed always to be most evident as the moon swelled and became more and more full. And one became quite frightened of them. There were certain Japanese who seemed to be more influenced by this phenomenon than others. There was one, for instance, whom the troops called 'Mad Harry', because you know that Latin for madness is 'lunatic'—touched by the moon. He ran amok sometimes, hitting and beating anyone in his way and generally acting so strangely.

I've seen the phenomenon in Africa. I have heard lions roar at the moon just as dogs bay at the moon. I heard a lion one night start as the moon came up at 8 o'clock and, so obsessed was he with it that he was still roaring at it in full daylight after it had set the next day. But this phenomenon I watched so closely and anxiously, seemed to wane with the moon, and a very pure, almost resolved kind of excitement and expectation built up within the Japanese. They were almost joyful and suddenly, when the new moon appeared in our sky, there was a feeling of catharsis, of having been cleansed, among them, as if somehow they had done the night journey themselves. You know, they had grown with the moon, they had waxed and they had gone back into the darkness and were emerging into the light again.

I can't really express it in any other way, because it was so mysterious. Most of the really bad excesses we encountered occurred really about the time when the moon started waning, when it started going back into the darkness.

But what kind of future do we prepare for our children—if we assume that they do have a future? With the advent of the nuclear age nothing and nobody can be the same as before. For our own good everything perhaps should be considered as atomized, even words. Don't you think all professionals in the use and exchange of words, such as politicians and journalists, should now treat words as if they were nuclear products, that is to say in a careful, meaningful and responsible way? In that sense the 'thousand suns' of Hiroshima and Nagasaki should have opened our eyes.

I certainly think that the lesson we learned from Hiroshima and Nagasaki could be used for the good of mankind, just as I think atomic energy can be used for the good of mankind. There is an enormous symbolic importance in the fact that the source of this destructive energy was nuclear—that it came from the atom—because it shows that the greatest energy in the physical world is in the smallest unit . . . Just as I have saying to you that the source of power, transforming power, in human society is in the smallest unity of human society, which is the individual. The individual is the atom of society and therefore these two symbols are in a sense complementary. What is most threatening and destructive in human society today is the human being who is split in his own nucleus: it is the fission in the modern soul which makes nuclear fission so dangerous—he is a split atom. He has got to heal himself, make himself whole.

So many things have been said and so many books have been written about the atomic bombing of Hiroshima and Nagasaki that, somehow, we tend to forget the context of it in the Pacific War. A sure fact is that that holocaust saved your life and the lives of hundreds of thousands of prisoners-of-war and civilians in countries occupied by the Japanese.

Yes, I know we were saved by it, because we have evidence of the fact that we were all due to have been killed by the Japanese. Actually the bomb was dropped in August, and the massacre was timed for when the real invasion of South-East Asia would begin. (See *The Night of the New Moon* by Laurence Van Der Post.) Mountbatten's forces were gathering to invade South-East Asia on the 2nd September. So we were only saved by a few weeks. But I am convinced that millions of other lives were saved too. Because if the war had gone on, hundreds of thousands of American lives would have been lost, millions of Japanese lives would have been lost—you can imagine the number of *seppukus*, the ritual suicides, that would have gone on, and the numbers that would have been killed in a last battle . . . It's unspeakable.

Do you agree with the argument that says if the Japanese had produced the atom bomb first they would have used it without hesitation?

Yes; you know them better than I do. I think that people were caught in such an extreme cycle of their own spirit that they could have done anything and believed it justified. It was an extraordinary war they fought; it was a sheer fantasy, you see, but in a way the same thing applied to Germany. I am certain that it was a *Göterdämmerung*, that Hitler conducted the war in such a way that he had to be defeated. If not, why did he ever invade Russia? Why did he invade Russia? He could not stop. It was just like Napoleon: why couldn't Napoleon stop? Why did he have to go on and on? It was this blind collective urge which once it is released is a form of madness, a collective madness, that only this deep mythological mechanism of proportion and self-correction can arrest and dispel, even in Hitler's as in Napoleon's case by unconsciously forcing them to conduct a war in a way that will defeat war and so make them instruments of their own destruction.

What is your opinion now about the bomb? Do you think the Americans were right to use it?

To me the interesting thing is that the bomb has only been used twice. You could have said that in the Korean War, which was a very dastardly war, another sort of Pearl Harbor was organized; I mean, when MacArthur's back was turned and the Americans were nearly pushed into the sea in Korea, there could have been a tremendous temptation and indeed argument to use the bomb, but it was not used. I am quite certain that what we call the western world will never drop an atom bomb first. But I feel it is important that the western world should have sufficient power to do so in self-defence, so that any country which may be tempted to use the bomb against us will know that it will get more in return. And we must not persist in thinking of nuclear problems as only a United States—Russian dimension. Soon all sorts of maverick states with money to burn are going to have atom bombs. The number who have them already or are about to get them is alarming. We must get away from looking at life partially and hysterically. We must, as the Greeks enjoined, look at it steadily and whole, and life will never forgive us if we neglect any defence reality demands of us, for the sake of a fine gesture that merely warms the egotistical lust for feeling ethical and superior; but the emphasis is always on defence, not aggression.

Remember, too, that in the psychology of war there is an element of proportion, diabolical proportion. You can see it, for instance, in the use of poison gas. In the 1914—18 war the Germans used poison gas with great initial success and everybody assumed in the 1939—45 war that it would be used again. We and the Americans had gases that went far beyond the original poison gas that was used. We were ready to use it in a big way against the Germans. But somehow, because everyone was conscious of it, it was never used.

How did you survive when you were a prisoner-of-war? What were the essential factors which contributed to your survival?

Well, it is a fact, it is a law of life that you should fight for life truthfully and honourably as long as you can, and that you as the individual cannot decide to abandon life—that is a thing which is left to God and therefore we had to do everything we could to go on living. The only weapon we had—because we were completely helpless—was to live truthfully and not to allow the madness which surrounded us to distort our vision of the truth. I could have been proved wrong at any moment, but I felt that as long as we lived truthfully we had a chance for survival. And the proof is that we did survive.

Your prison camp in Java was a microcosm of the world with Dutch, British, Australians, New Zealanders, Indonesians, Chinese and, of course, the Japanese and Koreans enrolled by force in the Japanese army. Was there any interaction, and did any changes take place in the hearts and minds of all these men?

Well, I described what happened in my books, (*The Night of the New Moon* and *The Seed and the Sower*) and what was interesting to me was the way in which the ordinary soldiers of all races and colours got on with one another, even when they could not speak the language. You'd see an English soldier and a Chinese walking about roaring with laughter at something they had seen, and having this feeling of togetherness that all prisoners tend to have. It was also interesting to me that the greatest problems we had were with people who were part of what you might describe as the intellectual classes. The people who had not lost contact with their instincts—they were our source of strength. They were the ones that sustained. The difficult people were among the officers—and I hasten to add how exceptional they were—because they felt some special treatment was due to their office, that they had privileges as officers necessary for the upholding of their rank and exercise of their command. And among the officers the trickiest were those who had been lawyers in private life.

They were excellent men but seemed to find it difficult ever to command or obey. Everything was a case to be argued. The wholeness of the thing tended to escape them. All was argument, counter-argument and special pleading. But for the most part everybody responded to leadership by example rather than command, and on the whole we were blessed in the quality of our officers and men. We came through, and though one would not like to repeat the experience, an enormous liberating influence for us all was the absence of possessions and the stark simplicity with which we had to lead our lives, so that only essentials mattered.

And everybody was forced to cling to one another, forced to be involved.

Oh yes, we did that, because our own command instinctively followed the great declaration of St. John, 'In the beginning was the Word, and the Word was with God, and the Word was God.'

For instance, I joined the prison camp later than anyone else because I was captured later, and when I did so I was horrified at the state of disorder and dissension there. So when Wing-Commander Nichols, a great prison commander, and I took over, I started by writing a letter and getting a man to help me make copies of it, and we posted it in all the different places where people could read it. Its message, in essence, was, 'We must look upon imprisonment not as a tragedy but as a great opportunity. This break of continuity which life in prison appears to be, is more apparent than real. We all carry our true and unassailable continuity within us and we have only to follow it and we shall come through.' I went on to outline what I thought the opportunity was; and that is how we lived it, as if this were a great opportunity for re-education. So I created an educational system in the camp and people had never been so busy. I meet people now who, I am sad to say, after the many years since they were in prison with Nichols and myself, get a look of intense nostalgia and they say, 'You know, those were the days . . .' It is rather tragic because it reflects the failure of so-called peace and its inadequacies which are the causes of war.

This experience of 'togetherness' can happen in time of war or in time of great urgency or emergency, but how can it happen in everyday life? How can we be wiser when money, power, status count for so much?

The only way you could do it would be by being an instrument of the truth, and then human beings would respond.

For instance, in the camp, one of the first things Nichols and I did was to confiscate all the money in the camp—and some of the officers parted with their money under protest. In fact, one of the most senior threatened to have us court-martialled after the war for what he called this insubordination. We used the money for the welfare of the camp as a whole. There was no private money henceforth. And in many ways like that we showed that an officer's condition was not created to give him special privileges. If anything, an officer in these circumstances should have less than his men. That is what being an officer meant: to lead by serving more than anyone else. That was why the British forces were for me so movingly called 'services' and why, contrary to their television image of today, they were not reflections of class and capitalistic systems but great brotherhoods; indeed monastic orders of sorts.

But to return to money, I can tell you an interesting story about money which reflects our prison approach to it. You see I had six weeks after the Japanese capitulation in which I had to represent the British Government in Java, and in all immediate issues, govern it through the Japanese, in a Java which was in a state of rebellion. And then the first contacts with Mountbatten came through an exceptional Admiral, Wilfred Patterson, a sensitive, humane and far-seeing serviceman. He was joined by General Christison, a soldier-statesman of a high order, who was going to take command when our troops arrived. I told him all I had learned, what I thought should be done, and how dangerous I thought the ignorance we seemed to fight in was, back at High Command. Characteristically, he made up his mind immediately, and said to me: 'You must go back and see Lord Mountbatten at once.' So, dressed in my old prison clothes, I was flown in a reconnaissance aircraft to Singapore. I arrived there late in the evening as everything was closing down at the airport. I told the RAF officer in control that I had most immediate authority from my Admiral and General to go in the first available transport to Ceylon the next day.

After a startled pause and a glance at the General's note written on a torn-out page of his pocket dispatch book, the officer said: 'That's all right, I can get you onto the transport but I am rather embarrassed, I don't know what to do with you for tonight because Singapore is full of ex POWs, full of people, I don't know where to put you . . .' I said: 'Do you mind if I just sleep on the floor of your office?' He said: 'No, but . . . what about food?' I said: 'That doesn't matter. I can wait until I get to Colombo.' 'But,' he said, 'that won't be for another twenty hours!' I said: 'I've gone without food for days in prison.' So he gave me some water to drink and left me. The next morning I flew to Colombo in Ceylon. I arrived there at four o'clock in the afternoon and found I had to wait for some hours for a plane to fly me on to Kandy where Lord Mountbatten's headquarters were. So I went into what we called a NAAFI, a restaurant organized by the services for people passing through. I went and sat at a table and a NAAFI girl in uniform came along and asked me what I would like to have. I was looking very odd in my improvised prison uniform with shaven head and emaciated features and she looked at me very strangely as I said, 'I'd love some eggs and bacon.'

So she went and got me eggs and bacon and toast and coffee. But then she came along and said, 'That will be five shillings.' And I looked at her in amazement and exclaimed, 'My God! Do people still use money?' 'Well, I'm afraid we do,' she replied.

I had not thought of equipping myself with money for this journey, for in our prison world private money had been so utterly abolished that it had been eliminated from our personal reckoning. So what could I do? Almost in a panic by the enormity not only of my thoughtlessness but this evidence of an abyss opening up between the values of our prison world and the 'free' world, I threw myself on the mercy of an officer sitting at a table near mine. I explained what had happened and said, 'Could you please pay for my tea. Give me your name and address and when I get back to London I will take you for dinner at Claridges.' He gave me one glance and said, 'Certainly,' and gave me my five shillings. I paid the waitress and went off on my journey to Lord Mountbatten.

But that shows you how we came out of prison and the way our lives had come to presuppose a world where these things were no longer necessary.

And did you also try—you yourself and the other six thousand prisoners with you—to understand your captors and tormentors, the Japanese?

I have often thought about this question. I realize that when I first went to Japan in 1926 I was really little more than a boy. I was tremendously changed at a very profound level, in my psyche, as it were, in my soul. That experience has been one of the great and most creative influences on my life, a meeting at a deep level of metamorphosis. And it has not come to an end yet. I notice changes are still going on. Today, I can see a lot of it consciously but I am not seeing anything that was not there unconsciously. So although this process of understanding started inevitably as an instinctive reaction, its conscious consequences were profound and have gone on all my life. Looking back on my encounter with the Japanese in Java I am amazed by how much was already unconsciously present in my imagination, which would have a decisive and protective fall-out in all my dealings and doings with the Japanese. I know, for instance, it saved my life that day in 1942 when I was caught by Japanese soldiers on the mountain, Djaja-Sempoer in Java, with almost all that I had known of the Japanese language forgotten—because unfortunately I could not read Japanese to keep it alive in my mind—and yet the right reaction came out of me in this moment of crisis, and I said to them, 'Would you please condescend to be so kind as to wait an honourable moment?'

In the best Japanese!

Yes! And from this little knowledge came more food for understanding. Particularly so when I came into contact with the Japanese again in prison and confronted their dark, shadow side. We all have a shadow within, but here I was meeting a specifically Japanese shadow, the aspect of their character aroused by the violence of their transition from the pre-Meiji Empire of Japan, moving overnight, as it were, from a medieval culture and structure into the modern age; and making the mistake we continue to make, in spite of all the evidence and warnings, of thinking that you can make men and their societies contemporary by merely heaping our terrifying technology and its horrendous power on them. They did not realize what damage they were doing to their instinctive selves. And here in the war it was bursting out, presenting itself in the most brutal way. yet it was never something which was totally inhuman to me. It seemed instinctively that I could understand it. Even in its most frightening forms, I could understand it in a way that I could not understand the Nazi phenomenon. It seemed important somehow that our salvation in prison depended on enlarging this process of understanding.

This is what I tried to do. I tried to tell people what I knew about Japan and Japanese history. I gave lectures in prison on these things, and then I relearnt, very rapidly, Japanese. I started teaching Japanese classes, and that was the biggest class that I had. Now this is a very strange phenomenon. To me it was profoundly symbolic that there were so many of the ordinary British soldiers who wanted to learn the language of the enemy. That was a tremendous bridge to understanding. I had these large classes and I found I only had to ask the Japanese and they gave us books in Dutch about the Japanese—and in Java there were a lot of people who knew Japan well. Holland had a very ancient connection with Japan; after the Portuguese were thrown out of Japan the Dutch were the only people allowed to trade with them, and there were a lot of books about it.

So that was strange. Everything that the Japanese inflicted on us was always balanced by something they gave us, through these books, out of their minds and their spirit. And I am certain that that is one of the reasons we came out of the experience with no bitterness. Very few people came out hating the Japanese. It was a remarkable achievement. Particularly when I hear what happened at other places where the bitterness was much greater. It was a great triumph really on both sides.

Of understanding.

Of understanding—I can only put it down to this fact. You see, if you meet something with truth, no matter how disagreeable the truth is, it is always a meaningful and creative experience. It seemed to be so not just for my own British soldiers, but also the Dutch, Menadonese, Ambonese—they all came through with this unique understanding which I think, looking back on it, is in a sense also a tribute to something in the Japanese—a sense that we were all victims in some cosmic process.

Yes, but on the other hand, didn't you feel that there was a pitiful lack of knowledge about the Japanese on the western side?

Oh yes.

And that you were trying to catch up with this lack of knowledge?

That too, yes, of course, there was that. But in the conditions in which we were, it was the human aspect—the human contact, you know. And after all, none of us was in our native country—we were all on foreign soil. We were condemned to play this role of people at war. And make no mistake about it, this is the most ancient theatre there is, where man dramatizes himself into a state of war.

And the paradox is, you felt freer than your captors.

Once we began to understand and to learn from the experience, yes.

Have you ever met any of your captors, after the war?

No, never again, because the military who ran the camps were immediately called up and sent back to their combat units. Although for about a year I saw quite a lot of the Japanese army people, they were not the people who had been involved with the prisoners. And I had a very remarkable experience with the Japanese army after the surrender. But I never had the chance to go back immediately to Japan because straight-away I went back into active service for about two years. Then the moment I returned hom I got involved in African matters. But I felt I could not abandon my relationship with Japan. I owed it to life to go and see Japan again and I did, I went back to see my Japanese friends.

And on that stage, of the camp and the war between the Japanese and you, you felt the experience had been positive on your side. But what about the other side? Did you have the impression that one of the Japanese, or two or three of them had somehow changed their behaviour, their psychology or psyche after being in contact with you, in relationship with you?

Yes! First of all, I think that if the Japanese had not been changed by their contact with us, our fate would have been much worse. I think that in putting understanding of the Japanese so much in the forefront of our prison lives we were in fact saving our lives all the time. Though that wasn't the object of the exercise, I think that had an enormous bearing on the way we were treated. That is the indirect evidence compared with other camps. There was, for instance, a young Japanese interpreter, who appeared towards the end of our captivity, and when I was being confronted on very critical occasions by the Japanese military and he was acting as interpreter, I always felt that he was on our side, and that in interpreting, as far as I could judge, he was improving on what I had to say. He was almost an accomplice after the fact. He was putting my case in the most convincing way possible.

Once the capitulation came about, I worked a great deal with him. One day he felt free to tell me what he had not been able to tell me before—he had an English mother. I saw then that it had been his mother who was always pleading for us on these occasions. How mysterious! Tears came to my eyes when he told me this and I said, 'Please thank your mother,' and he said gravely, 'I will do so next time I go to her shrine.' Another interesting thing was that he had heard from the Japanese how much they had respected us really. Apparently ours was the most unusual camp they had come across on the island. He said they had picked up a lot of things from us. He did not want me to think it was just the Japanese who had an effect on us—we had had a very strong effect on them. That was very nice to hear.

I seem to remember other examples of how understanding the Japanese character helped, particularly after the surrender.

Yes. One in particular stays with me. I had to order the Japanese General to use his forces to protect the Dutch against the Indonesians. I remember his look of horror and the anguish of his reply, 'But it would be dishonourable for me now to fight against people I myself urged to rebel.'

'You can have no honour rooted in dishonour,' I told him simply. 'You will have to discover, as I did under you, that there is a way in life of losing all in such a manner that it becomes a way of winning.'

Deeply moved, he bowed, hissed between his teeth and said almost in tears, 'That is a very Japanese thought.'

And from then on I had their full co-operation.

You suffered at the hands of the Japanese, but you still make a distinction between the Germans and the Japanese. Why?

Yes, I always distinguish between the Germans and the Japanese in the war, although there are resemblances. I think the problem was totally different. You know, Japan was thrown so quickly to the West that it really had a modern, western technology and power before it had the psychology to go with it. They were people who had not cut the umbilical cord between themselves and their medieval past; they were caught in their own history. Whereas the Germans had all the illumination possible but they deliberately rejected the light that we all shared, for this mission of darkness, this discredited, primitive, collective upsurge. And this was the terrifying thing about the Germans to me, and this in a sense makes the Nazi phenomenon different from the Russian one, although the Russian is also a totalitarian phenomenon. There is a certain natural element in the Russian collective vision. That is why it has gone on for so long, because the Russians are a primitive people, pliant to command and in a way trusting of authority. The Russians do not have the German enlightenment, or the German philosophic and scientific structure. They are very largely a tribal people. They had collective values in their villages. I describe in my book on Russia how the elders of the village controlled the life of the individual, whom he should marry, whom he should not marry. It was a collective existence so one cannot quite compare it with German life. But I think what one can compare with the Nazis are the leaders in Russia who make use of this natural primitiveness for their own ends.

Isn't it a bit strange that you admire, respect and even love the Japanese who were your enemies and inflicted pain and torture on you?

It is a paradox, we are all paradoxes, and when I first came to Japan I saw it all the time. I had the feeling that all that I loved was not the whole story. It was a great source of strength to me in prison to draw on my first experience of Japan and I think that made the difference between life and death, not only for me but for thousands of other prisoners, because I kept saying to myself, 'If I remember this other Japan very, very clearly, the Japanese who come in contact with me here will also have to remember it.'

And you know—the modern concept of 'love' is in any case restricted, sloppy and debased. It is really an heroic dominant in life. Those who experience it are almost always in battle with the 'not love' in themselves first, and then in their life and time. And the core of this love is a form of total and truthful knowing which is unshakeable and unswerving, perceiving the faults of its objects as precisely as its virtues but yet coming out of that difficult and contradictory perception intact.

What is your explanation for the cruelty of the Japanese during the Pacific War? Were they conscious of evil and their evil acts, or were they victims?

I think they were really caught in a trap of their own history. Really it is almost as if they were asking the world to stop them. They behaved in such a way that they had to lose, which is almost proof to me that unconsciously they wanted to lose the war. This is the only way in which they could get rid of the dark side of themselves. And I have Japanese friends; they do not talk much about the war but when they do talk about it, they talk about it as their revolution, they see it as a kind of evolutionary revolution.

What happened during the surrender of the Japanese Imperial Army in Indonesia?

We could not occupy Java immediately. Demobilization was going on, everybody wanted to get home, and the ships were full of troops going home. Java, Indonesia and Sumatra—indeed the whole of the Dutch Empire, which was the third biggest empire in the world—was made Mountbatten's responsibility overnight. He was not prepared for it, but he sent a cruiser, the *Cumberland*, under Admiral Patterson, to accept the Japanese formal surrender. He could not have chosen a finer or more imaginative officer. One day I hope to write about him properly and how invaluable his Celtic sensibility and sense of politics was to us.

Now he asked me to sit next to him when he was taking the surrender. I sat there on his quarter-deck in my old, tattered prison clothes and my shaven head. The Japanese general came and bowed to him, and I could see the somewhat startled look in his eye when he saw me sitting there. He came out of his bow and told the admiral that they had come to surrender, but he had one request: the admiral must know how much their swords meant to them, how they were the most treasured and revered possession for every Japanese officer. Would the admiral therefore please allow them to keep their swords? And Admiral Patterson—who had very blue eyes, which then became stern and full of a light that was not inhuman but as firm as the occasion demanded—replied, 'It is the irrevocable command of the Supreme-O, Lord Mountbatten, that you will surrender the swords you have done so much to dishonour.'

And I saw a tremendous rush of emotion into the Japanese general's face, and the faces of all his officers. I felt desperately full of pity for them, they could hardly contain themselves. But they made an enormous effort and unbuckled their swords and laid them down.

What were the true feelings of Lord Mountbatten towards the Japanese? It's notorious that he did not want any Japanese to attend his funeral. He could not forgive them, offically at least. This is the general opinion. Do you share it?

No, I do not, and I did not know that. I was abroad when he was assassinated, and I did not know he had put that in his will. But it was quite a common phenomenon that the people who had not suffered under the Japanese were more bitter than those of us who had gone through the experience and lived through it. People who came out from England after the war, like the War Crimes Officers, were much more bloodthirsty than we were. I would find it odd if Lord Mountbatten thought of them as beyond forgiveness because he was a magnanimous man. Yes, I would find it most strange . . . Mind you, you should have seen the prisoners when they came out of prison. Lady Mountbatten went round among them, helping them, and the stories they told about the way they had been treated and the numbers who had died of neglect and cruelty would have shaken anybody except the people concerned, because we were used to it, we had an immunity to it, but people seeing it from the outside were very upset and shocked. That may have been the cause of it.

I always think of Churchill's words: 'In defeat, defiance; in victory, magnanimity; in peace, unity.' 'In victory, magnanimity' are striking words. It seems to me you want to make a new beginning at the moment of victory when you have won apparently all you have fought for, and you want to start afresh. One must not keep the past alive by giving it a place in the future through punishment. My own instinct would be to wipe the slate clean and say it was a moment of madness in life and let us get back to sanity and re-begin as soon as we can.

You know, listening to you, I am more and more convinced that the British as well as the Bretons in France are quite close to the Japanese. They share the same feelings, especially towards nature. The Japanese love ghosts and what is boiling in a witch's cauldron. Shakespeare, of course, is universal, but he sounds so sure, so real and so frightening a Japanese context.

Well, I was only saying to a friend the other day that I think the two nations in the world who have been most influenced by nature are the English and the Japanese. English poetry is absolutely full of nature and a love of nature, a love of birds, grass and flowers, and even the common fly is 'gilded' as it 'lechers' in Shakespeare's sight. Wherever you go in London you see that everybody has a window-box with flowers in it; even if they cannot have a garden, they have a window-box at least.

There are many problems with Japan today on the economic front. The Japanese can be hard to deal with and they seem to understand us better than we understand them, so it is surprising to find that they can be sentimental.

I agree with you. I think our whole approach is based on European rational values that we should throw aside. We should look at the authentic symbolism of meaning which motivates us all. I am certain that if we direct ourselves to the Japanese in that area, we would get a very interesting and overwhelming response. However skilful they are technologically, in building trains, wireless sets, cars and so on, their personalities contain an area of doubting. One of my most acute reminders of how deep this unconscious—and sometimes conscious—sense of doubt among the Japanese, particularly young Japanese, could go, was through my friendship with Yukio Mishima.

I met Yukio Mishima in the United States. He and I went to the University of California and a series of colleges where we talked about Japan together, and

I was amazed to find he was a wonderful companion, with a great sense of humour. He spoke beautiful English. He was a connoisseur of European wine and food, and he was in a sense westernized, just as some of us feel that the Japanese civilization is for us a valid alternative civilization. We could, if pushed out of Europe, feel there was a civilization, with which we could identify. I think Yukio felt this about western civilization, that in some way it was an alternative, but nevertheless he was horrified that Japan was picking up all that was negative and materialistic in European civilization, that it was losing something of its honour, of its self-respect and the spirit of the Japan that mattered to him above all else. We talked about it a great deal. He was extraordinarily worried about the obsession with radio sets and motor cars and this whole way of living, although he enjoyed those things himself.

I think ultimately his death was of a special significance and truly Japanese. I saw him here in Europe not long before his death and I noticed the change in him since I'd last seen him in the United States of America. He looked to me not discouraged but very sombre. Later, after his death, I met a Japanese lady who's married to an eminent English theatrical producer. She is a friend of Mishima's wife and she told me that in Mishima's diaries after his death they found that, two years before he committed his form of *seppuku*, the date for it had already been set down. He knew that he was entering the last two years of his life and that ultimately the Japanese would not accept his message unless he could prove to them it mattered so much to him that he would die for it. He believed very profoundly in this thing that one picks up over and over again in Japan—that when life fails you, the only way to resurrect life and give it another chance was by giving up your own life and dying. He took death very seriously—not in a negative sense, but in a positive sense. This is one of the very difficult things that Europeans have to learn to understand about Japan; the extreme seriousness with which death is treated as something which is purely an end or purely negative. It is something for which one needs almost as much preparation, ceremonial, devotion and love as for marriage. I have always been deeply stirred by the great Feast of the Dead—Japan's All Saints' Day—when everyday life stops and minds and houses are opened wide to welcome the dead. This is one of the most joyful acts of remembrance I have ever encountered.

Yes, the Japanese seem to have a feeling almost of the 'romance of death'. What experience of that did you have among the Japanese soldiers in the war?

We had very little contact with the Japanese soldiers, so we did not really know what happened outside the prison camp. They very often said to me in moments of rage when they got drunk: 'We like you, but how can we like you—you are disgraced in being still alive. We would like you much better if you were dead!' I have seen them do extraordinary things—for instance, execute somebody in prison and then after the execution they would say, 'We will now show you Japanese morality towards the dead', and all the troops were paraded and made to present arms to the decapitated body lying there, then they would blow their bugles and truly honour the life they had despised when living.

You see, there are always so many different ways of approaching life, and I think that there is something valid in their approach to death. We no longer take it seriously enough in western civilization. The subject is avoided for as long as possible. People are sent off to die in hospitals; they are not with their own families and friends when they die. Animals are killed out of sight, so that nobody should see this unpleasant thing called death. We try to live as though death did not exist. I have often wondered if the very great extension of the years of life of the average European has not had a profound effect on the European spirit, because in the Elizabethan age a person was old at fifty. People did not expect to live much beyond fifty. Charles the Great at the age of fifty was rehearsing his own funeral in Paris, by lying in his coffin. Death was much more of an imminent reality. Michelangelo said that it is true that death destroyed all men, but that the thought made the man. But it is true the Japanese have a romantic affair with death; it is as if death really holds the romance for them that life lacks.

Quite often, for the Japanese, suicide means fulfilment and may have an erotic undertone. But could it not also be a form of escapism? For a Westerner it is odd to imagine that a Japanese prefers to commit suicide instead of speaking out, instead of attempting a dialogue.

Yes, there is something mysterious about that. I think it is the shadow side of the Japanese; and if they were to look into it very deeply they could make this compulsion contemporary, because it is an outmoded way of behaving. It is an archaic, built-in reaction, not an illuminated compulsion but a collective one, which the individual should face up to and break free from.

Other nations do resent the great success of the Japanese. How should they approach Japan and have a fair and balanced view of them?

I think there are two aspects to this question. There is the defensive reaction which says this is the Japanese way of continuing the war they lost, only now they are making war on our economy. I think that is the wrong reflex. On the other hand, the Japanese see this kind of hostility to their economic and technological success as the revival of the ancient forces that hemmed them in and would not let them expand into the modern world. This would be a very dangerous repeat performance of history in another dimension. My own feeling about it has been that somehow, in a non-rational more than a rational way, we have got an enormous area of sympathy for each other, the Japanese and ourselves. We ought to try and explore this through friendships. My Japanese friendships have been amongst the most meaningful ones in my life. Through our Japanese friends we must sit down and explore it together and find where we can bring each other closer to understanding one another. I think there is a great readiness for it. Of all the variations of the western spirit I think the United States of America, to the Japanese, is a country with which their relationship is still more technological and commercial than warm and spontaneous like the feeling they have for, say, the culture of France. They really seem to appreciate the ancient values of Europe as much as we do.

And look at the way they have taken European music into themselves. Through culture, through art, through religion, through studying the language, we can foster these bridges. I think it is most encouraging that the various Japanese firms who have started small enterprises here in Britain, with Japanese managing British workmen, have been eminently successful. People like them and they get on. Japan has got an enormous contribution of its own to make which we value and we want to take along with us.

In 'The Other 100 Years War 1941—2041' Russell Braddon wrote

In 1965 I wrote a book postulating America's defeat in Vietnam by 1972, thus leaving the whole of Asia and Australasia defenceless before the mighty sisterhood of China and a remilitarised Japan; but it was 1968 before I began to realise that I had completely misread Hirohito's Rescript—that the second stage of her Hundred Years War was to be fought not on battlefields but on the factory floor.

The question then became, could she beat the West at its own industrial game? And if she could, with how great a victory would she be satisfied? Or would she demand, as the West had demanded of her, nothing less than unconditional surrender?

There were too many stories, none of them denied by the Japanese who claimed that those who surrendered were so dishonoured as to be fortunate when they were subsequently put to death. That, they explained was bushido. We were to hear a lot about the code of bushido in the next three and a half years, but were never, to our host's disgust, to be converted, difficult though it was to dispute the sincerity of those who preached it. None of them had surrendered to us; and their wounded had even chosen to kill themselves rather than delay their comrades' advance.

It was to come as something of a shock, four decades later, when Wastaru Tajitsu—perched like an ancient child on one of Mitsubishi's huge armchairs—told me that Japan had vanquished the world in the trade war of the 1960s to the 1980s by running its industries 'in accordance with the rules of bushido'.

I had instant visions of captains of Mitsubishi vessels committing seppuki because they had docked late, of Mitsubishi pilots turned kamikazes and crashing their Mitsubishi freight planes on to the decks of rival tankers, of Mitsubishi employees by the thousand hurling themselves to their death off the summit of Fujiyama because Mitsubishi annual profits had grown by only five per cent instead of the stipulated six.

'You know my history, don't you?' I at once asked Mr. Tajitsu. He waited for me to elaborate. 'I surrendered to the Japanese Army in Malaya,' I told him.

'Very sorry,' he said—which, from the polite mouth of a Japanese, means 'Too bad'. But he seemed in no way shocked. 'Before the war,' he explained, 'if the

President of one of Mitsubishi's companies found it was not doing well, he would resign. Immediately after the war, that Mitsubishi spirit saw a decline; but now it's in the ascendant again.'

As the world switched from electricity stations powered by coal to stations powered mainly by oil, and the industry's demand for power increased, Britain fell farther and farther behind. By 1965 Japan was producing three and a half million tons of shipping a year (which included the first 150,000 ton tanker) and had cornered 31% of the world's shipbuilding orders.

In 1966 her output was almost seventeen million tons (including tankers of 209,000 tons). She had raised her share of the world's total orders to 40% (including six vessels of 276,000 tons) and could afford to gaze complacently back at Britain, Sweden and Germany, who had produced only three million tons between them.

From 1967 (when she cut the time she needed to build a 100,000 ton tanker from seven months to less than five) she consistently built 40% or more of the ships launched throughout the world in any one year. At various times new rivals, like Sweden or Brazil, would emerge; but only briefly. In 1971, she collected orders for no less than 1061 vessels—mainly tankers, containers and bulk carriers—and her rivals were left gasping. By 1978 her lead over Russia, Britain and Brazil, both in output and orders, was massive. It remains unassailable; and her rivals are bankrupt.

In the motor industry her success has been more phenomenal both because she entered the race late and because she challenged not only America but Britain and Europe as well. In 1962 she was not even listed as one of the world's eight leading producers of automobiles. Significantly, however, she was already seventh among the world's *exporters* of cars and commercial vehicles—with 16,000 of the former and 33,000 of the latter.

But as a manufacturer of motor cycles, Honda (the nattily dressed commoner who believes he owes everything to Japan's defeat and MacArthur's purge of the Zaibatsu) startled the world by producing more than a million motor cycles in 1962, and increasing his exports by 117% over 1961. Supported by his Japanese rivals in the industry, he had made his country the world's largest producer of two-wheeled vehicles.

It was in the field of four-wheeled vehicles that their real ambition lay, however; and one after the other Japanese firms began to manufacture them, each confident that it could outsell the other in a suddenly car-conscious and more affluent domestic market.

Able to pick and choose, the Japanese consumer imposed upon these rival manufacturers much higher standards than would otherwise have been provided; and when the domestic market became saturated, these same rivals had either to export their surplus production or go bankrupt. For the rest of the world's car makers the effect of this was to be deadly. Most of *them* went bankrupt.

In 1963, Japan produced a mere 407,000 motor cars and 875,000 commercial vehicles, and exported about 10% of each. Britain exported about ten times as many of both, and America manufactured about fifteen times as many.

The story of the succeeding eighteen years is more succinctly told by combining and approximating the total output of both cars and commercial vehicles. It makes sombre reading—unless one is Japanese.

From two million vehicles in 1968 (which exceeded Britain's output, but was a million less than Germany's, and seven million less than America's) Japan's production leapt to six and a half million in 1974 (not to mention six million motor cycles) and America, now less than two million in the lead, and her sales falling, had become anxious.

'Workers will find true happiness through work, for work will always be the basis of society,' says a slogan pasted on a Toyota factory wall.

'Work together to serve the company and the state with diligence and a strong spirit,' is the motto of Yamaha. Japanese production and sales, unlike America's, increased in the ensuing twelve months.

In November of 1981, as the Japanese produced more than eleven million vehicles, and the United States output had declined even further, the Americans sullenly admitted defeat. Despite the fact that Japan had voluntarily curbed her exports to all her foreign competitors (especially America), that France and Italy were refusing to move her cars from their docks to the sale rooms, that Britain was exhorting its people to 'Buy British', not one of them had escaped a mauling. But at the very moment when all of them were finding it impossible to sell sufficient of their products to their own people, the Japanese were opening up factories, or launching joint projects, in one enemy camp after the other, and succeeding.

Morals were invented by the Chinese because they were an immoral people', wrote the Shintoist philosopher Motoori two centuries ago. 'In Japan there was no need for any moral code,' because, to live a moral life, a man needed, 'only to consult his heart.'

His heart, however, was governed by his innumerable obligations—to his Emperor, his Lord, his master, his village, his group, his parents, his family—and to fail in any one of them was to offend so unpardonably that only death could exonerate him.

'If Japan were to behave again as she behaved in the past,' Shigemitsu warned his compatriots in 1960, 'her victory will turn to ashes once more.' Obviously he regarded that victory as inevitable; and patently Japan has achieved it without inflicting economic atrocities on her rivals.

Just as Japan opened up a world-wide network of spies in 1934 (to prepare for military conquest) so—since 1960—has a network of salesmen, trading companies and tourists provided her with a ceaseless flow of world-wide up-to-date data for her economic conquests.

Expert as she was, during World War II, at infiltration, she has contrived both to prevent foreigners from infiltrating her present industrial base and to seize beach-heads in almost any foreign market she chose, so desperate has been each host nation's need to find jobs for its millions of unemployed.

Miyoshi, the diplomat of the Keidanren, hurriedly glosses over this bushido anathema. 'It is our national tradition to worship perfection,' he reminds. 'It is a reverence we inherit from our ancestors, whether they were samurai or commoners. And after the war we combined that perfectionist spirit with the spirit of competition, and spread it over a much wider field of industry than we had ever done before.

'Absolute equality between either individuals or trading nations is, of course, impossible. One cannot change a people's genes or biological structure. But we Japanese are as egalitarian as the biological and genetic facts permit—and you can see the virtues of that egalitarianism in all our factories.'

'Also,' Hiraizumi concurred, 'we do not consume so much as other nations. We are *savers* of money—the highest by far in the world—and the extra power of those savings is being lent by banks to industry, which translates it into the extra power of our exports.

'Our life style is frugal. The Japanese were born poor, and they think poor. They don't, and won't, spend unnecessarily.

'Our whole infra-structure of roads, railways, factories and so on is based on plans and instructions taken from imported books.

'We have been, and still are, the biggest importers of books in the history of the literate world; and one of the main reasons why we are so successful in industry, and the West so unsuccessful, is that the West's labour force is simply not literate enough to be taught the required technology.'

No one in any industry is unaware of the methods the Japanese have employed. Everyone can reel them off: high productivity, constant automation and heavy investment. Plus their work ethic, minus our labour disputes. Toyota, they tell you, had its last strike more than a dozen years ago.

'But we're too civilized to have a work ethic like theirs,' I was assured. 'And the day I have to come in here, bow to the manager and recite the company prayer, this lot can say goodbye to me.'

It is also pointed out that the materials out of which cars are made (despite the fact that they have to be imported raw, and then reprocessed) are cheaper in Japan than they are in Europe. Nor does Western management deny that its labour force is worse trained, less educated, less versatile, three to six times larger, and less conscientious than Japan's. And only the labour force has yet to be convinced that, in any industry that finds itself competing with the Japanese, the guiding principle must be, '*Fewer* jobs, or *no* jobs'.

Compare that with Matsushita's nostrum, 'A firm will soon lose its vitality if it fails to provide its employees with dreams.' Or his advice to statesmen: 'To inspire its people and instil optimism, it is government's task to promote strong ideals and prospect of grandeur.'

No one in Western management denies that the Japanese have harnessed productivity to a daily continuity of supplies, which we have not; and that components are delivered from one factory to the assembly line of another as often as three times a day over distances of twenty kilometres or more, which we would not dare to do.

No one in Western management denies that a change-over of dies which takes our skilled workers three to four hours is performed by Japanese skilled workers in five to six minutes.

No one in Japanese management denies that to depend on supplies of components arriving daily at the assembly line, or thrice daily, makes them vulnerable to strikes in the factory manufacturing the components; but all Japanese managers know that such strikes will not happen—because the company's profits would suffer if they did; and when the company's profits suffer so does the worker's twice yearly, very substantial bonus.

When asked the secret of their non-strike record, Toyota reply with a typically Japanese parable. 'Three hundred years ago,' they say, 'if a bird would not sing, one killed it. Realizing that this hardly remedied our songless situation, we switched to a second policy: if the bird would not sing, we made it. But today, if a bird won't sing, we wait a while.'

'What does it mean?' a British marketing expert asked me. I told him that it meant that three hundred years ago, if a man wouldn't do what his master wanted him to do, his master chopped off his head. Later, if a man won't do what his employer wants him to do, the employer waits for a consensus.

'Seems ludicrous to me,' he commented.

All say, 'We must improve our productivity and, at the same time, cut down on our work force, or we won't survive.'

But none say, 'As well as improving our productivity, and reducing our work force, we must aspire to a work ethic like theirs.' A work ethic like theirs, say the British, is not only unattainable, it is even, in some indefinable way, undesirable. Yet in reality (as has been proved by a number of Japanese-owned, locally manned factories in the United Kingdom, America and Europe) it involves no greater sacrifice than membership of a house union and the willingness, having changed a die in five minutes instead of four hours, to man another machine rather than stand idle, or even to sweep the floor.

Furthermore, the West should abandon the American premise that, 'They like us'. Except that they believe us to be in a state of decline, and that some of them still harbour an understandable longing for revenge, they have no feeling for 'us' of any kind. To the Japanese, the West is merely an agglomeration of customers.

Malaysia in 1982 blatantly obstructed every British attempt to win contracts anywhere in her federation of sultanates—and awarded most of them to Japanese companies instead; and the Philippines' Foreign Minister openly berated Britain's Foreign Secretary for staying at the British Embassy during a 1982 conference instead of a government Rest House.

In the world of the twenty-first century, as the Ibukas and Matsushitas and Hondas of Japan see it, there will be only a small part for the West to play. Should Tojo's envisaged war between Russia and America come to pass, Japan plans to stand aside from it, convinced that there will be nothing left of either once it is over. Should it not come to pass, Asia's thousands of millions, fully 'electronified', importing from and exporting to one another, powered and motivated by Japan, and protected from Russia by China, will be rich beyond all imagining—and the West will buy from them whatever it can afford, and work for them in *their* European and American factories.

At the moment that is no more than a Japanese scenario—as was General Taro's plan to capture South East Asia in 1900. At least, though, they have a scenario: the West has only science fiction. For Europe and America, the alternatives are either a second industrial revolution, based on a new technology which it will refuse to sell to Japan, or conversion to the Japanese spirit of industry, so that an exports war can be waged, as the Battle of Midway was waged, on almost equal terms. Neither, as yet, is even, as Matsushita would put it, a dream.

Let it not be imagined, however, that the Japanese are content merely to dream. Already they have bred a better nourished and healthier generation of five to twenty-year-olds whose IQ, according to Professor Richard Lynn of Ulster's New University, is significantly higher than that of the same generation in America, Britain, France and other industrial countries.

Already, as Professor Edward Feigenbaum of Stanford University, California, warned a London conference on computers in July 1982, they have bred a new and privileged generation of computer programmers, dubbed 'knowledge engineers'.

Already they have announced to the world that their government has set aside £200 million, and that Japanese industry will contribute £600 million, to expedite the construction by these knowledge engineers of a fifth generation of computers that will be more intelligent than people—that will be able to see, hear, talk and think. Such a fifth generation, which the Japanese promise will be on the market within fifteen years, will sweep much of the West's high technology into oblivion. It will result, Professor Feigenbaum said in 'an electronic Pearl Harbour'; and the loss of face that would ensue from a failure to fulfil their promise means that the Japanese are confident of their ability—indeed are obliged—to launch just such an electronic onslaught upon all their rivals before the end of the twentieth century.

It is to be hoped that America's magnanimity to her in 1945 has convinced her that such a virtue exists. It is also to be feared that America's inability to compete with the beneficiary of *her* post-war magnanimity will have convinced the Japanese that it is a virtue that yields no dividends.

'We will be able to use our own computer-ware to change the world,' promised Mr. Ibuka of Sony. And added, 'Once our techniques are completed, we will transfer them to less developed countries.'

Among those less developed countries, Mr. Matsushita foretold, will be America and all the nations of Western Europe—between whom they will be able to pick and choose.

This they are already doing. Britain hoped desperately that the Nissan Motor Company would set up a plant in the United Kingdom to produce cars and provide jobs. But: 'There is strong opinion within our company,' Nissan's President Takashi Ishihara announced on 2 July 1982, 'that the project is very risky. We cannot push a project for which we cannot obtain consensus.'

'We must decide *now* how best we can help other nations redress their problems,' Mr. Honda insisted for the benefit of Western ears. But was his insistence genuine? 'I am pleased to find that you are in general keeping discipline and working diligently,' Colonel Nakamura politely congratulated the Allied prisoners of war who built the railway through Thailand as badly as possible while they died of starvation, disease and brutality. 'At the same time,' he added, 'regret to find seriousness in health matter . . . due mainly to the fact for absence of such firm belief as, "Japanese health follows will" and "Cease only when the enemy annihilated".'

That was as close as he could bring himself to saying that we had lost, we were wrong and we deserved every misfortune then befalling us. In victory again today, Japanese health continues to follow will; but this time *our* seriousness in health matters is the result not of their brutality but of our lack of will. What remains to be seen is whether, this time, Japan will cease only when her one-time enemies, real and prospective, are annihilated. I am not convinced that they will so cease because I am not convinced that they can. I am not even convinced that they should, because they have earned the right to a total victory. I simply hope that they will look into their hearts and decide—by consensus, of course—that they must.

That, though, will depend on tomorrow's Japanese than today's: upon those like the eleven hundred students who graduated from the Soka University in March 1982 and were exhorted by their Honorary President, Daisaku Ikeda, 'The world you are about to enter is not an easy one. In order to become victorious in life, you must be healthy, you must have tenacity and a persevering spirit, and you must have the will-power not to succumb to hardship.'

Extracts from 'The Japanese Mind' by Robert C. Christopher

Robert C. Christopher, Administrator of the Pulitzer Prizes, one time editor of 'Time', 'Newsweek' and 'Newsweek International' has written a most enlightening book, ***The Japanese Mind****. I have only been granted permission to use a limited number of words, so I have selected the following:*

When her children misbehave or disappoint her in any way, the typical Japanese mother does not get angry and shout. She forgives—and by making her children feel guilty about letting her down gains the psychological upper hand.

I have heard it argued by Japanese that relations between their country and the

United States are still heavily colored by Japan's national sense of guilt over the unexpectedly benevolent treatment it received from the United States following World War II.

In a survey which Tokyo's Nikko Research Center conducted among Japanese companies with US operations, 65 per cent of the respondents said that productivity in their American plants was lower than in their Japanese plants. And without exception they blamed that fact in large part on the inferior education and job skills of American workers.

It has become almost second nature to me not to extend any significant courtesy to a Japanese without first reckoning what kind of obligation it is likely to impose upon him . . .

Over-insistence on the unique nature of Japanese culture can lead to self-delusion: one of the reasons that Japan's World War II leaders never faced up to the rather obvious fact that the United States was reading their military and diplomatic codes lay in their unwarranted assumption that the Japanese language in itself constituted a code that very few *gaijin* were capable of penetrating.

. . . direct Japanese investment abroad, which amounted to barely $2 billion as late as 1968, had soared to more than $36 billion by 1980. This, however, has to be put in perspective: US direct investment abroad as of 1980 was nearly ten times the Japanese figure, and even Britain, with an economy considerably smaller than Japan's, had roughly twice as much invested overseas.

Japanese industry, in short, is still far from being truly multinational, and it seems clear that it will be hobbled in its efforts to become so as long as most Japanese corporations continue to be as culture-bound as they now are. Thus, the reluctance of Japanese management to deal with anything but co-operative Japanese-style trade unions has been a major inhibition to the establishment of US plants by the Japanese steel and auto industries. Similarly, insistence upon staffing middle management posts in the United States exclusively with Japanese males has created legal problems for the US subsidiaries of two big Japanese trading companies. Perhaps most crippling of all, however, is the fact that few if any Japanese companies are psychologically capable of granting foreigners, even foreigners fluent in Japanese, full-fledged membership in their top management councils. This inevitably makes it difficult for them to recruit outstanding local nationals to run their overseas operations—a practice which the best-run US multinationals long ago concluded constitutes the only formula for successful long-term operation abroad.

. . . there are now a significant number of young Japanese who not only have acquired first-hand familiarity with a foreign society but actively enjoyed that experience and, as a result, find the traditional restrictiveness of their own society a bit ridiculous and embarrasing.

That Japanese have in the past committed acts of unspeakable awfulness is a simple fact: besides such horrors as the Rape of Nanking and the Philippine Death March, there is a long, ugly roll call of less well-known atrocities, including the infamous medical experiments carried out upon prisoners of war by Japanese Army doctors in China. At the same time, it is difficult to think of many nations, large or small, whose citizens have not been guilty of indefensible cruelties within reasonably recent history. Frenchmen in Algeria, Americans in Vietnam, Russians in half a dozen countries including their own, Hindus and Moslems in the Indian sub-continent—all these and too many other 'civilized' people to list have shown themselves capable of barbarity on a massive scale. And while comparisons are even more odious in this connection than in most others, no excess ever committed by Japanese rivals what Germans did in the Holocaust. Nor is there any real parallel in contemporary Japanese society to the random violence and savagery now so prevalent in the great cities of the United States. But to say that there is nothing in the nature of social conditioning of Japanese that renders them as individuals any more predisposed to cruelty than other peoples does not totally dispose of the problems raised by Japan's behaviour as a nation before and during World War II. All imperialisms are brutal, but Japanese imperialism in its heyday was markedly so. To my mind, the most convincing explanation for this fact is that group orientation, latent xenophobia and the concept of morality as relative rather than absolute all conspired to make it comparatively easy for Japanese to be mobilized for ventures in which violence and brutality were presented as means to a glorious end.

The course taken by Japan in the aftermath of World War II was an extraordinary one for a proud nation to adopt: as a people, the Japanese quite consciously decided to restructure their society, modelling it as closely as practicable upon that of the United States. At bottom, the collective reasoning of the Japanese was very straightforward: because the United States had so clearly established itself as the world's strongest power, it followed that American practices and institutions must be superior to any others. Up till now, that reasoning, however simplistic it may appear, has paid off handsomely for Japan. But only if it continues to pay off will there be solid reason to hope that the first and infinitely more desirable of my two broad scenarios concerning Japan's future will become reality. It cannot be overstressed that there is one indispensable precondition to Japan's continued stability—and that is for the United States itself to maintain a healthy economy and enough national power and resolution to defend both its own vital interests and those of its principal allies.

From AB Walter Powell, Australia

I am still interested in all matters Naval and try to visit any visiting British ships which happen to call here. I did get a good look at *Invincible* when she was here. In Port Kembla I was rather disgusted, when I visited a British frigate, I couldn't resist telling the Quartermaster that I was once in the RN. He asked me what ship I was on, and when I said *Indefatigable*, he replied 'Never 'eard of it mate'!

Article from the Camden New Journal, dated 7th September 1989

HOME OF THE BRAVE

The battle ensign of a famous British aircraft carrier in the last war, HMS *Indefatigable*, was officially given a home in a Holborn church on Sunday.

At the 'Laying-up' ceremony at St. Giles-in-the-Fields Church in St. Giles High Street, were survivors of the ship which was adopted by the old Holborn Council in 1943. The mayor of Camden, Barbara Hughes, who wore the Holborn chain for the unique occasion, also attended.

From 1946 the ship's ensign was displayed in the Holborn Town Hall where it fell into disrepair until Camden took control of the borough and restored the flag at a cost of £300. Now, the ensign officially belongs to St. Giles-in-the-Fields Church.

A veteran of the ship, Stuart Eadon and writer of the book **Sakishima**, which tells the story of the 'floating fortress', commented: 'Seafarers can look upon the church as a focal point to pay tributes to dead shipmates.'

Built in 1941 the 36,000 ton *Indefatigable* 'patrolled the North Atlantic' *(Incorrect. She took part in the* Tirpitz *strikes and was in the Arctic as far north as Bear Island.—Ed.)* before eventually joining the American Fleet at the Pacific island of Okinawa. It was there that it made history by becoming the first British ship to be hit by a Japanese kamikaze plane. Fortunately, its revolutionary new armoured flight deck allowed the ship to function as normal within an hour.

On August 15 1945 the *Indefatigable* became the last ship in the Royal Navy to be attacked in the war.

'In the Newspapers'—September 1990

Mr. Takashi Ishihara, Chairman of Nissan, has received the same accolade as Bob Geldof and Ronald Reagan. He has been made an Honorary Knight for his contribution to economic relations between the United Kingdom and Japan, which includes the building of a car factory in Tyne and Wear.

This news reminded me of an ex-sailor who, while out driving with his wife, was overtaken by a dangerous young driver as they approached a bend. 'Gosh,' said his wife, 'he's driving dangerously. What sort of car is that?' 'It's a Mitsubishi,' replied Jack. 'We used to shoot 'em down during the war.'

From 'A Portrait of Japan', by Laurens van der Post

Since 1945 when it was a heap of rubble, Nagoya has performed the miracle of resurrection twice in a few years—in 1959 it was wrecked again by typhoon and flood . . . I have been alarmed by the tendency of the human being to form a mass impression of a foreign country and then to fit its individuals into a collective abstract, which is at best wildly approximate and as a rule wholly unreal. . . .

Haiku (a form of poetry in brief verse)

e.g. I thought I saw the fallen flower
Returning to its branch
Only to find it was a butterfly.

'Fore 'n Aft', the official publication of the Honolulu Council, US Navy League, carried a large photograph of HMS *Indefatigable* on the front cover of the October issue and an article

HMS *Indefatigable* Remembered
by Geoffrey G. Patterson

Each year on Veterans Day the Hawaii Chapters of Disabled American Veterans, known commonly as DAV, organize the Annual Massing of the Colors Ceremony at the Punchbowl Cemetery of the Pacific. DAV is a national organization of wartime disabled veterans that is funded entirely from dues and contributions. The total membership here in Hawaii stands at over four thousand veterans belonging to several chapters that represent all the major islands. Its members include veterans from both the World Wars, the Korean and Vietnam conflicts with about one third of the present members being disabled Vietnam veterans.

The Hawaii Branch of DAV, through its Commander James R. Mitchell, has this year invited the *Indefatigable* Association to be the first British Ships Organization to be included in the traditional Massing of the colours Ceremony to be held at Punchbowl Cemetery on November Eleventh. The total number of former *Indefatigable* shipmates and their wives visiting Honolulu is expected to number about fifty people who will be coming from the United Kingdom and Australia. Hospitality is also being extended to them through R. H. Brady, public affairs officer to Admiral Chadwick who has arranged a guided tour of the Pearl Harbor Naval Base on November 14th.

The visitors will be led by Gerry Purnell, secretary and treasurer of the *Indefatigable* Association and the driving force behind the visit. The one day's journey from England to the Pacific is a far cry from the two months it took the fleet to travel twenty-five thousand miles in 1945 in ships that were not designed for tropical climates.

Although most reference books continue to refer to *Implacable* and

Indefatigable as ships of the third group of the earlier *Illustrious* class they were in fact a greatly improved and modified design that generated greater speed and could accommodate up to eighty aircraft compared to fifty-six in their predecessors.

Indefatigable was laid down at the famed John Brown shipyard on Clydebank, Scotland in November 1939. Due to wartime delays that included bombing raids and the diversion of materials to ships of higher priority she was not launched until nearly three years later and was finally completed in May 1944 nearly five years after the laying of her keel.

In a personal letter, written recently to the *Indefatigable* Association the Duke of Edinburgh recollected the carrier with the following: 'I feel I have a rather special connection with *Indefatigable*. She was launched by my Grandmother. I was serving in the British Pacific Fleet at the same time and I was watching from the bridge when she was hit by the kamikaze. Our USN Liaison Officer was sure she was done for and could hardly believe his eyes when the part of the watch appeared on the flight deck and swept the remains over the side.'

The most significant Japanese reaction to the assault on Okinawa was demonstrated by the ferocity of the famed kamikaze suicide planes which rained down continuously on the Allied ships. Aircraft carriers, because of their size and direct threat to the Japanese homeland, became favourite targets.

Her first baptism in active combat took place in July and August 1944 when together with three other carriers, her Barracuda bombers attacked the German battleship *Tirpitz* which had been holed up in a Norwegian fiord making repairs from an earlier air raid in the spring. She was still considered a serious threat to the Arctic convoys and her destruction was a major priority. Unfortunately because of the combination of bad weather and effective German smokescreens the operation was not a success and the task was transferred to the heavy bombers of the Royal Air Force. In November an attack was made with Lancaster bombers which scored several hits with twelve thousand pound bombs causing the great ship to capsize and sink with nearly one thousand crew trapped inside.

The main advantage the British carriers held over their American counterparts was the use of steel rather than wooden decks. The naval architects of the United States had long favoured the traditional wooden deck mainly because of a saving in weight, whereas the designers of the British flattops had opted for steel decks. Samuel Eliot Morrison, in his epic book 'The Two Ocean War', emphasized the difference when he stated in part . . . 'A Kamikaze crashing a steel flattop crumpled up like a scrambled egg, and did no damage beyond its immediate vicinity; but a Kamikaze crashing onto an American wooden deck started serious fires and its bombs penetrated the ship's interior.'

The advantage gained by the British carriers' steel decks was offset by the need to refuel more often than their American counterparts. This fact was brought to light at the Big Three summit meeting in Quebec in September 1944.

With the war in Europe moving towards a total victory for the Allies, the British military leaders were anxious to play a major role in the final assault on Japan. Up until that time the Pacific operation had been largely an American effort with strong support from Australia and New Zealand.

But Admiral King strongly resisted the proposals for the Royal Navy to join the action in the Central Pacific, preferring that mopping up exercises in Japan's fast disintegrating empire to the south would be a more appropriate assignment. King's objections were not so much a question of being anti-British but rather a matter of logistics. His reasoning focussed on the fact that the British ships were not at that time capable of refuelling at sea and would therefore have to withdraw from the battlezone from time to time to reprovision and make necessary repairs. The American Navy on the other hand had developed an efficient auxiliary fleet that was able to provide the fighting units with everything they needed in the way of fuel, spare parts and minor repairs while staying at sea.

It was President Roosevelt, long renowned for his reputation of fostering good Anglo-American relations, who overruled Admiral King and paved the way for the Royal Navy to play a major role in supporting the Okinawa campaign and launching subsequent attacks on the Japanese homeland. Finally the details were agreed upon and Task Force 57 was formed and proceeded to Sydney, Australia for final tuning up and exercises. It was an impressive array of ships led by the battleships *King George The Fifth* and *Howe*, the carriers *Indomitable, Victorious, Illustrious* and *Indefatigable*, together with five cruisers, eleven destroyers and an assorted group of escort and supply ships.

The British task force was under the command of Admiral Rawlings who received a warm greeting from Admiral Nimitz which read: 'The British Carrier Task Force and attached units will greatly increase our striking power and demonstrate our unity of purpose against Japan. The United States Pacific Fleet welcomes you.' Several days later Rawlings reported to Admiral Spruance, commander of the American Fifth Fleet, that his ships were ready for active duty, and received the reply 'Welcome Task Force Fifty Seven and Good Hunting.'

Following several attacks on Japanese oil fields in Sumatra in early 1945 the air squadrons of *Indefatigable* were now poised for the final assault and ready to give support to their allies in the invasion of Okinawa.

The Okinawa expedition became a mammoth display of sea and air power. Admiral Spruance had more than twelve hundred ships under his command, and the British contingent, although small in number, played a vital role in the fierce fighting that took place in March and April 1945.

It was in April that *Indefatigable* took her first hit from a kamikaze, killing or wounding thirty men while leaving the flightdeck, sickbay and briefing room in a shambles. Within one hour the ship was again operational and able to receive her returning aircraft. *Victorious* was hit by a suicide plane later that day and five days later *Illustrious* was the victim. The planes from the British carriers continued to attack enemy airfields in Formosa and the Sakishima Islands.

Following two weeks of repair and replenishment in Leyte in late April the fleet was back among the Sakishima Islands by May 4th and ready to renew the attacks on the enemy. This second spell of service saw considerable damage to *Indomitable, Formidable* and *Victorious* but they continued to operate, although not at full capacity, until May 25th when the second tour of duty ended. As the British ships turned away and headed for Australia Admiral Spruance signalled to Admiral Rawlings: 'I would express to you, to your officers and men, after two months operations as a Fifth Fleet Task Force, my appreciation of your fine work and co-operative spirit. Task Force Fifty Seven has mirrored the great traditions of the Royal Navy to the American Task Forces.'

After spending a month in Sydney the British ships joined up with Admiral 'Bull' Halsey's Third Fleet for the final assault on Japan. And finally the battle was won and there were accolades from the highest brass of Britain and America.

The earlier doubts in the minds of some Americans as to whether the British Fleet had the ability to operate in Pacific waters had long been dispelled. Perhaps the most visible hero in the minds of the British sailors was Admiral Sir Philip Vian. Admiral Rawlings noted in his diaries that the achievements of the carriers 'derived directly from the sustained determination and leadership of Admiral Vian himself, for to him fell the conduct and handling of the fleet during its most active periods.'

Most of the British ships sailed south to Australia in late August but the Battleship *KG 5* and *Indefatigable* remained in Tokyo Bay for the surrender ceremonies. On Sunday September 2nd at Morning Colors on USS *Missouri* the flag that had flown above the Capitol in Washington on December 7th, 1941 was raised to the great battleship's flagstaff; a fitting symbol in the final act of a bitter struggle that had lasted for nearly five years.

On November 11th this year the same flag that flew nearby that day on HMS *Indefatigable* will be present along with some of her surviving shipmates at the Annual Massing of the Colors Ceremony at Punchbowl. And perhaps, to complete the picture, the USS *Missouri* just might be making one of her regular visits to Pearl Harbor. The sight of her, still vibrant and battle-ready after all those years, would indeed be a moving experience for the men of *Indefatigable* who have come half way around the world to pay their respects to their fallen comrades in that long ago war in the Pacific."

So the BPF was truly remembered and honoured by our American Cousins—news which will lift many a stout heart on this side of the Atlantic and in Southern Waters!

From Jack Hibberd re 'Pilgrimage' made by members of *Indefatigable* Association to Punchbowl Pacific Memorial, Honolulu

This took place on November 11th 1989 at the invitation of the Disabled American Veterans of Hawaii on what they call 'Veterans Day', it seemed very appropriate to us that it was our 'Remembrance Day'.

Our journey there and return was a catalogue of disasters but we didn't let that spoil the occasion for us. We were made most welcome by our American friends and by the brothers of one of our members. Geoffrey Paterson, brother to James Paterson paved the way for us, he has lived in Honolulu for many years and is a successful architect. He arranged a reception on the Friday after we arrived which allowed us to mingle with many who were to become good friends. On Saturday Gerry Purnell and I, as standard bearers, arrived early at the cemetery and met more who were to take part, in a truly impressive, shallow volcanic crater which had been transformed into the last resting place for ex-servicemen and their kin.

The ceremony which lasted quite some time, took place at the base of a long flight of steps leading up to the memorial colonnade at the top. At the start of the ceremony, the people were informed that we were attending from UK and Australia and we had to stand to be seen. Honolulu Police Pipe Band played marches etc. and the US Navy band played the hymns and anthems, American and British.

There was a 'missing man' formation of jet fighters which flew over right on time, one peeling off and leaving the rest. There were many observers and TV and Press reps who reported locally the next day. After we were bussed to the DAV Club House where we were 'fed and watered' and plaques were presented to them, one from our Association and another from the Ex Services Club, Southampton. A beautiful turned and ascribed wooden bowl was in return presented to Gerry for our Association.

On the Tuesday we were taken to Pearl Harbour Naval yard and in the office of Admiral Chadwick we were received by Capt. Webster who graciously received a plaque from the Association presented by Gerry Purnell and also a plaque from the Burma Star Association from myself. In return the Association received mounted pictures of Pearl Harbour. After a guided tour of the Naval Base and lunch we went to the *Arizona* Memorial. We were taken across by US Navy launch to the structure spanning the sunken remains of the ship sunk by the Japanese on the Sunday of the first day of the war for the United States.

The outlines of the ship are still visible and occasional spots of oil break the surface, coming from the grave of 1177 US Seamen from the Admiral down, their names are carved on marble tables above them.

The days not spent with our American hosts were taken up with sight seeing and one evening a mini re-union at our hotel in Honolulu. There was much to see and a round trip by coach of the Island took a whole day and was most enjoyable. I think the thing I missed most was a decent pint of beer! However

11th November 1989. Jack Hibberd, HMS Indefatigable, *Standard Bearer, represents the ship and the BPF at the National memorial Cemetery of the Pacific. Photo: J. Hibberd*

we made do as we always have.

On the last Saturday we again went to the DAV clubhouse and were entertained by them to food and drinks, also some impromptu entertainment. In return some of us performed for them and they seemed to enjoy it. Altogether a trip to remember, making good friends and meeting old comrades. I can't remember a single sour note in the whole trip, excepting of course the journey there and return, but that's an unfinished story!

PO Electrical Artificer Les Bancroft wrote to me from Bomaderry, NSW recently about his visit to The Punchbowl Cemetery of the Pacific 11 Nov. 1989. Part of his letter said

For Chris and I it was terrific. We had a fantastic time in a fabulous setting. Admittedly we had some problems, mobility being difficult on crutches for short distances but we found that wheelchairs were available at most places for longer distances—even in Pearl Harbour when visiting the *Arizona* memorial, the *Arizona* being one of the US Battleships sunk during the Pearl Harbour attack 7th December 1941 by the Japanese. The US authorities have made the *Arizona* the central memorial as the ship suffered the most casualties, 1100 ship's company being entombed in the sunken battleship. For the boat trip and memorial I travelled in a wheelchair loaned by the US Navy. At one stage when about to ascend the dozen steps inside the memorial I did say, 'Look, they are wide steps, I can manage on my crutches.' The prompt answer from our burly US navy guide and from a delicious coloured female US Navy Officer was, 'Stay in that wheelchair. Do as you are told, we are looking after you.' Said with smiles of course, but I just had to reply 'Yes Sir, Yes Madam' and then sit quietly as the wheelchair and I were taken up the steps by a rail mounted electric platform—in a memorial would you believe? The Americans think of everything. We had a wonderful and very emotionally moving day.

I quote a further passage from his letter

There are now 120 million Japanese occupying a very small and apparently highly polluted, Fatherland. They could, and eventually must, want to expand if their population continues its present rapid growth. Therein lies the problem, expand to where? World domination, no, but surrounding areas aggressive expansion, well? Especially if the US considered it was not in their interest to stop them. No one else would—they would leave China alone, the mineral and oil wealth plus land for expansion is to the south. I am conscious that last year, Japan became the world's 3rd largest spender on defence behind Russia and the USA and they wanted to start building aircraft carriers! The US said 'No', but, a few years back the US initially said 'No' to Japan building submarines. They now have 22—30 plus hundreds of planes and tanks and destroyers—all for defence? I'm philosophising Stuart, but it all makes one think. Japan could now be in a similar position to Germany in the 1930s. It would only require a military leader like Hitler to come forward and take over and then, who knows? Enough, the future is not ours to see, but unfortunately, history damned well keeps repeating itself.

(This letter made me think. After all, every Empire there has ever been, has been built on aggression and many atrocities—including The British Empire. So where does the answer lie?—Ed.)

Also from Les Bancroft, an article from The Week End Australian Review, dated 4th August 1990 by Phillip Adams, which concludes

I have lost count of the times I've circumnavigated the globe and of the countries I've visited. But nowhere do I feel as foreign as in Japan. For all the familiarity of the gadgety and brand names, for all the refinement of their culture, they seem to me the truly inscrutable orientals.

I don't have that feeling in China where, within a few days, the teeming millions begin to emerge as individual, idiosyncratic human beings. But Japan still remains, to me, an unfathomable mystery.

Koestler's point about 'face' versus 'guilt' addresses a part of it. It begins to explain why a people whose arts are so subtle, refined and delicate can suddenly be so savage, so brutal. But paradoxes abound. On the one hand, the Japanese decided that Hirohito was some sort of God but on the other they remain curiously agnostic. While they embrace just about everything the West had to offer they remain deeply unimpressed with Christianity, thus escaping the burden of guilt. But even their own indigenous religions, Buddhism and Shinto, are superficially embraced. They'll swap from one religion to another, depending on its suitability for a given ceremony. How does it go? Buddhism for birth and Shinto for funerals? The only thing they borrow from Christianity is the white dress for the wedding.

Another paradox is the way in which the Japanese are both writing history and rewriting it. They have a firm grip on the agenda for the future while, at the same time, they continue to print school texts that conveniently forget innumerable wartime atrocities. In recent years the world (and in particular China and Korea) has been demanding that the Japanese face the facts of the past and stop obscuring them with cherry blossom and colour tellies.

As well as telling their students the truth in history classes, it's time for them to learn that they very nearly had an A-bomb 'made in Japan'.

Extract from The South China Morning Post and the Hong Kong Telegraph, Monday September 17, 1945

The Atomic Bomb
How the Allies Won the War
Before Time
CENSORED NORWAY STORY

Discussions about how the war was won will occupy many an hour in the lives of ex-soldiers during the years to come, says 'Maptalk'. Arguments and claims will be hurled in all directions. But when one considers the terrible implications of the atomic bomb, it may well be that the decisive, critical action was an unheralded feat such as the one that came to light in a press release recently.

Except for a daring raid by four Norwegian youths through a wall of swirling snow, New York and London instead of Hiroshima and Nagasaki, might have been pulverized by atomic bombs, and Hitler might have been strutting in Washington.

Three years ago intrepid Norwegian partisans learned that the Germans were using a factory in Rhukan to produce 'heavy water'. A Norwegian chemical engineer who had worked in the captured factory, guessed that the 'heavy water' was being used for research on the atom, and his suspicions were confirmed by friends inside the plant.

Relaying their story to England, the Norwegians were dropped by parachute from a plane by the alarmed British in October, 1942. But it was four months before a wind 'so strong that it blew trains off their rails', let up long enough to permit them to blow up the plant. It took the Nazis nine months to rebuild it. And this time a force of American bombers swept in between the canyoned mountains to wreck the factory.

Fortunately no such sabotage hampered the Anglo-American researches on the atomic bombs.

The story was suppressed by the censorship which cloaked all research on the atomic bomb with impenetrable secrecy until the Allies were ready for the big strike.

Extracts from 'Out in the Midday Sun' by Kate Caffrey

The Japanese appear to have been quite unpredictable in their reactions, a blaze of anger was quite frequently followed by a relatively humane comment or the gift of a cigarette, and what would cause a towering rage one day would produce an indifferent shrug the next. Those who had direct dealings with them, wrote Major Peacock, 'found them interesting, neurotic, imponderable, and frequently crazy'.

Captain Gordon agreed with this. He also pointed out that during the years of their military success and its slow decline, the Japanese violated every civilised code, murdering the prisoners at first hand by bayonetting, shooting, drowning, beating or decapitation, and at second hand by denial of medical care, torture, starvation, and work beyond the limit of human endurance. He refers to the overall statistics, the four per cent death rate among prisoners held by the Germans and Italians as compared with the twenty-seven per cent scored by the Japanese, adding that on the Kwai the percentage was much higher. He summed up the railway as 'that human rubbish-heap' where the

Japanese cared nothing for human life. Just how cheap they held it, is illustrated in the true story of one Japanese engineer who carefully explained to two prisoners how to make a dynamite charge and while they were still working on it set off the charge and blew them to pieces.

There were plenty of chilling incidents elsewhere. There was, for instance, one guard at Changi, known as the Ice Cream Man because he always wore a white coat (he got to know of this in time and then the Australians called him Mr. Peters and the British called him Mr. Lyons which amounted to the same thing) who beat six or seven prisoners unconscious every day for not saluting him with the proper greeting. There were also the tortures of the Kempei-Tai (the secret police) when they suspected that someone had a secret radio, but it was on the Kwai that the health and morale were lowest and that punishments seemed worst.

Quite often a prisoner was hit or beaten for no better reason than that the Japanese guard concerned had been slapped or kicked by his superior officer and wanted to restore 'face'. Some would hit out with any object to hand, but others carried their 'trade mark' with them: a pick handle, a bamboo rod, a length of fencing wire or barbed wire nailed to a stick. One guard carried a saw, with which he would strike, invariably at the head and face, with the flat of it 'in his more benevolent moments', but 'when irritated he would use the blunt edge, or, if highly offended, the cutting edge'. On one occasion a Japanese guard knocked an Australian prisoner unconscious for not bowing deeply enough when passing, and when a complaint was made the Japanese commandant, regardless of the fact that the Australian still lay in front of him on the ground, stated calmly, 'No one has been struck.' Another guard, when an English soldier collapsed and fell down the embankment where they were shooting rubble, pulled the lever and let a ton of stones fall on the prisoner, burying him. Some of the other prisoners whose morale was at its lowest were heard to murmur: 'Half his luck', though others more stoutly commented: 'Your turn'll come.'

Omori camp, seven and a half miles south of the Imperial Palace, had five wooden barrack blocks, each a hundred feet by twenty-four, with eight-by-four bed space for each of the five hundred and twenty men who slept in double-deck bunks with an eight-foot passage down the middle. At each end were two twelve-by-ten cubicles for the officers. In the perishing cold of winter, the water froze in the three twenty-foot wash racks which only managed a faint trickle of water in the summer. The latrines were overflowing concrete pits swarming with white maggots. The food was vile, the morning roll call was at five in summer and six-thirty in winter, and the evening one at any time between six and ten according to the whim of the officer in charge.

'It is a pity,' wrote Captain James, after he found himself at four in the morning on August 30, 1945, a free man on board an American ship, 'that their heroism contrasts so strangely with their atrocious behaviour to their captives.' It was a generous statement. He had witnessed many horrors.

Extracts from 'The Night of the New Moon' by Laurens van der Post

Both animals and furniture, I had learnt, were proxies in their imaginations for the prisoners they guarded. For instance, some weeks before, one of the worst 'blitzes' on us had been preceded by this sort of dress rehearsal in which our proxies had been some rats caught by our Korean guards. They had amused themselves torturing the rats, among other ways, by blowing them up with bicycle pumps from behind until they were swollen almost like toy balloons. Laughingly, they would watch the rats stagger painfully around until the release of air brought them relief and enabled them to try and escape, when they would be recaptured, the process repeated and so on again and again until they died. Seeing this, I had known that something evil was in store for us as well. . . .

I knew of no nation at the time for whom honour, however perverted, was so great a necessity as for the Japanese. Honour, and a life in which they did not lose honour with themselves seemed to them as important as if not more important than, food. I knew their history and their literature well. I needed no reminders, even in prison, of the destructive forms their individual and collective sense of honour could assume. . . .

I felt strongly that if war had had any justification at all it was only in the sense that at its end, it should leave victors and vanquished free for a moment from the destructive aspects of their past. Modern war appeared to me as a grim autonomous state of life carrying within itself its own harsh system of reward and punishment for those who waged it. It was as if war today were a bitter form of penance for all our inadequate yesterdays. Once this terrible penance had been paid, my own experience suggested, it re-established men in a brief state of innocence which, if seized with imagination, could enable us to build better than before. To go looking for particular persons and societies to blame and punish at the end of war seemed to me to throw men back into the negative aspects of the past from which they had been trying to escape, and to deprive them of the opportunity they had so bitterly earned in order to begin afresh.

Extracts from 'The Seed and the Sower' by Laurens van der Post

I have selected two extracts from 'The Seed and the Sower' by Laurens van der Post—a harrowing but beautiful book, which illustrates the power of the spirit of man. He, more than most, has the experience of being a POW and the gift of a great brain. I respect his wisdom and his compassion. He wrote:

It was John Lawrence, who suffered more at Hara's hands than any of us except those whom he killed, who first drew our attention to his eyes. I remember so clearly his words one day after a terrible beating in prison. 'The thing you mustn't forget about Hara,' he had said, 'is that he is not an individual or for that matter even really a man.' He had gone on to say that Hara was the living myth, the expression in human form, the personification of the intense, inner vision which, far down in their unconscious, keep the Japanese people together and shapes and compels their thinking and behaviour. We should not forget two thousand and seven hundred full cycles of his sun-goddess's rule burnt in him. He was sure no one could be more faithful and responsive to all the imperceptible murmurings of Japan's archaic and submerged racial soul than he. Hara was humble enough to accept implicitly the promptings of his national spirit. He was a simple, uneducated country lad with a primitive integrity unassailed by higher education, and really believed all the myths and legends of the past so deeply that he did not hesitate to kill for them. Only the day before he had told Lawrence how in Manchuria the sun-goddess had once lifted a train full of soldiers over an undetected Chinese mine laid for them on the track and put them all down again safely on the other side.

'But just look in his eyes,' Lawrence had said: 'there is nothing ignoble or insincere there: only an ancient light, refuelled, quickened and brightly burning. There is something about the fellow I rather like and respect.'

This last sentence was such heresy among us at the time that I protested at once. Nothing Lawrence could say or explain could wash our *bête noir blanc* or even *jaune* for that matter, and I would have none of it.

'The troops do not call him "Rotang" for nothing,' I had reminded him severely. 'Rotang' is the Malay for the kind of cane Hara was seldom without. The troops christened him that because he would at times, seemingly without cause, beat them over the head and face with it.

'He can't help himself,' John Lawrence had said. 'It is not he but an act of Japanese gods in him, don't you see? You remember what the moon does to him!'

Three days later the end came and we all went our inevitable ways. Lawrence did not see Hara again for nearly two years. When he saw Hara then it was in dock at his trial. Yes! Hadn't I heard? Hara was sought out and brought to trial before one of our War Crimes Tribunals. It was largely Hicksley-Ellis's doing of course. I could have no idea how bitter that mild, lisping, sensitive fellow had become. It was understandable, of course, after what he had suffered, that he should be truly, implacably and irretrievably bitter and vengeful, and he gave his evidence at the trial with such a malign relish and fury that Hara never had a hope of a mitigated sentence, let alone acquittal. But what was not so understandable was the bitterness of the official prosecution, for bitter as Hicksley-Ellis was, his temper was more than matched by that of the war-crimes sleuths.

'And that,' Lawrence exclaimed, incomprehension on his broad brow, 'was very odd to me. After all, none of them had suffered under the Japanese. As far as I know, not one of the particular bunch on Hara's trail had even been on active service but they were none-the-less a bloodthirsty lot. They were more vengeful on behalf of our injuries than I myself could ever be.'

He said all this in such a way that I gathered he had tried to plead for Hara and had failed. It certainly seemed highly significant to me that when Lawrence held his hand out after the trial to say good-bye, Hicksley-Ellis had refused to take it and silently turned a neat, tense Air-Force back on him. I could not resist asking therefore:

'Did you tell the Court that Hara saved your life?'

'Indeed I did,' he replied, surprised that I should have found the question necessary. 'I did that and the judge-advocate looked me up and down over a pair of the most unmilitary glasses and said in a slow, precise voice, each syllable as distinct and pointed as a letter pen-pricked on a blank sheet of paper, a trace of ponderous irony, for which I can't blame him, in his voice: "That, of course, Colonel Lawrence, is a valuable consideration—most valuable, indeed hardly less valuable to this court than it must be to you; but it must not be overlooked that there are many others for whom life would have been no less valuable who are not here today as a direct result of the accused's actions." '

No, there was obviously nothing to be done. Hara was inevitably condemned to be hanged.

'How did he take it?' I asked with the memory of the way others had marched to the fall of Hara's keen two-headed sword on the backs of their necks as fresh in my mind as if it were a picture painted that morning.

'Without a tremor or change of expression, as you would have expected,' Lawrence said. 'After all, he had pleaded guilty from the start, said, as that hopelessly inadequate interpreter told the Court: "I am wrong for my people and ready to die!" He made no effort to defend himself except to say that he tried never to do more nor less than his duty. He called no witnesses, asked no questions even of me, and just went on standing silently and rigidly to attention in the box right to the end. Besides, all that too had been foreseen.'

'Foreseen?' I asked, surprised.

'Yes!' He explained Hara had never expected anything except death of some kind in the war. In fact, in an unconscious way, perhaps he had even longed for death. I must please not be too sceptical but try and follow what he was trying to say with intuition rather than with conscious understanding. This was the other half of what he'd been trying to say in the beginning. It was most important, most relevant and the one foundation whereon his understanding either stood erect or fell . . . He had always felt even when he was in Japan that the Japanese were a people in a profound, inverse, reverse, or if I preferred it, even perverse sense, more in love with death than living. As a nation they romanticized death and self-destruction as no other people. The romantic fulfilment of the national ideal, of the heroic thug of tradition, was often a noble and stylized self-destruction in a selfless cause. It was as if the individual at the start, at birth even, rejected the claims of his own individuality. Henceforth he was inspired not by individual human precept and example so much as by his inborn sense of the behaviour of the corpuscles in his own blood dying every split second in millions in defence of the corporate whole. As a result they were socially not unlike a more complex extension of the great insect societies in life. In fact in the days when he lived in Japan, much as he liked the people and country, his mind always returned involuntarily to this basic comparison: the just parallel was not an animal one, was not even the most tight and fanatical horde, but an insect one: collectively they were a sort of super-society of bees with the Emperor as a male queen-bee at the centre. He did not want to exaggerate these things but he knew of no other way of making me realize how strangely, almost cosmically, propelled like an eccentric and dying comet on an archaic, anti-clockwise and foredoomed course, Hara's people had been. They were so committed, blindly and mindlessly entangled in their real and imagined past that their view of life was not synchronized to our urgent time. Above all they could not respond to the desperate twentieth-century call for greater and more precise individual differentiation. Their view of life refused to be individual and to rise above their own volcanic and quaking earth, as if there was always a dark glass or the shadow of the great dragon's wings of their submerged selves between them and the light of individual mind, a long blackness of their own spinning globe between them and the sun, darkening the moon for which they yearned so eagerly, and some of the finest stars. He was sorry if it sounded fantastic but he could put it no other way.

Thereupon, he broke off the apparent continuity of his thought at once and asked me if I knew how the Japanese calculated the age of an individual? I said 'No' and he explained that at birth they added nine months to a person's life, counted in all the days between his conception and emergence from the womb. Didn't I see the significance of that? Didn't I realize that such a system of reckoning life was not just an artless and naïve accident of minds more primitive than ours? If I paused to reflect how biology clearly establishes that we recapture and relive in the womb the whole evolution of life from amoeba to pithecanthropus erectus, surely I too would recognize implicit in this sytem of reckoning a clear instinctive acknowledgment of the importance of the dim past to the Japanese character. He certainly looked at it that way and until now he had been forced to think of them as a people whose spiritual and mental umbilical cord with the past was uncut; as a people still tied by the navel to the mythical mother and begetter of their race, the great sun-goddess Ama-terasu. Even in that they were characteristically perverse, reversed and inside out, for to most races in the past the sun was a bright and shining masculine deity, but to them only a great, darkly glittering mother. While the moon, so beloved and eternally feminine to the rest of mankind, was pale and masculine to them. Perhaps it was that inside-out, upside-down subjection to the past which gave them their love of death.

If I had ever attended a feast of the dead in Japan as he had often done, I would not be surprised at his use of so strange a word as love to illustrate his meaning. That feast was the gayest and most cheerful of all Japanese celebrations. Their dead were happy, cheerful, contented and benevolent spirits. Why? Because the living, one felt, really preferred dying to living as they had to live; not only preferred it but also thought it nobler to die than to live for their country. Not life but death was romantic to them and Hara was no exception. He had all this and more, deeply ingrained in him, underneath and beyond conscious thinking; he had more because above all he was a humble, simple and believing country fellow as well.

The night before he left home to join the army at the age of seventeen, that is after nine months in the womb and sixteen years and three months on earth, he had gone to a little shrine in the hills nearby to say good-bye to life, to tell the spirits of his ancestors that he was dying that day in his heart and spirit for his country so that when death came to claim him in battle it would be a mere technicality, so that far from being surprised he would greet it either like a bosom friend, long expected and overdue, or merely accept it as formal confirmation of a state which had long existed. To hear him one would have thought that this bow-legged boy, with his blue-shaven head, yellow face and shuffling walk, had gone to report to his ancestors his decision to enter one of the grimmer monastic orders like the Grande Chartreuse, rather than to announce his banal intention of joining a regiment of infantry. But you see what I mean, when I say the end too had been foreseen? . . .

Poor devil: as I watched and listened to him trying to break into verse, suddenly I saw our roles reversed. I saw as if by a flash of lightning in the darkness of my own mind that I was really the free man and Hara, my gaoler, the prisoner. I had once in my youth in those ample, unexacting days before the war when the coining of an epigram had looked so convincingly like a discovery of wisdom, defined individual freedom to myself as freedom to choose one's own cage in life. Hara had never known even that limited freedom. He was born in a cage, a prisoner in an oubliette of mythology, chained to bars welded by a great blacksmith of the ancient gods themselves. And I felt an immense pity for him. And now four years later, Hara was our kind of prisoner as well and in the dock for the last time, with sentence of death irrevocably pronounced.

Here is the second incident which helps us to understand:

I stood there in the full glare of sunlight beside Celliers on that terrible morning uncomforted by his belief that he was listening to a tidal harmony of sounds and voices. I said nothing because I felt he had already suffered enough and if he found comfort, like Joan of Arc, in hearing heavenly voices he deserved to be allowed to cling to it. Nor had I time to say anything for a series of commands had rung out at the gate and the guard was rushing to present arms. Yonoi, followed by his warrant officer, a veteran of the wars in Manchuria and China, together with an interpreter walked in. He barely acknowledged the salute of the sentries and came straight to the centre of the parade ground looking neither to left nor right of him. Once there he turned to face our ranks, placed his supple legs in shining jack-sboots wide apart and firm on the ground, his hands clasped behind his back. He was almost directly opposite us and about fifty yards away. I was dismayed to note from the angle of his head that, although he was facing us, his eyes were glancing over our heads.

'I ordered you,' he told us through the interpreter, his voice tight and thin like the lash of a whip and the s's hissing like a serpent on his tongue, 'to parade all your men. You not only lie to me but are disobedient and wilful as well. You will parade all your men.'

Before I could stop him, Hicksley-Ellis stepped out of the ranks and said: 'But we are all here.'

Without waiting for the interpreter, Yonoi, his handsome face almost aglitter with the resentment of a whole people and the outrage of a long history, hissed: 'Come here!'

We watched the tall knock-kneed officer walk awkwardly to within a yard of Yonoi and then stop to stand facing him.

'I'm afraid that's done it,' I whispered out of the corner of my mouth, my heart dark with dismay.

I had barely finished when Yonoi, quite beside himself, shrieked: 'You! You lie again! I said all, all people! Where are hospital people?'

I thought he was going to draw his sword and stick Hicksley-Ellis there and then, but he just slashed him about the head and neck a dozen times with his cane before commanding: 'Now fetch all, all people!'

The order was instantly repeated by the interpreter. We were forced to get our doctors to move all the sick out of their improvised hospital and on to the parade ground into the most cruel of suns. They had tried to do so in a way most considerate to the sick, the orderlies carrying the worst cases out on stretchers. But Yonoi would have none of that. Incensed with a sense of injury against both us and life he walked down to the doctors and ordered all the sick to their feet. The senior medical officer protested and was immediately knocked senseless for his pains. Yonoi shrieking: 'You not sick, you lie! You, you all lie. Your spirit bad, very bad. You not sick!'

Fortunately we had no operation cases in hospital that day. Even so it was as bad as it could be. There were men with temperatures close on hundred and five from the fever which took such a heavy toll among a community as consistently under-nourished as we were. They stood swaying like drunkards on their feet and before long several of them fainted and lay moaning on the ground where they had fallen. At first Yonoi tried to prod them to their feet but when they failed to respond he just stamped his feet in disgust and left them lying there for he was eager to get to the climax of his affair with us.

Yonoi had summoned Hicksley-Ellis to him in the centre of the parade ground.

'Ask him,' Yonoi told his interpreter, 'how many armourers and armaments officers he has in his group?'

Of course Hicksley-Ellis, as arranged, answered 'None.'

Then, Yonoi, being what he was, cracked inside. He had Hicksley-Ellis tied with hands behind his back and made to kneel bare-headed on the ground near him. Yonoi then stepped back, drew his sword, raised it flashing in the sun and with his lips to the naked steel said a prayer to it as I had seen other officers do before executions. The machine-gun crews released their safety catches and all four guns clicked loudly as they rammed the first bullet into the firing breech. Nothing could prevent it coming now, I thought. One by one the heads would fall until someone broke—and even then it would not be the end. This appetite for disaster would have to be fed, and not until it was sated would the devourer in Yonoi and others desist. Whatever we did from now on would be wrong and only make it worse for those who survived the day—if any did.

In my despair I turned openly to Celliers.

Before I could speak he spoke to me in a low and reassuring voice as if he were still hearing the music in his ear. He said 'I'm going to stop it now. It'll be all right. But whatever happens do nothing about me. Remember, nothing. Good-bye.'

I did not have time or mind to take in the significance of that 'good-bye', nor recognize it then as a clear indication of his knowledge of what the end was going to be for him for as he spoke he stepped out of the ranks, his new hat at a rakish angle on his head and the sun flashing on its mutilated badge. He walked, as Lawrence had already remarked, most beautifully. Without hurry he advanced on Yonoi as if he were going across a paddock at home to do no more than take a high-spirited stallion in hand.

The effect among our prison ranks was startling. No sound broke from us but the atmosphere became unlocked and flowing. I knew that without even looking round. Celliers's reputation had already spread throughout the camp and hope flared up in our ranks again. Even I, though I had no idea what he could or would do, found a too-sweet excitement going through me as I watched his easy almost nonchalant approach. It was truly wonderful; perfectly timed and executed. Anything faster would have alarmed them. Anything slower given them time to recover. Anything before that moment would have failed, for Yonoi and his men still would have been free to rush forward and stop him. But finding themselves abandoned by the conclusion they thought foregone, they hesitated and just gaped at Celliers, waiting for Yonoi to give them a lead.

When Yonoi opened his eyes again after his short prayer to the spirit, the Maru of his sword, Celliers was barely fifteen yards away. Amazement like the shock of a head-long collision went through him. Going white in the process he stared in a blank unbelieving way at Celliers. For the first time in days he was compelled, because of the unfathomed identification between Celliers and himself, to see someone outside himself.

Amazement then gave way to consternation and he cried out a command in English that was also a plea: 'You—officer—go—back, go back, go back!'

Celliers shook his head quietly and went on staring at him steadily as a disarmed hunter might stare a growling lion straight in the face. Perhaps more in terror than in anger, Yonoi raised his sword and knocked Celliers down with the flat of it. The crack on his head rang out like a pistol-shot to be followed by another exhortation to Celliers to go back. Dazed, Celliers struggled to his feet, swayed and half-turned as if to obey—then swung around suddenly. He took a couple of paces back towards Yonoi, put his hands on Yonoi's arms and embraced him on both cheeks rather like a French general embracing a soldier after a decoration for valour.

The shock of this strange action was unbelievable. I do not know who apart from Yonoi was shocked the most: the Japanese or ourselves.

'My God, what a bastard!' an Australian infantry officer behind me exclaimed bitterly.

Celliers had stepped back a pace from Yonoi and stood once more silently facing him. Of course, none of us will ever know what went on in Yonoi's mind but for the only time I had ever known he, who always had been so quick and in command of all situations, obviously did not know what to do. He looked as if lightning had struck him. His face had lost its colour and was like death with dismay. He trembled on his feet and might even have fallen to the ground if his warrant officer had not acted for him. It was this old veteran of several long wars who now suddenly uttered the anthropoidal yell which always preceded a Japanese bayonet charge, jumped forward and began beating up Celliers. His example was inevitably followed by the NCO, Commanders of the Machine-Gun Sections and the Corporal of the Guard. Our prison in the light of the high-noon sun sailing serene and indifferent overhead was filled with the noises I have only heard in a jungle trying to maul out of existence its fear of the falling night. Most strangely one and all tried to outdo one another in beating up the already half-senseless Celliers.

Yet not so strange, Lawrence commented here, for the whole incident would have become immediately an affair of honour. Did I not realize that Celliers had insulted Yonoi before his men? Did I not remember how kissing between men and women, even in the most natural forms, was regarded by the Japanese as the most obscene of gestures? Did I not remember how Hara censored the few novels we had had in camp by ordering that all the pages with a mention of kisses and kissing should be torn out of the defaulting books? Surely knowing that I could see now how deeply Yonoi must have lost face, so deeply that even the right to avenge the insult must have gone as well. Now only his men could do that for him and, in their code, that was what they would have had to do if they were not also to lose all honour with themselves. But what was far more important, Lawrence went on, could I understand that in doing this to Yonoi, Celliers had made both us and the Japanese free of whatever it was that locked our spirits so fatally together? We had been there as two halves of the same thing, two opposites darkly dependent on each other, two ends of electricity equally inducing each other, until Celliers bridged the gap and released the fatal charge?

Indeed, I agreed with Lawrence, it was most noticeable how this whole situation immediately had become an issue between Celliers and the rest. The crisis that had brought us all out into the parade ground seemed to vanish behind us like waste thrown over the stern of a ship in a fast receding wake. Only one thing obsessed both Japanese and ourselves: the odd, unpredictable thing Celliers had done to Yonoi.

It wasn't so much Celliers versus the rest as Celliers versus Yonoi. He'd forced Yonoi to face up to his identification with him. It was no longer a thing between races but a thing between two individual men.

On the morning of the third day after the scene with Yonoi we were ordered to dig a hole in the centre of the parade ground. At once I feared that it was Celliers's grave we were digging. That done, our own carpenters were made to construct a stout wooden fence in a circle thirty yards in diameter round it and to put rolls of dannert wire against it as well. Immediately I knew I had been wrong and that the hole could not possibly be a grave. But for what else then?

We found out the truth in the afternoon when we were ordered to parade as before. There Celliers, more or less cleaned up but black in the face from his beating, doubled over and hardly able to walk, was brought out of his cell into the midst of a whole platoon of guards with fixed bayonets, who half-marched, half-dragged him right to the edge of the hole in the circle of steel and wood.

Just for a moment his hands were freed and, incredibly, he seized the opportunity to straighten his body and wave one trembling hand at us while he tried to smile. His hand however was instantly seized by a guard, jerked down, and then tightly tied with rope behind his back to the other hand. His feet were similarly bound and two guards then seized him and forced him upright into the hole. They held him thus, like two foresters transplanting a sapling, while some of their comrades piled their rifles and took up spades to shovel the earth, that rich, midnight earth of the central plateau of Java, back into the hole. They did this carefully and with a studied, ritualistic eagerness, pausing every now and then to stamp down the earth with their feet firmly all round Celliers until he was buried up to the neck with not the least chance of being able to make any movement. Only his bare head, chin, and neck showed above the ground but it was noticeable that the head was erect and that the face for all its bruising looked strangely composed as if it saw something beyond that moment which caused it, from time to time, to try and smile.

The living grave complete at last, two guards with fixed bayonets were posted at the entrance to the enclosure around it. Our new prison commander then read us a lecture exhorting us to look on Celliers and reflect on the consequences of our impurities of spirit and wrong-thinking. Then he dismissed us disdainfully from his sight. Not the least macabre of the many sinister touches to that terrible afternoon was the music which suddenly blared out from the loudspeakers of the wireless turned on in the guard room when the prison gates closed on the new commander. Broadcast from a worn-out record, Rene Clair's nostalgic accordion music 'Sous les toits de Paris' rang out loud and clear from one end of the camp to the other. I nearly broke down at this gratuitous refinement of tragedy for the tortured Celliers.

However, I could safely leave to Lawrence's imagination the terrible toll in the feelings of men like ourselves who were so keenly aware of our utter powerlessness to help Celliers in the days that followed. No one in our midst could move on their normal duties about camp without seeing the bare yellow head and bruised face exposed all day long to the tropical sun. I said 'yellow head' but it would be more accurate to say white because so fierce was the sun on Celliers's last days in the earth that his hair became as bleached as a desert bone. Fortunately, or perhaps unfortunately, we could not get near enough again to see the expression on his face. The guards whose awareness of the terrible punishment inflicted on the man showed itself in a marked fear that we might be provoked into rushing them, kept us henceforth at a safe distance. Even so after the first day we could tell from the fallen angle of Celliers's head that he could not possibly last very long in those conditions. The second evening after his living interment, the Padres of all nationalities held a special service for him, the whole camp joining in. The service ended with the singing together in many tongues of the hymn 'Abide with me'. The Ambonese and Menadonese sang with moving fervour and at the end of the service there was hardly a dry eye in camp.

Dangerous as the consequences could be for my fellow-prisoners I went straight from the service to the Camp Commander's headquarters to plead for mercy for Celliers. The reaction however was so outraged in every way (even an appeal for him to be given some water provoked a dangerous outburst) that I nearly revived the situation from which Celliers had rescued us. I remembered how he had beseeched me in that vital moment on the parade ground to do 'nothing about him' and felt forced not to repeat my approach to our new Commander. We had to watch him slowly dying the most painful of deaths. Yet he himself seemed in no hurry to die, or rather that tenacious, resourceful body of his was in no hurry to depart. However, from the motionless drop of his head I felt that his spirit was not there at all and I hoped with all my heart that it was out of reach of the pain. No moan, complaint or cry ever came from him but the evening after the service, the guard having just gone to the gate for his relief, some Dutch soldiers felt compelled to go nearer Celliers, and they said they thought they heard him trying to sing.

Significant too in those final hours was the manner in which the guards themselves changed in their attitude to Celliers. At first they had looked at him without pity and turned to stand sentry with their back to him. After the first day however, I was astonished to see that each guard coming for his turn of duty to the living grave would first face the buried man, come to attention and bow his head respectfully to Celliers. Finally, at the end of the third day the night-watch on duty in the barracks nearest Celliers reported the strangest thing of all.

The moon was full at the time and the parade ground brilliant with its light. At three in the morning our watch was startled to see Yonoi's elegant figure appear at the enclosure and send away the guard to the gate. For a moment he thought he was seeing ghosts because like many he believed Yonoi had committed *hara-kiri* some days before. Yet it was Yonoi, for his walk and build were unmistakable.

After standing in front of Celliers and looking at him for long in silence, Yonoi put his hand in his pocket and produced something which flashed like silver in the moonlight. Strange as it might seem, our watch was convinced that it was a pair of scissors, for Yonoi appeared to bend down over Celliers, take his long hair in his hand and snip some of it off . . .

For a while longer Yonoi remained there in deep thought before bowing low to Celliers in the same way that the watch had seen him bow to the rising sun on the day of his Emperor's birthday. That done he walked slowly to the gate where he re-summoned the guard. And that was the last we saw of Yonoi.

By morning Celliers was dead. We were summoned to the camp headquarters after morning gruel to be told that we could have the body for burial. The new Commander could not have been more considerate at the interview. He looked us straight in the eye with an expression of someone who had suddenly been absolved from all sin and restored to an innocent vision of life. His gods had had their sacrifice and for the moment he was profoundly content. As pleased as a child before a feast he informed us: 'I'll now show you typical Japanese morality for dead.' A bugler and a military firing-party of infantry were ordered to do honours at the cemetery, The Tanah Abang, 'the dead earth' as the Javanese called it, and so we buried Celliers that afternoon to the sound of the thunder he had loved so well rumbling over the purple citadel of Malabar.

When he was arrested and searched in one of our prisons after the war something Yonoi valued more than anything in the world was found on him and taken away. Could Lawrence get it back for him? Lawrence had asked what it was.

Instead of answering, Yonoi had looked him straight in the eyes and pleaded instead: 'I am an officer and ready to die. Could you please be so good as to tell me the honourable truth. Am I to be hanged like the rest?'

'I don't know,' Lawrence had answered. 'I fear the chances are you may.'

'In that case,' Yonoi begged, 'you understand us Japanese and will know how important it is to me. As my last wish would you recover this thing for me and send it to my home to be offered to the spirit of the ancestors in the shrine of my fathers?'

'I will if I can but you mustn't expect me to be definite until I know what it is,' Lawrence replied.

Yonoi had paused, clearly aware that this might be his last chance to achieve a result of such overwhelming importance to him. But then he had explained in detail. This thing was a strand of yellow hair. The British soldier who had found it on him, fed on stories of Yonoi's brutality to women prisoners, had thought Yonoi had cut it from the head of one of his victims, and had snatched it from him and hit him with his fist. Yonoi did not complain of that. All that mattered was the fact that the soldier was wrong. It was a man's not a women's hair. It was a lock of hair from the head of the most remarkable man he had ever met, an enemy and now a dead enemy, but nonetheless a man so remarkable that he would never forget him.

He had cut that strand of hair from the dead head purely so that the spirit of the man should be honoured and given a proper home in the hereafter. It was his intention when the war was over to give a place in the inmost hall of his own ancestors to that strand of hair. But alas, from what Lawrence now had told him, he could not hope to do it that way. Instead, would Lawrence please do it for him, for only then could Yonoi die as he ought to die?

Lawrence had promised, but in the end as Yonoi was given seven years in prison instead of the expected death sentence, he had recovered the hair from the other articles of evidence produced against Yonoi and kept it for him. When after four years Yonoi was pardoned and released, Lawrence had sent the hair to him in Japan. Yonoi had written back immediately with immense gratitude. The hair had been dedicated in the sacred fire of his people's shrine. It was, Yonoi wrote, a beautiful place at the end of a long cryptomeria avenue and among steep hills covered with maples burning like a forest fire on the autumn day of the ceremony. A long elegant waterfall poured out of the heights above the clouds and fed the stream and pools full of carp and wing-swift trout at the foot of the shrine. The air there was fragrant with the scent of pine and purified with so much water. He hoped Lawrence would agree that it was a suitable home for such a spirit. Finally he, Yonoi, had written a poem for the occasion.

Presenting himself at the shrine, bowing low and clapping his hands sharply to ensure that the spirits knew he was there, he had deposited this verse for the ancestors to read:

> '*In the spring,*
> Obeying the August spirits
> I went to fight the enemy.
> In the Fall,
> Returning I beg the spirits,
> To receive also the enemy.'

'You see,' Lawrence said to me now, his voice low with feeling: 'the seed sown by brother in brother in that far-off homeland was planted in many places. It was planted that day in your prison in Java. Yes, even in the manner they killed Celliers, his enemies acted out their unwitting recognition of the seed of his deed, for they did not only bury him alive but planted him upright like a new young growth in the earth. Even the manner of their denial of the deed was confirmation of what was rejected. He was planted again by Yonoi in the hills and spirit of his native country, and here again the seed is alive and growing in you and me.

Recently I came across a booklet entitled 'Towards a Theology for Inter-Faith dialogue'. It was published in 1984 for the Board for Mission and Unity of the General Synod of the Church of England.

One paragraph seemed so relevant that I thought you might like to read it also.

The situation in which relationships between those of different religious persuasions have to be worked out is delicate and complicated. The fact that those of other cultures and religions are British citizens, with the same rights, privileges and duties, is an important change in the context. It is no longer with someone out there, at a distance, that we engage in conversation, but with those with whom we share in a way quite other than any previous generation.

A recent (14 Aug. '90) ITV programme on 'Power in the Pacific' ended with the words—'International responsibility is the new price of power.'

It made me think that the USA have done a very good job. I just wonder what will happen if and when they ever pass over the torch of leadership to another nation and, if they do, to which nation it will be.

From my readings of books such as 'The Japanese Mind', edited by Charles A. Moore, and 'The Religions of Man', by J. R. S. Whiting, certain insights into that mind are revealed.

It is evident that the wide variety of religions in Japan—some 600 came into being between 1946 and 1956—have one thing in common. This is based on an empirical trait of Japanese culture; how to remove anxieties, remoulding the mind by mental training. He/she may go to a shrine (there are 100,000), sanctuary or quiet place, clap his hands to attract the attention of the spirit or spirits and feel their presence. The Japanese believe that the answer to life's problems is in how they accept them, so Shinto and Buddhism are mainly concerned with 'here and now'. By controlling their emotions, they aim for tranquility, which brings respect. So happiness, sadness, fear etc. are difficult to detect. In spite of inner conflict, they dig deep into their history to control it, even to facing up to death, which is not the end of life. I suppose it is something similar to our saying, 'In the midst of life, we are in death', or, 'Death, where is thy sting?' The difference is that they really believe it, and live it. So, taking one's own life—hara kiri—for a good cause or with good reason, is an honourable goal. Now maybe we can just begin to understand the mind of the kamikaze.

The Bushido vows, made every morning and evening, to die willingly at a moment's notice, become part of his very existence, so that to die the death of a Samurai is being actually practised or rehearsed daily to condition the mind to cope with it, thus enabling the mind to reach the heights of possibility.

Of course, I have to over-simplify this extremely complex subject, because I can only glimpse an element of its truth, but it is a beginning. Meanwhile, as the Japanese infiltrate the world, we do have an opportunity to influence their way of thinking. This however, may show cause for our own need to raise our level of thinking within our

Christian heritage. In fact Christianity does now have a foothold in Japan for the second time in history.

In Western minds, the word 'Kamikaze' usually refers to the death-diving planes of the Special Attack Force, but 'Kamikaze' is really a Japanese religion meaning 'The Way of the Gods' (Shin) which evolved about 650 BC. The Shintoists pay homage to some eight million 'Kami' and, because of its wide interpretation, 'Kami' can mean a wide range of things, from the sun or mountains to the spirits of the dead, including certain animals and objects. In short, anything or anyone who is or was held in reverence is a 'Kami' and it is everyone's aim to become one. They do not have a bible or guide book, only a 'Kojiki' which contains myths and legends, mainly about the creation of the universe.

Buddhism is the other great religion in Japan, Buddha meaning 'The Enlightened One', and it has become both diverse and yet entwined with Shintoism. Its basic principle is self-enlightenment by gradual improvement through dealing with life's problems and learning from them. To reach the truth may require many reincarnations. Their 'book of rules' is called the 'Tupitaka' and there are numerous versions, so that no one has ever read all the contents. Even so, their objective is to help all human beings to be 'saved'. The Karma, or driving force, is all that remains after death, to be carried forward into the next life on earth. This process, they believe, goes on and on until we reach perfection.

I suspect that Western materialism and its emotional freedom is already having an effect on the younger generation of Japanese, so forming an old and new outlook, as in our own country. We, I know, ponder the effects of this trend, for both extremes result in imbalance, and yet a middle road breeds apathy. Perhaps we have no option now but to try to understand other cultures, once we have removed 'the beam from our own eye' to improve our own eyesight.

The first Commanding Officer of HMS *Illustrious* was Captain Frank H. Shaw. In 1950, he wrote, 'When tomorrow's Navy goes paying courtesy visits to Java, it will find an undercurrent of sadness beneath the gaiety, for the Javanese have long memories, and they will remember the days of slavery under the Nipponese yoke for many a year to come. The brown, hairy men spread terror grimly through the lands they conquered and though the physical scars of that occupation may heal and be lost to sight, in the hearts of the gentle people memories will surge and bite like corrosive acid for generations still to come.'

Captain Shaw forecast that the future of the Navy would be safe in the hands of aircraft carriers, but he was not to know of the tremendous advances in the world of guided missiles and of the technology which we currently term 'modern'.

So many forecasts are made in good faith in the light of present knowledge, whereas men and women of vision are frequently ridiculed.

Although history and genetics are the basic materials for human survival, there is now undoubtedly a great need for democracy and the need for freedom in order that lives may be fulfilled, which is felt by the vast majority of the world's population.

Just one thought disturbs me. With authority comes responsibility for others. If and when this enthusiastic spirit of the people attains the goal of democratic societies, what will they do with it?

What does it profit a man if he gains the whole world—and loses his soul?

Bibliography

The Night of the New Moon, Laurens van der Post — Chatto & Windus and the Hogarth Press.
The Seed and the Sower, Laurens van der Post — Chatto & Windus and the Hogarth Press.
A Walk with a White Bushman, Laurens van der Post — Chatto & Windus and the Hogarth Press.
Japan and her Destiny, Manoru Shigemitsu — Random Century Group.
The Menacing Rise of Japan, A. Howard & E. Newman — Harrap Publishing Group Ltd.
The Kamikazes, Edwin P. Hoyt — Robert Hale Ltd.
The War with Japan, Charles Bateson — Barrie & Jenkins Ltd.
The Japanese Mind, Robert C. Christopher — Pan Books Ltd.
Carrier Operations in WW II, J. D. Brown — Ian Allan Ltd.
The Other Hundred Years War 1941—2041, Russell Braddon — Collins Publishers.
The Naked Island, Russell Braddon — Pan Books Ltd. & Michael Joseph Ltd.
The Rise and Fall of the Japanese Empire, David H. James — Unwin Hyman Ltd., © George Allan & Unwin 1951.
A Portrait of Japan, Laurens van der Post.
Java Nightmare, Daphne Jackson — Grafton Books.
The British Aircraft Carrier, Paul Beaver — Thorsons.
Escort Carriers in the Second World War, Kenneth Poolman — Leo Cooper.
United States Fleet Carriers of World War II, Richard Humble — Cassell PLC.
Okinawa 1945. Gateway to Japan, Ian Gow — Grub St. Publishers.
The Brave Japanese, Kenneth Harrison — Angus and Robertson.
Wings of War, Edited by Laddie Lucas — Hutchinson & Co. Ltd.
Dry Ginger, Richard Baker — W. H. Allen & Co. Ltd.
The Battle of Leyte Gulf, Stan Smith — Balmont Productions Inc.
Avenger from the Sky, Lt. Cdr. (A) D. M. Judd DSC — Wm. Kimber & Co. Ltd.
Out in the Midday Sun, Kate Caffrey — Andre Deutsch Ltd.

I have of course written to all publishers from whose books and articles I have quoted. However, four of these have been returned to me by the GPO marked 'Gone Away' or 'Not Known'. One publisher limited my extract to 500 words, one to 1,000 words, one requested payment at a reduced fee, and two did not reply.

All the others have given permission to quote without special conditions or cost. To all I am truly grateful.

THE AIRCRAFT OF THE BRITISH PACIFIC FLEET

Photos: By courtesy of the FAA Museum

Grumman Avenger Mk I (FN767)

Grumman Avenger of 854 Sqd

Firefly I Z2035

Supermarine Walrus of 1700 Squadron, HMS Ameer *8.7.45. Lt (A) F. Lawrence lands back on board after rescuing an 896 Sqd pilot 200 yds off Jap held Nicobar*

Corsairs of 1834 and 1836 Squadrons 47 Naval Fighter Wing HMS Victorious

Chance-Vought Corsair, 1842 Sqd. HMS Rajah, *1944. Flown by Lt. Gray who was later awarded the VC*

Seafire landing on HMS Indomitable

Hellcat

APPENDIX I

Summary of Japanese Aggression/Acquisitions since 1899

1899	Formosa ceded to Japan
1910	Korea ceded to Japan
1919	Marianne, Caroline and Marshall Islands mandated to Japan by the League of nations
1931—32	Conquest of Manchukuo
1937—38	Further Chinese territories conquered
1938	Canton Taken
7 Dec. 1941	Pearl Harbour attacked. Mindanao attacked
8 Dec. 1941	Thailand taken
10 Dec. 1941	Kata Bharu taken
11 Dec. 1941	Guam taken
12 Dec. 1941	Burma invaded
16 Dec. 1941	Sarawak taken
20 Dec. 1941	Penang taken
23 Dec. 1941	Wake Island invaded
25 Dec. 1941	Hong Kong taken. Gilbert Islands attacked
30 Dec. 1941	Corregidor Islands attacked
2 Jan. 1942	Manila taken

TABLE OF JAPANESE HISTORY

(According to the official Japanese chronology—NOT according to modern investigation, 1943)

BC 660	Coronation of Kimmu, the first emperor, at Yamato.
300	Legendary date of earthquake supposed to have formed Mount Fuji and Land Biwa.
AD 200	Empress Jingo leads an army to conquer Korea.
540	Chinese and Koreans emigrate to Japan.
552	Buddhism first introduced from Korea.
572	Shotoku Taishi born. Great reformer and Buddhist apostle. During his life (died 621) Chinese system of government and civilization adopted.
681	Costumes of every class regulated by the Emperor Temmu.

900—1100 Taira and Minamoto clans become rivals in terrible civil wars.
1192 Yoritomo Minamoto establishes Shogunate at Kamakura.
1205—33 Hojo family exercise political control of Empire.
1274—81 Kublai Kahn, founder of Mongol dynasty, repulsed at attempts at invasion.
1298 Name of Japan first made known to Europe by Marco Polo.
1330—1500 Renewal of civil wars.
1338—1565 Ashikaga dynasty of shoguns govern Empire.
1549 Christianity introduced by St. Francis Xavier, Portuguese Jesuit.
1564 Ota Nobunaga becomes military dictator.
1582 Hideyoshi becomes military dictator.
1598 First European Christian martyrs crucified at Nagasaki.
1600 Tokugawa Shogunate founded. Will Adams, the first Englishman (in Dutch employ) to land in Japan. At Emperor's request, remains as shipbuilder and adviser.
1613 First English ship reaches Japan. English factory established.
1614 Edict against Christianity. Expulsion of Jesuits.
1624 Christianity persecuted and Japan closed to all but the Dutch.
1638 Massacre of Christians.
1639 Dutch confined to small island in Nagasaki harbour.
1640 Portuguese embassy appeal against expulsion. All but 13 beheaded.
1672 British Ship—*Return*—refused entry.
1707 Last eruption of Mount Fuji.
1853 Commodore Perry visits Japan, resulting in:
1854 First Treaty between US and Japan.
1857—59 Commercial treaties with United States, Great Britain and other European Powers.
1861 British Legation in Tokyo attacked by conservative fanatics.
1862 British subject Richardson, murdered. British fleet bombard Kagoshima.
1864 Bombardment of Shimonoseki by fleets of Great Britain, France, Holland and United States.
1867 Yoshinobu, last Shogun resigns. Beginning of reign of the Mutsuhito, Meiji Emperor.
1871 Feudalism abolished by Imperial decree. European reforms introduced.
1880 New codes of law founded on Code Napoléon.
1885 New system of local government inaugurated.
1889 Proclamation by Emperor of new Constitution.
1894 Sino-Japanese war commences. Invasion of Manchuria.
1895 Peace treaty with China signed at Shimonoseki.
1902 First treaty of alliance concluded between Great Britain and Japan.
1904 War with Russia. Japanese land in Korea.

1905 Russia cedes half Sahhalien and evacuates Manchuria. Korea recognised under Japanese influence. Alliance with Great Britain renewed.
1911 Alliance with Great Britain renewed.
1912 Meiji Emperor dies. Taisho Emperor succeeds.
1914 War with Germany.
1921 Anglo-Japanese alliance ended. Naval Armaments Treaty.
1924 American immigration law excludes Japanese.
1926 Taisho Emperor dies; Showa period begins.
1932 Japan invades China.
1933 Japan withdraws from League of Nations.
1936 Nationalist purge. Military government formed. German-Japanese anti-Comintern pact.
1937 Hostilities with China begin.
1939 Border clashes with Russia. Japan scraps anti-Comintern pact.
1940 Occupation 'by treaty' of Indo-China.
1941 Non-aggression treaty with Russia. Pearl Harbour attacked. Japan declares war on United States and Great Britain.

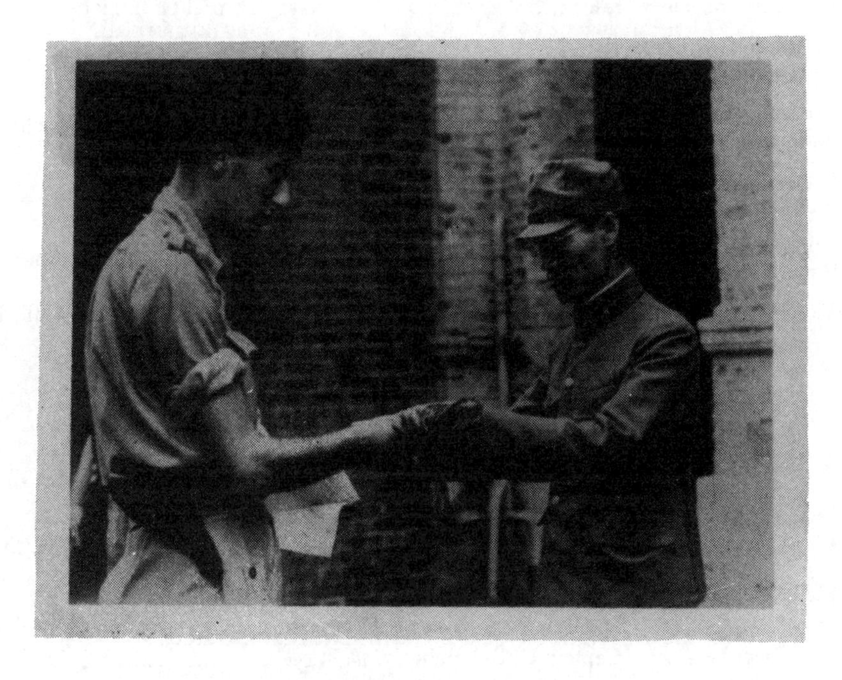

Surrender of sword—Hong Kong. Photo: J. R. Northeast, HMS Indomitable

APPENDIX II

The BPF
July—September 1945

Commander in Chief: .... Admiral Sir Bruce Fraser, GCB, KBE

Second in Command: .... Vice Admiral Sir Bernard Rawlings, KCB, KBE

Commanding First Aircraft)
Carrier Squadron:) .... Vice Admiral Sir Philip Vian, KCB, KBE, DSO

Rear Admiral Fleet Train: .... Rear Admiral D. B. Fisher, CB, CBE

Commanding Eleventh)
Aircraft Carrier Squadron:) .... Rear Admiral C. H. J. Harcourt, CB

Commanding Fourth Cruiser)
Squadron:) .... Rear Admiral E. J. P. Brind, CB, CBE

Commanding Destroyer)
Flotillas:) .... Rear Admiral J. H. Edelsten, CB, CBE

Commanding Third Cruiser)
Squadron:) .... Rear Admiral R. M. Servaes, CBE

Vice Admiral (Administration): .... Vice Admiral C. S. Daniel, CBE, DSO

January—June 1945

BATTLESHIPS

King George V ....Captain V. T. E. Halsey *Howe* .... Captain H. W. V. McCall

FLEET CARRIERS

Indomitable .... Captain J. A. S. Eccles *Victorious* .... Captain M. M. Denny

Illustrious .... Captain C. E. Lambe *Indefatigable* .... Captain Q. D. Graham

LIGHT CRUISERS

Swiftsure .... Captain P. V. MacLaughlin *Gambia* .... Captain R. A. B. Edwards

Black Prince .... Captain G. V. Gladstone *Argonaut* .... Captain W. P. McCathy

Euryalus .... Captain R. Oliver-Bellasis

DESTROYERS

Grenville .... Captain H. P. Henderson
Ulster .... Lt. Cdr. R. J. Harrison
Undine .... Cdr. T. C. Robinson
Urania .... Lt. Cdr. D. H. P. Gardiner
Undaunted .... Lt. Cdr. T. C. E. R. Sharp
Quickmatch .... Cdr. O. Becker
Quiberon .... Lt. Cdr. G. F. E. Knox
Quality .... Lt. Cdr. The Viscount Jocelyn
Queenborough .... Cdr. P. L. Saumarez
Kempenfelt .... Captain E. G. MacGregor
Whirlwind .... Cdr. W. A. F. Hawkins
Wessex .... Lt. Cdr. R. Horncastle
Whelp .... Cdr. G. A. F. Norfolk
Wager .... Lt. Cdr. R. C. Watkin

The Fleet Train
May 1945

Escort Carriers (Replenishment): *Striker, Speaker, Ruler, Slinger.*
Escort Carriers (Ferry Duties): *Fencer. Chaser.*
Destroyers: *Napier, Nizam, Nepal, Norman.*
Escort Vessels: *Crane, Pheasant, Woodcock, Whimbrel, Avon, Findhorn, Parret.*
Landing Ship: *Lothian.*
LSI: *Empire Spearhead, Glenearn, Lamont.*
Repair Ships: *Artifex, Resource.*
Light Fleet Carrier (Repair & Maintenance Carrier): *Unicorn.*
Oilers: *Brown Ranger, Dingledale, San Ambrosio, Cedardale, Arndale, San Adolpho, Wave King, Aese Maersk.*
Naval Store Issuing Ship: *Bacchus.*
Victualling Vessels: *Denbighshire, Fort Alabama, City of Dieppe.*
Distilling Ship: *Stagpool.*
Netlayer: *Guardian.*
Armament Issuing Ships: *Corinda, Darvel, Hermelin, Heron, Kheti, Pacheco, Prince de Liege, Princess Maria Pia, Robert Maersk, Thyras.*
Hospital Ship: *Tjitjalengka.*

The BPF
July—Sept. 1945

BATTLESHIPS

Duke of York .... Captain A. D. Nicholl, CBE, DSO
Anson .... Captain A. C. G. Madden
King George V ...... Captain B. B. Schofield, CBE
Howe .... Captain H. W. V. McCall, DSO

FLEET AIRCRAFT CARRIERS

Formidable .... Captain P. Ruck Keene CB, CBE, DSO
Indomitable .... Captain J. A. S. Eccles, CBE
Implacable ... Captain C. C. Hughes-Hallet, CBE
Indefatigable .... Captain Q. D. Graham, CBE, DSO
Illustrious .... Captain C. E. Lambe, KCB, CVO
Victorious ...... Rear Admiral M. M. Denny CB, CBE

LIGHT FLEET CARRIERS

Colossus .... Captain G. H. Stokes, CB, DSC

Glory .... Captain A. W. Buzzard, DSO, OBE

Venerable .. Captain W. A. Dallmeyer, DSO

Vengeance ... Captain D. M. L. Neave, DSO

ESCORT AIRCRAFT CARRIERS (Replenishment)

Striker .... Captain W. P. Carne

Arbiter . Captain D. H. Everett, DSO, MBE

Chaser .... Captain R. G. Poole

Ruler .... Captain H. P. Currey, OBE

Slinger .... Lt. Cdr. J. G. Hopkins

Speaker .... Captain U. H. R. Jones

ESCORT AIRCRAFT CARRIERS (Ferry)

Vindex .... Cdr. J. D. L. Willians, DSC

Fencer .... Lt. Cdr. A. M. Harris

Reaper .... Cdr. I. T. Clark, OBE

LIGHT CRUISERS

Bermuda .... Captain J. S. Bethell, CBE

Belfast ...... Captain R. M. Dick, CBE, DSC

Euryalus .... Captain R. S. Warne, CBE

Swiftsure .... Captain P. V. McLaughlin

Gambia (RNZN) .... Captain R. A. B. Edwards, CBE

Achilles (RNZN) .... Captain F. J. Butler, MBE

Argonaut .... Captain W. P. McCarthy

Black Prince .... Captain G. V. Gladstone

Newfoundland ..... Captain R. W. Ravenhill, CBE, DSC

Ontario (RCN) .... Captain H. T. W. Grant, DSO, RCN

Uganda .... Captain E. R. Mainguy, OBE, RCN

FAST MINELAYERS

Apollo .... Captain L. N. Brownfield

Ariadne .... Captain F. F. Lloyd, OBE

Manxman ..... Captain G. Thistleton-Smith GM

AUXILIARY A/A SHIP

Prince Robert (RCN) .... Captain W. B. Creasey, RCN

DESTROYER DEPOT SHIPS

Montclare ...... Captain G. W. Hoare-Smith

Tyne .... Captain S. Boucher

FLEET DESTROYERS

D13 *Napier* (RAN) .... Captain H. J. Buchanan, DSO, RAN

D14 *Nepal* (RAN) .... Lt. Cdr. C. J. Stephenson, RAN (7th DF-RAN)

D15 *Nizam* (RAN) .... Cdr. C. H. Brooks, RAN

D16 *Norman* .... Ltd. Cdr. J. Plunkett-Cole, RAN

D22 *Quilliam* .... Lt. J. R. Stephens

D17 *Quadrant* .... Lt. Cdr. P. C. Hopkins

D18 *Quality* .... Cdr. Viscount Jocelyn (4th DF)

D19 *Queenborough* .... Cdr. P. L. Saumarez, DSC

D20 *Quiberon* (RAN) ... Cdr. G. S. Stewart, RAN

D21 *Quickmatch* (RAN) .... Ltd. Cdr. O. H. Becher, DSC, RAN

D49 *Troubridge* ..... Captain G. F. Burghard

D45 *Teazer* .... Lt. Cdr. T. F. Taylor, DSC

D46 *Tenacious* ...... Lt. Cdr. G. C. Crowley, DSC (24th DF)

D48 *Terpsichore* ..... Cdr. R. T. White, DSO

D50 *Tumult* .. Lt. Cdr. A. S. Pomeroy, DSC

D51 *Tuscan* ... Lt. Cdr. P. B. N. Lewis, DSC

D52 *Tyrian* .... Cdr. R. H. Mills

D47 *Termagant* . Lt. Cdr. D. C. Beatty, DSC

D11 *Grenville* .... Captain R. G. Onslow, DSO

D23 *Ulster* .... Lt. Cdr: R. J. Hanson, DSO, DSC

D24 *Ulysses* ...... Lt. Cdr. P. J. Bordes, DSC

D25 *Undaunted* ..... Lt. Cdr. C. E. R. Sharp (25th DF)
D36 *Undine* ..... Cdr. T. C. Robinson, DSC
D27 *Urania* ..... Lt. Cdr. D. H. P. Gardiner, DSC
D28 *Urchin* .... Lt. Cdr. A. F. Harkness, OBE, DSC, RD, RNR
D29 *Ursa* .... Lt. Cdr. D. B. Wyburd, DSO, DSC
D12 *Kempenfelt* ... Captain E. G. McGregor, DSO
D31 *Wakeful* .... Lt. Cdr. G. D. Pound, DSC
D34 *Whirlwind* ..... Cdr. W. A. F. Hawkins, DSO, OBE, DSC (27th DF)
D32 *Wessex* .... Lt. Cdr. R. Horncastle
D30 *Wager* .... Lt. Cdr. R. C. Watkin
D33 *Whelp* .... Cdr. G. A. F. Norfolk
D35 *Wizard* .... Lt. Cdr. R. H. Hodgkinson, DSC
D36 *Wrangler* .... Lt. Cdr. E. G. Warren
D73 *Armada* .... Lt. Cdr. R. A. Fell
D61 *Barfleur* .... Cdr. M. S. Townsend, DSO, OBE, DSC
D62 *Camperdown* ..... Lt. Cdr. J. J. S. Yorke, DSC
D75 *Trafalgar* .... Captain A. F. Pugsley, CB, DSO
D70 *Penn* .... Lt. Cdr. A. H. Diack (BPF Aircraft Target Ship)
D68 *Lewes* .... Lt. Cdr. M. H. Grylle (BPF Aircraft Target Ship)
Algonquin (RCN) ...... Lt. Cdr. D. W. Piers, DSC, RCN
Hogue .... Cdr. A. St. Clair-Ford, DSO

ESCORT VESSELS (Frigates, Sloops, etc.)

Pheasant .... Cdr. J. B. Palmer
Crane .... Lt. Cdr. R. J. Jenkins, DSC
Redpole .... Lt. Cdr. E. J. Lee
Whimbrel .... Lt. Cdr. N. R. Murch
Woodcock .... Lt. Cdr. S. J. Parson, DSC
Avon .... Cdr. P. G. A. King, DSC, RD, RNR
Findhorn ...... Lt. Cdr. J. P. Burnett, RNVR
Parret .... Lt. Cdr. T. Hood, RNR
Helford .... Cdr. C. G. Cuthbertson, DSC, RD, RNR
Barle .... Lt. Cdr. J. Duncan, DSC, RNR
Derg .... Lt. Cdr. N. P. J. Stapleton, RD, RNR
Odzani ..... Lt. Cdr. J. N. Burgess, RANVR
Plym .... Lt. Cdr. A. Foxall, RNR
Usk .... Lt. Cdr. G. B. Medlycott, RNR
Widemouth Bay ... Lt. Cdr. J. H. MacAlister, RNVR
Bigbury Bay .... Lt. Cdr. G. P. D. Hall, DSC
Veryan Bay .... Lt. J. S. Brownrigg, DSC
Whitesand Bay .. Lt. Cdr. B. C. Longbottom
Alacrity .... Lt. Cdr. J. Chatton-Baker, DSC
Amethyst ...... Lt. Cdr. N. Scott-Elliot, DSC
Black Swan .... Lt. Cdr. A. D. Inglis
Erne .... Lt. Cdr. P. S. Evans
Hart .... Cdr. H. F. G. Leftwich
Hind .... Lt. Cdr. A. D. White, RD, RNR
Cygnet ... Lt. Cdr. A. H. Pierce, OBE, RNR
Flamingo .... Lt. A. Traill, RNR
Opossum .... Lt. Cdr. E. F. Hollins
Starling ... Lt. Cdr. G. C. Julian, RNZNVR
Stork .... Lt. Cdr. D. E. Mansfield, DSC
Wren . Cdr. S. R. J. Woods, DSC, RD, RNR

SUBMARINES

Taciturn, Tapir, Taurus, Thorough, Thule, Tiptoe, Trenchant, Totem, Trump, Turpin, Terrapin, Tudor, Scotsman, Seascout, Selene, Sidon, Sleuth, Solent, Spearhead, Stubborn, Supreme, Sanguine, Sea Devil, Sea Nymph, Spark, Stygian.
(Training) *Voracious, Vox, Virtue.*

FLEET MINESWEEPERS

Coquette, Rowena, Mary Rose, Moon, Providence, Seabear, Thisbe, Courier, Felicity, Hare, Liberty, Michael, Minstrel, Wave, Welcome.

AIRCRAFT TARGET SHIP: *Lewes.*
DANLAYERS: *Shillay, Trodday.*
BOOM CARRIERS: *Fernmoor, Leonian.*
LSI: *Lothian, Glenearn.*

FLEET ACCOMMODATION SHIPS: *Aorangi, Lancashire.*
REPAIR SHIPS: *Artifex, Resource, Berry Head, Flamborough Head, Dullisk Cove, Assistance, Diligence, Springdale, Kelantan* (RNZN), *Arbutus* (RNZN).
COMMAND SHIP LOGISTIC SUPPLY GROUP: *Aire.*
AIR MAINTENANCE SHIPS: *Pioneer, Unicorn, Deer Sound.*
AIRCRAFT STORE SHIPS: *Fort Colville, Fort Langley.*
FLEET OILERS: *Olna, Arndale, Bishopdale, Cedardale, Dingledale, Eaglesdale, Wave Emperor, Wave Governor, Wave King, Wave Monarch, Green Ranger, Rapidol, Serbol, Aase Maersk, Carelia, Can Adolpho, San Amado, San Ambrosio, Darst Creek, Golden Meadow, Iere, Loma Nova.*
WATER CARRIERS: *Empire Cres, Vacport, Brown Ranger, Seven Sisters.*
DISTILLING SHIPS: *Bacchus* (RFA), *Stagpool.*
NET LAYER: *Guardian.*
SALVAGE VESSELS: *King Salvador, Salvestor, Salvictor.*
HOSPITAL SHIPS, *Empire Clyde, Gerusalemme, Maunganui, Oxfordshire, Tjitjalengka, Vasna.*
STORE SHIPS: *Corinda, Darvel, Hermelin, Heron, Kheti, Kistna, Pacheco, Prince de Liege, Princess Maria Pia, Robert Maersk, Thyra S, Hickory Burn, Hickory Dale, Hickory Glen, Hickory Stream, City of Dieppe, Fort Alabama, Fort Constantine, Fort Dunvegan, Fort Edmonton, Fort Wrangell, Prome, Gudrun Maersk, Kola, Bosphorus, Jaarstroom, Marudu, San Andres, Schlesvig, Fort Providence, Edna* (Collier).
SUBMARINE DEPOT SHIPS: *Adamant, Maidstone, Bonaventure.*
MINESWEEPERS (RAN): *Ballarat, Bendigo, Burnie, Goulburn, Maryborough, Toowoomba, Whyalla, Cessnock, Gawler, Geraldton, Ipswich, Launceston, Pirie, Tamworth, Woolongong, Kalgoorlie, Lismore, Cairns.*

Disposition of Vessels and Squadrons
Sumatra—January 1945

Indomitable—Flag Rear Admiral Vian
1839 Squadron .... 14 Hellcats
1844 Squadron .... 14 Hellcats
857 Squadron .... 21 Avengers

Victorious
1834 Squadron .... 14 Corsairs
1836 Squadron .... 14 Corsairs
849 Squadron .... 21 Avengers
Ship's Flight ..... 2 Walruses (Search and Rescue)

Illustrious
1830 Squadron .... 14 Corsairs
1833 Squadron .... 14 Corsairs
854 Squadron .... 21 Avengers

Indefatigable
877 Squadron .... 20 Seafires
894 Squadron .... 20 Seafires
1770 Squadron .... 12 Fireflies
820 Squadron .... 21 Avengers
888 Squadron .... 6 Hellcats

APPENDIX III

BPF Carriers and FAA Squadrons 1945/6

HMS *Formidable*		UP TO
848 Squadron	Avenger	18 aircraft
1841 Squadron	Corsair	18 aircraft
1842 Squadron	Corsair	18 aircraft
1844 Squadron	Hellcats	6 night-fighters
HMS *Illustrious*		
854 Squadron	Avenger	16 aircraft
1830 Squadron	Corsair	18 aircraft
1833 Squadron	Corsair	18 aircraft
HMS *Victorious*		
849 Squadron	Avenger	21 aircraft
1834 Squadron	Corsair	19 aircraft
1836 Squadron	Corsair	18 aircraft
Ships Flight	Walrus	2 aircraft
HMS *Implacable*		
828 Squadron	Avenger	21 aircraft
801 Squadron	Seafire	24 aircraft

HMS *Implacable* (contd)		UP TO
880 Squadron	Seafire	24 aircraft
1771 Squadron	Firefly	12 aircraft
HMS *Indefatigable*		
820 Squadron	Avenger	21 aircraft
888 Squadron	Hellcat (Sumatra only)	6 aircraft
887 Squadron	Seafire	20 aircraft
894 Squadron	Seafire	20 aircraft
1770 Squadron	Firefly	12 aircraft
1772 Squadron	Firefly	12 aircraft
HMS *Indomitable*		
857 Squadron	Avenger	16 aircraft
899 Squadron	Seafire	12 aircraft
1839 Squadron	Hellcat	15 aircraft
1844 Squadron	Hellcat	18 aircraft

1945/46 Escort Aircraft Carriers/Squadrons

Vengeance	
802 Squadron	Seafires
812 Squadron	Barracudas
1831 Squadron	Corsairs
1850 Squadron	Corsairs
Colossus	
827 Squadron	Barracudas
1846 Squadron	Corsairs

Venerable	
814 Squadron	Barracudas
1851 Squadron	Corsairs
Ocean	
892 Squadron	Hellcats
Ruler	
885 Squadron	Hellcats

Slinger

1845 Squadron	Corsairs to *Formidable* and *Victorious* 5th April '45

Glory

837 Squadron	Barracudas
1831 Squadron	Corsairs

Ameer

Hellcats.	Penang etc.

Stalker

Seafires.	Re-occupation of Rangoon

Empress

888 Squadron	Hellcats. Penang etc.

Arbiter

899 Squadron	Seafires. Training

Vindex

1790 Squadron	Fireflies. Working up as night CAP.

APPENDIX IV

Top Secret
Extract from British Pacific State No. 12 dated 11/4/45

Ship	*Location*	*Remarks*
1st Battle Squadron		
King George V (BS1)	At sea (POA)	
Howe	At sea (POA)	
Anson	UK	Joins BPF June
Duke of York	UK	Joins BPF June
Aircraft Carriers		
Indomitable (AC1)	At sea (POA)	
Victorious	At sea (POA)	
Illustrious	At sea (POA)	
Indefatigable	At sea (POA)	
Formidable	At sea (POA)	
Implacable	EIS	Joins BPF May
Escort Carriers		
Striker (AC30)	At sea (POA)	
Fencer	Leyte	
Slinger	At sea	ETA Manus 13th April
Speaker	At sea (POA)	
Ruler	Sydney	L for Leyte 16th April
Chaser	EIS	Joins BPF late April
Arbiter	EIS	Joins BPF early May
Cruisers		
Swiftsure (CS4)	At sea (POA)	
Argonaut	At sea (POA)	
Black Prince	At sea (POA)	
Euryalus	At sea (POA)	
Achilles	Auckland (refit) Completes 18 April	
Gambia	At sea (POA)	
Uganda	At sea (POA)	
Newfoundland	At sea	ETA Fremantle 15 April
Ceylon	EIS	Joins BPF after refit
Bermuda	UK	Joins BPF June
Cleopatra	UK	Joins BPF June

Ship	*Location*	*Remarks*
Depot Ship		
Tyne (RAD, BPF)	Leyte	
4th Destroyer Flotilla		
Quilliam	Sydney (defects) Complete 16 April	
Quality	At sea (POA)	
Quadrant	Auckland	
Quiberon	At sea (POA)	
Quickmatch (D4)	At sea (POA)	
Queenborough	At sea (POA)	
7th Destroyer Flotilla		
Napier D7)	At sea	ETA Leyte 15th April
Nizam	At sea	ETA Leyte 12th April
Norman	At sea	ETA Leyte 12th April
Nepal	At sea	ETA Leyte 15th April
24th Destroyer Flotilla		
Troubridge (D24)	At sea	ETA Fremantle 17 April
Tenacious	At sea	ETA Fremantle 17 April
Termagent	At sea	ETA Fremantle 17 April
Terpsichore	EIS	Joins BPF May
Tumult	EIS	Joins BPF May
Teazer	Med	Joins BPF May
Tuscan	UK	Joins BPF June
Tyrian	UK	Joins BPF June
25th Destroyer Flotilla		
Grenville (D25)	At sea (POA)	
Ulster	Leyte	Damaged
Undine	At sea (POA)	
Ulysses	Med	Joins BPF May
Ursa	At sea (POA)	
Urania	At sea (POA)	
Undaunted	At sea (POA)	
Urchin	At sea (POA)	
28th Destroyer Flotilla		
Kempenfelt (D27)	At sea (POA)	
Wessex	At sea (POA)	
Wager	At sea (POA)	
Whelp	At sea (POA)	
Whirlwind	At sea (POA)	
Wrangler	Bombay	Completes mid May
Wizard	UK	Joins BPF July
Wakeful	Auckland	Refit

Ship	Location	Remarks
A/S Training Submarines		
Voracious	Sydney	
Vox	Sydney	
Virtue	Melbourne	L13 April for Sydney
21st Minesweeping Flotilla		
Ballarat	Leyte	
Maryborough	Adelaide (refit)	
Lisomore	Leyte	
Whyalla	At sea	ETA Manus 13 April
Burnie	At sea	ETA Leyte 12 April
Goulburn	At sea	ETA Townsville 17 April
Kalgoorlie	At sea	ETA Manus 13 April
Toowoomba	At sea	ETA Manus 21 April
Bendigo	Leyte	
22nd Minesweeping Flotilla		
Geraldton	Fremantle (refitting)	
Gawler	Adelaide	L12 April for Manus
Cessnock	At sea	ETA Manus 15 April
Cairns	Leyte	
Ipswich	Leyte	
Tamworth	Leyte	
Woolongong	Leyte	
Pirie	Leyte	
Launceston	At sea	ETA Leyte 12 April
Escort Force		
Pheasant	At sea (POA)	
Woodcock	At sea (POA)	
Whimbrel	At sea (POA)	
Crane	At sea (POA)	
Redpole	Auckland (refit)	
Parrett	At sea (POA)	
Findhorn	At sea (POA)	
Avon	At sea (POA)	
Usk	At sea	ETA Fremantle 12 April
Barle	At sea	ETA Fremantle 12 April
Odzani	EIS	Joins BPF May
Derg	EIS	Joins BPF May
Helford	At sea	ETA Darwin mid May
Plym	At sea	ETA Darwin mid May
Target Ship		
Lewes	Sydney	
Base and Depot Ships		
Montclare	At sea	ETA Fremantle 12 April
Lothian (RAFT)	Leyte	
Lamont	Manus	
Empire Spearhead	Leyte	

APPENDIX V

Acknowledgements

I am indebted to the following—and to those I may have inadvertently omitted, for their stories and encouragement in the compilation of **Kamikaze**.

BATTLESHIPS

HMS *Duke of York*: Bob Boon, Bert Crane, Albert Moss, Ralph Beanland
HMS *KGV*: Ron Padgett, Tony Jenner, H. V. Heal, Joe Sharp, Bob Putland
HMS *Anson*: John Haddock, Fred Martin
HMS *Howe*: Stan Ward, Eddie Mosling

AIRCRAFT CARRIERS

HMS *Formidable*: Edward Clarke, Tom Blurton, Richard Bigg-Wither, Ray Head, John Holloway, David Nash, Roy Forrest, Norman Coombs, Wilf Biggs, Arthur Camfield, F. W. Jones, Wilf Gillard, George Parker, Joe Doyle, Stanley Chatterton, Arthur Hovell, Ron English, Les Banks, John Blade, Norman King, Dick Sweet, Joseph Jones, Rear Admiral D. G. Parker, George Davies, Phil Evans, Ron Tovey, Dennis Edwards, Geoffrey Brooke, Bill Russell, George Bullamore, F. T. J. Johns.

HMS *Illustrious*: Gordon Aitken, Roy Wood, R. E. Hartley, Jack Gardiner, J. A. Hans-Hamilton.

HMS *Indefatigable*: Reg Beaver, Ian Darby, Jack Hibberd, Ted Tisdale, Teddy Key, Jim Shaw, Roger McCahey, Ben Pearce, Ivor Morgan, Michael Davey, Roy Gibson, Rear Admiral Anthony Davies, Les Bancroft, George Colling, Wal Powell, 'Cheese' Cheesman, Colin Mackenzie, John Birtle, Norman Smith, Dickie Walker, Alan Rogers, Bob Bowie, James Paterson, Arthur Bradley, John Thompson, Frank Grainer, Bill Daniel, Norman Gray, Bill Jones, George Turner, Mike Brown, Ray Gibbs, Roy Hawkes, Bill Coster, Cliff Miseldine, Den Gregory (deceased), John Baggs, Peter Bonney, Don Willstead, 'Brad' Bradley, Jeff Chittle, Jack Smith, Les Wills, Rear Admiral Terence Ridley, Colin Freeman, Eric Back, Denis Cowley, Cyril Painter, Ray Battison, Fred Piper, Don Banks, Dennis Hickman, Douglas Rathbone, Tom Jeans, Owen Lawrence-Jones, Alan Robers, George Carpenter,

Malcolm Williams, Reg Davies, George Raby, Michael Croft, P. W. Hall, Dick Douglas-Boyd, John MacLauchlan, George Hunn, R. Jenkins, Roy Hawker, Michael Cobb, David Colvan, Gerry Purnell, Cecil Golightly, Ron Pankhurst.

HMS *Indomitable*: Frank Stovin-Bradford, Bob Spurway, George Milcoy, Denis Moore, Fred Clark, Ron Barnett, J. M. Montgomery, Ronald Fidler, John Northeast.

HMS *Implacable*: Roy Merry, Harry Thomas, R. Lynch, Tony Britton, Vic Spencer, D. R. Wells.

HMS *Victorious*: Eric Such, M. Evans, Ern Crimp, Sam Porter, Michael Hancock, George Parkinson, Bill Fenwick-Smith, Jim Dodds, W. M. Taylor, Phil Davis, Arthur Groom, Lloyd Davies.

HMS *Chaser*: G. Tomlinson.

HMS *Speaker*: J. R. Murphy.

HMS *Slinger*: John Lawson, John Dunn, Jack Hill, Gordon Showell, Richard Brooke, John Howse, Clive Oakes, Richard Rowell.

HMS *Ruler*: George Luscombe.

HMS *Arbiter*: George Luscombe.

HMS *Vengeance*: Reg Parton.

HMS *Unicorn*: J. W. Sturrock.

CRUISERS, DESTROYERS, ESCORTS and OTHERS

HMS *Jamaica*: Kenneth Peberdy.

HMS *Newfoundland*: Gwyn Evans, Tom Roxby.

HMS *Black Prince*: Harold Johnson, Doug High, H. W. Lemming, Ingli Morgan, Ralph Beanland, Gwyn Evans.

HMNZS *Gambia*: N. J. Taylor.

HMS *Swiftsure*: Roger Kittering, Bill Shipp, John Deneulain, Ron Dovey, Paddy Vincent, J. Short, John Corbishley.

HMS *Argonaut*: Bill Proctor, Harry James.

HMS *Tyne*: Ian Garnett (also in *Euryalus, Whirlwind, Barfleur, Lothian*).

HMS *Quality*: Jack Collins, Len Walters.

HMS *Queenborough*: Joe Higham.

HMS *Quadrant*: Harry Lock.

HMS *Barfleur*: Geoff Postlethwaite, Joe Mole.

HMS *Tyrian*: R. Scott.

HMS *Tenacious*: Rear Admiral George C. Crowley.

HMS *Termagent*: George Lancaster.

HMS *Undine*: Bill McCullock.

HMS *Ulster*: A. L. Potts.

HMS *Ulysses*: Fred Fallows.

HMS *Urania*: A. Swift.

HMS *Undaunted*: Harry Chapman.

HMS *Urchin*: J. Banks.

HMS *Grenville*: Walter Uden, Roy Durber, J. Slade, Eric Heyward.

HMS *Wakeful*: Albert Scott.

HMS *Kempenfelt*: Thomas Tatler.
HMS *Crane*: Ron Blacker.
HMS *Barle*: Peter Longhurst.
HMS *Glenearn*: Lawrence Curtis.
HMS *Pheasant*: John Gillis.
HMS *Saumarez*: Bert Crisp.
HMAS *Shropshire*: R. J. Murray.
HMAS *Warrego*: George Ashton.
HMAS *Warramunga*: E. E. Fernandez.
HMS *Welcome*: George Burton.
HMS *Raider*: Derek Leaman.
HMS *Royalist*: Fred Caffrey.
HMS *Maidstone*: William Capseed.
HMS *Lothian*: Bill Cardew.
TSMV *Menestheus*: Les Hunt, Dr. Tony Ferguson, Nick Knight, John Haddock.
HMS *Golden Hind*: E. J. Foster.
HMS *Tamar*: A. L. Davies.
HMHS *Oxfordshire*: Harry Mitchell, Mrs. M. Clive (neé Pinson).
HMHS *Tjitjalengka*: Norman Burt.
SS *San Ambrosio*: J. Jenkinson.
SS *City of Dieppe*: Frank Manning.
SS *Empire Spearhead*: Fred Brown.
VSIS *Fort Wrangell*: Ray Hill.
SS *Empire Salvage*: Gerald Barcock.
LST(3) 3029: Clayton Maxwell.
USS *St. Louis*: Captain J. Q. Edwards USN.
Molcab: Kenneth Millar.

I should also like to express my gratitude to:

Mrs. Doris Dew, Aunt; Mrs. Deidre Thompson, Secretary; Upton-upon-Severn British Legion Secretary, Roger Slater; Upton-upon-Severn Library, Mrs. Jenny Ross; POW Changi Captain Richard Laird RASC; POW Peter Dunstan RM; Lt. Cdr. T. W. Ferrers-Walker; Admiral Vian's Staff, George Chere; Mrs. Sheila Whitfeld, widow of Captn. John Whitfeld; Matthew Taylor RM; Ken Tongue; Mrs. M. Ruck-Keene; Agnes Gibson; Walter Pritchard; Charles Birch, Canada; Lt. Cdr. Paul Housden; Mrs. Dorothy Wort; Mrs. Marion Percy; Mrs. St. Leger-Chambers; John Talbot-Cooper for photographic advice; FAA Museum Yeovilton; Graham Mottram; Anne Bell; David Richardson.

Appendix VI

Obituaries

Admiral Sir Ian Easton KCB.DSC who wrote the Foreword to 'Sakishima' has died. The Obituary Column in The Daily Telegraph dated Friday 16th June 1989 included the following:

'Ian Easton was born on November 27 1917 and joined the Navy in 1931, going to Dartmouth as a naval cadet . . .

He qualified as a pilot in 1939 and served in the carriers *Glorious* and *Ark Royal* in the Norwegian campaign in 1940, taking part in strikes against shipping and military targets on shore, and being twice rescued from the sea after his Skua dive-bomber ditched.

Flying a Fulmar fighter from *Ark Royal*, he took part in operations against French warships at Oran in North Africa to prevent them falling into Vichy hands after the fall of France in the summer of 1940. Later flying from *Formidable*, he ran out of fuel near Freetown and had to land in French West Africa.

He endured imprisonment in harsh conditions in a camp in Timbuktu where the Vichy French—as was their usual custom—ignored all civilised conventions for the treatment of prisoners of war.

Released after the Allied invasion of North Africa in November 1942 he went to *HMS Dryad*, the navigation school outside Portsmouth where he qualified in what was then the new naval art of fighter direction.

Easton went as Direction Officer to the aircraft carrier *Indefatigable* in 1943 and served in her in the campaign of air strikes mounted by the Fleet Air Arm against the German battleship *Tirpitz*, then lying in a Norwegian fjord, during the summer of 1944. Later that year *Indefatigable* went out to the Far East to join the British Pacific Fleet . . .

Early on the morning of 1st April 1945 a Japanese kamikaze bomber crashed on the flight deck about the island superstructure. Its 500lb bomb, which did extensive damage and caused casualties of 14 killed and 16 wounded, detonated almost below Easton in the air direction room.

Although he was dazed by the explosion and blinded by steam and smoke, he remained outwardly unruffled. Pilots in the air at the time said afterwards that they would never have guessed from his voice that anything untoward had happened to their ship.

His peacetime appointments included a stint on the staff of the British Joint Services Mission in Washington; an exchange service with the Royal Australian Navy in command of the Naval Direction and Torpedo School in Sydney; the directorship of the Naval Tactical Weapons Policy Division; and the command of the converted carrier *Triumph* in the Far East.

Then Easton was Assistant Chief of Naval Staff (Policy) and afterwards President of the Admiralty Interview Board. In 1973 he went back to Washington as head of the British Defence Staff and Defence Attaché and finally from 1976 to 1977, he was Commandant of The Royal College of Defence Studies.' . . .

I hope that I thanked him sufficiently, not only for his help with 'Sakishima', but for his wonderful encouragement and advice.

So many have cause to be grateful to him.

Stuart Eadon

I was sent the following obituary recently. It serves to illustrate the calibre of men who served in the BPF.

CAPT WALTER ELLIOT, who has died aged 78, had a long and distinguished career with the Fleet Air Arm and was then a Stalwart Conservative backbench MP.

Elliot was a superb athlete. He excelled at fencing and lawn tennis, was welterweight champion of the Navy in 1929, played at outside half for the Navy Rugby XV and then for England, being capped seven times in the 1930s. He might have won more caps, but in 1937 he went to the China Station to serve in the aircraft carrier *Eagle*.

In early 1942, he was appointed CO of 820 Squadron, serving in the carrier *Formidable* with the Eastern Fleet against the Japanese in the Indian Ocean.

Already mentioned in dispatches, he was awarded a DSC in 1946 for his distinguished service in the Far East.

I learned from The Fleet Air Arm Officers' Association News Sheet:

Admiral Sir Frank Hopkins KCB. DSO. DSC. DL—Died 14th April 1990. Lent to the U.S. Pacific Fleet serving in the carriers *Intrepid* and *Hancock* and witnessed the defeat of the Japanese Navy in the Battle of Leyte Gulf.

Captain U. James CBE. RN —Aged 87. Died 1990.

He will be remembered as the Captain of the Escort Carrier *Speaker* which was the first British warship to take released prisoners of war out of Tokyo Bay on 3rd September 1945. When *Speaker* sailed with nearly 500 men on board Captain James had been asked to sail close to the larger ships. Knowing that the upper decks of all the ships present were crammed with men all bursting to cheer, he took *Speaker* to sea by what he called "a most tortuous route". As the carrier steamed up and down the anchorage, her sailors were joined by hundreds of ex-POWs on her flight deck, while the Navy gave her a send-off which no one who saw it will ever forget.

Extracts from an article in the Daily Telegraph dated 28th July 1990.

Judge Desmond Vowden, who has died aged 69, brought to his judicial duties on the Western Circuit something of the robust, salty tang of his earlier career in the Royal Navy and the Royal Marines.

A clergyman's son, Captain Desmond Harvey Weight Vowden was born on Jan. 6 1921 and educated at Clifton. He joined the Royal Navy straight out of school, and later transferred to the Marines; but an accident sustained while serving in *Indomitable* in the Second World War left him with a spinal injury which afflicted him for the rest of his life.

From The Daily Telegraph, Friday February 24, 1989.

IN MEMORIUM
"THEIR NAME LIVETH FOR EVER MORE"

F.E.P.O.W.—Remembering in particular on this day the Servicemen and Nurses also Civilian Internees who died in captivity and those who have died since as a result of their brutal treatment by the Japanese.

READ—RICHARD GEORGE, Capt. RA
Died Sept, 1947, as a result of ill treatment in Changi, Singapore.

BRITISH COMMONWEALTH AND ALLIED SERVICEMEN, WOMEN AND CIVILIANS —Who lost their lives in action with the Imperial Japanese Forces, or as a result of it, and in the brutal Japanese POW camps throughout SE Asia, 1941—1945, are especially remembered today.

Tribute is also paid to all who served in the Far East, survived and returned, having given years of their youth for King, Country and Freedom in the struggle against the Emperor's evil regime, PT 67.

Sent to The Daily Telegraph by Lieut. (E) Dennis Edwards RN. Retd. President of the HMS Formidable *Association (at no cost to the association). PT 67 = HMS* Formidable—*Ed.*

Copy of letter from Mrs. Shelia Whitfeld who has since died aged 79, widow of Captain J. Whitfeld, Commander HMS *Indefatigable*

November 14th 1988. Cirencester, Glos.

Dear Stuart,

I must write to tall you how much I have enjoyed your book and how interesting I found it. I had no idea what an awful time you all went through.

John never told me a thing about it. I think that you were all incredibly brave and your endurance marvellous. How lucky I was that he came through unscathed and how sad that so many young lives were lost.

Thank you so much for all the kind words you and others say about John. It makes me very proud to be his wife and I shall always treasure them.

If I may I would like to correct you on a couple of points. He was not at the Christmas Island tests. His last two years we were in New Zealand and he retired in December 1955. He died on 12th May 1959 of Leukemia.

Thank you for writing the book which my children will also treasure I know.

Yours sincerely,

Shelia Whitfeld.

RM Peter Dunstan of HMS *Prince of Wales* has been researching POW graves and discovered that three *Indefatigable* aircrew are buried in Djakata:

	Died	*Age*	*Grave*
Pilot CPO Mitchel H.G.	24.1.45	24	6J4-6K3
Sub/Lt. Hemington A.	24.1.45	21	6J4-6K3
L/Airman Harris C.L.	24.1.45	20	6J4-6K3

The total of 12 names in the mass grave includes 9 RAF from a Liberator which crashed while dropping supplies to a POW Camp just after the end of the war. *(See **Sakishima** re 'Mitch' and crew.—Ed.)*

From an evacuee on board HMS *Colossus*

On Tuesday 11 December 1945 the British Aircraft Carrier *Colossus* left Tandjoeng Priok with 418 evacuees on board, to pick up 347 more at Semarang. They consisted of women, children, some elderly gentlemen and sick who had to be taken to Ceylon to wait there at Kandy in the mountains, for further transport to the Netherlands.

Now we are approaching this first destination and will be leaving this ship within a few hours, we wish to express in a few words our gratitude for the way in which we were taken care of during the voyage. Words are insufficient to describe how the Commanding Officer, Officers and Ship's Company did their utmost to make this week for ever memorable to us.

. . . It was a relief and a boon to us, after months of hardship and misery followed by months of terror and danger, to be a guest on board this ship, at the same time it made it easier to leave our beautiful, for many of us, Indies, which gave and took so much from us. In short, the *Colossus* did honour to its name and in a word, it has been 'colossal' . . .

Extract from The Manchester Guardian Weekly, Friday 10th August 1945

'By God's mercy, British and American science outpaced all German efforts,' says the ex-Prime Minister. And President Truman: 'We may be grateful to Providence that the Germans got V1 and V2 late and in limited quantities, and even more grateful that they did not get the atomic bomb at all.'

Article in The Sunday Times, June 1, 1952

ADMIRAL OF THE FLEET SIR PHILIP VIAN

His own Service, justly proud of tradition, has cast tradition aside to emphasise the honour paid to a great sailor. For his 'distinguished and outstanding services' in the last war, Sir Philip Vian is promoted, out of the strict run of seniority, to Admiral of the Fleet.

To the world at large his name symbolises daring and resolution. He was at sea throughout the war. From the fjords of Norway to the Mediterranean, he fought his most brilliant action; from the Channel on 'D' Day to the vast reaches of the Pacific, he made his mark on naval history.

Yet, to those who have served with him, Philip Vian has always been, and will remain, something of an enigma. He is intensely, surprisingly shy, and his shyness manifests itself in an aggressive brusqueness which can be highly disconcerting and on occasion has given offence. Neither studious nor analytical, he has an inborn faculty for taking the right course; generally it is the bold one. The same uncanny intuition which used to prompt the correct snap decision on the bridge enabled him to sense at a glance the soundness of an intricate operational plan. With this instinct Vian couples a quick brain and a remarkably retentive memory.

His searching steadfast gaze belies an innate restlessness which has beset him all his days. Never sparing himself, he expects an equally high standard from others. Demanding efficiency and inspiring it by his own example, he is a great leader in a crisis; yet, the crisis over, he withdraws behind a barrier of reserve which few have been encouraged to penetrate. His is a complex character. If his natural severity of manner and stiff formality reject easy companionship, his courage and his quite singular modesty are a shining example to lesser men.

'It takes three years to build a ship,' said Admiral Cunningham amid the disasters of Crete, 'but three hundred years to rebuild a naval tradition.' Admiral of the Fleet Sir Philip Vian, victor of Sirte, has enhanced that tradition.

'LOCAL GOSSIP'

HMS *GIPSY*

'On the 22nd November 1939, HMS *Gipsy* was on patrol off Harwich when she espied a German Dornier. Although at extreme range, she opened fire and shot it down. Three German airmen, who had just dropped mines, parachuted down and the *Gipsy* picked them up.

Soon afterwards, the *Gipsy* hit one of the mines and 31 officers and men lost their lives—including the three German airman who had 'laid' the mines!'

Related by Ian Lewis, son of George Tudor Lewis, one of the *Gipsy*'s crew who survived.

Although this story is not related to the BPF, it is indicative of the memories aroused when friends know that you are writing a book—and I couldn't resist including it. It is also an example of what some of the men had been doing before joining the BPF.—Ed.

While discussing my first book ***Sakishima*** *with the local Secretary of the British Legion, Roger Slater, he told me how Upton-upon-Severn had contributed to the efforts of the BPF. Later he wrote this for me:*

WAR WORK IN UPTON-UPON-SEVERN

Frederick George Patey (George) was a local self taught engineer and millwright. During the first war 1914—18 he was engaged on small scale munition work in his own workshop, machining fuses for shells. After the war he purchased an ex-army Foden FWD and carried on a part-time occupation of haulage contractor, travelling all over England and Wales, right up to the Scottish border. He was also a pioneer in the early radio age, making and selling locally 'wireless' sets. He continued working in his 'Ancona Works' and also carried out electrical work.

At the outbreak of the second war 1939, he and his works were taken over for war work, much of which was classified, at that time. Again munition work was carried out for a short time. Then a consultant engineer who lived in Hanley Swan (Mr. Dimbelby) brought the plans for a number of projects, and began to carry out experiments, and make wooden models and patterns. Among the projects worked on at the 'Ancona Works' were the *couplings for arrester wires on aircraft carriers*, many dozens of drawings, and wooden patterns were prepared, then these were taken away for castings to be made, the rough casts were then worked up in the works, fastened onto wire cables, set up on a test rig, and tested to destruction. Other types of coupling were also tested here, as it was the only test rig in the country, capable of doing the tests, and had been made especially for that purpose. It was constructed in the workshop top floor, down through the next floor, and into the basement. The base was about five feet square, and about four foot thick of reinforced concrete. Large cast iron weights some two feet square and two inches thick, were placed upon the bottom of the cables, the top end secured upstairs, and the machine started, it was a snatching action, up and down. A test may take only a few minutes before the wire came out of the coupling, the wire broke, or the coupling came apart, but sometimes the test would go on all day, and sometimes longer. The tests were recorded on yards of paper graph, on which the pens left an inky path. A Mr. Armison was also engaged in these works, and during the period a number of 'Boffins' also made visits.

Many BPF pilots have cause to be grateful to George Patey and his colleagues.—Ed.

STOP PRESS!

Extract from: FLY NAVY, Autumn 1990

ANOTHER FAA 'FIRST' OVER JAPAN

In FLY NAVY, Summer 1988, Doug Parker claimed that his Corsair Squadron, 1942, was the first British unit to strike the Japanese home islands. This was a correction to the previously published view in 'The Forgotten Fleet' and in Mike Crosley's book 'They Gave Me a Seafire'. Now Dick 'Biggy' Bigg-Wither supplies a further first-hand amendment to aviation history.

When *Formidable* joined the British Pacific Fleet in April, 1945, our first task was to continue neutralising the airfields of the Sakishima Gunto group of islands to prevent Kamikaze aircraft landing and refuelling there in order to attack the American fleet and support vessels off Okinawa, about 150 miles to the north.

'Judy' Garland, among others, was shot down by ground fire during these operations and was replaced by Doug Parker as CO 1942 for a short period before *Formidable* returned to Sydney to re-equip after being hit amidships by two Kamikazes and subsequently surviving a serious hangar fire when most of our aircraft with cockpit hoods open were sprayed with salt water.

Captain Ruck-Keene of *Formidable* invited me to his cabin for a drink two days before 'J-Day' July 17, and 'requested' me to lead the second ramrod, saying that he wished his new and less experienced CO, Doug Parker, to have the benefit of a surprise attack. I was to follow with twelve Corsairs two hours later to the same target. How could I refuse?

I was none too happy about it, but comforted myself with the thought that we would have an extra two hours in our bunks. I told only my senior pilot, Hammy Gray.

We duly took off at 0830, two hours after 1842, flying just under cloud base at 500 feet, not knowing of the hot reception they had encountered. As we approached the coast, the fog thickened to such an extent it would have been suicide to proceed so we climbed in open sections of fours in close formation to 10,000 feet. At that point, one of my flight, Sub. Lt. Maitland (subsequently shot down on August 10th), reported his oxygen u/s so we were unable to go higher to break cloud.

Half an hour or so later, we came out of it and to my utter amazement and delight I saw the other two flights a few hundred yards away on either side and our secondary target, Niigata airfield, dead ahead. Unlike 1842 Squadron, we achieved complete surprise and were able to carry out three strafing runs accounting for about 17 Jap aircraft 'flamers' plus one steam locomotive blown up.

It rather shook me when, in September 1945, I met an Australian Army officer in the Union Club, Sydney, just repatriated as a POW, who had been in prison camp on the edge of Niigata airfield. We were the first allied aircraft they had seen. He told me the whole camp was cheering us on but that a hail of small arms fire had been directed at us after the first run. We never saw it and fortunately no one was hit.

So perhaps, after conceding to 1842 a first in reaching the east coast, I may claim for 1841 a first to straddle Japan. However, I would prefer that any honours should go to every single fine pilot and crew member in all BPF squadrons who gave their all and many their lives for the final victory in which the Fleet Air Arm played such an heroic part in the last naval battle of the war.

Extract from a national newspaper—Nov. 1990

Emperor Akihito of Japan seems a shy and well-meaning man. Yet there was something sinister about the whole ceremony when he was installed on the Chrysanthemum Throne on Monday. The living doll courtiers, the echoes of a warlike past, the worshipping roar of 'banzai' ('may the emperor live for 10,000 years')—all of it left me squirming with unease.

Isn't there something chilling and alien about the whole Japanese way of life, with its over-formal code of manners, its early-morning physical jerks in the factory and unquestioning obedience to authority?

British politicians are constantly urging us to learn from the Japanese. Otherwise, they tell us, we seriously risk being 'left behind'.

If avoiding being left behind means adopting the Japanese outlook on life and work, I am not at all sure that I wish to join the race . . .

LAST WORDS

Well Fleetmates—Stand Easy. You've deserved it. There are still so many stories untold, but you've got the message, haven't you? Whatever the tale, 'It could have been *my* story,' someone will say—even if you weren't mentioned by name.

Let's put it to bed now, shall we? We did as we were asked.

As my wife Rosamund said, 'No one can take away what we have had.' How true, but we want more, don't we? Our love and compassion, especially because of our friends who didn't come home—is so intense. We do so want the youngsters to learn from our mistakes—and sacrifices—but that we must now leave in the hands of the Almighty.

Who better?

For there are Dragons still!

Stuart Eadon. September 1990

'There are Dragons Still' are the words inscribed at the foot of a carved statue of St. George and the Dragon which forms the War Memorial at Lawrence Sheriff School, Rugby, where I spent my early years.

INDEX TO THE MEMORIES OF THE MEN OF THE BRITISH PACIFIC FLEET

THE BRITISH PACIFIC FLEET

This memorial was erected by
The Naval Historical Society of Australia
to commemorate the service of the British Pacific Fleet
in the war of 1939 - 1945.
The treadplate and ship's badge were removed
in the year 1958 from the battleship
H.M.S. DUKE OF YORK, last flagship of the Fleet.

UNVEILED BY REAR-ADMIRAL G.D. MOORE C.B.E.
ON THE 2ND OF DECEMBER 1973.

Photographs of BPF Memorial in Sydney. The Badge and Treadplate were provided by Lieut-Cdr T.W. Ferrers-Walker RN